1989 Annual Edition

West's Federal Taxation:

Corporations, Partnerships, Estates, and Trusts

1989 Annual Edition

West's Federal Taxation:

Corporations, Partnerships, Estates, and Trusts

General Editors William H. Hoffman, Jr., J.D., Ph.D., C.P.A.

William A. Raabe, Ph.D., C.P.A.

Associate Editor Mary Sue Gately, Ph.D., C.P.A.
Texas Tech University

Contributing Authors D. Larry Crumbley, Ph.D., C.P.A.
Texas A & M University

Steven C. Dilley, J.D., Ph.D., C.P.A.
Michigan State University

Patrica C. Elliott, D.B.A., C.P.A.
University of New Mexico

William H. Hoffman, Jr., J.D., Ph.D., C.P.A.
University of Houston

Jerome S. Horvitz, J.D., LL.M. in Taxation
University of Houston

Marilyn Phelan, J.D., Ph.D., C.P.A.
Texas Tech University

William A. Raabe, Ph.D., C.P.A.
University of Wisconsin-Milwaukee

Boyd C. Randall, J.D., Ph.D.
Brigham Young University

W. Eugene Seago, J.D., Ph.D., C.P.A.
Virginia Polytechnic Institute and State University

James E. Smith, Ph.D., C.P.A.
College of William and Mary

Willis C. Stevenson, Ph.D., C.P.A.
University of Wisconsin-Madison

Eugene Willis, Ph.D., C.P.A.
University of Illinois at Urbana

West Publishing Company

St. Paul • New York • Los Angeles • San Francisco

Copy editor: Deborah Cady

Library of Congress Cataloging in Publication Data

Hoffman, William H.
  West's Federal taxation.
  Includes index.
  1. Taxation—United States—Law. I. Title.

KF6335.H63   343'.73'04   76–54355

ISBN 0–314–65769–X

ISSN 0270–5265

1989 ANNUAL EDITION

Preface

This work was inspired by and designed to relieve the absence, perceived by the authors, of suitable textual material for a second course in Federal taxation—the follow-up to a course outlining the Federal income taxation of individuals. This text, as the basis for a second course offered at either the undergraduate or graduate level or as a tool for self-study, contains an introduction to tax research and discussions of the Federal income tax treatment of taxpayers other than individuals and the treatment of those property transfers subject to Federal and state gift and death taxes.

Throughout the text the authors stress the practical application of the materials through a liberal use of examples, most of which have been classroom tested and found to be effective learning devices. At the same time, the evolution of specific statutory provisions through the interaction of case law, political compromise, and economic considerations is discussed to offer the student a broad base for understanding and applying the tax law. Our text does not purport to be a treatise on historical and fiscal policy considerations; its primary concern is tax practice. For this reason, such discussions of the law's development were minimized. In our opinion, this minimization does not compromise the subject matter's presentation.

At the center of the practical application of tax law is tax planning—the legal minimization of the tax burden. The authors are sensitive to this facet of tax law education; therefore, all chapters conclude with a special section—"Tax Planning Considerations."

The authors are of the opinion that any advanced Federal tax course should offer the student the opportunity to learn and utilize the methodology of tax research; therefore, Chapter 1 is devoted in part to this topic, and each Chapter contains several research projects. The effectiveness of the text does not, however, depend upon the use of these research materials. They may be omitted without diminishing the presentation of all other topics.

Many of our users are not aware of the useful material contained in the appendixes to the text. In addition to the usual Subject Index, the following items are included: Tax Rates and Tables (Appendix A); Tax Forms (Appendix B); Glossary of Tax Terms (Appendix C); Table of Code Sections Cited (Appendix D-1); Table of Regulations Cited (Appendix D-2); Table of Revenue Procedures and Revenue Rulings Cited (Appendix D-3); and, Table of Cases Cited (Appendix E).

We are delighted to have the opportunity, as editors, to coordinate the efforts of our authors in this, the 1989 Annual Edition of *West's Federal Taxation: Corporations, Partnerships, Estates and Trusts.* The more than ten years that have elapsed since our text first was made available to the academic and professional communities has more than justified the hope that it would fulfill a real need.

The 1989 Annual Edition incorporates the major changes to the tax law made by the Revenue Act of 1987. It also includes other recent developments, many of which clarified and refined the provisions of the Tax Reform Act of 1986.

Accompanying the text, is a separate *Instructor's Guide*. The so-called "IG" contains the following materials:

—Instructor's Summaries that can be used as lecture outlines and provide the instructor with teaching aids and information not contained in the text.

—Incorporated as part of the Instructor's Summaries are selected queries that facilitate the use of WESTLAW, a computerized compilation of legal sources (judicial, legislative, and administrative) pertinent of the area of taxation. WESTLAW, a service available from West Publishing Co., provides a sophisticated short cut for carrying out in-depth analysis of various tax issues.

—Improved and additional Examination Questions with solutions thereto.

—The solutions to the Research Problems contained in the text.

—The solutions to the Comprehensive Tax Return Problems contained in the text.

A separate *Solutions Manual* contains the answers to the Discussion Questions and Problems.

In addition, we make available to the user the following instructional aids:

—WEST–TAX Planner, a Lotus-based tax computation and planning spreadsheet template for non-individual taxpayers.

—Computerized testing (Microtest II for microcomputers, and WEST-TEST II for mainframes).

We are extremely grateful to the users of our text who were kind enough to provide us with constructive comments concerning its effectiveness both as a teaching and as a learning device. In particular, we express out gratitude to the following professors who extensively critiqued the WEST–TAX Planner material: Scott N. Cairns, James Madison University; Karen S. Hreha, University of Illinois; Cherie J. O'Neil, Virginia Polytechnic Institute and State University; and, James P. Trebby, Marquette University.

Lastly, we appreciate the invaluable assistance provided to us by Bonnie S. Hoffman, C.P.A. and William H. Hoffman III, C.P.A.

William H. Hoffman, Jr.
William A. Raabe

March, 1988

Contents in Brief

Table of Contents

Corporations: Organization
3 and Capital Structure

Corporate Distributions Not
████████ 4 ## in Complete Liquidation

Corporations: Distributions
████████ 5 ## in Complete Liquidation

6 Corporations: Reorganizations

7 Corporate Accumulations

8 Partnerships: Formation and Operation

Partnerships: Transfer of Partnership Interests; 9 Family and Limited Partnerships

10 S Corporations

11 The Federal Gift and Estate Taxes

14 Tax Administration and Practice

Appendixes

1989 Annual Edition

West's Federal Taxation:

Corporations, Partnerships, Estates, and Trusts

1 Understanding and Working with the Federal Tax Law

The Whys of the Tax Law

The Federal tax law is a mixture of statutory provisions, administrative pronouncements, and court decisions. Anyone who has attempted to work with this body of knowledge would have to admit to the law's disturbing complexity. For the person who has to wade through rule upon rule to find the solution to a tax problem, it may be of some consolation to know that the law's complexity can be explained. There is a reason for the formulation of every rule. Knowing these reasons, therefore, is a considerable step toward understanding the Federal tax law.

At the outset one should stress that the major objective of the Federal tax law is the raising of revenue. Although the fiscal needs of the government are important, other considerations exist that explain certain portions of the law. Economic, social, equity, and political factors also play a significant role. Added to these factors is the marked impact the Internal Revenue Service and the courts have had and will continue to have on the evolution of Federal tax law. These matters are treated in the first part of this chapter, and wherever appropriate, the discussion is related to subjects covered later in the text.

Revenue Needs

The foundation of any tax system has to be the raising of revenue to absorb the cost of government operations. Ideally, annual outlays should not be expected to exceed anticipated revenues, thereby leading to a balanced budget with no resulting deficit. Many states have achieved this objective by passing laws or constitutional amendments precluding deficit spending. Unfortunately, the Federal government has no such prohibition, and mounting annual deficits have become an increasing concern for many. This concern has had a definite impact on the Federal tax system as evidenced by recent legislation enacted by Congress. The Deficit Reduction Act of 1984, for example, made modest inroads on the deficit by modifying certain income exclusions and deductions and by strengthening penalties for taxpayer noncompliance.

When finalizing the Tax Reform Act (TRA) of 1986, a deficit-conscious Congress was guided by the concept of revenue neutrality which means that the changes made will neither increase nor decrease the net result previously reached under the prior rules. It does not mean that any one taxpayer's tax liability will remain the same, since this would depend upon the circumstances involved. Thus, one taxpayer's increased tax liability could be another's tax saving. Although revenue neutral tax reform does not reduce deficits, at least it does not aggravate the problem.

One can expect budget deficit considerations to play an ever-increasing role in shaping future tax policy. It is not inconceivable, for example, to expect some of the transitional rules provided for in TRA of 1986 to be modified so as to generate additional revenue. Also, any reinstatement of lost taxpayer benefits (e.g., the investment tax credit and favorable treatment for net capital gains) probably will be carried out on a revenue neutral basis.

Economic Considerations

The use of the tax system in an effort to accomplish economic objectives has become increasingly popular in recent years. Generally, this involves utilization of tax legislation to amend the Internal Revenue Code [1] and looks toward measures designed to help control the economy or to encourage certain activities and businesses.

Control of the Economy.   One of the better known provisions of the tax law that purported to aid in controlling the economy was the investment tax credit. By providing a tax credit for investment in qualified property, so the logic went, businesses would be encouraged to expand. The resulting expansion would stimulate the economy and generate additional employment. As a safety valve against overexpansion, the investment tax credit had been suspended for a period of time, repealed, reinstated, expanded, and again repealed.

TRA of 1986 revoked the investment tax credit retroactively for property placed in service after 1985. Purportedly, the repeal was motivated by revenue considerations and the notion that the credit, as then constituted, unduly favored capital-intensive industries over those that were labor-intensive. Probably the main reason for repeal was that the credit, at that time, was not needed to stimulate the economy. Should a downturn in the economy occur in the future, however, no one would be surprised if some form of the credit is restored. Certainly, past history reflects an on-and-off attitude on the part of Congress in using the credit as a means of controlling the economy.

Even if the repeal of the credit proves to be permanent, taxpayers who have claimed past investment tax credits will have to be aware of the recapture rules. Because the credit allowed was based on varying time periods, early disposition of the property will trigger recapture of some or all of the credit previously claimed.

Similar to its use of the investment tax credit, Congress has used depreciation write-offs as a means of controlling the economy. Theoretically, shorter class lives and accelerated methods should encourage additional investment in depreciable property acquired for business use. Conversely, longer class lives and the required use of the straight-line method of depreciation dampens the tax incentive for capital outlays.

Compared to past law, TRA of 1986 generally retrenches on faster write-offs as to property acquired after 1986. Particularly hard hit is most depreciable real estate where class lives have been extended from 19 years to as long as $31\frac{1}{2}$ years and the straight-line method is made mandatory. These changes were made in the interest of revenue neutrality and in the belief that the current economy is stable.

Of more immediate impact on the economy is a change in the tax rate structure. By lowering tax rates, taxpayers are able to obtain additional spendable funds. Generally, TRA of 1986 lowered tax rates for most taxpayers. But with the reduction or elimination of many deductions and credits, lower rates may not lead to lower tax liabilities. Thus, only time will tell what effect the tax rate changes made by TRA of 1986 will have on the economy.

---

1. The Internal Revenue Code is a compilation of Federal tax legislation.

Encouragement of Certain Activities.   Without passing judgment on the wisdom of any such choices, it is quite clear that the tax law does encourage certain types of economic activity or segments of the economy. If, for example, one assumes that technological progress is fostered, the favorable treatment allowed research and development expenditures can be explained. Under the tax law, such expenditures can be deducted in the year incurred or, as an alternative, capitalized and amortized over a period of 60 months or more. In terms of timing the tax saving, such options usually are preferable to a capitalization of the cost with a write-off over the estimated useful life of the asset created.[2]

Recent legislation further recognized the need to stimulate, through the use of the tax laws, technological progress. In addition to the favorable write-off treatment noted above, certain incremental research and development costs now qualify for a 20 percent tax credit.

Example 1   In 1988, T Corporation (a 34% bracket taxpayer) incurs incremental research and development expenditures of $100,000. If the proper election is made, these expenses can be written off in 1988 with a tax saving of $34,000 [$100,000 (expenses incurred) × 34% (applicable tax bracket)]. To this can be added the tax credit of $20,000 [$100,000 (qualifying incremental expenses) × 20%] for an overall tax benefit of $54,000 ($34,000 + $20,000). □

The encouragement of technological progress also can explain why the tax law places the inventor in a special position. Not only can patents qualify as capital assets, but under certain conditions their disposition automatically carries long-term capital gain treatment.[3]

Is it desirable to encourage the conservation of energy resources? Considering the world energy situation and our own reliance on the consumption of foreign oil, the answer to this question has to be in the affirmative. The concern over energy usage was a prime consideration that led to the enactment of legislation to make available to taxpayers various tax savings (in the form of tax credits) for energy conservation expenditures.

Are ecological considerations a desirable objective? If they are, it explains why the tax law permits a 60-month amortization period for costs incurred in the installation of pollution control facilities.

Would it be advantageous to the economy to stimulate the development and rehabilitation of low-income rental housing? The tax law definitely favors these activities, since taxpayers incurring such costs are allowed generous tax credits.

Is saving desirable for the economy? Saving leads to capital formation and thus makes funds available to finance home construction and industrial expansion. The tax law provides incentives to encourage savings through preferential treatment accorded to private retirement plans. Not only are contributions to Keogh (H.R. 10) plans and certain Individual Retirement Accounts (IRAs)

---

2. If the asset developed has no estimated useful life, no write-off would be available without the two options allowed by the tax law.
3. At this point, a long-term capital gain has lost its favorable tax treatment. It would, however, be advantageous if Congress saw fit to restore the net capital gain deduction.

deductible, but income from such contributions accumulates on a tax-free basis. As noted in a following section, the encouragement of private-sector pension plans can be justified under social considerations as well.

Is it wise to stimulate U.S. exports of goods and services abroad? Considering the pressing and continuing problem of a deficit in the U.S. balance of payments, the answer should be clear. Along this line, Congress has created a unique type of organization designed to encourage domestic exports of goods, called Foreign Sales Corporations (FSCs). A portion of the export income from such eligible FSCs is exempt from Federal income taxes. Further, a domestic corporation is allowed a 100 percent dividends received deduction for distributions from an FSC out of earnings attributable to certain foreign trade income. In another international setting, Congress has deemed it advisable to establish incentives for those U.S. citizens who accept employment in overseas locations. Such persons receive generous tax breaks through special treatment of their foreign-source income and certain housing costs.

An item previously mentioned can be connected to the encouragement of U.S. foreign trade. Because one of this country's major exportable products is its technology, can it not be said that the favoritism accorded to research and development expenditures (see above) also serves to foster international trade?

Encouragement of Certain Industries.   No one can question the proposition that a sound agricultural base is necessary for a well-balanced national economy. Undoubtedly this can explain why farmers are accorded special treatment under the Federal tax system. Among these benefits are the election to expense rather than capitalize certain soil and water conservation expenditures and fertilizers and the election to defer the recognition of gain on the receipt of crop insurance proceeds.

The tax law also operates to favor the development of natural resources by permitting the use of percentage depletion on the extraction and sale of oil and gas and specified mineral deposits and a write-off (rather than a capitalization) of certain exploration costs. The railroad and bank industries also are singled out for special tax treatment. All of these provisions can be explained, in whole or in part, by economic considerations.

Encouragement of Small Business.   At least in the United States, a consensus exists that what is good for small business is good for the economy as a whole. This assumption has led to a definite bias in the tax law favoring small business. One provision of the tax law allows a taxpayer to expense (rather than capitalize and depreciate) up to $10,000 of property placed in service each year. Thus, the capital expenditure is recovered immediately as a tax deduction and is not deferred through the depreciation process. The expense option is reduced, however, on a dollar-for-dollar basis for amounts invested in business property in excess of $200,000 per year.

Example 2   During 1988, T, a calendar year taxpayer, acquires $201,000 in machinery and equipment for use in his business. If T so elects, he may expense $9,000 [$10,000 − ($201,000 − $200,000)]. The balance of the cost ($192,000) will have to be capitalized and depreciated. ☐

Clearly, then, the expense option favors small business.

In the corporate tax area, several provisions can be explained by their motivation to benefit small business. One provision, for example, enables a shareholder in a small business corporation to obtain an ordinary deduction for any loss recognized on a stock investment. Normally, such a loss would receive the less attractive capital loss treatment. This apparent favoritism is to encourage additional equity investments in small business corporations.[4] Another provision permits the shareholders of a small business corporation to make a special election that generally will avoid the imposition of the corporate income tax.[5] Furthermore, such an election enables the corporation to pass through to its shareholders any of its operating losses.[6]

The tax rates applicable to corporations tend to favor small business insofar as size is relative to the amount of taxable income generated in any one year. Since the full corporate tax rate of 34 percent applies only to taxable income in excess of $75,000, corporations that stay within this limit are subject to lower average tax rates.

Example 3

For calendar year 1988, X Corporation has taxable income of $75,000 and Y Corporation has taxable income of $100,000. Based on this information, the corporate income tax is $13,750 for X Corporation and $22,250 for Y Corporation (see Chapter 2). By comparison, then, X Corporation is subject to an average tax rate of 18.33% (i.e., $13,750/$75,000), while Y Corporation is subject to an average rate of 22.25% ($22,250/$100,000). □

Furthermore, if a corporation has taxable income in excess of $100,000, the benefits of the lower brackets are phased out until all income is taxed at the maximum rate of 34 percent.

Another provision specifically designed to aid small business involves the LIFO inventory procedures. Simplified procedures are available only to those businesses with average gross receipts of five million dollars or less.

One of the justifications given for the enactment of the tax law governing corporate reorganizations (see Chapter 6) was the economic benefit it would provide for small businesses. By allowing corporations to combine without adverse tax consequences, small corporations would be in a position to compete more effectively with larger concerns.

Social Considerations

Some of the tax laws can be explained by looking to social considerations. This is particularly the case when dealing with the Federal income tax of individuals. Notable examples and the rationale behind each are summarized as follows:

—The nontaxability of certain benefits provided to employees through accident and health plans financed by employers. It would appear socially desir-

---

4. Known as Section 1244 stock, this subject is covered in Chapter 3.
5. Known as the S corporation election, the subject is discussed extensively in Chapter 10.
6. In general, an operating loss can benefit only the corporation incurring the loss through a carryback or carryover to profitable years. Consequently, the shareholders of the corporation usually cannot take advantage of any such loss.

able to encourage such plans, since they provide medical benefits in the event of an employee's illness or injury.

—The nontaxability to the employee of some of the premiums paid by an employer for group term insurance covering the life of the employee. These arrangements can be justified in that they provide funds for the family unit to help it readjust following the loss of wages caused by the employee's death.

—The tax treatment to the employee of contributions made by an employer to qualified pension or profit sharing plans. The contribution and any income it generates will not be taxed to the employee until the funds are distributed. Private retirement plans should be encouraged, since they supplement the subsistence income level the employee otherwise would have under the Social Security system.[7]

—The deduction allowed for contributions to qualified charitable organizations. The deduction attempts to shift some of the financial and administrative burden of socially desirable programs from the public (the government) to the private (the citizens) sector.

—The credit allowed for amounts spent to furnish care for certain minor or disabled dependents to enable the taxpayer to seek or maintain gainful employment. Who could deny the social desirability of encouraging taxpayers to provide care for their children while they work?

—The disallowance of a tax deduction for certain expenditures that are deemed to be contrary to public policy. This disallowance extends to such items as fines, penalties, illegal kickbacks, and bribes to government officials. Public policy considerations have also been used to disallow gambling losses in excess of gambling gains and political campaign expenditures in excess of campaign contributions. Social considerations dictate that these activities should not be encouraged by the tax law. Permitting the deduction would supposedly encourage the activities.

—The imposition of the Federal estate tax on large estates. From one viewpoint, it would be socially undesirable to permit large accumulations of wealth to pass by death from generation to generation without being subject to some type of transfer tax.[8]

Many other examples could be included, but the conclusion would be unchanged: Social considerations do explain a significant part of the Federal tax law.

Equity Considerations

The concept of equity is, of course, relative. Reasonable persons can, and often do, disagree about what is fair or unfair. In the tax area, moreover, equity is most often tied to a particular taxpayer's personal situation. To illustrate, it

---

7. The same rationale explains the availability of similar arrangements for self-employed persons (the H.R. 10, or Keogh, plan).
8. Portions of Chapter 11 are devoted to procedures that formerly permitted taxpayers to pass wealth from one generation to another with minimal tax consequences.

may be difficult for Ms. Jones to understand why none of the rent she pays on her apartment is deductible when her brother, Mr. Jones, is able to deduct a large portion of the monthly payments he makes on his personal residence in the form of interest and taxes.[9]

In the same vein, compare the tax treatment of a corporation with that of a partnership. Although the two businesses may be of equal size, similarly situated, and competitors in the production of goods or services, they are not comparably treated under the tax law. The corporation is subject to a separate Federal income tax; the partnership is not. Whether the differences in tax treatment logically can be justified in terms of equity is beside the point. The point is that the tax law can and does make a distinction between these business forms.

Equity, then, is not what appears fair or unfair to any one taxpayer or group of taxpayers. It is, instead, what the tax law recognizes. Some recognition of equity does exist, however, and offers an explanation of part of the law. The concept of equity appears in tax provisions that alleviate the effect of multiple taxation, postpone the recognition of gain when the taxpayer lacks the ability or wherewithal to pay the tax, mitigate the effect of the application of the annual accounting period concept, and help taxpayers to cope with the eroding result of inflation.

Alleviating the Effect of Multiple Taxation. The same income earned by a taxpayer may be subject to taxes imposed by different taxing authorities. If, for example, the taxpayer is a resident of New York City, income might generate Federal, State of New York, and City of New York income taxes. To compensate for this apparent inequity, the Federal tax law allows a taxpayer to claim a deduction for state and local income taxes. The deduction, however, does not neutralize the effect of multiple taxation, since the benefit derived depends on the taxpayer's Federal income tax bracket.[10]

Equity considerations can explain the Federal tax treatment of certain income from foreign sources. Since double taxation results when the same income is subject to both foreign and U.S. income taxes, the tax law permits the taxpayer to choose either a credit or a deduction for the foreign taxes paid.

The imposition of a separate income tax on corporations also leads to multiple taxation of the same income.

Example 4   During the current year M Corporation has net income of $100,000, of which $5,000 was received as dividends from stock it owns in Xerox Corporation. Assume M Corporation distributes the after-tax income to its shareholders (all individuals). At a minimum, the distribution received by the shareholders will be subject to two income taxes: the corporate income tax when the income is earned by M Corporation and the individual income tax when the balance is distributed to the shareholders as a dividend. The $5,000 M Corporation receives from Xerox Corporation

---

9. The encouragement of home ownership can be justified both on economic and social grounds. In this regard, it is interesting to note that some state income tax laws allow a form of relief (e.g., tax credit) to the taxpayer who rents his or her personal residence.
10. A tax credit, rather than a deduction, would eliminate the effects of multiple taxation on the same income.

fares even worse. Because it is paid from income earned by Xerox Corporation, it has been subjected to a third income tax (i.e., the corporate income tax imposed on Xerox Corporation).[11] ☐

For corporate shareholders, for whom triple taxation is possible, the law provides a deduction for dividends received from certain domestic corporations. The deduction, usually 70 percent of the dividends, would be allowed to M Corporation for the $5,000 it received from Xerox Corporation. (See the discussion in Chapter 2.)

In the area of the Federal estate tax, several provisions reflect attempts through the law to compensate for the effect of multiple taxation. Some degree of equity is achieved, for example, by allowing a limited credit against the estate tax for foreign death taxes imposed on the same transfer. Other estate tax credits are available and can be explained on the same grounds.[12]

The Wherewithal to Pay Concept.   Quite simply, the wherewithal to pay concept recognizes the inequity of taxing a transaction when the taxpayer lacks the means with which to pay the tax. It is particularly suited to situations when the taxpayer's economic position has not changed significantly as a result of a transaction.

Example 5   T Corporation holds unimproved land held as an investment. The land has a basis to T Corporation of $60,000 and a fair market value of $100,000. The land is exchanged for a building (worth $100,000) that the corporation will use in its business.[13] ☐

Example 6   T Corporation owns a warehouse that it uses in its business. At a time when the warehouse has an adjusted basis of $60,000, it is destroyed by fire. T Corporation collects the insurance proceeds of $100,000 and, within two years of the end of the year in which the fire occurred, uses all of the proceeds to purchase a new warehouse.[14] ☐

Example 7   T, a sole proprietor, decides to incorporate his business. In exchange for the business's assets (adjusted basis of $60,000 and a fair market value of $100,000), T receives all of the stock of X Corporation, a newly created corporation.[15]   The X Corporation stock is worth $100,000. ☐

Example 8   R, S, and T want to develop unimproved land owned by T. The land has a basis to T of $60,000 and a fair market value of $100,000. The RST Partnership is formed with the following investment: land worth $100,000 trans-

---

11. The result materializes because the tax law permits no deduction to a corporation for the dividend distributions it makes. See Chapter 2.
12. See Chapter 11.
13. The nontaxability of like-kind exchanges applies to the exchange of property held for investment or used in a trade or business for property to be similarly held or used.
14. The nontaxability of gains realized from involuntary conversions applies when the proceeds received by the taxpayer are reinvested within a prescribed period of time in property similar or related in service or use to that converted. Involuntary conversions take place as a result of casualty losses, theft losses, and condemnations by a public authority.
15. Transfers of property to controlled corporations are discussed in Chapter 3.

ferred by T, $100,000 cash by R, and $100,000 cash by S. Each party receives a one-third interest in the RST Partnership.[16] ☐

Example 9   A Corporation and B Corporation decide to consolidate to form C Corporation.[17] Pursuant to the plan of reorganization, T exchanges her stock in A Corporation (basis of $60,000 and fair market value of $100,000) for stock in C Corporation worth $100,000. ☐

In all of the preceding examples, either T Corporation or T had a realized gain of $40,000 [i.e., $100,000 (fair market value of the property received) − $60,000 (basis of the property given up)].[18] It would seem inequitable to force the taxpayer to recognize any of this gain for two reasons. First, without disposing of the property or interest acquired, the taxpayer would be hard-pressed to pay the tax.[19] Second, the taxpayer's economic situation has not changed significantly. To illustrate by referring to Example 7, can it be said that T's position as sole shareholder of X Corporation is much different from his prior status as owner of a sole proprietorship?

Several warnings are in order concerning the application of the wherewithal to pay concept. Recognized gain is merely postponed and not necessarily avoided. Because of the basis carryover to the new property or interest acquired in these nontaxable transactions, the gain element is still present and might be recognized upon a subsequent taxable disposition of the property. Referring to Example 7, suppose T later sold the stock in X Corporation for $100,000. Because T's basis in the stock is $60,000 (the same basis as in the assets transferred), the sale results in a recognized gain of $40,000. Also, many of the provisions previously illustrated prevent the recognition of realized losses. Since such provisions are automatic in application (i.e., not elective with the taxpayer), they could operate to the detriment of a taxpayer who wishes to obtain a deduction for a loss. The notable exception deals with involuntary conversions (Example 6). Here, nonrecognition treatment is elective with the taxpayer and will not apply to a realized loss if it is otherwise deductible.

One last comment about the wherewithal to pay concept is in order. Although it has definitely served as a guideline in shaping part of the tax law, it is not a hard and fast principle that is followed in every case. Only when the tax law specifically provides for no tax consequences will this result materialize.

Example 10   T exchanges stock in A Corporation (basis of $60,000 and fair market value of $100,000) for stock in B Corporation (fair market value of $100,000). The exchange is not pursuant to a reorganization. Under these

---

16. The formation of a partnership is discussed in Chapter 8.
17. Corporate reorganizations are discussed in Chapter 6.
18. Realized gain can be likened to economic gain. However, the Federal income tax is imposed only on that portion of realized gain considered to be recognized under the law. Generally, recognized (or taxable) gain can never exceed realized gain.
19. If the taxpayer ends up with other property (boot) as part of the transfer, gain may be recognized to this extent. The presence of boot, however, helps solve the wherewithal to pay problem, since it provides property (other than the property or interest central to the transaction) with which to pay the tax.

circumstances, T's realized gain of $40,000 is recognized for Federal income tax purposes.[20] ☐

The result reached in Example 10 seems harsh in that the exchange does not place T in a position to pay the tax on the $40,000 gain. How can this result be reconciled with that reached in Example 9 when the exchange was nontaxable? In other words, why does the tax law apply the wherewithal to pay concept to the exchange of stock pursuant to a corporate reorganization (Example 9) but not to certain other stock exchanges (Example 10)?

Recall that the wherewithal to pay concept is particularly suited to situations in which the taxpayer's economic position has not changed significantly as a result of a transaction. In Example 9, T's stock investment in A Corporation really continues in the form of the C Corporation stock, since C was formed through a consolidation of A and B Corporations.[21] However, continuation of investment is not the case in Example 10. Here T's ownership in A Corporation has ceased, and an investment in an entirely different corporation has been substituted.

Mitigating the Effect of the Annual Accounting Period Concept.   For purposes of effective administration of the tax law, it is necessary for all taxpayers to report to and settle with the Federal government at periodic intervals. Otherwise, taxpayers would remain uncertain as to their tax liabilities, and the government would have difficulty judging revenues and budgeting expenditures. The period selected for final settlement of most tax liabilities, in any event an arbitrary determination, is one year. At the close of each year, therefore, a taxpayer's position becomes complete for that particular year. Referred to as the annual accounting period concept, its effect is to divide, for tax purposes, each taxpayer's life into equal annual intervals.

The finality of the annual accounting period concept could lead to dissimilarity in tax treatment for taxpayers who are, from a long-range standpoint, in the same economic position.

Example 11   R and S are two sole proprietors and have experienced the following results during the past four years:

	Profit (or Loss)	
Year	R	S
1985	$50,000	$150,000
1986	60,000	60,000
1987	70,000	70,000
1988	50,000	(50,000)

Although R and S have the same profit of $230,000 over the period from 1985–1988, the finality of the annual accounting period concept places S at

20. The exchange of stock does not qualify for nontaxable treatment as a like-kind exchange (refer to Example 5).
21. This continuation is known as the continuity of interest concept. It forms the foundation for all nontaxable corporate reorganizations. The concept is discussed at length in Chapter 6.

a definite disadvantage for tax purposes. The net operating loss procedure offers S some relief by allowing him to apply some or all of his 1988
loss to the earliest profitable years (in this case 1985). Thus, S would be in
a position with a net operating loss carryback to obtain a refund for some
of the taxes he paid on the $150,000 profit reported for 1985. ☐

The same reasoning used to support net operating losses can be applied to
explain the special treatment accorded by the tax law to excess capital losses
and excess charitable contributions. Carryback and carryover procedures help
mitigate the effect of limiting a loss or a deduction to the accounting period in
which it is realized. With such procedures, a taxpayer may be able to salvage a
loss or a deduction that might otherwise be wasted.

The installment method of recognizing gain on the sale of property allows a
taxpayer to spread tax consequences over the payout period.[22]   The harsh
effect of taxing all the gain in the year of sale is thereby avoided. The installment method can also be explained by the wherewithal to pay concept, since
recognition of gain is tied to the collection of the installment notes received
from the sale of the property. Tax consequences, then, tend to correspond to
the seller's ability to pay the tax.

Example 12   In 1986, T sold unimproved real estate (cost of $40,000) for $100,000. Under
the terms of the sale, T receives two notes from the purchaser, each for
$50,000 (plus interest). One note is payable in 1987 and the other note in
1988. Without the installment method, T would have to recognize and pay
a tax on the gain of $60,000 for the year of the sale (i.e., 1986). This is a
rather harsh result, since none of the sale proceeds will be received until
1987 and 1988. With the installment method, and presuming the notes are
paid when each comes due, T recognizes half of the gain (i.e., $30,000) in
1987 and the remaining half in 1988. ☐

The annual accounting period concept also has been modified to apply to
situations in which taxpayers may have difficulty in accurately assessing their
tax positions by year-end. In many such cases, the law permits taxpayers to
treat transactions taking place in the next year as having occurred in the prior
year.

Example 13   T, a calendar year individual taxpayer, is a participant in an H.R. 10
(Keogh) retirement plan. (See Appendix C for a definition of a Keogh
plan.) Under the plan, T contributes 20% of her net self-employment
income, such amount being deductible for Federal income tax purposes.
On April 10, 1988, T determines that her net self-employment income for
calendar year 1987 was $80,000, and consequently, she contributes
$16,000 (20% × $80,000) to the plan. Even though the $16,000 contribution
was made in 1988, the law permits T to claim it as a deduction for tax
year 1987. Requiring T to make the contribution by December 31, 1987, in
order to obtain the deduction for that year would place the burden on her

22. Under the installment method, each payment received by the seller represents a return of basis
(the nontaxable portion) and profit from the sale (the taxable portion).

of arriving at an accurate determination of net self-employment income long before her income tax return needs to be prepared and filed. □

Similar exceptions to the annual accounting period concept cover certain charitable contributions by accrual basis corporations (Chapter 2), dividend distributions by S corporations (Chapter 10), and the dividend deduction allowed in applying the tax on unreasonable accumulation of corporate earnings and the tax on personal holding companies (Chapter 7).

Coping with Inflation.   During periods of inflation, bracket creep has plagued the working person. Because of the progressive nature of the income tax, any wage adjustment to compensate for inflation can increase the income tax bracket of the recipient. The overall impact is an erosion of purchasing power. Congress recognized this problem and began to adjust various income tax components (the indexation procedure) in 1985, based upon the rise in the consumer price index over the prior year. For example, because of the inflation factor, the amount of a personal and dependency exemption, previously set at $1,000, was raised to $1,040 for 1985 and to $1,080 for 1986.

Because TRA of 1986 significantly raised the amount of each exemption and the standard deduction (previously the zero bracket amount) and lowered the tax rates, the indexation procedure has been temporarily suspended. However, indexation is scheduled to resume beginning in 1990 as to personal and dependency exemptions and beginning in 1989 as to dollar amounts of the tax brackets and the standard deduction.

Political Considerations

A large segment of the Federal tax law is made up of statutory provisions. Since these statutes are enacted by Congress, is it any surprise that political considerations do influence tax law? For purposes of discussion, the effect of political considerations on the tax law is divided into the following topics: special interest legislation, political expediency, and state and local influences.

Special Interest Legislation.   There is no doubt that certain provisions of the tax law can be explained largely by looking to the political influence some pressure groups have exerted on Congress. Is there any other reason why, for example, prepaid subscription and dues income are not taxed until earned while prepaid rents are taxed to the landlord in the year received?

Along the same line are those tax provisions sponsored by individual members of Congress for the obvious benefit of a constituent. TRA of 1986 is replete with special interest legislation, an example of which would have allowed a charitable deduction for contributions to institutions of higher learning even though the contributor, because of the donation, is entitled to special seating at athletic events. However, the institution must have been mandated by a state constitution in 1876, established by a state legislature in March 1881, and located in a state capital pursuant to a statewide election held in September 1881; must have a campus that was formally opened on September 15, 1883; and must be operated under the authority of a nine-member board of regents appointed by the governor. Needless to say, only one such institution exists that meets these requirements.

Special interest legislation is not necessarily to be condemned if it can be justified on economic or social grounds. At any rate, it is an inevitable product of our political system.

Political Expediency. Various tax reform proposals rise and fall in favor, depending upon the shifting moods of the American public. That Congress is sensitive to popular feeling is an accepted fact. Therefore, certain provisions of the tax law can be explained on the basis of political necessity existing at the time of enactment. Once the general public became aware that certain large and profitable corporations were able to avoid the corporate income tax, Congress responded in TRA of 1986 with a new alternative minimum tax. By making a portion of a corporation's pretax book income a tax preference item, many such corporations no longer will escape taxation (see Chapter 2).

Measures that deter more affluent taxpayers from obtaining so-called preferential tax treatment have always had popular appeal and, consequently, the support of Congress. Provisions such as the alternative minimum tax, the imputed interest rules, and the limitation on the deductibility of interest on investment indebtedness can be explained on this basis. In the same vein are the provisions imposing penalty taxes on corporations that unreasonably accumulate earnings or that are classified as personal holding companies (see Chapter 7).

Other changes partially founded on the basis of political expediency include lowering individual income tax rates, increasing the amount of the dependency exemption, and increasing the earned income credit.

State and Local Influences. Political considerations have played a major role in the exclusion from gross income of interest received on state and local obligations. In view of the furor that has been raised by state and local political figures every time any kind of modification of this tax provision has been proposed, one might well regard it as sacred.

Somewhat less apparent has been the influence state law has had in shaping our present Federal tax law. Of prime importance in this regard has been the effect of the community property system employed in nine states.[23] At one time, the tax position of the residents of these states was so advantageous that many common law states actually adopted community property systems.[24] Needless to say, the political pressure placed on Congress to correct the disparity in tax treatment was considerable. To a large extent, this was accomplished in the Revenue Act of 1948, which extended many of the community

---

23. The states with community property systems are Louisiana, Texas, New Mexico, Arizona, California, Washington, Idaho, Nevada, and Wisconsin (effective January 1, 1986). The rest of the states are classified as common law jurisdictions. The difference between common law and community property systems centers around the property rights possessed by married persons. In a common law system, each spouse owns whatever he or she earns. Under a community property system, one half of the earnings of each spouse is considered owned by the other spouse. Assume, for example, H and W are husband and wife and their only income is the $40,000 annual salary H receives. If they live in New York (a common law state), the $40,000 salary belongs to H. If, however, they live in Texas (a community property state), the $40,000 salary is divided equally, in terms of ownership, between H and W.
24. Such states included Michigan, Oklahoma, and Pennsylvania.

property tax advantages to residents of common law jurisdictions.[25]   Thus, common law states avoided the trauma of discarding the time-honored legal system familiar to everyone. The impact of community property law on the Federal estate and gift taxes is further explored in Chapters 11 and 12.

Influence of the Internal Revenue Service

The influence of the IRS is recognized in many areas beyond its obvious role in the issuance of the administrative pronouncements that make up a considerable portion of our tax law. In its capacity as the protector of the national revenue, the IRS has been instrumental in securing the passage of much legislation designed to curtail the most flagrant tax avoidance practices (to close tax loopholes). In its capacity as the administrator of the tax laws, the IRS has sought and obtained legislation to make its job easier (to attain administrative feasibility).

The IRS as Protector of the Revenue.   Innumerable examples can be given of provisions in the tax law that stemmed from the direct influence of the IRS when it was applied to preclude the use of a loophole as a means of avoiding the tax consequences intended by Congress. Working within the letter of existing law, ingenious taxpayers and their advisers devise techniques that accomplish indirectly what cannot be accomplished directly. As a consequence, legislation is enacted to close the loophole that taxpayers have located and exploited. The following summarizes some tax law that can be explained in this fashion and that is discussed in the chapters to follow:

—The use of a fiscal year by personal service corporations, partnerships, S corporations, and trusts to defer income recognition to the owners (see Chapters 2, 8, 10, and 13).

—The use of the cash basis method of accounting by certain large corporations (see Chapter 2).

—The deduction of passive investment losses and expenses against other income (see Chapter 9).

—The shifting of income to lower bracket taxpayers through the use of reversionary trusts (see Chapter 13).

In addition, the IRS has secured from Congress legislation of a more general nature that enables it to make adjustments based upon the substance, rather than the formal construction, of what a taxpayer has done. One provision, for example, authorizes the IRS to establish guidelines on the thin capitalization issue—when will corporate debt be recognized as debt for tax purposes, and when will it be reclassified as equity or stock (see the discussion of thin capitalization in Chapter 3). Another provision permits the IRS to make adjust-

---

25. The major advantage extended was the provision allowing married taxpayers to file joint returns and compute the tax liability as if the income had been earned one-half by each spouse. This result is automatic in a community property state, since half of the income earned by one spouse belongs to the other spouse. The income-splitting benefits of a joint return are now incorporated as part of the tax rates applicable to married taxpayers.

ments to a taxpayer's method of accounting when the method used by the taxpayer does not clearly reflect income. The IRS also has been granted the authority to allocate income and deductions among businesses owned or controlled by the same interests when the allocation is necessary to prevent the evasion of taxes or to clearly reflect the income of each business.

Example 14   X Corporation and Y Corporation are brother-sister corporations (i.e., the stock of each is owned by the same shareholders), and both use the calendar year for tax purposes. For tax year 1988, each has taxable income as follows: $335,000 for X Corporation and $50,000 for Y Corporation. Not included in X Corporation's taxable income, however, is $10,000 of rent income usually charged Y Corporation for the use of some property owned by X Corporation. Since the parties have not clearly reflected the taxable income of each business, the IRS can allocate $10,000 of rent income to X Corporation. After the allocation, X Corporation has taxable income of $345,000 and Y Corporation has taxable income of $40,000.[26] □

Also of a general nature is the authority Congress has given the IRS to prevent taxpayers from acquiring corporations to obtain a tax advantage when the principal purpose of such acquisition was the evasion or avoidance of the Federal income tax. The provision of the tax law that provides this authority is discussed briefly in Chapter 6.

Administrative Feasibility.   Some of the tax law is justified on the grounds that it simplifies the task of the IRS in collecting the revenue and administering the law. With regard to collecting the revenue, the IRS long ago realized the importance of placing taxpayers on a pay-as-you-go basis. Elaborate withholding procedures apply to wages, while the tax on other types of income may have to be paid at periodic intervals throughout the year. The IRS has been instrumental in convincing the courts that accrual basis taxpayers should pay taxes on prepaid income in the year received and not when earned. The approach may be contrary to generally accepted accounting principles, but it is consistent with the wherewithal to pay concept.

Of considerable aid to the IRS in collecting revenue are the numerous provisions that impose interest and penalties on taxpayers for noncompliance with the tax law. Provisions such as the penalties for failure to pay a tax or to file a return that is due, the negligence penalty for intentional disregard of rules and regulations, and various penalties for civil and criminal fraud serve as deterrents to taxpayer noncompliance. This aspect of the tax law is discussed in Chapter 14.

One of the keys to an effective administration of our tax system is the audit process conducted by the IRS. To carry out this function, the IRS is aided by provisions that reduce the chance of taxpayer error or manipulation and therefore simplify the audit effort that is necessary. An increase in the amount of the standard deduction, for example, reduces the number of individual taxpayers

26. By shifting $10,000 of income to X Corporation (which is in the 34% bracket), the IRS gains $3,400 in taxes. Allowing the $10,000 deduction to Y Corporation (which is in the 15% bracket) costs the IRS only $1,500. See Chapter 2 for a further discussion of the income tax rates applicable to corporations.

who will be in a position of claiming itemized deductions. With fewer deductions to check, therefore, the audit function is simplified.[27] The same objective can be used to explain the $192,800 unified estate and gift tax credit in 1987 and thereafter and the $10,000 annual gift tax exclusion (see Chapter 11). These provisions decrease the number of tax returns that must be filed (as well as reduce the taxes paid) and thereby save audit effort.[28]

The audit function of the IRS has been simplified by provisions of the tax law dealing with the burden of proof. Suppose, for example, the IRS audits a taxpayer and questions a particular deduction. Who has the burden of proving the propriety of the deduction? Except in the case of fraud (see Chapter 14), the burden is always on the taxpayer.

Influence of the Courts

In addition to interpreting statutory provisions and the administrative pronouncements issued by the IRS, the Federal courts have influenced tax law in two other respects.[29] First, the courts have formulated certain judicial concepts that serve as guides in the application of various tax provisions. Second, certain key decisions have led to changes in the Internal Revenue Code. Understanding this influence helps to explain some of our tax law.

Judicial Concepts Relating to Tax Law.   It is difficult to rank the tax concepts developed by the courts in order of importance. If this were done, however, one must place near the top of the list the concept of substance over form. Variously described as the "telescoping" or "collapsing" process or the "step transaction approach," it involves determining the true substance of what occurred. In a transaction involving many steps, any one step may be collapsed (or disregarded) to arrive directly at the result reached.

Example 15   In 1988, Mrs. G, a widow, wants to give $20,000 to S without incurring any gift tax liability.[30] She knows that the law permits her to give up to $10,000 each year per person without any tax consequences (the annual exclusion). With this in mind, the following steps are taken: a gift by Mrs. G to S of $10,000 (nontaxable because of the $10,000 annual exclusion), a gift by Mrs. G to B of $10,000 (also nontaxable), and a gift by B to S of $10,000 (nontaxable because of B's annual exclusion). Regarding only the form of what Mrs. G and B have done, all appears well from a tax standpoint. In substance, however, what has happened? By collapsing the steps involving B, it is apparent that Mrs. G has made a gift of $20,000 to S and therefore has not avoided the Federal gift tax. □

---

27. The same justification was given by the IRS when it proposed to Congress the $100 per event limitation on personal casualty and theft losses. Imposition of the limitation eliminated many casualty and theft loss deductions and, as a consequence, saved the IRS considerable audit time. Also, an additional limitation equal to 10% of adjusted gross income applies to the total of nonbusiness losses after reduction by the floor of $100 for each loss.
28. Particularly in the case of nominal gifts among family members, taxpayer compliance in reporting and paying a tax on such transfers would be questionable. The absence of the $10,000 gift tax exclusion would therefore create a serious enforcement problem for the IRS.
29. A great deal of case law is devoted to ascertaining Congressional intent. The courts, in effect, ask: What did Congress have in mind when it enacted a particular tax provision?
30. The example assumes that Mrs. G has exhausted her unified tax credit. See Chapter 11.

The substance over form concept plays an important role in transactions involving corporations. The liquidation-reincorporation problem, discussed in Chapter 6, is an ideal example of its possible application.

Another leading tax concept developed by the courts deals with the interpretation of statutory tax provisions that operate to benefit taxpayers. The courts have established the rule that these relief provisions are to be narrowly construed against taxpayers if there is any doubt about their application. Suppose, for example, X Corporation wants to be treated as an S corporation (see Chapter 10) but has not literally satisfied the statutory requirements for making the required election. Because S corporation status is a relief provision favoring taxpayers, chances are the courts will deny X Corporation this treatment.

Important in the area of corporate-shareholder dealings (see the discussion of constructive dividends in Chapter 4) and in the resolution of valuation problems for estate and gift tax purposes (see Chapter 12) is the arm's length concept. Particularly in dealings between related parties, transactions can be tested by questioning whether the taxpayers acted in an "arm's length" manner. The question to be asked is: Would unrelated parties have handled the transaction in the same way?

Example 16   The sole shareholder of a corporation leases property to the corporation for a monthly rental of $50,000. To test whether the corporation should be allowed a rent deduction for this amount, the IRS and the courts will apply the arm's length concept. Would the corporation have paid $50,000 a month in rent if the same property had been leased from an unrelated party (rather than from the sole shareholder)? □

The continuity of interest concept originated with the courts but has, in many situations, been incorporated into statutory provisions of the tax law. Primarily concerned with business readjustments, the concept permits tax-free treatment only if the taxpayer retains a substantial continuing interest in the property transferred to the new business. Because of the continuing interest retained, tax consequences should not result from the transfer, because the position of the taxpayer has not changed. This concept applies to transfers to controlled corporations (Chapter 3), corporate reorganizations (Chapter 6), and transfers to partnerships (Chapter 8). The continuity of interest concept helps explain the results reached in Examples 7 through 9 of this chapter. This concept is further discussed in Chapter 6.

Also developed by the courts, the business purpose concept has principal application to transactions involving corporations. Under this concept, some sound business reason must be present that motivates the transaction in order for the prescribed tax treatment to ensue. The avoidance of taxation is not considered to be a sound business purpose.

Example 17   B and C are equal shareholders in X Corporation. They have recently had a disagreement and have therefore reached an impasse on how the future operations of X Corporation are to be conducted. This shareholder disagreement on corporate policy constitutes a sound business purpose and would justify a division of X Corporation in a way that will permit B and C to go their separate ways. Whether or not the division of X Corporation would be nontaxable to the parties involved would depend on compliance with the applicable statutory provisions dealing with corporate reorganizations. The point is, however, that compliance with statutory provisions would not be enough to insure nontaxability without a business purpose for the transaction. ☐

The business purpose concept is discussed further in Chapter 6.

Judicial Influence on Statutory Provisions.   Some court decisions have been of such consequence that Congress has incorporated them into statutory tax law. One illustration of this influence appears in Example 18.

Example 18   In 1980, T claimed a capital loss of $100,000 for Z Corporation stock that had become worthless during the year. Because of the absence of any offsetting gains, the capital loss deduction produced no income tax savings for T either in 1980 or in future years. In 1985, T institutes a lawsuit against the former officers of Z Corporation for their misconduct that resulted in the corporation's failure and thereby led to T's $100,000 loss. In settlement of the suit, the officers pay $50,000 to T. The IRS argued that the full $50,000 should be taxed as gain to T. Because the stock in Z Corporation was written off in 1980, it had a zero basis for tax purposes. The $50,000 recovery received by T on the stock was, therefore, all gain. Although the position of the IRS was logical, it was not equitable. The court stated that T should not be taxed on the recovery of an amount previously deducted unless the deduction produced a tax savings. Since the $100,000 capital loss deduction in 1980 produced no tax benefit, none of the $50,000 received in 1985 results in gain. ☐

The decision reached by the courts in Example 18, known as the tax benefit rule, is part of the statutory tax law. The tax benefit rule is discussed later in connection with transfers to controlled corporations (Chapter 3).

Court decisions sometimes produce uncertainty in the tax law. Although such decisions may reach the right result, they do not produce the guidelines necessary to enable taxpayers to comply. In many situations, then, Congress may be compelled to add certainty to the law by enacting statutory provisions specifying when a particular tax consequence will or will not materialize. Illustrations of this type of judicial "cause" and the statutory "effect" are as follows:

—When a stock redemption will be treated as an exchange or as a dividend (see Chapter 4).

—Whether the liquidating corporation, in substance, made the sale of property distributed to its shareholders (see Chapter 5).

—What basis a parent corporation will have in the assets received from a subsidiary that is liquidated shortly after its acquisition (see Chapter 5).

Some of the statutory provisions can be explained by the negative effect a particular court decision has had on Congress. In one decision, for example, it was held that the transfer of a liability to a controlled corporation should be treated as boot received by the transferor (see Chapter 3). Congress apparently disagreed with this treatment and promptly enacted legislation to change the result.

Summary

In addition to its obvious revenue-raising objective, the Federal tax law has developed in response to several other factors:

—*Economic considerations.* Here, the emphasis is on tax provisions that help regulate the economy and encourage certain activities and types of businesses.

—*Social considerations.* Some tax provisions are designed to encourage or discourage certain socially desirable or undesirable practices.

—*Equity considerations.* Of principal concern in this area are tax provisions that alleviate the effect of multiple taxation, recognize the wherewithal to pay concept, mitigate the effect of the annual accounting period concept, and recognize the eroding effect of inflation.

—*Political considerations.* Of significance in this regard are tax provisions that represent special interest legislation, reflect political expediency, and illustrate the effect of state law.

—*Influence of the IRS.* Many tax provisions are intended to aid the IRS in the collection of the revenue and in the administration of the tax law.

—*Influence of the Courts.* Court decisions have established a body of judicial concepts relating to tax law and have, on occasion, led Congress to enact statutory provisions to either clarify or negate their effect.

These factors explain various tax provisions and thereby help in understanding why the tax law developed to its present state. The next step involves learning to work with the tax law.

Working with the Tax Law— Tax Sources

Learning to work with the tax law involves the following three basic steps:

1. Familiarity with the sources of the law.
2. Application of research techniques.
3. Effective use of planning procedures.

Statutory, administrative, and judicial sources of the tax law are considered first.

Statutory Sources of the Tax Law

Origin of the Internal Revenue Code.   Before 1939, the statutory provisions relating to tax were contained in the individual revenue acts enacted by Congress. Because of the inconvenience and confusion that resulted from dealing with many separate acts, in 1939, Congress codified all of the Federal tax laws. Known as the Internal Revenue Code of 1939, the codification arranged all Federal tax provisions in a logical sequence and placed them in a separate part of the Federal statutes. A further rearrangement took place in 1954 and resulted in the Internal Revenue Code of 1954.

Perhaps to emphasize the magnitude of the changes made by TRA of 1986, Congress has redesignated the Internal Revenue Code of 1954 as the Internal Revenue Code of 1986. This is somewhat deceiving, since a recodification of the tax law, as was true in 1954, did not take place. TRA of 1986 merely amends, deletes, or adds provisions to what was the Internal Revenue Code of 1954. For example, before TRA of 1986, § 336 provided the general rule that no gain or loss would be recognized by a corporation when it distributed assets in kind to its shareholders in complete liquidation (see Chapter 5). After the effective date of TRA of 1986, § 336 provides that gain or loss will be recognized upon the same distributions.

The following observations will help clarify the significance of the three Codes:

—Neither the 1939, the 1954, nor the 1986 Code changed all of the tax law existing on the date of enactment. Much of the 1939 Code, for example, was incorporated into the 1954 Code. The same can be said for the transition from the 1954 to the 1986 Code. This point is important in assessing judicial and administrative decisions interpreting provisions under prior Codes. For example, a decision interpreting § 121 of the Internal Revenue Code of 1954 will have continuing validity, since this provision is carried over unchanged to the Internal Revenue Code of 1986.

—Statutory amendments to the tax law are integrated into the existing Code. Thus, any future tax legislation will become part of the Internal Revenue Code of 1986.

The Legislative Process.   Federal tax legislation generally originates in the House of Representatives, where it is first considered by the House Ways and Means Committee. Tax bills originate in the Senate when they are attached as riders to other legislative proposals.[31] If acceptable to the House Ways and Means Committee, the proposed bill is referred to the entire House of Representatives for approval or disapproval. Approved bills are sent to the Senate, where they are referred to the Senate Finance Committee for further consideration.

Disagreement is frequently the case with major tax bills. One factor contributing to a different Senate version is the latitude each individual senator has to make amendments to a bill when the Senate as a whole is voting on a bill referred to it by the Senate Finance Committee. Less latitude is allowed in

---

31. The Tax Equity and Fiscal Responsibility Act of 1982 originated in the Senate; its constitutionality was unsuccessfully challenged in the courts. The Senate version of the Deficit Reduction Act of 1984 was attached as an amendment to the Federal Boat Safety Act.

the House of Representatives. Thus, the entire House either accepts or rejects what is proposed by the House Ways and Means Committee, and changes from the floor are not commonplace. The result of the Joint Conference Committee, usually a compromise of the two versions, is then voted on by both the House and the Senate. Acceptance by both bodies precedes referral to the President for approval or veto.

The typical legislative process dealing with tax bills is summarized as follows:

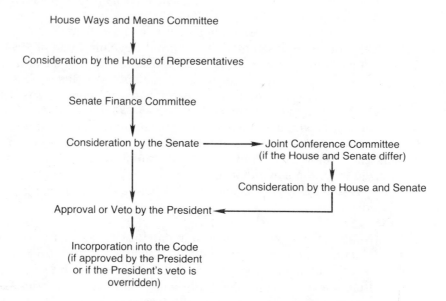

Some tax provisions are commonly referred to by the number of the bill designated in the House when first proposed or by the name of the member of Congress sponsoring the legislation. For example, the Self-Employed Individuals Tax Retirement Act of 1962 is popularly known as H.R. 10 (i.e., the House of Representatives Bill No. 10) or as the Keogh Act (i.e., Keogh being one of the members of Congress sponsoring the bill).

The next step in the legislative process involves referral from the Senate Finance Committee to the whole Senate. Assuming no disagreement between the House and the Senate, passage by the Senate means referral to the President for approval or veto. If the bill is approved or if the President's veto is overridden, the bill becomes law and part of the Internal Revenue Code.

When the Senate version of the bill differs from that passed by the House, the Joint Conference Committee, which includes members of both the House Ways and Means Committee and the Senate Finance Committee, is called upon to resolve these differences.

Referrals from the House Ways and Means Committee, the Senate Finance Committee, and the Joint Conference Committee are usually accompanied by Committee Reports. Because these Committee Reports often explain the provisions of the proposed legislation, they are a valuable source in ascertaining the intent of Congress. What Congress has in mind when it considers and enacts tax legislation is, of course, the key to interpreting such legislation by taxpayers, the IRS, and the courts. Since Regulations normally are not issued immediately after a statute is enacted, taxpayers often look to legislative history materials to ascertain congressional intent.

The role of the Joint Conference Committee indicates the importance of compromise to the legislative process. The practical effect of the compromise process can be illustrated by reviewing what happened in TRA of 1986 (H.R. 3838) with respect to the maximum income tax rates applicable to corporations beginning in 1988.

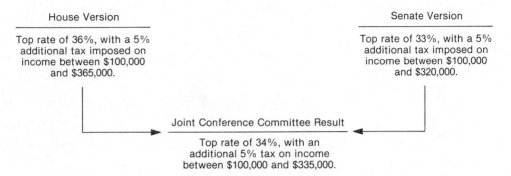

House Version		Senate Version
Top rate of 36%, with a 5% additional tax imposed on income between $100,000 and $365,000.		Top rate of 33%, with a 5% additional tax imposed on income between $100,000 and $320,000.

Joint Conference Committee Result

Top rate of 34%, with an additional 5% tax on income between $100,000 and $335,000.

Arrangement of the Code.   In working with the Code, it helps to understand the format followed. Note, for example, the following partial table of contents:

Subtitle A.   Income Taxes

> Chapter 1.   Normal Taxes and Surtaxes

>> Subchapter A.   Determination of Tax Liability

>>> Part I.   Tax on Individuals

>>>> Sections 1–5

>>> Part II.   Tax on Corporations

>>>> Sections 11–12

* * *

In referring to a provision of the Code, the key is usually the Section number involved. In designating Section 2(a) (dealing with the status of a surviving spouse), for example, it would be unnecessary to include Subtitle A, Chapter 1, Subchapter A, Part I. Merely mentioning Section 2(a) will suffice, since the Section numbers run consecutively and do not begin again with each new Subtitle, Chapter, Subchapter, or Part. However, not all Code Section numbers are used. Note that Part I ends with Section 5 and Part II starts with Section 11 (i.e., at present there are no Sections 6, 7, 8, 9, and 10).[32]

Among tax practitioners, a common way of referring to some specific area of income taxation is by Subchapter designation. More common Subchapter designations include Subchapter C (Corporate Distributions and Adjustments), Subchapter K (Partners and Partnerships), and Subchapter S (Tax Treatment of S Corporations and Their Shareholders). Particularly in the last situation, it is much more convenient to describe the effect of the applicable Code provisions

---

32. When the 1954 Code was drafted, the omission of Section numbers was intentional. This provided flexibility to incorporate later changes into the Code without disrupting its organization. When Congress does not leave enough space, subsequent Code Sections are given A, B, C, etc., designations. A good example is the treatment of §§ 280A through 280H.

involved (Sections 1361 through 1379) as S corporation status rather than as the "Tax Treatment of S Corporations and Their Shareholders."

Citing the Code.   Code Sections often are broken down into subparts.[33] Section 2(a)(1)(A) serves as an example.

Broken down as to content, § 2(a)(1)(A) becomes:

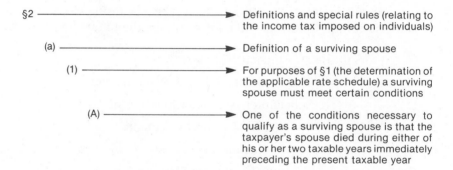

Throughout the remainder of the text, references to Code Sections are in the form just given. The symbols "§" and "§§" are used in place of "Section" and "Sections." Unless otherwise stated, all Code references are to the Internal Revenue Code of 1986. The format followed in the remainder of the text is summarized as follows:

Complete Reference	*Text Reference*
Section 2(a)(1)(A) of the Internal Revenue Code of 1986	§ 2(a)(1)(A)
Sections 1 and 2 of the Internal Revenue Code of 1986	§§ 1 and 2
Section 2 of the Internal Revenue Code of 1954	§ 2 of the Internal Revenue Code of 1954
Section 12(d) of the Internal Revenue Code of 1939 [35]	§ 12(d) of the Internal Revenue Code of 1939

---

33. Some Code Sections do not necessitate subparts. See, for example, § 482.
34. Some Code Sections omit the subsection designation and use, instead, the paragraph designation as the first subpart. See, for example, §§ 212(1) and 1221(1).
35. Section 12(d) of the Internal Revenue Code of 1939 is the predecessor to § 2 of the Internal Revenue Code of 1954. Keep in mind that the 1954 Code superseded the 1939 Code.

Administrative Sources of the Tax Law

The administrative sources of the Federal tax law can be grouped as follows: Treasury Department Regulations, Revenue Rulings and Procedures, and other administrative pronouncements. All are issued either by the U.S. Treasury Department or by one of its instrumentalities [e.g., the Internal Revenue Service (IRS) or a District Director]. The role played by the IRS in this process is considered in greater depth in Chapter 14.

Treasury Department Regulations.   Regulations are issued by the U.S. Treasury Department under authority granted by Congress. Interpretative by nature, they provide taxpayers with considerable guidance on the meaning and application of the Code. Although not issued by Congress, Regulations do carry considerable weight and are an important factor to consider in complying with the tax law.

Since Regulations interpret the Code, they are arranged in the same sequence. Regulations are, however, prefixed by a number that designates the type of tax or administrative, procedural, or definitional matter to which they relate. For example, the prefix 1 designates the Regulations under the income tax law. Thus, the Regulations under Code § 2 would be cited as Reg. § 1.2, with subparts added for further identification. However, these subparts often have no correlation in their numbering with the Code subsections. The prefix 20 designates estate tax Regulations; 25 covers gift tax Regulations; 31 relates to employment taxes; and 301 refers to Regulations dealing with procedure and administration. This listing is not all-inclusive.

New Regulations and changes to existing Regulations usually are issued in proposed form before they are finalized. The time interval between the proposal of a Regulation and its finalization permits taxpayers and other interested parties to comment on the propriety of the proposal. Proposed Regulations under Code § 2, for example, would be cited as Prop.Reg. § 1.2.

Sometimes temporary Regulations are issued by the Treasury Department relating to elections and other matters where speed is critical. Temporary Regulations usually are necessitated because of legislation recently enacted by Congress that takes effect immediately.

Proposed and final Regulations are published in the *Federal Register* and are reproduced in major tax services. Final Regulations are issued as Treasury Decisions (T.D.).

Revenue Rulings and Revenue Procedures.   Revenue Rulings are official pronouncements of the National Office of the IRS and, like Regulations, are designed to provide interpretation of the tax law. However, they do not carry the same legal force and effect of Regulations and usually deal with more restricted problems. Both Revenue Rulings and Revenue Procedures serve an important function in that they afford guidance to both IRS personnel and taxpayers in handling routine tax matters.

Although letter rulings (discussed below) are not the same as Revenue Rulings, a Revenue Ruling often results from a specific taxpayer's request for a letter ruling. If the IRS believes that a taxpayer's request for a letter ruling deserves official publication because of its widespread impact, the holding will be converted into a Revenue Ruling. In making this conversion, names, identifying facts, and money amounts will be changed to disguise the identity of the requesting taxpayer. The IRS then will issue what would have been a letter ruling as a Revenue Ruling.

Revenue Procedures are issued in the same manner as are Revenue Rulings, but they deal with the internal management practices and procedures of the IRS. Familiarity with these procedures can increase taxpayer compliance and assist the efficient administration of the tax laws by the IRS.

Both Revenue Rulings and Revenue Procedures are published weekly by the U.S. Government in the *Internal Revenue Bulletin* (I.R.B.). Semiannually, the bulletins for a six-month period are gathered together, reorganized by Code Section classification, and published in a bound volume designated *Cumulative Bulletin* (C.B.).[36] The proper form for citing Rulings and Procedures depends on whether the item has been published in the *Cumulative Bulletin* or is available in I.R.B. form. Consider, for example, the following transition:

Temporary Citation
- Rev.Rul. 86–151, I.R.B. No. 52, 4.
- *Explanation:* Revenue Ruling Number 151, appearing on page 4 of the 52d weekly issue of the *Internal Revenue Bulletin* for 1986.

Permanent Citation
- Rev.Rul. 86–151, 1986–2 C.B. 29.
- *Explanation:* Revenue Ruling Number 151, appearing on page 29 of volume 2 of the *Cumulative Bulletin* for 1986.

Since the second volume of the 1986 *Cumulative Bulletin* was not published until November of 1987, the I.R.B. citation had to be used until that time. After the publication of the *Cumulative Bulletin,* the C.B. citation became proper. The basic portion of both citations (i.e., Rev.Rul. 86–151) indicates that this was the 151st Revenue Ruling issued by the IRS during 1986.

Revenue Procedures are cited in the same manner, except that "Rev.Proc." is substituted for "Rev.Rul." Procedures, like Rulings, are published in the *Internal Revenue Bulletin* (the temporary source) and later transferred to the *Cumulative Bulletin* (the permanent source).

Other Administrative Pronouncements.   Treasury Decisions (T.D.s) are issued by the Treasury Department to promulgate new Regulations, to amend or otherwise change existing Regulations, or to announce the position of the Government on selected court decisions. Like Revenue Rulings and Revenue Procedures, T.D.s are published in the *Internal Revenue Bulletin* and subsequently transferred to the *Cumulative Bulletin.*

---

36. Usually only two volumes of the *Cumulative Bulletin* are published each year. However, when major tax legislation has been enacted by Congress, other volumes might be published containing the Congressional Committee Reports supporting the Revenue Act. See, for example, the two extra volumes for 1984 dealing with the Deficit Reduction Act of 1984. The 1984–3 *Cumulative Bulletin,* Volume 1, contains the text of the law itself; 1984–3, Volume 2, contains the Committee Reports. This makes a total of four volumes of the *Cumulative Bulletin* for 1984: 1984–1; 1984–2; 1984–3, Volume 1; and 1984–3, Volume 2.

Technical Information Releases (T.I.R.s) are usually issued to announce the publication of various IRS pronouncements (e.g., Revenue Rulings, Revenue Procedures).

Individual rulings are issued upon a taxpayer's request and describe how the IRS will treat a proposed transaction for tax purposes. They apply only to the taxpayer who asks for and obtains the ruling.[37] Though this procedure may sound like the only real way to carry out effective tax planning, the IRS limits the issuance of individual rulings to restricted, preannounced areas of taxation. Thus, it is not possible to obtain a ruling on many of the problems that are particularly troublesome for taxpayers.[38] For example, the IRS will not issue a ruling as to whether compensation paid to shareholder-employees is reasonable (see Chapter 4) or whether § 269 applies [i.e., the acquisition of a corporation to evade or avoid income tax (see Chapter 6)]. The main reason the IRS will not rule in certain areas is that such areas involve fact-oriented situations.

Individual rulings are not published by the government and, at one time, were "private" (i.e., the content of the ruling was made available only to the taxpayer requesting the ruling). However, Federal legislation and the courts have forced the IRS to modify its position on the confidentiality of individual rulings.[39]

The IRS must make individual rulings available for public inspection after identifying details are deleted. Published digests of private letter rulings can be found in *Private Letter Rulings* (published by Prentice-Hall), *BNA Daily Tax Reports,* and Tax Analysts & Advocates *TAX NOTES. IRS Letter Rulings Reports* (published by Commerce Clearing House) contains both digests and full texts of all letter rulings.

The National Office of the IRS releases Technical Advice Memoranda (TAMs) weekly. Although letter rulings are responses to requests by taxpayers, Technical Advice Memoranda are initiated by IRS personnel during audits. Technical Advice Memoranda give the IRS's determination of an issue somewhat like letter rulings. They deal with completed rather than proposed transactions and are often requested in relation to exempt organizations and employee plans. However, TAMs are issued by the National Office of the IRS to field personnel, whereas letter rulings are issued to taxpayers at their request. TAMs are not officially published and may not be cited or used as precedent according to § 6110(j)(3).

Both letter rulings and Technical Advice Memoranda are issued with multi-digit file numbers. Consider, for example, the following Technical Advice Memorandum dealing with a formula for the maximum marital deduction clause: DOC. 8708003. The first two digits refer to the year (87 = 1987), the next two digits indicate the week of issuance (08 = the eighth week), and the last three digits represent the number of the ruling issued during such week (003 = the third ruling during the eighth week).

---

37. In this regard, individual rulings differ from Revenue Rulings, which are applicable to *all* taxpayers.
38. Rev.Proc. 88–3, I.R.B. No. 1, 29, contains a listing of areas in which the IRS will not issue advance rulings. From time to time, subsequent Revenue Procedures are issued that modify or amplify Rev.Proc. 88–3.
39. The Freedom of Information Act as interpreted by *Tax Analysts and Advocates v. U.S.,* 74–2 USTC ¶ 9635, 34 AFTR2d 74–5731, 505 F.2d 350 (CA–DC, 1974), and *Tax Analysts and Advocates v. U.S.,* 75–2 USTC ¶ 9869, 37 AFTR2d 76–352, 405 F.Supp. 1065 (D.Ct.D.C., 1975).

Like individual rulings, determination letters are issued at the request of taxpayers and provide guidance concerning the application of the tax law. They differ from individual rulings in that the issuing source is the District Director rather than the National Office of the IRS. Also, determination letters usually involve completed (as opposed to proposed) transactions. Determination letters are not published but are made known only to the party making the request.

The following examples illustrate the distinction between individual rulings and determination letters:

Example 19 The shareholders of X Corporation and Y Corporation want assurance that the consolidation of the corporations into Z Corporation will be a nontaxable reorganization (see Chapter 6). The proper approach would be to request from the National Office of the IRS an individual ruling concerning the income tax effect of the proposed transaction. □

Example 20 T operates a barber shop in which he employs eight barbers. To properly comply with the rules governing income tax and payroll tax withholdings, T wants to know whether the barbers working for him are employees or independent contractors. The proper procedure would be to request from the appropriate District Director a determination letter on the status of such persons. □

Judicial Sources of the Tax Law

The Judicial Process in General.   After a taxpayer has exhausted some or all of the remedies available within the IRS (i.e., no satisfactory settlement has been reached at the agent or at the conference level discussed in Chapter 14), the dispute can be taken to the Federal courts. The dispute is first considered by a court of original jurisdiction (known as a trial court) with any appeal (either by the taxpayer or the IRS) taken to the appropriate appellate court. In most situations, the taxpayer has a choice of any of four trial courts: a Federal District Court, the U.S. Claims Court, the U.S. Tax Court, or the Small Claims Division of the U.S. Tax Court. The trial and appellate court scheme for Federal tax litigation is illustrated in Figure I.

The broken line between the U.S. Tax Court and the Small Claims Division indicates that there is no appeal from the Small Claims Division. Currently, the jurisdiction of the Small Claims Division of the U.S. Tax Court is limited to $10,000 or less. The proceedings of the Small Claims Division are informal, and its decisions are not precedents for any other court decision and are not reviewable by any higher court. Proceedings can be more timely and less expensive in the Small Claims Division.

American law, following English law, is frequently "made" by judicial decisions. Under the doctrine of *stare decisis,* each case (except in the Small Claims Division) has precedential value for future cases with the same controlling set of facts. Most Federal and state appellate court decisions and some decisions of trial courts are published. More than 3,000,000 judicial opinions have been published in the United States; over 30,000 cases are published each

Figure I   Federal Judicial Tax Process

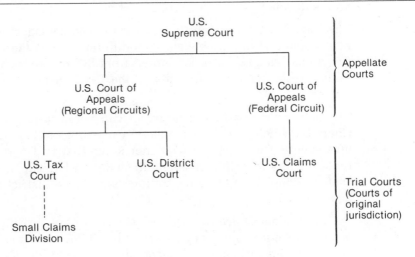

year.[40] Published court reports are organized by jurisdiction (Federal or state) and level of court (appellate or trial).

Trial Courts.   Differences between the various trial courts (courts of original jurisdiction) are summarized as follows:

—There is only one Claims Court and only one Tax Court, but there are many Federal District Courts. The taxpayer does not select the District Court that will hear the dispute but must sue in the one that has jurisdiction.

—The U.S. Claims Court has jurisdiction in judgment upon any claim against the United States that is based on the Constitution, any Act of Congress, or any regulation of an executive department.

—Each District Court has only one judge, the Claims Court has 16 judges, and the Tax Court has 19. In the case of the Tax Court, however, the whole court will decide a case (i.e., the court sits *en banc*) only when more important or novel tax issues are involved. Most cases will be heard and decided by one of the 19 judges.

—The Claims Court meets most often in Washington, D.C., while a District Court meets at a prescribed seat for the particular district. Since each state has at least one District Court and many of the more populous states have more, the problem of travel inconvenience and expense for the taxpayer and counsel (present with many suits in the Claims Court) is largely eliminated. Although the Tax Court is officially based in Washington, D.C., the various judges travel to different parts of the country and hear cases at predetermined locations and dates. Although this procedure eases the distance prob-

---

40. Jacobstein and Mersky, *Fundamentals of Legal Research,* 3rd Edition (Mineola, N.Y.: The Foundation Press, Inc. 1985).

lem for the taxpayer, it could mean a delay before the case comes to trial and is decided.

—The Tax Court hears only tax cases; the Claims Court and District Courts hear nontax litigation as well. This difference, plus the fact that many Tax Court justices have been appointed from IRS or Treasury Department positions, has led some to conclude that the Tax Court has more expertise in tax matters.

—The only court in which a taxpayer can obtain a jury trial is in a District Court. But since juries can decide only questions of fact and not questions of law, even those taxpayers who choose the District Court route often do not request a jury trial. In such event, the judge will decide all issues. Note that a District Court decision is controlling only in the district in which the court has jurisdiction.

—For the Claims Court or a District Court to have jurisdiction, the taxpayer must pay the tax deficiency assessed by the IRS and sue for a refund. If the taxpayer wins (assuming no successful appeal by the Government), the tax paid plus appropriate interest thereon will be recovered. For the Tax Court, however, jurisdiction is usually obtained without first paying the assessed tax deficiency. In the event the taxpayer loses in the Tax Court (and no appeal is taken or any appeal is unsuccessful), the deficiency must be paid with appropriate interest.

—Appeals from a District Court or a Tax Court decision are to the appropriate U.S. Court of Appeals. Appeals from the Claims Court go to the Court of Appeals for the Federal Circuit.

Appellate Courts. Regarding appeals from a trial court, the following list indicates the Court of Appeals of appropriate jurisdiction. Two of these Courts of Appeals are of recent vintage and may cause some confusion for one who conducts tax research. The Eleventh Court of Appeals came into being in late 1981 and comprises states (i.e., Alabama, Florida, and Georgia) that formerly were within the jurisdiction of the Fifth Court of Appeals. The reason for the division was the increase in population in some of the Sun Belt states and the enormity of the geographical area previously covered by the Fifth Court of Appeals. The Court of Appeals for the Federal Circuit was created in late 1982 and was given jurisdiction over all appeals from the U.S. Claims Court. Previously, such appeals went directly to the U.S. Supreme Court, thus bypassing the Court of Appeals level. As a matter of identification, the same legislation that established the Court of Appeals for the Federal Circuit changed the name of what used to be the U.S. Court of Claims to the U.S. Claims Court.

JURISDICTION OF THE COURTS OF APPEALS

First
Maine
Massachusetts
New Hampshire
Rhode Island
Puerto Rico

Second
Connecticut
New York
Vermont

Third

Delaware
New Jersey
Pennsylvania
Virgin Islands

District of Columbia

Washington, D.C.

Fourth

Maryland
North Carolina
South Carolina
Virginia
West Virginia

Fifth

Canal Zone
Louisiana
Mississippi
Texas

Sixth

Kentucky
Michigan
Ohio
Tennessee

Seventh

Illinois
Indiana
Wisconsin

Eighth

Arkansas
Iowa
Minnesota
Missouri
Nebraska
North Dakota
South Dakota

Ninth

Alaska
Arizona
California
Hawaii
Idaho
Montana
Nevada
Oregon
Washington
Guam

Tenth

Colorado
Kansas
New Mexico
Oklahoma
Utah
Wyoming

Eleventh

Alabama
Florida
Georgia

Federal Circuit

All of the jurisdictions (where the case
originates in the Claims Court)

If the Government loses at the trial court level (i.e., District Court, Tax Court, or Claims Court), it need not (and frequently does not) appeal. The fact that an appeal is not made, however, does not indicate that the IRS agrees with the result and will not litigate similar issues in the future. There could be a number of reasons for the Service's failure to appeal. First, the current litigation load may be heavy, and as a consequence, the IRS may decide that available personnel should be assigned to other, more important, cases. Second, the IRS may determine that this is not a good case to appeal. Such might be true if the taxpayer is in a sympathetic position or the facts are particularly strong in his or her favor. In such event, the IRS may wait to test the legal issues involved with a taxpayer who has a much weaker case. Third, if the appeal is from a District Court or the Tax Court, the Court of Appeals of jurisdiction could have some bearing on whether or not the decision is made to go forward with an appeal. Based on past experience and precedent, the IRS may conclude that the chance for success on a particular issue might be more promising in another Court of Appeals. The IRS will wait for a similar case to arise in a different appellate court.

District Courts, the Tax Court, and the Claims Court must abide by the precedents set by the Court of Appeals of jurisdiction. A particular Court of Appeals need not follow the decisions of another Court of Appeals. All courts, however, must follow the decisions of the U.S. Supreme Court.

Because the Tax Court is a national court (i.e., it hears and decides cases from all parts of the country), the observation made in the previous paragraph has caused problems. For many years, the Tax Court followed a policy of deciding cases based on what it thought the result should be, even though the appeal of its decision might have been to a Court of Appeals that had previously decided a similar case differently. A few years ago, this policy was changed. Now the Tax Court will still decide a case as it feels the law should be applied *only* if the Court of Appeals of appropriate jurisdiction has not yet passed on the issue or has previously decided a similar case in accordance with the Tax Court's decision.[41] If the Court of Appeals of appropriate jurisdiction has previously held otherwise, the Tax Court will conform under the *Golsen* rule even though it disagrees with the holding.

Example 21 Taxpayer T lives in Texas and sues in the Tax Court on Issue A. The Fifth Court of Appeals, the appellate court of appropriate jurisdiction, has already decided, based on similar facts and involving a different taxpayer, that Issue A should be resolved against the Government. Although the Tax Court feels that the Fifth Court of Appeals is wrong, under the *Golsen* rule, it will render judgment for T. Shortly thereafter, Taxpayer U, a resident of New York, in a comparable case, sues in the Tax Court on Issue A. Assume that the Second Court of Appeals, the appellate court of appropriate jurisdiction, has never expressed itself on Issue A. Presuming the Tax Court has not reconsidered its position on Issue A, it will decide against Taxpayer U. Thus, it is entirely possible for two taxpayers suing in the same court to end up with opposite results merely because they live in different parts of the country. □

Appeal to the U.S. Supreme Court is by Writ of Certiorari. If the Court accepts jurisdiction, it will grant the Writ (i.e., *Cert. Granted*). Most often, it will deny jurisdiction (i.e., *Cert. Denied*). For whatever reason or reasons, the Supreme Court rarely hears tax cases. The Court usually grants certiorari to resolve a conflict among the Courts of Appeals (e.g., two or more appellate courts have assumed opposing positions on a particular issue). The granting of a Writ of Certiorari indicates that at least four members of the Supreme Court believe that the issue is of sufficient importance to be heard by the full court.

The role of appellate courts is limited to a review of the record of trial compiled by the trial courts. Thus, the appellate process usually involves a determination of whether or not the trial court applied the proper law in arriving at its decision. Rarely will an appellate court disturb a lower court's fact-finding determination.

The result of an appeal could be any of a number of possibilities. The appellate court could approve (affirm) or disapprove (reverse) the lower court's finding, and it could also send the case back for further consideration (re-

---

41. *Jack E. Golsen,* 54 T.C. 742 (1970).

mand). When many issues are involved, it is not unusual to encounter a mixed result. Thus, the lower court could be affirmed (i.e., *aff'd.*) on Issue A and reversed (i.e., *rev'd.*) on Issue B, and Issue C could be remanded (i.e., *rem'd.*) for additional fact finding.

When more than one judge is involved in the decision-making process, disagreement is not uncommon. In addition to the majority view, there could be one or more judges who concur (i.e., agree with the result reached but not with some or all of the reasoning) or dissent (i.e., disagree with the result). In any one case it is the majority view that controls. But concurring and dissenting views can have influence on other courts or, at some subsequent date when the composition of the court has changed, even on the same court.

Having concluded a brief description of the judicial process, it is appropriate to consider the more practical problem of the relationship of case law to tax research. As previously noted, court decisions are an important source of tax law. The ability to cite a case and to locate it is therefore a must in working with the tax law. The usual pattern for a judicial citation is as follows: case name, volume number, reporter series, page or paragraph number, and court (where necessary).

Judicial Citations—The U.S. Tax Court.   A good starting point is with the U.S. Tax Court (formerly the Board of Tax Appeals). The Court issues two types of decisions: Regular and Memorandum. The distinction between the two involves both substance and form. In terms of substance, Memorandum decisions deal with situations necessitating only the application of already established principles of law. However, Regular decisions involve novel issues not previously resolved by the Court. In actual practice, this distinction is not always preserved. Not infrequently, Memorandum decisions will be encountered that appear to warrant Regular status and vice versa. At any rate, do not conclude that Memorandum decisions possess no value as precedents. Both represent the position of the Tax Court and, as such, can be relied upon.

Another important distinction between the Regular and Memorandum decisions issued by the Tax Court arises in connection with form. The Memorandum decisions officially are published in mimeograph form only, but Regular decisions are published by the U.S. Government in a series designated *Tax Court of the United States Reports.* Each volume of these reports covers a six-month period (January 1 through June 30 and July 1 through December 31) and is given a succeeding volume number. But, as was true of the *Cumulative Bulletin,* there is usually a time lag between the date a decision is rendered and the date it appears in bound form. A temporary citation might be necessary to aid the researcher in locating a recent Regular decision. Consider, for example, the temporary and permanent citations for *James L. Rose,* a decision filed on February 5, 1987:

Temporary   *James L. Rose,* 88 T.C. ___, No. 18 (1987).
Citation   *Explanation:* Page number left blank because not yet known

Permanent   *James L. Rose,* 88 T.C. 386 (1987).
Citation   *Explanation:* Page number now available

Both citations tell us that the case ultimately will appear in Volume 88 of the *Tax Court of the United States Reports.* But until this volume is bound and made available to the general public, the page number must be left blank. Instead, the temporary citation identifies the case as being the 18th Regular decision issued by the Tax Court since Volume 87 ended. With this information, the decision can be easily located in either of the special Tax Court services published by Commerce Clearing House or Prentice-Hall. Once Volume 88 is released, the permanent citation can be substituted and the number of the case dropped.

Before 1943, the Tax Court was called the Board of Tax Appeals, and its decisions were published as the *United States Board of Tax Appeals Reports* (B.T.A.). These forty-seven volumes cover the period from 1924 to 1942. For example, the citation *Karl Pauli,* 11 B.T.A. 784 (1928) refers to the eleventh volume of the *Board of Tax Appeals Reports,* page 784, issued in 1928.

One further distinction between Regular and Memorandum decisions of the Tax Court involves the IRS procedure of acquiescence (i.e., "A" or "Acq.") or nonacquiescence (i.e., "NA" or "Nonacq."). If the IRS loses in a Regular decision, it will usually indicate whether it agrees or disagrees with the result reached by the Court. The acquiescence or nonacquiescence will be published in the *Internal Revenue Bulletin* and the *Cumulative Bulletin.* The procedure is not followed for Memorandum decisions or for the decisions of other courts. The IRS can retroactively revoke an acquiescence. The IRS sometimes issues an announcement that it will *or* will not follow a decision of another Federal court on similar facts.

Although Memorandum decisions are not published by the U.S. Government, they are published by Commerce Clearing House (CCH) and Prentice-Hall (P-H). Consider, for example, the three different ways that *Walter H. Johnson* can be cited:

Walter H. Johnson, T.C.Memo. 1975–245
> The 245th Memorandum decision issued by the Tax Court in 1975.

Walter H. Johnson, 34 TCM 1056
> Page 1056 of Vol. 34 of the *CCH Tax Court Memorandum Decisions.*

Walter H. Johnson, P-H T.C.Mem.Dec. ¶ 75,245
> Paragraph 75,245 of the *P-H T.C. Memorandum Decisions.*

Note that the third citation contains the same information as the first. Thus, ¶ 75,245 indicates the following information about the case: year 1975, 245th T.C.Memo. decision.[42]

Judicial Citations—The U.S. District Court, Claims Court, and Court of Appeals. District Court, Claims Court, Court of Appeals, and Supreme Court decisions dealing with Federal tax matters are reported in both the CCH *U.S. Tax Cases* (USTC) and the P-H *American Federal Tax Reports* (AFTR) series.

---

42. In this text, the Prentice-Hall citation for Memorandum decisions of the U.S. Tax Court is omitted. Thus, *Walter H. Johnson* would be cited as: 34 TCM 1056, T.C.Memo. 1975–245.

Federal District Court decisions, dealing with *both* tax and nontax issues, are also published by West Publishing Company in its Federal Supplement Series. Examples of how a District Court case can be cited in three different forms appear as follows:

Simons-Eastern Co. v. U.S., 73–1 USTC ¶ 9279 (D.Ct.Ga., 1972).

> *Explanation:* Reported in the first volume of the *U.S. Tax Cases* (i.e., USTC) published by Commerce Clearing House for calendar year 1973 (i.e., 73–1) and located at paragraph 9279 (i.e., ¶ 9279).

Simons-Eastern Co. v. U.S., 31 AFTR2d 73–640 (D.Ct.Ga.,1972).

> *Explanation:* Reported in the 31st volume of the second series of the *American Federal Tax Reports* (i.e., AFTR2d) published by Prentice-Hall and beginning on page 640. The "73" preceding the page number indicates the year the case was published but is a designation used only in recent decisions.

Simons-Eastern Co. v. U.S., 354 F.Supp. 1003 (D.Ct.Ga., 1972).

> *Explanation:* Reported in the 354th volume of the *Federal Supplement Series* (i.e., F:Supp.) published by West Publishing Company and beginning on page 1003.

In all of the preceding citations, note that the name of the case is the same (Simons-Eastern Co. being the taxpayer), as is the reference to the Federal District Court of Georgia (i.e., D.Ct.Ga.,) and the year the decision was rendered (i.e., 1972).[43]

Beginning in October of 1982, decisions of the new Claims Court are reported by West Publishing Company in a series designated *Claims Court Reporter.* Thus, the Claims Court decision in *Recchie v. U.S.* appears as follows:

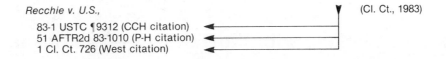

Decisions of the Claims Court (previously called the Court of Claims) and the Courts of Appeals are published in the USTCs, AFTRs, and a West Publishing Company reporter designated as the Federal Second Series (F.2d). Illustrations of the different forms follow:

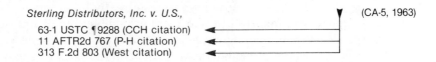

---

43. In this text, the case will be cited in the following form: *Simons-Eastern Co. v. U.S.,* 73–1 USTC ¶ 9279, 31 AFTR2d 73–640, 354 F.Supp. 1003 (D.Ct.Ga., 1972).

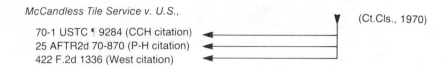

McCandless Tile Service v. U.S.,

   70-1 USTC ¶ 9284 (CCH citation)
   25 AFTR2d 70-870 (P-H citation)
   422 F.2d 1336 (West citation)

(Ct.Cls., 1970)

Note that *Sterling Distributors, Inc.* is a decision rendered by the Fifth Court of Appeals in 1963 (i.e., CA–5, 1963) while *McCandless Tile Service* is one rendered in 1970 by the Court of Claims (i.e., Ct.Cls., 1970), the predecessor of the Claims Court.

Judicial Citations—The U.S. Supreme Court. Like all other Federal tax cases (except those rendered by the U.S. Tax Court), Supreme Court decisions are published by Commerce Clearing House in the USTCs and by Prentice-Hall in the AFTRs. The U.S. Government Printing Office also publishes these decisions in the *United States Supreme Court Reports* (i.e., U.S.) as does West Publishing Company in its *Supreme Court Reporter* (i.e., S.Ct.) and the Lawyer's Co-Operative Publishing Company in its *United States Reports, Lawyer's Edition* (i.e., L.Ed.). The following is an illustration of the different ways the same decision can be cited:

(USSC, 1969)

U.S. v. The Donruss Co.,

   69-1 USTC ¶9167 (CCH citation)
   23 AFTR2d 69-418 (P-H citation)
   89 S.Ct. 501 (West citation)
   393 U.S. 297 (U.S. Government Printing Office citation)
   21 L.Ed.2d 495 (Lawyer's Co-Operative Publishing Co. citation)

The parenthetical reference (USSC, 1969) identifies the decision as having been rendered by the U.S. Supreme Court in 1969. The citations given in this text for Supreme Court decisions will be limited to the CCH (i.e., USTC), P-H (i.e., AFTR), and the West (i.e., S.Ct.) versions.

Working with the Tax Law—Tax Research

Tax research is the method whereby one determines the best available solution to a situation that possesses tax consequences. In other words, it is the process of finding a competent and professional conclusion to a tax problem. The problem might originate either from completed or proposed transactions. In the case of a completed transaction, the objective of the research would be to determine the tax result of what has already taken place. For example, was the expenditure incurred by the taxpayer deductible or not deductible for tax purposes? When dealing with proposed transactions, however, the tax research process is directed toward the determination of possible tax consequences. To the extent that tax research leads to a choice of alternatives or otherwise influences the future actions of the taxpayer, it becomes the key to effective tax planning.

Tax research involves the following procedures:

—Identifying and refining the problem.

—Locating the appropriate tax law sources.

—Assessing the validity of the tax law sources.

—Arriving at the solution or at alternative solutions with due consideration given to nontax factors.

—Effectively communicating the solution to the taxpayer or the taxpayer's representative.

—Following up on the solution (where appropriate) in light of new developments.

These procedures are diagrammed in Figure II. The broken lines reflect those steps of particular interest when tax research is directed toward proposed, rather than completed, transactions.

Identifying the Problem

Problem identification must start with a compilation of the relevant facts involved.[44] In this regard, *all* of the facts that might have a bearing on the problem must be gathered, because any omission could modify the solution to be reached. To illustrate, consider what appears to be a very simple problem.

Figure II   Tax Research Process

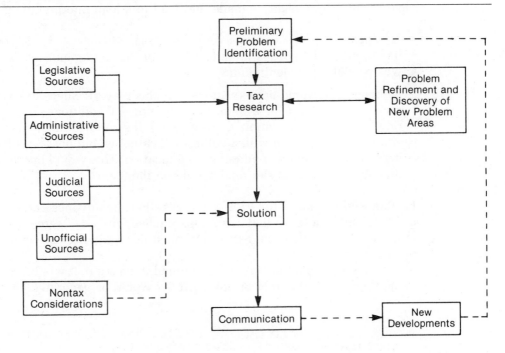

44. For an excellent discussion of the critical role of facts in carrying out tax research, see Ray M. Sommerfeld and G. Fred Streuling, *Tax Research Techniques,* Tax Study No. 5 (New York, N.Y.: The American Institute of Certified Public Accountants, 1981), Chapter 2.

Example 22   A widowed mother advances $52,000 to her son in 1981 to enable him to attend a private college. Seven years later, the mother claims a bad debt deduction for $42,000 that the son has not repaid. The problem: Is the mother entitled to a bad debt deduction? ☐

Refining the Problem.   Before a bad debt deduction can arise, it must be established that a debt really existed. In a related-party setting (e.g., mother and son), the IRS may contend that the original advance was not a loan but, in reality, a gift. Of key significance in this regard would be whether or not the lender (i.e., the mother) had an honest and real expectation of payment by the borrower (i.e., the son).[45] Indicative of this repayment expectation is whether or not the parties preserved the formalities of a loan, including the following:

—The borrower issued a written instrument evidencing the obligation.

—Interest was provided for as part of the loan arrangement.

—The note specified a set due date.

—Collateral was available to the lender in the event of default by the borrower.[46]

The very presence of some or all of the above formalities does not, however, guarantee that a bona fide loan will be found. By the same token, the absence of some or all of such formalities does not condemn the advance to a gift classification. Applying the formalities criteria to Example 22 is not possible, since key facts (e.g., the presence or absence of a written note) are not given. Nevertheless, several inferences might be made that lead to a loan interpretation:

—It appears that the son has repaid at least $10,000 of the $52,000 that he borrowed. If the parties intended a gift of the full amount of the loan, why was partial repayment made?

—Although one would not expect a son on his way to college to have assets to serve as collateral for a loan, the obtaining of additional education could reinforce any expectation of repayment the mother might have. In most situations, the person with a college education would possess a higher earning potential than one without such education. This would improve the son's financial ability to make repayments on the loan.

Further Refinement of the Problem.   Whether the advance constitutes a loan or a gift may be a result that cannot be reached with any degree of certainty. In either event, however, the researcher must ascertain the tax consequences of each possibility.

If the advance ultimately is determined to be a gift, it will be subject to the Federal gift tax.[47] Whether or not a gift tax would be generated because of the

---

45. *William F. Mercil,* 24 T.C. 1150 (1955), and *Evans Clark,* 18 T.C. 780 (1952), *aff'd.* 53–2 USTC ¶ 9452, 44 AFTR 70, 205 F.2d 353 (CA–2, 1953).
46. *Arthur T. Davidson,* 37 TCM 725, T.C.Memo. 1978–167.
47. The transfer does not fall within the unlimited gift tax exclusion of § 2503(e)(2)(A), since the mother did not pay the amount directly to an educational institution. Besides, the exclusion covers only tuition payments and not other costs attendant to going to college (e.g., room and board).

transfer would depend upon how much of the unified tax credit the mother has available to absorb the gift tax on $42,000 [$52,000 (total gift) — $10,000 (annual exclusion)].[48] But whether the transfer results in a gift tax or not, it would have to be reported on Form 709 (United States Gift Tax Return), since the amount of the gift exceeds the annual exclusion.

Even if it is assumed that the mother made a gift to the son in 1981, does not the intervention of seven years preclude the IRS from assessing any gift tax that might be due as a result of such transfer? [49] Further research would indicate that the statute of limitations on assessments does not begin to run when a tax return was due but not filed.[50]

To complete the picture, what are the tax consequences if the advance is treated as a bona fide loan? Aside from the bad debt deduction aspects (covered later in the chapter), the tax law provides more immediate tax ramifications, summarized as follows: [51]

—If interest is not provided for, interest will be imputed with the following effect:

   a. The lender (i.e., the mother) must recognize interest income as to the imputed value.

   b. Since the lender has not received the interest, a gift of such interest is deemed to have taken place from the lender to the borrower.

   c. The borrower (i.e., son) is entitled to deduct (as an itemized expense) a portion of the amount of interest deemed paid to the lender (i.e., mother).

—If interest is provided for but the rate is lower than market (as determined by the yield on certain U.S. government securities), the differential will be treated as noted above.

—For gift loans of $100,000 or less, the imputed element cannot exceed the net investment income of the borrower.

Locating the Appropriate Tax Law Sources

Once the problem is clearly defined, what is the next step? Although this is a matter of individual judgment, most involved tax research begins with the index volume of the tax service. If the problem is not complex, the researcher may bypass the tax service and turn directly to the Internal Revenue Code and the Treasury Regulations. For the beginner, this procedure saves time and will solve many of the more basic problems. If the researcher does not have a personal copy of the Code or Regulations, resorting to the appropriate volume(s) of a tax service will be necessary. Several of the major tax services

---

48. This, in turn, depends upon the amount of taxable gifts the mother has made in the past. For a discussion of the mechanics of the Federal gift tax, see Chapter 11.

49. Throughout the discussion of Example 22, the assumption has been made that if a gift occurred, it took place in 1981. Such need not be the case. Depending upon the mother's intent, she could have decided to make a gift of the unpaid balance anytime after the loan was made (e.g., 1982, 1983, etc.)

50. See § 6501(c)(3) and the discussion of the statute of limitations in Chapter 14.

51. § 7872.

publish paperback editions of the Code and Treasury Regulations which can be purchased at modest prices. These editions are usually revised twice each year. The major services available are as follows:

Standard Federal Tax Reporter, Commerce Clearing House.

Federal Taxes, Prentice-Hall.

Mertens Law of Federal Income Taxation, Callaghan and Co.

Tax Coordinator, Research Institute of America.

Tax Management Portfolios, Bureau of National Affairs.

Rabkin and Johnson, *Federal Income, Gift and Estate Taxation*, Matthew Bender, Inc.

Working with the Tax Services. In this text, it is not feasible to teach the use of any particular tax service; this can be learned only by practice. The representatives of the various tax services are prepared to provide the users of their services with printed booklets and individual instruction on the utilization of such materials. However, several important observations can be made about the use of tax services that cannot be overemphasized. First, never forget to check for current developments. The main text of any service is not revised frequently enough to permit reliance on that portion as the *latest* word on any subject. Where such current developments can be found depends, of course, on which service is being used. Both the Commerce Clearing House and Prentice-Hall services contain a special volume devoted to current matters. Second, when dealing with a tax service synopsis of a Treasury Department pronouncement or a judicial decision, remember there is no substitute for the original source.

To illustrate, do not base a conclusion solely on a tax service's commentary on *Simons-Eastern Co. v. U.S.*[52] If the case is vital to the research, look it up. It is possible that the facts of the case are distinguishable from those involved in the problem being researched. This is not to say that the case synopsis contained in the tax service is wrong; it might just be misleading or incomplete.

Tax Periodicals. Additional sources of tax information are the various tax periodicals. The best means of locating a journal article pertinent to a tax problem is through Commerce Clearing House's *Federal Tax Articles*. This three-volume service includes a subject index, a Code Section number index, and an author's index. Also, the P-H tax service has a topical "Index to Tax Articles" section that is organized using the P-H paragraph index system.

The following are some of the more useful tax periodicals:

The Journal of Taxation
Warren, Gorham and Lamont
210 South Street
Boston, MA 02111

Tax Law Review
Warren, Gorham and Lamont
210 South Street
Boston, MA 02111

---

52. Cited in Footnote 43.

Taxation for Accountants
Warren, Gorham and Lamont
210 South Street
Boston, MA 02111

The Tax Executive
1300 North 17th Street
Arlington, VA 22209

TAXES—The Tax Magazine
Commerce Clearing House, Inc.
4025 West Peterson Avenue
Chicago, IL 60646

National Tax Journal
21 East State Street
Columbus, OH 43215

The Tax Adviser
1211 Avenue of the Americas
New York, NY 10036

The Practical Accountant
Institute of Continuing Professional
  Development
964 – 3rd Avenue
New York, NY 10155

Journal of Corporate Taxation
Warren, Gorham and Lamont
210 South Street
Boston, MA 02111

Trusts and Estates
Communication Channels, Inc.
6255 Barfield Road
Atlanta, GA 30328

Estate Planning
Warren, Gorham and Lamont
210 South Street
Boston, MA 02111

Journal of Partnership Taxation
Warren, Gorham and Lamont
210 South Street
Boston, MA 02111

Oil and Gas Tax Quarterly
Matthew Bender & Co.
235 East 45th Street
New York, NY 10017

The International Tax Journal
Panel Publishers
14 Plaza Road
Greenvale, NY 11548

The Tax Lawyer
American Bar Association
1800 M Street, N.W.
Washington, DC 20036

Journal of the American Taxation Association
American Accounting Association
5717 Bessie Drive
Sarasota, FL 33583

Assessing the Validity of Tax Law Sources

After a source has been located, the next procedure is to assess such source in light of the problem at hand. Proper assessment involves careful interpretation of the tax law with consideration as to the law's relevance and validity. In connection with validity, an important step is to check for recent changes in the tax law.

Interpreting the Internal Revenue Code.   The language of the Code can be extremely difficult to comprehend fully. For example, a subsection [§ 341(e)] relating to collapsible corporations contains *one* sentence of more than 450 words (twice as many as in the Gettysburg Address). Within this same subsection are two other sentences of 300 and 270 words. One author has noted 10 common pitfalls in interpreting the Code: [53]

1. Determine the limitations and exceptions to a provision. Do not permit the language of the Code Section to carry greater or lesser weight than was intended.

---

53. H.G. Wong, "Ten Common Pitfalls in Reading the Internal Revenue Code," *The Practical Accountant* (July-August 1972), pp. 30–33.

2. Just because a Section fails to mention an item does not necessarily mean that the item is excluded.
3. Read definitional clauses carefully. Note, for example, that § 7701(a)(3) defines a corporation as including "associations." This inclusion (further developed in Chapter 2) becomes essential in determining how professional associations are to be treated for Federal income tax purposes.
4. Do not overlook small words such as "and" and "or." There is a world of difference between these two words.
5. Read the Code Section completely; do not jump to conclusions.
6. Watch out for cross-referenced and related provisions, since many Sections of the Code are interrelated.
7. Congress is at times not careful when reconciling new Code provisions with existing Sections. Conflicts among Sections, therefore, do arise.
8. Be alert for hidden definitions; terms in a particular Code Section may be defined in the same Section *or in a separate Section.*
9. Some answers might not be found in the Code; therefore, a researcher may have to consult the Regulations and/or judicial decisions.
10. Take careful note of measuring words such as "less than 50 percent," "exceeds 35 percent," "at least 80 percent," and "more than 80 percent."

Assessing the Validity of a Treasury Regulation. It is often stated that Treasury Regulations have the force and effect of law. This statement is certainly true for most Regulations, but there have been judicial decisions that have held a Regulation or a portion thereof invalid, usually on the grounds that the Regulation is contrary to the intent of Congress upon the enactment of a particular Code Section.

Keep in mind the following observations when assessing the validity of a Regulation:

—In a challenge, the burden of proof is on the taxpayer to show that the Regulation is wrong. However, a court may invalidate a Regulation that varies from the language of the statute and has no support in the Committee Reports.

—If the taxpayer loses the challenge, the imposition of the negligence penalty can result. This provision deals with the "intentional disregard of rules and regulations" on the part of the taxpayer and is further explained in Chapter 14.

—Some Regulations merely reprint or rephrase what Congress has stated in its Committee Reports issued in connection with the enactment of tax legislation. Such Regulations are "hard and solid" and almost impossible to overturn, because they clearly reflect the intent of Congress.

—In some Code Sections, Congress has given to the "Secretary or his delegate" the authority to prescribe Regulations to carry out the details of administration or to otherwise complete the operating rules. Under such circumstances, it could almost be said that Congress is delegating its legislative powers to the Treasury Department. Regulations issued pursuant to this type of authority truly possess the force and effect of law and are often called "legislative Regulations." They are to be distinguished from "interpretative" Regulations, which purport to reflect the meaning of a particular Code Section. Examples of legislative Regulations would be those dealing with consolidated returns issued under §§ 1501 through 1505. As a further example, note the authority granted to the Treasury Department by § 385 to issue Regulations setting forth guidelines on when corporate debt can be reclassified as equity (see Chapter 3).

Assessing the Validity of Other Administrative Sources of the Tax Law.   Revenue Rulings issued by the IRS carry less weight than Treasury Department Regulations. Rulings are important, however, in that they reflect the position of the IRS on tax matters. In any dispute with the IRS on the interpretation of tax law, therefore, taxpayers should expect agents to follow the results reached in any applicable Rulings.

Revenue Rulings further tell the taxpayer the IRS's reaction to certain court decisions. Recall that the IRS follows a practice of either acquiescing (i.e., agreeing) or nonacquiescing (i.e., not agreeing) with the *Regular* decisions of the U.S. Tax Court. This practice does not mean that a particular decision of the Tax Court is of no value if, for example, the IRS has nonacquiesced in the result. It does, however, indicate that the IRS will continue to litigate the issue involved.

The validity of individual letter rulings issued by the IRS is discussed in Chapter 14.

Assessing the Validity of Judicial Sources of the Tax Law.   The judicial process as it relates to the formulation of tax law has already been described. How much reliance can be placed on a particular decision depends upon the following variables:

—The level of the court. A decision rendered by a trial court (e.g., a Federal District Court) carries less weight than one issued by an appellate court (e.g., the Fifth Court of Appeals). Unless Congress changes the Code, decisions by the U.S. Supreme Court represent the last word on any tax issue.

—The legal residence of the taxpayer. If, for example, a taxpayer lives in Texas, a decision of the Fifth Court of Appeals means more than one rendered by the Second Court of Appeals. This result occurs because any appeal from a U.S. District Court or the U.S. Tax Court would be to the Fifth Court of Appeals and not to the Second Court of Appeals.

—Whether the decision represents the weight of authority on the issue. In other words, is it supported by the results reached by other courts?

—The outcome or status of the decision on appeal. For example, was the decision appealed and, if so, with what result?

In connection with the last two variables, the use of a manual citator or a computer search is invaluable to tax research.[54] Such use of a manual citator is illustrated in the appendix to this chapter.

---

54. The major manual citators are published by Commerce Clearing House, Prentice-Hall, and Shepard's Citations, Inc.

Assessing the Validity of Other Sources. Primary sources of tax law include the Constitution, legislative history materials, statutes, treaties, Treasury Regulations, IRS pronouncements, and judicial decisions. The IRS considers only primary sources to constitute substantial authority. However, a researcher might wish to refer to secondary materials such as legal periodicals, treatises, legal opinions, general counsel memoranda, technical memoranda, and written determinations. In general, secondary sources are not authority. Reg. § 1.6661–3(b)(2) summarizes the opinion of the IRS as follows:

> In determining whether there is substantial authority (other than in cases described in paragraph (b)(4)(i) of this section), only the following will be considered authority: Applicable provisions of the Internal Revenue Code and other statutory provisions; temporary and final regulations construing such statutes; court cases; administrative pronouncements (including revenue rulings and revenue procedures); tax treaties and regulations thereunder, and Treasury Department and other official explanations of such treaties; and Congressional intent as reflected in committee reports, joint explanatory statements of managers included in conference committee reports, and floor statements made prior to enactment by one of a bill's managers. Conclusions reached in treatises, legal periodicals, legal opinions or opinions rendered by other tax professionals, descriptions of statutes prepared after enactment (such as "General Explanations" prepared by the Staff of the Joint Committee on Taxation), general counsel memoranda, (other than those published in pre-1955 volumes of the Cumulative Bulletin), actions on decisions, technical memoranda, written determinations (except as provided in paragraph (b)(4)(i) of this section), and proposed regulations are not authority. The authorities underlying such expressions of opinion where applicable to the facts of a particular case, however, may give rise to substantial authority for the tax treatment of an item.

An individual ruling or determination letter is substantial authority only to the taxpayer to whom it is issued.

Arriving at the Solution or at Alternative Solutions

Returning to Example 22, assume the researcher decides that the loan approach can be justified from the factual situation involved. Does this lead to a bad debt deduction for the mother? Before this question can be resolved, the loan needs to be classified as either a business or a nonbusiness debt. One of the reasons this classification is important is that a nonbusiness bad debt cannot be deducted until it becomes entirely worthless. Unlike a business debt, no deduction for partial worthlessness is allowed.[55]

It is very likely that the loan the mother made in 1981 falls into the nonbusiness category. Unless exceptional circumstances exist (e.g., the lender was in the trade or business of lending money), loans in a related-party setting invari-

---

55. See § 166 and the discussion on "Investor Losses" in Chapter 3.

ably are treated as nonbusiness. The probability is therefore high that the mother would be relegated to nonbusiness bad debt status.

The mother has the burden of proving that the remaining unpaid balance of $42,000 is *entirely* worthless.[56] In this connection, what collection effort, if any, has the mother made? But would any such collection effort be fruitless? Perhaps the son is insolvent, ill, unemployed, or has disappeared for parts unknown.

Even if the debt is entirely worthless, one further issue remains to be resolved. In what year did the worthlessness occur? It could be, for example, that worthlessness took place in a year before it was claimed.[57]

A clear-cut answer may not be possible as to a bad debt deduction for the mother as to year 1988 (seven years after the advance was made). This does not, however, detract from the value of the research. Often a guarded judgment is the best possible solution to a tax problem.

Communicating Tax Research

Once satisfied that the problem has been researched adequately, the researcher may need to prepare a memo setting forth the result. The form such a memo takes could depend on a number of considerations. For example, is any particular procedure or format recommended for tax research memos by either an employer or an instructor? Is the memo to be given directly to the client, or will it first pass to the researcher's employer? Whatever form it takes, a good research memo should contain the following elements:

—A clear statement of the issue.

—In more complex situations, a short review of the factual pattern that raises the issue.

—A review of the tax law sources (e.g., Code, Regulations, Rulings, judicial authority).

—Any assumptions made in arriving at the solution.

—The solution recommended and the logic or reasoning in its support.

—The references consulted in the research process.

In short, a good tax memo should tell the reader what was researched, the results of that research, and the justification for the recommendation made.

Working with the Tax Law— Tax Planning

Tax research and tax planning are inseparable. The primary purpose of effective tax planning is to reduce the taxpayer's total tax bill. This does not mean

56. Compare *John K. Sexton,* 48 TCM 512, T.C.Memo. 1984–360, with *Stewart T. Oatman,* 45 TCM 214, T.C.Memo. 1982–684.
57. *Ruth Wertheim Smith,* 34 TCM 1474, T.C.Memo. 1975–339.

that the course of action selected must produce the lowest possible tax under the circumstances. The minimization of tax payments must be considered in context with the legitimate business goals of the taxpayer.

A secondary objective of effective tax planning works toward a deferment or postponement of the tax. Specifically, this objective aims to accomplish any one or more of the following: eradicating the tax entirely; eliminating the tax in the current year; deferring the receipt of income; proliferating taxpayers (i.e., forming partnerships and corporations or making lifetime gifts to family members); eluding double taxation; avoiding ordinary income; or creating, increasing, or accelerating deductions. However, this second objective should be pursued with considerable reservation. Although the maxim "A bird in the hand is worth two in the bush" has general validity, there are frequent cases in which the rule breaks down. For example, a tax election in one year, although it accomplishes a current reduction in taxes, could saddle future years with a disadvantageous tax position.

Nontax Considerations

There is an honest danger that tax motivations can take on a significance that is not in conformity with the true values involved. In other words, tax considerations can operate to impair the exercise of sound business judgment by the taxpayer. Thus, the tax planning process can become a medium through which to accomplish ends that are socially and economically objectionable. Ostensibly, a pronounced tendency exists for planning to move toward the opposing extremes of either not enough or too much emphasis on tax considerations. The happy medium—a balance that recognizes the significance of taxes, but not beyond the point at which planning serves to detract from the exercise of good business judgment—turns out to be the promised land that is seldom reached.

The remark is often made that a good rule to follow is to refrain from pursuing any course of action that would not be followed were it not for certain tax considerations. This statement is not entirely correct, but it does illustrate the desirability of preventing business logic from being "sacrificed at the altar of tax planning." In this connection, the following comment is significant:

> The lure of a quick tax dollar is often the only justification for a transaction that might have been accomplished with much sounder economic results and equivalent tax savings if more careful and deliberate consideration had been given to the problem. Certainly in this atmosphere of the tax-controlled economy a very heavy obligation is cast upon the tax adviser to give serious consideration as to whether a proposed action achieves a desirable economic result apart from tax savings or whether the immediate tax advantages may be more than offset by later economic or personal disadvantage. We cannot afford to develop successful cures that are killing our patients.[58]

---

58. Norris Darrell, "Some Responsibilities of the Tax Adviser in Regard to Tax Minimization Devices," *Proceedings of the New York University Eighth Annual Institute on Federal Taxation* (Albany, N.Y.: Matthew Bender & Co., 1950), pp. 988–989.

Tax Avoidance and Tax Evasion

A fine line exists between legal tax planning and illegal tax planning—tax avoidance versus tax evasion. Tax avoidance is merely tax minimization through legal techniques. In this sense, tax avoidance becomes the proper objective of all tax planning. Evasion, although also aimed at the elimination or reduction of taxes, connotes the use of subterfuge and fraud as a means to an end. Popular usage, probably because of the common goals that are involved, has linked these two concepts to the extent that any true distinctions have been obliterated in the minds of many. Consequently, the taint created by the association of tax avoidance and tax evasion has deterred some taxpayers from properly taking advantage of the planning possibilities. The now-classic verbiage of Judge Learned Hand in *Commissioner v. Newman* reflects the true values the individual should have:

> Over and over again courts have said that there is nothing sinister in so arranging one's affairs as to keep taxes as low as possible. Everybody does so, rich or poor; and all do right, for nobody owes any public duty to pay more than the law demands: taxes are enforced extractions, not voluntary contributions. To demand more in the name of morals is mere cant.[59]

Follow-Up Procedures

Because tax planning usually involves a proposed (as opposed to a completed) transaction, it is predicated upon the continuing validity of the advice based upon the tax research. A change in the tax law (either legislative, administrative, or judicial) could alter the original conclusion. Additional research may be necessary to test the solution in light of current developments.

Under what circumstances does a tax practitioner have an obligation to inform a client as to changes in the tax law? The legal and ethical aspects of this question are discussed in Chapter 14.

Tax Planning—A Practical Application

Returning to the facts in Example 22, what should be done to help protect the mother's bad debt deduction?

—All formalities should be present as to the loan (e.g., written instrument, definite and realistic due date).

—Upon default, the lender (mother) should make a reasonable effort to collect from the borrower (son). If not, the mother should be in a position to explain why any such effort would be to no avail.

—If interest is provided for, it should be paid.

—Any interest paid (or imputed under § 7872) should be recognized as income by the mother.

---

59. *Comm. v. Newman*, 47–1 USTC ¶ 9175, 35 AFTR 857, 159 F.2d 848 (CA–2, 1947).

—Because of the annual exclusion of $10,000, it appears doubtful that actual (or imputed) interest would necessitate the filing by the mother of a Federal gift tax return. But should one be due, it should be filed.

—If § 7872 applies (not enough or no interest is provided for), the son should keep track of his net investment income. This is advisable, since the income the mother must recognize might be limited by such amount.

Throughout the text, each chapter concludes with observations on Tax Planning Considerations. Such observations are not all-inclusive but are intended to illustrate some of the ways in which the material covered can be effectively utilized to minimize taxes.

Computer-Assisted Tax Research

The computer is being used more and more frequently in the day-to-day practice of tax professionals, students, and educators. Many software vendors offer tax return software programs for individual, corporate, partnership, and fiduciary returns. The use of computers, however, is not limited to the role of batch-processed tax returns and computer timesharing for quantitative tax and problem-solving planning and calculations.

Predictions are that the microcomputer will become the revolutionary tool of the future—much like the electronic calculator did in the seventies. Electronic spreadsheets are being used to replace the 14-column worksheet. The electronic spreadsheet approach can be used for retirement planning, Form 1040 projections, real estate projections, partnership allocations, consolidated tax return problems, compensation planning—anytime projections and calculations are needed. Internally prepared tax-related programs are used by many public accounting firms. Software is available for the microcomputer for estate planning calculations.

LEXIS, a computerized legal data bank, has been available since 1973 as a complement to the conventional manual research approach (available in many of the more than 97 graduate tax programs). WESTLAW, a competitive system from West Publishing Company, has been operational since 1975. Prentice-Hall has a national computer network, called PHINet, which makes its looseleaf service accessible by computer. WESTLAW, LEXIS, and PHINet are in actuality document retrieval systems that cannot interpret the law.

Users have access to these computerized data banks through special terminals and long-distance telephone lines. A user selects key words, phrases, or numbers and types the search request on the keyboard on the terminal. A display screen then shows the full text or portions of the various documents containing the words, phrases, or numbers in the search request. A printer can be used to obtain hard copy of any documents or portions of a document. For example, a researcher can obtain the decisions of a particular judge or court over a specified time period. It is also possible to access judicial opinions containing specific words or phrases of statutory language. These computer-assisted tax systems can be used as a citator by collecting all judicial decisions that have cited a particular decision or statute as well as all decisions that have a specific combination of two or more earlier decisions or statutes.

Computer-assisted tax research is useful in searching for facts, because human indexing evolves around legal theories rather than fact patterns. Computer searching also is useful in finding new court decisions not yet in the printed indexes. Because computer searching probably does not find as many relevant cases as does manual searching, a combination of manual and computer searching can be quite effective.[60]

▬▬▬ Use of the P-H Citator

ILLUSTRATION OF THE USE OF THE P-H CITATOR

Background

The Prentice-Hall *Federal Tax Citator* is a separate multi-volume service with two looseleaf current matters sections. Cases that are reported by the *Citator* are divided into the various issues involved. Since the researcher may be interested in only one or two issues, only those cases involving the particular issue need to be checked.

The volumes of the P-H *Federal Tax Citator* and the period of time covered by each are as follows:

Volume 1 (1863–1941)

Volume 2 (1942–1948)

Volume 3 (1948–1954)

Volume 1, Second Series (1954–1977)

Looseleaf, two volumes (1977 to present)

Through the use of symbols, the *Citator* indicates whether a decision is followed, explained, criticized, questioned, or overruled by a later court decision. These symbols are reproduced in Figure III.

Example

Determine the background and validity of *Adda v. Comm.,* 37 AFTR 654, 171 F.2d 457 (CA–4, 1948).

Solution

Turning directly to the case itself (reproduced as Figure IV), note the two issues involved (i.e., "1." and "2."). For purposes of emphasis, these issues have been bracketed and identified as such by a marginal notation added to Figure IV. The reason for the division of the issues becomes apparent when the case is traced through the *Citator.*

Refer to Volume 3 for the AFTR Series (covering the period from October 7, 1948, through July 29, 1954) of the P-H *Federal Tax Citator.* Reference to the case is located on page 5505 (reproduced in Figure V).

Correlating the symbols reproduced in Figure III with the shaded portion of Figure V reveals the following information about *Adda v. Comm.:*

---

60. For more detail, see W.A. Raabe, G.E. Whittenburg, and J.C. Bost, *West's Federal Tax Research,* 1st Edition (St. Paul: West Publishing Co., 1987), Chapter 13.

Figure III

Prentice-Hall Citator Symbols*

COURT DECISIONS

Judicial History of the Case

a	affirmed (by decision of a higher court)
d	dismissed (appeal to a higher court dismissed)
m	modified (decision modified by a higher court, or on rehearing)
r	reversed (by a decision of a higher court)
s	same case (e. g., on rehearing)
rc	related case (companion cases and other cases arising out of the same subject matter are so designated)
x	certiorari denied (by the Supreme Court of the United States)
(C or G)	The Commissioner or Solicitor General has made the appeal
(T)	Taxpayer has made the appeal
(A)	Tax Court's decision acquiesced in by Commissioner
(NA)	Tax Court's decision nonacquiesced in by Commissioner
sa	same case affirmed (by the cited case)
sd	same case dismissed (by the cited case)
sm	same case modified (by the cited case)
sr	same case reversed (by the cited case)
sx	same case-certiorari denied

Syllabus of the Cited Case

iv	four (on all fours with the cited case)
f	followed (the cited case followed)
e	explained (comment generally favorable, but not to a degree that indicates the cited case is followed)
k	reconciled (the cited case reconciled)
n	dissenting opinion (cited in a dissenting opinion)
g	distinguished (the cited case distinguished either in law or on the facts)
l	limited (the cited case limited to its facts. Used when an appellate court so limits a prior decision, or a lower court states that in its opinion the cited case should be so limited)
c	criticized (adverse comment on the cited case)
q	questioned (the cited case not only criticized, but its correctness questioned)
o	overruled

* Reproduced from the Federal Taxes Citator with the permission of the publisher, Prentice-Hall, Inc., Englewood Cliffs, N. J. 07632

—Application for certiorari (i.e., appeal to the U.S. Supreme Court) filed by the taxpayer (T) on March 1, 1949.

—Certiorari was denied (x) by the U.S. Supreme Court on April 18, 1949.

—The trial court decision is reported in 10 T.C. 273 and was affirmed on appeal (sa) to the Fourth Court of Appeals.

—During the time frame of Volume 3 of the *Citator* (October 7, 1948, through July 29, 1954), one decision (*Milner Hotels, Inc.*) has agreed "on all fours with

Figure IV

**ADDA v. COMMISSIONER OF INTERNAL
REVENUE.**

No. 5796.

United States Court of Appeals
Fourth Circuit.

Dec. 3, 1948.

1. Internal revenue ☞792

ISSUE 1

Where nonresident alien's brother residing in United States traded for alien's benefit on commodity exchanges in United States at authorization of alien, who vested full discretion in brother with regard thereto, and many transactions were effected through different brokers, several accounts were maintained, and substantial gains and losses realized, transactions constituted a "trade or business," profits of which were "capital gains" taxable as income to the alien. 26 U.S.C.A. § 211(b).

See Words and Phrases, Permanent Edition, for other judicial constructions and definitions of "Capital Gains" and "Trade or Business".

2. Internal revenue ☞792

ISSUE 2

The exemption of a nonresident alien's commodity transactions in the United States provided for by the Internal Revenue Code does not apply where alien has agent in United States using his own discretion in effecting transactions for alien's account. 26 U.S.C.A. § 211(b).

———◆———

On Petition to Review the Decision of The Tax Court of the United States.

Petition by Fernand C. A. Adda to review a decision of the Tax Court redetermining a deficiency in income tax imposed by the Commissioner of Internal Revenue.

Decision affirmed.

Rollin Browne and Mitchell B. Carroll, both of New York City, for petitioner.

Irving I. Axelrad, Sp. Asst. to Atty. Gen. (Theron Lamar Caudle, Asst. Atty. Gen., and Ellis N. Slack and A. F. Prescott, Sp. Assts. to Atty. Gen., on the brief), for respondent.

Before PARKER, Chief Judge, and SOPER and DOBIE, Circuit Judges.

PER CURIAM.

[1, 2] This is a petition by a non-resident alien to review a decision of the Tax Court. Petitioner is a national of Egypt, who in the year 1941 was residing in France. He had a brother who at that time was residing in the United States and who traded for petitioner's benefit on commodity exchanges in the United States in cotton, wool, grains, silk, hides and copper. This trading was authorized by petitioner who vested full discretion in his brother with regard thereto, and it resulted in profits in the sum of $193,857.14. The Tax Court said: "While the number of transactions or the total amount of money involved in them has not been stated, it is apparent that many transactions were effected through different brokers, several accounts were maintained, and gains and losses in substantial amounts were realized. This evidence shows that the trading was extensive enough to amount to a trade or business, and the petitioner does not contend, nor has he shown, that the transactions were so infrequent or inconsequential as not to amount to a trade or business." We agree with the Tax Court that, for reasons adequately set forth in its opinion, this income was subject to taxation, and that the exemption of a non-resident alien's commodity transactions in the United States, provided by section 211(b) of the Internal Revenue Code, 26 U.S.C.A. § 211(b), does not apply to a case where the alien has an agent in the United States using his own discretion in effecting the transactions for the alien's account. As said by the Tax Court, "Through such transactions the alien is engaging in trade or business within the United States, and the profits on these transactions are capital gains taxable to him." Nothing need be added to the reasoning of the Tax Court in this connection, and the decision will be affirmed on its opinion.

Affirmed.

Figure V

ADAMSON, JAMES H. & MARION C. v
U. S., — F Supp —, 36 AFTR 1529, 1946
P.-H. ¶ 72,418 (DC Calif) (See Adamson
v U. S.)

ADAMSON, R. R., MRS., — BTA —, 1934 (P.-
H.) BTA Memo. Dec. ¶ 34,370

ADAMSON v U. S., 26 AFTR 1188 (DC Calif,
Sept 8, 1939)
iv—Coggan, Linus C., 1939 (P.-H.) BTA
Memo. Dec. page 39—806

ADAMSON; U. S. v, 161 F(2d) 942, 35 AFTR
1404 (CCA 9)
1—Lazier v U. S., 170 F(2d) 524, 37 AFTR
545, 1948 P.-H. page 73,174 (CCA 8)
1—Grace Bros., Inc. v Comm., 173 F(2d)
178, 37 AFTR 1014, 1949 P.-H. page 72,433
(CCA 9)
1— Briggs; Hofferbert v, 178 F(2d) 744, 38
AFTR 1219, 1950 P.-H. page 72,267 (CCA
4)
1—Rogers v Comm., 180 F(2d) 722, 39 AFTR
115, 1950 P.-H. page 72,531 (CCA 3)
1—Lamar v Granger, 99 F Supp 41, 40
AFTR 270, 1951 P.-H. page 72,945 (DC Pa)
1—Herbert v Riddell, 103 F Supp 383, 41
AFTR 975, 1952 P.-H. page 72,383 (DC
Calif)
1—Hudson, Galvin, 20 TC 737, 20-1953
P.-H. TC 418

ADAMSON v U.S., — F Supp —, 36 AFTR
1529, 1946 P.-H. ¶ 72,418 (DC Calif, Jan
28, 1946)

ADAMS-ROTH BAKING CO., 8 BTA 458
1—Gunderson Bros. Engineering Corp., 16
TC 129, 16-1951 P.-H. TC 72

ADAMSTON FLAT GLASS CO. v COMM.,
162 F(2d) 875, 35 AFTR 1579 (CCA 6)
4—Forrest Hotel Corp. v. Fly, 112 F Supp
789, 43 AFTR 1080, 1953 P.-H. page 72,856
(DC Miss)

ADDA v COMM., 171 F(2d) 457, 37 AFTR 654,
1948 P.-H. ¶ 72,655 (CCA 4, Dec 3, 1948)
Cert. filed, March 1, 1949 (T)
No cert. (G) 1949 P-H ¶ 71,050
x—Adda v Comm., 336 US 952, 69 S Ct 883,
93 L Ed 1107, April 18, 1949 (T)
sa—Adda, Fernand C. A., 10 TC 273 (No.
33), ¶ 10.33 P.-H. TC 1948
iv—Milner Hotels, Inc., N. Y., 173 F (2d)
567, 37 AFTR 1170, 1949 P.-H. page 72,528
(CCA 6)
1—Nubar; Comm. v, 185 F(2d) 588, 39 AFTR
1315, 1950 P.-H. page 73,423 (CCA 4)
g-1—Scottish Amer. Invest. Co., Ltd.,
The, 12 TC 59, 12-1949 P.-H. TC 32
g-1—Nubar, Zareh, 13 TC 579, 13-1949
P.-H. TC 318

ADDA, FERNAND C. A., 10 TC 273 (No.
33), ¶ 10.33 P.-H. TC 1948 (A) 1918-2 CB 1
a—Adda v Comm., 171 F(2d) 457, 37 AFTR
654, 1948 P.-H. ¶ 72.655 (CCA 4)
1—Nubar; Comm. v, 185 F(2d) 588, 39 AFTR
1315, 1950 P.-H. page 73,423 (CCA 4)
g-1—Scottish Amer. Invest. Co., Ltd.,
The, 12 TC 59, 12-1949 P.-H. TC 32
g-1—Nubar, Zareh, 13 TC 579, 13-1949
P.-H. TC 318

ADDA, FERNAND C. A., 10 TC 1291 (No.
168), ¶ 10.168 P.-H. TC 1948 (A) 1953-1
CB 3, 1953 P.-H. ¶ 76.453 (NA) 1948-2
CB 5, 1948 P.-H. ¶ 76,434 withdrawn
1—Scottish Amer. Invest. Co., Ltd., The,
12 TC 59, 12-1949 P.-H. TC 32

ADDA INC., 9 TC 199 (A) 1949-1 CB 1, 1949
P.-H. ¶ 76,260 (NA) 1947-2 CB 6 withdrawn
a—Adda, Inc.; Comm. v, 171 F(2d) 367, 37
AFTR 641, 1948 P.-H. ¶ 72,654 (CCA 2)
a—Adda, Inc.; Comm. v, 171 F(2d) 367, 37
AFTR 641, 1949 P.-H. ¶ 72,303 (CCA 2)
e-1—G.C.M. 26069, 1949-2 CB 38, 1949 P.-H.
page 76,226
3—Koshland, Execx.; U.S. v, 208 F(2d)
640, — AFTR —, 1953 P.-H. page 73,597
(CCA 9)
4—Kent, Otis Beall, 1954 (P. H.) TC
Memo. Dec. page 54—47

ADDA, INC.; COMM. v, 171 F(2d) 367, 37
AFTR 641, 1948 P.-H. ¶ 72,654 (CCA 2, Dec
6, 1948)
sa—Adda, Inc., 9 TC 199
s—Adda, Inc.; Comm. v, 171 F(2d) 367, 37
AFTR 641, 1949 P.-H. ¶ 72,303 (CCA 2) reh.
den.
e-1—G.C.M. 26069, 1949-2 CB 39, 1949 P.-H.
page 76,227
e-2—G.C.M. 26069, 1949-2 CB 39, 1949 P.-H.
page 76,227

ADDA, INC.; COMM. v, 171 F(2d) 367, 37
AFTR 641, 1949 P.-H. ¶ 72,303 (CCA 2, Dec
6, 1948) reh. den.
sa—Adda, Inc., 9 TC 199
s—Adda, Inc.; Comm. v, 171 F(2d) 367, 37
AFTR 641, 1918 P.-H. ¶ 72,654 (CCA 2)

ADDISON-CHEVROLET SALES, INC. v
CHAMBERLAIN, L. A. & NAT. BANK
OF WASH., THE, — F Supp —, — AFTR
—, 1954 P.-H. ¶ 72,550 (DC DC) (See
Campbell v Chamberlain)

ADDISON v COMM., 177 F(2d) 521, 38 AFTR
821, 1949 P.-H. ¶ 72,637 (CCA 8, Nov 3,
1949)
sa—Addison, Irene D., — TC —, 1948
(P.-H.) TC Memo. Dec. ¶ 48,177
1—Roberts, Supt. v U. S., 115 Ct Cl 439,
87 F Supp 937, 38 AFTR 1314, 1950 P.-H.
page 72,292
1—Cold Metal Process Co., The, 17 TC
934, 17-1951 P.-H. TC 512
1—Berger, Samuel & Lillian, 1954 (P.-H.)
TC Memo. Dec. page 54—232
2—Urquhart, George Gordon & Mary F.,
20 TC 948, 20-1953 P.-H. TC 536

ADDISON, IRENE D., — TC —, 1948 (P.-
H.) TC Memo. Dec. ¶ 48,177
App (T) Jan 14. 1949 (CCA 8)
a—Addison v Comm., 177 F(2d) 521, 38
AFTR 821, 1949 P.-H. ¶ 72,637 (CCA 8)
1—Urquhart, George Gordon & Mary F.,
20 TC 948, 20-1953 P.-H. TC 536

ADDITON, HARRY L. & ANNIE S., 3
TC 427
1—Lum, Ralph E., 12 TC 379, 12-1949 P.-H.
TC 204
1—Christie, John A. & Elizabeth H., —
TC —, 1949 (P.-H.) TC Memo. Dec.
page 49—795

ADDRESSOGRAPH - MULTIGRAPH
CORP., 1945 (P.-H.) TC Memo. Dec.
¶ 45,058
f-10—Rev. Rul. 54-71, 1954 P.-H. page
76.453

ADDRESSOGRAPH-MULTIGRAPH CORP.
v U. S., 112 Ct Cl 201, 78 F Supp 111, 37
AFTR 53, 1948 P.-H. ¶ 72,504 (June 1, 1948)
No cert (G) 1949 P.-H. ¶ 71,041
1—New Oakmont Corp., The v U. S., 114
Ct Cl 686, 86 F Supp 901, 38 AFTR 924, 1949
P.-H. page 73,181

ADELAIDE PARK LAND, 25 BTA 211
g—Amer. Security & Fidelity Corp., — BTA
—, 1940 (P.-H.) BTA Memo. Dec. page
40—571

ADELPHI PAINT & COLOR WORKS,
INC., 18 BTA 436
1—Neracher, William A., — BTA —, 1939
(P.-H.) BTA Memo. Dec. page 39—69
1—Lyman-Hawkins Lumber Co., — BTA —,
1939 (P.-H.) BTA Memo. Dec. page 39—350

ADEMAN v U. S., 174 F(2d) 283, 37 AFTR
1406 (CCA 9, April 25, 1949)

ADICONIS, NOELLA L. (PATNAUDE),
1953 (P.-H.) TC Memo. Dec. ¶ 53,305

ADJUSTMENT BUREAU OF ST. LOUIS
ASSN., OF CREDIT MEN, 21 BTA 232
1—Cook County Loss Adjustment Bureau,
— BTA —, 1940 (P.-H.) BTA Memo. Dec.
page 40—331

ADKINS, CHARLES I., — BTA —, 1933
(P.-H.) BTA Memo. Dec. ¶ 33,457

ADLER v COMM., 77 F(2d) 733, 16 AFTR 162
(CCA 5)
g-2—McEuen v Comm., 196 F(2d) 130, 41
AFTR 1172, 1952 P.-H. page 72,604 (CCA 5)

Figure VI

ADASKAVICH—ADELSON   25

ADASKAVICH, STEPHEN A. v U.S., 39 AFTR2d
77-517, 422 F Supp 276 (DC Mont) (See Wiegand,
Charles J., Jr. v U.S.)
AD. AURIEMA, INC., 1943 P-H TC Memo ¶ 43,422
e-1—Miller v U.S., 13 AFTR2d 1515, 166 Ct Cl 257, 331
F2d 859
ADAY v SUPERIOR CT. OF ALAMEDA COUNTY, 8
AFTR2d 5367, 13 Cal Reptr 415, 362 P2d 47 (Calif,
5-11-61)
ADCO SERVICE, INC., ASSIGNEE v CYBERMATICS,
INC., 36 AFTR2d 75-6342 (NJ) (See Adco Service,
Inc., Assignee v Graphic Color Plate)
ADCO SERVICE, INC., ASSIGNEE v GRAPHIC
COLOR PLATE, 36 AFTR2d 75-6342 (NJ, Supr Ct,
11-10-75)
ADCO SERVICE, INC., ASSIGNEE v GRAPHIC
COLOR PLATE, INC., 36 AFTR2d 75-6342 (NJ) (See
Adco Service, Inc., Assignee v Graphic Color Plate)
ADDA v COMM., 171 F2d 457, 37 AFTR 654 (USCA 4)
Rev. Rul. 56-145, 1956-1 CB 613
1—Balanovski: U.S. v, 236 F2d 304, 49 AFTR 2013
(USCA 2)
1—Liang, Chang Hsiao, 23 TC 1045, 23-1955 P-H TC
624
f-1—Asthmanefrin Co., Inc., 25 TC 1141, 25-1956 P-H
TC 639
g-1—de Vegvar, Edward A. Neuman, 28 TC 1061,
28-1957 P-H TC 599
g-1—Purvis, Ralph E. & Patricia Lee, 1974 P-H TC
Memo 74-669
k-1—deKrause, Piedad Alvarado, 1974 P-H TC Memo
74-1291
1—Rev. Rul. 56-392, 1956-2 CB 971
ADDA, FERNAND C.A., 10 TC 273, ¶ 10,133 P-H TC
1948
1—Balanovski; U.S. v, 236 F2d 303, 49 AFTR 2012
(USCA 2)
1—Liang, Chang Hsiao, 23 TC 1045, 23-1955 P-H TC
624
g-1—de Vegvar, Edward A. Neuman, 28 TC 1061,
28-1957 P-H TC 599
g-1—Purvis, Ralph E. & Patricia Lee, 1974 P-H TC
Memo 74-669
k-1—deKrause, Piedad Alvarado, 1974 P-H TC Memo
74-1291
ADDA, INC., 9 TC 199
Pardee, Marvin L., Est. of, 49 TC 152, 49 P-H TC 107
[See 9 TC 206-208]
f-1—Asthmanefrin Co., Inc., 25 TC 1141, 25-1956 P-H
TC 639
1—Keil Properties, Inc. (Dela), 24 TC 1117, 24-1955 P-H
TC 615
1—Saffan, Samuel, 1957 P-H TC Memo 57—701
1—Rev. Rul. 56-145, 1956-1 CB 613
1—Rev. Rul. 56-392, 1956-2 CB 971
4—Midler Court Realty, Inc., 61 TC 597, 61 P-H TC
368
ADDA, INC.; COMM. v, 171 F2d 367, 37 AFTR 641
(USCA 2)
1—Pardee, Marvin L., Est. of, 49 TC 152, 49 P-H TC
107
1—Saffan, Samuel, 1957 P-H TC Memo 57-701
2—Midler Court Realty, Inc., 61 TC 597, 61 P-H TC
368
ADDELSTON, ALBERT A. & SARAH M., 1965 P-H TC
Memo ¶ 65,215
ADDISON v COMM., 177 F2d 521, 38 AFTR 821 (USCA
8)
g-1—Industrial Aggregate Co. v U.S., 6 AFTR2d 5963,
284 F2d 645 (USCA 8)
1—Sturgeon v McMahon, 155 F Supp 630, 52 AFTR
789 (DC NY)
1—Gilmore v U.S., 16 AFTR2d 5211, 5213, 245 F Supp
384, 386 (DC Calif)
1—Waldheim & Co., Inc., 25 TC 599, 25-1955 P-H TC
332
g-1—Galewitz, Samuel & Marian, 50 TC 113, 50 P-H TC
79
1—Buder, G. A., Est. of, 1963 P-H TC Memo 63-345
e-1—Rhodes, Lynn E. & Martha E., 1963 P-H TC
Memo 63-1374
2—Shipp v Comm., 217 F2d 402, 46 AFTR 1170 (USCA
9)

ADDISON—Contd.
g-2—Industrial Aggregate Co. v U.S., 6 AFTR2d 5964,
284 F2d 645 (USCA 8)
e-2—Buder, Est. of v Comm., 13 AFTR2d 1238, 330
F2d 443 (USCA 8)
2—Iowa Southern Utilities Co. v Comm., 14 AFTR2d
5063, 333 F2d 385 (USCA 8)
2—Kelly, Daniel, S.W., 23 TC 687, 23-1955 P-H TC 422
f-2—Morgan, Joseph P., Est. of, 37 TC 36, 37, 37-1961
P-H TC 26, 27
n-2—Woodward, Fred W. & Elsie M., 49 TC 385, 49
P-H TC 270
ADDISON, IRENE D., 1948 P-H TC Memo ¶ 48,177
1—Waldheim & Co., Inc., 25 TC 599, 25-1955 P-H TC
332
f-1—Morgan, Joseph P., Est. of, 37 TC 36, 37, 37-1961
P-H TC 26, 27
1—Buder, G. A., Est. of, 1963 P-H TC Memo 63-345
e-1—Rhodes, Lynn E. & Martha E., 1963 P-H TC
Memo 63-1374
ADDISON, JOHN MILTON, BKPT; U.S. v, 20 AFTR2d
5630, 384 F2d 748 (USCA 5) (See Rochelle Jr., Trtee:
U.S. v)
ADDRESSOGRAPH - MULTIGRAPH CORP., 1945
P-H TC Memo ¶ 45,058
Conn. L. & P. Co., The v U.S., 9 AFTR2d 679, 156 Ct
Cl 312, 314, 299 F2d 264
Copperhead Coal Co., Inc., 1958 P-H TC Memo 58-33
1—Seas Shipping Co., Inc. v Comm., 19 AFTR2d 596,
371 F2d 529 (USCA 2)
e-1—Hitchcock, E. R., Co., The v U.S., 35 AFTR2d
75-1207, 514 F2d 487 (USCA 2)
f-2—Vulcan Materials Co. v U.S., 25 AFTR2d 70-446,
308 F Supp 57 (DC Ala)
f-3—Marlo Coil Co. v U.S., 1969 P-H 58,133 (Ct Cl
Comr Rep)
4—United Gas Improvement Co. v Comm., 240 F2d 318,
50 AFTR 1354 (USCA 3)
10—St. Louis Co. (Del) (in Dissolution) v U.S., 237 F2d
156, 50 AFTR 257 (USCA 3)
ADDRESSOGRAPH - MULTIGRAPH CORP. v U.S.,
112 Ct Cl 201, 78 F Supp 111, 37 AFTR 53
f-1—St. Joseph Lead Co. v U.S., 9 AFTR2d 712, 299
F2d 350 (USCA 2)
e-1—Central & South West Corp. v U.S., 1968 P-H
58,175 (Ct Cl Comr Rep)
1—Smale & Robinson, Inc. v U.S., 123 F Supp 469, 46
AFTR 375 (DC Calif)
1—St. Joseph Lead Co. v U.S., 7 AFTR2d 401, 190 F
Supp 640 (DC NY)
1—Eisenstadt Mfg. Co., 28 TC 230, 28-1957 P-H TC 132
f-2—St. Joseph Lead Co. v U.S., 9 AFTR2d 712, 299
F2d 350 (USCA 2)
f-3—Consol. Coppermines Corp. v U.S., 8 AFTR2d
5873, 155 Ct Cl 736, 296 F2d 745
ADELAIDE PARK LAND, 25 BTA 211
g—Custom Component Switches, Inc. v U.S., 19
AFTR2d 560 (DC Calif) [See 25 BTA 215]
O'Connor, John C., 1957 P-H TC Memo 57-190
ADELBERG, MARVIN & HELEN, 1971 P-H TC Memo
¶ 71,015
ADELMAN v U.S., 27 AFTR2d 71-1464, 440 F2d 991
(USCA 9, 5-3-71)
sa—Adelman v U.S., 24 AFTR2d 69-5769, 304 F Supp
599 (DC Calif)
ADELMAN v U.S., 24 AFTR2d 69-5769, 304 F Supp 599
(DC Calif, 9-30-69)
a—Adelman v U.S., 27 AFTR2d 71-1464, 440 F2d 991
(USCA 9)
ADELSON, SAMUEL; U.S. v, 52 AFTR 1798 (DC RI)
(See Sullivan Co., Inc.: U.S. v)
ADELSON v U.S., 15 AFTR2d 246, 342 F2d 332 (USCA
9, 1-13-65)
sa—Adelson v U.S., 12 AFTR2d 5010, 221 F Supp 31
(DC Calif)
g-1—Greenlee, L. C. & Gladys M., 1966 P-H TC Memo
66-985
f-1—Cochran, Carol J., 1973 P-H TC Memo 73-459
f-1—Marchionni, Siro L., 1976 P-H TC Memo 76-1321
f-2—Krist, Edwin F. v Comm., 32 AFTR2d 73-5663, 483
F2d 1351 (USCA 2)
f-2—Fugate v U.S., 18 AFTR2d 5607, 259 F Supp 401
(DC Tex) [See 15 AFTR2d 249, 342 F2d 335]

the cited case" (iv). One decision (*Comm. v. Nubar*) has limited the cited case to its facts (l), and two decisions (*The Scottish American Investment Co., Ltd.* and *Zareh Nubar*) have distinguished the cited case on issue number one (g–1).

Reference to Volume 1 of the *Citator* Second Series (covering the period from 1954 through 1977) shows the *Adda v. Comm.* case on page 25. This page is reproduced in Figure VI.

Correlating the symbols reproduced in Figure III with the shaded portion of Figure VI reveals the following additional information about *Adda v. Comm.:*

—The case was cited without comment in two rulings and two cases: *Rev.Rul. 56–145* and *Rev.Rul. 56–392, Balanovski* and *Liang.*

—It was followed in *Asthmanefrin Co.* (f–1).

—It was distinguished in *deVegvar* and *Purvis* (g–1).

—It was reconciled in *deKrause* (k–1).

Reference to the "Court Decisions" section of the looseleaf Volume 1 for the *Citator* covering the period from 1977 to the present shows that *Adda v. Comm.* was cited in *Robert E. Cleveland* and *Judith C. Connelly*, each case limited to its facts (l). The looseleaf Volume 2 contains a "Supplementary Compilation" section and a "Current Monthly Supplement" section. When using the looseleaf volumes for the *Citator,* be sure to refer to the "Current Monthly Supplement" in Volume 2. Otherwise, very recent citations might be overlooked.

Except as otherwise noted, it would appear that *Adda v. Comm.* has withstood the test of time.

Problem Materials

Discussion Questions

1. For what reason(s) was the investment tax credit repealed by TRA of 1986?

2. What is meant by revenue neutral tax reform?

3. In what manner does the tax law encourage technological progress?

4. Does the tax law provide any stimulus for the development of international trade? Explain.

5. What purpose is served by provisions in the tax law that encourage private sector pension plans?

6. TRA of 1986 eliminated many low-income persons from being subject to the Federal income tax. On what grounds can this be justified?

7. State the manner in which the following tax provisions encourage small business:

   a. Expensing capital acquisitions.

   b. The nature of a shareholder's loss on a stock investment.

   c. The tax rates applicable to corporations.

   d. Nontaxable corporate reorganizations.

8. Although death taxes imposed on large estates can be justified on the grounds of social desirability, can such taxes carry economic implications? Explain.

9. What purpose is served by the credit allowed for certain child or disabled dependent care expenses?

10. Why should the deductibility of excess political campaign expenditures be contrary to public policy?

11. In the past, proposals have been before Congress that would allow a taxpayer to claim a tax credit for tuition paid to send a dependent to a private school. Is there any justification for such a proposal?

12. What purpose is served by allowing a deduction for home mortgage interest and property taxes?

13. Some states that impose a state income tax allow the taxpayer a deduction for any Federal income taxes paid. What is the justification for such an approach?

14. A provision of the Code allows a taxpayer a deduction for Federal income tax purposes for state and local income taxes paid. Does this provision eliminate the effect of multiple taxation of the same income? Why or why not? In this connection, consider the following:

   a. Taxpayer, an individual, has itemized deductions less than the standard deduction.

   b. Taxpayer is in the 15% tax bracket for Federal income tax purposes. The 28% tax bracket.

15. T operates a profitable sole proprietorship. Because the business is expanding, she would like to transfer it to a newly created corporation. T is concerned, however, over the possible tax consequences that would result from incorporating. Please comment.

16. Assume the same facts as in Question 15. T is also worried that once she incorporates, the business will be subject to the Federal corporate income tax. Any suggestions?

17. In situations in which the tax law recognizes the wherewithal to pay concept, discuss the effect of the following:

   a. The basis to the transferor of property received in an exchange.

   b. The recognition by the transferor of any realized loss on the transfer.

   c. The receipt of boot or other property by the transferor.

18. Can it be said that the application of the wherewithal to pay concept permanently avoids the recognition of any gain or loss by a transferor? Explain.

19. T, an individual, exchanges 100 shares of X Corporation stock for 100 shares of Y Corporation stock. Such exchange is not pursuant to a nontaxable reorganization. Does the wherewithal to pay concept shield T from the recognition of gain or loss? Why?

20. U, a calendar year cash basis taxpayer, is a participant in an H.R. 10 (Keogh) retirement plan for self-employed persons. To get the deduction for 1987, U makes his contribution on December 30, 1987.

   a. Why was there an element of urgency in U's action?

   b. Was U misinformed about the tax law? Explain.

21. What purpose is served by the indexation procedure?

    a. What is the current status of this procedure?

    b. To what items is indexation made applicable?

22. Give an example of how the community property system has affected the Federal tax law.

23. W operates a service business as a sole proprietor. For tax purposes, she recognizes income using the cash method but deducts expenses as they accrue.

    a. What is W trying to accomplish?

    b. Is this procedure proper?

    c. Does the IRS have any recourse?

24. In what way does the wherewithal to pay concept aid the IRS in the collection of tax revenue?

25. Describe how administrative feasibility is achieved for the IRS by each of the following tax provisions:

    a. The standard deduction allowed to individual taxpayers.

    b. The $192,800 unified tax credit allowed for estate tax purposes in 1988.

    c. The $10,000 annual exclusion allowed for gift tax purposes.

    d. The burden of proof in the audit of a taxpayer.

26. What is meant by the concept of substance over form? Why is it variously described as the "telescoping," "collapsing," or "step transaction" approach?

27. What is meant by the concept that statutory relief provisions of the tax law are to be narrowly construed? Where did the concept originate?

28. When does the tax benefit rule apply? With what effect?

29. W Corporation loans $10,000 to Z Corporation with no provision for interest. W Corporation and Z Corporation are owned by the same shareholders. In what manner might the IRS restructure this transaction with adverse tax consequences to W Corporation?

30. Under what circumstances can court decisions lead to changes in the Code?

31. Judicial decisions interpreting a provision of the Internal Revenue Code of 1939 are no longer of any value in view of the enactment of the Internal Revenue Code of 1986. Assess the validity of this statement.

32. Trace through Congress the path usually followed by a tax bill.

33. What is the function of the Joint Conference Committee of the House Ways and Means Committee and the Senate Finance Committee?

34. Why are Committee Reports of Congress important as a source of tax law?

35. What is a Proposed Regulation? How would a Proposed Regulation under § 541 be cited?

36. Distinguish between Treasury Regulations and Revenue Rulings, between Revenue Rulings and Revenue Procedures, and between Revenue Rulings and individual (i.e., private) rulings.

37. What is the difference, if any, between the *Internal Revenue Bulletin* (I.R.B.) and the *Cumulative Bulletin* (C.B.)?

38. Explain the fact-finding determination of a Federal Court of Appeals.

39. Taxpayer lives in Michigan. In a controversy with the IRS, taxpayer loses at the trial court level. Describe the appeal procedure under the following different assumptions:

    a. The trial court was the Small Claims Division of the U.S. Tax Court.

    b. The trial court was the U.S. Tax Court.

    c. The trial court was a U.S. District Court.

    d. The trial court was the U.S. Claims Court.

40. Suppose the U.S. Government loses a tax case in the U.S. District Court of Idaho but does not appeal the result. What does the failure to appeal signify?

41. Because the U.S. Tax Court is a national court, it always decides the same issue in a consistent manner. Assess the validity of this statement.

42. Explain the following abbreviations:

a. CA–2	d. *rev'd.*	g. *acq.*	j. AFTR	m. USSC
b. Cls.Ct.	e. *rem'd.*	h. B.T.A.	k. F.2d	n. S.Ct.
c. *aff'd.*	f. *Cert. denied*	i. USTC	l. F.Supp.	o. D.Ct.

43. What is the difference between a Regular and a Memorandum decision of the U.S. Tax Court?

44. What is a legislative Regulation?

45. In assessing the validity of a court decision, discuss the significance of the following:

    a. The decision was rendered by the U.S. District Court of Wyoming. Taxpayer lives in Wyoming.

    b. The decision was rendered by the U.S. Claims Court. Taxpayer lives in Wyoming.

    c. The decision was rendered by the Second Court of Appeals. Taxpayer lives in California.

    d. The decision was rendered by the U.S. Supreme Court.

    e. The decision was rendered by the U.S. Tax Court. The IRS has acquiesced in the result.

    f. Same as (e) except that the IRS has issued a nonacquiescence as to the result.

46. Is tax avoidance illegal? Explain.

Problems

1. T owns some real estate (basis of $100,000 and fair market value of $60,000) that she would like to sell to her son, S, for $60,000. T is aware, however, that losses on sales between certain related parties are disallowed for Federal income tax purposes [§ 267(a)(1)]. T therefore sells the property to P (an unrelated party) for $60,000. On the same day, P sells the same property to S for the same amount. Is T's realized loss of $40,000 deductible? Explain.

2. P exchanges some real estate (basis of $80,000 and fair market value of $100,000) for other real estate owned by R (basis of $120,000 and fair market value of $90,000) and $10,000 in cash. The real estate involved is unimproved and is held by P and R, before and after the exchange, as investment property.

    a. What is P's realized gain on the exchange? Recognized gain?

    b. What is R's realized loss? Recognized loss?

    c. Support your results to (a) and (b) under the wherewithal to pay concept as applied to like-kind exchanges (§ 1031).

3. In 1988, T (an individual) incurred and paid personal medical expenses of $3,400 and reported adjusted gross income of $40,000. Because of the 7.5% limitation of § 213, T deducted only $400 of these medical expenses [$3,400 − (7.5% × $40,000)] on her 1988 tax return. In 1989, T is reimbursed by her insurance company for $1,200 of the $3,400 medical expenses paid in 1988. How much, if any, of the reimbursement is income to T in 1989?

4. In late 1988, T, a cash basis and calendar year individual, received a state income tax refund for tax year 1987. On his Federal income tax return for 1987, T itemized his deductions and was able to deduct the full amount of state income taxes paid. Comment on the treatment of the refund in connection with the following alternatives:

   a. T should file an amended Federal income tax return for 1987 and reduce his itemized deductions by the amount of the refund.

   b. T should offset his income tax refund against any state income taxes he pays in 1988.

   c. T should include the refund in his gross income for 1988.

   d. T should disregard the refund for income tax purposes.

5. T sells property (basis of $20,000) to V Corporation for $30,000. Based on the following conditions, how could the IRS challenge this transaction?

   a. T is the sole shareholder of V Corporation.

   b. T is the son of the sole shareholder of V Corporation.

   c. T is neither a shareholder in V Corporation nor related to any of V's shareholders.

6. Using the legend provided, classify each of the following statements (Note: more than one answer per statement may be appropriate):

Legend
D = Applies to the U.S. District Court
T = Applies to the U.S. Tax Court
C = Applies to the U.S. Claims Court
A = Applies to the U.S. Court of Appeals
U = Applies to the U.S. Supreme Court
N = Applies to none of the above

   a. Decides only Federal tax matters.

   b. Decisions are reported in the F.2d Series.

   c. Decisions are reported in the USTCs.

   d. Decisions are reported in the AFTRs.

   e. Appeal is by Writ of Certiorari.

   f. Court meets generally in Washington, D.C.

   g. A jury trial is available.

   h. Trial courts.

   i. Appellate courts.

   j. Appeal is to the U.S. Court of Appeals for the Federal Circuit.

   k. Has a Small Claims Division.

   l. The only trial court where the taxpayer does not have to first pay the tax assessed by the IRS.

7. Identify the governmental unit that produces the following tax sources:

    a. Proposed Regulations.

    b. Revenue Procedures.

    c. Letter rulings.

    d. Determination letters.

    e. Technical Advice Memoranda.

8. Locate the following Internal Revenue Code citations and give a brief description of each:

    a. § 55(b)(1)(A).

    b. § 317(a).

    c. § 469(c)(1).

9. Locate the following Regulation citations and give a brief description of each:

    a. Reg. § 1.381(c)(3)–1(e)(3).

    b. Reg. § 1.543–1(b)(4).

    c. Reg. § 1.1502–1(b).

10. What is the subject matter of Revenue Ruling 464 that begins on page 115 of the 1976–2 *Cumulative Bulletin*?

11. Determine the acquiescence/nonacquiescence position of the IRS with respect to the following decisions:

    a. *Virginia Metal Products, Inc.*, 33 T.C. 788 (1960).

    b. *Naeter Bros. Publishing Co.*, 42 T.C. 1 (1964).

12. Locate the following tax services in your library and indicate the name of the publisher and whether the service is organized by topic or by Code Section:

    a. *Federal Taxes*.

    b. *Standard Federal Tax Reporter*.

    c. *Tax Coordinator 2d*.

    d. *Mertens Law of Federal Income Taxation*.

    e. *Tax Management Portfolios*.

    f. Rabkin & Johnson, *Federal Income, Gift and Estate Taxation*.

Research Problems

Research Problem 1. Determine the reliability of the following items:

    a. Rev.Rul. 69–502, 1969–2 C.B. 89.

    b. Rev.Rul. 73–206, 1973–1 C.B. 192.

    c. Rev.Rul. 72–201, 1972–1 C.B. 271.

Research Problem 2. Must the Internal Revenue Service treat similarly situated taxpayers consistently?

Research Problem 3. Determine the disposition of the following decisions at the Supreme Court level:

a. *International Business Machines Corp. v. U.S.*, 343 F.2d 914 (Ct.Cls., 1965).

b. *Knetsch v. U.S.*, 348 F.2d 932 (Ct.Cls., 1965).

c. *American Society of Travel Agents, Inc. v. Blumenthal*, 566 F.2d 145 (CA–D.C., 1977).

d. *Litchfield Securities v. U.S.*, 325 F.2d 667 (CA–2, 1963).

e. *Wilson Bros. & Co. v. Comm.*, 170 F.2d 423 (CA–9, 1948).

Research Problem 4. Did the IRS agree or disagree with the following court decisions:

a. *Joseph Weidenhoff, Inc.*, 32 T.C. 1222 (1959).

b. *Daron Industries, Inc.*, 62 T.C. 847 (1974).

c. *Harvey Coal Corp.*, 12 T.C. 596 (1949).

d. *Burke Concrete Accessories, Inc.*, 56 T.C. 588 (1971).

Research Problem 5. T is a participating physician in a medical plan offered by the SC Corporation. Under a deferred compensation plan, T enters into a supplemental agreement designating 30% of his scheduled fees to be paid to him and the remainder to go into the deferred compensation plan. SC has established a trust with itself as the settlor (i.e., grantor) and beneficiary, and three physicians (including T) as trustees. The trustees purchased retirement annuity policies to provide for the payment of benefits under the plan. These benefits become payable to T (or his beneficiaries) when he retires, dies, becomes disabled, or leaves SC. Are the 70% amounts placed into the trust taxable to T under the constructive receipt doctrine or the economic benefit doctrine?

Research Problem 6. In December of last year, T, a cash basis and calendar year taxpayer, embezzles $200,000 from a bank where he is employed as an assistant cashier. T disappears for parts unknown and goes on a three-month spending spree. In the current year, T is apprehended by law enforcement authorities and forced to make restitution of the $150,000 still not spent. Comment on T's income tax position, with special reference to the mitigation of the annual accounting period concept.

Partial list of research aids:

Code §§ 61, 172, and 1341.

Bernard A. Yerkie, 67 T.C. 388 (1976).

Research Problem 7. Complete the following citations to the extent the research materials are available to you:

a. Rev.Proc. 88–___, I.R.B. No. 1, 36.

b. Rev.Rul. ___, 1981–2 C.B. 243.

c. *Rutkin v. U.S.*, ___ S.Ct. ___ (___, 1952).

d. _____, 40 B.T.A. 333 (1939).

e. *C.F. Kahler*, 18 T.C. ___ (___).

f. *Cowden v. Comm.*, 289 F.2d ___ (CA–___, 1961).

g. *Wolder v. Comm.*, 74–1 USTC ¶ ___ (CA–2, ___).

h. *Harry H. Goldberg*, 29 TCM ___ T.C.Memo. 1970–___.

i. *Shopmaker v. U.S.*, 119 F.Supp. ___ (D.Ct.___1953).

Research Problem 8. By using the research materials available to you, answer the following questions:

a. Has Prop.Reg. § 1.79–1(d)(7) been finalized?

b. What happened to *Barry D. Pevsner,* P-H T.C.Mem.Dec. ¶ 79, 311, on appeal?

c. Does Rev.Rul. 60–97 still represent the position of the IRS on the issue involved?

d. What is the underlying Code Section for Reg. § 1.9101–1? Summarize this Regulation.

2 Corporations: Introduction and Operating Rules

Objectives

Summarize the income tax treatment of various forms of conducting a business.

Determine when an entity will be treated as a corporation for Federal income tax purposes.

Review the general income tax provisions applicable to individuals.

Establish the tax rules peculiar to corporations.

Illustrate the computation of the corporate income tax.

Explain the alternative minimum tax applicable to corporations.

Describe the procedural aspects of filing and reporting for corporate taxpayers.

Evaluate the corporate form as a means of conducting a trade or business.

Outline

Tax Treatment of Various Business Forms

What Is a Corporation?

An Introduction to the Income Taxation of Corporations

An Overview of Corporate Versus Individual Income Tax Treatment

Specific Provisions Compared

Accounting Periods and Methods

Capital Gains and Losses

Recapture of Depreciation

Charitable Contributions

Net Operating Losses

Deductions Available Only to Corporations

Determining the Corporate Income Tax Liability

Corporate Income Tax Rates

Alternative Minimum Tax

Procedural Matters

Filing Requirements for Corporations

Reconciliation of Taxable Income and Financial Net Income

Form 1120–A Illustrated

Tax Planning Considerations

Corporate Versus Noncorporate Forms of Business Organization

The Association Route

Operating the Corporation

ot needed.

Tax Treatment of
Various Business Forms

Business operations can be conducted in a number of different forms. Among the various possibilities are the following:

—Sole proprietorships.

—Partnerships.

—Trusts and estates.

—Subchapter S corporations (also known as S corporations).

—Regular corporations (also called Subchapter C or C corporations).

For Federal income tax purposes the distinction between these forms of business organizations becomes very important. A summary of the tax treatment of each form will highlight these distinctions.

1. Sole proprietorships are not separate taxable entities from the individual who owns the proprietorship. The owner of the business will therefore report all business transactions on his or her individual income tax return.
2. Partnerships are not subject to the income tax. Under the conduit concept, the various tax attributes of the partnership's operations flow through to the individual partners to be reported on their personal income tax returns (see Example 1). Although a partnership is not a tax-paying entity, it is a reporting entity. Form 1065 is used to aggregate partnership transactions for the tax year and to allocate their pass-through to the individual partners. The tax consequences of the partnership form of business organization are outlined in Subchapter K of the Internal Revenue Code and are the subject of Chapters 8 and 9.
3. The income tax treatment of trusts and estates is in some respects similar and in others dissimilar to the partnership approach. In terms of similarity, income is taxed only once. However, tax may be imposed on the entity. Unlike a partnership, therefore, a trust or an estate may be subject to the Federal income tax. Whether the income will be taxed to a trust or an estate or to its beneficiaries generally depends on whether the income is retained by the entity or distributed to the beneficiaries. In the event of distribution, a modified form of the conduit principle is followed to preserve for the beneficiary the character of certain income (e.g., nontaxable interest on municipal bonds). The income taxation of trusts and estates is treated in Chapter 13.[1]
4. Subchapter S of the Code permits certain corporations to elect special tax treatment. Such special treatment generally means avoidance of any income tax at the corporate level. Subchapter S corporations, called S corporations, are treated like partnerships in that the owners of the entity report most of

---

1. The tax treatment of Real Estate Investment Trusts (REIT's) presents peculiar problems and is not covered in this text. See §§ 856–859.

the corporate tax attributes (e.g., income, losses, capital gains and losses, § 1231 gains and losses, charitable contributions, tax-exempt interest) on their individual returns. S corporations and their shareholders are the subject of Chapter 10.

5. The regular corporate form of doing business carries with it the imposition of the corporate income tax. For Federal income tax purposes, therefore, the corporation is recognized as a separate tax-paying entity. This produces what is known as a double tax effect. Income is taxed to the corporation as earned and taxed again to the shareholders as dividends when distributed. Also, the tax attributes of various types of income lose their identity as they pass through the corporate entity. In other words, the corporation does not act as a conduit when making distributions to its shareholders.

Example 1   During the current year, X Company receives tax-exempt interest, which is distributed to its owners. If X Company is a regular corporation, the distribution to the shareholders constitutes a dividend. The fact that it originated from tax-exempt interest is of no consequence.[2] On the other hand, if X Company is a partnership or an S corporation, the tax-exempt interest retains its identity and passes through to the individual partners.

☐

The tax consequences of operating a business in the regular corporate form fall within Subchapter C of the Code and are the subject of this chapter and Chapters 3 through 6.[3] Corporations that either unreasonably accumulate earnings or meet the definition of a personal holding company may be subject to further taxation. These so-called penalty taxes are imposed in addition to the corporate income tax and are discussed in Chapter 7.

Clearly, then, the form of organization chosen to carry on a trade or business has a significant effect on Federal income tax consequences. Though tax considerations may not control the choice, it could be unfortunate if they are not taken into account.

What Is a Corporation?

The first step in any discussion of the Federal income tax treatment of corporations must be definitional. More specifically, what is a corporation? At first glance, the answer to this question would appear to be quite simple. Merely look to the appropriate state law to determine whether the entity has satisfied the specified requirements for corporate status. Have articles of incorporation been drawn up and filed with the state regulatory agency? Has a charter been granted? Has stock been issued to shareholders? These are all points to consider.

---

2. As noted in Chapter 4, such items will, however, affect the distributing corporation's earnings and profits.
3. Special rules apply to cooperative organizations (§ 521), banking institutions (Subchapter H), insurance companies (Subchapter L), and regulated investment companies (Subchapter M). In the interest of space and because of limited applicability, these rules are not discussed in this text.

Compliance with state law, although important, may not tell the full story as to whether or not an entity is to be recognized as a corporation for tax purposes. On the one hand, a corporation qualifying under state law may be disregarded as a taxable entity if it is a mere sham. On the other hand, an organization not qualifying as a regular corporation under state law may be taxed as a corporation under the association approach. These two possibilities are discussed in the following sections.

Disregard of Corporate Entity.   In most cases, the IRS and the courts will recognize a corporation legally constituted under state law. In exceptional situations, however, the corporate entity may be disregarded because it lacks substance.[4] The key to such treatment rests with the degree of business activity conducted at the corporate level. Thus, the more the corporation does in connection with its trade or business, the less likely it will be treated as a sham and disregarded as a separate entity.

Example 2   C and D are joint owners of a tract of unimproved real estate that they wish to protect from future creditors. Consequently, C and D form R Corporation, to which they transfer the land in return for all of the latter's stock. The corporation merely holds title to the land and conducts no other activities. In all respects, R Corporation meets the requirements of a corporation under applicable state law. □

Example 3   Assume the same facts as in Example 2. In addition to holding title to the land, R Corporation leases the property, collects rents, and pays the property taxes thereon. □

R Corporation probably would not be recognized as a separate entity under the facts set forth in Example 2. In Example 3, however, the opposite should prove true. It appears that enough activity has taken place at the corporate level to warrant the conclusion that R Corporation should be treated as a real corporation for Federal income tax purposes.[5]

Whether the IRS or the taxpayers will attempt to disregard the corporate entity must depend on the circumstances of each particular situation. More often than not, the IRS may be trying to disregard (or "collapse") a corporation to make the corporation's income taxable directly to the shareholders. In other situations, a corporation might be trying to avoid the corporate income tax or permit its shareholders to take advantage of excess corporate deductions and losses.[6]

---

4. The reader should bear in mind that the textual discussion relates to the classification of an entity for *Federal* income tax purposes. State corporate income taxes or other corporate taxes (e.g., franchise taxes) may still be imposed. An entity may quite possibly be treated as a corporation for state tax purposes and not for Federal and vice versa. This will become even more apparent when dealing with S corporations (Chapter 10), such status not being recognized by some states.

5. A classic case in this area is *Paymer v. Comm.*, 45–2 USTC ¶9353, 33 AFTR 1536, 150 F.2d 334 (CA–2, 1945). Here, two corporations were involved. The Court chose to disregard one corporate entity but to recognize the other.

6. An election under Subchapter S would accomplish this if it were timely made and the parties qualified. See Chapter 10.

Theoretically speaking, the disregard-of-corporate-entity approach should be equally available to both the IRS and the taxpayers. From a practical standpoint, however, taxpayers have enjoyed considerably less success than has the IRS. Courts generally conclude that since the taxpayers created the corporation in the first place, they should not be permitted later to disregard it in order to avoid taxes.

Associations Taxed as Corporations.   Section 7701(a)(3) defines a corporation to include "associations, joint stock companies, and insurance companies." What Congress intended by the inclusion of associations in the definition has never been entirely clear. Judicial decisions have clarified the status of associations and the relationship between associations and corporations.

The designation given to the entity under state law is not controlling. In one case, what was a business trust under state law was deemed to be an association (and therefore taxable as a corporation) for Federal income tax purposes.[7] In another case, a partnership of physicians was held to be an association even though state law prohibited the practice of medicine in the corporate form.[8] The partnership was thus subject to the Federal income tax rules applicable to corporations.

Whether or not an entity will be considered an association for Federal income tax purposes depends upon the number of corporate characteristics it possesses. According to court decisions and Reg. § 301.7701–2(a), corporate characteristics include the following:

1. Associates.
2. An objective to carry on a business and divide the gains therefrom.
3. Continuity of life.
4. Centralized management.
5. Limited liability.
6. Free transferability of interests.

The Regulations state that an unincorporated organization shall not be classified as an association unless it possesses more corporate than noncorporate characteristics. In making the determination, the characteristics common to both corporate and noncorporate business organizations shall be disregarded.

Both corporations and partnerships generally have associates (i.e., shareholders and partners) and an objective to carry on a business and divide the gains. In testing whether a particular partnership is an association, these criteria would be disregarded. It then becomes a matter of determining whether the partnership possesses a majority of the remaining corporate characteristics (items 3 through 6). Does the partnership terminate upon the withdrawal or death of a partner (i.e., no continuity of life)? Is the management of the partnership centralized, or do all partners participate therein? Are all partners individually liable for the debts of the partnership, or is the liability of some limited to their actual investment in the partnership (i.e., limited partnership)? May a

---

7. *Morrissey v. Comm.*, 36–1 USTC ¶9020, 16 AFTR 1274, 56 S.Ct. 289 (USSC, 1936).
8. *U.S. v. Kintner*, 54–2 USTC ¶9626, 47 AFTR 995, 216 F.2d 418 (CA–9, 1954).

partner freely transfer his or her interest without the consent of the other partners? Courts have ruled that any partnership lacking two or more of these characteristics will not be classified as an association. Conversely, any partnership having three or more of these characteristics will be classified as an association.[9]

For trusts, the first two characteristics would have to be considered in testing for association status. The conventional type of trust often does not have associates and usually restricts its activities to investing rather than carrying on a trade or business. These characteristics, however, are common to corporations. Consequently, whether a trust qualifies as an association depends upon the satisfaction of the first two corporate characteristics.

From a taxpayer's standpoint, the desirability of association status turns on the tax implications involved. In some cases, the parties may find it advantageous to have the entity taxed as a corporation while in others they may not. These possibilities are explored at length under Tax Planning Considerations in this chapter.

An Introduction to the Income Taxation of Corporations

An Overview of Corporate Versus Individual Income Tax Treatment

In any discussion of how corporations are treated under the Federal income tax, the best approach is to compare such treatment with that applicable to individual taxpayers.

Similarities. Gross income of a corporation is determined in much the same manner as it is for individuals. Thus, gross income includes compensation for services rendered, income derived from a business, gains from dealings in property, interest, rents, royalties, dividends—to name only a few such items [§ 61(a)]. Both individuals and corporations are entitled to exclusions from gross income. However, fewer exclusions are allowed for corporate taxpayers. Interest on municipal bonds is excluded from gross income whether the bondholder is an individual or a corporate taxpayer.

Gains and losses from property transactions are handled similarly. For example, whether a gain or loss is capital or ordinary depends upon the nature of the asset in the hands of the taxpayer making the taxable disposition. Code § 1221, in defining what is not a capital asset, makes no distinction between corporate and noncorporate taxpayers. In the area of nontaxable exchanges, corporations are like individuals in that they do not recognize gain or loss on a like-kind exchange (§ 1031) and they may defer recognized gain on an involuntary conversion of property (§ 1033).[10] The nonrecognition of gain provisions dealing with the sale of a personal residence (§§ 121 and 1034) do not apply to

---

9. See *Zuckman v. U.S.*, 75–2 USTC ¶9778, 36 AFTR2d 6193, 524 F.2d 729 (Ct.Cls., 1975), and *P. G. Larson*, 66 T.C. 159 (1976).

10. For definitions of terms such as "like-kind exchange" and "involuntary conversion," see the Glossary of Tax Terms in Appendix C.

corporations. Both corporations and individuals are vulnerable, however, to the disallowance of losses on sales of property to related parties [§ 267(a)(1)] or on the wash sales of securities (§ 1091). The wash sales rules do not apply to individuals who are traders or dealers in securities or to corporations that are dealers if the sales of the securities are in the ordinary course of the corporation's business.

Upon the sale or other taxable disposition of depreciable property, the recapture rules (e.g., §§ 1245 and 1250) generally make no distinction between corporate and noncorporate taxpayers. [However, § 291(a) does cause a corporation to have more recapture on § 1250 property. This difference is discussed later in the chapter.]

The business deductions of corporations also parallel those available to individuals. Therefore, deductions will be allowed for all ordinary and necessary expenses paid or incurred in carrying on a trade or business under the general rule of § 162(a). Specific provision is made for the deductibility of interest, certain taxes, losses, bad debts, accelerated cost recovery, charitable contributions, net operating losses, research and experimental expenditures, and other less common deductions. No deduction will be permitted for interest paid or incurred on amounts borrowed to purchase or carry tax-exempt securities. The same holds true for expenses contrary to public policy and certain unpaid expenses and interest between related parties.

Many of the tax credits available to individuals also can be claimed by corporations. This is the case with the foreign tax credit. Not available to corporations are certain credits that are personal in nature, such as the child care credit, the credit for the elderly, and the earned income credit.

Dissimilarities. Significant variations exist, however, in the income taxation of corporations and individuals. A major variation is that different tax rates apply to corporations (§ 11) and to individuals (§ 1). Corporate tax rates are discussed later in the chapter.

All allowable corporate deductions are treated as business deductions. Thus, the determination of adjusted gross income (AGI), so essential for individual taxpayers, has no relevance to corporations. Taxable income simply is computed by subtracting from gross income all allowable deductions and losses. Corporations need not be concerned with itemized deductions or the standard deduction, nor is the deduction for personal and dependency exemptions available to them.

Because corporations can have only business deductions and losses, the $100 floor on the deductible portion of personal casualty and theft losses and the limitation that nonbusiness casualty losses will be deductible only to the extent such losses exceed 10 percent of AGI do not apply.

Example 4 During 1988, X, a calendar year taxpayer with AGI of $10,000, suffers a casualty loss of $4,000. If X is an individual, only $2,900 ($4,000 − $100 − $1,000) of the casualty loss can be deducted (assuming the loss is personal and there has been no actual insurance recovery and none is reasonably anticipated). Chances are the casualty loss can be claimed only as an itemized deduction and would not be available if X chose not to itemize. On the other hand, if X is a corporation, the item would be deductible in full as a business expense under § 162. □

Specific Provisions Compared

In comparing the tax treatment of individuals and corporations, the following areas warrant special discussion:

—Accounting periods and methods.

—Capital gains and losses.

—Recapture of depreciation.

—Charitable contributions.

—Net operating losses.

—Special deductions available only to corporations.

Accounting Periods and Methods

Accounting Periods.   Corporations generally have the same choices of accounting periods as do individual taxpayers. Like an individual, a corporation may choose a calendar year or a fiscal year for reporting purposes. Corporations, however, enjoy greater flexibility in the selection of a tax year. For example, corporations usually can have different tax years from those of their shareholders. Also, newly formed corporations (as new taxpayers) usually have a choice of any approved accounting period without having to obtain the consent of the IRS.

Personal service corporations (PSCs) and S corporations are subject to severe restrictions in the use of a fiscal year. The rules applicable to S corporations are discussed in Chapter 10. A PSC, often an association treated as a corporation (refer to the earlier discussion in the chapter), is one of which the principal activity is the performance of personal services and such services are substantially performed by owner-employees. The performance of services must be in the fields of health, law, engineering, architecture, accounting, actuarial science, performing arts, or consulting.[11]

By placing the PSC on a fiscal year and retaining a calendar year for the employee-owner, a significant deferral of income could take place.

Example 5 On February 1, 1985, Dr. T (a calendar year taxpayer) incorporates his practice and the corporation adopts a fiscal year of February 1–January 31. The corporation's monthly earnings (before Dr. T's salary) during 1985–1986 are $10,000. In January 1986, the corporation pays Dr. T a salary of $120,000. For fiscal year 1985–1986, therefore, the corporation has no taxable income and pays no income tax. Although Dr. T would have some of his salary withheld for taxes, the full amount of his income tax liability would not be due until April 15, 1987. □

Congress was concerned with the deferral potential of a situation such as the one in Example 5. To cure this perceived abuse, the Tax Reform Act (TRA) of 1986 required all PSCs to change to a calendar year for tax purposes.[12] After considerable controversy led by tax practitioners (whose workload would be seriously bunched), Congress created an exception. Under the Revenue Act of 1987, PSCs can retain a fiscal year, without penalties, provided the corporation

11. § 448(d).
12. § 441(i).

pays the shareholder-employee's salary during the portion of the calendar year after the close of the fiscal year. The amount that has to be paid must be proportionate to the employee's salary received for the previous fiscal year.[13]

Example 6   Assume the same facts as in Example 5, except that fiscal 1987–1988 is involved. Dr. T's PSC can retain its fiscal year without penalty, provided Dr. T receives as salary during the period February 1, 1987, through December 31, 1987, at least $110,000 [(11 months/12 months) × $120,000]. ☐

If the salary test is not satisfied, the PSC can retain the fiscal year, but the corporation's deduction for salary for such year is limited by the following formula:

$$A + A \left(\frac{12 - N}{N}\right)$$

where A is the amount paid after the close of the previous fiscal year and N is the number of months from the end of the fiscal year to the end of the ongoing calendar year.

Example 7   Assume the same facts as in Example 5, except that fiscal 1988–1989 is involved. The PSC paid Dr. T a salary of $77,000 during the period February 1–December 31, 1988. Applying the formula:

$$A = \$77,000$$
$$N = 11$$

the corporation's deduction for Dr. T's salary for fiscal 1988–1989 is limited to $84,000 ($77,000 + [$77,000 $\left(\frac{12 - 11}{11}\right)$]] = $77,000 + $7,000). ☐

Another exception to the prohibition on the use of a fiscal year by PSCs deals with situations involving a business purpose. If the taxpayer is able to convince the IRS that a fiscal year is supported by a business purpose (e.g., it coincides with a natural business cycle), the change to a calendar year is not necessary.

Example 8   R & T is a professional association of public accountants. Because over 40% of its gross receipts are received in March and April of each year from the preparation of tax returns, R & T has a May 1 to April 30 fiscal year. Under these circumstances, one would expect the IRS to permit R & T to continue to use the fiscal year chosen, since it reflects a natural business cycle (i.e., the end of tax season). ☐

Accounting Methods. Effective for taxable years beginning after 1986, the cash method of accounting will be unavailable to regular corporations.[14] Exceptions apply in the following situations:

—S corporations.

—Corporations engaged in the trade or business of farming and timber.

—Qualified personal service corporations.

---

13. §§ 444 and 280H.
14. § 448.

—Corporations with average annual gross receipts of $5 million or less. (In determining the $5 million or less test, the corporation would use the average of the three prior taxable years.)

For corporations that are forced to change from cash to accrual accounting, a four-year transition period is provided to avoid duplication of income or omission of expenses. The transition period begins with the first year of the change.

Example 9
X Corporation, a cash basis regular corporation with a fiscal year of May 1 to April 30, is forced to convert to the accrual basis as of May 1, 1987. As of that date, X Corporation's unrealized accounts receivable exceed its accounts payable by $400,000. For fiscal year May 1, 1987, through April 30, 1988, X Corporation must recognize $100,000 of the $400,000 as income. The remaining $300,000 will be allocated over the next three fiscal years in the amount of $100,000 per year. □

Example 10
Assume the same facts as in Example 9, except that as of May 1, 1987, X Corporation's accounts payable exceed its unrealized accounts receivable by $400,000. For fiscal year May 1, 1987, through April 30, 1988, X Corporation should claim a deduction of $100,000. The remaining $300,000 will be allocated over the next three fiscal years in the amount of $100,000 per year. □

Both individuals and corporations that maintain inventory for sale to customers are required to use the accrual method of accounting for determining sales and cost of goods sold.

Capital Gains and Losses

Capital gains and losses result from the taxable sales or exchanges of capital assets. Whether such gains and losses would be long-term or short-term depends upon the holding period of the assets sold or exchanged. Each year, a taxpayer's long-term capital gains and losses are combined, and the result is either a *net* long-term capital gain or a *net* long-term capital loss. A similar aggregation is made with short-term capital gains and losses, the result being a *net* short-term capital gain or a *net* short-term capital loss. The following combinations and results are possible:

1. A net long-term capital gain and a net short-term capital loss. These are combined, and the result is either a net capital gain or a net capital loss.
2. A net long-term capital gain and a net short-term capital gain. No further combination is made.
3. A net long-term capital loss and a net short-term capital gain. These are combined, and the result is either capital gain net income or a net capital loss.
4. A net long-term capital loss and a net short-term capital loss. No further combination is made.

Capital Gains. Before TRA of 1986, long-term capital gains (combination 2 and, possibly, combination 1) enjoyed favorable tax treatment. Individuals were allowed a 60 percent deduction, which meant that only 40 percent of net capital gains were subject to the income tax. For corporations, the gains were subject to either the applicable corporate rate or an alternative rate of 28 percent.

While retaining the capital gain and loss classification, TRA of 1986 eliminates the preferential treatment previously allowed for net capital gains. Barring certain transitional rules, such gains will therefore be taxed at ordinary income tax rates.[15]

Capital Losses.   Differences exist between corporate and noncorporate taxpayers in the income tax treatment of net capital losses (refer to combinations 3 and 4 and, possibly, to combination 1). Generally, noncorporate taxpayers can deduct up to $3,000 of such net losses against other income.[16] Any remaining capital losses can be carried forward to future years until absorbed by capital gains or by the $3,000 deduction.[17] Carryovers do not lose their identity but remain either long-term or short-term.

Example 11   T, an individual, incurs a net long-term capital loss of $7,500 for calendar year 1988. Assuming adequate taxable income, T may deduct $3,000 of this loss on his 1988 return. The remaining $4,500 (i.e., $7,500 − $3,000) of the loss is carried to 1989 and years thereafter until completely deducted. The $4,500 will be carried forward as a long-term capital loss. □

Unlike individuals, corporate taxpayers are not permitted to claim any net capital losses as a deduction against ordinary income. Capital losses, therefore, can be used only as an offset against capital gains. Corporations may, however, carry back net capital losses to three preceding years, applying them first to the earliest year in point of time. Carryforwards are allowed for a period of five years from the year of the loss. When carried back or forward, a long-term capital loss becomes a short-term capital loss.

Example 12   Assume the same facts as in Example 11, except that T is a corporation. None of the $7,500 long-term capital loss incurred in 1988 can be deducted in that year. T Corporation may, however, carry the loss back to years 1985, 1986, and 1987 (in this order) and apply it to any capital gains recognized in these years. If the carryback does not exhaust the loss, it may be carried forward to calendar years 1989, 1990, 1991, 1992, and 1993 (in this order). Either a carryback or a carryforward of the long-term capital loss converts the loss to a short-term capital loss. □

Recapture of Depreciation

Corporations have more recapture of depreciation under § 1250 than do individuals. Depreciation recapture for § 1245 property is computed in the same manner for individuals and for corporations. However, under § 291(a)(1) for sales of depreciable real estate that is § 1250 property, 20 percent of the excess of any

---

15. For individuals, § 1(j) prevents the net capital gains from being taxed at a rate higher than 28%. For corporations, § 1201(a) limits the maximum rate to 34%.
16. The limitations on capital losses for both corporate and noncorporate taxpayers are contained in § 1211.
17. Carryback and carryover rules for both corporate and noncorporate taxpayers can be found in § 1212.

Section ↓

amount that would be treated as ordinary income under § 1245 over the amount treated as ordinary income under § 1250 is additional ordinary income.

Example 13   A corporation purchased an office building on January 3, 1984, for $300,000. Accelerated depreciation was taken in the amount of $117,000 before the building was sold on January 5, 1988, for $250,000. Straight-line depreciation would have been $80,000 (using a 15-year recovery period under ACRS). Because the building is § 1245 recovery property, the gain of $67,000 [$250,000 − ($300,000 − $117,000)] is recaptured to the extent of all depreciation taken. Thus, all gain is ordinary income under § 1245. □

Example 14   Assume the building in Example 13 is residential rental property, making it § 1250 property. Thus, gain recaptured under § 1250 is $37,000 ($117,000 − $80,000). For an individual taxpayer, the remaining gain of $30,000 would be § 1231 gain. However, for a corporate taxpayer, § 291(a)(1) causes additional § 1250 ordinary income of $6,000, computed as follows:

Section 1245 recapture	$67,000
Less gain recaptured under § 1250	37,000
Excess § 1245 gain	$30,000
Percentage that is ordinary gain	20%
Additional § 1250 gain	$ 6,000
Ordinary income ($37,000 + $6,000)	$43,000
Section 1231 gain ($67,000 − $37,000 − $6,000)	24,000
Total gain	$67,000

□

Example 15   Assume the building in Example 13 is commercial property and straight-line depreciation was used. An individual would report all gain of $30,000 [$250,000 − ($300,000 − $80,000 depreciation)] as § 1231 gain. However, a corporate taxpayer would recapture as ordinary income (under § 291) 20% of the depreciation recapture under § 1245 (20% of $30,000). Thus, $6,000 would be ordinary income, and $24,000 would be § 1231 gain. □

Charitable Contributions

No deduction will be allowed to either corporate or noncorporate taxpayers for a charitable contribution unless the recipient is a qualified charitable organization. Generally, a deduction will be allowed only for the year in which the payment is made. However, an important exception is made for *accrual basis corporations*. Here the deduction may be claimed in the year preceding payment if the contribution has been authorized by the board of directors by the end of that year and is, in fact, paid on or before the fifteenth day of the third month of the next year.[18]

Example 16   On December 28, 1988, XYZ Company, a calendar year accrual basis taxpayer, authorizes a $5,000 donation to the Atlanta Symphony Associa-

---

18. § 170(a)(2).

tion (a qualified charitable organization). The donation is made on March 14, 1989. If XYZ Company is a partnership, the contribution can be deducted only in 1989.[19] ☐

Example 17   Assume the same facts as in Example 16, except that XYZ Company is a corporation. Presuming the December 28, 1988, authorization was made by its board of directors, XYZ Company may claim the $5,000 donation as a deduction for calendar year 1988. If it was not, the deduction may still be claimed for calendar year 1989. ☐

Property Contributions.   For both corporate and noncorporate taxpayers, the amount that can be claimed as a charitable deduction for a noncash contribution generally is measured by the fair market value of the property contributed. If the property has appreciated in value, however, the tax law makes a distinction between ordinary income and capital gain property. If the property had been sold and would have yielded ordinary income, the deduction is limited to the adjusted basis of the property contributed. Only when the property would have yielded a long-term capital gain is a deduction allowed for any appreciation thereon. Section 1231 property (i.e., depreciable property and real estate used in a trade or business and held for the long-term holding period) would not be ordinary income property except to the extent of its recapture potential under §§ 1245 and 1250.

Not all capital gain property is treated alike for purposes of the charitable contribution deduction. The appreciation is not deductible in the following two situations:

1. Tangible personal property is involved, and the use of the property by the charitable organization is unrelated to the purpose or function constituting the basis for exemption under § 501.
2. The donation is to a private foundation [as defined in § 509(a)].

In situation 1, tangible personalty does not include real estate and intangible property (e.g., stocks and bonds).

Example 18   In the current year, X (a retail grocer) contributes the following items to qualified charitable organizations:

	Adjusted Basis	Fair Market Value
Canned food products given to the local Salvation Army soup kitchen	$ 4,000	$ 4,400
Rare gem collection given to the Civic Symphony Association	50,000	120,000
Texaco stock held for two years as an investment and given to the Methodist Church building fund	20,000	25,000

---

19. Each partner will pick up his or her allocable portion of the charitable contribution deduction as of December 31, 1989 (the end of the partnership's tax year). See Chapter 8.

Since the canned food products were inventory to X (i.e., ordinary income property), the deduction is limited to $4,000. Because of situation 1, none of the appreciation on the rare gem collection can be claimed. Thus, the deduction is limited to $50,000. As to the Texaco stock, it is a capital asset and if sold would have yielded a long-term capital gain of $5,000. Consequently, the $5,000 appreciation is allowable resulting in a deduction of $25,000. Situation 1 does not apply, since stock is an intangible. As noted later in the chapter, the $5,000 amount is a tax preference item for purposes of the alternative minimum tax. □

Corporations enjoy two special exceptions where 50 percent of the appreciation (but not to exceed twice the basis) on property will be allowed on certain contributions. The first exception concerns inventory if the property is used in a manner related to the exempt purpose of the donee and the donee uses the property solely for the care of the ill, the needy, or infants.

Example 19   Assume the same facts as in Example 18, except that X is a regular corporation. Under the exception, the donation to the Salvation Army would increase by $200 [50% × ($4,400 − $4,000)] for a total of $4,200. All other allowable contribution amounts would remain the same. □

The second exception deals with gifts of scientific property to colleges and certain scientific research organizations for use in research, provided certain conditions are met.[20] As was true of the inventory exception, 50 percent of the appreciation on such property will be allowed as an additional deduction.

Limitations Imposed on Charitable Contribution Deductions.   Like individuals, corporations are not permitted an unlimited charitable contribution deduction.[21] For any one year, a corporate taxpayer is limited to 10 percent of taxable income, computed without regard to the charitable contribution deduction, any net operating loss carryback or capital loss carryback, and the dividends received deduction. Any contributions in excess of the 10 percent limitation may be carried forward to the five succeeding tax years. Any carryforward must be added to subsequent contributions and will be subject to the 10 percent limitation. In applying this limitation, the current year's contributions must be deducted first, with excess deductions from previous years deducted in order of time.[22]

Example 20   During 1988, T Corporation (a calendar year taxpayer) had the following income and expenses:

Income from operations	$140,000
Expenses from operations	110,000
Dividends received	10,000
Charitable contributions made in May 1988	5,000

---

20. These conditions are set forth in § 170(e)(4). For the inventory exception, see § 170(e)(3).
21. The percentage limitations applicable to individuals and corporations are set forth in § 170(b).
22. The carryover rules relating to all taxpayers are in § 170(d).

For purposes of the 10% limitation *only*, T Corporation's taxable income is $40,000 [$140,000 − $110,000 + $10,000]. Consequently, the allowable charitable deduction for 1988 is $4,000 (10% × $40,000). The $1,000 unused portion of the contribution can be carried forward to 1989, 1990, 1991, 1992, and 1993 (in that order) until exhausted. □

Example 21   Assume the same facts as in Example 20. In 1989, T Corporation has taxable income (for purposes of the 10% limitation) of $50,000 and makes a charitable contribution of $4,500. The maximum deduction allowed for 1989 would be $5,000 (10% × $50,000). The first $4,500 of the allowed deduction must be allocated to the contribution made in 1989, and $500 of the balance is carried over from 1988. The remaining $500 of the 1988 contribution may be carried over to 1990, etc. □

Net Operating Losses

The net operating loss of a corporation may be carried back three years and forward 15 to offset taxable income for those years and is not subject to the adjustments required for individual taxpayers. A corporation does not adjust its tax loss for the year for capital losses as do individual taxpayers. This is true because a corporation is not permitted a deduction for net capital losses. A corporation does not make adjustments for nonbusiness deductions as do individual taxpayers. Further, a corporation is allowed to include the dividends received deduction (discussed below) in computing its net operating loss.[23]

Example 22   In 1988, X Corporation has gross income (including dividends) of $200,000 and deductions of $300,000 excluding the dividends received deduction. X Corporation had received taxable dividends of $100,000 from Exxon stock. X Corporation has a net operating loss computed as follows:

Gross income (including dividends)		$ 200,000
Less:		
Business deductions	$300,000	
Dividends received deduction		
(70% of $100,000)	70,000	370,000
Taxable income (or loss)		$(170,000)

The net operating loss is carried back three years to 1985. (X Corporation may forgo the carryback option and elect instead to carry forward the loss.) Assume X Corporation had taxable income of $40,000 in 1985. The carryover to 1986 is computed as follows:

---

23. The modifications required to arrive at the amount of net operating loss that can be carried back or forward are in § 172(d).

Taxable income for 1985	$ 40,000
Less net operating loss carryback	170,000
Taxable income for 1985 after net operating loss carryback (carryover to 1986)	$(130,000)

Deductions Available Only to Corporations

Dividends Received Deduction. The purpose of the dividends received deduction is to prevent triple taxation. Absent the deduction, income paid to a corporation in the form of a dividend would be subject to taxation for a second time (once to the distribution corporation) with no corresponding deduction to the distributing corporation. Later, when the recipient corporation paid the income to its individual shareholders, such income would again be subject to taxation with no corresponding deduction to the corporation. The dividends received deduction alleviates this inequity by causing only some or none of the dividend income to be subject to taxation at the corporate level.

The amount of the dividends received deduction depends upon the percentage of ownership the recipient corporate shareholder holds in a domestic corporation making the dividend distribution.[24] For dividends received (or accrued) after 1987, the deduction percentage is summarized as follows:

Percentage of Ownership by Corporate Shareholder	Deduction Percentage
Less than 20%	70%
20% or more (but less than 80%)	80%
80% or more *	100%

* The payor corporation must be a member of an affiliated group with the recipient corporation.

For dividends received (or accrued) during 1987, the deduction was 80 percent as long as the ownership percentage was less than 80 percent.

Example 23 During 1987 and 1988, U Corporation (a calendar year cash basis taxpayer) owned 18% of the stock in W Corporation. During these years, W Corporation distributed cash dividends to U Corporation as follows: $100,000 in 1987 and $100,000 in 1988. U Corporation's dividends received deduction is $80,000 for 1987 and $70,000 for 1988. □

The dividends received deduction is limited to a percent of the taxable income of a corporation computed without regard to the net operating loss, the dividends received deduction, and any capital loss carryback to the current tax year. The percentage of taxable income limitation corresponds to the deduc-

---

24. § 243(a).

tion percentage. Thus, if a corporate shareholder owns less than 20 percent of the stock in the distributing corporation, the dividends received deduction is limited to 70 percent of taxable income. However, the taxable income limitation does not apply if the corporation has a net operating loss for the current taxable year.[25]

In working with this myriad of rules, the following steps need to be taken:

1. Multiply the dividends received by the deduction percentage.
2. Multiply the taxable income by the deduction percentage.
3. The deduction is limited to the lesser of Step 1 or Step 2, unless subtracting the amount derived in Step 1 from 100 percent of taxable income generates a loss. If so, the amount derived in Step 1 should be used.

Example 24   P, R, and T Corporations are three unrelated calendar year corporations and for 1988 have the following transactions:

	P Corporation	R Corporation	T Corporation
Gross income from operations	$400,000	$320,000	$260,000
Expenses from operations	(340,000)	(340,000)	(340,000)
Dividends received from domestic corporations (less than 20% ownership)	200,000	200,000	200,000
Taxable income before the dividends received deduction	$260,000	$180,000	$120,000

In determining the dividends received deduction, use the step procedure just described:

Step 1 (70% × $200,000)	$140,000	$140,000	$140,000
Step 2			
70% × $260,000 (taxable income)	$182,000		
70% × $180,000 (taxable income)		$126,000	
70% × $120,000 (taxable income)			$ 84,000
Step 3			
Lesser of Step 1 or Step 2	$140,000	$126,000	
Generates a net operating loss			$140,000

□

R Corporation is subject to the 70 percent of taxable income limitation. It does not qualify for loss rule treatment, since subtracting $140,000 (Step 1) from $180,000 (100 percent of taxable income) does not yield a negative figure. T Corporation does qualify for loss rule treatment, because subtracting $140,000 (Step 1) from $120,000 (100 percent of taxable income) does yield a negative figure. In summary, the dividends received deduction for each corporation for

---

25. § 246(b).

1988 is as follows: $140,000 for P Corporation, $126,000 for R Corporation, and $140,000 for T Corporation.

If a corporation already has a net operating loss before any dividends received are claimed, the taxable income limitation would not apply. Consequently, the full dividends received deduction is allowed.

Deduction of Organizational Expenditures.   Expenses incurred in connection with the organization of a corporation normally are chargeable to a capital account. That they benefit the corporation during its existence seems clear. But how can they be amortized when most corporations possess unlimited life? The lack of a determinable and limited estimated useful life would therefore preclude any tax write-off. Code § 248 was enacted to solve this problem.

Under § 248, a corporation may elect to amortize organizational expenditures over a period of 60 months or more. The period begins with the month in which the corporation begins business.[26] Organizational expenditures subject to the election include legal services incident to organization (e.g., drafting the corporate charter, bylaws, minutes of organizational meetings, terms of original stock certificates), necessary accounting services, expenses of temporary directors and of organizational meetings of directors or shareholders, and fees paid to the state of incorporation. Expenditures that do not qualify include those connected with issuing or selling shares of stock or other securities (e.g., commissions, professional fees, and printing costs) or with the transfer of assets to a corporation. Such expenditures reduce the amount of capital raised and are not deductible at all.

To qualify for the election, the expenditure must be *incurred* before the end of the taxable year in which the corporation begins business. In this regard, the corporation's method of accounting is of no consequence. Thus, an expense incurred by a cash basis corporation in its first tax year would qualify even though not paid until a subsequent year.

The election is made in a statement attached to the corporation's return for its first taxable year. The return and statement must be filed no later than the due date of the return (including any extensions). The statement must set forth the description and amount of the expenditure involved, the date such expenditures were incurred, the month in which the corporation began business, and the number of months (not less than 60) over which such expenditures are to be deducted ratably.

If the election is not made on a timely basis, organizational expenditures cannot be deducted until the corporation ceases to do business and liquidates. These expenditures will be deductible if the corporate charter limits the life of the corporation.

Example 25   T Corporation, an accrual basis taxpayer, was formed and began operations on May 1, 1988. The following expenses were incurred during its first year of operations (May 1–December 31, 1988):

---

26. The month in which a corporation begins business may not be immediately apparent. See Reg. § 1.248–1(a)(3). For a similar problem in the Subchapter S area, see Chapter 10.

Expenses of temporary directors and of organizational meetings	$500
Fee paid to the state of incorporation	100
Accounting services incident to organization	200
Legal services for drafting the corporate charter and bylaws	400
Expenses incident to the printing and sale of stock certificates	300

Assume T Corporation makes a timely election under § 248 to amortize qualifying organizational expenses over a period of 60 months. The monthly amortization would be $20 [($500 + $100 + $200 + $400) ÷ 60 months], and $160 ($20 × 8 months) would be deductible for tax year 1988. Note that the $300 of expenses incident to the printing and sale of stock certificates does not qualify for the election. These expenses cannot be deducted at all but reduce the amount of the capital realized from the sale of stock. □

Organizational expenditures are to be distinguished from start-up expenditures covered by § 195. Start-up expenditures refer to various investigation expenses involved in entering a new business, whether incurred by a corporate or a noncorporate taxpayer. Such expenditures (e.g., travel, market surveys, financial audits, legal fees), at the election of the taxpayer, can be amortized over a period of 60 months or longer rather than capitalized as part of the cost of the business acquired.

Determining the Corporate Income Tax Liability

Corporate Income Tax Rates

Pre-TRA of 1986 Rates.   Before TRA of 1986, corporate income tax rates were as follows:

Taxable Income	Rates
$ 1–$ 25,000	15%
25,001– 50,000	18
50,001– 75,000	30
75,001– 100,000	40
Over $100,000	46
Excess over $1,000,000	For tax years beginning after 1983, an additional tax of 5% of the excess (but not to exceed $20,250)

Current Rates.   TRA of 1986 reduces the income tax brackets from five to three, as follows:

Taxable Income	Tax Rate
$50,000 or less	15%
Over $50,000 but not over $75,000	25
Over $75,000	34

For a corporation that has taxable income in excess of $100,000 for any taxable year, the amount of the tax shall be increased by the lesser of (1) five percent of such excess or (2) $11,750. In effect, the additional tax means a 39 percent rate for every dollar of taxable income from $100,000 to $335,000.[27]

Example 26 X Corporation, a calendar year taxpayer, has taxable income of $90,000 for 1988. Its income tax liability will be $18,850 determined as follows: $7,500 (15% × $50,000) + $6,250 (25% × $25,000) + $5,100 (34% × $15,000). □

Example 27 Y Corporation, a calendar year taxpayer, has taxable income of $335,000 for 1988. Its income tax liability will be $113,900 determined as follows: $7,500 (15% × $50,000) + $6,250 (25% × $25,000) + $88,400 (34% × $260,000) + $11,750 (5% × $235,000). Note that the tax liability of $113,900 is 34% of $335,000. Thus, the benefit of the lower rates on the first $75,000 of taxable income completely phases out at $335,000. □

Under the Revenue Act of 1987 and effective for taxable years beginning after December 31, 1987, qualified personal service corporations will be taxed at a flat 34 percent rate on all taxable income. Thus, PSCs will not enjoy the tax savings of 15 percent (on the first $50,000) and 25 percent (on the next $25,000) lower brackets. For this purpose, a qualified personal service corporation is one that is substantially employee owned and engages in one of the following activities: health, law, engineering, architecture, accounting, actuarial science, performing arts, or consulting.

Transitional Rules. The current corporate income tax rates are effective for taxable years beginning on or after July 1, 1987. Blended rates (i.e., a combination of prior and current rates) must be applied for taxable years that include July 1, 1987.[28] In determining the tax liability under blended rates, the instructions to Form 1120 (U.S. Corporation Income Tax Return) contain a useful worksheet.

Example 28 Z Corporation, a calendar year corporation, has taxable income of $1,500,000 for 1987. Under § 15, Z Corporation will determine its tax for the year by prorating a tax for the period before July 1, 1987, and for the period beginning on July 1, 1987, using the tax rates in effect for each period.

Tax on taxable income of $1,500,000 at rates in effect before July 1, 1987, is as follows:

---

27. § 11(b).
28. § 15.

$ 25,000 × 15%	= $ 3,750
25,000 × 18%	= 4,500
25,000 × 30%	= 7,500
25,000 × 40%	= 10,000
1,400,000 × 46%	= 644,000
5% of excess over $1,000,000 but limited to	20,250
Total tax	$690,000

Tax on taxable income of $1,500,000 at rates in effect on and after July 1, 1987, is as follows:

$ 50,000 × 15%	= $ 7,500
25,000 × 25%	= 6,250
1,425,000 × 34%	= 484,500
5% of excess over $100,000 but limited to	11,750
Total tax	$510,000
No. of days 1/1/87 to 6/30/87 = 181	
No. of days 7/1/87 to 12/31/87 = 184	

1987 tax:

$690,000 × (181/365) =	$342,164
510,000 × (184/365) =	257,096
Total tax	$599,260

The total tax of $599,260 approximates 40% of taxable income of $1,500,000. ☐

Alternative Minimum Tax

In General. The alternative minimum tax (AMT) applicable to corporations is quite similar to that applicable to individuals.[29] Many of the adjustments and tax preference items necessary to arrive at alternative minimum taxable income (AMTI) are the same. The rates and exemptions are different, but the objective is identical. The objective is to force taxpayers who are more profitable than their taxable income reflects to pay additional income taxes.

The formula for determining the AMT liability of corporate taxpayers appears in Figure I and follows the format of Form 4626 (Alternative Minimum Tax—Corporations).

---

29. The alternative minimum tax provisions are contained in §§ 55 through 59.

AMT Adjustments. Figure I reflects that the starting point for computing AMTI is the taxable income of the corporation before any net operating loss deduction. To this amount, certain adjustments must be made. Unlike tax preference items, which are always additions, the adjustments may either increase or decrease taxable income.

Although net operating losses are separately stated in Figure I, they are, in fact, negative adjustments. They are separately stated in Figure I and on Form 4626 because they may not exceed more than 90 percent of AMTI. Thus, such adjustments cannot be determined until all other adjustments and tax preference items are considered. Other adjustments include the following:

—A portion of accelerated depreciation on property placed in service after 1986. For realty, the adjustment amount will be the difference between accelerated and straight-line depreciation using a 40-year life. For personalty, the adjustment is the excess of accelerated depreciation over the amount determined using the 150 percent declining-balance method switching to straight-line.

—The excess of mining exploration and development costs over what would have resulted if the costs had been capitalized and written off over 10 years.

—For contracts entered into on or after March 1, 1986, the requirement that the percentage of completion method be used for AMTI purposes. Thus, corporations using the completed contract method must make the appropriate adjustment.

—For AMTI purposes, denial to dealers of the use of the installment method in accounting for sales. Consequently, gain must be reflected in the year the property is disposed of.

—A portion of business untaxed reported profits.

Figure I   AMT Formula for Corporations

Regular taxable income before NOL deduction

Plus/minus: AMT adjustments

Plus: Tax preferences

Equals: AMTI before AMT NOL deduction

Minus: AMT NOL deduction

Equals: Alternative minimum taxable income (AMTI)

Minus: Exemption

Equals: Alternative minimum tax base

Times: 20% rate

Equals: AMT before AMT foreign tax credit

Minus: AMT foreign tax credit

Equals: Tentative minimum tax

Minus: Regular tax liability before credits minus regular foreign tax credit

Equals: Alternative minimum tax (AMT)

Business Untaxed Reported Profits.   An additional adjustment is included in determining AMTI with respect to those corporations whose taxable income differs from income used for financial accounting purposes. Because of the notoriety received by the news that some large corporations were able to enjoy large book profits but paid little, if any, Federal income tax, Congress decided to make sure some of these book profits would be subject to tax. At least for 1987 through 1989, this is done by making one half of the excess of pretax book income over AMTI a positive adjustment.

Example 29   Z Corporation's pretax book income is $1,000,000, and its AMTI (before including the adjustment for business untaxed reported profits) is $200,000. The adjustment is $400,000 [50% $\times$ ($1,000,000 − $200,000)]. Thus, total AMTI becomes $600,000 ($200,000 + $400,000). □

In the determination of book income, Congress provided the order of priority (i.e., if item 1 exists, it is to be used), summarized as follows:

1. Financial statements filed with the Securities and Exchange Commission.
2. Certified audited financial statements prepared for nontax purposes (e.g., reporting to shareholders).
3. Financial statements that must be filed with any Federal or other governmental agency (e.g., state railroad commission).
4. Financial statements used for credit purposes.
5. Financial statements provided to shareholders.
6. Financial statements used for other substantial nontax purposes.
7. The corporation's earnings and profits for the year.

Many accountants are fearful that the motivation to reduce book income to avoid the AMT may lead to manipulation of sound accounting standards for financial reporting. If this fear is justified, using book income as the base for any tax may be an undesirable approach in the long run.

After 1989, the use of pretax book income is to be replaced by a concept based on earnings and profits. However, the corporation currently may elect to use current earnings and profits in determining the business untaxed reported profits adjustment if items 1, 2, or 3 (as noted above) do not exist. Such an election is irrevocable, but it may be attractive where the earnings and profits amount is closer to AMTI than to book income.

Tax Preferences.   AMTI includes designated tax preference items. In many cases, this has the effect of subjecting nontaxable income to the AMT. Some of the most common tax preferences include the following:

—Amortization claimed on certified pollution control facilities.

—Accelerated depreciation on real property in excess of straight-line.

—Tax-exempt interest on state and local bonds where the generated funds are not used for an essential function of the government.

—Percentage depletion claimed in excess of the adjusted basis of property.

—The excess of intangible drilling costs over 10-year amortization if in excess of 65 percent of net oil and gas income.

—Untaxed appreciation on property donated to charity.

Example 30   For 1988, W Corporation (a calendar year taxpayer) had the following transactions:

Taxable income	$200,000
Mining exploration costs	50,000
Percentage depletion claimed (the property has a zero adjusted basis)	70,000
Donation of land held since 1980 as an investment (basis of $40,000 and fair market value of $50,000) to a qualified charity	50,000
Interest on City of Elmira (Michigan) bonds. The proceeds were used for nongovernmental purposes	20,000

W Corporation's AMTI for 1988 is determined as follows:

Taxable income		$200,000
Adjustments		
Excess mining exploration costs [$50,000 (amount expensed) − $5,000 (amount allowed over a 10-year amortization period)]		45,000
Tax preferences		
Excess depletion	$70,000	
Untaxed appreciation on charitable contribution ($50,000 − $40,000)	10,000	
Interest on bonds	20,000	100,000
AMTI		$345,000

Exemption.   The AMT is 20 percent of AMTI that exceeds the exemption amount. The exemption amount for a corporation is $40,000 reduced by 25 percent of the amount by which AMTI exceeds $150,000.

Example 31   Y Corporation has AMTI of $180,000. Since the exemption amount is reduced by $7,500 [25% × ($180,000 − $150,000)], the amount remaining is $32,500 ($40,000 − $7,500). Thus, Y Corporation's alternative minimum tax base (refer to Figure I) is $147,500 ($180,000 − $32,500). □

Note that the exemption phases out entirely when AMTI reaches $310,000.

Other Aspects of AMT.   Investment tax credit carryovers under the regular tax can offset 25 percent of AMT liability. Only 90 percent of foreign tax credits can be applied against AMT liability.

Because it is possible for a taxpayer to be subject to the AMT in one year and the regular tax in a later year, the minimum credit was devised. This would mitigate the double tax effect of taxing a deferred preference (e.g., percentage depletion) under both the AMT and the regular income tax. Thus, a portion of the earlier AMT could be used as a credit against the later regular tax.

Unfortunately, the law does not cover the reverse situation (i.e., preference item generates a regular tax in one year and results in an AMT in a later year). An example could be unearned income that is taxed in the year of receipt but is not recognized for book income purposes until the year earned. Consequently, it is entirely possible that the same income could be taxed twice.

In addition to paying their regular tax liability, corporations will have to make estimated tax payments of the AMT liability. Even for corporations that prepare quarterly financial statements, this requirement could add to compliance costs. Unfortunately, the estimated tax payment dates will not coincide with the dates of the financial statements. It may, therefore, be difficult to estimate book income accurately for AMT purposes from the usual information available.

For taxable years beginning after December 31, 1986, the tax law imposes an environmental tax on corporations with large amounts of AMTI. The tax is 0.12 percent on the excess of modified AMTI over $2,000,000.[30] Modified AMTI is AMTI determined without regard to any AMT NOL adjustment and the environmental tax deduction. No tax credits are allowed against the tax, and the corporation must include the tax in its quarterly estimated payments. A corporation may be subject to the environmental tax even though it owes no AMT (i.e., the regular corporate income tax is larger).

Both the AMT and the environmental tax can be computed and reported by completing Form 4626 [Alternative Minimum Tax—Corporations (Including Environmental Tax)].

Procedural Matters

Filing Requirements for Corporations

A corporation must file a return whether or not it has taxable income.[31] A corporation that was not in existence throughout an entire annual accounting period is required to file a return for that fraction of the year during which it was in existence. In addition, the corporation must file a return even though it has ceased to do business if it has valuable claims for which it will bring suit. It is relieved of filing returns once it ceases business and dissolves, retaining no assets, whether or not under state law it is treated as a corporation for certain limited purposes connected with the winding up of its affairs, such as for suing and being sued.

The corporate return is filed on Form 1120 unless the corporation is a small corporation entitled to file the shorter Form 1120–A. Corporations having gross receipts or sales, total income (gross profit plus other income including gains

---

30. § 59A.
31. § 6012(a)(2).

on sales of property), or total assets not exceeding $250,000 each may file Form 1120–A if the following additional requirements are met: The corporation may not be involved in a dissolution or liquidation, be a member of a controlled group under §§ 1561 and 1563, file a consolidated return, have ownership in a foreign corporation, and have foreign shareholders who directly or indirectly own 50 percent or more of its stock. Corporations electing under Subchapter S (see Chapter 10) file on Form 1120S. Forms 1120, 1120–A, and 1120S are reproduced in Appendix B.

The return must be filed on or before the fifteenth day of the third month following the close of a corporation's tax year. Corporations can receive an automatic extension of six months for filing the corporate return by filing Form 7004 by the due date for the return.[32] However, the IRS may terminate the extension by mailing a 10-day notice to the taxpayer corporation.

A corporation must make payments of estimated tax unless its tax liability can reasonably be expected to be less than $500. The payments must be at least 90 percent of the corporation's final tax.[33] These payments can be made in four installments due on or before the fifteenth day of the fourth month, the sixth month, the ninth month, and the twelfth month of the corporate taxable year. The full amount of the unpaid tax is due on the due date of the return.

A corporation failing to pay 90 percent of its final tax liability as estimated tax payments will be subjected to a nondeductible penalty on the amount by which the installments are less than 90 percent of the tax due unless the installments are based on (1) tax liability for the prior year, (2) tax liability on the prior year's income computed using tax rates for the current year, or (3) 90 percent of the tax that would be due on its income computed on an annualized basis.

A *large* corporation (defined as one with taxable income in excess of one million dollars in any of three preceding taxable years) cannot rely on exceptions (1) and (2).

Reconciliation of Taxable Income and Financial Net Income

Taxable income and financial net income for a corporation are seldom the same amount. For example, a difference may arise if the corporation uses accelerated cost recovery system (ACRS) for tax purposes and straight-line depreciation for financial purposes. Consequently, cost recovery allowable for tax purposes may differ from book depreciation.

Many items of income for accounting purposes, such as proceeds from a life insurance policy on the death of a corporate officer and interest on municipal bonds, may not be taxable income. Some expense items for financial purposes, such as expenses to produce tax-exempt income, estimated warranty reserves, a net capital loss, and Federal income taxes, may not be deductible for tax purposes.

Schedule M–1 on the last page of Form 1120 is used to reconcile financial net income (net income after Federal income taxes) with taxable income (as computed on the corporate tax return before the deduction for a net operating

---

32. § 6081.
33. § 6655(b).

loss and for the dividends received deduction). In the left-hand column of Schedule M–1, net income per books is added to the Federal income tax liability for the year, the excess of capital losses over capital gains (which cannot be deducted in the current year), taxable income that is not income in the current year for financial purposes, and expenses recorded on the books that are not deductible on the tax return. In the right-hand column, income recorded on the books that is not currently taxable or is tax-exempt and deductions for tax purposes that are not expenses for financial purposes are deducted from the left-hand column total to arrive at taxable income (before the net operating loss deduction and the dividends received deduction).

Example 32   During 1988, T Corporation had the following transactions:

Net income per books (after tax)	$92,400
Taxable income	50,000
Federal income tax liability (15% × $50,000)	7,500
Interest income from tax-exempt bonds	5,000
Interest paid on loan, the proceeds of which were used to purchase the tax-exempt bonds	500
Life insurance proceeds received as a result of the death of a key employee	50,000
Premiums paid on keyman life insurance policy	2,600
Excess of capital losses over capital gains	2,000

For book and tax purposes, T Corporation determines depreciation under the straight-line method. T Corporation's Schedule M–1 for the current year is as follows:

Schedule M-1	**Reconciliation of Income per Books With Income per Return** You are not required to complete this schedule if the total assets on line 14, column (d), of Schedule L are less than $25,000.			
1 Net income per books	92,400	7 Income recorded on books this year not included in this return (itemize)		
2 Federal income tax	7,500	a Tax-exempt interest $ 5,000		
3 Excess of capital losses over capital gains	2,000	Life insurance proceeds on keyman $50,000		55,000
4 Income subject to tax not recorded on books this year (itemize) _____		8 Deductions in this tax return not charged against book income this year (itemize)		
_____		a Depreciation $ _____		
5 Expenses recorded on books this year not deducted in this return (itemize)		b Contributions carryover $ _____		
a Depreciation $ _____		_____		
b Contributions carryover $ _____				
Int. on tax exempt bonds $ 500				
Prem. on keyman insurance $ 2,600	3,100	9 Total of lines 7 and 8		55,000
6 Total of lines 1 through 5	105,000	10 Income (line 28, page 1)—line 6 less line 9		50,000

□

Schedule M–2 reconciles unappropriated retained earnings at the beginning of the year with unappropriated retained earnings at year-end. Beginning balance plus net income per books, as entered on line 1 of Schedule M–1, less dividend distributions during the year equals ending retained earnings. Other sources of increases or decreases in retained earnings are also listed on Schedule M–2.

Example 33   Assume the same facts as in Example 32. T Corporation's beginning balance in unappropriated retained earnings is $125,000. During the year, T Corporation distributed a cash dividend of $30,000 to its shareholders.

Based on these further assumptions, T Corporation's Schedule M–2 for the current year follows:

Schedule M-2	Analysis of Unappropriated Retained Earnings per Books (line 24, Schedule L) You are not required to complete this schedule if the total assets on line 14, column (d), of Schedule L are less than $25,000.				
1 Balance at beginning of year	125,000	5 Distributions: **a** Cash	30,000
2 Net income per books	92,400	**b** Stock	
3 Other increases (itemize)		**c** Property	
		6 Other decreases (itemize)	
		7 Total of lines 5 and 6	30,000
4 Total of lines 1, 2, and 3	217,400	8 Balance at end of year (line 4 less line 7)	187,400

Form 1120–A Illustrated

The Cash-Carry Flower Shop, Inc., was incorporated on July 1, 1982. All of its stock is owned by various unrelated parties. The corporation is engaged in the business of selling fresh cut flowers and plants. Its employer identification number is 10–2134657, and its business address is 1349 Brentwood Lane, Fairfield, MD 20715. The corporation uses the accrual method of accounting and reports on a calendar year basis for tax purposes. For 1987, the corporation made estimated tax payments of $6,000 and had no 1986 overpayments that could be allowed as a credit.

The corporate books and records reflect the following profit and loss items for 1987:

Account	Debit	Credit
Gross sales		$248,000
Sales returns and allowances	$ 7,500	
Cost of goods sold	144,000	
Interest income (taxable)		942
Compensation of officers	23,000	
Salaries and wages	24,320	
Rents	6,000	
Taxes	3,320	
Interest expense	1,340	
Contributions	1,820	
Advertising	3,000	
Federal income tax accrued	5,340	
Net income per books after tax	29,302	
Total	$248,942	$248,942

In arriving at cost of goods sold, the purchases amount was $134,014. Also considered were other costs of $9,466 for items relating to the sale of flowers and plants, such as flower pots, vases, stands, boxes, wire strands, and tissue paper.

Comparative balance sheets for the Cash-Carry Flower Shop, Inc., are presented at the bottom of the next two pages:

Form 1120-A

Department of the Treasury
Internal Revenue Service

U.S. Corporation Short-Form Income Tax Return
To see if you qualify to file Form 1120-A, see instructions.

1235

OMB No. 1545-0890

1987

For calendar 1987 or tax year beginning _____, 1987, ending _____, 19__

See Instructions for list of principal business

A Activity: Flower sh
B Product or service: Flowers
C Code: 5995

Use IRS label. Otherwise, please type or machine print

Name: Cash-Carry Flower Shop, Inc.
Number and street: 1349 Brentwood Lane
City or town, state, and ZIP code: Fairfield, MD 20715

D Employer identification number (EIN): 10-2134657
E Date incorporated: 7/1/82
F Total assets (See Specific Instructions.)
Dollars: $ 65,987   Cents:

G Check method of accounting: (1) ☐ Cash (2) ☒ Accrual (3) ☐ Other (specify) ▶ _____
H Check applicable boxes: (1) ☐ Initial return (2) ☐ Change in address

Income

1a	Gross receipts or sales	248,000	b Less returns and allowances 7,500	Balance ▶ 1c	240,500
2	Cost of goods sold and/or operations (see instructions)		2	144,000
3	Gross profit (line 1c less line 2)		3	96,500
4	Domestic corporation dividends subject to the Section 243(a)(1) deduction		4	
5	Interest		5	942
6	Gross rents		6	
7	Gross royalties		7	
8	Capital gain net income (attach separate Schedule D (Form 1120))		8	
9	Net gain or (loss) from Form 4797, line 18, Part II (attach Form 4797)		9	
10	Other income (see instructions)		10	
11	TOTAL income—Add lines 3 through 10		11	97,442

Deductions (See Instructions for limitations on deductions)

12	Compensation of officers (see instructions)		12	23,000
13a	Salaries and wages 24,320	b Less jobs credit	Balance ▶ 13c	24,320
14	Repairs		14	
15	Bad debts (see instructions)		15	
16	Rents		16	6,000
17	Taxes		17	3,320
18	Interest		18	1,340
19	Contributions (see instructions for 10% limitation)		19	1,820
20	Depreciation (attach Form 4562)	20		
21	Less depreciation claimed elsewhere on return	21a	21b	
22	Other deductions (attach schedule) (Advertising)		22	3,000
23	TOTAL deductions—Add lines 12 through 22		23	62,800
24	Taxable income before net operating loss deduction and special deductions (line 11 less line 23)		24	34,642
25	Less: a Net operating loss deduction (see instructions)	25a		
	b Special deductions (see instructions)	25b	25c	
26	Taxable income (line 24 less line 25c)		26	34,642
27	TOTAL TAX (from Part I, line 6 on page 2)		27	5,340

Tax and Payments

28	Payments:			
a	1986 overpayment allowed as a credit			
b	1987 estimated tax payments	6,000		
c	Less 1987 refund applied for on Form 4466	( )	6,000	
d	Tax deposited with Form 7004			
e	Credit from regulated investment companies (attach Form 2439)			
f	Credit for Federal tax on gasoline and special fuels (attach Form 4136)		28	6,000
29	Enter any PENALTY for underpayment of estimated tax—Check ▶ ☐ if Form 2220 is attached		29	
30	TAX DUE—If the total of lines 27 and 29 is larger than line 28, enter AMOUNT OWED		30	
31	OVERPAYMENT—If line 28 is larger than the total of lines 27 and 29, enter AMOUNT OVERPAID		31	660
32	Enter amount of line 31 you want: Credited to 1988 estimated tax ▶ 660 Refunded ▶		32	

Please Sign Here

Under penalties of perjury, I declare that I have examined this return, including accompanying schedules and statements, and to the best of my knowledge and belief, it is true, correct, and complete. Declaration of preparer (other than taxpayer) is based on all information of which preparer has any knowledge.

Signature of officer: *George Rose*   Date: 2/14/88   Title: President

Paid Preparer's Use Only

Preparer's signature ▶ _____ Date _____ Check if self-employed ▶ ☐   Preparer's social security number _____
Firm's name (or yours if self-employed) and address ▶ _____   E.I. No. ▶ _____   ZIP code ▶ _____

For Paperwork Reduction Act Notice, see page 1 of the instructions.

Form **1120-A** (1987)

Assets	January 1, 1987	December 31, 1987
Cash	$20,540	$18,498
Inventories	2,530	2,010
Federal bonds	13,807	45,479
Total assets	$36,877	$65,987

Form 1120-A (1987)   Page 2

Part I	Tax Computation (See Instructions.) Enter EIN ▶	10-2134657		
1	Income tax (See instructions to figure the tax. Enter lesser of this tax or alternative tax from Schedule D.) Check if from Schedule D ▶ ☐	1	5,340	
2	Credits. Check if from: ☐ Form 3800 ☐ Form 3468 ☐ Form 5884 ☐ Form 6478 ☐ Form 6765 ☐ Form 8586	2		
3	Line 1 less line 2	3	5,340	
4	Tax from recomputing prior-year investment credit (attach Form 4255)	4		
5	Alternative minimum tax (see instructions—attach Form 4626)	5		
6	Total tax—Add lines 3 through 5. Enter here and on line 27, page 1	6	5,340	

Additional Information (See instruction F.)

I Was a deduction taken for expenses connected with:

(1) An entertainment facility (boat, resort, ranch, etc.)? Yes ☐ No ☒

(2) Employees' families at conventions or meetings? Yes ☐ No ☒

J Did any individual, partnership, estate, or trust at the end of the tax year own, directly or indirectly, 50% or more of the corporation's voting stock? (For rules of attribution, see section 267(c).) If "Yes," complete (1) and (2) . . . . Yes ☐ No ☒

(1) Attach a schedule showing name, address, and identifying number.

(2) Enter "highest amount owed;" include loans and accounts receivable/payable:

(a) Enter highest amount owed by the corporation to such owner during the year ▶

(b) Enter highest amount owed to the corporation by such owner during the year ▶

K Enter the amount of tax-exempt interest received or accrued during the tax year ▶

L (1) If an amount for cost of goods sold and/or operations is entered on line 2, page 1, complete (a) through (c):

(a) Purchases ▶	134,014	
(b) Additional sec. 263A costs (see instructions) ▶		
(c) Other costs (attach schedule) ▶	9,466	

(2) Do the rules of section 263A (with respect to property produced or acquired for resale) apply to the corporation? . . . . Yes ☐ No ☒

M At any time during the tax year, did you have an interest in or a signature or other authority over a financial account in a foreign country (such as a bank account, securities account, or other financial account)? (See instruction F for filing requirements for Form TD F 90-22.1.) . . . . Yes ☐ No ☒

If "Yes," write in the name of the foreign country
▶

N During this tax year was any part of your accounting/tax records maintained on a computerized system? . . . . Yes ☐ No ☒

O Enter amount of cash distributions and the book value of property (other than cash) distributions made in this tax year ▶

Part II	Balance Sheets	(a) Beginning of tax year	(b) End of tax year
Assets	1 Cash	20,540	18,498
	2 Trade notes and accounts receivable		
	a Less: allowance for bad debts	( )	( )
	3 Inventories	2,530	2,010
	4 Federal and state government obligations	13,807	45,479
	5 Other current assets (attach schedule)		
	6 Loans to stockholders		
	7 Mortgage and real estate loans		
	8 Depreciable, depletable, and intangible assets		
	a Less: accumulated depreciation, depletion, and amortization	( )	( )
	9 Land (net of any amortization)		
	10 Other assets (attach schedule)		
	11 Total assets	36,877	65,987
Liabilities and Stockholders' Equity	12 Accounts payable	6,415	6,223
	13 Other current liabilities (attach schedule)		
	14 Loans from stockholders		
	15 Mortgages, notes, bonds payable		
	16 Other liabilities (attach schedule)		
	17 Capital stock (preferred and common stock)	20,000	20,000
	18 Paid-in or capital surplus		
	19 Retained earnings	10,462	39,764
	20 Less cost of treasury stock	( )	( )
	21 Total liabilities and stockholders' equity	36,877	65,987

Part III	Reconciliation of Income per Books With Income per Return (Must be completed by all filers)

1 Enter net income per books	29,302	5 Income recorded on books this year not included in this return (itemize)		
2 Federal income tax	5,340			
3 Income subject to tax not recorded on books this year (itemize)		6 Deductions in this tax return not charged against book income this year (itemize)		
4 Expenses recorded on books this year not deducted in this return (itemize)		7 Income (line 24, page 1). Enter the sum of lines 1, 2, 3, and 4 less the sum of lines 5 and 6	34,642	

Liabilities and Equity	January 1, 1987	December 31, 1987
Accounts payable	$ 6,415	$ 6,223
Capital stock	20,000	20,000
Retained earnings	10,462	39,764
Total liabilities and equity	$36,877	$65,987

The completed Form 1120-A for the Cash-Carry Flower Shop, Inc., is reproduced above.

Although most of the entries of Form 1120-A for Cash-Carry Flower Shop, Inc., are self-explanatory, the following additional comments should be helpful:

—To arrive at the cost of goods sold figure appearing on line 2 (page 1), the instructions require that the preparer answer item L in Part I (page 2). Other costs (e.g., flower pots, vases, stands) relating to cost of goods sold should be added to purchases and supported by a schedule. Thus, $2,530 (beginning inventory) + $134,014 (purchases) + $9,466 (other costs) − $2,010 (ending inventory) = $144,000 (cost of goods sold).

—The charitable contributions listed on line 19 (page 1) are within the 10 percent limitation imposed on corporations. Therefore, the $1,820 amount is allowed in full.

—Lines 1 through 6 of Part I (page 2) are used for tax computation purposes. The § 11(b) tax on taxable income of $34,642 (see line 26 of page 1) is $5,340 and is entered on line 27 of page 1. The income was determined by using blended rates (refer to Example 28 for an illustration of the procedure used). Because $6,000 was prepaid, the overpayment of $660 can either be claimed as a refund or be credited towards the 1988 estimated tax (line 32 of page 1).

—Part III (page 2), although not designated as such, serves the same function as the Schedule M-1 to Form 1120 previously illustrated in Example 32 by reconciling net income per books with income per return (i.e., taxable income).

Concept Summary

Income Taxes of Individuals and Corporations Compared

	Individuals	Corporations
Computation of Gross Income	§ 61.	§ 61.
Computation of Taxable Income	§§ 62, 63(b) through (h).	§ 63(a). Concept of AGI has no relevance.
Deductions	Trade or business (§ 162); non-business (§ 212); some personal and employee expenses (generally deductible as itemized deductions).	Trade or business (§ 162).
Charitable Contributions	Limited in any tax year to 50% of AGI; 30% for long-term capital gain property unless election is made to reduce fair market value of gift; 20% for private nonoperating foundations.	Limited in any tax year to 10% of taxable income computed without regard to the charitable contribution deduction, net operating loss, and dividends received deduction.

	Individuals	Corporations
	Excess charitable contributions carried over for five years.	Same as for individuals.
	Amount of contribution is the fair market value of the property; if lower, ordinary income property will be limited to adjusted basis; capital gain property will be treated as ordinary income property if certain tangible personalty is donated to a nonuse charity or a private foundation is the donee.	Same as individuals, but exceptions allowed for certain inventory and for scientific property where one half of the appreciation will be allowed as a deduction.
	Time of deduction—year in which payment is made.	Time of deduction—year in which payment is made unless accrual basis taxpayer. Accrual basis corporation can take deduction in year preceding payment if contribution was authorized by board of directors by end of year and contribution is paid by fifteenth day of third month of following year.
Casualty Losses	$100 floor on personal casualty and theft losses; personal casualty losses deductible only to extent losses exceed 10% of AGI.	Deductible in full.
Depreciation Recapture Under § 1250	Recaptured to extent accelerated depreciation exceeds straight-line.	20% of excess of amount that would be recaptured under § 1245 over amount recaptured under § 1250 is additional ordinary income.
Net Operating Loss	Adjusted for nonbusiness deductions over nonbusiness income and personal exemptions.	Generally no adjustments.
	Carryback period is 3 years while carryforward period is 15 years.	Same as for individuals.
Dividend Exclusion and Deduction	None	Generally 70% of dividends received.
Net Capital Gains	Taxed in full, but rate cannot exceed 28%.	Taxed in full, but rate cannot exceed 34%.
Capital Losses	Only $3,000 of capital loss per year can offset ordinary income; loss is carried forward indefinitely to offset capital gains or ordinary income up to $3,000; carryovers remain long-term or short-term (as the case may be).	Can offset only capital gains; carried back three years and forward five; carryovers and carrybacks are short-term losses.

	Individuals	Corporations
Tax Rates	Mildly progressive with five rates for 1987 (11%, 15%, 28%, 35%, and 38.5%) and two rates for 1988 (15% and 28%); phase-out of 15% bracket begins in 1988 as taxpayers (depending on filing status) reach a certain level of taxable income.	Mildly progressive with three rates (15%, 25%, and 34%) starting July 1, 1987; blended rates apply to tax years straddling this date; lower brackets phased out between $100,000 and $335,000 of taxable income.
Alternative Minimum Tax	Applied at a 21% rate to AMTI; exemption allowed depending on filing status (e.g., $40,000 for married filing jointly); exemption phases out when AMTI reaches a certain amount (e.g., $150,000 for married filing jointly).	Applied at a 20% rate on AMTI (taxable income as modified by certain adjustments plus preference items); $40,000 exemption allowed but phases out once AMTI reaches $150,000; adjustments and tax preference items similar to those applicable to individuals but also include one half of pretax book profits over AMTI.

✓ Tax Planning Considerations

Corporate Versus Noncorporate Forms of Business Organization

The decision to use the corporate form in conducting a trade or business must be weighed carefully. Besides the nontax considerations attendant to the corporate form (i.e., limited liability, continuity of life, free transferability of interest, and centralized management), tax ramifications will play an important role in any such decision. Close attention should be paid to the following:

1. The regular corporate form means the imposition of the corporate income tax. Corporate-source income will be taxed twice—once as earned by the corporation and again when distributed to the shareholders. Since dividends are not deductible, a strong incentive exists in a closely-held corporation to structure corporate distributions in a deductible form. Thus, profits may be bailed out by the shareholders in the form of salaries, interest, or rents. Such procedures lead to a multitude of problems, one of which, the reclassification of debt as equity, is discussed in Chapter 3. The problems of unreasonable salaries and rents are covered in Chapter 4 in the discussion of constructive dividends.

2. Assuming the current tax rates remain in effect, the top rates definitely favor the noncorporate taxpayer over the corporate taxpayer. For example, the top rate for individuals is 28 percent for 1988. For corporations, the top rate is 34 percent. The differential is not so pronounced, however, if one presumes a shareholder with a top rate of 28 percent and a corporation that limits its taxable income to $100,000 to avoid the phase-out of the 15 percent and 28 percent lower brackets. Here, the time value of the taxes saved (by

not distributing dividends and postponing the effect of the double tax that otherwise results) could make operating a business in the corporate form advantageous.

3. Corporate source income loses its identity as it passes through the corporation to the shareholders. Thus, items possessing preferential tax treatment (e.g., interest on municipal bonds) are not taxed as such to the shareholders.

4. As noted in Chapter 4, it may be difficult for shareholders to recover some or all of their investment in the corporation without an ordinary income result, since most corporate distributions are treated as dividends to the extent of the corporation's earnings and profits.

5. Corporate losses cannot be passed through to the shareholders.[34]

6. The liquidation of a corporation may generate tax consequences to both the corporation and its shareholders (see Chapter 5).

7. The corporate form provides the shareholders with the opportunity to be treated as employees for tax purposes if the shareholders, in fact, render services to the corporation. Such status makes a number of attractive tax-sheltered fringe benefits available. They include, but are not limited to, group term life insurance (§ 79), the $5,000 death gratuity [§ 101(b)(1)], and meals and lodging (§ 119). These benefits are not available to partners and sole proprietors.

The Association Route

Consideration 7 in the preceding section led to the popularity of the professional association. The major tax incentive involved was to cover the shareholder-employees under a qualified pension plan. Professionals, particularly physicians, who were not permitted to form regular corporations either because of state law prohibitions or ethical restrictions, created organizations with sufficient corporate attributes to be classified as associations. The position of the IRS on the status of these professional associations (whether or not they should be treated as corporations for tax purposes) vacillated over a period of years. After a series of judicial losses, however, the IRS has accepted their association status, assuming certain conditions are satisfied.[35]

Over recent years, the popularity of the association approach has diminished significantly. Changes in the tax law have curtailed the deferral opportunities of qualified pension and profit sharing plans available to employees. At the same time, improvements were made to H.R. 10 (i.e., Keogh) plans available to self-employed taxpayers. By placing the two types of plans on a parity with each other, one of the major incentives to achieve employee status through association status no longer exists.

Operating the Corporation

Tax planning to reduce corporate income taxes should occur before the end of the tax year. Effective planning can cause income to be shifted to the next tax

---

34. Points 1, 2, and 5 could be resolved through a Subchapter S election (see Chapter 10), assuming the corporation qualifies for such an election. In part, the same can be said for point 3.

35. See, for example, *U.S. v. Empey*, 69–1 USTC ¶9158, 23 AFTR2d 69–425, 406 F.2d 157 (CA–10, 1969).

year and can produce large deductions by incurring expenses before year-end. Attention should especially be focused on the following.

Charitable Contributions.   Recall that accrual basis corporations may claim a deduction for charitable contributions in the year preceding payment if the contribution has been authorized by the board of directors by the end of the tax year and is paid on or before the fifteenth day of the third month of the following year. Even though the contribution may not ultimately be made, it might well be authorized. A deduction cannot be thrown back to the previous year (even if paid within the 2½ months) if it has not been authorized.

Timing of Capital Gains and Losses.   The corporation should consider offsetting profits on the sale of capital assets by selling some of the depreciated securities in the corporate portfolio. In addition, any already realized capital losses should be carefully monitored. Recall that corporate taxpayers are not permitted to claim any net capital losses as deductions against ordinary income. Capital losses can be used only as an offset against capital gains. Further, net capital losses can only be carried back three years and forward five. Gains from the sales of capital assets should be timed to offset any capital losses. The expiration of the carryover period for any net capital losses should be watched carefully so that sales of appreciated securities occur before that date.

Net Operating Losses.   In some situations the election to forgo a net operating loss carryback and utilize the carryforward option might generate greater tax savings. In this regard, one must take into account three considerations. First, the time value of the tax refund that is lost by not using the carryback procedure must be considered. Second, the election to forgo a net operating loss carryback is irrevocable. Thus, one cannot later choose to change if the future high profits predicted do not materialize. Third, one must consider the future increases (or decreases) in corporate income tax rates that can reasonably be anticipated. This last consideration undoubtedly will be the most difficult to work with. Although corporate tax rates have remained relatively stable in past years, the changes made by TRA of 1986 and projected budget deficits do little to assure taxpayers that future rates will remain constant.

Dividends Received Deduction.   Although the dividends received deduction normally is limited to the lesser of 70 percent of the qualifying dividends or 70 percent of taxable income, an exception is made when the full deduction yields a net operating loss. In close situations, therefore, the proper timing of income or deductions may yield a larger dividends received deduction.

Organizational Expenditures.   To qualify for the 60-month amortization procedure of § 248, only organizational expenditures incurred in the first taxable year of the corporation can be considered. This rule could prove to be an unfortunate trap for corporations formed late in the year.

Example 34   T Corporation is formed in December 1988. Qualified organizational expenditures are incurred as follows: $2,000 in December 1988 and $3,000 in January 1989. If T Corporation uses the calendar year for tax purposes, only $2,000 of the organizational expenditures can be written off over a period of 60 months. ☐

The solution to the problem posed by Example 34 is for T Corporation to adopt a fiscal year that ends beyond January 31. All organizational expenditures will then have been incurred before the close of the first taxable year.

Shareholder-Employee Payment of Corporate Expenses. In a closely-held corporate setting, shareholder-employees often pay corporate expenses (e.g., travel and entertainment) for which they are not reimbursed by the corporation. The IRS often disallows the deduction of these expenses by the shareholder-employee, since the payments are voluntary on the part of such shareholder-employee. If the deduction is more beneficial at the shareholder-employee level, a corporate policy against reimbursement of such expenses should be established. Proper planning in this regard would be to decide before the beginning of each tax year where the deduction would do the most good. Any corporate policy regarding reimbursement of such expenses could be modified on a year-to-year basis depending upon the varying circumstances.

In deciding whether corporate expenses should be kept at the corporate level or shifted to the shareholder-employee, the impact of TRA of 1986 will have to be considered. One important point is the treatment of unreimbursed employee expenses after 1986. First, since employee expenses are now itemized deductions, they will be of no benefit to the taxpayer who chooses the standard deduction option. Second, these expenses will be subject to the two percent of AGI limitation. No such limitation will be imposed if the expenses are claimed by the corporation.

Problem Materials

Discussion Questions

1. Briefly discuss the income tax consequences of the various forms of business organization in relation to the following:

   a. The tax treatment of sole proprietorships.

   b. Partnerships and the conduit concept.

   c. Partnerships as reporting entities.

   d. The similarities and dissimilarities between the tax treatment of partnerships, trusts, and estates.

   e. The similarities between S corporations and partnerships.

   f. The dissimilarities between S corporations and regular corporations.

   g. The similarities and dissimilarities between the tax treatment of individuals and regular corporations.

2. What effect does state law have in determining whether an entity is to be treated as a corporation for Federal income tax purposes?

3. Under what circumstances may a corporation legally constituted under state law be disregarded for Federal income tax purposes?

4. Why might the IRS attempt to disregard a legally constituted corporate entity? Why might the shareholders attempt such?

5. Evaluate the disadvantages of using the corporate form in carrying on a trade or business in light of the following:

    a. No deduction is permitted for dividend distributions.

    b. The conduit concept does not apply.

6. What is an association? How is it taxed?

7. Under what circumstances might the owners of a business wish to have the business classified as an association? Not be so classified?

8. In testing for association status, what criteria are considered for partnerships? For trusts?

9. Compare the income tax treatment of corporations and individuals in the following respects:

    a. Applicable tax rates.

    b. Adjusted gross income determination.

    c. The deduction for casualty losses.

    d. Allowable tax credits.

    e. Recapture of depreciation.

    f. Dividends received from domestic corporations.

    g. Net operating losses.

    h. The alternative minimum tax.

10. Beginning after 1986, personal service corporations will have to adopt a calendar year for tax purposes. Is this statement entirely correct? What is a personal service corporation?

11. Effective for taxable years beginning after 1986, the cash method of accounting will be unavailable to corporations. Is this a correct statement? Why or why not?

12. Compare the tax treatment of corporate and noncorporate taxpayers' capital gains and losses with respect to the following:

    a. Net capital gains.

    b. A net long-term capital loss.

    c. A net short-term capital loss.

    d. Capital loss carrybacks.

    e. Capital loss carryovers.

13. What is the justification for the dividends received deduction?

14. The amount of the dividends received deduction may depend on the percentage of ownership held by the corporate shareholder. Explain.

15. Compare the tax treatment of corporate and noncorporate taxpayers' charitable contributions with respect to the following:

    a. The year of the deduction for an accrual basis taxpayer.

    b. The percentage limitations on the maximum deduction allowed for any one year.

    c. The amount of the deduction allowed for the donations of certain inventory.

16. In connection with organizational expenditures, comment on the following:

    a. Those that qualify for amortization.

    b. Those that do not qualify for amortization.

    c. The period over which amortization can take place.

    d. Expenses incurred but not paid by a cash basis corporation.

    e. Expenses incurred by a corporation in its second year of operation.

    f. The alternative if no election to amortize is made.

    g. The timing of the election to amortize.

17. Effective for tax years beginning on or after July 1, 1987, the corporate income tax can be expressed by use of the following formula: $13,750 + 34% of taxable income in excess of $75,000.

    a. Do you agree? Explain.

    b. When would the formula work?

18. Qualified personal service corporations need not be concerned about keeping taxable income at $100,000 or less. Please comment.

19. For AMTI purposes, what is the difference between adjustments and tax preferences?

20. As it relates to the alternative minimum tax, what purpose does the business untaxed reported profits concept serve?

21. When should a corporation consider an election to use earnings and profits in its computation of the business untaxed reported profits AMT adjustment?

22. What are the conditions for filing a Form 1120–A?

23. What purpose is served by Schedule M–1 of Form 1120? By Schedule M–2?

Problems

1. Z Corporation, a cash basis regular corporation with a fiscal year of July 1 to June 30, is forced to convert to the accrual basis as of July 1, 1987. As of that date, Z Corporation's unrealized accounts receivable exceed its accounts payable by $440,000. Describe the tax effect of the conversion.

2. XYZ Corporation incurred net short-term capital gains of $30,000 and net long-term capital losses of $80,000 during 1988. Taxable income from other sources was $400,000. Prior years' transactions included the following:

1984	Net long-term capital gains	$80,000
1985	Net short-term capital gains	20,000
1986	Net long-term capital gains	10,000
1987	Net long-term capital gains	10,000

    a. How are the capital gains and losses treated on the 1988 tax return?

    b. Compute the capital loss carryback to the carryback years.

    c. Compute the amount of capital loss carryover, if any, and designate the years to which the loss may be carried.

3. X Corporation acquired residential rental property on January 3, 1985, for $100,000. The property was depreciated using the accelerated method and a 15-year recovery period under ACRS. Depreciation in the amount of $31,000 was claimed. X Corporation sold the property on January 1, 1988, for $110,000. What is the gain on the sale, and how is it taxed?

4. Assume the property in Problem 3 was a commercial building and X Corporation used the straight-line method of depreciation with a 15-year recovery period under ACRS. What would be the gain on the sale, and how would it be taxed?

5. T, a calendar year taxpayer engaged in the catering business, makes the following donations to qualified charitable organizations during 1988:

	Adjusted Basis	Fair Market Value
Used delivery van to half-way house, which sold it immediately	$3,200	$2,900
IBM stock held two years as an investment to Goodwill, which sold it immediately	3,000	9,500
Dry groceries to Catholic Meals for the Poor	4,000	4,100

What is the amount of the charitable contribution deduction if T is an individual? A corporation?

6. During 1988, T Corporation (a calendar year taxpayer) had the following income and expenses:

Income from operations	$225,000
Expenses from operations	165,000
Qualifying dividends from domestic corporations	15,000
Net operating loss carryover from 1987	4,500

On June 3, 1988, T Corporation made a contribution to a qualified charitable organization of $10,500 in cash (not included in any of the above items).

a. Determine T Corporation's charitable contribution deduction for 1988.

b. What happens to any excess charitable contribution deduction not allowable for 1988?

7. Pursuant to a resolution adopted by its board of directors, X Corporation, a calendar year accrual basis taxpayer, authorizes a $50,000 donation to City University (a qualified charitable organization) on December 20, 1988. The donation is made on March 10, 1989. Is the corporation correct in claiming a deduction (subject to statutory limitations) in 1988? What if the donation were made on April 10, 1989?

8. During 1988, a corporation has $100,000 of gross income and $125,000 in allowable business deductions. Included in gross income is $30,000 in qualifying dividends from less than 20% owned domestic corporations.

a. Determine the corporation's net operating loss for 1988.

b. What happens to the loss if the corporation was newly created in 1988? In 1985?

9. In each of the following independent situations, determine the dividends received deduction. Assume that none of the corporate shareholders own 20% or more of the stock in the corporations paying the dividends.

	E Corporation	F Corporation	G Corporation
Income from operations	$700,000	$800,000	$700,000
Expenses from operations	(600,000)	(900,000)	(740,000)
Qualifying dividends	100,000	200,000	200,000

10. P Corporation was formed on December 1, 1988. Qualifying organizational expenses were incurred and paid as follows:

Incurred and paid in December 1988	$10,000
Incurred in December 1988 but paid in January 1989	5,000
Incurred and paid in February 1989	3,000

Assume P Corporation makes a timely election under § 248 to amortize organizational expenditures over a period of 60 months. What amount may be amortized in the corporation's first tax year under each of the following assumptions:

a. P Corporation adopts a calendar year and the cash basis of accounting for tax purposes.

b. Same as (a), except that P Corporation chooses a fiscal year of December 1–November 30.

c. P Corporation adopts a calendar year and the accrual basis of accounting for tax purposes.

d. Same as (c), except that P Corporation chooses a fiscal year of December 1–November 30.

11. T Corporation, an accrual basis taxpayer, was formed and began operations on July 1, 1988. The following expenses were incurred during the first tax year (July 1 to December 31, 1988) of operations:

Expenses of temporary directors and of organizational meetings	$2,500
Fee paid to the state of incorporation	300
Accounting services incident to organization	600
Legal services for drafting the corporate charter and by-laws	1,400
Expenses incident to the printing and sale of stock certificates	500
	$5,300

Assume T Corporation makes an appropriate and timely election under § 248(c) and the Regulations thereunder.

a. What is the maximum organizational expense T may write off for tax year 1988?

b. What would be the result if a proper election had not been made?

12. In each of the following independent situations, determine the corporation's income tax liability. Assume that all corporations use a calendar year for tax purposes and that the tax year involved is 1988.

	Taxable Income
J Corp.	$ 40,000
K Corp.	120,000
L Corp.	380,000
M Corp.	70,000

13. In each of the following independent situations, determine the tentative minimum tax:

	AMTI (before the exemption amount)
Q Corp.	$150,000
R Corp.	160,000
T Corp.	320,000

14. For 1988, P Corporation (a calendar year taxpayer) had the following transactions:

Taxable income	$100,000
Accelerated depreciation on realty in excess of straight-line	150,000
Amortization of certified pollution control facilities	10,000
Tax-exempt interest on municipal bonds (funds were used for nongovernmental purposes)	30,000
Untaxed appreciation on property donated to charity	8,000
Percentage depletion in excess of the property's adjusted basis	60,000

a. Determine P Corporation's AMTI for 1988.

b. Determine the alternative minimum tax base (refer to Figure I).

c. Determine the tentative minimum tax.

d. What is the amount of the AMT?

15. L Corporation's current year AMTI is $1,000,000, and its book income for the period is $300,000. L Corporation is considering whether to invest in a municipal bond (where the issuing city put the funds to a nonessential use) that would generate $50,000 of interest income for L Corporation this year. What is the marginal rate of tax on the interest income if the AMT applies to L Corporation this year? If it does not apply?

16. U Corporation's pretax book income is $1,100,000, and its AMTI (before including business untaxed reported profits) is $300,000. What is U Corporation's total AMTI?

17. Indicate in each of the following independent situations whether the corporation may file Form 1120–A:

	A Corporation	B Corporation	C Corporation
Sales of merchandise	$300,000	$200,000	$150,000
Total assets	100,000	180,000	200,000
Total income (gross profit plus other income, including gains)	240,000	245,000	190,000
Member of controlled group	no	yes	no
Ownership in foreign corporation	no	no	no
Entitled to file Form 1120–A (Circle Y for yes or N for no)	Y N	Y N	Y N

18. For 1988, T Corporation, an accrual basis calendar year taxpayer, had net income per books of $172,750 and the following special transactions:

Life insurance proceeds received through the death of the corporation president	$100,000
Premiums paid on the life insurance policy on the president	10,000
Prepaid rent received and properly taxed in 1987 but credited as rent income in 1988	15,000
Rent income received in 1988 ($10,000 is prepaid and relates to 1989)	25,000
Interest income on tax-exempt bonds	5,000
Interest on loan to carry tax-exempt bonds	3,000
ACRS depreciation in excess of straight-line (straight-line was used for book purposes)	4,000
Capital loss in excess of capital gains	6,000
Federal income tax liability for 1988	22,250

Using Schedule M–1 of Form 1120 (the most recent version available), compute T Corporation's taxable income for 1988.

19. Using the legend provided, classify each of the following statements:

Legend

I Applies only to individual taxpayers
C Applies only to corporate taxpayers
B Applies to both individual and corporate taxpayers
N Applies to neither individual nor corporate taxpayers

a. A net capital loss can be carried back.

b. Net long-term capital losses are carried forward as short-term capital losses.

c. A $4,000 net short-term capital loss in the current year can be deducted against ordinary income only to the extent of $3,000.

d. The carryforward period for net capital losses is five years.

e. The alternative minimum tax does not apply.

f. Net operating losses are not allowed to be carried back.

g. The retirement income credit applies.

h. The carryback period for excess charitable contributions is three years.

i. Excess charitable contributions can be carried forward indefinitely.

j. On the disposition of certain depreciable real estate, more ordinary income may result.

k. Percentage limitations may restrict the amount of charitable deductions that can be claimed in any one tax year.

l. Casualty losses are deductible in full.

m. More adjustments are necessary to arrive at a net operating loss deduction.

n. Maximum income tax rate for 1988 is 28%.

o. The AMT rate is 21%.

p. The AMT exemption is phased out when AMTI reaches a certain amount.

Comprehensive Tax Return Problem

Novelco Corporation was formed on October 1, 1974, by Jim and Anne Adams to manufacture and assemble novelty items (mainly key chains, ballpoint pens, and campaign buttons). These items usually are customized with the client's name (and/or logo) for distribution as promotional material. Pertinent information regarding Novelco is summarized as follows:

—The business address is 5210 Union Street, Leesville, IL 60930.

—Employer identification number is 71–0395674; the principal business activity code is 3998.

—Jim and Anne Adams, brother and sister, each own one half of the outstanding common stock, and no other class of stock is authorized. Every three years, they rotate the positions of president and vice president. Currently, Anne is the president and Jim the vice president. Both are full-time employees, and the corporation has no other officers. Each receives a salary of $60,000. Jim's Social Security number is 581–00–0836; Anne's is 581–00–2604.

—The corporation uses the accrual method of accounting and reports on a fiscal year (October 1 through September 30) basis. The specific chargeoff method is used in handling bad debt losses, and inventories are determined under the lower of cost or market method with full absorption of cost. For book and tax purposes, the straight-line method of depreciation is used.

FOOTNOTE ON BALANCE SHEET

—During 1987–1988, the corporation distributed a cash dividend of $50,000. Because a customer was injured on the business premises and has threatened legal action for personal damages, a reserve for contingencies is to be established in the amount of $40,000.

—In November 1987, the corporation received from the IRS a refund of $24,000 due to overpayment on its 1986–1987 estimated income tax liability.

Selected portions of Novelco's profit and loss statement reflect the following debits and credits:

Account	Debit	Credit
Gross sales		$2,500,000
Sales returns and allowances	$ 20,000	
Cost of goods sold	1,450,000	
Dividends received from stock investments in less than 20% owned U.S. corporations ($7,000 accrued in Oct.–Dec. of 1987)		30,000
Interest income		
Certificates of Deposit	$12,000	
State bonds	14,000	26,000
Premiums on term life insurance (the policies are owned by the corporation and cover Jim and Anne Adams; the corporation is the designated beneficiary)	14,000	
Compensation of officers	120,000	
Salaries and wages—indirect	70,000	
Repairs	4,000	
Bad debts	5,000	
Rental expense	12,000	
Taxes (state, local, payroll—indirect)	23,000	
Interest expense		
Loan to purchase state bonds	$ 2,000	
Other business loans and mortgages	27,000	29,000
Charitable contributions	31,000	
Depreciation—indirect	5,000	
Advertising in trade journals	10,000	

Account	Debit	Credit
Other expenses (e.g., office expenses, sales commissions, legal and accounting fees)	$ 60,000	
Long-term loss from the sale of stock held as an investment—no carryback was available	4,000	

Information regarding the cost of goods sold is as follows:

Beginning inventory (10/1/87)	$ 120,000
Ending inventory (9/30/88)	160,000
Purchases (including subcontracted parts and raw materials)	900,000
Cost of labor—direct	450,000
Other costs [e.g., utilities, small tools, depreciation—direct ($14,000)]	140,000

Net income per books (before any income tax accrual) is $699,000.

A comparative balance sheet for Novelco reveals the following information:

Assets	October 1, 1987	September 30, 1988
Cash	$ 28,682	$ 53,360
Trade notes and accounts receivable	125,000	140,000
Inventories	120,000	160,000
Federal and state government bonds	140,000	140,000
Other current assets	18,000	24,000
Other investments	108,000	240,000
Buildings and other depreciable assets	304,000	304,000
Accumulated depreciation	(105,000)	(124,000)
Land	115,000	165,000
Other assets	17,000	24,000
Total assets	$870,682	$1,126,360

Liabilities and Equity		
Accounts payable	$ 24,000	$ 12,000
Other current liabilities	11,000	6,000
Mortgages	168,000	—
Capital stock	200,000	200,000
Retained earnings (appropriated and unappropriated)	467,682	908,360
Total liabilities and equity	$870,682	$1,126,360

During 1987–1988, Novelco made estimated tax payments to the IRS of $240,000.

Prepare a Form 1120 for Novelco for tax year 1987–1988.

Research Problems

Research Problem 1. In 1980, several unrelated individuals created Joya Trust with a transfer of undeveloped real estate located near a large metropolitan area. In return for the transfer, the grantors received beneficial interests in Joya that were of a stated value and freely transferable. Under the trust instrument, the trust was to last 25 years or until dissolution by the trustees, whichever occurred sooner. The trust was not to terminate upon the death of a trustee, and the trustees were empowered to appoint their own successors. The trustees were authorized to call annual meetings of the beneficiaries, but the votes of such beneficiaries were advisory only. Under applicable state law, the liability of the beneficiaries was limited to their investment in the trust.

Pursuant to authority granted by the trust instrument, Joya Trust arranged for the development of the real estate into recreational facilities (e.g., golf courses, tennis courts) and luxury housing units. When developed, the real estate was either sold or leased to the general public. Joya continued to manage the unsold and leased units as well as the recreational facilities until it was dissolved by action of its trustees in 1988. During its existence, how should Joya Trust be treated for Federal income tax purposes? Why?

Research Problem 2. U and V are brothers and equal shareholders in X Corporation, a calendar year taxpayer. In 1987, and as employees, they incurred certain travel and entertainment expenditures on behalf of X Corporation. Because X Corporation was in a precarious financial condition, U and V decided not to seek reimbursement as to these expenditures. Instead, each brother deducted what he spent on his own individual return (Form 1040). Upon audit of the returns filed by U and V for 1987, the IRS disallowed these expenditures. Do you agree? Why or why not?

3

Corporations: Organization and Capital Structure

Objectives

Describe the tax consequences of incorporating a new or an existing business.

Explain how to deal with subsequent property transfers to a controlled corporation.

Describe the capital structure of a corporation and explain what it means for tax purposes.

Discuss the advantages and disadvantages of preferring debt over an equity investment.

Describe the nature and treatment of shareholder debt and stock losses.

Describe the tax rules unique to multiple corporations that are controlled by the same shareholders.

Establish some fundamental concepts relating to the consolidated return procedure.

Outline

Chapter 2 dealt with three principal areas fundamental to working with corporations: (1) the recognition of an entity as a corporation for Federal income tax purposes, (2) the tax rules applicable to the day-to-day operation of a corporation, and (3) the filing and reporting procedures governing corporations.

Chapter 3 addresses more sophisticated problems in dealing with corporations, summarized as follows:

—The tax consequences to the shareholders and the corporation upon the organization of the corporation.

—Once the corporation has been formed, the tax result that ensues when shareholders make later transfers of property.

—The capital structure of a corporation, including the treatment of capital contributions by nonshareholders and shareholders and the handling of investor losses suffered by shareholders.

—Selected problems that arise when dealing with related corporations. Here, some ground rules are established for dealing with consolidated returns.

Organization of and Transfers to Controlled Corporations

In General

Absent special provisions in the Code, a transfer of property to a corporation in exchange for stock would be a sale or exchange of property and would constitute a taxable transaction. Gain or loss would be measured by the difference between the tax basis of the property transferred and the value of the stock received. Section 351 provides for the nonrecognition of gain or loss upon the transfer of property to a corporation solely in exchange for stock or securities if the persons transferring such property are in control of the corporation immediately after the transfer. The nonrecognition of gain or loss reflects the principle of continuity of the taxpayer's investment. There is no real change in the taxpayer's economic status. The investment in certain properties carries over to the investment in corporate stock or securities. The same principle governs the nonrecognition of gain or loss on like-kind exchanges under § 1031. [Note: § 1031(a) covers the exchange of property held for productive use in a trade or business or for investment, but it specifically excludes stocks, bonds, or other securities.] Gain is postponed until a substantive change in the taxpayer's investment occurs (i.e., a sale to or a taxable exchange with outsiders). This approach can be justified under the wherewithal to pay concept discussed in Chapter 1.

Section 351(a) provides that gain or loss is not recognized upon the transfer by one or more persons of property to a corporation solely in exchange for stock or securities in that corporation if, immediately after the exchange, such person or persons are in control of the corporation to which the property was transferred. Section 351(b) provides that if property or money other than stock or securities is received by the transferors, gain will be recognized to the extent of the lesser of the gain realized or boot received (i.e., the amount of money and the fair market value of other property received). The gain is characterized by reference to the type of asset transferred.[1] Loss is never recognized. The nonrecognition of gain or loss is accompanied by a carryover of basis.[2]

Example 1   A and B, individuals, form X Corporation. A transfers property with an adjusted basis of $30,000, fair market value of $60,000, for 50% of the stock. B transfers property with an adjusted basis of $40,000, fair market value of $60,000, for the remaining 50% of the stock. Gain is not recognized on the transfer because it qualifies under § 351. The basis of the stock to A is $30,000, while the basis of the stock to B is $40,000. X Corporation has a basis of $30,000 in the property transferred by A and a basis of $40,000 in the property transferred by B. ☐

There are three requirements for nonrecognition of gain or loss: (1) a transfer of property for (2) stock or securities if (3) the transferors are in control of the transferee corporation.

Transfer of Property

Questions concerning exactly what constitutes property for purposes of § 351 have arisen. Services rendered are specifically excluded by the Code from the definition of property. With this exception, the definition of property is comprehensive. Unrealized receivables for a cash basis taxpayer and installment obligations are considered property, for example.[3] Thus, the transfer of an installment obligation in a transaction qualifying under § 351 would not be a disposition of the installment obligation, and gain would not be recognized to the transferor. Secret processes and formulas, as well as secret information in the general nature of a patentable inventory, also qualify as property under § 351.[4]

Stock and Securities

If property is transferred to a corporation in exchange for any property other than stock and securities, the property constitutes boot. Such property is taxable to the transferor shareholder to the extent of any realized gain. The Regulations state that stock rights and stock warrants are not included in the term "stock or securities." [5] Generally, however, the term "stock" needs no clarification. On the other hand, the definition of a security can be a problem. A security is an obligation of the corporation. However, courts have required that the definition of security be limited to long-term obligations and exclude short-term notes. Courts have held short-term notes to be the equivalent of cash.[6]

---

1. Rev.Rul. 68–55, 1968–1 C.B. 140.
2. §§ 358(a) and 362(a). See the discussion preceding Example 9.
3. *Hempt Brothers, Inc. v. U.S.*, 74–1 USTC ¶9188, 33 AFTR2d 74–570, 490 F.2d 1172 (CA–3, 1974), and Reg. § 1.453–9(c)(2).
4. Rev.Rul. 64–56, 1964–1 C.B. 133.
5. Reg. § 1.351–1(a)(1)(ii).
6. *Turner v. Comm.*, 62–1 USTC ¶9488, 9 AFTR2d 1528, 303 F.2d 94 (CA–4, 1962). But compare *U.S. v. Mills, Jr.*, 68–2 USTC ¶9503, 22 AFTR2d 5302, 399 F.2d 944 (CA–5, 1968).

No definite length of time to maturity has been established to draw a line between long-term and short-term securities. Some courts would draw the line at five years; others at ten years. In *Camp Wolters Enterprises, Inc.*,[7] the Court stated:

> The test as to whether notes are securities is not a mechanical determination of the time period of the note. Though time is an important factor, the controlling consideration is an overall evaluation of the nature of the debt, degree of participation and continuing interest in the business, the extent of proprietary interest compared with the similarity of the note to a cash payment, the purpose of the advances, etc.

Control of the Transferee Corporation

To qualify as a nontaxable transaction under § 351, the transferor must be in control of the transferee corporation immediately after the exchange. Control for these purposes requires the person or persons transferring the property to own, immediately after the transfer, stock possessing at least 80 percent of the total combined voting power of all classes of stock entitled to vote and at least 80 percent of the total *number* of shares of all other classes of stock of the corporation.[8] Control can apply to a single person or to several individuals if they are all parties to an integrated transaction. If more than one person is involved, the Regulations affirm that the exchange does not necessarily require simultaneous exchanges by two or more persons. They do, however, comprehend situations in which the rights of the parties have been previously defined and the execution of the agreement proceeds "... with an expedition consistent with orderly procedure."[9]

Example 2   A exchanges property, which cost him $60,000 but which has a fair market value of $100,000, for 70% of the stock of X Corporation. The other 30% is owned by B, who acquired it several years ago. The fair market value of the stock is $100,000. A realizes a taxable gain of $40,000 on the transfer. If A and B had transferred property to X Corporation in a simultaneous transaction or in separate transactions, both of which related to the execution of a previous agreement, with A receiving 70% of the stock and B receiving 30%, gain would not have been recognized to either party. □

Stock or securities need not be issued to the transferring parties in proportion to the interest each held in the transferred property. However, when stock and securities received are not proportionate to the value of the property transferred, the transaction could produce a gift from one transferor to the other.

Example 3   C and D organize a corporation with 500 shares of stock. C transfers property worth $10,000 for 100 shares, and D transfers property worth

---

7. 22 T.C. 737 (1955), *aff'd.* in 56–1 USTC ¶9314, 49 AFTR 283, 230 F.2d 555 (CA–5, 1956).
8. § 368(c).
9. Reg. § 1.351–1.

$5,000 for 400 shares. The transaction qualifies under § 351; however, if C did in fact make a gift to D, the transfer might be subject to a gift tax (see Chapter 11). ☐

Section 351 treatment will be lost if stock is transferred to persons who did not contribute property, causing those who did to lack control immediately after the exchange. However, a person who performs services for the corporation in exchange for stock and also transfers some property is treated as a member of the transferring group, although he or she is taxed on the value of the stock issued for services.

To be a member of the group and aid in qualifying all transferors under the 80 percent test, the person contributing services must transfer property having more than a relatively small value in relation to the services performed. Stock or securities issued for property of relatively small value compared with the value of the stock and securities already owned (or to be received for services rendered) by the person transferring such property will not be treated as issued in return for property if the primary purpose of the transfer is to qualify the transaction under § 351 for concurrent transferors.[10]

Example 4   A and B, individuals, transfer property to X Corporation, each in exchange for one-third of the stock. C, an individual, receives the other one-third of the stock for services rendered. The transaction will not qualify under § 351, because C is not a member of the group transferring property and A and B together received only 66⅔% of the stock. The post-transfer control requirement is not met. If C also transferred property, he would then be a member of the group, and the transaction would qualify under § 351. C would be taxed on the value of the stock issued for services, but the remainder of the transaction would be tax-free, assuming no boot was received. However, if the property transferred by C was of a relatively small value in comparison to the stock he received for his services, and the primary purpose for including the property was to cause the transaction to be tax-free for A and B, the exchange will not qualify under § 351. Gain or loss would be recognized by all parties. ☐

Control is not lost if stock received by shareholders in a § 351 exchange is sold to persons who are not parties to the exchange shortly after the transaction, unless the plan for ultimate sale of the stock existed before the exchange.[11]

Section 351 is mandatory and not elective. If a transaction falls within the provisions of § 351, neither gain nor loss is recognized on the transfer (except that realized gain is recognized to the extent of boot received), and there is a carryover of basis.

---

10. Reg. § 1.351–1(a)(1)(ii).
11. *Wilgard Realty Co. v. Comm.*, 42–1 USTC ¶9452, 29 AFTR 325, 127 F.2d 514 (CA–2, 1942).

Assumption of Liabilities—§ 357

Absent § 357 of the Code, the transfer of mortgaged property to a controlled corporation could trigger gain to the extent of the mortgage whether the controlled corporation assumed the mortgage or took property subject to it. This is the case in nontaxable like-kind exchanges under § 1031. Liabilities assumed by the other party are considered the equivalent of cash and treated as boot. Section 357(a) provides, however, that the assumption of a liability by the acquiring corporation or the corporation taking property subject to a liability will not produce boot to the transferor shareholder in a § 351 transaction. Nevertheless, liabilities assumed by the transferee corporation are treated as "other property or money" as far as basis of stock received in the transfer is concerned. The basis of the stock received must be reduced by the amount of the liabilities assumed by the corporation.

Example 5   C transfers property with an adjusted basis of $60,000, fair market value of $100,000, to X Corporation for 100% of the stock in X. The property is subject to a liability of $25,000 which X Corporation assumes. The exchange is tax-free under §§ 351 and 357. However, under § 358(d), the basis to C of the stock in X Corporation is only $35,000 (basis of property transferred, $60,000, less amount of mortgage assumed, $25,000). The basis of the property to X Corporation is $60,000. □

The rule of § 357(a) has two exceptions. Section 357(b) provides that if the principal purpose of the assumption of the liabilities is to avoid tax *or* if there is no bona fide business purpose behind the exchange, the liabilities, in total, will be treated as money received and taxed as boot. Further, § 357(c) provides that if the sum of the liabilities exceeds the adjusted basis of the properties transferred, the excess is taxable gain.

Tax Avoidance or No Bona Fide Business Purpose Exception.   Section 357(b)(1)(A) generally poses few problems. A tax avoidance purpose for transferring liabilities to a controlled corporation would seem unlikely in view of the basis adjustment necessitated by § 358(d). Since the liabilities transferred reduce the basis of the stock or securities received for the property, any realized gain is merely deferred and not avoided. Such gain would materialize when and if the stock is disposed of in a taxable sale or exchange.

Satisfying the bona fide business purpose will not be difficult if the liabilities were incurred in connection with the transferor's normal course of conducting his or her trade or business. But the bona fide business purpose requirement will cause difficulty if the liability is taken out shortly before the property is transferred and the proceeds therefrom are utilized for personal purposes.[12] This type of situation seems akin to a distribution by the corporation of cash, which would be taxed as boot.

Example 6   D transfers real estate (basis of $40,000 and fair market value of $90,000) to a controlled corporation in return for stock in such corpora-

---

12. See, for example, *Campbell, Jr. v. Wheeler*, 65–1 USTC ¶9294, 15 AFTR2d 578, 342 F.2d 837 (CA–5, 1965).

tion. Shortly before the transfer, D mortgages the real estate and uses the $20,000 proceeds to meet personal obligations. Along with the real estate, the mortgage is transferred to the corporation. In this case, it would appear that the assumption of the mortgage lacks a bona fide business purpose within the meaning of § 357(b)(1)(B). Because the amount of the liability is considered boot, D has a taxable gain on the transfer of $20,000.[13] □

Liabilities in Excess of Basis Exception.   Unlike § 357(b), § 357(c) has posed numerous problems in § 351 transfers. Much litigation has centered around this provision of the Code in recent years, particularly with respect to cash basis taxpayers who incorporate their businesses. Section 357(c) states that if the sum of liabilities assumed and the liabilities to which transferred property is subject exceeds the total of the adjusted bases of the properties transferred, the excess is taxable gain. Absent this provision, if liabilities exceed basis in property exchanged, a taxpayer would have a negative basis in the stock or securities received in the controlled corporation.[14] Section 357(c) alleviates the negative basis problem; the excess over basis is gain to the transferor.

Example 7   A, an individual, transfers assets with an adjusted tax basis of $40,000 to a newly formed corporation in exchange for 100% of the stock. The corporation assumes liabilities on the transferred properties in the amount of $50,000. Absent § 357(c), A's basis in the stock of the new corporation would be a negative $10,000 (basis of property transferred, $40,000, plus gain recognized, $0, less boot received, $0, less liabilities assumed, $50,000). Section 357(c) causes A to recognize a gain of $10,000. The stock will have a zero basis in A's hands, and the negative basis problem is eliminated (basis of property transferred, $40,000, plus gain recognized, $10,000, less boot received, $0, less liabilities assumed, $50,000). □

Accounts payable of a cash basis taxpayer that give rise to a deduction and amounts payable under § 736(a) (payments to a retiring partner or payments in liquidation of a deceased partner's interest) are not considered to be liabilities for purposes of § 357(c).

Example 8   T, a cash basis individual, incorporates her sole proprietorship. In return for all of the stock of the new corporation, she transfers the following items:

---

13. § 351(b). The effect of the application of § 357(b) is to taint *all* liabilities transferred even though some may be supported by a bona fide business purpose.
14. *Easson v. Comm.*, 33 T.C. 963 (1960), *rev'd.* in 61–2 USTC ¶9654, 8 AFTR2d 5448, 294 F.2d 653 (CA–9, 1961).

	Adjusted Basis	Fair Market Value
Cash	$10,000	$10,000
Unrealized accounts receivable (i.e., amounts due to T but not yet paid to her)	–0–	40,000
Trade accounts payable	–0–	30,000
Note payable	5,000	5,000

Unrealized accounts receivable and trade accounts payable have a zero basis, because under the cash method of accounting, no income is recognized until the receivables are collected and no deduction materializes until the payables are satisfied. The note payable has a basis, because it was issued for consideration received.

The accounts receivable and the trade accounts payable are disregarded. Thus, T has only transferred cash ($10,000) and a note payable ($5,000) and does not have a problem of liabilities in excess of basis. □

The definition of liabilities under § 357(c) excludes those obligations that would have been deductible to the transferor had he or she paid such obligations before the transfer. Consequently, T, in Example 8, would have no gain.

If §§ 357(b) and (c) both apply to the same transfer (i.e., the liability is not supported by a bona fide business purpose and also exceeds the basis of the properties transferred), § 357(b) predominates.[15] This could be significant, because § 357(b) does not create gain on the transfer, as does § 357(c), but merely converts the liability to boot. Thus, the realized gain limitation continues to apply to § 357(b) transactions.

Basis Determination

Recall that § 351(a) postpones gain until the taxpayer's investment changes substantially. Postponement of the realized gain is accomplished through a carryover of basis pursuant to §§ 358(a) and 362(a).

Section 358(a). For a taxpayer transferring property to a corporation in a § 351 transaction, basis of stock or securities received in the transfer is the same as the basis the taxpayer had in the property transferred, increased by any gain recognized on the exchange and decreased by boot received.

Section 362(a). The basis of properties received by the corporation is determined under § 362(a), which provides that basis to the corporation is the basis in the hands of the transferor increased by the amount of any gain recognized to the transferor shareholder.

Example 9   C and D form Y Corporation with the following investment: C transfers property (basis of $30,000 and fair market value of $70,000), and D transfers cash of $60,000. Each receives 50 shares of the Y Corporation stock, but C also receives $10,000 in cash. Assume each share of the Y Corpora-

---

15. § 357(c)(2)(A).

tion stock is worth $1,200. Although C's realized gain is $40,000 [i.e., $60,000 (the value of 50 shares of Y Corporation stock) + $10,000 (cash received) − $30,000 (basis of the property transferred)], only $10,000 (the amount of the boot) is recognized. C's basis in the Y Corporation stock becomes $30,000 [$30,000 (basis of the property transferred) + $10,000 (gain recognized by C) − $10,000 (cash received)]. Y Corporation's basis in the property transferred by C is $40,000 [$30,000 (basis of the property to C) + $10,000 (gain recognized to C)]. D neither realizes nor recognizes gain or loss and will have a basis in the Y Corporation stock of $60,000. □

Example 10   Assume the same facts as in Example 9, except that C's basis in the property transferred is $68,000 (instead of $30,000). Because recognized gain cannot exceed realized gain, the transfer generates only $2,000 of gain to C. The basis of the Y Corporation stock to C becomes $60,000 [$68,000 (basis of property transferred) + $2,000 (gain recognized) − $10,000 (cash received)]. Y Corporation's basis in the property received from C is $70,000 [$68,000 (basis of the property to C) + $2,000 (gain recognized by C)]. □

Recapture Considerations

Recapture of Accelerated Cost Recovery (Depreciation).   In a pure § 351(a) nontaxable transfer (i.e., no boot involved) to a controlled corporation, the recapture of accelerated cost recovery rules do not apply.[16] Moreover, any recapture potential of the property carries over to the corporation as it steps into the shoes of the transferor-shareholder for purposes of basis determination.

Example 11   T transfers to a controlled corporation equipment (basis of $30,000 and a fair market value of $100,000) in return for additional stock. If sold by T, the property would have yielded a gain of $70,000, all of which would be recaptured as ordinary income under § 1245. If the transfer comes within § 351(a) because of the absence of boot, T has no recognized gain and no accelerated cost recovery to recapture. Should the corporation later dispose of the real estate in a taxable transaction, it will have to take into account the § 1245 recapture potential originating with T. □

Recapture of Investment Tax Credit.   Although the investment tax credit has been repealed, recapture of some of the prior credit taken on § 38 property (i.e., property that yielded an investment tax credit on its acquisition) will apply if the § 38 property is disposed of prematurely (before the end of the recapture period). In this regard, two problems arise with the transfer of § 38 property. First, does the transfer to a controlled corporation trigger a recapture of the credit to the transferor-shareholder? Second, will a subsequent and premature disposition of the property by the transferee-corporation cause recapture, and from whom will the credit be recaptured?

---

16. §§ 1245(b)(3) and 1250(d)(3).

In answer to the first question, § 47(b) precludes recapture with respect to a taxpayer who merely changes "the form of conducting the trade or business so long as the property is retained in such trade or business as § 38 property and the taxpayer retains a substantial interest in such trade or business." What is meant by the retention of a substantial interest in the business is not entirely clear. The Regulation in point does not offer much guidance when it suggests that the exchange of a five percent interest in a partnership for a five percent interest in a corporation constitutes the retention of a substantial interest.[17] But what about a 50 percent interest in a partnership for a 20 percent interest in a corporation? These are close judgment questions that eventually will have to be resolved by the courts.[18]

One should note that the recapture of the investment tax credit can operate independent of § 351. Thus, recapture of the credit can take place on a transfer of § 38 property to a controlled corporation even though no gain is recognized to the transferor under § 351(a). In this regard, the investment tax credit recapture rules differ from those applicable to depreciation and cost recovery. The recapture of depreciation and cost recovery comes into play only if the transfer results in recognized gain to the transferor.

Even if the recapture of the investment tax credit is avoided on the transfer of property to a controlled corporation, the transferor-shareholder does not cease to be vulnerable. Unlike the recapture of depreciation, the potential stays with the transferor-shareholder. Consequently, recapture can take place at the shareholder level if the corporation prematurely disposes of the property *or* if the shareholder terminates his or her substantial interest in the business through disposition of stock.[19]

Example 12   In 1984, T (an individual) purchased § 38 property for $12,000. T claimed an investment tax credit of $1,200 based on a recovery period of five years. In 1985, T forms X Corporation through the incorporation of his sole proprietorship. In return for all of the stock in the corporation, T transfers all of his assets (including the § 38 property). In 1988, four years after T purchased the § 38 property, X Corporation sells it at a loss. Under these circumstances, T must recapture $240 of the credit previously claimed.[20] The fact that the property was sold at a loss by X Corporation makes no difference in the recapture of the investment tax credit. No recapture of the credit occurred upon the property's transfer to X Corporation because T retained a substantial interest in the business. □

Example 13   Assume the same facts as in Example 12 except that X Corporation does not sell the § 38 property but continues to use it in its trade or business for the full five years. In 1988, however, T makes gifts to family members of 75% of the stock he holds in X Corporation. These gifts terminate T's

---

17. Reg. § 1.47–3(f)(2)(ii).
18. In *James Soares*, 50 T.C. 909 (1968), the Court found that the exchange of a 48% interest in a partnership for a 7.22% interest in a corporation was not the retention of a substantial interest in the business. Thus, recapture of the investment tax credit took place on the transfer to the corporation.
19. Reg. § 1.47–3(f)(5) and *W. F. Blevins*, 61 T.C. 547 (1974).
20. Recapture is reduced by 2% for each full year the property is held before disposition (2% × 4 years = 8%, in this case). Hence, only 2% (10% minus 8%) of the credit is subject to recapture.

substantial interest in the business, and T must recapture some of the investment tax credit previously claimed. ☐

Tax Benefit Rule

A taxpayer may have to take into income the recovery of an item previously expensed. Such income, however, will be limited to the amount of the deduction that actually produced a tax saving. The relevance of the tax benefit rule to transfers to controlled corporations under § 351 was first apparent in connection with accounts receivable and the reserve for bad debts.

Example 14   T, an accrual basis individual, incorporates her sole proprietorship. In return for all of the stock of the corporation, T transfers, among other assets, accounts receivable with a face amount of $100,000 and a reserve for bad debts of $10,000 (i.e., book value of $90,000). T had previously deducted the addition to the reserve. The $10,000 deduction resulted in a tax benefit to T. ☐

The IRS took the position that § 351 did not insulate the transfer from the tax benefit rule.[21] Since T had previously deducted the reserve for bad debts and such reserve was no longer necessary to her, the full $10,000 should be taken into income. In *Nash v. U.S.*,[22] the Supreme Court disagreed. Operating on the assumption that the stock T received must be worth only $90,000 (the book value of the receivables), the situation was compared to a sale. Because no gain would have resulted had the receivables been sold for $90,000, why should it matter that they were transferred to a controlled corporation under § 351?

The Supreme Court decision in *Nash*, however, does not imply that the tax benefit rule is inapplicable to transfers to controlled corporations when no gain is otherwise recognized under § 351(a). Returning to the facts in Example 14, suppose T was one of several transferors and the value of the stock she received exceeded the book value of the receivables (i.e., $90,000). Could the excess be subject to income recognition by virtue of the application of the tax benefit rule? The answer to this question has not been specifically passed upon by the courts.

Capital Structure of a Corporation

Capital Contributions

The receipt of money or property in exchange for capital stock (including treasury stock) produces neither gain nor loss to the recipient corporation [§ 1032]. Gross income of a corporation also does not include shareholders' contributions of money or property to the capital of the corporation. Additional funds received from shareholders through voluntary pro rata payments are not

---

21. Rev.Rul. 62–128, 1962–2 C.B. 139.
22. 70–1 USTC ¶9405, 25 AFTR2d 1177, 90 S.Ct. 1550 (USSC, 1970).

income to the corporation even though there is no increase in the outstanding shares of stock of the corporation. Such payments represent an additional price paid for the shares held by the shareholders and are treated as additions to the operating capital of the corporation.[23]

Contributions by nonshareholders, such as land contributed to a corporation by a civic group or a governmental group to induce the corporation to locate in a particular community, are also excluded from the gross income of a corporation.[24] Property that is transferred to a corporation by a nonshareholder for services rendered or for merchandise does constitute taxable income to the corporation.[25]

The basis of property received by a corporation from a shareholder as a contribution to capital is the basis of the property in the hands of the shareholder increased by any gain recognized to the shareholder. For property transferred to a corporation by a nonshareholder as a contribution to capital, the basis of the property is zero. If money is received by a corporation as a contribution to capital from a nonshareholder, the basis of any property acquired with the money during a 12-month period beginning on the day the contribution was received is reduced by the amount of the contribution. The excess of money received over the cost of new property is used to reduce the basis of other property held by the corporation. The excess is applied in reduction of basis in the following order: (a) depreciable property, (b) property subject to amortization, (c) property subject to depletion, and (d) all other remaining properties. The reduction of the basis of property within each category is made in proportion to the relative bases of the properties.[26]

Example 15 Assume a television company charges its customers an initial fee to hook up to a new television system installed in the area. These contributions will be used to finance the total cost of constructing the television facilities. The customers will then make monthly payments for the television service. Even though the initial payments were for capital expenditures, they still represent payments for services to be rendered by the television company, and as such, they are taxable income and not contributions to capital by nonshareholders. ☐

Example 16 A city donates land to X Corporation as an inducement for X to locate in the city. The receipt of the land does not represent taxable income. However, the land's basis to the corporation is zero. Assume the city also pays the corporation $10,000 in cash. The money is not taxable income to the corporation. However, if the corporation purchases property with the $10,000 within the next 12 months, the basis of such property is reduced by $10,000. ☐

---

23. § 118 and Reg. § 1.118–1.
24. See *Edwards v. Cuba Railroad Co.*, 1 USTC ¶139, 5 AFTR 5398, 45 S.Ct. 614 (USSC, 1925).
25. Reg. § 1.118–1. See also *Teleservice Co. of Wyoming Valley v. Comm.*, 27 T.C. 722 (1957), *aff'd.* in 58–1 USTC ¶9383, 1 AFTR2d 1249, 254 F.2d 105 (CA–3, 1958), *cert. den.* 78 S.Ct. 1360 (USSC, 1958).
26. § 362 and Reg. § 1.362–2(b).

Debt in the Capital Structure

Advantages of Debt.   In forming a corporation, shareholders should consider the relationship between debt and equity in the capital structure. Section 351 provides for nonrecognition of gain on a transfer for either stock or securities (i.e., long-term debt). Consequently, a shareholder can transfer property and receive both stock and long-term debt tax-free. The advantages of receiving long-term debt are numerous. Interest on debt is deductible by the corporation, whereas dividend payments are not. Further, the shareholders are not taxed on loan repayments made to them unless the repayments exceed basis. As long as a corporation has earnings and profits (see Chapter 4), an investment in stock cannot be withdrawn tax-free. Any withdrawals will be deemed to be taxable dividends to the extent of earnings and profits of the distributing corporation.

Example 17   A, an individual, transfers assets with a tax basis of $100,000 to a newly formed corporation for 100% of the stock. The basis of the assets to the corporation is $100,000. In the first year of operations, the corporation has net income of $40,000. Such earnings are credited to the earnings and profits account of the corporation. If the corporation distributes $10,500 to A, the distribution will be a taxable dividend with no corresponding deduction to the corporation. Assume A transferred the assets for stock and debt in the amount of $50,000, payable in equal annual installments of $5,000 and bearing interest at the rate of 11%. The transfer would still be tax-free because the securities—the long-term debt—have a maturity date of 10 years. At the end of the year, the corporation would pay A $5,500 interest, which would be tax deductible. The $5,000 principal repayment on the loan would not be taxed to A. □

Reclassification of Debt as Equity.   In certain instances, the IRS will contend that debt is really an equity interest and will deny the shareholders the tax advantages of debt financing. If the debt instrument has too many features of stock, it may be treated as a form of stock, and principal and interest payments will be considered dividends.

Though the form of the instrument will not assure debt treatment, the failure to observe certain formalities in the creation of the debt may lead to an assumption that the purported debt is, in fact, a form of stock. The debt should be in proper legal form, should bear a legitimate rate of interest, should have a definite maturity date, and should be repaid on a timely basis. Payments should not be contingent upon earnings. Further, the debt should not be subordinated to other liabilities, and proportionate holdings of stock and debt should be avoided. Thin capitalization, which occurs when there is a high ratio of shareholder debt to shareholder equity, creates a substantial risk that debt will be reclassified as equity.

Section 385 was added to the Internal Revenue Code in 1969. This section lists several factors that *may* be used to determine whether a debtor-creditor relationship or a shareholder-corporation relationship exists. The obvious thrust of § 385, however, is to turn the matter over to the U.S. Treasury Department to prescribe Regulations that would provide more definite guidelines as to when a corporation is or is not thinly capitalized. After a wondrous deliberation of more than a decade, such Regulations were proposed and, with significant modifications, scheduled to be completed in 1980. However, the effective date of such Regulations had been repeatedly postponed, causing further modification. The Treasury concluded that neither the final regulations, as published in December 1980, nor the proposed revisions, as published in January 1982, fully reflected the position of either the IRS or the Treasury on debt/equity matters. Consequently, the final regulations and the proposed revisions have been withdrawn. It is unlikely that the Treasury will adopt a new set of regulations.

Investor Losses

The choice between debt and equity financing entails a consideration of the tax treatment of worthless stock and securities versus the treatment of bad debts.

Stock and Security Losses. If stocks and bonds are capital assets in the hands of the holder, losses from their worthlessness will be governed by § 165(g)(1). Under this provision, a capital loss will materialize as of the last day of the taxable year in which the stocks or bonds become worthless. Because no deduction is allowed for a mere decline in value, the burden of proving complete worthlessness will be on the taxpayer claiming the loss. One way to recognize partial worthlessness would be to dispose of the stocks or bonds in a taxable sale or exchange.[27] But even then, the loss may be disallowed under § 267(a)(1) if the sale or exchange is to a related party.

When the stocks or bonds are not capital assets, worthlessness thereof would yield an ordinary loss under § 165(a).[28] Usually, however, stocks and bonds are held as investments and will be deemed capital assets. If, on the other hand, the stocks or bonds are an integral part of a taxpayer's trade or business, they are not capital assets. One example would be stocks and bonds held by a broker for resale to customers in the normal course of business. Other possibilities are more subtle.

Example 18
T Corporation manufactures a product from raw materials purchased from S Corporation. Because S Corporation also sells the materials to other concerns, T Corporation is sometimes unable to satisfy its needs. Consequently, to assure itself of a steady source of supply for its manufacturing operations, T Corporation acquires a controlling interest in S Corporation. Since the acquisition was not motivated by investment considerations, the S Corporation stock is not a capital asset in the hands of T Corporation. Thus, if the stock were to become worthless, the loss would be ordinary and not capital.[29] □

Under certain circumstances involving stocks and bonds of affiliated corporations, an ordinary loss also would be allowed upon worthlessness. These

---

27. Reg. § 1.165–4(a).
28. Reg. § 1.165–5(b).
29. See *Corn Products Refining Co. v. Comm.*, 55–2 USTC ¶9746, 47 AFTR 1789, 76 S.Ct. 20 (USSC, 1955).

conditions are set forth in § 165(g)(3). The possibility of an ordinary loss on the stock of small business corporations (i.e., § 1244) is discussed later in the chapter.

Business Versus Nonbusiness Bad Debts.   In addition to leading to the possible worthlessness of stocks and bonds, the financial demise of a corporation can lead to bad debt deductions. Such deductions can be either business bad debts or nonbusiness bad debts. The distinction between the two types of deductions becomes important for tax purposes in the following respects:

—Business bad debts are deducted as ordinary losses; nonbusiness bad debts are treated as short-term capital losses.[30] Thus, a business bad debt can generate a net operating loss while a nonbusiness bad debt cannot.[31]

—A deduction is allowed for the partial worthlessness of a business debt. Nonbusiness debts, however, can be written off only when they become entirely worthless.[32]

—Nonbusiness bad debt treatment is limited to noncorporate taxpayers. All of the bad debts of a corporation will qualify as business bad debts.[33]

But when is a debt business or nonbusiness? Unfortunately, since the Code sheds little light on the matter, the distinction has been left to the courts.[34] In a leading decision, the Supreme Court somewhat clarified the picture when it held that being an investor does not constitute, by itself, a trade or business.[35] Consequently, if an individual shareholder loans money to a corporation in his or her capacity as an investor, any resulting bad debt will be classified as nonbusiness. Nevertheless, the Court did not preclude the possibility of a shareholder-creditor's incurring a business bad debt. If the loan was made in some capacity that does qualify as a trade or business, nonbusiness bad debt treatment can be avoided. For example, was the loan made to protect the shareholder's employment with the corporation? Employee status is a trade or business, and a loss on a loan made for this purpose will qualify for business bad debt treatment.[36] Shareholders may also receive business bad debt treatment if they are in the trade or business of loaning money or of buying, promoting, and selling corporations.

Suppose, however, the shareholder has multiple motives for making the loan. Again the Supreme Court was called upon to resolve the problem.[37] According to the Court the "dominant" or "primary" motive for making the loan should control the classification of the loss.

---

30. Compare § 166(a) with § 166(d)(1)(B).
31. Note the adjustments necessitated by § 172(d)(2).
32. Compare § 166(a)(2) with § 166(d)(1)(A).
33. § 166(d)(1).
34. For definitional purposes, § 166(d)(2) might be regarded as almost as worthless as the debt it purports to describe.
35. *Whipple v. Comm.*, 63–1 USTC ¶9466, 11 AFTR2d 1454, 83 S.Ct. 1168 (USSC, 1963).
36. *Trent v. Comm.*, 61–2 USTC ¶9506, 7 AFTR2d 1599, 291 F.2d 669 (CA–2, 1961).
37. *U.S. v. Generes*, 72–1 USTC ¶9259, 29 AFTR2d 72–609, 92 S.Ct. 827 (USSC, 1972).

Example 19   T owns 48% of the stock of X Corporation, acquired several years ago at a cost of $100,000. T is also employed by the corporation at an annual salary of $40,000. At a time when X Corporation is experiencing financial problems, T loans it $50,000. Subsequently, the corporation becomes bankrupt, and both T's stock investment and his loans become worthless.

☐

Granted that T's stock investment will be treated as a long-term capital loss (absent the application of § 1244 discussed below), but how will the bad debt be classified? If T can prove that the dominant or primary reason for making the loan was to protect his salary, a business bad debt deduction results. If not, it will be assumed that T was trying to protect his stock investment, and nonbusiness bad debt treatment results. Factors to be considered in the resolution of this matter include the following:

—A comparison of the amount of stock investment with the trade or business benefit to be derived. In Example 19, this entails comparing the stock investment of $100,000 with the annual salary of $40,000. In this regard, the salary should be considered as a recurring item and not viewed in isolation. Obviously, $40,000 each year could mean a great deal to one who has no other means of support and who may have difficulty obtaining like employment elsewhere.

—A comparison of the amount of the loan with the stock investment and the trade or business benefit to be derived.

—The percentage of ownership held by the shareholder. A minority shareholder, for example, may be under more compulsion to loan the corporation money to protect his or her job than one who is in control of corporate policy.

In summary, it would be impossible to conclude whether the taxpayer in Example 19 suffered a business or nonbusiness bad debt without additional facts. Even with such facts, the guidelines are vague, as they must be when a taxpayer's intent or motivation is at issue. For this reason, this problem is the subject of frequent litigation.[38]

Section 1244 Stock.   Section 1244 permits ordinary loss treatment up to a maximum of $50,000 per year ($100,000 if a joint return is filed) for losses on the sale or worthlessness of stock of so-called small business corporations. By placing shareholders on a more nearly equal basis with proprietors and partners as to the tax treatment of losses, the provision encourages investment of capital in small corporations. Gain on the sale of § 1244 stock remains capital. Consequently, the shareholder has nothing to lose and everything to gain by complying with § 1244.

Only a small business corporation may issue qualifying § 1244 stock. The total amount of stock that can be offered under the plan to issue § 1244 stock

38. See, for example, *Kelson v. U.S.*, 74–2 USTC ¶9714, 34 AFTR2d 74–6007, 503 F.2d 1291 (CA–10, 1974).

cannot exceed $1,000,000. For these purposes, property received in exchange for stock is valued at its adjusted basis, reduced by any liabilities assumed by the corporation or to which the property is subject. Fair market value of the property is not considered. The $1,000,000 limitation is determined by property and money received for the stock as a contribution to capital and as paid-in capital on the date the stock is issued. Consequently, even though a corporation fails to meet these requirements when the stock is sold, the stock can still qualify as § 1244 stock if the requirements were met on the date the stock was issued.

The corporation must have derived more than 50 percent of its aggregate gross receipts from sources other than royalties, rents, dividends, interest, annuities, and sales and exchanges of stock or securities (only the gains are considered) for the corporation's most recent five tax years. This gross receipts requirement applies only if the corporation's receipts equal or exceed its deductions other than a net operating loss deduction or the dividends received deduction.

The amount of ordinary loss deductible in any one year on § 1244 stock is limited to $50,000 for a taxpayer filing a separate return and $100,000 for husband and wife filing a joint return. If the amount of the loss sustained in the taxable year exceeds these amounts, the remainder is considered a capital loss.

Example 20   A taxpayer acquires § 1244 stock at a cost of $100,000. He sells the stock for $10,000 in one tax year. He has an ordinary loss (on a separate return) of $50,000 and a capital loss of $40,000. On a joint return the entire $90,000 loss would be ordinary. □

Only the original holder of § 1244 stock, whether an individual or a partnership, qualifies for ordinary loss treatment. Should the stock be sold or donated, it loses its § 1244 status. If a partnership is involved, the individual must have been a partner at the time the partnership acquired the stock. Each partner's share of partnership tax attributes includes the share of the loss the partnership sustains on the stock.

Recall the advantages of issuing some debt to shareholders in exchange for capital contributions to a corporation. A disadvantage occurs in issuing debt, because debt does not qualify under § 1244. Should the debt become worthless, the taxpayer will generally have a short-term capital loss rather than the ordinary loss (up to $50,000 per year, or $100,000 if a joint return is filed) for § 1244 stock.

The basis of § 1244 stock issued by a corporation in exchange for property that has an adjusted basis above its fair market value immediately before the exchange is reduced to the fair market value of the property on the date of the exchange for the purpose of determining ordinary loss upon a subsequent sale.

Example 21   A taxpayer transfers property with a basis of $10,000 and a fair market value of $5,000 to a corporation in exchange for shares of § 1244 stock. Assuming the transfer qualifies under § 351, the basis of the stock would be $10,000, the same as the taxpayer's basis in the property. For purposes of § 1244, the basis is only $5,000. If the stock is later sold for $3,000, the total loss sustained is $7,000 ($10,000 − $3,000); however, only $2,000 is ordinary loss ($5,000 − $3,000). The remaining portion, $5,000, is capital loss. □

If a shareholder contributes additional property or money to a corporation after he or she acquires § 1244 stock, the amount of ordinary loss upon a sale of the § 1244 stock is limited to his or her original contribution.

Problems of Related Corporations

When the same group of owners operate a business in the corporate form, there could be a distinct advantage to making use of multiple corporations. Consider, for example, a business that annually yields taxable income of $300,000. The corporate income tax on this amount would be $7,500 (tax on the first $50,000) plus $6,250 (tax on the next $25,000) plus $86,500 [34% of $225,000 (the excess over $75,000) plus 5% of $200,000 (excess over $100,000)], or $100,250. If, however, this income could be divided equally among four corporations, the total tax would be $55,000 [$13,750 (the tax on $75,000) × 4 (the number of corporations)] for an overall savings of $45,250 ($100,250 − $55,000). The use of multiple corporations (unless otherwise proscribed) could generate additional accumulated earnings tax credits (currently $250,000) to help avoid the tax on unreasonable accumulations of earnings (discussed in Chapter 7) and additional exemptions for purposes of computing the amount of the alternative minimum tax.

Controlled Groups

To preclude the abuse with the use of multiple corporations, § 1561(a) requires special treatment for controlled groups of corporations. Controlled groups are limited to taxable income in each of the first two tax brackets as though they were one corporation. Referring to the previous illustration and presuming the controlled corporation rules apply, each of the four corporations would have only $12,500 (one-fourth of the first $50,000 of taxable income) subject to tax at 15 percent and $6,250 (one-fourth of the next $25,000 of taxable income) taxed at 25 percent. This will be the required allocation unless all members of the controlled group consent to an apportionment plan providing for an unequal allocation of these amounts.

Similar procedures are required for the $250,000 accumulated earnings credit for controlled groups and for the $40,000 exemption amount for purposes of computing the alternative minimum tax. In addition, members of a controlled group are treated as one taxpayer for purposes of the election to expense certain depreciable business assets under § 179. [A controlled group for purposes of § 179 has the same meaning as in § 1563(a), except that "more than 50 percent" is substituted for the "at least 80 percent" control prescribed by § 1563(a)(1)].

A controlled group of corporations includes parent-subsidiary corporations, brother-sister groups, combined groups, and certain insurance companies.

Parent-Subsidiary Corporations.   A parent-subsidiary controlled group includes one or more corporations connected through stock ownership with a common parent corporation. A parent-subsidiary controlled group exists if (a) stock possessing at least 80 percent of the total combined voting power of all classes of stock entitled to vote or at least 80 percent of the total value of shares of all classes of stock of each of the corporations, except the common parent, is owned by one or more of the other corporations and (b) the common parent corporation owns stock possessing at least 80 percent of the total combined voting power of all classes of stock entitled to vote or at least 80 percent of the total value of shares of all classes of stock of at least one of the other corporations, excluding stock owned directly by such other corporations. (See Figure I and Figure II.)

Figure I

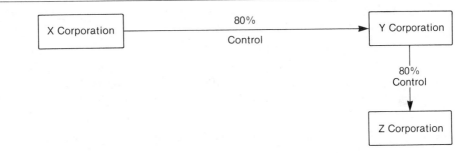

X is the common parent of a parent-subsidiary
controlled group consisting of X, Y, and Z Corporations

Figure II

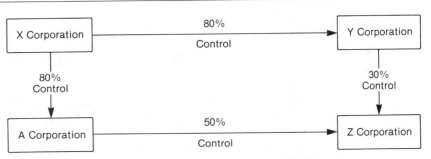

X is the common parent of a parent-subsidiary
controlled group consisting of X, Y, Z, and A Corporations.[39]

Brother-Sister Corporations.   A brother-sister controlled group exists if two or more corporations are owned by five or fewer persons (individuals, estates, or trusts) who (a) possess stock representing at least 80 percent of the total combined voting power of all classes of stock entitled to vote or at least 80 percent of the total value of shares of all classes of stock of each corporation and (b) have a common ownership of more than 50 percent of the total combined voting power of all classes of stock entitled to vote or more than 50 percent of the total value of shares of all classes of stock of each corporation.

39. Reg. § 1.1563–1(a)(2).

The stock held by each such person is considered only to the extent that such stock ownership is identical with respect to each corporation.

Example 22

The outstanding stock of Corporations W, X, Y, and Z, each of which has only one class of stock outstanding, is owned by the following unrelated individuals:

Individuals	Corporations				Identical Ownership
	W	X	Y	Z	
A	40%	30%	60%	60%	30%
B	50%	20%	30%	20%	20%
C	10%	30%	10%	10%	10%
D		20%		10%	
Total	100%	100%	100%	100%	60%

Five or fewer individuals (A, B, and C) with more than a 50% common ownership own at least 80% of all classes of stock in W, X, Y, and Z. They own 100% of W, 80% of X, 100% of Y, and 90% of Z. Consequently, W, X, Y, and Z are regarded as members of a brother-sister controlled group. □

Example 23

Changing the facts in Example 22, assume the ownership is as follows:

Individuals	Corporations				Identical Ownership
	W	X	Y	Z	
A	20%	10%	5%	60%	5%
B	10%	20%	60%	5%	5%
C	10%	70%	35%	25%	10%
D	60%			10%	
Total	100%	100%	100%	100%	20%

In this instance, the identical ownership is only 20%. Consequently, the four corporations are not members of a brother-sister controlled group. X and Y would be brother-sister corporations. □

Example 24

The outstanding stock of Corporations X and Y, each of which has only one class of stock outstanding, is owned as follows:

Individuals	Corporations		Identical Ownership
	X	Y	
A	55%	100%	55%
B	45%		
Total	100%	100%	55%

Although the 50% common ownership test would have been met, the 80% test would not, as there is no common ownership in Y Corporation. Are X and Y brother-sister corporations? No, according to the U.S. Supreme Court. □

The Regulations took the position that persons in a shareholder group (as in Example 24) could hold stock singly or in combination. However, in *U.S. v. Vogel Fertilizer Co.*,[40] the U.S. Supreme Court sided with the taxpayer and declared Reg. § 1.1563–1(a)(3) to be an unwarranted interpretation of the Internal Revenue Code. The Treasury Department has issued proposed regulations that would amend the current regulations to comply with the conclusions reached in *Vogel*.[41]

Combined Groups.   A group of three or more corporations form a combined group if each corporation is a member of either a parent-subsidiary controlled group or a brother-sister controlled group and if at least one of the corporations is the common parent of a parent-subsidiary controlled group and is also a member of a brother-sister controlled group.

Example 25   A, an individual, owns 80% of all classes of stock of X and Z Corporations. X Corporation, in turn, owns 80% of all classes of stock of Y Corporation. Z owns all the stock of W Corporation. X, Y, Z, and W are members of the same combined group. As a result, X, Y, Z, and W are limited to taxable income in the first two tax brackets and the $250,000 accumulated earnings credit as though they were one corporation. This is also the case as to the election to expense certain depreciable business assets under § 179 and as to the $40,000 exemption for purposes of computing the alternative minimum tax. □

Consolidated Returns

Corporations that are members of a parent-subsidiary affiliated group, as defined in § 1504(a) of the Code,[42] may file a consolidated income tax return for a taxable year. Each corporation that has been a member of the group during any part of the taxable year for which the consolidated return is to be filed must consent by filing Form 1122.[43] It may also consent by the actual filing of a consolidated return on Form 1120 with an affiliations schedule on Form 851 that includes all the member corporations. Once a consolidated return is filed, the controlled group must continue to file consolidated returns unless it has secured permission from the IRS to discontinue the filing of such returns.[44] Applications for discontinuance of such filing are made to the IRS by the ninetieth day preceding the return's due date. A corporation that ceases to be a member of a consolidated group must generally wait five years before it can again file on a consolidated basis.

---

40. 82–1 USTC ¶9134, 49 AFTR2d 82–491, 102 S.Ct. 821 (USSC, 1982).
41. See Prop. Reg. § 1.1563–1(a)(3), 1982–2 C.B. 735.
42. An affiliated group for this purpose is one or more chains of includible corporations connected through stock ownership with a common parent but only if (1) the common parent owns stock that represents at least 80% of the total voting power *and* 80% of the total value of stock of at least one of the includible corporations and (2) stock representing at least 80% of the total voting power *and* 80% of the total value of stock in each of the includible corporations (except the common parent) is owned directly by one or more of the includible corporations.
43. § 1501 and Reg. §§ 1.1502–75(a) and (b).
44. Reg. § 1.1502–75(c).

The privilege of filing a consolidated return is based on the concept that the affiliated group constitutes a single taxable entity despite the existence of technically separate businesses. By filing a consolidated return, the corporations can eliminate intercompany profits and losses on the principle that tax liability should be based on transactions with outsiders rather than on intragroup affairs.

Filing a consolidated return has distinct advantages. Income of a profitable company is offset by losses of another. Capital losses of one corporation can offset capital gains of another. Without this possibility, net capital losses cannot be deducted currently, as noted previously. Further, there is no § 482 problem (allocation of income and deductions among related corporations, discussed in Chapter 6).

Filing a consolidated return has certain disadvantages. Losses on intercompany transactions must be deferred. Accounting for consolidated taxable income and deferral of intercompany transactions can become perplexing. Another problem is that consolidated returns filed for tax purposes might not include the same corporations as included in the consolidated financial statements. For example, most foreign corporations cannot be consolidated for Federal income tax purposes but should be consolidated when preparing financial statements. This variance will cause some degree of compliance grievance in computing the alternative minimum tax (AMT). Under the AMT, a new preference item is a portion of a business's untaxed reported profits. For this purpose, pretax book income must be determined only for those corporations included in the consolidated tax return. In certain cases, therefore, the financial statements may have to be unconsolidated to obtain the appropriate book income amount.

Example 26 X Corporation, Y Corporation, and Z Corporation prepare financial statements that reflect their consolidated activities. For tax purposes, however, only X Corporation and Y Corporation can file a consolidated return. Under the AMT, the parties involved will have to break out Z Corporation from their financial statements. This is required, since only the pretax book income of X Corporation and Y Corporation can be considered in the determination of business untaxed reported profits. □

The filing of consolidated returns is available only to parent-subsidiary affiliated groups; it is not available to brother-sister corporations.

Computation of Consolidated Income.   Sections 1501–1504 and 1552, and the Regulations pursuant thereto, prescribing the manner of computing consolidated income, are quite complex. The rules to determine consolidated taxable income of the group are summarized in the following paragraph. The complicated accounting adjustments required to determine consolidated taxable income are beyond the scope of this text.

The consolidated return is filed using the parent corporation's taxable year, with the parent being responsible for filing the return. Each subsidiary must adopt the parent's accounting period the first year its income is included in the consolidated return. Consolidated net taxable income is computed by aggregating the separate taxable incomes for each corporation in the controlled group with certain adjustments. Net operating losses, capital gains and losses, § 1231 gains and losses, charitable contributions, unrealized profits and losses from intercompany transactions, and dividends paid and received are eliminated. These items are then aggregated separately, with required adjustments, to compute consolidated taxable income.

Limitation of Net Operating Loss Deductions.   A net operating loss (NOL) deduction for the controlled group may be used to offset consolidated income of the group with the following exceptions. If the loss year was a separate return limitation year (an SRLY), the loss may be carried over only against income of the loss corporation. An SRLY is any year in which a member of the group filed a separate return. However, a separate return year of a member is not an SRLY if such member corporation was a member of the affiliated group for each day of such year. The separate return year of a corporation that is the common parent of the group is not an SRLY unless the corporation, while nominally the common parent, is not treated as the parent because of a reverse acquisition. (A reverse acquisition occurs when shareholders in the acquired corporation obtain more than 50 percent of the stock ownership in the acquiring corporation as a result of the acquisition.) A loss corporation can acquire a profitable subsidiary and apply its loss carryovers against the profits of that corporation unless a consolidated return change of ownership (a CRCO) accompanied the acquisition or a reverse acquisition occurred. A CRCO is a change of control in the corporate group, measured as at least a 50 percent change in the ownership of the corporation's outstanding stock since the beginning of the present or prior taxable year. If there has been a CRCO, carryover losses may offset income of the original group only.

Section 382 (discussed in Chapter 6) applies to NOL carryovers by the controlled group. If these limitations apply, the NOL carryovers are reduced accordingly. Section 269 can apply to disallow such carryovers altogether (see Chapter 6).

Built-in Deductions.   Certain built-in deductions, acquired by a subsidiary in an SRLY but realized in a consolidated return year, are treated as sustained by the subsidiary before the consolidated return year. Such built-in deductions may then be deducted only against income of the subsidiary that sustained the deductions.

Example 27   Beta Corporation is the common parent of a controlled group. Beta purchased the stock of Alpha Corporation on December 30, 1987. Alpha owned a capital asset with an adjusted basis of $20,000 but with a fair market value of $10,000 on December 30, 1987. The asset was sold in 1988 for $9,000. If the group files a consolidated return for 1988, $10,000 of the $11,000 loss is a built-in deduction, because it was economically accrued in an SRLY. This portion of the loss can be deducted only against the separate income of Alpha. □

Example 28   Assume the asset in Example 27 was depreciable property. Depreciation deductions attributable to the $10,000 difference between basis and fair market value on December 30, 1987, are treated as built-in deductions and are limited to deductions against separate income of Alpha. □

The rules relating to built-in deductions do not apply once the assets of the acquired subsidiary have been held by the controlled group for more than 10 years or if the total adjusted basis of all assets of the acquired subsidiary (other than cash, certain marketable securities, and goodwill) does not exceed the fair market value of all such assets by more than 15 percent.[45] Built-in deductions will be completely eliminated if the corporation was acquired to obtain such deductions.[46]

Intercompany Transactions.   Intercompany transactions are divided into deferred intercompany transactions and transactions that are not deferred. Those transactions that are not deferred are taken into income and expense by the separate corporations in the same tax year so that there is a "wash" for purposes of computing consolidated taxable income. The deferred intercompany transactions are placed in a suspense account, and profits and losses are deferred until either the assets are sold to a taxpayer outside the controlled group or one of the parties to the transaction leaves the controlled group.

Summary of Steps in Calculating Consolidated Taxable Income.   Briefly, the steps in calculating consolidated taxable income are as follows:

1. Combine the separately computed taxable income for each member of the controlled group.
2. Eliminate from the combined taxable income of the group any intercompany dividends and any built-in deductions. (Dividends paid to minority shareholders are not eliminated.)
3. Eliminate from the combined taxable income of the group, and then adjust to reflect a consolidated figure, the following items:

   a. Any NOL deduction for each affiliate. [Any NOL deduction for an affiliate is subject to the SRLY and CRCO limitation rules. In addition, §§ 382 and 269 are applicable to a recently acquired subsidiary to cause a possible disallowance of all or part of the loss carryover. (See Chapter 6.)]

   b. Capital gains and losses for each affiliate.

   c. Section 1231 gains and losses for each affiliate.

   d. Charitable contribution deductions for each affiliate. [The consolidated charitable contribution deduction is limited to ten percent of the adjusted consolidated taxable income (consolidated taxable income computed without regard to the dividends received deduction and any consolidated NOL or capital loss carrybacks).]

45. Reg. § 1.1502–15(a)(4).
46. Reg. §§ 1.269–3(a) and (c).

4. Transfer from combined taxable income certain intercompany transactions. [Intercompany transactions such as sales or exchanges of property or the performance of services where the amount of the expenditure for such services is capitalized (or any other expenditure where the amount of the expenditure is capitalized) among members of the controlled group are transferred to a deferred account.]

   a. Intercompany gains or losses on such deferred transactions are postponed until the property is sold to a third party.

   b. Generally, noncapitalized intercompany transactions are not deferred.

   c. The group may elect not to defer gain or loss on any otherwise deferred intercompany transactions.

Example 29   X, Y, and Z Corporations are members of a controlled group that has elected to file a consolidated return. In the fiscal year beginning July 1, 1987, the corporations have separate taxable income as follows: S, $50,000 taxable income from operations plus a § 1231 gain of $60,000; Y, $50,000 taxable income representing $80,000 taxable income from operations minus a § 1231 loss of $30,000; Z, taxable income from operations of $200,000. Consolidated taxable income for the group would be $330,000 plus a net § 1231 gain of $30,000, computed as follows: $300,000 (combined separately computed taxable income for X, Y, and Z Corporations) + $30,000 (§ 1231 loss deducted by Y in arriving at its separate taxable income) + net § 1231 gain of $30,000 [$60,000 (§ 1231 gain for X) − $30,000 (§ 1231 loss for Y)]. Tax liability for the group would be $122,400, determined as follows:

Tax on first $75,000	$ 13,750
Tax on $285,000 at 34%	96,900
Tax on $260,000 [excess over $100,000 at 5% (limited to $11,750)]	11,750
	$122,400

Tax Planning Considerations

Working with § 351

Effective tax planning with transfers of property to corporations involves a clear understanding of § 351 and its related Code provisions. The most important question in planning is simply: Does compliance with the requirements of § 351 yield the desired tax result?

Utilizing § 351.   In using § 351(a), one should insure that all parties transferring property (which includes cash) receive control of the corporation. Although simultaneous transfers are not necessary, a long period of time between transfers could be vulnerable if the transfers are not properly documented as part of a single plan.

Example 30   C, D, and E decide to form the X Corporation with the following investment: cash of $100,000 from C, real estate worth $100,000 (basis of $20,000) from D, and a patent worth $100,000 (basis of zero) from E. In return for this investment, each party is to receive one-third of the corporation's authorized stock of 300 shares. On June 1, 1988, after the corporate charter is granted, C transfers cash of $100,000 in return for 100 shares. Two months later, D transfers the real estate for another 100 shares. On December 3, 1988, E transfers the patent for the remaining 100 shares. □

   Taken in isolation, the transfers by D and E would result in recognized gain to each. Section 351 would not be applicable, because neither D nor E achieves the required 80 percent control. If, however, the parties are in a position to prove that all transfers were part of the same plan, C's transfer can be counted and the 80 percent requirement is satisfied. To do this the parties should document and preserve evidence of their intentions. Also, it would be helpful to have some reasonable explanation for the delay in D's and E's transfers.

   To meet the requirements of § 351, mere momentary control on the part of the transferor may not suffice if loss of control is compelled by a prearranged agreement.[47]

Example 31   For many years T operated a business as a sole proprietor employing R as manager. To dissuade R from quitting and going out on her own, T promised her a 30% interest in the business. To fulfill this promise, T transfers the business to newly formed X Corporation in return for all its stock. Immediately thereafter, T transfers 30% of the stock to R. Section 351 probably would not apply to the transfer by T to X Corporation; it appears that T was under an obligation to relinquish control. If this is not the case and such loss of control was by voluntary act on the part of T, momentary control would suffice.[48] □

   Be sure that later transfers of property to an existing corporation satisfy the control requirement if recognition of gain is to be avoided. In this connection, a transferor's interest cannot be counted if the value of stock or securities received is relatively small compared with the value of stock or securities already owned and the primary purpose of the transfer is to qualify other transferors for § 351 treatment.[49] For purposes of issuing advance rulings, the IRS policy is to treat the amount transferred as *not* being relatively small in value if such amount is equal to, or in excess of, 10 percent of the fair market value of the stock and securities already owned by such person.[50]

---

47. Rev.Rul. 54–96, 1954–1 C.B. 111.
48. Compare *Fahs v. Florida Machine and Foundry Co.*, 48–2 USTC ¶9329, 36 AFTR 1151, 168 F.2d 957 (CA–5, 1948), with *John C. O'Connor*, 16 TCM 213, T.C.Memo. 1957–50, *aff'd.* in 58–2 USTC ¶9913, 2 AFTR2d 6011, 260 F.2d 358 (CA–6, 1958).
49. Reg. § 1.351–1(a)(1)(ii). Refer to Example 4 of this chapter.
50. Rev.Proc. 77–37, 1977–2 C.B. 568.

Example 32   At a point when R Corporation has 800 shares outstanding (owned equally by T and her son) and worth $1,000 each, it issues an additional 200 shares to T in exchange for land (basis of $20,000 and fair market value of $200,000). Presuming the son makes no contribution, T's transfer does not meet the requirements of § 351. Since the son's ownership interest cannot be counted (he was not a transferor), T must satisfy the control requirement on her own. In this regard, she falls short, since she ended up with 600 shares [400 shares (originally owned) + 200 shares (newly received)] out of 1,000 shares now outstanding for only a 60% interest.[51] Thus, T must recognize a gain of $180,000 on the transfer. ☐

To make the transfer in Example 32 fall under § 351, what needs to be done? One possibility would be to include the son as a transferor so that his ownership interest can be counted in meeting the control requirement. In using the IRS guidelines to avoid the "relatively small in value" hurdle, this would entail an investment on the part of the son (for additional stock) of at least $40,000 in cash or property [10% × $400,000 (fair market value of the shares already owned)]. If this approach is taken, § 351 will apply to T, and none of her realized gain of $180,000 will be recognized.

To keep the matter in perspective, be in a position to recognize when § 351 is not relevant.

Example 33   Assume the same facts as in Example 32, except that T receives no additional shares in R Corporation in exchange for the transfer of the land. Because T has made a contribution to capital, compliance with § 351 is of no consequence. No gain will be recognized by T due to such contribution, although a basis adjustment is in order as to her original 400 shares.[52] Other tax consequences, however, may materialize.[53] ☐

Avoiding § 351.   Because § 351(a) provides for the nonrecognition of gain on transfers to controlled corporations, it is often regarded as a relief provision favoring taxpayers. There could be situations, however, where the avoidance of § 351(a) produces a more advantageous tax result. The transferors might prefer to recognize gain on the transfer of property if they cannot be particularly harmed by the gain because they are in low tax brackets. Further, the gain might be capital gain from which the transferors may be able to offset substantial capital losses.

Another reason that a particular transferor might wish to avoid § 351 concerns possible loss recognition. Recall that § 351(a) refers to the nonrecognition of both gains and losses. In a boot situation, § 351(b)(2) specifically states: "No loss to such recipient shall be recognized." The course of action for

---

51. The stock attribution rules of § 318 (see Chapter 4) do not apply to § 351 transfers. Consequently, the shares held by the son are not treated as being constructively owned by the mother.

52. If R Corporation is a foreign corporation, the result (in terms of recognition of gain) may well be different. See § 367(c)(2).

53. Because the son has benefited from T's capital contribution (i.e., his shares are, as a result, worth more), a gift has taken place. It could be, therefore, that T's capital contribution could lead to the imposition of a gift tax liability. In this connection, see Chapter 11.

a transferor who wishes to recognize loss on the transfer of property with a basis in excess of fair market value could be any of several alternatives:

—Sell the property to the corporation for its stock. However, the IRS could attempt to collapse the "sale" by taking the approach that the transfer really falls under § 351(a).[54] If the sale is disregarded, the transferor ends up with a realized, but unrecognized, loss.

—Sell the property to the corporation for other property or boot. Because the transferor receives no stock or securities, § 351 is inapplicable.

—Transfer the property to the corporation in return for securities. Surprisingly, the IRS has held that § 351 does not apply to a transferor who receives only securities and no stock.[55] In both this and the previous alternatives, one would have to watch for the possible disallowance of the loss under § 267.

Suppose, however, the loss property is to be transferred to the corporation and no loss is recognized by the transferor due to § 351(a). This could present an interesting problem in terms of assessing the economic realities involved.

Example 34   E and F form X Corporation with the following investment: property by E (basis of $40,000 and fair market value of $50,000) and property by F (basis of $60,000 and fair market value of $50,000). Each receives 50% of the X Corporation stock. Has F acted wisely in settling for only 50% of the stock? At first blush, it would appear so, since E and F each invested property of the same value ($50,000). But what about the tax considerations? Due to the basis carryover of § 362(b), the corporation now has a basis of $40,000 in E's property and $60,000 in F's property. In essence, then, E has shifted a possible $10,000 gain to the corporation while F has transferred a $10,000 potential loss. (The higher basis in F's property has value to the corporation either in the form of higher depreciation deductions or less gain on a later sale.) With this in mind, an equitable allocation of the X Corporation stock would call for F to receive a greater percentage interest than E. □

Investor Losses

Even though the Tax Reform Act of 1986 made significant changes in the treatment of capital gains and losses, the disadvantages of capital losses are largely retained. Except for the elimination of the $2 for $1 rule applicable to individuals deducting up to $3,000 of net long-term capital losses, the limitations on capital losses are unchanged. Thus, net capital gains may be treated as ordinary income, but net capital losses are by no means the equivalent of ordinary losses.

The premium on categorizing investor losses as ordinary losses rather than capital losses definitely continues to exist. In this regard, using § 1244 (when available) and other approaches (e.g., noninvestment motives for acquiring

---

54. *U.S. v. Hertwig*, 68–2 USTC ¶9495, 22 AFTR2d 5249, 398 F.2d 452 (CA–5, 1968).
55. Rev.Rul. 73–472, 1973–2 C.B. 115. But compare Rev.Rul. 73–473, 1973–2 C.B. 115.

stock or trade or business reasons for making loans) will not be changed as a result of the Tax Reform Act of 1986.

Related Corporations

Controlled Groups.   Recall that § 1561 was designed to prevent the abuse of operating a business as multiple corporations to obtain lower tax brackets and multiple minimum accumulated earnings tax credits. Corporations in which substantially all the stock is held by five or fewer persons are subject to the provisions of § 1561. Therefore, if ownership of voting stock is divided so that control of each corporation lies with the different individuals rather than with the individuals having a common control of all the corporations, the prohibitions of § 1561 can be avoided.

Example 35   A, B, and C, individuals, have voting stock in Corporations X, Y, and Z as follows:

Shareholder	X	Y	Z	Common Ownership
A	40	30	30	30
B	40	20	30	20
C	20	50	40	20
Total	100	100	100	70

Because the total combined ownership is more than 50% and the three individuals own at least 80% of the combined voting power, X, Y, and Z are treated as a controlled group and are subject to § 1561. Thus, Corporations X, Y, and Z are limited to taxable income in the first two tax brackets and to the $250,000 accumulated earnings tax credit as though they were one corporation. ☐

Assume, however, that voting stock is divided differently so that each of the individuals—A, B, and C—control one of the corporations rather than having common control of all the corporations.

Example 36   A, B, and C hold voting stock in Corporations X, Y, and Z in the following percentages:

Shareholder	X	Y	Z	Common Ownership
A	80	10	10	10
B	10	80	10	10
C	10	10	80	10
Total	100	100	100	30

Now the total combined ownership is less than 50%. Consequently, the corporations are not treated as a controlled group, since the prohibitions of § 1561 are not applicable. ☐

The differences in ownership in the corporations could be alleviated somewhat by issuing nonvoting preferred stock to those shareholders with the 10 percent ownership. (Nonvoting stock is not considered to be stock for purposes of § 1563.)

Consolidated Returns. Effective tax planning for affiliated corporations (recall that brother-sister controlled groups cannot file consolidated returns) requires a determination of whether to file a consolidated return for the group. Because of the complex accounting required to compute consolidated taxable income, computations should be made initially to determine whether the tax savings from filing a consolidated return will be significant enough to warrant making the election. An incorrect decision can cause problems; once a consolidated return is filed, the affiliated group must continue to file such a return until it has secured permission from the IRS to discontinue doing so.

The principal advantage of filing a consolidated return is that the losses of one corporation may be used to offset the income of other corporations.

Example 37

In 1988, X Corporation has taxable income from operations in the amount of $50,000 and has incurred a short-term capital gain of $10,000 and a long-term capital gain of $20,000. Its tax liability would be $15,450 [$13,750 (tax on first $75,000) + $1,700 (34% of $5,000)]. X owns 80% of the voting stock of Y Corporation, which had a tax loss from operations in 1988 of $30,000 plus a net short-term capital loss of $40,000. Y Corporation would have no tax liability filing a separate return. If X and Y file a consolidated return, tax liability would be only $3,000 [15% of $20,000 ($50,000 income from operations for X less $30,000 loss from operations for Y)]. The net short-term capital loss of $40,000 incurred by Y would offset the capital gains of $30,000 incurred by X. Consequently, there would be a tax savings of $12,450 [$15,450 (income tax liability for X if a separate return is filed) − $3,000 (liability on a consolidated return)]. □

Filing a consolidated return can have disadvantages. Although gain on intercompany transactions is deferred when a consolidated return is filed, intercompany losses are also deferred. In addition, the accounting for deferred transactions can become quite complex. (Because of the accounting complexity, an affiliated group may elect not to defer such gains and losses.) The accounting problems relating to built-in deductions and SRLY and CRCO limitations can be extensive.

Although the advantages of filing consolidated returns can be substantial, the filing of a consolidated return does eliminate the flexibility of corporate planning on a separate return basis. With the additional concern that filing a consolidated return can be disadvantageous, the election to file such a return should not be made if the tax advantages in doing so are small.

Problem Materials

Discussion Questions

1. In terms of justification and effect, § 351 (transfer to corporation controlled by transferor) and § 1031 (like-kind exchanges) are much alike. Explain.

2. F and S (father and son) form a corporation with a transfer of property valued at $200,000 and $100,000, respectively. In return for this property, F and S each receive 50% of the corporation's stock. Explain the tax consequences of these transfers as to F and to S.

3. What does the term "property" include for purposes of § 351?

4. Is the transfer of an installment obligation in a § 351 transaction a disposition of the installment obligation so that gain is triggered on the transfer? Explain.

5. If gain is recognized in a § 351 transfer because of the receipt of boot, how is the gain characterized?

6. In arriving at the basis of stock received by a shareholder in a § 351 transfer, describe the effect of the following:

   a. The receipt of other property (boot) in addition to stock by the shareholder.

   b. Transfer of a liability to the corporation, along with the property, by the shareholder.

   c. The shareholder's basis in the property transferred to the corporation.

7. How does a corporation determine its basis in property received pursuant to a § 351 transfer?

8. What are "securities" for purposes of § 351? What difference does it make if debt instruments do or do not qualify as securities?

9. What is the control requirement of § 351? Describe the effect of the following in satisfying this requirement:

   a. A shareholder renders services to the corporation for stock.

   b. A shareholder both renders services and transfers property to the corporation for stock.

   c. A shareholder has only momentary control after the transfer.

   d. A long period of time elapses between the transfers of property by different shareholders.

10. Assuming a § 351(a) nontaxable transfer, explain the tax effect, if any, of the following transactions:

    a. The transfer of depreciable property with recapture potential under § 1245 or § 1250.

    b. The later sale of such property by the corporation.

    c. The transfer of property upon which an investment tax credit has previously been claimed by the transferor.

    d. The later sale of such property by the corporation.

11. At a point when X Corporation has been in existence for six years, shareholder T transfers real estate (adjusted basis of $20,000 and fair market value of $100,000) to the corporation for additional stock. At the same time, P, the other shareholder, purchases one share of stock for cash. After the two transfers, the percentage of stock ownership is as follows: 79% by T and 21% by P.

    a. What were the parties trying to accomplish?

    b. Will it work? Explain.

    c. Would the result change if T and P are father and son?

12. Assume the same facts as in Question 11, except that T receives nothing from X Corporation for the transfer of the real estate to the corporation. Does this change the tax result as to T?

13. Before incorporating her apartment rental business, B takes out second mortgages on several of the units. B uses the mortgage funds to make capital improvements to her personal residence. Along with all of the rental units, B transfers the mortgages to the newly formed corporation in return for all of its stock. Discuss the tax consequences to B of the procedures followed.

14. K's sole proprietorship includes assets that, if sold, would yield a gain of $100,000. It also includes assets that would yield a loss of $30,000. K incorporates his business using only the gain assets. Two days later, K sells the loss assets to the newly formed corporation.

    a. What was K trying to accomplish?

    b. Will it work? Explain.

15. The recapture of the investment tax credit can operate independent of § 351. Explain.

16. In structuring the capitalization of a corporation, what are the advantages of utilizing debt rather than equity?

17. Presuming § 1244 does not apply, what is the tax treatment of stock that has become worthless?

18. Under what circumstances, if any, may a shareholder deduct a business bad debt on a loan he or she has made to the corporation?

19. T, an unmarried individual taxpayer, had invested $75,000 in the stock of X Corporation, which recently declared bankruptcy. Although T is distressed over the loss of her investment, she is somewhat consoled by the fact that the $75,000 will be an ordinary (rather than a capital) loss. Is T fully apprised of the tax result? Why or why not?

20. Several years ago, M purchased stock in Y Corporation for $40,000. Such stock has a current value of $5,000. Consider the following alternatives:

    a. Without selling the stock, M deducts $35,000 for partial worthlessness of the Y Corporation investment.

    b. M sells the stock to his son for $5,000 and deducts a $35,000 long-term capital loss.

    c. M sells the stock to a third party and deducts a $35,000 long-term capital loss.

    d. M sells the stock to a third party and deducts a $35,000 ordinary loss.

21. How does treatment as a controlled group of corporations work to the disadvantage of the corporate group?

22. What is the difference between a brother-sister controlled group and a parent-subsidiary controlled group?

23. Assume an individual, A, owns 80% of all classes of stock of two corporations, X and Y. X Corporation, in turn, owns all the stock of Z Corporation, and Y Corporation owns 80% of the stock of W Corporation. Would X, Y, Z, and W Corporations be members of a combined group? Explain.

24. What groups of corporations may file consolidated returns?

25. What are the advantages and disadvantages of filing a consolidated return?

26. Assume a parent corporation uses the calendar year as its taxable year. It owns 80% of all classes of stock in two subsidiary corporations that use a fiscal year for their tax years. The corporations wish to file a consolidated return. What tax year should be used?

27. When may a net operating loss for a controlled group be used to offset consolidated taxable income?

28. What is a built-in deduction of a controlled group?

29. What is the significance of a deferred intercompany transaction?

Problems

1. G and H form Z Corporation with the following investment:

	Basis to Transferor	Fair Market Value	Number of Shares Issued
From G—			
Cash	$ 60,000	$ 60,000	
Installment obligation	40,000	140,000	50
From H—			
Cash	25,000	25,000	
Machinery	50,000	75,000	50
Equipment	80,000	100,000	

The installment obligation has a face amount of $140,000 and was acquired last year from the sale of land held for investment purposes (adjusted basis of $40,000).

a. How much gain, if any, must G recognize?

b. What will be G's basis in the Z Corporation stock?

c. What will be Z Corporation's basis in the installment obligation?

d. How much gain, if any, must H recognize?

e. What will be H's basis in the Z Corporation stock?

f. What will be Z Corporation's basis in the machinery and equipment?

2. A, B, C, and D (all individuals) form W Corporation with the following investment:

	Basis to Transferor	Fair Market Value	Number of Shares Issued
From A—			
Personal services rendered to W Corporation	$ 0	$ 10,000	10
From B—			
Equipment	115,000	100,000	90 *
From C—			
Cash	20,000	20,000	
Unrealized accounts receivable	0	30,000	50
From D—			
Land & building	70,000	150,000	
Mortgage on land & building	100,000	100,000	50

* B receives $10,000 in cash in addition to the 90 shares.

The mortgage transferred by D is assumed by W Corporation. The value of each share of W Corporation stock is $1,000.

a. What, if any, is A's recognized gain or loss?

b. What basis will A have in the W Corporation stock?

c. How much gain or loss must B recognize?

d. What basis will B have in the W Corporation stock?

e. What basis will W Corporation have in the equipment?

f. What, if any, is C's recognized gain or loss?

g. What basis will C have in the W Corporation stock?

h. What basis will W Corporation have in the unrealized accounts receivable?

i. How much gain or loss must D recognize?

j. What basis will D have in the W Corporation stock?

k. What basis will W Corporation have in the land and building?

3. J, K, L, and M form V Corporation with the following investment:

	Property Transferred		Number of Shares Issued
	Basis to Transferor	Fair Market Value	
From J—			
Inventory	$ 10,000	$ 32,000	30 *
From K—			
Equipment ($10,000 of depreciation taken by K in prior years)	15,000	33,000	30 **
From L—			
Secret process	5,000	30,000	30
From M—			
Cash	10,000	10,000	10

* J receives $2,000 in cash in addition to the 30 shares.

** K receives $3,000 in cash in addition to the 30 shares.

Assume the value of each share of V Corporation stock is $1,000.

a. What, if any, is J's recognized gain or loss? How is any such gain or loss treated?

b. What basis will J have in the V Corporation stock?

c. What basis will V Corporation have in the inventory?

d. How much gain or loss must K recognize? How is the gain or loss treated?

e. What basis will K have in the V Corporation stock?

f. What basis will V Corporation have in the equipment?

g. What, if any, is L's recognized gain or loss?

h. What basis will L have in the V Corporation stock?

i. What basis will V Corporation have in the secret process?

j. How much income, if any, must M recognize?

k. What basis will M have in the V Corporation stock?

4. A and B organize X Corporation by transferring the following property:

| | Property Transferred | | Number of |
	Basis to Transferor	Fair Market Value	Shares Issued
From A—			
Unimproved land	$ 10,000	$100,000	
Mortgage on land	50,000	50,000	50
From B—			
Receivables	60,000	50,000	50

Assume the value of each share of X Corporation stock is $1,000.

a. What, if any, is A's recognized gain or loss?

b. What basis will A have in the X Corporation stock?

c. What basis will X Corporation have in the land?

d. What, if any, is B's recognized gain or loss?

e. What basis will B have in the X Corporation stock?

f. What basis will X Corporation have in the receivables?

5. A and B, individuals, formed X Corporation by each investing property with a fair market value of $100,000. The assets had a tax basis to A of $30,000 and a tax basis of $50,000 to B. A received stock in X Corporation consisting of 1,000 shares with a par value of $100. B received 10-year notes executed by X Corporation in the amount of $100,000, bearing 10% interest. What gain, if any, will A and B recognize on the transfer?

6. A organized Y Corporation 10 years ago by contributing property worth $500,000, basis of $100,000, for 2,000 shares of stock in Y, representing 100% of the stock in Y Corporation. A later gave each of his children, B and C, 500 shares of stock in Y Corporation. In the current year, A transfers property worth $160,000, basis of $50,000, to Y Corporation for 500 shares in Y Corporation. What gain, if any, will A recognize on this transfer?

7. In 1985, T, an individual, purchased § 38 property for $20,000. T claimed an investment tax credit of $2,000, based on a recovery period of five years. In 1986, T transferred all of her assets (including the § 38 property) to X Corporation for all the stock in X. In 1987, two years after T purchased the § 38 property, X Corporation sold the § 38 property. What, if any, are the tax consequences to T as a result of the sale by X Corporation?

8. T organized X Corporation and transferred land with a basis of $200,000, value of $600,000, and subject to a mortgage of $150,000. A month before incorporation, T borrowed $100,000 for personal purposes and gave the bank a lien on the land. X Corporation issued stock worth $350,000 to T and assumed the loans in the amount of $150,000 and $100,000. What are the tax consequences of the incorporation to T and to X Corporation?

9. Indicate whether the following statements are true or false:

a. If both § 357(b) and § 357(c) apply, the latter will control.

b. For § 357(b) to apply, the transfer of the liability must be for the purpose of tax avoidance *and* must lack a bona fide business purpose.

c. Section 357(c) will not apply if there is no realized gain on the transfer.

d. The application of § 357(b) to a transfer to a controlled corporation would not affect the basis of the stock received by the transferor.

e. T transfers property (upon which an investment tax credit has previously been claimed) to a controlled corporation. A later sale of the property by the corporation could trigger recapture of the credit to T.

f. Same as (e). A later sale of the stock by T could trigger recapture of the credit to T.

g. T transfers depreciable property to a controlled corporation. The property possesses a recapture potential under § 1245. A later sale of the property by the corporation could trigger recapture of depreciation to T.

h. T transfers supplies (tax basis of zero, fair market value of $10,000) for stock in a controlled corporation worth $10,000. Under these circumstances, the tax benefit rule will not cause any recognition of gain to T.

i. P Corporation owns 80% of X Corporation and 90% of Y Corporation. X owns 30% of Z Corporation, and Y owns 50% of Z Corporation. Z owns 85% of W Corporation and 90% of A Corporation. A owns 80% of B Corporation and 85% of C Corporation. P, X, Y, Z, W, A, B, and C Corporations are all members of a controlled group and may file a consolidated return.

10. A city donates land to X Corporation as an inducement for X to locate there. The land is worth $100,000. The city also donates $50,000 in cash to X.

a. What income, if any, must X recognize as a result of the transfer of land and cash to it by the city?

b. What basis will X have in the land?

c. If X purchases property with the $50,000 cash, what basis will it have in the property?

 11. T, an individual, transfers assets with a tax basis of $400,000 to a newly formed corporation for 100% of the stock. In the first year of operations, the corporation has net taxable income of $90,000. If the corporation distributes $74,000 to T, how will the distribution be treated for tax purposes to T? To the corporation?

 12. Assume in Problem 11 that T transferred the assets for stock in the amount of $200,000 and debt in the amount of $200,000, payable in equal annual installments of $50,000 plus interest at the rate of 12%. Assume again that the corporation has net taxable income of $90,000. If the corporation distributes $74,000 to T as payment on the debt, how will the distribution be treated for tax purposes to T? To the corporation?

13. T forms X Corporation with an investment of $200,000, for which he receives $20,000 in stock and $180,000 in 8% interest-bearing bonds maturing in nine years. Several years later, T loans the corporation an additional $50,000 on open account. X Corporation subsequently becomes insolvent and is adjudged bankrupt. During the corporation's existence, T was paid an annual salary of $40,000. How might T's losses be treated for tax purposes?

14. Stock in X Corporation is held equally by A, B, and C. X seeks additional capital to construct a building in the amount of $900,000. A, B, and C each propose to loan X Corporation $300,000, taking from X Corporation a $300,000 four-year note with interest payable annually at two points below the prime rate. X Corporation has current taxable income of $2,000,000. How might the payments on the notes be treated for tax purposes?

15. T, an individual taxpayer who files a joint return with her spouse, acquired § 1244 stock at a cost of $200,000 two years ago. She sells the stock for $20,000 in the current tax year. How will the loss be treated for tax purposes?

16. T, a single taxpayer, acquired stock in a corporation that qualified as a small business corporation under § 1244, at a cost of $100,000 three years ago. He sells the stock for $10,000 in the current tax year. How will the loss be treated for tax purposes?

17. Assume that T in Problem 16 gave the stock to his brother a few months after he acquired it. The stock was worth $100,000 on the date of the gift. T's brother sells the stock for $10,000 in the current tax year. How will the loss be treated for tax purposes?

18. T, an individual, transfers property with a basis of $40,000 and a fair market value of $20,000 to X Corporation in exchange for shares of § 1244 stock. (Assume the transfer qualifies under § 351.)

    a. What is the basis of the stock to T?

    b. What is the basis of the stock for purposes of § 1244 to T?

    c. If T sells the stock for $10,000 two years later, how will the loss be treated for tax purposes?

19. X Corporation owns 80% of the total combined voting power of all classes of stock entitled to vote in Y Corporation. Y Corporation owns 20% of the stock in Z Corporation. X Corporation owns 90% of W Corporation, while the latter owns 60% of Z Corporation. Which corporations are part of a controlled group?

20. An individual, A, owns 20% of X Corporation. X Corporation owns 90% of all classes of stock in Y Corporation. Another individual, B, owns 30% of X Corporation and 40% of Z Corporation. A owns 10% of W Corporation. C, an individual, owns 20% of X Corporation and 10% of W Corporation. D, an individual, owns 10% of W Corporation, 10% of X Corporation, and 20% of Z Corporation. A owns 5% of Z Corporation, and C owns 15% of Z Corporation. W Corporation owns 85% of all classes of stock in U Corporation. B owns 50% of W Corporation. Which, if any, of the above corporations are members of a controlled group?

21. The outstanding stock in X and Y Corporations, each of which has only one class of stock, is owned by the following unrelated individuals:

Shareholders	Corporations	
	X	Y
A	20	16
B	5	54
C	75	30
Total	100	100

    a. Determine if a brother-sister controlled group exists.

    b. Assume that B owns no stock in X Corporation and C owns 80 shares. Would a brother-sister controlled group exist? Why or why not?

22. X Corporation owns 100% of Y Corporation. For the taxable fiscal year beginning August 1, 1987, X Corporation had taxable income from operations of $60,000 and incurred a § 1231 gain of $30,000 and a net long-term capital gain of $10,000. Y had taxable income from operations of $80,000 for the same taxable year plus a short-term capital loss of $5,000 and a § 1231 loss of $15,000. Compute tax liability for X Corporation and Y Corporation if a consolidated income tax return is filed.

23. Assume the following transactions occurred in the current calendar year for Corporations X, Y, and Z. X owns 100% of Y Corporation, and Y Corporation owns 100% of Z Corporation.

Corporation	§ 1231 Gain or (Loss)	Deferred Gain or (Loss)	Capital Gain or (Loss) Short-term	Long-term
X	$3,000	–0–	$5,000	$10,000
Y	2,000	$20,000	4,000	(8,000)
Z	(9,000)	–0–	(6,000)	(12,000)

Income (loss) from business operations was as follows:
X	$110,000
Y	58,000 (includes deferred gain of $20,000)
Z	(40,000)

Compute consolidated taxable income for X, Y, and Z Corporations.

24. X Corporation is the common parent of a controlled group. X purchased stock of Y Corporation on December 20, 1986. Y Corporation owned a capital asset with an adjusted basis of $50,000, fair market value of $10,000, on December 20, 1986. The asset was sold in 1988 for $5,000. The controlled group filed a consolidated return for 1988. What amount of the loss on the sale of the asset can be used to offset capital gains on a consolidated basis?

25. Assume the asset in Problem 24 was not sold until 12 years after the purchase of the stock in Y Corporation. How much of the loss can be used to offset consolidated income?

Research Problems

Research Problem 1. A cash basis partnership is incorporated. The newly formed corporation elects the cash method of accounting. The partnership transfers $30,000 of accounts receivable along with equipment, land, and cash. The corporation also agrees to pay accounts payable of the partnership in the amount of $40,000. The corporation files its return for its first year of operation and does not report the $30,000 received on accounts receivable of the partnership as income. It does deduct the $40,000 it paid on the partnership's accounts payable. The IRS disallows the deductions totaling $40,000 and increases the corporation's taxable income by $30,000, which represents the collection of partnership accounts receivable. What is the result?

Research Problem 2. A, a wealthy farmer, wants to take advantage of gift tax exclusions and give some of his property to his children. He decides to incorporate his farm operation in order to donate the property to his children more easily in the form of shares of stock. He transfers his property to a newly formed corporation for 100% of the stock. He gives 30% of the stock to his children immediately upon receipt. The IRS asserts upon audit that A is to be taxed on the initial transfer of property to the corporation because he failed to gain control of 80% of the stock. What is the result?

Research Problem 3. Individuals A, B, C, and D organize T Corporation with 100 shares of common stock. Each individual receives 25 shares in T Corporation in exchange for $60,000 worth of stock in different corporations. All of the stock transferred to T Corporation is listed on the New York Stock Exchange and is readily marketable. A transferred stock in X Corporation; B transferred stock in Y Corporation; C transferred stock in Z Corporation; and D transferred stock in several corporations. The stock will be held by T Corporation for investment purposes. A, B, C, and D each have a low basis in the stock they transferred to T Corporation. Will they recognize gain on the transfer? Assume A, B, C, and D form a partnership rather than T Corporation and transfer their readily marketable stock to the partnership. The partnership will hold the stock for investment purposes. Will gain be recognized on the transfer?

Research Problem 4. A and B, two doctors, form W, a professional association, to engage in the practice of medicine. W purchases X-ray equipment to be used in the business. A and B later form Y, an S corporation, to perform X-ray services for W. All the stock in Y is transferred by A and B to their children. W transferred the X-ray equipment to Y, with Y executing a note payable to W for the equipment. Y then hires an X-ray technician to perform the X-ray services for W. The X-ray equipment and the X-ray technician's office are located in the building owned by W. W does all the billing for X-ray services and then remits a percentage of its collections to Y. Y then pays the technician for his services, pays rent to W for use of the building, and pays W on the note it executed for payment of the X-ray equipment. During the tax year, Y had a profit that the children of A and B reported on their individual income tax returns. Upon audit, the IRS assessed a deficiency against W, asserting that all income and expenses of Y must be attributed to W, because Y was a sham corporation. The IRS also assessed a deficiency against A and B, stating that all distributions from Y to A's and B's children are constructive dividends to A and B from W Corporation. What are the results?

Partial list of research aids:

§§ 61 and 482.

Edwin D. Davis, 64 T.C. 1034 (1975).

Engineering Sales, Inc. v. U.S., 75–1 USTC ¶9347, 35 AFTR2d 75–1122, 510 F.2d 565 (CA–5, 1975).

Research Problem 5. T owned and operated a farm producing cotton and grain sorghum. T transferred all the farm assets except the land and a portion of the equipment to a newly formed corporation for 100% of the stock. Before incorporation, T had paid farm expenses of $30,000 incurred in connection with planting the crops. T deducted the $30,000 on his individual income tax return; however, income from the crops was reported by the corporation, because the crops were harvested and sold after incorporation. Upon audit, the IRS disallowed the $30,000 deduction to T, reallocating it to the corporation under § 482. T challenges the reallocation. What is the result?

Research Problem 6. T purchased 100 shares of stock in X Corporation at a cost of $20,000, relying on a magazine advertisement regarding X Corporation and on information furnished by his friend F, who owned some stock in X Corporation. T then purchased another 200 shares in X Corporation from F at a cost of $40,000. During the tax year, X Corporation became bankrupt, and T lost his entire investment. T deducted the $60,000 in full as a theft loss rather than reporting it as a capital loss, contending that the president of X Corporation and his friend F had defrauded him and other investors in that they knew the claims they made about X Corporation were erroneous. T thus claimed that the money was stolen from him. Is T correct in reporting the loss as a theft loss?

Partial list of research aids:

Perry A. Nichols, 43 T.C. 842 (1965).

Research Problem 7. T, a partner in a law firm, had represented a large corporation as its general counsel. This contact had brought large legal fees to the law firm. The corporation found itself in need of additional new financing and proposed a plan whereby substantial blocks of stock would be sold to a company that would loan additional funds to the corporation. T feared that the sale of the stock would cause a change in management of the corporation and that the legal work for the corporation would be transferred to another law firm. As a result, to protect his firm's retainer fee with the corporation, T purchased a large number of shares in the corporation for himself, paying a total of $100,000 for the shares. In 1986, the corporation found itself in further financial difficulties, and the stock in the corporation became worthless. T deducted the $100,000 he paid for the then worthless stock in 1986 as an ordinary loss. In 1988, T's return was audited. The IRS contends that the $100,000 is a capital loss because the stock was a capital asset.

    a. What argument can be made in defense of T's position?

    b. How successful will it be?

Partial list of research aids:

John A. Kuhnen, 42 TCM 1438, T.C.Memo. 1981–600.

4 Corporations: Distributions *dividends* Not in Complete Liquidation

Objectives

Distinguish between corporate distributions not in complete liquidation and those in complete liquidation of the corporation.

Explain the concept of earnings and profits and its importance in measuring dividend income.

Discuss the tax consequences of a property dividend to the recipient shareholder and to the corporation making the distribution.

Differentiate between taxable and nontaxable stock dividends.

Describe the various stock redemptions that qualify for sale or exchange treatment and thereby avoid dividend treatment.

Review the tax rules governing the distribution of stock and securities of a controlled corporation.

Outline

Dividend Distributions
Taxable Dividends—In General
Earnings and Profits
Property Dividends—Effect on the Shareholder
Property Dividends—Effect on the Corporation
Constructive Dividends
Stock Dividends and Stock Rights

Stock Redemptions—Exchange Treatment
Historical Background and Overview
Stock Attribution Rules
Not Essentially Equivalent to a Dividend Stock Redemptions
Substantially Disproportionate Redemptions

Complete Termination of a Shareholder's Interest Redemptions
Redemptions in Partial Liquidation
Redemptions to Pay Death Taxes
Effect on the Corporation Redeeming Its Stock

Stock Redemptions—No Exchange Treatment
Preferred Stock Bailouts
Redemptions Through Use of Related Corporations

Distribution of Stock and Securities of a Controlled Corporation

Tax Planning Considerations
Corporate Distributions
Constructive Dividends
Stock Redemptions

A working knowledge of the rules pertaining to corporate distributions is essential for anyone dealing with the tax problems of corporations and their shareholders. The form of such distributions is important because it can produce varying tax results to shareholders. Dividends are taxed as ordinary income to the recipient shareholder (however, stock dividends may not be taxed at all); stock redemptions (qualifying under § 302) generally receive capital gain or loss treatment after allowing the shareholder to recover basis in the redeemed stock; corporate spin-offs or split-offs under § 355 do not represent a taxable event to the shareholder.

Dividend Distributions

Taxable Dividends—In General

Distributions by a corporation to its shareholders are presumed to be dividends unless the parties can prove otherwise. Section 316 makes such distributions, whether in the form of cash or other property, ordinary dividend income to a shareholder to the extent of the distribution's pro rata share of earnings and profits (E & P) of the distributing corporation accumulated since February 28, 1913, or to the extent of corporate earnings and profits (E & P) for the current year.

Under § 301(c), the portion of a corporate distribution that is not taxed as a dividend (because of insufficient E & P) will be nontaxable to the extent of the shareholder's basis in the stock and will reduce that basis accordingly. The excess of the distribution over the shareholder's basis is treated as a capital gain if the stock is a capital asset.

Example 1

C & D each get $20,000

At the beginning of the year, X Corporation (a calendar year taxpayer) has accumulated E & P of $30,000. During the year, the corporation distributes $40,000 to its *equal* shareholders, C and D. Only $30,000 of the $40,000 distribution is a taxable dividend. Suppose C's basis in his stock is $8,000, while D's basis is $4,000. Under these conditions, C must recognize a taxable dividend of $15,000 and reduce the basis of the stock from $8,000 to $3,000. The $20,000 D receives from X Corporation will be accounted for as follows: a taxable dividend of $15,000, a reduction in stock basis from $4,000 to zero, and a capital gain of $1,000. □

Since earnings and profits (E & P) is the key to dividend treatment of corporate distributions, its importance cannot be emphasized enough. After 1989, E & P will assume added importance, since it will replace pretax book income in the determination of business untaxed reported profits for purposes of the alternative minimum tax (refer to discussion in Chapter 2).

Earnings and Profits (E & P)—§ 312

The term "earnings and profits" is not defined by the Code. Although § 312 lists certain transactions that affect E & P, it stops short of a complete definition. E & P does possess similarities to the accounting concept of retained earnings (i.e., earnings retained in the business); however, E & P and retained earnings are often not the same. For example, although a stock dividend is treated for financial accounting purposes as a capitalization of retained earnings (i.e., it is debited to the retained earnings account and credited to a capital stock account), it does not decrease E & P. Similarly, the elimination of a deficit in a quasi-reorganization increases retained earnings but does not increase E & P.

To fully understand the concept of E & P, it is helpful to keep several observations in mind. First, E & P might well be described as the factor that fixes the upper limit on the amount of dividend income shareholders would have to recognize as a result of a distribution by the corporation. In this sense, E & P represents the corporation's economic ability to pay a dividend without impairing its capital. Therefore, the effect of a specific transaction on the E & P account can be determined simply by considering whether or not the transaction increases or decreases the corporation's capacity to pay a dividend.

Computation of E & P.   Barring certain important exceptions, E & P is increased by earnings for the taxable year computed in the same manner as is used in determining taxable income. If the corporation uses the cash method of accounting in computing taxable income, it must also use the cash method to determine the changes in E & P.[1]

E & P is increased for all items of income. Interest on municipal bonds, for example, though not taxed to the corporation, would increase the corporation's E & P. The dividends received deduction under § 243 is added back to compute E & P. Gains and losses from property transactions generally affect the determination of E & P only to the extent they are recognized for tax purposes. Thus, a gain on an involuntary conversion not recognized by the corporation because the insurance proceeds are reinvested in property that is similar or related in service or use to the property converted (§ 1033) would not affect E & P. But the E & P account can be affected by both deductible and nondeductible items. Consequently, excess capital losses, expenses incurred to produce tax-exempt income, and Federal income taxes all reduce E & P, although such items do not enter into the calculation of taxable income.

The E & P account can be reduced only by cost depletion, even though the corporation may be using percentage (i.e., statutory) depletion for income tax purposes. E & P cannot be reduced by accelerated depreciation.[2] However, if a depreciation method such as units-of-production or machine hours is used, the adjustment to E & P can be determined on this basis.[3]

The alternative ACRS system must be used for purposes of computing E & P.[4] Thus, if cost recovery is figured under ACRS, E & P must be computed using the straight-line recovery method over a recovery period equal to the asset's Asset Depreciation Range (ADR) midpoint life.[5] Later, when the asset is sold,

---

1. Regulations relating to E & P begin at Reg. § 1.312–6.
2. § 312(k).
3. Reg. § 1.312–15(a)(2).
4. § 312(k)(3)(A).
5. See § 168(g)(2). The ADR midpoint life for most assets is set out in Rev.Proc. 87–56, I.R.B. No. 42, 4. The recovery period is 5 years for automobiles and light-duty trucks and 40 years for real property. For assets with no class life, the recovery period is 12 years. Any amount expensed under § 179 is deducted over a period of five years in computing E & P. See § 312(k)(3)(B).

the increase or decrease in E & P is determined by using the adjusted basis of the asset for E & P purposes.[6]

A corporation's E & P for the year in which it sells property on the installment basis will be increased by the amount of any deferred gain. This is accomplished by treating all principal payments as having been received in the year of sale.[7]

A corporation that accounts for income and expenses attributable to a long-term contract on the completed contract method of accounting must use the percentage of completion basis in arriving at E & P.[8]

Intangible drilling costs [allowable as a deduction under § 263(c)] and mine exploration and development costs [allowable under § 616(a) or § 617] are required to be capitalized for purposes of computing E & P. Once capitalized, these expenditures can be charged to E & P over a specified period: 60 months for intangible drilling costs and 120 months for mine exploration and development costs.[9]

Example 2   A corporation sells property (basis of $10,000) to its sole shareholder for $8,000. Because of § 267 (i.e., disallowance of losses on sales between related parties), the $2,000 loss cannot be deducted in arriving at the corporation's taxable income for the year. But since the overall economic effect of the transaction is a decrease in the corporation's assets by $2,000, the loss will reduce the current E & P for the year of sale. □

Example 3   A corporation pays a $10,000 premium on a keyman life insurance policy (i.e., the corporation is the owner and beneficiary of the policy) covering the life of its president. As a result of the payment, the cash surrender value of the policy is increased by $7,000. Although none of the $10,000 premium would be deductible for tax purposes, current E & P would be reduced by $3,000. □

Example 4   A corporation collects $100,000 on a keyman life insurance policy. At the time the policy matured on the death of the insured-employee, it possessed a cash surrender value of $30,000. None of the $100,000 will be included in the corporation's taxable income [see § 101(a)], but $70,000 would be added to the current E & P account. □

Example 5   During 1988, a corporation makes charitable contributions, $12,000 of which cannot be deducted in arriving at the taxable income for the year because of the 10% limitation. However, pursuant to § 170(d)(2), the $12,000 is carried over to 1989 and fully deducted in that year. The excess charitable contribution would reduce the corporation's current E & P for

---

6. § 312(f)(1).

7. Under prior law, gains from installment sales were not included in E & P until recognized for purposes of computing taxable income for the year. Thus, gain deferred for purposes of computing taxable income was also deferred for purposes of computing E & P.

8. Under prior law, income from long-term contracts accounted for under the completed contract method of accounting was included in E & P when such income was recognized for tax purposes, generally in the year in which the contract was completed.

9. Under prior law, these costs were charged against E & P in the same manner as they were treated for purposes of computing taxable income.

1988 by $12,000 and increase its current E & P for 1989, when the deduction is allowed, by a like amount. The increase in E & P in 1989 is necessitated by the fact that the charitable contribution carryover reduces the taxable income for that year (the starting point for computing E & P) and already has been taken into account in determining the E & P for 1988. □

Example 6

On January 2, 1987, X Corporation purchased equipment with an alternative recovery period of 10 years for $30,000 that was then depreciated under MACRS. The asset was sold on January 2, 1989, for $27,000. For purposes of determining taxable income and E & P, cost recovery claimed on the machine and the machine's adjusted basis are summarized as follows:

	Cost Recovery	Adjusted Basis
Taxable Income		
1987: $30,000 × 14.29%	$4,287	$25,713
1988: $30,000 × 24.49%	7,347	18,366
E & P		
1987: $30,000 ÷ 10-year recovery period ÷ ½ (half year for first year of service)	$1,500	$28,500
1988: $30,000 ÷ 10-year recovery period	3,000	25,500

Gain on the sale for purposes of determining taxable income and increase (decrease) in E & P is computed as follows:

	Taxable Income	E & P
$27,000 − $18,366 (adjusted basis)	$8,634	
$27,000 − $25,500 (adjusted basis)		$1,500

□

Example 7

In 1988, X Corporation, a calendar year taxpayer, sells unimproved real estate (basis of $20,000) for $100,000. Under the terms of the sale, X Corporation will receive two annual payments, beginning in 1989, of $50,000 each with interest of 12%. X Corporation does not elect out of the installment method. Although X Corporation's taxable income for 1988 will not reflect any of the gain from the sale, the corporation must increase E & P for 1988 by $80,000 (the deferred profit component). □

Summary of E & P Adjustments. Recall that E & P serves as a measure of the earnings of the corporation that are treated as available for distribution as taxable dividends to the shareholders. Although E & P is initially increased by the corporation's taxable income, certain adjustments must be made to taxable income with respect to various transactions in determining the corporation's current E & P. Those adjustments are reviewed in the Concept Summary that follows. Other items that affect E & P, such as property dividends and stock redemptions, are covered later in the chapter and are not incorporated in the Concept Summary.

Concept Summary

E & P Adjustments

Nature of the Transaction	Effect on Taxable Income in Arriving at Current E & P
Tax-exempt income	Add
Federal income taxes	Subtract
Loss on sale between related parties	Subtract
Payment of premiums on insurance policy on life of corporate officer	Subtract
Collection of proceeds of insurance policy on life of corporate officer	Add
Excess charitable contribution (over 10% limitation)	Subtract
Deduction of excess charitable contribution in succeeding taxable year (increase E & P because deduction reduces taxable income while E & P was reduced in a prior year)	Add
Realized gain (not recognized) on an involuntary conversion	No effect
Percentage depletion (only cost depletion can reduce E & P)	Add
Accelerated depreciation (E & P is reduced only by straight-line, units-of-production, or machine hours depreciation)	Add
Deferred gain on installment sale (all gain is added to E & P in year of sale)	Add
Long-term contract reported on completed contract method (use percentage of completion method)	Add
Intangible drilling costs deducted currently (reduce E & P in future years by amortizing costs over 60 months)	Add
Mine exploration and development costs (reduce E & P in future years by amortizing costs over 120 months)	Add

The Source of the Distribution.   In determining the source of a dividend distribution, a dividend is deemed to have been made first from current E & P and then from E & P accumulated since February 28, 1913.[10]

Example 8   At the beginning of the current year, Y Corporation has a deficit in accumulated E & P of $30,000. For the year, it has current E & P of $10,000 and distributes $5,000 to its shareholders. The $5,000 distribution will be treated as a taxable dividend, since it is deemed to have been made from current E & P. This will be the case even though Y Corporation

---

10. Regulations relating to the source of a distribution are at Reg. § 1.316–2.

will still have a deficit in its accumulated E & P at the end of the current year. □

If distributions made during the year exceed the current year's E & P, the portion of each distribution deemed to have been made from current E & P is that percentage that the total E & P for the year bears to the total distributions for that year. This can make a difference if any of the shareholders sell their stock during the year and total distributions exceed current E & P.

Example 9

As of January 1, 1988, Z Corporation has two *equal* shareholders, E and F, and accumulated E & P of $10,000. Current E & P for 1988 amounts to $30,000. On August 1, 1988, E sells all of his stock to G. Distributions during 1988 are as follows: $40,000 to E and F ($20,000 to each) on July 1 and $40,000 to F and G ($20,000 to each) on December 1. The allocation result is summarized as follows:

	Source of Distribution	
	Current E & P	Accumulated E & P
July 1 distribution ($40,000)	$15,000	$10,000
December 1 distribution ($40,000)	15,000	—

½ yr. figures

The end result in terms of tax consequences to the shareholders is as follows:

	Shareholder		
	E	F	G
July distribution ($40,000)			
Dividend income—			
From current E & P ($15,000)	$ 7,500	$ 7,500	$ 0
From accumulated E & P ($10,000)	5,000	5,000	0
Return of capital ($15,000)	7,500	7,500	0
December distribution ($40,000)			
Dividend income—			
From current E & P ($15,000)	0	7,500	7,500
From accumulated E & P ($0)	0	0	0
Return of capital ($25,000)	0	12,500	12,500
Total dividend income	$12,500	$20,000	$ 7,500
Nontaxable return of capital (presuming sufficient basis in the stock investment)	$ 7,500	$20,000	$12,500

Note that the current E & P was allocated between both distributions, while the accumulated E & P was applied to and exhausted by the first distribution. □

Distinguishing between Current and Accumulated E & P.   Accumulated E & P can be defined as the total of all previous years' current E & P as computed on the first day of each taxable year in accordance with the tax law in effect during that year. The factors that affect the computation of the current E & P for any one year have been discussed previously. Why must the distinction be drawn between current and accumulated E & P when it is clear that distributions are taxable if and to the extent that current *and* accumulated E & P exist?

1. When a deficit exists in accumulated E & P and a positive balance exists in current E & P, distributions will be regarded as dividends to the extent of the current E & P. Refer to Example 8.
2. Current E & P is allocated on a pro rata basis to the distributions made during the year; accumulated E & P is applied (to the extent necessary) in chronological order beginning with the earliest distributions. Refer to Example 9.
3. Unless and until the parties can show otherwise, it is presumed that any distribution is covered by current E & P.
4. When a deficit exists in current E & P (i.e., a current loss develops) and a positive balance exists in accumulated E & P, the accounts are netted at the date of distribution. If the resulting balance is zero or a deficit, the distribution is a return of capital. If a positive balance results, the distribution will represent a dividend to such extent. Any loss is allocated ratably during the year unless the parties can show otherwise.

Distinctions 3 and 4 are illustrated as follows:

Example 10   Q Corporation uses a fiscal year of July 1 through June 30 for tax purposes; T, Q Corporation's only shareholder, uses a calendar year. As of July 1, 1988, Q Corporation has a zero balance in its accumulated E & P account. For fiscal year 1988–1989 the corporation suffers a $5,000 operating loss. On August 1, 1988, Q Corporation distributes $10,000 to T. The distribution represents dividend income to T and must be reported as such when she files her income tax return for calendar year 1988 on or before April 15, 1989. Because T cannot prove until June 30, 1989, that the corporation had a deficit for fiscal 1988–1989, she must assume the $10,000 distribution was fully covered by current E & P. When T learns of the deficit, she can file an amended return for 1988 showing the $10,000 as a return of capital. ☐

Example 11   At the beginning of the current year, R Corporation (a calendar year taxpayer) has accumulated E & P of $10,000. During the year, the corporation incurs a $15,000 net loss from operations that accrued ratably. On July 1, R Corporation distributes $6,000 in cash to H, its sole shareholder. The balance of both accumulated and current E & P as of July 1, must be determined and netted because of the deficit in current E & P. The balance at this date would be $2,500 [$10,000 (accumulated E & P) − $7,500 (one half of the current deficit of $15,000)]. Of the $6,000 distribution, $2,500 would be taxed as a dividend and $3,500 would represent a return of capital. ☐

Property Dividends—Effect on the Shareholder

When a corporation distributes property rather than cash to a shareholder, the amount distributed is measured by the fair market value of the property on the date of distribution. Section 301(c) is applicable to such distributions. Thus, the portion of the distribution covered by existing E & P is a dividend, and any excess is treated as a return of capital. If the fair market value of the property distributed exceeds the corporation's E & P and the shareholder's basis in the stock investment, a capital gain would result. The amount distributed is reduced by any liabilities to which the distributed property is subject immediately before and immediately after the distribution and by any liabilities of the corporation assumed by the shareholder in connection with the distribution.[11] The basis in the distributed property is the fair market value of the property on the date of the distribution.

Example 12   P Corporation has E & P of $60,000. It distributes land with a fair market value of $50,000 (adjusted basis of $30,000) to its sole shareholder, T. The land is subject to a liability of $10,000, which T assumes. T would have a taxable dividend of $40,000 [$50,000 (fair market value) − $10,000 (liability)]. The basis of the land to T is $50,000. □

always subtract the liability

Example 13   Ten percent of X Corporation is owned by Y Corporation. X Corporation has ample E & P to cover any distributions made during the year. One such distribution made to Y Corporation consists of a vacant lot with adjusted basis of $5,000 and a fair market value of $3,000. Y Corporation has a taxable dividend of $3,000, and its basis in the lot becomes $3,000. □

Property that has depreciated in value is usually not a suitable subject for distribution as a property dividend. Note what has happened in Example 13. The loss of $2,000 (adjusted basis $5,000, fair market value $3,000), in effect, disappears. If, instead, the lot had first been sold and the $3,000 proceeds distributed, the loss would have been preserved for X Corporation.

Property Dividends—Effect on the Corporation

A property distribution by a corporation to its shareholders poses two questions. Does the distribution result in recognized gain or loss to the corporation making the distribution? What effect will the distribution have on the corporation's E & P? These questions are answered in the following discussion.

Recognition of Gain or Loss.   All distributions of appreciated property cause gain to the distributing corporation.[12] In effect, the corporation that makes a property dividend will be treated as if it had sold the property to the shareholder for its fair market value. However, no loss is recognized to the distributing corporation on distributions of property with a tax basis in excess of fair market value.

---

11. § 301(b)(2).
12. Code § 311 covers taxability of a corporation on distributions.

Example 14   X Corporation distributes land (basis of $10,000 and fair market value of $30,000) to T, an individual shareholder. X Corporation must recognize a gain of $20,000. ☐

Example 15   Assume the property in Example 14 has a fair market value of $10,000 and a basis of $30,000. X Corporation would not recognize a loss on the distribution. ☐

If the distributed property is subject to a liability in excess of basis or the shareholder assumes such a liability, the fair market value of the property for purposes of determining gain on the distribution is treated as not being less than the amount of the liability.

Example 16   Assume the land in Example 14 is subject to a liability of $35,000. X Corporation must recognize gain of $25,000 on the distribution. ☐

Effect of Corporate Distributions on E & P.   In the event of a corporate distribution, the E & P account is reduced by the amount of money distributed or by the greater of the fair market value or the adjusted basis of property distributed, less the amount of any liability on the property.[13] E & P is increased by gain recognized on appreciated property distributed as a property dividend.[14]

Example 17   M Corporation distributes property (basis of $10,000 and fair market value of $20,000) to T, its shareholder. M Corporation recognizes a gain of $10,000, which would be added to its E & P.   E & P would then be reduced by $20,000, the fair market value of the property. T would have dividend income of $20,000. ☐

Example 18   Assume the same facts as in Example 17, except that the fair market value of the property is $15,000 and the adjusted basis in the hands of M Corporation is $20,000. Because loss is not recognized and the adjusted basis is greater than fair market value, E & P is reduced by $20,000. T must report dividend income of $15,000. ☐

Example 19   Assume the same facts as in Example 18, except that the property is subject to a liability of $6,000. E & P would now be reduced by $14,000 [$20,000 (adjusted basis) − $6,000 (liability)]. T would have a dividend of $9,000 [$15,000 (amount of the distribution) − $6,000 (liability)], and T's basis in the property is $15,000. ☐

Under no circumstances can a distribution, whether cash or property, either generate a deficit in E & P or add to a deficit in E & P. Deficits can arise only through corporate losses.

---

13. §§ 312(a), (b), and (c).
14. § 312(b).

Constructive Dividends

A distribution by a corporation to its shareholders can be treated as a dividend for Federal income tax purposes even though it is not formally declared or designated as a dividend or issued pro rata to all shareholders.[15] Nor must the distribution satisfy the legal requirements of a dividend as set forth by applicable state law. The key factor determining dividend status is a measurable economic benefit conveyed to the shareholder. This benefit, often described as a constructive dividend, is distinguishable from actual corporate distributions of cash and property in form only.

Constructive dividend situations usually arise in the context of the closely-held corporation. Here, the dealings between the parties are less structured, and frequently, formalities are not preserved. The constructive dividend serves as a substitute for actual distributions and is intended to accomplish some tax objective not available through the use of direct dividends. The shareholders may attempt to bail out corporate profits in a form deductible to the corporation (see, for example, items 6 through 9 below). Recall that dividend distributions do not provide the distributing corporation with an income tax deduction, although they do reduce E & P. Alternatively, the shareholders may be seeking benefits for themselves while avoiding the recognition of income (see, for example, items 1 through 6 below). Constructive dividends are, in reality, disguised dividends.

Do not conclude, however, that all constructive dividends are deliberate attempts to avoid actual and formal dividends. Often, constructive dividends are inadvertent; and consequently, a dividend result may come as a surprise to the parties (see, for example, item 1 below). For this reason, if for none other, an awareness of the various constructive dividend situations is essential to protect the parties from unanticipated tax consequences. The types of constructive dividends most frequently encountered are summarized as follows:

1. Personal use by a shareholder of corporate-owned property (e.g., company-owned automobiles, airplanes, yachts, fishing camps, hunting lodges).[16] The measure of dividend income to the shareholder would be the fair rental value of the property for the period of its personal use.[17]
2. A bargain sale of corporate property to the shareholders. The measure of the constructive dividend is the difference between amounts paid for the property and the property's fair market value on the date of sale.[18] Such questionable situations might be avoided by appraising the property on or about the date of sale. The appraised value becomes the price to be paid by the shareholders.
3. A bargain rental of corporate property to the shareholders. The measure of the constructive dividend would be the excess of the property's fair rental

---

15. See *Lengsfield v. Comm.*, 57–1 USTC ¶9437, 50 AFTR 1683, 241 F.2d 508 (CA–5, 1957).
16. See, for example, *Ray R. Tanner*, 45 TCM 1419, T.C.Memo. 1983–230.
17. This result presumes the ownership of the property to be in the corporation. If not, and the ownership can be attributed to the shareholder, the measure of the constructive dividend would be the cost of the property. In this regard, bare legal title at the corporate level may not suffice. See, for example, *Raymond F. Daly*, 37 TCM 15, T.C.Memo. 1978–5.
18. Reg. § 1.301–1(j). In *Claud E. Lynch*, 45 TCM 1125, T.C.Memo. 1983–173, the arm's length standard was not satisfied.

value over the rent actually paid. As in item 2, the importance of appraisal data to avoid any questionable situations should be readily apparent.

4. The satisfaction by the corporation of a shareholder's personal obligation to a third party.[19] The obligation involved need not be legally binding on the shareholder but may, in fact, be a moral obligation.[20] Forgiveness by the corporation of shareholder indebtedness can create an identical problem.[21]
5. Advances by a corporation to a shareholder that are not bona fide (i.e., real) loans.[22] Whether an advance qualifies as a bona fide loan is a question of fact to be determined in light of the particular circumstances.
6. Interest-free (or below-market) loans by a corporation to a shareholder.[23]
7. Interest and principal payments made by a corporation where debt is reclassified as equity (refer to Chapter 3).[24]
8. Excessive rentals paid by a corporation for the use of shareholder property.[25]
9. Compensation paid to shareholder-employees that is deemed unreasonable.[26]

As noted in item 9, excessive salary payments to shareholder-employees are usually termed "unreasonable compensation." The excess over reasonable compensation is frequently deemed a constructive dividend and therefore is not deductible by the corporation. In determining the reasonableness of salary payments, factors to be considered are the employee's qualifications; a comparison of salaries with dividend distributions; the prevailing rates of compensation for comparable positions in comparable business concerns; the nature and scope of the employee's work; the size and complexity of the business; a comparison of salaries paid to both gross and net income; the salary policy of the taxpayer with respect to all employees; and, for small corporations with a limited number of officers, the amount of compensation paid the particular employee in previous years.[27]

Advances to shareholders that are not bona fide loans are also deemed to be constructive dividends as noted in item 5. Factors considered in determining whether an advance qualifies as a bona fide loan include whether the advance is on open account or is evidenced by a written instrument; whether the shareholder furnished collateral or other security for the advance; how long the advance has been outstanding; whether any payments have been made, excluding dividend sources; the shareholder's financial capability to repay the advance; the shareholder's use of the funds (e.g., payment of routine bills

19. See, for example, *William D. Garner*, 35 TCM 1592, T.C.Memo. 1976–349.
20. *Montgomery Engineering Co. v. U.S.*, 64–2 USTC ¶9618, 13 AFTR2d 1747, 230 F.Supp. 838 (D.Ct. N.J., 1964); *aff'd.* in 65–1 USTC ¶9368, 15 AFTR2d 746, 344 F.2d 966 (CA–3, 1965).
21. Reg. § 1.301–1(m).
22. See, for example, *Richard B. Busch, Jr.*, 45 TCM 772, T.C.Memo. 1983–98.
23. See § 7872.
24. See, for example, *Smithco Engineering, Inc.*, 47 TCM 966, T.C.Memo. 1984–43. However, compare *Electronic Modules Corporation v. U.S.*, 83–1 USTC ¶9113, 51 AFTR2d 83–614, 695 F.2d 1367 (CA–Fed. Cir., 1983), wherein the taxpayer was successful.
25. See, for example, *Scott C. Rethorst*, 31 TCM 1101, T.C.Memo. 1972–222; *aff'd.* in 75–1 USTC ¶9111, 35 AFTR2d 75–394, 509 F.2d 623 (CA–9, 1975).
26. See, for example, *Roth Properties Co. v. Comm.*, 75–1 USTC ¶9337, 35 AFTR2d 75–1093, 511 F.2d 527 (CA–6, 1975).
27. *Mayson Manufacturing Co. v. Comm.*, 49–2 USTC ¶9467, 38 AFTR 1028, 178 F.2d 115 (CA–6, 1949).

versus nonrecurring, extraordinary expenses); the regularity of such advances; and the dividend-paying history of the corporation.

If a corporation succeeds in getting past the hurdle of proving that an advance to a shareholder is a bona fide loan so that the advance is not deemed to be a constructive dividend as noted in item 5, the shareholder will still have a constructive dividend in the amount of the forgone interest as noted in item 6. However, the shareholder may also have a corresponding interest deduction. The problem relates to the corporation. The imputed interest element, which is a constructive dividend to the shareholder, is interest income to the corporation; however, because it is deemed to be a constructive dividend to the shareholder, there is no corresponding deduction to the corporation.

Constructive distributions possess the same tax attributes as actual distributions.[28] Thus, a corporate shareholder would be entitled to the dividends received deduction of § 243. The constructive distribution would be a taxable dividend only to the extent of the corporation's current and accumulated E & P. As usual, the task of proving that the distribution constitutes a return of capital because of inadequate E & P rests with the taxpayer.[29]

Stock Dividends and Stock Rights

Stock Dividends—§ 305. Because no change occurs in a shareholder's proportionate interest in a corporation upon receipt of a stock dividend, such distributions were initially accorded tax-free treatment.[30] Subsequently, the test for taxability of a stock dividend was based on change in the proportionate interest of a shareholder following the distribution. The 1954 Code simply stated that stock dividends would not be taxable unless (a) the shareholder could elect to receive either stock or property or (b) the stock dividends were in discharge of preference dividends. In response, corporations devised various methods to distribute stock dividends that would change the shareholder's interest and still qualify as tax-free.[31]

The provisions of § 305 that currently govern the taxability of stock dividends are based on the proportionate interest concept. Stock dividends are not taxable if they are pro rata distributions of stock, or stock rights, on common stock. The general rule that stock dividends are nontaxable has five exceptions, summarized as follows:

1. Distributions payable either in stock or property.
2. Distributions resulting in the receipt of property by some shareholders and an increase in the proportionate interest of other shareholders in the assets or E & P of the distributing corporation.
3. Distributions that result in the receipt of preferred stock by some common stock shareholders and the receipt of common stock by other shareholders.
4. Distributions on preferred stock other than an increase in the conversion ratio of convertible preferred stock made solely to take account of a stock dividend or stock split with respect to stock into which the preferred is convertible.

---

28. *Simon v. Comm.*, 57–2 USTC ¶9989, 52 AFTR 698, 248 F.2d 869 (CA–8, 1957).
29. *DiZenzo v. Comm.*, 65–2 USTC ¶9518, 16 AFTR2d 5107, 348 F.2d 122 (CA–2, 1965).
30. See *Eisner v. Macomber*, 1 USTC ¶32, 3 AFTR 3020, 40 S.Ct. 189 (USSC, 1920).
31. See "Stock Dividends," Senate Report 91–552, 1969–3 C.B. 519.

5. Distributions of convertible preferred stock, unless it can be shown that the distribution will not result in a disproportionate distribution.

Note that the exceptions to nontaxability of stock dividends deal with various disproportionate distribution situations.

Because holders of convertible securities are considered shareholders, payment of interest on convertible debentures will cause stock dividends paid on common stock to be taxable unless an adjustment is made on the conversion ratio or conversion price to reflect the stock dividend.[32]

If stock dividends are not taxable, there is no reduction in the corporation's E & P.[33] If the stock dividends are taxable, the distribution is treated by the distributing corporation in the same manner as any other taxable property dividend.

If stock dividends are taxable, basis to the shareholder-distributee is fair market value, and the holding period starts on the date of receipt. If a stock dividend is not taxable, § 307 requires that the basis of the stock on which the dividend is distributed be reallocated. If the dividend shares are identical to these formerly held shares, basis in the old stock is reallocated by dividing the taxpayer's cost in the old stock by the total number of shares. If the dividend stock is not identical to the underlying shares (a stock dividend of preferred on common, for example), basis is determined by allocating cost of the formerly held shares between the old and new stock according to the fair market value of each. Holding period will include the holding period of the formerly held stock.[34]

Example 20   A, an individual, bought 1,000 shares of stock two years ago for $10,000. In the current tax year, A received 10 shares of common stock as a nontaxable stock dividend. A's basis of $10,000 would be divided by 1,010; consequently, each share of stock would have a basis of $9.90 instead of the pre-dividend $10 basis. □

Example 21   Assume A received, instead, a nontaxable preferred stock dividend of 100 shares. The preferred stock has a fair market value of $1,000, and the common stock, on which the preferred is distributed, has a fair market value of $19,000. After the receipt of the stock dividend, the basis of the common stock is $9,500, and the basis of the preferred is $500, computed as follows:

Fair market value of common	$19,000
Fair market value of preferred	1,000
	$20,000
Basis of common: 19/20 × $10,000	$ 9,500
Basis of preferred: 1/20 × $10,000	$ 500

□

---

32. See Reg. § 1.305–3(d) for illustrations on how to compute required adjustments on conversion ratios or prices.
33. § 312(d)(1).
34. § 1223(5).

Stock Rights.   The rules for determining taxability of stock rights are identical to those determining taxability of stock dividends. If the rights are taxable, the recipient has income to the extent of the fair market value of the rights. The fair market value then becomes the shareholder-distributee's basis in the rights.[35] If the rights are exercised, the holding period for the new stock is the date the rights (whether taxable or nontaxable) are exercised. The basis of the new stock is the basis of the rights plus the amount of any other consideration given.

If stock rights are not taxable and the value of the rights is less than 15 percent of the value of the old stock, the basis of the rights is zero unless the shareholder elects to have some of the basis in the formerly held stock allocated to the rights.[36] If the fair market value of the rights is 15 percent or more of the value of the old stock and the rights are exercised or sold, the shareholder must allocate some of the basis in the formerly held stock to the rights. When the value is less than 15 percent of the value of the stock and the shareholder makes an election to allocate basis to the rights, such an election is made in the form of a statement attached to the shareholder's return for the year in which the rights are received.[37]

Example 22   A corporation with common stock outstanding declares a nontaxable dividend payable in rights to subscribe to common stock. Each right entitles the holder to purchase one share of stock for $90. One right is issued for every two shares of stock owned. T owns 400 shares of stock purchased two years ago for $15,000. At the time of the distribution of the rights, the market value of the common stock is $100 per share and the market value of the rights is $8 per right. T receives 200 rights. He exercises 100 rights and sells the remaining 100 rights three months later for $9 per right. T need not allocate the cost of the original stock to the rights, because the value of the rights is less than 15% of the value of the stock ($1,600 ÷ $40,000 = 4%).

If T does not allocate his original stock basis to the rights, the tax consequences are as follows:

—Basis in the new stock will be $9,000 ($90 × 100). The holding period of the new stock begins on the date the stock was purchased.

—Sale of the rights would produce long-term capital gain of $900 ($9 × 100). The holding period of the rights starts with the date the original 400 shares of stock were acquired.

If T elects to allocate basis to the rights, the tax consequences are as follows:

—Basis in the stock would be $14,423 [$40,000 ÷ $41,600 (value of rights and stock) × $15,000 (cost of stock)].

---

35. Reg. § 1.305–1(b).
36. § 307(b)(1).
37. Reg. § 1.307–2.

—Basis in the rights would be $577 [$1,600 (value of rights) ÷ $41,600 (value of rights and stock) × $15,000 (cost of stock)].

—When T exercises the rights, his basis in the new stock would be $9,288.50 [$9,000 (cost) + $288.50 (basis in 100 rights)].

—Sale of the rights would produce a long-term capital gain of $611.50 [$900 (selling price) − $288.50 (basis in the remaining 100 rights)]. ☐

Stock Redemptions— Exchange Treatment

Section 302 provides that if a corporation redeems its stock within the meaning of § 317 and pursuant to §§ 302(b)(1), (2), (3), or (4), the redemption will be treated as a distribution in part or full payment of a shareholder's stock. Section 317 defines a stock redemption as an *exchange* between a corporation and its shareholder of that corporation's stock for property. Section 303 provides that certain distributions of property to a shareholder in exchange for certain stock that was included in a decedent's estate will be treated as a stock redemption. Before the Tax Reform Act (TRA) of 1986, there were two major tax advantages to successful stock redemptions under §§ 302 and 303. First, the shareholder was able to recover the amount invested in the redeemed stock without dividend consequences. Second, any amount received over basis generally was treated as long-term capital gain.

TRA of 1986 has not had an impact on the first advantage. Thus, a successful redemption will continue to provide a viable way for a shareholder to recoup the amount invested in stock without tax consequences. By deleting the preferential treatment accorded to long-term capital gains, however, Congress has largely eliminated the second advantage. Any premium paid by the corporation on stock it redeems will, in essence, be taxed at ordinary income rates to the shareholder. Still, classification of the gain as a capital gain does provide a benefit to a taxpayer who has substantial capital losses. The capital losses can be used in full to offset capital gains.

Example 23
In 1986, X Corporation redeems a substantial portion of Ms. T's stock under § 302(b)(2) for its fair market value of $200,000. The redeemed stock had been acquired by Ms. T several years ago as an investment at a cost of $150,000. As a result of the transaction, Ms. T will treat the $200,000 redemption proceeds as follows: $150,000 (tax-free return of basis) and $50,000 (long-term capital gain). Because of the 60% capital gain deduction, $30,000 of the $50,000 is not taxed. Thus, only $20,000 is subject to tax. Had the distribution not qualified for redemption treatment, and presuming adequate E & P on the part of X Corporation, the full $200,000 would have been dividend income. ☐

Example 24
Assume the same facts as in Example 23, except that the redemption takes place in 1987. The result would be the same [i.e., $150,000 (return of basis) and $50,000 (long-term capital gain)]. What changes, however, is the absence of the 60% capital gain deduction. Consequently, the $50,000

is taxed in full at ordinary income rates. (Note: A special transitional rule applicable to 1987 keeps long-term capital gains from being taxed at no more than 28%.) Again, if the redemption provisions do not apply, Ms. T has dividend income of $200,000. □

Although rare, some stock redemptions may yield a loss. Any such losses will continue to be classified as capital losses. Except for the removal of the $2 for $1 rule, the $3,000 annual limit still applies. By dropping the capital gain deduction and retaining the capital loss limitation, TRA of 1986 has lessened some of the tax glitter of the stock redemption procedure for bailing out funds invested in the corporate form.

Nonetheless and to the extent that a shareholder can recoup an investment in stock without tax consequences, a stock redemption can still be advantageous. The problem in achieving a successful stock redemption comes with structuring the distribution so that it qualifies under one of the types of stock redemptions stipulated in the Code as being entitled to *exchange* treatment. Failure to qualify means the distribution will be treated as a dividend. In this regard, it does not matter whether the parties intended a stock redemption to take place or whether the transfer is considered a stock redemption under applicable state law.

Historical Background and Overview

Before the 1954 Code, stock redemptions that constituted ordinary taxable dividends were distinguished from those qualifying for capital gain treatment by the so-called dividend equivalency rule. When a redemption was essentially equivalent to a dividend, it would not qualify as a stock redemption; the entire amount received by the shareholder would be subject to taxation as ordinary income to the extent of the corporation's E & P.

Example 25   A, an individual, owns 100% of the stock of X Corporation. X Corporation has E & P of $50,000. A sells one half of his shares to the corporation for $50,000. His basis in one half of the stock is $10,000, and he has held the stock for five years. If the sale of the stock to X Corporation qualified as a stock redemption, A would have a long-term capital gain of $40,000. However, such a distribution is essentially equivalent to a dividend. A's percentage of ownership of the corporation has not changed. Consequently, he is deemed to have received a taxable dividend of $50,000. □

Under the present Code, the following major types of stock redemptions qualify for exchange treatment and will, as a result, avoid dividend income consequences:

—Distributions not essentially equivalent to a dividend [§ 302(b)(1)].

—Distributions substantially disproportionate in terms of shareholder effect [§ 302(b)(2)].

—Distributions in complete termination of a shareholder's interest [§ 302(b)(3)].

—Distributions in partial liquidation of a corporation, but only to a noncorporate shareholder when (a) the distribution is not essentially equivalent to a dividend or (b) an active business is terminated [§ 302(b)(4)].

—Distributions to pay a shareholder's death taxes [§ 303].

Stock Attribution Rules

To deter the use of certain qualifying stock redemptions for related parties, § 318 imposes constructive ownership of stock (i.e., stock attribution) rules. In testing for a stock redemption, therefore, a shareholder may have to take into account the stock owned by others who fall within the definition of related parties. Related parties include immediate family, specifically, spouses, children, grandchildren, and parents. Attribution also takes place *from* and *to* partnerships, estates, trusts, and corporations (50 percent or more ownership required in the case of corporations).

Example 26   T, an individual, owns 30% of the stock in X Corporation, the other 70% being held by her children. For purposes of § 318, T is treated as owning 100% of the stock in X Corporation. She owns 30% directly and, because of the family attribution rules, 70% indirectly. □

Example 27   C, an individual, owns 50% of the stock in Y Corporation. The other 50% is owned by a partnership in which C has a 20% interest. C is deemed to own 60% of Y Corporation: 50% directly and, because of the partnership interest, 10% indirectly. □

The stock attribution rules of § 318 do not apply to stock redemptions to pay death taxes. Under certain conditions, the *family* attribution rules (refer to Example 26) do not apply to stock redemptions in complete termination of a shareholder's interest.

Not Essentially Equivalent to a Dividend
Stock Redemptions—§ 302(b)(1)

Section 302(b)(1) provides that a redemption will be treated as a distribution in part or full payment in exchange for the stock if it is "not essentially equivalent to a dividend." A distribution is not essentially equivalent to a dividend when there has been a meaningful reduction of the shareholder's proportionate interest in the redeeming corporation. The facts and circumstances of each case will determine whether a distribution in redemption of stock is essentially equivalent to a dividend within the meaning of § 302(b)(1).[38] Courts have considered a decrease in the redeeming shareholder's voting control to be the most significant indicator of a meaningful reduction.[39] Other factors considered are reductions in the rights of redeeming shareholders to share in corporate earnings or to receive corporate assets upon liquidation.[40]

---

38. Reg. § 1.302–2(b). See *Mary G. Roebling*, 77 T.C. 30 (1981).
39. See *Jack Paparo*, 71 T.C. 692 (1979), and *Blanche S. Benjamin*, 66 T.C. 1084 (1976).
40. See *Grabowski Trust*, 58 T.C. 650 (1972).

Example 28   A, an individual, owns 58% of the common stock of Y Corporation. After a redemption of part of A's stock, A owns 51% of the stock of Y Corporation. A would continue to have dominant voting rights in Y; thus, the redemption would be treated as "essentially equivalent to a dividend," and A would have ordinary income on the entire amount of the distribution. □

Example 29   X Corporation redeems 2% of the stock of B, a minority shareholder. Before the redemption, B owned 10% of X Corporation. In this case, the redemption may qualify as "not essentially equivalent to a dividend." B experiences a reduction in her voting rights, her right to participate in current earnings and accumulated surplus, and her right to share in net assets upon liquidation. □

Few objective tests exist to determine when a redemption is or is not essentially equivalent to a dividend. This provision was specifically added to provide for redemptions of preferred stock.[41] Often, such stock is called in by the corporation without the shareholders exercising any control over the redemption. Some courts interpreted § 302(b)(1) to mean a redemption would be granted capital gain treatment if the redemption had a business purpose and no tax avoidance scheme existed to bail out dividends at favorable tax rates.[42] The real question was whether the stock attribution rules of § 318(a) applied to this provision. However, some courts appeared to be less concerned with the application of § 318(a) and more concerned with the presence of a business purpose for the redemption.

The question of the applicability of § 318 was presumably settled by the Supreme Court in *U.S. v. Davis*.[43] In *Davis*, the taxpayer, who with his wife and children owned all of the common stock of a corporation, made an additional contribution of $25,000 for 1,000 shares of preferred stock, purchasing the preferred stock to increase the company's working capital so that the company might qualify for a government loan. It was understood that the corporation would redeem the preferred stock after the loan was repaid. At such time, the corporation did indeed redeem the taxpayer's preferred stock for $25,000. Taxpayer did not report the $25,000 on his personal income tax return, concluding it was a stock redemption under § 302 and did not exceed his stock basis. The Supreme Court agreed with the IRS that the redemption was essentially equivalent to a dividend and was taxable as ordinary income under §§ 301 and 316. The Court stated that § 318(a) applies to § 302(b)(1). Consequently, taxpayer was deemed the owner of all the common stock either directly or indirectly. Accordingly, to qualify for a stock redemption under § 302(b)(1), there must be ". . . a meaningful reduction of the shareholder's proportionate interest in the corporation." [44]

---

41. See S.Rept. No. 1622, 83d Cong., 2d Sess., at 44.
42. See, for example, *Kerr v. Comm.*, 64–1 USTC ¶9186, 13 AFTR2d 386, 326 F.2d 225 (CA–9, 1964).
43. 70–1 USTC ¶9289, 25 AFTR2d 70–827, 90 S.Ct. 1041 (USSC, 1970).
44. Later cases have addressed the issue of whether family discord should be considered in the application of § 318 in factual situations similar to those in *U.S. v. Davis*. In *Robin Haft Trust*, 75–1 USTC ¶9409, 35 AFTR2d 75–750, 510 F.2d 43 (CA–1, 1975), the First Court of Appeals said yes; the attribution rules should not be mechanically applied. However, the IRS refused to follow the *Robin Haft Trust* case. In *David Metzger Trust*, 82–2 USTC ¶9718, 51 AFTR2d 83–

If a redemption is treated as an ordinary dividend, the shareholder's basis in the stock redeemed attaches to the remaining stock. According to the Regulations, this basis would attach to other stock held by the taxpayer (or to stock he or she owns constructively).[45]

Example 30   Husband and wife each own 50 shares in X Corporation, representing 100% of the stock of X. All the stock was purchased for $50,000. The corporation redeems husband's 50 shares. Assuming the rules governing the complete termination of a shareholder's interest under § 302(b)(3) would not apply, such a redemption would be treated as a taxable dividend. Husband's basis in the stock, $25,000, would attach to wife's stock so that wife would have a basis of $50,000 in the 50 shares she currently owns in X Corporation. □

Substantially Disproportionate Redemptions—§ 302(b)(2)

A redemption of stock qualifies for capital gain treatment under § 302(b)(2) if two conditions are met.

1. The distribution must be substantially disproportionate. To be substantially disproportionate, the shareholder must own, after the distribution, less than 80 percent of total interest in the corporation before his or her redemption. For example, if a shareholder has a 60 percent ownership in a corporation that redeems part of the stock, the redemption is substantially disproportionate only if the percentage of ownership after the redemption is less than 48 percent (80 percent of 60 percent).
2. The shareholder must own, after the distribution, less than 50 percent of the total combined voting power of all classes of stock entitled to vote.

In determining the percentage of ownership of the shareholder, it must be remembered that the constructive ownership rules of § 318(a) apply.

Example 31   A, B, and C, unrelated individuals, own 30 shares, 30 shares, and 40 shares, respectively, in X Corporation. X Corporation has E & P of $200,000. The corporation redeems 20 shares of C's stock for $30,000. C paid $200 a share for the stock two years ago. After the redemption, C has a 25% interest in the corporation [20 shares of a total of 80 shares (100 − 20)]. This represents less than 80% of his original ownership (40% × 80% = 32%) and less than 50% of the total voting power. Consequently, the distribution qualifies as a stock redemption. C has a long-term capital gain of $26,000 [$30,000 − $4,000 (20 shares × $200)]. □

Example 32   Given the situation in Example 31, assume in addition, that B and C are father and son. The redemption described previously would not qualify for exchange treatment. C is deemed to own the stock of B so that after

---

376, 693 F.2d 459 (CA–5, 1982), the Fifth Court of Appeals agreed with the IRS, stating that family discord should not be taken into account in applying the attribution rules.

45. Reg. § 1.302–2(c).

the redemption, he would have 50 shares of a total of 80 shares, more than 50% ownership. He would also fail the 80% test. Before the redemption, C is deemed a 70% owner (40 shares owned by him and 30 shares owned by B, his son). After the redemption, he is deemed a 62.5% owner (20 shares owned directly by him and 30 shares owned by B from a total of 80 shares). C has a taxable dividend of $30,000. □

Complete Termination of a Shareholder's Interest Redemptions—§ 302(b)(3)

If a shareholder terminates his or her entire stock ownership in a corporation through a stock redemption, the redemption generally will qualify for exchange treatment under § 302(b)(3). Such a complete termination may not meet the substantially disproportionate rules of § 302(b)(2) if the constructive ownership rules of § 318(a)(1) are applied. The difference in the two provisions is that the constructive ownership rules of § 318(a)(1) do not apply to § 302(b)(3) if (1) the former shareholder has no interest, other than that of a creditor, in the corporation after the redemption (including an interest as an officer, director, or employee) for at least 10 years, and (2) the former shareholder files an agreement to notify the IRS of any acquisition within the 10-year period and to retain all necessary records pertaining to the redemption during this time period.

A shareholder can reacquire an interest in the corporation by bequest or inheritance, but in no other manner. The required agreement should be in the form of a separate statement signed by the shareholder and attached to the return for the year in which the redemption occurred. The agreement should recite that the shareholder agrees to notify the appropriate District Director within 30 days of a reacquisition of an interest in the corporation occurring within 10 years from the redemption.

A redeemed estate or trust may waive family attribution if, after the redemption, neither the entity nor its beneficiaries hold an interest in the corporation or acquire such an interest within the 10-year period and all parties involved file an agreement to be jointly and severally liable for any taxes due if a reacquisition occurs.[46]

Example 33   In 1988, D, a 40% shareholder in X Corporation, dies; his will designates W as his sole beneficiary. The remaining interest in X Corporation is held as follows: 35% by X (D's son) and 25% by E (a key employee). After the executor of D's estate redeems all that is permissible under § 303 [i.e., the sum total of death taxes and administrative expenses (see later discussion)], a 10% interest remains in the estate. The remaining 10% interest can be redeemed under § 302(b)(3) if both the entity (D's estate) and the beneficiary (W) terminate all interest in the corporation and do not reacquire an interest within a 10-year period and if the parties (D's estate and W) agree to be jointly and severally liable for any taxes due in the event of a reacquisition. □

---

46. § 302(c)(2)(C).

Redemptions in Partial Liquidation—§ 302(b)(4)

Recall that sale or exchange treatment for each of the previously discussed types of stock redemptions [§§ 302(b)(1), (2), and (3)] was dependent on share-holder—not corporate—considerations. The application of § 302(b)(4) is determined by corporate conditions.

Section 302(b)(4) permits sale or exchange treatment as to noncorporate shareholders for partial liquidations, defined in § 302(e) to include either of the following:

—A distribution not essentially equivalent to a dividend.

—A distribution pursuant to the termination of an active business.

To qualify as a partial liquidation, however, any distributions must be made within the taxable year in which the plan is adopted or within the succeeding taxable year. The not essentially equivalent to a dividend approach is determined at the corporate level. Presumably, it encompasses prior case law, which basically required a genuine contraction of the business of the corporation.[47]

Example 34   X Corporation owned a building with seven stories. Part of the building was rented, and part was used directly in X Corporation's business. A fire destroyed the two top floors, and X Corporation received insurance proceeds. For business reasons, X Corporation did not rebuild the two floors. With excess funds collected as insurance proceeds from the fire, the corporation purchased some stock from its shareholders. The distribution qualified as a partial liquidation.[48] □

The genuine contraction of a corporate business concept has been difficult to apply, because it has no objective tests. The IRS has ruled that proceeds from the sale of excess inventory distributed to shareholders in exchange for a part of their stock will not qualify.[49] Because of the subjectiveness of the genuine contraction of a corporate business test, it should not be relied upon without a favorable ruling from the IRS.

The requirements are objective with respect to the complete termination of a business test. If a corporation has more than one trade or business, both of which have been in existence for more than five years, and terminates one while continuing the other, the proceeds from the sale of the one trade or business can be distributed as a stock redemption to the shareholders so long as the trade or business was not acquired in a taxable transaction within such period. The five-year requirement prevents the bailout of E & P by the acquisition and distribution of another business within a short period of time.

---

47. Section 302 presents a true paradox for the reader. First, there is the not essentially equivalent to a dividend of § 302(b)(1), which is tested at the shareholder level. Second, there is the not essentially equivalent to a dividend of § 302(e), which looks to the effect of the distribution on the corporation. Thus, identical terminology in the same Code Section carries different meanings.
48. See *Joseph W. Imler*, 11 T.C. 836 (1948).
49. Rev.Rul. 60–322, 1960–2 C.B. 118.

Example 35   X Corporation has been selling a single product to its customers. It loses its major customer, and a severe drop in sales results. The corporation reduces its inventory investment and has substantial cash on hand. It redeems 20% of its outstanding stock as a liquidating dividend. A, an individual shareholder, receives $10,000 for stock that cost $5,000 two years ago. The distribution will not qualify under § 302; there was only one business activity, and the distribution is not a disproportionate redemption. Consequently, the $10,000 is a taxable dividend to A assuming adequate E & P. (Such a distribution would not qualify as a genuine contraction of a corporate business, because it is simply a reduction of excess inventory.) ☐

Example 36   X Corporation, the owner and operator of a wholesale grocery business, acquired a freight-hauling concern. The acquisition was by purchase and therefore constituted a taxable transaction. Three years later, the freight-hauling concern is distributed in kind on a pro rata basis to all of the shareholders of X Corporation. The distribution does not satisfy the requirements of § 302(e)(3) for two reasons. First, the business distributed had not been conducted for five years. Second, it was acquired by X Corporation in a taxable transaction. Since the distribution was pro rata among the shareholders, none of the regular types of stock redemptions [i.e., § 302(b)(1), (2), or (3)] should come into play. All other alternatives having been exhausted, X Corporation's distribution must fall into the classification of a dividend distribution. ☐

Redemptions to Pay Death Taxes—§ 303

Section 303 provides an executor the opportunity to redeem stock in a closely-held corporation when the stock represents a substantial amount of the gross estate of the shareholder-decedent. The redemption is effected to provide the estate with liquidity. Stock in a closely-held corporation is generally not readily marketable; however, it could be redeemed if § 302 would not cause ordinary dividend treatment. Section 303, to an extent, alleviates this problem.

Section 303 is, in effect, an exception to § 302(b). If a stock redemption qualifies under § 303, the rules of § 302(b) do not apply. The distribution will qualify as a stock redemption regardless of whether it is substantially disproportionate or not essentially equivalent to a dividend.

A redemption under § 303 should remain largely immune from the capital gain or loss changes under TRA of 1986. In a § 303 redemption, the redemption price generally equals the basis of the stock that qualifies. This is so because under § 1014, the income tax basis of property owned by a decedent becomes the property's fair market value on the date of death (or alternate valuation date if available and if elected). If, as is usually the case, this so-called step-up or step-down in basis that occurs at death (see Chapter 12) equals the redemption price, the exchange is free of any income tax consequences to the shareholder's estate.

Section 303 applies when a distribution is made with respect to stock of a corporation, the value of which stock, in the gross estate of a decedent, is in excess of 35 percent of the value of the adjusted gross estate of the decedent.

(For a definition of "gross estate" and "adjusted gross estate," see the Glossary of Tax Terms in Appendix C.) In determining the 35 percent requirement, stock of two or more corporations is treated as the stock of a single corporation if 20 percent or more in value of the outstanding stock of each corporation is included in the decedent's gross estate.[50]

Example 37   The adjusted gross estate of a decedent is $300,000. The gross estate includes stock in X and Y Corporations valued at $100,000 and $80,000, respectively. Unless the two corporations can be treated as a single corporation, § 303 will not apply to a redemption of the stock. Assume the decedent owned all the stock of X Corporation and 80% of the stock of Y. Section 303 would then apply, because 20% or more of the value of the outstanding stock of both corporations would be included in the decedent's estate. The 35% test would be met when the stock is treated as that of a single corporation. ☐

Example 38   The adjusted gross estate of D, decedent, was $900,000. The death taxes and funeral and administration expenses of the estate totaled $200,000. Included in the estate was stock in X Corporation, a closely-held corporation, valued at $340,000. D had acquired the stock years ago at a cost of $60,000. X Corporation redeems $200,000 of the stock from D's estate. The redemption would qualify under § 303 and thus would not represent a dividend to D's estate. In addition, § 1014 would apply to give the stock a step-up in basis. Consequently, there would be no tax on the redemption. ☐

The use of § 303 is subject to time limitations. Section 303 applies only to redemptions made within 90 days after the expiration of the period of limitations for the assessment of the Federal estate tax. If a petition for a redetermination of an estate tax deficiency is timely filed with the U.S. Tax Court, the applicable period for a § 303 redemption is extended to 60 days after the decision of the Court becomes final.[51]

Section 303 applies only to the extent of the sum of the estate, inheritance, legacy, and succession taxes imposed by reason of the decedent's death and to the extent of the amount of funeral and administration expenses allowable as deductions to the estate.[52] Stock must be redeemed from a shareholder whose interest in the estate is reduced by the payment of these taxes and expenses.

Effect on the Corporation Redeeming Its Stock

Having considered the different types of stock redemptions that will receive exchange treatment, what is the tax effect to the corporation redeeming its stock? If the corporation uses property to carry out the redemption, is gain or

---

50. § 303(b)(2)(B).
51. § 303(b)(1). The latter extension of time applies only to bona fide contests in the Tax Court. It does not apply to a petition initiated solely for the purpose of extending the time period under § 303.
52. § 303(a).

loss recognized on the distribution? Furthermore, one needs to determine what effect, if any, the redemption will have on the corporation's E & P. These matters are discussed in the following paragraphs.

Recognition of Loss by the Corporation.   The purchase of stock, including the repurchase by an issuing corporation of its own stock, generally is treated as a capital transaction that does not give rise to a loss. In addition, all expenses a corporation incurs in redeeming its stock are nonamortizable capital expenditures. Payments that are not deductible include stock purchase premiums; amounts paid to a shareholder for the shareholder's agreement not to reacquire stock in the corporation for a specified time; and legal, accounting, transfer agent, brokerage, and appraisal fees.

Recognition of Gain by the Corporation.   Section 311 provides that corporations will be taxed on all distributions of appreciated property whether in the form of a property dividend or a stock redemption. Before TRA of 1986, an important exception to the recognition of gain by a corporation carrying out a stock redemption with appreciated property involved § 303 situations. If a redemption was to pay death taxes and administration expenses and qualified under § 303, the appreciation was not taxed at the corporation level. TRA of 1986 eliminated this exception.[53]

Example 39   To carry out a § 303 redemption, Y Corporation transfers land (basis of $80,000, fair market value of $300,000) to a shareholder's estate. If this redemption occurred in 1986, Y Corporation would have no recognized gain as a result of the distribution. If it occurs in 1987 or thereafter, Y Corporation has a recognized gain of $220,000 ($300,000 − $80,000). □

Effect on Earnings and Profits.   The E & P account of a corporation is reduced as a result of a stock redemption in an amount not in excess of the ratable share of the E & P of the distributing corporation attributable to the stock redeemed.[54]

Example 40   X Corporation has 100 shares of stock outstanding. It redeems 30 shares for $100,000 at a time when it has paid-in capital of $120,000 and E & P of $150,000. The charge to E & P would be 30% of the amount in the E & P account ($45,000), and the remainder of the redemption price ($55,000) would be a reduction of the capital account. □

---

53. The § 303 exception served a meaningful purpose. In a closely-held corporation, carrying out a stock redemption from a deceased shareholder's estate most often will necessitate the use of corporate property. If such property has appreciated in value, forcing the corporation to recognize a gain merely compounds the corporation's obligation of coming up with the necessary funds. If one assumes that § 303 has a desirable objective (i.e., to provide liquidity for the estate of a deceased shareholder), making it more difficult for the corporation to carry out the redemption impedes this objective.

54. § 312(n)(7).

Stock Redemptions—
No Exchange Treatment

Stock redemptions that do not fall under any of the four major types provided for in the Code will be treated as dividend distributions to the extent of E & P. Resourceful taxpayers, however, found two ways to circumvent the redemption provisions. Both involved structuring as a sale of the stock what was, in effect, a stock redemption or a dividend distribution. The widespread use of these approaches to obtain the favorable capital gain treatment available in the past led to the enactment of § 306 dealing with preferred stock bailouts and § 304 dealing with transfers of stock to related corporations.

Preferred Stock Bailouts—§ 306

The Problem. Suppose a shareholder would like to bail out corporate profits as a long-term capital gain rather than as a dividend. Several possibilities exist:

—A sale of stock to the corporation that qualifies as a stock redemption under the four types provided for by § 302 or the one type allowed under § 303.

—A complete liquidation of the corporation under § 331.

—A sale of stock to third parties.

As noted previously, a stock redemption under § 302 may be difficult to carry out successfully in the case of a family corporation unless the shareholder completely terminates his or her interest in the corporation. A redemption of stock under § 303 would not be available until after the death of a shareholder. Partial liquidations are limited to peculiar circumstances and may be hard to arrange. Also, complete liquidations may not be feasible for going concerns with good present and future profit potential. Lastly, the sale of stock to third parties may not be desirable if a shareholder wishes to maintain voting power in the corporation at its present level.

Clever taxpayers devised the following scheme to bail out corporate profits: [55]

First, the corporation issues a nontaxable preferred stock dividend on common stock [§ 305(a)]. The preferred stock is nonvoting.
Second, the shareholder assigns to the preferred stock an appropriate portion of the basis of the common stock [§ 307(a)].
Third, the shareholder sells the preferred stock to a third party for the stock's fair market value. If the stock is a capital asset, the spread between the selling price and the assigned basis will be a capital gain. The holding period of the common stock can be counted [§ 1223(5)] to determine the nature of the gain—either short-term or long-term capital gain.

---

55. *Chamberlin v. Comm.*, 53–2 USTC ¶9576, 44 AFTR 494, 207 F.2d 462 (CA–6, 1953), *cert. den.*, 74 S.Ct. 516 (USSC, 1954).

Fourth, the third party holds the preferred stock for a suitable period of time (at least more than one year) and then returns it to the corporation for redemption at a premium. If the requirements of § 302(b)(3) are met (i.e., complete termination of a shareholder's interest), the difference between the purchase price and the redemption proceeds (i.e., the premium) will be taxed as a long-term capital gain.

Note what has been accomplished. The original shareholder obtains the bailout of corporate profits as a long-term capital gain. No diminution in the control of the corporation occurs; the voting common stock has remained intact throughout. The third party purchaser of the preferred stock is rewarded for its cooperation by the premium paid upon the ultimate redemption of the stock.

The Solution of § 306.   Because of the tax avoidance possibilities of the preferred stock bailout approach, Congress enacted § 306, which in essence produces the following tax consequences:

—The shareholder will have ordinary income on the sale (but not the receipt) of the preferred stock to a third party to the extent that the fair market value of the preferred stock (on the date of distribution) would have been a dividend had the corporation distributed cash in lieu of stock [§ 306(a)(1)]. But such income is *not a dividend* and therefore has no effect on the issuing corporation's E & P.[56] In this respect, § 306 leads to a harsher result than does a taxable dividend distribution.

—No loss is recognized on any sale of the preferred stock by the shareholder.

—If the shareholder does not sell the preferred stock to a third party but chooses, instead, to have it redeemed by the issuing corporation, the redemption proceeds will constitute dividend income to the extent of the corporation's E & P on the date of the redemption [§ 306(a)(2)].

Example 41   As of January 1 of the current year, Z Corporation has E & P of $150,000. T, the sole shareholder of Z Corporation, owns all of Z's common stock (100 shares) with a basis of $60,000. On that date, Z Corporation declares and pays a preferred stock dividend [nontaxable under § 305(a)] of 100 shares. After the dividend, the fair market value of one share of common is $2,000 and the fair market value of one share of preferred is $1,000. Two days later, T sells the 100 shares of preferred to V for $100,000. Section 306 produces the following results:

—After the distribution and before the sale, the preferred stock will have a basis to T of $20,000 [($100,000 ÷ $300,000) × $60,000 (the original basis of the common stock)].

—The sale of the preferred stock generates $100,000 of ordinary income to T. This would have been the amount of dividend income T would recognize had cash instead of preferred stock been distributed.

---

56. Reg. § 1.306–1(b)(1).

—The $20,000 basis allocated to the preferred stock is not lost but should be returned to the common stock account.

—Z Corporation's E & P account remains unaffected by either the stock distribution or its subsequent sale. □

Example 42   Assume the same facts as in Example 41 with this exception: Z Corporation's E & P was only $50,000 on the date the preferred stock was distributed. Under these circumstances, the $100,000 sale proceeds would be accounted for as follows: $50,000 ordinary income under § 306, $20,000 applied against the basis of the preferred stock, and $30,000 capital gain. Whether the capital gain was long-term or short-term would depend upon the holding period of the underlying common stock. □

What Is § 306 Stock?   Section 306 stock is stock other than common that (1) is received as a nontaxable stock dividend, (2) is received tax-free in a corporate reorganization or separation to the extent that either the effect of the transaction was substantially the same as the receipt of a stock dividend or the stock was received in exchange for § 306 stock, or (3) has a basis determined by reference to the basis of § 306 stock. Stock rights are treated as stock for these purposes. Stock acquired through the exercise of such rights is treated as § 306 stock to the extent of the fair market value of the rights at the time of their distribution. If a corporation has no E & P on the date of distribution of a nontaxable preferred stock dividend, the stock will not be § 306 stock.

Exceptions to § 306.   Section 306(b) specifically excepts the following transactions from the general rule:

1. A shareholder sells *all* (i.e., both common and preferred) of the stock interest to an unrelated third party. To determine what is a related or an unrelated party, refer to the constructive ownership rules of § 318(a).
2. A corporation redeems *all* (i.e., both common and preferred) of the stock of a shareholder if such redemption qualifies under § 302(b)(3) (i.e., complete termination of a shareholder's interest).
3. Stock is turned in to the corporation pursuant to a complete liquidation or a qualified partial liquidation.
4. Stock on which gain or loss is not recognized is disposed of. For example, death of a shareholder is an exception; the preferred stock passes to the estate or heirs free of any taint.
5. The transfer is not in pursuance of a plan having as one of its principal purposes the avoidance of the Federal income tax. What this means in actual practice is not entirely clear.[57] The Regulation in point refers to isolated dispositions of preferred stock by minority shareholders or a sale by a shareholder of all the preferred stock subsequent to a disposition of all the common stock.[58]

---

57. *Fireoved v. U.S.*, 72–2 USTC ¶9485, 30 AFTR2d 72–5043, 462 F.2d 1281 (CA–3, 1972), and S.Rept. No. 1622, 83d Cong., 2d Sess.
58. Reg. § 1.306–2(b)(3).

Most of the preceding exceptions can be understood by recalling the basic objective of the preferred stock bailout scheme—to bail out corporate profits at capital gain rates with no loss of control. One can hardly accomplish such an objective if, for example, *all* of the stock is sold to a third party or redeemed by the corporation (refer to exceptions 1 and 2).

Example 43   D makes a gift of § 306 stock to her son, S. Although the transfer will not trigger ordinary income to D because no gain is recognized on a gift, the stock will be § 306 stock in the hands of S. One might say that the § 306 ordinary income taint is transferred from D to S. □

Example 44   T transfers cash to a newly created corporation in return for all its stock (1,000 shares of common and 500 shares of preferred). The preferred stock will not be § 306 stock; it was not issued as a nontaxable dividend. Even if the stock were so issued, it would escape the § 306 taint, because no E & P existed at the time of issuance. □

Redemptions Through Use of Related Corporations—§ 304

Without § 304, the rules of § 302 (detailing when a stock redemption is treated as a taxable dividend) could be circumvented if a shareholder had a controlling interest in more than one corporation. For example, a shareholder could sell the stock in X Corporation to Y Corporation and receive capital gain treatment regardless of whether or not the proportionate interest in X Corporation changed substantially as a result of the sale. Section 304 closes this loophole. When a shareholder sells stock of one corporation to a related corporation, the sale is treated as a redemption subject to §§ 302 and 303.

Section 304 applies to a corporation's acquisition from a shareholder of stock of another corporation in exchange for property when the shareholder has at least a 50 percent ownership in both corporations. Section 317(a) defines property to mean money, securities, and any other property, except that stock (or rights to acquire stock) in the corporation making the distribution is specifically excluded. This means, then, that most tax-free corporate reorganizations involving the exchange of stock for stock would generally avoid the consequences of § 304.[59]

Control for the purpose of § 304 is defined as the ownership of stock possessing at least 50 percent of the total combined voting power of all classes of stock entitled to vote, or at least 50 percent of the total value of all classes of stock. Section 304 also applies if an individual has a 50 percent interest in a corporation that, in turn, has control (as defined above) of another corporation. For purposes of determining the 50 percent control, the constructive ownership rules of § 318(a) apply.[60]

Transfers Involving Brother-Sister Corporations.   If an individual controls two corporations[61] and transfers stock in one corporation to the other for

---

59. However, there might be a problem when a subsidiary distributes stock of the parent.
60. § 304(c)(2).
61. Control being determined under § 304 for these purposes.

property, the exchange is treated as a redemption of the stock of the *acquiring* corporation. If the distribution is treated as a dividend under § 301, the stock received by the acquiring corporation is treated as a contribution to the corporation's capital. In that event, basis of the stock is the basis the shareholder had in the stock, and the individual's basis in the stock of the acquiring corporation is increased by the basis of the stock he or she surrendered. In applying the provisions of § 302(b) to the exchange, reference is made to the shareholder's ownership of stock in the issuing corporation and not to his or her ownership of stock in the acquiring corporation.[62] The amount of dividend income is determined as if the property were distributed by the acquiring corporation to the extent of its E & P and then by the issuing corporation to the extent of its E & P.[63]

Example 45   A owns 100 shares of X Corporation stock and 200 shares of Y Corporation stock, representing 50% ownership in both corporations. A sells 20 shares of stock in X Corporation to Y Corporation for $30,000. X Corporation has E & P of $100,000; Y Corporation has E & P of $20,000. The stock was purchased by A two years ago for $5,000. □

What are the results of the sale in Example 45? Section 304 applies to the transaction; therefore, the sale is treated as a redemption of the stock of Y Corporation. If the redemption qualifies under § 302(b), A will have a long-term capital gain of $25,000 on the sale. If not, the transaction will be considered to be a dividend under § 301.

—To determine whether the sale qualifies as a stock redemption, reference is made to A's ownership in X Corporation before and after the redemption. Assuming the not essentially equivalent to a dividend provision of § 302(b) (1) is inapplicable, the substantially disproportionate redemption provisions of § 302(b)(2) are considered.

—Before the sale, A owned 100 shares, or 50 percent, of X Corporation. After the sale, A owns 90 shares in X Corporation [100 shares originally owned − 20 shares transferred to Y Corporation + 10 shares (constructive ownership of one half of the shares transferred to Y Corporation)]. The constructive ownership of 10 shares results because A owns 50 percent of Y Corporation and, thus, is deemed to own 50 percent of the stock that Y Corporation owns in X Corporation. Of the 200 shares outstanding in X Corporation, A's 90 shares now result in a 45 percent interest in X Corporation. Since A, following the sale, does not own less than 80 percent of his interest in X Corporation before the sale, the sale does not qualify as a stock redemption.

—Because the sale does not qualify as a stock redemption, A will have dividend income of $30,000. A's basis in his Y Corporation stock will be increased by $5,000.

—Y Corporation will have a basis of $5,000 in the X Corporation stock it acquired from A.

---

62. See Reg. § 1.304–2(a).
63. § 304(b)(2).

Example 46   Assume A in Example 45 sells 60 (instead of 20) of his shares in X Corporation to Y Corporation for $90,000. His basis in the 60 shares is $15,000. After the sale, A owns 70 shares in X Corporation (100 − 60 + 30 shares owned constructively). This represents a 35% ownership in X Corporation. Both the 50% ownership and the 80% ownership tests of § 302(b) (2) are satisfied. Consequently, A has a long-term capital gain of $75,000. The basis of the stock in X Corporation received by Y Corporation is $90,000. A's basis in the Y Corporation stock remains the same. □

Parent-Subsidiary Situations.   If a subsidiary corporation acquires stock in its parent from a shareholder owning at least 50 percent of the parent corporation, § 304 applies to the transaction. However, the acquisition is treated as though the parent had *redeemed* its own stock.[64] The transaction is construed as a distribution from the subsidiary to the parent and a subsequent distribution from the parent to the individual shareholder.[65] The transfer is treated as a redemption of the parent corporation stock (rather than that of the acquiring corporation as would be the case in transactions involving brother-sister corporations). If the transaction does not qualify as a stock redemption, the shareholder's basis in the stock sold to the subsidiary attaches to the remaining stock owned in the parent.

Example 47   A, an individual, owns 50% of X Corporation, which, in turn, owns 50% of Y Corporation. X Corporation has 200 shares of stock outstanding, 100 of which are owned by B (no relationship to A). A sells 20 of his 100 shares to Y Corporation for $40,000. He purchased the 20 shares two years ago for $10,000. After the sale, A is considered to own 84 shares in X Corporation (100 − 20 + 4 shares owned constructively through Y Corporation). Y Corporation acquired 20 shares, of which 50% are constructively owned by X Corporation (10 shares). Of these 10 shares, 40% are now owned constructively by A (4 shares). A's 84 shares represent a 42% ownership in X Corporation, which does not meet the 80% ownership test of § 302(b) (2); consequently, the $40,000 is treated as a dividend to A to the extent of the E & P of Y Corporation and then to the extent of the E & P of X Corporation. The cost of the 20 shares, $10,000, attaches to A's basis in his remaining shares in X Corporation. X Corporation is deemed to have received a dividend from Y Corporation in the amount of $40,000. □

Distribution of Stock and Securities of a Controlled Corporation

If a corporation has control [80 percent control as defined in § 368(c)] of another corporation, stock in the subsidiary corporation can be distributed to the shareholders of the parent corporation tax-free if the requirements of § 355 are met. When a subsidiary is newly formed to perfect a corporate division, § 355 applies through § 368(a)(1)(D) (i.e., a corporate divisive reorganization

---

64. Reg. § 1.304–3(a).
65. § 304(b)(2).

provision discussed in Chapter 6). However, when a subsidiary already exists, § 355 alone applies. Although Section 355 is discussed further in Chapter 6 in connection with the corporate reorganization provisions, it is mentioned here because applied alone, it involves a transaction resembling a dividend or a stock redemption.

Section 355 applies only (1) to distributions that involve all the stock of the subsidiary, or a sufficient amount to give control [as defined in § 368(c)] to the shareholders of the parent, (2) when both the parent and the subsidiary, following the distribution, are engaged in a trade or business in which they had been so engaged for at least five years before the distribution and (3) when the parent has held stock in the subsidiary for at least five years before the distribution (unless the stock was acquired in a nontaxable transaction). The distribution can take the form of a spin-off, a split-off, or a split-up.

A spin-off is a distribution of subsidiary stock to the shareholders of the parent corporation giving them control of that subsidiary. The shareholders of the parent do not surrender any of their stock for the subsidiary stock. This distribution resembles an ordinary dividend distribution. A split-off is identical to a spin-off, except that the shareholders in the parent corporation exchange some of their parent corporation stock for the subsidiary stock. It more nearly resembles a stock redemption. A split-up is the distribution of the stock of two subsidiaries to shareholders of the parent in complete liquidation of the parent.

Section 355 requires that both the controlled corporation and the parent corporation be engaged in the active conduct of a trade or business for at least five years before the distribution. This requirement also appears in § 302(b)(4) with respect to partial liquidations.[66] If a corporation discontinues a trade or business that it has conducted for at least five years, it can distribute the assets pertaining to such business to the shareholders in exchange for their stock as a partial liquidation, but the shareholders must recognize capital gain. In the distributions of stock of a controlled corporation, pursuant to § 355, the shareholder recognizes no gain or loss.

What constitutes an active trade or business is often the subject of litigation. The Regulations take the position that the holding of stock, securities, land, or other property, including casual sales of such properties, is not an active trade or business.[67] The problem of defining an active trade or business is discussed in more detail in Chapter 6 in connection with the application of § 355 to a divisive reorganization.

Example 48 X Corporation has operated an active business for the past 10 years. Six years ago it acquired all of the stock of Y Corporation, which has been engaged in an active business for eight years. X Corporation distributes all the stock of Y Corporation to its shareholders. Both corporations continue to operate their separate businesses. Assuming a business reason exists for the distribution, the distribution qualifies under § 355, and the receipt of the Y Corporation stock is tax-free to the shareholders of X Corporation. This is a spin-off. ☐

66. The five-year requirement was added to both §§ 302(b)(4) and 355 to deter the bailout of E & P by the acquisition and distribution of another business within a short span of time.
67. Regulations covering distributions of stock and securities of controlled corporations, including examples and limitations, are at Reg. §§ 1.355–1 to –5.

A shareholder can receive only stock or securities tax-free. If other property is received, it is considered boot and is subject to taxation under § 356. To further qualify the exchange, it is tax-free only if securities are surrendered in a principal amount that is the same as the principal amount of the securities received. If the principal amount of the securities received is greater than the principal amount of the securities surrendered or if no securities are surrendered, the shareholder has boot to the extent of the fair market value of the excess principal amount measured on the date of the exchange.

Example 49   T, an individual, exchanges stock in X Corporation (the parent corporation) for stock and securities in Y Corporation (the subsidiary corporation) pursuant to § 355. The exchange is a tax-free split-off except to the extent of the securities received. The securities in Y have a principal amount of $1,000 and a fair market value of $950 on the date of the exchange. T has boot of $950. □

Example 50   Assume in Example 49 that T also surrenders securities in X for the securities in Y. The securities in X have a principal amount of $600. T has boot of $380, the fair market value of the excess principal of $400 [($950 ÷ $1000) × $400 = $380]. □

A distribution under § 355 must not be used principally as a device for the distribution of the E & P of either the distributing corporation or the controlled corporation. If the stock or securities of the controlled corporation are sold shortly after the exchange, the sale is evidence that the transaction was used as a device to distribute E & P. There must also be a business purpose for a distribution made pursuant to § 355. The reason for this requirement is to limit § 355 to distributions incident to any readjustment of corporate structure "... as is required by business exigencies and which, in general, effect only a readjustment of continuing interests in property under modified corporate forms." Problems with the antitrust laws would be an example of a business reason justifying the distribution of a subsidiary's stock to the parent's shareholders.

Every taxpayer who receives a distribution of stock or securities of a corporation controlled by a second corporation in which is held stock or securities must attach to the return for the year in which the distribution is received a detailed statement giving appropriate information to show the application of § 355. The statement must include a description of the stock and securities surrendered (if any) and received and the names and addresses of all the corporations involved in the transaction.[68]

The basis of stock received by a shareholder pursuant to § 355 is determined by §§ 358(b) and (c). Basis of the stock held before the exchange is allocated among the stock of all classes held immediately after the transaction in proportion to the fair market value of the stock of each class.[69] The rule is the same regardless of whether a spin-off, split-off, or split-up is involved. Regarding a spin-off (i.e., wherein stock is received in the subsidiary without

---

68. Reg. § 1.355–5(b). See Rev.Proc. 81–41, 1981–2 C.B. 605, for a checklist of information to be included in a request for a ruling under § 355.
69. Reg. § 1.358–2(a)(2).

the shareholder's surrendering stock in the parent), § 358(c) states that such a distribution is nonetheless treated as an exchange. A portion of the basis in the old stock is allocated to the new shares.

E & P of the distributing corporation is decreased by a distribution of stock in its subsidiary. The decrease is the lesser of (1) an amount determined by multiplying the distributing corporation's E & P by a fraction, the numerator of which is the fair market value of the subsidiary's stock and the denominator of which is the fair market value of all the parent corporation's assets, or (2) the net worth of the subsidiary. If this decrease is more than the E & P of the subsidiary, the E & P account of the subsidiary is increased to equal this decrease. If the subsidiary's E & P exceeds the decrease in the E & P of the parent, the subsidiary's E & P account will remain the same.[70]

If a distribution pursuant to § 355 fails to meet the requirements of this Section, such a distribution would become taxable. If a spin-off is involved, the stock distributed to the parent corporation's shareholders would be treated as an ordinary dividend. If a split-off is involved, the distribution would be treated as a stock redemption subject to the provisions of § 302 to determine whether it qualified as a capital gain or whether it would be treated as a dividend. If a split-up is involved, the transaction would be treated as a complete liquidation of the parent corporation.

Concept Summary

1. Without a special provision, corporate distributions are taxed as dividend income to the recipient shareholders to the extent of the distributing corporation's E & P accumulated since February 28, 1913, or to the extent of current E & P. Any excess is treated as a return of capital to the extent of the shareholder's basis in the stock and, thereafter, as capital gain. See §§ 301 and 316.

2. Property distributions are considered dividends (taxed as noted in item 1) in the amount of their fair market value. The amount deemed distributed is reduced by any liabilities on the property distributed. The shareholder's basis in such property is the fair market value.

3. Earnings and profits of a corporation are increased by corporate earnings for the taxable year computed in the same manner as the corporation computes its taxable income. As a general rule, the account is increased for all items of income, whether taxed or not, and reduced by all items of expense, whether deductible or not. See § 312. Refer to the Concept Summary on page 4–6 of this chapter for a summary of the effect of certain transactions on taxable income and current E & P.

4. A corporation recognizes gain, but not loss, on distributions of property to its shareholders. E & P of the distributing corporation is reduced by the amount of money distributed or by the greater of the fair market value or the adjusted basis of property distributed less the amount of any liability applicable to the distributed property.

5. As a general rule, stock dividends or stock rights (representing stock in the distributing corporation) are not taxed, with five exceptions: (1) distributions payable in either stock or property; (2) distributions that have the result of the receipt of property by some shareholders and an increase in the proportionate interest of other shareholders in the assets or E & P of the distributing corporation; (3) distributions that result in the

---

70. Reg. § 1.312–10.

receipt of preferred stock by some common shareholders and the receipt of common stock by other shareholders; (4) distributions on preferred stock other than an increase in the conversion ratio of convertible preferred stock made solely to take account of a stock dividend or stock split with respect to stock into which the preferred is convertible; and (5) distributions of convertible preferred stock, unless it can be shown that the distribution will not result in a disproportionate distribution. Changes in conversion ratios, changes in redemption prices, and differences between issue price and redemption price are taxable dividends. See § 305.

6. Stock redemptions that qualify under § 302(b) are given capital gain treatment. Section 302(b) requires that such distributions either be substantially disproportionate, be not essentially equivalent to a dividend, or be a distribution to a noncorporate shareholder in a qualified partial liquidation. In making a determination of substantially disproportionate or not essentially equivalent to a dividend under §§ 302(b)(1), (2), and (3), the rules of § 318(a) determining the constructive ownership of stock apply, unless the shareholder redeems all of his or her interest in the corporation and does not reacquire (other than by bequest or inheritance) any interest (except as a creditor) for 10 years after the redemption.

7. Redemptions that are qualified partial liquidations must be made to noncorporate shareholders. A qualified partial liquidation occurs when the distribution is not essentially equivalent to a dividend (i.e., there is a genuine contraction of a corporate business) or when a corporation has had two or more trades or businesses for at least five years and discontinues one of the businesses, distributing all the assets of such business to its shareholders. It must continue the other business or businesses. Any distributions must be made within the taxable year in which the plan is adopted or within the succeeding taxable year. See § 302(b)(4).

8. If stock included in a decedent's estate represents more than 35 percent of the adjusted taxable estate, it may upon redemption qualify for capital gain treatment separate and apart from § 302(b). Section 303 provides automatic exchange treatment on the redemption of such stock.

9. A corporation is taxed on the appreciation of property distributed in redemption of its stock.

10. A distribution of preferred stock as a nontaxable stock dividend to common shareholders is subject to special treatment outlined in § 306. The proceeds of a sale of § 306 stock or the redemption of such stock results in ordinary income to the extent of the distributing corporation's E & P (1) on the date of the distribution for a *sale* of such stock or (2) on the date of the redemption for the *redemption* of such stock.

11. The sale of stock in a controlled corporation (50 percent control) to another corporation controlled by the shareholder (also 50 percent control) is deemed a stock redemption and must be tested by § 302(b) or § 303 to determine if the shareholder will receive exchange treatment or dividend treatment. See § 304.

12. The E & P account of the distributing corporation is reduced in a stock redemption in proportion to the amount of the corporation's outstanding stock that is redeemed.

13. Distributions of stock in a subsidiary corporation (80 percent controlled by the parent) are not taxed to the shareholders if the distribution is pursuant to § 355. To qualify under § 355, stock representing this ''control'' must be distributed to the parent's shareholders. The parent must have owned stock in the subsidiary for at least five years unless the stock was acquired in a nontaxable transaction. Both the parent and subsidiary must continue a trade or business after the distribution. Further, each must have actively conducted this trade or business for at least five years before the redemption. The distribution must be motivated by a sound business purpose and not by a scheme to avoid Federal taxes.

✓ Tax Planning Considerations

Corporate Distributions

In connection with the preceding discussion of corporate distributions, the following points might well need reinforcement:

—Because E & P is the measure of dividend income, its periodic determination is essential to corporate planning. Thus, an E & P account should be established and maintained, particularly if the possibility exists that a corporate distribution might represent a return of capital.

—Accumulated E & P is the sum of all past years' current E & P. No statute of limitations exists on the computation of E & P. The IRS could, for example, redetermine a corporation's current E & P for a tax year long since passed. Such a change would affect accumulated E & P and would have a direct impact on the taxability of current distributions to shareholders.

—Taxpayers should be aware that manipulating distributions to avoid or minimize dividend exposure is possible.

Example 51   Q Corporation has accumulated E & P of $100,000 as of January 1, 19X5. During 19X5, it expects to have earnings from operations of $80,000 and to make a cash distribution of $60,000. Q Corporation also expects to sell a particular asset for a loss of $100,000. Thus, it anticipates incurring a deficit of $20,000 for the year. The best approach would be to recognize the loss as soon as possible and immediately thereafter make the cash distribution to its shareholders. Suppose these two steps took place on January 1, 19X5. Because the current E & P for 19X5 will have a deficit, the accumulated E & P account must be brought up to date (refer to Example 11 in this chapter). Thus, at the time of the distribution, the combined E & P balance is zero [i.e., $100,000 (beginning balance in accumulated E & P) − $100,000 (existing deficit in current E & P)], and the $60,000 distribution to the shareholders constitutes a return of capital. Current deficits are allocated pro rata throughout the year unless the parties can prove otherwise. Here they can. □

Example 52   After several unprofitable years, Y Corporation has a deficit in accumulated E & P of $100,000 as of January 1, 19X5. Starting in 19X5, Y Corporation expects to generate annual E & P of $50,000 for the next four years and would like to distribute this amount to its shareholders. The corporation's cash position (for dividend purposes) will correspond to the current E & P generated. Compare the following possibilities:

1. On December 31 of 19X5, 19X6, 19X7, and 19X8, Y Corporation distributes a cash dividend of $50,000.
2. On December 31 of 19X6 and 19X8, Y Corporation distributes a cash dividend of $100,000.

The two alternatives are illustrated as follows:

Year	Accumulated E & P (First of Year)	Current E & P	Distri-bution	Amount of Dividend
		Alternative 1		
19X5	($100,000)	$50,000	$ 50,000	$50,000
19X6	(100,000)	50,000	50,000	50,000
19X7	(100,000)	50,000	50,000	50,000
19X8	(100,000)	50,000	50,000	50,000
		Alternative 2		
19X5	($100,000)	$50,000	$ –0–	$ –0–
19X6	(50,000)	50,000	100,000	50,000
19X7	(50,000)	50,000	–0–	–0–
19X8	–0–	50,000	100,000	50,000

Alternative 1 leads to an overall result of $200,000 in dividend income, since each $50,000 distribution is fully covered by current E & P. Alternative 2, however, results in only $100,000 of dividend income to the shareholders. The remaining $100,000 is a return of capital. Why? At the time Y Corporation made its first distribution of $100,000 on December 31, 19X6, it had a deficit of $50,000 in accumulated E & P (the original deficit of $100,000 is reduced by the $50,000 of current E & P from 19X5). Consequently, the $100,000 distribution yields a $50,000 dividend (the current E & P for 19X6) and $50,000 as a return of capital. As of January 1, 19X7, Y Corporation's accumulated E & P now has a deficit balance of $50,000 (a distribution cannot increase a deficit in E & P). Add in $50,000 of current E & P from 19X7, and the balance as of January 1, 19X8, is zero. Thus, the second distribution of $100,000 made on December 31, 19X8, also yields $50,000 of dividends (the current E & P for 19X8) and $50,000 as a return of capital. □

Constructive Dividends

Tax planning can be particularly effective in avoiding constructive dividend situations.

—Shareholders should try to structure their dealings with the corporation on an arm's length basis. For example, reasonable rent should be paid for the use of corporate property, or a fair price should be paid for its purchase. Needless to say, the parties should make every effort to support the amount involved with appraisal data or market information obtained from reliable sources at or close to the time of the transaction.

—Dealings between shareholders and a closely-held corporation should be formalized as much as possible. In the case of loans to shareholders, for example, the parties should provide for an adequate rate of interest, written evidence of the debt, and a realistic repayment schedule that is not only arranged but also followed.

—If corporate profits are to be bailed out by the shareholders in a form deductible to the corporation, a balanced mix of the different alternatives could lessen the risk of disallowance by the IRS. Rent for the use of shareholder property, interest on amounts borrowed from shareholders, or salaries for services rendered by shareholders are all feasible substitutes for dividend distributions. But overdoing any one approach may well attract the attention of the IRS. Too much interest, for example, might mean the corporation is thinly capitalized, and some of the debt therefore really represents equity investment.

—Much can be done to protect against the disallowance of corporate deductions for compensation that is determined to be unreasonable in amount. Example 53 is an illustration, all too common in a family corporation, of what *not* to do.

Example 53   Z Corporation is wholly owned by T. Corporate employees and annual salaries include Mrs. T ($15,000), T, Jr. ($10,000), T ($80,000), and E ($40,000). The operation of Z Corporation is shared about equally between T and E (an unrelated party). Mrs. T (T's wife) performed significant services for the corporation during the corporation's formative years but now merely attends the annual meeting of the board of directors. T, Jr. (T's son), is a full-time student and occasionally signs papers for the corporation in his capacity as treasurer. Z Corporation has not distributed a dividend for 10 years, although it has accumulated substantial E & P. What is wrong with this situation?

—Mrs. T's salary seems vulnerable unless one can prove that some or all of the $15,000 annual salary is payment for services rendered to the corporation in prior years (i.e., she was underpaid for those years).[71]

—T, Jr.'s, salary is also vulnerable; he does not appear to earn the $10,000 paid to him by the corporation. True, neither T, Jr., nor Mrs. T is a shareholder, but each one's relationship to T is enough of a tie-in to raise the unreasonable compensation issue.

—T's salary appears susceptible to challenge. Why, for instance, is he receiving $40,000 more than E when it appears each shares equally in the operation of the corporation?

—No dividends have been distributed by Z Corporation for 10 years, although the corporation is capable of doing so. □

Stock Redemptions

Several observations come to mind in connection with tax planning for stock redemptions.

—The § 302(b)(1) variety (i.e., not essentially equivalent to a dividend) provides minimal utility and should be relied upon only as a last resort. Instead, the redemption should be structured to fit one of the safe harbors of either § 302(b)(2) (i.e., substantially disproportionate), § 302(b)(3) (i.e., complete termination), or § 303 (i.e., to pay death taxes).

—For a family corporation in which all of the shareholders are related to each other, the only hope of a successful redemption might lie in the use of

---

71. See, for example. *R. J. Nicoll Co.*, 59 T.C. 37 (1972).

§ 302(b)(3) or § 303. But in using § 302(b)(3), be careful that the family stock attribution rules are avoided. Here, strict compliance with § 302(c)(2) (i.e., the withdrawing shareholder does not continue as an employee of the corporation, etc., and does not reacquire an interest in the corporation within 10 years) is crucial.

—The alternative to a successful stock redemption or partial liquidation is dividend treatment of the distribution under § 301. But do not conclude that a dividend is always undesirable from a tax standpoint. Suppose the distributing corporation has little, if any, E & P. Or the distributee-shareholder is another corporation. In this latter regard, dividend treatment might well be preferred due to the availability of the dividends received deduction.

—When using the § 303 redemption, the amount to be sheltered from dividend treatment is the sum of death taxes and certain estate administration expenses. Nevertheless, a redemption in excess of the limitation will not destroy the applicability of § 303. Even better, any such excess (if properly structured) might qualify under § 302. Thus, § 302 can be used to pick up where § 303 left off.

—The timing and sequence of a redemption should be carefully handled.

Example 54   P Corporation's stock is held as follows: R (60 shares), S (20 shares), and T (20 shares). R, S, and T are all individuals and are not related to each other. The corporation redeems 24 of R's shares. Shortly thereafter, it redeems five of S's shares. Does R's redemption qualify as substantially disproportionate? Taken in isolation, it would appear to meet the requirements of § 302(b)(2)—the 80% and 50% tests have been satisfied. Yet, if the IRS takes into account the later redemption of S's shares, R has not satisfied the 50% test; he still owns $^{36}/_{71}$ of the corporation after both redemptions. A greater time lag between the two redemptions, would have placed R in a better position to argue against collapsing the series of redemptions into one. □

Problem Materials

Discussion Questions

1. What is meant by the term "earnings and profits"?

2. Why is it important to distinguish between current and accumulated E & P?

3. Describe the effect of a distribution in a year when the distributing corporation has—

    a. A deficit in accumulated E & P and a positive amount in current E & P.

    b. A positive amount in accumulated E & P and a deficit in current E & P.

    c. A deficit in both current and accumulated E & P.

    d. A positive amount in both current and accumulated E & P.

4. Five years ago, a corporation determined its current E & P to be $100,000. In the current year, it makes a distribution to its shareholders of $200,000. The IRS contends that the current E & P of the corporation five years ago really was $150,000.

a. Can the IRS successfully make this contention?

b. What difference would the additional $50,000 in E & P make?

5. If a corporation is chartered in a state that prohibits the payment of dividends that impair paid-in capital, is it possible for the corporation to pay a dividend that is a return of capital for tax purposes and yet comply with state law? Discuss.

6. The suggestion is made that any distributions to shareholders by a calendar year corporation should take place on January 1 before the corporation has developed any current E & P. Assess the validity of this suggestion.

7. T, an individual shareholder, receives a distribution from X Corporation and treats it as a return of capital. Upon audit by the IRS, he tells the agent: "Show me that X Corporation had adequate E & P to cover the distribution, and I will report the distribution as dividend income." Please comment.

8. X Corporation has no current or accumulated E & P. It distributes inventory (fair market value of $50,000 and basis of $10,000) to A, its sole shareholder. Does A recognize any dividend income? Explain.

9. A corporation with no E & P distributes a property dividend. Can it be said that the shareholders need not recognize any dividend income? Explain.

10. A corporation distributed property (adjusted basis of $100,000 and fair market value of $80,000) to its shareholders. Has the corporation acted wisely? Why or why not?

11. Does the distributing corporation recognize gain or loss when it distributes property as a dividend to its shareholders? Explain.

12. When are stock dividends taxable?

13. How are nontaxable stock rights handled for tax purposes? Taxable stock rights?

14. X Corporation sells its plant and equipment to its shareholders. Shortly thereafter, X Corporation enters into a long-term lease for the use of these assets. In connection with the possible tax ramifications of these transactions, consider the following:

a. The sale of the assets for less than their adjusted basis to X Corporation.

b. The amount of rent X Corporation has agreed to pay.

15. Why is it important that an advance from a corporation to a shareholder be categorized as a bona fide loan? With regard to the resolution of this issue, comment on the relevance of the following factors:

a. The corporation has never paid a dividend.

b. The advance is on open account.

c. The advance provides for 2% interest.

d. No date is specified for the repayment of the advance.

e. The advance was used by the shareholder to pay personal bills.

f. The advance is repaid by the shareholder immediately after the transaction was questioned by the IRS on audit of the corporate income tax return.

16. How can shareholders bail out corporate profits in such a manner as to provide the corporation with a deduction? What are the risks involved?

17. Whether compensation paid to a corporate employee is reasonable is a question of fact to be determined from the surrounding circumstances. How would the resolution of this problem be affected by each of the following factors:

a. The employee is not a shareholder but is related to the sole owner of the corporate-employer.

b. The employee-shareholder never completed high school.

c. The employee-shareholder is a full-time college student.

d. The employee-shareholder was underpaid for her services during the formative period of the corporate-employer.

e. The corporate-employer pays a nominal dividend each year.

f. Year-end bonuses are paid to all shareholder-employees.

18. What problems exist with respect to a corporation's redemption of its preferred stock?

19. Can a shareholder incur ordinary gain on a stock redemption that is not treated as a dividend? Explain.

20. Can a shareholder incur a loss on a stock redemption? Explain.

21. It has been said that a shareholder in a family corporation may have difficulty effectively utilizing § 302(b)(2) (i.e., substantially disproportionate) as a means of carrying out a stock redemption. Why? What other alternatives are available?

22. When does a so-called partial liquidation qualify for exchange treatment?

23. Compare a stock redemption under §§ 302(b)(1), (2), and (3) with a stock redemption pursuant to a partial liquidation under § 302(b)(4).

24. Under what circumstances does § 303 apply to a stock redemption? What is the tax effect of the application of § 303?

25. "A § 303 stock redemption usually results in no gain or loss being recognized by the estate." Evaluate this statement.

26. A corporation distributes $100,000 to a shareholder in complete redemption of the shareholder's stock. Can the corporation reduce its E & P by this amount? Explain.

27. What is a preferred stock bailout?

28. T, a 30% shareholder in X Corporation, sells one half of his preferred stock and one half of his common stock to a third party. Is there any danger that § 306 could apply to the sale of the preferred stock? Why or why not?

29. It has been said that the operation of § 306 to a sale of preferred stock could have a harsher tax effect than if the corporation had distributed a taxable dividend in the first place. Explain.

30. What problems arise when a shareholder sells stock he or she owns in one corporation to a related corporation?

31. What is an active trade or business?

32. Why does the requirement that a corporation be engaged in two active trades or businesses for at least five years before a qualified partial liquidation or that both the controlled corporation and the parent corporation be engaged in an active trade or business for at least five years before a distribution pursuant to § 355 exist as a condition for qualifying such distributions for special tax treatment?

33. Describe a spin-off, a split-off, and a split-up.

34. X Corporation, a manufacturing concern, maintains an investment portfolio in publicly traded securities. During the current year, it distributes some of these securities to its shareholders. Presuming the distribution is deemed to be a property dividend, what is the tax effect to X Corporation and to X Corporation's shareholders?

35. Referring to Question 34, comment on the following:

    a. The possibility that the distribution would qualify as a stock redemption.

    b. The possibility that the distribution would qualify as a qualified partial liquidation.

    c. The possibility that the distribution would qualify under § 355.

Problems

1. Complete the following schedule for each case:

	Accumulated E & P Beginning of Year	Current E & P	Cash Distributions (all on last day of year)	Amount Taxable	Return of Capital
a.	$40,000	($10,000)	$50,000	$____	$____
b.	(50,000)	30,000	40,000	____	____
c.	30,000	50,000	70,000	____	____
d.	60,000	(20,000)	45,000	____	____

    e. Same as (d), except the distribution of $45,000 is made on June 30 and the corporation uses the calendar year for tax purposes. ____ ____

2. Complete the following schedule for each case:

	Accumulated E & P Beginning of Year	Current E & P	Cash Distributions (all on last day of year)	Amount Taxable	Return of Capital
a.	$75,000	$20,000	$ 60,000	$____	$____
b.	20,000	40,000	45,000	____	____
c.	(90,000)	50,000	30,000	____	____
d.	60,000	(55,000)	40,000	____	____

    e. Same as (d), except the distribution of $40,000 is made on June 30 and the corporation uses the calendar year for tax purposes. ____ ____

3. Indicate in each of the following independent situations the effect on taxable income and E & P, stating the amount of any increase or (decrease), as a result of the transaction. (In determining the effect on E & P, assume E & P has already been increased by current taxable income.)

Transaction	Taxable Income Increase (Decrease)	E & P Increase (Decrease)
a. Receipt of $15,000 tax-exempt income	_____	_____
b. Payment of $15,150 Federal income taxes	_____	_____
c. Collection of $100,000 on life insurance policy on corporate president	_____	_____
d. Charitable contribution, $30,000, $20,000 allowable as a deduction in the current tax year	_____	_____
e. Deduction of remaining $10,000 charitable contribution in succeeding year	_____	_____
f. Realized gain on involuntary conversion of $200,000 ($30,000 of gain is recognized)	_____	_____

4. Indicate in each of the following independent situations the effect on taxable income and E & P, stating the amount of any increase or (decrease) as a result of the transaction. (In determining the effect on E & P, assume E & P has already been increased by current taxable income.)

Transaction	Taxable Income Increase (Decrease)	E & P Increase (Decrease)
a. Intangible drilling costs incurred in the current tax year and deductible from current taxable income in the amount of $50,000	_____	_____
b. Sale of unimproved real estate, basis of $200,000, fair market value of $800,000 (no election out of installment basis; payments in year of sale total $40,000)	_____	_____
c. Accelerated depreciation of $70,000 (straight-line would have been $40,000)	_____	_____
d. Long-term contract begun in current year (income to be reported on completed contract method; estimated profit on total contract is $350,000; percentage completed in current tax year is 30%)	_____	_____
e. Sale of equipment to 100% owned corporation (adjusted basis was $120,000 and selling price was $50,000)	_____	_____

5. Equipment with a useful life of seven years under MACRS and an ADR midpoint life of ten years was purchased on January 3, 1987, at a cost of $100,000. A § 179 deduction to expense was not elected. The equipment had an adjusted basis of $61,220 on January 3, 1989, when it was sold for $70,000. What are the tax consequences on the sale, and what adjustment is made to E & P?

6. X Corporation sells property, adjusted basis of $200,000, fair market value of $180,000, to its sole shareholder for $160,000. How much loss can the corporation deduct as a result of this transaction? What is the effect on the corporation's E & P for the year of sale?

7. M Corporation has beginning E & P of $60,000. Its current taxable income is $30,000. During the year it distributed land (not used in the active conduct of its business) worth $100,000, adjusted basis of $30,000, to T, one of its individual shareholders. T assumes a liability on the property in the amount of $10,000. The corporation had tax-exempt interest income of $2,000 and received $40,000 on a term life insurance policy on the death of a corporate officer. Premiums on the policy for the year were $1,000.

   a. What is the amount of taxable income to T?

   b. What is the amount of E & P for M Corporation after the property distribution?

   c. What is T's tax basis in the property he received?

   (Note: Disregard the effect of the corporate income tax.)

8. X Corporation, with E & P of $300,000, distributes property worth $70,000, adjusted tax basis of $100,000, to Y, a corporate shareholder. The property is subject to a liability of $15,000, which Y assumes.

    a. What is the amount of dividend income to Y?

    b. What is Y's basis in the property received?

    c. How does the distribution affect X Corporation's E & P account?

9. R & D Corporation had E & P of $45,000 when it made a current distribution of inventories with a cost of $60,000 and a fair market value of $105,000. Determine a sole shareholder's taxable income from the distribution.

10. A corporation distributes inventory to its shareholders. Basis of the inventory is $16,000, and fair market value is $32,000. What is the effect of this distribution on the corporation's taxable income and on its E & P?

11. AB Corporation distributes to its shareholders realty not used in the active conduct in its business with an adjusted basis of $5,000 and fair market value of $10,000. The realty is subject to a liability of $17,500. What is the effect of this distribution on taxable income of the corporation?

12. X Corporation, a cash method, calendar year taxpayer, had the following income and expenses in the current year: net profit from sales, $40,000; salaries paid to employees, $20,000; tax-exempt interest, $5,000; dividends from a corporation in which X Corporation holds a 5% interest, $8,000; STCL on the sale of stock, $6,000; estimated Federal income taxes paid, $2,300. X Corporation purchased five-year MACRS property in the current year for $28,000; no § 179 election was made. The property has a seven-year class life. Compute taxable income and E & P for X Corporation.

13. X Corporation distributes property not used in the active conduct of its business to A, an individual, as a property dividend. The property has a basis of $25,000 and a fair market value of $50,000. What are the tax consequences to X Corporation and to A?

14. What are the tax consequences to X Corporation and to A if instead of a property dividend, the distribution in Problem 13 were a stock redemption qualifying under § 302(b)(3)? A has a basis in her stock in X Corporation of $20,000.

15. X Corporation advances $60,000 as an interest-free loan to its shareholder, A (an individual). X Corporation can prove the advance is a bona fide loan. What are the tax consequences of the loan to X Corporation and to A?

16. A paid $30,000 for 15 shares of stock in XY Corporation five years ago. In November 1988, she received a nontaxable stock dividend of five additional shares in XY Corporation. She sells the five shares in March 1989 for $10,000. What is her gain, and how is it taxed?

17. AB Corporation declares a nontaxable dividend payable in rights to subscribe to common stock. One right and $60 entitles the holder to subscribe to one share of stock. One right is issued for each share of stock owned. T, a shareholder, owns 100 shares of stock that she purchased two years ago for $3,000. At the date of distribution of the rights, the market value of the stock was $80 and the market value of the rights was $20 per right. T received 100 rights. She exercises 60 rights and purchases 60 additional shares of stock. She sells the remaining 40 rights for $750. What are the tax consequences of these transactions to T?

18. V Corporation has 1,000 shares of common stock outstanding. The shares are owned by unrelated shareholders as follows: H, 400 shares; J, 400 shares; and K 200 shares. The corporation redeems 100 shares of the stock owned by K for $45,000. K paid $100 per share for her stock two years ago. The E & P of V Corporation was $100,000 on the date of redemption. What is the tax effect to K of the redemption?

19. In Problem 18, assume H is the father of K. How would this affect the tax status of the redemption? What if H were K's brother instead of her father?

20. X Corporation has 100 shares of common stock and 150 shares of preferred stock outstanding. A owns 60 shares of common stock of X Corporation and 75 shares of its preferred stock. B, unrelated, owns the remaining 40 shares of common stock and 75 shares of preferred stock. Determine whether the following redemptions would qualify under § 302(b)(2):

    a. X Corporation redeems all of A's preferred stock.

    b. X Corporation redeems all of A's preferred stock and 10 shares of A's common stock.

    c. X Corporation redeems 50 shares of A's preferred stock and 30 shares of A's common stock.

    d. X Corporation redeems 50 shares of A's preferred stock and 30 shares of A's common stock; it also redeems 20 shares of B's common stock.

21. Y Corporation is owned by A, S (A's son), and D (A's daughter). A owns 50 shares in Y, S owns 25, and D owns 25. In the current year, Y Corporation redeems all of A's shares. Determine whether the redemption qualifies under § 302(b)(3) under the following circumstances:

    a. A acquires 25 shares in Y Corporation when S dies two years later and leaves his property to A.

    b. A does not file an agreement with her tax return to notify the IRS of any acquisition of stock in Y Corporation in the next 10 years.

    c. A remains as a director in Y Corporation.

    d. A resigns as director of Y Corporation; D becomes a director of Y Corporation to replace A.

22. X Corporation has 200 shares of common stock outstanding, owned as follows: A, 100 shares; B (unrelated to A), 50 shares; estate of F (A's father), 50 shares. Determine whether the following redemptions of X Corporation stock qualify for exchange treatment:

    a. X Corporation redeems the stock of the estate of F. A is the beneficiary of F's estate.

    b. X Corporation redeems all of A's 100 shares. A is the beneficiary of F's estate.

    c. X Corporation redeems all of A's 100 shares and all of the 50 shares of the estate of F.

23. X Corporation, which has E & P of $6,000,000 manufactures widgets. In addition it operates a separate division that sells farm machinery. X Corporation also owns stock in several corporations which it purchased for investment purposes. The stock in X Corporation is held by A, an individual; and Y Corporation. Both A and Y Corporation own 100 shares in X Corporation purchased 10 years ago at a cost of $10,000 per share. Determine whether the following transactions qualify as partial liquidations under § 302(b)(4). In each transaction, determine the tax consequences to X Corporation, to Y Corporation, and to A, including the tax basis of any property received by the shareholders, A and Y Corporation.

    a. The division selling farm machinery was destroyed by fire. X Corporation decided to discontinue the business and distributed all the insurance collected as a result of the fire to A and to Y Corporation in redemption of 20 shares from each shareholder. The assets in the farm machinery division that were destroyed by fire had a basis to X Corporation of $1,000,000 and a fair market value of $5,000,000. The insurance recovery was $4,000,000.

b. X Corporation has manufactured widgets and sold farm machinery for 10 years. It decided in the current year to discontinue selling farm machinery and distributed all the assets of the farm machinery division to A and Y Corporation, equally, in redemption of 20 shares from each shareholder. The assets in the farm machinery division had a basis of $1,000,000 to X Corporation and a fair market value of $5,000,000 on the date of the distribution.

c. Assume that X Corporation had manufactured widgets for only two years but had sold farm machinery for the past ten years. It distributed the farm machinery equally to A and to Y Corporation as in (b) for half the shares A and Y Corporation held in X Corporation.

d. X Corporation distributed the stock it held in other corporations equally to A (an individual) and to Y Corporation in exchange for 10 shares of stock that A and Y Corporation held in X Corporation. The stock had a basis to X Corporation of $100,000 and a fair market value of $500,000 on the date of the distribution.

24. The adjusted gross estate of D, decedent, is $1,000,000. D's estate will incur death taxes and funeral and administration expenses of $120,000. D's gross estate includes stock in X Corporation (fair market value of $120,000, basis of $10,000) and stock in Y Corporation (fair market value of $200,000, basis of $50,000). D owned 25% of the stock in X Corporation and 40% of the stock in Y Corporation. If X Corporation redeems all of D's stock from D's estate, will the redemption qualify under § 303? Why or why not?

25. The gross estate of D, decedent, includes stock in A Corporation and B Corporation valued at $150,000 and $250,000, respectively. The adjusted gross estate of D is $900,000. D owned 30% of A stock and 60% of B stock. Death taxes and funeral and administration expenses for D's estate were $100,000. D had a basis of $60,000 in the A stock and $90,000 in the B stock. What are the tax consequences to D's estate if A Corporation redeems one third of D's stock for $50,000 and B Corporation redeems one fifth of D's stock for $50,000?

26. On December 31, 1987, prior to a stock redemption, TB Corporation had accumulated E & P of $50,000 and paid-in capital from the 1,000 shares outstanding of $150,000. One half of the stock was purchased by the corporation on that date for $75,000 cash in a redemption that was not equivalent to a dividend. In 1988, the corporation had current E & P of $25,000 and distributed $50,000 in cash to the shareholders on December 31. How much taxable income did the shareholders realize from the $50,000 distribution?

27. X Corporation has 500 shares of stock outstanding. It redeems 50 shares for $90,000 when it has paid-in capital of $300,000 and E & P of $400,000. What is the reduction in the E & P of X Corporation as a result of the redemption?

28. X Corporation has 100 shares of common stock outstanding owned as follows: A, 50 shares, and B (an unrelated party), 50 shares. A and B each paid $1,000 per share for the X Corporation stock 10 years ago. X Corporation has $100,000 accumulated E & P and $20,000 current E & P. X distributes land held as an investment (fair market value of $80,000, adjusted basis of $30,000) to A in redemption of 25 of A's shares.

a. What are the tax results to A on the redemption of A's stock in X Corporation?

b. What are the tax results to X Corporation on the redemption?

c. What is E & P of X Corporation after the redemption?

29. C and D are the sole shareholders of TZ Corporation, which has E & P of $500,000. C and D each have a basis in their 100 shares of TZ stock of $50,000. TZ Corporation issued an 8% preferred stock dividend on the common shares of C and D in 19X8. C and D each received 100 shares of preferred stock with a par value of $200 per share.

Fair market value of one share of common was $300, and fair market value of one share of preferred was $200.

a. What are the tax consequences of the distribution to C and D?

b. What are the tax consequences to C if he later sells his preferred stock to A for $40,000? A is unrelated to C.

c. What are the tax consequences to D if she subsequently sells all her stock (both common and preferred) to B for $80,000? B is unrelated to D.

d. What are the tax consequences to C and his son, S, if C dies and bequeaths his stock to S, who later sells the preferred stock to A for $50,000. The preferred stock had a fair market value of $45,000 on the date of C's death.

e. What are the tax consequences to D if she makes a gift to her daughter of the preferred stock?

30. T owns 200 shares of X Corporation and 100 shares of Y Corporation, representing 100% ownership of X and 50% ownership of Y. T sells 60 shares of Y Corporation to X Corporation for $90,000. T purchased the stock in Y Corporation three years ago at a cost of $1,000 per share. What are the tax consequences of the sale, assuming X Corporation has E & P of $80,000 and Y Corporation has E & P of $100,000?

31. A, an individual, owns 50% of T Corporation, which in turn owns 70% of Y Corporation. A sells 60 of his 100 shares in T Corporation to Y Corporation for $30,000. A purchased the 60 shares two years ago for $10,000. What are the tax consequences of the sale assuming T Corporation has E & P of $120,000 and Y Corporation has E & P of $50,000?

32. B owns 250 shares of stock in X Corporation and 200 shares of stock in Y Corporation, representing an 80% interest in both corporations. B sells 20 shares of Y stock to X Corporation for $20,000. The Y stock was acquired 10 years ago; the tax basis to B of these 20 shares is $2,000. B's share of the E & P of X Corporation is $10,000 on the date of sale; his share of the E & P of Y Corporation is $15,000. What are the tax consequences of this transaction?

33. T, an individual shareholder in P Corporation, exchanges stock in P (the parent corporation) for all the stock and some securities in S Corporation. The transaction meets the requirement of § 355. The stock in P that T exchanged had a fair market value of $120,000 and a tax basis of $80,000. The stock he received in S had a fair market value of $100,000; the securities had a fair market value of $20,000 and a principal amount of $22,000. What gain, if any, is recognized by T?

34. T Corporation has been engaged in the manufacture of farm equipment for over five years. The stock in T Corporation is held by W Corporation, which has sold automobiles for the past 10 years. W Corporation acquired the T Corporation stock eight years ago. A shareholder dispute occurred in the previous year. In the current year with the dispute still unresolved, W Corporation distributes all its stock in T Corporation to its shareholders.

a. What are the tax consequences of the distribution to R, an individual shareholder, who receives stock in T Corporation worth $60,000? R does not surrender any of her stock in W Corporation.

b. What would be the tax consequences to R if T Corporation had been in existence for only two years before the distribution?

Research Problems

Research Problem 1. The stock of X Corporation is held 10% by Y and 90% by Z. W would like to purchase all of this stock but has the cash to pay for only 60%. X Corporation has enough cash on hand to redeem 40% of its shares. Consider and evaluate, in terms of X Corporation, Y, Z, and W, the following alternatives:

a. X Corporation redeems 40% of the shares from Z. W purchases the remaining 50% held by Z and the 10% owned by Y.

b. W borrows enough money from a bank to purchase all of Y's and Z's shares. Later, W has X Corporation redeem 40% of the shares purchased to pay off the bank loan.

c. X Corporation redeems all of Y's shares. W purchases 60% of the shares held by Z. X Corporation then redeems the remainder of Z's 30% interest.

d. X Corporation distributes 90% of its cash to Z and 10% to Y. This reduces the value of the stock to a level where W's cash is adequate to purchase all of Z's and Y's shares.

Partial list of research aids:

Television Industries, Inc. v. Comm., 60–2 USTC ¶9795, 6 AFTR2d 5864, 284 F.2d 322 (CA–2, 1960).

Zenz v. Quinlivan, 54–2 USTC ¶9445, 45 AFTR 1672, 213 F.2d 914 (CA–6, 1954).

U.S. v. Carey, 61–1 USTC ¶9428, 7 AFTR2d 1301, 289 F.2d 531 (CA–8, 1961).

Research Problem 2. T is the president and majority shareholder of X Corporation. During 19X0, T was paid a salary of $50,000 and received a year-end bonus of $200,000. Upon audit in 19X1 of X Corporation, $150,000 of the amount paid to T was disallowed by the IRS as being unreasonable. Pursuant to a repayment agreement, T reimbursed X Corporation for the $150,000 in 19X2. On his 19X0 return, T had included the $150,000 in gross income. On his 19X2 return, he deducted none of the repayment but elected the option set forth in § 1341(a)(5). Thus, T claimed a credit for the amount of tax that was generated by the inclusion of the $150,000 on his 19X0 return. Upon audit of his 19X2 return in 19X3, the IRS did not accept the credit approach but did permit a deduction of $150,000 for 19X2. Because T was in a higher tax bracket in 19X0, a deficiency resulted for 19X2. T comes to you for advice. Should he challenge the tax deficiency for tax year 19X2?

Research Problem 3. J, the principal shareholder of X Corporation, diverted sums totaling $60,000 from the corporation during tax year 19X3. Upon audit of J's return, the IRS contended these sums were taxable income to J under § 61 of the Code. J disagrees, stating that such sums represent constructive dividends and are taxable only to the extent of X Corporation's E & P, which J argues had a deficit in 19X2. The IRS contends that should § 61 not apply, the $60,000 would still be taxable income because X Corporation had income in 19X3. X Corporation is on the cash basis. It had a deficit in its E & P account as of January 1, 19X3. However, it had E & P in 19X3 of $65,000. Its income tax liability for 19X3 was $31,500. The IRS argues that $31,500 cannot be a charge against current E & P, because the tax was not paid until 19X4 and the corporation was on the cash basis. Consequently, the $60,000 would be taxable income to J in 19X3, regardless of whether it is income under § 61 or under § 301. J comes to you for advice. What advice would you give him?

Research Problem 4. A, an individual, owned 80% of the common stock of XY Corporation. In 19X7, when XY Corporation had E & P of $300,000, it issued a pro rata dividend of preferred stock on common stock. As a result of the distribution, A received 100 shares of preferred stock which he did not report as income. In 19X7, A donated the preferred stock to his favorite charity, his alma mater. A deducted $100,000, the amount he determined to be the fair market value of the stock on the date of the gift, as a charitable contribution on his 19X7 income tax return. A's adjusted gross income for 19X7 was $500,000. Upon audit of A's return in 19X9, the IRS disallowed the deduction contending that the preferred stock was § 306 stock. Thus, according to the IRS, the gift was subject to the provisions of § 170(e)(1)(A) of the Code. A seeks your advice.

Research Problem 5. A owns 40% of X Corporation; his father owns the remaining 60%. A also owns 70% of Y Corporation, with the remaining 30% being owned by his wife. A terminates his entire interest in X Corporation through a stock redemption that he reports as a long-term capital gain pursuant to § 302(b)(3). Three years later, Y Corporation enters into a contract with X Corporation whereby Y Corporation is given exclusive management authority over X Corporation's operations. Upon audit, the IRS disallowed long-term capital gain treatment on the stock redemption in X Corporation contending that A acquired an interest in X within 10 years from the date of the redemption because of Y's management contract with X. What is the result?

Research Problem 6. X Corporation is controlled by H. As part of a property settlement incident to a divorce between H and W, X Corporation agrees to redeem the shares held by W (H's ex-wife). Because of cash-flow problems, the stock is to be redeemed in annual increments over a period from 19X1 to 19X6. Although the agreement is mandatory in its terms, no redemptions were carried out in 19X1 or 19X2; however, redemptions were effected in 19X3. W reports the gain on the redemption of her stock as a capital gain under § 302(b)(1) in 19X3. The IRS contends the redemption in 19X3 is a dividend, as there has not been a "meaningful reduction" in W's stock interests. W contends that although the redemption in 19X3 does not represent a meaningful reduction, when the redemptions are taken as a whole, the effect of all the redemptions does satisfy the meaningful reduction test. What is the result?

Research Problem 7. The stock of Y Corporation was owned equally by 20 individuals. It became necessary for Y to borrow money to purchase inventory and to pay its operating expenses. Y Corporation was able to obtain loans for three years but only on the condition that individuals with substantial net worth guarantee the loans. Three of Y's shareholders agreed to guarantee the loans. They were paid a fee for the guaranty in the amount of 5% of the average outstanding indebtedness, prorated among the guarantors in proportion to the sum each personally guaranteed. Y Corporation deducted these fees—$30,000 in 1981 and $35,000 in 1982. Upon audit of Y's return in 1984, the IRS disallowed the deductions, reclassifying them as dividends. What is the result if Y challenges the tax deficiency?

5 Corporations: Distributions in Complete Liquidation

Objectives

Contrast property dividends and stock redemptions with distributions in complete liquidation of a corporation.

Review the tax effect on the shareholders of a corporation being liquidated.

Review the tax effect of a complete liquidation on the corporation being liquidated.

Recognize the tax planning opportunities available to minimize the income tax result in the complete liquidation of a corporation.

Outline

When a stock redemption is transacted or a dividend is distributed, the assumption usually is that the corporation will continue as a separate entity. With complete liquidation, however, corporate existence terminates. In view of the difference in the result, the tax rules governing this type of distribution differ from those relating to a dividend distribution or to a stock redemption.

Recall that a property distribution, whether in the form of a dividend or a stock redemption, produces gain (but not loss) to the distributing corporation. For the shareholder, the fair market value of a property dividend produces ordinary income to the extent of the corporation's E & P. A stock redemption qualifying under § 302 or § 303 is afforded exchange treatment.

The tax effects to the corporation of a complete liquidation vary somewhat. With the exception of certain distributions to related parties (in which case loss recognition is limited) and the liquidation of an 80 percent or more controlled subsidiary, a liquidating corporation recognizes gain *and* loss upon distribution of its assets. The shareholders receive exchange treatment on receipt of the property from the liquidating corporation. The distribution of assets is treated as payment for the shareholders' stock, resulting in either a gain or a loss.

Liquidations and stock redemptions parallel each other as to the effect of E & P on such distributions. For the corporation undergoing liquidation, E & P has no tax impact on the gain or loss to be recognized by the shareholders. This is so because § 301 (governing dividend distributions) is specifically made inapplicable to complete liquidations.[1]

Example 1   Z Corporation, with E & P of $40,000, makes a cash distribution of $50,000 to its sole shareholder. Assume the shareholder's basis in the Z Corporation stock is $20,000 and the stock is held as an investment. If the distribution is not in complete liquidation or if it does not qualify as a stock redemption, the shareholder must recognize dividend income of $40,000 (i.e., the amount of Z Corporation's E & P) and must treat the remaining $10,000 of the distribution as a return of capital. On the other hand, if the distribution is pursuant to a complete liquidation or qualifies for exchange treatment as a stock redemption, the shareholder will have a recognized capital gain of $30,000 [$50,000 (the amount of the distribution) − $20,000 (the basis in the stock)]. In the latter case, note that Z Corporation's E & P is of no consequence to the tax result. □

In the event the distribution results in a *loss* to the shareholder, an important distinction could exist between stock redemptions and liquidations. The distinction could arise because § 267 (i.e., disallowance of losses between related parties) is applicable to stock redemptions but generally not to liquidations.

Example 2   The stock of P Corporation is owned equally by three brothers, R, S, and T. At a point when T's basis in his stock investment is $40,000, the corporation distributes $30,000 to him in cancellation of all his shares. If the distribution is a stock redemption, the $10,000 realized loss is not

---

1. § 331(b).

recognized.[2] T and P Corporation are related parties because T is deemed to own more than 50% in value of the corporation's outstanding stock. Although T's direct ownership is limited to 33⅓%, through his brothers he owns indirectly another 66⅔% for a total of 100%. Had the distribution qualified as a complete liquidation, T's $10,000 realized loss would be recognizable. ☐

With reference to the basis of noncash property received from the corporation, the rules governing liquidations and stock redemptions are identical. Section 334(a) specifies that the basis of such property distributed pursuant to a complete liquidation under § 331 shall be the fair market value on the date of distribution.

The tax consequences of a complete liquidation of a corporation are examined in this chapter from the standpoint of the effect on the distributing corporation and on the shareholder. Tax rules differ when a controlled subsidiary is liquidated. Thus, the rules relating to the liquidation of a controlled subsidiary receive separate treatment.

Effect on the Distributing Corporation

For the corporation in the process of complete liquidation, §§ 336 and 337 as amended by the Tax Reform Act (TRA) of 1986 govern the tax results. The general rules relating to complete liquidations are covered in § 336, wherein gain or loss is recognized to the distributing corporation. However, for certain distributions to related shareholders, loss is not recognized. Under § 337, no gain or loss is recognized to a subsidiary corporation for distributions to a parent corporation that owns 80 percent or more of the stock of the subsidiary.

Background

Originally, a corporate distribution of property, whether a liquidating or a nonliquidating distribution, produced neither gain nor loss to the distributing corporation. This nonrecognition concept was sometimes referred to as the *General Utilities* rule.[3] The doctrine was codified in 1954 with the enactment of § 311 for nonliquidating distributions (refer to Chapter 4) and § 336 for liquidating distributions. Both of these Sections provided for nonrecognition of gain or loss on corporate distributions. Later, § 337 was added to the Code to

---

2. *McCarthy v. Conley, Jr.,* 65–1 USTC ¶ 9262, 15 AFTR2d 447, 341 F.2d 948 (CA–2, 1965).
3. The doctrine was attributed to the 1935 Supreme Court decision in *General Utilities & Operating Co. v. Helvering,* 36–1 USTC ¶ 9012, 16 AFTR 1126, 56 S.Ct. 185 (USSC, 1935). Actually, the case involved a dividend distribution. In *General Utilities,* the Supreme Court rejected the contention of the IRS that distribution of a dividend to a corporation's shareholders was the equivalent of a sale in that it satisfied a corporate debt that the corporation owed to its shareholders as a result of the dividend declaration. The opinion actually ignored the other contention of the IRS that a corporation realizes the appreciation on property it distributes to its shareholders. Nonetheless, the case was regarded as providing the general rule that no gain was recognized by a corporation upon the distribution of property to shareholders in complete liquidation.

continue the rule of § 336 for sales during a 12-month period by a corporation in complete liquidation.

Despite the breadth of the nonrecognition language of §§ 336 and 337 for corporations in complete liquidation, the rule of nonrecognition was not without exception. Statutory and judicial modifications and interpretations had, over the years, significantly increased the number of recognition situations. For example, §§ 336 and 337 did not bar the recapture of depreciation taken on distributed assets[4] or the recapture of investment tax credit.[5] Under the tax benefit rule, a corporation had to take into income any assets distributed to the shareholders for which it had previously claimed a deduction.[6] The assignment of income doctrine was applied to distributions in liquidation and to sales by the liquidating corporation despite § 337.[7] Gain resulted from the distribution or sale of LIFO inventory[8] and installment notes receivable.[9] The sale of inventory (unless it was sold in bulk to one person in one transaction) was excepted from the nonrecognition provisions of § 337.[10] Because of the many modifications, §§ 336 and 337 clearly did not shield the liquidating corporation from recognition of all income.

With the many statutory and judicial inroads, there was actually not much left of the *General Utilities* doctrine in 1986 when it was repealed. Foremost among those transfers that did remain, wherein the doctrine insulated the liquidating corporation from a recognition result, were the following: distributions in kind and sale of investment assets (e.g., marketable securities and land), distributions in kind and bulk sales of non-LIFO inventory, and the § 1231 element as to assets used in a trade or business.

By amending §§ 336 and 337, effective for liquidations completed after July 31, 1986, TRA of 1986 rescinded what was left of the *General Utilities* rule. As a consequence, the corporation being liquidated will, as a general rule, recognize gains and losses on distributions of property.

Example 3   Pursuant to a complete liquidation, R Corporation (not a closely-held corporation) distributes the following assets to its shareholders: land held as an investment (basis of $150,000, fair market value of $300,000), non-LIFO inventory (basis of $50,000, fair market value of $40,000), and marketable securities (basis of $100,000, fair market value of $120,000). If the liquidation were completed in 1985, R Corporation would recognize no gain or loss as a result of the distribution. However, if the liquidation were completed in 1987, R Corporation would have a gain of $170,000 ($150,000 + $20,000) and a loss of $10,000. □

---

4. §§ 1245(d), 1250(i), and 291(a).
5. § 47(a).
6. *Bliss Dairy, Inc. v. Comm.,* 83–1 USTC ¶ 9229, 51 AFTR2d 83–874, 103 S.Ct. 1134 (USSC, 1983).
7. *Pridemark, Inc. v. Comm.,* 65–1 USTC ¶ 9388, 15 AFTR2d 853, 345 F.2d 35 (CA–4, 1965), and *Standard Paving Co. v. Comm.,* 51–2 USTC ¶ 9376, 40 AFTR 1022, 190 F.2d 330 (CA–10, 1951).
8. §§ 336(b) and 337(f) before amendment by TRA of 1986.
9. § 453B(a).
10. § 337(b) before amendment by TRA of 1986.

General Rule after TRA of 1986

Section 336 now provides that with the exception of property distributed to a parent in complete liquidation of a subsidiary (covered by § 337 as amended and discussed later in the chapter), gain or loss is recognized to a liquidating corporation on the distribution of property in complete liquidation as if such property were sold to the distributee at the fair market value. This Section, which has repealed the *General Utilities* doctrine, strengthens the notion of double taxation that is inherent with operating a business in the corporate form. As a result, liquidating distributions are subject to tax both at the corporate level and at the shareholder level.

When property distributed in a complete liquidation is subject to a liability of the liquidating corporation, the fair market value of that property cannot be less than the amount of the liability.

Example 4   Pursuant to a complete liquidation, T Corporation (not a closely-held corporation) distributes to its shareholders land held as an investment (basis of $200,000, fair market value of $300,000). The land is subject to a liability in the amount of $350,000. T Corporation has a gain of $150,000 on the distribution. □

Limitation on Losses.   Because the abolition of the *General Utilities* rule opens the door for recognition of losses in a liquidation, Congress was concerned that taxpayers might attempt to avoid the repeal of the rule by creating artificial losses at the corporate level. Taxpayers could accomplish this by contributing property with built-in losses to the corporation before a liquidation. Recall from Chapter 3 that in § 351 transfers (i.e., nontaxable transfers to a corporation in exchange for stock when the transferor is in control of the corporation) and contributions to capital, the transferor's income tax basis carries over to the transferee corporation. Thus, high basis, low fair market value property could be transferred to a corporation contemplating liquidation with the expectation that such built-in losses might neutralize expected gains from appreciated property distributed or sold in the liquidation process. Section 336(d) closes this possibility by imposing restrictions on the deductibility of losses in related party situations (those covered by § 267). A corporation and a shareholder are related parties if the shareholder owns (directly or indirectly) more than 50 percent in value of the corporation's outstanding stock.

Once the related party situation is present, losses will be disallowed on distributions to the related parties in either of the following cases: (1) the distribution is not pro rata or (2) the property distributed is disqualified property (property acquired by the liquidating corporation in a § 351 transaction or as a contribution to capital during a five-year period ending on the date of the distribution).

Important →

Example 5   Z Corporation's stock is held equally by three brothers. One year before Z's liquidation, the shareholders transfer property (basis of $150,000, fair market value of $100,000) to Z Corporation in return for stock (i.e., a § 351 transaction). In liquidation, Z Corporation transfers the property (still worth $100,000) to the brothers. Because § 267 applies (each brother owns directly and indirectly 100% of the stock) and disqualified property is involved, none of the $50,000 realized loss may be recognized by Z Corporation.

If a liquidating corporation acquired property in a § 351 transaction or as a contribution to capital as part of a plan, the principal purpose of which was to recognize loss by the corporation in connection with the liquidation, losses are disallowed even on distributions to shareholders who are not related parties. Such a purpose will be presumed if the transfer occurs within two years of the adoption of the plan of liquidation. However, it may be possible for a liquidating corporation to recognize some loss on disqualified property. The basis of such property (for liquidation loss purposes) is reduced by the excess of the property's basis on the contribution date over the property's fair market value on such date.[11] Thus, any subsequent decline in value to the point of the liquidating distribution results in a deductible loss.

Example 6   Z Corporation's stock is held 60% by A and 40% by B. One year before Z's liquidation, property (basis of $150,000, fair market value of $100,000) is transferred to Z Corporation as a contribution to capital. In liquidation, Z Corporation transfers the property (now worth $90,000) to B. Because the distribution was to an unrelated party, the basis is reduced to $100,000 for liquidation purposes [$150,000 (carryover basis under § 362)–$50,000 (difference between carryover basis of $150,000 and fair market value of $100,000)]. A loss of $10,000 ($100,000–$90,000) can be recognized. (If the property had been distributed to A, a related party, even the $10,000 loss would be disallowed.) □

Small Corporation Exception. An exception to the general rule under § 336 exists for certain small closely-held corporations if the liquidation of such a corporation is completed before January 1, 1989. In such cases, some of the gain or loss is not recognized to the liquidating corporation. But even if the exception applies, gains and losses on ordinary income property and short-term capital gains and losses are recognized.

To qualify for the exception, a corporation must satisfy two conditions. First, more than 50 percent in value of the stock of the corporation must be held by 10 or fewer noncorporate shareholders on August 1, 1986, and at all times thereafter. Value refers to the fair market value of all of the stock of the corporation on the date of adoption of the plan of liquidation (or, if greater, on August 1, 1986). Second, the value of the corporation must not exceed $10,000,000.

If the value of the corporation does not exceed $5,000,000, 100 percent of the insulated gain or loss is not recognized. If the value ranges from $5,000,000 to $10,000,000, the percentage of the insulated gain or loss is 100 percent reduced by 100 percent multiplied by a fraction, the numerator of which is the value of the corporation in excess of $5,000,000 and the denominator of which is $5,000,000.

---

11. § 336(d)(2).

Example 7   X Corporation has been in existence since 1980 and has had five share-holders, all of whom are individuals. A plan of liquidation is adopted in 1988, at which time X's stock has a value of $7,500,000, and the liquidation is completed in the same year. X Corporation's assets consist of a tract of land (basis of $1,000,000, fair market value of $4,000,000) and inventory property (basis of $50,000, fair market value of $90,000). Tax consequences of the liquidation are as follows:

—X Corporation qualifies for the small corporation exception to the general rule under § 336. More than 50 percent of the value of the stock was held by 10 or fewer shareholders who held the stock on August 1, 1986. Value of the corporate stock does not exceed $10,000,000, and the liquidation was completed before January 1, 1989.

—Even though X Corporation qualifies for the small corporation exception, it must recognize gain on ordinary income property and thus must recognize $40,000 gain on the inventory property.

—Because the value of the corporate stock exceeds $5,000,000, only a portion of the $3,000,000 appreciated value of the land is insulated. The insulated gain of $1,500,000 that must be recognized is computed as follows: $3,000,000 $\times$ 50%. The applicable percentage (50%) is 100% minus [100% $\times$ ($2,500,000/$5,000,000)]. [The numerator of the fraction is $7,500,000 (value of the corporation)–$5,000,000.]

—X Corporation recognizes a total gain of $1,540,000 on the liquidation—$40,000 (gain on distribution of the inventory) plus $1,500,000 (gain recognized on distribution of the land). □

Expenses of Liquidation.   The general expenses involved in liquidating a corporation are deductible to the corporation as business expenses under § 162. Examples include the legal and accounting cost of drafting a plan of liquidation and the cost of revocation of the corporate charter. Liquidation expenses relating to the disposition of corporate assets are also deductible. Expenses relating to the sale of corporate assets, including a brokerage commission for the sale of real estate and a legal fee to clear title, are offset against the selling price of the assets.

Example 8   During its liquidation, R Corporation incurs the following expenses:

General liquidation expenses	$12,000
Legal expenses to effect a distribution of property	200
Sales commissions to sell inventory	3,000
Brokerage fee on sale of real estate	8,000

R Corporation can deduct $12,200 (i.e., $12,000 + $200). The $3,000 commission and the $8,000 brokerage fee are applied against the selling price of the inventory and the real estate. □

Filing Requirements for Corporate Liquidations.   A copy of the minutes of the shareholders' meeting in which the plan of liquidation was adopted must be attached to the income tax return for the liquidating corporation. In addition, a statement must be included listing the assets sold, with dates of sales given. The statement should include computations of gain or loss both realized and recognized on the sales. Form 966, Corporate Dissolution or Liquidation, must be filed with the IRS within 30 days after the adoption of the plan of liquidation. Notification of this type is also required by some states. Information returns (Form 1099–DIV, transmitted to each shareholder on or before January 31 of the year following the liquidation, and Form 1096, sent to the IRS by February 28) notify shareholders of their respective gains or losses.

Effect on the Shareholder— The General Rule under § 331

The tax consequences to the shareholders of a corporation in the process of liquidation are governed by the general rule under § 331 and two exceptions under §§ 332 and 338 (both exceptions relating to the liquidation of a subsidiary). Section 333, repealed by TRA of 1986, is available as an exception until January 1, 1989, for those corporations subject to the small corporation exception and whose assets principally consist of long-term capital gain assets.

The General Rule under § 331

In the case of a complete liquidation, the general rule under § 331(a)(1) provides for exchange treatment. Since § 1001(c) requires the recognition of gain or loss on the sale or exchange of property, the end result is to treat the shareholder as having sold his or her stock to the corporation being liquidated. Thus, the difference between the fair market value of the assets received from the corporation and the adjusted basis of the stock surrendered (i.e., realized gain or loss) becomes the amount that is recognized. If the stock is a capital asset in the hands of the shareholder, capital gain or loss results.[12] As is usually true, the burden of proof is on the taxpayer to furnish evidence on the adjusted basis of the stock. In the absence of such evidence, the stock will be deemed to have a zero basis, and the full amount of the liquidation proceeds represents the amount of the gain to be recognized.[13]

Section 334(a) provides that under the general rule of § 331, the income tax basis to the shareholder of property received in a liquidation will be the property's fair market value on the date of distribution. The general rule follows the same approach taken with stock redemptions that qualify for exchange treatment (refer to Chapter 4).

Special Rule for Certain Installment Obligations

Section 453(h) provides some relief from the bunching of gain problem encountered when a liquidating corporation sells its assets. Although the liquidating

---

12. For insight as to what represents a capital asset, see § 1221 and *Corn Products Refining Co. v. Comm.*, 55–2 USTC ¶ 9746, 47 AFTR 1789, 76 S.Ct. 20 (USSC, 1955).
13. *John Calderazzo*, 34 TCM 1, T.C. Memo. 1975–1.

corporation must recognize all gain on such sales (unless it is a qualifying small corporation and completes the liquidation before January 1, 1989), the shareholders' gain on the receipt of notes obtained by the corporation on the sale of its assets may be deferred to the point of collection.[14] Such treatment will require the shareholders to allocate their bases in the stock among the various assets received from the corporation.

Example 9   In 1988, after a plan of complete liquidation has been adopted, X Corporation sells its only asset—unimproved land held as an investment that has appreciated in value—to P (an unrelated party) for $100,000. Under the terms of the sale, X Corporation receives cash of $25,000 and P's notes for the balance of $75,000. The notes are payable over 10 years ($7,500 per year) and carry an 11% rate of interest. Immediately after the sale, X Corporation distributes the cash and notes to S, an individual and sole shareholder. Assume that S has an adjusted basis in the X Corporation stock of $20,000 and that the installment notes possess a value equal to the face amount (i.e., $75,000). The tax result of these transactions is summarized as follows:

—No gain is recognized to X Corporation on the sale of the land, because X Corporation qualifies as a small corporation. (Refer to the discussion under Effect on the Distributing Corporation—General Rule After TRA of 1986, Small Corporation Exception.)

—S must allocate the adjusted basis in the stock ($20,000) between the cash and the installment notes. Using the relative fair market value approach, 25% [$25,000 (amount of cash)/$100,000 (total distribution)] of $20,000 (adjusted basis in the stock), or $5,000, is allocated to the cash, and 75% [$75,000 (FMV of notes)/$100,000 (total distribution)] of $20,000 (adjusted basis in the stock), or $15,000, is allocated to the notes.

—S must recognize $20,000 [$25,000 (cash received) − $5,000 (allocated basis of the cash)] in the year of the liquidation.

—Since S's gross profit on the notes is $60,000 [$75,000 (contract price) − $15,000 (allocated basis of the notes)], the gross profit percentage is 80% [$60,000 (gross profit)/$75,000 (contract price)]. Thus, S must report a gain of $6,000 [$7,500 (amount of note) × 80% (gross profit percentage)] on the collection of each note over the next 10 years. The interest element would be accounted for separately. □

If distributions are received by the shareholder in more than one taxable year, basis reallocations may necessitate the filing of amended returns.[15]

---

14. Section 453(h) does not apply to the sale of inventory property and property held by the corporation primarily for sale to customers in the ordinary course of its trade or business unless such property is sold in bulk to one person.

15. § 453(h)(2). For an example of such a possibility, see the Finance Committee Report on H.R. 6883 (reported with amendments on September 26, 1980), the Installment Sales Revision Act of 1980.

Special rules apply if the installment obligations arise from sales between certain related parties.[16]

Effect on the Shareholder— Election under § 333

Section 333 was an exception to the general rule that a shareholder has a gain or loss upon a corporate liquidation. This provision permitted qualified shareholders to postpone some or all of the gain on a complete liquidation. Although § 333 was repealed by TRA of 1986, qualified shareholders of corporations subject to the small corporation exception may elect under § 333 if the liquidation of such corporation is completed before January 1, 1989. Benefits of the election will phase out for corporations with a value between $5,000,000 and $10,000,000 in the same manner as discussed under Effect on the Distributing Corporation—General Rule After TRA of 1986, Small Corporation Exception.

If shareholders elect and the liquidation is completed within some one calendar month, § 333 postpones the recognition of gain on assets with substantial appreciation unrealized by the corporation on the date of liquidation, but only as to those assets that would generate a long-term capital gain if they were sold. The shareholder does have recognized gain in an amount equal to the greater of (1) the shareholder's share of E & P accumulated after February 28, 1913, or (2) the amounts received by the shareholder consisting of money and stock and securities acquired by the corporation after 1953. In no event may recognized gain exceed realized gain. Only qualifying electing shareholders are entitled to the benefits of § 333.

A corporate shareholder owning 50 percent or more of the stock of a liquidating corporation cannot qualify under § 333. The remaining shareholders are divided into two groups: (1) noncorporate shareholders and (2) those corporate shareholders owning less than 50 percent of the stock in the liquidating corporation. Owners of stock possessing at least 80 percent of the total combined voting power of all classes of stock owned by shareholders in one of the two specified groups must elect the provisions of § 333. If the 80 percent requirement is not met, the one-month liquidation treatment is not available to any member of that group. If owners of 80 percent of the stock in a particular group have elected § 333 and if a particular shareholder involved has also elected, such party becomes a qualifying electing shareholder. Shareholders not qualifying for or electing § 333 would come under the general rule of § 331, and their gain or loss would be determined by the difference between the fair market value of the assets received in the liquidation and the adjusted basis of the stock investment.

An election to have liquidation proceeds taxed under § 333 is made on Form 964, Election of Shareholder Under Section 333 Liquidation. The form must be filed by the shareholder within 30 days after the adoption of a plan of liquidation or the election is not available. But even if the election is properly made and timely filed, § 333 will not apply unless the corporation is liquidated

---

16. §§ 453(h)(1)(C) and (D). For this purpose, related parties are defined in § 1239(b).

within one calendar month. However, the month chosen to carry out the liquidation need not be the same month in which the election is made.

Gain on each share of stock held by a qualified electing shareholder at the time of adoption of a plan of liquidation is recognized under § 333 only to the extent of the *greater* of the following:

1. The shareholder's ratable portion of E & P of the corporation accumulated after February 28, 1913, computed as of the last day of the month of liquidation, without reduction for distributions made during that month and including all items of income and expense accrued to the date on which the transfer of all property under the liquidation is completed, plus or minus the gain or loss recognized upon the liquidation to a qualified small corporation from ordinary-income producing assets and those assets that would produce a short-term capital gain or loss.
2. The shareholder's ratable portion of the sum of cash and the fair market value of all stock or securities (acquired by the corporation after December 31, 1953) received by the shareholder.

Dividend income to noncorporate shareholders is that portion of recognized gain not in excess of the shareholder's ratable share of E & P. To those noncorporate shareholders who hold the corporation's stock as an investment, the remainder of the gain is either short-term or long-term capital gain, depending on the length of time the stock has been held. A qualified electing corporate shareholder has no dividend income, and all recognized gain is capital gain.

Because gain is recognized to those small closely-held corporations on assets that would produce ordinary income or short-term capital gain in spite of the small corporation exception, that income is added to the corporation's E & P. If E & P is substantial, no benefit is attached to an election under § 333. For that reason, the benefits of § 333 are limited to those small corporations whose assets consist principally of assets that would produce a long-term capital gain upon a sale.

Basis of property received in a liquidation wherein a shareholder elects under § 333 is the same as the basis of the shares redeemed decreased by the amount of money received and increased by gain recognized and liabilities assumed by the shareholder.

Effect on the Shareholder— Liquidation of a Subsidiary

Section 332 is an exception to the general rule that the shareholder recognizes gain or loss on a corporate liquidation. If a parent corporation liquidates a subsidiary corporation in which it owns at least 80 percent of the voting stock, no gain or loss is recognized for distributions to the parent.[17]

The requirements for application of § 332 are (1) the parent must own at least 80 percent of the voting stock of the subsidiary and at least 80 percent of

17. § 337(a).

the total value of the subsidiary's stock, (2) the subsidiary must distribute all its property in complete redemption of all its stock within the taxable year or within three years from the close of the tax year in which a plan was adopted and the first distribution occurred, and (3) the subsidiary must be solvent.[18] If these requirements are met, § 332 becomes mandatory.

When a series of distributions occurs in the liquidation of a subsidiary corporation, the parent corporation must own the required amount of stock (80 percent) on the date of adoption of a plan of liquidation and at all times until all property has been distributed.[19] If the parent fails to qualify at any time, the provisions for nonrecognition of gain or loss do not apply to any distribution.[20] If a liquidation is not completed within one taxable year, for each taxable year that falls wholly or partly within the period of liquidation, the parent corporation shall file with its income tax return a waiver of the statute of limitations on assessment. The parent corporation may be forced to file a bond with the District Director to insure prompt payment of taxes should § 332 not apply.[21]

For the taxable year in which the plan of liquidation is adopted and for all taxable years within the period of liquidation, the parent corporation must file with its return a statement of all facts pertaining to the liquidation including a copy of the plan, a list of all properties received showing cost and fair market value, a statement of indebtedness of the subsidiary corporation to the parent, and a statement of ownership of all classes of stock of the liquidating corporation.[22]

Tax Treatment When a Minority Interest Exists

A distribution to a minority shareholder in a § 332 liquidation is treated in the same manner as one made pursuant to a nonliquidating redemption. Accordingly, gain (but not loss) is recognized to the distributing corporation on the property distributed to the minority shareholder.

Example 10   The stock of S Corporation is held as follows: 80% by P Corporation and 20% by T, an individual. S Corporation is liquidated on December 10, 1987, pursuant to a plan adopted on January 10, 1987. At the time of its liquidation, S Corporation had assets with a basis of $100,000 and fair market value of $500,000. S Corporation will have to recognize gain of $80,000 [($500,000 fair market value − $100,000 basis) × 20% minority interest]. The remaining gain of $320,000 will be sheltered by § 337(a). □

The minority shareholder is subject to the general rule of § 331. Accordingly, the difference between the fair market value of the assets distributed and the basis of the minority shareholder's stock is the amount of gain or loss recognized by the minority shareholder. The tax basis of property received by

---

18. Reg. §§ 1.332–2(a) and (b).
19. The date of the adoption of a plan of complete liquidation could be crucial in determining whether § 332 applies. See, for example, *George L. Riggs, Inc.,* 64 T.C. 474 (1975).
20. Reg. § 1.332–2(a).
21. Reg. § 1.332–4(a).
22. Reg. § 1.332–6.

the minority shareholder will be the property's fair market value as of the date of distribution.[23]

Indebtedness of Subsidiary to Parent

If a subsidiary satisfies a debt owed to the parent with appreciated property, it must recognize gain on the transaction unless § 332 applies. When § 332 is applicable, gain or loss is not recognized by the subsidiary upon the transfer of properties to the parent even though some properties are transferred to satisfy the subsidiary's indebtedness to the parent.[24]

Example 11   S Corporation owes its parent, P Corporation, $20,000. It satisfies the obligation by transferring land (worth $20,000 with a tax basis of $8,000). Normally, S Corporation would recognize a gain of $12,000 on the transaction. However, if the transfer is made pursuant to a liquidation under § 332, S Corporation would not recognize a gain. □

Realized gain or loss is recognized by the parent corporation on the satisfaction of indebtedness, even though property is received during liquidation of the subsidiary. The special provision noted above does not apply to the parent corporation.

Example 12   P Corporation purchased bonds of its subsidiary S at a discount. Upon liquidation of the subsidiary pursuant to § 332, P received payment in the face amount of the bonds. The transaction has no tax effect on S Corporation. However, P Corporation must recognize gain in the amount of the difference between its basis in the bonds and the amount received in payment. □

If a parent corporation does not receive at least partial payment for its stock in a subsidiary corporation upon liquidation of the subsidiary, § 332 will not apply.[25] The parent corporation would then have a bad debt deduction for the difference between the value of any properties received from the subsidiary and its basis in the subsidiary debt.

Section 332 does not apply to the liquidation of an insolvent subsidiary corporation. If the subsidiary is insolvent, the parent corporation would have a loss deduction for its worthless stock in the subsidiary. The loss would be ordinary if more than 90 percent of the gross receipts for all tax years of the subsidiary were from sources other than passive sources.[26] Otherwise, the loss would be a capital loss.

Example 13   P Corporation paid $100,000 for all the stock of S Corporation 15 years ago. At present, S has a deficit of $600,000 in E & P. If P liquidates S, § 332 would not apply, because S is insolvent. P Corporation would have a loss deduction for its worthless stock in S Corporation. If more than 90% of the

---

23. § 334(a).
24. § 337(b).
25. Reg. § 1.332–2(b).
26. See § 165(g) and Reg. § 1.165–5.

gross receipts of S Corporation for all tax years were from sources other than passive sources, the loss would be ordinary. Otherwise, it would be a capital loss. Assume P also loaned S Corporation $50,000. Since the assets are not sufficient to pay the liabilities, P would also have a loss on the note. Upon liquidation, the basis of the assets of S to P would be the fair market value. P's loss would be measured by the fair market value of S's assets less the liabilities payable to third parties less P's basis in the S stock and note. □

Basis of Property Received by the Parent Corporation

The General Rule of § 334(b)(1). Unless a parent corporation elects under § 338, property received by the parent corporation in a complete liquidation of its subsidiary under § 332 has the same basis it had in the hands of the subsidiary.[27] The parent's basis in stock of the liquidated subsidiary disappears. This is true even though some of the property was transferred to the parent in satisfaction of debt owed the parent by the subsidiary.

Example 14   P, the parent corporation, has a basis of $20,000 in stock in S Corporation, a subsidiary in which it owns 85% of all classes of stock. P Corporation purchased the stock of S Corporation 10 years ago. In the current year, P Corporation liquidates S Corporation and acquires assets worth $50,000 with a tax basis to S Corporation of $40,000. P Corporation would have a basis of $40,000 in the assets, with a potential gain upon sale of $10,000. P Corporation's original $20,000 basis in S Corporation's stock disappears. □

Example 15   P Corporation has a basis of $60,000 in stock in S Corporation, a subsidiary acquired 10 years ago. It liquidates S Corporation and receives assets worth $50,000 with a tax basis to S Corporation of $40,000. P Corporation again has a basis of $40,000 in the assets it acquired from S Corporation. If it sells the assets, it will have a gain of $10,000 in spite of the fact that its basis in S Corporation stock was $60,000. P Corporation's loss will never be recognized. □

Because the parent corporation takes the subsidiary's basis in its assets, the carryover rules of § 381 apply (see Chapter 6). The parent would acquire a net operating loss of the subsidiary, any investment credit carryover, capital loss carryover, and a carryover of E & P of the subsidiary. Section 381 applies to most tax-free reorganizations and to a tax-free liquidation under § 332 if the subsidiary's bases in its assets carry over to the parent.

The Election of § 338. Under the general rule of § 332(b)(1), problems developed when a subsidiary was liquidated shortly after acquisition by a parent corporation.

---

27. § 334(b)(1) and Reg. § 1.334–1(b).

1. When the basis of the subsidiary's assets was in excess of the purchase price of the stock, the parent received a step-up in basis in such assets at no tax cost. If, for example, the parent paid $100,000 for the subsidiary's stock and the basis of the assets transferred to the parent was $150,000, the parent enjoyed a $50,000 benefit without any gain recognition. The $50,000 increase in basis of the subsidiary's assets could have led to additional depreciation deductions and either more loss or less gain upon the later disposition of the assets by the parent.
2. If the basis of the subsidiary's assets were below the purchase price of the stock, the parent suffered a step-down in basis in such assets with no attendant tax benefit. Return to Example 15. If the situation is changed slightly—the subsidiary's stock is not held for 10 years, but the subsidiary is liquidated shortly after acquisition—the basic inequity of the "no loss" situation is apparent. (Any number of reasons that one corporation would pay more for the stock in another corporation than the latter's basis in the assets could exist. For one, the basis of the assets has no necessary correlation to the fair market value. For another, the acquiring corporation might have no choice in the matter if it really wants the assets. The shareholders in the acquired corporation might prefer to sell their stock rather than the assets of the corporation. Tax consequences would undoubtedly have some bearing on such a decision.)

In the landmark decision of *Kimbell-Diamond Milling Co. v. Comm.,*[28] the courts finally resolved these problems. When a parent corporation liquidates a subsidiary shortly after the acquisition of its stock, the parent is really purchasing the assets of the subsidiary. Consequently, the basis of such assets should be the cost of the stock. Known as the "single transaction" approach, the basis determination is not made under the general rule of § 334(b)(1). The *Kimbell-Diamond* problem ultimately led to the enactment of § 338.

Section 338 provides that for a qualified stock purchase as defined below, an acquiring corporation may, by the fifteenth day of the ninth month beginning after the month in which the qualified stock purchase occurs, make an irrevocable election to treat the acquisition as a purchase of the assets of the acquired corporation. If the parent elects under § 338, the purchasing corporation will have a basis in the subsidiary's assets equal to its basis in the subsidiary's stock. The subsidiary need not be liquidated.

A purchasing corporation makes a qualified stock purchase if it acquires at least 80 percent of the voting power and at least 80 percent of the value of the acquired corporation within a 12-month period beginning with the first purchase of stock. The stock must be acquired in a taxable transaction (e.g., § 351 and other nonrecognition provisions do not apply). An acquisition of stock by any member of an affiliated group, including the purchasing corporation, is considered to be an acquisition by the purchasing corporation.

Under § 338, the acquired corporation is deemed to have sold its assets for an amount equal to the purchasing corporation's grossed-up basis in the subsidiary's stock adjusted for liabilities of the subsidiary corporation. The

---

28. 14 T.C. 74 (1950), *aff'd.* in 51–1 USTC ¶ 9201, 40 AFTR 328, 187 F.2d 718 (CA–5, 1951), *cert. den.* 72 S.Ct. 50 (USSC, 1951).

grossed-up basis is the basis in the subsidiary stock multiplied by a fraction having 100 percent as its numerator and the percentage of value of the subsidiary's stock held by the purchasing corporation on the acquisition date as its denominator.[29] This amount is allocated among the subsidiary's assets using the residual method as described later.

Except for small closely-held corporations (refer to discussion under Effect on the Distributing Corporation—General Rule After TRA of 1986, Small Corporation Exception), the election of § 338 produces gain or loss to the subsidiary being purchased. The subsidiary is treated as having sold all of its assets at the close of the acquisition date in a single transaction at the fair market value.[30] The subsidiary is then treated as a new corporation that purchased all of the assets as of the beginning of the day after the acquisition date.

For small closely-held corporations, some or all of the gain or loss will not be recognized if the acquisition occurs before January 1, 1989. The rules insofar as they apply to these acquisitions are similar to those relating to qualified small corporations. Gain and losses on ordinary income property and short-term capital gains and losses *are* recognized. Other gains and losses are insulated from recognition under the following circumstances:

—If 100 percent of the stock is purchased, 100 percent of the insulated gain or loss is not recognized if the value of the subsidiary does not exceed $5,000,000. If the value of the corporation ranges from $5,000,000 to $10,000,000, the applicable percentage of the insulated gain or loss is 100 percent reduced by 100 percent multiplied by a fraction, the numerator of which is the value of the corporation in excess of $5,000,000 and the denominator of which is $5,000,000.

—If less than 100 percent of the stock is purchased, the insulated gain or loss is limited to the acquiring company's percentage ownership.[31] The insulated gain or loss is further limited to the applicable percentage noted above if the value of the subsidiary corporation exceeds $5,000,000.

—If less than 100 percent of the stock is purchased but the acquired corporation is liquidated during a one-year period beginning on the acquisition date of the qualified stock purchase, 100 percent of the insulated gain is not recognized if the value of the subsidiary does not exceed $5,000,000. But, again, if the value exceeds $5,000,000, the insulated gain is limited to the applicable percentage that applies under the small corporation exception. These rules also apply if the stock of the minority interest is obtained by the acquired corporation in a complete redemption of the minority stock that qualifies under § 302(b)(3), complete termination of shareholder's interest.

Example 16   S Corporation (not a closely-held corporation) has an $800,000 basis in its assets and liabilities totaling $500,000. It has E & P of $200,000 and assets worth $2,000,000. P Corporation purchases 80% of the stock of S on March 10, 1988, for $1,200,000 [($2,000,000 less liabilities of $500,000) × 80%]. Because the purchase price of the S stock exceeds S's basis in its assets,

---

29. § 338(b)(4).
30. § 338(a).
31. § 338(c) before its repeal by TRA of 1986.

and to eliminate S's E & P, P may choose to elect by December 15, 1988, to treat the acquisition as a purchase of the assets of S under § 338. S need not be liquidated for § 338 to apply. If P elects § 338, the tax consequences are as follows:

—S will be deemed to have sold its assets for an amount equal to the grossed-up basis in the S stock.

—The grossed-up basis in the S stock would be computed as follows: The basis of the S stock would be multiplied by a fraction, with 100% the numerator and 80% the denominator. Thus, the basis of the S stock, $1,200,000, is multiplied by 100/80. The result is $1,500,000, which is adjusted for liabilities of S Corporation of $500,000 for a deemed selling price of $2,000,000.

—The selling price of $2,000,000 less the basis of S's assets of $800,000 produces a recognized gain to S Corporation of $1,200,000. ☐

Because P did not purchase 100% of the stock of S, different results occur depending on whether or not S is liquidated. If S is not liquidated, it is treated as a new corporation as of March 11, 1988. The basis of S's assets would be $2,000,000, and the E & P would be eliminated. If S Corporation is liquidated, P Corporation would have a basis of $1,600,000 in S's assets, representing 80% of S's assets. S's E & P would not carry over to P.

Note the results of the § 338 election. The assets of S Corporation receive a stepped-up basis but at a substantial tax cost. S Corporation must recognize all of its realized gain. Because of the tax liability to S Corporation on its recognized gain, P Corporation should reduce the amount paid for the assets of S Corporation.

Example 17   Assume the same facts as in Example 16, except that S Corporation has five shareholders, all individuals, and its value is $1,500,000. Of the $1,200,000 realized gain, $300,000 is ordinary income, $400,000 is a short-term capital gain, and the remaining $500,000 is a long-term capital gain. The entire $300,000 of ordinary income and $400,000 short-term capital gain are recognized. If S Corporation is liquidated or the minority stock is redeemed, none of the $500,000 long-term capital gain would be recognized. However, if S Corporation is not liquidated and the minority interest remains, 20% of the $500,000 long-term capital gain, or $100,000, would also be recognized. That portion of the long-term capital gain represented by the purchased interest, 80%, would not be recognized. ☐

The new stepped-up basis of the assets of a subsidiary when a § 338 election is in effect is allocated among the assets by use of the residual method,[32] which requires that the amount of the purchase price of the assets that exceeds the aggregate fair market values of the tangible and identifiable intangible assets (other than goodwill and going concern value) must be allo-

---

32. § 1060.

cated to goodwill or going concern value. Neither goodwill nor going concern value can be amortized for tax purposes.

Example 18   For $4,000,000, P Corporation acquires all of the stock of S Corporation and elects to liquidate pursuant to an election under § 338. If the fair market value of S Corporation's physical assets is $3,500,000, P must allocate $500,000 of the purchase price either to goodwill or to going concern value. ☐

In Example 18, none of the purchase price would have to be allocated to goodwill or going concern value if the physical assets were worth $4,000,000. However, the burden of proof of showing no residual amount will be on the taxpayer and not on the IRS.

A consistency requirement under § 338 insures that the acquiring corporation does not pick and choose which of the acquired subsidiary corporations are to be covered by the § 338 election. For a one-year period before and after the acquisition of the subsidiary (the consistency period), the parent is deemed to have made an election under § 338 if it makes a direct purchase of assets from the subsidiary or from an affiliate of the subsidiary during that period.[33] (Exceptions exist, such as for asset purchases in the ordinary course of a business.)

Example 19   On June 15, 1988, P Corporation purchases all of the stock of T Corporation. Shortly thereafter, P Corporation purchases all of the assets of S Corporation, a subsidiary of T Corporation. P Corporation will be deemed to have made the election as to T Corporation. ☐

In addition, during the consistency period, tax treatment of acquisitions of stock of two or more other companies that are members of an affiliated group must be consistent.[34]

Example 20   On June 1, 1988, P Corporation purchases all of the stock in T Corporation and makes a timely election under § 338. If T Corporation owns all the stock in S Corporation, the § 338 election also applies to S Corporation. This is so even though P Corporation never made an election as to S Corporation. On the other hand, if P Corporation does not make an election as to T Corporation, it cannot make the election as to S Corporation. ☐

A Comparison of §§ 334(b)(1) and 338.   Under the general rule of § 334(b)(1), a subsidiary's basis in its assets carries over to the parent corporation upon liquidation. The recapture rules of §§ 1245, 1250, and 1252 do not apply to liquidations of subsidiary corporations when basis is determined under § 334(b)(1). Nor does the provision for investment credit recapture under § 47 apply. These Sections except such liquidations from their provisions.[35] Consequently, a subsidiary liquidation pursuant to §§ 332 and 334(b)(1) is completely

---

33. § 338(e).
34. § 338(f).
35. See, for example, §§ 1245(b)(3), 1250(d)(3), and 47(b)(2).

tax-free (except for any minority interest). On the other hand, a liquidation pursuant to § 338, while tax-free to the parent, is taxable to the subsidiary.

If a liquidation under § 332 qualifies under § 338 and a timely election is made, the holding period of the property received by the parent corporation begins on the date the parent acquired the subsidiary's stock. If the corporation is not liquidated, the holding period of the assets to the subsidiary would start anew on the acquisition date, because the subsidiary is treated as having sold the assets as of that date.[36] In a liquidation under § 334(b)(1), the holding period of the subsidiary carries over to the parent.

Concept Summary

Summary of Liquidation Rules

Effect on the Shareholder	Basis of Property Received	Effect on the Corporation
§ 331—The general rule provides for capital gain treatment on the difference between the FMV of property received and the basis of the stock in the corporation. (Gain on installment obligations resulting from sales of noninventory property or inventory property sold in bulk to one person by the corporation may, however, be deferred to the point of collection.)	§ 334(a)—Basis of assets received by the shareholder will be the FMV on the date of distribution (except for installment obligations in which gain is deferred to the point of collection).	§ 336—Gain or loss is recognized for distributions in kind and for sales by the liquidating corporation. Losses are not recognized for distributions to related parties (shareholders who own, directly or indirectly, more than 50 percent of the corporation's stock) if the distribution is not pro rata or disqualified property is distributed.
§ 333—Elective provision available to shareholders of qualified small closely-held corporations until 1/1/89. Gain to qualified electing shareholders is recognized only to the extent of the *greater* of (1) E & P computed as of the last day of the month of the liquidation and including all gains recognized by the corporation being liquidated or (2) cash and securities acquired after 1953.		Some gain or loss is not recognized for the liquidation of a qualified small closely-held corporation if the liquidation is completed before 1/1/89.

---

36. § 338(a).

Effect on the Shareholder	Basis of Property Received	Effect on the Corporation
§ 332—Liquidation of a subsidiary in which the parent owns 80 percent of the voting stock and 80 percent of the value of the subsidiary stock. No gain or loss is recognized to the parent corporation. Subsidiary must distribute all of its property within the taxable year or within three years from the close of the taxable year in which the plan is adopted.	§ 334(b)(1)—Property has the same basis as it had in the hands of the subsidiary. Parent's basis in the stock disappears. Carryover rules of § 381 apply.	§ 337—No gain or loss is recognized to the subsidiary on distributions to an 80% or more parent. Gain (but not loss) is recognized on distributions to minority shareholders.
	§ 338—Basis of assets takes the basis that the parent held in the stock in the subsidiary. Basis is allocated to assets using the residual method. Carryover rules of § 381 do not apply. (Subsidiary need not be liquidated.)	§ 338—Gain or loss is recognized to the subsidiary corporation. Some or all of the gain or loss will not be recognized for a subsidiary that is a qualified small closely-held corporation if acquisition occurs before 1/1/89.

✓ Tax Planning Considerations

Effect on the Corporation

With the repeal of the *General Utilities* rule, liquidating distributions are taxed at both the corporate level and at the shareholder level. But recall the important exception for certain small closely-held corporations. Managers of those closely-held corporations that qualify under the exception should plan now whether a liquidation is in order. Recall that the exception will not apply for liquidations that are not completed before January 1, 1989.

When would liquidation of a closely-held corporation timed to take advantage of the exception be beneficial?

—A corporation that has substantial ordinary-income producing assets would not benefit from an immediate liquidation. Most of its gain would be recognized despite the exception.

—A corporation that has substantially appreciated assets that are either capital assets or § 1231 assets should consider the exception.

Example 21   X Corporation, with five noncorporate shareholders, has a value of $4,000,000. Its only asset is unimproved land (basis of $500,000, fair market value of $4,700,000). X corporation has liabilities of $700,000. Each shareholder has a basis of $100,000 in the X Corporation stock. Assuming the land is sold after 1988, what are the tax consequences (1) if X Corporation liquidates before January 1, 1989, and (2) if X Corporation waits until the land is sold to liquidate?

1. If X Corporation liquidates before January 1, 1989, there will be no gain to X Corporation, assuming the land was a capital asset or a § 1231 asset. Each shareholder will have recognized gain of $700,000 [$800,000 ($4,000,000 value of the corporation/5) − $100,000 basis of the X Corporation stock] *unless* the shareholders elect under § 333. (The shareholders could elect under § 333 and postpone recognition of gain until the land is sold.) If § 333 is elected, the basis of the land to the shareholders is the basis each shareholder has in the X Corporation stock as adjusted for any gain or liabilities on the property.
2. If X Corporation is not liquidated until the land is sold, X will have a recognized gain of $4,200,000. After payment of X's tax liability, one fifth of the remaining cash distributed to the five shareholders less the $100,000 basis each shareholder has in the X Corporation stock will also be taxed to the shareholders.

It appears that X Corporation should use the exception and liquidate before January 1, 1989. But what if X Corporation had been in the business of buying and selling land? The land would be an ordinary-income producing asset. In that case, use of the exception would be of no benefit, because all of the realized gain would be recognized to X Corporation despite the exception. □

Assets that have depreciated in value should not be distributed in the form of a property dividend before liquidation. Although losses on disqualified property and non pro rata distributions to related shareholders are not recognized (refer to the discussion under Effect on the Distributing Corporation— General Rule After TRA of 1986, Limitation on Losses), losses are otherwise recognized in complete liquidations. Thus, potential loss from such assets can be used to offset gains recognized upon a complete liquidation. On the other hand, if assets that have depreciated in value are distributed as property dividends, the corporation will receive no tax benefit from the potential loss. Recall that losses on nonliquidating distributions are not recognized.

Effect on the Shareholder

Under the general rule of § 331, shareholders will have recognized gain or loss measured by the difference between the liquidation proceeds and the basis of the stock given up. When the gain is large, a shareholder may wish to consider shifting it to others. One approach is to give the stock to family members or donate it to charity. Whether or not this procedure will be successful depends on the timing of the transfer. If the donee of the stock is not in a position to prevent the liquidation of the corporation, the donor will be deemed to have made an anticipatory assignment of income. As a result, the gain will still be taxed to the donor. Hence, advance planning becomes crucial in arriving at the desired tax result.

Recall that § 453(h) provides some relief from the general rule of § 331 that all gain is to be recognized by the shareholder upon the shareholder's receipt of the liquidation proceeds. If the payment for the sale of corporate assets after a plan of liquidation has been adopted is by installment notes, the shareholders receiving such notes as liquidation distributions may be able to report the gain on the installment method. Hence, some gain can be deferred to the point of collection of such notes.

The use of § 332 for the liquidation of a subsidiary is not elective. Nevertheless, some flexibility may be available.

—Whether § 332 applies depends on the 80 percent stock ownership test. Given some substance to the transaction, § 332 may well be avoided if a parent corporation reduces its stock ownership in the subsidiary below this percentage. On the other hand, the opposite approach may be desirable. A parent could make § 332 applicable by acquiring enough additional stock in the subsidiary to meet the 80 percent test.

—Once § 332 becomes operative, less latitude is present in determining the parent's basis in the subsidiary's assets. If § 334(b)(1) applies, the subsidiary's basis carries over to the parent. If § 338 applies and a timely election is made, the parent's basis becomes the cost of the stock. (If the subsidiary is not liquidated, the basis of the assets to the subsidiary is the parent's cost of the stock.) Presumably, § 338 can be avoided by failing to make a timely election.

—If a timely election is made under § 338, the parent corporation's basis in the stock of the subsidiary is allocated among the assets of the subsidiary by use of the residual method.

—Because the residual method requires the parent corporation's basis in excess of the aggregate fair market value of the physical assets to be allocated to goodwill or going concern value (which cannot be amortized for tax purposes), appraisal data relating to the physical assets should be retained to minimize the amount the IRS might otherwise allocate to goodwill or going concern value. Recall that the burden of proof as to the value of the physical assets will be on the taxpayer.

—A § 338 election should be carefully weighed. Unless the corporation whose stock is being purchased is a qualified closely-held corporation *and* has few ordinary-income producing assets, such an election can be detrimental. Any stepped-up basis in the subsidiary's assets will produce immediate taxable gain to the subsidiary.

Problem Materials

Discussion Questions

1. Compare stock redemptions and liquidations with other corporate distributions in terms of the following:

   a. Recognition of gain to the shareholder.

b. Recognition of gain or loss by the distributing corporation.

c. Effect on the distributing corporation's E & P.

2. Compare stock redemptions with liquidations in terms of the following:

a. Possible disallowance of a loss (i.e., § 267) to a shareholder.

b. Basis of noncash property received from the corporation.

3. What is the *General Utilities* rule?

4. Explain the provisions of the 1954 Code that represented a codification of the *General Utilities* rule.

5. What exceptions were applicable to the *General Utilities* rule before being repealed in 1986?

6. What were the principal transfers that were subject to the *General Utilities* rule just before its repeal?

7. What is the tax consequence of the repeal of *General Utilities*?

8. How does a liability in excess of basis on property distributed in a complete liquidation affect recognized gain?

9. What losses are not recognized to the liquidating corporation in a complete liquidation?

10. What are related-party situations?

11. What is disqualified property in a liquidating distribution?

12. Can losses ever be recognized in a complete liquidation if disqualified property is involved? Explain.

13. What corporations qualify for an exception to the repeal of *General Utilities*?

14. If a corporation is a qualified closely-held corporation, what gain or loss is recognized to the corporation upon complete liquidation?

15. What percentage of insulated gain or loss is recognized when a qualified closely-held corporation is worth more than $5,000,000?

16. Discuss the tax treatment of liquidation expenses in connection with the following:

a. General liquidation expenses.

b. Expenses relating to a distribution of assets in kind.

c. Expenses relating to the sale of assets.

17. Explain the tax consequences to a shareholder of a corporation in the process of liquidation under the general rule of § 331.

18. In terms of the applicability of § 332, describe the effect of each of the following factors:

a. The adoption of a plan of complete liquidation.

b. The period of time in which the corporation must liquidate.

c. The amount of stock held by the parent corporation.

d. The solvency of the subsidiary being liquidated.

19. What are the tax consequences of a § 332 liquidation when a minority interest is involved?

20. Under § 332, how is the satisfaction by a subsidiary of a debt owed to its parent treated for tax purposes?

21. Could a liquidation of one corporation involve §§ 331 and 332?

22. Describe the problem that led to the enactment of § 338.

23. What are the requirements for the application of § 338?

24. Under what circumstances could the application of § 338 be beneficial to the parent corporation? Detrimental?

25. How can a small closely-held corporation avoid recognition of gain when its assets are purchased by a corporation and the corporation elects under § 338?

26. Explain the residual method of allocating basis to assets in a § 338 election.

27. Compare §§ 334(b)(1) and 338 with respect to the following:

    a. Carryover to the parent of the subsidiary's corporate attributes.

    b. Recognition by the subsidiary of gain or loss on distributions to its parent.

28. Will the application of § 331 to a liquidation always result in capital gain or loss being recognized by a shareholder? Why or why not?

29. "The E & P of the corporation being liquidated will disappear."

    a. Do you agree with this statement?

    b. Why or why not?

30. Is it possible to have a complete liquidation where the existence of the corporation being liquidated is not terminated? Elaborate.

Problems

1. In 1988, T Corporation, a qualified closely-held corporation with E & P of $50,000, distributes unimproved land with a basis of $60,000 and a fair market value of $150,000 to its shareholder, A. A has a $30,000 basis in her 1,000 shares in T Corporation.

   a. What are the tax consequences to T if the distribution is made pursuant to a complete liquidation of T?

   b. What are the tax consequences to T if the distribution is made pursuant to a redemption of A's stock wherein A owned 80% of T before the redemption and 75% after?

   c. What are the tax consequences to A under each alternative?

2. Pursuant to a complete liquidation, ZX Corporation distributes the following assets to its shareholders: marketable securities (basis of $30,000, fair market value of $80,000), non-LIFO inventory property (basis of $20,000, fair market value of $60,000), building (adjusted basis of $15,000, fair market value of $90,000 with $20,000 of potential §§ 1250 and 291 recapture), land used in its trade or business (basis of $100,000, fair market value of $200,000). ZX is not a qualified closely-held corporation. What gain or loss would ZX Corporation recognize as a result of the distribution if the liquidation was completed in 1985? In 1988?

3. XY Corporation is owned equally by A and B, who are not related. Each has a stock basis of $500,000. XY Corporation has the following assets and no liabilities:

	Basis to XY Corporation	Fair Market Value
Cash	$ 50,000	$ 50,000
Inventory	200,000	300,000
Equipment ($100,000 depreciation has been taken)	50,000	250,000
Building	200,000	600,000
Land	50,000	100,000
Stock in TS Corporation (10% interest)	400,000	1,000,000
Total	$950,000	$2,300,000

Compute the tax liability to XY Corporation and the taxable gain to A and B if XY Corporation is liquidated in 1989 after XY Corporation sells each asset for its fair market value and distributes the after-tax proceeds to A and B. Straight-line depreciation of $300,000 had been claimed on the building. The land was used in XY Corporation's business.

4. S Corporation, not a qualified closely-held corporation, distributes to its shareholders land held as an investment (basis of $100,000, fair market value of $600,000) pursuant to a complete liquidation. The land is subject to a liability of $700,000. How much gain does S Corporation have on a distribution of the land in 1988?

5. On July 1, 1988, T Corporation's stock is held equally by F and D, father and daughter. One year before liquidation, F transfers property (basis of $200,000, fair market value of $60,000) to T Corporation in return for stock. In liquidation, T Corporation transfers the property to D. At the time of the liquidation, the property is worth $50,000. How much loss would T Corporation recognize on the distribution?

6. X Corporation has the following assets on January 10, 1989:

	Basis to X Corporation	Fair Market Value
Cash	$150,000	$150,000
Inventory	50,000	150,000
Equipment	530,000	300,000
Building	200,000	380,000
Land	20,000	20,000

The inventory had been purchased by X Corporation; the remaining assets were acquired seven years ago. X Corporation adopted a plan of liquidation in January 1989 and distributed its assets that same year to its shareholders, A (70%) and B (30%). A and B are unrelated. What are the tax consequences to X Corporation under the following independent circumstances:

a. The assets are distributed to A and B in proportion to their stock interests (i.e., 70% interest in each asset to A and 30% interest in each asset to B).

b. The equipment, building, and land are distributed to A, and the cash and inventory are distributed to B.

c. The equipment is distributed to B, and the remaining assets are distributed to A.

d. What is the result in (a) if the equipment had been transferred to X Corporation in a § 351 transaction 10 months before the liquidation when the equipment had a basis of $530,000 and a fair market value of $330,000?

7. Y Corporation has four shareholders, all individuals, and is worth $6,000,000. Y adopts a plan of liquidation in 1988 and completes the liquidation that same year. Its assets consist of marketable securities (basis of $500,000, fair market value of $1,000,000), land (basis of $1,000,000, fair market value of $4,800,000), and inventory property (basis of $30,000, fair market value of $200,000). How much gain must Y Corporation recognize on the liquidation?

8. In 1988, after a plan of complete liquidation has been adopted, W Corporation sells its only asset, unimproved land, to T (an unrelated party) for $100,000. Under the terms of the sale, W Corporation receives cash of $20,000 and T's note in the amount of $80,000. The note is payable in five years ($16,000 per year) and carries an interest rate of 11%. In 1988, immediately after the sale, W Corporation distributes the cash and notes to S, an individual and sole shareholder. Assume that S has an adjusted basis in the W Corporation stock of $20,000 and that the installment notes possess a value equal to the face amount. What are the tax results to S if the choice is to defer as much gain as possible on the transaction?

9. A, an individual and the sole shareholder of YZ Corporation, has a basis in her stock of $80,000. The corporation's only asset is an apartment building valued at $150,000 with an adjusted basis of $50,000. Potential § 1250 depreciation recapture is $30,000. Section 1245 recapture would have been $50,000. YZ sells the building for $150,000 in 1988 and distributes the cash to A. What is the taxable gain to YZ Corporation? To A?

10. A, an individual, has 40 shares of stock in X Corporation, 20 of which were acquired in 1981 at a cost of $25,000 and 20 of which were acquired on January 10, 1988, at a cost of $10,000. X Corporation liquidates on July 1, 1988, and distributes $1,000 per share to its shareholders in complete liquidation. How will A be taxed on the distribution?

11. The stock of S Corporation is held as follows: 85% by P Corporation and 15% by T, an individual. S Corporation is liquidated on October 1, 1988, pursuant to a plan of liquidation adopted on January 15, 1988. At the time of its liquidation, S Corporation's assets had a basis of $1,000,000 and fair market value of $9,000,000. P Corporation has a basis of $400,000 in its S Corporation stock. The basis of the stock in S Corporation to T is $40,000.

  a. How much gain, if any, must S Corporation recognize on the liquidation?

  b. How much gain, if any, is recognized by the receipt of property from S Corporation to P Corporation? To T?

12. X Corporation has been in existence for several years. A, an individual and X's sole shareholder, wants to liquidate the corporation in 1988. X Corporation has the following assets and no liabilities:

	Basis to X Corporation	Fair Market Value
Non-LIFO inventory	$20,000	$35,000
Equipment ($30,000 of depreciation taken)	15,000	60,000
Supplies	–0–	5,000
Land	30,000	120,000
Installment notes with a face value of $80,000 (received from sale of inventory last year)	20,000	70,000

A has a $30,000 basis in her stock investment. Compare the tax results to X Corporation and to A under the following circumstances:

a. The assets of X Corporation are distributed to A, who continues to operate the business as a sole proprietorship.

b. X Corporation sells the assets for fair market value and distributes the cash to A.

 13. S Corporation is owned 90% by P Corporation. The parent is contemplating a liquidation of S Corporation and the acquisition of its assets. P Corporation purchased the stock of S from S's two individual shareholders a month ago on January 1, 1988, for $200,000. The financial statement of S Corporation as of January 1, 1988, is as follows:

Assets

	Basis to S Corporation	Fair Market Value
Cash	$ 20,000	$ 20,000
Inventory	40,000	30,000
Accounts receivable	80,000	50,000
Equipment	200,000	160,000
Land	260,000	140,000
	$600,000	$400,000

Liabilities and Shareholders' Equity

	Basis to S Corporation	Fair Market Value
Accounts payable	$ 60,000	$ 60,000
Mortgages payable	100,000	100,000
Common stock	500,000	240,000
Retained earnings	(60,000)	
	$600,000	$400,000

The management of P Corporation asks your advice on the feasibility of an election under § 338. How will you advise your client?

14. At the time of its liquidation under § 332, S Corporation had the following assets and liabilities:

	Basis to S Corporation	Fair Market Value
Cash	$ 240,000	$ 240,000
Marketable securities	180,000	480,000
Unimproved land	300,000	600,000
Unsecured bank loan	(60,000)	(60,000)
Mortgage on land	(180,000)	(180,000)

P Corporation, the sole shareholder of S Corporation, has a basis in its stock investment of $720,000. At the time of its liquidation, S Corporation's E & P was $960,000.

a. How much gain (or loss) will S Corporation recognize if it distributes all of its assets and liabilities to P Corporation?

b. How much gain (or loss) will P Corporation recognize?

c. If § 334(b)(1) applies, what will be P Corporation's basis in the marketable securities it receives from S Corporation?

d. What will be P's basis in the unimproved land?

15. P Corporation paid $900,000 for all the stock of S Corporation 10 years ago. S Corporation's balance sheet is as follows:

Assets

Cash	$ 22,500
Inventory	67,500
Accounts receivable	45,000
Equipment	180,000
Land	225,000
	$ 540,000

Liabilities and Shareholders' Equity

Accounts payable	$ 360,000
Payable to P Corporation	540,000
Common stock	900,000
Deficit	(1,260,000)
	$ 540,000

What are the tax consequences to P Corporation if it liquidates S Corporation?

16. S Corporation is owned by W, an individual, who is interested in selling either his stock in S Corporation or S's assets. The financial statement of S Corporation as of December 31, 1987, is as follows:

Assets

	Basis to S Corporation	Fair Market Value
Cash	$ 7,500	$ 7,500
Accounts receivable	5,000	5,000
Inventory	7,500	12,500
Equipment (depreciation allowed of $20,000)	25,000	50,000
Land	50,000	100,000
	$95,000	$175,000

Liabilities and Shareholders' Equity

Accounts payable	$20,000	$ 20,000
Mortgages payable	25,000	25,000
Common stock	12,500	130,000
Retained earnings	37,500	
	$95,000	$175,000

P Corporation is interested in purchasing S Corporation. Should P Corporation purchase the stock for $130,000 or the assets for $175,000? If stock is purchased for $130,000, what steps should P Corporation take to secure maximum tax benefits?

17. S Corporation, owned by two individual shareholders, has a basis of $450,000 (fair market value of $1,000,000) in its assets and has E & P of $80,000. Its liabilities total $100,000. If the assets were sold, all gain would be long-term capital gain or § 1231 gain. P Corporation purchases 20% of all the stock of S Corporation for $180,000 on

March 1, 1988; 15% for $135,000 on September 20, 1988; and 60% for $540,000 on December 1, 1988, or a total consideration of $855,000.

a. Is P Corporation entitled to make an election under § 338?

b. Assume P Corporation may make an election under § 338. Should P do so? When must P make such an election?

c. What are the tax consequences to S Corporation and to P Corporation if P Corporation makes a valid election under § 338 but does not liquidate S Corporation?

d. What is the tax result if S Corporation is liquidated four months after a valid § 338 election? A, an individual who holds the 5% minority interest in S Corporation, has a $10,000 basis in his stock in S. What is the tax result to A upon the liquidation?

18. T and S formed the TS Corporation in 1970. T transferred assets worth $100,000 with an adjusted basis of $50,000 to TS for 1,000 shares of common stock of TS with a par value of $50 per share. S, T's son, transferred cash of $50,000 to TS for 1,000 shares of common stock of TS. TS Corporation made substantial profits from 1970 to the present and had an E & P of $400,000 on December 31, 1987, the close of its tax year. XY Corporation purchased all the stock of TS on January 10, 1988, at a cost of $550,000. What steps should XY take to obtain the maximum tax benefits? Explain.

19. S Corporation is wholly owned by A, an individual, who has a basis in the S stock of $50,000. S Corporation has the following assets and no liabilities:

	Basis to S Corporation	Fair Market Value
Inventory	$50,000	$ 80,000
Equipment (§ 1245 depreciation recapture potential of $100,000)	40,000	150,000
Building (no recapture potential)	30,000	200,000

P Corporation wants to buy the assets of S Corporation or the stock in S.

a. What are the tax results to S Corporation, to P Corporation, and to A under the following circumstances:

—P purchases the S stock in 1988 for $430,000 and makes an election under § 338.

—S Corporation adopts a plan of complete liquidation, sells all its assets to P Corporation, and distributes the cash of $430,000 to A.

b. Which alternative is preferable to P Corporation?

20. S Corporation has assets with a basis of $700,000 and fair market value of $1,500,000 and liabilities totaling $500,000. S has E & P of $150,000. S Corporation has two individual shareholders. Of the $800,000 appreciated value of S's assets, $100,000 represents ordinary income, $50,000 represents a short-term capital gain, $30,000 represents an ordinary loss, $600,000 represents § 1231 gain, and $80,000 represents a long-term capital gain. P Corporation purchases 85% of the stock of S Corporation on June 10, 1988, for $850,000 and makes a proper election to treat the acquisition as a purchase of the assets of S Corporation under § 338. S is not liquidated.

a. What will be the tax basis of the assets of S Corporation?

b. What, if any, gain must S Corporation recognize upon the transaction?

c. What will be the E & P of S Corporation after P's purchase of 85% of the S stock?

■■■■■■   ## Research Problems

Research Problem 1. Before the liquidation of X Corporation, T, one of the shareholders, sells her stock (basis of $50,000) to a newly created T Trust for the stock's fair market value of $140,000. Under the sales agreement, T Trust is to pay $14,000 in the year of sale and $12,600 in each of the next 10 years. Interest of 10% is provided for on the notes T Trust issues for the deferred balance of $126,000. Shortly after the sale, X Corporation liquidates and distributes to T Trust cash and property worth $140,000 in exchange for its stock.

The trust department of a local bank is the trustee of T Trust, and T's son and grandchildren are the designated holders of the life estate and remainder interests. (Note: See the Glossary of Tax Terms in Appendix C for a definition of these terms.)

    a. What is T trying to accomplish by the creation and use of T Trust?

    b. Will it work?

Research Problem 2. YZ Corporation was liquidated in 1987. In the year of liquidation, YZ Corporation reported taxable gain of $8,000,000, based upon a value in its assets of $10,000,000 and a basis of $2,000,000. After paying its tax liability of $2,720,000, YZ Corporation distributed its remaining assets, valued at $7,280,000 ($10,000,000 less the tax paid of $2,720,000), to its 10 shareholders. Shareholder A received $728,000 and reported a long-term capital gain in 1987 of $628,000 ($728,000 distribution − $100,000 stock basis). In 1988, the IRS audited YZ Corporation and determined that the corporation had an additional gain of $1,000,000 in the year of liquidation. The IRS assessed additional tax of $340,000 plus penalties and interest against YZ Corporation and then against A, based on transferee liability. A comes to you for advice. He is not certain where the other shareholders are located.

    a. If A is required to pay all of the tax liability, will he·be entitled to deduct the amount paid as a loss?

    b. What is the nature of the loss—capital or ordinary?

    c. Would § 1341 apply?

    d. How can a shareholder be protected from the problem facing A?

Research Problem 3. T, an individual, was the sole shareholder of W Corporation, which was liquidated in 1981. All of the assets of W Corporation were distributed to T in 1981. Included in the assets that T received in liquidation was a 1978 license agreement between W Corporation and a third party to whom was given the right to use the taxpayer's name in connection with the sale of electrical appliances in return for royalties payable to W Corporation. In 1981, T reported property valued at $500,000, from which he deducted his stock basis of $50,000, reporting a net capital gain of $450,000. T received royalties under the license agreement which by the end of 1984 had amounted to $500,000. In 1985, he received an additional $30,000. In 1986, royalties were $20,000. T reported these amounts as long-term capital gains. Upon audit of T's tax returns for 1985 and 1986, the IRS determined that these amounts were ordinary income. T asks your advice.

Partial list of research aids:

Stephen H. Dorsey, 49 T.C. 606 (1968).

6 Corporations: Reorganizations

A corporate combination, usually referred to as a "reorganization," can be either a taxable or a nontaxable transaction. Assuming a business combination is taxable, § 1001 of the Code provides that the seller's gain or loss is measured by the difference between the amount realized and the basis of property surrendered. The purchaser's basis for the property received is the amount paid for such property, and the holding period begins on the date of purchase.

Certain exchanges are specifically excepted from tax recognition by the Code. For example, § 1031 provides that no gain or loss shall be recognized if property held for productive use or for investment is exchanged solely for property of a like kind. If elected by the taxpayer, § 1033 provides for partial or complete nonrecognition of gain if property destroyed, seized, or stolen is compulsorily or involuntarily converted into similar property. Further, § 351 provides for nonrecognition of gain upon the transfer of property to a controlled corporation. Finally, §§ 361 and 368 provide for nonrecognition of gain in certain corporate reorganizations. The Regulations state the underlying assumption behind such nonrecognition of gain or loss—

> ... the new property is substantially a continuation of the old investment still unliquidated; and, in the case of reorganizations, ... the new enterprise, the new corporate structure, and the new property are substantially continuations of the old still unliquidated.[1]

Summary of the Different Types of Reorganizations

Section 368(a) of the Code specifies seven reorganizations that will qualify as nontaxable exchanges. It is important that the planner of a nontaxable business combination determine well in advance that the proposed transaction falls specifically within one of these seven described types. If the transaction fails to qualify, it will not be granted special tax treatment. In certain situations, the parties contemplating a corporate reorganization should obtain a letter ruling from the IRS that the proposed combination qualifies as a tax-free reorganization under § 368.

Section 368(a)(1) states that the term "reorganization" means the following:

A. A statutory merger or consolidation.

B. The acquisition by one corporation, in exchange solely for all or a part of its voting stock (or in exchange solely for all or a part of the voting stock of a corporation that is in control of the acquiring corporation), of stock of another corporation if, immediately after the acquisition, the acquiring corporation has control of such other corporation (whether or not such acquiring corporation had control immediately before the acquisition).

---

1. Reg. § 1.1011–2(c).

C. The acquisition by one corporation, in exchange solely for all or a part of its voting stock (or in exchange solely for all or a part of the voting stock of a corporation that is in control of the acquiring corporation), of substantially all of the properties of another corporation. But in determining whether the exchange is solely for stock, the assumption by the acquiring corporation of a liability of the other or the fact that property acquired is subject to a liability shall be disregarded.

D. A transfer by a corporation of all or a part of its assets to another corporation if, immediately after the transfer, the transferor or one or more of the shareholders (including persons who were shareholders immediately before the transfer), or any combination thereof, is in control of the corporation to which the assets are transferred; but only if, in pursuance of the plan, stock or securities of the corporation to which the assets are transferred are distributed in a transaction that qualifies under § 354, § 355, or § 356.

E. A recapitalization.

F. A mere change in identity, form, or place of organization, however effected.

G. A transfer by a corporation of all or a part of its assets to another corporation in a bankruptcy or receivership proceeding but only if in pursuance of the plan, stock and securities of the transferee corporation are distributed in a transaction that qualifies under § 354, § 355, or § 356.

These seven different types of tax-free reorganizations are designated by the letters identifying each: "Type A," "Type B," "Type C," "Type D," "Type E," "Type F," and "Type G" reorganizations. Basically, excepting the recapitalization (E), the change in form (F), and the insolvent corporation (G) provisions, a tax-free reorganization is (1) a statutory merger or consolidation, (2) an exchange of stock for voting stock, (3) an exchange of assets for voting stock, or (4) a divisive reorganization (the so-called spin-off, split-off, or split-up).

General Consequences of Tax-Free Reorganizations

Generally, the security holders of the various corporations involved in a tax-free reorganization do not recognize a gain or a loss in the exchange of their stock and securities [2] except when they receive cash or other consideration in addition to stock and securities.[3] As far as securities (long-term debt) are concerned, however, gain is not recognized if securities are surrendered in the

---

2. The term "securities" includes bonds and long-term notes. Short-term notes are not considered to be securities. The problem of drawing a line between short-term and long-term notes was discussed in Chapter 3.
3. § 358(a).

same principal amount (or a greater principal amount) as the principal amount of the securities received.

If additional consideration is received, gain is recognized but not in excess of the sum of money and the fair market value of other property received. If the distribution has the effect of the distribution of a dividend, any recognized gain is a taxable dividend to the extent of the shareholder's share of the corporation's earnings and profits. The remainder is treated as an exchange of property.[4] Loss is never recognized. The tax basis of stock and securities received by a shareholder pursuant to a tax-free reorganization will be the same as the basis of those surrendered, decreased by the amount of boot received and increased by the amount of gain and dividend income, if any, recognized on the transaction.[5]

Example 1

A, an individual, exchanges stock he owns in X Corporation for stock in Y Corporation plus $2,000 cash. The exchange is pursuant to a tax-free reorganization of both corporations. A paid $10,000 for the stock in X two years ago. The stock in Y has a fair market value of $12,000. A has a realized gain of $4,000 ($12,000 + $2,000 − $10,000), which is recognized to the extent of the boot received, $2,000. Assume the distribution has the effect of a dividend. If A's share of earnings and profits in X is $1,000, that amount would be a taxable dividend. The remaining $1,000 would be treated as a gain from the exchange of property. A's basis in the Y stock would be $10,000 [$10,000 (basis in stock surrendered) − $2,000 (boot received) + $2,000 (gain and dividend income recognized)]. □

Example 2

Assume A's basis in the X stock was $15,000. A would have a realized loss of $1,000 on the exchange, none of which would be recognized. His basis in the Y stock would be $13,000 [$15,000 (basis in stock surrendered) − $2,000 (boot received)]. □

Because there is a substituted basis in tax-free reorganizations, the unrecognized gain or loss will be recognized when the new stock or securities are disposed of in a taxable transaction.

No gain or loss is recognized to the acquired corporation on the exchange of property pursuant to a tax-free reorganization.[6] If the acquired corporation receives cash or other property in the exchange as well as stock or securities in the acquiring corporation, gain is recognized to the corporation on such other property only if the corporation fails to distribute the "other property" to its shareholders. If the acquired corporation distributes boot received in a tax-free reorganization, the shareholders, and not the corporation, are taxed on any recognized gain occasioned by the receipt of boot.

If the acquired corporation has sufficient earnings and profits and the shareholders receive pro rata distributions as boot, the position of the IRS is

4. § 356(a).
5. § 358.
6. § 361(a).

that the boot is treated as a dividend and taxed as ordinary income and not as capital gain. Various courts are divided on this issue.[7]

Gain or loss also is not recognized by the acquiring corporation.[8] Property received from the acquired corporation retains the basis it had in the hands of the acquired corporation, increased by the amount of gain recognized to the acquired corporation on the transfer.[9]

If a corporate exchange qualifies as a tax-free reorganization under one of the seven types mentioned, the tax consequences described are automatic regardless of the intent of the parties involved.

Types of Tax-Free Reorganizations

Type A

Although the terms are not analogous, "Type A" reorganizations include both mergers and consolidations. A merger has been defined as the union of two or more corporations in which one of the corporations retains its corporate existence and absorbs the other or others. These other corporations lose their corporate existence by operation of law. A consolidation, on the other hand, is effected when a new corporation is created to take the place of two or more constituent corporations, which consequently lose their corporate existence by operation of law.

Example 3 Beta Corporation acquires all the properties of Alpha Corporation in exchange for 5,000 shares of stock in Beta Corporation. The Beta stock is distributed to Alpha's shareholders in complete liquidation of Alpha Corporation. This transaction qualifies as an "A" reorganization (assuming the requirements of state law are met). It is a statutory merger. □

Example 4 Alpha and Beta Corporations are consolidated under state law into a new corporation, Zeta Corporation. Zeta stock is distributed to the shareholders of Alpha and Beta in complete liquidation of each. This is an "A" reorganization, a consolidation. □

The "Type A" reorganization is illustrated in Figure I.

Advantages and Disadvantages. The "A" reorganization allows greater flexibility than is present in other types of reorganizations, because there is no requirement that consideration be voting stock. (This is a requirement for both the "B" and "C" reorganizations.) Further, the "A" reorganization allows money or property to change hands without disqualifying the business combination as a tax-free reorganization. The money or property will

---

7. Compare *Shimberg v. U.S.*, 78–2 USTC ¶9607, 42 AFTR2d 78–5575, 577 F.2d 283 (CA–5, 1978), with *Clark v. Comm.*, 87–2 USTC ¶ 9504, 60 AFTR2d 87–5592, 828 F.2d 221 (CA–4, 1987).
8. § 361(a).
9. § 362(b).

Figure I   "A" Reorganization

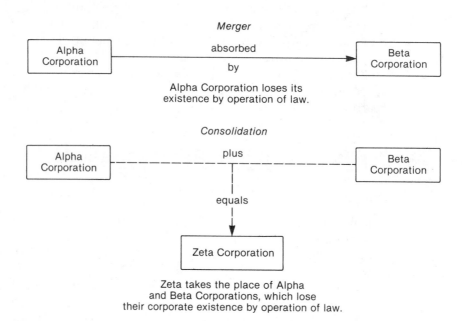

Merger

Alpha Corporation — absorbed by → Beta Corporation

Alpha Corporation loses its
existence by operation of law.

Consolidation

Alpha Corporation · · · plus · · · Beta Corporation

equals

Zeta Corporation

Zeta takes the place of Alpha
and Beta Corporations, which lose
their corporate existence by operation of law.

constitute boot, and some gain may be recognized. However, the receipt of this boot will not destroy the tax-free treatment of receiving stock as consideration. If consideration other than stock is to be used, the tax planners must be careful that they do not run afoul of the continuity of interest test. This test, promulgated by the courts, requires that at least 50 percent of the consideration used in a reorganization be stock or the reorganization will be treated as a taxable transaction.

Definite disadvantages need to be considered before an "A" reorganization is activated. Because the "A" reorganization is statutory, compliance with applicable state law is required to perfect the acquisition. In almost all states, shareholders of all corporations participating in a merger or consolidation are granted the right to dissent and have their shares appraised and bought. The problems in meeting the demands of objecting shareholders can become so cumbersome that the planners may be forced to abandon the "A" reorganization. In addition, because a majority of the shareholders of all corporations involved must approve the transaction, all of the problems inherent in shareholder meetings are brought to the fore. These problems are magnified if the stock of either of the corporations is widely held.

Another disadvantage of the "A" reorganization is the required assumption by the acquiring corporation of *all* liabilities of the acquired corporation. The surviving corporation assumes these liabilities of the acquired corporation as a matter of law. Though the legal procedure required to transfer assets and liabilities is not complex when a merger or consolidation occurs, the fact that all liabilities (including unknown and contingent liabilities) pass to the transferee corporation as a matter of law is a distinct disadvantage.

The Use of a Subsidiary in a "Type A" Reorganization.   Many of the problems of compliance with state law in the "Type A" reorganization can be reduced if a subsidiary becomes the acquiring corporation. When a subsidiary acquires the assets of another corporation and gives its own voting stock as consideration, for the most part, any problem regarding the validity of the stock transfer ends. However, the parent corporation might want the shareholders of the acquired corporation to hold the parent's stock rather than the stock of the subsidiary to enable the parent to retain control over the subsidiary. The parent does not want to be the acquiring corporation, because it does not want to assume the liabilities of the acquired corporation. (If the subsidiary becomes the acquiring corporation, it will assume the liabilities of the acquired corporation, and the assets of the parent will be protected.) Further, a major problem of the "A" reorganization—securing the approval of a majority of the shareholders of the acquiring corporation—is removed, because the parent corporation is the majority shareholder.[10] Consequently, only the approval of the board of directors of the parent corporation need be obtained. This also eliminates the possibility that the parent's shareholders might exercise their right to dissent. For these reasons, the use of a subsidiary corporation to effect the "A" reorganization should not be overlooked.

The exchange of a parent's stock by a subsidiary in a statutory merger qualifies the reorganization as a tax-free "A" reorganization if (1) no subsidiary stock is used and (2) the exchange would have been an "A" reorganization had the merger been into the parent.[11]

Further, under § 368(a)(2)(E), a so-called reverse merger is permitted. To qualify as a tax-free reorganization under this provision, the surviving corporation must hold, in addition to its own properties, substantially all of the properties of the merged corporation. Further, the former shareholders of the surviving corporation must receive voting stock of the controlling corporation in exchange for control (80 percent) of the surviving corporation.

The following examples demonstrate the use of a subsidiary in an "A" reorganization.

Example 5   Beta Corporation is a subsidiary of Parent Corporation. It also holds some stock in Parent. Beta transfers the Parent stock it owns to the shareholders of Alpha Corporation for substantially all the assets of Alpha. Alpha is liquidated. This is an "A" reorganization using parent company stock. If Parent Corporation is the only shareholder of Beta, the merger can be effected by securing approval of Parent's board of directors. Because the vote of Parent's shareholders is not required, considerable time and expense are avoided. Further, Parent's assets are protected from Alpha Corporation's creditors. □

Example 6   In a reverse merger, Alpha Corporation, rather than Beta Corporation, would survive. Further, the stock in Parent Corporation must be voting stock only. The shareholders of Alpha must surrender their stock representing 80% control of Alpha to Parent for its voting stock. Beta Corpora-

---

10. The approval of a majority of the shareholders of the acquired corporation would still be required.
11. § 368(a)(2)(D).

tion would transfer all its assets to Alpha and be liquidated. Alpha Corporation then becomes the subsidiary of Parent Corporation. □

The use of a subsidiary in an "A" reorganization and a reverse merger are illustrated in Figure II.

A disadvantage of the reverse merger is the requirement that voting stock of the parent corporation be used and that at least 80 percent of the stock of the acquired corporation be obtained. These requirements severely limit the flexibility present in the regular "A" reorganization. Indeed, the provision is drafted to correspond more closely with a "Type B" than with a "Type A" reorganization.

Before attempting an "A" reorganization by having a subsidiary corporation exchange parent stock for assets of another corporation or by utilizing the reverse merger provisions, state law must be examined to determine whether the use of parent corporation stock is permitted in a statutory merger. Recall that because the "A" reorganization is a statutory merger, state law requirements must be met.

Other problems must be considered in the use of a subsidiary. Assume the parent corporation exchanges its stock for stock in the subsidiary before the reorganization. Does the parent increase its basis in the subsidiary's stock?

Figure II Use of a Subsidiary in the "A" Reorganization

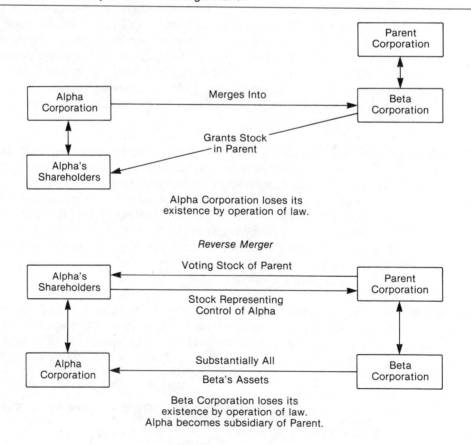

Alpha Corporation loses its existence by operation of law.

Reverse Merger

Beta Corporation loses its existence by operation of law.
Alpha becomes subsidiary of Parent.

The basis of the parent's stock to the parent is zero. Consequently, the parent could not increase the basis of the subsidiary's stock unless the receipt can be tied to the subsidiary's later acquisition of assets in the reorganization. If it can, the parent's basis in the subsidiary's stock is equal to the acquired corporation's basis in the assets less the acquired corporation's liabilities. The concept behind this assumption is that the assets of the acquired corporation are treated as having been first acquired by the parent and then transferred to the subsidiary for the subsidiary stock. What if the parent transfers its stock to the subsidiary in a separate transaction before the subsidiary acquires the assets of another corporation? Would it receive an increase in its basis in the subsidiary's stock after the reorganization? This question remains unanswered.

Type B

A "Type B" reorganization involves the acquisition by a corporation of the stock of another corporation solely in exchange for its voting stock. Immediately after the acquisition, the acquiring corporation must be in control of the acquired corporation. This is, in simple terms, a transaction in the form of an exchange of stock for voting stock. Voting stock must be the sole consideration, and this requirement is strictly construed.

Example 7   Alpha Corporation exchanges 20% of its voting stock for stock representing 80% of all classes of stock in Beta Corporation. The exchange qualifies as a "B" reorganization. Alpha becomes the parent of Beta. It should be noted that this type of reorganization precludes the use of boot. Consequently, gain would never be recognized in a "B" reorganization. □

Example 8   If, in the previous example, Alpha Corporation exchanges nonvoting preferred stock or bonds in addition to voting stock, the transaction would not qualify as a "B" reorganization. □

The "Type B" reorganization is illustrated in Figure III.

The Eighty Percent Control Requirement. Stock may be acquired from the shareholders or directly from the corporation. If A Corporation has 100 shares outstanding, for example, B Corporation must acquire, in exchange for its voting stock, at least 80 of those shares. It could also acquire 400 newly issued

Figure III   "B" Reorganization

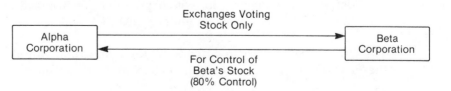

Alpha Corporation becomes the parent
and Beta Corporation, the subsidiary.

shares directly from A Corporation. It would then own 400 shares of 500 outstanding shares, an 80 percent ownership.

The control level that must be reached by the parent, or acquiring corporation, is at least 80 percent of the total combined voting power of all classes of stock entitled to vote and at least 80 percent of the total number of shares of all other classes of stock of the corporation. This requirement does not mean that the acquiring corporation must actually "acquire" 80 percent of the acquired corporation, but rather that, after the acquisition, it must have an 80 percent ownership. As a consequence, certain problems arise. Alpha Corporation, in Example 7, might have earlier acquired 30 percent of Beta Corporation for cash. It now acquires another 50 percent through the issuance of voting stock. It is possible that the transaction will not be tax-free, because if both transactions are a continuing effort to gain control, Alpha Corporation has attained such control of Beta through the use of both cash and stock. However, the Regulations state that the acquisition of stock of another corporation by the acquiring corporation solely for its voting stock can be tax-free even though the acquiring corporation already owns stock of the other corporation.[12] Suppose, for example, 10 years ago Alpha Corporation acquired 30 percent of Beta Corporation's stock for cash. In the current year, it acquires another 50 percent, but this time the acquisition is made through the use of Beta Corporation's voting stock. Under these circumstances, it seems unlikely that the two acquisitions were part of the same plan to gain control of Beta Corporation. Even though some of the shares were acquired with cash, the requirements of a "B" reorganization are still satisfied.

Example 9 Beta has assets with an adjusted basis of $400,000 and liabilities of $100,000. Its common stock consists of 2,000 shares with a par value of $100 per share. It has no other classes of stock and has E & P of $100,000. Beta's assets are worth $500,000. Should Alpha acquire the assets and liabilities of Beta in a tax-free "A" reorganization, Alpha would have a basis of $400,000 in Beta's assets. [Property received from an acquired corporation has a carryover basis to the acquiring corporation. Basis in the hands of the acquired corporation carries over to the acquiring corporation. See § 362(b).] If Alpha acquires Beta by exchanging with Beta's shareholders 30% of its voting stock (worth $320,000) for 1,600 shares of Beta stock, the reorganization would qualify as a "B" reorganization. Beta would become the subsidiary of Alpha. Alpha's basis in the Beta stock would be the basis Beta's shareholders had in the stock. [Section 362(b) would again apply.] However, Beta's shareholders would have a substituted basis in the Alpha stock (their basis in the Alpha stock will have the basis they had in the Beta stock). (Basis for the shareholders of Beta is determined under § 358, which provides for a substituted basis rather than a carryover basis as under § 362.) ☐

The Use of a Subsidiary in a "Type B" Reorganization.   In the "Type B" as in the "Type A" reorganization, voting stock of the acquiring corporation's parent

---

12. Reg. § 1.368–2(c).

may be used. The following example demonstrates the use of a subsidiary in a "B" reorganization.

Example 10   P Corporation is the parent of Alpha Corporation. Alpha Corporation also owns some stock in P. It exchanges stock (voting stock only) in P for control of the stock in Beta Corporation. This qualifies as a "B" reorganization. Beta would become the subsidiary of Alpha Corporation. ☐

The use of a parent's stock by a subsidiary in a "Type B" reorganization is illustrated in Figure IV.

The "Solely for Voting Stock" Requirement.   The "B" reorganization is limited in that the *sole* consideration must be voting stock. Voting stock plus some other consideration does not meet the statutory requirement.[13] This limitation on consideration is a great disadvantage of the "B" reorganization.

Absent the voting stock problem, the stock for voting stock acquisition has the advantage of simplicity. Because, generally, the shareholders of the acquired corporation act individually in transferring their stock, the affairs of the corporation itself are not directly involved. Consequently, no formal action is required of the shareholders of the acquired corporation, at least not in their capacity as shareholders. Further, no formal action is required of the shareholders of the acquiring corporation (assuming there are sufficient treasury or unissued shares to effect the transaction without any formal shareholder action to increase authorized shares).[14] Thus, much of the shareholder problem presented in the "A" reorganization is eliminated. However, there can be disadvantages to a "B" reorganization. Assuming the acquiring corporation does not obtain a 100 percent control of the acquired corporation, problems may arise with respect to the minority interest remaining in the acquired corporation.

Figure IV   Use of a Subsidiary in a "B" Reorganization

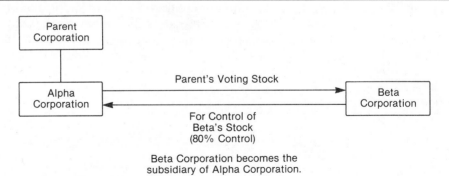

Beta Corporation becomes the
subsidiary of Alpha Corporation.

13. See *Helvering v. Southwest Consolidated Corporation*, 41–1 USTC ¶9402, 27 AFTR 160, 119 F.2d 567 (CA–5, 1941), *rev'd.* in 42–1 USTC ¶9248, 28 AFTR 573, 62 S.Ct. 546 (USSC, 1942).
14. Though shareholders in the "B" reorganization normally do not act through the corporation, this is subject to legal or other restrictions on transfers of shares.

Type C

The "Type C" reorganization involves the acquisition by the acquiring corporation of substantially all of the assets of the acquired corporation solely in exchange for voting stock. It is basically an exchange of assets for voting stock.

A transaction will not qualify as a "C" reorganization unless the acquired corporation distributes to its shareholders the stock, securities, and other properties it receives in the reorganization as well as any of its own properties.[15]

Example 11   Alpha Corporation transfers voting stock representing a 30% interest in the corporation to Beta Corporation for substantially all of the assets of Beta. After the exchange, Beta's only assets are the voting stock in Alpha Corporation. This exchange qualifies as a "C" reorganization if Beta distributes the voting stock to its shareholders. □

The "Type C" reorganization is illustrated in Figure V.

"Type A" and "Type C" Reorganizations Compared.   The "Type C" reorganization has almost the same consequences as the "Type A," but the rule with respect to consideration is more exacting for the "Type C." On the other hand, the "C" reorganization is preferable to the "A" in many circumstances. In the "C" reorganization, unlike the "A," the acquiring corporation assumes only those liabilities it chooses to assume. It is normally not liable for unknown or contingent liabilities. Further, in the "C" reorganization, in some states, only the approval of the shareholders in the acquired corporation is required. This considerably diminishes the magnitude of the problem involved in the "A" reorganization. In addition, dissenters' rights are generally given only to the shareholders of the acquired corporation in a "C" reorganization, whereas these rights must be recognized in both the acquired and the acquiring corporation in a statutory merger or consolidation.

The "C" reorganization can also be effected by the use of a subsidiary, as demonstrated in the following examples.

Example 12   Parent Corporation is in control of Alpha Corporation. Alpha also owns some stock in Parent. It transfers the Parent stock (voting stock) to Beta Corporation for substantially all of the assets of Beta. Beta is then liquidated. The transaction qualifies as a "C" reorganization. □

Figure V   "C" Reorganization

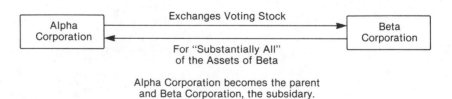

Alpha Corporation becomes the parent
and Beta Corporation, the subsidary.

---

15. § 368(a)(1)(G).

Example 13   The acquiring corporation could be the parent corporation even though the subsidiary ultimately acquires the assets of the acquired corporation. Parent Corporation could acquire the assets of Beta for its voting stock and then transfer the assets to Alpha Corporation. ☐

The use by a subsidiary corporation of its parent's stock in carrying out a "Type C" reorganization is illustrated in Figure VI.

Consideration in the "Type C" Reorganization.   Consideration in the "C" reorganization normally would consist of voting stock, as in the "B" reorganization. However, there are exceptions to this rule. Section 368(a)(2)(B) provides that cash and other property will not destroy the tax-free status of the reorganization if at least 80 percent of the fair market value of all the property of the acquired corporation is obtained by the use of voting stock. In addition, an assumption of the liabilities of the acquired corporation is disregarded in determining whether the transaction is solely for voting stock.[16]

The "C" reorganization, then, is given a slight degree of freedom in reference to consideration, whereas the "B" is not. But in making the statutory computation that "other property" does not exceed 20 percent of the fair market value of the property transferred, liabilities assumed by the acquiring corporation are, if the corporation receives other consideration, treated as "other property." As a practical matter, because liabilities assumed by the acquiring corporation normally exceed 20 percent of the fair market value of the assets acquired, the provision relaxing the requirement of "solely" for voting stock in the "C" reorganization is limited in its application. The following examples illustrate this problem.

Example 14   Beta Corporation transfers assets with a fair market value of $200,000 to Alpha Corporation for voting stock valued at $160,000 and cash of $40,000. No liabilities are assumed. Beta uses the $40,000 to pay its liabilities, distributes the stock to its shareholders, and liquidates. The transaction qualifies as a "C" reorganization, because "other property" received is exactly 20% of $200,000. ☐

Figure VI   Use of a Subsidiary in a "C" Reorganization

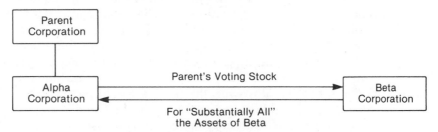

After the reorganization, Beta Corporation's
only asset would be Alpha's voting stock.
Alpha's stock must be distributed to Beta's shareholders.

---

16. § 368(a)(1)(C).

Example 15   Assume in Example 14 that Beta's assets have a basis of $100,000. Beta would have no gain on the exchange pursuant to § 361(a). Beta's basis in the voting stock in Alpha would be $100,000 (its $100,000 basis in its assets). Alpha's basis in the Beta assets will be $100,000 (Beta's basis of $100,000). (Recall that basis for the acquiring corporation is determined under § 362, which provides for a carryover basis rather than a substituted basis as under § 358. Basis in property received by the acquiring corporation is the same basis as in the hands of the acquired corporation increased for any gain recognized to the acquired corporation on the transfer.) ☐

Example 16   Assume Beta has no liabilities. It liquidates and distributes the Alpha stock plus the $40,000 cash to X and Y, its shareholders. X has a basis of $60,000 in the Beta stock, and Y has a basis of $90,000 in the Beta stock. Now § 358 applies to determine basis. Gain of $40,000 will be reported by X and Y. If each has a 50% ownership in Beta, each will have a gain of $20,000. Basis in the Alpha stock will be $60,000 for X ($60,000 basis in the Beta stock plus $20,000 gain recognized minus $20,000 boot received) and $90,000 for Y ($90,000 basis in the Beta stock plus $20,000 gain recognized minus $20,000 boot received). ☐

Example 17   Assume in Example 14 that Beta transferred assets for stock valued at $140,000, cash of $40,000, and the assumption of $20,000 of its liabilities by Alpha. Liabilities would be counted as "other property," because Beta also received cash. "Other property" amounts to $60,000, which exceeds 20% of the fair market value of Beta Corporation's assets. The transaction does not qualify as a "C" reorganization. ☐

Example 18   Assume Alpha Corporation gives Beta Corporation voting stock worth $120,000 and assumes $80,000 of Beta Corporation's liabilities. The transaction would qualify as a "C" reorganization. Liabilities assumed by the acquiring corporation are disregarded if no additional consideration (other than stock) is used. ☐

Asset Transfers.   The "C" reorganization requires that substantially all of the assets of the acquired corporation be transferred. There are numerous problems in determining whether the "substantially all" requirement has been met. There is no statutory definition of "substantially all." If a favorable ruling is to be obtained from the Internal Revenue Service, assets representing at least 90 percent of the fair market value of the net assets and at least 70 percent of the fair market value of the gross assets held by the acquired corporation must be transferred.[17] Smaller percentages than this rule of thumb adopted by the IRS may still qualify. However, the parties would have to rely on case law inasmuch as a favorable ruling could not be obtained.[18]

The results of a statutory merger and an asset acquisition, the "C" reorganization, are almost identical if the acquired corporation is liquidated in a "C"

---

17. Rev.Rul. 77–37, 1977–2 C.B. 568, amplified by Rev.Proc. 86–42, 1986–2 C.B. 722.
18. See, for example, *National Bank of Commerce of Norfolk v. U.S.*, 58–1 USTC ¶9278, 1 AFTR2d 894, 158 F.Supp. 887 (D.Ct. Va., 1958).

reorganization. In both situations, the acquiring corporation will receive the assets of the acquired. Because all the properties of the acquired corporation must be distributed, the acquired corporation generally is liquidated in a "C reorganization, and the shareholders of the acquired will receive stock in the acquiring corporation. However, the methods used to achieve these almost identical results as well as the legal consequences of the two are considerably different. These differences make the choice of the preferable form of acquisition highly pertinent.

Type D

The first three types of tax-free corporate reorganizations were designed for corporate combinations. The "D" reorganization differs from them in that it is a mechanism for corporate division. The "D" reorganization involves the transfer of all or part of the assets of one corporation to another corporation when the transferor corporation or one or more of its shareholders (or any combination thereof) are in control of the transferee corporation. The transaction must meet the requirements of § 354, § 355, or § 356. Section 354 requires that substantially all of the property of one corporation be transferred to the second corporation. All property received in the exchange by the transferor corporation must be distributed to the transferor's shareholders. If assets remain in the transferor corporation, the requirements of § 354 are not met. Section 355 requires that upon the transfer of a part of the assets of one corporation for control of another corporation, stock and securities received by the transferor corporation be distributed to its shareholders. Further, the requirements (noted in Chapter 4) that both corporations be actively engaged in a trade or business after the exchange, that only assets of an active trade or business be transferred, and that there be a business purpose for the exchange must be met. Section 356 applies only when a distribution pursuant to § 354 or § 355 involves property other than qualifying stock or securities. The "other property" becomes boot and is taxed pursuant to § 356.

The "D" reorganization can be a corporate combination. Section 354 applies to a transfer of all or substantially all of the assets of one corporation to another corporation for control (50 percent) of the second corporation. This transaction can also meet the requirements of a "C" reorganization. If a transaction can be both a "C" and a "D" reorganization, § 368(a)(2)(A) provides that it be treated as a "D" reorganization. This will insure that the distribution of stock or securities be made pursuant to § 354 or § 355. This type of "D" reorganization is essentially a transfer of parent corporation assets to the subsidiary. The parent is liquidated, with all the stock in the subsidiary being distributed to the parent's shareholders.

Example 19   Alpha Corporation transfers all of its assets to a newly formed corporation, Beta, for all of Beta's stock. The Beta stock is then transferred to Alpha's shareholders, and Alpha is liquidated. The transaction qualifies as a "D" reorganization. It is equivalent to an "E" or an "F" reorganization. In essence, it is a new corporate shell around an old body. □

Control in a "D" reorganization has different meanings depending upon whether the reorganization is a corporate combination or a corporate division.

If it is a corporate combination, control is ownership of at least 50 percent of the total voting stock *or* 50 percent of the total *value* of all classes of stock.[19] If the reorganization is a corporate division, control is ownership of at least 80 percent of the total voting stock *and* at least 80 percent of the total *number* of shares of all other classes of stock.[20]

Spin-Offs, Split-Offs, and Split-Ups.   The more typical "D" reorganization involves a corporate division. One corporation transfers a part of its assets to another corporation for stock in that corporation. To qualify as a tax-free reorganization, the transferor corporation must obtain stock representing control (80 percent) in the transferee corporation and must distribute that stock to its shareholders pursuant to § 355. Section 355 (discussed in Chapter 4) permits stock to be received tax-free by shareholders in a qualifying spin-off, split-off, or split-up. Consequently, the stock received in the new corporation must be distributed to the shareholders of the transferor corporation either as a spin-off, wherein the shareholders do not surrender any stock in the distributing corporation, or as a split-off, wherein the shareholders do surrender stock in the distributing corporation. A split-up involves the transfer of the assets of one corporation to two or more new corporations. Stock in the new corporations is distributed to the transferor's shareholders. The transferor corporation is liquidated. The spin-off, split-off, and split-up are illustrated in Figure VII.

Shareholders of a corporation may wish to divide the corporate assets and split up the business of a corporation for several reasons. Antitrust problems may arise. The shareholders may have differences of opinion. Family planning may enter the picture. The old corporation could be liquidated with the assets distributed to the various shareholders. Those wishing to continue the business in corporate form could then establish a new corporation. Assets can be transferred to a controlled corporation tax-free under § 351. However, there are problems upon liquidation of the old corporation. Shareholders will normally recognize gain upon the liquidation, and § 336 will generate tax at the corporate level. Consequently, this route may not be the best. A stock redemption under § 302, either a substantially disproportionate distribution or a qualified partial liquidation, is a possibility. Again, however, gain will normally be recognized both at the shareholder level and at the corporate level. The better alternative is to effect a split-up under § 368(a)(1)(D) and distribute stock and securities in the new corporation pursuant to § 355.

Example 20   A and B, individuals, are the sole shareholders of Alpha Corporation. Alpha Corporation was organized 10 years ago and has been actively engaged in the manufacturing business. Alpha manufactures two major products, Product 1 and Product 2. Considerable friction has developed between A and B, who wish to divide the business. A wants the assets used for the manufacture of Product 1, and B wants to continue the manufacture of Product 2. Two new corporations are formed, Beta and Zeta Corporations. All of the assets relating to the manufacture of Product 1 are transferred to Beta Corporation. The remaining assets are trans-

---

19. § 368(a)(2)(H).
20. § 368(c).

Figure VII   "D" Reorganization

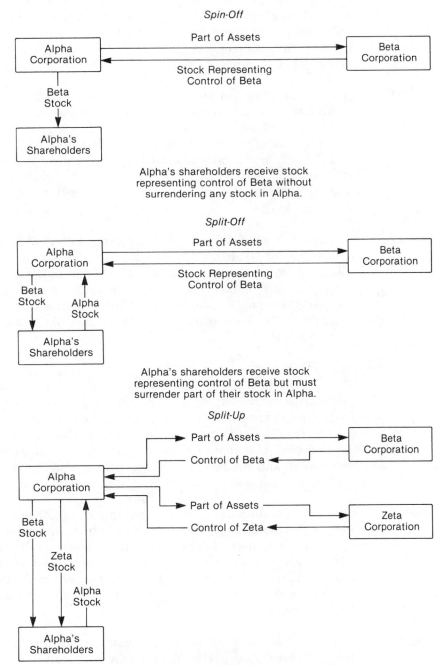

Spin-Off

Alpha's shareholders receive stock
representing control of Beta without
surrendering any stock in Alpha.

Split-Off

Alpha's shareholders receive stock
representing control of Beta but must
surrender part of their stock in Alpha.

Split-Up

A part of Alpha's assets are transferred to Beta; the
remainder of the assets are transferred to Zeta. Stock in
Beta and Zeta is transferred to Alpha's shareholders
for their stock in Alpha, and Alpha is liquidated.

ferred to Zeta Corporation. The stock in Beta is transferred to A for his
stock in Alpha, while the stock in Zeta is transferred to B for his stock in
Alpha. Alpha is liquidated. The transaction qualifies as a "D" reorganiza-

tion. Neither gain nor loss is recognized to either A or B upon the exchange of their stock in Alpha for stock in the new corporations by virtue of § 355. Gain or loss is not recognized to Alpha Corporation under § 361. Beta and Zeta Corporations receive the assets of Alpha tax-free under § 1032 (i.e., no gain or loss is recognized to a corporation on the receipt of money or other property in exchange for its stock). ☐

Example 21 A owns 200 shares of R Corporation stock with a basis of $40,000 (value of $60,000). In a "D" reorganization (a spin-off), she receives a distribution of 50 shares of S Corporation stock valued at $20,000. A surrenders none of her R stock. The basis she had in her R stock is allocated to the R stock and S stock on the basis of the fair market value of each. Thus, $20,000/$80,000 of the $40,000 basis, or $10,000, will be allocated to the S stock, and $60,000/$80,000 of the $40,000 basis, or $30,000, will be allocated to the R stock. ☐

Example 22 Assume that a split-off occurred in Example 21. A surrenders 100 shares of R stock for 50 shares of S stock. Again, her basis of $40,000 will be allocated among the R and S stock on the basis of the fair market value of each. The fair market value of the retained R stock is $30,000. Thus, $30,000/$50,000 of the $40,000, or $24,000, will be allocated to the R stock A retained, and $20,000/$50,000 of the $40,000, or $16,000, will be allocated to the S stock. ☐

Requirements of § 355. The "D" reorganization requires that the provisions of § 355 be met if the transfer is to be considered tax-free. All the requirements of § 355 discussed in Chapter 4 come into play. Stock representing control [control being 80 percent as defined in § 368(c)(1)] of the transferee corporation must be distributed to the shareholders of the transferor corporation. The assets transferred (plus those retained) must represent an active business that has been owned and conducted by the transferor corporation for at least five years before the transfer.

Example 23 Alpha Corporation has been engaged in the manufacture of certain products. It also owns investment securities. It transfers the investment securities to a newly formed corporation and distributes the stock of the new corporation to its shareholders. The transaction does not qualify as a "D" reorganization. The holding of investment securities does not constitute a trade or business. The shareholders of Alpha Corporation will be taxed on the receipt of the stock. ☐

Example 24 Assume Alpha Corporation has a separate research department. It transfers the research department to a new corporation and distributes the stock of the new corporation to its shareholders. The activities of the research department do not constitute a trade or business. Consequently, the transaction does not qualify as a "D" reorganization. ☐

Example 25 Alpha Corporation manufactures a single product, but it has had two plants for the past 10 years. It transfers one plant and related activities to a new corporation and distributes the stock of the new corporation to its shareholders. The activities of each plant constitute a trade or business. Consequently, the transaction qualifies as a "D" reorganization. □

Example 26   Assume one of the plants in Example 25 has been in existence for only two years. Alpha Corporation transfers one plant and related activities to a new corporation and distributes the stock of the new corporation to its shareholders. Though the activities of each plant constitute a trade or business, one has not been in existence for at least five years. Consequently, the transaction does not qualify as a "D" reorganization. (It does not matter which plant is transferred, since both—the one transferred and the one retained—must have been in existence for at least five years before the transfer.) □

As noted in Chapter 4, § 355 requires a business purpose for the transfer and the absence of a tax avoidance scheme. However, there is no requirement that the distribution of stock and securities be pro rata if all the other requirements of § 355 are satisfied.[21]

Example 27   A and B, individuals, own all the stock of Alpha Corporation, which has operated two active businesses for the past 10 years. Alpha transfers the assets representing one business to a newly formed corporation, Beta Corporation. The stock of Beta is distributed to B only, in exchange for a part of B's stock in Alpha Corporation. The transaction qualifies as a "D" reorganization. □

Although the Regulations[22] state that a single trade or business cannot be divided or separated and consequently effect a tax-free distribution of stock in the newly formed corporation, the IRS has conceded that a single business can be subject to split-off or spin-off treatment.[23]

Type E

The "Type E" reorganization is a recapitalization—a major change in the character and amount of outstanding capital stock or paid-in capital of a corporation. The transaction is significant only as far as shareholders who exchange stock or securities are concerned. The corporation itself receives no property and, consequently, should have no tax problems.

The Regulations give several examples of recapitalizations:[24]

1. A corporation with $100,000 par value bonds outstanding will, instead of liquidating the bonds for cash, discharge them by issuing preferred shares to the bondholders.
2. Twenty-five percent of a corporation's preferred stock is surrendered to the corporation for cancellation in exchange for no par value common stock.

---

21. Reg. § 1.355–3(a).
22. Reg. § 1.355–1(a).
23. Rev.Rul. 64–147, 1964–1 C.B. 136.
24. Reg. § 1.368–2(e).

3. A corporation issues preferred stock, previously authorized but unissued, for outstanding common stock.

4. An exchange is made of a corporation's outstanding preferred stock that possesses certain priorities with reference to the amount and time of payment of dividends and the distribution of the corporate assets upon liquidation for a new issue of the corporation's common stock having no such rights.

If a shareholder exchanges his or her stock for bonds in the corporation, the former shareholder is in receipt of boot, taxable under § 356, unless bonds are also surrendered either in the same amount as or in a greater principal amount than the bonds received.

Type F

The "Type F" reorganization is "a . . . mere change in identity, form or place of organization, however effected." [25] The IRS has ruled that if a reorganization qualifies as an "A," "C," or "D" reorganization and, at the same time, as an "F" reorganization, "Type F" reorganization treatment will predominate.[26]

Example 28   X Corporation changes its name to Y Corporation. This is an "F" reorganization. □

Example 29   X Corporation, a corporation organized in New Mexico, incorporates Y Corporation in Delaware and transfers all its assets to Y in exchange for all of Y's stock. X is to be liquidated. Its shareholders surrender all their X stock for a pro rata distribution of the Y stock. This transaction can be an "A," a "C," or a "D" reorganization. It also satisfies the requirements of an "F" reorganization. Consequently, it will be treated as an "F" reorganization. □

The surviving corporation in an "F" reorganization is actually the same corporation as its predecessor. Consequently, the tax characteristics of the predecessor carry over to the successor. Because such a reorganization is a mere change in identity or form, net operating losses can be carried back as well as forward.

An "F" reorganization is restricted to a single operating corporation. Even though there may be uninterrupted business continuity and substantially the same ownership before and after the reorganization of a number of operating companies, such a reorganization must be considered under the other applicable reorganization provisions.

An "F" reorganization will not jeopardize the status of § 1244 stock, nor will it terminate a valid Subchapter S election.[27] This is true because there can be no significant change in stock ownership in the "F" reorganization.[28]

---

25. § 368(a)(1)(F).
26. Rev.Rul. 57–276, 1957–1 C.B. 126.
27. Reg. § 1.1244(d)–3(d)(1) and Rev.Rul. 64–250, 1964–2 C.B. 333.
28. Rev.Rul. 66–284, 1966–2 C.B. 115.

Type G

The Bankruptcy Act of 1980 created the "G" reorganization, which is a transfer of all or a part of the assets of a debtor corporation in a bankruptcy, receivership, foreclosure, or similar proceeding in a Federal or state court to an acquiring corporation wherein stock or securities of the acquiring corporation are distributed in a transaction that qualifies under § 354, § 355, or § 356. The debtor corporation's creditors must receive voting stock of the acquiring corporation equal to 80 percent or more of the total fair market value of the debt of the debtor corporation.

▬▬▬ Judicial Conditions

A discussion of the reorganization concept must consider certain basic conditions that pervade the entire field of corporate reorganizations. Various judicially created doctrines—sound business purpose, continuity of interest, and continuity of business enterprise—have become basic requirements for the tax-free status of corporate reorganizations. In addition, the courts have formulated the so-called step transaction doctrine to determine tax status of a reorganization effected through a series of related transactions. It is further required that a plan of reorganization exist before tax-free status will be granted an exchange. In essence, these requirements have prescribed additional requirements for tax-free status of corporate reorganizations.

Sound Business Purpose

Even though the reorganization statutes have been literally followed, a transaction will not be tax-free unless it exhibits a bona fide business purpose.[29]

Example 30   T, an individual, owns all of the stock of YZ Corporation, which holds, along with its operating assets, some appreciated stock in X Corporation. T would like to sell the X Corporation stock and some of the operating assets of YZ Corporation and retain the proceeds. How might this objective be carried out with the minimum of tax consequences?

—A direct distribution of the X Corporation stock and some of the operating assets to T would result in dividend income to T to the extent of the lesser of (1) the fair market value of the X Corporation stock and the portion of operating assets distributed or (2) YZ Corporation's E & P (refer to Chapter 4).

—A redemption of part of T's stock in YZ in return for the X Corporation stock and some of YZ's operating assets would also produce dividend income, because T is the sole shareholder of YZ Corporation (refer to Chapter 4).

---

29. See *Gregory v. Helvering*, 35–1 USTC ¶9043, 14 AFTR 1191, 55 S.Ct. 266 (USSC, 1935).

—A complete liquidation would cause T to have a long-term capital gain with a step-up in basis in the assets of YZ Corporation. However, T does not want a complete liquidation of YZ Corporation.

—As a solution, YZ Corporation forms a new corporation, W Corporation. YZ transfers part of its operating assets and the X Corporation stock to W Corporation in exchange for all of the stock of W Corporation. Immediately after the transfer, YZ distributes the W Corporation stock to T. An allocable portion of T's basis in the YZ Corporation stock is assigned to the W Corporation stock. The holding period of the W Corporation stock includes the holding period T has in the YZ stock. T then sells the stock in W Corporation and reports as a long-term capital gain the amount of the difference between the sales proceeds and the basis in the W Corporation stock. A tax savings results based on the amount of T's original basis in the YZ Corporation stock that was allocated to the W Corporation stock. T's argument is that the original transfer from YZ Corporation to W Corporation has no adverse tax consequences, since it qualifies as a nontaxable "D" reorganization. ☐

Although the transfer in Example 30 may meet the literal definition of a "D" reorganization, no business purpose existed for the creation of W Corporation. It was, instead, a mere device through which T could avoid dividend income. Because the substance of the transaction was a direct distribution to T by YZ Corporation of a portion of its assets (the X Corporation stock plus some of YZ's operating assets), T would be taxed accordingly, and the various intervening steps would be disregarded.

The requirement that a reorganization must exhibit a bona fide business purpose is a judicially created doctrine.[30] Moreover, the Regulations have followed the courts in recognizing the requirement.[31]

The test of business purpose, and whether it may reflect the shareholder's purpose rather than that of the corporation, is not well-defined. In one case, the Court implied that the benefit to the corporation must be direct and substantial.[32] However, in more recent cases, courts have conceded that it is sometimes impossible to draw a line between the purpose of the corporation and the purpose of the shareholders.[33]

Cases indicate that the business purpose doctrine does not operate in reverse. It is normally the revenue agent who asserts lack of business purpose to deny tax-free status to a corporate reorganization. Occasionally, however, the taxpayer may want the transaction to be taxable in order to receive a step-up in basis in assets or to recognize a loss. In some cases, taxpayers have attempted to employ the business purpose doctrine to prevent the transaction

30. The doctrine as developed in the *Gregory* case became a precedent for all transactions that might be shams devised merely for tax avoidance purposes. It brought about the principle of substance over form. The IRS and the courts will look through the form of a transaction to determine what really took place. All business transactions must have a sound business purpose.
31. Reg. § 1.368-1(c).
32. *Bazley v. Comm.*, 47-1 USTC ¶9288, 35 AFTR 1190, 67 S.Ct. 1489 (USSC, 1947).
33. See *Estate of Parshelsky v. Comm.*, 62-1 USTC ¶9460, 9 AFTR2d 1382, 303 F.2d 14 (CA-2, 1962).

from being considered a reorganization. In those instances, however, the courts have required the taxpayers to abide by the form of the transaction and have upheld the contention of the IRS that such transaction was a reorganization.[34] One reason for giving the IRS this benefit is that the taxpayer is initially in command of tax consequences. Generally, "business purpose" is devised in the offices of the taxpayer's attorneys. Consequently, taxpayers should not be allowed to benefit from the option of producing or failing to produce documentation of a sufficient purpose.

Continuity of Interest

The continuity of interest doctrine is founded in the basic philosophy of the tax-free reorganization (i.e., if a shareholder or corporation has substantially the same investment after a corporate exchange as before, no tax should be imposed upon the transaction). For the "A" reorganization, however, the Code imposes no limitations on consideration. Consequently, a purchase of the properties of one corporation could qualify as a reorganization even if the consideration were cash or short-term notes.[35] Without some restrictions on consideration, the reorganization provisions would be an avenue for unwarranted tax avoidance. Thus, courts imposed what has been termed the "continuity of interest" test. To qualify for tax-free status, the seller must acquire an equity interest in the purchasing corporation.[36]

The Internal Revenue Service has attempted to define exactly how much equity shareholders of the acquired corporation must receive in the acquiring corporation to satisfy the continuity of interest test. For purposes of issuing an advance ruling, the IRS will deem the continuity of interest test to be met if shareholders of the acquired corporation, in the aggregate, receive stock in the acquiring corporation equal in value to at least 50 percent of all formerly outstanding stock of the acquired corporation.[37] Not all shareholders of the acquired corporation need to have a proprietary interest in the surviving corporation. The requirement is applied to the total consideration given in the acquisition and would be met if one or more of the acquired corporation's shareholders retain a sufficient proprietary interest in the continuing corporation.

Example 31 Alpha Corporation, with 50 shareholders, merges into Beta Corporation pursuant to state statute. Under the plan of merger, the shareholders of Alpha can elect to receive either cash or stock in Beta. Thirty of the shareholders (holding 40% of Alpha's outstanding stock) elect to receive cash; the remaining 20 shareholders of Alpha (holding 60% of the stock) elect to receive stock in Beta. This plan satisfies the continuity of interest

34. *Survaunt v. Comm.*, 47–2 USTC ¶9344, 35 AFTR 1557, 162 F.2d 753 (CA–8, 1947).
35. The use of short-term notes was first disallowed in *Cortland Specialty Co. v. Comm.*, 3 USTC ¶980, 11 AFTR 857, 60 F.2d 937 (CA–2, 1932), *cert. den.* 53 S.Ct. 316 (USSC, 1933). In *Cortland*, the Court stated that there must be some continuity of interest on the part of the transferor corporation or its shareholders to secure tax exemption.
36. *Pinellas Ice & Cold Storage v. Comm.*, 3 USTC ¶1023, 11 AFTR 1112, 53 S.Ct. 257 (USSC, 1933), and *LeTulle v. Scofield*, 40–1 USTC ¶9150, 23 AFTR 789, 60 S.Ct. 313 (USSC, 1940). In *LeTulle*, a corporation transferred all its assets to another corporation for cash and bonds. The Court held that the transaction was not a tax-free reorganization if the transferor's only retained interest was that of a creditor.
37. Rev.Proc. 74–26, 1974–2 C.B. 478, § 3.02, updated by Rev.Proc. 77–37, 1977–2 C.B. 568.

test. The shareholders receiving cash would be taxed on the transaction. Those receiving stock would not. ☐

Example 32   A and B, individuals, each hold 50% of the stock of Alpha Corporation. Alpha merges into Beta Corporation. A receives cash for his stock in Alpha, while B receives stock in Beta. This should also qualify as a tax-free merger. B receives stock in Beta equal in value to at least 50% of the formerly outstanding stock in Alpha. A will be taxed on the transaction, but B will not. ☐ ·

The continuity of interest requirement presents complications principally for the "A" reorganization. The other reorganization provisions have statutory limitations on consideration that surpass the requirements of the continuity of interest test as defined by the IRS. Consequently, this test generally presents no problem for other reorganizations.

Continuity of Business Enterprise

The Regulations refer to a "continuity of business enterprise under the modified form" as a prerequisite for a tax-free reorganization.[38] This requirement is an expansion of the sound business purpose principle.[39] However, it is a separate test. Originally, it was interpreted to mean that the acquiring corporation must conduct business activities of the same type as did the acquired corporation.[40] Amendments to the Regulations provide that this test is satisfied only if the transferee continues the historic business of the transferor or, if the business is not continued, uses a significant portion of the assets of the transferor in the transferee's business.[41]

Step Transaction

The court-imposed step transaction doctrine is employed to determine whether a reorganization is tax-free when a series of related transactions are involved. The courts look at the conditions before and after the change in ownership and, assuming the series of transactions are related, will consider all such transactions to be one for tax purposes. In one case, the Court proffered a test for determining whether a series of steps is to be treated as a single indivisible transaction.[42] The Court stated that such a test is one of mutual interdependence: "Were the steps so interdependent that the legal relations created by one transaction would have been fruitless without a completion of the series?"

The step transaction presents complications for reorganizations when "unwanted" assets are involved. If the acquired corporation attempts to dispose of its unwanted assets before a reorganization, the doctrine might be utilized to defeat tax-free status of the reorganization on the contention that substantially

---

38. Reg. § 1.368–1(b).
39. See *Gregory v. Helvering*, cited in Footnote 29.
40. Rev.Rul. 56–330, 1956–2 C.B. 204.
41. Reg. § 1.368–1(d).
42. *American Bantam Car Co.*, 11 T.C. 397 (1948), *aff'd.* in 49–2 USTC ¶9471, 38 AFTR 820, 177 F.2d 513 (CA–3, 1949), *cert. den.* 70 S.Ct. 622 (USSC, 1950).

all of the properties were not transferred. The "substantially all" requirement is present in the "C" reorganization, the "D" reorganization, and the subsidiary "A" reorganization. Assuming application of the step transaction is sustained, a prior nontaxable disposition of unwanted assets and a later reorganization would be treated as a single transaction. Consequently, the acquiring corporation would have failed to acquire substantially all of the acquired corporation's assets.

Example 33 Alpha Corporation wants to acquire certain, but not all, of the assets of Beta Corporation. A direct conveyance of the desired property to Alpha Corporation will not be a tax-free reorganization, because the unwanted assets are a substantial portion of Beta's total assets. Thus, a valid "C" reorganization is not possible; substantially all of Beta's assets will not be conveyed. A possible solution would be to organize a new corporation, transfer the unwanted assets to the new corporation for all of its stock, and distribute the stock to Beta's shareholders. The remaining assets in Beta Corporation would then be transferred to Alpha Corporation in return for stock. What has been accomplished?

—The first transfer would be tax-free under § 351 as a transfer to a corporation in exchange for at least 80 percent of the new company's stock.

—The second transfer of Beta's remaining assets to Alpha Corporation in return for stock is a tax-free "C" reorganization. What could go wrong with the results? ☐

In a case [43] with facts similar to those in Example 33, the Supreme Court agreed with the IRS that the first transfer was equivalent to a retention of assets by Beta Corporation. If the unwanted assets had remained in Beta, the transfer to Alpha Corporation would not have met the "substantially all" test. A transfer to cause the reorganization provisions to be available in situations such as in Example 33 was held to be unwarranted tax avoidance.

Example 33 involved two nontaxable events. If unwanted assets are sold to an unrelated purchaser in a taxable transaction, a later transfer of the remaining assets for stock might qualify as a "C" reorganization. Further, a dividend distribution to shareholders of the transferor corporation should not affect the tax-free nature of a subsequent reorganization. On the other hand, if a transfer to shareholders is in connection with a stock redemption wherein the shareholders receive capital gain treatment, there might again be a question as to the tax-free status of a subsequent reorganization.

The IRS generally views any transaction occurring within one year of the reorganization as part of the acquisition, assuming there is no proof the transaction was, in fact, unrelated.[44] The application of the step transaction doctrine to such a transaction can bring the continuity of interest test into prominence

43. *Helvering v. Elkhorn Coal Co.*, 38–1 USTC ¶9238, 20 AFTR 1301, 95 F.2d 732 (CA–4, 1938), *cert. den.* 59 S.Ct. 65 (USSC, 1938).
44. In Rev.Rul. 69–48, 1969–1 C.B. 106, the IRS applied the step transaction doctrine to transactions that were 22 months apart.

in a "B" or "C" reorganization should shareholders of the transferor corporation immediately dispose of stock received in the transferee corporation. In the case of an "A" reorganization, the application of the doctrine can cause an otherwise tax-free reorganization to be deemed a purchase. This is possible if the shareholders do not retain their equity interests for a reasonable period of time.

Liquidation-Reincorporation

As noted in Chapter 5, gain on a distribution to shareholders is capital gain in a complete liquidation pursuant to § 331. Further, assets received in a liquidation receive a step-up in basis, and the accumulated earnings and profits account of the distributing corporation is closed. Before repeal of the *General Utilities* rule, the liquidated corporation had limited recognition of gain. Under § 351, assets can be transferred to a new, controlled corporation tax free. The tax benefits of these two Code Sections made the liquidation of a corporation with high earnings and profits appealing. The assets would have a step-up in basis from the liquidation. This step-up in basis could then be transferred to a new, controlled corporation. The cash in the old corporation would have been removed at capital gain rates because of the liquidation.

Although the liquidation-reincorporation has limited tax benefit with the repeal of the *General Utilities* rule and the elimination of the favorable tax treatment of long-term capital gains, it could still produce favorable tax consequences for a qualified closely-held corporation if the shareholder has a high tax basis in his or her stock in the liquidated corporation.

The Regulations address the problem of a liquidation-reincorporation. According to Reg. § 1.331–1(c), a liquidation followed by a transfer to another corporation, or a liquidation preceded by such a transfer, may have the effect of a dividend distribution. Regulation § 1.301–1(l) states that a distribution to shareholders is a dividend distribution, even though taking place at the same time as certain other transactions, if it is in substance a separate transaction. The Regulation mentions, as examples, distributions to shareholders in connection with a recapitalization, a reincorporation, or a merger of one corporation with a newly organized corporation possessing little or no property. These provisions in the Regulations are an attempt to eliminate tax advantages of a liquidation-reincorporation.

The Internal Revenue Service often relies on the reorganization provisions to prevent tax advantages inherent in a liquidation-reincorporation. The IRS has attempted to classify a liquidation-reincorporation as either an "E" or an "F" reorganization on the theory that the shareholders' proportionate interests in the new corporation are the same as in the old.[45] The IRS has also attempted to bring such transactions within the provisions of the "D" reorganization. If a liquidation followed by a reincorporation can be validly labeled a reorganization, there is no step-up in basis in any of the assets. Further, accumulated earnings and profits carry over to the new corporation pursuant to § 381. Any assets retained by shareholders of the liquidated corporation constitute boot

---

45. Rev.Rul. 61–156, 1961–2 C.B. 2, and *Davant v. Comm.*, 66–2 USTC ¶9618, 18 AFTR2d 5523, 366 F.2d 874 (CA–5, 1966), *cert. den.* 87 S.Ct. 1370 (USSC, 1967).

and are taxed to the shareholders as such. If the distributions are pro rata, § 356 would cause such distributions to be treated as ordinary dividends to the extent of earnings and profits of the distributing corporation.

The control test for "D" reorganizations that are corporate combinations conforms to that of § 304. Thus, the transferor corporation or its shareholders are treated as having control of the transferee corporation if the transferor corporation or its shareholders own stock possessing at least 50 percent of the total combined voting stock or 50 percent of the total value of all classes of stock. In addition, the constructive ownership rules of § 318(a) apply in determining control. Thus, a liquidation-reincorporation transaction can be treated as a "D" reorganization if the shareholders of the liquidated corporation have a 50 percent control of the newly formed corporation.

If the business of the liquidated corporation is not continued by the new corporation, the IRS's assertion that the liquidation-reincorporation is in reality a reorganization can more easily be rebutted.[46]

Example 34

X Corporation has assets with a fair market value of $100,000 and a tax basis of $60,000. X is liquidated. A, the sole shareholder of X, has a basis of $20,000 in his stock in X. A retains $10,000 cash and transfers the remaining assets received in the liquidation to a newly formed corporation, Y, for all the stock in Y. If the first transaction qualifies as a liquidation pursuant to § 331, A would have a capital gain of $80,000. There would be no tax on the transfer of the assets to Y, and Y would have a basis of $90,000 in assets received. A would have a $90,000 basis in his stock in Y. If the IRS successfully contends the transaction is a "D" reorganization, the $10,000 cash would be an ordinary dividend to A to the extent of the earnings and profits of X. The assets acquired by Y would have a basis of $50,000, and the earnings and profits of X (less the $10,000 dividend distributed to A) would carry over to Y. A would have a basis of $20,000 in his stock in Y. □

Other Considerations

Plan of Reorganization and Parties Thereto

Section 361 states that a party to a reorganization recognizes neither gain nor loss if it exchanges property under a plan of reorganization for stock or securities in another corporation also a party to the reorganization. Section 354 provides that gain or loss will not be recognized if stock or securities in a corporation that is a party to the reorganization are exchanged solely for stock or securities in the same corporation or in another corporation also a party to the reorganization. Section 368 does not mention "plan of reorganization," and the term is not defined in the Code. The Regulations state that plan of reorganization refers to a consummated transaction specifically defined as a reorgani-

---

46. See *Pridemark v. Comm.*, 65–1 USTC ¶9388, 15 AFTR2d 853, 345 F.2d 35 (CA–4, 1965), in which the Court stated that there is a complete liquidation of the first corporation if the newly formed corporation does not resume the business of the liquidated corporation.

zation under § 368.[47] The Regulations take the position that the term limits rather than enlarges the definition of "reorganization." Only those exchanges or distributions that are directly a part of transactions described in § 368 produce nonrecognition of gain or loss.

The connotation placed upon "plan of reorganization" is essentially the same concept applicable to the step transaction doctrine. Acts would normally be included in the "plan" if their consummation was contemplated when the first step was begun and if their absence would have resulted in none of the acts being performed. Both the requirement that the transaction be pursuant to a plan of reorganization and the step transaction doctrine refer to a series of steps or acts.

The requirement that there be a plan of reorganization implies that a formal, written document is essential. The Regulations, in fact, refer to the adoption of a plan of reorganization.[48] Though the courts have not required a written plan, it is preferable that the parties execute a formal document, which would serve to delineate the rights of all parties and enumerate the required steps to perfect the exchange.

The parties to a reorganization are defined in §§ 368(b)(1) and (2). Parties to a reorganization include a corporation resulting from the reorganization, both corporations in an acquisition by one corporation of stock or properties of another, and the parent of the acquiring corporation when parent stock is exchanged for property in an "A," a "B," or a "C" reorganization.

Example 35
A parent corporation, Alpha, uses stock of its subsidiary, Beta, as consideration for the acquisition of assets in Zeta Corporation. The transaction will not qualify as a tax-free reorganization, because Beta is not a party to the reorganization. (Refer to Figures II, IV, and VI. Parent stock can be exchanged by a subsidiary in a reorganization, but a parent that is a party to a reorganization cannot use subsidiary stock to effect a reorganization. The parent must use its own stock.) □

Assumption of Liabilities

Because a corporate reorganization normally results in a continuation of the business activities of the previous corporations, liabilities are seldom liquidated. The acquiring corporation will either assume liabilities of the acquired organization or take property subject to liabilities. In a regular sale or purchase of properties, the assumption of liabilities by the purchaser is part of the selling price.[49] As noted in Chapter 3, in some nonrecognition transactions, assumption of liabilities is considered boot and hence taxable. This is not true in a § 351 transaction because of § 357. Also, in a tax-free reorganization pursuant to §§ 357 and 368(a)(1)(C), assumed liabilities are, for the most part, disregarded in computing taxable gain to the transferor corporation. At first glance, then, assumption of liabilities in a corporate reorganization would seem to present few problems. Troublesome areas exist, however.

47. Reg. § 1.368–2(g).
48. Reg. § 1.368–3(a).
49. *Crane v. Comm.*, 47–1 USTC ¶9217, 35 AFTR 776, 67 S.Ct. 1047 (USSC, 1947).

Section 357(c), which, irrespective of § 357(a), provides that liabilities in excess of basis are taxable gain, was discussed in Chapter 3 in connection with a § 351 transaction. This provision supposedly has no effect on tax-free reorganizations other than the "D" reorganization. Section 357(c) specifically states that it is applicable to exchanges "... to which § 351 applies, or to which § 361 applies by reason of a plan of reorganization within the meaning of § 368(a)(1)(D) ..." The "D" reorganization alone would be affected. However, § 368(a)(2)(A) provides that if a transaction qualifies both as an acquisition of assets for stock under § 368(a)(1)(C) and as a transfer to a controlled corporation under § 368(a)(1)(D), it is treated as a § 368(a)(1)(D) transaction. Consequently, taxpayers might be misled as to the application of § 357(c).

Section 368(a)(1), which discusses the acquisition of another corporation's properties solely in exchange for all or a part of the acquirer's voting stock, specifically states that the assumption of a liability of the acquired corporation will be disregarded. Congress added this provision to the predecessor of § 368(a)(1)(C) to eliminate any "solely for voting stock" problem in the "C" reorganization. However, § 368(a)(1)(B) contains no similar provision. Thus, any assumption of a liability by the transferor corporation in a "B" reorganization presumably will violate the "solely for voting stock" requirement. Normally, however, the assumption of liabilities is not present in a "B" reorganization inasmuch as "Type B" is simply a change in stock ownership.

Carryover of Corporate Tax Attributes

In General

The determination of the tax features of an acquired corporation to be carried over to the acquiring or successor corporation is a significant problem in a corporate acquisition and in the liquidation of a subsidiary corporation. Some tax features of an acquired corporation (the carryover of losses, tax credits, and deficits) will be welcomed by a successor corporation. Others may prove less welcome. It is immaterial whether the acquiring corporation desires the carryover of certain tax attributes of its acquired predecessor inasmuch as the carryover rules, if applicable, are mandatory. Thus, the carryover rules should be carefully considered in every corporate acquisition; they may, in fact, determine the form of the acquisition. This is particularly true in the liquidation of a subsidiary pursuant to § 332. The carryover rules apply in the liquidation of a controlled subsidiary under § 332 if the basis of the transferred assets carries over to the parent. If basis of assets is determined pursuant to the single transaction approach of § 338, the carryover rules do not apply.

Theory of Carryovers

Before the advent of § 381, case law determined the aggregate tax benefits of an acquired corporation that could be carried over to the successor. With respect to net operating losses, general theory held that only the corporation sustaining the loss could take the deduction. Because of this theory, the form of a corporate acquisition largely determined whether a tax loss could be carried over to the acquiring corporation. If a statutory merger or consolidation occurred, the courts permitted the carryover of the predecessor corporation's deductions. Because there was an amalgamation of assets and liabilities of the two corporations through operation of law, a carryover was justified. On the other hand, carryovers were not permitted in other forms of corporate acquisitions.[50]

With respect to the carryover of earnings and profits of a predecessor corporation, the courts held that although a credit balance in earnings and profits of the acquired corporation would carry over to the successor corporation, a deficit would not.[51] This rule was supposedly grounded on the desire to prevent escape of earnings and profits from taxation.

Although § 381 now determines which tax benefits of an acquired corporation can be carried over to the successor, it does not apply to all transactions. In instances where it does not apply, case law presumably is still applicable.

Allowance of Carryovers

Section 381 provides for the carryover of various specific tax attributes from one corporation to another in certain tax-free liquidations and reorganizations. It permits the successor corporation "... to step into the 'tax shoes' of its predecessor corporation." [52]

Though § 381 presumably solves the problem of carryovers in many instances, it does not apply to all tax items nor does it apply to all transactions. Section 381(c) lists the tax features of an acquired corporation that can be carried over to a successor corporation. Section 381 does not apply to any other items. Further, only the following transactions are covered: the "A," the "C," the "F," the nondivisive "D" and "G" reorganizations, and the liquidation of a controlled subsidiary under § 332 wherein the subsidiary's basis in its assets carries over to the parent. As to other tax items and transactions, the tax practitioner must use the case law.

Net Operating Loss Carryovers. A net operating loss carryover, as determined under § 172, is permitted as a deduction of the successor corporation under § 381(c)(1). However, there are limitations on the amount of the carryover. Sections 381(c)(1)(B) and 382(b) limit the aggregate deduction the successor corporation can obtain from net operating losses of the predecessor corporation or corporations, while § 269 will deny the deduction altogether if a tax avoidance scheme exists. Section 384, added by the Revenue Act of 1987, limits the amount of preacquisition loss an acquiring corporation can use to offset built-in gains of the acquired corporation.

Under § 381(c)(1)(B), the amount of a net operating loss that can be carried to the first tax year ending after the transfer date is limited to a percentage representing the remaining days in that tax year. For example, if two calendar year corporations merged on July 1, only a portion of a net operating loss of the acquired corporation could be used to offset income for that tax year. The amount would be limited to one half of the taxable income of the acquiring corporation. This limitation applies only for the purpose of computing the net operating loss

50. *New Colonial Ice Co. v. Helvering,* 4 USTC ¶1292, 13 AFTR 1180, 54 S.Ct. 788 (USSC, 1934).
51. *Comm. v. Sansome,* 3 USTC ¶978, 11 AFTR 854, 60 F.2d 931 (CA–2, 1931), *cert. den.* 53 S.Ct. 291 (USSC, 1932), and *Comm. v. Phipps,* 49–1 USTC ¶9204, 37 AFTR 827, 69 S.Ct. 616 (USSC, 1949).
52. S. Rept. 1622, 83d Cong., 2d Sess. (1954).

deduction of the successor corporation for the successor's first taxable year ending after the date of the transfer. The limitation does not apply for purposes of determining the portion of any net operating loss that may be carried to any taxable year of the successor corporation after the first taxable year.

Example 36   Alpha Corporation merges into Beta Corporation on December 16, 1987. Alpha Corporation had a net operating loss of $73,000, while Beta Corporation had taxable income for 1987 of $100,000. Only $4,110 ($100,000 × 15/365 = $4,110) of the $73,000 net operating loss can be used to offset Beta's taxable income. Beta would have taxable income of $95,890 ($100,000 − $4,110). The remainder of the loss carryover from Alpha Corporation, $68,890, would be carried forward to offset Beta's 1988 taxable income.

If the merger had taken place on December 31, there would have been no net operating loss deduction for 1987 ($100,000 × 0/365 = $0). The entire loss of $73,000 would be carried to 1988. □

The taxable years to which a net operating loss can be carried back or forward are prescribed by § 172(b)(1), which contains the general rules for net operating losses.[53]

Timing is important if a net operating loss carryover is possible. Section 381(b)(1) states that the taxable year of the transferor corporation will end on the date of distribution or transfer (except in the case of an "F" reorganization).[54] Section 381(c)(1)(A) states that the net operating loss carryovers are carried to the first taxable year of the acquiring corporation ending after the date of the transfer, subject to the limitation noted above. If the transfer should not be completed by the last day of the taxable year of both corporations, the application of the first rule will produce a short taxable year for the loss corporation (it will end on the date of transfer) which will be counted as a full year for purposes of the 15-year carryover period. The portion of the taxable year of the acquiring corporation beginning on the date of transfer will count as a full year in computing the carryover period. Thus, a full year could be lost. For example, a transferor corporation's net operating loss for 1988 would be spread over only 14 years if it is merged into a calendar year transferee corporation on any day in 1988 other than December 31. Two taxable years would occur in 1988 so that the carryover would apply to years 1988 through 2002.

Section 382 imposes limitations on the carryover of a net operating loss of an acquired corporation. Before 1987, § 382(a) provided that a net operating loss carryover of a purchased corporation was eliminated if there was a change of at least 50 percent in the ownership of the corporation's outstanding stock since the beginning of the present or prior taxable year *and* if the acquired corporation did not continue to carry on substantially the same trade or business as that conducted before the ownership change. This provision applied to a purchase of stock through which one or more of the 10 principal

53. See Reg. § 1.381(c)(1)–1(e)(3) for the application of this Section to corporate reorganizations.
54. In the "F" reorganization, the transferor corporation's year does not end on the transfer date. Carryovers are considered as though there had been no reorganization. A net operating loss could thus be carried back as well as forward. (This assumes that a single corporation is involved in the merger, as the "F" reorganization is not applicable in the case of multiple corporations.)

shareholders obtained a percentage of the total value of the outstanding stock that was at least 50 percentage points above the interest held at the beginning of the present or prior taxable year.

As for a tax-free reorganization, § 382(b) provided that a net operating loss carryover was limited when the shareholders of the loss corporation owned less than 20 percent of the fair market value of the outstanding common stock in the acquiring corporation immediately after the reorganization. If shareholders of the loss corporation owned less than 20 percent of the stock of the successor corporation, the loss carryover was reduced proportionately. The percent of reduction was determined by multiplying the percent of the stock of the successor corporation owned by shareholders of the loss corporation by 5 and subtracting the product from 100%.

Example 37   Alpha Corporation acquires the assets of Beta Corporation, the loss corporation, in 1986. Beta has a net operating loss of $100,000. Immediately after the acquisition, the shareholders of Beta own 12% of the fair market value of the stock of Alpha. The 12% figure reduces the net operating loss of Beta Corporation (to be carried over) to $60,000, computed as follows: The 12% figure would be multiplied by 5, and the product (60%) would be subtracted from 100%. Thus, 40% of the loss would be eliminated. Sixty percent, or $60,000, of the loss can be used to offset Alpha Corporation's net income. □

The Tax Reform Act of 1986 amended § 382 both for ownership changes under § 382(a) and for tax-free reorganizations under § 382(b). For 1987 and thereafter, the limitations on net operating loss carryovers under § 382 are triggered only if there is (1) an owner shift or (2) an equity structure shift. If neither an owner shift nor an equity structure shift occurs, § 382 is not applicable and no limitation is placed on the amount of the net operating loss carryover. If either an owner shift or an equity structure shift occurs, the net operating loss carryover is subject to what is termed a "§ 382 limitation."

—An owner shift generally is any change in the respective ownership of stock by a five percent shareholder. The change is determined by looking to a testing period that is the shorter of the prior three years or the period following the most recent ownership change. (The testing period does not start before May 6, 1986.) Stock changes do not include stock acquired by gift, death, or divorce or pursuant to certain employee stock ownership plan (ESOP) transactions. Holdings of nonvoting preferred stock are not considered in determining whether an ownership change has occurred. All less-than-five percent shareholders are treated as a single five percent shareholder. If a 50 percent shareholder treats his stock as being worthless during a tax year and holds it at year-end, the shareholder is treated as having acquired the stock on the first day of the succeeding tax year in determining whether there has been a more-than-50 percent change in stock ownership. The shareholder is regarded as not having owned the stock previously. The result is that claiming a worthless stock deduction by a 50 percent shareholder can cause an owner shift.

—An equity structure shift is a tax-free reorganization other than a divisive reorganization or an "F" reorganization.

—If either the owner shift or the equity structure shift causes a more-than-50 percent change in the ownership of the loss corporation, the net operating loss carryover is subject to the § 382 limitation.

—The § 382 limitation provides that the taxable income of the new loss or the surviving corporation may be reduced each year by the net operating loss carryover only to the extent of the value of the loss corporation's stock on the date of the ownership change multiplied by the long-term tax-exempt rate. The long-term tax-exempt rate is the highest of the Federal long-term rates in effect in the three calendar month period before the stock change. (This information is available on a monthly basis in revenue rulings published by the IRS in Internal Revenue Bulletins.) [55]

—Any § 382 limitation not used because of insufficient taxable income may be carried forward to future years.

Example 38   The stock of L Corporation is publicly traded, and no shareholder holds 5% or more of the stock. During the three-year period between January 1, 1987, and January 1, 1990, numerous trades are made involving the stock of L Corporation, but no person (or persons) becomes a 5% shareholder (either directly or indirectly) and increases his or her (or their) ownership by more than 50 percentage points. No ownership change takes place, therefore, that will result in § 382 limitations to any net operating loss carryovers. Note that no ownership shift has occurred, since the less-than-5% shareholders are aggregated, thereby owning 100% before the trades and 100% after the trades. □

Example 39   U Corporation, a calendar year taxpayer, has a more-than-50 percent ownership change on January 1, 1988. At this point, it has a net operating loss carryover of $500,000. Also, the value of the U Corporation stock is $1,000,000, and the long-term tax-exempt rate is 10%. Thus, U Corporation's § 382 limitation for 1988 is $100,000 ($1,000,000 × 10%). If in calendar year 1988, U Corporation has taxable income of $70,000 (before any NOL carryover), $70,000 of the loss can be used. The $30,000 remaining portion ($100,000 − $70,000) can be carried over and will increase the § 382 limitation for 1989 to $130,000 ($30,000 + $100,000). □

Example 40   On July 1, 1988, X Corporation is merged into P Corporation in an "A" reorganization. At the time of the merger, X Corporation had a net operating loss of $100,000. Pursuant to the merger, the shareholders of X Corporation receive 40% of the stock of P Corporation. An equity structure shift (an "A" reorganization) has taken place with a more-than-50% change over the lowest percentage of X Corporation stock owned by such shareholders at any time during the testing period. If the value of X Corporation is $50,000 and the applicable rate is 10%, the § 382 limitation on X Corporation's net operating loss is $5,000 ($50,000 × 10%). □

55. The objective of the § 382 limitation is to restrict the use of net operating losses to a hypothetical future income stream. This income stream is to be measured by the yield that would have been received had the value of the stock been invested in long-term securities. Although the long-term tax-exempt rate will be readily available in determining the § 382 limitation, ascertaining the value of the acquired corporation's stock could prove troublesome.

Example 41   Assume in Example 40 that the shareholders of X Corporation receive 50% of the stock of P Corporation. There has not been a more-than-50% change over the lowest percentage of X Corporation owned by such shareholders during the testing period. Consequently, the entire $100,000 will carry over with no § 382 limitation. □

Example 42   On July 1, 1988, Y Corporation is owned by two unrelated shareholders, C (70%) and D (30%). Y Corporation redeems all of C's stock in exchange for nonvoting preferred stock. Following this recapitalization, an ownership change in Y Corporation has occurred, because the percentage of Y stock owned by D during the testing period has increased by more than 50 percentage points. For this purpose, the preferred stock issued to C is not counted. Thus, any net operating losses Y Corporation might have will be subject to the § 382 limitation. □

An owner shift or an equity structure shift often does not occur on the last day of the tax year. In such case, the annual § 382 limitation is allocated based on the number of days in the tax year before and after the change.

Net operating loss carryforwards are disallowed completely if the new loss or surviving corporation fails to satisfy the continuity of business enterprise requirement, as discussed previously, for a two-year period following any ownership change or equity structure shift.

Because it will be of benefit to the parties to increase the value of the loss corporation, certain capital contributions (including § 351 transfers) are to be disregarded if they are tax motivated. Capital contributions (including § 351 transfers) are presumed to be tax motivated if they occur within the two years preceding the ownership change.

If at least one third of the fair market value of a corporation's assets consists of nonbusiness assets, the value of the loss corporation is reduced by the excess of the value of the nonbusiness assets over the corporation's indebtedness attributable to such assets. Nonbusiness assets include any assets held for investment, including cash, marketable securities, and investments in subsidiaries.

The corporation having a net operating loss may be the acquiring corporation. If an acquired corporation has a built-in gain (wherein fair market value of its assets exceeds the aggregate adjusted bases of its assets immediately before the gain), § 384, added by the Revenue Act of 1987, prevents the acquiring corporation with an NOL from offsetting the loss against any built-in gain of the acquired corporation, that is recognized during the five-year period following the acquisition. Section 384 is applicable to a gain corporation acquired by a loss corporation in a § 332 liquidation or in an "A", a "C", or a "D" reorganization.

Earnings and Profits.   The Supreme Court held in an early case [56] that the earnings and profits of an acquired corporation carries over to a successor corporation. However, the Court later held that a successor corporation was not permitted to apply a deficit in the acquired corporation's earnings and

---

56. *Comm. v. Sansome*, cited in Footnote 51.

profits against its own earnings and profits.[57] There was confusion in applying these general rules. Section 381(c)(2) clarifies these rules with respect to the carryover of earnings and profits of a predecessor corporation. Earnings and profits of a predecessor corporation is deemed to have been received by the successor corporation as of the date of the distribution or transfer. A deficit, on the other hand, may be used to offset earnings and profits accumulated by the successor corporation only after the date of the transfer. Thus, both earnings and profits and deficits carry over, but deficits reduce earnings and profits only after the date of transfer.

If one corporation has accumulated earnings and profits and the other has a deficit, the deficit can be used only to offset earnings and profits accumulated after the date of the transfer. If this is the case, the acquiring corporation will be considered as maintaining two separate earnings and profits accounts after the date of transfer, the first containing the total accumulated earnings and profits as of the date of the transfer and the second containing total deficits as of such date.[58] The deficit in one account may not be used to reduce accumulated earnings and profits in the other account.

Capital Loss Carryovers.   Section 381(c)(3) prescribes the same limitations for the carryover of capital losses of the predecessor corporation as those imposed on the carryover of net operating losses. The taxable year of the acquiring corporation to which a capital loss is carried is the first taxable year ending after the date of transfer. The capital loss carryover is a short-term capital loss to the acquiring corporation, and the amount deductible in the year of transfer is limited to a percent of the net capital gains of the successor corporation computed with reference to the number of days remaining in the tax year.

Example 43   Beta Corporation, the acquired corporation, has a capital loss in the amount of $30,000. Beta transfers all its assets to Alpha Corporation on July 1. Alpha Corporation files its return on the basis of a calendar year. Alpha Corporation has net capital gains (computed without regard to any capital loss carryovers) for that year of $40,000. The amount of capital loss carryover would be $20,000 ($40,000 $\times$ 1/2). □

Section 382(b), which limits the carryover of a net operating loss if an owner shift or an equity structure shift causes a more-than-50 percent change in the ownership of the loss corporation, is, pursuant to § 383, applicable to the capital loss carryover. The limitation is computed in the same manner as the limitation on a net operating loss.

Method of Accounting.   Section 381(c)(4) provides that the acquiring corporation must use the method of accounting used by the acquired corporation on the date of transfer unless different methods were employed by the acquired and the acquiring corporations. If different methods were used, the Code requires the acquiring corporation to use different methods if the business of the acquired corporation is operated as a separate and distinct business after the reorganization.[59]

---

57. *Comm. v. Phipps*, cited in Footnote 51.
58. Reg. § 1.381(c)(2)–1(a)(5).
59. Reg. § 1.381(c)(4)–1(c)(4).

Other Carryovers.   Numerous other carryover items are prescribed by § 381. The successor corporation would determine depreciation on acquired assets in the same manner as did the predecessor corporation. Should installment obligations pass to a transferee corporation in a reorganization, the transferee corporation would also report income from such obligations on the installment method. Should there be an involuntary conversion, the successor corporation is treated as the predecessor. The successor corporation also stands in the tax shoes of the predecessor with respect to unused investment credits and recapture of the investment tax credit should there be early dispositions. Section 383 limits the amount of unused investment tax credits (as well as foreign tax credits and other credits) that may be carried over if an owner shift or an equity structure shift causes a more-than-50 percent change in the ownership of the loss corporation. The limitation under § 383 is applied to these credits in the same manner as it is applied to capital loss carryovers.

Though the carryover items under § 381 are numerous, those remaining have limited applicability and are not discussed in this text.

Disallowance of Carryovers

Irrespective of § 381, § 269 can be utilized by the Internal Revenue Service to disallow the carryover of tax benefits if a tax avoidance scheme is apparent. Section 269 states that if a corporation acquires property of another corporation primarily to evade or avoid Federal income tax by securing the benefit of a deduction, credit, or other allowance that the acquiring corporation would not otherwise enjoy, the deduction, credit, or other allowance will be disallowed. Whether or not the principal purpose is the evasion or avoidance of taxes becomes a question of fact. If the business of the loss corporation is promptly discontinued after a corporate reorganization, § 269 will undoubtedly be asserted by the IRS in an attempt to disallow the loss carryover.

Section 269 may be applied to disallow a net operating loss carryover even though such carryover might be limited pursuant to § 382.[60]

Example 44   Alpha Corporation, which has a net operating loss of $100,000, is merged into Beta Corporation. Beta acquires Alpha for the principal purpose of utilizing the net operating loss. After the merger, the former shareholders of Alpha own 10% of the fair market value of the stock in Beta. Pursuant to § 382, the loss is limited to the value of Alpha stock multiplied by the long-term exempt rate. However, pursuant to § 269, none of the loss can be used by Beta. □

✓ Tax Planning Considerations

Assessing the Possible Alternatives

The various types of corporate reorganizations should not be considered in isolation. Often the parties involved can achieve the desired tax result through more than one type of reorganization.

---

60. Reg. § 1.269–6.

Example 45   X Corporation operates two businesses, each of which has been in existence for five years. One business is a manufacturing operation, the other is a wholesale distributorship. Z Corporation wishes only to acquire the former business and not to purchase all the assets of X Corporation. X Corporation has a net operating loss, a deficit in earnings and profits, and a basis in its assets in excess of their fair market value. □

What course of action might be advisable to transfer the manufacturing operation from X to Z with the least, if any, tax consequences? Compare the following three possibilities:

1. X Corporation transfers the manufacturing operation to Z Corporation in return for some of the latter's stock.
2. X Corporation forms Y Corporation to which it transfers the wholesale distributorship in return for all of Y's stock. The Y stock is then distributed to X's shareholders. This portion of the arrangement represents a nontaxable spin-off. X Corporation now transfers the manufacturing operation to Z Corporation in exchange for some of the latter's stock.
3. The nontaxable spin-off described in possibility 2 is followed by Z Corporation's acquisition of all the X Corporation stock in exchange for some of Z's stock. The end result is that X Corporation becomes a subsidiary of Z Corporation.

Possibility 1 probably would not fit within the definition of a "C" reorganization, because substantially all of the assets were not transferred by X Corporation in return for Z Corporation stock. Although the manufacturing operation (i.e., the "wanted" assets) was transferred, the wholesale distributorship (i.e., "unwanted" assets) was not.

Possibility 2 suffers from these same shortcomings. If the spin-off is disregarded, the transaction becomes an unsuccessful attempt to carry out a "C" reorganization (i.e., possibility 1). Disregarding the spin-off would be the natural result of following the step transaction doctrine.[61]

Possibility 3 follows a different approach. Though starting with the spin-off of the "unwanted" assets, the "wanted" assets are obtained by Z Corporation through the purchase of the X stock. Taken by itself, this last step satisfies the stock for stock requirement of a "B" reorganization. If, however, the step transaction doctrine is applied and the spin-off is disregarded, the Y Corporation stock distributed to X's shareholders might be considered as property *other than voting stock* in Z Corporation. The IRS has not chosen to take this position and probably will recognize the nontaxability of a spin-off of "unwanted" assets followed by a "B" reorganization.[62]

Resolving Shareholder Disputes

The use of a split-off under the "D" reorganization should not be overlooked as a means of resolving shareholder disputes.

---

61. *Helvering v. Elkhorn Coal Co.*, cited in Footnote 43.
62. Rev.Rul. 70–434, 1970–2 C.B. 83.

Example 46   Alpha Corporation was organized 10 years ago and since that time has operated retail and wholesale businesses. Alpha's two shareholders, R and S, each manage one of the businesses. Due to a difference of opinion between R and S over corporate policy, R and S decide to separate the two businesses. ☐

Presuming R and S plan to continue operating each business in the corporate form, the way to avoid any tax consequences on the division would be to pursue a "D" reorganization. Alpha Corporation could form Beta Corporation by transferring to it one of the businesses, say the wholesale operation, in return for all the Beta stock. Next the Beta stock would be distributed to the manager of the wholesale business, R, in exchange for all of his stock in Alpha Corporation. After the nontaxable split-off, S has the retail business through his sole ownership in Alpha Corporation, and R has control of the wholesale operation through the ownership of Beta Corporation.

Reorganizations Compared with Stock Redemptions and Liquidations

Example 46 presents an opportunity to review certain other possibilities discussed in previous chapters.

1. If, for example, one of the shareholders, say S, wishes to continue operating in the corporate form while the other does not, the stock redemption approach should be considered (refer to Chapter 4). Thus, R could exchange all of his stock in Alpha Corporation for the wholesale business. This would qualify as a complete termination of a shareholder's interest under § 302(b)(3) and as a partial liquidation under § 302(b)(4). R would recognize a capital gain or loss measured by the difference between the fair market value of the wholesale business and his basis in the Alpha stock surrendered. As noted in Chapter 4, gain would be recognized by Alpha Corporation because of the redemption.
2. If both shareholders are indifferent about whether the businesses should continue to operate in the corporate form, some thought should be given to a complete liquidation of Alpha Corporation. The liquidation could be carried out by making a distribution in kind of the wholesale business to R and of the retail business to S. As was true with reference to the stock redemption alternative, the shareholders would recognize a capital gain or loss measured by the difference between the fair market value of the property received and the basis of the stock given up, and gain would be recognized by Alpha Corporation because of the liquidation (refer to Chapter 5).

The stock redemption and liquidation approaches produce gain at both the corporate level and the shareholder level. The "D" reorganization, on the other hand, postpones the recognition of *any* gain on the division of the businesses. In a purely tax-free exchange, moreover, no change will take place in income tax basis. Thus, S's basis in the Alpha Corporation stock remains the same, while R's basis in the Alpha stock surrendered carries over to the new Beta Corporation stock received. At the corporate level, Alpha will retain the same basis it had in the retail business, and Beta will assume Alpha's basis in the wholesale operation.

Carryover Considerations. The tax differences between corporate reorganizations and liquidations become pronounced in other respects.

Example 47 P Corporation wants to acquire the assets of S Corporation. These assets have a basis to S Corporation of $300,000 and a fair market value of $200,000. Further, S Corporation has incurred losses in its operations during the past several years and possesses unabsorbed net operating losses. P Corporation plans to continue the business conducted by S, hoping to do so on a profitable basis. □

To carry out the acquisition planned by P Corporation, one must assess the tax consequences of various available alternatives. In this connection, consider the following:

1. Using cash and/or other property, P Corporation purchases the assets directly from S Corporation. Following the purchase, S Corporation liquidates and distributes the cash and/or property to its shareholders.
2. P Corporation purchases all of the stock in S Corporation from its shareholders. Shortly thereafter, P liquidates S.
3. Utilizing an "A" reorganization, S Corporation merges into P Corporation. In exchange for their stock, the shareholders of S Corporation receive stock in P Corporation.
4. Under a "C" reorganization, S Corporation transfers all of its assets to P Corporation in return for the latter's voting stock. S then distributes the P stock to its shareholders.

A satisfactory resolution must center around the preservation of S Corporation's favorable tax attributes—the high basis in the assets and the net operating loss carryovers. In this regard, alternative 1 is highly unsatisfactory. The purchase price (probably $200,000) becomes the basis of the assets in the hands of P Corporation. Further, any unused net operating losses will disappear upon the liquidation of S Corporation. It is true, however, that S Corporation will have a realized loss of $100,000 [$300,000 (basis in the assets) − $200,000 (sale proceeds)] from the sale of its assets. Even so, the realized loss may generate little, if any, tax savings to S Corporation because of either of two possibilities. First, the realized loss may not be recognizable if the sale took place after the adoption of a plan of complete liquidation and S Corporation is a qualified closely-held corporation (refer to Chapter 5). Second, even if the loss is recognizable, it means little, absent offsetting gains. In view of S Corporation's past history (i.e., unabsorbed net operating loss carryovers), it appears doubtful that such gains would be present in the year of sale.

Alternative 2 suffers from the same shortcomings as alternative 1. When the liquidation of a subsidiary under § 332 occurs, the basis of property received by the parent corporation is determined under either § 334(b)(1) or § 338 (assuming it applies and a timely election is made). In this case, if the parent elects under § 338, the assumed cost of the S Corporation stock ($200,000) becomes P's basis in the assets received from S (refer to Chapter 5).

Consequently, the $100,000 built-in loss S Corporation had in its assets disappears and benefits neither P nor S. Likewise, S Corporation's unused net operating loss carryovers disappear.

If an election under § 338 is not made, the general rule of § 334(b)(1) applies for basis determination purposes. Thus, S Corporation's basis in its assets carries over to P Corporation. In this regard, what P Corporation paid for the S stock becomes irrelevant. Other tax attributes of S Corporation (e.g., net operating losses) will, under certain circumstances, carry over to P Corporation. There are certain tax risks, however. Section 269 (dealing with the disallowance of any deduction or credit when the acquisition was made to evade or avoid income tax) could present a problem. Section 269(b) specifically applies to a liquidation within two years after the acquisition date of a qualified stock purchase when an election is not made under § 338. Section 269(b)(1)(D) provides that if the principal purpose of the liquidation is the evasion or avoidance of income tax by securing the benefit of a deduction, credit, or other allowance, the items involved may be disallowed.

Alternatives 3 and 4 should accomplish the same tax result as not electing under § 338 but with less tax risk. Presuming P Corporation can establish a business purpose for the "A" or "C" reorganization, § 269 can be avoided.

The preservation of favorable tax attributes, such as the net operating loss carryover and any capital loss or investment credit carryovers, should be considered in the context of the sale of a small corporation.

Example 48 X Corporation, worth $200,000, has a net operating loss of $150,000. The stock in X Corporation is owned by two individuals as follows: A, 55%, and B, 45%. A wants to sell his interest in X Corporation and retire. But what happens to the net operating loss if A sells his entire interest? There would be a more-than-50% change in the ownership of X Corporation. Therefore, the § 382 limitation would be $200,000 times the long-term tax-exempt rate. Assume the rate is 10%. The loss of $150,000 would now be limited to $20,000 annually. Can a sale be structured so that the net operating loss is not so limited? □

An owner shift is determined by looking to a three-year testing period. A could sell 15 percent of his stock in Year 1, 15 percent in Year 2, 15 percent in Year 3, and 10 percent in Year 4. Note that in neither of the three-year testing periods (Years 1 through 3 or Years 2 through 4) was there a more-than-50 percent change in the ownership of X Corporation. Result: There is no § 382 limitation. X Corporation can deduct the entire $150,000 net operating loss sooner rather than later.

The Role of the Letter Ruling

Before leaving the area of corporate reorganizations, one further point needs emphasis. When feasible, the parties contemplating a corporate reorganization should apply for and obtain from the IRS a letter ruling concerning the income tax effect of the transaction(s). Assuming the parties carry out the transfers as proposed in the ruling request, a favorable ruling provides, in effect, an insurance policy leading to the desired tax result. If the tax implications are significant, as they often are with corporate reorganizations, the advantage of obtaining prior IRS approval should be apparent. The pros and cons of letter rulings and the procedures by which they are obtained are discussed in Chapter 14.

Problem Materials

Discussion Questions

1. What is the theory underlying nonrecognition of gain or loss in a corporate reorganization?

2. Briefly explain the seven forms of corporate reorganizations that qualify for nonrecognition treatment.

3. How does the receipt of boot affect the tax-free status of a corporate reorganization?

4. What are the advantages of effecting a business combination through a "Type A" reorganization?

5. What problems exist in effecting a business combination through a "Type A" reorganization?

6. How can the use of a subsidiary corporation in a "Type A" reorganization solve some of the problems inherent in such a reorganization?

7. What is a reverse merger?

8. What is the principal limitation of the "Type B" reorganization?

9. In what instances will a "Type C" reorganization be more beneficial than a "Type A" reorganization?

10. X Corporation transfers all of its assets to a newly formed corporation, Y, for all of Y's stock. The Y Stock is exchanged with X's shareholders for all of their stock in X. X is then liquidated. Does the exchange qualify as a tax-free reorganization? Explain.

11. What is the difference between a spin-off pursuant to § 355 and a spin-off coupled with a "Type D" reorganization?

12. In what instances is a "Type D" reorganization accompanied by transfer of only part of the assets of the transferor corporation beneficial?

13. Can a corporation divide a single trade or business and qualify the transaction for tax-free status as a "Type D" reorganization?

14. When is the receipt of bonds tax-free in a "Type E" reorganization?

15. Why can a "Type F" reorganization give the surviving corporation more tax benefits in certain instances than can an "A" or a "C" reorganization?

16. How does the business purpose requirement affect a tax-free reorganization?

17. What is the continuity of interest test?

18. What is the continuity of business enterprise test?

19. How does the step transaction doctrine affect the tax consequences of corporate combinations?

20. What is the liquidation-reincorporation doctrine?

21. Does the assumption of liabilities of an acquired corporation by the acquiring corporation trigger gain recognition to the acquired corporation?

22. What reorganizations are not covered by the carryover provisions of § 381?

23. What is the status of a net operating loss carryover if the assets of the loss corporation are purchased by another corporation?

24. How does an owner shift affect a net operating loss carryover?

25. How does an equity structure shift affect a net operating loss carryover?

26. What is the § 382 limitation on a net operating loss?

27. How does the long-term tax-exempt rate affect a net operating loss?

28. How will a deficit in earnings and profits of an acquired corporation carry over to offset earnings and profits of the acquiring corporation?

29. Do capital loss carryovers survive in a tax-free reorganization? Investment credit carryovers?

30. X Corporation is interested in acquiring the assets of Y Corporation. Y has a basis of $400,000 in its assets (fair market value of Y's assets is $250,000). Y has incurred substantial losses in the last few years and has a $175,000 net operating loss carryover. X believes it could make some changes in operations and could make Y a successful corporation. What is the best alternative for tax purposes in acquiring either the assets or the stock of Y Corporation?

Problems

1. What type of reorganization is effected in the following transactions:

   a. XY Corporation acquires all the assets of T Corporation in exchange for newly issued nonvoting preferred stock of XY Corporation. T Corporation distributes the preferred stock in XY Corporation to its shareholders in exchange for their common stock in T Corporation. T is then dissolved.

   b. P Corporation transfers P voting stock to S Corporation in exchange for preferred stock in S Corporation. P owns 85% of the voting stock in S Corporation. S exchanges the voting stock in P Corporation with shareholders in T Corporation holding 95% of the stock in T Corporation.

   c. The shareholders of X and Y Corporations agree to form W Corporation. All the assets of X and Y Corporations are transferred to W Corporation in exchange for common stock in W Corporation. The common stock in W Corporation is then distributed to the shareholders of X and Y Corporations in exchange for all their stock in X and Y. X and Y Corporations are then dissolved.

   d. Assume in (c) that the shareholders of X and Y Corporations receive stock in W Corporation worth $400,000 and long-term bonds worth $200,000.

   e. Assume in (c) that the shareholders of X and Y Corporations receive stock in W Corporation worth $100,000 and long-term bonds worth $300,000.

   f. S Corporation transfers voting stock in P Corporation, its parent, to A Corporation for substantially all of A's assets. A then distributes the P stock to its shareholders.

   g. S Corporation transfers all its assets to X Corporation. P, the parent of S, transfers its voting stock to the shareholders of X for 80% control of X Corporation. S Corporation is then liquidated.

   h. X Corporation transfers assets worth $300,000 to Y Corporation for voting stock worth $200,000, the assumption of liabilities in the amount of $40,000, and cash of $60,000.

   i. A Corporation has been actively engaged in two businesses for the past 10 years. It transfers assets of one business to a newly formed corporation and distributes stock in the new corporation, representing control of such corporation, to the shareholders of A.

j. A Corporation manufactures a single product but has two plants. One plant was established three years ago; the other has been in existence since the corporation was organized eight years ago. A transfers the older plant to a new corporation and distributes stock in the new corporation to one half its shareholders in exchange for all of their A stock.

k. Common shares in A Corporation are owned by father and son. The father exchanges his common stock in A for newly issued nonvoting cumulative preferred stock.

l. A, a New York corporation, incorporates B in Delaware and transfers all its assets to B in exchange for B's stock. A is subsequently liquidated.

m. A parent corporation exchanges stock in its subsidiary for substantially all of the assets of X Corporation.

2. a. T, a shareholder of X Corporation, exchanges his X Corporation stock for stock in Y Corporation. The exchange is pursuant to a tax-free reorganization of X and Y. T paid $50,000 for his stock in X Corporation three years ago. The X stock is worth $100,000, and the stock T receives in Y is worth $80,000. What is T's basis in the Y Corporation stock?

    b. Assume T receives $20,000 cash in addition to the Y stock. What are the tax consequences to T, and what basis does he have in the Y Corporation stock?

3. C, an individual, exchanges stock she owns in Y Corporation for stock in X Corporation and additionally receives $10,000 cash. The exchange is pursuant to a tax-free reorganization of both corporations. C paid $15,000 five years ago for the stock in Y Corporation. The stock in X Corporation has a fair market value of $60,000. C's share of E & P of Y Corporation is $5,000. How will C treat this transaction for tax purposes?

4. Assume the same facts as in Problem 3, except that C paid $80,000 (instead of $15,000) for her stock in Y Corporation. How would C treat the transaction for tax purposes?

5. Pursuant to a plan of reorganization, X Corporation's shareholders deposit all their stock in X with X Corporation. X then exchanges its shareholders' stock with Y Corporation for 30% of the voting stock of Y. X Corporation delivers the Y stock to its shareholders.

    a. What are the tax results of the transaction?

    b. Assume Y also transferred 10% of its nonvoting preferred stock to X, with X then delivering the preferred stock as well as the voting stock to its shareholders. What is the tax result?

6. P Corporation transfers part of its voting stock to Y Corporation's only shareholders, A and B, who then transfer all their stock in Y to S Corporation, a subsidiary of P. Does this qualify as a tax-free reorganization? Why or why not?

7. X Corporation has assets with a basis of $600,000 (fair market value of $900,000) and liabilities of $200,000. Its common stock consists of 20,000 shares at a par value of $15 per share. X has E & P of $100,000. Y Corporation exchanges with X's shareholders 1,000 shares of its voting stock (worth $560,000) for 16,000 shares of common stock in X. What are the tax results of the exchange?

8. S Corporation owns 20% of the voting stock of its parent, P Corporation. P owns 100% of S Corporation. S Corporation acquired 40% of the stock of T Corporation three years

ago in a cash tender offer. P would like to acquire control of T Corporation in a tax-free reorganization. Can this be done? Explain.

9. X Corporation transfers assets with a fair market value of $50,000 to Y Corporation and receives voting stock valued at $40,000 and cash of $10,000. No liabilities are assumed. X distributes the cash and the stock in Y to its shareholders and is liquidated. Does this transaction qualify as a tax-free reorganization?

10. T Corporation transfers assets with a fair market value of $600,000 to W Corporation and receives voting stock valued at $400,000 and cash of $80,000. W Corporation assumes $120,000 of T Corporation's liabilities. T distributes the cash and stock in W and is liquidated. Would this transaction qualify as a "C" reorganization?

11. A and B formed XY Corporation in January 1986 by each investing $50,000 in cash and receiving 5,000 shares of $10 par value common stock in XY. XY acquired operating assets with the $100,000 cash and continued in business until December 31, 1988, at which time the basis in its assets was $80,000. XY Corporation had a net operating loss carryover of $20,000 as of the end of that tax year. On December 31, 1988, XY transferred all its assets to C Corporation for $100,000 worth of stock in C and $20,000 cash. XY then distributed the C stock and $20,000 cash to its shareholders, A and B, in exchange for A's and B's stock in XY. XY was then liquidated. A received $60,000 worth of C stock, and B received $40,000 of stock and the $20,000 cash. The C stock transferred to XY represented a 55% ownership in C. What are the tax consequences of the transaction to C, XY, A, and B?

12. X Corporation transfers assets with a tax basis of $100,000, fair market value of $150,000, to Y Corporation for voting stock in Y worth $130,000 and $20,000 cash. X uses the $20,000 to pay its liabilities in the amount of $20,000, distributes the Y stock to its shareholder, and is liquidated. What are the tax consequences of the transfer? What are the basis of the assets to Y and the basis of the Y Corporation stock to X?

13. Assume the same facts as Problem 12, except the consideration given by Y consists of voting stock worth $100,000 and the assumption of $50,000 of X Corporation's liabilities. What are the tax consequences and the bases of assets and stock transferred?

14. X Corporation transfers 30% of its voting stock to Y Corporation for Y's assets worth $2,000,000. X also assumes liabilities of Y in the amount of $500,000. Y transfers the X stock to its shareholders for their Y stock. Y Corporation is then liquidated. Does this qualify as a tax-free reorganization? Suppose X transferred its voting stock plus $500,000 cash for Y's assets worth $2,000,000. Y distributes the cash and voting stock to its shareholders and is liquidated. Does this qualify as a tax-free reorganization?

15. X Corporation wishes to acquire control of T Corporation. X Corporation transfers 200 shares of newly issued voting stock to the shareholders of T Corporation in exchange for all their stock in T Corporation. However, X Corporation also pays reorganization expenses and attorney's fees incurred by the shareholders of T Corporation in connection with the transaction. Does the transaction qualify as a tax-free reorganization? Explain.

16. T Corporation has assets with a basis of $200,000. T transfers the assets (worth $400,000) to W Corporation for voting stock valued at $320,000, cash of $30,000, and the assumption of $50,000 of T's liabilities. T distributes the voting stock in W and the cash of $30,000 to A, its sole shareholder, and liquidates. A had a basis of $80,000 in his stock in T. What are the tax consequences of the transfer to T, W, and A?

17. C, an individual shareholder in T Corporation, has 50 shares of stock in T Corporation which she purchased two years ago for $60 per share. The stock is now worth $200 per share. Pursuant to a tax-free split-off, C received 100 shares of stock in W Corporation in exhange for 10 shares in T Corporation. The stock in W Corporation was worth $20 per share. What are the tax consequences of the exchange to C?

18. X Corporation has 1,000 shares of $100 par value preferred stock and 2,000 shares of $100 par value common stock outstanding. A, a highly valued employee of X, owns 200 shares of preferred stock and 400 shares of common, or 20% of each. B owns the remaining shares, or 80% of each. To retain A in the corporation, B agrees to surrender 1,000 of his shares of common stock for 1,000 shares of preferred stock to give A a 40% ownership in X. Will this transaction qualify as a tax-free reorganization? Why or why not? What are some possible tax problems that could arise?

19. T, an individual, is a 10% shareholder in X Corporation. X Corporation, with E & P of $150,000 and assets worth $750,000, is merged into Y Corporation. T receives cash of $5,000, common stock in Y Corporation worth $60,000, and preferred stock in Y worth $10,000. T's basis in her X Corporation stock was $14,000. Assuming that the merger qualifies as an ''A'' reorganization, what are the tax consequences to T? To X Corporation? To Y Corporation?

20. Alpha Corporation has assets with a basis of $200,000 and a fair market value of $300,000, liabilities of $40,000, and E & P of $160,000. Beta Corporation, with E & P of $100,000, acquires all the assets of Alpha Corporation in a ''C'' reorganization. Beta transfers cash of $40,000 and voting stock worth $260,000 to Alpha in exchange for all of Alpha's assets. Alpha uses the cash to pay off its liabilities, distributes the voting stock in Beta to its two shareholders, A and B, and liquidates. A and B have an aggregate basis of $30,000 in their Alpha stock. What are the tax consequences to A and B? To Alpha Corporation? To Beta Corporation?

21. X Corporation is merged into Y Corporation in a statutory merger. X Corporation had 5,000 shares of common stock, with a fair market value of $100 a share, outstanding. One of X's shareholders exchanges his X stock (50 shares) for which he paid $80 per share for five 10% debenture bonds in Y Corporation (face value *and* fair market value of $1,000 per bond). What are the tax consequences to the shareholder?

22. Assume the shareholder in Problem 21 exchanges his stock for 100 shares of stock in W Corporation. Y Corporation was holding the W stock as an investment. The stock was worth $50 per share.

23. X Corporation is owned 100% by A, an individual, who purchased the stock in X 10 years ago at a cost of $20,000. X Corporation has assets with a basis of $110,000, fair market value of $220,000, no liabilities, and E & P of $160,000. X Corporation is liquidated in the current tax year. A retains $90,000 of the cash distributed upon X Corporation's liquidation and transfers the remaining assets, worth $130,000, to Y, a newly formed corporation, for 100% of the stock in Y Corporation. What are the tax consequences to A? To Y?

24. T Corporation merges into A Corporation on June 30, 1988. Both corporations have a calendar year. T has a net operating loss of $150,000. A's taxable income for 1988 is $180,000. How much of the loss can be used to offset A's 1988 taxable income? (Assume § 382 is not applicable.)

25. In 1986, X Corporation acquires the assets of Y Corporation in a statutory merger. Y Corporation has a net operating loss of $400,000. Immediately after the transfer, the shareholders of Y own 15% of the fair market value of X's stock. How much of Y's net operating loss can be used by X?

26. T Corporation is merged into X Corporation on June 1, 1988. At the time of merger, T Corporation had a net operating loss of $150,000. Pursuant to the merger, the shareholders of T Corporation receive 30% of the stock of X Corporation. T Corporation has a value of $100,000 on the date of the merger, and the long-term tax-exempt rate is 10%. How much of T Corporation's net operating loss can be used to offset X Corporation's taxable income of $500,000 in 1988?

27. Assume the shareholders in Problem 26 receive 60% of the stock of X Corporation. How much of T Corporation's net operating loss can be used to offset X Corporation's taxable income in 1988?

28. XY Corporation is owned equally by 10 shareholders and has a net operating loss of $200,000. Determine whether the § 382 loss limitation will apply in the following transactions:

    a. Six of the shareholders sell their stock to a third party, A.

    b. Four of the shareholders sell their stock to a third party, A.

    c. Assume in (b) that XY Corporation redeems the stock of three other shareholders in the following year.

29. T Corporation has a net operating loss of $800,000. The net operating loss was incurred in 1986. T Corporation has assets worth $600,000 and liabilities of $400,000 on January 1, 1988, when A Corporation acquires all the assets of T Corporation in a statutory merger. A Corporation exchanged stock worth $200,000 for the assets of T Corporation. The stock in A Corporation was distributed to the shareholders of T Corporation. The shareholders in T Corporation acquired a 10% interest in A Corporation. The tax-exempt rate on January 1, 1988, was 8%.

    a. If A Corporation continues the business of T Corporation, how much of T Corporation's net operating loss can be used to offset A Corporation's taxable income in 1988?

    b. How much of the $800,000 net operating loss of T Corporation will A Corporation be able to use in future years assuming A Corporation has adequate taxable income in each year after 1988?

    c. How much of the net operating loss of T Corporation will A Corporation be able to use if A Corporation does not continue the business of T Corporation?

    d. Assume that the assets of T Corporation (worth $600,000) include equipment with a value of $100,000 that was transferred to T Corporation in 1987. How much of the net operating loss of T Corporation can be used to offset A Corporation's taxable income in 1988?

    e. Assume the assets of T Corporation consist of cash and marketable securities worth $250,000. Indebtedness attributable to the marketable securities is $150,000. How much of the net operating loss of T Corporation can be used to offset A Corporation's taxable income in 1988?

30. X Corporation has a deficit in earnings and profits of $60,000. It acquires the assets of Y Corporation in a statutory merger. Y has earnings and profits of $300,000. After the merger, X distributes $180,000 to its shareholders. How will the $180,000 be treated for tax purposes?

31. X Corporation uses the cash method of accounting for computing taxable income for its service business. X acquires the assets of Y Corporation in a statutory merger. Y has been using the accrual method of accounting for its retail boat business. X continues both the retail and service operations after the merger as separate businesses. What accounting method must be used to compute taxable income?

Research Problems

Research Problem 1. N Insurance Company acquired S Insurance Company in a tax-free reorganization. S Insurance Company had a net operating loss carryover of $200,000. S Insurance Company acquired stock in N Insurance Company as consideration for the transfer of its assets to N. It did not liquidate and retained the stock in N as its principal asset. N Insurance Company deducted S Insurance Company's net operating loss carryover on its income tax return. The IRS disallowed the deduction under Reg. § 1.382(b)–1(a)(2). The Regulation states that shareholders of a loss corporation do not own stock in the acquiring corporation for purposes of determining the amount of a net operating loss of the acquired corporation that can be carried over to the acquiring corporation unless there is an actual distribution of that stock to the individual shareholders. N Insurance Company contends that it is entitled to all the loss carryover because the stock it transferred to S represented 50% of the value of all of its outstanding stock and it had no control over the disposition of that stock by S Insurance Company. N Insurance Company seeks your advice. What would you advise the corporation?

Research Problem 2.   P owned all the stock of XY Corporation on May 1, 1987. XY Corporation operated several fast-food restaurants. W Corporation was interested in acquiring the restaurants operated by XY Corporation and thus proposed a merger of XY Corporation into W Corporation. W Corporation entered into a contract with XY Corporation and P on May 1, 1987, in which P would exchange all of his stock in XY Corporation for unregistered stock in W Corporation. The assets of XY Corporation would be transferred to W Corporation, and XY Corporation would be liquidated. Under the terms of the contract, P would be employed by W Corporation. The contract included a covenant by P not to compete in the restaurant business with W Corporation for a period of two years. The contract also gave P a right to have the stock in W Corporation registered. Because stock in W Corporation was publicly traded, the unregistered stock could not be sold for a period of two years under SEC rules. In June of 1987, P purchased three fast-food restaurants in nearby cities and began to operate the restaurants by employing members of his family. The directors of W Corporation terminated P's employment as a result of P's breach of the covenant not to compete. P then demanded that W Corporation register the stock P received in the exchange so that P might sell the stock. W Corporation registered the stock on February 1, 1988, at which time P sold all his stock in W Corporation.

Upon audit of the tax returns of XY Corporation and P for 1987, the IRS contended that the exchange of P's stock in XY Corporation for the stock in W Corporation was a taxable exchange. The IRS contended that the step transaction doctrine should be applied to the exchange, since P sold all the stock he acquired in W Corporation for cash less than a year later. P contended that the parties intended that the exchange be a tax-free "A" reorganization and that the sale of the stock in W Corporation was caused by subsequent events not related to the original transaction. Does the exchange of stock in XY Corporation for stock in W Corporation qualify as an "A" reorganization?

Research Problem 3.   The former shareholders of R Corporation exchanged all their shares in R for voting stock in M Corporation. The agreement provided that a sufficient number of shares in M, valued at $20 per share, would be issued to the shareholders of R to equal the value of R shares. In the event the purchase price was not evenly divisible by shares at $20 per share, the difference would be paid in cash. The value of shares was not so divisible. Therefore, each shareholder was paid an additional $40 in lieu of fractional shares. The shareholders of R did not report any gain on their income tax returns with respect to the stock exchange. The IRS contends there is a taxable gain to each shareholder based on the difference between the fair market value of shares in M plus the $40 cash and the tax basis of the stock in R. The IRS is of the opinion the exchange is not nontaxable. It is an exchange for stock and cash and hence does not qualify as a "B" reorganization. The shareholders seek your advice. What would you advise?

Research Problem 4.   A state-chartered savings and loan association merges with a Federal savings and loan association. The shareholders of the state-chartered savings and loan exchange their guaranty stock in the savings and loan for passbook savings accounts and certificates of deposit in the Federal savings and loan association. The savings accounts and certificates of deposit were the only form of equity in the Federal savings and loan association. Does the merger qualify as an "A" reorganization? Why or why not?

Research Problem 5. X Corporation and Y Corporation are brother-sister corporations and are engaged in similar activities, although X Corporation is much smaller than Y Corporation. X Corporation holds a valuable franchise issued by W Corporation. W Corporation is acquired by Z Corporation. Z Corporation then informs X Corporation that X Corporation has too small a capitalization to hold the franchise. Z Corporation proposes to transfer the franchise to a larger corporation but would agree to accept Y Corporation as a qualified holder. Consequently, X Corporation, with approval of its shareholders, transfers the franchise to Y Corporation and then adopts a plan of complete liquidation, since X's major source of income no longer exists. X Corporation then sells its remaining assets to Y Corporation and distributes the sale proceeds to its shareholders. X Corporation is then formally dissolved, and the shareholders of X treat their distribution as one in complete liquidation and recognize a long-term capital gain on the transaction. Upon audit, the IRS disallows the long-term capital gain and substitutes dividend income stating that the transactions, when viewed as a whole, constituted a "D" reorganization. The shareholders of X Corporation seek your advice.

Research Problem 6. T Corporation had a large net operating loss. A, an individual who was the sole shareholder and president of W Corporation, purchased all the stock of T on January 10. On December 15, of the same year, W adopted a plan to merge T and W. After the merger on January 5, of the following year, T was liquidated. W Corporation offset the net operating loss of T against its income from operations in the latter year. Upon audit of W's return, the IRS disallowed the carryover of T's loss to W. A seeks your advice. A's argument is that she was the sole shareholder of both T and W on the date of the merger. Thus, the provisions of § 382 provide that all the loss of T can be carried over to W. What would you advise A?

Research Problem 7. A and B, individuals, each own 20% of the voting stock of X Corporation. A owns 40% of Y Corporation, and B owns 60% of Y. On December 30, 1987, X Corporation transferred all its assets to Y Corporation in consideration of the transfer of an additional 40 shares in Y Corporation to A and an additional 60 shares in Y Corporation to B. Y Corporation used X Corporation's bases in its assets for purposes of calculating its depreciation deduction on those assets for tax year 1988 and deducted a net operating loss of X Corporation on its 1988 return, contending that the transfer between X Corporation and Y Corporation was a "D" reorganization. As a result, the bases of X's assets and X's net operating loss carried over to Y Corporation pursuant to § 381. Upon audit of Y Corporation's return for 1988, the IRS disallowed a carryover of X Corporation's bases in its assets and X's net operating loss, contending that the transfer between X and Y Corporations was a sale of X's assets to Y. According to the IRS, the transfer did not qualify as a "D" reorganization, because the requirements of § 354(b)(1) were not met. The IRS contended that the stock of Y Corporation must have been received by X Corporation and then distributed to X Corporation's shareholders. The corporate officers of Y Corporation contend that this would have been a mere formality. They seek your advice regarding the audit.

Partial list of research aids:

South Texas Rice Warehouse Co., 43 T.C. 540 (1965).

Rose v. U.S., 81–1 USTC ¶9271, 47 AFTR2d 81–1070, 640 F.2d 1030 (CA–9, 1981).

7 Corporate Accumulations

Chapter 10 discusses one major technique for minimization of the tax liability of closely-held corporations: the S corporation election. However, some of the corporations that fall into the closely-held category either may not qualify for the election or may find it unattractive. For these other taxpayers, how can corporate earnings be transmitted to the shareholders while insuring a deduction for the corporation? One method is to reduce the amount of equity capital invested in a controlled corporation by increasing the debt obligations. In other words, convert dividends into interest payments deductible by the corporation. This method has limits. The Internal Revenue Service may contend that the capital structure is unrealistic and the debt is not bona fide. For these reasons, the IRS will disallow the corporate deduction for interest expense (refer to Chapter 3).

An alternative possibility is to convert the earnings of the closely-held corporation into compensation to the officers, generally the major shareholders. The compensation is a deductible expense. If it were not for the reasonableness requirement, officer-shareholders could withdraw all corporate profits as salaries and thereby eliminate the corporate tax (refer to Chapter 4). However, the reasonableness requirement prevents a corporation from deducting as salaries what are, in fact, nondeductible dividends.

Another approach entails the lease of shareholder-owned property to the corporation. The corporation (the lessee) deducts the lease payment from gross income and saves taxes at the corporate level. Although the shareholders must recognize the rental payments as ordinary income, there is an overall tax savings, because the corporation obtains deductions for what are essentially dividend payments. However, the IRS may classify such payments as disguised dividends and disallow the rental deductions (refer to Chapter 4).

A fourth method is simply to accumulate the earnings at the corporate level. A temporary or permanent accumulation of earnings in a corporation results in a deferral of the second tax at the shareholder level. Further, the corporation can invest such funds in tax-free vehicles or invest in other corporations taking advantage of the dividends received deduction. Congress took steps to stem such accumulations as early as the first income tax law enacted under the Sixteenth Amendment. Today, in addition to the usual corporate income tax, an extra tax is imposed on earnings accumulated beyond the reasonable needs of the business. Also, a penalty tax may be imposed on undistributed personal holding company income.

This chapter demonstrates how the accumulation of earnings can be employed without leading to adverse tax consequences—the imposition of additional taxes.

Penalty Tax on Unreasonable Accumulations

One method of optimizing the distribution of earnings in a corporation is to accumulate the earnings until the most advantageous time is reached to distribute them to shareholders. If the board of directors is aware of the tax problems of the shareholders, it can channel earnings into the shareholders' pockets with a minimum of tax cost by using any of several mechanisms. The corporation can distribute dividends only in years when the major shareholders are in lower tax brackets. Alternatively, dividend distributions might be curtailed causing the value of the stock to increase, in a manner similar to that of a savings account, as the retained earnings (and the earnings and profits account) increase. Later, the shareholders can sell their stock in the year of their choice at an amount that reflects the increased retained earnings. In this manner, the capital gain could be postponed to years when less tax ensues (e.g., the shareholders have capital losses to offset the gains). Or, the shareholders can choose to retain their shares. Upon death, the estate or heirs would receive a step-up in basis equal to the fair market value of the stock on date of death or, if elected, on the alternate valuation date. As a result, the increment in value represented by the step-up in basis would be largely attributable to the earnings retained by the corporation and would not be subject to income taxation.

However, there are problems involved in any situation in which corporate earnings are accumulated. As previously mentioned, a penalty tax may be imposed on accumulated taxable earnings, or a personal holding company tax may be levied on certain accumulated passive income. Consider first the accumulated earnings tax. Accumulation can be accomplished. However, the tax law is framed to discourage the retention of earnings that are unrelated to the business needs of the company. Earnings retained in the business to avoid the imposition of the tax that would have been imposed on distributions to the shareholder are subject to a penalty tax.

The Element of Intent

Although the penalty tax is normally applied against closely-held corporations, a corporation is not exempt from the tax merely because its stock is widely held.[1] For example, in a Second Court of Appeals decision,[2] the tax was imposed upon a widely-held corporation with over 1,500 shareholders. However, a much smaller group of shareholders actually controlled the corporation. As a practical matter, the presence of the required tax avoidance purpose may not exist in the case of a widely-held corporation in which no small group has legal or effective control of the corporation.

The key to imposition of the tax is not the number of the shareholders in the corporation but whether a shareholder group controls corporate policy. If such a group does exist and withholds dividends to protect its own tax position, an accumulated earnings tax (§ 531) problem might materialize.

When a corporation is formed or availed of to shield its shareholders from individual taxes by accumulating rather than distributing earnings and profits, the "bad" purpose for accumulating earnings is considered to exist under § 532(a). This subjective test, in effect, asks, Did the corporation and/or shareholder(s) *intend* to retain the earnings in order to avoid the tax on dividends? According to the Supreme Court, this tax avoidance motive need *not* be the dominant or controlling purpose for accumulating the earnings to trigger application of the penalty tax; it need only be a contributing factor to the retention

---

1. § 532(c).
2. *Trico Products v. Comm.*, 43–2 USTC ¶9540, 31 AFTR 394, 137 F.2d 424 (CA–2, 1943).

of earnings.[3] If a corporation accumulates funds beyond its reasonable needs, such action is determinative of the existence of a "bad" purpose, unless the contrary can be proven by the preponderance of the evidence. The fact that the business is a mere holding or investment company is *prima facie* evidence of this tax avoidance purpose.[4]

Imposition of the Tax and the Accumulated Earnings Credit

The tax is imposed in addition to the regular corporate tax and the 20 percent alternative minimum tax. The rates are $27\frac{1}{2}$ percent on the first $100,000 of accumulated taxable income and $38\frac{1}{2}$ percent on all accumulated taxable income in excess of $100,000.

Most corporations are allowed a minimum $250,000 credit against accumulated taxable income, even though it might be accumulating earnings beyond its reasonable business needs. However, certain personal service corporations in health, law, engineering, architecture, accounting, actuarial science, performing arts, and consulting are limited to a $150,000 accumulated earnings credit. Moreover, a nonservice corporation (other than a holding or investment company) may retain more than $250,000 ($150,000 for a service organization) of accumulated earnings if the company can justify that the accumulation is necessary to meet the reasonable needs of the business.[5]

The accumulated earnings credit is the greater of the following:

1. The current earnings and profits for the tax year that are needed to meet the reasonable needs of the business (see the subsequent discussion) less the net long-term capital gain for the year (net of any tax thereon). In determining the reasonable needs for any one year, the accumulated earnings and profits of past years must be taken into account.
2. The amount by which $250,000 exceeds the accumulated earnings and profits of the corporation at the close of the preceding tax year (designated the "minimum credit").

Example 1   T Corporation, a calendar year manufacturing concern, has accumulated E & P of $120,000 as of December 31, 1987. For 1988, it has no capital gains and current E & P of $140,000. A realistic estimate places T Corporation's reasonable needs of the business for 1988 at $200,000. Under item 1, T Corporation's accumulated earnings credit based on the reasonable needs of the business would be $80,000 [$200,000 (reasonable needs of the business) − $120,000 (accumulated E & P)]. Pursuant to item 2, the minimum accumulated earnings credit would be $130,000 [$250,000 (minimum credit allowed for nonservice corporations) − $120,000 (accumulated E & P as of the close of the preceding tax year)]. Thus, the credit becomes $130,000 (i.e., the greater of $80,000 or $130,000). □

---

3. *U.S. v. The Donruss Co.*, 69–1 USTC ¶9167, 23 AFTR2d 69–418, 89 S.Ct. 501 (USSC, 1969).
4. § 533. See, for example, *H. C. Cockrell Warehouse Corp.*, 71 T.C. 1036 (1979).
5. §§ 535(c) and 537 and Reg. § 1.537–1.

Several observations should be made about the accumulated earnings credit. First, the minimum credit of $250,000 is of no consequence as long as the prior year's ending balance in accumulated E & P is $250,000 or more. Second, when the credit is based on reasonable needs, the credit is the amount that exceeds accumulated E & P. Third, a taxpayer must choose between the reasonable needs credit (item 1) and the minimum credit (item 2). Combining the two in the same year is not permissible. Fourth, although the § 531 tax is not imposed on accumulated E & P, the amount of the credit depends upon the balance of this account as of the end of the preceding year.

Reasonable Needs of the Business

It has been firmly established that if a corporation's funds are invested in assets essential to the needs of the business, the IRS will have a difficult time imposing the accumulated earnings tax. "Thus, the size of the accumulated earnings and profits or surplus is not the crucial factor; rather it is the reasonableness and nature of the surplus." [6] What are the reasonable business needs of a corporation? This is precisely the point upon which difficulty arises and which creates controversy with the IRS.

Justifiable Needs—In General.   The reasonable needs of a business include the business's reasonably anticipated needs.[7] These anticipated needs must be specific, definite, and feasible. A number of court decisions illustrate that indefinite plans referred to only briefly in corporate minutes merely provide a false feeling of security for the taxpayer.[8]

The Regulations list some legitimate reasons that could indicate that the earnings of a corporation are being accumulated to meet the reasonable needs of the business. Earnings may be allowed to accumulate to provide for bona fide expansion of the business enterprise or replacement of plant and facilities as well as to acquire a business enterprise through the purchase of stock or assets. Provision for the retirement of bona fide indebtedness created in connection with the trade or business (e.g., the establishment of a sinking fund for the retirement of bonds issued by the corporation) is a legitimate reason for accumulating earnings under ordinary circumstances. Providing necessary working capital for the business (e.g., to acquire inventories) and providing for investment or loans to suppliers or customers (if necessary to maintain the business of the corporation) are valid grounds for accumulating earnings.[9] Funds may be retained for self-insurance [10] and realistic business contingencies (e.g., lawsuits, patent infringement).[11] Accumula-

---

6. *Smoot Sand & Gravel Corp. v. Comm.*, 60–1 USTC ¶9241, 5 AFTR2d 626, 274 F.2d 495 (CA–4, 1960).
7. § 537(a)(1).
8. See, for example, *Fine Realty, Inc. v. U.S.*, 62–2 USTC ¶9758, 10 AFTR2d 5751, 209 F.Supp. 286 (D.Ct. Minn., 1962).
9. Reg. § 1.537–2(b).
10. *Halby Chemicals Co., Inc. v. U.S.*, 67–2 USTC ¶9500, 19 AFTR2d 1589 (Ct.Cls., 1967).
11. *Dielectric Materials Co.*, 57 T.C. 587 (1972).

tions to avoid an unfavorable competitive position [12] and to carry keyman life insurance policies [13] are justifiable.

The reasonable business needs of a company also include the post-death § 303 redemption requirements of a corporation.[14] Accumulations for such purposes are limited to the amount needed (or reasonably anticipated to be needed) to effect a redemption of stock included in the gross estate of the decedent-shareholder.[15] This amount may not exceed the sum of the death taxes and funeral and administration expenses allowable under §§ 2053 and 2106.[16]

Section 537(b) provides that reasonable accumulations to pay future product liability losses shall represent a reasonable anticipated need of the business. Guidelines for the application of this change are prescribed in Proposed Regulations.

Justifiable Needs—Working Capital Requirements for Inventory Situations. For many years the penalty tax on accumulated earnings was based upon the concept of retained earnings. The courts generally looked at retained earnings alone to determine whether there was an unreasonable accumulation. However, a corporation may have a large retained earnings balance and yet possess no liquid assets with which to pay dividends. Therefore, the emphasis should more appropriately be placed upon the liquidity of a corporation. Does the business have liquid assets *not* needed that could be used to pay dividends? It was not until 1960, however, that the courts began to use this liquidity approach.[17]

Over the years, greater recognition has been placed on the liquidity needs of the corporation. The reasonable needs of the business can be divided into two categories:

1. Working capital needed for day-to-day operations.
2. Expenditures of a noncurrent nature (extraordinary expenses).

The operating cycle of a business is the average time interval between the acquisition of materials (or services) entering the business and the final realization of cash. The courts seized upon the operating cycle, because it had the advantage of objectivity for purposes of determining working capital. A normal business has two distinct cycles:

1. Purchase of inventory → the production process → finished goods inventory
2. Sale of merchandise → accounts receivable → cash collection

---

12. *North Valley Metabolic Laboratories*, 34 TCM 400, T.C.Memo, 1975–79.
13. *Emeloid Co. v. Comm.*, 51–1 USTC ¶66,013, 40 AFTR 674, 189 F.2d 230 (CA–3, 1951). Keyman life insurance is a policy on the life of a key employee that is owned by and made payable to the employer. Such insurance would enable the employer to recoup some of the economic loss that could materialize upon the untimely death of the key employee.
14. The § 303 redemption to pay death taxes and administration expenses of a deceased shareholder is discussed in Chapter 4.
15. §§ 537(a)(2) and (b)(1).
16. § 303(a).
17. See *Smoot Sand & Gravel Corp. v. Comm.*, cited in Footnote 6.

A systematic operating cycle formula was developed in *Bardahl Manufacturing Co.* and *Bardahl International Corp.*[18] The technique became known as the *Bardahl* formula.

The standard method now used to determine the reasonable working capital needs for a corporation can be outlined as follows:

$$\text{Inventory Cycle} \quad = \quad \frac{\text{Average Inventory}}{\text{Cost of Goods Sold}}$$

Plus

$$\text{Accounts Receivable Cycle} \quad = \quad \frac{\text{Average Accounts Receivable}}{\text{Net Sales}}$$

Minus

$$\text{Accounts Payable Cycle} \quad = \quad \frac{\text{Average Accounts Payable}^{[19]}}{\text{Purchases}}$$

Equals

A Decimal Percentage

This formula assumes that working capital needs are computed on a yearly basis. However, this may not provide the most favorable result. A business that experiences seasonally based high and low cycles illustrates this point. For example, a construction company can justify a greater working capital need if computations are based on a cycle that includes the winter months only and not on an annual average.[20] In the same vein, an incorporated CPA firm would choose a cycle during the slow season.

Both of the original *Bardahl* decisions used the so-called peak cycle approach, whereby the inventory and accounts receivable figures are the amounts for the month-end during which the total amount in inventory and accounts receivable were the greatest. In fact, the *Bardahl International* decision specifically rejected the average cycle approach. However, some courts have rejected the peak cycle approach,[21] which probably should be used where the business of the corporation is seasonal.[22]

The decimal percentage derived above, when multiplied by the cost of goods sold plus general, administrative, and selling expenses (not including Federal income taxes and depreciation),[23] equals the working capital needs of the business.

If the statistically computed working capital needs plus any extraordinary expenses are more than the current year's net working capital, no penalty tax is imposed. Working capital is the excess of current assets over current liabilities. This amount is the relatively liquid portion of the total business capital

---

18. *Bardahl Manufacturing Co.*, 24 TCM 1030, T.C.Memo. 1965–200; *Bardahl International Corp.*, 25 TCM 935, T.C.Memo. 1966–182. See also *Apollo Industries, Inc. v. Comm.*, 66–1 USTC ¶9294, 17 AFTR2d 518, 358 F.2d 867 (CA–1, 1966).
19. The accounts payable cycle was developed in *Kingsbury Investments, Inc.*, 28 TCM 1082, T.C. Memo. 1969–205.
20. See *Audits of Construction Contracts*, AICPA, 1965, p. 25.
21. See, for example, *W. L. Mead, Inc.*, 34 TCM 924, T.C.Memo. 1975–215.
22. *Magic Mart, Inc.*, 51 T.C. 775 (1969).
23. In *W. L. Mead, Inc.*, cited in Footnote 21, the Tax Court allowed depreciation to be included in the expenses of a service firm with no inventory. Likewise, in *Doug-Long, Inc.*, 72 T.C. 158 (1979), the Tax Court allowed a truck stop to include quarterly estimated tax payments in operating expenses.

that is a buffer for meeting obligations within the normal operating cycle of the business.

However, if working capital needs plus any extraordinary expenses are less than the current year's net working capital, the possibility of the imposition of a penalty tax does exist.[24]

In *Bardahl Manufacturing Corp.*, the costs and expenses used in the formula were those of the following year, whereas in *Bardahl International Corp.*, costs and expenses of the current year were used. Use of the subsequent year's expected costs seems to be the more equitable position.

The IRS normally takes the position that the operating cycle should be reduced by the accounts payable cycle, since the payment of such expenses may be postponed by various credit arrangements that will reduce the operating capital requirements. However, a number of court decisions have omitted such a reduction. In any case, a corporate tax planner should not have to rely on creditors to avoid the accumulated earnings penalty tax. The corporation with the most acute working capital problem will probably have a large accounts payable balance. If the previously outlined formula for determining reasonable working capital needs is used, a large accounts payable balance will result in a sizable reduction in the maximum working capital allowable before the tax is imposed. For tax planning purposes, a corporation should hold accounts payable at a reduced level.

Justifiable Needs—Working Capital Requirements for Noninventory Situations. In a service business, inventories are not purchased, and part of the operating cycle is missing in the *Bardahl* formula. However, certain costs such as salaries and overhead are incurred by a service business for a period of time before billing customers for services. Some courts have used a rough rule of thumb to determine an inventory equivalent cycle. Under certain circumstances, a human resource accounting (HRA) approach may be used to determine the working capital needs of a noninventory corporation. The use of an HRA approach is based on the contention that the strength of a service business—and its major asset—is its highly educated, skilled technicians. Such individuals must be available first to attract clients and second to execute their projects efficiently. It would be foolish to abruptly discharge highly paid specialists, recruited and trained at considerable expense, because of a business decline that might, in fact, prove to be of brief duration.

One court [25] allowed an engineering firm to add to the IRS's *Bardahl*-calculated operating reserve the reasonable professional and technical payroll for an additional period of two months (or 60 days). The Court felt that this extra amount would "... allow sufficient reserve for one cycle of full operation plus a reasonable period, i.e., 60 days, of curtailed operation to recapture business or, in the alternative, to face up to hard decisions on reducing the scope of the entire operation or abandoning it." Further, the Court expressed its opinion that a multiple of reasonable professional and technical salaries is

---

24. *Electric Regulator Corp. v. Comm.*, 64–2 USTC ¶9705, 14 AFTR2d 5447, 336 F.2d 339 (CA–2, 1964) used "quick assets" (current assets less inventory).

25. *Simons-Eastern Co. v. U.S.*, 73–1 USTC ¶9279, 31 AFTR2d 73–640, 354 F.Supp. 1003 (D.Ct. Ga., 1972). See also *Delaware Trucking Co., Inc.*, 32 TCM 105, T.C.Memo. 1973–29, and *Magic Mart, Inc.*, cited in Footnote 22.

a useful method for determining the amount to be included in an operating reserve. However, the Court did not indicate why it selected two months as the magic number. It can be anticipated that the courts will continue to evolve a *Bardahl*-like formula for noninventory corporations.

No Justifiable Needs.   Certain situations do *not* call for the accumulation of earnings. For example, accumulating earnings to make loans to shareholders [26] or brother-sister corporations is not considered within the reasonable needs of the business.[27] Accumulations to retire stock without curtailment of the business and for unrealistic business hazards (e.g., depression of the U.S. economy) are invalid reasons for accumulating funds,[28] as are accumulations made to carry out investments in properties or securities unrelated to the corporation's activity.[29]

Example 2   For a period of years, M, Inc., a trucking company, has considered the purchase of various vehicles and other facilities directly related to its business. It has, during the same time, also invested in oil and gas drilling projects (mostly wildcats). Despite substantial accumulated earnings, the corporation made no distributions of dividends during the same period of years. The Claims Court imposed the penalty tax, because the plan to acquire vehicles and facilities was not supported by documents in existence or prepared during the taxable years at issue. Furthermore, accumulations to further the oil and gas investments were unjustified. (The company was not in the oil and gas business, and the corporation was only a minority investor.)[30] □

Measuring the Accumulation.   Should the cost or fair market value of assets be used to determine whether a corporation has accumulated earnings and profits beyond its reasonable needs? This issue remains unclear. The Supreme Court has indicated that fair market value is to be used when dealing with marketable securities.[31] Although the Court admitted that the concept of earnings and profits does not include unrealized appreciation, it asserted that to determine if accumulated earnings are reasonable, the current asset ratio must be considered. Thus, the Court looked to the economic realities of the situation and held that fair market value is to be used with respect to readily marketable securities. The Court's opinion did not address the proper basis for valuation of assets other than marketable securities. However, the IRS may assert that this rule should be extended to include other assets. Therefore, tax advisers and corporate personnel should regularly check all security holdings to guard against accumulations caused by the appreciation of investments.

Example 3   C Company had accumulated earnings and profits of approximately $2,000,000. Five years ago, the company invested $150,000 in various

26. Reg. §§ 1.537–2(c)(1), (2), and (3).
27. See *Young's Rubber Corp.*, 21 TCM 1593, T.C.Memo. 1962–300.
28. *Turnbull, Inc. v. Comm.*, 67–1 USTC ¶9221, 19 AFTR2d 609, 373 F.2d 91 (CA–5, 1967), and Reg. § 1.537–2(c)(5).
29. Reg. § 1.537–2(c)(4).
30. *Cataphote Corp. of Miss. v. U.S.*, 75–2 USTC ¶9753, 36 AFTR2d 75–5990 (Ct.Cls., 1975).
31. *Ivan Allen Co. v. U.S.*, 75–2 USTC ¶9557, 36 AFTR2d 75–5200, 95 S.Ct. 2501 (USSC, 1975).

stocks and bonds. At the end of the current tax year, the fair market value of these securities approximated $2,500,000. Two of C Company's shareholders, father and son, owned 75% of the stock. If these securities are valued at cost, current assets minus current liabilities are deemed to be equal to the reasonable needs of the business. However, if the marketable securities are valued at their $2,500,000 fair market value, the value of the liquid assets would greatly exceed the corporation's reasonable needs. Under the Supreme Court's economic reality test, the fair market value must be used. Consequently, the corporation would be subject to the § 531 penalty tax. □

Mechanics of the Penalty Tax

The taxable base of the accumulated earnings tax is a company's accumulated taxable income (ATI). Taxable income of the corporation is modified as follows: [32]

$$\text{ATI} = \text{taxable income} \pm \text{certain adjustments} - \text{the dividends paid deduction} - \text{the accumulated earnings credit}$$

The "certain adjustments" include the following items (for a corporation not a mere holding or investment company):

As deductions—

1. Corporate income tax accrued.
2. Charitable contributions in excess of 10 percent of adjusted taxable income.
3. Capital loss adjustment.[33]
4. Excess of net long-term capital gain over net short-term capital loss, diminished by the capital gain tax and reduced by net capital losses from earlier years.

And as additions—

5. Capital loss carryovers and carrybacks.
6. Net operating loss deduction.
7. The dividends received deduction.

Note that item 4, in effect, allows a corporation to accumulate any capital gains without a penalty tax.

Payment of dividends reduces the amount of accumulated taxable income subject to the penalty tax. The dividends paid deduction includes those dividends paid during the tax year that the shareholders must report as ordinary income *and* any dividends paid within two and one-half months after the close

---

32. § 535(a).
33. The capital loss adjustment is calculated by reducing the net capital loss for the current taxable year by the lesser of (a) the nonrecaptured capital gain deduction or (b) the corporation's accumulated earnings and profits as of the close of the preceding tax year. The term "nonrecaptured capital gain deduction" is the total amount of net capital gains (less attributable taxes) deducted from ATI for preceding years beginning after July 18, 1984, in excess of total prior reductions already made by the corporation under (a) or (b). This deduction (item 3) and item 4 are either/or deductions, since a corporation would not have both in the same year.

of the tax year.[34] Further, a shareholder may file a consent statement to treat as a dividend the amount specified in such consent. A consent dividend is taxed to the shareholder even though it is not actually distributed. However, the consent dividend is treated as a contribution to the capital of the corporation (i.e., paid-in capital) by the shareholder.[35]

Example 4

A nonservice closely-held corporation that had no capital gains or losses in prior years has the following financial transactions for calendar year 1988:

Taxable income	$300,000
Tax liability	100,250
Excess charitable contributions	22,000
Short-term capital loss	(40,000)
Dividends received (less than 20% owned)	100,000
Research and development expenses	46,000
Dividends paid in 1988	40,000
Accumulated earnings (1/1/88)	220,000

Presuming the corporation is subject to the § 531 tax and has *no* reasonable business needs that would justify its accumulations, the accumulated taxable income is calculated as follows:

Taxable income		$300,000
Plus: 70% dividends received deduction		70,000
		$370,000
Less: Tax liability	$100,250	
Excess charitable contributions	22,000	
Net short-term capital loss adjustment	40,000	
Dividends paid	40,000	
Accumulated earnings minimum credit ($250,000 − $220,000)	30,000	232,250
Accumulated taxable income		$137,750

Thus, the accumulated earnings penalty tax for 1988 would be $42,033.75 [($100,000 × 27$\frac{1}{2}$%) + ($37,750 × 38$\frac{1}{2}$%)]. □

Example 5

In Example 4, assume that the reasonable needs of the business of § 535(c) amount to $270,000 in 1988. The current year's accumulated earnings would be reduced by $50,000, rather than the $30,000, of accumulated earnings minimum credit. Thus, accumulated taxable income would be $117,750, and the penalty tax would be $34,333.75. Note that the first $220,000 of accumulated earnings *cannot* be omitted in determining

---

34. §§ 535(a), 561(a), and 563(a).
35. §§ 565(a) and (c)(2). The consent dividend procedure would be appropriate if the corporation is not in a position to make a cash or property distribution to its shareholders. The dividends paid deduction is discussed more fully later in the chapter.

whether taxable income for the current year is reasonably needed by the enterprise. ☐

Personal Holding Company Penalty Tax

The personal holding company (PHC) tax was enacted to discourage the sheltering of certain types of passive income in corporations owned by high tax bracket individuals. These "incorporated pocketbooks" were frequently found in the entertainment and construction industries. For example, a taxpayer could shelter the income from securities in a corporation, which would pay no dividends, and allow the corporation's stock to increase in value. Thus, as with the accumulated earnings tax, the purpose of the PHC tax is to force the distribution of corporate earnings to the shareholders. However, in any one year, the IRS cannot impose both the PHC tax and the accumulated earnings tax.[36]

Example 6
A great deal of tax savings could be achieved by incorporating a "pocketbook" if § 541 did not exist. Assume that investments that yield $50,000 a year are transferred to a corporation by a 38½% income tax bracket shareholder. A tax savings of $11,750 would occur each year if no dividends were paid to the shareholder. With no corporation, there would be a total tax liability of $19,250, but with a corporation the tax liability would be only $7,500 in 1988 (15% × $50,000). Further, if the yield of $50,000 were in the form of dividends, the corporate tax would be even less because of the dividends received deduction. ☐

Whether a corporation will be included within the statutory definition of a personal holding company for any particular year depends upon the facts and circumstances in evidence during that year.[37] Therefore, PHC status may be conferred even in the absence of any such active intent on the part of the corporation. In one situation,[38] a manufacturing operation adopted a plan of complete liquidation, sold its business, and invested the proceeds of the sale in U.S. Treasury bills and certificates of deposit. During the liquidating corporation's last tax year, 100 percent of the corporation's adjusted ordinary gross income was interest income. Since the corporation was owned by one shareholder, the corporation was a PHC, even though in the process of liquidation.

Certain types of corporations are expressly excluded from PHC status in § 542(c):

—Tax-exempt organizations under § 501(a).

—Banks and domestic building and loan associations.

—Life insurance companies.

---

36. § 532(b)(1) and Reg. 1.541–1(a).
37. *Affiliated Enterprises, Inc. v. Comm.*, 44–1 USTC ¶9178, 32 AFTR 153, 140 F.2d 647 (CA–10, 1944).
38. *Weiss v. U.S.*, 75–2 USTC ¶9538, 36 AFTR2d 75–5186 (D.Ct. Ohio, 1975). See also *O'Sullivan Rubber Co. v. Comm.*, 41–2 USTC ¶9521, 27 AFTR 529, 120 F.2d 845 (CA–2, 1941).

—Surety companies.

—Foreign personal holding companies.

—Lending or finance companies.

—Foreign corporations.

—Small business investment companies.

Absent these exceptions, the business world could not perform necessary activities without a high rate of taxation. For example, a legitimate finance company should not be burdened by the personal holding company tax, because it is performing a valuable business function of loaning money, whereas an incorporated pocketbook's major purpose is to shelter the investment income from possible higher individual tax rates.

Definition of a Personal Holding Company

Two tests are incorporated within the PHC provisions:

1. Was more than 50 percent of the *value* of the outstanding stock owned by five or fewer individuals at any time during the *last half* of the taxable year?
2. Is a substantial portion (60 percent or more) of the corporate income (adjusted ordinary gross income) composed of passive types of income such as dividends, interest, rents, royalties, or certain personal service income?

If the answer to both of these questions is affirmative, the corporation is classified as a PHC. Once classified as a PHC, the corporation is required to pay a penalty tax in addition to the regular corporate income tax. This penalty tax is 50 percent before 1987, 38.5 percent for 1987, and 28 percent for taxable years beginning after 1987.

Stock Ownership Test.   To meet the stock ownership test, more than 50 percent *in value* of the outstanding stock must be owned, directly or indirectly, by or for not more than five individuals sometime during the last half of the tax year. Thus, if the corporation has nine or fewer shareholders, it automatically meets this test. If 10 unrelated individuals own an *equal* portion of the value of the outstanding stock, the stock ownership requirement would not be met. However, if these 10 individuals do not hold equal value, the test would be met.

Note that this ownership test is based on fair market value and not on the number of shares outstanding. Fair market value is determined in light of all the circumstances and is based on the company's net worth, earning and dividend paying capacity, appreciation of assets, and other relevant factors. If there are two or more classes of stock outstanding, the total value of all the stock should be allocated among the various classes according to the relative value of each class.[39]

---

39. Reg. § 1.542–3(c).

In determining the stock ownership of an individual, very broad constructive ownership rules are applicable. Under § 544, the following attribution rules determine indirect ownership:

1. Any stock owned by a corporation, partnership, trust, or estate is considered to be owned proportionately by the shareholders, partners, or beneficiaries.
2. The stock owned by the members of an individual's family (brothers, sisters, spouse, ancestors, and lineal descendants) or by the individual's partner is considered to be owned by such individual.
3. If an individual has an option to purchase stock, such stock is regarded as owned by that person.[40]
4. Convertible securities are treated as outstanding stock.

Example 7   A and B, two individuals, are the equal beneficiaries of a trust that owns the entire capital stock of M Corporation. M Corporation owns all of the stock of N Corporation. Here, all of the stock of M Corporation and N Corporation is considered to be owned equally by A and B by reason of indirect ownership under § 544(a)(1). ☐

Example 8   During the last half of the tax year, X Corporation had 1,000 shares of outstanding stock, 499 of which were held by various individuals having no relationship to one another and none of whom were partners. The remaining 501 shares were held by seven shareholders as follows:

H	100
H's spouse	50
H's brother	20
H's sister	70
H's father	120
H's son	80
H's daughter	61

Under the family attribution rules of § 544(a)(2), H is considered to own 501 shares of X for purposes of determining stock ownership in a personal holding company. ☐

Attribution rules 2, 3, and 4 are applicable only for the purpose of classifying a corporation as a PHC and cannot be used to avoid the application of the PHC provisions. Basically, these broad constructive ownership rules make it difficult for a closely-held corporation to avoid application of the stock ownership test. For example, convertible securities would be treated as outstanding stock only if the effect of the inclusion is to make the corporation a PHC (and not to expand the total amount of stock in order to avoid PHC classification).

---

40. For examples of how these constructive ownership rules operate, see Reg. §§ 1.544–2, –3(a), and –4.

Gross Income Test.   The gross income test is met if 60 percent or more of the corporation's adjusted ordinary gross income (AOGI) is composed of certain passive income items (i.e., PHC income). AOGI is calculated by subtracting the following from gross income (as defined by § 61):

—Gains from the sale or disposition of capital assets.

—Section 1231 gains.

—Expenditures attributable to income from rents and mineral royalties (such as depreciation, property taxes, interest expense, and rental payments).[41]

The deduction of the first two items from gross income results in the intermediate concept, ordinary gross income (OGI), the use of which is noted subsequently. The starting point, gross income, is not necessarily synonymous with gross receipts. In fact, for transactions in stocks, securities, and commodities, the term "gross income" includes only the excess of gains over any losses.[42]

PHC income includes income from dividends; interest; royalties; annuities;[43] rents; mineral, oil, and gas royalties; copyright royalties; produced film rents; and amounts from certain personal service contracts. Any amount from personal service contracts is classified as PHC income only if (1) some person other than the corporation has the right to designate, by name or by description, the individual who is to perform the services and (2) the person so designated owns, directly or indirectly, 25 percent or more in value of the outstanding stock of the corporation at some time during the taxable year.[44] (See Example 25 later in the chapter.)

Example 9   M Corporation has four shareholders, and its AOGI is $95,000, composed of gross income from a merchandising operation of $40,000, interest income of $15,000, dividend income of $25,000, and adjusted income from rents of $15,000. Total passive income is $55,000 ($15,000 + $25,000 + $15,000). Since 60% of AOGI (i.e., $57,000) is greater than the passive income ($55,000), this corporation is not a personal holding company. □

Example 10   Assume in Example 9 that the corporation received $21,000 in interest income rather than $15,000. Total passive income is now $61,000 ($21,000 + $25,000 + $15,000). Since 60% of AOGI (i.e., $60,600) is less than passive income of $61,000, this corporation is a personal holding company. □

Although rental income is normally classified as PHC income, it can be excluded from that category if two tests are met. The first test is met if a corporation's adjusted income from rents is 50 percent or more of the corporation's AOGI. The second test is satisfied if the total dividends paid for the tax year, dividends considered as paid on the last day of the tax year, and consent

---

41. §§ 543(b)(1) and (2).
42. Reg. § 1.542–2. See also Reg. § 1.543–2(b) wherein net gain on transactions in stocks and securities is not reduced by a net loss on commodities futures transactions.
43. § 543(a)(1).
44. § 543(a)(7). For an application of the "right to designate," see *Thomas P. Byrnes, Inc.*, 73 T.C. 416 (1979).

dividends are equal to or greater than the amount by which the nonrent PHC income exceeds 10 percent of OGI.[45] The taxpayer wishes to meet both tests so that the rent income can be excluded from PHC income for purposes of the gross income test referred to above. (See Figure III later in the chapter.)

With respect to this 50 percent test, "adjusted income from rents" is defined as gross income from rents reduced by the deductions allowable under § 543(b)(3). These deductions are depreciation, property taxes, interest, and rent. Generally, compensation is not included in the term "rents" and is not an allowable deduction. The final amount included in AOGI as adjusted income from rents cannot be less than zero.

Example 11   Assume that Z Corporation has rental income of $10,000 and the following business deductions:

Depreciation on rental property	$1,000
Interest on mortgage	2,500
Real property taxes	1,500
Salaries and other business expenses (§ 162)	3,000

The adjusted income from rents included in AOGI is $5,000 (i.e., $10,000 − $1,000 − $2,500 − $1,500). Salaries and other § 162 expenses do not affect the calculation of AOGI. □

A company deriving its income primarily from rental activities can avoid PHC status by merely distributing as dividends the amount of nonrental PHC income that exceeds 10 percent of its OGI.

Example 12   During the tax year, N Corporation receives $15,000 in rental income, $4,000 in dividends, and a $1,000 long-term capital gain. Corporate deductions for depreciation, interest, and real estate taxes allocable to the rental income amount to $10,000. The company paid a total of $2,500 in dividends to its eight shareholders. To determine whether or not rental income is PHC income, OGI, AOGI, and adjusted income from rents must be calculated.

Rental income	$15,000
Dividends	4,000
Long-term capital gain	1,000
Gross income	$20,000
Deduct: Gains from sale or disposition of capital assets	1,000
OGI	$19,000
Deduct: Depreciation, interest, and real estate taxes	10,000
AOGI	$ 9,000

---

45. § 543(a)(2).

First, adjusted income from rents must be 50% or more of AOGI.

Rental income	$15,000
Deduct: Depreciation, interest, and real estate taxes	10,000
Adjusted income from rents	$ 5,000
50% of AOGI	$ 4,500

N Corporation has satisfied the first test.

Second, total dividends paid for the year amount to $2,500. This figure must be equal to or greater than the amount by which nonrent PHC income exceeds 10% of OGI.

Nonrent PHC income	$4,000
Less: 10% of OGI	1,900
Excess	$2,100

N Corporation meets both tests; the adjusted income from rents is not classified as PHC income. ☐

Similar to rental income, adjusted income from mineral, oil, and gas royalties can be excluded from PHC income classification if three tests are met.[46] First, adjusted income from such royalties must constitute 50 percent or more of AOGI. Second, nonroyalty PHC income may not exceed 10 percent of OGI. Note that this 10 percent test is not accompanied by the dividend escape clause previously described in relation to rental income. Therefore, corporations receiving income from mineral, oil, or gas royalties must be careful to minimize nonroyalty PHC income. Furthermore, adjusted income from rents and copyright royalties is considered to be nonroyalty PHC income whether or not treated as such by §§ 543(a)(2) and (4). Third, the company's business expenses under § 162 (other than compensation paid to shareholders) must be at least 15 percent of AOGI.

Example 13   P Corporation has gross income of $4,000, which consists of gross income from oil royalties in the amount of $2,500, $400 of dividends, and $1,100 from the sale of merchandise. The total amount of the deductions for depletion, interest, and property and severance taxes allocable to the gross income from oil royalties equals $1,000. Deductions allowable under § 162 amount to $450. P Corporation's adjusted income from oil royalties will not be PHC income if the three tests are met. Therefore, OGI, AOGI, and adjusted income from oil royalties must be determined:

---

46. § 543(a)(3).

Oil royalties income	$2,500
Dividends	400
Sale of merchandise	1,100
Gross income (*and* OGI)	$4,000
Deduct: Depletion, interest, and property and severance taxes	1,000
AOGI	$3,000

Adjusted income from oil royalties must be 50% or more of AOGI.

Oil royalties income	$2,500
Deduct: Depletion, interest, and property and severance taxes	1,000
Adjusted income from oil royalties	1,500
50% of AOGI	$1,500

Test one is met. Since nonroyalty PHC income is $400 (composed solely of the $400 of dividends) and this amount is not more than 10% of OGI, the second test is also satisfied. The third requirement is satisfied if deductible expenses under § 162 amount to at least 15% of AOGI.

§ 162 expenses	$450
15% of $3,000 (AOGI)	$450

P Corporation's adjusted income from oil royalties is not PHC income. □

As in the case of income from mineral, oil, and gas royalties and rents, copyright royalties and produced film rents are not categorized as PHC income if certain tests are met.[47]

Before amendment by TRA of 1986, § 543 had been interpreted to include as PHC income computer software royalties. This was a harsh result for those corporations that received such royalties on software developed in connection with the active conduct of a trade or business. If the stock ownership test was met, the only way these corporations could avoid the PHC tax was through the dividends paid deduction. Needless to say, this created cash flow problems for developing businesses in which cash needs were already critical.

Royalties received from licensing computer software are excluded from the definition of PHC income [48] if the following conditions are satisfied:

—The corporation must be actively engaged in the business of developing computer software.

—The royalties must constitute at least 50 percent of OGI.

---

47. §§ 543(a)(4) and (5).
48. Section 543(d) is retroactive to all past years not barred by the statute of limitations.

—Business-related deductions equal or exceed 25 percent of OGI.

—Passive income (other than computer software royalties) in excess of 10 percent of OGI must be distributed as a dividend.

Calculation of the PHC Tax

To this point, the discussion has focused on the determination of personal holding company status. If an entity is classified as a PHC, a new set of computations is relevant in determining the amount upon which the penalty tax is imposed. This tax base is called undistributed PHC income (UPHC income). Basically, this amount is taxable income, subject to certain adjustments, minus the dividends paid deduction.

The starting point is corporate taxable income as determined for income tax purposes. To this amount the following adjustments must be made:

—The Federal income tax accrual (other than the PHC tax and the accumulated earnings tax) for the tax year is deductible. The deduction is determined under the accrual method even though the corporation may actually use the cash receipts and disbursements method. Any contested, unpaid tax is not considered accrued until the issue is resolved.

—Excess charitable contributions beyond the corporate limitation of 10 percent of taxable income can be deducted up to the 20 percent, 30 percent, or 50 percent limitations imposed upon individuals.[49]

—The excess of long-term capital gain over short-term capital loss (net of tax) is deducted from taxable income. Thus, long-term capital gains can be accumulated in a corporation and are not subject to the PHC tax.

—The dividends received deduction and other special deductions allowed by §§ 241 through 250 (other than the organizational expense deduction) are not available. Such amounts must be added back to taxable income to determine the penalty tax base.

—Any net operating loss, except for the preceding year, must be added back.

—Under certain conditions, business expenses and depreciation attributable to nonbusiness property owned by the corporation that exceed the income derived from such property must be added back to taxable income to determine UPHC income.[50]

Dividends Paid Deduction.   Since the purpose of the PHC penalty tax is to force a corporation to pay dividends, five types of dividends paid deductions reduce the amount subject to the penalty tax. (See Figure I on page 7–21.) First, dividends actually paid during the tax year ordinarily reduce UPHC income.[51] However, such distributions must be pro rata. They must exhibit no preference to any shares of stock over shares of the same class or to any class of stock over other classes outstanding.[52] This prohibition is especially harsh when

---

49. Reg. § 1.545–2.
50. § 545(b).
51. §§ 561(a)(1) and 562.
52. § 562(c).

portions of an employee-shareholder's salary are declared unreasonable and classified as a disguised or constructive dividend.[53] In the case of a property dividend of appreciated property, the dividends paid deduction should be the fair market value of the property (not adjusted basis). The Regulations, however, hold to the contrary.[54]

Example 14   Three individuals are equal shareholders in a personal holding company. A property dividend is paid to the three shareholders in the following proportion: 25%, 35%, and 40%. This is not a pro rata distribution, and the dividends are not deductible from UPHC income. □

A two and one-half month grace period exists following the close of the tax year. Dividends paid during this period may be treated as paid during the tax year just closed. However, the amount allowed as a deduction from UPHC income cannot exceed either (1) the UPHC income for the tax year or (2) 20 percent of the total dividends distributed during the tax year.[55] Reasonable cause may not be used to overcome the 20 percent limitation even if the taxpayer relied upon incorrect advice given by an accountant.[56]

The consent dividend procedure [57] involves a hypothetical distribution of the corporate income taxed to the shareholders. Since the consent dividend is taxable, a dividends paid deduction is allowed. The shareholder's basis in his or her stock is increased by the consent dividend (i.e., a contribution to capital), and a subsequent actual distribution of the consent dividend might be taxed. The consent election is filed by the shareholders at any time not later than the due date of the corporate tax return. The consent dividend is considered distributed by the corporation on the last day of the tax year and is included in the gross income of the shareholder in the tax year in which or with which the tax year of the corporation ends. The obvious disadvantage of this special election is that the shareholders must pay taxes on dividends they do not actually receive. However, if cash is not available for dividend distributions, the consent dividend route is a logical alternative.

Example 15   Q Corporation, a calendar year taxpayer solely owned by T, is a PHC. Dividends of $30,000 must be paid to avoid the PHC tax, but the company has a poor cash position. T elects the consent dividend treatment under § 565 and is taxed on $30,000 of dividends. The shareholder's basis in Q Corporation stock is increased by $30,000 as a result of this special election. Thus, the corporation does not incur the PHC tax, but T is taxed even though he receives no cash from the corporation with which to pay such tax. □

Even after a corporation has been classified as a PHC, a belated dividend distribution made in a subsequent tax year can avoid the PHC penalty tax.

---

53. Refer to Chapter 4 and *Henry Schwartz Corp.*, 60 T.C. 728 (1973).
54. Reg. § 1.562–1(a). This Regulation was promulgated when most property dividends were non-taxable to the distributing corporation.
55. §§ 563(b) and 543(a)(2)(B)(ii).
56. *Kenneth Farmer Darrow*, 64 T.C. 217 (1975).
57. Reg. § 1.565–1.

This deficiency dividend provision [58] allows the payment of a dividend within 90 days after the determination of the PHC tax deficiency for a prior tax year. A determination occurs when a decision of a court is final, a closing agreement under § 7121 is signed, or a written agreement is signed between the taxpayer and a District Director. Note that the dividend distribution cannot be made before the determination or after the running of the 90-day time period. Furthermore, the deficiency dividend procedure does not relieve the taxpayer of interest, additional amounts, or assessable penalties computed with respect to the PHC tax.

A dividend carryover from two prior years may be available to reduce the UPHC income. When the dividends paid by a company in its prior years exceed the company's UPHC income for such years, the excess amount may be deducted in the current year. See § 564(b) for the manner of computing this dividend carryover and Figure I for a summary of dividends paid deductions.

Figure I   Dividends Paid Deduction

Type of Dividend	Availability	Timing	Statutory Location	Effect on Shareholders
Current year	Both § 531 and § 541	By end of year.	§ 561(a)(1)	Reduction in ATI and UPHC income.
Two and one-half month grace period*	Both § 531 and § 541	On or before the 15th day of the 3rd month after end of year.	§§ 563(a) and (b)	Reduction in ATI and UPHC income.
Consent dividend	Both § 531 and § 541	Not later than due date of corporate tax return.	§ 565(a)	Treated as a dividend as of end of tax year and given back as a contribution to capital.
Dividend carryover	§ 541	Not later than due date of the corporate tax return.	§ 564	Reduction in UPHC income.
Deficiency dividend	§ 541	Within 90 days after determination of PHC tax deficiency.	§ 547	Treated as if dividend paid in offending year. No impact on interest and penalties.

* Under the § 531 tax, dividends paid within the first two and one-half months of the succeeding year must be carried back to the preceding year. In the case of the § 541 tax, the carryback is optional—some or all of the dividends can be deducted in the year paid. The 20% limit on carrybacks applicable to § 541 [see § 563(a)] does not cover § 531 situations.

---

58. § 547.

Personal Holding Company Planning Model. Some of the complex PHC provisions may be developed into a flow chart format. Figure II and Figure III provide a PHC planning model and the rules for the rent exclusion test, respectively.

Computations Illustrated. After the appropriate adjustments have been made to corporate taxable income and the sum of the dividends paid has been subtracted, the resulting figure is UPHC income, which is multiplied by the appropriate penalty tax rate to obtain the PHC tax. Although the tax revenue from the PHC tax may be small, the mere threat of this confiscatory tax prompts owners to monitor their corporations and take the necessary steps to avoid the tax.

Example 16   X Corporation had the following items of income and expense in 1988:

Dividend income (less than 20% owned)	$ 40,000
Rent income	150,000
Depreciation expense	40,000
Mortgage interest	30,000
Real estate taxes	30,000
Salaries	20,000
Dividends paid (three shareholders)	20,000
Corporate income tax liability (§ 11)	6,300

OGI would be $190,000 ($40,000 + $150,000), and AOGI would be $90,000 ($190,000 − $40,000 − $30,000 − $30,000). Taxable income is $42,000, computed as follows:

Rent income		$150,000
Dividend income		40,000
		$190,000
Less: Depreciation expense	$40,000	
Mortgage interest	30,000	
Real estate taxes	30,000	
Salaries	20,000	(120,000)
		$ 70,000
Less: Dividends received deduction		
($40,000 × 70%)		(28,000)
Taxable income		$ 42,000

The adjusted income from rents is $50,000 ($150,000 − $100,000). The corporation does meet the 50% rental income test, since $50,000 is greater than 50% of AOGI ($90,000 × 50% = $45,000). But the corporation did not pay at least $21,000 of dividends (nonrental PHC income $40,000 − $19,000 = $21,000). Therefore, the 10% rental income test is not met, and the rental income is classified as PHC income. Since all income is passive, this corporation is a PHC. The PHC tax of $12,236 would be calculated as follows:

Taxable income	$42,000
Plus: Dividends received deduction ($40,000 × 70%)	28,000
	$70,000
Less: § 11 tax	(6,300)
	$63,700
Less: Dividends paid	(20,000)
UPHC income	$43,700
	× .28
PHC tax liability	$12,236

Example 17   Assume in Example 16 that $22,000 of dividends are paid to the shareholders (instead of $20,000). In this case, the rental income is not PHC income, because the 10% test is met ($22,000 is equal to or greater than the nonrental PHC income in excess of 10% of OGI). Thus, an increase of at least $2,000 in the dividends paid in Example 16 avoids the $12,236 PHC tax liability. □

Figure II   Personal Holding Company Planning Model*

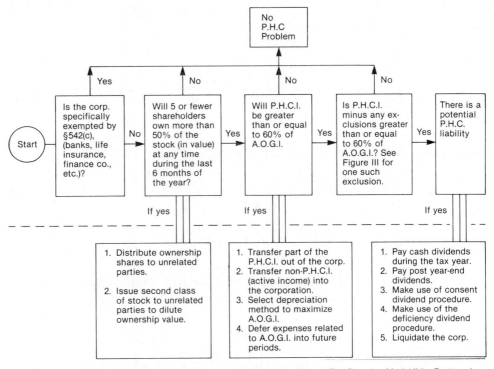

* from "Understanding and Avoiding the Personal Holding Company Tax: A Tax Planning Model," by Pratt and Whittenburg, which appeared in the June 1975 issue of *Taxes — the Tax Magazine* published and copyrighted 1975 by Commerce Clearing House, Inc., and appears here with their permission.

Figure III   Rent Exclusion Test*

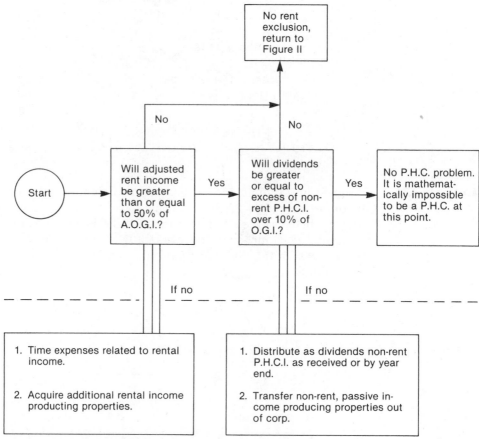

*from "Understanding and Avoiding the Personal Holding Company Tax: A Tax Planning Model," by Pratt and Whittenburg, which appeared in the June 1975 issue of *Taxes — the Tax Magazine* published and copywrited 1975 by Commerce Clearing House, Inc., and appears here with their permission.

Comparison of Sections 531 and 541

A review of several important distinctions between the penalty tax on the unreasonable accumulation of earnings (§ 531) and the tax on personal holding companies (§ 541) will set the stage for the presentation of tax planning considerations applicable to the § 541 tax.

—Unlike § 531, there is no element of intent necessary for the imposition of the § 541 tax.[59] This makes § 541 a real trap for the unwary.

---

59. In light of the Supreme Court decision in *Donruss* (refer to Footnote 3 and the text thereto), one wonders what role, if any, intent will play in the future in aiding taxpayers to avoid the § 531 tax. In this connection, see the dissenting opinion in this decision issued by Justice Harlan.

—The imposition of the § 541 tax is not affected by the past history of the corporation. Thus, it could be just as applicable to a newly formed corporation as to one that has been in existence for many years. This is not the case with the § 531 tax. Past accumulations have a direct bearing on the determination of the accumulated earnings credit. In this sense, younger corporations are less vulnerable to the § 531 tax, since complete insulation generally is guaranteed until accumulations exceed $250,000.

—Although one could conclude that both taxes pose threats for closely-held corporations, the stock ownership test of § 542(a)(2) makes this very explicit with regard to the § 541 tax. However, publicly held corporations can be subject to the § 531 tax if corporate policy is dominated by certain shareholders who are using the corporate form to avoid income taxes on dividends through the accumulation of corporate profits.[60]

—Sufficient dividend distributions can negate both taxes. In the case of § 531, however, such dividends must be distributed on a timely basis. Both taxes allow a two and one-half month grace period and provide for the consent dividend procedure.[61] Only the § 541 tax allows the deficiency dividend procedure.

—Differences in reporting procedures arise, because the § 541 tax is a self-assessed tax and the § 531 tax is not. For example, if a corporation is a personal holding company, it must file a Schedule PH along with its Form 1120 (the corporate income tax return) for the year involved. Failure to file the Schedule PH can result in the imposition of interest and penalties and also brings into play a special six-year statute of limitations for the assessment of the § 541 tax.[62] On the other hand, the § 531 tax is assessed by the IRS and consequently requires no reporting procedures on the part of the corporate taxpayer.

✓ Tax Planning Considerations

The elimination of favorable capital gain rates has made most corporate distributions less attractive, and many companies will prefer permanent rather than temporary deferral of accumulated earnings. Even with higher corporate rates than individual rates, a corporation can invest accumulated funds in tax-free securities or purchase high-yield corporate stocks to take advantage of the dividends received deductions. Thus, the threat of the accumulated earnings tax and the personal holding company tax continues to be a prime concern of many corporations.

---

60. § 532(c).
61. Under the § 531 tax, dividends paid within the first two and one-half months of the succeeding year *must* be carried back to the preceding year. In the case of the § 541 tax, the carryback is optional—some or all of the dividends can be deducted in the year paid. The 20% limit on carrybacks applicable to § 541 [see § 563(a)] does not cover § 531 situations.
62. § 6501(f). Refer also to Chapter 14.

The § 531 Tax

Justifying the Accumulations. The key defense against imposition of the § 531 tax is a successful assertion that the accumulations are necessary to meet the reasonable needs of the business. Several points should be kept in mind:

—To the extent possible, the justification for the accumulation should be documented. If, for example, the corporation plans to acquire additional physical facilities for use in its trade or business, the minutes of the board of directors' meetings should reflect the decision. Furthermore, such documentation should take place during the period of accumulation. This planning may require some foresight on the part of the taxpayer, but meaningful planning to avoid a tax problem should not be based on what happens after the issue has been raised by an agent as the result of an audit. In the case of a profitable closely-held corporation that accumulates some or all of its profits, the parties might well operate under the assumption that § 531 is always a potential issue. Recognition of a tax problem at an early stage is the first step in a satisfactory resolution.

—Keep in mind that multiple reasons for making an accumulation are not only permissible but invariably advisable. Suppose, for example, a manufacturing corporation plans to expand its plant. It would not be wise to stop with the cost of such expansion as the only justification for all accumulations. What about further justification based on the corporation's working capital requirements as determined under the *Bardahl* formula or some variation thereof? Other reasons for making the accumulation may well be present and should be recognized.

—The reasons for the accumulation should be sincere and, once established, pursued to the extent feasible.

Example 18
In 1983, the board of directors of W Corporation decide to accumulate $1,000,000 to fund the replacement of W's plant. Five years pass, and no steps are taken to initiate construction. ☐

Example 19
In 1983, the board of directors of Y Corporation decide to accumulate $1,000,000 to fund the replacement of Y's plant. In the ensuing five-year period, the following steps are taken: a site selection committee is appointed (1984); a site is chosen (1985); the site (i.e., land) is purchased (1986); an architect is retained, and plans are drawn up for the new plant (1987; bids are requested and submitted for the construction of the new plant (1988). ☐

Compare Examples 18 and 19. Y Corporation is in a much better position to justify the accumulation. Even though the plant has not yet been replaced some five years after the accumulations began, the progress toward its ultimate construction speaks for itself. On the other hand, W Corporation may be hard pressed to prove the sincerity of its objective for the accumulations in light of its failure to follow through on the projected replacement.

—The amount of the accumulation should be realistic under the circumstances.

Example 20   W Corporation plans to replace certain machinery at an estimated cost of $500,000. The original machinery was purchased for $300,000 and, because of $250,000 in depreciation deducted for tax purposes, possesses a present book value of $50,000. How much of an accumulation can be justified for the replacement to avoid the § 531 tax? At first blush, one might consider $500,000 as the appropriate amount, since this represents the estimated replacement cost of the machinery. But what about the $250,000 in depreciation that W Corporation has already deducted? If it is counted again as part of a reasonable accumulation, a double tax benefit results. Only $250,000 [i.e., $50,000 (the unrecovered cost of the old machinery) + $200,000 (the additional outlay necessary)] can be justified as the appropriate amount for an accumulation.[63] □

Example 21   During the current year, a competitor files a $2,000,000 patent infringement suit against Z Corporation. Competent legal counsel advises Z Corporation that the suit is groundless. Under such conditions, the corporation can hardly justify accumulating $2,000,000 because of the pending lawsuit. □

—Since the § 531 tax is imposed on an annual basis, justification for accumulations may vary from year to year.[64]

Example 22   For calendar years 1986 and 1987, R Corporation was able to justify large accumulations due to a pending additional income tax assessment. In early 1988, the assessment is settled and paid. After the settlement, R Corporation can no longer consider the assessment as a reasonable anticipated need of the business. □

Danger of Loans to Shareholders.   The presence of loans made by a corporation to its shareholders often raises the § 531 issue. If this same corporation has a poor dividend-paying record, it becomes particularly vulnerable. When one recalls that the avowed goal of the § 531 tax is to force certain corporations to distribute dividends, the focus becomes clear. If a corporation can spare funds for loans to shareholders, it certainly has the capacity to pay dividends. Unfortunately, the presence of such loans can cause other tax problems for the parties.

Example 23   During the year in question, Q Corporation made advances of $120,000 to its sole shareholder, T. Although prosperous and maintaining substantial accumulations, Q Corporation has never paid a dividend. Under these circumstances, the IRS could move in either of two directions. The Service could assess the § 531 tax against Q Corporation for its unreasonable accumulation of earnings. Alternatively, the IRS could argue that the

---

63. *Battelstein Investment Co. v. U.S.*, 71–1 USTC ¶9227, 27 AFTR2d 71–713, 442 F.2d 87 (CA–5, 1971).
64. Compare *Hardin's Bakeries, Inc. v. Martin, Jr.*, 67–1 USTC ¶9253, 19 AFTR2d 647, 293 F.Supp. 1129 (D.Ct.Miss., 1967), with *Hardin v. U.S.*, 70–2 USTC ¶9676, 26 AFTR2d 70–5852 (D.Ct.Miss., 1970), *aff'd., rev'd., rem'd.* by 72–1 USTC ¶9464, 29 AFTR2d 72–1446, 461 F.2d 865 (CA–5, 1972).

advances were not bona fide loans but, instead, taxable dividends.[65] Such a dual approach places the taxpayers in a somewhat difficult position. If, for example, they contend that the advance was a bona fide loan, T avoids dividend income but Q Corporation becomes vulnerable to the imposition of the § 531 tax.[66] On the other hand, a concession that the advance was not a loan hurts T but helps Q Corporation avoid the penalty tax. □

Role of Dividends.   The relationship between dividend distribution and the § 531 tax needs further clarification. It would be helpful to pose and answer several questions. First, can the payment of enough dividends completely avoid the § 531 tax? The answer must be in the affirmative because of the operation of § 535. Recall that this provision defines accumulated taxable income as *taxable income* (adjusted by certain items) *minus the sum of the dividends paid deduction and the accumulated earnings credit.* Since the § 531 tax is imposed on accumulated taxable income, no tax would be due if the dividends paid and the accumulated earnings credit are large enough to offset taxable income. Sufficient dividends, therefore, will avoid the tax.[67] Second, can the payment of *some* dividends completely avoid the § 531 tax? As the question is worded, the answer must be *no*. Theoretically, even significant dividend distributions will not insulate a corporation from the tax.[68] From a practical standpoint, however, the payment of dividends indicates that the corporation is not being used exclusively to shield its shareholders from tax consequences. To the extent that this reflects the good faith of the parties and the lack of tax avoidance motivation, it is a factor the IRS will consider with regard to the § 531 issue.

Role of the S Corporation Election.   An S corporation election will circumvent the application of the § 531 tax.[69] However, the protection only covers the period of S corporation status and is not retroactive to years during which the entity was a regular corporation.

Example 24   P Corporation, a calendar year taxpayer, makes a timely and proper election under Subchapter S effective for tax year 1988. Since its formation in 1980, P Corporation has accumulated significant earnings and has never paid a dividend. The election protects the corporation from the imposition of the § 531 tax for year 1988 and for whatever subsequent years it remains in effect. It would not, however, preclude the IRS from assessing the tax on P Corporation for those years open under the statute of limitations in which it qualified as a regular corporation. □

---

65. Refer to the discussion of constructive dividends in Chapter 4.
66. *Ray v. U.S.*, 69–1 USTC ¶9334, 23 AFTR2d 69–1141, 409 F.2d 1322 (CA–6, 1969).
67. Such dividends must, however, be taxable to the shareholders. Nontaxable stock dividends issued under § 305(a) do not affect the dividends paid deduction.
68. In *Henry Van Hummell, Inc. v. Comm.*, 66–2 USTC ¶9610, 18 AFTR2d 5500, 364 F.2d 746 (CA–10, 1966), the § 531 tax was imposed even though the corporation paid out over 60% of its taxable income as dividends.
69. See Chapter 10.

Avoiding the § 541 Tax

The classification of a corporation as a personal holding company requires the satisfaction of *both* the stock ownership and the gross income tests. Failure to meet either of these two tests will avoid PHC status and the § 541 tax.

—The stock ownership test can be handled through a dispersion of stock ownership. Success might not be achieved, however, unless the tax planner watches the application of the stock attribution rules.

—Remember the following relationship when working with the gross income test:

$$\frac{\text{PHC income}}{\text{AOGI}} = 60\% \text{ or more}$$

Decreasing the numerator (PHC income) or increasing the denominator (AOGI) of the fraction will reduce the resulting percentage. Keeping the resulting percentage below 60 percent precludes classification as a personal holding company. To control PHC income, investments in low-yield growth securities are preferable to those that generate heavy interest or dividend income. Capital gains from the sale of such securities will not affect PHC status, since they are not included in either the numerator or the denominator of the fraction. Investments in tax-exempt securities are also attractive, because the interest income therefrom, like capital gains, carries no effect in applying the gross income test.

—Income from personal service contracts may, under certain conditions, constitute PHC income.

Example 25   B, C, and D (all attorneys) are equal shareholders in X Company, a professional association engaged in the practice of law. E, a new client, retains X Company to pursue a legal claim. Under the terms of the retainer agreement, E designates B as the attorney who will perform the legal services. The suit is successful, and 30% of the judgment E recovers is paid to X Company as a fee. Since the parties have met all of the requirements of § 543(a)(7), the fee received by X Company is PHC income.[70] □

The result reached in Example 25 could have been avoided had B not been specifically designated in the retainer agreement as the party to perform the services.

—Rent income may or may not be PHC income. The relative amount of rent income is the key consideration. If

$$\frac{\text{Adjusted income from rents}}{\text{AOGI}} = 50\% \text{ or more}$$

---

70. The example presumes X Company will be treated as a corporation for Federal tax purposes. As noted in Chapter 2, this is the usual result of professional association status.

and nonrent PHC income less 10 percent of OGI is distributed dividend, rent income will not be PHC income. Maximizing adjusted income from rents clearly will improve the situation for taxpayers. Since adjusted income from rents represents gross rents less expenses attributable thereto, a conservative approach in determining such expenses would be helpful. The taxpayer should be encouraged to minimize depreciation (e.g., choose straight-line over accelerated cost recovery method). This approach to the handling of expenses attributable to rental property has to be confusing to many taxpayers, because it contradicts what is normally done to reduce income tax consequences.

—In some cases, it may be possible to reduce PHC exposure by readjusting corporate structures.

Example 26   P Corporation carries on two principal activities: a rental business (approximately 49% of total gross receipts) and a finance operation (approximately 51% of total gross receipts). As presently constituted, P Corporation could well be classified as a personal holding company. (One cannot be sure without applying the stock ownership tests.) The gross income test is probably satisfied, since interest income from the finance operation and rents from the rental business are PHC income.[71] The separation of these two activities into multiple corporations would solve the problem.[72] The rents no longer are PHC income due to the 50% or more of AOGI test. The finance operation would be an excepted corporation to which the PHC tax does not apply.[73] □

In the same vein, business combinations (e.g., mergers and consolidations) or the filing of a consolidated return by an affiliated group of corporations could be used to dilute the PHC income of one corporation with the income from operations of another to avoid meeting the gross income test.

Corporations in the process of liquidation could be particularly susceptible to the PHC tax for two reasons. Operating income may be low because the corporation is in the process of winding up its business. If passive investment income remains at the level maintained during periods of normal operations or perhaps increases, the corporation might satisfy the gross income test.[74] In addition, the parties may never realize that the corporation was a PHC until it has been completely liquidated. At this point, the tax can no longer be neutralized through the issuance of a deficiency dividend.[75] The apparent solution to the problem is to recognize the vulnerability of the corporation and keep it on the safe side of the gross income test. Good control can be obtained over the situation if the earlier corporate distributions in liquidation include those assets that generate PHC income.

---

71. See, for example, *Hilldun Corp.* v. *Comm.*, 69–1 USTC ¶9319, 23 AFTR2d 69–1090, 408 F.2d 1117 (CA–2, 1969).
72. The separation could be carried out as a nontaxable reorganization. Refer to Chapter 6.
73. Pursuant to § 542(c)(6), a lending or finance company is excepted under certain circumstances.
74. Investment or PHC income might increase if the corporation, pending complete dissolution, invested some or all of the proceeds from the sale of its operating assets.
75. *Michael C. Callan*, 54 T.C. 1514 (1970), and *L. C. Bohart Plumbing & Heating Co., Inc.*, 64 T.C. 602 (1975).

PHC status need not carry tragic tax consequences if the parties are aware of the issue and take appropriate steps. Since the tax is imposed on UPHC income, properly timed dividend distributions will neutralize the tax and avoid interest and penalties. Also, as long as a corporation holds PHC status, the § 531 tax cannot be imposed.

Example 27   X Corporation is owned entirely by two sisters, R and S (ages 86 and 88, respectively). X Corporation's major assets comprise investments in low-yield and high-growth securities, unimproved real estate, and tax-exempt bonds, all of which have a realizable value of $500,000. The basis of the stock in X Corporation to each sister is $50,000. ☐

The liquidation of X Corporation (a frequent solution to undesired PHC status) would be disastrous to the two sisters. As noted in the discussion of § 331 in Chapter 5, such liquidation would result in the recognition of a capital gain of $400,000. In this case, therefore, it would be preferable to live with PHC status. Considering the nature of the assets held by X Corporation, this may not be difficult to do. Keep in mind that the interest from the tax-exempt bonds is not PHC income. Should X Corporation wish to sell any of its investments, the long-term capital gain that would result is not PHC income. The PHC tax on any other income (i.e., the dividends from the securities) can be controlled through enough dividend distributions to reduce UPHC income to zero. Furthermore, as long as X Corporation remains a PHC, it is insulated from the § 531 tax (the imposition of which would be highly probable in this case).

The liquidation of X Corporation should await the deaths of R and S and consequently should be carried out by their estates or heirs. By virtue of the application of § 1014 (see Chapter 12), the income tax basis in the stock would be stepped up to the fair market value of the stock on the date of death. Much, if not all, of the capital gain potential presently existing at the shareholder level would thus be eliminated.

Problem Materials

Discussion Questions

1. List some valid business reasons for accumulating funds in a closely-held corporation.
2. Explain the purpose(s) underlying the creation of the accumulated earnings penalty tax and the personal holding company tax.
3. Explain the consent dividend provision.
4. A merger of two corporations could result in the imposition of the accumulated earnings tax on the surviving corporation. Is this possible? Explain.
5. Explain the *Bardahl* formula. How could it be improved?
6. Why might a corporation not wish to include Federal income taxes into the calculation of the *Bardahl* formula (i.e., the accounts payable turnover)?
7. Why is it desirable for a closely-held corporation to maintain a good dividends record (i.e., pay some dividends each year)?

8. May a holding or investment company accumulate more than $250,000 of earnings if the company can justify that such excess is necessary to meet the reasonable needs of the business?

9. How can human resource accounting be used in an accumulated earnings situation?

10. A holding company's only income item during its first taxable year is a $300,000 long-term capital gain. Calculate any accumulated earnings tax.

11. Can the IRS impose both the PHC tax and the accumulated earnings tax upon a construction company?

12. ATI = taxable income ± certain adjustments + the dividends paid deduction − the accumulated earnings credit. Please comment.

13. In making the "certain adjustments" (refer to Question 12) necessary in arriving at ATI, which of the following items should be added (+), should be subtracted (−), or will have no effect (NE) on taxable income:

    a. A nontaxable stock dividend distributed by the corporation to its shareholders.

    b. Corporate income tax incurred and paid.

    c. Charitable contributions paid in the amount of 10% of taxable income.

    d. A net operating loss carried over from a prior year that was deducted.

    e. The dividends received deduction.

14. If a corporation has a Federal income tax of 34% and also incurs an accumulated earnings tax of 27.5%, what is the aggregate tax rate? An accumulated earnings tax of 38.5%?

15. Ms. J (a widow) and Mr. K (a bachelor) are both shareholders in H Corporation (closely-held). If they elope during the year, what possible effect, if any, could it have on H Corporation's vulnerability to the PHC tax?

16. M Corporation is a consulting firm. Its entire outstanding stock is owned by three individuals. M Corporation entered into a contract with T Corporation to perform certain consulting services in consideration of which T was to pay M $65,000. The individual who was to perform the services was not designated by name or description in the contract, and no one but M had the right to designate such person. Does the $65,000 constitute PHC income?

17. Why is the designation of capital gain income still important for PHC purposes?

18. Which of the following income items could be PHC income:

    a. Dividends.

    b. Interest.

    c. Rental income.

    d. Sales of merchandise.

    e. Annuities.

    f. Mineral royalties.

    g. Copyright royalties.

    h. Produced film rents.

    i. Gain from sale of securities.

19. D, a shareholder in H Corporation, dies, and under his will, the stock passes to his children. If H Corporation is a personal holding company, what effect, if any, will D's death have on the continuation of this status?

20. How is AOGI calculated?

21. Diagram (or flow chart) the rent exclusion tests for purposes of the PHC tax.

22. The election to capitalize (rather than to depreciate) certain expenses to rental property could make a difference in determining whether or not the corporate lessor is a personal holding company. How could this be so?

23. If the 50% test as to rents is satisfied, the PHC tax cannot be imposed upon the corporation. Do you agree? Why or why not?

24. General Motors Corporation has no difficulty avoiding either the accumulated earnings tax or the PHC tax. Explain.

25. TRA of 1986 excluded from the definition of PHC income certain active business computer software royalties. Why?

26. The payment of enough dividends can avoid either the accumulated earnings tax or the PHC tax. Explain.

27. Explain the deficiency dividend procedure.

28. If a corporation has a Federal income tax of 34% and also incurs a PHC tax, what is the aggregate tax rate in 1988?

29. Relate the following points to the avoidance of the accumulated earnings tax:

    a. Documentation of justification for the accumulation.

    b. Multiple justifications for the accumulation.

    c. Follow-up on the established justification for the accumulation.

    d. Loans by the corporation to its shareholders.

    e. The corporation's record of substantial dividend payments.

    f. An S corporation election.

30. Relate the following points to the avoidance of the PHC tax:

    a. Sale of stock to outsiders.

    b. An increase in AOGI.

    c. A decrease in PHC income.

    d. Long-term capital gains recognized by the corporation.

    e. Corporate investment in tax-exempt bonds.

    f. Income from personal service contracts.

    g. The choice of straight-line depreciation for rental property owned by the corporation.

    h. A merger of several corporations.

    i. The liquidation of a corporation.

31. Compare the accumulated earnings tax to the PHC tax on the basis of the following items:

    a. The element of intent.

    b. Applicability of the tax to a newly created corporation.

    c. Applicability of the tax to a publicly held corporation.

   d. The two and one-half month rule with respect to the dividends paid deduction.

   e. The availability of the deficiency dividend procedure.

   f. Procedures for reporting and paying the tax.

Problems

1. A calendar year consulting corporation has accumulated earnings and profits of $80,000 on January 2, 1988. For the calendar year 1988, the corporation has taxable income of $100,000. This corporation has no reasonable needs that justify an accumulation of its earnings and profits. Calculate the amount vulnerable to the accumulated earnings penalty tax.

2. A nonservice corporation has accumulated earnings and profits of $225,000 as of December 31, 1987. The company has earnings for the taxable year 1988 of $100,000 and has a dividends paid deduction of $30,000. The corporation determines that the earnings for the tax year that may be retained for the reasonable needs of the business amount to $65,000 and that it is entitled to a $5,000 deduction for net capital gain (after adjustment for attributable tax and prior capital losses). Calculate the accumulated earnings credit for the tax year ending December 31, 1988.

3. In 1988, P Corporation, a manufacturing company, retained $60,000 for its reasonable business needs. The company had a long-term capital gain of $20,000 and a net short-term capital loss of $15,000, with a resulting capital gain tax of $1,250. The accumulated earnings and profits at the end of 1987 was $260,000. On January 25, 1988, a taxable dividend of $90,000 was paid. Calculate the accumulated earnings credit for 1988.

4. A retail corporation had accumulated earnings and profits on January 1, 1988, of $250,000. Its taxable income for the year 1988 was $75,000. The corporation paid no dividends during the year. There were no other adjustments to determine accumulated taxable income. Assume that a court determined that the corporation is subject to the accumulated earnings tax and that the reasonable needs of the business required retained earnings in the total amount of $266,500. Determine the accumulated earnings tax and explain your calculations.

5. A construction corporation is accumulating a significant amount of earnings and profits. Although the corporation is closely-held, it is not a personal holding company. The following facts relate to the tax year 1988:

    —Taxable income, $450,000.

    —Federal income tax, $153,000.

    —Dividend income from a qualified domestic corporation (less than 20% owned), $30,000.

    —Dividends paid in 1988, $70,000.

    —Consent dividends, $35,000.

    —Dividends paid on 2/1/89, $5,000.

    —Accumulated earnings credit, $10,000.

    —Excess charitable contributions of $9,000 (i.e., the portion in excess of the amount allowed as a deduction in computing the corporate income tax).

    —Net capital loss adjustment of $3,000.

    Compute the accumulated earnings tax, if any.

6. The following facts relate to a closely-held legal services corporation's 1988 tax year:

Net taxable income	$400,000
Federal income taxes	136,000
Excess charitable contributions	20,000
Capital loss adjustment	20,000
Dividends received (less than 20% owned)	120,000
Dividends paid	60,000
Accumulated earnings, 1/1/88	130,000

a. Assume that this is not a personal holding company. Calculate any accumulated earnings tax.

b. Can the deficiency dividend procedure be applicable to the accumulated earnings tax?

7. Which of the following purposes can be used by a corporation to justify accumulations to meet the reasonable needs of the business:

a. X Corporation creates a reserve for a depression that might occur in 1990.

b. P Corporation has an extraordinarily high working capital need.

c. Q Corporation, a manufacturing company, invests in several oil and gas drilling funds.

d. N, a hotel, is being sued because of a structural accident that injured 32 people.

e. M Corporation is considering establishing a sinking fund to retire some bonds.

f. Z Corporation carries six keyman life insurance policies.

g. T Corporation makes loans to R Corporation, an unrelated party who is having financial problems and who is a key customer.

h. B Corporation agrees to retire 20% of its outstanding stock without curtailment of its business.

8. A wholly owned motor freight corporation has permitted its earnings to accumulate. The company has no inventory but wishes to use the *Bardahl* formula to determine the amount of operating capital required for a business cycle. The following facts are relevant:

Yearly revenues	$3,300,000
Average accounts receivable	300,000
Yearly expenses	3,500,000
Average accounts payable	213,000

a. Determine the turnover rate of average accounts receivable.

b. Determine the number of days in the accounts receivable cycle.

c. Determine the expenses for one accounts receivable cycle.

d. Determine the number of days in the accounts payable cycle.

e. Determine the operating capital needed for one business cycle.

f. Explain why the time allowed a taxpayer for the payment of accounts payable should be taken into consideration in applying the *Bardahl* formula.

9. Indicate in each of the following independent situations whether or not the corporation involved has any accumulated taxable income and, if so, the amount (assume the corporation is not a mere holding or investment company):

	F Corporation	G Corporation
Taxable income	$150,000	$500,000
Accrued Federal income taxes	41,750	170,000
Capital loss adjustment	1,000	
Net LTCG		42,000
Tax on LTCG		14,280
Contributions in excess of 10%	10,000	
NOL deduction	24,000	
70% dividends received deduction		35,000
Dividends paid deduction	4,000	8,000
Accumulated earnings credit	135,000	102,000

10. March is the longest operating cycle for U Corporation, which has reasonable business needs of $30,000 in addition to the working capital required for one operating cycle. Certain additional information is provided as follows:

Accounts receivable—March	$ 120,000
Inventory—March	160,000
Accounts payable—March	101,000
Cost of goods sold	1,000,000
Other expenses (less depreciation)	100,000
Depreciation	90,000
Sales	2,000,000
Dividends paid	7,000
Accumulated earnings (beginning)	180,000
Accrued Federal income taxes	228,000

Determine the operating cycle needs of U Corporation without considering accrued Federal income taxes as an operating expense.

11. N Corporation is having accumulated earnings problems but has no accounts receivable. C, the corporate controller, provides you with the following information:

Year-end balances:		
Current assets		
Cash	$ 25,000	
Inventory (average)	72,000	
	$ 97,000	
Current liabilities	17,000	
Working capital available	$ 80,000	
Income statement:		
Gross sales		$330,000
Less: Sales returns and allowances		30,000
		$300,000
Less: Cost of goods sold	$170,000	
Sales and administrative expenses	45,000	
Depreciation	20,000	
Income taxes	9,000	244,000
Net income		$ 56,000

Calculate the working capital *required* for the corporation if purchases total $120,000.

12. Determine whether the following factors or events will increase (+), decrease (−), or have no effect (NE) on the working capital needs of a corporation when calculating the *Bardahl* formula:

    a. Decrease in depreciation deduction.

    b. Use of peak inventory figure rather than average inventory.

    c. An increase in the annual cost of goods sold.

    d. Purchase of a tract of land for a future parking lot.

    e. Use of average receivables rather than peak receivables.

    f. An increase in annual net sales.

    g. An increase in accounts payable.

    h. An increase in the annual expenses.

    i. Gain on the sale of treasury stock.

13. The stock of P Corporation is owned as follows:

S Corporation (wholly owned by K)	100 shares
K's wife	100 shares
K's partner	100 shares
K's wife's sister	100 shares
A	50 shares
B	30 shares
C	20 shares
Unrelated individuals with 10 or fewer shares	500 shares
Total	1,000 shares

    Do five or fewer individuals own more than 50% of P Corporation?

14. N Corporation, at some time during the last half of the taxable year, had 1,800 shares of outstanding stock, 450 of which were held by various individuals having no relationship to one another and none of whom were partners. The remaining 1,350 shares were held by 51 shareholders as follows:

Relationship		Shares		Shares		Shares		Shares		Shares
An individual	A	100	B	20	C	20	D	20	E	20
His father	AF	10	BF	10	CF	10	DF	10	EF	10
His wife	AW	10	BW	40	CW	40	DW	40	EW	40
His brother	AB	10	BB	10	CB	10	DB	10	EB	10
His son	AS	10	BS	40	CS	40	DS	40	ES	40
His daughter by former marriage (son's half-sister)	ASHS	10	BSHS	40	CSHS	40	DSHS	40	ESHS	40
His brother's wife	ABW	10	BBW	10	CBW	10	DBW	160	EBW	10
His wife's father	AWF	10	BWF	10	CWF	110	DWF	10	EWF	10
His wife's brother	AWB	10	BWB	10	CWB	10	DWB	10	EWB	10
His wife's brother's wife	AWBW	10	BWBW	10	CWBW	10	DWBW	10	EWBW	110
His partner	AP	10	—	—	—	—	—	—	—	—

    Is the stock ownership test of § 544 met for determining whether this corporation is a personal holding company?

15. A corporation has gross income of $20,000, which consists of $11,000 of rental income and $9,000 of dividend income. The corporation has $3,000 of rental income adjustments and pays $8,000 of dividends to its nine shareholders.

    a. Calculate adjusted income from rents.

    b. Calculate AOGI.

    c. Is the so-called 50% test met? Show calculations.

    d. Is the 10% rental income test met? Show calculations.

    e. Is the corporation a personal holding company?

16. Assume one change in the situation in Problem 15. Rental income adjustments are decreased from $3,000 to $2,000. Answer the same questions as in Problem 15.

17. X Corporation has $10,000 of interest income, $40,000 of gross income from rents, and $30,000 of personal service income (not PHC income). Expenses in the amount of $20,000 relate directly to the rental income. Assume there are six shareholders and the 10% test is met. Is this corporation a PHC? Explain.

18. P Corporation has dividend income of $20,000, rental income of $60,000, and income from an operating business (not PHC income) of $30,000. Expenses in the amount of $14,000 relate directly to the rental income. Assume there are eight shareholders and the 10% test is met. Is this corporation a PHC? Explain.

19. C Corporation has gross income of $200,000, which consists of gross income from rent of $150,000, dividends of $15,000, a capital gain from the sale of securities of $10,000, and $25,000 from the sale of merchandise. Deductions directly related to the rental income total $100,000.

    a. Calculate OGI.

    b. Calculate AOGI.

    c. Calculate adjusted income from rents.

    d. Does the rental income constitute PHC income? Explain.

    e. Is this corporation a PHC (assuming there are five shareholders)?

20. Assume the same facts as in Problem 19, except that dividend income is $25,000 (rather than $15,000) and the corporation pays $5,000 of dividends to its shareholders. Answer the same questions as in Problem 19.

21. T is the sole owner of a corporation. The following information is relevant to the corporation's tax year just ended:

Capital gain	$ 20,000
Dividend income	30,000
Rental income	130,000
Rental expenses	40,000
Section 162 business expenses	15,000
Dividends paid	12,000

    a. Calculate OGI.

    b. Calculate AOGI.

    c. Calculate adjusted income from rents.

    d. Calculate nonrental PHC income.

    e. Does this corporation meet the 50% rental income test? Explain.

f. Does this corporation meet the 10% rental income test? Explain.

g. Is this company a PHC?

h. Would your answers change if $15,000 of dividends are paid?

22. X Corporation has the following financial data for the tax year 1988:

Rental income	$430,000
Dividend income	2,900
Interest income	50,000
Operating income	9,000
Depreciation (rental warehouses)	100,000
Mortgage interest	125,000
Real estate taxes	35,000
Officers' salaries	85,000
Dividends paid	2,000

a. Calculate OGI.

b. Calculate AOGI.

c. Does X Corporation's adjusted income from rents meet the 50% or more of AOGI test?

d. Does X Corporation meet the 10% dividend test?

e. How much in dividends could X Corporation pay within the two and one-half month grace period during 1989?

f. If the 1988 corporate income tax return has not been filed, what would you suggest for X Corporation?

23. Using the legend provided, classify each of the following statements accordingly:

Legend

A = relates only to the tax on unreasonable accumulation of earnings (i.e., the § 531 tax)
P = relates only to the personal holding company tax (i.e., the § 541 tax)
B = relates to both the § 531 tax and the § 541 tax
N = relates to neither the § 531 tax nor the § 541 tax

a. The tax is applied to taxable income after adjustments are made.

b. The tax is a self-assessed tax.

c. An accumulation of funds for reasonable business purposes will help avoid the tax.

d. A consent dividend mechanism can be used to avoid the tax.

e. If the stock of the corporation is equally held by 10 unrelated individuals, the tax cannot be imposed.

f. Any charitable deduction in excess of the 10% limitation is allowed as a deduction before the tax is imposed.

g. Gains from the sale or disposition of capital assets are not subject to the tax.

h. A sufficient amount of rental income will cause the tax not to be imposed.

i. A life insurance company would not be subject to the tax.

j. A corporation with only dividend income would avoid the tax.

24. The PHC tax is computed on an amount called undistributed personal holding company (UPHC) income. To arrive at UPHC income, certain adjustments are made to taxable income. Determine whether the following independent items are positive (+), negative (−), or no adjustment (NA):

    a. Federal income taxes on the accrual basis.

    b. Tax-free interest from municipal bonds.

    c. Charitable deductions in excess of 10%.

    d. Net capital gain minus any taxes.

    e. Dividends paid during the taxable year.

    f. Dividends received deduction.

    g. NOL carryforward from two tax years ago.

    h. Consent dividends under § 565.

25. Indicate in each of the following independent situations whether or not the corporation involved is a PHC (assume the stock ownership test is met):

	A Corporation	B Corporation	C Corporation	D Corporation
Sales of merchandise	$ 8,000	$ 0	$ 0	$ 2,500
Capital gains	0	0	0	1,000
Dividend income	15,000	5,000	1,000	2,500
Gross rental income	10,000	5,000	9,000	15,000
Expenses related to rents	8,000	2,500	8,000	10,000
Dividends paid	0	0	0	500
Personal holding company? (Circle Y for yes or N for no)	Y N	Y N	Y N	Y N

26. Indicate in each of the following independent situations whether or not the corporation involved is a PHC (assume the stock ownership test is met):

	E Corporation	F Corporation	G Corporation	H Corporation
Sales of merchandise	$ 0	$3,000	$ 0	$ 0
Capital gains	0	0	1,000	0
Interest income	20,000	4,800	2,000	60,000
Gross rental income	80,000	1,200	20,000	50,000
Expenses related to rents	60,000	1,000	10,000	0
Dividends paid	12,000	0	0	20,000
Personal holding company? (Circle Y for yes or N for no)	Y N	Y N	Y N	Y N

 27. Calculate in each of the following independent situations the PHC tax liability in 1988:

	M Corporation	N Corporation
Taxable income	$140,000	$580,000
Dividends received deduction	37,000	70,000
Contributions in excess of 10%	4,000	10,000
Federal income taxes	37,850	197,200
Net capital gain	70,000	40,000
Capital gain tax	25,350	13,600
NOL under § 172		12,000
Current year dividends	12,000	120,000
Consent dividends		25,000
Two and one-half month dividends	4,000	

Research Problems

Research Problem 1. In 1988, X Corporation lost a Tax Court decision upholding the following deficiencies in income tax and accumulated earnings tax:

Year	Deficiency in Income Tax	Accumulated Earnings Tax
1978	$360,000	$ 0
1979	200,000	450,000
1980	201,000	600,000

May X Corporation deduct the deficiency in income taxes for 1979 and 1980 from accumulated taxable income in order to determine the accumulated earnings tax in 1979 and 1980?

Research Problem 2. Dr. B owns 90% of the stock of Dental Services, Inc. Dr. B performs medical services under an employment contract with the corporation. He is the only dentist employed and is the only officer of the corporation actively engaged in the production of income. Dental Services, Inc., furnishes office space and equipment and employs a dental hygienist and a receptionist to assist Dr. B.

a. Various patients receive dental care from Dr. B. Does Dental Services have PHC income under § 543(a)(7)?

b. Suppose Patient J secures an absolute binding promise from Dr. B that the dentist will personally perform a root canal operation and that the dentist has no right to substitute another dentist. Would your answer change?

Research Problem 3. X owns 100% of both A and B Corporations. A Corporation's accumulated earnings for 1985, 1986, 1987, and 1988 were reflected almost entirely in liquid assets, which were used to obtain bonding on the construction work of the sister corporation, B. A Corporation itself undertook no construction work as a general contractor and paid no dividends during the three-year period. Both corporations entered into an indemnity agreement under which both would be liable to the bonding company for any loss suffered by the bonding company from the issuance of a bond to either of the corporations. A Corporation was merged into B Corporation in early January 1987. Assume that A Corporation would be subject to the accumulated earnings tax if the reasonable business needs of B Corporation are not considered. Would A Corporation be subject to the accumulated earnings tax in 1985, 1986, 1987, and 1988?

Research Problem 4. N is a U.S. corporation wholly owned by B, a nonresident alien individual. Ninety-two percent of N's gross income consists of interest from loans to U.S. individuals and corporations. The remainder of N's gross income is derived from buying, selling, and leasing U.S. real property. In 1988, N's entire gross income consists of rents and interest received from sources within the United States. N is neither a lending nor a finance company under § 542(c)(6). Does the exception in § 542(c)(7) protect this corporation from the PHC penalty tax?

Research Problem 5.   During early 1989, P Corporation's controller discovers that the corporation is a personal holding company for 1988. He decides to use the deficiency dividend procedure under § 547 for avoiding the PHC tax. The company is short of cash. Can a consent dividend qualify for deficiency dividend treatment? Should the controller make a full disclosure of the liability for the PHC tax on the 1988 corporate tax return by filing a Schedule PH?

Research Problem 6.   A, Inc., has six shareholders, and most of its income is from a grant of a trademark by A, Inc., to Pac Company. The contract grant can be summarized as follows:

a. The grant of the trademark by A, Inc., to Pac was exclusive, worldwide, and forever, so long as Pac made the required production payments.

b. At such time as Pac had made production payments to A of $1,000,000, A was required to transfer legal title to the trademark to Pac (as distinguished from a mere option in Pac to acquire such title).

c. A had no right to terminate the agreement except upon the failure of Pac to make the required periodic payments. Furthermore, after the transfer of title to the trademark from A to Pac, such termination rights no longer applied even if Pac failed to make the required continuing payments.

d. Although Pac was not permitted to dispose of the portion of the business using the trademark "MYCLO" separately from a sale of Pac's entire business without A's prior approval, "said approval shall not be unreasonably withheld."

e. A retained the right to inspect the business operations of Pac to ensure continuing quality control.

f. A agreed that it would not use the trademark any further or engage in any business involving the products covered by the trademark that was conveyed to Pac.

If most of A, Inc., income is from the trademark, would A be subject to the personal holding company tax?

Research Problem 7.   V and S are equal shareholders of P Corporation. In 1988, the corporation received gross rent of $5,000 from a 30-unit apartment building it owned. The company incurred depreciation, interest, and property tax expenses in the amount of $900 that were attributable to the building. The company also received $500 rent from a duplex it leased to V and S. The company incurred depreciation, interest, and property tax expenditures in the amount of $200 (attributable to the duplex). The company also had $3,000 gross income from a bookstore it owned and operated, and the company received dividend income of $1,000 from R Corporation. Discuss.

8

Partnerships: Formation and Operation

Objectives

Define a partnership.

Discuss the tax ramifications of forming and operating a partnership.

Explain how nonliquidating distributions to the partners are handled.

Provide insight as to when the partnership form of doing business is advisable.

Outline

Overview
Taxation of Partnership Income
What Is a Partnership?
Publicly Traded Partnerships
Exclusion from Partnership Treatment
Who Is a Partner?

Formation
Taxable Year
Contributions to Partnership
Basis of Partnership Interest
Basis and Nature of Contributed Property
Organization and Syndication Costs

Operation
Measuring and Reporting Income
Loss Limitations
Allocating Partnership Income
Partners and Related Parties
Close of Final Tax Year

Nonliquidating Distributions

Tax Planning Considerations
Selecting the Partnership Form
Formation and Operation

Overview

This chapter introduces the first of two statutory provisions meant to counteract the possibilities for the double taxation of corporate income, namely, partnerships and S corporations. In each case, the owner of a trade or business elects to avoid the treatment of the enterprise itself as a separate C corporation taxable entity. The owners of the business are taxed on a proportionate share of the entity's taxable income at the end of each of its taxable years, regardless of the magnitude of distributions that the owners received therefrom during the year. The entity serves merely as an information provider to the IRS with respect to such proportionate income shares that its owners have received. In this manner, the tax falls directly upon the owners of the enterprise, and no double taxation occurs.

A partnership is not a taxable entity. Rather, the taxable income or loss of the entity, and any other receipts or expenditures that receive special tax treatment under the Code when they relate to an individual taxpayer, flow through to the partners at the end of the entity's tax year. Each partner receives his or her allocable share of the partnership's ordinary income for the year and any other such specially treated items. As a result, although the partnership itself pays no Federal income tax on its income, the partners' own individual tax liabilities are affected by the activities of the entity. For instance, if the partnership enjoys a profitable year and generates ordinary taxable income of $100,000, a 25 percent partner must increase his or her adjusted gross income for the year by $25,000, regardless of the extent of property distributions received from the partnership during the year.

With the enactment of the Tax Reform Act of 1986 and the lower rates for individuals relative to C corporations, the importance of the partnership as an operating form is likely to increase. This chapter addresses the basic elements of partnership formations, operations, and nonliquidating distributions. Chapter 9 focuses on dispositions of partnership interests, liquidating and disproportionate distributions, optional basis adjustments, and special problems associated with family and limited partnerships.

Taxation of Partnership Income

Unlike corporations, estates, and trusts, partnerships are not considered separate tax entities for purposes of determining and paying Federal income taxes. Instead, partnership members are subject to tax on their distributive share of partnership income, even if an actual distribution is not made.[1] Thus, the partnership tax return (Form 1065) serves only as an information device to determine the character and amount of each partner's distributive share of partnership income and expense.[2] Although a partnership is not considered a separate tax entity for purposes of determining and paying Federal income taxes, it is treated as such for other tax purposes. Moreover, a partnership is

---

1. Section 701 contains the statutory rule that partners are liable for income tax in their separate or individual capacities. The partnership itself cannot be subject to the income tax on its earnings.
2. § 6031.

usually treated as a separate legal entity under civil law, with the right to own property and transact business in its own name.[3]

The unique treatment of partners and partnerships under the Code's Subchapter K can be traced to two general concepts that evolved long before its enactment: the *entity concept* and the *aggregate* or *conduit concept*. Both concepts have been applied in civil and common law, and their influence can be seen in practically every related statutory tax rule. With some rules directed toward the entity concept, others based solely on the conduit concept, and still others containing a mixture of both, an individual studying the partnership provisions for the first time might find the rules difficult to grasp. However, by concentrating on the basic purpose underlying each rule, one can better understand each rule's rationale and general approach.

Entity Concept. The entity concept treats partners and partnerships as separate units and gives the partnership its own tax "personality." The right of the entity to select its own MACRS method for tangible personal property and other accounting methods is a direct reflection of this concept.

The entity concept is embodied in the statutory rules (1) requiring a partnership to file an information tax return and (2) treating partners as separate and distinct parties from the partnership in certain transactions between them.

Aggregate or Conduit Concept. Using the perspective of the aggregate or conduit concept, the partnership is merely a channel through which income, credits, deductions, etc., flow to the partners for their own tax consideration. Under this concept, a partnership is considered as nothing more than a collection of taxpayers joined in an agency relationship with one another. Imposition of the income tax on individual partners rather than the partnership and the disallowance of certain deductions and tax credits reflect the influence of this concept.

Combined Concepts. Many Code Sections contain a blend of both the entity and aggregate concepts, such as the statutory provisions concerning the formation, operation, and liquidation of a partnership.

What Is a Partnership?

The Uniform Partnership Act defines a partnership as "an association of two or more persons to carry on as co-owners a business for profit." Similarly, a common law definition considers a partnership to be the contractual relationship between two or more persons who join together to carry on a trade or business, each contributing money, property, labor, or skill, and all with the expectation of sharing in the profits and losses of the business. The definition of a partnership for Federal income tax purposes is much broader than the state law definition.

Sections 761(a) and 7701(a)(2) define a partnership as a syndicate, group, pool, joint venture, or other unincorporated organization, through which any business, financial operation, or venture is carried on and which is not other-

---

3. See the Uniform Partnership Act and the Uniform Limited Partnership Act.

wise classified as a corporation, trust, or estate. This definition of a partnership provides adequate guidance in the classification of many typical partnerships. However, certain unincorporated businesses have been classified as corporations for Federal income tax purposes, as pointed out in Chapter 2. If the organization exhibits the characteristics of an *association*, it will be classified as a corporation regardless of its owners' intent. Thus, classification as a partnership for tax purposes can be more complex than the basic Code definition might indicate.[4]

Avoiding the corporate classification does not automatically qualify an organization for partnership status. For instance, a joint undertaking to share the expenses of constructing and maintaining a ditch to drain surface water from properties does not qualify the owners as partners. Likewise, the mere co-ownership of property that is maintained, kept in repair, and rented or leased does not constitute a partnership. If co-owners of farm property lease the land to a farmer for cash or a share of the crops, they do not necessarily create a partnership. The Regulations provide that co-owners may be partners if they actively carry on a trade, business, financial operation, or venture and divide the profits. Thus, a partnership would exist if the co-owners of an apartment building leased space and, in addition, provided services to the occupants either directly or through an agent.[5]

Publicly Traded Partnerships

For tax year 1988, only two tax rates will apply to individuals (15 percent and 28 percent), with a phase-out of the lower rate as taxable income rises, so that individuals with high incomes will be subject to a flat tax of 28 percent. The maximum corporate tax rate will be 34 percent. If an organization is operated as a partnership rather than as a corporation, not only can a lower tax rate prevail, but the double tax on corporate earnings can be avoided. Moreover, if the limited partnership form is utilized, liability protection for the owners who are limited partners is available.

One business form that takes advantage of these provisions is the master limited partnership, or MLP. Although the provisions of § 469 restrict loss deductions from passive activities, investors in publicly traded partnerships (PTPs), including MLPs, which were "publicly traded" on December 17, 1987, can use their passive activity losses to shelter PTP income if the partnership's taxable year begins before 1998. Generally, PTPs that were not publicly traded on December 17, 1987, are treated as corporations unless 90% or more of their gross income consists of qualifying income. Income from a PTP which is treated as a corporation is not passive activity income, it is portfolio income.

---

4. See W. S. McKee, W. F. Nelson, and R. L. Whitmire, *Federal Taxation of Partnerships and Partners* (Boston, Mass.: Warren, Gorham & Lamont, Inc., with current updates), Chapter 3, for an excellent analysis of the criteria used in determining the existence of a partnership for Federal tax purposes.
5. Reg. §§ 1.761–1(a) and 301.7701–3(a).

Exclusion from Partnership Treatment

Certain unincorporated organizations may be excluded, completely or partially, from treatment as partnerships for Federal income tax purposes. The exclusion applies to organizations that are used (1) for investment purposes rather than for the active conduct of a business; (2) for the joint production, extraction, or use of property, but not for the purpose of selling services or products produced or extracted; or (3) by dealers in securities for a short period for purposes of underwriting, selling, or distributing a particular security issue.[6]

Who Is a Partner?

Section 761(b) defines a partner simply as one who is a member of a partnership. For instance, an individual, estate, trust, corporation, or another partnership can be a partner in the same partnership. However, certain problems can arise when a minor child is a member of a family partnership or when a corporation is the general partner in a limited partnership. These problems are discussed in Chapter 9 under Special Problems—Family Partnerships and Limited Partnerships.

Formation

The general provisions that relate to partnership formation are contained in §§ 721 through 723. Like their counterparts in Subchapter C, the statutes provide for tax-free partnership formations and admissions of new partners. The provisions also contain the rules used to determine the basis of a partner's interest and of transferred property. Standing alone, they do not, in all situations, assure the nonrecognition of gain or loss upon formation of a partnership. Therefore, other provisions that supplement these rules must be examined.

Taxable Year

In computing a partner's taxable income for a specific year, § 706(a) requires that each partner's distributive share include partnership income and guaranteed payments for the partnership year that ends with or within the partner's taxable year. (Guaranteed payments are discussed under Operation—Partners and Related Parties.) Generally, guaranteed payments are includible in the partner's income only for the partnership year in which the partnership deducted them *under the partnership's method of accounting.*[7]

With two exceptions, § 706(b)(1) indicates that the tax year of a partnership must be determined by reference to the tax years (usually calendar years) of the partners. One exception allows the partnership to establish to the IRS's satisfaction that a business purpose exists for selecting another tax year. Another exception allows a partnership that recognizes 25 percent or more of

---

6. See Reg. §§ 1.761–2(a) and (b) for a discussion of investing partnerships and operating agreements. Both may be excluded from application of the partnership provisions of Subchapter K.
7. Reg. § 1.707–1(c).

its gross receipts in the last two months of a 12-month period for three consecutive years to adopt an alternative 12-month period as its fiscal year.[8]

If neither of the exceptions is met, the partnership's tax year is determined as follows:

1. The tax year of the majority partners, if they use the same tax year, is adopted. This rule refers to partners with more than a 50 percent aggregate interest in the partnership's capital and profits.
2. If a common tax year does not exist for the majority partners, the tax year of all principal partners (i.e., partners with a five percent or greater interest in capital or profits) is used.
3. If a common tax year does not exist for the majority partners or all principal partners, a calendar year is used.

However, under § 444, a partnership may elect to use a tax year other than the required tax year if the deferral period is three months or less. Retention of the last tax year which started in 1986 also is available if an election was made to use such year for the first tax year which started after 1986. If a partnership is changing its tax year, an election is available only if the new deferral period (relative to the required tax year) is the shorter of three months or the old deferral period. To obtain these benefits, the partnership (not the partners) must make additional estimated tax payments to account for the revenue deferral.

When a partnership tax year change is required after 1986, any partner who must include items from more than one tax year of the partnership in any one of his or her own tax years will include only a one-fourth share of net partnership income for the short tax year in each of the first four tax years after the change (including the short tax year). By election, though, the partner may choose to include all such net income in the short tax year.

Contributions to Partnership

The aggregate concept is reflected in the general rule of § 721: No gain or loss is recognized by a partnership or any of its partners upon the contribution of property in exchange for a partnership interest. In addition to initial formation transfers, this rule applies to all subsequent contributions of property. Thus, the partners of an existing partnership are insulated from gain or loss recognition upon the admission of a new partner if the partnership interest is in exchange for a property contribution. Although cash and most other contributions of tangible or intangible assets are covered by the general rule, several circumstances exist where it does not apply.

Consideration Received for Transfers.   When a partner transfers property to a partnership and the partnership directly or indirectly transfers property to a partner, the transfers when viewed together may be characterized as a sale rather than as a contribution and an unrelated distribution. In such a case, the transfers are treated as occurring between the partner (acting in his or her capacity as a nonpartner) and the partnership.[9] To receive favorable contribution treatment,

---

8. Rev.Proc. 83–25, 1983–1 C.B. 689.
9. § 707(a)(2)(B).

the partner transferring the cash or other property must receive an appropriate interest in the partnership, and the partnership must not make inappropriate transfers to the partner (or another partner). Care is advised in planning such transfers in this regard, especially in planning for the lead or lag time between the property contribution date and the partnership allocation and distribution dates.

Interest for Services.   Another situation in which the general rule of § 721 does not apply concerns the exchange of a partnership interest for services. The fair market value of any part of an interest in partnership capital transferred to a partner for services is considered as compensation for such services.[10] The recipient must recognize the amount so determined as ordinary income in the year actually or constructively received. If a profits interest in a partnership is received for services, generally it is taxed immediately. When the received interest is subject to a substantial risk of forfeiture, the partner receiving it still has ordinary income. However, determining the amounts and timing of income with respect to such an interest can be difficult.

Example 1   C received a 20% interest in capital and profits in the current year for services rendered to the AB Partnership. The interest was not subject to a substantial risk of forfeiture. At the time of transfer, the aggregate fair market value and adjusted basis of the partnership's assets were $50,000 and $30,000, respectively, and the partnership was subject to no liabilities. C recognizes $10,000 ordinary income for the current year, the fair market value of the capital interest received. Since the value of the profits interest cannot be determined immediately, C's share of such future profits is included in ordinary income as they are reported by the partnership. □

Collapsible Transactions.   The nonrecognition provision of § 721 will not apply if the partnership is used solely to effect a tax-free exchange of assets. For example, assume that two partners in the same partnership have appreciated assets they wish to exchange free of tax. Assume further that the assets involved cannot qualify under any other nonrecognition provision of the Code (e.g., a like-kind exchange). Each partner contributes his or her appreciated property to the partnership. Shortly thereafter, each receives what is hoped to be a nontaxable distribution of the property contributed by the other. Under these circumstances, the IRS may collapse the transactions into a single taxable exchange. It is also possible that the transfers will be treated as occurring between the partnership and the partners acting in nonpartner capacities.[11]

Investment Companies.   Section 721(b) provides another exception to the general rule of nonrecognition of gain on the contribution of property to a partnership. The contributing partner is required to recognize any gain realized on the transfer of property to a partnership that would be treated as an investment company if the partnership were incorporated. A partnership will be considered an investment company if, after the transfer, more than 80 percent of the value of its assets (excluding cash and nonconvertible debt obligations) is held for investment and

---

10. Reg. § 1.721–1(b)(1). See also *F. G. McDougal*, 62 T.C. 720 (1974), *acq.* 1975–1 C.B. 2.
11. § 707(a)(2)(B).

8-8 Partnerships: Formation and Operation

consists of readily marketable stocks or securities. The purpose of this provision is to prevent investors from using the partnership form to diversify their investment portfolios or exchange stocks or securities on a tax-free basis.

Basis of Partnership Interest

The tax basis of a partnership interest acquired in a nontaxable transfer of property to a partnership is determined under § 722. Generally, the contributing partner's interest basis equals the sum of money contributed plus the adjusted basis of any other property transferred. However, if gain is recognized under § 721(b), the partner's basis must be increased accordingly.

Note that the basis of a partner's interest may or may not equal the partner's capital account per books. Moreover, throughout this text, any reference to a capital interest percentage implies an equal profits interest percentage unless otherwise specified.

Inside/Outside Basis. When discussing the basis of a partner's interest, the terms "inside basis" and "outside basis" are frequently used. In this regard, inside basis refers to the partnership's basis in the partner's share of the entity's assets. On the other hand, one's outside basis relates to the magnitude of after-tax assets that have been invested in the partnership interest.

Generally, the initial inside and outside bases of a partner's interest equal either the price paid for the interest or the adjusted basis of property contributed for it. If an interest is purchased from another partner, the purchasing partner generally takes the same inside interest basis as the selling partner. However, the outside basis of this partner generally equals the price paid for the interest. When the partnership realizes profits or losses, the partner's inside and outside bases increase or decrease proportionately. When profits are withdrawn, inside and outside bases decrease proportionately.

Since each partner is generally liable for a portion of the partnership's debts, each partner's inside and outside interest bases increase or decrease by the partner's proportionate share of any debt change. The following section illustrates the computations associated with a partner's original inside and outside interest bases. Additional illustrations of the terms are presented throughout this chapter and in Chapter 9.

Contributed Property. When property is contributed to a partnership for a capital interest, generally it is recorded for financial accounting purposes at its fair market value with a corresponding offset to the partner's capital account. Some partnerships maintain their accounting books on a tax basis.[12] Nonetheless, the following examples assume that all property contributions are recorded at fair market value.

Example 2   U and R form an equal partnership with a cash contribution of $30,000 from U and a land contribution (adjusted basis of $18,000 and fair market value of $30,000) from R. Although the books of the UR Partnership reflect

---

12. Reg. § 1.704–1(b)(2)(iv)(b) requires the capital accounts of partners to be increased by the fair market value of contributed property (net of related liabilities) so that substantial economic effect is achieved for partnership allocations.

a credit of $30,000 in each partner's capital account, only U will have a tax basis of $30,000. R's tax basis will be $18,000, the tax basis of the contributed property. Immediately after formation, the partnership books and tax basis are as follows:

	Books	Tax Basis
Cash	$30,000	$30,000
Land	30,000	18,000
Total	$60,000	$48,000

	Capital Accounts	Interest Basis
U	$30,000	$30,000
R	30,000	18,000
Total	$60,000	$48,000

At this point, the inside basis and outside basis of each partner are equal (i.e., $30,000 for U and $18,000 for R). If R's interest now is sold to M for its fair market value of $30,000, M's inside basis would remain at $18,000, because there was no transaction that affected the partnership's accounting or tax books. However, M's outside basis would be $30,000, the price paid to R. □

Example 3   In return for having rendered services and contributed property (basis of $50,000, fair market value of $80,000) to the KLM Partnership, A receives a 25% unrestricted interest, valued at $100,000, in the capital contributed by all KLM partners. The contribution of property is nontaxable under § 721. However, the receipt of a partnership interest for services results in compensation to A of $20,000 (value of partnership interest of $100,000 less value of property contributed of $80,000). A's tax basis in the KLM Partnership is $70,000 (basis of the property contributed of $50,000 plus ordinary income recognized of $20,000). For financial accounting purposes, A's capital account immediately after acquisition of the partnership interest is $100,000. □

Example 4   The KLM Partnership in Example 3 was formed with separate $105,333 cash contributions from individuals K, L, and M. The partners agreed to share all profits and losses equally. After KLM was formed, it purchased land for $16,000. At the time of A's admission to the partnership, the land had appreciated in value and was worth $20,000. Immediately before A's admission, each partner's inside basis, outside basis, and capital account equaled $105,333.

The land was transferred to A as payment for professional services rendered. On the transfer, K, L, and M each recognized a gain of $1,333 [($20,000 fair market value of the land — $16,000 adjusted basis) ÷ 3], and each partner generated a business expense deduction of $6,666 ($20,000 ÷ 3). A recontributed the land along with other property, with an adjusted basis of $50,000, fair market value of $80,000, for a 25% fair market value interest. The preceding transactions are summarized as follows:

	Before A's Admission	Payment for Services, Deductible Expense, & Gain Recognized	Contribution to Partnership by A	After A's Admission	Fair Market Values
Cash	$300,000			$300,000	$300,000
Land	16,000	($16,000)	$20,000	20,000	20,000
Other	–0–		50,000	50,000	80,000
Total	$316,000	($16,000)	$70,000	$370,000	$400,000
K capital	$105,333	($ 6,667) 1,334		$100,000	$100,000
L capital	105,333	(6,667) 1,334		100,000	100,000
M capital	105,334	(6,666) 1,332		100,000	100,000
A capital	–0–		$70,000	70,000	100,000
Total	$316,000	($16,000)	$70,000	$370,000	$400,000

Since the land transaction was between A and the KLM Partnership, and since the appropriate amount of gain and deductible expense has been recorded on the partnership books, the inside basis, outside basis, and capital account of K, L, and M after A's partnership admission are each equal to $100,000. Although A's inside basis and outside basis equal $70,000, A's capital account equals $100,000 (the aggregate fair market value of contributed property). ☐

Contributed Property with Debt. Under § 721, no gain or loss is recognized to a partner upon the contribution of property for a partnership interest. However, this provision may not protect the contributing partner from recognizing a gain when the contributed property is subject to a liability that exceeds its basis.

When property subject to a liability is contributed to a partnership or if the partnership assumes any of the transferor partner's liabilities, the basis of the partnership interest is reduced by the amount of the liabilities effectively assumed by the other partners.[13] Debt on property that is not assumed directly is treated as assumed by the partnership to the extent of the property's fair market value.[14] All such debt on contributed property must be considered when determining the basis of a partner's interest.[15]

Correspondingly, the noncontributing partners increase their basis by that portion of the liabilities assumed directly or indirectly on the transfer. Generally, each partner's loss-sharing ratio is used to determine the amount of liabilities assumed. Absent some specific reference to the contrary, it is assumed that the partners share losses in the same ratio as they share

---

13. Reg. § 1.722–1.
14. § 752(c) and Reg. § 1.752–1(c).
15. § 704(c).

profits.[16] These adjustments to the basis of a partnership interest result from the application of §§ 752(a) and (b). An increase in a partner's share of partnership liabilities is treated as a contribution of money by the partner to the partnership. Likewise, a decrease in a partner's share of partnership liabilities is treated as a distribution of money by the partnership.

Example 5   X, Y, and Z form the XYZ Partnership with the following contributions: cash of $50,000 from X for a 50% interest in capital and profits, cash of $25,000 from Y for a 25% interest, and property valued at $33,000 from Z for a 25% interest. The property contributed by Z has an adjusted basis of $15,000 and is subject to a mortgage of $8,000 which is assumed by the partnership. Z's interest basis in the XYZ Partnership is $9,000, determined as follows:

Adjusted basis of Z's contributed property	$15,000
Increase in Z's share of partnership debt (25% of $8,000)	2,000
Subtotal	$17,000
Decrease in Z's individual debt	8,000
Basis of Z's interest in XYZ Partnership	$ 9,000

The same result will occur if the basis of the contributed property is decreased by the portion of Z's debt assumed by X and Y ($15,000 less 75% of $8,000). ☐

Example 6   Assuming the same facts as in Example 5, X and Y will have a basis in their partnership interest of $54,000 and $27,000, respectively.

	X	Y
Cash contribution	$50,000	$25,000
Plus portion of mortgage assumed and treated as an additional cash contribution:		
(50% of $8,000)	4,000	
(25% of $8,000)		2,000
Basis of interest in XYZ Partnership	$54,000	$27,000

☐

---

16. In the case of a limited partnership, only the general partner(s) would be entitled to this treatment. However, if the debt involved was a nonrecourse liability (i.e., where none of the partners are personally liable), all of the partners (including limited partners) are treated as sharing such a liability in the same proportion as they share profits. Chapter 9 further addresses nonrecourse liabilities. .

The basis of a contributing partner's interest may be reduced to zero if the property transferred is subject to a liability in excess of its basis. The basis of a partnership interest, however, like the basis of any other kind of property, never can be negative. Thus, if the portion of the liability assumed by the noncontributing partners exceeds the contributing partner's basis, *recognized* gain results.[17] Such a gain is considered as being from the sale of a partnership interest, which usually is classified as a capital gain.[18] However, ordinary income may result if the transferred property were subject to depreciation recapture.[19] Thus, a proper determination of the partnership's capital gains and losses is essential.

Example 7   Assume the same facts as in Example 5, except that the property contributed by Z is land held for investment with a fair market value of $49,000 that is subject to a mortgage of $24,000 (instead of $8,000). Z's interest basis is zero, and a $3,000 gain must be recognized.

Adjusted basis of the land to Z	$15,000
Plus recognized capital gain	3,000
Less portion of mortgage assumed by X and Y and treated as a distribution of money to Z (75% of $24,000)	(18,000)
Basis of Z's interest in the XYZ Partnership	$ –0–

If the $3,000 gain recognized by partner Z in Example 7 appears to be harsh treatment, consider the tax consequences if the property had been contributed to a corporation. Under § 357(c), the *entire* excess of the liability over Z's basis in the property (i.e., $9,000) would have resulted in a taxable gain. Thus, the use of the partnership form in this instance results in a tax benefit to Z.

Partnership Debt. Changes in partnership liabilities (including trade accounts payable and bank loans) also affect the basis of a partner's interest. For instance, a partner's basis is *increased* by the pro rata share of liabilities incurred by the partnership and is *decreased* by the pro rata share of decreases in partnership liabilities.[20] Thus, when the acquisition of partnership assets is financed by creditors, the partners generally are treated as if they each borrowed proportionate amounts of money and contributed them to the partnership, which then used the money to purchase the assets. If partnership assets are used to satisfy creditor obligations, the partners are treated as if they constructively received a distribution of money from the partnership and then satisfied the obligations. Consequently, applying the aggregate concept, as the

---

17. Reg. § 1.752–1(c).
18. §§ 731 and 741. Arthur B. Willis, John S. Pennell, and Phillip F. Postlewaite, *Partnership Taxation*, Third Edition (Colorado Springs, Colo.: McGraw-Hill Book Company, with current updates), §§ 24.02 and 112.05.
19. Reg. § 1.1245–4(c)(4) (Ex. 3).
20. Reg. § 1.752–1.

partnership's pool of assets increases or decreases, the partners' bases in the partnership increase or decrease simultaneously.

Example 8   A and B are equal partners in AB Partnership. To purchase a parcel of real estate to be used as a potential office site, the partnership borrows $50,000 from a local savings and loan association. As a result of the loan, the basis of A's and B's partnership interests is increased by $25,000 each. ☐

Example 9   Assume the same facts as in Example 8, except that AB Partnership repays $20,000 of the loan. The repayment decreases A's and B's partnership interests by $10,000 each. ☐

Example 10   Assume the same facts as in Example 8, except that the partnership decides not to use the real estate after all. Instead, the property is distributed to A. At the time of distribution, the property has an adjusted basis and fair market value of $50,000 and is subject to a mortgage of $30,000. As a result of the distribution, A's interest is decreased by $35,000.

Decrease equal to the adjusted basis of property distributed	$ 50,000
Decrease as a result of the reduction in A's share of partnership liabilities (½ of $30,000)	15,000
Increase as a result of the assumption of a partnership liability	(30,000)
Net decrease	$ 35,000

☐

Example 11   Assume the same facts as in Example 10. What effect will the distribution of the real estate to A have on B's interest? B's interest is decreased by $15,000, since the distribution decreased B's share of partnership liabilities. ☐

Continuous Fluctuation.   In addition to being affected by partnership debt, a partner's interest is influenced continuously by a number of transactions. It is *increased* by any additional capital contributions and by each partner's distributive share of the following:

—Taxable income of the partnership, including capital gains.

—Tax-exempt income of the partnership.

—The excess of the deduction for depletion over the basis of the corresponding property.

Similarly, the basis of a partner's interest is *decreased*, but not below zero, by the partner's limited depletion deduction (i.e., limited by the partner's proportionate share of the partnership's adjusted basis in oil and gas property) and by the sum of the distributive share of the following:

—Partnership losses, including capital losses.

—Partnership expenditures that are not capital expenditures (e.g., expenses incurred to produce tax-exempt income, personal living expenses of partners, and contributions to charities).[21]

A partner's interest can be viewed as a segmented bar chart, with the bottom layer being the partner's original capital contribution. If the partner makes additional contributions to the partnership during its first time period, another segment is added to the bar. If the partnership has taxable income during this period, the partner's share of the income also is added to the bar. The aggregate height of the bar represents the partner's interest basis at any time. Since there is no real separation of capital forms in a partnership, the imaginary segment lines disappear before distributions are considered. Distributions to a partner reduce that partner's aggregate interest basis and, in turn, the aggregate height of the bar.

Example 12

Assume that a new partnership is formed and that X contributes $5 to the partnership at the formation date (situation 1) and $10 more in six months (situation 2). Also assume that X's share of the partnership profits for the first time period equals $20 (situation 3). Situation 4 represents the merging of all capital forms. Assume that at the end of the first period, X receives a $15 distribution (situation 5). The following bars illustrate X's interest basis in the partnership at various times:

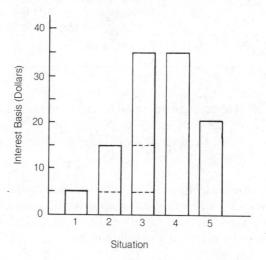

Situation

Holding Period. Generally, the holding period of a partner's interest acquired by a noncash property contribution includes the holding period of the contributed property. However, if the contributed property is neither a capital asset nor a § 1231 asset in the hands of the transferor-partner (e.g., inventory), the holding period starts on the day the interest is acquired. The holding period of an interest acquired by a cash contribution or by purchase is determined under

21. § 705(a) and Reg. § 1.705–1(a).

the general holding period rules. The holding period of an interest acquired by gift or by inheritance is determined under related rules.[22]

Contributed ITC Property.   An early disposal of contributed investment tax credit (ITC) property will trigger the recapture provisions, which are still in effect. However, § 47(b) provides that the ITC is not recaptured "by reason of a mere change in the form of conducting the trade or business so long as the property is retained in such trade or business as section 38 property and the taxpayer retains a substantial interest in such trade or business."

Basis and Nature of Contributed Property

Under § 723, the basis of property contributed to a partnership is the adjusted basis of such property to the contributing partner at the time of contribution. If the partnership is classified as an investment company, § 721(b) allows the partnership to increase the basis of contributed property by any gain recognized by the contributing partner.

Gain Effect.   When the partnership is not an investment company, gain is still recognized on contributed property, but the partnership's basis is not increased when liabilities assumed by the noncontributing partners exceed the contributing partner's basis in the property.

Example 13   K and L form an equal partnership with a contribution of land valued at $100,000 from K and a contribution of equipment valued at $150,000 from L. K's basis in the land is $30,000. The equipment contributed by L has an adjusted basis of $20,000 and is subject to a mortgage of $50,000 which is assumed by the partnership. K's inside basis and outside basis are both $55,000 ($30,000 basis in the contributed land plus 50% of the $50,000 mortgage on the equipment). L's inside basis and outside basis are both zero ($20,000 basis in the contributed equipment decreased, but not below zero, by 50% of the $50,000 mortgage on the equipment treated as assumed by K). In addition, L recognizes a taxable gain of $5,000, because the debt share treated as assumed by K exceeded L's contributed basis by this amount. Since the partnership is not an investment company, it has a $30,000 basis in the land and a $20,000 basis in the equipment. □

Holding Period.   The partnership's holding period for contributed property includes the period the property was held by the contributing partner, since the property's basis is determined by reference to the contributing partner's basis.[23]

Depreciation Method and Period.   Although the contributing partner's property basis and holding period carry over to the partnership, the transfer of certain depreciable property could result in unfavorable tax consequences to the partnership. For instance, a partnership is not allowed to expense immediately any

---

22. § 742.
23. § 1223(2) and Reg. § 1.723–1.

part of the cost of § 179 property that it receives from the transferor partner.[24] In addition, § 168(f)(7) prohibits a partnership from using an accelerated cost recovery method or holding period that differs from that of the transferor partner.

Receivables, Inventory, and Losses. Section 724 assigns ordinary income treatment to any gain or loss recognized by the partnership on the disposition of contributed receivables that were unrealized in the contributing partner's hands immediately before the contribution. These receivables include such things as the right to receive payment for goods or services delivered or to be delivered to the extent that they were not previously included in the partner's income.

Ordinary income treatment is also assigned to any gain or loss by the partnership on the disposition of contributed inventory during the five-year period starting on the contribution date if the assets were inventory in the contributor's hands immediately before the contribution. For this provision, inventory includes all property that is neither a capital asset nor a § 1231 asset.

Section 724 also indicates that when capital loss property is contributed to a partnership, any subsequent loss on the property's disposal during the five-year period starting on the contribution date will be a capital loss to the extent of any existing loss at that date. This provision is aimed at taxpayers who try to convert a capital loss into an ordinary loss by contributing real estate to a real estate partnership that holds the property as inventory.

Example 14 D operates a cash basis retail clothing store as a sole proprietor. The DEF Partnership is formed by D and two other proprietors, both of whom manufacture plastic products for home use. DEF will manufacture and sell plastic containers for packaging retail products.

D contributes receivables with a $1,500 fair market value and zero basis, land used as an employee parking lot and held four months with a $1,000 fair market value and $800 adjusted basis, inventory with a $5,000 basis and $7,500 fair market value, and a two-year-old personal use computer. The computer's fair market value is $1,600, and its original cost was $2,300. No cost recovery deductions have been claimed.

Within two months of DEF's formation, the entity collects the receivables and sells the inventory and computer for their contribution date fair market values. It uses the land contributed by D as a parking lot for 12 months and then sells it for $1,300.

DEF realizes the following gains and losses from these transactions:

—$1,500 gain from the receivables.

—$2,500 gain from the sale of inventory.

—$700 disallowed loss on the computer.

—$500 gain on the land sale.

---

24. § 179(d)(2)(C).

Under § 724(a), the receivables create ordinary income when collected. The inventory falls under § 724(b) and also creates ordinary income. Although the computer falls under § 724(c), the loss is disallowed as relating to a personal use asset. Because the land was used in D's business immediately before its contribution to the partnership, it was not a capital asset at that time. Since it was held for only four months at the contribution date, neither is it a § 1231 asset. However, at the sale date, the land was being used in the partnership's business; it had been held long-term. Thus, the land meets the definitional requirements of a § 1231 asset, and gain on its sale is so treated. ☐

Organization and Syndication Costs

Section 709(a) provides the general rule that amounts paid or incurred to organize a partnership or to promote the sale of (or to sell) a partnership interest are not deductible by the partnership. However, § 709(b) provides an exception that permits a ratable amortization of some of these costs.

Organization Costs.   Organization costs may, at the irrevocable election of the partnership, be amortized ratably over a period of not less than 60 months, starting with the month in which the partnership began business. The signing of the partnership agreement may not be the point at which the partnership began business. The election must be made by the due date (including extensions) of the partnership return for the year it began business, simply by claiming the deduction.[25] Although an amended return may be used to add qualified expenditures not included on the original election return, generally it may not be used to make the election.

Amortizable organizational costs include expenditures that are (1) incident to the creation of the partnership; (2) chargeable to a capital account; and (3) of a character which, if incident to the creation of a partnership having an ascertainable life, would be amortized over such a life. These expenditures include filing, accounting, and legal fees incident to the partnership's organization. Such expenditures must be incurred within the period that starts a reasonable time before the partnership begins business and ends with the due date (without extensions) of the tax return for that year.

Cash method partnerships are not allowed to deduct *in the year incurred* a portion of such expenditures that are paid after that year's end. The portion of such expenditures that would have been deductible in a prior year, if paid before that year's end, is deductible in the year of payment. A corporation can amortize such items beginning in the year in which it begins business, regardless of its accounting method.

The following items are not organization costs: expenses associated with acquiring assets for or transferring assets to the partnership, expenses associated with the admission or removal of partners other than at the time the partnership is first organized, expenses associated with a contract relating to the operation of the partnership trade or business (even where the

---

25. Reg. § 1.709–1(c).

contract is between the partnership and one of its members), and syndication costs.

Example 15   The ABC Partnership was formed on May 15 of the current year and immediately started business. Since its partners all use the calendar year, ABC uses the calendar year. ABC incurred $720 in legal fees for drafting the partnership agreement and $480 in accounting fees for tax advice, as well as other matters of an organizational nature. The legal fees were paid in October of the current year, and the accounting fees were paid in January of the following year. The partnership selected the cash method of accounting and made a proper election to amortize its organization costs.

On its first tax return, ABC deducts $96 of organization costs [($720 legal fees/60 months) $\times$ 8 months]. No deduction is allowed for the accounting fees on the first return, since the fees were paid the following year. On its tax return for next year, ABC deducts organization costs of $304 {[($720 legal fees/60 months) $\times$ 12 months] + [($480 accounting fees/60 months) $\times$ 20 months]}. The $64 portion of the accounting fees [($480/60) $\times$ 8] that could have been deducted on ABC's first tax return if the fees had been paid by that year's end is properly added to the return for the second year. $\square$

Syndication Costs.   Unlike the allowed treatment of organization costs, § 709(a) requires syndication costs to be capitalized, but no amortization is allowed. Syndication costs are those expenditures incurred in connection with promoting and marketing interests in partnerships [e.g., brokerage fees; registration fees; related legal fees for the underwriter, placement agent, and issuer (the general partner or partnership) for securities advice and for advice pertaining to the adequacy of tax disclosures in the prospectus or placement memo for securities law purposes; accounting fees related to offering materials; and printing costs of prospectus, placement memo, and materials for selling and promotion].[26]

Fees incurred for tax advice regarding partnership operation and projections or forecasts used to plan operations and structure transactions are not syndication costs and should be deductible either as amortized organization costs or as general business start-up expenditures. In either case, they would be amortized over a period of 60 months or more.

■■■■ Operation

The statutory provisions that govern the operation of a partnership are contained in §§ 701 through 708. The rules govern who is taxed on partnership income, how such income is determined, and how and when it is reported. The provisions also include the rules governing the determination of a partner's interest basis and the effect of transactions among a partnership, partners, and related parties.

---

26. Reg. § 1.709–2(b).

Measuring and Reporting Income

Although a partnership is not subject to Federal income taxation, it must determine its taxable income and file an income tax return for information purposes.[27] Under the conduit concept, the tax is imposed on partners in their separate capacities. A partnership is, however, subject to other Federal taxes, such as the unemployment tax and the employer's share of Social Security taxes. Moreover, it must withhold taxes on its employees' salaries and wages.

Tax Return and Schedule K–1.   The principal purpose of the partnership return (Form 1065) is to provide information necessary for determining the character and amount of each partner's distributive share of partnership income, expenses, and credits (an application of the aggregate or conduit concept of partnerships). Usually, one general partner must sign the return. If a receiver, trustee in bankruptcy, or assignee controls the partnership property or business, that person must sign the return. The return is due on the fifteenth day of the fourth month following the close of the partnership's taxable year. Concurrent with this filing, the partnership is required to provide each partner with a Schedule K–1, which indicates each partner's distributive share of all items of income, deductions, and credits and enables the partners to timely file their own personal income tax returns.

Elections.   In addition to the reporting function, Form 1065 is used to make various elections. With few exceptions, the partnership must make the elections affecting the computation of its taxable income. For instance, selection of the method of accounting or an election not to use the installment method of reporting sales must be made by the partnership and will apply to all partners in all partnership transactions.[28] The electing capacity of the partnership is an expression of the entity concept.

Measurement and Reporting.   The measurement and reporting of partnership income requires a two-step approach. First, § 702(a) requires certain transactions to be segregated and reported separately on the partnership return (and on each partner's Schedule K–1):

1. Gains and losses from sales or exchanges of capital assets, segregated by the long-term holding period requirement (short-term and long-term capital gains and losses).
2. Gains and losses from sales or involuntary conversions of real or depreciable property used in the business meeting the long-term holding period requirement (i.e., § 1231 gains or losses).
3. Charitable contributions.
4. Dividends that qualify for the dividends received deduction allowed to corporate partners.
5. Taxes paid or accrued to foreign countries and to possessions of the United States that can be claimed as a credit.

---

27. § 6031.
28. Reg. § 1.703–1(b)(1).

6. Other items of income, gain, loss, deduction, or credit to the extent provided by the Regulations.
7. Taxable income or loss, exclusive of the preceding items.

The Regulations expand the list of items in category 6 to be segregated and reported separately:

—Recovery of tax benefit items (§ 111).

—Gains and losses from wagering transactions [§ 165(d)].

—Soil and water conservation expenditures (§ 175).

—Nonbusiness expenses (§ 212).

—Medical and dental expenses (§ 213).

—Alimony payments (§ 215).

—Intangible drilling and development costs [§ 263(c)].

—Income, gain, or loss to the partnership arising from a distribution of unrealized receivables [§ 751(b)].

—Partially tax-exempt interest on obligations of the United States or its instrumentalities.

—Any items of income, gain, loss, deduction, or credit subject to a special allocation under the partnership agreement that differ generally from the allocation of partnership taxable income or loss.

In addition, the Regulations require that the partners separately take into account their distributive share of any partnership item that would result in an income tax liability for a partner different from that which would result if the item were not taken into account separately.[29] Thus, the partners must separately take into account such things as their share of all partnership items that would be considered tax preference items for purposes of the alternative minimum tax and their share of any § 179 immediate expensing amounts. Passive activity income or loss from rental real estate activities is passed through separately, as is portfolio income (e.g., interest, dividends, and royalties).

Although § 1231 gains and losses must be separately stated so that they can be netted with each partner's § 1231 gains and losses to determine if the partner has a net § 1231 gain or loss, ordinary income via the recapture provisions of §§ 1245 and 1250 generally does not require such treatment. However, segregation should be indicated when the related property is sold for a gain and a special allocation agreement exists for the recapture element or when the recapture element existed at the time the property was contributed to the partnership.

The reason for the required segregation and direct allocation to the individual partners of the preceding items is rooted in the aggregate or conduit concept. This first stage of measuring and reporting partnership income is

---

29. Reg. § 1.702–1(a)(8)(ii).

necessary, because the items subject to this treatment affect the computation of various exclusions, deductions, and credits at the partner level. Thus, these items must pass through to the individual partners without loss of identity.

The second stage of the measuring and reporting process deals with all partnership items not segregated or directly allocated as previously described.[30] All items not separately stated under § 702(a) are netted at the partnership level. In this process, the taxable income of a partnership is computed in the same manner as the taxable income of an individual taxpayer, except that a partnership is not allowed certain deductions:[31]

—The deduction for personal exemptions.

—The deduction for taxes paid to foreign countries or possessions of the United States.

—The deduction for charitable contributions.

—The deduction for net operating losses.

—Certain itemized deductions for individuals (e.g., alimony, medical expense, moving expense, and individual retirement savings).

—The deduction for depletion with respect to oil and gas interests.

The result of this second measuring stage is the partnership's ordinary income or loss that is reported on the first page (line 21) of Form 1065. This amount and each of the items that must be segregated and listed separately are reported on Schedule K of Form 1065 and then allocated and reported on a Schedule K–1 for each partner. The partners must then report their distributive share of these items on their own tax return, regardless of whether an actual distribution is made.

Return Illustrated.   A better understanding of the measuring and reporting process may be obtained by examining the presentation of a few transactions on selected portions of a partnership return.

Example 16   Completed page 1 of Form 1065 and Schedule K for the equal XY Partnership for the current year and Schedule K–1 for partner Franklin C. Xenia are presented on the following pages. These items were prepared by Jay L. Bing, a local accountant. XY had cash receipts of $52,175 from consulting fees and $100 from interest on its bank account. It had the following cash payments:

---

30. § 702(a)(8).
31. § 703(a).

Form **1065**	**U.S. Partnership Return of Income**	OMB No. 1545-0099
Department of the Treasury Internal Revenue Service	▶ For Paperwork Reduction Act Notice, see Form 1065 Instructions. For calendar year 1987, or fiscal year beginning _____ 1987, and ending _____ 19 ___	**1987**

A Principal business activity	Use IRS label. Other-wise, please print or type.	Name XY Partnership	**D** Employer identification number 22-6872310
B Principal product or service		Number and street (or P.O. Box number if mail is not delivered to street address) 700 North High Street	**E** Date business started 1/1/85
C Business code number		City or town, state, and ZIP code Columbus, Ohio 43210	**F** Enter total assets at end of tax year $ 25,000

G Check accounting method: (1) ☒ Cash (2) ☐ Accrual (3) ☐ Other
H Check applicable boxes: (1) ☐ Final return (2) ☐ Change in address (3) ☐ Amended return

		Yes	No
I	Number of partners in this partnership ▶ ......2....		
J	Is this partnership a limited partnership (see the Instructions)? . .		X
K	Is this partnership a partner in another partnership?		X
L	Are any partners in this partnership also partnerships?		X
M	Does the partnership meet **all** the requirements shown in the Instructions for **Question M**?		X
N	Was there a distribution of property or a transfer (for example, by sale or death) of a partnership interest during the tax year? If "Yes," see the Instructions concerning an election to adjust the basis of the partnership's assets under section 754		X

		Yes	No
O	At any time during the tax year, did the partnership have an interest in or a signature or other authority over a financial account in a foreign country (such as a bank account, securities account, or other financial account)? (See the Instructions for exceptions and filing requirements for Form TD F 90-22.1.) If "Yes," write the name of the foreign country. ▶ _____		X
P	Was the partnership the grantor of, or transferor to, a foreign trust which existed during the current tax year, whether or not the partnership or any partner has any beneficial interest in it? If "Yes," you may have to file Forms 3520, 3520-A, or 926		X
Q	Was this partnership in operation at the end of 1987?	X	
R	Number of months in 1987 that this partnership was in operation ▶ ....12....		
S	Check this box if the partnership has filed or is required to file Form 8264, Application for Registration of a Tax Shelter . . . . ☐		
T	Check this box if this is a partnership subject to the consolidated partnership audit procedures of TEFRA. (See page 7 of the Instructions.) . . . . . . ☐		

Caution: *Include only trade or business income and expenses on lines 1a–21 below. See the instructions for more information.*

Income

1a	Gross receipts or sales $ .... **1b** Minus returns and allowances $............. Balance ▶	**1c**	52,175
2	Cost of goods sold and/or operations (Schedule A, line 7)	**2**	
3	Gross profit (subtract line 2 from line 1c)	**3**	
4	Ordinary income (loss) from other partnerships and fiduciaries (attach schedule)	**4**	
5	Net farm profit (loss) (attach Schedule F (Form 1040))	**5**	
6	Net gain (loss) (Form 4797, line 18)	**6**	
7	Other income (loss)	**7**	
8	**TOTAL** income (loss) (combine lines 3 through 7)	**8**	52,175

Deductions (see instructions for limitations)

9a	Salaries and wages (other than to partners) $............. **9b** Minus jobs credit $............. Balance ▶	**9c**	
10	Guaranteed payments to partners	**10**	
11	Rent	**11**	20,000
12	Deductible interest expense not claimed elsewhere on return (see Instructions)	**12**	
13	Taxes	**13**	1,600
14	Bad debts	**14**	250
15	Repairs	**15**	425
16a	Depreciation from Form 4562 (attach Form 4562) $ .... **16b** Minus depreciation claimed on Schedule A and elsewhere on return $ .... Balance ▶	**16c**	
17	Depletion (**Do not deduct oil and gas depletion.**)	**17**	
18a	Retirement plans, etc.	**18a**	
b	Employee benefit programs	**18b**	
19	Other deductions (attach schedule)	**19**	2,450
20	**TOTAL** deductions (add amounts in column for lines 9c through 19)	**20**	24,725
21	Ordinary income (loss) from trade or business activity(ies) (subtract line 20 from line 8)	**21**	27,450

Please Sign Here
Under penalties of perjury, I declare that I have examined this return, including accompanying schedules and statements, and to the best of my knowledge and belief, it is true, correct, and complete. Declaration of preparer (other than taxpayer) is based on all information of which preparer has any knowledge.

▶ *Franklin C. Xenia*
Signature of general partner
▶ Date *4/1/88*

Paid Preparer's Use Only

Preparer's signature ▶ *Jay L. Bing*	Date 4-1-88	Check if self-employed ▶ ☒	Preparer's social security no. 282 : 12 : 1236
Firm's name (or yours if self-employed) and address ▶ Jay L. Bing 190 Capitol Square, Columbus, OH		E.I. No. ▶ 38 : 8226910	ZIP code ▶ 43211

Form 1065 (1987)

Schedule K   Partners' Shares of Income, Credits, Deductions, etc.

	(a) Distributive share items		(b) Total amount	
Income (Loss)	**1** Ordinary income (loss) from trade or business activity(ies) (page 1, line 21)	**1**	27,450	
	2 Net income (loss) from rental real estate activity(ies) (Schedule H, line 17)	**2**		
	3a Gross income from other rental activity(ies)	**3a** $		
	b Minus expenses (attach schedule)	**3b** $		
	c Balance net income (loss) from other rental activity(ies) . . . . ▶	**3c**		
	4 Portfolio income (loss):			
	a Interest income	**4a**	100	
	b Dividend income	**4b**		
	c Royalty income	**4c**		
	d Net short-term capital gain (loss) (Schedule D, line 4)	**4d**		
	e Net long-term capital gain (loss) (Schedule D, line 9)	**4e**		
	f Other portfolio income (loss) (attach schedule)	**4f**		
	5 Guaranteed payments	**5**		
	6 Net gain (loss) under section 1231 (other than due to casualty or theft) . . .	**6**		
	7 Other (attach schedule)	**7**		
Deduc-tions	**8** Charitable contributions (attach list)	**8**	200	
	9 Expense deduction for recovery property (section 179)	**9**		
	10 Deductions related to portfolio income (do not include investment interest expense) . . .	**10**		
	11 Other (attach schedule) . . . . . Medical expense: F. Xenia	**11**	80	
Credits	**12a** Credit for income tax withheld	**12a**		
	b Low-income housing credit (attach Form 8586)	**12b**		
	c Qualified rehabilitation expenditures related to rental real estate activity(ies) (attach schedule)	**12c**		
	d Credit(s) related to rental real estate activity(ies) other than 12b and 12c (attach schedule)	**12d**		
	e Credit(s) related to rental activity(ies) other than 12b, 12c, and 12d (attach schedule) . .	**12e**		
	13 Other (attach schedule)	**13**		
Self-Employ-ment	**14a** Net earnings (loss) from self-employment	**14a**	27,450	
	b Gross farming or fishing income	**14b**		
	c Gross nonfarm income	**14c**		
Tax Preference Items	**15a** Accelerated depreciation of real property placed in service before 1/1/87	**15a**		
	b Accelerated depreciation of leased personal property placed in service before 1/1/87	**15b**		
	c Depreciation adjustment on property placed in service after 12/31/86	**15c**		
	d Depletion (other than oil and gas)	**15d**		
	e (1) Gross income from oil, gas, and geothermal properties	**15e(1)**		
	(2) Deductions allocable to oil, gas, and geothermal properties	**15e(2)**		
	f Other (attach schedule)	**15f**		
Invest-ment Interest	**16a** Interest expense on investment debts	**16a**		
	b (1) Investment income included on lines 4a through 4f, Schedule K	**16b(1)**		
	(2) Investment expenses included on line 10, Schedule K	**16b(2)**		
Foreign Taxes	**17a** Type of income _			
	b Foreign country or U.S. possession _ _ _ _ _ _ _ _ _ _ _ _ _ _ _ _ _ _			
	c Total gross income from sources outside the U.S. (attach schedule)	**17c**		
	d Total applicable deductions and losses (attach schedule)	**17d**		
	e Total foreign taxes (check one): ▶ ☐ Paid ☐ Accrued	**17e**		
	f Reduction in taxes available for credit (attach schedule)	**17f**		
	g Other (attach schedule)	**17g**		
Other	**18** Attach schedule for other items and amounts not reported above. See Instructions . .			

SCHEDULE K-1 (Form 1065) Department of the Treasury Internal Revenue Service	**Partner's Share of Income, Credits, Deductions, etc.** For calendar year 1987 or fiscal year beginning _____, 1987, and ending _____ 19 ___ .	OMB No. 1545-0099 **1987**

Partner's identifying number ▶   **Partnership's identifying number ▶**

Partner's name, address, and ZIP code	Partnership's name, address, and ZIP code
Franklin C. Xenia 3407 Morse Road Columbus, OH 43216	XY Partnership 700 North High Street Columbus, OH 43210

A(1) Is this partner a general partner? . . . ⊠ Yes ☐ No
   If "yes" to Question A(1):
(2) Did this partner materially participate in the trade or business activity(ies) of the partnership? (See page 12 of the Form 1065 Instructions. Leave blank if no trade or business activities.). · . . . ⊠ Yes ☐ No
(3) Did this partner actively participate in the rental real estate activity(ies) of the partnership? (See page 13 of the Form 1065 Instructions. Leave blank if no rental real estate activities.). . . . ☐ Yes ☐ No
B Partner's share of liabilities
   Nonrecourse. . . . . $ _____
   Other . . . . $ 12,000
C What type of entity is this partner? ▶ Individual

D Enter partner's percentage of: **(i)** Before decrease or termination   **(ii)** End of year
   Profit sharing . . . . ____% __50__%
   Loss sharing . . . . ____% __50__%
   Ownership of capital . . . . . . ____% __50__%
E IRS Center where partnership filed return ▶ _____
F Tax Shelter Registration Number ▶ _____
G(1) Did the partner's ownership interest in the partnership increase after Oct. 22, 1986? . . . . . ☐ Yes ⊠ No
   If yes, attach statement. (See page 13 of the Form 1065 Instructions.)
(2) Did the partnership start or acquire a new activity after Oct. 22, 1986? . . . . ☐ Yes ⊠ No
   If yes, attach statement. (See page 14 of the Form 1065 Instructions.)
H Check here ▶ ☐ if this Schedule K-1 is for a short tax year required by section 706(b).

I Reconciliation of partner's capital account:

(a) Capital account at beginning of year	(b) Capital contributed during year	(c) Income (loss) from lines 1, 2, 3, and 4 below	(d) Income not included in column (c), plus nontaxable income	(e) Losses not included in column (c), plus unallowable deductions	(f) Withdrawals and distributions	(g) Capital account at end of year
500		13,775		180	13,700	395

Caution: *Refer to attached Partner's Instructions for Schedule K-1 (Form 1065) before entering information from this schedule on your tax return.*

	(a) Distributive share Item	(b) Amount	(c) 1040 filers enter the amount in column (b) on:
Income (Loss)	**1** Ordinary income (loss) from trade or business activity(ies)	13,725	⎱ (See Partner's Instructions for Schedule K-1 (Form 1065))
	2 Income or loss from rental real estate activity(ies)		
	3 Income or loss from other rental activity(ies)		
	4 Portfolio income (loss):	▨▨▨▨▨	
	a Interest	50	Sch. B, Part I, line 2
	b Dividends		Sch. B, Part II, line 4
	c Royalties		Sch. E, Part I, line 5
	d Net short-term capital gain (loss)		Sch. D, line 5, col. (f) or (g)
	e Net long-term capital gain (loss)		Sch. D, line 12, col. (f) or (g)
	f Other portfolio income (loss) (attach schedule)		(Enter on applicable lines of your return)
	5 Guaranteed payments		⎱ (See Partner's Instructions for Schedule K-1 (Form 1065))
	6 Net gain (loss) under section 1231 (other than due to casualty or theft)		
	7 Other (attach schedule)		(Enter on applicable lines of your return)
Deductions	**8** Charitable contributions . . . . · .	100	See Form 1040 Instructions
	9 Expense deduction for recovery property (section 179)		
	10 Deductions related to portfolio income		⎱ (See Partner's Instructions for Schedule K-1 (Form 1065))
	11 Other (attach schedule)	80	
Credits	**12a** Credit for income tax withheld		See Form 1040 Instructions
	b Low-income housing credit		Form 8586, line 8
	c Qualified rehabilitation expenditures related to rental real estate activity(ies) (attach schedule)	▨▨▨▨▨	
	d Credit(s) related to rental real estate activity(ies) other than 12b and 12c (attach schedule)	▨▨▨▨▨	⎱ (See Partner's Instructions for Schedule K-1 (Form 1065))
	e Credit(s) related to rental activity(ies) other than 12b, 12c, and 12d (attach schedule).	▨▨▨▨▨	
	13 Other credits (attach schedule)		

For Paperwork Reduction Act Notice, see Form 1065 Instructions.   Schedule K-1 (Form 1065) 1987

Schedule K-1 (Form 1065) (1987)   Page **2**

	(a) Distributive share item	(b) Amount	(c) 1040 filers enter the amount in column (b) on:
Self-employment 14a	Net earnings (loss) from self-employment	13,725	Sch. SE, Part I
b	Gross farming or fishing income		(See Partner's Instructions for Schedule K-1 (Form 1065))
c	Gross nonfarm income		
Tax Preference Items 15a	Accelerated depreciation of real property placed in service before 1/1/87		Form 6251, line 5a
b	Accelerated depreciation of leased personal property placed in service before 1/1/87		Form 6251, line 5b
c	Depreciation adjustment on property placed in service after 12/31/86		Form 6251, line 4g
d	Depletion (other than oil and gas)		Form 6251, line 5h
e	(1) Gross income from oil, gas, and geothermal properties		See Form 6251 Instructions
	(2) Deductions allocable to oil, gas, and geothermal properties . . .		See Form 6251 Instructions
f	Other (attach schedule)		(See Partner's Instructions for Schedule K-1 (Form 1065))
Investment Interest 16a	Interest expense on investment debts		Form 4952, line 1
b	(1) Investment income included in Schedule K-1, lines 4a through 4f .		(See Partner's Instructions for Schedule K-1 (Form 1065))
	(2) Investment expenses included in Schedule K-1, line 10		
Foreign Taxes 17a	Type of income _____		Form 1116, Check boxes
b	Name of foreign country or U.S. possession _____		Form 1116, Part I
c	Total gross income from sources outside the U.S. (attach schedule) .		Form 1116, Part I
d	Total applicable deductions and losses (attach schedule)		Form 1116, Part I
e	Total foreign taxes (check one): ▶ ☐ Paid ☐ Accrued		Form 1116, Part II
f	Reduction in taxes available for credit (attach schedule)		Form 1116, Part III
g	Other (attach schedule)		See Form 1116 Instructions
Other 18	Other items and amounts not included in lines 1 through 17g and 19 that are required to be reported separately to you		(See Partner's Instructions for Schedule K-1 (Form 1065))

	19 Properties:	A	B	C	
Property Subject to Recapture of Investment Credit	a Description of property (State whether recovery or nonrecovery property. If recovery property, state whether regular percentage method or section 48(q) election used.) .				Form 4255, top
	b Date placed in service .				Form 4255, line 2
	c Cost or other basis . .				Form 4255, line 3
	d Class of recovery property or original estimated useful life .				Form 4255, line 4
	e Date item ceased to be investment credit property				Form 4255, line 8

Other Information Provided by Partnership:

Line 11 - Medical Expense: F. Xenia $80

Contribution to United Way	$ 200
Electricity	1,500
Medical expense: F. Xenia	80
Real estate taxes, building site	1,600
Rents for office space and equipment	20,000
Repairs to leased equipment	425
Supplies	950
Withdrawal: F. Xenia	13,700

Frank C. Xenia's capital balance at the beginning of the year was $500. During the year, XY wrote off a $250 bad debt due from a business-related loan to a client who went bankrupt. □

In comparing Schedules K and K–1, note that each line on Schedule K is reflected on Schedule K–1. Schedule K–1 also provides instructions for partners filing as individual taxpayers as to the tax return form and place to report their respective shares of items. Line I of Schedule K–1 is a reconciliation of the partner's capital account. The aggregate in each Line I column for all partners should agree with the totals in each column of Schedule M (not shown) on page 2, Form 1065. Schedule M reconciles the aggregate balances in the partners' capital accounts at the beginning and end of the tax year presented on the partnership's balance sheet in Schedule L (not shown) on page 2, Form 1065. Columnar headings for both reconciliations are the same. The amounts in columns (a) and (g) represent the beginning and ending balances in the capital account. A brief explanation of the contents of columns (b) through (f) for Line I of Schedule K–1 follows.

Column   **Purpose**

b. Cash and property contributions of the partner during the year are reported here. Fair market values are entered when used for accounting purposes. Otherwise, adjusted basis is used.

c. The partner's income or loss share as reported on Lines 1 through 4 of Schedule K–1 is reported here.

d. In this column, the partner's share of all income not included in column (c) plus nontaxable income is reported.

e. This column includes the partner's share of all losses not included in column (c) plus unallowable deductions.

f. The partner's capital withdrawals are reported here.

Impact of Withdrawals. Actual capital withdrawals by a partner during the year do not affect the partnership's income measuring and reporting process but are treated as distributions made on the last day of the partnership's tax year.[32] Furthermore, when partner withdrawals exceed the partners' shares of partnership income, the partners may be required to recognize the excess as income unless repayment is required.[33] Distributions are discussed later in the chapter, under Nonliquidating Distributions.

---

32. Reg. § 1.731–1(a)(1)(ii).
33. Reg. § 1.731–1(c)(2).

Penalties.   Each partner's share of partnership items must be reported on the partner's individual tax return in the same manner as presented on Schedule K–1, Form 1065, or the IRS must be notified of any inconsistent treatment at the time of such reporting.   A partnership with 10 or fewer partners, all of whom are either estates or natural persons (other than nonresident aliens), where each partner's share of partnership items is the same for all items is automatically excluded from this rule.   If a partner fails to comply with this reporting requirement because of negligence or intentional disregard of rules or regulations, a negligence penalty may be added to the tax due.

To encourage the filing of a partnership return, a penalty is imposed on the partnership of $50 per month (or fraction thereof), but not to exceed five months, for failure to file a complete and timely information return without reasonable cause.   Every general partner is personally liable for the entire penalty.

Loss Limitations

Partnership losses flow through to the partners for use on their individual tax returns. However, for any given year, the amount and nature of the losses that may be used by a partner for tax computational purposes may be limited. When the limitations apply, all or a portion of the losses are held in suspension until a triggering condition occurs. At that time, the losses can be used to determine the partner's tax liability.

Overall Limitation.   Section 704(d) limits the amount of partnership losses a partner can deduct. Specifically, a partner's deduction of partnership losses (including capital losses) is limited to the adjusted basis of the partner's interest at the end of the partnership year before considering any losses for that year. Distributions during the year are taken into account before losses are applied against basis. Losses that cannot be deducted by a partner because of the limitation are suspended and carried forward for use against future increases in the partner's interest basis. Such increases might result from additional capital contributions, additional liabilities, or future income.

Example 17   C and D do business as the CD Partnership, sharing profits and losses equally. All parties use the calendar year. At the start of the current year, C's partnership interest is $25,000. The partnership sustained an operating loss of $80,000 in the current year and earned a profit of $70,000 in the next year. For the current year, only $25,000 of C's $40,000 distributive share of the partnership loss (one half of $80,000 loss) can be deducted. As a result, the basis of C's partnership interest is zero as of January 1 of the following year, and C must carry forward the remaining $15,000 of partnership losses. ☐

Example 18   Assume the same facts as in Example 17. Since the partnership earned a profit of $70,000 for the next calendar year, C will report net partnership income of $20,000 ($35,000 distributive share of income less the $15,000 carryover loss). The adjusted basis of C's partnership interest now becomes $20,000. ☐

C's entire $40,000 share of the current year partnership loss could have been deducted in the current year if C had contributed an additional $15,000 or more in capital by December 31. Likewise, if the partnership had incurred additional debt of $30,000 or more by the end of the current year, C's basis would have been increased to permit the entire share of the distributive loss to be deducted in that year. Thus, if partnership losses are projected for a given year, careful tax planning can ensure the deductibility of a partner's distributive share of such losses.

Nature Limitation. If ordinary losses, short-term and long-term capital losses, and § 1231 losses exist and the amount of interest basis needed to absorb the partner's aggregate share is insufficient, the amount of each item used on the partner's individual tax return is limited.

Example 19

E and Z are equal partners in the EZ Partnership. For the current year, the partnership had an ordinary loss from operations of $20,000, a long-term capital gain of $2,000, and a short-term capital loss of $8,000. Z's distributive share of these items is $10,000 of the operating loss, $1,000 of the long-term capital gain, and $4,000 of the short-term capital loss. The partnership had no other transactions for the current year. At the start of the current year, Z's interest basis in the partnership was $6,000. How much of each loss can Z claim as a deduction in the current year? First, Z's interest basis at the end of the current year before considering the partnership losses must be determined. Then, Z's deductible share of each loss must be computed.

At the end of the current year, *before* considering Z's share of the losses but *after* considering the income items, Z's interest basis is $7,000. This amount represents the maximum amount of partnership losses Z can deduct in the current year. The portion of each loss that is deductible is determined by the ratio of the specific loss to the aggregate losses. Thus, $5,000 of the ordinary loss ($10/14 \times \$7,000$) and $2,000 of the short-term capital loss ($4/14 \times \$7,000$) can be deducted in the current year.

After the deduction, Z's interest basis is zero. The losses that cannot be deducted in the current year are carried forward until Z has a sufficient year-end interest basis to absorb them and future losses. Related computations are as follows:

Z's interest basis at start of year			$6,000
Add: Share of long-term capital gain			1,000
Z's year-end interest basis before losses			$7,000
Ordinary loss	$10,000	10/14 × $7,000 = $5,000	
Short-term loss	4,000	4/14 × 7,000 = 2,000	7,000
Total	$14,000		
Z's year-end interest basis after deducting losses			$-0-

Losses carried forward to next year:

	Ordinary Loss	Short–Term Capital Loss
Current year losses	$10,000	$4,000
Deducted in current year	5,000	2,000
Carryover losses	$ 5,000	$2,000

Several points should be noted about losses and carryover period limitations. The first guidepost is the partner's interest basis at year-end before considering any losses. In the aggregate, the losses that exceed this basis are carried forward indefinitely, awaiting the time when the partner has a positive year-end basis in the partnership interest.

Second, the partner's separate limitation rules come into play. These rules may relate to statutory limits on the use of capital, casualty, passive, or portfolio losses to reduce taxable income.

Finally, special at-risk (§ 465) and passive loss (§ 469) limitations may apply. Generally, a partner is at risk to the extent of his or her economic investment in the partnership (i.e., adjusted basis of contributed property, cash contributions, debt for which the partner is personally liable or has pledged other property as security, and the earnings share that has not been withdrawn or used to absorb losses). Passive losses generally arise where the taxpayer does not participate in the activity on a regular, continuous, and substantial basis. These items and their limitations are discussed in Chapter 9 under Special Problems—Limited Partnerships. For now, though, it is worth mentioning that the at-risk rules also apply to general partnerships with nonrecourse debt, and the passive loss limitation rules apply in a variety of situations.

Allocating Partnership Income

Under § 704(a), a partner's distributive share of partnership items is determined by the partnership agreement. Under § 704(b), the partnership agreement may provide different ratios for sharing items of income, gain, loss, deductions, or credits among the individual partners. However, retroactive allocations to partners according to their interests at year-end are not permitted. When there is a change in any partner's ownership interest during the year, § 706(d)(1) indicates that, with the exception of cash basis items, the entity can use any allocation method approved by forthcoming Regulations that takes into account the varying interests of partners. Until the Regulations are issued, Treasury News Release 84–129 indicates that for partnerships using an interim closing of the books a semimonthly convention will be permitted. Under this convention, partners entering the partnership during the first 15 days of the month generally will be treated as if they entered the partnership on the first day of the month. Partners entering after the fifteenth day of the month generally will be treated as entering the partnership on the sixteenth day of the month. Partnerships that do not use an interim closing but prorate partnership items will be required to use a daily convention.

Cash Basis Items.   Cash basis items must be allocated first to each day in the partnership's tax year and then to partners in proportion to their interests in the partnership at the close of each day. Allocable cash basis items include interest, taxes, service payments, lease and rental payments, and other items specified in the Regulations.

Substantial Economic Effect.   If the partnership agreement does not provide for determining a partner's distributive share of income, gain, loss, deduction or credit, or the specified allocation lacks any substantial economic effect, § 704(b) indicates that a partner's share is to be determined in accordance with the partner's interest in the partnership (determined by taking into account all of the facts and circumstances). The Regulations provide that the manner in which profits or losses are actually recorded on the partnership books (i.e., their division between the partners' accounts) generally determines the profit- and loss-sharing ratios in the absence of a partnership agreement. Additionally, in determining whether an allocation has substantial economic effect, the Regulations [34] indicate that the allocation must affect the dollar amount of a partner's share of income or loss, independent of the tax consequences. A two-part analysis is required to determine if an allocation has substantial economic effect: (1) economic effect test and (2) substantiality test.

Although each test for substantial economic effect has several parts, only the main elements are summarized here. To meet the economic effect test, an allocation must do the following:

1. Be consistent with the economic arrangement of the partners so that the partner receiving the allocation also receives the economic benefit or bears the economic risk or burden.
2. Affect the dollar amount received by the partners to the same extent as the allocation.

To meet the substantiality test, a reasonable possibility must exist that the allocation will substantially affect the dollar amount to be received by the partners independent of the tax consequences.

Required Allocations.   A special allocation that results in the shifting of tax benefits to partners who could take full advantage of selected items would be subject to close IRS scrutiny. However, Congress provided for required allocations of income, gain, loss, and deductions with respect to contributed property to mitigate the inequities that might arise because of the differing nature of property contributed to a partnership by individual partners.[35]

The Code provides that the IRS will prescribe Regulations so that income, gain, loss, and deductions with respect to property contributed to a partnership are shared among the partners in a manner that will take into account the discrepancy between the basis of the property to the partnership and the property's fair market value at the time of contribution. Until the new Regulations are issued, the old ones may be relied upon. There, the amount allocated

---

34. Reg. § 1.704–1(b).
35. § 704(c).

to the partners for any one item cannot exceed the total amount properly allowable to the partnership.[36] The illustration in Example 20 is based on the old Regulations.

Example 20   A and B form an equal partnership on January 1 of the current year. A contributes cash of $95,000, and B contributes land with an adjusted basis of $7,000 and fair market value of $95,000. The land was held as inventory by B's proprietorship real estate business. Immediately after formation, each partner has an undivided fair market value interest in each asset of $47,500.

	Adjusted Basis	FMV	One-Half FMV
Cash	$ 95,000	$ 95,000	$47,500
Land	7,000	95,000	47,500
Totals	$102,000	$190,000	$95,000

Assume the partnership has no business use for the land. Consequently, the land is a capital asset when received. Two months after the partnership is formed, the land is sold for $100,000.

For accounting purposes, the land generally is recorded at its fair market value of $95,000, and for tax purposes, at its carryover basis of $7,000. Thus, for accounting purposes, when the land is sold, a $5,000 gain results which is divided equally between A and B ($2,500 to each).

Selling price	$100,000
Land (FMV basis to AB Partnership)	95,000
Gain	$ 5,000

For tax purposes, the gain on the sale is $93,000, and it is divided so that A receives $2,500 and B receives $90,500 ($88,000 + $2,500).

Selling price	$100,000
Land	7,000
Taxable gain	$ 93,000
Unrealized appreciation at contribution, allocated to B	88,000
Split equally between A and B	$ 5,000

Since B's real estate business held the land as inventory, all the gain is ordinary income, because it was sold within five years of the contribution date.

---

36. Reg. § 1.704–1(c)(2)(i).

The capital account and interest basis of A are equal before and after the land sale, but for B they are equal only after the sale (i.e., after the unrealized appreciation at the contribution date has been recognized).

	A		B	
	Capital Account	Interest Basis	Capital Account	Interest Basis
Before sale	$95,000	$95,000	$95,000	$ 7,000
Gains from sale	2,500	2,500	2,500	90,500
After sale	$97,500	$97,500	$97,500	$97,500

Partners and Related Parties

The entity theory of a partnership has been adopted in the general rule governing transactions between a partner and the partnership. Thus, under § 707(a), a partner engaging in a transaction with the partnership can be regarded as a nonpartner or outsider. Applications of this rule include the following:

1. Loans of money or property by the partnership to the partner or by the partner to the partnership.
2. The sale of property by a partner to the partnership or the purchase of property by the partner from the partnership.
3. The rendition of services by the partnership to the partner or by the partner to the partnership.[37]

Losses and Deferred Expenses.   Transactions between a partner or a related party and the partnership are subject to close scrutiny. An accrual basis partnership that makes expense and interest payments to related cash basis payees can deduct such payments only when the payees include them in gross income. Such payments are not disallowed, they are only deferred. Items such as interest accrued on partner loans to the partnership and accrued rents to a partner for leased property are covered by this provision. However, losses from sales or exchanges between a partner or related party and a partnership or between two partnerships are covered by § 707(b)(1). Guaranteed payments to partners also are exempt from coverage.[38]

Related parties for purposes of § 267 include any person—as well as anyone related to this person—who owns directly or indirectly any capital or profits interest in either of the following:

1. The partnership.
2. A partnership in which the first partnership owns directly or indirectly any capital or profits interest.

---

37. Reg. § 1.707–1(a).
38. § 267(e)(5)(C).

Interests owned by or for a C corporation are considered as owned by the shareholders who hold five percent or more in value of the corporation's stock. Finally, related parties include a corporation and a partnership in which the same person owns more than 50 percent in value of the corporation's stock (a controlled corporation) *and also owns* more than a 50 percent interest in the partnership's capital or profits (a controlled partnership).

Example 21   The BOQ Partnership uses the accrual method of accounting. At the start of last year, Q, a cash basis individual who owns a 30% interest in BOQ's capital and profits, loaned BOQ $5,000 at 12%, compounded annually, for business purposes. At the end of last year, BOQ had accrued and unpaid interest on this loan of $600. On December 31 of the current year, Q received a $1,272 check from BOQ. The accompanying remittance advice indicated that the check included $600 for last year's interest (12% × $5,000) and $672 for the current year's interest (12% × $5,600). Both parties use the calendar year. Q includes the $1,272 in gross income of the current year, and BOQ deducts the full $1,272 as interest expense for the current year. BOQ could not deduct the $600 of interest due to Q last year, though, since Q did not include it in last year's gross income. □

Losses Disallowed.   Losses from the sale or exchange of property are disallowed if they arise in either of the following cases:

1. Between a partnership and a person whose direct or indirect interest in the capital or profits of the partnership is more than 50 percent.
2. Between two partnerships in which the same persons own more than a 50 percent interest in the capital or profits.

If one of the purchasers later sells the property, any gain realized will be recognized only to the extent that it exceeds the loss previously disallowed.[39] The offset of the disallowed loss is available only to the original transferee who acquired the property by purchase or exchange.[40] Although the disallowed loss may be used by the transferee to offset any subsequent gain on the property's disposal, it cannot be used to increase or create a loss.

Example 22   R owns a 35% interest in the capital and profits of the RST Partnership. On September 1 of the current year, R sells property with an adjusted basis of $50,000 to the partnership for the property's fair market value of $35,000. Assuming R is not related to any partners (within the meaning of § 267), a recognized loss of $15,000 is to be reported. □

Example 23   Assume the same facts as in Example 22, except that R's brother owns a 40% interest in the capital and profits of the partnership. Under § 267, constructive ownership takes place between brothers and sisters. Thus, R is deemed to own a 75% interest in the partnership (35% direct ownership

---

39. Reg. § 1.707–1(b)(1)(ii).
40. Reg. § 1.267(d)–1(a)(3).

plus the 40% interest owned by R's brother). Consequently, R's $15,000 loss is disallowed. □

Example 24   Assume the same facts as in Example 23. If the RST Partnership later sells the property for $40,000, none of the $5,000 gain (sale price of $40,000 less adjusted basis to partnership of $35,000) will be recognized. The partnership can offset any subsequent gain by the loss previously disallowed. The unused $10,000 of R's disallowed loss disappears. □

Conversion of Capital Gain.   Under § 707(b)(2), gains are treated as ordinary income in a sale or exchange of property between a person and partnership (or between two partnerships) if more than 50 percent of the partnership or partnerships is owned by the same person. This rule does not apply, however, if the property is a capital asset in the hands of the transferee (purchaser) immediately after the transfer.

Through § 1239, gains may be treated as ordinary income on the sale or exchange of property between a partner or related party and a partnership (or between two partnerships). Ordinary income results if the transferred property is depreciable in the hands of the transferee and the partner or related party owns more than 50 percent of the partnership or partnerships. Finally, unless it can be proven that unwarranted tax avoidance is not a principal purpose, § 453 prohibits the use of the installment method for sales of depreciable property between a partner or related party and a partnership (or between two partnerships) when the more-than-50 percent test is met.

Related Parties.   In evaluating the 50 percent test for gains and losses under § 707 and for gains under §§ 453 and 1239, the following rules apply:

1. Any interest owned by or for a corporation, partnership, estate, or trust is considered to be owned proportionately by or for the shareholders, partners, or beneficiaries.
2. An individual is considered as owning the interest owned by or for family members.
3. The family of an individual includes only brothers and sisters (whether by the whole or half blood), spouse, ancestors, and lineal descendants.
4. An interest constructively owned by a person under rule 1 is treated, for applying rules 1 and 2, as actually owned by that person. However, an interest constructively owned by an individual under rule 2 is not treated as owned by the individual for purposes of again applying rule 2 to make another party the constructive owner of the interest.[41]

Guaranteed Payments.   Payments made by a partnership to one of its partners for services rendered or for the use of capital, determined without regard to the income of the partnership, are treated by the partnership in the same manner as payments made to a person who is not a partner. Referred to as "guaranteed payments" under § 707(c), such payments generally are deductible by the partnership as a business expense and must be reported as ordinary

---

41. Reg. §§ 1.707–1(b)(3) and 1.267(c)–1(b).

income by the receiving partner. Their deductibility distinguishes guaranteed payments from a partner's distributive share of income.

A guaranteed payment is deductible by a partnership if it is not a capital expenditure and if it meets the tests of an ordinary and necessary business expense. Typically, it is deductible to the partnership and includible in the partner's gross income only after payment.

Example 25   Under the terms of the LMN Partnership agreement, N is entitled to a fixed annual salary of $18,000 without regard to partnership income. L, M, and N share profits and losses equally. After deducting the guaranteed payment, the partnership has $36,000 of ordinary income. N reports $30,000 of ordinary income for the partnership tax year that ends with or within N's tax year ($18,000 guaranteed payment plus his one-third distributive share of partnership income of $12,000). L and M each report $12,000 of ordinary income (a one-third share of the partnership's ordinary income of $36,000). If N were not entitled to a salary, the partnership's ordinary income would be $54,000 ($36,000 + $18,000), and each partner's share would be $18,000. Thus, the salary paid to N reduced the income of L and M by $6,000 each. From an operating viewpoint, if the salary to N represented compensation for managing the business, L and M may have gained via a higher net income from the partnership.

	L	M	N
Salary	$ –0–	$ –0–	$18,000
Income share after salary	12,000	12,000	12,000
Total	$12,000	$12,000	$30,000
Less income share without salary	18,000	18,000	18,000
Gain (loss) to partner	($ 6,000)	($ 6,000)	$12,000

Minimum Guaranteed Payment. If a partner is to receive a percentage of partnership income with a stipulated minimum payment, the guaranteed payment is the amount by which the minimum guarantee exceeds the partner's share of partnership income before taking into account the minimum guaranteed amount.

Example 26   Assume that the LMN Partnership from Example 25 does not have any separately stated items. Under the partnership agreement, M is to receive 40% of partnership income, but in no event less than $10,000. In the current year, the partnership has income of $15,000 before considering M's guaranteed payment. M's share is $6,000 (40% of $15,000). Thus, the guaranteed payment that may be deducted by the partnership is $4,000 (excess of $10,000 minimum guarantee over $6,000 share of partnership income before considering the guaranteed payment). M's ordinary income from the partnership is $10,000, and the remaining $5,000 of income is reported by the other partners in proportion to their profit shares under the agreement. Note that M's share of partnership income after deducting the guaranteed payment is 54.55% [$6,000 ÷ ($15,000 − $4,000)].[42] ☐

Losses and Guaranteed Payments. When the partnership agreement provides for a guaranteed payment and such payment results in a partnership loss, the partner must report the full guaranteed payment and separately account for the distributive share of the loss. This reporting assumes the partnership agreement provides for the partner receiving the guaranteed payment to share in partnership losses resulting from such payment.

Example 27 Partner T of the STP Partnership is to receive a payment of $20,000 for services, plus 20% of the partnership income or loss. After deducting the $20,000 payment to T, the partnership has a loss of $10,000. Of this amount, $2,000 (20% of $10,000) is T's distributive share which, subject to the limitation imposed by § 704(d), is to be reported on T's tax return. In addition, T must report the guaranteed payment of $20,000 as ordinary income. ☐

Example 28 Assume the same facts as in Example 27, except that instead of a $10,000 loss, the partnership has $40,000 of capital gains and no deductions or income items other than the $20,000 paid to T as a guaranteed payment. Since the items of partnership income or loss must be segregated under § 702(a), the partnership has a $20,000 ordinary loss and $40,000 in capital gains. T's 20% distributive share of these items is a $4,000 ordinary loss and an $8,000 capital gain. Additionally, T must report the $20,000 guaranteed payment as ordinary income.[43] ☐

Partners as Employees. A partner generally does not qualify as a partnership employee for tax purposes. Accordingly, a partner receiving guaranteed payments will not be regarded as an employee of the partnership for the purposes of withholding taxes or for qualified pension and profit sharing plans.

Close of Final Tax Year

When does a partnership's final tax year end? Technically, it closes at the time at which the partnership itself terminates, which is when either of the following events occurs:

1. No part of any business, financial operation, or venture of the partnership continues to be carried on by any of the partners in a partnership.
2. Within a 12-month period, there is a sale or exchange of 50 percent or more of the total interest in partnership capital and profits.[44]

A partnership's tax year generally does not close upon the death of a partner; the entry of a new partner; or the liquidation, sale, or exchange of an existing partnership interest. In the case of the sale or liquidation of an entire

---

42. Reg. § 1.707–1(c) (Ex. 2) and Rev.Rul. 69–180, 1969–1 C.B. 183.
43. Reg. § 1.707–1(c) (Ex. 4).
44. §§ 708(b)(1)(A) and (B).

interest, the partnership's tax year will close only as to the partner who disposed of the partnership interest.[45] Additionally, the taxable year of the partnership will close as to a deceased partner if there is a sales agreement among the partners that the deceased partner's interest is immediately sold to the remaining partners for a formula or fixed price on the date of the deceased partner's death.

Such an agreement, though, is not without problems. If the deceased partner owned 50 percent or more of the total interest in the partnership's capital and profits, the entire partnership would terminate when the interest is sold. Termination would also occur under the sales agreement if the deceased partner's interest in capital and profits equaled or exceeded 50 percent of total capital and profits when added to the other interests in the partnership that were sold or exchanged within a 12-month period.

An unplanned close of the partnership's tax year usually should be avoided because of the potentially problematic bunching of income (partnership income from more than 12 months being included in one taxable year).

Example 29
Partner R, who held a one-third interest in the RST Partnership, died on November 20 of the last calendar year. The partnership uses an IRS-approved business purpose fiscal year, ending September 30. R used a calendar year. The partnership agreement does not contain a sales provision that is triggered upon the death of a partner. Under these circumstances, the partnership's tax year does not close with R's death. Instead, income from the fiscal year ending September 30 of the current calendar year will be taxed to R's estate or other successor. Income from the fiscal year ending September 30 of the last calendar year must be reported on R's final income tax return, covering the period from January 1 to November 20.

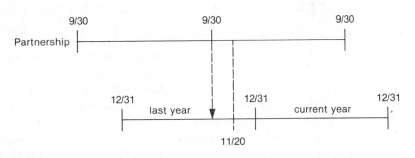

Example 30
Assume the same facts as in Example 29, except that the partnership agreement contained a provision that triggered the sale of the deceased partner's interest to the remaining partners for a fixed price immediately upon the death of the partner. Although R's death will not affect the surviving partners, it will close the partnership's tax year as to R. Thus, R's final income tax return for the last calendar year must include R's share of partnership income both for the fiscal year ending September 30 of the last calendar year and for the period from October 1 to R's death. □

---

45. § 706(c)(2)(B). Even this does not occur if less than the partner's entire interest is transferred.

Example 31   Assume the same facts as in Example 29, except that on November 20 of the last calendar year R's entire partnership interest is sold to a third party. Again, the partnership's tax year will not close with respect to the remaining partners. However, R's share of partnership income for the fiscal year ending September 30 of the last calendar year and for the short period ending on the sale date must be reported on R's tax return for the last year.[46] ☐

Example 32   Assume the same facts as in Example 31, except that R's entire interest represents 60% of the partnership rather than a one-third interest. Although the result of the disposition of this 60% interest does not change as to R, the same is not true for the remaining partners. Since an interest of 50% or more in the partnership has changed hands, the partnership's tax year is closed as of November 20 of the last calendar year for all partners. The RST Partnership is considered to be terminated on that date. ☐

Nonliquidating Distributions

Three basic types of distributions from a partnership exist, and a different set of rules governs the income tax consequences of each:

1. Distributions of cash and other property that will not result in the liquidation of the distributee partner's interest (i.e., a current distribution).
2. Liquidating distributions of money and other property.
3. Distributions that affect the partner's proportionate interests in the partnership's § 751 property (disproportionate distributions).

Section 751 property is sometimes called a "hot asset," because it includes various types of property that cause ordinary income to be recognized. The tax consequences of the last two types of distributions are discussed in Chapter 9 under Liquidating and Disproportionate Distributions.

Section 731(b) states that no gain or loss shall be recognized by a partnership on the distribution of money or other property to a partner. Similarly, § 731(a) provides the general rule that no gain or loss is recognized by a partner receiving such distributions. However, gain is recognized when *money* received in a distribution exceeds the basis of the partner's interest immediately preceding the distribution. Thus, current distributions of property other than money never result in gain or loss recognition to the partner unless they involve disproportionate distributions of hot assets. Any recognized gain is treated as being from the *sale* or *exchange* of a partnership interest. The character of such gain is determined under § 741, discussed in Chapter 9 under Sale of Partnership Interest.

---

46. Reg. § 1.706–1(c)(2)(i) and (ii).

Section 733 provides that nonliquidating distributions from a partnership reduce the distributee partner's interest basis (but not below zero) by (1) the sum of money distributed and (2) the basis to such partner of distributed property other than money. Additionally, § 732 provides that the basis of property (other than money) distributed to a partner in a nonliquidating distribution is the adjusted basis to the partnership immediately before the distribution. However, the basis of the property may not exceed the adjusted basis of the partner's interest in the partnership reduced by any money received in the same transaction.

When the bases of distributed properties are limited by the basis of the partner's interest, an allocation of basis must be made under § 732(c). However, when no § 751 property or inventory is involved, the "remaining" basis of the partner's interest is allocated among the assets in the ratio of their adjusted bases to the partnership. Section 735(b) states that the holding period of the property received as a distribution includes that of the partnership.

Example 33   D, a partner in the DEF Partnership, receives a nonliquidating distribution of land, which has a basis to the partnership of $5,000, and cash of $3,000. If D's adjusted basis before the distribution is $7,000, no gain is recognized. However, the land has a basis of $4,000, and D's interest basis is reduced to zero. The cash received reduced D's interest basis first. The $4,000 remaining basis was then allocated to the land. □

Example 34   Assume the same facts as in Example 33, except that the cash distribution amounts to $9,000. Under these circumstances, D recognizes a gain of $2,000. The gain is considered to be from the sale or exchange of a partnership interest. The basis of the land in D's hands and D's interest basis are both reduced to zero. □

Example 35   R receives a nonliquidating distribution from the RST Partnership when the basis of R's interest is $30,000. The distribution consists of $5,000 of cash and land with an adjusted basis to the partnership of $15,000 and a fair market value of $20,000. R's basis in the land is $15,000, and R's interest basis is reduced to $10,000. □

Concept Summary

1. Under the entity concept, partners and partnerships are treated as separate units, with the nature of gains and losses determined at the partnership level.
2. Under the aggregate concept, a connecting pipeline between the partners and the partnership exists that allows income, credits, deductions, etc., to flow to the partners for separate reporting on their tax returns.
3. Sometimes both concepts apply, such as when land formerly held as inventory by a contributing partner is sold within five years of the contribution date. Here, the aggregate concept prevails, causing ordinary treatment for all gain or loss.

4. A partnership uses the common tax year of the majority partners, if there is such a year, or that of the principal partners if a common tax year exists for them but not for the majority partners. In the absence of any common year, the calendar year is used unless an exception is met or a § 444 election is made.

5. Generally, no gain or loss is recognized by the partner or partnership on a contribution of property for a capital interest. If the entity is not an investment partnership, though, gain may be recognized if the transfer is subject to debt.

6. A partner who contributes property for a partnership interest generally takes the contributed property's adjusted basis as his or her inside and outside interest basis. Recognized gain may increase this amount.

7. The holding period of a partner's interest generally includes that of the contributed property if the property is a § 1231 or capital asset. If not, the holding period starts on the day the interest is acquired. An interest acquired by a cash contribution starts on the acquisition date.

8. To the partnership, contributed property generally takes a carryover basis.

9. The partnership's holding period for contributed property includes the contributing partner's holding period.

10. Organization costs may be amortized over a period of 60 months or more. Syndication costs must be capitalized.

11. Partner capital withdrawals do not affect partnership income but are treated as distributions made on the last day of the partnership's tax year.

12. Losses from a partnership may be used on the partner's separate tax return to the extent of the partner's interest basis in the partnership, determined at the end of the partnership's tax year (before considering any losses). Flow-through losses that are limited because of the partner's year-end interest must be divided by types, based on the partner's aggregate loss share of each loss.

13. Partners can transact business with their partnerships in nonpartner capacities, such as through the lease or sale of property.

14. Losses are disallowed between a partner or related party and a partnership when the partner or related party owns more than a 50 percent interest in the partnership's capital or profits. Ordinary income results if the property is depreciable or if the property is a capital asset to the partner but not to the partnership.

15. Guaranteed payments to partners generally are deductible to the partnership in determining the partnership's taxable income and includible in the partner's gross income for the partnership tax year that ends with or within the partner's tax year under the partnership's method of accounting. Such payments are not deductible immediately, though, if they are capital in nature.

16. A partnership's final tax year closes when no part of the business continues to be carried on by any of the partners in a partnership or when, within a 12-month period, there is a sale or exchange of 50 percent or more of the total interest in capital and profits.

17. Generally, the partnership tax year of a deceased partner does not close with the partner's death. If the partners have a fixed-price or formula agreement to purchase the deceased partner's interest at death, the partnership's tax year could close.

18. Generally, no gain or loss is recognized on a nonliquidating (current) distribution that is proportional as to hot assets. However, if the distributed cash exceeds the partner's outside interest, gain is recognized.

19. Distributed property usually takes the same basis that it had to the partnership. With respect to a current distribution wherein the adjusted basis of distributed property exceeds the partner's outside interest (and unrealized receivables and inventory are not present), the interest is allocated among the assets.

✓ Tax Planning Considerations

The principal factors contributing to the popularity of the partnership form of conducting a business are the ease with which a partnership can be formed and the flexibility allowed under the Federal income tax law for allocating items of income, loss, deductions, or credits among the partners. The partnership form is not free of uncertain tax consequences. Conflicting concepts of partnership taxation and the lack of judicial interpretations of the partnership provisions of the Code require careful and continuous planning to ensure expected income tax results.

Selecting the Partnership Form

The decision to use the partnership form in conducting a trade or business should be made only after a careful consideration of both tax and nontax differences among alternative forms of business organization. Nontax considerations, such as the need to raise more capital or the desire to share the burden of losses, generally eliminate sole proprietorships as alternatives. Thus, when two or more persons are faced with the decision of selecting a form of doing business together, the comparison will be between a partnership and a corporation. The major differences between these alternative business forms are as follows:

—Unlike corporations, partnerships generally involve unlimited liability, lack continuity of life, and have restrictions on the free transferability of ownership interests. The free transferability of a partnership interest may not exist if, under local law, the partnership is dissolved when an interest is transferred or if the general partners must accept a transferee as a partner before such status is conferred. Although the general partners may not formally approve a transferee as a partner, informal approval may take place via the general partners' actions or inactions. When the nontax considerations mentioned here are important, the corporate form may be preferable.

—Unlike partnerships, corporations are taxable entities separate and apart from their owners. Thus, unless S corporation status is elected (see Chapter 10), any corporate-source income may be taxed twice.

—Corporate income loses its identity when distributed to shareholders. Consequently, income eligible for preferential tax treatment at the corporate level (e.g., tax-exempt interest) does not receive preferential treatment at the shareholders' level unless an S election is made.

—Corporate losses cannot be passed through to shareholders unless S corporation status is elected.

—The sale of corporate stock usually results in capital gain or loss. The sale of a partnership interest can result in both ordinary income and capital gain or loss. This distinction is addressed in Chapter 9 under Sale of a Partnership Interest.

—As a separate entity, a corporation is free to select any fiscal year for tax purposes. An S corporation must use a calendar year unless it can convince the IRS that it has a legitimate business purpose for adopting a different tax year. Except for the 12-month rule or a business purpose tax year sanctioned by the IRS, a partnership must adopt a tax year based on a specific order. If the majority partners do not have a common tax year, the common tax year of the principal partners is used. If the principal partners do not have a common tax year, the calendar year or year specified in the Regulations is used unless a § 444 election is made.

—Corporate ownership allows more flexibility for income splitting among family members through gifts of ownership interests. As discussed in Chapter 9 under Special Problems—Family Partnerships, such partnerships are carefully scrutinized by the IRS to prevent the assignment of income among family members.

—Partners report their distributive share of partnership income for the partnership tax year that ends with or within the partners' tax year. The method of accounting used by the partnership for measuring income (i.e., cash, hybrid, or accrual) controls. Cash basis shareholders generally report salaries, interest, rents, or dividends from the corporation when received. Thus, any income accumulated by a corporation is not taxed to shareholders (unless it is an S corporation) until distributed. Partners are taxed on their respective shares of partnership income whether or not distributed.

Formation and Operation

In connection with the formation and operation of a partnership, the following points merit close attention:

—If a joint venture is formed solely for investment purposes, for the joint production, extraction, or use of property, or for purposes of underwriting, selling, or distributing a particular security issue by dealers, consideration should be given to electing exclusion from the partnership provisions of Subchapter K. In many situations, taxpayers may be uncertain as to whether they have formed a partnership and could be treated as such for income tax purposes. If the partnership form is undesirable and the possibility exists that the organization may be a partnership for tax purposes, the election procedures under § 761 should be followed.

—Recall that the contribution of property to a partnership subject to a liability in excess of its basis may result in gain recognition to the contributing partner. If the contributed property were subject to depreciation recapture, ordinary income would result. Unless the partnership is considered the original user of depreciable property, it will not be allowed to deviate from the contributing partner's recovery period or method elected for such property under the cost recovery rules. In situations such as these, thought should be given to retaining ownership of the property and leasing it to the partnership.

—Although the Code does not require a written partnership agreement, many of the statutory provisions governing the tax consequences to partners and their partnerships refer to such an agreement. Remember, for instance, that § 704(a) provides for the determination of a partner's distributive share of income, gain, loss, deduction, or credit in accordance with the partnership agreement. Consequently, if taxpayers operating a business in partnership form want a measure of certainty as to the tax consequences of their activities, a carefully drafted partnership agreement is crucial. If such an agreement contains the obligations, rights, and powers of the partners, it should prove invaluable in settling controversies among partners and providing some degree of certainty as to the tax consequences of the partners' actions.

—Taxpayers also should be alert to the potential advantages and pitfalls of special allocation agreements. If one or more partners assume all of the economic risks associated with the formative years of the partnership, it seems logical that these partners should be entitled to the tax benefits. A special allocation agreement can be used to assign all losses to these partners until such time as the partners have recouped their investment. Recall, however, that such arrangements are subject to careful IRS scrutiny and must have substantial economic effect. As a result, great care should be exercised in drafting such agreements, and adequate documentation should be drawn up and preserved to ensure the desired tax results.

—Caution should be exercised when sales or exchanges are contemplated between a partnership and a related party. Losses from such transactions will be disallowed, and certain gains may be treated as ordinary income (rather than as capital gain).

Tax planning considerations for partnership distributions are presented in Chapter 9.

Problem Materials

Discussion Questions

1. Distinguish between the entity concept and the aggregate or conduit concept of a partnership.

2. What is a partnership for Federal income tax purposes?

3. Under what circumstances can organizations elect to be excluded from the partnership tax provisions? Why would an organization wish to be excluded?

4. Compare the nonrecognition of gain or loss provision on contributions to a partnership with the similar provision found in corporate formation (§ 351). What are the major differences and similarities?

5. When a partner transfers property to a partnership with a fair market value of $1,000 and receives a cash distribution of $1,000, will the transfer be treated as a contribution to capital?

6. How is the basis of a contributing partner's interest determined?

7. If appreciated property is contributed to a partnership in exchange for a partnership interest, what basis does the partnership take in such property?

8. How is the holding period of a partnership interest determined? The partnership's holding period in contributed property?

9. What effect does the contribution of property subject to a liability have on the basis of the contributing partner's interest? What is the effect on the basis of the other partners' interests?

10. What is the effect to the partner of a contribution of property subject to a liability in excess of the partner's basis in the property? To the partnership?

11. What transactions or events will cause a partner's interest to continuously fluctuate?

12. Why is a partnership required to file an information return (Form 1065)?

13. Describe the two-step approach used to determine partnership income. Why is this computation necessary?

14. Under what circumstances can an allocation of income or expense to a partner differ from the general profit- and loss-sharing ratios? Under what circumstances would such an allocation be justified? What could go wrong?

15. To what extent can partners deduct their distributive share of partnership losses? What happens to any unused losses?

16. When can a partnership have a taxable year different from its principal partners? When must partners report their share of partnership income?

17. Under what circumstances will a partnership's tax year close?

18. When may a partner engage in a transaction with the partnership without tax difficulties? What could go wrong?

19. What are guaranteed payments? When might such payments be used?

20. When will a nonliquidating distribution result in a gain to the recipient partner? How is the recipient partner's basis in any property received determined? How is the recipient partner's basis in the partnership determined after the distribution?

Problems

1. L and K form an equal partnership with a cash contribution of $60,000 from L and a property contribution (adjusted basis of $30,000 and a fair market value of $60,000) from K.

   a. How much gain, if any, must L recognize on the transfer? Must K recognize any gain?

   b. What is L's interest basis in the partnership?

   c. What is K's interest basis in the partnership?

   d. What basis will the partnership have in the property transferred by K?

2. L, B, and R form the LBR Partnership on January 1 of the current year. In return for a 30% capital interest, L transfers property (basis of $24,000, fair market value of $37,500) subject to a liability of $15,000. The liability is assumed by the partnership. B transfers property (basis of $37,500, fair market value of $22,500) for a 30% capital interest, and R transfers cash of $30,000 for the remaining 40% interest.

   a. How much gain must L recognize on the transfer?

   b. What is L's interest basis in the partnership?

   c. How much loss may B recognize on the transfer?

   d. What is B's interest basis in the partnership?

e. What is R's interest basis in the partnership?

f. What basis will the LBR Partnership have in the property transferred by L?

g. What is the partnership's basis in the property transferred by B?

 3. Assume the same facts as in Problem 2, except that the property contributed by L has a fair market value of $67,500 and is subject to a mortgage of $45,000.

a. How much gain must L recognize on the transfer?

b. What is L's interest basis in the partnership?

c. What is B's interest basis in the partnership?

d. What is R's interest basis in the partnership?

e. What basis will the LBR Partnership have in the property transferred by L?

f. If the partnership borrows $200,000 to purchase an office building, what effect, if any, will the loan have on each partner's interest in the partnership? What effect will the loan *repayment* have on each partner's interest?

4. X and Y are equal members of the XY Partnership. They are real estate investors who formed the partnership two years ago with equal cash contributions. The XY Partnership purchased a piece of land. On January 1 of the current year, Z contributed to the partnership some land he held for investment with a fair market value of $20,000 for a one-third interest. Z purchased the land three years ago for $25,000. No special allocation agreements were in effect before or after Z was admitted to the partnership. The XYZ Partnership holds all land for investment. Immediately before Z's property contribution, the balance sheet of the XY Partnership was as follows:

	Basis	FMV		Basis	FMV
Land	$5,000	$40,000	X	$2,500	$20,000
			Y	2,500	20,000
	$5,000	$40,000		$5,000	$40,000

a. At the contribution date, what is Z's date basis and interest basis in the XYZ Partnership?

b. On June 30 of the current year, the partnership sold the land contributed by Z for $20,000. How much is the loss, and how is it allocated among the partners?

c. Prepare a balance sheet for the XYZ Partnership immediately after the land sale.

5. Assume the same facts as in Problem 4, with the following exceptions:

—The fair market value of the land contributed by Z declined after Z joined the partnership.

—XYZ sold the land contributed by Z for $17,000.

a. How much is the loss, and how is it allocated among the partners?

b. Prepare a balance sheet for the XYZ Partnership immediately after the land sale, along with schedules that support the amount in each partner's account.

6. Assume the same facts as in Problem 4, with the following exceptions:

—The fair market value of the land not contributed by Z declined after Z joined the partnership.

—XYZ sold the land for $17,000.

a. How much is the gain, and how is it allocated among the partners?

b. Prepare a balance sheet for the XYZ Partnership immediately after the land sale, along with schedules that support the amount in each partner's account.

7. Q is a cash basis sole proprietor whose business is the buying, holding, and selling of real estate. S is a small cash basis manufacturer of specialty candies. Last year, S served as a consultant to a small candy manufacturer in another state and billed the manufacturer $10,000 for her services. B is employed by a local manufacturer and is a casual investor in real estate. Q, S, and B form the QSB Partnership, which will buy, hold, and sell real estate parcels. On January 2 of the current year, the three individuals contributed the following items to the newly formed partnership, each for a one-third interest in capital and profits:

	Adjusted Basis	Fair Market Value
Q contributes land held as inventory	$ 5,000	$10,000
S contributes the receivable for her consulting activities	–0–	10,000
B contributes land held as a long-term capital asset	15,000	10,000

Since the partnership needs cash for working capital, shortly after formation it sells both land parcels for their contribution date fair market values and collects the receivable contributed by S.

a. What is the nature of the gain on the sale of the land contributed by Q, and how is the gain allocated among the partners?

b. What is the nature of the income from the collection of the receivable contributed by S, and how is the income allocated among the partners?

c. What is the nature of the loss on the sale of the land contributed by B, and how is the loss allocated among the partners?

8. As of January 1 of last year, the basis of D's 25% capital interest in the DEF Partnership was $24,000. D and the partnership use the calendar year for tax purposes. The partnership incurred an operating loss of $100,000 for last year and a profit of $8,000 for the current year.

a. How much loss, if any, may D recognize for last year?

b. How much net reportable income must D recognize for the current year?

c. What is D's interest in the partnership as of January 1 of the current year?

d. What is D's interest in the partnership as of January 1 of the next year?

e. What year-end tax planning would you suggest to ensure that partners can deduct their share of partnership losses?

9. LM and KM are equal partners in the calendar year M & M Partnership. For the current year, the partnership had an operating loss of $60,000, a long-term capital loss of $4,000, and a short-term capital gain of $9,000. The partnership had no other transactions for the current year. At the start of the current year, LM's interest basis in the M & M Partnership was $28,000 and KM's was $19,500.

a. How much short-term capital gain must LM report on her tax return for the current year?

b. How much short-term capital gain must KM report on her tax return for the current year?

c. How much of the operating loss and the long-term capital loss must LM report on her tax return for the current year?

d. How much of the operating loss and the long-term capital loss must KM report on her tax return for the current year?

e. What is LM's partnership interest at the start of the next calendar year? KM's partnership interest at the start of the next calendar year?

10. CUGO is a 20-year-old, four-partner, equal capital and equal profit-sharing general partnership. Since formation, it has used a June 30 fiscal year. The four individuals that started the partnership have remained with CUGO since its formation and are partners today. Each partner has a different tax year that ends between July 1 and December 31. Partner C uses the calendar year. For its fiscal year ending in 1987, CUGO's ordinary income was $100,000, earned at an equal monthly rate, which reflects all partnership transactions. For the following two June 30 fiscal years, CUGO's ordinary annual income is projected to be as follows:

1988   120,000
1989   160,000

CUGO's projections are based on equal monthly earnings and include all estimated transactions of the partnership. No § 444 election is in effect.

a. Assuming that CUGO "cannot" justify using a fiscal year for business purposes and that C wants to avoid income bunching as much as possible, what should C do to minimize the bunching? How much of CUGO'S income will be reported on C's tax returns for 1987–1988 if the above projections are realized? (Changing the partnership agreement and C's tax year are not possibilities.)

b. If C prefers to have as much income as possible reported in the calendar year that includes CUGO's short period year, what should C do relative to CUGO? If C is successful and the above projections are realized, how much of CUGO's income will be reported on C's tax returns for 1987–1988? (Changing the partnership agreement and C's tax year are not possibilities.)

c. If U, G, and O each use a September 30 fiscal year and C uses a December 31 year, how much of CUGO's income is reported on C's tax returns for 1987–1988 if the above projections are realized? Assume that C wants to minimize the effects of income bunching and that changing the partnership agreement and C's tax year are not possibilities.

11. Four Lakes Partnership is owned by four sisters (25% interest each). One sister sells investment property to the partnership for its fair market value of $54,000 (basis of $72,000).

a. How much loss, if any, may this sister recognize?

b. If the partnership later sells the property for $81,000, how much gain must it recognize?

c. If the sister's basis in the investment property were $20,000 instead of $72,000, how much, if any, capital gain would she recognize on the sale?

12. Under a partnership agreement, Q, the owner of a 30% interest in the QPD Partnership, is entitled to a 30% interest in partnership profits. In no event will Q receive less than $100,000. For the current year, the partnership had ordinary income of $200,000 before any adjustment for the minimum payment to Q. As of January 1 of the current year, Q's interest was $30,000. On January 1 of the next year, the partnership distributed the $100,000 promised to Q. All parties use the calendar

year for tax purposes. The partnership uses the accrual method of accounting, and Q uses the cash method.

a. How much income must Q recognize for the current year?

b. What is the nature of Q's income?

c. What will be Q's partnership interest as of December 31 of the current year, assuming the partnership agreement indicates that all unpaid guaranteed payments at year-end are to be treated as a capital contribution by the partner to whom due?

d. Assuming that partners P and D each own a 35% interest in the capital and profits of the partnership, how much income must each report for the current year, and what is the nature of the income?

13. N, an equal partner in the MN Partnership, is to receive a payment of $20,000 for services plus 50% of the partnership's profits or losses. After deducting the $20,000 payment to N, the partnership has a loss of $12,000.

a. How much, if any, of the $12,000 partnership loss will be allocated to N?

b. What is the net income from the partnership that N must report on his personal income tax return?

14. X, who has a partnership interest of $23,000, receives a nonliquidating distribution that consists of cash of $3,000, land parcel A with an adjusted basis of $4,000 and a fair market value of $5,000, and land parcel B with an adjusted basis of $8,000 and a fair market value of $15,000.

a. How much gain, if any, must X recognize on the distribution?

b. What basis will X have in the distributed land parcels?

c. What is X's basis in the partnership interest after the distribution?

15. Assume the same facts as in Problem 14, except that the cash distribution amounts to $13,000 instead of $3,000.

a. How much gain, if any, must X recognize on the distribution?

b. What basis will X have in the land parcels?

c. What is X's basis in the partnership interest after the distribution?

16. FM and FT are equal partners in the calendar year F & F Partnership. FM uses a fiscal year ending June 30, and FT uses a calendar year. FM is paid an annual calendar year salary of $50,000. For the last calendar year, F & F Partnership's taxable income was $40,000. For the current calendar year, the partnership's taxable income is $50,000.

a. What is the aggregate amount of income from the partnership that must be reported by FM for his tax year that ends within the current calendar year?

b. What is the aggregate amount of income from the partnership that must be reported by FT for the current calendar year?

c. If FM's annual salary is increased to $60,000 starting on January 1 of the current calendar year and the taxable income of the partnership for the last year and the current year are the same (i.e., $40,000 and $50,000), what is the aggregate amount of income from the partnership that must be reported by FM for his tax year that ends within the current calendar year?

17. On October 1 of the last calendar year, T is invited to join the partnership of PFK & Associates, a local certified public accounting firm. In exchange for a cash contribution of $10,000 to the partnership, T receives a 5% partnership interest. Before admission, T was employed as one of the partnership's salaried managers and received $2,500

monthly as compensation. As a new partner, T is entitled to monthly cash drawings of $4,000. The partnership has an October 1 to September 30 fiscal year, which the IRS has approved as appropriate for business purposes. It reports profits of $800,000 and $1,000,000, respectively, for its fiscal years ending September 30 of the current and next calendar years.

a. Assuming partner T is a cash basis calendar year taxpayer who withdraws $4,000 per month, how much income from the partnership must he report for the last calendar year?

b. For the current calendar year?

18. Assume that the PFK & Associates partnership described in Problem 17 purchased $100,000 of new equipment on December 1 of the last calendar year and the property was to be assigned a five-year cost recovery life. No other § 179 assets were acquired.

a. If the partnership properly elects to treat $10,000 of the investment in the new equipment as a § 179 deduction, what will be T's share of the qualifying investment in § 179 property?

b. On which personal income tax returns of T must the above item be reported?

19. For each of the following independent statements, indicate whether the statement is true or false:

a. The principal purpose for requiring a partnership to file a tax return is to make certain the partnership pays all income taxes that are due.

b. Dividends received by a partnership from a domestic corporation, when all of the partners are individuals, are excluded from the computation of the partnership's ordinary income on page 1 of Form 1065 and are separately reported on Schedule K–1.

c. When a partner's cash withdrawals exceed the partner's interest basis, determined at the end of the year before considering the withdrawals, the partner must recognize a gain.

d. A new partner that acquired a 20% interest in the partnership on the last day of the partnership's tax year is entitled to deduct 20% of the partnership's loss for the year, assuming the partner's interest basis is sufficient to absorb the partner's share of the loss.

e. When a partner contributes appreciated land to a partnership for a capital interest and the partnership at a later date sells the land for an amount above the partnership's basis in the land but less than the land's fair market value on the day it was contributed to the partnership, generally all of the gain is allocated to the partner that contributed the property.

f. When the majority partners are on different tax years, the taxable year of a partnership must be the same as that of the principal partners when they are all on the same tax year.

g. With respect to a partner who dies, the partnership's tax year closes on the date of the partner's death unless the partnership agreement contains a clause that prevents the closing.

h. T, the son of a 52% partner in the XYZ Partnership, sells property to the partnership at a loss of $2,000. The son is not a partner in the partnership. All of the loss from the sale is disallowed to the son.

20. For each of the following independent statements, indicate whether the tax attribute is applicable to regular corporations (C), partnerships (P), both business forms (B), or neither business form (N):

    a. Restrictions are placed on the type and number of owners.

    b. Business income will be taxable to the owners rather than to the entity.

    c. Distributions of earnings to the owners will result in a tax deduction to the entity.

    d. The source characteristics of an entity's income flow through to the owners.

    e. Capital gains are subject to tax at the entity level.

    f. Organization costs can be amortized over a period of 60 months or more.

21. R, M, and T formed the RMT Partnership at the start of the current year to operate a bookstore in a local shopping mall. Each individual contributed cash of $50,000 for a one-third interest in the partnership's capital, profits, and losses. The partnership agreement indicated that the partners would earn interest on their beginning capital contributions of 4% and that for subsequent years they were to earn interest on their beginning-of-the-year capital balances at this same rate. So that RMT would have sufficient working capital, the partnership borrowed another $50,000 from the bank. The books and records of RMT for the current year disclosed the following items of income and expense:

Book sales	$250,000
Returns	(5,000)
Cost of goods sold	177,500
Depreciation of store equipment	15,000
Interest on loan	5,000
Interest on partners' capital accounts	6,000
Rental of office space	14,400
Utilities	9,000
Charitable contribution to Salvation Army	3,000
Interest earned on bank passbook account	1,400
Interest on City of Chicago tax-exempt bonds	900
Gain on sale of equipment held seven months	300

    a. What was the aggregate amount of gross income of RMT for the current year?

    b. What was the taxable income of RMT for the current year?

    c. How is R's share of the partnership items reported on R's Schedule K–1 of Form 1065?

22. E and Z are equal partners in the EZ Partnership. At the beginning of the current year, E's capital account has a balance of $10,000, and the partnership has debts of $30,000 payable to unrelated parties. The following information about EZ's operations for the current year is obtained from the partnership's records:

Taxable income	$48,000
Tax-exempt interest income	5,000
§ 1245 gain	4,000
§ 1231 gain	6,200
Long-term capital gain	500
Long-term capital loss	100
Short-term capital loss	250
Charitable contribution to Girl Scouts	800
Cash distribution to E	10,000

Assume none of the property was contributed by the partners and year-end partnership debt payable to unrelated parties is $24,000.

a.   What is E's basis in the partnership interest at the beginning of the year?

b.   What is E's basis in the partnership interest at the end of the current year?

23. R, A, and M, each a calendar year taxpayer, together form the equal RAM Partnership on January 1 of the current year to manufacture wooden toys. R and A each contribute $25,000 for their partnership interest, and M contributes land held for investment. The land, which was encumbered by a $9,000 first mortgage, was purchased by M two years ago for $15,000 and had a fair market value at the contribution date of $34,000. RAM elects to use the cash method of accounting for everything except its inventories, for which it uses the accrual method of accounting.

Each partner agrees to work 40 hours per week without pay at the partnership's manufacturing and selling activities. However, the three agree that R is to handle the accounting aspects of the business and is to be paid a salary of $100 per month for this work. R's accounting work assignment started the moment the partnership was formed. No other salaries are to be paid to partners.

Shortly after formation, RAM opens a checking account and deposits $50,000. It then sells the land for $34,000, pays off the mortgage, and places the net proceeds in the checking account. It rents an old store building, a vacant lot next to the building, display cases and racks, woodworking equipment, and a cash register. It makes arrangements with the telephone, electric, and water companies for the installation and turn-on of appropriate utilities. Finally, it purchases $10,000 of wood for proposed toy projects, and the partners start making and selling toys.

The first year's operations are more successful than the partners had imagined. The following information summarizes RAM's transactions for the current year:

Contribution of wood to Salvation Army for small building project:	
Cost of wood	$ 6,000
Fair market value	6,500
Rental expenses	4,500
Sales	150,000
Sales returns	500
Supplies used	800
Utilities	3,200
Wood purchases (including initial $10,000 purchase)	90,000
Wood taken home by M for personal use project	100
Miscellaneous expenses	900

At the end of the year, RAM has on hand $7,000 of raw lumber and $4,000 of finished and unsold toys. No work is in process at year-end. The bank reconciliation indicates that the cash balance in the checking account at year-end is $36,000. M's salary had been paid regularly on the 28th of every month. The remaining cash had been withdrawn in equal amounts by each partner at the same time each month. All sales had been for cash, and no unpaid invoices for wood exist at year-end.

a. What is each partner's interest in RAM immediately after formation?

b. What is each partner's interest in RAM immediately after the land contributed by R is sold and the debt is paid?

c. What is RAM's ordinary income for the current year as reported on page 1, line 21, of Form 1065?

d. What is each partner's interest in RAM at the end of the current year?

e. Prepare RAM's financial balance sheet at the end of the current year.

Comprehensive Tax Return Problem

Arden B. Boulder (221–01–9991), Tricia Q. Adams (283–23–8873), and Frank R. Smithy (338–45–6035) are equal general partners in the BAS Partnership, a manufacturer of wooden toys. The partnership's Standard Industrial Classification Code is 2400 (manufacturing-lumber and wood products except furniture), and its employer ID number is 89–672083. The plant and office are located at 2222 West Water Street, Erie, PA 16510. The partnership was formed 10 years ago and started business on March 1 of that year. At that time, it decided to use the calendar year and a hybrid accounting method (i.e., the accrual method of accounting for inventories, payables related to inventory items, sales, and accounts receivables and the cash method of accounting for all other items). For bad debts it uses the direct charge-off method. Under the recovery of capital concept, a deduction for depreciation on its manufacturing and office building is allowable for tax purposes.

BAS does not own an interest in another partnership, nor does it have any investments in foreign countries. Each partner is a designer of toys and a supervisor of production. Thus, BAS is not a passive activity for the three partners.

Since Arden Boulder agreed to keep the partnership's books, prepare financial statements, and prepare and file all tax returns, the partners agreed that he would be paid a salary. The following information was taken from the books and records of BAS for the current year:

Toy sales	$402,780
Toy returns from retailers for credit	4,220
Cost of goods sold	241,668
Dividends received on General Motors stock	550
Salaries and wages to factory employees	55,000
Salary to Arden Boulder for keeping books	10,000
Rent for manufacturing equipment	8,000
Total depreciation on building	6,500
Depreciation on building which is part of the cost of goods sold	4,200
Bad debts	1,000
Utilities (90% for factory)	6,000
Insurance expense for current year (90% for factory)	3,200
Real estate taxes (90% for factory)	3,000
Charitable contribution to Distressed Orphans Fund, an approved public charity	2,000
Gain on sale of General Motors stock held long-term	900
Miscellaneous expenses	350

The following balances were noted in the accounts of BAS for the current year:

	Start of Year	End of Year
Cash	$ 7,800	?
Accounts receivable from sales	8,350	$ 7,100
Inventories (at cost)	33,000	30,000
General Motors stock (cost)	3,700	–0–
Land	10,000	10,000
Building	100,000	100,000
Accumulated depreciation	52,000	58,500
Accounts payable for inventory items	2,550	2,900
Boulder, capital	36,100	?
Adams, capital	36,100	?
Smithy, capital	36,100	?

The records disclosed that each partner withdrew $25,000 in cash during the current year. Other than the $25,000 withdrawal by each partner and the salary payment to Arden Boulder of $10,000, no other cash or property payments were made to the partners during the current year. The partnership tax return (Form 1065) is filed with the IRS Service Center in Cincinnati, Ohio.

Required:

a. Prepare Form 1065 and Schedule K for the BAS Partnership for the current year. Do not supply answers to questions where appropriate data is not supplied.

b. Prepare Schedule K–1 for Arden B. Boulder for the current year.

Research Problems

Research Problem 1. XL was the promoter of a new indoor lobster-growing and harvesting business in northern Minnesota. He decided that the business should operate as a general partnership. With two other individuals, he formed the GP Partnership.

The partnership agreement provided that XL was to receive 20% of GP's profits, acquire appropriate assets for partnership operations, oversee the development and operation of the properties, and bear 100% of the cost of organizing and syndicating the partnership. The agreement also indicated that subscriptions and additional contributions for the partnership should be made by selected broker-dealers on a best efforts basis, for commissions of 3% of the amount secured, and that XL was to bear all sales commissions. For providing these services to GP, the partnership agreement indicated that XL would receive a management fee equal to the cost of the services provided. The management fee is to be in addition to 20% of the profits after deducting the management fee.

During the first and second year of GP's life, XL incurred several expenditures related to the partnership's organization and syndication, including the following payments:

	Year	
	First	Second
Legal and professional fees	$ 5,000	$ 5,000
Commissions to broker-dealers	15,000	25,000
XL's share arrangement	7,500	7,500

The legal and professional fees represent organization expenses of the partnership. The other items represent syndication expenses incurred in the solicitation of subscriptions to the partnership.

XL prepared his own tax returns and those of the partnership for the first and second tax years. On his own Form 1040 tax returns for these years, he reported the full amount of the payments received from the partnership and claimed deductions for like amounts, since the partnership agreement stated that he was to bear all of these costs. On the partnership return (Form 1065), he deducted the same amounts as management fees.

In the third year, XL has started to be concerned that he didn't report the above items properly on his tax returns and those of the partnership. He has contacted you, a local tax adviser, to determine if he properly reported the items for the first and second years on both his own tax returns and those of the partnership. If the tax adviser determines that there is a problem with his reporting, XL wants to know about all available elections for himself and the partnership and what he should do from a Federal income tax standpoint to correct the situation.

Partial list of research aids:

§§ 707(a) and (c) and § 709.

Reg. § 1.709–2(a).

Cagle v. Comm., 76–2 USTC ¶9672, 38 AFTR2d 76–5834, 539 F.2d 409 (CA–5, 1976).

Research Problem 2.   R contributed $50,000 for an interest in the RM Partnership. In its first year of operations, RM incurred legal fees of $2,000 for services incident to the organization of the partnership. R's share of these legal fees was $1,000. On its tax return for the first year of operations, RM did not elect to amortize the legal fees as organization expense under § 709. Toward the end of the third year of operations, RM decided to wind up the business and liquidate. Based on R's capital account at the end of the third operating year, RM made a final liquidating distribution to R of $90,000. In determining RM's taxable income for its final tax year (the third year), its accountant deducted the $2,000 of organization legal fees on Form 1065 as a § 165 loss. R has asked you, her tax adviser, to determine how she should handle her $1,000 share of these legal fees on her Form 1040.

Partial list of research aids:

§§ 165 and 709.

Reg. §§ 1.709–1(b)(2) and 1.709–1(c).

Research Problem 3.   X is a partner in the two-person general partnership of XY which started business five years ago. The partners have agreed to share all profits and losses equally. The partnership and the partners use the cash basis and calendar year. The accounting books and records of the partnership are maintained by an employee. All sales of the partnership are for cash. X and Y participate in the management and operations of the business, and each sells goods to customers and makes cash collections.

Two years ago, Y sold goods to customers and collected related cash which was not reported to the partnership's bookkeeper. These sales and collections amounted to $100,000. Y used some of the embezzled funds to cover his living expenses on a winter vacation to Mexico and Las Vegas. Y lost the remainder of the funds while gambling in Las Vegas. For the year of the embezzlement, the partnership's bookkeeper prepared the tax returns of the partnership and the two partners, and reviewed the returns with them before they were signed, dated, and filed. These returns did not include the embezzled funds.

In the current year, the IRS was auditing the records of the XY Partnership and its partners and discovered the unreported sales. The IRS claims that X must include $50,000 (50% of $100,000) in his income for the year the embezzlement took place. X does not feel that he is receiving fair treatment from the IRS and contacts you for tax advice as to whether he must report $50,000 of additional partnership income from the embezzlement year.

Partial list of research aids:

U.S. v. Basye, 73–1 USTC ¶ 9250, 31 AFTR2d 73–802, 93 S.Ct. 1080 (USSC, 1973).

9 Partnerships: Transfer of Partnership Interests; Family and Limited Partnerships

Objectives

Explain the tax consequences that result from the sale or exchange of a partnership interest.

Compare the disposition of interest by gift, by death, and by abandonment.

Explain how the liquidation of a partnership is treated.

Describe the special constraints that exist in a family partnership and in a limited partnership.

Outline

Sale of a Partnership Interest
General Rules
Effect of § 751 Assets

Exchange of Partnership Interests
Transfers to Controlled Corporations
Like-Kind Exchanges

Other Dispositions
Gift
Death of a Partner
Abandonment or Forfeiture

Liquidating and Disproportionate Distributions
Review of Nonliquidating Distributions
Nature of Liquidating Distributions

Liquidating Distributions of Money
Liquidating Distributions of Property
Disproportionate Distributions

Optional Adjustments to Property Basis
Sale or Exchange of an Interest
Partnership Distributions
Making the Election

Special Problems
Family Partnerships
Limited Partnerships

Tax Planning Considerations
Sales and Exchanges of Interests
Planning Distributions
Other Partnership Interests

Chapter 9 reviews the tax consequences of partnership interest transfers and the special problems confronted by family and limited partnerships.

Sale of a Partnership Interest

A partner's interest, much like a shareholder's corporate holdings, can be sold or exchanged in whole or in part. As a result of applying both the entity and aggregate concepts, the gain or loss that results from a disposition of a partnership interest may be fragmented into capital gain or loss and ordinary income or loss.

General Rules

Under § 741, a partnership interest is a capital asset, the sale or exchange of which results in capital gain or loss. Such gain or loss is measured by the difference between the amount realized and the selling partner's adjusted basis in the partnership.

Liabilities.   In computing both the amount realized on the sale of a partner's interest and the adjusted basis of the sold interest, the selling partner takes into account partnership liabilities. The effect of changes in partnership liabilities was discussed in Chapter 8 under Formation—Basis of Partnership Interest. Likewise, the purchasing partner includes any assumed indebtedness as a part of the consideration paid for the partnership interest.

Example 1   C originally invested $50,000 in cash for a one-third interest in the accrual basis CDE Partnership. During the aggregate period of membership, C's share of partnership income was $90,000. Over that same period, C withdrew $60,000. C's capital account balance is now $80,000, and partnership liabilities are $45,000, of which C's share is $15,000. Thus, C's inside and outside bases in the partnership are $95,000 ($80,000 capital account plus $15,000 share of partnership debts). C sells his partnership interest to F for $110,000 cash, with F assuming C's share of partnership liabilities. The total amount realized by C is $125,000 ($110,000 cash received plus $15,000 of partnership debts transferred to F). C's gain on the sale is $30,000 ($125,000 realized less adjusted basis of $95,000). □

Example 2   Assuming the same facts as in Example 1, what is F's outside basis in the new DEF Partnership? Since F did not contribute money or other property to the partnership, § 722 does not apply. F's outside basis equals $125,000 (cash paid of $110,000 plus assumed partnership debt of $15,000). Since there were no transactions with the partnership other than a name change, F's inside basis equals C's old inside basis of $95,000. □

Several related effects that result from the sale or exchange of a partnership interest are discussed in the following sections.

Variance in Basis.   In Example 2, F's outside basis in the DEF Partnership is $30,000 greater than F's proportionate share of the basis in underlying partnership assets (i.e., an amount equal to F's $95,000 inside basis and the basis used to measure C's gain on the sale). To correct this discrepancy, F may be entitled to a special basis adjustment under § 743(b). The requirements and procedures for making such an adjustment are discussed under Optional Adjustments to Property—Sale or Exchange of an Interest.

Tax Years That Close.   For the partner disposing of an entire interest, the partnership's tax year closes as of the sale date. If the partnership uses an IRS-approved business purpose fiscal year and the partner uses a calendar year, income bunching may take place, because the selling partner's distributive share of partnership income for the closed tax year is reported in that partner's tax year that includes the sale date.

Example 3   Assume the same facts as in Example 1, except that the CDE Partnership had earned income of $12,000 as of the sale date of C's entire interest. Since the partnership's tax year closes with respect to C, $4,000 of partnership income is reported in C's tax year that includes the sale date, plus the income share from the last partnership year that may have closed in this tax year. C's capital account and interest basis are both increased by $4,000, and gain on the sale is reduced correspondingly. □

Additionally, the sale or exchange of a partnership interest may result in a termination of the entire partnership. Recall from Chapter 8 under Operation—Close of Tax Year, that the sale or exchange of 50 percent or more of the total interest in partnership capital and profits within any 12-month period terminates the partnership. As a result, the partnership's tax year ends and income bunching may take place, because all partners are required to report their share of profits up to the date of termination. If the reconstituted partnership wants to use the same fiscal year as did the previous entity, it must apply for IRS permission, although approval is not guaranteed. Thus, great care should be exercised in effecting the disposition of a partner's interest if it represents a 50 percent or greater interest in capital and profits or if the sum of the transfers within any 12-month period is expected to do so.

Example 4   Assume the same facts as in Example 1, except that three months after C's interest is sold to F, D's one-third interest is sold to G. As a result of D's sale, two thirds of the interest in capital and profits of the old CDE Partnership has been sold within a 12-month period, and the DEF Partnership is deemed to have terminated when D's interest is sold. D, E, and F must report their ratable share of partnership income or loss on termination. However, if, three months after F acquired C's interest in the CDE Partnership, F sold this interest to G (rather than D's sale to G), the DEF Partnership would not terminate.[1] □

ITC Recapture.   The selling partner's share of the investment tax credit (ITC) that was passed through from the partnership may be recaptured in whole or in part because the appropriate holding period for related property has not been met.

---

1. Reg. § 1.708–1(b)(ii).

Under the aggregate concept of partnerships, the selling partner is treated as having sold an undivided interest in each partnership asset. If the selling partner's interest in the general profits of the partnership or in the particular item of property on which the ITC was claimed is reduced below two thirds of the partner's interest determined at the time the property was placed in service, the selling partner is considered to have disposed of a like portion of the ITC property, and the recapture rules are triggered. An exception to these recapture rules exists for a partnership interest transferred between corporate partners who are members of the same affiliated group filing a consolidated tax return.[2]

Effect of § 751 Assets

A major exception to capital gain or loss treatment on the sale or exchange of a partnership interest arises when the partnership possesses hot assets. Recall from Chapter 8 that hot assets cause ordinary income to be recognized.

Technically, § 751 provides that an amount realized from the sale of a partnership interest attributable to *unrealized receivables* or *substantially appreciated inventory* is treated as received from the sale of a noncapital asset. The principal purpose of this provision is to prevent the conversion of ordinary income into capital gain through the sale of a partnership interest. It also applies to partnership distributions that have the effect of a disposition of ordinary income assets.

Unrealized Receivables. The term "unrealized receivables" generally includes receivables from the sales of ordinary income property and rights to payments for services. Sometimes the method of accounting, the nature of the property, or the property's holding period affects whether an item is an unrealized receivable. For instance, under the cash method of accounting, trade receivables from inventory sales and from services rendered (including related notes receivable) are included in the term, while under the accrual method they are not. The gain element in installment receivables from the sale of capital assets or § 1231 assets is excluded, but that which relates to ordinary income is included in unrealized receivables.

The term "unrealized receivables" includes, in addition to the preceding items, the recapture potential from the assumed disposition at fair market value of the following items, and other, less commonly encountered, recapture provisions:

1. Mining property, to the extent of recaptured exploratory expenditures.
2. Real and personal property, to the extent of recaptured depreciation.
3. Oil, gas, and geothermal property, to the extent of recaptured intangible drilling and development costs.

Substantially Appreciated Inventory. The term "substantially appreciated inventory" includes virtually all partnership property except money, capital assets, and § 1231 property.[3] Specifically, the term includes inventory and

---

2. Reg. §§ 1.47–6 and 1.1502–3(f)(2)(i).
3. Reg. § 1.751–1(d).

other similar noncapital and non-Section 1231 assets. Accounts and notes receivable of an accrual basis partnership are included in the definition of inventory under § 751(d), since they are neither capital assets nor § 1231 assets.

Note that this definition is broad enough to include all items considered to be unrealized receivables. The disadvantage of including unrealized receivables in inventory can be seen when a determination is made as to whether the inventory is substantially appreciated. Because unrealized receivables usually are included at a zero basis in the tests to determine if the inventory is substantially appreciated, they greatly enhance the possibility of this event's occurring.

Inventory items are considered to be substantially appreciated if, at the time of their sale or distribution, their aggregate fair market value exceeds 120 percent of their total adjusted basis to the partnership *and* if their fair market value is more than 10 percent of the fair market value of all partnership property other than money.[4] In applying these tests, inventory items are evaluated as a group rather than individually. If there is substantial appreciation of all inventory items taken collectively, each item will be treated as substantially appreciated, even if a specific item has not appreciated at all.

Section 751 Applied. The application of § 751 to the sale of a partner's interest is illustrated in Examples 5 through 8, and its effect upon certain partnership distributions is discussed under Liquidating and Disproportionate Distributions.

Example 5   XYZ is a cash basis calendar year partnership that provides educational consulting services. The three equal partners of XYZ are full-time employees of a local university. None of the partners contributed property to the partnership for a capital interest. They did, however, agree to share all profits and losses equally, since all services provided by the partnership are rendered equally by the partners. The following balance sheet represents the status of the partnership at the end of last year:

	Adjusted Basis Per Books	Market Value
Receivable for services rendered	$ –0–	$30,000
Total	$ –0–	$30,000
Capital accounts		
X	$ –0–	$10,000
Y	–0–	10,000
Z	–0–	10,000
Total	$ –0–	$30,000

---

4. Reg. § 1.471–4. For this purpose, use original asset costs, without regard to special partnership basis adjustments, and inventory bid prices for quantities representing typical purchases.

Z has accepted a position at another university and wants to sell his interest in XYZ to R for its fair market value. X and Y agree to accept R as a partner. On January 5 of the current year, R pays Z $10,000 in cash for the partnership interest. At the sale date, and at the end of the last year, XYZ had no debts outstanding. Section 751 applies to the sale because the partnership's one and only asset is hot (i.e., it will generate ordinary income when it is collected). Although the sale of a partnership interest generally results in a capital gain or loss, the $10,000 gain on the sale of Z's interest (selling price of $10,000 less outside basis of $0) is all ordinary income. If Z had remained in the partnership and the partnership had collected the receivable, Z would have realized ordinary income of $10,000 [($30,000 less zero basis) × ⅓]. Via § 751, the ordinary income goes to the partner that earned it. □

Example 6

C's interest in the equal ABC Partnership is sold to D for $17,000 cash. On the sale date, the partnership's cash basis balance sheet reflects the following:

Assets	Adjusted Basis Per Books	Market Value
Cash	$10,000	$10,000
Accounts receivable (for services)	–0–	30,000
Other assets	14,000	20,000
Total	$24,000	$60,000

Liabilities and Capital		
Liabilities	$ 9,000	$ 9,000
Capital accounts		
A	5,000	17,000
B	5,000	17,000
C	5,000	17,000
Total	$24,000	$60,000

Section 751(a) applies to the sale, because the partnership has unrealized receivables. The total amount realized by C is $20,000 (cash price of $17,000 plus $3,000 of debt assumed by D). C's one-third interest includes $10,000 of market value in the receivables. Consequently, $10,000 of the $20,000 realized from the sale must be considered as received in exchange for C's interest in the receivables. The remaining $10,000 is treated as received in exchange for a capital asset.

C's inside basis is $8,000 (capital account of $5,000 plus $3,000 debt share). No portion of this basis can be attributed to the unrealized receivables, since they have a zero basis to the partnership. Thus, the full

$10,000 received for the receivables is ordinary income ($10,000 less related zero basis).

C's entire basis of $8,000 is treated as being in non-Section 751 property and is applied against the remaining $10,000 received from the sale (amount realized of $20,000 less $10,000 allocated to hot assets). Thus, C also incurs a $2,000 capital gain ($10,000 less related $8,000 basis).[5] ☐

Example 7

Assume the same facts as in Example 6, except that C's basis in partnership property (other than unrealized receivables) is $10,000 instead of $8,000. Under these circumstances, C's capital gain or loss is zero. C still has $10,000 of ordinary income because of the unrealized receivables.

If C's basis in the partnership interest is $11,000 (instead of $10,000), C incurs a capital loss of $1,000 which should not be combined with the $10,000 of ordinary income from the sale of unrealized receivables. In this situation, the total gain on the sale of $9,000 ($20,000 amount realized less C's basis of $11,000) is fragmented into two distinct parts—ordinary income and capital loss. ☐

Example 8

Q sells his one-third interest in QPD, a cash basis calendar year partnership, to V for $10,000 cash. The balance sheet of QPD immediately before the sale is as follows:

	Adjusted Basis Per Books	Market Value
Cash	$ 3,000	$ 3,000
Land	3,000	6,000
Receivable	–0–	7,000
Inventory	12,000	14,000
Total	$18,000	$30,000
Capital accounts		
Q	$ 6,000	$10,000
P	6,000	10,000
D	6,000	10,000
Total	$18,000	$30,000

If § 751 is to apply to the sale, the partnership must have unrealized receivables, substantially appreciated inventory, or both. The receivable qualifies as a hot asset by itself, but the *inventory standing alone does not pass the two tests for substantial appreciation.* However, when the receivable is added to the inventory, the aggregate fair market value of the assets is $21,000 (account receivable of $7,000 + inventory of $14,000) and the two tests are passed. Thus, the inventory is a hot asset.

---

5. Reg. § 1.751–1(g) (Ex. 1).

	Market Value	Adjusted Basis			Market Value
Receivable	$ 7,000	$ –0–		All assets	$30,000
Inventory	14,000	12,000		Less: Cash	3,000
Total	$21,000	$12,000		Noncash assets	$27,000
		×120%			× 10%
		$14,400			$ 2,700

Test passed because	Test passed because
$21,000 > $14,400	$21,000 > $2,700

At this point, all assets can be classified as either § 751 or non-Section 751.

	§ 751 Assets	Non- § 751 Assets	Adjusted Basis Per Books	Total Market Value	Q's One-Third Share
Cash		$ 3,000	$ 3,000	$ 3,000	$ 1,000
Land		3,000	3,000	6,000	2,000
Receivable	$ –0–		–0–	7,000	2,333
Inventory	12,000		12,000	14,000	4,667
Total	$12,000	$ 6,000	$18,000	$ 30,000	
Q's one-third share	$ 4,000	$ 2,000	$ 6,000	$ 10,000	$10,000

Q allocates the $10,000 amount realized from the sale between § 751 and non-Section 751 assets and compares the allocated amounts with his share of the related adjusted basis. As a result, Q has ordinary income of $3,000 and a $1,000 capital gain.

	§ 751 Assets	Non- § 751 Assets	Total
Selling price	$ 7,000	$ 3,000	$10,000
Q's one-third share	4,000	2,000	6,000
	$ 3,000	$ 1,000	$ 4,000
	Ordinary Income	Capital Gain	

Tax Reporting.   When a partnership owns hot assets, partners who sell or exchange a partnership interest must promptly notify the partnership of such transfers. After the notification is received, the partnership must file an information return with the IRS for the calendar year in which such transfers took place. The return will contain the names and addresses of the transferors and transferees and such other information prescribed by statutory Regulations. In addition, each person whose name is shown on the calendar year return is to be furnished the name and address of the partnership making the return and the information shown on the return with respect to such person. To avoid incurring any reporting penalties, Regulations under §§ 6050K and 6678 should be consulted when hot assets are present and a partnership interest changes hands.

Exchange of Partnership Interests

On occasion, partnership property or one's partnership interest might be involved in an exchange rather than a sale, such as when a partnership incorporates or when partners in more than one entity swap interests therein. The tax consequences of an exchange usually are the same as those of a sale. The distinction between sales and exchanges is important, because certain exchanges qualify as nontaxable events.

Transfers to Controlled Corporations

Section 351(a) provides that gain or loss is not recognized on the transfer by one or more persons of property to a corporation solely in exchange for stock or securities in that corporation if, immediately after the exchange, such person or persons are in control of the corporation to which the property was transferred.

Partner's Interest Basis.   The transfer of a partnership interest to a corporation will be treated as a nontaxable exchange if the conditions of § 351 are met. The transferor partner generally recognizes gain to the extent that any debt assumed by the corporation or debt to which the partner's interest is subject exceeds the interest.

All items of partnership income or loss, deduction, or credit attributable to the transferred interest are apportioned between the transferor partner and the corporation. Moreover, if the partnership interest transferred represented 50 percent or more of the total interest in capital and profits, the partnership is terminated. When gain is recognized in the transfer of a partnership interest to a controlled corporation, determining its character requires an allocation similar to that presented in Example 8 in connection with the sale of a partnership interest.

Incorporation.   When a cash basis partnership incorporates and normal operating debts (e.g., salaries and wages due employees, unpaid utilities, and rents due for the use of property) exist that exceed the basis of transferred property, the general rules of § 351 trigger gain recognition. However, if such debt constitutes either ordinary payments to a partner or an item that otherwise would be deductible, no gain is recognized.

Incorporation Methods.   If the partners decide to incorporate their business, at least three alternative methods might be used to accomplish the desired change in form:

1. Each partner's interest is transferred to the corporation in exchange for stock under § 351. As a result, the partnership terminates, and the corporation owns all partnership assets.
2. The partnership transfers all of its assets to the corporation in exchange for stock and the assumption of partnership liabilities. The stock then is distributed to the partners in proportion to their partnership interests.
3. The partnership makes a pro rata distribution of all of its assets and liabilities to its partners in complete liquidation. The partners then transfer their undivided interests in the assets and liabilities to the corporation in exchange for stock under § 351.

Assuming that existing partnership debt was not created in an unwarranted tax avoidance scheme and that it does not exceed the basis of transferred assets, none of the three incorporation methods generate a recognized gain or loss. They do, however, cause different tax results.[6] Thus, selecting the appropriate incorporation method is crucial.

If the corporation plans to issue § 1244 stock, the original shareholders, not the partnership, must be partners. Otherwise, any ordinary loss benefits of the stock issue will be forfeited when the partners become shareholders. If an S election is to be made by the corporation after the partnership's assets are received, such an election will be invalid if the partnership is the shareholder.[7] If the corporation is already in existence and operates under an S election, the election will terminate if the partnership is a shareholder. Consequently, when a partnership is to be incorporated with § 1244 stock or an S election is desirable, the partnership should undertake method 3 and make a pro rata distribution of all of its assets and liabilities to its partners in a complete liquidation. The partners then should transfer these items to the corporation in a § 351 exchange. Transfers to controlled corporations and § 1244 stock are discussed in Chapter 3. S corporations are discussed in Chapter 10.

Like-Kind Exchanges

Another attempt to achieve nonrecognition treatment involves the exchange of an interest in one partnership for an interest in another partnership. If the partnership interests exchanged could qualify as like-kind property, no gain or loss would be recognized.

The like-kind exchange rules do not apply to the exchange of interests in different partnerships. However, these rules can apply to exchanges of interests in the same partnership. Moreover, according to the IRS, under certain circumstances, a general partnership interest may be converted into a limited partnership interest in the same partnership without gain or loss recognition (and vice versa).[8]

---

6. Rev.Rul. 84–111, 1984–2 C.B. 88.
7. Reg. § 1.1371–1(e).
8. § 1031(a)(2)(D) and Rev.Rul. 84–52, 1984–1 C.B. 157.

Other Dispositions

Gift

Generally, the gift of a partnership interest results in neither gain nor loss recognized to the donor. If the donor's entire interest in the partnership is transferred, all items of partnership income, loss, deduction, or credit attributable to the interest transferred are prorated between the donor and donee in accordance with § 706(d).

Several exceptions exist to the general rule of treating gifts as nontaxable transfers. If the partnership uses the cash method of accounting and has accounts receivable at the time of transfer, the gift may be considered an anticipatory assignment of income by the donor. Similarly, if the partnership has installment notes receivable, the gift of an interest may be considered a disposition thereof.[9] In addition, if the donor's share of partnership liabilities exceeds the donor's basis in the partnership, the gift will be treated as part gift and part sale.[10] Because of these possibilities for gain or loss recognition, the donor should exercise caution in transferring a partnership interest by gift.

Death of a Partner

Many of the tax issues associated with the death of a partner were discussed in Chapter 8 under Operation—Close of Tax Year. Recall that unless there is a sales agreement among the partners that the deceased partner's interest be sold immediately to the remaining partners for a formula or fixed price on the date of the deceased partner's death, the partnership's tax year does not close. Furthermore, the transfer of a partnership interest to a deceased partner's estate or other successor is not considered a sale or exchange. Even if the deceased partner's interest is 50 percent or more of the total interest in partnership capital and profits, § 708(b)(1) does not terminate the entire partnership. The death of a partner does not trigger recapture of the investment tax credit or result in a taxable disposition of installment obligations.

In certain professional partnerships, local law prohibits an estate or other successor from continuing as a partner (beyond a certain time period). In other cases, the remaining partners may wish to buy out or liquidate the deceased partner's interest in the partnership. In such situations, usually there is a provision in the partnership agreement specifying a valuation method and the manner in which the deceased partner's interest will be terminated.

If the remaining partners choose to purchase the deceased partner's interest, basis is determined under § 1014. The purchasing partners may be entitled to a special basis adjustment under § 743 for their respective shares of the interest acquired. If the partnership interest is to be liquidated, decisions regarding the form and time of liquidating distributions must be made. If the estate or other successor is to continue as a partner, a special basis adjustment may be available to reflect the difference between the fair market value of its share of partnership assets and the partnership's basis in these assets.

9. Rev.Rul. 60–352, 1960–2 C.B. 208.
10. Rev.Rul. 75–194, 1975–1 C.B. 180.

Abandonment or Forfeiture

Historically, an abandonment or forfeiture of a partnership interest is a rare event. The abandonment or forfeiture of a partnership interest results in an ordinary loss deduction when the partner's share of partnership debt is zero.[11] Although a partnership interest is a capital asset, the abandonment loss generates an ordinary loss, because an abandonment is not a sale or exchange.[12]

Liquidating and Disproportionate Distributions

Nonliquidating distributions of money and other property from a partnership were examined in Chapter 8. Distributions that result in the liquidation of a partner's interest or that affect the distributee partner's proportionate interest in hot assets are discussed in the following sections.

Review of Nonliquidating Distributions

No gain or loss is recognized by a partnership on the distribution of money or other property to a partner. Similarly, no gain or loss generally is recognized by a partner receiving such distributions. Specifically, loss is never recognized, and gain is recognized only if *money* received in a distribution exceeds the basis of the partner's interest immediately preceding the distribution. Distributions of property other than money will not result in the recognition of gain or loss to the partner unless they involve disproportionate distributions of hot assets. Any gain recognized is treated as gain from the *sale* or *exchange* of a partnership interest. The character of such gain is determined under rules previously discussed governing the sale of a partnership interest.

Nonliquidating distributions from a partnership reduce the distributee partner's interest (but not below zero) by (1) the sum of money distributed and (2) the basis to such partner of distributed property other than money. The basis of property (other than money) distributed to a partner in a nonliquidating distribution is the asset's adjusted basis to the partnership immediately before the distribution. However, the basis of the property may not exceed the adjusted basis of the partner's interest reduced by any money received in the same transaction.

When the basis of distributed assets is limited by the partner's interest, an allocation of basis must be made. The manner of allocation is discussed in the section of this chapter dealing with liquidating distributions. When unrealized receivables or inventory is not involved, the remaining basis of the partner's interest is allocated to the assets in the ratio of their adjusted bases to the partnership. The holding period of the property received as a distribution includes that of the partnership. Examples 33 to 35 in Chapter 8 illustrate these rules.

---

11. *Gaius G. Gannon,* 16 T.C. 1134 (1951), *acq.,* and *Palmer Hutcheson,* 17 T.C. 14 (1951), *acq.* However, partnership debt was not a problem in these cases.
12. *Edward H. Pietz,* 59 T.C. 207 (1972), and *Milledge L. Middleton,* 77 T.C. 310 (1981), *aff'd per curiam* in 82–2 USTC ¶ 9713, 51 AFTR2d 83–353, 693 F.2d 124 (CA–11, 1982). When the partner holds a share of the entity's debt, the abandonment is treated as a constructive distribution.

The previous discussion of dispositions of partnership interests noted that some distributions can have the effect of a sale or exchange of hot assets. In such cases, § 751 produced a recognition of all ordinary income. When a partner's proportionate share of the hot assets is received in a distribution, § 751 does not apply, and the rules previously outlined generally control the tax consequences of the distribution.

Although a proportionate distribution of hot assets may not immediately result in income recognition, any subsequent disposition of unrealized receivables by the distributee partner triggers full ordinary gain or loss recognition. Similarly, a subsequent sale or exchange of inventory items triggers ordinary gain or loss recognition if the partner sells or exchanges such items within five years of the distribution date.[13] This rule applies to all inventory items regardless of whether they were substantially appreciated.

Example 9   B receives a proportionate share of inventory items (basis of $16,000) in a nonliquidating distribution from the partnership. Fourteen months later, B sells the property for $20,000. Even though the inventory is a capital asset in B's hands and the long-term holding period is met, the $4,000 recognized gain is taxed as ordinary income. ☐

Example 10   Assume the same facts as in Example 9, except that the five-year holding period is met. The $4,000 gain constitutes a long-term capital gain. ☐

Nature of Liquidating Distributions

Distributions in liquidation of partnership interests have a multiple character. First, they are similar to all partnership distributions and generally are treated as a tax-free return of capital. Unlike corporate shareholders, partners may be able to withdraw their investment without tax consequences. Under the general rule, unrealized appreciation or depreciation in the market value of distributed partnership property is not recognized. Consequently, the basis of such property is determined by reference to the property's basis in the hands of the partnership and the basis of the distributee partner's interest before the distribution.

Second, depending upon how the transaction is structured, a liquidating distribution may have the same effect as the sale of a partnership interest. Here, the parties may be required to recognize gain or loss. Third, there are two overriding considerations. All income and expense (or loss) should be recognized at some time, and ordinary income should not be converted into capital gain. Finally, § 761(e) treats any distribution of a partnership interest as an exchange for purposes of the continuation of a partnership, optional adjustments to the basis of partnership property, and any other provision specified in the Regulations.

Liquidating distributions can take several forms. A partner's interest can be liquidated by a series of cash payments or a lump-sum distribution in kind. The cash payments may be based on the partnership's annual income or may

---

13. Reg. § 1.735–1(a)(2). When the distributed inventory is held over five years, the character of any gain or loss is determined by the character of the property in the hands of the distributee.

be a guaranteed payment. Distributions in kind may be a lump sum or one of a series in liquidation of a partnership interest. Since the statutory rules differ with respect to liquidating distributions of money and distributions of other property, the money distributions are given separate treatment.

Liquidating Distributions of Money

The character and treatment of liquidating distributions of money are governed by § 736. Money payments are allocated between amounts paid for the partner's interest in partnership property under § 736(b) and other payments under § 736(a).[14] This allocation generally is made in accordance with the partnership agreement.

Section 736(a) Payments. The receiving partner recognizes ordinary income relative to payments for unrealized receivables and to cash payments for goodwill in excess of the partner's share of the goodwill's basis to the partnership that have not been specifically provided for in the partnership agreement. Such payments are treated in one of the following ways:

—As income distributions, if they are determined by reference to the partnership income, thus reducing the amount of partnership income available to the continuing partners.

—As guaranteed payments, if they are *not* determined by reference to the partnership income, thus producing a deduction from gross income to arrive at the partnership's taxable income.

The receiving partner includes the payments in gross income for the related partnership year that ends with or within the partner's year. As a result, ordinary income is earned on all unrealized receivables as they are realized or collected. For example, depreciation recapture potential is undiminished and results in ordinary income to the partnership when and if the related asset is sold or exchanged.

Section 736(b) Payments. Cash payments for a partner's interest in partnership property are essentially the same as current (nonliquidating) distributions. Such payments do not include the following:

—Payments for unrealized receivables.

—Payments for goodwill in excess of the partner's share of the goodwill's basis to the partnership that have not been specifically provided for in the partnership agreement.

If the partnership agreement provides for goodwill payments to a partner in excess of the partner's share of the partnership basis, such payments consti-

---

14. Reg. § 1.736–1(a)(2).

tute a capital gain. Liquidating cash payments under § 736(b) are generally considered a return of capital to the extent of the partner's basis in the partnership, and gain is recognized to the extent of any excess. If substantially appreciated inventory is present, ordinary income is created in the year received.[15]

Liabilities.   In making computations under § 736, partnership liabilities forgiven or assumed by another party (or by the partnership) are treated as cash withdrawals. Normally, the amount included in the partner's basis for liabilities is the same as the amount considered withdrawn, and the two amounts "wash." When a partner's share of partnership liabilities exceeds the basis of the partner's interest, gain recognized can exceed the cash actually received. This occurs when loan proceeds have been withdrawn by the partners or when cumulative partnership losses have exceeded the partner's capital investment (exclusive of debts).

Lump-sum Payment.   Examples 11 and 12 illustrate the application of § 736 when a lump-sum cash payment is made to eliminate a partner's entire interest and when liabilities are present.

Example 11   At the time T decides to withdraw from the ACT Partnership, the partnership's balance sheet for tax purposes includes the following:

	Adjusted Basis Per Books	Market Value
Assets		
Cash	$ 60,000	$ 60,000
Equipment	30,000	24,000
Building	90,000	120,000
Total	$180,000	$204,000
Liabilities and Capital		
Mortgage payable	$ 60,000	$ 60,000
Capital accounts		
A	40,000	48,000
C	40,000	48,000
T	40,000	48,000
Total	$180,000	$204,000

T's entire interest is liquidated by a lump-sum cash distribution of $48,000 and the assumption of T's share of partnership liabilities by the remaining partners. T's realized gain is computed as follows:

---

15. Reg. § 1.736–1(a)(5).

Amount realized	
Cash	$48,000
Liabilities assumed by other partners ($\frac{1}{3}$ of $60,000), treated as money distributed	20,000
Total realized	$68,000
Less: Basis of partnership interest	
Capital account of $40,000 plus $\frac{1}{3}$ of partnership liabilities	(60,000)
Gain realized	$ 8,000

Assuming no depreciation recapture potential exists for the equipment or building, no hot asset is involved in the liquidation. Thus, T's $8,000 gain is a capital gain from the sale of a partnership interest. If there were any recapture potential, it would be considered an unrealized receivable, and the amount attributable to T's interest therein would be treated as ordinary income under § 736(a). ☐

Example 12   Assume the same facts as in Example 11, except that $15,000 of § 1250 recapture potential exists on the building. T's share, $5,000, is treated as a guaranteed payment, deductible by the partnership. T's realized capital gain is $3,000. Under the general rule, the basis of the building to the partnership is still $90,000, and the recapture potential remains at $15,000. The partnership may elect to adjust its basis in the remaining assets to reflect the gain recognized by the withdrawing partner. ☐

Series of Payments.   When liquidating cash distributions are spread over a number of years, it is necessary to allocate the total amounts paid between § 736(a) and § 736(b) payments. If the partners have dealt at arm's length and specifically agreed to the allocation and timing of each class of payment, such an agreement normally controls the tax consequences.

Example 13   Partner X retires from the equal XYZ Partnership at a time when partnership debt is $90,000. It has been agreed among all of the partners that X's interest in partnership assets, exclusive of unrealized receivables and goodwill, is worth $105,000. To totally liquidate X's interest, it is further agreed that X will be paid $15,000 in cash per year for 10 years and the remaining partners will assume X's share of partnership liabilities, for a total consideration of $180,000 (cash of $150,000 plus $30,000 debt assumption). If the partners agree that the assumption of X's share of liabilities and the first $75,000 of cash payments made by the partnership are to be treated as consideration for X's interest in partnership assets (exclusive of unrealized receivables and goodwill), this agreement controls for tax purposes.

For the first five years, the $105,000 of payments (including the assumption of partnership debts) is treated as liquidating distributions under § 736(b). X recognizes a gain when these payments exceed the basis of his interest, but the partnership is not entitled to any deduction. In each of the next five years, X recognizes ordinary income of $15,000, and the partnership deducts the same amount as a guaranteed payment. □

If the partners do not enter into a specific agreement as to the timing of payments for the two classes, a pro rata part of each payment is treated as a § 736(b) payment and the balance is treated as a § 736(a) payment.

Example 14 Assume the same facts as in Example 13, except that the partners agree to a value of $120,000 (instead of $105,000) for X's interest in partnership assets, exclusive of unrealized receivables and goodwill. Further assume that there is no specific agreement as to the timing of the payments for each class, except that the liabilities are assumed immediately. In this situation, all payments are allocated between § 736(a) and § 736(b). This allocation is made for the cash payments as well as for the debt assumption.

Two thirds ($120,000/$180,000) of each payment is treated as a distribution under § 736(b), and the balance is treated as a guaranteed payment under § 736(a). Relative to the cash payments, $10,000 is treated as a § 736(b) payment, and $5,000 is treated as a § 736(a) payment. □

For a series of § 736 liquidating payments that eliminate a partner's entire interest, the question of imputed interest may arise. If unpaid amounts due to a partner are related to an arm's length loan to the partnership, the rules for below-market rate loans could apply. However, if none of the payments are related to such a loan, apparently the unpaid amounts simply will constitute a § 736(b) distribution or a § 736(a) guaranteed payment.[16]

Contingent Payments. If the total amount of the liquidating payments is contingent on future events, absent a specific agreement to the contrary, all payments are considered as payments for an interest in partnership property under § 736(b) until the total value of such interest has been paid.[17] As in Example 14, if the partners agree on the value of the retiring partner's interest in partnership property, the agreement normally controls for tax purposes.

Example 15 Assume the same facts as in Example 14, except that instead of receiving $15,000 per year, X receives 20% of partnership profits for a period of 10 years. The cash amounts paid under the agreement are as follows:

Year 1—$20,000	Year 6—$ 4,000
Year 2—$35,000	Year 7—$ 9,000
Year 3—$15,000	Year 8—$18,000
Year 4—$10,000	Year 9—$31,000
Year 5—$23,000	Year 10—$26,000

Assuming that the agreed value of X's interest in partnership assets other than unrealized receivables and goodwill was $120,000 less the assumed

16. Prop.Reg. §§ 1.7872–2(a)(1), (b)(3), –4(c)(1), and (c)(2) and Reg. §§ 1.731–1(a)(1) and (c)(2).
17. Reg. §§ 1.736–1(a)(1)(ii) and (b)(5)(ii).

liabilities of $30,000, all payments made for the first four years, plus $10,000 paid in Year 5, are § 736(b) payments. All amounts paid in Years 6 through 10, plus $13,000 paid in Year 5, are treated as ordinary income under § 736(a). ☐

As stated earlier, § 736(b) payments generally are treated in the same manner as current (nonliquidating) cash distributions. They reduce the liquidating partner's basis dollar for dollar and result in income recognition only to the extent of the excess. Such excess is treated as capital gain, except to the extent it is attributable to substantially appreciated inventory. Moreover, liquidating payments for a withdrawing partner's share of unrealized receivables also are treated as ordinary income.

Example 16   Assume the same facts as in Example 15. X's basis in the partnership is $95,000. Since the payments are not fixed or stated in amount, X must use the cost recovery method of accounting for the liquidating payments. The $20,000 of cash received and debt relief of $30,000 in Year 1, plus the $35,000 received in Year 2, and $10,000 of the $15,000 received in Year 3 are treated as a return of capital. This is the same treatment as that given to current cash distributions. Assuming that none of the gain is attributable to substantially appreciated inventory, X recognizes capital gain of $5,000, $10,000, and $10,000 in Years 3, 4, and 5, respectively. [Total § 736(b) payments $120,000 − Basis $95,000 = Capital gain $25,000]. ☐

As an alternative to the cost recovery method described in Example 16, the Regulations allow a withdrawing partner to recognize the gain from a partnership interest in much the same manner as though it were an installment sale.[18] Such treatment is allowed only if the total of § 736(b) payments is a fixed sum *and* the partner elects such treatment for the first taxable year in which such payments are received.

Example 17   Assume the same facts as in Example 16, except that the basis of X's interest is $60,000. X makes the special election. The total § 736(b) payments to be received are $120,000. X treats 50% of each payment as gain and the remaining 50% as a return of capital. This election could also be made for the § 736(b) payments in the circumstances described in Examples 13 through 15. ☐

Liquidating Distributions of Property

In some situations, partnerships find it impractical or undesirable to liquidate a retiring partner's interest solely by cash distributions. Instead, some or all of the withdrawing partner's interest is liquidated through other property distributions. If the partnership does not have § 751 property or if the distributions do not change the proportionate ownership of such property, the tax treatment of liquidating property distributions is essentially the same as current (nonliq-

---

18. Reg. § 1.736–1(b)(6).

uidating) distributions. However, recall that losses are recognized under certain circumstances in liquidating distributions.

Basis of Distributed Property.   Cash distributions reduce the withdrawing partner's basis dollar for dollar and are taken into account before subsequent or contemporaneous distributions of other property. The partner's remaining basis, after reduction by cash distributions, first is allocated to the distributed unrealized receivables and inventory (whether or not substantially appreciated) in an amount equal to the partnership's adjusted basis in such property. If the partnership's bases in the receivables and inventory exceed the partner's remaining interest, the latter is allocated to such assets in the ratio of their adjusted bases to the partnership. Next, if the withdrawing partner has any basis remaining in the partnership after reductions for cash distributions and unrealized receivables and inventory, that basis is allocated to any other assets received in the ratio of their adjusted bases to the partnership.

Gain or Loss Recognition.   Gain is recognized only when the cash received exceeds the partner's interest. Loss is recognized only if the sum of the cash received plus the basis of distributed unrealized receivables and inventory is less than the adjusted basis of the partner's interest before the liquidating distribution and no other property is distributed.

Example 18   When T's basis in her partnership interest is $25,000, T receives cash of $15,000 and a proportionate share of inventory and buildings in a liquidating distribution. The inventory has a basis to the partnership of $20,000 and a fair market value of $30,000. The building's basis is $8,000, and the fair market value is $12,000. The building was depreciated under the straight-line method. Under these circumstances, T does not recognize any gain or loss. After reducing T's basis by the cash received, the remaining $10,000 is allocated to the inventory. The basis of the inventory in T's hands is $10,000, and the basis of the building is zero. Note that $10,000 of the inventory's original basis in the hands of the partnership appears to have been *lost* in the liquidating distribution. As discussed under Optional Adjustments to Property, the partnership may be able to "save" this portion of the inventory's basis by making an election to adjust the basis of its remaining inventory. ☐

Example 19   Assume the same facts as in Example 18, except that there was no inventory and T received two buildings (both of which were depreciated under the straight-line method). Building 1 had a basis of $6,000 to the partnership, and Building 2 had a basis of $9,000. Again, no gain or loss is recognized. The $10,000 basis of T's interest remaining after reduction for the cash received is allocated to the buildings in the ratio of their bases to the partnership. T's basis in Building 1 is $4,000 (6/15 × $10,000) and in Building 2 is $6,000 (9/15 × $10,000). The $5,000 of partnership basis in the buildings that could not be passed on to T may be *lost* in the distribution. ☐

Example 20   When R's basis is $15,000, R receives a liquidating distribution of $7,000 cash and a proportionate share of inventory having a partnership basis of

$3,000 and a fair market value of $10,000. Since R cannot allocate to the inventory more than $3,000 of the $8,000 remaining basis after reduction for cash, he recognizes a $5,000 capital loss on the liquidation. The basis of the inventory is $3,000. □

Example 21   Assume the same facts as in Example 20, except that R receives $19,000 of cash in addition to the inventory. Under these circumstances, R recognizes a capital gain of $4,000 (cash of $19,000 less $15,000 basis), and the inventory is assigned a zero basis. □

Gain realized by the withdrawing partner on the subsequent disposition of inventory is ordinary income unless the disposition occurs more than five years after the distribution. Presumably, anyone who receives the inventory from the withdrawing partner as a gift or inheritance is not bound by the five-year holding period requirement. The withdrawing partner's holding period of all other property received in a liquidating distribution includes the partnership's related holding period.

Disproportionate Distributions

A disproportionate distribution occurs when either less than or more than the partner's proportionate share of the partnership's unrealized receivables and substantially appreciated inventory is received. Recall that absent a special allocation agreement that has economic substance, each partner has an interest in each asset of the partnership (the aggregate concept). Although a partnership interest is a capital asset, remember that gain on the disposition of an interest attributable to unrealized receivables and substantially appreciated inventory is treated as ordinary income. To the extent (1) a partner receives hot assets in exchange for the partner's interest in other property *or* (2) a partner receives other property in exchange for the partner's interest in hot assets, the distribution is treated as a taxable exchange of assets between the partner and the partnership (the entity concept).

Purpose Behind § 751(b).   Section 751(b) was placed in the Code to prevent an arbitrary allocation of ordinary income and capital gain items among partners. For example, substantially appreciated inventory (property with ordinary income potential) might be distributed to a partner in a low tax bracket. At the same time, property with capital gain potential might be retained by the partnership primarily to benefit partners in a higher tax bracket. This example is, in fact, a disproportionate distribution.

Transactions: Real and Fictional.   To understand the tax consequences of a disproportionate distribution of hot assets that terminates a partner's entire interest, it should be noted that two distributions must be considered: a real distribution and a fictional nonliquidating (current) distribution that precedes the real one. In these distributions, the income-generating event takes place when some or all of the assets in the real distribution are transferred to the leaving partner. No income is generated when the fictional distribution takes place.

The starting point in analyzing a disproportionate distribution is to determine the nature and amount of the assets received by the leaving partner in the real distribution. The second step is to determine if the leaving partner's fair market value share of the hot assets received in the real distribution (if any) is equal to, greater than, or less than this partner's undivided fair market value share of the hot assets in the partnership's hands immediately before the fictional and real distributions take place. Ignoring the fictional distribution, if the leaving partner's fair market value ownership in the hot assets is the same before and after the real distribution, the disproportionate distribution rules of § 751 do not apply.

Example 22   The LMN Partnership owns the following:

Assets		
	Adjusted Basis Per Books	Market Value
Trade accounts receivable	$ –0–	$18,000
Land	18,000	36,000
Total	$18,000	$54,000

Liabilities and Capital		
Capital accounts		
L	$ 6,000	$18,000
M	6,000	18,000
N	6,000	18,000
Total	$18,000	$54,000

LMN distributes $18,000 worth of land (non-hot assets) in liquidation of M's entire interest. This is a *disproportionate* distribution, subject to the provisions of § 751. In the fictional distribution, M's share of the accounts receivable is treated as being distributed to M. M is then treated as having sold these receivables to the remaining partnership for an additional $6,000 of land. The partnership is considered to have exchanged $6,000 of land for M's interest in the receivables. M recognizes ordinary income of $6,000 ($6,000 fair market value of land received – $0 basis of M's share of accounts receivable surrendered). M takes a basis of $12,000 in the land.

The partnership recognizes a gain of $3,000 on the exchange ($6,000 fair market value of the excess share of accounts receivable retained by the partnership – $3,000 basis of the portion of land exchanged), and after the distribution, it holds receivables included in the fictional transactions with a basis of $6,000 and land with a basis of $9,000. The capital accounts of L and N are $7,500 each. In addition, the partnership holds $12,000 of other zero-basis receivables. The effect of the liquidation can be analyzed as follows:

M's Proportionate Share	Assets FMV	FMV Received	Fictional Dist. Basis	Sale FMV	Gain (Loss)
Accounts receivable	$ 6,000	$ –0–	$ –0–	$6,000	$6,000*
Land	12,000	18,000	–0–	–0–	N/A
	$18,000	$18,000		$6,000	

* Ordinary income to M under § 751.

L's & N's Proportionate Shares	Assets FMV	FMV Received	Fictional Paid Basis	Received FMV	Gain (Loss)
Accounts receivable	$12,000	$18,000	$ –0–	$ –0–	$ N/A
Land	24,000	18,000	3,000	6,000	3,000**
	$36,000	$36,000		$6,000	

** Nature of gain depends on the nature of assets given up.

Exceptions. A distribution to a partner of property that the partner contributed to the partnership is not considered a § 751 distribution, notwithstanding that the distribution is otherwise disproportionate.

Example 23 Assume the same facts as in Example 22, except that the $18,000 worth of other property distributed to M was originally contributed by M. In this case, neither M nor the partnership recognizes gain or loss. M has a basis of $6,000 in the property distributed. The partnership holds $18,000 of receivables with a basis of zero and other property worth $18,000 with a basis of $9,000. The capital accounts of L and N are $6,000 each. In this case, there appears to have been a "loss" of basis of $3,000 to the partnership without tax benefit ($18,000 original basis – $6,000 basis to withdrawing partner M – $9,000 basis left with the partnership). □

Additionally, § 736(a) distributions are treated as a distribution of profit or as a guaranteed payment, and they are already subject to ordinary income treatment.

Optional Adjustments to Property Basis

Except to the extent that § 751 applies, the basis of property in the hands of a continuing partnership is not adjusted as a result of the transfer of a partnership interest or on account of current or liquidating distributions. In some situations, though, this rule produces inequitable results.

Example 24 A partnership owns a building with an adjusted basis of $300,000 and a fair market value of $900,000. T, an individual, buys a one-third interest in the partnership for $300,000 (an amount equal to one third of the value of the building). Although the price T paid for the interest was based on fair market value, the building's depreciation continues to be determined on the partnership's related adjusted basis of $300,000, of which T's share is only $100,000. ☐

Example 25   To illustrate contrasting results, assume that the building in Example 24 had an adjusted basis of $600,000 and a fair market value of $300,000. Assume also that T purchased the one-third interest for $100,000 (an amount equal to one third of the value of the building). Although the purchase price was based on fair market value, T obtains the benefit of *double* depreciation deductions, since these deductions are calculated on the adjusted basis of the depreciable property ($600,000), which is twice the property's market value. ☐

A result similar to that presented in Example 25 can take place when a partnership redeems a partner's interest with a cash payment that is less than the retiring partner's share of the adjusted basis of the partnership assets. Here, the partnership does not reduce the adjusted basis of its assets for the excess share *not* paid to the retiring partner. If some of the remaining assets are depreciable, the remaining partners will receive larger depreciation deductions (i.e., they will receive depreciation deductions based on their old share of these assets, plus deductions based on the excess share *not* paid to the retiring partner).

In other situations, an effective loss of basis without tax benefits results.

Example 26   Consider again Example 23, where M's interest in the LMN Partnership (which possessed hot assets) was liquidated with a distribution of non-hot assets. Here, L and N have effectively exchanged property with a basis of $9,000 for a partnership interest with a basis of $6,000. Since no gain or loss was recognized, $3,000 of basis was *lost*. However, the bases of the remaining partners' (L and N) interests are not diminshed; each retains a balance of $6,000. Partnership income may be overstated, since it reflects depreciation on $9,000 of other assets instead of the true investment of L and N of $12,000. This point would be even more evident if the partnership had liquidated M's interest for a cash payment of $18,000. The partnership effectively would have paid the full fair market value for M's interest of $6,000 in receivables and $12,000 in other property. Nevertheless, under the general rule, the basis of the receivables is zero and the basis of the other property is $18,000. ☐

To prevent or alleviate the results presented in Examples 24 through 26, § 754 permits partnerships to make a special election under which the basis of partnership assets may be adjusted following either a sale or exchange of an interest or a distribution of partnership property.

Sale or Exchange of an Interest

If an election under § 754 is in effect and if a partner's interest is sold or exchanged, the partner dies, or a § 761(e) distribution of a partnership interest is made, § 743(b) provides that the partnership shall effect one of the following:

1. *Increase* the adjusted basis of partnership property by:

Transferee's interest basis in partnership	$XXX
Less: Transferee's share of adjusted basis of all partnership property	(XXX)
Increase	$XXX

2. *Decrease* the adjusted basis of partnership property by:

Transferee's share of adjusted basis of all partnership property	$XXX
Less: Transferee's interest basis in partnership	(XXX)
Decrease	$XXX

The amount of the increase or decrease constitutes an adjustment affecting the basis of partnership property with respect to the transferee partner only. For purposes of depreciation, depletion, gain or loss, and distributions, the transferee partner has a special basis for those partnership assets whose bases are adjusted. This special basis is the partner's share of the common partnership basis (i.e., the adjusted basis of such assets to the partnership without regard to any special basis adjustment of any transferee) *plus or minus* any special basis adjustments.

Example 27   R is a member of the RST Partnership, and all partners have equal interests in capital and profits. The partnership has made a § 754 election. R's interest is sold to U for $76,000. The balance sheet of the partnership at the date of the sale shows the following:

	Assets Adjusted Basis Per Books	Market Value
Cash	$ 15,000	$ 15,000
Depreciable assets	150,000	213,000
Total	$165,000	$228,000
	Capital	
Capital accounts		
R	$ 55,000	$ 76,000
S	55,000	76,000
T	55,000	76,000
Total	$165,000	$228,000

The § 743(b) adjustment is the difference between the basis of the transferee's interest in the partnership and the transferee's share of the adjusted basis of partnership property. The basis of U's interest is $76,000. U's share of the adjusted basis of partnership property is $55,000. The amount of the adjustment (to be added to the basis of partnership property) is $21,000:

Transferee's interest basis in partnership	$76,000
Less: Transferee's share of adjusted basis of all partnership property	(55,000)
Increase	$21,000

This amount is allocated to partnership property in accordance with the rules set forth in § 755 and the Regulations thereunder.[19] ☐

Partnership Distributions

If an election under § 754 is in effect, the basis of partnership property is increased upon a distribution to a partner under § 734 by the following:

—Any gain recognized by a distributee partner.

—The excess of the adjusted basis of any distributed property to the partnership over the adjusted basis of that property in the hands of the distributee.

Conversely, the basis of partnership property is decreased by the following:

—Any loss recognized by a distributee partner.

—In the case of a liquidating distribution, the excess of the distributee's adjusted basis of any distributed property over the basis of such property to the partnership.

Example 28   R has a partnership basis of $50,000 and receives a building having an adjusted basis to the partnership of $120,000, which terminates R's interest. The building's basis in R's hands is $50,000. If a § 754 election is in effect, the partnership increases the basis of its remaining property by $70,000.

Partnership's adjusted basis in distributed property	$120,000
Less: Distributee's basis in distributed property	(50,000)
Total	$ 70,000

☐

Example 29   Assume the same facts as in Example 28, except that the partnership's basis in the building was $40,000. R's basis in the building is still $50,000,

---

19. Reg. § 1.743–1(b)(1) (Ex. 1).

and the partnership reduces the basis of its remaining property by $10,000:

Distributee's basis in distributed property	$50,000
Less: Partnership's adjusted basis in distributed property	(40,000)
Total	$10,000

Making the Election

An election can be made under § 754 for any year in which a transfer or distribution occurs by attaching a statement to a timely filed partnership return (including extensions). An election is binding for the year for which it is made and for all subsequent years unless the IRS consents to its revocation. Permission to revoke generally is granted for business reasons, such as a change in the nature of the business or an increase in the frequency of interest transfers. Permission is not granted if it appears the primary purpose is to avoid downward adjustments to basis otherwise required under the election.[20]

Special Problems

Family Partnerships

Family partnerships require special treatment because of abuses that may arise from the close association of partners. Distributive shares of partnership income may be channeled to low tax bracket partners (e.g., children) who perform little, if any, real service for the partnership.

Family Members.   The family, for purposes of § 704(e), includes only husband and wife, ancestors, lineal descendants, and any trusts for the primary benefit of such persons. Brothers and sisters are not included. A family member will be recognized as a partner in either of the following cases:

—Capital is a material income-producing factor and the family member's capital interest is acquired in a bona fide transaction (even if by gift or purchase from another family member) in which ownership and control are received.

—Capital is not a material income-producing factor but the family member contributes substantial or vital services.[21]

Capital.   If a substantial portion of the partnership's gross income results from the use of capital, such as substantial inventories or investments in plant, machinery, or equipment, it is considered to be a material income-producing factor. If most of the partnership's capital results from borrowings, however, the anticipated allocation of partnership profits might be disallowed.

---

20. Reg. § 1.754–1.
21. § 704(e).

Ordinarily, capital is not a material income-producing factor if the income of the business consists principally of fees, commissions, or other compensation for personal services performed by members or employees of the partnership. To alleviate the uncertainty of whether capital is a material income-producing factor in family partnerships, many taxpayers and their advisers might be inclined to request an individual ruling from the IRS. Unfortunately, the IRS has indicated it will not rule on this issue.[22]

Children as Partners.   When capital is a material income-producing factor and a partnership interest is transferred by gift to a child who is under age 14 and is eligible to be claimed as a dependent by the parent-partner, the child's distributive share of income in excess of $1,000 will be taxed at the parent's tax rate unless the income share constitutes earned income. Regardless of age, if the child provides bona fide services to the partnership and the income share constitutes earned income, the parent-partner's tax rate will be avoided, and the child's full standard deduction (to the extent of the earned income) can be used.

Gift of Capital Interest.   If a family member acquires a capital interest by gift in a family partnership in which capital is a material income-producing factor, limitations exist on the amount of income that may be allocated to this interest. First, the donor of the interest must be allocated an amount of partnership income that represents reasonable compensation for services to the partnership. Then, the remaining income generally is divided among the partners. An interest purchased by one family member from another is considered to be created by gift for the purpose of reallocation.[23]

Example 30   A partnership in which a 50% interest was transferred by sale between a parent and child (considered a gift) had a profit of $90,000 in the current year. Capital is a material income-producing factor. The parent performed services valued at $20,000. The child performed no services. Under these circumstances, $20,000 must be allocated to the parent as compensation. Of the remaining $70,000 of income attributable to capital, at least 50%, or $35,000, must be allocated to the parent.   □

Limited Partnerships

Before 1987, limited partnerships were used to generate and pass through losses from a variety of activities to shelter a partner's other income. The Internal Revenue Code of 1986 essentially eliminated such sheltering for non-corporate taxpayers, personal service corporations, and pass-through entities such as partnerships and S corporations; reduced it for closely-held corporations; and made it difficult for corporations that are not closely-held. For the last group, the new alternative minimum tax is probably the greatest barrier to such sheltering. For other taxpayers, the main difficulties are found in the at-risk rules and passive activity provisions.

---

22. Rev.Proc. 88–3, I.R.B. No. 1, 29.
23. § 704(e).

At-Risk Rules. Section 465 generally limits the loss deduction of individuals and closely-held corporations from business and income-producing activities to amounts that are economically invested in an activity (i.e., adjusted basis of contributed property, cash contributions, debt for which investors are personally liable or have pledged other property as security, and the earnings share that has not been withdrawn or used to absorb losses). Closely-held corporations exist when five or fewer individuals own more than 50 percent of a corporation's stock under the attribution and ownership rules of §§ 318 and 542(a)(2).

Before 1976, losses from limited partnerships in excess of a partner's economic investment could be deducted for two reasons. First, the Regulation permitted (and still does permit) limited and general partners to include a portion of the partnership's nonrecourse debt in their interest basis.[24] Second, under § 704(d) partnership losses generally were deductible on a partner's tax return (and still are) to the extent of the partner's interest in the partnership, determined at the partnership's year-end before considering any losses.

Essentially, losses from business or income-producing activities are now deductible only to the extent a partner has amounts at economic risk. Since nonrecourse debt carries no financial risk to investing partners, it is not at risk.

Before the Tax Reform Act of 1986, real estate activities were exempted from the at-risk rules. Thereafter, real estate financing secured only by an activity's underlying assets generally will not be considered at risk. Generally, though, if such financing is provided by someone who is actively and regularly engaged in the business of lending money and who is not the property's seller or promoter, or by a Federal, state, or local government or its instrumentality, the activity is considered at risk and flow-through losses are allowed.

When determining a partner's loss deduction, first, the general loss limitation rule is invoked (i.e., the deduction is limited to the partner's interest at the end of the partnership year before considering any losses). Then, the at-risk provisions are applied to see if the remaining loss is still deductible. Suspended losses are carried forward until a partner has a sufficient amount at risk in the activity to absorb them. When the at-risk amount at the end of any tax year is less than zero, the excess amount must be included in the partner's gross income (i.e., losses for which deductions were previously allowed are recaptured). Negative amounts at risk can occur as a result of a distribution or conversion of recourse debt to nonrecourse debt.

Example 31   U invests $5,000 in the CC Limited Partnership in the current year for an interest in capital and profits as a general partner. Shortly thereafter, the partnership acquires the master recording of a well-known vocalist for $250,000 ($50,000 from the partnership and $200,000 secured from a local bank via a *recourse* mortgage). U's share of the recourse debt is $10,000, and his interest basis is $15,000 ($5,000 cash investment + $10,000 debt share). Since the debt is recourse, U's at-risk amount is also $15,000. U's share of partnership losses in the first year of operations (due principally to depreciation of the master recording) is $11,000. Under these circum-

---

24. Reg. § 1.752–1(e).

stances, U is entitled to deduct $11,000 of partnership losses, because this amount is less than both his interest basis and at-risk amount. □

Example 32   Assume the same facts as in Example 31. After deducting his share of losses from the partnership, U's interest basis is $4,000 ($15,000 − $11,000). If the *recourse* debt is converted to *nonrecourse* debt in the second year of operations, U is required to include $6,000 of excess losses in his gross income. This amount represents the negative amount of capital U has at risk in the activity ($5,000 cash investment − $11,000 of deducted losses). U can, however, carry this amount forward and deduct it in a subsequent year when his at-risk amount is sufficient to absorb it.
□

Passive Activity Provisions.   A partnership loss share also may be disallowed under the § 469 passive activity provisions. Although these provisions are not applicable per se to partnerships, they most assuredly affect how and when a partner's loss can be deducted. The provisions require taxpayers to separate their activities into three groups:

Active: Earned income, such as salary and wages; income or loss from a trade or business in which the taxpayer materially participates on a regular, continuous, and substantial basis; and guaranteed payments from a partnership for services (but not guaranteed payments for interest on capital).

Portfolio: Annuity income, interest, dividends, guaranteed payments from a partnership for interest on capital, royalties not derived in the ordinary course of a trade or business, and gains and losses from disposal of related assets (e.g., those held for investment).

Passive: Income from a trade or business in which the taxpayer does not participate on a regular, continuous, and substantial basis (including nonbusiness activities under § 212).

Active participation in an activity is determined annually. The burden of proving active participation rests with the taxpayer. Thus, a Maine vacation resort operator investing in a California grape farm or an electrical engineer employed in Virginia investing in an Iowa corn and hog farm may have difficulty proving material participation (i.e., regular, continuous, and substantial involvement with daily farming operations).

Rental income from real or personal property generally is passive income, regardless of the taxpayer's level of participation. Exceptions are made for rental income from activities where substantial services are provided (i.e., hotel, motel, or other transient lodging and income from equipment rentals to various users for short periods). Limited partnership income is conclusively presumed to be passive income for a limited partner.

Usually, passive activity losses can be offset only against passive activity income. In determining the net passive activity loss for a year, losses and income from all passive activities are aggregated. The amount of suspended losses carried forward from a particular activity is determined by the ratio of the net loss from that activity to the aggregate net loss from all passive activities for that year. A special rule for rental real estate (discussed in the following section) allows a limited $25,000 offset against nonpassive income.

A taxpayer making a taxable disposition of an entire interest in a passive activity generally takes a full deduction for suspended losses in the year of disposal. Suspended losses are deductible against income in the following order: income or gain from the passive activity, net income or gain from all passive activities, and other income. When a passive activity is transferred in a nontaxable exchange (e.g., a like-kind exchange or contribution to a partnership), suspended losses are deductible only to the extent of recognized gains. Remaining losses may be deducted on disposal of the received property.

Example 33   B is an individual who has several investments in passive activities that generate aggregate losses of $10,000 in the current year. B wants to deduct all of these losses in the current year. To assure a loss deduction, B needs to invest in some passive activities that generate income. One of her old friends, an entrepreneur in the women's apparel business, is interested in opening a new apparel store in a nearby community. B is willing to finance a substantial part of the expansion but doesn't want to get involved with day-to-day operations. B also wants to limit any possible loss to her initial investment.

After substantial discussions, B and her friend decide to form a limited partnership, which will own the new store. B's friend will be the general partner, and B will be a limited partner. B invests $100,000, and her friend invests $50,000 and sweat equity (i.e., provides managerial skills and knowhow). Each has a 50% interest in profits and losses. In the first year of operations, the store generates a profit of $30,000. Since B's share of the profit ($15,000) is passive activity income, it can be fully utilized against any passive activity losses. Thus, via her share of the apparel store profits, B assures a full deduction of her $10,000 of passive activity losses. □

Rental Real Estate Losses. Up to $25,000 of passive losses from rental real estate can be offset by individuals against active and portfolio income in any one year. The $25,000 maximum is reduced by 50 percent of the difference between the taxpayer's modified adjusted gross income (AGI) and $100,000. Thus, when the taxpayer's AGI reaches $150,000, the offset is eliminated.

The offset is available to those who actively (rather than materially) participate in rental real estate activities. Active participation is an easier test to meet. It does not require regular, continuous, and substantial involvement with the activity, as does material participation. However, the individual must own at least 10 percent of the fair market value of all interests in the rental property and either contribute to the activity in a significant and bona fide way regarding management decisions or actively participate in arranging for others to make such decisions. Limited partners cannot meet the active participation test.

Example 34   R invests $5,000 in the ARX Limited Partnership for an overall 10% interest in capital and profits as a general partner. R's interest in items to be shared exclusively among the general partners is 20%. R makes no other investments in passive activities during the year and has no carryover losses from prior years.

Shortly after R's investment, ARX acquires rental real estate for $50,000 cash and a $100,000 recourse mortgage from a commercial bank. R's share of the recourse debt (a general partner item) is $20,000, and her basis in the partnership interest is $25,000. R's share of the partnership loss in the first year of operations is $18,000. R's adjusted gross income before considering the loss is $75,000.

R does not meet the requirements for material participation in ARX, but she does meet the requirements for active participation. R's loss deduction is not restricted by her interest basis, the general loss limitation rule, or the at-risk provisions. Therefore, R may deduct the $18,000 loss against nonpassive income. □

Example 35 X invests $10,000 cash in the AXE Limited Partnership in the current year for a 10% limited liability interest in capital and profits. Shortly thereafter, the partnership purchases rental real estate subject to a nonconvertible qualified nonrecourse mortgage of $150,000 obtained from a commercial bank. X has no other passive loss activities during the current year.

X's share of losses from AXE's first year of operations is $27,000. Before considering the loss, X's partnership interest is $25,000 [$10,000 cash plus (10% × $150,000 debt)], and the loss deduction is limited to this amount. X's adjusted gross income before considering the loss is $60,000. The debt is exempted from the at-risk provisions, and it seems that X should be allowed to deduct the $25,000 loss share from portfolio or active income. However, the loss may not be offset against this income, since X is a limited partner and can never satisfy the active participation requirement for the passive activity loss deduction of $25,000. □

Corporate General Partner. Another problem confronting limited partnerships is the required assumption of unlimited liability by the general partner or partners. A variation of the limited partnership that is used to solve this problem is to make the general partner a corporation. Whether such an arrangement is recognized for tax purposes depends upon the application of Rev. Proc. 72–13.[25] A limited partnership with a corporation as the sole general partner is recognized as a partnership only if the following requirements are met:

1. The limited partners do not own directly or indirectly, individually or in the aggregate, over 20 percent of the corporate general partner's stock, including the stock of any of its affiliates.
2. If the corporate general partner has an interest in only one limited partnership and total contributions to that partnership are under $2,500,000, the net worth of such partner at all times must be at least 15 percent of that total or $250,000, whichever is less. If total contributions are $2,500,000 or more, the net worth of such a partner must at all times be at least 10 percent of total contributions.

25. 1972–1 C.B. 735.

3. If the corporate general partner has an interest in more than one limited partnership, the above net worth requirements are applied separately for each limited partnership.

Concept Summary

1. A partner's partnership interest is a capital asset and generally results in a capital gain or loss on disposal.

2. The basis of a partner's partnership interest includes a share of the partnership debt. Generally, the debt share is determined by the partner's loss sharing ratio. When the debt of a limited partnership is *recourse,* only the general partners share in it. If the debt is *nonrecourse,* the general and limited partners share in it according to their profit sharing ratios.

3. The interest bases of the selling and buying partners include an appropriate share of the partnership debt. The selling price and purchase price also include such a debt share.

4. When hot assets are present, ordinary income may be recognized on the disposal of a partner's interest or when partnership property is distributed to a partner. Hot assets include unrealized receivables and substantially appreciated inventory.

5. Unrealized receivables include amounts earned by a cash basis taxpayer from services rendered and inventory sales. Unrealized receivables include depreciation recapture potential under §§ 1245 and 1250 that would result if the underlying asset were sold. The basis of this recapture potential is zero.

6. Substantially appreciated inventory includes virtually all property except money, capital assets, and § 1231 property. Inventory is considered to be substantially appreciated if at the time of its sale or distribution its aggregate fair market value exceeds 120 percent of its adjusted basis and if its fair market value is more than 10 percent of the fair market value of all partnership property, exclusive of cash. This definition encompasses unrealized receivables.

7. If a partnership has hot assets and a distribution causes the interests of the partners in these assets to change (i.e., a disproportionate distribution takes place), ordinary income is recognized. Sometimes this income is recognized by the partnership, and at other times it is recognized by the distributee partner.

8. The partnership recognizes ordinary income from the disproportionate distribution of hot assets when the partners who did not receive the assets have their fair market value interests in the assets reduced. The distributee partner recognizes ordinary income when his or her fair market value interest in these assets is reduced.

9. When a partnership is incorporated, it is important to select the appropriate incorporation method to prevent potentially disastrous results. If the corporation plans to issue § 1244 stock, the original shareholders and not the partnership must be the partners. If an S corporation election is to be made, the election will be invalid if the partnership is a shareholder.

10. If a partner's interest is liquidated by a distribution of money, cash payments in excess of the partner's share of the recorded goodwill basis generally constitute ordinary income. If the partnership agreement calls for goodwill payments in excess of the partner's share of its recorded basis, such payments are generally treated as a capital gain to the extent of the excess.

11. Cash payments for a partner's interest in partnership property essentially are treated as current (nonliquidating) distributions. Such payments do not include payments for the partner's interest in the partnership's goodwill (to the extent not provided for in the

partnership agreement) or in unrealized receivables. If substantially appreciated inventory is present, ordinary income is created.

12. When a partnership interest is sold and the outside basis of the incoming partner's interest does not equal that partner's inside basis, or if a distribution of partnership assets is made and the basis of the assets to the distributee is not a carryover basis but is determined by reference to the partner's outside interest basis, a special basis adjustment is possible.

Tax Planning Considerations

Sales and Exchanges of Interests

Delaying Ordinary Income

A partner planning to dispose of a partnership interest in a taxable transaction might consider either an installment sale or a pro rata distribution of the partner's share of hot assets, followed by a sale of the remaining interest in the partnership. Although the subsequent disposition of the hot assets usually results in ordinary income, the partner can spread the income tax consequences over more than one tax year.

Bunching of Income

The sale or exchange of a partner's entire interest in a partnership can result in an unexpected bunching of income. Keep in mind that the partnership's tax year closes as of the date of the transfer, and as a result, the transferor partner's distributive share of partnership income may be recognized as of that date. Proper timing of the sale or exchange could alleviate the bunching problem. The sale or exchange can also result in a complete termination of the partnership. Such an event could have devastating effects on both the transferor partner and the remaining partners. If the transaction results in the sale or exchange of 50 percent or more of the total interest in partnership capital and profits within any 12-month period, the partnership is deemed to terminate. This possibility can be avoided by prohibiting any potential terminating sales or exchanges under the partnership agreement.

Basis Adjustment for Transferee

If a partnership interest is acquired by purchase, the partner may want to condition such acquisition on the partnership's promise to make an election under § 754. Such an election would adjust the basis in the partner's ratable share of partnership assets to reflect the difference between the purchase price and the selling partner's share of the basis in partnership assets. Failure to do so could result in the loss of future depreciation deductions as well as the conversion of ordinary losses into capital losses.

Timing Other Dispositions

The disposition of a partnership interest by gift or abandonment can result in unexpected recognition of gain. If the partner's share of partnership liabilities exceeds the adjusted basis of the partnership interest, the operation of §§ 752 and 731 causes such transfers to be treated as taxable sales. The only major relief from these provisions is to time the disposition to occur in a tax year in which the partner has other losses to offset the gain that results.

Death and Partnership Agreement

A limited possibility exists to effectively plan for the disposition of a partnership interest as a result of death. The bunching of income in the deceased partner's final tax year can be avoided or accomplished by means of the partnership agreement. More important, the remaining partners can avoid unnecessary and unpleasant problems of dealing with the deceased partner's successor by implementing a well-planned and carefully drafted partnership agreement. If the successor continues as a member of the partnership, an election under § 754 should be considered. This would enable the transferee's basis in the partnership's assets to be adjusted to reflect the difference in the deceased partner's basis in the interest and the successor's basis in the partnership interest.

Planning Distributions

General Rules

In planning for any partnership distributions, taxpayers should be alert to the following rules:

—Gain is recognized by the distributee receiving *either* current *or* proportionate liquidating distributions *only* to the extent that any money distributed exceeds the partner's basis in the partnership.

—Loss is never recognized on current distributions. However, the distributee may recognize a loss on a liquidating distribution if *only* money and/or inventory and/or unrealized receivables are distributed, *and* only then if the basis of this property is less than the withdrawing partner's basis in the partnership interest.

—Gain or loss recognized by the distributee is a capital gain or loss in both current and liquidating distributions, *except* when a portion of the gain must be treated as ordinary income to the extent it is attributable to hot assets.

—The distributee's basis in property received in a current distribution is the basis of the property to the partnership, *except* that it cannot exceed the partner's interest reduced by any money received in the same distribution.

—The basis of property received in a liquidating distribution is dependent upon the type of property distributed. The distributee partner's basis in inventory and unrealized receivables is the same basis the property had to the partnership, but it cannot exceed the partner's interest basis reduced by any money distributed. Any other distributed property is assigned the withdrawing partner's remaining interest basis.

—If a partner receives inventory or unrealized receivables in either a current or liquidating distribution, ordinary income results when a disposition of such property occurs. Recall that if the inventory items are held for at least five years before being sold, capital gain treatment might be achieved.

—Gain or loss is not recognized by a partnership on either current or liquidating distributions, except on a disproportionate distribution of hot assets.

—The holding period of property received in either a current or liquidating distribution includes the holding period of the partnership.

Valuation Problems

The value of a partner's interest or any partnership assets agreed upon by all partners usually is considered to be correct by both the IRS and the courts. Thus, in planning the sale or liquidation of a partnership interest, it is advisable to document the results of the bargaining process. To avoid valuation problems on liquidation, it would be extremely helpful to have some formula or agreed-upon procedure incorporated in the partnership agreement.

Other Partnership Interests

The following elements are essential for the recognition of the family partnership:

—A genuine intent of the parties to conduct the business as a partnership.

—Contribution of capital or vital services by each partner to the partnership.

When capital is a material income-producing factor and a partnership interest is transferred to a child of the taxpayer under age 14 for whom a dependency exemption can be claimed, income in excess of $1,000 that is not earned income may be taxed at the parent's tax rate.

The at-risk rules and passive activity loss provisions have virtually eliminated the opportunity to shelter nonpassive income via losses from a limited partnership. General partners who actively participate in the management of rental real estate can shelter up to $25,000 annually. However, such loss deductions are eliminated when the partner's modified adjusted gross income reaches $150,000.

Problem Materials

Discussion Questions

1. What is the nature of a partnership interest under the entity concept of partnerships? Under the aggregate or conduit concept?

2. What is the character of a gain or loss recognized on the sale or exchange of a partnership interest?

3. What are unrealized receivables of a partnership? Substantially appreciated inventory items?

4. Discuss the possible collateral effects of a sale or exchange of a partnership interest.

5. Under what circumstances will the transfer of a partnership interest to a controlled corporation for stock result in taxable gain?

6. Describe the alternative methods of incorporating a partnership. Which method is recognized by the IRS?

7. What are the collateral effects of incorporating a partnership?

8. Discuss the problems involved in attempting a nontaxable like-kind exchange of partnership interests.

9. Under what circumstances will the gift of a partnership interest result in a taxable sale?

10. What are the anticipated income tax results of an abandonment or forfeiture of a partnership interest? What can go wrong?

11. Discuss the various types of distributions from a partnership and the tax consequences of each.

12. Distinguish between a sale of a partnership interest and a liquidation. Specifically, discuss the tax consequences of a sale of a partnership interest to the selling partner, the purchaser, and the partnership itself. What type of liquidation could be used to avoid immediate gain recognition by the withdrawing partner?

13. Distinguish between § 736(a) payments and § 736(b) payments. What are the tax consequences of such payments to the remaining partners and the partnership?

14. If liquidating payments are to be spread over a number of years, how are the payments to be allocated between §§ 736(a) and (b)?

15. Under what circumstances is a loss recognized by a withdrawing partner whose entire interest is liquidated in a proportionate distribution of assets?

16. Distinguish between the basis adjustments allowed under §§ 734 and 743. Why are such adjustments allowed? When could an unfavorable result occur?

17. What is a family partnership? Under what circumstances can a family member be a partner in such a partnership? What income allocation is required?

18. What is a limited partnership? What types of related tax shelters have been developed? What could go wrong?

19. Discuss the applicability of § 465 to limited partnerships.

20. What is the special recapture rule of § 465? Under what circumstances will it become applicable?

Problems

1. At the end of the current year, K, an equal partner in the four-person KLOM Partnership, has an interest basis of $18,000 in the partnership, including a $40,000 share of partnership debt. On December 1 of last year, the partnership purchased and immediately placed in service five-year MACRS property qualifying for $10,000 of rapid expensing under § 179, which it elected to take. K last year properly claimed the § 179 amount. At the end of the current year, K's share of the partnership's § 1245 recapture potential (including K's share of the § 179 expensed amount) is $12,000. The partnership did not have any taxable income or loss in the current year, and all parties use the

calendar year. Describe the income tax consequences to K in each of the following situations that take place at the end of the current year:

a. K sells the partnership interest to T for $25,000 cash and the assumption of the appropriate share of partnership liabilities.

b. K exchanges the 25% partnership interest for a 25% limited partnership interest in the continuing KLOM Partnership valued at $30,000. L, O, and M remain general partners, each with a 25% interest in partnership capital and profits.

c. Faced with the possibility of having to contribute an additional $50,000 to the partnership to keep it operating, K abandons the partnership interest, and the remaining partners assume K's share of existing partnership liabilities.

d. K dies after a lengthy illness on December 31 of the current year. K's widow becomes the immediate successor in interest.

2. Briefly discuss changes to the responses given in Problem 1 if the KLOM Partnership had $88,000 of unrealized receivables at the end of the current year, including any recapture potential under § 1245 of the Code.

3. L, a partner in the cash basis LAM Partnership, has a 30% interest in partnership profits and losses. The partnership's balance sheet at the end of the current year is as follows:

	Basis	FMV		Basis	FMV
Cash	$ 25,000	$ 25,000	L, Capital	$ 54,000	$135,000
Receivables	–0–	240,000	A, Capital	63,000	157,500
Land	155,000	185,000	M, Capital	63,000	157,500
Totals	$180,000	$450,000	Totals	$180,000	$450,000

Assume that L sells her interest in the LAM Partnership to J at the end of the current year for cash of $135,000.

a. How much income must L report on her tax return for the current year from the sale, and what is its nature?

b. If the partnership did not make a § 754 election or have one in effect, what is the type and amount of income that J must report in the next year when the receivables are collected? Assume no other transactions in the next year.

c. If the partnership did make a § 754 election, what is the type and amount of income that J must report in the next year when (assuming no other transactions in the next year) the receivables are collected? The land (which is used in the LAM Partnership's business) is sold for $205,000?

 4. X's interest in the equal HEX Partnership is sold to Y for $47,000 cash and the assumptions of X's share of partnership liabilities. On the sale date, the partnership's cash basis balance sheet reflects the following:

	Assets	
	Adjusted Basis	Fair Market Value
Cash	$27,000	$ 27,000
Accounts receivable	–0–	90,000
Section 1231 assets	33,000	33,000
Total	$60,000	$150,000

Liabilities and Capital

	Adjusted Basis	Fair Market Value
Note payable	$ 9,000	$ 9,000
Capital accounts		
H	17,000	47,000
E	17,000	47,000
X	17,000	47,000
Total	$60,000	$150,000

a. What is the total amount realized by X on the sale?

b. How much, if any, ordinary income must X recognize on the sale?

c. How much capital gain to X?

d. What will be Y's basis in the partnership interest acquired?

e. If the partnership makes an election under § 754 to adjust the bases of the partnership assets to reflect the sale, what adjustment must be made?

5. Assume in Problem 4 that X's partnership interest is not sold to an outsider. Instead, the partnership makes a proportionate liquidating distribution to X, and the remaining partners assume X's share of the liabilities. X receives cash of $6,000, accounts receivable of $30,000, and a § 1231 asset worth $11,000.

a. How much gain or loss must X recognize?

b. What basis will X have in the accounts receivable?

c. What basis will X have in the § 1231 asset?

6. Suppose that X's partnership interest in Problem 5 is terminated with a distribution of $47,000 of accounts receivable instead of the proportionate distribution described.

a. How much gain or loss, if any, must X recognize?

b. What basis will X have in the receivables?

c. How much gain or loss, if any, must the partnership recognize on the distribution? Will this be ordinary or capital gain or loss?

d. What basis will the partnership have in the § 1231 assets as a result of the distribution?

7. Suppose that X in Problem 6 receives cash of $14,000 and all the § 1231 assets worth $33,000 instead of the accounts receivable in a disproportionate distribution in termination of X's entire interest.

a. How much gain or loss, if any, must X recognize? Will it be ordinary or capital gain or loss?

b. What basis will X have in the § 1231 assets after the distribution?

c. How much gain or loss, if any, must the partnership recognize on the distribution?

d. What basis will the partnership have in the accounts receivable as a result of the distribution?

8. D's 25% interst in the CADE Partnership is sold to G for $15,000 cash and assumption of partnership liabilities. At the date of the sale, the partnership's cash basis balance sheet reflects the following:

Assets

	Adjusted Basis	Fair Market Value
Cash	$10,000	$10,000
Accounts receivable	–0–	20,000
Depreciable assets	16,000	24,000
Capital assets	14,000	18,000
Total	$40,000	$72,000

Liabilities and Capital

	Adjusted Basis	Fair Market Value
Notes payable	$12,000	$12,000
Capital accounts		
C	7,000	15,000
A	7,000	15,000
D	7,000	15,000
E	7,000	15,000
Total	$40,000	$72,000

a. What is the amount realized by D on the sale?

b. If there is $4,000 of § 1245 depreciation recapture potential associated with the partnership's assets, how much ordinary income must D recognize on the sale?

c. How much of this amount is capital gain to D?

d. What will be G's basis in the acquired partnership interest?

e. Assuming that a § 754 election is in effect at the time of the sale, what effect will it have on G's basis in the partnership interest acquired?

9. In addition to assuming the facts in Problem 8, assume that E's partnership interest is sold to G after D's interest is sold to G.

a. What effect, if any, will this transaction have on the existing partnership?

b. What unfavorable tax consequences could result from E's sale?

c. If the partnership did not intend to make an election under § 754 and it did not have one in effect at the date of G's acquisition, what effect will these facts have on G's basis in the partnership interest acquired?

10. QRX, an equally owned general partnership involved in the development of real estate, had the following balance sheet at the beginning of the current tax year:

Assets

	Adjusted Basis	Fair Market Value
Cash	$ 10,000	$ 10,000
Accounts receivable	60,000	60,000
Land	120,000	40,000
Total	$190,000	$110,000

Liabilities and Capital

	Adjusted Basis	Fair Market Value
Qualified nonrecourse debt	$121,000	$121,000
Capital accounts		
Q	23,000	(3,667)
R	23,000	(3,667)
X	23,000	(3,666)
Total	$190,000	$110,000

Assume that the three partners have actively participated in the management of QRX, that none of them owns an interest in any other partnership or passive activity, and that Q's interest is abandoned at the start of the current year.

a. How much gain or loss must Q recognize on the abandonment, and what is its nature?

b. If the accounts receivable were unrealized with a zero basis and the totals for the adjusted basis balance sheet were $130,000 rather than $190,000, and if the nonrecourse debt remains at $121,000, how much gain or loss does Q recognize on the abandonment, and what is its nature?

c. If Q were a limited partner rather than a general partner and did not actively participate in the management of QRX, would your answer to (b) change? If so, how?

d. If the partnership was formed in 1987 and Q's share of partnership losses from prior years totaled $40,000, would your answer to (c) change? If so, how?

11. The basis of L's partnership interest is $17,080. L receives a pro rata liquidating distribution consisting of $9,760 cash and L's share of inventory having a basis of $12,200 to the partnership and a fair market value of $18,300.

a. How much gain or loss, if any, must L recognize as a result of the distribution?

b. What basis will L have in the inventory?

c. If the inventory is sold two years later for $18,000, what are the tax consequences to L?

d. As a result of the liquidating distribution, what are the tax consequences to the partnership?

12. Assume the same facts as in Problem 11, except that L's basis in the partnership is $24,400 instead of $17,080.

a. How much gain or loss, if any, must L recognize on the distribution?

b. What basis will L have in the inventory?

c. What are the tax consequences to the partnership?

13. D's partnership basis is $64,500. In a pro rata distribution in liquidation of the partnership, D receives $12,900 cash and two parcels of land having bases of $17,200 and $12,900 to the partnership. Each parcel of land was held by the partnership for investment, and the parcels had fair market values of $32,250 and $43,000.

a. How much gain or loss, if any, must D recognize on the distribution?

b. What basis will D have in each parcel?

c. If the land had been held as inventory by the partnership, what effect, if any, would it have on the responses to (a) and (b)?

14. Assume the same facts as in Problem 13, except that D received $21,500 cash and an old truck having a basis of $430 to the partnership and a fair market value of $215.

a. How much loss, if any, may D recognize on the distribution?

b. What basis will D have in the truck?

c. Suppose D's son drives the truck for personal use for one year before selling it for $100. How much loss may D recognize on the sale of the truck? What tax planning procedure could have prevented this result?

15. S is an equal partner in the SWJ Partnership and has an interest basis of $225,000 at the end of the partnership's current year. S receives the following distribution from the partnership in complete termination of his interest: cash of $112,500 and two pieces of property with partnership bases and fair market values as follows:

	Partnership Basis		FMV	
	Amount	Fraction	Amount	Fraction
Land A	$ 90,000	$^2/_3$	$135,000	$^3/_5$
Land B	45,000	$^1/_3$	90,000	$^2/_5$
Totals	$135,000		$225,000	

Both pieces of property were used in the partnership in connection with its business. No § 751 assets are present.

a. How much income is recognized by S on the liquidating distribution, and what is its nature?

b. What is the basis of Land A and of Land B to S?

c. If S had received cash of $67,500 (instead of $112,500) and the two land parcels, what would be the basis of Land A and of Land B to S?

d. If S had received cash of $230,000 (instead of $112,500 or $67,500) and the two land parcels, what would be the basis of Land A and of Land B to S?

e. For (d), if the partnership had previously made a § 754 election, what would be the aggregate amount of the adjustment under § 734 and its direction (i.e., upward or downward adjustment of basis)?

16. At the time J decides to retire from the JET Partnership, JET's balance sheet for tax purposes contains the following:

	Assets Adjusted Basis Per Books	Market Value
Cash	$193,500	$193,500
Section 1231 assets	64,500	64,500
Investment in land	77,400	193,500
Total assets	$335,400	$451,500

	Liabilities and Capital	
Mortgage payable	$ 64,500	$ 64,500
Capital accounts		
J	90,300	129,000
E	90,300	129,000
T	90,300	129,000
Total	$335,400	$451,500

It has been agreed by all partners that J's interest in the partnership assets, exclusive of goodwill, is worth $129,000. To totally liquidate J's interest, it is further agreed that J will be paid $64,500 per year for three years and J's share of partnership liabilities will be assumed immediately by the remaining partners.

   a. How should the total payments be allocated between § 736(a) and § 736(b) payments?

   b. What are the tax consequences to J for the current and next two years?

   c. What are the tax consequences to the partnership of each of the three payments?

17. Assume the same facts as in Problem 16, except that instead of receiving $64,500 per year for three years, J is to receive 30% of partnership profits for five years. The amounts paid to J are as follows:

Year 1—$43,000	Year 4—$30,100
Year 2—$34,400	Year 5—$64,500
Year 3—$51,600	

   a. What are the tax consequences to J of each of the five payments?

   b. What are the tax consequences to the partnership upon making each of the payments?

18. In each of the following proportionate liquidating distributions, determine the amount and character of any gain or loss to be recognized by each partner and the basis of each asset (other than cash) received. Indicate the amount of any optional basis adjustments available to the distributing partnership if a § 754 election is in effect.

   a. R has a partnership basis of $18,000 and receives a distribution of $25,000 in cash.

   b. S has a partnership basis of $9,000 and receives $3,000 cash and a capital asset with a basis to the partnership of $4,000 and a fair market value of $12,000.

   c. T has a partnership basis of $15,000 and receives $4,000 cash, inventory with a basis to the partnership of $8,000, and a capital asset with a partnership basis of $10,000. The inventory and capital asset have fair market values of $5,000 and $7,000, respectively.

19. P and C, parent and child, operate a local apparel shop as a partnership. The PC Partnership earned a profit of $20,000 in the current year. C's equal partnership interest was acquired by purchase from the parent. Assume that capital is a material income-producing factor and that P manages the day-to-day operations of the shop without any help from C. Further assume that $8,000 is reasonable compensation for P's services.

   a. How much of the partnership income must be allocated to P?

   b. What is the maximum amount of partnership income that can be allocated to C?

   c. Assuming the child is five years old, has no other income, and is claimed as a dependency exemption by the parent, how is the child's income from the partnership taxed?

20. T invests $25,000 cash in the CP Limited Partnership for a 5% limited liability interest in capital and profits. Shortly thereafter, the partnership acquires a completed 10-story office building for a cash down payment of $500,000 and subject to a qualified nonrecourse mortgage of $1,500,000. T has a 10% limited liability interest in another limited real estate partnership that has burned out (i.e., the partnership is now profitable). T's share of the other partnership's net income is $22,000, and T has no other passive investments.

   a. What is T's basis in CP after the acquisition of the office building?

b. Assuming that T's share of CP's losses for the first year of operation is $35,000, how much of the loss is T allowed to recognize?

c. What is T's basis in CP after deducting T's allowed loss?

21. S has an equal interest in the profits and losses of the SIE Partnership. During the current year, S agrees to retire from the partnership just before the current year ends and receive the following cash payments for his entire partnership interest: $30,600 just before the end of the current year and payments aggregating $68,000 over the following two years. The partners agree that the partnership's goodwill is worth $30,600 at the instant of S's retirement and that the payments to S for his partnership interest cover his share of the goodwill. The closing balance sheet of the partnership *just before* the first cash payment to S is as follows:

	Books	FMV		Books	FMV
Cash	$ 44,200	$ 44,200	Debt	$ 10,200	$ 10,200
Unrealized receivables	—0—	102,000	Capital, S	34,000	71,400
			Capital, I	34,000	71,400
Capital and § 1231 assets	68,000	78,200	Capital, E	34,000	71,400
Totals	$112,200	$224,400	Totals	$112,200	$224,400

In addition, before the current year ends, the remaining partners agree to assume S's share of partnership debt existing just before the first payment.

a. What is the basis of S's partnership interest just before the first payment?

b. What is S's aggregate interest in § 736(b) property just before the first payment?

c. In the aggregate, how much in the way of § 736(a) payments will be received by S?

d. Assuming no other partnership provisions regarding S's retirement, how will S be taxed on all retirement amounts for the current year?

e. In (d), could S do anything to change the way the retirement amounts are taxed?

22. On January 1 of the current year, Z purchased, as a limited partner, three separate 10% interests in rental real estate limited partnerships for $10,000 apiece. The operating profit and loss for each partnership for the current year, along with its qualified nonrecourse debt at the end of the year, is as follows:

	Profit (Loss)	Qualified Debt
ABC Partnership	($ 40,000)	$100,000
DEF Partnership	50,000	100,000
RST Partnership	(120,000)	100,000

Before considering the profits and losses from the partnerships, Z's modified adjusted gross income for the current year is $140,000.

a. In the aggregate, how much of the losses from the three partnerships may Z use to offset his other taxable income?

b. What is Z's partnership interest in each partnership at the end of the current year, assuming no other transactions took place?

c. How much is the suspended loss carryover from each partnership?

d. If the acquired interests were general partnership interests, would your answer to (a) change if Z actively participated in the management of each partnership. If so, how?

e. Based on the assumptions in (d), how much is the suspended loss carryover from each partnership?

23. The balance sheet of the equal BAS Partnership at the end of the current year before any distributions during the year is as follows:

Assets

	Adjusted Basis	Fair Market Value
Cash	$40,000	$ 40,000
Accounts receivable	–0–	30,000
Inventory	15,000	51,000
Land used for parking	8,000	11,000
Total	$63,000	$132,000

Liabilities and Capital

Accounts payable	$12,000	$ 12,000
Capital accounts		
B	17,000	40,000
A	17,000	40,000
S	17,000	40,000
Total	$63,000	$132,000

Assume the land meets the long-term holding period requirement. For each of the following independent assumptions, determine the impact of the stated distribution on the partnership and the receiving partner:

a. Immediately before the end of the current year, BAS made a current cash and land distribution to B. The distributed cash was $20,000, and the land had an adjusted basis of $2,000 and fair market value of $2,750. Assume BAS had a § 754 optional basis adjustment election in effect.

b. Immediately before the end of the year, BAS made the following distribution, which eliminated A's entire interest in the partnership:

	Adjusted Basis	Market Value
Cash	$ 9,333	$ 9,333
Receivable	–0–	10,000
Inventory	5,000	17,000
Land	2,667	3,667
Total	$17,000	$40,000

c. Immediately before the end of the year, BAS made the following distribution, which eliminated S's entire interest in the partnership. The partners agreed that all of the land distributed to S and some of the cash was used to purchase S's interest in hot assets.

	Adjusted Basis	Market Value
Cash	$36,000	$36,000
Land	2,910	4,000
Total	$38,910	$40,000

Research Problems

Research Problem 1. Assume that all transactions in this problem take place after 1986. Five years ago, an enterprising group of young real estate developers, with a substantial list of financial successes in residential apartments and shopping centers in the northwest continental United States, organized Harpervalley Development Formations (HDF), a general real estate development and management partnership located in Harpervalley, Oregon. At that time, these men and women together had invested $25,000 in HDF, and the partnership had acquired an option to buy some choice land on the southwest side of Harpervalley, adjacent to Interstate Highway 90 near the airport. The partners planned to sell another $475,000 of general partnership units in HDF and secure about $5,000,000 of recourse/nonrecourse financing. The funds would be used to purchase the optioned land and construct a showcase apartment-shopping center complex with appropriate landscaping. At the start of the fifth year of operations, the partners planned that any obtained recourse debt would automatically convert to nonrecourse status. JP, the leading sparkplug behind HDF, had made an impressive loan presentation request to the board of directors of the Ranchers Insurance Group (RIG). BM, then president of RIG, was fairly certain the board would approve the $5,000,000 loan to HDF on a recourse/nonrecourse basis with the land (to be purchased) and the apartment-shopping center complex (to be constructed) pledged as collateral. RIG has several existing loans to real estate developers that its board feels are wise investments. This loan to HDF (if approved) would be another that the board feels would be a wise investment and in which RIG would not acquire an equity interest.

At a cocktail party at his country club the Saturday evening before the RIG board was to approve the loan to HDF, BM mentioned to his childhood sweetheart, SA, that HDF planned to construct an apartment-shopping center complex on the southwest side of the city. He suggested that SA consider making an investment in HDF and hinted that RIG would likely be a substantial participant. SA, about 50, with two married children, had made her own fortune in the stock market before marrying the late JA, a wealthy rancher in the valley area. She told BM, whose advice she valued highly, that she had discussed the project with JP the prior weekend over dinner and was seriously considering such an investment. On Monday morning, SA telephoned JP and informed him that she had placed her check in the mail to him along with the necessary signed papers to make her a general partner in HDF. JP informed SA that as a general partner, she must actively participate in HDF's management activities. He also indicated that SA would not participate in the partnership's daily management decisions on a regular, continuous, and substantial basis, since the selected management group would perform these functions. On Wednesday of the same week, the RIG board approved the loan as requested. HDF immediately purchased the optioned land and constructed the apartment-shopping center complex. After all the general partnership units in HDF were sold, SA's $100,000 investment provided SA with a 20% interest in capital, profits, and losses.

Although SA had not received any cash from the HDF Partnership during the past four years, she did receive the following share of partnership losses:

Year	Loss
1	$ 20,000
2	40,000
3	40,000
4	100,000

Toward the middle part of last year, the economy took a deep downturn. Several of the mines and factories in the area closed down, and many local ranchers had to lay off a substantial number of their workhands. These events had a drastic effect on the revenues and operations of the HDF apartment-shopping center complex.

By late October of the current year, it was evident that the partnership would be unable to make the loan and interest payment due to RIG on January 15 of next year. A meeting of the partners was called for November 5, at which time the complete situation was explained. None of the local partners wanted HDF to default on the loan to RIG. It was decided that the management group of HDF would try to find a buyer for all partnership interests who would be willing to assume the loan to RIG. On November 30, each partner received a letter indicating that a potential buyer had been located. This potential buyer was in the process of having the properties appraised. On December 20, each partner received a letter indicating that the appraisals had been completed and that the average of the three independent appraisals was $3,000,000, with a variance between the high and low appraisals of $30,000. The letter also announced that there would be a partners' meeting on December 30 of the current year, at which time the full offer from the potential buyer would be disclosed and each partner's share of the loss for the year would be announced.

At the December 30 meeting, SA learned that her share of the current year's operating loss was $200,000 (her share of the loss for the fifth year of operations). RE, a real estate investor from Denver, was introduced. JP indicated that RE would be willing to assume the debt to RIG and reimburse each partner for his or her share of the selling expenses, which included the finder's fee paid to locate RE. SA's share of these expenses would be $500. JP indicated the importance of making a quick decision, because the next payment to RIG was due on January 15. JP indicated that if the payment were not made on time, HDF would be in default on the unpaid loan principal of $4,500,000 plus interest. After much discussion, it was decided to accept RE's offer. On December 31, the transfer contract was signed and each partner received a check from RE as reimbursement for the selling expenses. SA received a check for $500 and a statement confirming that her share of the operating loss for the year was $200,000.

SA has contacted you, a local CPA, to determine how the above facts should be presented on her tax return for the current year. SA's other investments are all in stocks and bonds traded on the New York Stock Exchange and have produced annual adjusted gross income, in the form of taxable dividends and interest, ranging from $250,000 to $375,000 for the past four years. In the current year, the investments produced an adjusted gross income of $210,000. From these facts you are to determine the following:

a. The basis of SA's interest in the HDF Partnership on December 31, the disposal date, ignoring any interest due for the use of money.

b. The amount of investment gain or loss from the disposal of SA's interest in HDF. Your answer should contain some general comments regarding the nature of the gain or loss.

c. The proper presentation for the $200,000 share of the current year loss.

Partial list of research aids:

§§ 61, 704, 752, and 1001.

Reg. §§ 1.61–12 and 1.752–1.

Gavins S. Millar, 67 T.C. 656 (1977).

Peninsula Properties Co., LTD, 47 B.T.A. 84 (1942).

Unique Art Manufacturing Co., Inc., 8 T.C. 1341 (1947).

Research Problem 2. RD was a 25% partner in the Pleasant View Partnership, which was organized 17 years ago to construct and manage an apartment building in Indianapolis, Indiana. Three years ago, RD and his partners disagreed on some management policies, and RD decided to retire from the partnership and move to Florida. The partners agreed on the value of RD's partnership interest and agreed that it would be liquidated by the immediate assumption of RD's share of the partnership's debt and a series of cash payments over the year of retirement and the next nine years.

In the year of RD's retirement and in each of the next two years, RD received a check from the partnership in liquidation of his partnership interest of $8,000. In the current year, he received the fourth $8,000 check from the partnership on December 15. However, on July 10 in the current year, RD received another check for $5,000 from the partnership. The letter that accompanied the $5,000 check indicated that the garage at the back of the apartment rental property had been destroyed by a fire, that no automobiles of tenants were in the garage at the time of the fire, and that the check represented RD's share of the insurance proceeds. The letter also indicated that RD's share of the garage's adjusted basis at the date of the fire was $2,000, that the garage had been depreciated by the straight-line method, and that the remaining partners had decided not to replace the garage.

RD was pleased when he received the $5,000 check, since he had recently been talking to the tenants of an apartment building he owned and managed in Sarasota, Florida, about plans for constructing a garage on the property in which they could rent space to house their cars. With the $5,000 and some other money, RD had a garage constructed on the property that was placed in service on September 25 of the current year.

Since RD's tax return for the current year will be due in a few months, RD has contracted with you to determine if he will be able to make an election under § 1033 to defer gain recognition from the proceeds he received from the garage fire in Indianapolis. He informs you that the garage destroyed in the fire was in existence at the date of his retirement from the Pleasant View Partnership and that all appropriate documentation is available for your examination, including a letter from his former partners that grants him the right to retain all tax elections he had in the partnership at the date of his retirement. Will RD be able to make an appropriate election under § 1033 to defer any income recognition on the $5,000 received from the garage fire?

Research Problem 3. SSH, a calendar year corporation located on the southwest side of Lincoln, Nebraska, near William Jennings Bryan's home, is owned by six calendar year shareholders. SSH was formed 10 years ago by its present shareholders, who are sole proprietors of businesses in a shopping mart, which is also located on the southwest side of Lincoln. SSH rents office space from the shopping mart owners and has assets consisting of a small amount of cash, a few pieces of office equipment, and six 15% general partner interests in the capital and profits of RP. RP is a calendar year general partnership that owns and operates residential property on the west side of Lincoln near the airport. RP took accelerated depreciation and statutory percentage accelerated cost recovery deductions in excess of related straight-line amounts on its real property. As a result of these deductions, RP had operating losses.

On November 15 of the current year, SSH adopted a plan of complete liquidation and on December 5 sold its office equipment to an unrelated party for book value. The aggregate fair market value of SSH's stock at the date the liquidation plan was adopted was $4,950,000. On December 31 of the current year, SSH made its one and only liquidating distribution, distributing to each shareholder in exchange for its stock an equal amount of cash and a 15% interest in RP. After the distribution, 90% of RP is owned by the former shareholders of SSH. The other 10% interest is owned by the same taxpayers who helped form the partnership several years ago.

The former treasurer of SSH, who was also a shareholder in SSH, has contracted with you to determine the answers to the following questions and report back to her before the tax returns for SSH and RP are due:

a. Must SSH report ordinary income under § 1250 for the excess depreciation taken by RP when it (SSH) distributed the six 15% interests in RP in a liquidating distribution?

b. Was RP terminated when the six 15% interests in it were distributed to SSH shareholders?

10 S Corporations

Objectives

Provide an in-depth discussion of the rules governing S corporation status.
Describe those corporations that qualify for the S election.
Discuss how the election must be made and, once made, how it can be lost.
Explain the effect of the S election on the corporation and its shareholders.
Describe the situations where S status is desirable or undesirable.
Compare the tax attributes of partnerships, S corporations, and C corporations.

Outline

General Considerations
Advantages of the Corporate Form
Disadvantages of the Corporate Form
Subchapter S in Perspective

Qualification for S Corporation Status
Definition of a Small Business Corporation
Making the Election
Loss of the Election

Operational Rules
Choice of Tax Year
Computation of Taxable Income
Tax Treatment to Shareholders of
  Distributions
Corporate Treatment of Certain Property
  Distributions
Shareholder's Tax Basis

Treatment of Losses
Tax Treatment of Preelection Built-in
  Gains
Tax Treatment of Long-Term Capital
  Gains
Passive Investment Income Penalty Tax
Fringe Benefit Rules
Other Operational Rules

Tax Planning Considerations
Determining When the Election Is
  Advisable
Making a Proper Election
Preserving the Election
Planning for the Operation of the
  Corporation

General Considerations

Subchapter S of the Internal Revenue Code of 1986 allows for the unique treatment of certain corporations for Federal income tax purposes.[1] Although this election essentially results in a tax treatment of the S corporation that resembles that of a partnership, the entity is still a corporation under state law and for many other tax purposes. Special provisions pertain to the entity, however, under the operational provisions of §§ 1361–1379. Since individual tax rates are now generally lower than corporate rates, both Subchapters S and K of the Code have taken on an added importance. Most businesses should reevaluate the desirability of using a C corporation as the means of conducting a trade or business.

Advantages of the Corporate Form

Operating a business in the corporate form entails numerous tax and nontax advantages. Among the more important nontax advantages are the attributes of continuity of existence, free transferability of ownership interests, and limited liability. The corporation, possessing continuity of existence, will survive the withdrawal or death of any of its owners (i.e., shareholders). Thus, the corporation normally will continue to exist until such time as the shareholders decide upon its liquidation. Free transferability of ownership interests permits shareholders to dispose of stock in whatever manner they desire. This flexibility can be crucial in a family setting in which an individual wishes to shift some of the income from the business to related parties in lower income tax brackets. As noted in Chapter 9, this may be impossible to accomplish if the business is being operated in the partnership form. Often, the key nontax advantage the corporate form offers is the limited liability characteristic. If a corporation fails, a shareholder's loss is limited to the amount of the stock investment. When one contrasts this result with what could happen in a partnership setting, where all of a partner's personal assets may be at the mercy of the partnership's creditors, the disparity in treatment becomes quite clear.

Disadvantages of the Corporate Form

Operating a business in the corporate form carries several distinct tax disadvantages. First, the system of double taxation materializes. Profits are taxed to the corporation as earned and to the shareholders when distributed as dividends. Second, losses suffered at the corporate level cannot be passed through to the shareholders. Such losses remain locked within the corporation and are unavailable to the shareholders.[2] This last disadvantage would be of considerable importance in the formation of a new business, wherein losses in the early

---

1. The Subchapter S Revision Act of 1982 labels a Subchapter S corporation as an "S corporation." It also designates regular corporations (i.e., those that have not elected S status) as "C corporations." C corporations are those that are governed by Subchapter C of the Code (§§ 301–386).
2. The losses might eventually materialize upon the sale of the stock or during the liquidation of the corporation. Such losses, however, probably would be capital and not ordinary.

years are often anticipated. In such situations, the owners of a business would like to receive the immediate tax deductions from such losses.

The advantage of a flow-through business entity, such as an S corporation or a partnership, over a C corporation is demonstrated in Example 1.

Example 1
Assume that an entity earns $300,000. Assume also that the applicable marginal individual tax rate is 28%, the applicable marginal corporate tax rate is 34%, and all after-tax income is distributed currently.

	C Corporation	S Corporation or Partnership
Earnings	$ 300,000	$ 300,000
Less: Corporate tax	(102,000)	–0–
Available for distribution	$ 198,000	$ 300,000
Less: Tax at shareholder level	(55,000)	(84,000)
Available after-tax earnings	$ 142,560	$ 216,000

The flow-through business entity generates an extra $73,440 of after-tax earnings compared to a C corporation. Moreover, the flow-through business entity avoids the corporate alternative minimum tax and the business untaxed reported profits AMTI adjustment (refer to Chapter 2). The C corporation might be able to reduce this disadvantage by paying out its earnings as compensation, rents, or interest expense. Tax at the owner level also can be avoided by not distributing after-tax earnings. ☐

Subchapter S in Perspective

Because of the tax disadvantages just noted, considerable support exists for the proposition that many persons have been deterred from using the corporation, although they may have had good reasons for preferring this form of operation. In the interest of preventing tax considerations from interfering with the exercise of sound business judgment (i.e., whether to operate a business in the corporate form), Congress in 1958 enacted Subchapter S of the Code.[3]

Subchapter S permits certain corporations to avoid the corporate income tax and enables them to pass through operating losses to their shareholders. It represents an attempt to achieve a measure of tax neutrality in resolving the difficult problem of whether a business should be conducted as a sole proprietorship, partnership, or corporation.

In dealing with the provisions of Subchapter S, certain observations should be kept in mind.

1. S corporation status is an elective provision. Failure to make the election will mean that the rules applicable to the taxation of corporations (i.e., Subchapter C status) and shareholders will apply (refer to Chapter 2).

---

3. The same justification applies to § 351, which permits tax-free incorporation of a new or existing business. Refer to Chapter 3.

2. S corporations are regular corporations in the legal sense. The S election affects only the Federal income tax consequences of electing corporations. In fact, a few states, including California and New Jersey, do not recognize the S election, and in such cases, such corporations are subject to the state corporate income tax and whatever other state corporate taxes are imposed.

3. S corporations are not treated by Federal income tax law as either partnerships or regular corporations. The tax treatment is almost like partnership taxation, but it involves a unique set of tax rules. However, Subchapter C controls unless Subchapter S otherwise provides a pertinent tax effect.

4. Because Subchapter S is an elective provision, strict compliance with the applicable Code requirements generally has been demanded by both the IRS and the courts. An unanticipated deviation from the various governing requirements therefore may lead to an undesirable and often unexpected tax result (e.g., the loss of the S election).

5. The S election is available only to small business corporations as they are defined in § 1361.[4]

Qualification for S Corporation Status

Definition of a Small Business Corporation

A small business corporation must possess the following characteristics:[5]

—Is a domestic corporation (i.e., is incorporated or organized in the United States).

—Is not otherwise ineligible for the election.

—Has no more than 35 shareholders. *70 because husband/wife = 1*

—Has as its shareholders only individuals, estates, and certain trusts.

—Does not have a nonresident alien shareholder.

—Issues only one class of stock. *no preffered stock all common*

Ineligible Corporation. Banks, insurance companies, Puerto Rico or possession corporations, and members of an affiliated group (as defined in § 1504) are not eligible to make an S election. Thus, an S corporation cannot own 80 percent or more of the stock of another corporation. Under certain conditions, however, a corporation can establish one or more inactive affiliates, looking to the possibility that such companies may be needed in the future. The "affiliat-

---

4. Somewhat confusing is the fact that the Code contains several definitions of small business corporation, each pertinent to a different tax consequence. For example, compare the definition in § 1361 with the one in § 1244(c)(1), which relates to ordinary loss treatment for stock losses. These provisions, however, are not mutually exclusive. Thus, a corporation can be a small business corporation for both purposes, if it satisfies both definitions.

5. § 1361(b)(1). Note that the definition of "small" for purposes of Subchapter S relates chiefly to the number of shareholders and not to the size of the corporation. This is in sharp contrast with § 1244, which looks to the capitalization of the corporation. Section 1244 is discussed in Chapter 3.

ed group" prohibition does not apply, though, as long as none of the affiliated corporations engage in business or produce gross income.[6]

Example 2   T Corporation is formed in Texas to develop and promote a new fast-food franchise system, namely, the "Texas Chicken Delight." If the entity is successful in Texas, the shareholders of T will expand the operation to New Mexico, Oklahoma, Arkansas, and Louisiana. With this in mind and with a view toward protecting the name and product identification of the parent corporation, T Corporation forms subsidiaries in each of these states. Although T Corporation and its subsidiaries now constitute an affiliated group, T can still qualify as an S corporation as long as the subsidiaries remain inactive and generate no gross income. If any of the subsidiaries begin conducting business, T Corporation can no longer maintain its S election. □

Number of Shareholders Limitation.   An electing corporation is limited to 35 shareholders. This number corresponds to the private placement exemption under Federal securities law. In testing for the 35 shareholder limitation, a husband and wife are treated as one shareholder as long as they remain married. Furthermore, the estate of a husband or wife and the surviving spouse are treated as one shareholder in § 1361(c)(1).

Example 3   H and W (husband and wife) jointly own 10 shares in S Corporation, with the remaining 90 shares outstanding owned by 34 other unmarried persons. H and W are divorced, and pursuant to the property settlement approved by the court, the 10 shares held by H and W are divided between them (five to each). Before the divorce settlement, S Corporation had only 35 shareholders. After the settlement, it has 36 shareholders and no longer can qualify as a small business corporation. □

Type of Shareholder Limitation.   All of an S corporation's shareholders must be either individuals, estates, or certain trusts.[7] Stated differently, none of the shareholders may be partnerships, corporations, or nonqualifying trusts. The justification for this limitation is related to the 35 shareholder restriction. If, for example, a partnership with 40 partners were qualified to be a shareholder, could it not be said that there would be at least 40 owners of the corporation? If this interpretation were permitted, the 35 shareholder restriction could be easily circumvented by indirect ownership. Keep in mind, though, that an S corporation can be a partner in a partnership, and it can own stock of another corporation or all the stock of an inactive subsidiary corporation.
The tax law permits a voting trust arrangement.

Example 4   A, B, and C (three individuals) each own one third of the stock of an S corporation. Because they cannot agree on major corporate policy, they transfer the voting rights of their stock to a specially created voting trust, with an independent third party as trustee. The trustee now holds all of the voting power of the stock and can establish and follow a consistent

---

6. § 1361(c)(6).
7. § 1361(b)(1)(B).

management policy for the corporation without the interference of A, B, or C. □

Moreover, other exceptions exist that mitigate the rule that a trust cannot be a shareholder in an S corporation. Since these exceptions are of limited applicability, they are not discussed in this text.

Nonresident Alien Prohibition. None of an S corporation's shareholders can be nonresident aliens.[8] In a community property jurisdiction where one of the spouses is married to a nonresident alien, this rule could provide a trap for the unwary.[9] A resident alien or a nonresident U.S. citizen is, however, a permissible S corporation shareholder.

One Class of Stock Limitation. An S corporation can have only one class of stock issued and outstanding.[10] Congress apparently felt that the capital structure of a small business corporation should be kept relatively simple. Allowing more than one class of stock (e.g., common and preferred) would complicate the pass-through to the shareholders of various corporate tax attributes. Authorized and unissued stock or treasury stock of another class does not disqualify the corporation. Likewise, unexercised stock options, warrants, and convertible debentures do not constitute a second class of stock, and differences in voting rights among shares of common stock are permitted.[11]

Straight debt is not treated as a second class of stock and cannot disqualify an S election.[12] Such a debt instrument entails a written unconditional promise to pay on demand or on a specified date a sum certain in money so long as the interest rate and payment date are fixed. These items are fixed if they are not contingent on the profits of the corporation, the discretion of the corporation, or other similar factors. However, the fact that the interest rate is dependent upon the prime rate or a similar measure not related to the debtor corporation does not disqualify the instrument from being treated under this safe harbor rule. Such a debt instrument must not be convertible into stock and must be held by a person eligible to hold S corporation stock.

Making the Election

If the corporation satisfies the definition of a small business corporation, the next step to achieving S status is a valid election. In this regard, key factors include who must make the election and when the election must be made.

Who Must Elect. The election is made by filing Form 2553, and all shareholders must consent thereto.[13] For this purpose, both husband and wife must file

---

8. § 1361(b)(1)(C).
9. See, for example, *Ward v. U.S.,* 81–2 USTC ¶ 9519, 48 AFTR2d 81–5337, 661 F.2d 226 (Ct.Cls., 1981), where the Court found that the stock was owned as community property. Since the taxpayer-shareholder (a U.S. citizen) was married to a citizen and resident of Mexico, the nonresident alien prohibition was violated. If the taxpayer-shareholder had held the stock as his separate property, the S election would have been valid.
10. § 1361(b)(1)(D).
11. § 1361(c)(4).
12. § 1361(c)(5)(A).
13. § 1362(a)(2). But see Example 7 for a situation where a nonshareholder may have to consent.

consents if their stock is held as joint tenants, tenants in common, tenants by the entirety, or community property. Since the husband and wife are generally considered as one shareholder for purposes of the 35 shareholder limitation, this inconsistency in treatment has led to considerable taxpayer grief—particularly in community property states where the spouses may not realize that their stock is jointly owned as a community asset.

The consent of a minor shareholder can be made by the minor or legal or natural guardian (e.g., parent). If the stock is held under a state Uniform Gifts to Minors Act, the custodian of the stock may consent for the minor, but only if the custodian is also the minor's legal or natural guardian. The minor would not be required to issue a new consent when he or she comes of age and the custodianship terminates.[14]

When the Election Must Be Made. To be effective for the following year, the election can be made at any time during the current year. To be effective for the current year, however, the election must be made on or before the fifteenth day of the third month of such current year. An election can be effective for a short tax year of less than two months and fifteen days, even if it is not made until the following tax year.[15]

Example 5   In 1987, X Corporation, a calendar year C corporation, decides to become an S corporation beginning January 1, 1988. An election made at any time during 1987 will accomplish this objective. If, however, the election is made in 1988, it must be made on or before March 15, 1988. An election after March 15, 1988, will not make X Corporation an S corporation until 1989. ☐

Although no statutory authority exists for obtaining an extension of time for filing an election or consent, permission may be obtained for an extension of time to file a consent if a timely election is filed, reasonable cause is given, and the interests of the government are not jeopardized.

An election cannot be made for an entity that does not yet exist.[16] For a newly created corporation, the question may arise as to when the 2½-month election period begins to run. Reg. § 1.1372–2(b)(1) specifies that the first month begins at the earliest occurrence of any of the following events: (1) when the corporation has shareholders, (2) when it acquires assets, or (3) when it begins doing business.[17]

Example 6   Several individuals acquire assets on behalf of T Corporation on June 29, 1988, and begin doing business on July 3, 1988. They subscribe to shares of stock, file articles of incorporation for T Corporation, and become shareholders on July 7, 1988. The S election must be filed no later than 2½ months from June 29, 1988 (i.e., on or before September 12) to be effective for 1988. ☐

14. Rev.Rul. 71–287, 1971–2 C.B. 317.
15. § 1362(b).
16. See, for example, *T.H. Campbell & Bros., Inc.,* 34 TCM 695, T.C.Memo. 1975–149.
17. For support of Reg. § 1.1372–2(b)(1) see, for example, *Nick A. Artukovich,* 61 T.C. 101 (1973).

Even if the 2½-month rule is met, a current election will not be valid until the following year under either of the following conditions:

—The eligibility requirements were not met during any part of the taxable year before the date of election.

—Persons who were shareholders during any part of the taxable year before the election date, but were not shareholders when the election was made, did not consent.

These rules prevent the allocation of income or losses to preelection shareholders who either were ineligible to hold S corporation stock or did not consent to the election.

Example 7   As of January 15, 1988, the stock of X Corporation (a calendar year C corporation) was held equally by three individual shareholders: U, V, and Z. On that date, Z sells his interest to U and V. On March 14, 1988, U and V make the S election by filing Form 2553. X Corporation cannot become an S corporation until 1989. Although the election was timely filed, Z did not consent thereto. Had all the shareholders (i.e., U, V, and Z) during the year signed Form 2553, S status would have taken effect as of January 1, 1988. ☐

Once an election is made, it does not have to be renewed; it remains in effect unless otherwise lost.

Loss of the Election

An S election can be lost in any of the following ways:

—A new shareholder owning more than one half of the stock affirmatively refuses to consent to the election.

—Shareholders owning a majority of shares (voting and nonvoting) voluntarily revoke the election.

—The number of shareholders exceeds the maximum allowable limitation.

—A class of stock other than voting or nonvoting common stock is created.   *↙ no preferred stock*

—A subsidiary (other than a nonoperating entity) is acquired.

—The corporation fails the passive investment income limitation.

—A nonresident alien becomes a shareholder.

Voluntary Revocation.   Section 1362(d)(1) permits a voluntary revocation of the election if shareholders owning a majority of shares consent. A revocation filed up to and including the fifteenth day of the third month of the tax year is effective for the entire tax year unless a prospective effective date is specified. A revocation made after the fifteenth day of the third month of the tax year is effective on the first day of the following tax year. However, if a prospective date is specified, the termination is effective as of the specified date.

Example 8
The shareholders of T Corporation, a calendar year S corporation, elect to revoke the election on January 5, 1988. Assuming the election is duly executed and timely filed, T Corporation will become a regular corporation for calendar year 1988. If, on the other hand, the election is not made until June 1988, T Corporation will not become a regular corporation until calendar year 1989. ☐

A revocation that designates a prospective effective date results in the splitting of the year into a short S corporation taxable year and a short C corporation taxable year. The day *before* the day on which the revocation occurs is treated as the last day of a short S corporation taxable year, and the day on which the revocation occurs is treated as the first day of the short regular corporate taxable year. The corporation allocates the income or loss for the entire year on a pro rata basis.

Example 9
Assume the same facts as in Example 8, except that the corporation designates July 1, 1988, as the revocation date. Accordingly, June 30, 1988, is the last day of the S corporation taxable year. The regular corporate taxable year runs from July 1, 1988, to December 31, 1988. Any income or loss for the entire year is allocated between the short years on a pro rata basis. ☐

Rather than elect a pro rata allocation, the corporation can elect (with the consent of *all* who were shareholders at any time during the S short year) to report the income or loss on each return on the basis of income or loss as shown on the corporate permanent records. Under this method, items are attributed to the short S corporation and C corporation years according to the time they were incurred (as reflected in the records).[18]

Cessation of Small Business Corporation Status. A corporation not only must be a small business corporation to make the S election but also must continue to qualify as such to keep the election. In other words, meeting the definition of a small business corporation is a continuing requirement for maintaining the S status. In the case of such an involuntary termination, the loss of the election applies as of the date on which the disqualifying event occurs.[19]

Example 10
T Corporation has been a calendar year S corporation for three years. On August 13, 1988, one of its 35 unmarried shareholders sells *some* of her stock to an outsider. T Corporation now has 36 shareholders, and it ceases to be a small business corporation. For calendar year 1988, T Corporation is an S corporation through August 12, 1988, and it is a C corporation from August 13 through December 31, 1988. ☐

Passive Investment Income Limitation. The Code provides a passive investment income limitation for an S corporation that possesses accumulated earnings and profits from years in which the entity was a C corporation. If such a

---

18. §§ 1362(e)(1)(2) and (3).
19. § 1362(d)(2)(B).

corporation has passive income in excess of 25 percent of its gross receipts for three consecutive taxable years, the S election is terminated as of the beginning of the following taxable year.[20]

Example 11   For 1986, 1987, and 1988, B Corporation, a calendar year S corporation, derived passive income in excess of 25% of its gross receipts. If B holds accumulated earnings and profits from years in which it was a C corporation, its S election is terminated as of January 1, 1989. □

Such damaging C corporation earnings and profits could be acquired by an S corporation from a regular corporation where earnings and profits carry over under § 381 (e.g., due to a merger), or they could be earned in years before the S election. S corporations themselves, however, never generate earnings and profits.[21]

Although this definition of passive investment income appears to parallel that of personal holding company income (refer to Chapter 7), the two types of income are not identical. For example, long-term capital gain from the sale of securities would be passive investment income but would not be personal holding company income. Moreover, there are no relief provisions for rent income similar to the personal holding company rules. The inclusion of gains from the sale of securities within the definition of passive investment income generally has made it difficult, if not impossible, for corporations that deal chiefly in security transactions to achieve S status if the harmful C corporation earnings and profits exist.

Rents present a unique problem. Although rents are classified by the Code as passive investment income, Reg. § 1.1372–4(b)(5)(vi) states that rents will not fall into this category if the corporation (landlord) renders significant services to the occupant (tenant).

Example 12   T Corporation owns and operates an apartment building. Although the corporation provides utilities for the building, maintains the lobby in the building, and furnishes trash collection for the tenants, this does not constitute the rendering of significant services for the occupants.[22] Thus, the rents paid by the tenants of the building constitute passive investment income to T Corporation. □

Example 13   Assume the facts as in Example 12, with one addition—T Corporation also furnishes maid services to its tenants. Now the services rendered are significant in that they go beyond what one might normally expect the landlord of an apartment building to provide. Under these circumstances, the rental income no longer constitutes passive investment income. □

Reelection After Termination.   After the election has been terminated, § 1362(g) enforces a five-year waiting period before a new election can be made. The Code does, however, allow for the IRS to make exceptions to this rule (i.e., to permit an earlier reelection by the corporation).[23]

20. § 1362(d)(3)(A)(ii).
21. § 1362(d)(3)(B).
22. *Bramlette Building Corp., Inc.,* 52 T.C. 200 (1969), *aff'd.* in 70–1 USTC ¶ 9361, 25 AFTR2d 70–1061, 424 F.2d 751 (CA–5, 1970).
23. § 1362(f).

Operational Rules

An S corporation is largely a tax-reporting, rather than a taxpaying, entity. In this respect, the entity is treated much like a partnership. Similar to the partnership conduit concept, the taxable income of an S corporation flows through to the shareholders, whether or not such income is distributed in the form of actual dividends. Likewise, losses of the entity are allocated to the shareholders, who deduct them on their individual tax returns. Other corporate transactions that flow through separately under the conduit concept include net long-term capital gains and losses, charitable contributions, tax-exempt interest, foreign tax credits, and business credits. Similar to the partnership rules, each shareholder of an S corporation takes into account separately his or her pro rata share of certain items of income, deductions, and credits. Under § 1366(b), the character of any item of income, expense, gain, loss, or credit is determined at the corporate level. These tax items pass through as such to each shareholder based on the prorated number of days during the relevant S year that each held stock in the corporation.

Choice of Tax Year

After 1986, all newly electing and existing S corporations must adopt a calendar year unless the corporation has a bona fide business purpose for a different tax year or elects under § 444 to retain the tax year used for its last tax year beginning in 1986. An S corporation may adopt or change to a tax year with a limited deferral period if the adoption or change does not result in a greater deferral than the year currently in use.

An S corporation may apply to the IRS for permission to use a fiscal year by demonstrating a valid business purpose. An S corporation may adopt, retain, or change to a fiscal year if the use of such year meets the 25 percent test of Rev.Proc. 83–25.[24] This opportunity is available if 25 percent or more of the corporation's gross receipts for the 12–month period is recognized in the last two months of such period and such requirement has been met for three consecutive 12–month periods.

According to Congressional Reports, a taxable year under the § 444 election is allowable only if such taxable year results in a deferral period of not longer than three months (i.e., a fiscal year ending no earlier than September 30). However, the Code seems to allow a firm to keep any year-end used before converting to S status.[25]

The penalty for a fiscal year under § 444 is that the S corporation must make a required payment for any tax year for which the election is in effect. This required payment is equal to the revenue the government would lose as a result of the S corporation's remaining on a fiscal year. Such payments are not deductible by the S corporation (or by any person) for Federal income tax purposes. They are refundable deposits that do not earn interest and do not pass through to the S shareholders.[26]

---

24. 1983–1 C.B. 689.
25. § 444(b)(3).
26. § 7519.

Example 14   X was a C corporation in 1986 with a September 30 fiscal year. During 1987 X elects S status and is unable to meet the business purpose exception for maintaining a fiscal year. For X Corporation to maintain a fiscal year, it must elect § 444 and make a required payment under § 7519. A failure to make this payment would result in the termination of the § 444 election, effective for the year in which the failure occurred. An electing corporation need not make a required payment until the amount for the current and all preceding election years exceeds $500. If X Corporation had made an S election in 1986, § 444 would not apply. However, the entity would be allowed to change to a taxable year under § 444 by treating the deferral period of the tax year being changed as the same as the deferral period of the last tax year of the C corporation. □

Computation of Taxable Income

Subchapter S taxable income or loss generally is determined in a manner similar to the tax rules that apply to partnerships, except that the amortization of organizational expenditures under § 248 is an allowable deduction.[27] Furthermore, salaries and payroll taxes are deductible by an S corporation in contrast to their nondeductibility for a greater than five percent partner. Finally, S corporations must recognize any gains (but not losses) under § 1363(d) on distributions of appreciated property to the shareholders.

Certain deductions not allowable for a partnership are not allowable for an S corporation, including the standard deduction, personal exemption, alimony deduction, personal moving expenses, and expenses for the care of certain dependents. Furthermore, provisions of the Code governing the computation of taxable income applicable only to corporations, such as the dividends received deduction, do not apply.[28]

In general, S corporation items are divided into (1) nonseparately computed income or losses and (2) separately stated income, losses, deductions, and credits that uniquely could affect the tax liability of any shareholders. In essence, nonseparate items are lumped together into an undifferentiated amount that constitutes Subchapter S taxable income or loss. For example, any net gains from the recapture provisions of § 1245 and §§ 1250 through 1255 constitute nonseparately computed income.

Each shareholder receives a pro rata portion of this nonseparately computed amount. Under § 1366(a)(1), for a shareholder who dies during the year, the share of the pro rata items up to the date of death must be reported on the shareholder's final individual income tax return. Tax accounting and other elections generally are made at the corporate level, except for those elections that partners may make separately (e.g., foreign tax credit election).

The following items, among others, are separately stated on Schedule K of the Form 1120S, and each shareholder takes into account his or her pro rata share (i.e., the share is passed through on a Schedule K–1): [29]

---

27. § 1363(b).
28. § 703(a)(2).
29. §§ 1366(a) and (b).

—Tax-exempt income.[30]
—Long-term and short-term capital gains and losses.
—Section 1231 gains and losses.
—Charitable contributions.
—Passive gains, losses, and credits under § 469.
—Certain portfolio income.
—Section 179 expense deduction.
—Tax preferences.
—Depletion.
—Foreign income or losses.
—Wagering gains or losses.
—Nonbusiness income or loss (§ 212).
—Recoveries of tax benefit items.
—Intangible drilling costs.
—Investment interest, income, and expenses.
—Total property distributions.
—Total dividend distributions from accumulated earnings and profits.

A comparison of Schedule K for Form 1120S and Schedule K for Form 1065 indicates several major differences. The S corporation's Schedule K contains a section for reporting distributions from both S and C corporation earnings. In addition, the S corporation form includes no listing of guaranteed salaries or self-employment income.

Example 15   The following is the income statement for B Company, an S corporation:

Sales		$ 40,000
Less cost of sales		(23,000)
Gross profit on sales		$ 17,000
Less: Interest expense	$1,200	
Charitable contributions	400	
Advertising expenses	1,500	
Other operating expenses	2,000	(5,100)
		$ 11,900
Add: Tax-exempt income	$ 300	
Dividend income	200	
Long-term capital gain	500	
	$1,000	
Less: Short-term capital loss	(150)	850
Net income per books		$ 12,750

Subchapter S taxable income for B Company is calculated as follows, using net income for book purposes as a point of departure:

30. Tax-exempt income passes through to the shareholders and increases their tax basis in the stock. A subsequent distribution does not result in taxation of the tax-exempt income.

Net income per books			$12,750
Separately computed items			
Deduct: Tax-exempt interest		$ 300	
Dividend income		200	
Long-term capital gain		500	
		$(1,000)	
Add: Charitable contributions	$400		
Short-term capital loss	150	550	
Net effect of separately computed items			(450)
Subchapter S taxable income			$12,300

The $12,300 of Subchapter S taxable income as well as the separately computed items is divided among the shareholders based upon their stock ownership. ☐

Tax Treatment to Shareholders of Distributions

The rules governing distributions to S shareholders blend the entity and conduit approaches. A distribution to a shareholder of a C corporation is treated as ordinary dividend income to the extent of earnings and profits, as a nontaxable return of capital until the stock basis reaches zero, and as a sale or exchange thereafter. To accommodate both pre-election and post-election earnings, there is effectively a dormant C corporation within the distribution framework of an S corporation.

The amount of any distribution to an S corporation shareholder is equal to the cash plus the fair market value of any other property distributed. Either of two sets of distribution rules applies, depending upon whether the electing corporation has accumulated earnings and profits (e.g., from Subchapter C years).

A distribution by an S corporation having no accumulated earnings and profits is not includible in gross income to the extent that it does not exceed the shareholder's adjusted basis in stock. When the amount of the distribution exceeds the adjusted basis of the stock, such excess is treated as a gain from the sale or exchange of property (i.e., capital gain in most cases).

Example 16   P, a calendar-year S corporation, has no accumulated earnings and profits. J, an individual shareholder, receives a cash dividend during 1988 of $12,200 from P Corporation. J's basis in his stock is $9,700. J recognizes a capital gain from the cash distribution of $2,500, the excess of the distribution over the stock basis ($12,200 − $9,700). The remaining $9,700 is tax-free, but it reduces J's basis in the stock to zero. ☐

An S corporation should maintain an accumulated adjustments account (AAA). Essentially, the AAA is a cumulative total of undistributed net income items for S corporation taxable years beginning after 1982. The AAA is adjusted in a similar fashion to the shareholder's stock basis, except there is no adjustment for tax-exempt income and related expenses and no adjustment for

Federal taxes attributable to a C corporation tax year. Further, any decreases in stock basis have no impact on AAA when the AAA balance is negative.

The AAA is a corporate account, whereas the shareholder basis in the stock investment is calculated at the shareholder level. Therefore, the AAA (unlike the stock basis) can have a negative balance. The AAA is determined at the end of the year of a distribution rather than at the time such distribution is made. A pro rata portion of each distribution is treated as made out of the AAA when more than one distribution occurs in the same year. The AAA is important in maintaining the treatment of a property distribution as tax-free. This AAA procedure provides the mechanism for taxing the income of an S corporation only once.

A shareholder has a proportionate interest in the AAA regardless of the size of his or her stock basis. However, since the AAA is a corporate account, no connection exists between the prior accumulated S corporation income and any particular shareholder. AAA is not a personal right. Thus, the benefits of AAA can be shifted from one shareholder to another. For example, when an S shareholder transfers stock to another shareholder, any AAA on the purchase date is fully available to the purchaser. Similarly, the issuance of additional stock to a new shareholder in an S corporation having AAA would cause a dilution of such account in relationship to the existing shareholders.

The treatment of a distribution from an S corporation with accumulated earnings and profits is summarized as follows:

1. Tax-free up to the amount in the AAA (limited to stock basis).

2. Any previously taxed income (PTI) [31] in the corporation under prior-law rules on a tax-free basis. However, PTI probably cannot be distributed in property other than cash [according to Reg. § 1.1375–4(b), effective under prior law].

3. The remaining distribution constitutes a dividend to the extent of accumulated earnings and profits. With the consent of all of its shareholders, an S corporation may elect to have a distribution treated as made from accumulated earnings and profits rather than from the AAA. This is known as an AAA bypass election. Otherwise, no adjustments are made to accumulated earnings and profits during S years except for distributions taxed as dividends; investment tax credit recapture applicable to the corporation; and adjustments from redemptions, liquidations, reorganizations, and divisions. For example, accumulated earnings and profits can be acquired in a reorganization.

4. Any residual amount is applied against the shareholder's remaining basis in the stock.[32] Such amount is considered to be a return of capital, which is not taxable. In this context, basis is reduced by the fair market value of the distributed asset.

5. Distributions that exceed the shareholder's tax basis for the stock are taxable as capital gains.

---

31. §§ 1368(c)(1) and (e)(1). Before 1983, an account similar to AAA was called previously taxed income (PTI). Any S corporations in existence before 1983 might have PTI, which, at this point, may be distributed tax-free.
32. § 1368(c).

These rules apply regardless of the manner in which the shareholder acquired the stock.

Example 17   T, a calendar year S corporation, distributes a $1,200 cash dividend to its only shareholder, X, on December 31, 1988. The shareholder's basis in the stock is $100 on December 31, 1987, and the corporation has no accumulated earnings and profits. For 1988, T Corporation had $1,000 of earnings from operations, $500 of deductions, and $500 of tax-exempt income.

X must report $1,000 of income and $500 of deductions. The tax-exempt income retains its character and is not taxed to the shareholder. X's stock basis is increased by the $500 tax-exempt income and the $1,000 taxable income, and it is decreased by the $500 of deductions. The results of current operations affect the shareholder's basis before the application of the distribution rule.

Immediately before the cash dividend, X's stock basis is $1,100. Thus, $1,100 of the dividend is tax-free (i.e., a tax-free recovery of basis), but X has a $100 gain from the sale or exchange of stock. X's basis in the stock is zero as of December 31, 1988. (Refer to Concept Summary 10–1, second column.) □

Example 18   Assume the same facts as in Example 17, except that T Corporation had Subchapter C earnings and profits of $750. T has an AAA of $500 ($1,000 − $500), which does not include the tax-exempt income. X's basis in the stock immediately before the distribution is $1,100, since X's basis

Concept Summary 10–1

Classification Procedures for Distributions from an S Corporation *

Where Earnings and Profits Exist	Where No Earnings and Profits Exist
1. Tax-free to the extent of accumulated adjustments account.**	1. Nontaxable to the extent of adjusted basis in stock.
2. Any PTI from pre-1983 tax years can be distributed tax-free.	2. Excess treated as gain from the sale or exchange of property (i.e., capital gain in most cases).
3. Ordinary dividend from accumulated earnings and profits.***	
4. Tax-free reduction in basis of stock.	
5. Any excess distribution treated as gain from the sale or exchange of stock (i.e., capital gain in most cases).	

* A distribution of appreciated property by an electing corporation results in a gain that first is allocated to and reported by the shareholders.

** Once stock basis reaches zero, any distribution from AAA is treated as a gain from the sale or exchange of stock. Thus, basis is an upper limit on what a shareholder may receive tax-free.

*** An AAA bypass election is available to pay out accumulated E & P before reducing the AAA [§ 1368(e)(3)].

is increased by the tax-exempt income. Therefore, X is not taxed on the first $500, which is a recovery of the AAA. The next $700 is a taxable dividend from the accumulated earnings and profits account. (Refer to the first column of Concept Summary I.)

X's basis in the stock is $600 ($1,100 − $500). Although the taxable portion of the distribution does not reduce X's basis in the stock, the nontaxable AAA distribution does. ☐

Schedule M on page 4 of Form 1120S (reproduced below) contains a column labeled "Other adjustments account." Essentially, this account is used to make the balance sheet balance; it includes items not used in the calculation of the AAA, such as tax-exempt income and any related nondeductible expenses. However, distributions from this "plug" account are not taxable. Once the earnings and profits account reaches zero, distributions fall under the two-tier system: (1) nontaxable to the extent of basis, then (2) capital gain. Moreover, there is no need for an "other adjustments account" when there is no accumulated earnings and profits.

Example 19   During 1988, S Corporation incurred the following items:

Accumulated adjustments account, beginning of year	$ 8,500
Prior-taxed income, beginning of year	6,250
Ordinary income	25,000
Tax-exempt interest	4,000
Life insurance proceeds received	5,000
Payroll penalty expense	2,000
Charitable contributions	3,000
Unreasonable compensation	5,000
Expenses related to tax-exempt interest	2,000
Distributions to shareholders	16,000

S Corporation's Schedule M for the current year appears as follows:

Schedule M Analysis of Accumulated Adjustments Account, Other Adjustments Account, and Shareholders' Undistributed Taxable Income Previously Taxed (If Schedule L, column (c), amounts for lines 23, 24, or 25 are not the same as corresponding amounts on line 9 of Schedule M, attach a schedule explaining any differences. See instructions.)

	Accumulated adjustments account	Other adjustments account	Shareholders' undistributed taxable income previously taxed
1 Balance at beginning of year	8,500		6,250
2 Ordinary income from page 1, line 21	25,000		
3 Other additions		9,000**	
4 Total of lines 1, 2, and 3	33,500	9,000	
5 Distributions other than dividend distributions	16,000		
6 Loss from page 1, line 21			
7 Other reductions	10,000*	2,000	
8 Add lines 5, 6, and 7	26,000	2,000	
9 Balance at end of tax year—Subtract line 8 from line 4	7,500	7,000	6,250

* $2,000 (payroll penalty) + $3,000 (charitable contributions) + $5,000 (unreasonable compensation)
** $4,000 (tax-exempt interest) + $5,000 (life insurance proceeds)

☐

Any distribution of cash by the corporation with respect to the stock during a post-termination transition period of approximately one year is applied against and reduces the adjusted basis of the stock to the extent that the amount of the distribution does not exceed the accumulated adjustments account.[33] Thus, a terminated S corporation should make a cash distribution during the one-year period following termination to the extent of all previously undistributed net income items for all S tax years.

Example 20   The sole shareholder of P, a calendar year S corporation during 1988, elects to terminate the S election, effective January 1, 1989. As of the end of 1988, P has an AAA of $1,300. P's sole shareholder, Q, can receive a nontaxable distribution of cash during a post-termination transition period of approximately one year to the extent of P's AAA. Although a cash dividend of $1,300 during 1989 would be nontaxable to Q, it would reduce the adjusted basis of Q's stock. □

Corporate Treatment of Certain Property Distributions

A gain is recognized by an S corporation on any distribution of appreciated property (other than in a reorganization) in the same manner as if the asset had been sold to the shareholder at its fair market value.[34] The corporate gain is passed through to the shareholders. There is an important reason for this rule. Otherwise, property might be distributed tax-free (other than for certain recapture items) and later sold without income recognition to the shareholder because of the stepped-up basis equal to the asset's fair market value. The character of the gain—capital gain or ordinary income—will depend upon the type of asset being distributed.

Example 21   Q, an S corporation for 10 years, distributes a tract of land held as an investment to its majority shareholder. The land was purchased for $22,000 many years ago and is currently worth $82,000. Q Corporation recognizes a capital gain of $60,000. □

A loss will not be recognized by the S corporation relative to assets that are worth less than their basis. Furthermore, when such depreciated property is distributed, the shareholder receives a basis in the asset equal to the asset's fair market value. Thus, the potential loss disappears.

Example 22   Assume the same facts as in Example 21, except that the land was purchased for $80,000 many years ago and is currently worth $30,000. The $50,000 realized loss would not be recognized at the corporate level, and the shareholder receives a $30,000 basis in the land. The $50,000 realized loss disappears. □

Shareholder's Tax Basis

The initial tax basis of stock in an S corporation is calculated similarly to the basis of stock in a regular corporation, depending upon the manner in which shares are acquired (e.g., gift, inheritance, purchase). Once the initial tax basis is

---

33. §§ 1371(e) and 1377(b).
34. § 1363(d).

determined, various transactions during the life of the corporation affect the shareholder's basis in the stock. See Concept Summary 10–2 on the next page.

A shareholder's basis is increased by further stock purchases and capital contributions. Operations during the year also cause the following upward adjustments to basis: [35]

—Nonseparately computed income.

—Separately stated income items (i.e., nontaxable income).

—Depletion in excess of basis in the property.

The following items cause a downward adjustment to basis (but not below zero):

—Nonseparately computed loss.

—Separately stated loss and deduction items.

—Distributions not reported as income by the shareholder (i.e., an AAA distribution).

—Nondeductible expenses of the corporation.

A shareholder's basis in the stock can never be reduced below zero, and any excess decrease is applied to reduce (but not below zero) the shareholder's basis in any indebtedness from the electing corporation. Once the basis of any debt is reduced, it is later increased (only up to the original amount) by subsequent net income items. The adjustment is made *before* any increase to the basis in the stock but only to the extent that the debt basis was reduced in a taxable year *after* 1983.[36]

Example 23 T, a sole shareholder, has a $7,000 stock basis and a $2,000 basis in a loan that he made to a calendar year S corporation at the beginning of 1988. Subchapter S net income during 1988 is $8,200. The corporation incurred a short-term capital loss of $2,300 and received $2,000 of tax-exempt interest income. Cash of $15,000 is distributed to T on November 15, 1988. As a result, T's basis in his stock is zero, and his loan basis is $1,900 ($2,000 − $100) at the end of 1988:

Beginning basis in the stock	$ 7,000
Separately computed income	8,200
Short-term capital loss	(2,300)
Tax-exempt interest income	2,000
	$ 14,900
Distribution received (to extent of basis)	− 14,900
Final basis in the stock	$ —0—

35. § 1367(a).
36. § 1367(b)(2).

Because stock basis cannot be reduced below zero, the $100 excess distribution reduces T's loan basis. □

The basis rules for an S corporation are somewhat similar to the basis rules for determining a partner's interest in a partnership. However, a partner's basis in the partnership interest includes the partner's direct investment plus a ratable share of any partnership liabilities.[37] Conversely, corporate borrowing has no effect on the stock basis of an S corporation shareholder. If a partnership borrows from a partner, the partner receives a basis increase as if the partnership had borrowed from an unrelated third party.[38] In a similar fashion, an S corporation shareholder has a tax basis in any loan made by the shareholder to the S corporation. Although S losses may be applied against such loan basis, partnership losses do not reduce a partner's loan basis.

Treatment of Losses

Net Operating Loss. One major advantage of an S election is the ability to pass through any net operating loss (NOL) of the corporation directly to the shareholders. Under § 1366(a)(1)(A), a shareholder can deduct such a loss for the year in which the corporation's tax year ends. The corporation is not entitled to any deduction for the NOL. The loss is deducted in arriving at adjusted gross income (i.e., it is a deduction *for* AGI). A sharehold-

Concept Summary 10–2

Adjustments to Stock Basis and AAA

	Stock Basis*	AAA
Original basis (e.g., purchase, inheritance, gift)	Increase	No effect
Stock purchases	Increase	No effect
Taxable income items	Increase	Increase
Nontaxable income	Increase	No effect
Capital gains	Increase	Increase
Deductible expenses	Decrease	Decrease
Expenses related to tax-exempt income	Decrease	No effect
Losses (ordinary and capital)	Decrease	Decrease
Depletion in excess of basis	Decrease	Decrease
Corporate distributions	Decrease**	Decrease**

* Can never go below zero.

** Only by tax-free distributions under § 1367(a)(2)(A).

37. § 752(a).
38. Reg. § 1.752–1(e).

er's basis in the stock is reduced to the extent of any pass-through of the net operating loss, and the shareholder's AAA is reduced by the same deductible amount.[39]

Net operating losses are allocated among shareholders in the same manner as is income. NOLs are allocated on a daily basis to all shareholders.[40] Presumably, transferred shares are considered to be held by the transferee (not the transferor) on the date of the transfer.[41]

Example 24   An S corporation incurs a $20,000 NOL for the current year. The stock was at all times during the tax year owned equally by the same 10 shareholders. Each shareholder is entitled to deduct $2,000 *for* adjusted gross income for the tax year in which the corporate tax year ends. □

Deductions for an S corporation's NOL pass-through cannot exceed a shareholder's adjusted basis in the stock plus the basis of any loans made by the shareholder to the corporation. If a taxpayer is unable to prove the tax basis, the NOL pass-through can be denied.[42] In essence, a shareholder's stock or loan basis cannot go below zero. As noted previously, once a shareholder's adjusted stock basis has been eliminated by an NOL, any excess net operating loss is used to reduce the shareholder's basis for any loans made to the corporation (but never below zero). The basis for loans is established by the actual advances made to the corporation and not by indirect loans.[43]

The fact that a shareholder has guaranteed a loan made to the corporation by a third party has no effect upon the shareholder's loan basis unless payments actually have been made as a result of the guarantee.[44] If the corporation defaults on an indebtedness and the shareholder makes good on the guarantee, the shareholder's indebtedness basis is increased to that extent.[45] Such a subsequent increase in basis has no influence on the results of a prior year in which an NOL exceeded a shareholder's adjusted basis.

A shareholder's share of an NOL may be greater than both the basis in the stock and the basis of the indebtedness. A shareholder is entitled to carry forward a loss to the extent that the loss for the year exceeds both the stock basis and the loan basis. Any loss carried forward may be deducted *only* by the same shareholder if and when the basis in the stock of or loans to the corporation is restored.[46]

Any loss carryover remaining at the end of a one-year post-termination transition period is lost forever.[47] The post-termination transition period ends on the later of (1) one year after the effective date of the termination of the S election or the due date for the last S return (whichever is later) or (2) 120 days after the determination that the corporation's S election had terminated for a previous year. Thus, if a shareholder has a loss carryover, he or she should

---

39. § 1368(e)(1)(A).
40. § 1377(a)(1).
41. Reg. § 1.1374–1(b)(3).
42. See *Donald J. Sauvigne,* 30 TCM 123, T.C.Memo. 1971–30.
43. *Ruth M. Prashker,* 59 T.C. 172 (1972).
44. See, for example, *B. James Parson,* 33 TCM 789, T.C.Memo. 1974–183.
45. Rev.Rul. 70–50, 1970–1 C.B. 178.
46. § 1366(d).
47. § 1377(b).

increase the stock or loan basis and flow through the loss before disposing of the stock.

Example 25 T, an individual, has a stock basis of $4,000 in an S corporation. He has loaned $2,000 to the corporation and has guaranteed another $4,000 loan made to the corporation by a local bank. Although his share of the S corporation's NOL for the current year is $9,500, T may deduct only $6,000 of the NOL on his individual tax return. T may carry forward $3,500 of the NOL, to be deducted when the basis in his stock or loan to the corporation is restored. T has a zero basis in both the stock and the loan after the flow-through of the $6,000 NOL. □

Net operating losses from regular-corporation years cannot be utilized at the corporate level (except with respect to built-in gains), nor can they be passed through to the shareholders. Further, the running of the carryforward period continues during S status.[48] Consequently, it may not be appropriate for a corporation that has unused net operating losses to make this election. When a corporation is expecting losses in the future, an election should be made before the loss year.

If a loan's basis has been reduced and is not restored, income will result when the loan is repaid. If the corporation issued a note as evidence of the debt, repayment constitutes an amount received in exchange for a capital asset, and the amount that exceeds the shareholder's basis is entitled to capital gain treatment.[49] However, if the loan is made on open account, the repayment constitutes ordinary income to the extent that it exceeds the shareholder's basis in the loan. Each repayment must be prorated between the gain portion and the repayment of the debt.[50] Thus, a note should be given to assure capital gain treatment for the income that results from a loan's repayment.

Passive Losses and Credits. Section 469 provides that net passive losses and credits are not deductible and must be carried over to a year when there is passive income. There are now three major classes of income and losses—active, portfolio, and passive. S corporations are not directly subject to the limits of § 469, but shareholders who do not materially participate in operating the business will be able to apply the corporate losses and credits only against income from other passive activities. In other words, flow-through income and deductions from an S corporation are considered as arising from a passive activity unless the shareholder materially participates in the corporate business. For example, a passive loss at the S corporation level could not be offset against the earned income of a nonparticipating shareholder. Regular, continuous, and substantial involvement in the S corporation is necessary to meet the material participation requirement.

Example 26 N is a 50% owner of an S corporation engaged in a passive activity under § 469 in 1988. N, a nonparticipating shareholder, receives a salary of

48. § 1371(b).
49. *Joe M. Smith,* 48 T.C. 872 (1967), *aff'd.* and *rev'd.* in 70–1 USTC ¶ 9327, 25 AFTR2d 70–936, 424 F.2d 219 (CA–9, 1970), and Rev.Rul. 64–162, 1964–1 C.B. 304.
50. Rev.Rul. 68–537, 1968–2 C.B. 372.

$6,000 for services as a result of the passive activity. This deduction creates a $6,000 passive loss at the corporate level. N will have $6,000 earned income as a result of the salary. The $6,000 salary creates a $6,000 deduction/passive loss, which flows through to the shareholders. N's $3,000 share of the loss may not be deducted against the $6,000 earned income; § 469(e)(3) indicates that earned income shall not be taken into account in computing the income or loss from a passive activity. □

At-Risk Provisions. The at-risk rules generally apply to S corporation shareholders. Essentially, the amount at risk is determined separately for each shareholder, and the amount of the losses of the corporation that are passed through and deductible by the shareholders is not affected by the amount the S corporation has at risk. A shareholder usually is considered at risk with respect to an activity to the extent of cash and the adjusted basis of other property contributed to the electing corporation, any amount borrowed for use in the activity with respect to which the taxpayer has personal liability for payment from personal assets, and the net fair market value of personal assets that secure nonrecourse borrowing.[51]

Hobby Loss Rules. The hobby loss provisions of § 183 also apply to S corporations. Although § 183 was enacted by the Tax Reform Act of 1969, prior case law precluded the pass-through of losses to the shareholders when the corporation was not deemed to be engaged in a trade or business.[52] Thus, if the corporation would have difficulty in establishing that its activities do constitute an active trade or business, its shareholders may be precluded from deducting the full amount of the flow-through loss.

Tax Treatment of Preelection Built-in Gains

Because Congress was concerned that certain C corporations would elect S status to avoid the corporate income tax on the sale or exchange of appreciated property (i.e., avoid a tax on such built-in gains), it completely revamped § 1374. A regular corporation converting to S status after 1986 generally incurs a corporate level tax on any built-in gains when an asset is disposed of at a gain by the S corporation in a taxable disposition within 10 years after the date on which the S election took effect.

The tax is applied to any unrealized gain attributable to appreciation in the value of an asset (e.g., real estate, cash basis receivables, goodwill) while held by the C corporation. The highest corporate tax rate (applicable to that type of income) is applied to the lesser of (1) the recognized built-in gains of the S corporation for the tax year or (2) the amount that would be the taxable income of the corporation for such tax year if it were a C corporation. The total amount of gain that must be so recognized is limited to the aggregate net built-in gains of the corporation at the time of conversion to S status. Thus, it may be advisable to obtain an independent appraisal when converting a C corporation to an S corporation.

---

51. The at-risk rules and their significance for income tax purposes are discussed in Chapter 9.
52. See, for example, *Arthur H. Eppler*, 58 T.C. 691 (1972).

When a C corporation converts to an S corporation after December 17, 1987, the C corporation must include in that year's income a LIFO recapture amount. Such amount increases the basis of the inventory and eliminates any built-in gain with respect to this item.

Gains on sales or distributions of all assets by an S corporation are presumed to be built-in gains unless the taxpayer can establish that the appreciation accrued after the conversion. This new § 1374 tax generally is avoided if the S election was made before 1987.[53] The old § 1374 tax may still apply to many grandfathered S corporations in each of the first three S years after the conversion.

To the extent that a tax is imposed on any built-in gain, under § 1366(f)(2), such tax reduces proportionately the amount of any built-in gain to pass through to the shareholder. Post-conversion appreciation is subject to the regular S corporation pass-through rules.

Example 27   M Corporation elects S status, effective for calendar year 1988. As of January 1, 1988, one of M Corporation's assets has a basis of $50,000 and a fair market value of $110,000. Early in 1989, the asset is sold for $135,000. M Corporation incurs a realized gain of $85,000, of which $60,000 is subject to the § 1374 penalty tax. If the corporation has taxable income between $100,000 and $335,000, the applicable tax rate would be 39%. The entire $85,000 gain is subject to the corporate pass-through rules (reduced by the § 1374 tax itself), but only $25,000 of the gain fully bypasses the corporate income tax. ☐

Normally, tax attributes of a C corporation do not carry over to a converted S corporation. For purposes of the tax on built-in gains, however, certain carryovers are allowed. An S corporation can offset these gains by related attributes from prior C corporation years such as unexpired net operating losses or business credit carryforwards.

Example 28   Assume the same facts as in Example 27, except that M also had a $10,000 net operating loss carryover when it elected S status. The NOL reduces M Corporation's built-in gain from $60,000 to $50,000. Thus, only $50,000 is subject to the § 1374 penalty tax. ☐

The IRS takes the position that the term "disposition" includes not only sales or exchanges but also other income-recognition events that dispose of or relinquish a taxpayer's right to claim or receive income.[54] For example, if a cash basis C corporation with accounts receivable converts to S status, the corporate level tax will be applied to the fair market value of the receivables when they are collected. Similarly, the completion of a long-term contract by a converted S corporation using the completed contract method might be subject to this rule.

Apparently, a like-kind exchange or reorganization exchange of built-in gain property may not avoid the corporate level tax. The IRS plans to issue

---

53. § 1362.
54. Announcement 86–128, I.R.B. No. 51, 22.

Regulations to the effect that property received in exchange for built-in gain property in carryover or substituted basis transactions inherits the built-in gain and recognition period that would be applicable to the original property.

Example 29   An S corporation transfers a built-in gain asset in a § 1031 like-kind exchange. The property received in exchange inherits the amount of built-in gain attributable to the transferred property along with the remainder of the original recognition period. The corporation can avoid this built-in gain tax if the exchange property is sold more than 10 years after the corporation converts to S status. □

The new § 1374 tax is applied to the net unrealized built-in gain of the former C corporation on the date of conversion to S status. Thus, loss assets on the date of conversion reduce the unrealized built-in gain and any potential tax under § 1374. However, the IRS indicates that contributions of loss property within two years before the earlier of the date of conversion or the date of filing an S election are presumed to have a tax avoidance motive and will not reduce the corporation's net unrealized built-in gain. Other losses incurred by the electing corporation during the year will offset any built-in gains in arriving at net unrealized gains. Advisably, built-in gains should be recognized in years in which there are such anticipated losses.

Tax Treatment of Long-Term Capital Gains

If the new § 1374 built-in gains tax is inapplicable, a tax under old § 1374 may be incurred. For example, if a C corporation made a valid S election in December 1986 to be effective January 1, 1987, such an S corporation could be subject to the old § 1374 penalty tax. If a new corporation makes an S election after 1986, the new § 1374 penalty tax does not apply. Since the new corporation never was a C corporation, the new built-in gains tax would not apply.

The effect of old § 1374 was to hinder the use of Subchapter S on a one-shot basis to avoid the tax on corporate capital gains. Before passage of the old corporate capital gains tax, a regular corporation could "save" its capital asset sales for several years, elect S corporation status, sell the capital assets, and pass such gains to the shareholders to avoid the capital gains tax at the corporate level.

Tax Consequences at the Corporation Level.   Under old § 1374(a), an S corporation is taxed on capital gains if it meets all of the following requirements. First, the taxable income of the corporation must exceed $25,000. Second, the excess of the net long-term capital gain (LTCG) over the net short-term capital loss must exceed $25,000. Third, this amount must exceed 50 percent of the corporation's taxable income for the year.

The corporation may, however, fall within the preceding requirements and still avoid the special tax at the corporate level because of two exceptions to the rules. Under old § 1374(c), the tax does not apply to those corporations that have had valid elections in effect for the three previous tax years. Moreover, a new corporation in existence for less than four tax years can avoid the tax if it has operated under Subchapter S since it was founded. An S corporation and a predecessor S corporation are treated as one corporation for purposes of determining whether either of these exceptions applies. Thus, the corporation that has elected S status for sound business reasons generally will find its pattern of taxation unaffected by the realization of capital gains.

The corporate capital gains rate is applied only to those gains that exceed $25,000. Pursuant to old § 1374(b), the total tax will be no more than the amount that would result from applying the standard corporate rates to the taxable income of the corporation were it not an S corporation. Taxable income is determined without regard to the net operating loss and the special deductions in §§ 241 through 250 (except for the amortization of organizational expenditures provided for in § 248).

Before 1987, any tax applied at the corporate level reduces the amount of the long-term capital gain to be passed through to the shareholders.[55]

Example 30   An S corporation has four equal shareholders. It is not subject to the new § 1374 penalty tax, and it fails to meet any of the exemptions from old § 1374. For the current year, it has taxable income of $90,000. The corporation also has a $100,000 net long-term capital gain taxable under old § 1374. The capital gains tax at the corporate level is $21,000, 28% of $75,000. The first $25,000 of net long-term capital gain is exempt from this tax. Since the amount that will be treated as long-term capital gain by the shareholders should be reduced by any tax paid at the corporate level, the amount that can be treated as long-term capital gain by each shareholder is $19,750. This amount is computed by subtracting the tax ($21,000) from $100,000 and dividing the amount into four equal parts. Thus, each shareholder would include $19,750 in long-term capital gains. □

Any capital gain subject to the passive investment income tax of § 1375 (see the following section) is not subject to either of the § 1374 penalty taxes.[56] Section 1231 gains are not aggregated with capital gains at the corporate level for this purpose but pass through separately.

Tax Consequences at the Shareholder Level.   A net long-term capital gain retains its character when passed through to the shareholders. Net capital gains are not offset by ordinary losses at the corporate level.

Example 31   An S corporation has three equal shareholders and realizes a net long-term capital gain of $9,000 for the current tax year. In the same year, the corporation has taxable income in excess of $9,000. If no distributions are made, each shareholder must include $3,000 in gross income as a long-term capital gain. □

Example 32   During 1988, S Corporation has a $20,000 ordinary loss and a net long-term capital gain of $30,000. T, the sole shareholder, must report a long-term capital gain of $30,000 and a $20,000 Subchapter S ordinary loss at the shareholder level. □

---

55. § 1366(f)(2) before amendment by TRA of 1986.
56. § 1375(c)(2).

The amount includible in the gross income of a shareholder as a pass-through item is treated as a long-term capital gain to the extent of the shareholder's pro rata share of the S corporation's net long-term capital gain for the year of distribution.

Example 33   An S corporation with one shareholder, T, has a net long-term capital gain of $48,000 and Subchapter S taxable income of $3,000. The corporation has no accumulated earnings and profits. Its AAA amounts to $12,200. During 1988, it made cash distributions of $56,000 to T. The corporation paid a $6,440 capital gains tax. T would treat $41,560 as a long-term capital gain ($48,000 − $6,440), $3,000 as ordinary income, and $11,440 as a tax-free distribution from the AAA. □

Passive Investment Income Penalty Tax

A tax is imposed on the excess passive income of S corporations that possess accumulated earnings and profits from Subchapter C years. The tax rate is the highest corporate rate for the year, and it is applied to that portion of the corporation's net passive income that bears the same ratio to the total net passive income for the tax year as excess gross passive income bears to the total gross passive income for the year. However, the amount subject to the tax may not exceed the taxable income of the corporation computed under § 1374(d)(4).[57]

$$\text{Excess net passive income} = \frac{\text{Passive investment income in excess of 25\% of gross receipts for the year}}{\text{Passive investment income for the year}} \times \text{Net passive investment income for the year}$$

For this purpose, passive investment income means gross receipts derived from royalties, rents, dividends, interest, annuities, and sales and exchanges of stocks and securities.[58] Only the net gain from the disposition of capital assets (other than stocks and securities) is taken into account in computing gross receipts. Net passive income means passive income reduced by any deductions directly connected with the production of such income. Any tax resulting from the application of § 1375 reduces the amount the shareholders must take into income.

The excess net passive income cannot exceed the corporate taxable income for the year before considering any net operating loss deduction or the special deductions allowed by §§ 241–250 (except the organizational expense deduction of § 248).

Example 34   At the end of 1988, B Corporation, an electing S corporation, has gross receipts totaling $264,000 (of which $110,000 is passive investment income). Expenditures directly connected to the production of the passive investment income total $30,000. Therefore, B Corporation has net passive

---

57. §§ 1375(a) and (b).
58. § 1362(d)(3)(D)(i).

investment income of $80,000 ($110,000 − $30,000), and the amount by which its passive investment income for tax year 1988 exceeds 25% of its gross receipts is $44,000 ($110,000 passive investment income less $66,000). Excess net passive income (ENPI) is $32,000, calculated as follows:

$$\text{ENPI} = \frac{\$44,000}{\$110,000} \times \$80,000 = \$32,000$$

B Corporation's passive investment income tax for 1988 is $10,800 ($32,000 × 34%). ☐

Fringe Benefit Rules

An S corporation cannot deduct its expenditures in providing certain fringe benefits to an employee-shareholder owning more than two percent of the stock of the S corporation. The constructive ownership rules of § 318 (refer to Chapter 4) are applicable in applying the two percent ownership test.[59] Such a shareholder-employee is restricted from receiving the following benefits, among others:

—Group term life insurance.

—The $5,000 death benefit exclusion.

—The exclusion from income of amounts paid for an accident and health plan.

—The exclusion from income of amounts paid by an employer to an accident and health plan.

—The exclusion from income of meals and lodging furnished for the convenience of the employer.

—Workers' compensation payments on behalf of the shareholder-employee.[60]

Example 35   P Corporation, an S corporation, pays for the medical care of two shareholder-employees during the current year. T, an individual owning 2% of the stock, receives $1,700 for this purpose. S, an individual owning 20% of the stock, receives $3,100. The $1,700 is deducted as a business expense by P Corporation. The $3,100 paid on behalf of S is not deductible by the corporation, because S owns more than 2% of the stock. S can deduct the $3,100, but only to the extent that personal medical expenses are allowable as an itemized deduction under § 213. ☐

Other Operational Rules

Investment Tax Credit.   Although the investment tax credit (ITC) was eliminated as of 1986, S corporations may still have ITC recapture potential. An S election is treated as a mere change in the form of conducting a trade or business for purposes of ITC recapture. However, an S corporation still contin-

---

59. §§ 1372(a) and (b).
60. Rev.Rul. 72–596, 1972–2 C.B. 395.

ues to be liable for any ITC recapture for Subchapter C taxable years upon early disposition of property.[61] Any premature disposition of the property results in ITC recapture at the shareholder level.

Since the investment in qualified property passed through to the shareholders, recapture falls upon the shareholders when the corporation prematurely disposes of the property (or ceases to use it as ITC property).[62] Recapture may also be required of any shareholder who prematurely disposes (by sale or otherwise) of too much of the stock. Any change in the shareholder's proportionate ownership below 66⅔ percent and 33⅓ percent of original investment triggers proportionate recapture at the shareholder level.[63] The purchaser of the stock is *not* allowed to claim the ITC on the amount of the purchase price of the stock allocated to the ITC property. Since the S corporation is still the user of the ITC property, this may be inequitable, but no ITC is available to the purchaser of the stock.

Example 36   In 1985, a C corporation purchased ITC property, upon which it properly claimed an investment tax credit. On January 1, 1988, the C corporation becomes an S corporation. Under present law, there is no recapture as a result of the election. Near the end of 1988, the company sells the property. The corporation will be subject to any recapture tax as a result of the disposition. ☐

Oil and Gas Producers.   Oil and gas producers seldom choose S status. The election by a C corporation of Subchapter S is treated as a transfer of oil and gas properties under § 613A(c)(13)(C). Therefore, as of the date of the election, neither the shareholders nor the electing corporation will be allowed to claim percentage depletion on production from proven oil or gas wells.

Miscellaneous Rules.   Several other points complete the discussion of the possible effects of various Code provisions on S corporations:

—An S corporation may own stock in another corporation, but an S corporation may not have a corporate shareholder. An S corporation is not eligible for a dividends received deduction.

—An S corporation is not subject to the 10 percent of taxable income limitation applicable to charitable contributions made by a C corporation.

—Foreign taxes paid by an electing corporation will pass through to the shareholders and should be claimed as either a deduction or a credit (subject to the applicable limitations).[64] However, an electing corporation is not eligible for the foreign tax credit with respect to taxes paid by a foreign corporation in which the S corporation is a shareholder.

—Any family member who renders services or furnishes capital to an electing corporation must be paid reasonable compensation or the IRS can make

---

61. § 1371(d).
62. Reg. § 1.47–4(a)(1).
63. Reg. § 1.47–4(a)(2)(ii) and *Charbonnet v. U.S.,* 72–1 USTC ¶ 9266, 29 AFTR2d 72–633, 455 F.2d 1195 (CA–5, 1972).
64. § 1373(a).

adjustments to reflect the value of such services or capital.[65] This rule may make it more difficult for related parties to shift Subchapter S taxable income to children or other family members.

Example 37   F and M each own one third of a fast-food restaurant, and their 14-year-old son owns the other shares. Both parents work full time in the restaurant operations, but the son works infrequently. Neither parent receives a salary during 1988, when the taxable income of the S corporation is $160,000. The IRS can require that reasonable compensation be paid to the parents to prevent the full one third of the $160,000 from being taxed to the son. Otherwise, this would be an effective technique to shift earned income to a family member to reduce the total family tax burden. With the new tax treatment of the unearned income of children, this shifting technique becomes much more valuable. □

—The depletion allowance is computed separately by each shareholder. Each shareholder is treated as having produced his or her pro rata share of the production of the electing corporation, and each is allocated a respective share of the adjusted basis of the electing corporation as to oil or gas property held by the corporation.[66]

—An S corporation is placed on the cash method of accounting for purposes of deducting business expenses and interest owed to a cash basis related party (including a shareholder who owns at least two percent of the stock in the corporation).[67] Thus, the timing of the shareholder's income and the corporate deduction must match.

—The 20 percent basic research credit is not available to an S corporation. A further limitation indicates that this credit may offset only the tax attributable to the S shareholder's interest in the trade or business that generated the credit.

—Although § 1366(a)(1) provides for a flow-through of S corporation items to a shareholder, it does not apply to self-employment income. Thus, a shareholder's portion of S corporation income is not self-employment income and is not subject to the self-employment tax. Compensation for services rendered to an S corporation is, however, subject to FICA taxes.

—An S corporation avoids the corporate alternative minimum tax (AMT) provisions and the adjustment for business untaxed reported profits. The adjustments and tax preference items flow through to the individual shareholders and are determined under the definition of individual (not corporate) AMT adjustments and preferences. This relief from the AMT may be offset by a capital gain or built-in gains tax.

—If alternative minimum taxable income (AMTI) exceeds $2 million, an S corporation will be subject to an environmental excise tax under § 59A. Beginning in 1987, this excise tax is computed as 0.12 percent of AMTI (12¢

65. § 1366(e). In addition, beware of an IRS search for the "real owner" of the stock, under Reg. § 1.1373–1(a)(2).
66. § 613A(c)(13).
67. §§ 267(b) and (f).

on every $100) in excess of $2 million. Even though an S corporation normally is not required to compute AMTI, it now must do so for this new consumption tax.

✓ Tax Planning Considerations

Determining When the Election Is Advisable

Effective tax planning with S corporations begins with determining whether the election is appropriate. In light of changes made by TRA of 1986, a reevaluation of the desirability of using a C corporation as a means of conducting a trade or business should be considered. In this context, one should consider the following factors:

—Are losses from the business anticipated? If so, the S election may be highly attractive, because these losses pass through to the shareholders.

—What are the tax brackets of the shareholders? If the shareholders are in high individual income tax brackets, it may be desirable to avoid S corporation status and have profits taxed to the corporation at lower rates (e.g., 15 percent or 25 percent). Individual income tax rates have been lowered, but a married couple with passive losses reporting between $100,000 and $149,250 of taxable income in 1988 may have a tax rate of 42.9 percent. When the passive loss rules are fully effective in 1991, the same couple may be in the 49.5 percent bracket.

—When the immediate pass-through of Subchapter S taxable income is avoided, profits of the corporation may later be taken out by the shareholders as capital gain income through stock redemptions, some liquidating distributions, or sales of stock to others; received as dividend distributions in low tax bracket years; or negated by a partial or complete step-up in basis upon the death of the shareholder.[68] On the other hand, if the shareholders are in low individual income tax brackets, the pass-through of corporate profits does not affect the decision so forcefully, and the avoidance of the corporate income tax becomes the paramount consideration. Under these circumstances, the S election could be highly attractive. Although an S corporation usually escapes Federal taxes, it may not be immune from state and local taxes imposed on corporations or from several Federal penalty taxes.

—Does a C corporation have a net operating loss carryover from a prior year? Such a loss cannot be used in an S year (except for purposes of the § 1374 tax). Even worse, S years count in the 15-year carryover limitation. Thus, even if the S election is made, one might consider terminating the election before the carryover limitation expires. This would permit utilization of the loss by what is now a C corporation.

—Both individuals and C corporations are subject to the alternative minimum tax. Many of the tax preference items are the same, but some apply only to

---

68. See the discussion of § 1014 in Chapter 12.

corporate taxpayers while others are limited to individuals. The corporate tax preference relating to business untaxed reported profits could create havoc with some C corporations (refer to Chapter 2). S corporations themselves are not subject to this tax.

—Some C corporations must convert from the cash method to the accrual method of accounting (refer to Chapter 2).

—S corporations and partnerships have lost some of the flexibility in the choice of their accounting period (see also Chapters 8 and 9).

—By taxing C corporations on nonliquidating and liquidating distributions of appreciated property (refer to Chapters 4 and 5), the effect of double taxation is reinforced.

—The modifications made to § 382 (refer to Chapter 6) have imposed severe restrictions on the carryover of net operating losses.

—Since the S election may or may not provide the shareholders with tax advantages, it is necessary to consider all of the provisions that will affect the owners.

Example 38   T has a basis of $500,000 in his business assets, including some land, which is subject to a liability of $700,000. T transfers all of the assets of the business to a newly formed corporation, X, in exchange for all of the stock in X Corporation. X elects to be taxed as an S corporation. X incurs ordinary losses as follows: Year 1, $50,000; Year 2, $80,000; Year 3, $90,000. T deducts the losses to offset income from other sources. X Corporation is audited in Year 3.

—The IRS asserts that T must recognize a $200,000 gain upon the incorporation of X Corporation under § 357(c), because the liabilities exceed T's basis in the assets. T's basis in the X stock is zero: $500,000 (basis of T's assets) − $700,000 (liabilities assumed by X Corporation) + $200,000 (gain recognized to T).

—Because T's basis in the X Corporation stock is zero, T is not entitled to deduct any of the losses for Year 1, Year 2, or Year 3.

—Because T was actively involved in his business, had he not incorporated, he could have offset total losses of $220,000 against other ordinary income, and he would have eliminated the $200,000 gain upon the incorporation of his business. The incorporation and S election, then, caused T to generate additional income for tax purposes of $420,000. ☐

The choice of the form of doing business often is dictated by other factors. For example, many businesses cannot qualify for the S election or would find the partnership form impractical. Therefore, freedom of action based on tax considerations may not be an attainable goal. Several tax attributes of partnerships, S corporations, and regular corporations are compared in Concept Summary 10–3.

Concept Summary 10–3

Tax Attributes of Different Forms of Business (Assume Partners and Shareholders Are All Individuals)

	Partnership*	S Corporation	Regular Corporation**
Restrictions on type or number of owners	None.	Only individuals, estates, and certain trusts can be owners. Maximum number of shareholders limited to 35.	None.
Incidence of tax	Entity not subject to tax. Partners in their separate capacity subject to tax on their distributive share of income.	Except for certain capital gains, built-in gains, and violations of passive investment income tests when accumulated earnings and profits are present from Subchapter C tax years, entity not subject to Federal income tax. Shareholders are subject to tax on income attributable to their stock ownership. C corporations that claimed an investment tax credit and elect S status remain liable for any ITC recapture potential.	Income subject to double taxation. Entity subject to tax, and shareholder subject to tax on any corporate dividends received.
Maximum tax rate	33 percent at partner level.	33 percent at shareholder level.	39 percent at corporate level plus 33 percent on any corporate dividends.
Choice of tax year	Selection generally restricted to coincide with tax year of majority partners or principal partners, or to calendar year.	Restricted to a calendar year unless IRS approves a different year for business purposes or other exceptions apply.	Unrestricted selection allowed at time of filing first tax return.
Timing of taxation	Partners report their share of income in their tax year with or within which the partnership's tax year ends. Partners in their separate capacity are subject to declaration and payment of estimated taxes.	Shareholders report their share of income in their tax year with or within which the corporation's tax year ends. Generally, the corporation uses a calendar year; but see "Choice of tax year" above. Shareholders may be subject to declaration and payment of estimated taxes.	Corporation subject to tax at close of its tax year. May be subject to declaration and payment of estimated taxes. Dividends will be subject to tax at the shareholder level in the tax year received.
Basis for allocating income to owners	Profit and loss sharing agreement. Cash basis items of cash basis partnerships are allocated on a daily basis. Other partnership items are allocated after considering varying interests of partners.	Pro rata share based on stock ownership. Shareholder's pro rata share is determined on a daily basis according to the number of shares of stock held on each day of the corporation's tax year.	Not applicable.

	Partnership*	S Corporation	Regular Corporation**
Character of income taxed to owners	Conduit—retains source characteristics.	Conduit—retains source characteristics.	All source characteristics are lost when income is distributed to owners.
Basis for allocating a net operating loss to owners	Profit and loss sharing agreement. Cash basis items of cash basis partnerships are allocated on a daily basis. Other partnership items are allocated after considering varying interests of partners.	Prorated among shareholders on a daily basis.	Not applicable.
Limitation on losses deductible by owners	Partner's investment plus share of liabilities. At-risk rules apply to liabilities. Indefinite carryover for excess loss.	Shareholder's investment plus loans made by shareholder to corporation. At-risk rules apply to liabilities. Indefinite carryover for excess loss.	Not applicable.
Tax consequences of earnings retained by entity	Taxed to partners when earned and increases their respective interests in the partnership.	Taxed to shareholders when earned and increases their respective basis in stock.	Taxed to corporation as earned and may be subject to penalty tax if accumulated unreasonably.
Nonliquidating distributions to owners	Not taxable unless money received exceeds recipient partner's basis in partnership interest. Existence of § 751 assets may cause tax problems. Refer to Chapter 9.	Generally not taxable unless the distribution exceeds the shareholder's AAA or stock basis. Existence of accumulated earnings and profits could cause some distributions to be dividends.	Taxable in year of receipt to extent of earnings and profits or if exceeds basis in stock.
Splitting of income among family members	Difficult—IRS will not recognize a family member as a partner unless certain requirements are met. Refer to Chapter 9.	Rather easy—gift of stock will transfer tax on a pro rata share of income to the donee. However, IRS can make adjustments to reflect adequate compensation for services.	Same as an S corporation, except that donees will be subject to tax only on earnings actually or constructively distributed to them. Other than unreasonable compensation, IRS generally cannot make adjustments to reflect adequate compensation for services and capital.
Organizational costs	Amortizable over 60 months.	Same as partnership.	Same as partnership.
Charitable contributions	Conduit—partners are subject to deduction limitations in their own capacity.	Conduit—shareholders are subject to deduction limitations in their own capacity.	Limited to 10 percent of taxable income before certain deductions.
Tax preference items	Conduit—passed through to partners who must account for such items in their separate capacity.	Conduit—passed through to shareholders.	Subject to alternative minimum tax at corporate level.
Capital gains	Conduit—partners must account for their respective shares.	Conduit, with certain exceptions (a possible penalty tax)—shareholders must account for their respective shares.	Taxed at corporate level.

	Partnership*	S Corporation	Regular Corporation**
Capital losses	Conduit—partners must account for their respective shares.	Conduit—shareholders must account for their respective shares.	Carried back three years and carried forward five years, deductible only to the extent of capital gains.
§ 1231 gains and losses	Conduit—partners must account for their respective shares.	Conduit—shareholders must account for their respective shares.	Taxable or deductible at corporate level only. Five-year lookback rule for § 1231 losses.
Foreign tax credits	Conduit—passed through to partners.	Generally conduit—passed through to shareholders.	Available at corporate level only.
§ 1244 treatment of loss on sale of interest	Not applicable.	Available.	Available.
Basis treatment of entity liabilities	Includible in interest basis.	Not includible in stock basis.	Not includible in stock basis.
Built-in gains	Not applicable.	Possible corporate tax.	Not applicable.
Special allocations to owners	Available if supported by substantial economic effect.	Not available.	Not applicable.
Availability of fringe benefits to owners	None.	None unless a two percent or less shareholder.	Available within antidiscrimination rules of § 89.
Effect of liquidation/ redemption/ reorganization on basis of entity assets	Usually, carried over from entity to partner unless a § 754 or § 743 election is made, excessive cash is distributed, or more than 50 percent of the capital interests are transferred within 12 months.	Taxable step-up to fair market value.	Taxable step-up to fair market value.
Investment tax credit recapture	Conduit—passed through to partners.	Conduit—passed through to shareholders.	Occurs at corporate level.

* Refer to Chapters 8 and 9 for details on partnerships.

** Refer to Chapters 2 through 6 for details on regular corporations.

Making a Proper Election

Once the parties have decided the election is appropriate, it becomes essential to ensure that the election is made properly.

—Make sure all shareholders consent thereto. If any doubt exists concerning the shareholder status of an individual, it would be wise to have such party issue a consent anyway.[69] Not enough consents will be fatal to the election; the same cannot be said for too many consents.

---

69. See *William B. Wilson,* 34 TCM 463, T.C. Memo. 1975–92.

—Be sure that the election is timely and properly filed. Along this line, either hand carry the election to an IRS office or send it by certified or registered mail. A copy of the election should become part of the corporation's permanent files.

—Regarding the preceding, be careful to ascertain when the timely election period begins to run for a newly formed corporation. Keep in mind that an election made too soon (i.e., before the corporation is in existence) is worse than one made too late. If serious doubts exist concerning when this period begins, more than one election might be considered a practical means of guaranteeing the desired result.

—It still is beneficial for an S corporation to issue § 1244 stock (refer to Chapter 3). This type of stock allows the original shareholder to obtain an ordinary deduction for a loss on sale or worthlessness of the stock rather than receive long-term capital loss treatment. Shareholders have nothing to lose and everything to gain by complying with § 1244.

—Because of the § 1374 built-in gains provision, proper tax planning dictates that all corporate properties be appraised on or about the effective date of the S election. Valuations made a number of years later (e.g., when the property is sold) may be difficult to justify to the IRS. With such contemporaneous appraisals in hand, an S corporation can provide evidence as to the appreciation of any assets after the effective date of the election. Especially for inventory items or goods in process on the conversion date, the S corporation has an incentive to maximize the portion of overall gain attributable to the post-conversion period. The corporation must keep records to show the assets that were purchased in a taxable acquisition after the election.

Example 39   X Corporation elects S status effective for calendar year 1988. As of January 1, 1988, X Corporation's only asset has a basis of $40,000 and a fair market value of $100,000. If, in 1989, this asset is sold for $120,000, X Corporation recognizes an $80,000 gain, of which $60,000 is subject to the corporate income tax. The other $20,000 of gain is subject to the S corporation pass-through rules and bypasses the corporate income tax. Unless the taxpayer can show otherwise, any appreciation existing at the sale or exchange will be presumed to be preconversion built-in gain. Therefore, X Corporation incurs a taxable gain of $80,000 unless it can prove that the $20,000 gain developed after the effective date of the election. □

To preclude deferral of gain recognition under LIFO, the Revenue Act of 1987 requires a LIFO recapture amount for an S election made after December 17, 1987. A C corporation using LIFO for its last year before making an S election must include in income the excess of the inventory's value under FIFO over the LIFO value. The increase in tax liability resulting from LIFO recapture is payable in four equal installments, with the first payment due on or before the due date for the corporate return for the last C corporation year (without regard to any extensions). The remaining three installments must be paid on or before the due dates of the succeeding corporate returns. No interest is due if payments are made by the due dates.

Preserving the Election

Recall how an election can be lost and that a five-year waiting period generally is imposed before another S election is available. To preserve an election, the following points should be kept in mind:

—As a starting point, all parties concerned should be made aware of the various transactions that lead to the loss of an election.

—Watch for possible disqualification as a small business corporation. For example, the divorce of a shareholder, accompanied by a property settlement, could violate the 35-shareholder limitation. The death of a shareholder could result in a nonqualifying trust becoming a shareholder. The latter circumstance might be avoided by utilizing a buy/sell agreement, binding the deceased shareholder's estate to turn in the stock to the corporation for redemption or, as an alternative, to sell it to the surviving shareholders.[70]

—Make sure a new majority shareholder (including the estate of a deceased shareholder) does not file a refusal to continue the election.

—Watch for the passive investment income limitation. Avoid a consecutive third year with excess passive income if a corporation has accumulated Subchapter C earnings and profits. In this connection, assets that produce passive investment income (e.g., stocks and bonds, certain rental assets) might be retained by the shareholders in their individual capacities and thereby kept out of the corporation.

—Do not transfer stock to a nonresident alien.

—Do not create an active affiliate.

Planning for the Operation of the Corporation

Operating an S corporation to achieve optimum tax savings for all parties involved requires a great deal of care and, most important, an understanding of the applicable tax rules.

AAA Considerations.   Although the corporate level accumulated adjustments account (AAA) is used primarily by an S corporation with accumulated earnings and profits from a Subchapter C year, all S corporations should maintain an accurate record of the AAA. Because there is a grace period for distributing the AAA after termination of the S election, the parties must be in a position to determine the balance of the account.

The AAA bypass election may be used to avoid the accumulated earnings tax or personal holding company tax in the year preceding the first tax year under Subchapter S. This bypass election allows the accumulated earnings and profits to be distributed instead.

---

70. See the discussion in Chapter 12 for the treatment of buy/sell agreements. Most such agreements do not create a second class of stock. Rev.Rul. 85–161, 1985–2 C.B. 191; *Portage Plastics Co. v. U.S.*, 72–2 USTC ¶ 9567, 30 AFTR2d 72–5229, 470 F.2d 308 (CA–7, 1973).

A net loss allocated to a shareholder reduces the AAA. This required adjustment should encourage an electing corporation to make annual distributions of net income to avoid the reduction of an AAA by a future net loss.

Salary Structure.   The amount of salary that a shareholder-employee of an S corporation is paid can have varying tax consequences and should be considered carefully. Larger amounts might be advantageous if the maximum contribution allowed under the retirement plan has not been reached. Smaller amounts may be beneficial if the parties are trying to shift taxable income to lower-bracket shareholders, lessen payroll taxes,[71] curtail a reduction of Social Security benefits, or reduce losses that do not pass through because of the basis limitation. Many of the problems that do arise in this area can be solved with proper planning. Most often, such planning involves making before-the-fact projections of the tax positions of the parties involved.

The IRS can require that reasonable compensation be paid to family members who render services or provide capital to the S corporation. Section 1366(e) allows the IRS to make adjustments in the items taken into account by family-member shareholders to reflect the value of services or capital provided by such parties. Refer to Example 37.

Loss Considerations.   A net loss in excess of tax basis may be carried forward and deducted only by the same shareholder in succeeding years. Thus, before disposing of the stock, one should increase the basis of such stock/loan to flow through the loss. The next shareholder does not obtain the carryover loss.

Any unused carryover loss in existence upon the termination of the S election may be deducted only in the next tax year and is limited to the individual's *stock* basis (not loan basis) in the post-termination year.[72] The shareholder may wish to purchase more stock to increase the tax basis in order to absorb the loss.

The NOL provisions create a need for sound tax planning during the last election year and the post-termination transition period. If it appears that the S corporation is going to sustain a net operating loss or use up any loss carryover, each shareholder's basis should be analyzed to determine if it can absorb the share of the loss. If basis is insufficient to absorb the loss, further investments should be considered before the end of the post-termination transition year. Such investments can be accomplished through additional stock purchases from the corporation, or from other shareholders, to increase basis. This action will insure the full benefit from the net operating loss or loss carryover.

Example 40   A calendar year C corporation has a net operating loss in 1988 of $20,000. A valid S election is made in 1989, and there is another $20,000 NOL in that year. The stock of the corporation was at all times during 1989 owned by the same 10 shareholders, each of whom owned 10% of the stock. T, one of the 10 shareholders, has an adjusted basis at the beginning of 1989 of $1,800. None of the 1988 NOL may be carried forward into the S year.

---

71. In this regard, see Rev.Rul. 74–44, 1974–1 C.B. 287.
72. § 1366(d)(3).

Although T's share of the 1989 NOL is $2,000, the deduction for the loss is limited to $1,800 in 1989 with a $200 carryover. ☐

Controlling Adjustments and Preference Items. The individual alternative minimum tax (AMT) affects more taxpayers because of tax base expansion, the personal exemption phase-out, and a narrowing of the difference between regular tax rates and the individual AMT rate. In an S corporation setting, tax preferences flow through proportionately to the shareholders, who, in computing the individual AMT, treat the preferences as if they were directly realized.

A flow-through of tax preferences can be a tax disaster for a shareholder who is an "almost-AMT taxpayer." Certain steps can be taken to protect such a shareholder from being pushed into the AMT. For example, a large donation of appreciated property by an S corporation could adversely affect an "almost-AMT taxpayer". Certain adjustment and preference items are subject to elections that can remove them from a shareholder's AMT computation. Preferences can be removed from a shareholder's AMTI base by the S corporation's electing to capitalize and amortize certain expenditures over a prescribed period of time. These expenditures include excess intangible drilling and development expenditures, research and experimental costs, mining exploration and development expenditures, and circulation expenses.

Other corporation choices can protect an "almost-AMT shareholder." Using the percentage of completion method of accounting (rather than the completed contract method) or the accrual method (rather than the installment method) of tax accounting can be beneficial to certain shareholders. Many of these decisions and elections, however, may generate conflicts of interest when some shareholders are not so precariously situated and would not suffer from the flow-through of adjustments and tax preference items.

Termination Aspects. It is advisable always to avoid accumulated earnings and profits. There is the ever-present danger of terminating the election because of excess passive investment income in three consecutive years. Further, there is the § 1375 penalty tax on excess passive net income. Thus, one should try to eliminate such accumulated earnings and profits through a dividend distribution or liquidation of the corporation with a subsequent reincorporation. If the accumulated earnings and profits account is small, to eliminate the problem, all the shareholders may consent under § 1368(e)(3) to have distributions treated as made first from accumulated earnings and profits rather than from the AAA (the AAA bypass election).

One should issue straight debt to avoid creating a second class of stock and establish an instrument with a written unconditional promise to pay on demand or on a specific date a sum certain in money with a fixed interest rate and payment date.

If the shareholders of an S corporation decide to terminate the election other than through voluntary revocation, they should make sure that the disqualifying act possesses substance. When the intent of the parties is obvious and the act represents a technical noncompliance rather than a real change, the IRS may be able to disregard it and keep the parties in S status.[73]

---

73. See *Clarence L. Hook,* 58 T.C. 267 (1972).

Liquidation of an S Corporation.   S corporations are subject to the same liquidation rules applicable to C corporations (refer to Chapter 5). With certain transitional protection and a small business exception, the distribution of appreciated property to S shareholders in complete liquidation is treated as if the property were sold to the shareholders in a taxable transaction. Unlike a C corporation, however, the S corporation incurs no tax on the liquidation gains, because such gains flow through to the shareholders subject only to the built-in gains tax of § 1374. Any corporate gain increases the shareholder's stock basis by a like amount and reduces any gain realized by the shareholder when he or she receives the liquidation proceeds. Thus, an S corporation usually avoids the double tax that is imposed on C corporations.

Problem Materials

Discussion Questions

1. What are the major advantages and disadvantages of an S election?

2. Which of the following items could be considered to be disadvantageous (or potential hazards) for S elections:

   a. The dividends received deduction is lost.

   b. Foreign tax credit is not available.

   c. Net operating loss at the corporate level cannot be utilized.

   d. Constructive dividends are not actually distributed.

   e. A locked-in AAA occurs after termination.

   f. An AAA is a personal right that cannot be transferred.

   g. Basis in stock is increased by constructive dividends.

   h. A trust is treated as a shareholder.

   i. Salaries of certain shareholders are not high enough.

3. Which, if any, of the following will prevent a corporation from making a valid S corporation election:

   a. There are 26 shareholders. 35 or 70

   b. One shareholder is a resident alien.

   c. One of the shareholders is a partnership.

   d. There is a net operating loss during the year.

   e. One half of the common stock does not have voting rights.

   f. One of the shareholders is an estate.

   g. One of the shareholders is a minor.

4. On February 23, 1988, the two 50% shareholders of a calendar year corporation decide to elect to be an S corporation. One of the shareholders had purchased her stock from a previous shareholder on January 18, 1988. Discuss any potential problems.

5. Q is the sole owner of a calendar year S corporation that manufactures water heaters. On March 9, Q realizes that the corporation is going to make a very large profit. Discuss how Q can terminate his corporation's S election.

6. A termination of the calendar year S corporation election is effective as of the first day of the following tax year in which of the following situations:

   a. A partnership becomes a shareholder on April 2.

   b. There is a failure of the passive investment income limitation.

   c. A new 45% shareholder affirmatively refuses to consent to the S election.

   d. Shareholders owning 57% of the outstanding stock file a formal revocation on February 23.

   e. A fatal second class of stock is issued on March 3.

   f. The electing corporation becomes a member of an affiliated group on March 10.

7. An S corporation recently had its S election involuntarily terminated. Must the corporation wait five years before making a new election?

8. What is the tax effect on its shareholders when an S corporation that has an AAA terminates its election and makes subsequent distributions?

9. K is considering creating an S corporation for her interior decorating business. She has a friend who has an S corporation with a January 31 fiscal year. K wishes to set up a similar fiscal year. Advise K.

10. In the current year, an S corporation distributes land worth $88,000 to a 33% shareholder. The land cost $22,000 three years ago. Discuss any tax impact on the corporation or the shareholder from this distribution. The corporation has no accumulated earnings and profits, and the stock basis is $102,000.

11. Y's basis in his S corporation is $5,500, but he anticipates that his share of the net operating loss for this year will be $7,400. The tax year is not closed. Advise Y.

12. What happens to net operating losses incurred in preelection years when an S corporation terminates its election?

13. How do the passive loss limitations of § 469 affect an S corporation?

14. X, Inc. (a calendar year corporation), has a $25,000 net operating loss for 1988. On January 10, 1989, the president contacts you for advice as to the practicality of an S election for 1989. X Inc. is expecting another $30,000 net operating loss this year. Discuss the possibility and effect of the election.

15. Discuss planning opportunities under the § 1374 built-in gains tax.

16. Does the old § 1374 penalty tax on capital gains apply after 1986?

17. Which of the following income items are considered generally to be passive investment income:

   a. Royalties from a book.

   b. Mineral royalties.

   c. Long-term capital gain from the sale of land held as an investment.

   d. Annuity income.

   e. Section 1245 gain from the sale of an automobile.

   f. Section 1231 gain from the sale of real estate.

   g. Receipts received from the liquidation of a 60%-owned subsidiary.

h. Dividend income from a domestic corporation.

i. Dividend income from a foreign corporation.

j. Rent income from an apartment unit.

k. Interest income.

l. Long-term capital gain from the sale of stock held as an investment.

18. T, a shareholder-employee, owns 11% of an S corporation that was incorporated in 1983. Which of the following items are deductible by this corporation if paid on behalf of T in 1988:

a. Salary of $22,000.

b. $370 paid under an accident and health plan.

c. Bonus of $9,050.

d. Premiums of $625 on the purchase of $45,000 of group term life insurance.

e. $2,075 of meals and lodging furnished to T for the convenience of the corporation.

f. $5,000 of employee death benefits paid to T's beneficiary (wife) on his death in November.

19. One of your clients is considering electing S status. T, Inc., is a six-year-old company with two equal shareholders who paid $30,000 each for their stock. In 1988, T, Inc., has a $90,000 NOL carryforward. Estimated income is $40,000 for 1988 and approximately $25,000 for each of the next three years. Should T, Inc., make an S election for 1988?

Problems

1. An S corporation's profit and loss statement for 1988 shows net profits of $80,000 (i.e., book income). The corporation has three equal shareholders. From supplemental data, you obtain the following information about the corporation for 1988:

Advertising expense	$11,000
Tax-exempt interest	1,500
Dividends received	9,000
Section 1231 gain	6,000
Section 1245 gain	20,000
Recovery of bad debts	3,500
Capital losses	6,000
Salary to owners (each)	8,000
Cost of goods sold	90,000

a. Compute Subchapter S taxable income or loss for 1988.

b. What would be one of the shareholders' portion of taxable income or loss?

2. An S corporation reports its income on a calendar year basis. On April 1, 1988, the corporation issues a second class of stock which terminates the election. Through March 31, the corporate records show that the corporation has $42,000 of income, $22,000 of deductions, and $18,000 of tax credits. On December 31, 1988, the tax records indicate that the corporation has earned $340,000 of income and has deductions of $180,000 and tax credits of $43,000. No special elections are made.

a. What amounts would the sole shareholder show on his individual return in 1988?

b. Compute taxable income of the C corporation.

3. Z purchased all of the stock of B Corporation on March 1, 1988, for $200,000. Throughout 1988 and 1989, the corporation was an S corporation. During 1988, the corporation did not make any distributions and reported a profit of $20,450, of which $5,000 was attributable to the period before Z acquired the stock. Because of illness, Z sold his stock in B Corporation on October 20, 1989. The corporation operated at a loss of $13,860 during 1989, but it did make a $4,000 dividend distribution on July 1, 1989. Four thousand dollars of the loss was sustained after Z sold his stock. (Assume no special election is made.)

   a. What amount, if any, of the corporation's income must Z include in his gross income for 1988?

   b. Determine the amount, if any, of the corporation's net operating loss for 1989 that Z may deduct.

   c. Calculate Z's gain or loss if he sells his entire interest in S Corporation for $225,000.

4. P owned 10% of the outstanding stock of a calendar year S corporation. P sold all of his stock to Q on July 1, 1988. At the end of 1988, the total AAA was $800,000 before considering any distributions, and the amount in the accumulated earnings and profits account was $800,000. The corporation made a distribution of $600,000 to the shareholders on April 1, 1988, which included a distribution of $60,000 to P. On October 1, 1988, another distribution of $600,000 was made to the shareholders, including $60,000 to Q. Determine the amounts taxable to P and Q.

5. A calendar year S corporation has no accumulated earnings and profits in the current year. The corporation pays a cash dividend of $90,000 to Q, an individual shareholder. Q's AAA is $40,000, and the adjusted basis in his stock is $70,000. Determine how this distribution should be taxed.

6. Assume the same facts as in Problem 5, except that Q's share of accumulated earnings and profits is $10,000.

7. Using the categories in the following legend, classify each transaction as a plus (+) or minus (−) on Schedule M on page 4 of Form 1120S:

   LEGEND
   PTI = Shareholders' undistributed taxable income previously taxed
   AAA = Accumulated adjustments account
   OAA = Other adjustments account
   NA = No impact directly on Schedule M

   a. Receipt of tax-exempt interest income.

   b. Unreasonable compensation determined.

   c. Ordinary income.

   d. Distribution of nontaxable income (PTI) from 1981.

   e. Nontaxable life insurance proceeds.

   f. Expenses related to tax-exempt securities.

   g. Charitable contributions.

   h. Gifts in excess of $25.

   i. Nondeductible fines.

   j. Organizational expenses.

8. X, an individual, owns 50% of an S corporation's stock with a basis of $40,000. X receives a corporate distribution of appreciated property with a fair market value of

$18,000 (adjusted basis of $4,000). Calculate X's stock basis *after* the property distribution.

9. Form 1120S of an S corporation shows a net loss of $9,200 for 1988. G, an individual, owns 30% of the stock throughout the year. While auditing the corporate books, you obtain the following information for 1988:

Salaries paid to the three owners	$42,000
Charitable contributions	6,000
Tax-exempt interest	1,500
Dividends received ($4,000 was from a foreign company)	9,000
Section 1231 losses	3,000
Section 1245 gain	15,000
Recoveries of prior property taxes	3,000
Cost of goods sold	64,000
Capital losses	4,500
Selling expenses	4,200
Long-term capital gain	15,000

a. Compute book income or loss.

b. If G's tax basis in his stock is $2,200 at year-end, what amount may he deduct for 1988 on his individual tax return?

10. Form 1120S of an S corporation shows taxable income of $70,000 for 1988. P, an individual, owns all of the shares throughout the year. The corporate books show the following information for 1988:

P's beginning stock basis	$ 2,000
Cash dividends to P	30,000
Tax-exempt interest	3,000
Net sales	182,000
Section 1245 gain	10,000
Section 1231 loss	8,000
Charitable contributions	7,000
Cost of goods sold	72,000
Capital loss	5,000
Overhead expenses	12,000
Long-term capital gain	9,000
Political contributions	2,000
P's loan to S corporation	12,000
P's additional stock purchases	4,000
P's beginning AAA	13,000

a. Compute P's stock basis at the end of 1988.

b. Compute P's ending AAA.

11. At the beginning of 1988, T, the sole shareholder of a calendar year S corporation, has a stock basis of $6,300. From supplemental data, you obtain the following information about the corporation for 1988:

Tax-exempt insurance proceeds	$10,000
Long-term capital gain	8,000
Section 1231 gain	4,000
Taxable income	23,000
Distribution to T	11,000
Charitable contributions	1,000
Section 1250 gain	4,000
Dividends received	6,000
Short-term capital loss	3,000
Long-term capital loss	2,000

Calculate T's ending stock basis.

12. In the following independent statements, indicate whether the transaction will increase (+), decrease (−), or have no effect (NE) on the adjusted basis of a shareholder's stock in an S corporation:

   a. Tax-exempt income.

   b. Long-term capital gain.

   c. Net operating loss.

   d. Section 1231 gain.

   e. Excess of percentage depletion over the basis of the property.

   f. Separately computed income.

   g. Nontaxable return-of-capital distribution by the corporation.

   h. Charitable contributions.

   i. Business gift in excess of $25.

   j. Section 1245 gain.

   k. Dividends received by the S corporation.

   l. Short-term capital loss.

   m. Recovery of a bad debt.

   n. Long-term capital loss.

13. A calendar year S corporation owes $90,000 to P, a calendar year shareholder. At the end of 1987, P's stock basis in the corporation is zero, and the debt basis is $70,000. In 1988, the corporation becomes bankrupt, and the debt to P becomes worthless. P's share of the corporation's ordinary losses for 1988 is $40,000, which is passed through and which P uses in computing his 1988 taxable income. These same losses reduce P's debt basis to $30,000. Determine any losses that P may recognize.

14. T owns stock in an S corporation. The corporation sustains a net operating loss during 1988, and T's share of the loss is $45,000. T's adjusted basis in the stock is $24,000, but she has a $5,000 loan outstanding to the corporation. What amount, if any, is T entitled to deduct with respect to the NOL?

15. A calendar year corporation has a net operating loss in 1987 of $20,000. It makes a valid S election in 1988 and again has a $20,000 NOL. The stock of the corporation is at all times during 1988 owned by the same 10 shareholders, each of whom own 10% of the stock. If W, one of the 10 shareholders, has an adjusted basis at the beginning of 1988 of $1,500, what amount, if any, may she deduct for 1988?

16. M owns 50% of the stock in an S corporation. The corporation sustains a $12,000 net operating loss and a $4,000 capital loss during 1988. M's adjusted basis in the stock is

$4,000, but she has a loan outstanding to the corporation for $3,000. What amount, if any, is M entitled to deduct with respect to these losses for 1988?

17. An S corporation had a net operating loss of $36,600 in 1988. E and B were the equal and only shareholders of the corporation from January 1 to January 21, 1988. On January 21, 1988, E sold his stock to B for $41,000. At the beginning of 1988, both E and B had a basis of $40,000 in the stock of the corporation.

    a. What amount, if any, of the NOL will pass through to E?

    b. What amount of the NOL will pass through to B?

    c. What gain, if any, will be taxable to E on the sale of his stock?

18. During 1986, N, an individual, loans $100,000 to his solely owned S corporation. During 1987, his basis in the debt is reduced to $60,000, because N recognized $40,000 of losses from the S corporation on his personal tax return. In March 1988, the corporation repays $50,000 of the loan to the shareholder. How much income, if any, does N recognize in 1988?

19. For 1986, a C corporation elects S status. Its only 1987 income is a $100,000 capital gain from the sale of stock. Calculate any § 1374 tax and the amount the sole shareholder will pay, assuming she has no other capital transactions and is in the 40% tax bracket.

20. Assume the same facts as in Problem 19. If the corporation had elected S treatment four years earlier, what would be the total 1987 tax for the corporation and the sole shareholder?

21. During February 1987, W, Inc., a C corporation, elects to become an S corporation at a time when its building and land are worth $2.2 million. The adjusted basis of the land is $200,000, and the tax book value of the building is $400,000. The company has some securities valued as of February at $260,000 (with an $80,000 cost basis). You are the accountant for a 40% shareholder. What happens at both the corporate and shareholder level in the following events?

    a. In November 1988, W, Inc., moves into a new building and sells the land and old building for $2.3 million (total tax basis of $500,000).

    b. The company sells one half of the securities in February 1989 for $145,000.

22. N Corporation elects S status effective for tax year 1988. As of January 1, 1988, N's assets were appraised as follows:

	Adjusted Basis	Fair Market Value
Cash	$ 10,220	$ 10,220
Accounts receivable	–0–	58,500
Inventory (FIFO)	72,000	90,000
Investment in land	110,000	190,000
Building	230,000	270,000
Goodwill	–0–	98,000

In the following situations, calculate any § 1374 tax, assuming that the highest corporate rate is 34%:

    a. During 1988, N Corporation collects $42,000 of the accounts receivable and sells 80% of the inventory for $98,000.

    b. In 1989, N Corporation sells the land held for investment for $197,000.

    c. In 1995, the building is sold for $310,000.

23. At the end of 1988, an S corporation has gross receipts of $190,000 and gross income of $170,000. The corporation has accumulated earnings and profits of $22,000 and taxable income of $35,000. It has passive investment income of $100,000, with $30,000 of expenses directly related to the production of passive investment income. Calculate the excess net passive income and any § 1375 penalty tax.

24. For each of the following independent statements, indicate whether the tax attribute is applicable to partnerships (P), S corporations (S), both business forms (B), or neither business form (N). (*Hint:* Refer to Concept Summary III in this chapter.)

    a. Flow-through to owners of net operating losses.

    b. Flow-through to owners of capital losses.

    c. Unrestricted selection of taxable year.

    d. An increase in the organization's trade accounts payable will increase the tax basis of the owner's interests.

    e. An owner's share of losses in excess of tax basis can be carried forward indefinitely.

    f. A nonliquidating distribution of money or other property is generally not taxable to the owners.

    g. Income retained in the business will not be taxed to the owners until distributed to them.

    h. Organizational costs can be amortized over a 60-month period.

25. For each of the following independent statements, indicate whether the tax attribute is applicable to nonelecting (regular) corporations (C), partnerships (P), both business forms (B), or neither business form (N):

    a. Restrictions are placed on the type and number of owners.

    b. Business income will be taxable to the owners rather than to the entity.

    c. Distributions of earnings to the owners will result in a tax deduction to the entity.

    d. The source characteristics of an entity's income flow through to the owners.

    e. Capital gains are subject to tax at the entity level.

    f. Organizational costs can be amortized over a period of 60 months or more.

    g. Foreign tax credits are passed through to the owners.

26. P is an accrual basis S corporation with three shareholders. The AAA is $72,000 at the beginning of 1988. P Corporation's three shareholders have the following stock ownership and basis at the beginning of 1988: A (50%), $45,000; B (30%), $19,000; and C (20%), $11,000. P Corporation has the following income and expenses during 1988:

Interest income	$ 10,000
Operating income	200,000
Tax-exempt income	10,000
Cost of goods sold	160,000
Shareholders' salaries	30,000
Other salaries	40,000
Other expenses	50,000

Calculate each shareholder's stock basis at the end of 1988.

Comprehensive Tax Return Problem

Jay Mitchell (243–58–8695) and Stan Marshall (221–51–8695) are 70% and 30% owners of Dana, Inc. (73–8264911), a service company located in Dime Box, Texas. The company's S corporation election was made on January 15, 1987. The following information was taken from the income statement for 1987:

Tax-exempt interest	$ 1,000
Gross rents	5,000
Gross royalties	10,000
Service income	110,000
Salaries and wages	55,000
Repairs	2,000
Officers' compensation	15,000
Bad debts	5,000
Rent expense	5,000
Taxes	5,000
Expenses relating to tax-exempt income	500
Charitable contributions	2,000
Payroll penalties	1,500
Advertising expenses	5,000
Other deductions	10,000

A partially completed comparative balance sheet appears as follows:

	Beginning of the year	End of the year
Cash	$6,000	$ 6,500
Accounts receivable	2,000	6,000
Loan to Jay Mitchell	0	2,000
Total	$8,000	$14,500
Accounts payable	$2,000	$ 1,800
Other current liabilities	0	1,200
Capital stock	6,000	6,000
Retained earnings	0	?
Previously taxed income	0	?
Accumulated adjustments account	0	?
Other adjustments account	0	?
Total liabilities/shareholders' equity	$8,000	$14,500

The corporation distributed $16,500 to the two shareholders during the year. From the available information, prepare Form 1120S and Schedule K–1 for Jay Mitchell. If any information is missing, make realistic assumptions.

Research Problems

Research Problem 1. In 1970, S Corporation is formed by T to engage in a new venture. Under its charter granted by the state of incorporation, S Corporation is authorized to issue both common and preferred stock. However, only common stock is issued to T. At the time of incorporation, a Form 2553 is properly executed and timely filed with the IRS.

After several years of operating losses and when it appears that S Corporation might generate a modest profit, the preferred stock is issued to T as a stock dividend. In the years following the dividend, S Corporation enjoys substantial taxable income, none of which is distributed as dividends. As a result of the undistributed profits, T is able to sell his preferred stock to an unrelated third party for $100,000 on April 14, 1987. In 1988, S Corporation redeems all of its outstanding preferred stock for $120,000.

Comment on these transactions in connection with the following:

a. The tax status of S Corporation from 1970 to present.

b. The tax consequences to T during this period.

c. The tax consequences to the third party upon the redemption of the preferred stock.

From a tax planning standpoint, assess the wisdom of the procedures that were carried out.

Research Problem 2. On March 14, 1988, a client indicates that her S corporation has $115,000 of previously taxed income. Upon further questioning, you learn that the corporation has accumulated earnings and profits of $76,000. Your new client wants to know how to get this PTI out of her solely owned corporation. Subsequent investigation indicates that her stock basis is $98,000 and her accumulated adjustments account has a balance of $71,000.

Research Problem 3. During 1988, S's share of his S corporation's net operating loss is $7,000. At the end of the year, the adjusted basis of his stock in the corporation is $2,500. In addition, he has loaned $2,000 to the corporation. During the next year, his share of taxable income is $800 before he sells his stock, and the corporation repays S the $2,000 loan. Discuss all tax considerations.

Partial list of research aids:

Code § 1366(d).

Byrne v. Comm., 66–2 USTC ¶ 9483, 17 AFTR2d 1272, 361 F.2d 939 (CA–7, 1966).

Sam Novell, 29 TCM 92, T.C.Memo. 1970–31.

Research Problem 4. For several years, a father and son held some oil and gas working interests in a general partnership. These working interests incur some losses before they are transferred to a newly created S corporation in early 1989. The corporation acquires some other oil and gas working interests that incur losses, and the original oil and gas interests have both income and losses in 1989. Although the father does not materially participate in the corporation, he draws a salary of $7,000 during 1989. The son materially participates and receives a salary of $26,000 from the corporation. The corporation receives a small amount of interest and dividend income. Discuss the tax ramifications of these transactions under § 469.

Research Problem 5. On February 10, 1989, a calendar year S corporation mistakenly issues a second class of stock, thereby terminating the S election. During 1989, the corporation had nonseparately computed income of $200,000, nonseparately computed deductions of $60,000, tax-exempt income of $20,000, and tax credits of $30,000. The corporate records indicate that through February 9, 1989, the S corporation earned $20,000 of nonseparately computed income, incurred $5,000 of nonseparately computed deductions, and had no tax-exempt income or tax credits. Discuss the annualization procedure for this corporation, including the special election provided for in § 1362(e)(3).

Research Problem 6. A calendar year S corporation is equally owned by A and B during the first half of 1989. B sells all of his stock to C on July 2, 1989. Up to the date of the sale, the corporation had incurred a $70,000 net operating loss. After the stock sale, the corporation had $20,000 of income from operations. Discuss the alternatives available to the three shareholders.

Research Problem 7. On July 19, 1988, several taxpayers as primary applicants and B as a secondary applicant apply for a loan of $725,000 from a local bank. On August 12, 1988, the taxpayers agree to buy some farm land and several pieces of farm equipment for $775,000. The next day, a warranty deed is issued by the sellers showing consideration of $775,000. The farm land is transferred to X, an S corporation organized by B. On August 19, 1988, B and X sign a variable interest rate loan for $700,000 on which they agree to be jointly and severally liable. This note is secured by a mortgage for the land owned by X. B and his spouse sign the mortgage and other loan documents on behalf of X Corporation. On August 23, 1988, the taxpayers sign the articles of incorporation that were filed with the state in which X was incorporated. In organizing the S corporation (X), the assets and liabilities are transferred under § 351. The $700,000 bank loan is included in the transfer. Do the shareholders receive an adjusted basis increase as a result of a third-party loan?

Research Problem 8. P makes a Subchapter S election on January 4, 1987, and meets the qualification requirements of § 633(d)(8) of the Tax Reform Act (TRA) of 1986. The corporation has recognized built-in gains of $20,000 as follows:

Capital Gain Property	Other Property
$10,000	$10,000

If the corporation has stock outstanding at a value of $8 million, determine the tax on the property using the partial relief of § 633(d)(8) of TRA of 1986.

11 The Federal Gift and Estate Taxes

Objectives

Illustrate the mechanics of the unified transfer tax.

Establish what persons are subject to this tax.

Review the formulas for the Federal gift and estate taxes.

Set forth what transfers are subject to the Federal gift or estate tax.

Describe the exclusions and the deductions available in arriving at a taxable gift or a taxable estate.

Illustrate the computation of the Federal gift or estate tax by making use of all available credits.

Explain the objective of a program of lifetime giving.

Show how the gift and estate taxes can be reduced.

Outline

Transfer Taxes—In General
Nature of the Taxes

The Federal Gift Tax
General Considerations
Transfers Subject to the Gift Tax
Annual Exclusion
Deductions
Computing the Federal Gift Tax
Procedural Matters

The Federal Estate Tax
Gross Estate

Taxable Estate
Computing the Federal Estate Tax
Estate Tax Credits
Procedural Matters

Tax Planning Considerations

The Federal Gift Tax

The Federal Estate Tax
Controlling the Amount of the Gross Estate
Proper Handling of Estate Tax Deductions

Transfer Taxes—In General

Until now, the text has dealt primarily with the various applications of the Federal income tax. Also important in the Federal tax structure are various excise taxes that cover transfers of property. Sometimes designated as transaction taxes, excise taxes are based on the value of the property transferred and not on the income derived therefrom. Two such taxes—the Federal estate tax and the Federal gift tax—are the central focus of Chapters 11 and 12.

Before the enactment of the Tax Reform Act of 1976, Federal law imposed a tax on the gratuitous transfer of property in one of two ways. If the transfer was during the owner's life, it was subject to the Federal gift tax. If, however, the property passed by virtue of the death of the owner, the Federal estate tax applied. Both taxes were governed by different rules including a separate set of tax rates. Because Congress felt that lifetime transfers of wealth should be encouraged, the gift tax rates were lower than the estate tax rates.

The Tax Reform Act of 1976 made significant changes to the approach taken by the Federal estate and gift taxes. Much of the distinction between life and death transfers was eliminated. Instead of subjecting these transfers to two separate tax rate schedules, the Act substituted a unified transfer tax to cover all gratuitous transfers. Thus, gifts are subject to a gift tax at the same rates as those applicable to transfers at death. In addition, current law eliminates the prior exemptions allowed under each tax and replaces them with a unified tax credit.

Nature of the Taxes

The Federal gift tax is imposed on the right to transfer property by one person (i.e., the donor) to another (i.e., the donee) for less than full and adequate consideration. The tax is payable by the donor.[1] If, however, the donor fails to pay the tax when due, the donee may be held liable for the tax to the extent of the value of the property received.[2] The gift tax is to be determined by using the fair market value of the property as of the date of the gift.

The Federal estate tax dates from 1916 and, as is true with the origin of many taxes, was enacted to generate additional revenue in anticipation of this country's entry into World War I. The tax is designed to tax transfers at death, although it may have some application to lifetime transfers that become complete upon the death of the donor or to certain gifts when made within three years of death. The tax is, in several respects, unlike the typical inheritance tax imposed by many states and some local jurisdictions. First, the Federal death tax is imposed on the decedent's entire estate. It is a tax on the right to pass property at death. Inheritance taxes are taxes on the right to receive property at death and are therefore levied on the beneficiaries. Second, the relationship of the beneficiaries to the decedent usually has a direct bearing on the inheritance tax determination. In general, the more closely related the parties, the larger the exemption and the lower the applicable

---

1. § 2502(c).
2. § 6324(b).

rates.[3] Except for transfers to a surviving spouse that may result in a marital deduction, the Federal death tax accords no difference in treatment based on the relationship of a decedent to his or her beneficiaries.

The Federal gift tax, enacted later, was designed to improve upon the effectiveness of the income and estate taxes. Apparently, Congress felt that one should not be able to give away property—thereby shifting the income tax consequences to others and further avoiding estate taxes on the death of the transferor—without incurring some tax liability. The answer, then, was the Federal gift tax, which covered inter vivos (i.e., lifetime) transfers.

Persons Subject to the Tax.   To determine whether a transfer is subject to the Federal gift tax, one must first ascertain if the donor is a citizen or resident of the United States. If the donor is not a citizen or a resident, it becomes important to determine whether the property involved in the gift was situated within the United States.

The Federal gift tax is applied to all transfers by gift of property wherever situated by individuals who, at the time of the gift, were citizens or residents of the United States. The term "United States" includes only the 50 states and the District of Columbia; it does not include U.S. possessions or territories. For a U.S. citizen, the place of residence at the time of the gift is immaterial.

For individuals who are neither citizens nor residents of the United States, the Federal gift tax is applied only to gifts of property situated within the United States.[4] A gift of intangible personal property (e.g., stocks and bonds) usually is not subject to the Federal gift tax when made by nonresident aliens.[5]

A gift by a corporation is considered a gift by the individual shareholders. A gift to a corporation is generally considered a gift to the individual shareholders, except that in certain cases, a gift to a charitable, public, political, or similar organization may be regarded as a gift to the organization as a single entity.[6]

The Federal death tax is applied to the entire estate of a decedent who, at the time of his or her death, was a resident or citizen of the United States.[7] If the decedent was a U.S. citizen, the residence at death makes no difference for this purpose.

If the decedent was neither a resident nor a citizen of the United States at the time of death, the Federal estate tax will nevertheless be imposed on the value of any property situated within the United States. In such case, the tax determination is controlled by a separate subchapter of the Internal Revenue

3. For example, one state's inheritance tax provides an exemption of $50,000 for surviving spouses, with rates ranging from 5% to 10% on the taxable portion. This is to be contrasted with an exemption of only $1,000 for strangers (persons unrelated to the deceased), with rates ranging from 14% to 18% on the taxable portion. Other exemptions and rates fall between these extremes to cover beneficiaries variously related to the decedent.
4. § 2511(a).
5. §§ 2501(a)(2) and (3). But see § 2511(b) and Reg. §§ 25.2511–3(b)(2), (3), and (4) for exceptions.
6. Reg. §§ 25.0–1(b) and 25.2511–1(h)(1). But note the exemption from the Federal gift tax for certain transfers to political organizations discussed later.
7. § 2001(a). The term "United States" includes only the 50 states and the District of Columbia; it does not include U.S. possessions or territories. § 7701(a)(9).

Code.[8] In certain instances, these tax consequences outlined in the Internal Revenue Code may have been modified by death tax conventions (i.e., treaties) between the United States and various foreign countries.[9] Further coverage of this area is beyond the scope of this text. The discussion to follow is limited to the tax treatment of decedents who were residents or citizens of the United States at the time of death.[10]

Formula for the Gift Tax.   Like the income tax, which uses taxable income (and not gross income) as a tax base, the gift tax rates do not usually apply to the full amount of the gift. Deductions and the annual exclusion may be allowed to arrive at an amount called the *taxable gift.* However, unlike the income tax, which does not take into account taxable income from prior years, *prior taxable gifts* must be added in arriving at the tax base to which the unified transfer tax is applied. Otherwise, the donor could start over again each year with a new set of progressive rates.

Example 1   D makes taxable gifts of $500,000 in 1985 and $500,000 in 1988. Presuming no other taxable gifts and *disregarding the effect of the unified tax credit,* D must pay a tax of $155,800 (see Appendix A, page A–8) on the 1985 transfer and a tax of $345,800 on the 1988 transfer (using a tax base of $1,000,000). Had not the 1985 taxable gift been included in the tax base for the 1988 gift, the tax would have been $155,800. One can easily see that the correct tax liability of $345,800 is more than twice $155,800. ☐

Because the gift tax is cumulative in effect, a credit is allowed against the gift taxes paid (or deemed paid) on prior taxable gifts included in the tax base. The deemed paid credit is explained later in the chapter.

Example 2   Assume the same facts as in Example 1. D will be allowed a credit of $155,800 against the gift tax of $345,800. Thus, D's gift tax liability for 1988 becomes $190,000 ($345,800 − $155,800). ☐

The formula for the gift tax is summarized below. [Note: Section (§) references are to the portion of the Internal Revenue Code involved.]

---

8. Subchapter B (§§ 2101 through 2108) covers the estate tax treatment of decedents who are neither residents nor citizens. Subchapter A (§§ 2001 through 2057) covers the estate tax treatment of those who are either residents or citizens.
9. At present, the United States has death tax conventions with the following countries: Australia, Austria, Denmark, Finland, France, Greece, Ireland, Italy, Japan, Netherlands, Norway, Republic of South Africa, Sweden, Switzerland, and the United Kingdom. At the time of this writing, a death tax treaty with West Germany was pending ratification by the U.S. Senate. The United States has gift tax conventions with Australia, France, Japan, and the United Kingdom.
10. Further information concerning Subchapter B (§§ 2101 through 2108) can be obtained by reading the Code Sections involved (and the Treasury Regulations thereunder). See also the Instructions to Form 706NA (U.S. Estate Tax Return of Nonresident Not a Citizen of the U.S.).

Determine whether the transfers are or are not covered by referring to §§ 2511 through 2519; list the fair market value of only the covered transfers		$xxx,xxx
Determine the deductions allowed by § 2522 (charitable) and § 2523 (marital)	$xx,xxx	
Claim the annual exclusion (per donee) under § 2503(b), if available	10,000	xx,xxx
Taxable gifts [as defined by § 2503(a)] for the current period		$ xx,xxx
Add: Taxable gifts from prior years		xx,xxx
Total of current and past taxable gifts		$ xx,xxx
Compute the gift tax on the total of current and past taxable gifts by using the rates in Appendix A		$ x,xxx
Subtract: Gift tax paid or deemed paid on past taxable gifts and the unified tax credit		xxx
Gift tax due on transfers during the current period		$ xxx

make this lowest number possible

The annual exclusion before 1982 was $3,000. The change to $10,000 was made to allow larger gifts to be exempt from the Federal gift tax. The increase improves taxpayer compliance and thereby eases the audit function of the IRS. It also recognizes the inflationary trend in the economy.

Formula for the Federal Estate Tax. The Federal unified transfer tax at death, commonly referred to as the Federal estate tax, is summarized below. [Note: Section (§) references are to the portion of the Internal Revenue Code involved.]

Gross estate (§§ 2031–2046)		$xxx,xxx
Subtract:		
Expenses, indebtedness, and taxes (§ 2053)	$xx	
Losses (§ 2054)	xx	
Charitable bequests (§ 2055)	xx	
Marital deduction (§ 2056)	xx	
ESOP deduction (§ 2057)	xx	x,xxx
Taxable estate (§ 2051)		$ xx,xxx
Add: Post-1976 taxable gifts [§ 2001(b)]		x,xxx
Tax base		$xxx,xxx
Tentative tax on total transfers [§ 2001(c)]		$ xx,xxx
Subtract:		
Unified transfer tax on post-1976 taxable gifts (i.e., gift taxes paid)	$xx	
Other tax credits (including the unified tax credit) [§§ 2010–2016]	xx	x,xxx
Estate tax due		$ xxx

The gross estate is determined by using the fair market value of the property on the date of the decedent's death (or on the alternate valuation date if applicable). Valuation considerations are discussed in Chapter 12.

The reason for adding post–1976 taxable gifts to the taxable estate to arrive at the tax base goes back to the scheme of the unified transfer tax. Starting in 1977, all transfers, whether lifetime or by death, are to be treated the same. Consequently, taxable gifts made after 1976 must be accounted for upon the death of the donor. Note, however, that the double tax effect of including these gifts is mitigated by allowing a credit against the estate tax for the gift taxes previously paid.

Role of the Unified Tax Credit.   Before the unified transfer tax, the gift tax allowed a $30,000 specific exemption for the lifetime of the donor. A comparable $60,000 exemption was allowed for estate tax purposes. The justification for these exemptions was to allow donors and decedents to transfer modest amounts of wealth without being subject to the gift and estate taxes. Unfortunately, inflation took its toll, and more taxpayers were being subject to these transfer taxes than Congress felt was appropriate. The congressional solution, therefore, was to rescind the exemptions and replace them with the unified tax credit.[11]

To curtail revenue loss, the credit was phased in as follows:

Year of Death	Amount of Credit	Amount of Exemption Equivalent
1977	$ 30,000	$120,667
1978	34,000	134,000
1979	38,000	147,333
1980	42,500	161,563
1981	47,000	175,625
1982	62,800	225,000
1983	79,300	275,000
1984	96,300	325,000
1985	121,800	400,000
1986	155,800	500,000
1987 & thereafter	192,800	600,000

The exemption equivalent is the amount of the transfer that will pass free of the gift or estate tax by virtue of the credit.

Example 3   In 1988, D makes a taxable gift of $600,000. Presuming she has made no prior taxable gifts, D will not owe any gift tax. Under the tax rate schedules (see Appendix A, page A–8), the tax on $600,000 is $192,800, which is the exact amount of the credit allowed.[12]   □

The Tax Reform Act of 1976 allowed donors one last chance to use the $30,000 specific exemption on lifetime gifts. If, however, such use occurred on gifts made after September 8, 1976 (and before January 1, 1977), the unified tax

---

11. §§ 2010 and 2505.
12. The rate schedules are contained in § 2001(c).

credit must be reduced by 20 percent of the exemption so utilized.[13] No adjustment is necessary for post-1976 gifts, since the specific exemption was no longer available for such transfers.

Example 4   Net of the annual exclusion, D, a widow, made gifts of $10,000 in June 1976 and $20,000 in December 1976. Assume D has never used any of her specific exemption and chooses to use the full $30,000 to cover the 1976 gifts. Under these circumstances, the unified tax credit will be reduced by $4,000 (i.e., 20% × $20,000). Note that the use of the specific exemption on transfers made before September 9, 1976, will have no effect on the credit. □

The Federal Gift Tax

General Considerations

Requirements for a Gift.   For a gift to be complete under state law, the following elements must be present:

—A donor competent to make the gift.

—A donee capable of receiving and possessing the property.

—Donative intent on behalf of the donor.

—Actual or constructive delivery of the property to the donee or the donee's representative.

—Acceptance of the gift by the donee.

What transfers are or are not gifts under state law is important in applying the Federal gift tax. But state law does not always control in this matter. For example, with reference to the element of donative intent, the Regulations make it quite clear that this is not an essential factor in the application of the Federal gift tax to the transfer.[14]

Example 5   B (age 24) consents to marry D (age 62) if D transfers $200,000 of his property to her. The arrangement is set forth in a prenuptial agreement, D makes the transfer, and B and D are married. D lacked donative intent, and in most states no gift has been made from D to B. Nevertheless, the transfer would be subject to the Federal gift tax. □

The key to the result reached in Example 5 and to the status of other types of transfers is whether full and adequate consideration in money or money's worth was given for the property transferred.[15] Although such consideration is present in Example 5 (i.e., property for marriage) for purposes of state law, Reg.

---

13. §§ 2010(c) and 2505(c). The adjustment to the credit because of the use of the specific exemption applies whether the gift tax or the estate tax is involved.

14. § 25.2511–1(g)(1).

15. § 2512(b).

§ 25.2512–8 reads: "A consideration not reducible to a value in money or money's worth, as love and affection, promise of marriage, etc., is to be wholly disregarded, and the entire value of the property transferred constitutes the amount of the gift."

Incomplete Transfers. The Federal gift tax does not apply to transfers that are incomplete. Thus, if the transferor retains the right to reclaim the property or, for all intents and purposes, has not really parted with the possession of the property, a taxable event has not taken place.

Example 6

LIFE
ESTATE

D creates a trust, income payable to S for life, remainder to R.[16] Under the terms of the trust instrument, D can revoke the trust at any time and repossess trust corpus and income therefrom. No gift takes place on the creation of the trust; D has not ceased to have dominion and control over the property. □

Example 7

Assume the same facts as in Example 6, except that one year after the transfer, D relinquishes his right to terminate the trust. At this point, the transfer becomes complete and the Federal gift tax applies. □

Business Versus Personal Setting. In a business setting, full and adequate consideration in money or money's worth is apt to exist. Reg. § 25.2512–8 provides that "a sale, exchange, or other transfer of property made in the ordinary course of business (a transaction that is bona fide, at arm's length, and free of any donative intent) will be considered as made for an adequate and full consideration in money or money's worth." If the parties are acting in a personal setting, however, a gift usually is the result.

Example 8

D loans money to S in connection with a business venture. About a year later, D forgives part of the loan. D probably has not made a gift to S if D and S are unrelated parties.[17] □

Example 9

Assume the same facts as in Example 8, except that D and S are father and son and no business venture is involved. If the loan itself was not, in fact, a disguised gift, the later forgiveness will probably be treated as a gift. □

Do not conclude, however, that the presence of *some* consideration may be enough to preclude Federal gift tax consequences. Again, the answer may rest on whether the transfer occurred in a business setting.

Example 10

D sells S some real estate for $40,000. Unknown to D, the property contains valuable mineral deposits and is really worth $100,000. D may have made a bad business deal, but he has not made a gift to S of $60,000. □

16. The holder of a life estate (called a life tenant) has the right to the use of the property (including the right to the income therefrom) for his or her life. On the death of the life tenant, the property (called the remainder interest) passes to the designated remainderperson.
17. The forgiveness could, however, result in taxable income to S under § 61(a)(12).

Example 11   Assume the same facts as in Example 10, except that D and S are father and son. In addition, D is very much aware of the fact that the property is worth $100,000. D has made a gift to S of $60,000. ☐

Certain Excluded Transfers.   Transfers to political organizations are exempt from the application of the Federal gift tax.[18] This provision in the Code made unnecessary the previous practice whereby candidates for public office established multiple campaign committees to maximize the number of annual exclusions available to their contributors. As noted later, an annual exclusion of $10,000 (previously $3,000) for each donee passes free of the Federal gift tax.

The Federal gift tax does not apply to tuition payments made to an educational organization (e.g., a college) on another's behalf. Nor does it apply to amounts paid on another's behalf for medical care.[19] In this regard, perhaps, the law is realistic, since most donors would not likely recognize these items as being transfers subject to the gift tax.

Lifetime Versus Death Transfers.   Be careful to distinguish between lifetime (i.e., inter vivos) and death (i.e., testamentary) transfers.

Example 12   D buys a U.S. savings bond, which he registers as follows: "D, payable to S upon D's death." No gift is made when D buys the bond; S has received only a mere expectancy (i.e., to obtain ownership of the bond at D's death). Anytime before his death, D may redeem or otherwise dispose of the bond and thereby cut off S's interest. On D's death, no gift is made, because the bond passes to S by testamentary disposition. As noted later, however, the bond will be included in D's gross estate as property in which the decedent had an interest (§ 2033). ☐

Example 13   D purchases an insurance policy on his own life (face value of $100,000) and designates S as the beneficiary. Until his death, D remains the owner of the policy and pays all premiums thereon. In accordance with the reasoning set forth in Example 12, no gift to S is made either when the policy is purchased or when D pays any of the premiums thereon. On D's death, the $100,000 proceeds pass to S as a testamentary and not as an inter vivos transfer. As mentioned later, the insurance proceeds will be included in D's gross estate under § 2042(2). ☐

Transfers Subject to the Gift Tax

Whether or not a transfer will constitute one subject to the Federal gift tax will depend upon the application of §§ 2511 through 2519 and the Regulations thereunder.

Gift Loans.   To understand legislation enacted by Congress, an illustration is helpful.

---

18. § 2501(a)(5).
19. § 2503(e).

Example 14   Before his daughter (D) leaves for college, F loans her $300,000. D signs a note that provides for repayment in five years. The loan, however, contains no interest element, and neither F nor D expects any interest to be paid. Following F's advice, D invests the loan proceeds in income-producing securities. During her five years in college, D uses the income from the investments to pay for college costs and other living expenses. On the maturity date of the note, D repays the $300,000 she owes F. □

Regarding the factual situation presented in Example 14, what were the parties trying to accomplish? Presuming the loan is recognized as valid, D and F would hope for the following results:

1. No gift has taken place as to the loan proceeds.
2. No gift has taken place as to the interest element. Although D enjoys the use of the loan funds interest-free, until recently no court had held that this was a benefit subject to the Federal gift tax.[20]
3. The income from the invested loan proceeds will be taxed to D. This will save income taxes for the family unit if one assumes that D is in a lower tax bracket than F.
4. No income will result to F as to the forgone interest element. Again, this result was based on a very solid judicial foundation.[21]

In 1984, Congress resolved to rectify what it considered to be an abusive situation (i.e., Example 14). In a gift loan arrangement, the following consequences now ensue:

—F will have made a gift to D of the interest element. The amount of the gift will be determined by the difference between the amount of interest charged (in this case, none) and the market rate (as determined by the yield on certain U.S. government securities). (Compare result 2.)

—The interest element must be included in F's gross income and will be subject to the Federal income tax. (Compare result 4.)

—D may be allowed an income tax deduction as to the interest element. This result may benefit D only if she is in a position to itemize her deductions *from* adjusted gross income.

Section 7872(f)(3) defines a gift loan as "any below-market loan where the foregoing [*sic*] of interest is in the nature of a gift." Unless tax avoidance was one of the principal purposes of the loan, special limitations apply if the gift loan does not exceed $100,000. In such a case, the interest element shall not exceed the borrower's net investment income.[22] Furthermore, if such net investment income does not exceed $1,000, it shall be treated as zero. Under the $1,000 de minimis rule, therefore, the interest element is to be disregarded.

---

20. The result reached in *Lester Crown*, 67 T.C. 1060 (1977), was thought to be valid until repudiated in *Dickman v. Comm.*, 84–1 USTC ¶ 9240, 53 AFTR2d 84–1608, 104 S.Ct. 1086 (USSC, 1984). In *Dickman*, the Supreme Court found that the interest element was subject to the Federal gift tax.
21. See, for example, *J. Simpson Dean*, 35 T.C. 1083 (1961), which negated imputed income as to the borrower.
22. Net investment income has the same meaning given to the term by § 163(d). Generally, net investment income is investment income (e.g., interest, dividends) less related expenses.

Certain Property Settlements (§ 2516).   Normally, the settlement of certain marital rights is not regarded as being for consideration in money or money's worth and is therefore subject to the Federal gift tax.[23] As a special exception to this general approach, Congress saw fit to enact § 2516. Under this provision, transfers of property interests made under the terms of a written agreement between spouses in settlement of their marital or property rights are deemed to be for adequate consideration and are thereby exempt from the Federal gift tax if a final decree of divorce is obtained within the three-year period beginning on the date one year before such agreement is entered into. Likewise excluded are transfers to provide a reasonable allowance for the support of minor children (including legally adopted children) of a marriage. The agreement need not be approved by the divorce decree.

Disclaimers (§ 2518).   A disclaimer is a refusal by a person to accept property that is designated to pass to him or her. The effect of the disclaimer is to pass the property to someone else.

Example 15   D dies intestate (i.e., without a will) and is survived by a son, S, and a grandson, GS.[24] At the time of his death, D owned real estate which, under the applicable state law of intestate succession, passes to the closest lineal descendant, S in this case. If, however, S disclaims his interest in the real estate, state law provides that the property would pass to the next lineal descendant, GS in this case. At the time of D's death, S has considerable property of his own although GS has none. □

Why might S want to consider issuing a disclaimer as to his inheritance and have the property pass directly from D to GS? By so doing, an extra transfer tax might be avoided. If the disclaimer does not take place, (i.e., S accepts the inheritance) and the property eventually passes to GS (either by gift or by death), the later transfer will be subject to the application of either the gift tax or the estate tax.

For many years, whether or not a disclaimer was effective to avoid a Federal transfer tax depended on the application of state law. To illustrate by using the facts of Example 15, if state law determined that a disclaimer by S after D's death still meant that the real estate was deemed to have passed through S, the Federal gift tax would apply. In essence, S would be treated as if he had inherited the property from D and then given it to GS. As state law was not always consistent in this regard and sometimes was not even known, the application or nonapplication of Federal transfer taxes could depend on where the parties lived. To remedy this situation and provide some measure of uniformity to the area of disclaimers, §§ 2046 (relating to disclaimers for estate tax purposes) and 2518 were added to the Code.

---

23. See Reg. § 25.2512–8 and Example 5 in this chapter.
24. All states provide for an order of distribution in the event someone dies without a will. After the surviving spouse who receives some or all of the estate, the preference is usually in the following order: down to lineal descendants (e.g., children, grandchildren), up to lineal ascendants (e.g., parents, grandparents), and out to collateral relations (e.g., brothers, sisters, aunts, and uncles).

In the case of the gift tax, meeting the requirements of § 2518 would treat a timely lifetime disclaimer by S (refer to Example 15) as if the property went directly from D to GS. Since it is not regarded as having passed through S (regardless of what state law holds), it will not be subject to the Federal gift tax.

The tax law also permits the avoidance of the Federal gift tax in cases of a partial disclaimer of an undivided interest.

Example 16   Assume the same facts as in Example 15, except that S wishes to retain one half of the real estate for himself. If S makes a timely disclaimer of an undivided one-half interest in the property, the Federal gift tax will not apply as to the portion passing to GS. ☐

Other Transfers Subject to Gift Tax.   Other transfers that may carry gift tax consequences (e.g., the exercise of a power of appointment, the creation of joint ownership) are discussed and illustrated in connection with the Federal estate tax.

Annual Exclusion

In General.   The first $10,000 of gifts made to any one person during any calendar year (except gifts of future interests in property) is excluded in determining the total amount of gifts for the year.[25] The annual exclusion is applied to all gifts of a present interest made during the calendar year in the order in which made until the $10,000 exclusion per donee is exhausted. For a gift in trust, each beneficiary of the trust is treated as a separate person for purposes of the exclusion.

A future interest may be defined as one that will come into being (as to use, possession, or enjoyment) at some future date. Examples of future interests would include such possessory rights, whether vested or contingent, as remainder and reversionary interests that are commonly encountered when property is transferred to a trust. On the other hand, a present interest is an unrestricted right to the immediate use, possession, or enjoyment of property or of the income therefrom.

Example 17   During the current year, D makes the following cash gifts: $8,000 to R and $12,000 to S. D may claim an annual exclusion of $8,000 with respect to R and $10,000 with respect to S. ☐

Example 18   By a lifetime gift, D transfers property to a trust with a life estate (with income payable annually) to R and remainder upon R's death to S. D has made two gifts: one to R of a life estate and one to S of a remainder interest. (The valuation of each of these gifts is discussed in Chapter 12.) The life estate is a present interest and therefore qualifies for the annual exclusion. The remainder interest granted to S is a future interest and does not qualify for the exclusion. Note that S's interest does not come into being until some future date (i.e., on the death of R). ☐

---

25. § 2503(b).

Although Example 18 indicates that the gift of an income interest is a present interest, this may not always prove to be the case. If a possibility exists that the income beneficiary may not receive the immediate enjoyment of the property, the transfer is one of a future interest.

Example 19   Assume the same facts as in Example 18, except that the income from the trust need not be payable annually to R but may, at the trustee's discretion, be accumulated and added to corpus. Since R's right to receive the income from the trust is conditioned on the trustee's discretion, it is not a present interest and no annual exclusion will be allowed. The mere possibility of diversion is enough. It would not matter if the trustee never exercised his or her discretion to accumulate and did, in fact, distribute the trust income to R annually. □

Trust for Minors.   Section 2503(c) offers an important exception to the future interest rules just discussed. Under this provision, a transfer for the benefit of a person who has not attained the age of 21 years on the date of the gift may be considered a gift of a present interest even though the minor is not given the unrestricted right to the immediate use, possession, or enjoyment of the property. For the exception to apply, the following conditions must be satisfied:

—Both the property and its income may be expended by or for the benefit of the minor before the minor attains the age of 21.

—Any portion of the property or its income not expended by the minor's attainment of age 21 shall pass to the minor at that time.

—If the minor dies before attaining the age of 21, the property and its income will be payable either to the minor's estate or as the minor may appoint under a general power of appointment (discussed later in the chapter).

Thus, the exception would allow a trustee to accumulate income on behalf of a minor beneficiary without converting the income interest to a future interest.

Example 20   D places property in trust, income payable to S until he reaches 21, remainder to S or S's estate. Under the terms of the trust instrument, the trustee is empowered to accumulate the trust income or apply it towards S's benefit. In either event, the accumulated income and corpus must be paid to S whenever he reaches 21 years of age or to whomever S designates in his will if he dies before reaching such age. The conditions of § 2503(c) are satisfied, and D's transfer qualifies for the annual exclusion. S's interest is a present interest. □

Deductions

In arriving at taxable gifts, a deduction is allowed for transfers to certain qualified charitable organizations. On transfers between spouses, a marital deduction may be available. Since both the charitable and marital deductions apply in determining the Federal estate tax, these deductions are discussed later in the chapter.

Computing the Federal Gift Tax

The Unified Transfer Tax Rate Schedule.   The top rates of the unified transfer tax rate schedule originally reached as high as 70 percent (see Appendix A, page A–5). To be consistent with the maximum income tax rate applicable to individuals which, until recently, was 50 percent, the top unified transfer tax rate was lowered to this amount. But the reduction was phased in, and the maximum of 50 percent is not scheduled to be reached until 1993 (see Appendix A, page A–9). For transfers (by gift or death) made from 1984 through 1992, the top rate is 55 percent (see Appendix A, page A–8). As noted later in the chapter, the benefits of the graduated rates are to be phased out for larger gifts beginning after 1987. Keep in mind that the unified transfer tax rate schedule applies to all transfers (by gift or death) after 1976. Different rate schedules apply for pre-1977 gifts (see Appendix A, page A–11) and pre-1977 deaths (see Appendix A, page A–10).

The Deemed Paid Adjustment.   Reviewing the formula for the gift tax (earlier in the chapter), note that the tax base for a current gift includes *all* past taxable gifts. The effect of such inclusion is to force the current taxable gift into a higher bracket because of the progressive nature of the unified transfer tax rates (refer to Example 1). To mitigate such double taxation, the donor is allowed a credit for any gift tax previously paid (refer to Example 2).

To limit the donor to a credit for the gift tax *actually paid* on pre-1977 taxable gifts would be unfair. Pre-1977 taxable gifts were subject to a lower set of rates (see Appendix A, page A–11) than those contained in the unified transfer tax rate schedule. As a consequence, the donor is allowed a "deemed paid" credit on pre-1977 taxable gifts. This is the amount that would have been due under the unified transfer tax rate schedule had it been applicable. Post-1976 taxable gifts do not need the deemed paid adjustment, since the same rate schedule is involved in all gifts.

Example 21   In early 1976, T made taxable gifts of $500,000, upon which a Federal gift tax of $109,275 (see Appendix A, page A–11) was paid. Assume T makes further taxable gifts of $700,000 in 1988. The unified transfer tax on the 1988 gifts would be determined as follows:

Taxable gifts made in 1988		$ 500,000
Add: Taxable gifts made in 1976		700,000
Total of current and past taxable gifts		$1,200,000
Unified transfer tax on total taxable gifts per Appendix A, page A–8 [$345,800 + (41% × $200,000)]		$ 427,800
Subtract:		
Deemed paid tax on pre-1977 taxable gifts per Appendix A, page A–8	$155,800	
Unified tax credit for 1988	192,800	(348,600)
Gift tax due on the 1988 taxable gift		$ 79,200

Note that the gift tax actually paid on the 1976 transfer was $109,275. Nevertheless, the deemed paid credit allowed T on the gift was $155,800, considerably more than what was paid. □

The Election to Split Gifts by Married Persons.   To understand the reason for the gift-splitting election of § 2513, consider the following situations:

Example 22   H and W are husband and wife and reside in Michigan, a common law state.[26] H has been the only breadwinner in the family, and W has no significant amount of property of her own. Neither has made any prior taxable gifts or has used the $30,000 specific exemption previously available for pre-1977 gifts. In 1988, H makes a gift to S of $1,220,000. Presuming the election to split gifts did not exist, H's gift tax is as follows:

Amount of gift	$1,220,000
Subtract: Annual exclusion	(10,000)
Taxable gift	$1,210,000
Gift tax on $1,210,000 per Appendix A, page A–8 [$345,800 + (41% × $210,000)]	$ 431,900
Subtract: Unified tax credit for 1988	(192,800)
Gift tax due on the 1988 taxable gift	$ 239,100

□

Example 23   Assume the same facts as in Example 22, except that H and W always have resided in California. Even though H is the sole breadwinner, since income from personal services generally is community property, the gift to S probably involves community property. If this is the case, the gift tax is worked out as follows:

	H	W
Amount of the gift (50% × $1,220,000)	$610,000	$610,000
Subtract: Annual exclusion	(10,000)	(10,000)
Taxable gifts	$600,000	$600,000
Gift tax on $600,000 per Appendix A, page A–8	$192,800	$192,800
Subtract: Unified tax credit for 1988	(192,800)	(192,800)
Gift tax due on the 1988 taxable gifts	$ –0–	$ –0–

□

By comparing the results of Examples 22 and 23, one can see that married donors residing in community property jurisdictions possessed a significant gift tax advantage over those residing in common law states. To rectify this

26. The following states have the community property system in effect: Louisiana, Texas, New Mexico, Arizona, California, Washington, Idaho, Nevada, and Wisconsin (effective January 1, 1986). All other states follow the common law system in ascertaining the rights of spouses to property acquired after marriage.

inequity, the Revenue Act of 1948 incorporated into the Code the predecessor to § 2513. Under this Section, a gift made by a person to someone other than his or her spouse may be considered, for Federal gift tax purposes, as having been made one-half by each spouse. Returning to Example 22, this means H and W could treat the gift passing to S as being made one-half by each of them in spite of the fact that the cash may have belonged to H. Consequently, the parties were able to achieve the same tax result as that outlined in Example 23.

To split gifts, the spouses must be legally married to each other at the time of the gift. If they are divorced later in the calendar year, they may still split the gift if neither marries anyone else during that year. They both must signify on their separate gift tax returns their consent to have all gifts made in that calendar year split between them. In addition, both must be citizens or residents of the United States on the date of the gift. A gift from one spouse to the other spouse cannot be split. Such a gift might, however, be eligible for the marital deduction.

The election to split gifts would not be necessary when husband and wife transfer community property to a third party. It would, however, be available if the subject of the gift consisted of the separate property of one of the spouses. Generally, separate property is property acquired before marriage and property acquired after marriage by gift or inheritance. The election, then, is not limited to residents of common law states.

Procedural Matters

Having determined what transfers are subject to the Federal gift tax and the various deductions and exclusions available to the donor, consideration should be accorded to the procedural aspects of the tax. The sections to follow discuss the return itself, the due dates for filing and paying the tax, and other related matters.

The Federal Gift Tax Return.   For transfers by gift, a Form 709 (U.S. Gift Tax Return) must be filed whenever the gifts for any one calendar year exceed the annual exclusion or involve a gift of a future interest. Regardless of amount, however, transfers between spouses that are offset by the unlimited marital deduction do not require the filing of a Form 709.[27]

Example 24   In 1988, D makes five gifts, each in the amount of $10,000, to his five children. If the gifts do not involve future interests, a Form 709 need not be filed to report the transfers. ☐

Example 25   During 1988, M makes a gift of $20,000 cash of her separate property to her daughter. To double the amount of the annual exclusion allowed, F (M's husband) is willing to split the gift. Since the § 2513 election can be made only on a gift tax return, a form needs to be filed. This is so in spite of the fact that no gift tax will be due as a result of the transfer. Useful for this purpose is Form 709–A (U.S. Short Form Gift Tax Return) available to simplify the gift-splitting procedure. ☐

---

27. § 6019(a)(2).

Presuming a gift tax return is due, it must be filed on or before the fifteenth day of April following the year of the gift.[28] As is the case with other Federal taxes, when the due date falls on Saturday, Sunday, or a legal holiday, the date for filing the return is the next business day. Note that the filing requirements for Form 709 have no correlation to the accounting year used by a donor for Federal income tax purposes. Thus, a fiscal year taxpayer would have to follow the April 15 rule as to any reportable gifts.

Extensions of Time and Payment of Tax. If sufficient reason is shown, the IRS is authorized to grant reasonable extensions of time for filing of the return.[29] Unless the donor is abroad, no extension in excess of six months may be granted. The application must be made before the due date of the return and must contain a full report of the causes for the delay. For a calendar year taxpayer, an extension of time for filing an income tax return also extends the time for filing the Form 709. An extension of time to file the return does not extend the time for payment of the tax.

The tax shown on the gift tax return is to be paid by the donor at the time and place fixed for the filing of the return.[30] A reasonable extension of time, not to exceed six months (unless the donor is abroad), may be granted by the IRS at the request of the donor for the payment of the tax shown on the return.[31]

Interest must be paid on any amount of tax that is not paid on or before the last date prescribed for the payment of the tax.[32] In addition, a penalty will be imposed unless the failure to pay was for reasonable cause. A penalty is also imposed for failure to file a gift tax return.[33]

Concept Summary

1. The Federal gift tax applies to all gratuitous transfers of property made by U.S. citizens or residents. In this regard, it does not matter where the property is located.
2. In the eyes of the IRS, a gratuitous transfer is one not supported by full and adequate consideration in money or money's worth. If the parties are acting in a business setting, such consideration usually will exist. If, however, purported sales are between family members, such transfers are suspect of a gift element.
3. If a lender loans money to another and intends some or all of the interest element to be a gift, the arrangement is categorized as a gift loan. To the extent that the interest provided for is less than the market rate, three tax consequences ensue. First, a gift has taken place between the lender and the borrower as to the interest element. Second, income may result to the lender. Third, an income tax deduction may be available to the borrower.
4. Property settlements can escape the gift tax if a divorce occurs within a prescribed period of time.

---

28. § 6075(b).
29. § 6081.
30. § 6151.
31. § 6161(a)(1).
32. § 6601.
33. §§ 6651(a)(1) and (2). These penalties are discussed in Chapter 14.

5. A disclaimer is a refusal by a person to accept property designated to pass to that person. The effect of a disclaimer is to pass the property to someone else. If certain conditions are satisfied, the issuance of a disclaimer will not be subject to the Federal gift tax.

6. Except for gifts of future interests, a donor will be allowed an annual exclusion of $10,000. The future interest limitation does not apply as to certain trusts created for minors.

7. By making the election to split a gift, a married couple will be treated as two donors. Such an election doubles the annual exclusion and makes available the unified tax credit to the nonowner spouse.

8. The election to split gifts would not be necessary if the property is jointly owned by the spouses. Such would be the case if the property is part of the couple's community.

9. In determining the tax base for computing the gift tax, all prior taxable gifts must be added to current taxable gifts. Thus, the gift tax is cumulative in nature.

10. Gifts are reported on Form 709 or Form 709–A. The return is due on April 15 following the year of the gift.

The Federal Estate Tax

The discussion of the estate tax that follows is developed to coincide with the pattern of the formula appearing earlier in the chapter. In brief, the formula for the estate tax is summarized as follows:

	Gross estate
—	Deductions allowed
	Taxable estate
+	Post-1976 taxable gifts
	Tax base
	Tentative tax on total transfers
—	Tax credits
	Estate tax due

The key components in the formula are the gross estate, the taxable estate, the tax base, and the credits allowed against the tentative tax.

Gross Estate

Simply stated, the gross estate comprises all property subject to the Federal estate tax. This in turn depends on the provisions of the Internal Revenue Code as supplemented by IRS pronouncements and the judicial interpretations of Federal courts.

Contrasted with the gross estate is the concept of the probate estate. Controlled by state (rather than Federal) law, the probate estate consists of all of a decedent's property subject to administration by the executor or administrator of the estate operating under the supervision of a local court of appropriate jurisdiction (usually designated as a probate court). An executor (or executrix) is the decedent's personal representative as appointed under the decedent's will. An administrator (or administratrix) is appointed by the local probate court of appropriate jurisdiction, usually because the decedent failed to appoint an executor in his or her will (or such designated person refused to serve) or the decedent died without a will.

The probate estate is frequently smaller than the gross estate, because it contains only property owned by the decedent at the time of death and passing to heirs under a will or under the law of intestacy (i.e., the order of distribution for those dying without a will). As noted later, such items as the proceeds of many life insurance policies become part of the gross estate but are not included in the probate estate.

Property Owned by the Decedent (§ 2033).   Property owned by the decedent at the time of death will be includible in the gross estate. The nature of the property or the use to which it was put during the decedent-owner's lifetime has no significance as far as the death tax is concerned. Thus, personal effects (such as clothing), stocks, bonds, furniture, jewelry, works of art, bank accounts, and interests in businesses conducted as sole proprietorships and partnerships are all included in the deceased owner's gross estate. In other words, no distinction is made between tangible and intangible, depreciable and nondepreciable, business and personal assets.

The application of § 2033 can be illustrated as follows:

Example 26   D dies owning some City of Denver bonds. The fair market value of the bonds plus any interest accrued to the date of D's death is includible in D's gross estate. Although interest on municipals is normally not taxable under the Federal income tax, it is, nevertheless, property owned by D at the time of D's death. □

Example 27   D dies on April 8, 1988, at a time when she owns stock in X Corporation and in Y Corporation. On March 1 of this year both corporations authorized a cash dividend payable on May 1. For X Corporation, the dividend was payable to shareholders of record as of April 1. Y Corporation's date of record is April 10. D's gross estate includes the following: the stock in X Corporation, the stock in Y Corporation, and the dividend on the X Corporation stock. It does not include the dividend on the Y Corporation stock. □

Example 28   D dies holding some promissory notes issued to him by his son. In his will, D forgives these notes, relieving the son of any obligation to make payments thereon. The fair market value of these notes will be included in D's gross estate. □

Example 29   D died while employed by Z Corporation. Pursuant to an informal but nonbinding company policy, Z Corporation awards one half of D's annual salary to D's widow as a death benefit. Presuming that D had no vested interest in and that the widow had no enforceable right to the payment, none of it will be includible in his gross estate.[34]   ☐

Dower and Curtesy Interests (§ 2034).   In its common law (nonstatutory) form, dower generally gave a surviving widow a life estate in a portion of her husband's estate (usually the real estate he owned) with the remainder passing to their children. Most states have modified and codified these common law rules, and variations between jurisdictions are not unusual. In some states, for example, a widow's statutory share of her deceased husband's property may mean outright ownership in a percentage of both his real estate and his personal property. Curtesy is a similar right held by the husband in his wife's property taking effect in the event he survives her. Most states have abolished the common law curtesy concept and have, in some cases, substituted a modified statutory version.

[handwritten margin note: Widow's Third]

Dower and curtesy rights are incomplete interests and may never materialize. Thus, if a wife predeceases her husband, her dower interest in her husband's property is lost.

Example 30   D dies without a will, leaving an estate of $900,000. Under state law, W (D's widow) is entitled to one third of D's property. The $300,000 W receives will be included in D's gross estate. Depending on the nature of the interest W receives in the $300,000, this amount could qualify D's estate for a marital deduction. (This possibility is discussed at greater length later in the chapter. For the time being, however, the focus is on what is or is not included as part of the decedent's gross estate.)   ☐

Adjustments for Gifts Made within Three Years of Death (§ 2035).   At one time, all taxable gifts made within three years of death were included in the donor's gross estate unless it could be shown that the gifts were not made in contemplation of death. The prior rule was designed to preclude tax avoidance, since the gift tax and estate tax rates were separate and the former was lower than the latter. However, when the gift and estate tax rates were combined into the unified transfer tax, the reason for the rule for gifts in contemplation of death largely disappeared. The three-year rule has, however, been retained for the following items:

[handwritten margin note: In contemplation of death]

—Inclusion in the gross estate of any gift tax paid on gifts made within three years of death. Called the gross-up procedure, it prevents the gift tax amount from escaping the estate tax.

—As to any property interests transferred by gift within three years of death that would have been included in the gross estate by virtue of the application of § 2036 (transfers with a retained life estate), § 2037 (transfers taking effect at death), § 2038 (revocable transfers), and § 2042 (proceeds of life insurance). (All except § 2037 are discussed later in the chapter.)

---

34. *Barr's Estate,* 40 T.C. 164 (1963).

Example 31   Before his death in 1988, D made the following taxable gifts:

Year of Gift	Nature of the Asset	Fair Market Value		Gift Tax Paid
		Date of Gift	Date of Death	
1983	X Corporation stock	$100,000	$150,000	$ –0–
1986	Policy on D's life	40,000	200,000	
		(cash value)	(face value)	–0–
1987	Land	400,000	410,000	8,200

D's *gross estate* includes $208,200 [$200,000 (life insurance proceeds) + $8,200 (gross-up for the gift tax on the 1987 taxable gift)] as to these transfers. Referring to the formula for the estate tax (see page 11–5), the other post-1976 taxable gifts are added to the *taxable estate* (at the fair market value on the date of the gift) in arriving at the tax base. D's estate will be allowed a credit for the $8,200 gift tax paid on the 1987 transfer. □

The three-year rule also applies in testing for qualification under § 303 (stock redemptions to pay death taxes and administration expenses), § 2032A (special valuation procedures), and § 6166 (extensions of time to pay death taxes), all of which are discussed in Chapter 12.

Transfers with a Retained Life Estate (§ 2036).   Code §§ 2036 through 2038 were enacted on the premise that the estate tax can be avoided on lifetime transfers only if the decedent does not retain control over the property. The logic of this approach is somewhat difficult to dispute—one should not be able to escape the tax consequences of property transfers at death while remaining in a position during life to enjoy some or all of the fruits of ownership.

Code § 2036 requires inclusion of the value of any property transferred by the deceased during lifetime for less than adequate consideration (in money or money's worth) if there was retained either of the following:

—The possession or enjoyment of, or the right to the income from, the property.

—The right, either alone or in conjunction with any person, to designate the persons who shall possess or enjoy the property or the income therefrom.

"The possession or enjoyment of, or the right to the income from, the property," as it appears in § 2036(a)(1), is considered to have been retained by or reserved to the decedent to the extent that such income, etc., is to be applied toward the discharge of a legal obligation of the decedent. The term "legal obligation" includes a legal obligation of the decedent to support a dependent during the decedent's lifetime.[35]

The practical application of § 2036 can best be explained by turning to two illustrations.

Example 32   F's will passes all of F's property to a trust, income to D for his life (i.e., D is given a life estate), and upon D's death, corpus (i.e., the principal) goes

---

35. Reg. § 20.2036–1(b)(2).

to R (i.e., R is granted a remainder interest). On D's death, none of the trust property will be included in D's gross estate. Although D held a life estate, § 2036 is inapplicable, because D was not the transferor (F was) of the property. Section 2033 (property owned by the decedent) would compel inclusion in D's gross estate of any income distributions D was entitled to receive at the time of his death. □

Example 33   By deed, D transfers the remainder interest in her ranch to S, retaining for herself the right to continue occupying the property until death. Upon D's death, the fair market value of the ranch will be included in D's gross estate under § 2036(a)(1). Furthermore, D is subject to the gift tax. The amount of the gift would be the fair market value of the ranch on the date of the gift less the portion applicable to D's retained life estate. (See Chapter 12 for the manner in which this gift is determined.) □

Revocable Transfers (§ 2038).   Another type of lifetime transfer that is drawn into a decedent's gross estate is covered by § 2038. Under this Section, the gross estate includes the value of property interests transferred by the decedent (except to the extent that the transfer was made for adequate and full consideration in money or money's worth) if the enjoyment of the property transferred was subject, at the date of the decedent's death, to any power of the decedent to alter, amend, revoke, or terminate the transfer. This includes the power to change the beneficiaries or the power to accelerate or increase any beneficiary's enjoyment of the property.

The capacity in which the decedent could exercise the power is immaterial. If the decedent gave property in trust, making himself or herself the trustee with the power to revoke the trust, the property would be included in his or her gross estate. If the decedent named another person as trustee with the power to revoke, but reserved the power to later appoint himself or herself trustee, the property would also be included in his or her gross estate. If, however, the power to alter, amend, revoke, or terminate was held at all times solely by a person other than the decedent and the decedent reserved no right to assume these powers, the property is not included in the decedent's gross estate under § 2038.

The Code and the Regulations make it quite clear that inclusion in the gross estate under § 2038 is not avoided by relinquishing a power within three years of death.[36] Recall from the previous discussion that § 2038 was one of several types of situations listed as exceptions to the usual rule excluding from the gross estate gifts made within three years of death.

In the event § 2038 applies, the amount includible in the gross estate is only the portion of the property transferred that is subject, at the decedent's death, to the decedent's power to alter, amend, revoke, or terminate.

The preceding rules can be illustrated as follows.

Example 34   D transfers securities to S under the state's Uniform Gifts to Minors Act designating himself as the custodian. Under the Act, the custodian has the authority to terminate the custodianship at any time and distribute the

---

36. § 2038(a)(1) and Reg. § 20.2038–1(e)(1).

proceeds to the minor. D dies four years later and before the custodianship is terminated.[37] Although the transfer is effective for income tax purposes, it runs afoul of § 2038.[38] Under this Section, the fair market value of the securities on the date of D's death will be included in D's gross estate for Federal estate tax purposes. ☐

Example 35   Assume the same facts as in Example 34, except that D dissolves the custodianship (thereby turning the securities over to S) within three years of death. The fair market value of the securities on the date of D's death will be includible in D's gross estate.[39] ☐

Example 36   Assume the same facts as in Example 34, except that S becomes of age and the custodianship terminates before D's death. Nothing will be included in D's gross estate upon D's death. ☐

Example 37   G transfers securities to S under the state's Uniform Gifts to Minors Act designating D as the custodian. Nothing relating to these securities will be included in D's gross estate upon D's death during the term of the custodianship. Code § 2038 is not applicable, because D was not the transferor. G's death during the custodianship should cause no estate tax consequences; G has retained no interest or control over the property transferred. ☐

In the area of incomplete transfers (i.e., §§ 2036 and 2038) there is much overlap in terms of application. It is not unusual, therefore, to find that either or both of these Sections apply to a particular transfer.

Annuities (§ 2039).   Annuities can be divided by their origin into commercial and noncommercial contracts. The noncommercial annuities are those issued by private parties and, in some cases, charitable organizations that do not regularly issue annuities. Although both varieties have much in common, noncommercial annuities present special income tax problems and are not treated further in this discussion.

Reg. § 20.2039–1(b)(1) defines an annuity as representing "one or more payments extending over any period of time." According to this Regulation, the payments may be equal or unequal, conditional or unconditional, periodic or sporadic. Most commercial contracts fall into one of four general patterns:

1. *Straight-life annuity.* The insurance company promises to make periodic payments to X (the annuitant) during his or her life. Upon X's death, the company has no further obligation under the contract.

---

37. The Uniform Gifts to Minors Act permits the ownership of securities to be transferred to a minor with someone designated as the custodian. The custodian has the right to sell the securities, collect any income therefrom, and otherwise act on behalf of the minor without court supervision. The custodianship arrangement is convenient and inexpensive. Under most state laws, the custodianship terminates when the minor reaches age 21.
38. If the minor is under the age of 14, net unearned income may be taxed at the parents' income tax rate. Net unearned income generally is passive income (e.g., dividends, interest) in excess of $1,000. §§ 1(i) and (j).
39. § 2035(d)(2).

2. *Joint and survivor annuity.* The insurance company promises to make periodic payments to X and Y during their lives with the payments to continue, usually in a diminished amount, for the life of the survivor.

3. *Self and survivor annuity.* The company agrees to make periodic payments to X during his or her life and, upon X's death, to continue these payments for the life of a designated beneficiary. This and the preceding type of annuity are most frequently used by married couples.

4. *Refund feature.* The company agrees to return to the annuitant's estate or other designated beneficiary a portion of the investment in the contract in the event of the annuitant's premature death.

larger payments

In the case of a straight-life annuity, nothing will be included in the gross estate of the annuitant at death. Section 2033 (i.e., property in which the decedent had an interest) does not apply, because the annuitant's interest in the contract is terminated by death. Section 2036 (i.e., transfers with a retained life estate) does not cover the situation; a transfer that is a "bona fide sale, for an adequate and full consideration in money or money's worth" is specifically excluded from § 2036 treatment. The purchase of a commercial annuity is presumed to entail adequate and full consideration unless some evidence exists to indicate that the parties were not acting at arm's length.

Example 38

D purchases a straight-life annuity that will pay him $6,000 a month when he reaches age 65. D dies at age 70. Except for the payments he received before his death, nothing relating to this annuity will affect D's gross estate. □

In the case of a survivorship annuity (classifications 2 and 3), the estate tax consequences under § 2039(a) are usually triggered by the death of the first annuitant. The amount included in the gross estate is the cost from the same company of a comparable annuity covering the survivor at his or her attained age on the date of the deceased annuitant's death.

Example 39

Assume the same facts as in Example 38, except that the annuity contract provides for W to be paid $3,000 a month for life as a survivorship feature. W is 62 years of age when D dies. Under these circumstances, D's gross estate will include the cost of a comparable contract that would provide an annuity of $3,000 per month for the life of a person (male or female, as the case may be) age 62. □

Full inclusion in the gross estate of the survivorship element is subject to the important exception of § 2039(b). Under this provision, the amount includible is to be based on the proportion of the deceased annuitant's contribution to the total cost of the contract. This can be expressed by the following formula:

$$\frac{\text{Decedent's contribution to purchase price}}{\text{Total purchase price of the annuity}} \times \frac{\text{Value of the annuity (or refund) at decedent's death}}{} = \frac{\text{Amount includible in the deceased annuitant's gross estate}}{}$$

Example 40   Assume the same facts as in Example 39, except that D and W are husband and wife and have always lived in a community property state. The premiums on the contract were paid with community funds. Because W contributed one half of the cost of the contract, only one half of the amount determined under Example 39 would be included in D's gross estate. ☐

The result reached in Example 40 is not unique to community property jurisdictions. For example, the outcome would have been the same in a noncommunity property state if W had furnished one half of the consideration from her own funds.

Joint Interests (§ 2040 and § 2511).   Assume that D and Y own an undivided but equal interest in a piece of property. Such joint ownership could fall into any one of four categories: joint tenancy, tenancy by the entirety, tenancy in common, or community property.

If D and Y hold ownership as joint tenants, the right of survivorship exists. If D predeceases Y, D's rights terminate and Y becomes the sole owner of the property. During his or her lifetime, a joint tenant usually possesses the right of severance—the right to have the property partitioned or to sell his or her interest to another. In the event of severance (either partition or sale), the right of survivorship ceases. If, for example, D sells his interest in a joint tenancy to Z, the joint tenancy terminates and Y and Z now hold the property as tenants in common.

A tenancy by the entirety is basically a joint tenancy between husband and wife. One important difference, however, is the absence of the right of severance except by divorce. D, for example, may transfer his interest to Y, but he cannot sell to another or secure a partition of the property.

Acting together, husband and wife can terminate the tenancy by transferring their interest to a third party. Thus, D and Y may join together to sell their interest to Z.

Under the tenancy in common and community property arrangements, the rights of each owner extend beyond the owner's death. Thus, if D predeceases Y, one half, or whatever interest he holds in the property, is included in his *probate* estate and passes to his heirs or other appointees. At least in the case of a tenancy in common, a tenant possesses the right to secure a partition of the property or to otherwise dispose of the interest. As to community property, however, partitions or other dispositions are not so easily accomplished, and state law should be checked carefully in this regard.

The Federal estate tax treatment of tenancies in common or of community property follows the logical approach of taxing only that portion of the property included in the deceased owner's probate estate. Thus, if D, X, and Z are tenants in common in a tract of land, each owning an equal interest, and D dies, only one third of the value of the property is included in the gross estate. This one third interest is also the same amount that will pass to D's heirs or appointees.

Example 41   D, X, and Z acquire a tract of land, ownership listed as tenants in common, each party furnishing $20,000 of the $60,000 purchase price. At a point when the property is worth $90,000, D dies. If D's undivided interest in the property is 33⅓%, the gross estate *and* probate estate would each include $30,000. ☐

Unless the parties have provided otherwise, each tenant will be deemed to own an interest equal to the portion of the original consideration he or she furnished. On the other hand, the parties in Example 41 could have provided that D would receive an undivided half interest in the property although he contributed only one third of the purchase price. In such case, X and Z have made a gift to D when the tenancy was created, and D's gross estate and probate estate would each include $45,000.

For certain joint tenancies, the tax consequences are different. All of the property is included in the deceased co-owner's gross estate unless it can be proven that the surviving co-owners contributed to the cost of the property.[40] If a contribution can be shown, the amount to be excluded is calculated by the following formula:

$$\frac{\text{Surviving co-owner's contribution}}{\text{Total cost of the property}} \times \text{Fair market value of the property}$$

In computing a survivor's contribution, any funds received as a gift *from the deceased co-owner* and applied to the cost of the property cannot be counted. However, income or gain from gift assets can be so counted.

If the co-owners receive the property as a gift *from another*, each co-owner will be deemed to have contributed to the cost of his or her own interest.

The preceding rules can be illustrated as follows.

Example 42   D and Y (father and son) acquire a tract of land, ownership listed as joint tenancy with right of survivorship, D furnishing $40,000 and Y $20,000 of the $60,000 purchase price. Of the $20,000 provided by Y, $10,000 had previously been received as a gift from D. At a point when the property is worth $90,000, D dies. Because only $10,000 of Y's contribution can be counted (the other $10,000 was received as a gift from D), Y has only furnished one sixth (i.e., $10,000/$60,000) of the cost. Thus, D's gross estate must include five sixths of $90,000, or $75,000. This presumes Y can prove that he did in fact make the $10,000 contribution. In the absence of such proof, the full value of the property will be included in D's gross estate. D's death makes Y the immediate owner of the property by virtue of the right of survivorship; therefore, none of the property will be part of D's probate estate. ☐

Example 43   F transfers property to D and Y as a gift listing ownership as joint tenancy with the right of survivorship. Upon D's death, one half of the value of the property will be included in the gross estate. Since the property was received as a gift and the donees are equal owners, each will be considered as having furnished one half of the consideration. ☐

40. § 2040(a).

To simplify the joint ownership rules for married persons, § 2040(b) provides for an automatic inclusion rule upon the death of the first joint-owner spouse to die. Regardless of the amount contributed by each spouse, one half of the value of the property will be included in the gross estate of the spouse that predeceases. This special rule eliminates the need to trace the source of contributions and recognizes that any inclusion in the gross estate will be neutralized by the marital deduction.

Example 44 In 1982, H purchases real estate for $100,000 using his separate funds and listing title as "H and W, joint tenants with the right of survivorship." H predeceases W four years later when the property is worth $300,000. If H and W are husband and wife, H's gross estate must include $150,000 ($\frac{1}{2}$ of $300,000) as to the property. □

Example 45 Assume the same facts as in Example 44, except that it is W (instead of H) who dies first. Presuming the date of death value to be $300,000, W's gross estate must include $150,000 as to the property. In this regard, it is of no consequence that W did not contribute to the cost of the real estate. □

In both Examples 44 and 45, inclusion in the gross estate of the first spouse to die will be neutralized by the unlimited marital deduction allowed for estate tax purposes (see the discussion of § 2056 later in the chapter). Recall that under the right of survivorship feature, the surviving joint tenant obtains full ownership of the property. The marital deduction generally is allowed for property passing from one spouse to another.

Whether or not a gift results when property is transferred into some form of joint ownership will depend on the consideration furnished by each of the contributing parties for the ownership interest thereby acquired.

Example 46 D and S purchase real estate as tenants in common, each furnishing $20,000 of the $40,000 cost. If each is an equal owner in the property, no gift has occurred. □

Example 47 Assume the same facts as in Example 46, except that of the $40,000 purchase price, D furnishes $30,000 and S furnishes only $10,000. If each is an equal owner in the property, D has made a gift to S of $10,000. □

Example 48 M purchases real estate for $240,000, the title to the property being listed as follows: "M, D, and S as joint tenants with the right of survivorship." If under state law the mother (M), the daughter (D), and the son (S) are deemed to be equal owners in the property and each has the right of severance, M will be treated as having made gifts of $80,000 to D and $80,000 to S. □

Several principal exceptions exist to the general rule that the creation of a joint ownership with disproportionate interests resulting from unequal consideration will trigger gift treatment. First, if the transfer involves a joint bank account, there is no gift at the time of the contribution.[41] If a gift occurs, it will

---

41. Reg. § 25.2511–1(h)(4).

be when the noncontributing party withdraws the funds provided by the other joint tenant. Second, the same rule applies to the purchase of U.S. savings bonds. Again, any gift tax consequences will be postponed until such time as the noncontributing party appropriates some or all of the proceeds for his or her individual use.

Example 49   D deposits $200,000 in a bank account under the names of D and S as joint tenants. Both D and S have the right to withdraw funds from the account without the other's consent or joinder. D has not made a gift to S when the account is established. □

Example 50   Assume the same facts as in Example 49. At some later date, S withdraws $50,000 from the account for her own use. At this point, D has made a gift to S of $50,000. □

Example 51   D purchases a U.S. savings bond that he registers in the names of D and S. After D dies, S redeems the bond. No gift takes place when D buys the bond. In addition, S's redemption is not treated as a gift, because the bond passed to her by testamentary disposition (i.e., S acquired the bond by virtue of surviving D) and not through a lifetime transfer. However, the fair market value of the bond would be included in D's gross estate under § 2040. □

Powers of Appointment (§ 2041 and § 2514).   A power of appointment is a power to determine who shall own or enjoy, presently or in the future, the property subject to the power. It must be created by another and therefore does not include a power created or retained by the decedent when he or she transferred his or her own property. The term "power of appointment" includes all powers that are in substance and effect powers of appointment regardless of the terminology used in a particular instrument and regardless of local property law. If, for example, a trust instrument provides that the income beneficiary may appropriate or consume the principal of the trust, this right is a power of appointment over the principal even though it may not be designated as such.

Powers of appointment fall into one of two classifications: general and special. A general power of appointment is one in which the decedent could have appointed himself, his creditors, his estate, or the creditors of his estate. On the other hand, a special power enables the holder to appoint to others but *not* to himself, his creditors, his estate, or the creditors of his estate. Assume, for example, that D has the power to designate how the principal of the trust will be distributed among X, Y, and Z. At this point, D's power is only a special power of appointment. If D were further given the right to appoint the principal to himself, what was a special then becomes a general power of appointment.

Three things can happen to a power of appointment: exercise, lapse, and release. To exercise the power would be to appoint the property to one or all of the parties designated. A lapse occurs upon failure to exercise a power. Thus, if a holder, D, failed to indicate how the principal of a trust will be distributed among X, Y, and Z, D's power of appointment would lapse and the principal would pass in accordance with the terms of the trust instrument. A release occurs if the holder relinquishes a power of appointment. A release should be distinguished from a disclaimer. In the former situation, the act follows after the acceptance of the power. If the designated holder decides he or she does not want the power, he or she may disclaim (i.e., refuse) and avoid the tax consequences attendant to a release. To constitute a disclaimer, the refusal must be made on a timely basis, be unequivocal, and be effective under applicable law.

The transfer tax consequences of powers of appointment can be summarized as follows:

1. No tax implications come about through the exercise, lapse, or release of a special power of appointment.
2. Only the exercise of a general power of appointment created before October 22, 1942, would result in a gift or cause inclusion in the holder's gross estate. The lapse or release of such powers during life or upon the death of the holder causes no tax consequences.
3. The exercise, lapse, or release of a general power of appointment created after October 21, 1942, during life or upon the death of the holder will cause the fair market value of the property (or income interest) subject to the power to be a gift or to be included in the holder's gross estate.
4. In connection with (3), a lapse of a general power is subject to gift or estate taxation only to the extent that the value of the property that could have been appointed exceeds the greater of either $5,000 or five percent of the aggregate value of the property out of which the appointment could have been satisfied.
5. In connection with (3), a holder is not considered to have had a general power of appointment if the power was exercisable only with the consent or joinder of the creator of the power or a person having a substantial adverse interest in the property subject to the power. For this purpose, the trustee administering a trust in his or her fiduciary capacity does not, by that fact alone, have an adverse interest in the trust.[42]
6. In connection with (3), a holder is not considered to have had a general power of appointment if he or she had a right to consume or invade for his or her own benefit, as long as such right is limited by an ascertainable standard relating to his or her health, education, support, or maintenance. A power to use the property for the "comfort, welfare, or happiness" of the holder is not an ascertainable standard and therefore is a general power of appointment.

These rules can be illustrated as follows (assume all powers were created after October 21, 1942).

Example 52 F, D's father, leaves his property in trust, life estate to D and remainder to whichever of D's children D decides to appoint under her will. D's power is not a general power of appointment, because she cannot exercise it in favor of herself, her creditors, her estate, or the creditors of her estate. Thus, regardless of whether or not D exercises the power, none of the trust property subject to the power will be included in her gross estate. □

---

42. See Reg. § 20.2041-3(c)(2) for examples of what constitutes a substantial adverse interest.

Example 53   Assume the same facts as in Example 52. In addition to having the testamentary power to designate the beneficiary of the remainder interest, D is given a power to direct the trustee to pay to D from time to time so much of corpus as she might request "for her support." Although D now has a power that she can exercise in favor of herself, it is not a general power of appointment, because it is limited to an ascertainable standard. Thus, none of the property subject to these powers will be subject to the gift tax or be included in D's gross estate at D's death. □

Life Insurance (§ 2042).   Under § 2042, the gross estate includes the proceeds of life insurance on the decedent's life if (1) they are receivable by the estate, (2) they are receivable by another for the benefit of the estate, or (3) the decedent possessed an incident of ownership in the policy.

Life insurance on the life of another owned by a decedent at the time of his or her death would be included in his or her gross estate under § 2033 (i.e., property in which the decedent had an interest) and not under § 2042. The amount includible is the replacement value of the policy.[43] Under these circumstances, inclusion of the face amount of the policy would be inappropriate; the policy has not yet matured.

Example 54   At the time of his death, D owned a life insurance policy on the life of S, face amount of $100,000 and replacement value of $25,000, with W as the designated beneficiary. Since the policy has not matured at D's death, § 2042 is inapplicable. However, § 2033 (i.e., property in which the decedent had an interest) would compel the inclusion of $25,000 (the replacement value) in D's gross estate. If the policy were owned by D and W as community property, only $12,500 would be included in D's gross estate. □

The term "life insurance" includes whole life policies, term insurance, group life insurance, travel and accident insurance, endowment contracts (before being paid up), and death benefits paid by fraternal societies operating under the lodge system.[44]

As just noted, proceeds of insurance on the life of the decedent receivable by the executor or administrator or payable to the decedent's estate are included in the gross estate. It is not necessary that the estate be specifically named as the beneficiary. For example, if the proceeds of the policy are receivable by an individual beneficiary and are subject to an obligation, legally binding upon the beneficiary, to pay taxes, debts, and other charges enforceable against the estate, the proceeds will be included in the decedent's gross estate to the extent of the beneficiary's obligation. If the proceeds of an insurance policy made payable to a decedent's estate are community assets and, under state law, one half belongs to the surviving spouse, only one half of the proceeds will be considered as receivable by or for the benefit of the decedent's estate.

Proceeds of insurance on the life of the decedent not receivable by or for the benefit of the estate are includible if the decedent possessed at his or her

---

43. Reg. § 20.2031–8(a)(1).
44. Reg. § 20.2042–1(a)(1). As to travel and accident insurance, see *Comm. v. Estate of Noel,* 65–1 USTC ¶ 12,311, 15 AFTR2d 1397, 85 S.Ct. 1238 (USSC, 1965).

death any of the incidents of ownership in the policy, exercisable either alone or in conjunction with any other person, even if acting as trustee. In this connection, the term "incidents of ownership" not only means the ownership of the policy in a technical legal sense. Generally speaking, the term has reference to the right of the insured or his or her estate to the economic benefits of the policy. Thus, it also includes the power to change beneficiaries, to revoke an assignment, to pledge the policy for a loan, or to surrender or cancel the policy.[45]

Example 55   At the time of death, D was the insured under a policy (face amount of $100,000) owned by S with W as the designated beneficiary. The policy originally was taken out by D five years ago and immediately transferred as a gift to S. Under the assignment, D transferred all rights in the policy except the right to change beneficiaries. D died without having exercised this right, and the policy proceeds are paid to W. Under § 2042(2), the retention of an incident of ownership in the policy (e.g., the right to change beneficiaries) by D forces $100,000 to be included in the gross estate. □

Assuming that the deceased-insured holds the incidents of ownership in a policy, how much will be includible in the gross estate if the insurance policy is a community asset? Only one half of the proceeds becomes part of the deceased spouse's gross estate.

In determining whether or not a policy is community property or what portion of it might be so classified, state law controls. In this regard, two general views appear to be followed. Under the inception of title approach, the key to classification depends on when the policy was originally purchased. If purchased before marriage, the policy will be separate property regardless of how many premiums were paid after marriage with community funds. However, in the event the noninsured spouse is not the beneficiary of the policy, he or she may be entitled to reimbursement from the deceased-insured spouse's estate for one half of the premiums paid with community funds. The inception of title approach is followed in at least three states: Louisiana, Texas, and New Mexico.

In some community property jurisdictions, the classification of a policy follows the tracing approach: The nature of the funds used to pay premiums controls. Thus, a policy paid for 20 percent with separate funds and 80 percent with community funds will be 20 percent separate property and 80 percent community property. At what point in time the policy was purchased should make no difference. Conceivably, a policy purchased after marriage with the premiums paid exclusively with separate funds would be classified entirely as separate property. The tracing approach appears to be the rule in California and Washington.

The mere purchase of a life insurance contract with the designation of someone else as the beneficiary thereunder does not constitute a gift. As long as the purchaser still owns the policy, nothing has really passed to the beneficiary. Even on the death of the insured-owner, no gift takes place. The pro-

---

45. Reg. § 20.2042–1(c)(2).

ceeds going to the beneficiary constitute a testamentary and not a lifetime transfer. But consider the following possibility:

Example 56   D purchases an insurance policy on his own life which he transfers to S. D retains no interest in the policy (such as the power to change beneficiaries or to revest in himself or his estate the economic benefits of the policy). Under these circumstances, D has made a gift to S. Furthermore, if D continues to pay the premiums on the transferred policy, each payment will constitute a separate gift. □

Under certain conditions, the death of the insured might represent a gift to the beneficiary of part or all of the proceeds. This may prove true when the owner of the policy is not the insured.

Example 57   D owns an insurance policy on the life of S, with T as the designated beneficiary. Up until the time of S's death, D retained the right to change the beneficiary of the policy. The proceeds paid to T by the insurance company by reason of S's death constitute a gift from D to T.[46] □

Example 58   H and W live in a community property state. With community funds, H purchases an insurance policy with a face amount of $100,000 on his own life and designates S as the revocable beneficiary. On H's death, the proceeds of the policy are paid to S. If under state law H's death makes the transfer by W complete, W has made a gift to S of $50,000. Since the policy was held as community property, W was deemed to be the owner of only one half of the policy. Furthermore, one half of the proceeds of the policy ($50,000) would be included in H's gross estate under § 2042. □

Taxable Estate

After the gross estate has been determined, the next step is to arrive at the taxable estate. By virtue of § 2051, the taxable estate is the gross estate less the following: expenses, indebtedness, and taxes (§ 2053); losses (§ 2054); charitable transfers (§§ 2055 and 2522); the marital deduction (§§ 2056 and 2523); and the ESOP deduction (§ 2057). As previously noted, the charitable and marital deductions also carry gift tax ramifications.

Expenses, Indebtedness, and Taxes (§ 2053).   A deduction is allowed for funeral expenses; expenses incurred in administering property; claims against the estate; and unpaid mortgages and other charges against property, the value of which is included in the gross estate without reduction for the mortgage or other indebtedness.

Expenses incurred in administering community property are deductible only in proportion to the deceased spouse's interest in the community.[47]

---

46. *Goodman v. Comm.,* 46–1 USTC ¶ 10,275, 34 AFTR 1534, 156 F.2d 218 (CA–2, 1946).
47. *U.S. v. Stapf,* 63–2 USTC ¶ 12,192, 12 AFTR2d 6326, 84 S.Ct. 248 (USSC, 1963).

Administration expenses include commissions of the executor or administrator, attorney's fees of the estate, accountant's fees, court costs, and certain selling expenses for disposition of estate property.

Claims against the estate include property taxes accrued before the decedent's death, unpaid income taxes on income received by the decedent in his or her lifetime, and unpaid gift taxes on gifts made by the decedent in his or her lifetime.

Amounts that may be deducted as claims against the estate are only for enforceable personal obligations of the decedent at the time of his or her death. Deductions for claims founded on promises or agreements are limited to the extent that the liabilities were contracted in good faith and for adequate and full consideration in money or money's worth. However, a pledge or subscription in favor of a public, charitable, religious, or educational organization is deductible to the extent that it would have constituted an allowable deduction had it been a bequest.[48]

Deductible funeral expenses include the cost of interment, the burial plot or vault, a gravestone, perpetual care of the grave site, and the transportation expense of the person bringing the body to the place of burial. If the decedent had, before death, acquired cemetery lots for himself or herself and his or her family, no deduction will be allowed, but such lots will not be included in the decedent's gross estate under § 2033 (i.e., property in which the decedent had an interest).

Losses (§ 2054).   Section 2054 permits an estate tax deduction for losses from casualty or theft incurred during the period of settlement of the estate. As is true with casualty or theft losses for income tax purposes, any anticipated insurance recovery must be taken into account in arriving at the amount of the deductible loss. Unlike the income tax, however, the deduction is not limited by a floor (i.e., $100) or a percentage amount (i.e., the excess of 10 percent of adjusted gross income). If the casualty occurs to property after it has been distributed to an heir, the loss belongs to the heir and not to the estate. If the casualty occurs before the decedent's death, it should be claimed on the appropriate Form 1040. The fair market value of the property (if any) on the date of death plus any insurance recovery would be included in the gross estate.

As is true of certain administration expenses, a casualty or theft loss of estate property can be claimed as an income tax deduction on the fiduciary return of the estate (Form 1041). But the double deduction prohibition of § 642(g) applies; claiming the income tax deduction requires a waiver of the estate tax deduction.

Transfers to Charity (§ 2055 and § 2522).   A deduction is allowed for the value of property in the decedent's gross estate that was transferred by the decedent through testamentary disposition to (or for the use of) any of the following:

1. The United States or any political subdivision therein.

---

48. § 2053(c)(1)(A) and Reg. § 20.2053–5.

2. Any corporation or association organized and operated exclusively for religious, charitable, scientific, literary, or educational purposes, as long as no benefit inures to any private individual and no substantial activity is undertaken to carry on propaganda or otherwise attempt to influence legislation or participate in any political campaign on behalf of any candidate for public office.
3. A trustee or trustees of a fraternal society, order, or association operating under the lodge system if the transferred property is to be used exclusively for religious, charitable, scientific, literary, or educational purposes, and no substantial activity is undertaken to carry on propaganda or otherwise attempt to influence legislation or participate in any political campaign on behalf of any candidate for public office.
4. Any veteran's organization incorporated by an Act of Congress (or any of its subdivisions) as long as no benefit inures to any private individual.

The organizations just described are identical to the ones that qualify for the Federal gift tax deduction under § 2522. With the following two exceptions, they are also the same organizations that will qualify a donee for an income tax deduction under § 170:

—Certain nonprofit cemetery associations qualify for income tax but not death and gift tax purposes.

—Foreign charities may qualify under the estate and gift tax but not under the income tax.

No deduction will be allowed unless the charitable bequest is specified by a provision in the decedent's will or the transfer was made before death and the property is subsequently included in the gross estate. Generally speaking, a deduction does not materialize when an individual dies intestate (i.e., without a will). The bequest to charity must be mandatory as to the amount involved and cannot be based on the discretion of another. It is, however, permissible to allow another—such as the executor of the estate—the choice of which charity will receive the specified donation. Likewise, a bequest may be expressed as an alternative and still be effective if the noncharitable beneficiary disclaims (i.e., refuses) the intervening interest before the due date for the filing of the estate tax return (i.e., nine months after the decedent's death plus any extensions of time granted for filing).

Marital Deduction (§ 2056 and § 2523).   The marital deduction originated with the Revenue Act of 1948 as part of the same legislation that permitted married persons to secure the income-splitting advantages of filing joint income tax returns. The purpose of these statutory changes was to eliminate the major tax variations that could develop between taxpayers residing in community property and common law states. The marital deduction was designed to provide equity in the estate and gift tax areas.

In a community property state, for example, no marital deduction generally was allowed, since the surviving spouse already owned one half of the community and such portion was not included in the deceased spouse's gross estate. In a common law state, however, most if not all of the assets often belonged to the breadwinner of the family. Upon such person predeceasing, all of these assets were included in his or her gross estate. [Recall that a dower or curtesy interest (regarding a surviving spouse's right to some of the deceased spouse's property) does not reduce the gross estate.] To equalize the situation, therefore, a marital deduction, usually equal to one half of all separate assets, was allowed upon the death of the first spouse.

Ultimately Congress decided to dispense with these historical justifications and recognize husband and wife as a single economic unit. Consistent with the approach taken under the income tax, spouses are to be considered as one for transfer tax purposes. By making the marital deduction unlimited in amount, neither the gift tax nor the estate tax will be imposed on outright interspousal transfers of property. Unlike prior law, the unlimited marital deduction even includes one spouse's share of the community property transferred to the other spouse.

Under § 2056, the marital deduction is allowed only for property included in the deceased spouse's gross estate and that passes or has passed to the surviving spouse. Property that passes from the decedent to the surviving spouse includes any interest received as (1) the decedent's legatee, devisee, heir, or donee; (2) the decedent's surviving tenant by the entirety or joint tenant; (3) the appointee under the decedent's exercise (or lapse or release) of a general power of appointment; or (4) the beneficiary of insurance on the life of the decedent.

Example 59 At the time of his death in the current year, D owned an insurance policy on his own life (face amount of $100,000) with W (his wife) as the designated beneficiary. D and W also owned real estate (worth $250,000) as tenants by the entirety (D having furnished all of the purchase price). As to these transfers, $225,000 ($100,000 + $125,000) would be included in D's gross estate, and this amount represents the property that passes to W for purposes of the marital deduction.[49] ☐

Under certain conditions, disclaimers of property by the surviving spouse in favor of some other heir will affect the amount that passes and therefore qualifies for the marital deduction. Thus, if W is entitled to $400,000 of H's property but disclaims $100,000 in favor of S, the residuary legatee under the will, the $100,000 will pass from H to S and not from H to W. Disclaimers by some other heir in favor of the surviving spouse may have a similar effect. Suppose W, as residuary legatee, will receive $300,000 under H's will, but the will also provides that S is to receive a specific bequest of $100,000. If S issues a timely disclaimer in favor of W, the amount passing from H to W for purposes of the marital deduction will be increased from $300,000 to $400,000.

When a property interest passes to the surviving spouse, subject to a mortgage or other encumbrance, or when an obligation is imposed upon the surviving spouse in connection with the passing of a property interest, only the net value of the interest after reduction by the amount of the mortgage or other encumbrance qualifies for the marital deduction. To allow otherwise would

---

49. Inclusion in the gross estate would fall under § 2042 (i.e., proceeds of life insurance) and § 2040 (i.e., joint interests). Although D provided the full purchase price for the real estate, § 2040(b) requires inclusion of only one half of the value of the property when one spouse predeceases the other.

result in a double deduction, since liabilities of a decedent are separately deductible under § 2053.

Example 60　In his will, H leaves real estate (fair market value of $200,000) to his wife. If the real estate is subject to a mortgage of $40,000 (upon which H was personally liable), the marital deduction is limited to $160,000 ($200,000 − $40,000). The $40,000 mortgage is deductible under § 2053 as an obligation of the decedent (H). □

However, if the executor is required under the terms of the decedent's will or under local law to discharge the mortgage or other encumbrance out of other assets of the estate or to reimburse the surviving spouse, the payment or reimbursement constitutes an additional interest passing to the surviving spouse.

Example 61　Assume the same facts as in Example 60, except that H's will directs that the real estate is to pass to H's wife free of any liabilities. Accordingly, H's executor pays off the mortgage by using other estate assets and distributes the real estate to H's wife. The marital deduction now becomes $200,000. □

Federal estate taxes or other death taxes that are paid out of the surviving spouse's share of the gross estate are not included in the value of property passing to the surviving spouse. Therefore, it is usually preferable for the deceased spouse's will to provide that death taxes be paid out of the portion of the estate that does not qualify for the marital deduction.

Certain interests in property passing from the deceased spouse to the surviving spouse are referred to as terminable interests. Such an interest is one that will terminate or fail after the passage of time, upon the happening of some contingency, or upon the failure of some event to occur. Examples are life estates, annuities, estates for terms of years, and patents. A terminable interest will not qualify for the marital deduction if another interest in the same property passed from the deceased spouse to some other person for less than adequate and full consideration in money or money's worth, and by reason of its passing, such other person or his or her heirs may enjoy part of the property after the termination of the surviving spouse's interest.[50]

Example 62　H's will places H's property in trust, life estate to W, remainder to S or his heirs. The interest passing from H to W does not qualify for the marital deduction. It will terminate on W's death, and S or his heirs will thereafter possess or enjoy the property. □

Example 63　Assume the same facts as in Example 62, except that the trust was created by H during his life. No marital deduction is available for gift tax purposes for the same reason given in Example 62.[51] □

---

50. §§ 2056(b)(1) and 2523(b)(1).
51. Both Examples 62 and 63 contain the potential for a qualified terminable interest property (QTIP) election discussed later in this section.

Example 64   During his life, H purchased a joint and survivor annuity providing for payments to himself for life and then to W for life should she survive him. All payments cease on the death of H or W, whoever dies later. If H dies first, the value of the survivorship annuity included in his gross estate under § 2039(a) and passing to W will qualify for the marital deduction. Although W's interest in the annuity will terminate on W's death, it is not a terminable interest. No other person may possess or enjoy the property after W's death. □

The justification for the terminable interest rule can be illustrated by examining more closely the possible result of Examples 62 and 63. Without the rule, H could have passed property to W at no cost because of the marital deduction. Yet, on W's death, none of the property would have been included in W's gross estate. Section 2036 (i.e., transfers with a retained life estate) would not apply to W, since she was not the original transferor of the property. Apparently, then, the marital deduction should not be available in situations where the surviving spouse can enjoy the property and still pass it to another without tax consequences. The marital deduction merely postpones the transfer tax on the death of the first spouse and operates to shift any such tax to the surviving spouse.

The terminable interest rule takes another form when one considers the power of appointment exception.[52] Under this provision, a property interest passing from the deceased spouse to the surviving spouse will qualify for the marital deduction (and not be considered a terminable interest) under the following conditions:

1. The survivor is entitled for life to all of the income from the entire interest.
2. Such income is payable annually or at more frequent intervals.
3. The survivor has the power, exercisable in favor of himself or herself (or his or her estate) to appoint the entire interest.
4. Such power is exercisable by the survivor alone and in all events (although it may be limited to exercise either during life or by will).
5. No part of the interest is subject to a power in any other person to appoint to anyone other than the surviving spouse.

Note that conditions 3. and 4. require the surviving spouse to be the holder of a general power of appointment over the property. The exercise, release, or lapse of the power during the survivor's life or at death would be subject to either the gift or the death tax.[53] Thus, if Examples 62 and 63 were modified to satisfy the preceding conditions, the life estate passing from H to W would not be a terminable interest and would qualify for the marital deduction.

As previously noted, the purpose of the terminable interest rule is to ensure that property not taxed to the transferor-spouse (due to the marital deduction) will be subject to the gift or the estate tax upon disposition by the transferee-spouse.

---

52. For the estate tax, see § 2056(b)(5). The gift tax counterpart is in § 2523(e).
53. §§ 2514 and 2041.

Consistent with the objective of the terminable interest rule, another provision of the tax law offers an alternative means for obtaining the marital deduction. Under this provision, the marital deduction will be allowed for transfers of qualified terminable interest property (commonly referred to as QTIP), defined as property that passes from one spouse to another by gift or at death and for which the transferee-spouse has a qualifying income interest for life.

For a donee or a surviving spouse, a qualifying income interest for life exists under the following conditions:

—Such person is entitled for life to all of the income from the property (or a specific portion thereof), payable at annual or more frequent intervals.

—No person (including the spouse) has a power to appoint any part of the property to any person other than the surviving spouse during his or her life.[54]

If these conditions are met, an election can be made to claim a marital deduction as to the qualified terminable interest property. For estate tax purposes, the election is made by the executor of the estate on Form 706 (the Federal estate tax return). For gift tax purposes, the election is made by the donor spouse on Form 709 (the Federal gift tax return). The election is irrevocable.

If the election is made, a transfer tax will be imposed upon the qualified terminable interest property when the transferee-spouse disposes of it by gift or upon death. If the disposition occurs during life, the gift tax applies measured by the fair market value of the property as of that time.[55] If no lifetime disposition takes place, the fair market value of the property on the date of death (or alternate valuation date if applicable) will be included in the gross estate of the transferee-spouse.[56]

Example 65　In 1988, H dies and provides in his will that certain assets (fair market value of $400,000) are to be transferred to a trust under which W (H's wife) is granted a life estate with the remainder passing to their children upon W's death. Presuming all of the preceding requirements are satisfied and H's executor so elects, H's estate will receive a marital deduction of $400,000. □

Example 66　Assume the same facts as in Example 65, with the further stipulation that W dies in 1995 when the trust assets are worth $900,000. This amount must be included in W's gross estate. □

Because the estate tax will be imposed on assets not physically included in the probate estate, the law provides for a shifting of the liability attributable thereto to the heirs. The amount that can be shifted is to be determined by comparing the estate tax liability both with and without the inclusion of the

---

54. §§ 2523(f) and 2056(b)(7).
55. § 2519.
56. § 2044.

qualified terminable interest property. This right of recovery can be negated by a provision in the deceased spouse's will.[57]

The major difference between the power of appointment and the QTIP exceptions to the terminable interest rules relates to the control the surviving spouse has over the principal of the trust. In the power of appointment situation, the surviving spouse can appoint the principal to himself or herself (or to his or her estate), and only if this power is not exercised will the property pass as specified in the deceased spouse's will. In the QTIP situation, however, no such control exists as to the surviving spouse. If the QTIP election is made, the principal must pass as prescribed by the transferor (i.e., the donor in the case of a lifetime transfer or the decedent in the case of a death transfer).

ESOP Deduction (§ 2057).   As amended by the Revenue Act of 1987, § 2057 allows an estate deduction of 50 percent of the proceeds from the sale of employer securities to an employee stock ownership plan (ESOP) or an eligible worker-owned cooperative.[58] The sale can only be of securities that are not publicly traded. The deduction is limited to 50 percent of the taxable estate (determined without regard to § 2057) and cannot reduce estate taxes by more than $750,000.

Holding period requirements are imposed to impede a planned sale in an imminent death situation. The deduction is not allowed unless the decedent has held the securities for at least the lesser of five years prior to death or the period from October 22, 1986 to the date of death.

The purchaser of the employer securities (i.e., ESOP or qualified cooperative) must allocate them (or hold them for future allocation) to the plan participants. The purchaser may be subject to a special excise tax if it fails to make the allocation or disposes of the securities within a prescribed period of time.

Computing the Federal Estate Tax

Once the taxable estate has been determined, post-1976 taxable gifts are added to arrive at the tax base. Note that pre-1977 taxable gifts do not enter into the computation of the tax base.

Example 67   D dies in 1988, leaving a taxable estate of $800,000. During her life, D made taxable gifts as follows: $50,000 in 1975 and $100,000 in 1982. For estate tax purposes, the Federal estate tax base becomes $900,000 determined as follows: $800,000 (taxable estate) + $100,000 (taxable gift made in 1982). □

With the unified transfer tax rate schedule contained in § 2001(c), the tentative tax on the tax base is then computed. Using the facts in Example 67, the tax on $900,000 is $306,800 [$248,300 + (39% × $150,000)]—see Appendix A, page A–8.

See the following discussion for the phase-out of the unified tax credit and the graduated tax rates for certain large estates.

---

57. § 2207A(a).
58. When first enacted by TRA of 1986, § 2037 was extremely liberal in its application. The Revenue Act of 1987 curtailed much of the original generosity.

All available estate tax credits are subtracted from the tentative estate tax to arrive at the estate tax (if any) that is due.

Estate Tax Credits

Unified Tax Credit (§ 2010). From previous discussion of this credit, recall that the amount of the credit allowed depends upon the year of the transfer. Returning to Example 67, the credit allowed on the gift in 1982 would be $62,800. Since the exemption equivalent of this amount is $225,000 (refer to the table preceding Example 3), no gift tax is due on the transfer. On D's death in 1988, however, the unified tax credit is $192,800, which is less than the tentative tax of $306,800 (refer to the discussion following Example 67). Disregarding the effect of any other estate tax credits, D's estate owes a tax of $114,000 [$306,800 (tentative tax on a tax base of $900,000) — $192,800 (unified tax credit for 1988)].

Recall also that an adjustment to the unified tax credit will be necessary if any portion of the specific exemption was utilized on gifts made after September 8, 1976, and before January 1, 1977. In this regard, refer to Example 4.

Under the Revenue Act of 1987 the benefit of the unified tax credit and of the graduated unified tax rates is phased out for taxable transfers exceeding a certain amount. The gift and estate tax liability for taxable transfers in excess of $10 million is increased by five percent of such excess until the benefit of the credit and graduated brackets is recaptured.

Credit for State Death Taxes (§ 2011). Section 2011 allows a limited credit for the amount of any death, inheritance, legacy, or succession tax actually paid to any state (or to the District of Columbia) attributable to any property included in the gross estate. Like the credit for foreign death taxes paid, this provision mitigates the harshness of subjecting the same property to multiple death taxes.

The credit allowed is limited to the lesser of the amount of tax actually paid or the amount provided for in a table contained in § 2011(b). (See Appendix A, page A–12.) The table amount is based on the adjusted taxable estate, which for this purpose is the taxable estate less $60,000. No credit is allowed if the adjusted taxable estate is $40,000 or less.

Example 68   D's taxable estate is $98,000, and the state of appropriate jurisdiction imposes a death tax of $1,500 on this amount. Since the adjusted taxable estate is $38,000 ($98,000 — $60,000), none of the $1,500 paid qualifies for the death tax credit. □

Example 69   D's taxable estate is $200,000, and the state of appropriate jurisdiction imposes a death tax of $3,000 on this amount. Because the adjusted gross estate is $140,000 ($200,000 — $60,000), the table amount limits the death tax credit to $1,200. □

As noted in Examples 68 and 69, it may be entirely possible that the credit allowed by § 2011 proves to be less than the amount of state death taxes paid. The reverse is possible but usually not the case. Most states insure that the minimum tax payable to the jurisdiction is at least equal to the credit allowed by the table. Sometimes this result is accomplished by a sponge tax superimposed on the regular inheritance tax. Thus, if the regular inheritance tax yielded $2,500, but the maximum credit allowed by the table is $3,200, a sponge tax would impose an additional $700 in state death taxes. In other states, the whole state death tax liability depends entirely upon the amount allowed for Federal death tax purposes as the credit under the table. Thus, in the previous illustration, the state death tax would be an automatic $3,200.

Credit for Gift Taxes (§ 2012).   A credit is allowed under § 2012 against the estate tax for any Federal gift tax paid on a gift of property subsequently included in the donor-decedent's gross estate.

Example 70   In 1965, D transfers a remainder interest in a farm to her children, retaining for herself a life estate. As a result of the transfer, D incurred and paid a Federal gift tax of $45,000. D dies in 1988 when the property is worth $400,000. Since the application of § 2036 (retention of a life estate) forces the inclusion of the farm in D's gross estate, a double tax effect results. To mitigate this effect, § 2012 allows D's estate a credit for some or all of the $45,000 in gift taxes previously paid. □

The adjustments that might be necessary in working out the amount of the credit could become somewhat complicated and are not discussed further.[59]

Only taxable gifts made after 1976 ill be added to the donor's taxable estate in arriving at the base for the application of the unified transfer tax at death. To the extent these gifts have exceeded the unified tax credit and have generated a tax, such tax should be credited against the transfer tax due at death.

Credit for Tax on Prior Transfers (§ 2013).   Suppose D owns some property that he passes at death to S. Shortly thereafter, S dies and passes the property to R. Assuming both estates are subject to the Federal estate tax, one can easily imagine the multiple effect involved in successive deaths. To mitigate the possible multiple taxation that might result, § 2013 provides relief in the form of a credit for a death tax on prior transfers. Thus, with regard to the preceding hypothetical case, S's estate may be able to claim as an estate tax credit some of the taxes paid by D's estate.

The credit is limited to the lesser of the following amounts:

1. The amount of the Federal estate tax attributable to the transferred property in the transferor's estate.
2. The amount of the Federal estate tax attributable to the transferred property in the decedent's estate.

To apply the preceding limitations, certain adjustments must be made that are not covered in this text.[60] One must note, however, that it is not necessary for the transferred property to be identified in the present decedent's estate or for it to be in existence at the time of the present decedent's death. It is sufficient that the transfer of property was subjected to the Federal estate tax in the

59. They are illustrated and explained in the instructions to Form 706 and in Reg. § 20.2012–1.
60. See the instructions to Form 706 and Reg. §§ 20.2013–2 and –3.

estate of the transferor and that the transferor died within the prescribed period of time.

If the transferor died within two years before or after the present decedent's death, the credit is allowed in full (subject to the preceding limitations). If the transferor died more than two years before the decedent, the credit is a certain percentage: 80 percent if the transferor died within the third or fourth year preceding the decedent's death, 60 percent if within the fifth or sixth year, 40 percent if within the seventh or eighth year, and 20 percent if within the ninth or tenth year.

Example 71   Pursuant to D's will, S inherits property. One year later S dies. Assume the estate tax attributable to the inclusion of the property in D's gross estate was $15,000 and that attributable to the inclusion of the property in S's gross estate is $12,000. Under these circumstances, S's estate may claim a credit against the estate tax of $12,000 (refer to limitation 2). □

Example 72   Assume the same facts as in Example 71, except that S dies three years after D's death. The applicable credit is now 80% of $12,000, or $9,600. □

Credit for Foreign Death Taxes (§ 2014).   Under § 2014, a credit is allowed against the estate tax for any estate, inheritance, legacy, or succession tax actually paid to any foreign country. For purposes of this provision, the term "foreign country" not only means states in the international sense but also refers to possessions or political subdivisions of foreign states and to possessions of the United States.

The credit is allowed for death taxes paid (1) with respect to property situated within the foreign country to which the tax is paid, (2) with respect to property included in the decedent's gross estate, and (3) with respect to the decedent's estate. No credit is allowed for interest or penalties paid in connection with foreign death taxes.

The credit is limited to the lesser of the following amounts:

1. The amount of the foreign death tax attributable to the property situated in the country imposing the tax and included in the decedent's gross estate for Federal estate tax purposes.
2. The amount of the Federal estate tax attributable to particular property situated in a foreign country, subject to death tax in that country, and included in the decedent's gross estate for Federal estate tax purposes.

Both of these limitations may require certain adjustments to arrive at the amount of the allowable credit. Such adjustments are illustrated in the Regulations and are not discussed in this text.[61] In addition to the credit for foreign death taxes under the provisions of Federal estate tax law, similar credits are allowable under death tax conventions with a number of foreign countries.[62] If a credit is allowed either under the provisions of law or under the provisions of a convention, that credit that is most beneficial to the estate is allowed.

---

61. Reg. §§ 20.2014–2 and –3.
62. For the list of countries with which the United States has death tax conventions, refer to Footnote 9.

Procedural Matters

A Federal estate tax return, if required, is due nine months after the date of the decedent's death.[63] This time limit applies to all estates regardless of the nationality or residence of the decedent. Not infrequently, however, an executor will request and obtain from the IRS an extension of time for filing Form 706 (estate tax return).[64]

For the estate of a citizen or resident of the United States dying after 1976, Form 706 must be filed by the executor or administrator under the following conditions: [65]

Year of Death	Gross Estate in Excess of
1977	$120,000
1978	134,000
1979	147,000
1980	161,000
1981	175,000
1982	225,000
1983	275,000
1984	325,000
1985	400,000
1986	500,000
1987 & thereafter	600,000

Note that the filing rquirements parallel the exemption equivalent amounts of the unified tax credit available for each year (refer to the table preceding Example 3). The filing requirements may be lower when the decedent has made taxable gifts after 1976 or has utilized any of the $30,000 specific gift tax exemption after September 8, 1976.

Example 73   D dies in 1988, leaving a gross estate of $595,000. If D has never made any post-1976 taxable gifts or used the specific gift tax exemption after September 8, 1976, Form 706 need not be filed by his estate. □

Example 74   Assume the same facts as in Example 73, except that D made a taxable gift of $20,000 in 1980. Since the filing requirement now becomes $580,000 [$600,000 (the regular filing requirement for 1988) − $20,000 (the post-1976 taxable gift)], Form 706 must be filed by D's estate. □

Form 706 must be filed with the IRS Service Center serving the district in which the decedent lived at the time of death. The return must be accompanied by various documents relevant to the determination of tax liability. Among items that must be included are statements on Form 712 to be obtained from the insurance companies involved for each insurance policy listed on the return.

---

63. § 6075(a).
64. § 6081.
65. § 6018(a).

Penalties are provided for willful failure to make and file a timely return and for willful attempts to evade or defeat payment of tax.[66]

Concept Summary

1. Both the Federal gift and estate taxes are excise taxes on the transfer of wealth.
2. The starting point for applying the Federal estate tax is to determine what assets are subject to tax. Such assets comprise a decedent's gross estate. The gross estate must be distinguished from the probate estate, since the latter classification includes those assets subject to administration by the executor of the estate.
3. Although the gross estate generally will not include any gifts made by the decedent within three years of death, it will include any gift tax paid on such transfers.
4. Based on the premise that one should not continue to enjoy or control property and not have it subject to the estate tax, certain incomplete transfers are subject to inclusion in the gross estate.
5. Upon the death of a joint tenant, the full value of the property will be included in the gross estate unless the survivor(s) made a contribution towards the cost of the property. Spouses are subject to a special rule that calls for automatic inclusion of one half of the value of the property in the gross estate of the first tenant to die. As to joint tenancies (or tenancies by the entirety) between husband and wife, it therefore makes no difference who furnished the original consideration. The creation of joint ownership will be subject to the gift tax when a tenant receives a lesser interest in the property than is warranted by the consideration furnished.
6. A power of appointment is the right to determine who shall own or enjoy, presently or in the future, the property subject to the power. The exercise, lapse, or release of a general power of appointment during the life of the holder will be subject to the gift tax. If the exercise, lapse, or release occurs at death, the property subject to the power will be included in the holder's gross estate. If, however, a special power of appointment is involved, no gift or estate tax consequences will result. Barring certain exceptions, a special power cannot be used to benefit the holder or his or her estate.
7. If the decedent is the insured, life insurance proceeds will be included in the gross estate if either of two conditions is satisfied. First, the proceeds are payable to the estate or for the benefit of the estate. Second, the decedent had possessed incidents of ownership (e.g., the right to change beneficiaries) over the policy. A transfer of an unmatured life insurance policy is subject to the gift tax. A gift also occurs when a policy matures and the owner of the policy is not the insured or the beneficiary.
8. In moving from the gross estate to the taxable estate, certain deductions are allowed. Under § 2053, deductions are permitted for various administration expenses (e.g., executor's commissions, funeral costs), debts of the decedent, and certain unpaid taxes. Casualty and theft losses incurred during the administration of an estate also can be deducted in arriving at the taxable estate.
9. Charitable transfers are deductible if the designated organization holds qualified status with the IRS at the time of the gift or upon death.
10. Transfers to a spouse qualify for the gift or estate tax marital deduction. Except as noted in (11), such transfers are subject to the terminable interest limitation.
11. The terminable interest limitation will not apply if the transferee-spouse is given a general power of appointment over the property or the QTIP election is made. In the case of a lifetime transfer, the donor-spouse makes the QTIP election. In the case of a

---

66. See, for example, §§ 6651, 6653, 6672, and 7203.

testamentary transfer, however, the executor of the estate of the deceased spouse has the election responsibility.

12. Subject to limitations, a deduction of one half of the selling price is allowed an estate for sale of employer stock to an ESOP.

13. The tax base for determining the estate tax is the taxable estate plus all post-1976 taxable gifts. From the tax so derived, all available credits are subtracted.

14. Of prime importance in the tax credit area is the unified tax credit. Except for large taxable transfers, the unified tax credit is $192,800 (exemption equivalent of $600,000).

15. Other Federal estate tax credits include credits for state death taxes, gift taxes, tax on prior transfers, and foreign death taxes.

16. If due, a Federal estate tax return (Form 706) must be filed within nine months of the date of the decedent's death. The IRS grants extensions for those estates that encounter difficulty in complying with this deadline.

Tax Planning Considerations

The Federal Gift Tax

Before 1977, two sets of tax rates applicable to transfers for insufficient consideration existed. Since the gift tax rates were lower than the estate tax rates, this, by itself, placed a premium on lifetime giving as a means of reducing the overall tax burden. After 1976, however, the estate tax savings from a lifetime gift usually is limited to the appreciation on the property that develops after the transfer is made. This result materializes because transfers by gift and by death are now subject to the same set of rates [i.e., the uniform transfer tax of § 2001(c)]. Also, taxable gifts made after 1976 must be added to the taxable estate in arriving at the amount of the estate tax.

As to taxable gifts that generate a tax, consideration must be given to the time value to the donor of the gift taxes paid. Since the donor loses the use of these funds, the expected interval between a gift (the imposition of the gift tax) and death (the imposition of the death tax) might make the gift less attractive from an economic standpoint. On the plus side, however, is the estate tax savings that would result from any gift tax paid. Since these funds are no longer in the gross estate of the donor (except for gifts within three years of death), the estate tax thereon is avoided.

Gifts made after 1976 do, nevertheless, possess distinct advantages. First, and often most important, income from the property will generally be shifted to the donee. If the donee is in a lower bracket than the donor, the family unit will save on income taxes. Second, the proper spacing of gifts can further cut down the Federal gift tax by maximizing the number of annual exclusions available. Third, all states but one impose some type of death tax, but only a minority impose a gift tax. Thus, a gift might completely avoid a state transfer tax.

In minimizing gift tax liability in lifetime giving, the optimum use of the annual exclusion can have significant results. Important in this regard are the following observations:

1. Because the annual exclusion is available every year, space the gifts over as many years as possible. To carry out this objective, start the program of lifetime giving as soon as is feasible. As an illustration, a donor could give as much as $100,000 to a donee if equally spaced over a 10-year period without using any of the unified tax credit and incurring any gift tax.
2. To the extent consistent with the wishes of the donor, maximize the number of donees. For example, a donor could give $500,000 to five donees over a 10-year period ($100,000 apiece) without using any of the unified tax credit and incurring any gift tax.
3. For the married donor, make use of the election to split gifts. As an example, a married couple can give $1,000,000 to five donees over a 10-year period (i.e., $20,000 per donee each year) without using any of their unified tax credit and incurring any gift tax.
4. Watch out for gifts of future interests. As noted earlier in the chapter, the annual exclusion is available only for gifts of a present interest.

Income tax considerations in lifetime giving are discussed under Tax Planning Considerations in Chapter 12.

The Federal Estate Tax

Controlling the Amount of the Gross Estate

Presuming an estate tax problem is anticipated, the starting point for planning purposes would be to reduce the size of the potential gross estate. Aside from initiating a program of lifetime giving, several other possibilities exist.

Incomplete Transfers. If property is to be excluded from a donee's gross estate by means of a lifetime transfer, the consequences of transfers deemed incomplete for estate tax purposes must be recognized. In general, transfers are considered incomplete if the transferor continues to exercise control over the property or to enjoy its use.

Example 75   Ten years ago, M transfers title to her personal residence to D, her daughter. Until the time of her death in the current year, M continues to live in the residence. ☐

In Example 75, the residence will be included in the gross estate of the donor (i.e., M) if an express or implied agreement exists between the donor and the donee for continued occupancy of the property.[67] This result is dictated by § 2036(a)(1); the transferor did not surrender the right to possession or enjoyment of the property.

If no express or implied agreement exists between the parties, may one be inferred by virtue of the fact that the transferor does not vacate the premises

---

67. See, for example, *Guynn v. U.S.*, 71–1 USTC ¶ 12,742, 27 AFTR2d 71–1653, 437 F.2d 1148 (CA–4, 1971).

after the gift but continues to live there until his or her death? In this regard, the situation described in Example 75 could be precarious, to say the least.

An implied agreement will probably be found in Example 75 unless the parties can produce some strong proof to show otherwise. An affirmative answer to any of the following questions would be helpful, though not controlling, in excluding the residence from M's gross estate:

—Did M report the transfer on a gift tax return and, if appropriate, pay a Federal gift tax thereon?

—Did M pay a reasonable rental to D for her continued occupancy of the premises?

—Did D, as any owner might be expected to do, absorb the cost of maintaining the property?

—If the property was income-producing (e.g., a farm or ranch), did D collect and report the income therefrom? [68]

Life Insurance. If the insured wants to keep the proceeds of a life insurance policy out of his or her gross estate, no incidents of ownership can be retained. All too often, a policy is transferred but the transferor has unsuspectingly retained some incident of ownership that may cause inclusion in the gross estate. The only way to prevent this from happening is to carefully examine the policy itself. Needless to say, only through this review procedure can one be assured that all incidents of ownership have been released.

Recall that a gift of a life insurance policy within three years of death of the owner-insured will be ineffective in terms of keeping the maturity value of the policy out of the gross estate. In this regard, refer to Example 31. To avoid this trap, as to gifts of life insurance policies, the sooner transferred the better, since death usually is an unpredictable event.

Proper Handling of Estate Tax Deductions

Estate taxes can be saved either by reducing the size of the gross estate or by increasing the total allowable deductions. Thus, the lower the taxable estate, the less the amount of estate tax generated. Planning in the deduction area generally involves the following considerations:

—Making proper use of the marital deduction.

—Working effectively with the charitable deduction.

—Handling properly other deductions and losses allowed under §§ 2053 and 2054.

The Marital Deduction in Perspective. When planning for the estate tax marital deduction, both tax and nontax factors have to be taken into account. In the

---

68. Compare, for example, *Estate of Ethel R. Kerdolff,* 57 T.C. 643 (1972) with *Estate of Roy D. Barlow,* 55 T.C. 666 (1971).

tax area, two major goals exist that guide planning. They are the equalization and the deferral approaches described as follows:

—Attempt to equalize the estates of both spouses. Clearly, for example, the estate tax on $2,000,000 is more than double the estate tax on $1,000,000 [compare $780,800 with $691,600 ($345,800 × 2)].

—Try to postpone estate taxation as long as possible. On a $1,000,000 amount, for example, what is the time value of $345,800 in estate taxes deferred for a period of, say, 10 years?

Barring certain circumstances, the deferral approach generally is preferable. By maximizing the marital deduction on the death of the first spouse to die, not only are taxes saved, but the surviving spouse is enabled to trim his or her future estate by entering into a program of lifetime giving. By making optimum use of the annual exclusion, considerable amounts can be gifted without incurring *any* transfer tax.

Tax planning must remain flexible and be tailored to the individual circumstances of the parties involved. Before the equalization approach is cast aside, therefore, consider the following variables:

—Both spouses are of advanced age and/or in poor health, and neither is expected to survive the other for a prolonged period of time.

—The spouse that is expected to survive has considerable assets of his or her own. To illustrate, a spouse that passes a $250,000 estate to the survivor who already has assets of $1,000,000 is trading a 32 percent bracket for a later 43 percent bracket.

—Because of appreciation, property worth $250,000 today when it passes to the surviving spouse may be worth $1,000,000 five years later when the survivor dies.

The Marital Deduction—Sophistication of the Deferral Approach. When the saving of estate taxes for the family unit is the sole consideration, the equalization and deferral approaches can be combined with maximum effect.

Example 76 At the time of his death in 1988, H had never made any post-1976 taxable gifts or used his specific exemption on any pre-1977 gifts. Under H's will, H's disposable estate of $1,100,000 passes to W, H's surviving spouse. For this purpose, the disposable estate means the gross estate less administration and other expenses and debts. ☐

Example 77 Assume the same facts as in Example 76, except that H's will provides as follows: $600,000 to the children and the remainder (i.e., $500,000) to W. ☐

From a tax standpoint, which is the better plan? Although no estate tax results from either arrangement, Example 76 represents overkill in terms of the marital deduction. Why place an additional $600,000 in W's potential estate when it can pass free of tax to the children through the application of the $192,800 unified tax credit available for 1988? (Keep in mind that the exemption equivalent of $192,800 is $600,000.) Clearly, then, the arrangement in Example 77 is to be preferred, as it avoids unnecessary concentration of wealth in W's estate.

On occasion the disclaimer procedure can be used to maximize the deferral approach.

Example 78   At the time of his death in 1988, H had never made any post-1976 gifts or used his specific exemption on pre-1977 gifts. Under H's will, H's disposable estate of $1,500,000 passes as follows: $700,000 to S (H's adult son) and the remainder ($800,000) to W (H's surviving spouse). Shortly after H's death, S issues a disclaimer as to $100,000 of his $700,000 bequest. Such amount, therefore, passes to W as the remainderperson under H's will. □

Because the unified tax credit for 1988 is $192,800 (with an exemption equivalent of $600,000), S's disclaimer avoids an estate tax on $100,000. The end result is to increase the marital deduction by $100,000 and eliminate *any* estate tax upon H's death.

Effectively Working with the Charitable Deduction.   As a general guide to obtain overall tax savings, lifetime charitable transfers are to be preferred over testamentary dispositions. For example, an individual who gave $10,000 to a qualified charity during his or her life would secure an income tax deduction, avoid any gift tax, and reduce the gross estate by the amount of the gift. By way of contrast, if the $10,000 had been willed to charity, no income tax deduction would be available and the amount of the gift would be includible in the decedent's gross estate (though later deducted for estate tax purposes). In short, the lifetime transfer provides a double tax benefit (i.e., income tax deduction plus reduced estate taxes) at no gift tax cost. The testamentary transfer merely neutralizes the effect of the inclusion of the property in the gross estate (i.e., inclusion under § 2033 and then deduction under § 2055).

To insure that an estate tax deduction will be allowed for a charitable contribution, the designated recipient must fall within the classifications set forth in § 2055. The status of the organization on the date the transfer becomes effective, and not on the date the will authorizing the transfer was executed, controls.

Example 79   In 1982, D drew up and executed a will in which he provided for $100,000 to pass to the XYZ Academy, a nonprofit educational organization described in § 2055(a)(2) and, at that time, approved by the IRS as a qualified recipient. In 1984, the qualified status of the XYZ Academy was revoked for practicing racial discrimination in the enrollment of its student body.[69] D dies in 1989, and the executor of his estate, being com-

---

69. Most of the organizations that are qualified recipients (which would permit the donor a charitable deduction) are listed in IRS Publication 78. This compilation, revised and supplemented from time to time, is designed to cover § 170 (i.e., the income tax deduction) transfers. Publication 78 will, with the exceptions noted in this chapter, also apply to § 2055 (estate tax deduction) and § 2522 (gift tax deduction) transfers.

pelled to satisfy the provisions of the will, transfers $100,000 to the XYZ Academy. □

Even though D may have been unaware of the action taken by the IRS in 1984, no charitable deduction will be allowed his estate, since the recipient was no longer qualified on the date of D's death. It may be that D, even if he had known about the probable loss of the charitable deduction, would still have wished the bequest carried out as originally conceived. If not, it is easy to say that the error was of D's own making because of his failure over this period of years to have his estate planning situation reviewed.

A possible way to circumvent the quandary posed by Example 79 (other than changing D's will before D's death) would be to express the charitable bequest in more flexible terms. The transfer to the XYZ Academy could have been conditioned on the organization's continued status as a qualified recipient at the time of D's death. Or D's will may grant D's executor the authority to substitute a different, but comparable, charitable organization *that is qualified* in the event of the disqualification of the named group.

On occasion, a charitable bequest may be dependent on the issuance of a disclaimer by a noncharitable heir. Such a situation frequently arises when special types of property or collections, which the decedent may feel a noncharitable heir should have a choice of receiving, are involved. If the charitable organization is the residuary legatee under a decedent's will, a disclaimer by a specific legatee passes the property by operation of the will to the holder of the residual interest and qualifies the estate for a charitable deduction under § 2055. Any exercise of such disclaimers in favor of charitable organizations should be carefully considered. Another course may be more advantageous from a tax standpoint.

Example 80 D specified in his will that his valuable art collection is to pass to his son or, if the son refuses, to a designated and qualified art museum. At the time the will was drawn, D was aware of the fact that his son was not interested in owning the art collection. If, after D's death, the son issues a timely disclaimer, the art collection will pass to the designated museum, and D's estate will be allowed a charitable deduction for its death tax value. □

Example 81 D's will specifies that one half of his disposable estate is to pass to his wife and the remainder of his property to a designated and qualified charitable organization. If the wife issues a timely disclaimer after D's death, all of the property will pass to the charity and will qualify for the § 2055 charitable deduction. □

Has the son in Example 80 acted wisely if he issued the disclaimer in favor of the museum? Although such a disclaimer would provide D's estate with a deduction for the value of the art collection, consider the income tax deduction alternative. If the son accepts the bequest, he can still dispose of the collection (and fulfill his father's philanthropic objectives) through lifetime donation to the museum and, at the same time, obtain for himself an income tax deduction under § 170. Whether this will save taxes for the family unit depends on a comparison of the father's estate tax bracket with the estimated income tax bracket of the son. If the value of the collection runs afoul of the percentage limitations of § 170(b)(1), the donations could be spread over more than one year. If this is done, and to protect against the contingency of the son's dying before donation of the entire collection, the son could neutralize any potential death tax consequences by providing in his will for the undonated balance to pass to the museum.

The use of a disclaimer in Example 81 would be sheer folly. It would not reduce D's estate tax; it would merely substitute a charitable deduction for the marital deduction. Whether the wife issues a disclaimer or not, no estate taxes will be due. The wife would be well-advised to accept her legacy and, if she is so inclined, to make lifetime gifts of it to a qualified charity. In so doing, she generates an income tax deduction for herself.

Proper Handling of Other Deductions and Losses under Code §§ 2053 and 2054. Many § 2053 and § 2054 deductions and losses may be claimed either as estate tax deductions or as income tax deductions of the estate on the fiduciary return (Form 1041), but a choice must be made.[70] In such a case, the deduction for income tax purposes will not be allowed unless the estate tax deduction is waived. It is possible for these deductions to be apportioned between the two returns. Certain expenses exist that do not follow this general rule. These variations are summarized as follows:

1. An expense deductible for estate tax purposes may not qualify as an income tax deduction. An example might be interest expense incurred to carry tax-exempt bonds that is disallowed for income tax purposes under § 265(a)(2). If this expense is not claimed under § 2053 for estate tax purposes, it will be completely lost.
2. Medical expenses incurred by the decedent but unpaid at the time of the decedent's death are covered by a special rule. If paid out of the estate during a one-year period beginning with the day after death, these expenses may be claimed as an income tax deduction in the year incurred or as an estate tax deduction, but not both.[71] Thus, the choice is between the decedent's appropriate Form 1040 and the estate's estate tax return. Such expenses may be split (i.e., divided in any way between Form 1040 and the estate tax return). Note that the estate's income tax return (Form 1041) is not involved.
3. Expenses in respect of a decedent fall into a special classification. Generally, they are expenses of a cash basis taxpayer, accrued at the time of the taxpayer's death but not deductible on the final Form 1040 by reason of the method of accounting.[72] Such deductions are allowed both for income tax and estate tax purposes. The deductions are available for income tax purposes to whoever is liable for and makes the payment. They include business and nonbusiness expenses (§§ 162 and 212), interest (§ 163), taxes (§ 164), and a possible credit for foreign taxes (§ 27). A deduction for depletion is allowed to the recipient of the income to which it relates.

---

70. § 642(g) and Reg. § 20.2053–1(d).
71. § 213(c).
72. § 691(b).

4. Brokerage commissions and other expenses relating to the sale of estate property can be offset against the sale price of the property in computing taxable income of the estate or can be deducted on the estate tax return. A choice will have to be made whether these expenses will be claimed as income tax or estate tax deductions.

The preceding rules can be illustrated by the following examples:

Example 82   The executor of D's estate is paid a proper commission (authorized under local law and approved by the probate court of appropriate jurisdiction) of $10,000 from estate assets. Such commission expense can be claimed on the estate tax return (Form 706) or on the income tax return of the estate (Form 1041) or split in any way between the two returns. However, no more than $10,000 can be claimed. □

Example 83   The executor of D's estate pays $5,000 in burial expenses (authorized under local law and approved by the probate court of appropriate jurisdiction) from estate assets. The $5,000 expense should be claimed on the estate tax return; it is not an item properly deductible for income tax purposes. □

Example 84   At the time of his death, D (a cash basis taxpayer) owed a local bank $10,000 on a loan due in several months. On the due date of the loan, the executor of D's estate pays the bank $10,800, which represents the principal amount of the loan ($10,000), interest accrued before D's death ($700), and interest accrued after D's death ($100). The amount deductible on the estate tax return (Form 706) is $10,700.[73] Because the interest accrued before D's death is an expense in respect of a decedent, it can also be claimed as an income tax deduction by whoever pays it. Since the interest was paid by the estate, it should be claimed on the estate's income tax return (Form 1041) along with the $100 of interest expense accrued after D's death. □

When a choice is available in the handling of §§ 2053 and 2054 expenses and losses, any decision must take into account different tax implications. A number of questions first have to be asked and satisfactorily resolved. Is the executor or executrix of the estate also the residuary legatee? If so, it would usually be rather pointless for him or her to claim any commissions due for serving in the capacity of executor or executrix. Although it would generate a § 2053 deduction (on Form 706) or an income tax deduction on the fiduciary return of the estate (on Form 1041), claiming the commission results in taxable income to the executor or executrix. If the commission is not claimed, the

---

73. The loan and interest accrued before death are deductible as a claim against the estate under § 2053(a)(3). This does not include any interest accrued after death. In this regard, it would not matter if the executor elected the alternate valuation date (see Chapter 12) for the estate. See Reg. § 20.2053–4 and Rev.Rul. 77–461, 1977–2 C.B. 324. Compare *Estate of Jane deP. Webster*, 65 T.C. 968 (1976).

amount involved should pass through to the executor or executrix tax-free by virtue of his or her rights as residuary legatee.[74]

Problem Materials

Discussion Questions

1. The unified transfer tax adopts a different approach to the taxation of life and death transfers after 1976. Explain.

2. Why can the unified transfer tax be categorized as an excise tax? In this regard, how does it differ from an income tax?

3. Upon whom is the Federal gift tax imposed? Suppose such party is unable to pay the tax.

4. What are the major differences between the Federal estate tax and the typical inheritance tax levied by many states?

5. T, a resident and citizen of Canada, owns real estate located in Rochester, New York.

    a. Would T be subject to the U.S. gift tax if she transferred this property as a gift to her Canadian son?

    b. Would T be subject to the U.S. estate tax if she died and left the property to her Canadian son?

6. Explain what is meant by the statement that the Federal gift tax is cumulative in nature.

7. What effect, if any, do prior gifts made by a decedent have on the determination of the decedent's estate tax liability?

8. What effect, if any, does prior utilization of the $30,000 specific exemption have on the unified tax credit currently available?

9. What is meant by the exemption equivalent of the unified tax credit?

10. Reg. § 25.2512–8 states: "A consideration not reducible to a value in money or money's worth, as love and affection, promise of marriage, etc., is to be wholly disregarded, and the entire value of the property transferred constitutes the amount of the gift."

    a. What does this Regulation mean?

    b. When might it apply?

11. X sells property to Y for $50,000. If the property is really worth $100,000, has X made a gift to Y? What additional facts would you want to know before answering this question?

12. In connection with gift loans, comment on the following points:

    a. Since any interest element recognized by the lender as income can be deducted by the borrower, the income tax effect is neutralized for the family unit.

    b. The borrower's net investment income for the year is less than $1,000.

    c. The gift loan involved only $95,000.

    d. The lender charged the borrower interest of 2%.

---

74. Section 102(a) specifies that a "bequest, devise, or inheritance" is excludible from gross income.

13. In the absence of § 2516, why would certain property settlements incident to a divorce be subject to the Federal gift tax?

14. In connection with § 2518 dealing with disclaimers, comment on the following:

    a. The role of state law.

    b. The avoidance of a Federal gift tax or the Federal estate tax.

    c. The disclaimer of only a partial interest.

15. What is the justification for the annual exclusion? In what manner does it resemble the gift tax treatment of the following:

    a. Tuition payments to an educational organization on behalf of another.

    b. Medical care payments on behalf of another.

16. What purpose is served by the § 2503(c) trust for minors?

17. In connection with the gift-splitting provision of § 2513, comment on the following:

    a. What it was designed to accomplish.

    b. How the election is made.

    c. Its utility in a community property jurisdiction.

18. D makes the following taxable gifts: $200,000 in 1975 and $450,000 in 1988. On the 1975 gift, D incurred and paid a Federal gift tax of $40,000. How should the gift tax be determined on the 1988 gift?

19. In connection with the filing of a Federal gift tax return, comment on the following:

    a. No Federal gift tax is due.

    b. The § 2513 election to split gifts is to be used.

    c. A gift of a future interest is involved.

    d. The donor uses a fiscal year for Federal income tax purposes.

    e. The donor obtained from the IRS an extension of time for filing his or her Federal income tax return.

20. Distinguish between the following:

    a. The gross estate and the taxable estate.

    b. The gross estate and the probate estate.

21. No taxable gifts made within three years of death will be included in the gross estate of the donor. Evaluate the soundness of this statement.

22. D transfers a remainder interest in her residence to her adult son and continues to occupy the premises until her death five years later. Will the property be included in D's probate estate? Gross estate?

23. Using community property, H creates a trust, life estate to W (H's wife), remainder to their children upon W's death.

    a. Is there any estate tax effect upon H's death four years later?

    b. Is there any estate tax effect upon W's death five years later?

24. It has been said that community property is much like a tenancy in common. Do you agree? Why or why not?

25. At the time of X's death, X was a joint tenant with Y in a parcel of real estate. With regard to the inclusion in X's gross estate under § 2040, comment on the following independent assumptions:

    a. The property was received by X and Y as a gift from D.

    b. Y provided all of the purchase price of the property.

    c. Y's contribution was received as a gift from X.

    d. X's contribution was derived from income generated by property received by X as a gift from Y.

26. Under what circumstances will the creation of a joint tenancy not constitute a gift when one of the tenants furnishes more of the consideration than the other (others)?

27. If the holder can use the power to appoint some of the property for his or her benefit, it is a general power of appointment. Do you agree? Why or why not?

28. T owns a policy on the life of S, with D as the designated beneficiary. Upon S's death, the insurance proceeds are paid to D.

    a. Are any of the proceeds included in S's gross estate?

    b. Does S's death generate any tax consequences to T?

29. What are expenses in respect of a decedent? How are they treated for tax purposes?

30. W, the surviving spouse of H, is the executrix of H's estate. Also, W is designated by H's will as the remainderperson of H's estate. In deciding whether W should claim or waive any commissions she might be entitled to for serving as executrix, what tax factors should be considered?

31. Unpaid medical expenses of a decedent are handled for tax purposes in the same manner as funeral expenses. Do you agree or disagree with this statement? Explain.

32. For tax purposes, what difference does it make whether a casualty loss occurs before or after the death of the owner of the property?

33. In terms of the QTIP (qualified terminable interest property) election, comment on the following:

    a. Who makes the election.

    b. What the election accomplishes.

    c. The tax effect of the election upon the death of the surviving spouse.

34. Explain the difference between the equalization and deferral approaches to the estate tax marital deduction.

35. For married persons, the real danger of an estate tax burden materializes upon the death of the surviving spouse. Do you agree or disagree with this observation? Why?

Problems

1. In each of the following independent situations, indicate whether or not the transfer by D is, or could be, subject to the Federal gift tax:

    a. D makes a contribution to an influential political figure.

    b. D makes a contribution to B Corporation, of which he is not a shareholder.

    c. In consideration of his upcoming marriage to B, D establishes a savings account in B's name.

d. Same as (c). After their marriage, D establishes a joint checking account in the names of "D and B."

e. Same as (d). One year after the checking account is established, B withdraws all of the funds.

f. D exercises a special power of appointment in favor of B.

g. D enters into an agreement with B whereby he will transfer property to her in full satisfaction of her marital rights. One month after the agreement, the transfer occurs. Later D and B are divorced.

h. D purchases U.S. savings bonds, listing ownership as "D and B." Several years later, and after D's death, B redeems the bonds.

2. In each of the following independent situations, indicate whether or not the transfer by D is, or could be, subject to the Federal gift tax:

a. D purchases real estate and lists title as "D and B as joint tenants." D and B are brothers.

b. Same as (a), except that D and B are husband and wife.

c. D creates a revocable trust with B as the designated beneficiary.

d. Same as (c). One year after creating the trust, D releases all power to revoke the trust.

e. D takes out an insurance policy on his life, designating B as the beneficiary.

f. Same as (e). Two years later, D dies and the policy proceeds are paid to B.

g. D takes out an insurance policy on the life of W and designates B as the beneficiary. Shortly thereafter, W dies and the policy proceeds are paid to B.

h. D pays for B's college tuition.

3. In 1976, R purchased real estate for $300,000, listing ownership as follows: "R and S, equal tenants in common." R predeceases S in 1988 when the property is worth $500,000. Before 1976, R had not made any taxable gifts or utilized the $30,000 specific exemption. Assume R and S are brothers.

a. Determine R's gift tax consequences, if any, in 1976.

b. How much, if any, of the property should be included in R's gross estate?

4. In 1982, T purchased real estate for $250,000, listing title to the property as follows: "T and U, joint tenants with the right of survivorship." Under applicable state law, both parties possess the right of severance. U predeceases T in 1988 when the real estate is worth $400,000. Assume T and U are brothers and that neither has made any other taxable gifts or utilized his $30,000 specific exemption.

a. Determine T's gift tax consequences, if any, in 1982.

b. How much, if any, of the property should be included in U's gross estate?

5. Assume the same facts as in Problem 4, except that T and U are husband and wife (rather than brothers).

a. Determine T's gift tax consequences, if any, in 1982.

b. How much, if any, of the property should be included in U's gross estate? Will any such inclusion generate an estate tax liability? Explain.

6. In January 1988, H and W enter into a property settlement under which H agrees to pay $500,000 to W in return for the release of her marital rights. At the time the agreement is signed, H pays W $100,000 as a first installment. Although the parties intended to

obtain a divorce, H dies in July 1988 before legal proceedings have been instituted. After H's death, the executor of H's estate pays to W the $400,000 remaining balance due under the property settlement.

a. What are the gift tax consequences of the $100,000 payment made upon the signing of the agreement? Why?

b. What are the estate tax consequences of the $400,000 paid to W from estate assets after H's death? Why?

7. In 1988, M makes a gift to her daughter of securities worth $700,000. M has never made any prior taxable gifts or utilized her $30,000 specific exemption. F (M's husband), however, made a taxable gift of $500,000 in early 1976 upon which he paid a gift tax of $109,275. At the time of F's gift, F was not married to M.

a. Determine M's gift tax liability on the 1988 transfer, assuming the parties chose not to make the election to split gifts under § 2513.

b. What would the liability be if the election to split the gift were made?

8. Before her death in 1988, D (a widow) made the following transfers:

—A gift of real estate (basis of $50,000 and fair market value of $200,000) to S (D's son). The gift was made in 1986 and resulted in a Federal gift tax of $10,000, which D paid. On the date of D's death, the property is worth $220,000.

—A gift of an insurance policy on D's life to B (the designated beneficiary). The policy was worth $10,000 but had a maturity value of $50,000. The gift was made in 1986 and resulted in no Federal gift tax liability.

—A gift of stock (basis of $40,000 and fair market value of $100,000) to R. The gift was made in 1980 and resulted in no Federal gift tax liability. On the date of D's death, the stock was worth $300,000.

Presuming the alternate valuation date is not elected, how much should be included in D's gross estate as to these transfers?

9. D dies on July 7, 1988, at a time when he owns stock in Z Corporation and W Corporation. On June 1 of the same year both corporations authorized cash dividends payable on August 1. For Z Corporation, the dividend was payable to shareholders of record as of July 1, and W Corporation's date of record was July 10. After D's death, the executor of the estate received dividends in the following amounts: $6,000 from Z Corporation and $8,000 from W Corporation. D also owned some City of Minneapolis tax-exempt bonds. As of July 7, the accrued interest on the bonds was $7,500. On December 1, the executor of the estate received $10,000 in interest ($2,500 accrued since D's death) from the bonds. Concerning the dividends and interest, how much should be included in D's gross estate?

10. G would like to make a lifetime transfer in trust of $300,000 to his son, S, and accomplish the following objectives:

—Avoid any death tax on the deaths of G, S, and W (S's wife).

—Give S the right to determine what portion of the remainder should be allocated between W and their children, A and B.

—Give S some additional security by allowing him to reach corpus should the need materialize.

—Prevent S from squandering all of corpus to the detriment of W, A, or B.

In light of § 2041, what do you suggest?

11. In each of the following independent situations, determine how much should be included in D's gross estate under § 2042 as to the various life insurance policies involved. Assume that none of the policies are community property.

    a. At the time of his death, D owned a paid-up policy on the life of B, with S as the designated beneficiary. The policy had a replacement cost of $80,000 and a maturity value of $300,000.

    b. W owns a policy on the life of D ($300,000 maturity value) with D's estate as the designated beneficiary. Upon D's death, the insurance company pays $300,000 to D's estate.

    c. Four years before his death, D transferred a policy on his life ($300,000 maturity value) to S as a gift. D retained the power to change beneficiaries. At the time of the transfer, the designated beneficiary was S. Because D had never exercised his right to change beneficiaries, the insurance company pays S $300,000 upon D's death.

    d. Same as (c), except that D releases the power to change beneficiaries one year before his death.

12. Comment on how each of the following independent situations should be handled for estate tax purposes:

    a. Before her death in 1988, D issued a note payable to her daughter in the amount of $100,000 for which no consideration was ever received by D. After D's death, the daughter files a claim against the estate and collects $100,000 on the note.

    b. At the time of her death, D (a widow) owned 10 cemetery lots (each worth $5,000), which she had purchased many years before for herself and her family.

    c. At the time of his death, D was delinquent in the payment of back Federal income taxes. Such taxes are paid by D's executor from assets of the estate.

13. Before his death in 1987, D donates stock held as an investment (basis of $8,000 and fair market value of $15,000) to his church. Under the same circumstances, E transfers an equal amount of property, except that such donation occurs pursuant to E's will. Assume that both taxpayers were in a 33% bracket for income tax purposes and that their estates will be subject to a top death tax rate of 40%. Which taxpayer is in a better tax position? Why?

 14. Four different persons (D, E, F, and G) die in 1988, each leaving a disposable estate of $1,100,000 and none having made any post-1976 taxable gifts. Each decedent leaves a surviving spouse and a will dictating the disposition of his or her property. From a tax standpoint, evaluate the following various testamentary schemes:

    a. Under D's will, the full disposable estate passes to a qualified charity.

    b. Under E's will, the full disposable estate passes to the surviving spouse.

    c. Under F's will, the disposable estate is to be divided between the surviving spouse and a qualified charitable organization.

    d. Under G's will, $600,000 passes to the children and the balance goes to the surviving spouse.

15. In 1988, H places in trust $500,000 worth of securities. Under the terms of the trust instrument, W (H's wife) is granted a life estate, and on W's death, the remainder interest passes to H and W's children (as W determines in her will). Upon W's death 18 years later, the trust assets are valued at $2,000,000.

    a. How much, if any, marital deduction will be allowed on the gift made in 1988?

    b. How much, if any, of the trust will be included in W's gross estate upon W's death?

16. Assume the same facts as in Problem 15, except that H made the qualified terminable interest property election when the trust was created. Further assume that W has no choice as to which of her children will receive the remainder interest upon her death.

    a. How much, if any, marital deduction will be allowed on the gift made in 1988?

    b. How much, if any, of the trust will be subject to the Federal estate tax upon W's later death?

17. In each of the following independent situations determine the decedent's final estate tax liability (net of any unified tax credit):

	Decedent			
	A	B	C	D
Year of death	1984	1985	1986	1988
Taxable estate	$500,000	$700,000	$900,000	$800,000
Pre-1977 taxable gift	—	250,000*	100,000*	—
Post-1976 taxable gift	200,000	—	—	250,000
Gift tax on pre-1977 taxable gift	—	49,725	15,525	—
Gift tax on post-1976 taxable gift	38,000	—	—	70,800

* The $30,000 specific exemption was used in full for each of these gifts. B's gift occurred on October 1, 1976, while C's took place in June of 1976.

18. In each of the following independent situations determine the decedent's final estate tax liability (net of any unified tax credit):

	Decedent			
	E	F	G	H
Year of death	1985	1986	1987	1988
Taxable estate	$900,000	$800,000	$1,000,000	$1,100,000
Pre-1977 taxable gift	250,000*	250,000*	—	—
Post-1976 taxable gift	—	—	500,000	80,000
Gift tax paid on post-1976 taxable gift	—	—	155,800	18,200
Gift tax paid on pre-1977 taxable gift	49,275	49,275	—	—

* The $30,000 specific exemption was used in full for each of these gifts. E's gift occurred in December 1976, while F's took place in December 1975.

19. In each of the following independent situations determine the decedent's final estate tax liability for 1988 (net of any unified tax credit and credit for gift taxes paid). (Note: In some cases, you will have to compute the gift tax that was paid.)

	Decedent			
	I	J	K	L
Taxable estate	$500,000	$300,000	$500,000	$600,000
Taxable gift made in:				
1981	200,000	—	—	—
1979	—	200,000	—	—
1982	—	—	300,000	—
1983	—	—	—	200,000

20. In each of the following independent situations determine the decedent's final estate tax liability for 1988 (net of any unified tax credit and credit for gift taxes paid), the year of death. (Note: In some cases, you will have to compute the gift tax that was paid.)

	Decedent			
	M	N	O	P
Taxable estate	$800,000	$300,000	$700,000	$900,000
Taxable gift made in:				
1980	200,000	—	—	—
1981	—	300,000	—	—
1982	—	—	150,000	—
1983	—	—	—	300,000

21. Assume the filing requirement for 1988 is a gross estate in excess of $600,000. What effect would each of the following transactions before the decedent's death in 1988 have on the filing requirement?

—Utilized $10,000 of the $30,000 specific gift tax exemption on a gift made in June 1976.

—Used the balance of the $30,000 specific gift tax exemption on a gift made in October 1976.

—Made a taxable gift of $100,000 in November 1976.

—Made a taxable gift of $100,000 in 1978.

Comprehensive Tax Return Problem

During 1987, Robert and Susan Brown (Social Security Nos. 463–04–7964 and 466–36–4596) resided at 4321 Mt. Vernon Place, Altview, VA 23284. In their 25 years of marriage, the Browns have always lived in common law states. Robert Brown practices internal medicine, and Susan Brown is a partner in a well-known architectural firm in Richmond, Virginia. Both practices have been highly successful.

During 1987, the Browns made the following transfers (without adjustment for the annual exclusion or the marital deduction):

	Robert Brown	Susan Brown
Cash gift to Susan Brown.	$150,000	
Payment to Oxford University for David Brown's (22-year-old son) tuition.	16,000	$ 2,000
Payment to Clinical Associates for psychiatric treatment rendered to Mildred Hogan. Mildred is Robert Brown's aunt and suffers from severe depression. For income tax purposes, she does not qualify as the Browns' dependent.	13,000	
Gift to David Brown of securities owned by Susan Brown. The securities had a basis to Susan Brown of $18,000 and a fair market value on the date of the gift of $100,000.		100,000

	Robert Brown	Susan Brown
Cash gift to Lea Brown (21-year-old daughter).	$130,000	$120,000
Cash gift to Mary Smith (the Browns' housekeeper).		4,000
Cash gift to Bonnie Davis (Susan Brown's sister) to enable her to cover certain personal debts.	9,000	11,000
A savings account established for James Brown (14-year-old son) under the Virginia Uniform Gifts to Minors Act. Robert Brown is designated as the custodian of the account.	100,000	100,000

In past years, the Browns have made the following taxable gifts:

Year	Robert Brown	Susan Brown
1981	$200,000	$200,000
1984	300,000	200,000
1985	100,000	200,000

As to all past gifts, the Browns have elected to use the gift-splitting provisions of § 2513.

Required:

a. Determine how much, if any, Federal gift tax will have been paid on the pre-1987 taxable gifts Robert and Susan Brown have made.

b. Complete Forms 709 (U.S. Federal Gift Tax Return) for the gifts made in 1987.

Research Problems

Research Problem 1. During the current year, D establishes a trust with 500 shares of D Corporation stock. Under the terms of the trust instrument, income from the stock is to be paid to or accumulated for S, D's son, until he reaches age 21. At this point, the trust is to terminate if S, by written request, so decides. If not, the trust will continue until S reaches age 30. Upon termination of the trust, all income and principal are to be paid to S. In the event S dies during the term of the trust, all accumulated income and principal are to be paid to S's estate or to whomever S may direct under a general power of appointment. Although the designated trustee, a local bank, is empowered to expend trust income for S's benefit, the trustee does not possess the right to dispose of the stock without D's consent.

After the transfer, the outstanding stock of D Corporation (5,000 shares of common) is held as follows: 500 shares by the trust and 4,500 shares by D. For the 10 years preceding the gift, no dividends were paid on the D Corporation stock.

a. Would D be allowed an annual exclusion for the gift in trust to S? Explain.

b. Assuming D dies while the trust was still in effect, could the trust be included in D's gross estate? Explain.

Partial list of research aids:

Code §§ 2035, 2036, 2038, and 2503.

Stark v. U.S., 73–1 USTC ¶ 12,921, 31 AFTR2d 1457, 477 F.2d 131 (CA–8, 1973).

Rev.Rul. 74–43, 1974–1 C.B. 285.

Estate of Arthur A. Chalmers, 31 TCM 792, T.C.Memo. 1972–158.

Research Problem 2. On October 1, 1976, H makes a gift of $66,000 to his son. In reporting the gift, W (H's wife) made the election under § 2513. As a result, no gift tax was due. W dies in 1988, and in completing Form 706, her executor claims a unified tax credit of $192,800.

    a. Why was no gift tax due on the 1976 gift?

    b. Did the executor of W's estate act correctly in claiming a unified tax credit of $192,800 on Form 706? Why or why not?

Research Problem 3. Before her death in 1988, D entered into the following transactions:

    a. In 1981, she borrowed $35,000 from a bank, which sum she promptly loaned to her controlled corporation. The executor of D's estate repaid the bank loan but never attempted to collect the amount due D from the corporation.

    b. In 1978, D promised her sister, S, a bequest of $200,000 if S would move in with her and care for her during an illness (which eventually proved to be terminal). D never kept her promise, as her will was silent on any bequest to S. After D's death, S sued the estate and eventually recovered $120,000 for breach of contract.

    c. One of the assets in D's estate was a palatial residence that passed to R under a specific provision of the will. R did not want the residence, preferring cash instead. Per R's instructions, the residence was sold. Expenses incurred in connection with the sale were claimed as § 2053 expenses on Form 706 filed by D's estate.

    d. Before her death, D incurred and paid certain medical expenses but did not have the opportunity to file a claim for partial reimbursement from her insurance company. After her death, the claim was filed by D's executor, and the reimbursement was paid to the estate.

Discuss the estate and income tax ramifications of each of these transactions.

Partial list of research aids:

Code §§ 61(a)(1) and (12), 111, 213, 691, 2033, and 2053.

Estate of Allie W. Pittard, 69 T.C. 391 (1977).

Estate of Myron M. Miller, 37 TCM 1547, T.C.Memo. 1978–374.

Joseph F. Kenefic, 36 TCM 1226, T.C.Memo. 1977–310.

Hibernia Bank v. U.S., 78–2 USTC ¶ 13,261, 42 AFTR2d 78–6510, 581 F.2d 741 (CA–9, 1978).

Rev.Rul. 78–292, 1978–2 C.B. 233.

Research Problem 4. On August 1, 1987, H transfers securities in X Corporation to his son, S, under the Florida Uniform Gifts to Minors Act. Under the transfer, W (H's wife and mother of S) is designated as the custodian of the stock. On September 3, 1987, W transfers securities in X Corporation to her son, S, under the Florida Uniform Gifts to Minors Act. Under the transfer, H is designated as the custodian of the stock. H dies in 1988 as a result of an accident. Will any of the securities in X Corporation be included in H's gross estate?

Partial list of research aids:

Exchange Bank and Trust Co. v. U.S., 82–2 USTC ¶ 13,505, 51 AFTR2d 83–1317, 694 F.2d 1261 (CA–Fed.Cir., 1982).

Estate of Herbert Levy, 46 TCM 910, T.C.Memo. 1983–453.

12 Valuation and Liquidity Problems

Objectives

Emphasize the importance of the valuation process in the estate and gift tax areas.
Review the rules governing the valuation of different assets and business interests.
Explain the purpose of the alternate valuation date and the rules governing its use.
Explain the purpose of the special use valuation method and its utility as a tax-saving procedure.
Summarize the income tax basis considerations of property acquired by gift or by inheritance.
Recognize and plan for the problem of estate liquidity.
Review the different provisions of the law whereby the payment of estate taxes can be extended beyond the normal due date.

Outline

Importance of Valuation

One essential element in working with the tax law concerns the satisfactory resolution of the valuation problem. Recall that the gift tax is predicated on the fair market value of the property on the date of the transfer. For the Federal estate tax, it is the fair market value on the date of the owner's death or alternate valuation date (if available and elected) that controls. Even more subtle are the income tax considerations inherent in this problem.

Example 1   D would like to give to S an unimproved tract of land that he inherited from his grandmother 20 years ago. Rather apparent is the importance of the value of the property on the date of the gift, since this is the starting point in determining the gift tax implications of the transfer. A less obvious but equally important consideration is the determination of S's income tax basis in the property. To determine S's basis, one must know D's adjusted basis in the property. Since D inherited the property, § 1014 controls, and D's basis will be the land's fair market value as of 20 years ago. □

The fair market value of the land transferred in Example 1 is important in at least two respects: D's gift tax consequences and S's income tax basis upon the later disposition of the property in a taxable sale or exchange. Not mentioned, but nevertheless consequential, would be the effect the fair market value of the land had on the death taxes paid by the grandmother's estate.

In the sections that follow, the question of valuation is discussed together with its tax implications.

The Valuation Process

Valuation in General

Although the Internal Revenue Code refers to "value" and even "fair market value," these terms are not considered at length.[1] Code § 2031(b) comes closest to a definition when it treats the problem of stocks and securities for which no sales price information (i.e., the usual case with closely-held corporations) is available. In such situations, "the value thereof shall be determined by taking into consideration, in addition to all other factors, the value of stock or securities of corporations engaged in the same or similar line of business which are listed on an exchange."

Reg. § 20.2031–1(b) is more specific in defining fair market value as "the price at which property would change hands between a willing buyer and a willing seller, neither being under any compulsion to buy or to sell and both having reasonable knowledge of relevant facts." The same Regulation makes it

---

1. See, for example, §§ 1001(b), 2031(a), and 2512(a). The exception might be the special use valuation procedures enacted by the Tax Reform Act of 1976. Under §§ 2032A(e)(7) and (8), certain valuation procedures are set forth for valuing farms and interests in closely-held businesses.

clear that the fair market value of an item of property is not to be determined by a forced sale price. Nor is the fair market value to be determined by the sale price of the item in a market other than that in which such item is most commonly sold to the public, taking into account the item's location whenever appropriate. Thus, for property that generally is obtained by the public in a retail market, the fair market value of such property is the price at which such property (or comparable items) would be sold at retail.

Example 2   At the time of his death, D owned three automobiles. These automobiles must be included in D's gross estate at their fair market value on the date of D's death or on the alternate valuation date (if available and elected). To arrive at the fair market value of these automobiles, look to the price for which automobiles of approximately the same description, make, model, age, condition, etc., could be purchased by a member of the general public. The price for which these automobiles would be purchased by a dealer in used automobiles would be inappropriate, because an automobile is an item generally obtainable by the public in a retail market. ☐

If tangible personalty [2] is sold as a result of an advertisement in the classified section of a newspaper and the property is of a type often sold in this manner, or if the property is sold at a public auction, the price for which it is sold will be presumed to be the retail sales price of the item at the time of the sale. This price also will be presumed to be the retail sales price on the applicable valuation date if the sale is made within a reasonable period following the valuation date and there is no substantial change in market conditions or other circumstances affecting the value of similar items. [3]

Valuation of Particular Types of Property

Before turning to a consideration of how tax planning can aid in resolving the valuation problem, some discussion of the rules applicable in valuing particular types of property interests is in order.

Stocks and Bonds.   If there is a market for stocks and bonds on a stock exchange, in an over-the-counter market, or otherwise, the mean between the highest and lowest quoted selling prices on the valuation date is the fair market value per unit. If there were no sales on the valuation date but there were sales on dates within a reasonable period before and after the valuation date, the fair market value is determined by taking a weighted average of the means between the highest and the lowest sales prices on the nearest date before and the nearest date after the valuation date. The average is to be weighted *inversely* by the respective number of trading days between the selling dates and the valuation date. [4]

---

2. Tangible personalty would include all property except real estate and intangible property. For this purpose, intangible property includes stocks and bonds.
3. Rev.Proc. 65–19, 1965–2 C.B. 1002.
4. Reg. §§ 20.2031–2(b) and 25.2512–2(b).

Example 3   D makes a gift to S of shares of stock in X Corporation. The transactions closest to the date of the gift that involve this stock took place two trading days before the date of the gift at a mean selling price of $10 and three trading days after the gift at a mean selling price of $15. The $12 fair market value of each share of X Corporation stock is determined by the following computation:

$$\frac{(3 \times \$10) + (2 \times \$15)}{5} = \$12 \qquad \square$$

[handwritten annotation: (days × mean) + (days × mean) / total days]

[handwritten annotation: 2, 3 above the numbers; days (3+2) → 5]

If no transactions occurred within a reasonable period before and after the valuation date, the fair market value may be determined by taking a weighted average of the means between the bona fide bid and asked prices on the nearest trading dates before and after the valuation date, if both such dates are within a reasonable period of time.

If no actual sales prices or bona fide bid and asked prices are available on a date within a reasonable period before the valuation date but are available on a date within a reasonable period after the valuation date, or vice versa, the mean between the highest and lowest available sales prices or bid and asked prices on that date may be taken as the value.

If selling prices or bid and asked prices are not available, as is typically the case with securities of a closely-held corporation, fair market value is to be determined by taking the following into account:

[handwritten annotation: acceptable to use like company on "Big Board"]

1. For bonds, the soundness of the security, the interest yield, the date of maturity, and other relevant factors.
2. For shares of stock, the corporation's net worth, prospective earning power, dividend-paying capacity, and other relevant factors.

Some of the "other relevant factors" are the goodwill of the business, the economic outlook in the particular industry, the company's position in the industry, and the value of securities of other corporations engaged in the same or similar lines of business.[5] The ramifications of these concepts as applied to the valuation of stock in a closely-held corporation are discussed later in the chapter.

Shares in an open-end investment company (i.e., mutual fund) are valued at the redemption, or bid, price of the security.

Interest in Businesses.   The fair market value of any interest in a business, whether a sole proprietorship or partnership, is the net amount that a willing purchaser would pay for the interest of a willing seller, neither being under any compulsion to buy or sell and both having reasonable knowledge of the relevant facts.

The relevant facts to be considered in valuing the business are (1) a fair appraisal of the assets of the business, (2) the demonstrated earning capacity of the business, and (3) certain other factors used in arriving at the valuation of

---

5. Reg. §§ 20.2031–2(f) and 25.2512–2(f). See also Rev.Rul. 59–60, 1959–1 C.B. 237, which discusses the subject at greater length than do the Regulations.

corporate stock to the extent applicable to the particular situation. Special attention should be given to the determination of an adequate value for the goodwill of the business if no bona fide purchase agreement exists.[6]

Notes Receivable.   The fair market value of notes, secured or unsecured, is presumed to be the amount of unpaid principal plus interest accrued to the valuation date unless the parties (e.g., executor, donor) establish a lower value or prove the notes are worthless. Factors such as a low interest rate and a distant maturity date would be relevant in showing that a note is worth less than its face amount. The key to proving that a note is entirely or partially worthless would be the financial condition of the obligor and the absence of any value as to property pledged or mortgaged as security for the obligation.[7]

Example 4   At the time of his death, D held a note (face amount of $5,000) issued by his son, S. Although S is solvent, he does not have to satisfy the obligation, because D forgives the note in his will. Presuming the note is payable on demand, it must be included in D's gross estate at $5,000 plus accrued interest. If not immediately due and/or the interest provided for is under the current rate, a discount may be in order, and the fair market value of the note would be less than $5,000. The burden of proof to demonstrate that less than the face amount of the note should be included in the gross estate is on the executor. ☐

Insurance Policies and Annuity Contracts.   The value of a life insurance policy on the life of a person other than the decedent or the value of an annuity contract issued by a company regularly engaged in the selling of contracts of that character is the cost of a comparable contract.[8]

Example 5   D purchased from an insurance company a joint and survivor annuity contract. Under the contract's terms, D is to receive payments of $9,600 per year for his life. Upon D's death, D's wife (W) is to receive $7,200 annually for her life. Ten years after the purchase of the annuity, and when W is 40 years of age, D dies. The value of the annuity contract on the date of D's death [and the amount includible in D's gross estate under § 2039(a)] will be the amount the insurance company would charge for an annuity providing for the payment of $7,200 annually for the life of a female 40 years of age. ☐

Example 6   At the time of his death, D owns an insurance policy (face amount of $100,000) on the life of his son, S. The policy is one on which no further payments need be made (e.g., single premium policy or a paid-up policy). The value of the policy on the date of D's death (and the amount includible in D's gross estate under § 2033 as property in which the decedent had an interest) will be the amount the insurance company would charge

6. Reg. §§ 20.2031–3 and 25.2512–3. But see the special use valuation procedures of § 2032A(e)(8) discussed later in the chapter.
7. Reg. §§ 20.2031–4 and 25.2512–4.
8. Reg. §§ 20.2031–8(a)(1) and 25.2512–6(a).

for a single premium contract (face amount of $100,000) on the life of a person the same age as S. ☐

The valuation of an insurance policy by determining the amount charged for a comparable policy is not readily ascertainable when, on the date of valuation, the contract has been in force for some time and further premium payments are to be made. In such a case, the value may be approximated by adding to the interpolated terminal reserve the proportionate part of the gross premium last paid before the valuation date that covers the period extending beyond that date.[9]

The valuation of annuities issued by parties not regularly engaged in the sale of annuities requires the use of special tables issued by the IRS. Which table must be used depends on whether the valuation date occurs before 1971, after 1970 and before December 1, 1983, or after November 30, 1983. These three sets of tables reflect an attempt on the part of the IRS to adjust for the increase in interest rates that has taken place over the years. The two most recent sets of tables are reproduced in Appendix A.

Example 7   Under the terms of F's will, D (F's son) is entitled to receive an annuity of $20,000 payable annually for life. When D is 50 in 1988, he assigns the annuity to S as a gift. Turning to column 2 of Table A, Reg. § 25.2512–5(f), the annuity factor for a person age 50 is 8.4743. Multiplying 8.4743 by the annual payment of $20,000 yields a fair market value of $169,486. Thus, when D assigns his annuity to S, he has made a gift of $169,486.[10]   ☐

Life Estates, Terms for Years, Reversions, and Remainders.   As was true with noncommercial annuities, the valuation of life estates, income interests for a term of years, reversions, and remainders involves the use of tables. Again, it is important to ascertain when the transfer occurred. The two most recent tables are reproduced in Appendix A.

Example 8   D transfers $100,000 in trust, life estate to W, remainder to S on W's death. At the time of the gift, W is a female, age 35. If the gift took place on November 30, 1983, Table A(2) of Reg. § 25.2512–9(f) yields a factor of 0.87593 (column 3) for a female, age 35.[11] [Note: The factor for a remainder interest is 0.12407 (column 4).] Thus, D has made a gift of $87,593 (i.e., 0.87593 × $100,000) to W and a gift of $12,407 (i.e., 0.12407 × $100,000) to S. ☐

Example 9   Assume the same facts as in Example 8, except that the transfer occurs in 1988. Referring to Table A of Reg. § 25.2512–5(f), a life estate for a person

---

9. The terminal reserve of a life insurance policy generally will approximate the policy's cash surrender value. For an illustration on how to arrive at the interpolated terminal reserve, see Reg. § 20.2031–8(a)(3) (Ex. 3).
10. The Regulations contain identical tables for estate tax situations. For transfers after November 30, 1983, see Reg. § 20.2031–7(f). For transfers after 1970 and before December 1, 1983, see Reg. § 20.2031–10(f).
11. The pre-1971 and the current tables are unisex (i.e., no distinction is made between male and female). The tables applicable to transfers after 1970 and before December 1, 1983, do make a distinction between the sexes.

age 35 shows a factor of 0.93868 [column (3)]; the factor for a remainder interest is 0.06132 [column (4)]. Consequently, D has made a gift of $93,868 (i.e., 0.93868 × $100,000) to W and a gift of $6,132 (i.e., 0.06132 × $100,000) to S. Note that the value of the life estate ($93,868) when added to the value of the remainder interest ($6,132) equals the total amount of the gift ($100,000). ☐

Example 10   In 1988, D transfers by gift $100,000 worth of securities. The securities were placed in trust, income payable to M for 11 years, remainder to S. Based on Table B of Reg. § 25.2512–5(f), the appropriate factor is 0.649506 [see column (3), term certain for 11 years]. Thus, D has made a gift to M of $64,950.60 (i.e., 0.649506 × $100,000) and a gift to S of $35,049.40 (0.350494 × $100,000). ☐

What is the significance of the division of a gift into several distinct parts? Such a division becomes important in determining the applicability of the annual exclusion and the marital deduction. Under the facts of Example 8, an annual exclusion probably would be allowed with respect to the gift to W and would not be allowed with respect to the interest passing to S (because of the future interest limitation). If W is D's wife, no marital deduction would be allowed, because the life estate she receives is a terminable interest. As noted in Chapter 11, however, this problem could be cured with a qualified terminable interest property (QTIP) election.

The Alternate Valuation Date

Under certain conditions, requiring the use of the date of death value for estate tax purposes could work a real hardship on the estate. Suppose, for example, the gross estate contained property that significantly decreased in value after the owner died but before the administration of his or her estate could be wound up and all charges against it satisfied. As happened during the Great Depression, it is entirely possible that the death tax liability alone (based on the date of death value) could wipe out the assets of an estate. In recognition of such a possibility, Congress enacted the predecessor of § 2032. Under this provision, the executor of the estate is given the option to value property included as of an alternate date that falls after the date of death but before the due date of the return.

Although the alternate valuation date was designed to reduce the amount of the gross estate, in practice the opposite effect was sometimes desirable. Based on the rule that the valuation used for estate tax purposes becomes the income tax basis of the property, a higher value could lead to potential income tax savings for the heirs. This would produce a very attractive result when the higher value yielded little, if any, estate tax liability.

Example 11   D dies in 1988 leaving a disposable estate valued at $1,000,000. During his life, D had never made any post-1976 taxable gifts or used his specific exemption of $30,000. Under D's will, $600,000 of the estate is to pass to his children, while the remainder goes to his surviving spouse, W. Because the estate has a large portfolio of marketable securities and the stock market rose after D's death, the disposable estate jumped to $1,200,000 in six months. ☐

Electing the alternate valuation date in Example 11 would be a win-win situation. The election does not increase estate taxes, because the additional $200,000 in value is neutralized by the marital deduction. The only result is positive, since the election gives W $200,000 more in income tax basis.

Congress finally decided to eliminate the windfall that was possible in Example 11. It amended § 2032 to permit the election only when the effect will be to reduce both the value of the gross estate *and* the Federal estate tax liability. Thus, the election of § 2032 in Example 11 no longer is possible for two reasons. First, the election would increase (rather than reduce) the value of the gross estate. Second, the election would not reduce the Federal estate tax liability. Because of the interplay of the unified tax credit exemption equivalent ($600,000 for 1988) and the marital deduction, the use of date of death or alternate valuation date does not carry any estate tax consequences. In either case, no estate tax is due.

Several observations can be made about the alternate valuation date that will aid in its understanding and application.

1. The choice of the alternate valuation date is elective with the executor or administrator of the estate. If no affirmative action is taken, the date of death value must be used. The election is made by checking the appropriate box on the Federal estate tax return and placing the alternate valuation date values in the corresponding column. Apparently, the failure to do the former is not disastrous as long as the alternate valuation date values are listed and used in completing the return.
2. The election may be made on an estate tax return filed no more than one year late. Once made, the election is irrevocable.[12]
3. The election cannot be made for Federal tax purposes unless a Federal estate tax return must be filed. The following schedule summarizes the filing requirements: [13]

Year of Death	Filing Required When Gross Estate Exceeds—
Before 1977	$ 60,000
1977	120,000
1978	134,000
1979	147,000
1980	161,000
1981	175,000
1982	225,000
1983	275,000
1984	325,000
1985	400,000
1986	500,000
1987 and later	600,000

12. § 2032(d).
13. § 6018.

For the post-1976 period, the preceding amounts must be reduced by taxable gifts made after 1976. This adjustment is consistent with the scheme of the unified transfer tax at death. Recall that in determining the estate tax, post-1976 taxable gifts must be added to the taxable estate.

4. The election covers *all* assets included in the gross estate and cannot be applied to only a portion of the property.
5. The use of the alternate valuation date may require adjustment for changes in value due to a mere lapse of time.
6. The alternate valuation date is the earlier of six months following the date of death or when the property is "distributed, sold, exchanged, or otherwise disposed of." [14]
7. Generally, any income generated by the property after the owner's death must be accounted for separately and has no effect on the amount determined as of the alternate valuation date.

The preceding observations can be illustrated as follows:

Example 12   D dies in January of 1986. Without obtaining an extension from the IRS, the executor of D's estate files the Federal estate tax return on February 3, 1987, and elects the alternate valuation date. On March 4, 1988, the executor files an amended return for the estate using the date of death valuation. Since the election of the alternate valuation date was valid (made within one year of the due date of the return), it is irrevocable. Therefore, the amended return switching to date of death valuation is not an acceptable procedure. ☐

Example 13   At the time of her death in 1988, D had a gross estate of $590,000 which six months later was valued at $585,000. In 1980, however, D made a taxable gift of $20,000. Since the filing requirement for 1988 now becomes $580,000 ($600,000 − $20,000) instead of $600,000, the alternate valuation date can be elected. ☐

It is not clear whether the election of the alternate valuation would be wise in the case presented in Example 13. Even though the gross estate would be $590,000 without the election, by the time it is reduced by any expenses and liabilities and the exemption equivalent of the unified tax credit is taken into account, how much, if any, estate tax would be due? Furthermore, using the date of death value would provide a higher income tax basis (i.e., $590,000 versus $585,000) for the assets of the estate.

Example 14   D's gross estate includes the following property:

	Value on Date of Death	Value on Alternate Valuation Date
Land	$380,000	$382,000
Stock in X Corporation	170,000	155,000
Stock in Y Corporation	190,000	198,000
Total	$740,000	$735,000

---

14. §§ 2032(a)(1) and (2) and Reg. § 20.2032–1(c).

If D's estate elected the alternate valuation date, the value to be used would be $735,000. It would not be permissible for the estate to use the lower of the date of death or the alternate valuation date values for each individual asset. Thus, the estate *could not* choose the $380,000 value for the land, $155,000 for the X Corporation stock, and $190,000 for the Y Corporation stock (thereby reflecting a total of $725,000). ☐

Example 15

On the date of death, D owned a patent (fair market value of $100,000) with a remaining life of 10 years. Six months later the patent possessed a fair market value of $90,000. Because some of the change in value of the patent must be due to the lapse of time (i.e., it has a remaining life of only nine and one-half years), the value of the patent on the alternate valuation date must be adjusted accordingly. Thus, dividing $90,000 by 0.95 (the ratio of the remaining life of the patent at the alternate date to the remaining life of the patent at the date of the decedent's death) yields a value of $94,736.84 on the alternate valuation date.[15] ☐

Example 16

At the time of his death, D held some stock in Z Corporation. In a will, D bequeathed the stock to S. The stock had a value as follows: $30,000 on the date of D's death, $28,000 four months later, and $27,000 six months after D's death. Four months after D's death, the executor satisfies the bequest by distributing the Z Corporation stock to S. If the estate elects the alternate valuation date, the stock should be included in the gross estate at $28,000. Although its value six months after D's death is $27,000, it was "distributed, sold, exchanged, or otherwise disposed of" before this date. ☐

Example 17

At the time of D's death, one of D's assets was rental property worth $320,000 with accrued rents of $13,000. Six months later the property is worth $330,000, the rents of $13,000 have been paid, and an additional $18,000 has been accrued. Whether the alternate valuation date is or is not elected will make no difference in the treatment of the accrued rents. In either case, $13,000 will be included in D's gross estate; this is the amount accrued to the point of death. The $18,000 accrued within the six-month period after death has no estate tax consequences. Thus, the election of the alternate date means the inclusion in D's gross estate of $13,000 of accrued rents and rental property worth $330,000. If D used the cash basis of accounting during life, the $13,000 would be income in respect of a decedent (see later in the chapter). As such, it would be subject to the income tax on the return of the recipient. Under the accrual basis of accounting, the $13,000 would be taxed to D and reported on D's final Form 1040. The $18,000 of rents accrued after D's death would also be subject to the income tax. If taxed to the estate, it would be reported on Form 1041. ☐

---

15. Reg. § 20.2032–1(f)(2).

The Special Use Valuation Method

Section 2032A permits an executor to elect to value certain classes of real estate used in farming or in connection with a closely-held business at its "current" use rather than the usual "highest," "best," or "most suitable" use. The major objective of this provision is to provide a form of limited relief against the possibility that a portion of the family farm might have to be sold by the heirs to pay death taxes.

Example 18   At the time of his death, D owned a farm on the outskirts of a large city that was used for truck farming. For farming purposes, the property would have a value of $300,000 (i.e., the current use value).[16] As a potential site for a shopping center, however, the property is worth $800,000 (i.e., the most suitable use value). The executor of D's estate could elect to include only $300,000 in the gross estate. The availability of the election presumes that the conditions set forth in § 2032A, and discussed below, are satisfied. □

The special use valuation election is available if *all* of the following conditions are satisfied:

1. At least 50 percent of the adjusted value of the gross estate consists of *real* or *personal* property devoted to a qualifying use (i.e., used for farming or used in a closely-held business) at the time of the owner's death.[17]
2. The *real* property devoted to a qualifying use comprises at least 25 percent of the adjusted value of the gross estate. For purposes of satisfying both the 50 percent test (condition 1) and the 25 percent test, the qualifying property is considered at its most suitable use value. Referring to Example 18, this means that the property would be treated as if it had a value of $800,000 (not $300,000). The adjusted value of the gross estate is the gross estate less certain unpaid mortgages and other indebtedness.
3. The qualifying property passes to a qualifying heir of the decedent. A qualifying heir includes certain family members as set forth in § 2032A(e)(2).
4. The *real* property has been owned by the decedent or the decedent's family for five out of the eight years ending on the date of the decedent's death and was devoted to qualifying use during such period of time.
5. The decedent or a member of the decedent's family has participated materially in the operation of the farm or business during the period specified under condition 4.[18]

The special use valuation procedure permits a reduction in estate tax valuation of no more than $750,000.

Example 19   At the time of his death in 1988, D owned a farm with a most suitable use value of $2,000,000 but a current use value of $1,000,000. Assuming the

---

16. Sections 2032A(e)(7) and (8) set forth various methods of valuation to be applied in arriving at current use value.
17. §§ 2032A(b)(1)(A) and (b)(2). For a definition of "farm" and "farming," see §§ 2032A(e)(4) and (5).
18. § 2032A(b)(1)(C)(ii). "Material participation" is defined in § 2032A(e)(6).

property qualifies under § 2032A and the special use valuation election is made, D's gross estate must include $1,250,000. Thus, only $750,000 in value can be excluded under § 2032A. ☐

The election of § 2032A will have an effect on the qualifying heir's income tax basis in the property. Referring to Example 19, the use of § 2032A means the heir will have an income tax basis of $1,250,000 in the farm. Had § 2032A not been elected and had the most suitable use value been included in D's gross estate, the income tax basis would have become $2,000,000.

Section 2032A(c) provides that the benefits (i.e., estate tax savings) derived from the special use valuation method will be recaptured as additional estate tax liability if the heir disposes of the property or ceases to use it as qualifying use property within a period of 10 years from the date of the decedent's death.

Example 20   Assume the same facts as in Example 19. Further assume that by electing § 2032A, D's estate tax liability was reduced by $245,000. Three years after D's death, H (the qualifying heir) sells the farm for $3,000,000. At this point, the $245,000 additional estate tax liability that would have been imposed had § 2032A not been utilized becomes due. ☐

Any additional tax liability due to the application of the recapture rules will be imposed upon the qualifying heir. In this connection, § 6324B gives the IRS security for compliance with the terms of § 2032A by placing a special lien on the qualifying property. The IRS may subordinate this special lien to third-party creditors if it feels its interest would otherwise be adequately secured.

In a recapture situation, an upward adjustment in income tax basis can be elected by the heir.[19] The adjustment is the difference between the value of the property that would have been included in the gross estate had § 2032A not been elected and the amount actually included under § 2032A.

Example 21   Assume the same facts as in Example 20. If H chooses to do so, he can add $750,000 to the basis in the farm in determining the gain or loss to be recognized on its sale. ☐

When a qualified heir makes the election to increase basis, he or she must pay interest on the amount of the estate tax that is recaptured. The interest is computed (at rates in effect during the period involved) beginning from nine months after the date of death to the due date of the recaptured estate tax.

Income Tax
Considerations in Valuation

Valuation is not only important for gift and estate tax determination but also crucial for income tax purposes. In the area of family tax planning, the focus generally is on the income tax basis a donee or an heir will receive as a result of lifetime or testamentary transfers.

---

19. §§ 1016(c)(1) and (5).

Basis of Property Acquired by Gift—§ 1015

The income tax basis of property acquired by gift could depend on whether the donee sells the property for a gain or for a loss and, in certain cases, on when the gift occurred.

—If the gift took place before 1921, the donee's basis for gain or loss will be the fair market value of the property on the date of the gift.[20]

—If the gift took place after 1920 and before 1977, the donee's basis for gain is the donor's adjusted basis plus any gift tax paid on the transfer (but not to exceed fair market value on the date of the gift). The basis for loss is the lower of the basis for gain or the fair market value of the property on the date of the gift.

—If the gift took place after 1976, the donee's basis for gain is the donor's adjusted basis plus only the gift tax attributable to the appreciation of the property to the point of the gift. The basis for loss is the lower of the basis for gain or the fair market value of the property on the date of the gift.[21]

These rules are illustrated by the following examples:

Example 22   In 1920, D received real estate as a gift from her grandfather. The property cost the grandfather $10,000 and was worth $25,000 on the date of the gift. D's income tax basis for gain or loss is $25,000. □

Example 23   In 1975, D receives stock as a gift from M. The stock cost M $10,000 and had a fair market value of $50,000 on the date of the gift. As a result of the transfer, M paid a gift tax of $5,000. D's income tax basis for gain and for loss is $15,000 [$10,000 (M's basis) + $5,000 (gift tax paid by M)]. D does not have a different basis for loss, since the fair market value of the property on the date of the gift (i.e., $50,000) is not lower than the basis for gain (i.e., $15,000). □

Example 24   Assume the same facts as in Example 23, except that the gift took place in 1988 (instead of 1975). D's income tax basis for gain is $14,000 determined as follows:

M's adjusted basis on the date of the gift	$10,000
Gift tax attributable to the $40,000 appreciation $\left(\dfrac{\$40,000}{\$50,000} \times \$5,000 \right)$	4,000
D's income tax basis for gain	$14,000

D's basis for loss would also be $14,000, based on the same reasoning set forth in Example 23. □

---

20. § 1015(c).
21. §§ 1015(a) and (d).

The effect of the rule illustrated in Example 24 is to deny a donee any increase in basis for the gift tax attributable to the donor's adjusted basis. In making the allocation, one has to assume that $1,000 of the gift tax paid related to M's $10,000 basis and $4,000 to the $40,000 appreciation in the property.

Basis of Property Acquired by Death—§ 1014

General Rule.   Except as otherwise noted in the following sections, the income tax basis of property acquired from a decedent will be the fair market value on the date of death or, if elected, on the alternate valuation date. As to property that has appreciated in value from point of acquisition to date of death, this result causes a step-up in income tax basis for the estate or heir of the deceased owner. A step-up in basis, then, means that appreciation existing at death escapes the application of the Federal income tax.

Example 25   At the time of his death in 1988, D owned real estate (adjusted basis of $100,000) worth $400,000 that he leaves to S. Presuming the alternate valuation date is not elected, S's income tax basis in the property becomes $400,000. Thus, a subsequent sale of the real estate by S for $400,000 would result in no gain or loss to S. □

Example 26   Assume the same facts as in Example 25, except that shortly before death, D sells the real estate for $400,000. Based on this assumption, D has a gain of $300,000 taxable under the income tax. □

By contrasting Examples 25 and 26, one can see that the rules place a premium on holding appreciated property until death to take advantage of the step-up in basis result. The same cannot be said for property that has declined in value. Here there is the danger that death would cause a step-down in basis—a result to be avoided if a sale of the property would have generated a deductible income tax loss.

Example 27   At the time of his death in 1988, D held stock as an investment with an adjusted basis of $50,000 and a fair market value of $30,000. Because only $30,000 is included in the gross estate, the basis of the stock to the estate or heir is this amount. Had D sold the stock before his death, some or all of the $20,000 loss might have been salvaged. Whether the sale would have helped D would have depended on D's capital gains position at the time of his death and whether he had lived long enough to take advantage of any unabsorbed loss. □

Community Property.   Although there is usually no change in basis for property not part of a decedent's gross estate, a special exception applies to community property. In such situations, the surviving spouse's half of the community takes on the same basis as the half included in the deceased spouse's gross estate.[22] The reason for and the effect of this special rule can be illustrated as follows:

---

22. § 1014(b)(6).

Example 28   D and W were husband and wife and lived in a common law state. At the time of D's death in 1988, D owned assets (worth $800,000 with a basis to him of $100,000), which he bequeathed to W. Presuming the transfer qualifies under § 2056, D's estate is allowed a marital deduction of approximately $800,000. As the property passes through D's estate, W would receive a step-up in basis to $800,000. □

Example 29   Assume the same facts as in Example 28, except that D and W had always lived in California (a community property state). If the $800,000 worth of property were community property, only one half of this value would be included in D's gross estate. Because the other half does not pass through D's estate (i.e., it already belongs to W), is it fair to deny W a new basis therein? Therefore, allowing the surviving spouse's share of the community to take on a basis equal to that half included in the deceased spouse's gross estate merely equalizes the income tax result generally achieved in common law states with the use of the marital deduction. By giving W an income tax basis of $800,000 (i.e., $400,000 for H's half passing to her plus $400,000 for her half) and including only $400,000 in D's gross estate, the tax outcome is essentially the same as that outlined in Example 28. □

Step-Up in Basis and the One-Year Rule.   To understand the exception of § 1014(e), consider the following situation:

Example 30   H and W are husband and wife and reside in a common law state. When the parties learn that W has a terminal illness, H transfers property (basis of $50,000 and fair market value of $200,000) to W as a gift. W dies shortly thereafter, and under the provisions of W's will, the property returns to H.
□

If it were not for § 1014(e), what have the parties accomplished? No gift tax occurs on the transfer from H to W because of the application of the marital deduction. Upon W's death, the bequest from W to H does not generate any estate tax, because the inclusion of the property in W's gross estate is offset by the marital deduction. Through the application of the general rule of § 1014, H would end up with the same property, the basis of which has been stepped up to $200,000. Thus, this procedure would enable H to get a "free ride" as to an increase in income tax basis of $150,000.

When applicable, § 1014(e) forces H (the original donor) to assume the property with the same basis it had to W immediately before W's death. Since W's basis would have been determined under § 1015 (basis of property acquired by gift), W's basis would have been $50,000 (donor's adjusted basis) plus any gift tax adjustment (none in this case) and any capital additions made by the donee (none in this case), or $50,000. If § 1014(e) applies to Example 30, H ends up where he started (i.e., with $50,000) in terms of income tax basis.

For § 1014(e) to be operative, the following conditions must be satisfied:

—The decedent must have received appreciated property as a gift during the one-year period ending with his or her death. Under § 1014(e)(2)(A), appreciated property is defined as property whose fair market value on the date of its transfer exceeded the adjusted basis in the hands of the donor.

—The property is acquired from the decedent by the donor (or the donor's spouse).

—The property must have been acquired after August 13, 1981, by persons dying after 1981.

Although Example 30 concerns a transfer between spouses, the application of § 1014(e) is not so limited. The provision would apply with equal effect if, for example, the donor-heir were a son of the donee-decedent. In such cases, moreover, the technique used in Example 30 might prove to be more susceptible to the imposition of transfer taxes (viz., gift and estate taxes) because of the unavailability of the marital deduction.

Income in Respect of a Decedent

Income in respect of a decedent can be defined as income earned by a decedent to the point of his or her death but not reportable on the final income tax return by virtue of the method of accounting used. Most frequently applicable to decedents using the cash basis of accounting, it will apply, for example, to an accrual basis taxpayer who held installment notes receivable at the time of death, the gain from which has been deferred.

For estate tax purposes, income in respect of a decedent will be included in the gross estate at its fair market value on the appropriate valuation date. For income tax purposes, however, the income tax basis of the decedent transfers over to the estate or heirs. Neither a step-up nor a step-down is possible as is true of property received by death.[23] Furthermore, the recipient of such income must classify it in the same manner (i.e., ordinary income, capital gain) as would have the decedent.[24]

Example 31   D, a cash basis taxpayer, made some loans before her death. At the time of her death, interest of $3,200 had accrued on the loans. This amount, plus the sum of $300 accrued after death, was collected by the executor of D's estate. Regardless of when D died, the $3,200 of interest is income in respect of a decedent and is includible in the gross estate. The $3,500 paid to the estate must be reported as interest income on the fiduciary return (Form 1041). □

Example 32   D, an accrual basis taxpayer, sold some undeveloped real estate held as an investment (basis of $40,000) for $100,000, receiving $30,000 in cash and an 8% interest-bearing note payable in two annual installments of $35,000 each. On a timely filed income tax return, D chose not to elect out from reporting the gain under the installment method. D dies before the first installment is due and at a time when the note possesses a fair market value (without interest) of $68,000. The note is collected (with accrued

23. § 1014(c).
24. § 691(a)(3).

interest) as follows: $35,000 by the executor of D's estate three months after D's death and $35,000 by S (D's heir) one year and three months after D's death. The note is includible in D's gross estate at a value of $68,000 plus accrued interest to date of death. Since the note represents income in respect of a decedent, the note's income tax basis remains the same as it was in the hands of D. Thus, when the estate collects the first installment of $35,000, it will recognize gain (for income tax purposes) of $21,000 based on a gross profit percentage of 60%.[25] The same gain must be recognized by S upon the collection of the remaining $35,000. Whether gain recognized by the estate and S will be ordinary or capital depends upon its character to D had he lived to collect the installments. □

Since denying a change in income tax basis for income in respect of a decedent (even though such income is included in the gross estate) has the effect of subjecting the same asset to both income and death taxes, § 691(c) provides a limited form of relief. Under this provision, the recipient of income in respect of a decedent is allowed an income tax deduction for the Federal death tax attributable to the inclusion of the income interest in the gross estate. To illustrate, in Example 31 recall that $3,200 of interest was income in respect of a decedent, and such interest later was paid to D's estate. To oversimplify the solution, assume further the inclusion of $3,200 in the gross estate resulted in an additional Federal death tax of $640. On its income tax return (Form 1041) for the year in which the interest income is reported, the estate may claim an income tax deduction of $640.

Estate Liquidity

Recognizing the Problem

Even with effective predeath family tax planning directed toward a minimization of transfer taxes, the smooth administration of an estate necessitates a certain degree of liquidity. After all, probate costs will be incurred, and most important of all, death taxes must be satisfied. In the meantime, the surviving spouse and dependent beneficiaries may have to be supported. Without funds to satisfy these claims, estate assets may have to be sold at sacrifice prices, and most likely, the decedent's scheme of testamentary disposition will be defeated.

Example 33   At the time of D's death, D's estate was made up almost entirely of a large ranch currently being operated by S, one of D's two sons. Because the ranch had been in the family for several generations and was a successful economic unit, it was D's hope that S would continue its operation and share the profits with R, D's other son. Unfortunately, R, on learning that his mother had died without a will, demanded and obtained a partition

---

25. The gross profit percentage is computed by dividing the gross profit by the selling price. D's gross profit on the sale was the selling price of $100,000 less his adjusted basis of $40,000, or $60,000. Thus, $60,000 divided by $100,000 yields 60%. The gain of $21,000 is determined by multiplying the $35,000 payment received by 60%.

and sale of his share of the property. Additional land was sold to pay for administration expenses and death taxes. After all of the sales had taken place, the portion remaining to S could not be operated profitably, and S subsequently was forced to give up the family ranch activity. □

What type of predeath planning might have avoided the result reached in Example 33? Certainly D should have recognized and provided for the cash needs of the estate. Life insurance payable to her estate, although it adds to the estate tax liability, could have eased or solved the problem. This presumes that D was insurable or that the cost of any such insurance would not be prohibitive. Furthermore, D made a serious error in dying without a will. A carefully drawn will could have precluded R's later course of action and perhaps kept much more of the ranch property intact. The ranch could have been placed in trust, life estate to S and R, remainder to their children. With such an arrangement, R would have been unable to sell corpus (i.e., the ranch). Also, D could have tried to arrange her estate so that it could qualify for the extension of time to pay death taxes under § 6166.

Extensions of Time for Payment of Death Taxes

Being able to defer the payment of death taxes may be an invaluable option for an estate that lacks cash or near-cash assets (e.g., marketable securities). In this connection, two major possibilities exist:

—The discretionary extension of time (§ 6161).

—The extension of time when the estate consists largely of an interest in a closely-held business (§ 6166).

Both of these aids to estate liquidity are discussed in the following sections.

Discretionary Extension of Time to Pay Estate Taxes—§ 6161. Currently, an executor or administrator may request an extension of time for paying the death tax for a period not to exceed 10 years from the date fixed for the payment. Such a request will be granted by the IRS whenever there is "reasonable cause." Reasonable cause is not limited to a showing of undue hardship. It includes cases in which the executor or administrator is unable to readily marshal liquid assets because they are located in several jurisdictions, or the estate is largely made up of assets in the form of payments to be received in the future (e.g., annuities, copyright royalties, contingent fees, or accounts receivable), or the assets that must be liquidated to pay the estate tax must be sold at a sacrifice or in a depressed market.

Extension of Time When the Estate Consists Largely of an Interest in a Closely-Held Business—§ 6166. By way of background, Congress always has been sympathetic to the plight of an estate that includes an interest in a closely-held business. The immediate imposition of the estate tax in such a situation may force the liquidation of the business at distress prices or cause the interest to be sold to outside parties. Congress also was mindful of the fact that the extension of time to pay taxes under § 6161 was not a complete solution, since it largely was discretionary with the IRS.

A possible resolution of the problem is § 6166 which, if applicable, requires the IRS to accept a 15-year payout procedure [5-year deferral (except for the interest element) followed by 10-year installment payments of the estate tax]. One would hope that this delay would enable the business to generate enough income with which to buy out the deceased owner's interest without disruption of operations or other financial sacrifice.

To meet the requirements of § 6166, the decedent's interest in a farm or other closely-held business must be more than 35 percent of the decedent's adjusted gross estate.[26] The adjusted gross estate is the gross estate less the sum allowable as deductions under § 2053 (i.e., expenses, indebtedness, and taxes) and § 2054 (i.e., casualty and theft losses during the administration of an estate).

An interest in a closely-held business includes the following: [27]

—A sole proprietorship.

—An interest in a partnership carrying on a trade or business if 20 percent of the capital interest in such partnership is included in the gross estate *or* the partnership has 15 or fewer partners.

—Stock in a corporation carrying on a trade or business if 20 percent or more in the value of the voting stock of such corporation is included in the gross estate *or* such corporation has 15 or fewer shareholders.

In meeting the preceding requirements, a decedent and his or her surviving spouse will be treated as one owner (i.e., shareholder or partner) if the interest is held as community property, tenants in common, joint tenants, or tenants by the entirety. Also, attribution from family members is allowed. In determining who is a family member, reference is made to § 267(c)(4).[28]

Example 34   At the time of his death, D held a 15% capital interest in the XYZ Partnership. D's son holds another 10%. The XYZ Partnership had 16 partners including D and his son. Since the son's interest is attributed to D, the estate is deemed to hold a 25% interest and the XYZ Partnership (for purposes of § 6166) has only 15 partners. ☐

In satisfying the more-than-35 percent test for basis qualification under § 6166 (see above), interests in more than one closely-held business can be aggregated when the decedent's gross estate includes 20 percent or more of the value of each such business.[29]

Example 35   D's estate includes stock in X Corporation and Y Corporation, each of which qualifies as a closely-held business. If the stock held in each corporation represents 20% or more of the total value outstanding, the stocks can be combined for purposes of the more-than-35% test. ☐

---

26. § 6166(a)(1).
27. § 6166(b)(1).
28. Section 267 deals with the disallowance of losses and expenses between related parties.
29. § 6166(c).

If the conditions of § 6166 are satisfied and the provision is elected, the following results transpire:

—No payments on the estate tax attributable to the inclusion of the interest in a closely-held business in the gross estate need be made for the first five years. After such five-year period, annual installments must be made over a period not longer than 10 years.

—From the outset, interest at the rate of four percent must be paid.[30] The rate is limited to the first $1,000,000 of estate tax value.

—Acceleration of deferred payments may be triggered upon the happening of certain subsequent events (e.g., disposition of the interest, failure to make scheduled principal or interest payments).[31]

In qualifying for § 6166, the main objective would be to prune the potential estate of those assets that may cause the 35 percent test not to be satisfied. In this regard, lifetime gifts of such assets as marketable securities and life insurance should be considered.[32]

✓ Tax Planning Considerations

In addition to the points already discussed, much can be done to minimize taxes while resolving the issue of valuation. Most often, this involves the determination of a value that will withstand challenge by the IRS without unduly compromising the tax position of the family unit.

Closely tied to the valuation issue are the basis ramifications of § 1015 (basis of property acquired by gift) and § 1014 (basis of property acquired through inheritance). Income tax considerations, moreover, could well make the basis rules a key factor in the valuation process. In this regard, the planning potential rests with the difference between transfers by gift and transfers at death.

General Planning Considerations

Somewhat basic but frequently overlooked are certain procedures that should be pursued in establishing a sound value for tax purposes. These procedures are summarized as follows:

1. Obtain competent appraisal information. Needless to say, such information should be in writing.
2. In obtaining appraisal data, be sure to choose the right expert for the job. Such assets as works of art, antique furniture, mineral deposits, and closely-held stock present special problems and require appraisals by persons with

---

30. § 6601(j)(1).
31. § 6166(g).
32. A gift within three years of death will not be effective for this purpose because of the operation of § 2035(d)(4).

special expertise. Rest assured that the IRS also has access to highly qualified valuation experts.

3. Obtain and preserve comparable sales information. It is never too early to
   start building a file on what is happening in the marketplace to property
   similar in nature and use. Such information may be difficult to reconstruct at
   some later time.
4. Maintain a record of the cost of property transferred as a gift. The donee
   will need this information for income tax purposes if the property is disposed of in a taxable exchange. If the fair market value of the property on
   the date of the gift might be less than the donor's basis, the property should
   be appraised. Recall that the income tax basis of the property to the donee
   for purposes of loss determination is the lesser of the donor's adjusted basis
   or the fair market value on the date of the gift.
5. All interested parties (i.e., donees and heirs) should have access to relevant
   valuation data. At a minimum, donees should be given copies of gift tax
   returns and heirs copies of death tax returns.

Transfers at Death and the Alternate Valuation Date.   In the event of transfers
at death, the same appraisal data just described should also cover the alternate valuation date. Further, when considering election of the alternate valuation date, one must be on the lookout for significant changes in value since the
decedent's death. When the gross estate includes a significant amount of
publicly traded investments, a sharp decline in the financial markets could
make the election of the alternate valuation date highly attractive.

When assessing the advisability of utilizing the alternate valuation date,
one has to consider the effect on income tax basis. Granted that the alternate
valuation date will reduce estate taxes, is the reduction worth the sacrifice in
income tax basis? Only by comparing the estate tax bracket of the decedent
with the potential income tax bracket of the estate or heirs can this question be
answered. In some cases, forgoing a lower alternate valuation amount in
favor of a higher date of death value would be more beneficial to the family
unit. Here, it has to be assumed that imminent income tax savings outweigh
the additional estate tax cost.

Special Use Valuation Procedure of § 2032A.   Because of the conditions imposed upon the application of the special valuation method, qualifying for its
use may be difficult. Also, the maximum gross estate reduction through the use
of the election is limited in amount. Unfortunately, the special valuation
method is limited to estate tax situations and is not available to reduce the
valuation of property transferred by gift.

Despite its shortcomings, the special use valuation will be highly advantageous under the proper circumstances. Such might be the case where there is
substantial appreciation in most suitable use value over current use value and
the heirs of the decedent wish to continue operating the qualifying business. In
such situations, it might be ruinous to the business not to make the election and
thereby avoid or reduce the transfer tax at death on the appreciation.

In planning for the future use of the special use valuation method, taxpayers should keep in mind both the 50 percent test and the 25 percent test relating
to the value of qualifying assets included in the adjusted value of the gross
estate. If difficulty is anticipated in satisfying these percentage requirements,

lifetime gifts of nonqualifying property should be carried out. Be careful, however, of gifts made within three years of the donor's death. Although such gifts usually are no longer included in the gross estate of the donor for estate tax purposes, they are counted when testing for the percentage requirements of § 303 (redemption to pay death taxes and administration expenses—refer to Chapter 4), § 2032A, and § 6166 (extension of time to pay estate taxes in installments).

Example 36

In planning to meet the percentage requirements of § 2032A, D transfers by gift marketable securities worth $200,000. If D dies within three years of the gift, the value of such securities must be included in D's gross estate in applying the 50% and 25% tests of § 2032A. This "as if" approach, however, does not have the effect of making such securities subject to actual inclusion in the gross estate. □

Lifetime Gifts—Income Tax Considerations

Income Tax Consequences to the Donor. Presuming lifetime giving is desired, great care should be exercised in selecting the property to be given away. Of initial importance might be any income tax consequences to the donor generated by the gift.

Example 37

Last year, D sold real estate (basis of $40,000) to P (an unrelated party) for $100,000, receiving $20,000 in cash and P's note for $80,000. On a timely filed return, D did not elect out of the installment method of reporting the gain on the sale. This year, when the note has a fair market value of $76,000, D gives it to his son, S. In addition to the gain of $12,000 (60% × $20,000) on the down payment, D must recognize $44,000 when he disposes of the note. This represents the difference between the fair market value of the note ($76,000) and D's unrecovered basis of $32,000 [$40,000 (original basis) − $8,000 (amount of basis applied against the down payment)]. The gift of an installment obligation is treated as a taxable disposition under § 453B(a). □

If the obligor and obligee are related persons, the tax law provides for a different result. In such cases, the entire unreported gain will be taxed on what, in effect, is a cancellation of the obligation. Referring to Example 37, assume the original sale was to S (a related party) and not to P (an unrelated party). Under § 453B(f)(2), when D (the obligee) gives (or otherwise cancels) the note to S (the obligor), D must recognize a gain of $48,000 [60 percent (gross profit percentage) × $80,000 (face amount of the note)]. In defining related party, § 453(f)(1) makes reference to the attribution rules of § 318(a) (refer to Chapter 4 and the discussion of certain stock redemptions).

Would there be any difference to D had the transfer outlined in Example 37 been testamentary? In other words, suppose the property had passed to S by virtue of D's death rather than by gift. The disposition of an installment note receivable by death is not a taxable event under the income tax; therefore, the results would have been different.[33] But in Example 37, the unrealized gain, though not taxed to D, will not go unrecognized. As income in respect of a decedent, it will be taxed to whoever collects the note. If the installment obligation passes to the obligor (or is otherwise cancelled by the obligee's will), it will be treated as a transfer by the obligee's estate and will trigger recognition of gain to the estate. If the parties are related persons [within the meaning of § 318(a)], the face amount of the obligation will be deemed to be the obligation's fair market value.[34]

Income Tax Consequences to the Donee.   What about the income tax position of the donee? Certainly this must be an important factor in the donor's choice of property to transfer as a gift.

Example 38   D makes a gift to S of depreciable tangible personalty (adjusted basis of $20,000 and a fair market value of $30,000) used in the trade or business. If D had sold the property for $30,000, he would have recognized a gain of $10,000, all of which would have been ordinary income under the recapture of depreciation provisions of § 1245. The gift does not generate income to D. Such transfers are excepted from the usual recapture of depreciation rules by § 1245(b)(1).[35] The recapture potential of the property is, however, transferred to the donee. As a consequence, if S sold the property for $30,000 immediately after the gift, he must recognize a gain of $10,000, all of which would be recaptured as ordinary income. □

In Example 38, any gain, including the ordinary income element, would go unrecognized if the property were passed by death.[36]

Just because a testamentary transfer might produce a more favorable income tax result does not mean this type of property is always unsuitable for gifts. The owner of the property (i.e., D) may be unable or unwilling to retain the property until death. If the property is to be disposed of before this time, shifting the income tax consequences to someone else (i.e., S) may be less costly to the family unit from a tax standpoint. Such might be the case if the donee (i.e., S) is in a lower tax bracket than the donor or has losses that will neutralize some or all of the gain on the later sale of the property. One must be wary of situations in which the sale by the donee has been prearranged by the donor or the sale takes place shortly after the gift of the property. If either happens, the IRS may try to collapse the gift and argue that the sale really was made by the donor and not the donee. If the argument is successful, the income tax consequences will be attributed to the donor and not the donee. On the other hand, the donee may not intend to sell the property. In this event, any built-in income tax potential should provide no real concern.

Example 39   D owns a summer home in Arkansas which, because of its location and accessibility to recreational facilities, has been used for many years by

---

33. § 453B(c).
34. § 691(a)(5).
35. With respect to depreciable real estate, see § 1250(d)(1) for a like exception.
36. § 1245(b)(2). Note that the income tax basis of the property to the estate or heirs will be determined under § 1014.

the family for vacation purposes. The property has an adjusted basis of only $40,000 but has appreciated to a present value of $110,000. D would like to exclude the property from his gross estate but still keep it in the family. S, D's son, plans to continue vacationing at the summer home and would make it available to the rest of the family in the event the property became his. □

Much can be said in favor of a gift of the summer home to S. Although S's basis for income tax purposes will be only $40,000, it creates no real problem, because S does not plan to dispose of the property.

Example 39 raises another interesting point. Aside from the gift tax liability, what has D really lost by making the transfer? One would hope the donee-son will permit his father (D) to use the property for its intended recreational purpose. As long as such use is by invitation only and no express or implied agreement exists requiring S to do so, the hoped-for estate tax result will be accomplished. After the transfer, the parties must be careful to treat S as the true owner of the summer home. If not, the IRS may contend that D has retained "the possession or enjoyment" of the property. If this were the case, the property would be includible in D's gross estate upon D's death by virtue of § 2036. (Refer to the discussion of incomplete transfers in Chapter 11.)

Other Considerations. In addition to the preceding, other considerations that might affect the type of property to be given include the following:

—Property that may be difficult to value for estate tax purposes. Though this substitutes one valuation problem for another, the gift tax valuation may be more easily resolved.

—Property located in other states and in foreign countries. Not only might this eliminate the possibility of multiple death taxes, but it could save on probate costs. Ancillary court proceedings may have to be instituted in the states or countries where the property is located to wind up the estate. This leads to additional court costs, legal fees, etc.

—Property with a high income yield. This is predicated on the assumption that the donor can spare the income from the gift property and is in a high personal income tax bracket. In terms of the objective of family tax planning, it should follow that the donee is in a lower income tax bracket than is the donor.

—The liquidity of the property. Because many estates encounter a problem of liquidity, at least some cash or near-cash assets (e.g., marketable securities) should be retained. Thus, an executor will not be forced to sell nonliquid assets at bargain prices in order to raise funds to meet pressing administration expenses.

Transfers by Death—Income Tax Considerations

General Guidelines. In some cases, it may be advisable to maximize death tax values in order to achieve a higher income tax basis for the estate or heirs. The option may be available when there is conflict as to the true value of an asset. This might be the case with hard-to-value property such as real estate, intangibles, interests in closely-held businesses, antiques, and valuable collections. Here, the true value of assets may fall within a range, and upon the high and low even expert appraisers may disagree. Under such circumstances, the executor of an estate may be in a position to select a realistic value that is most beneficial for tax purposes to the parties involved. Whether such value will be acceptable to the IRS is another problem.

Whether or not it is wise to increase death tax values in order to add to income tax basis is a matter that must be considered carefully. Some of the variables that will enter any such decision follow:

1. The effect that the increase in death value will have on the income tax basis of the property.
2. The additional death taxes that will result from the increased valuation. In light of the unified tax credit, it may well be that many small or modest estates would incur little, if any, additional death taxes by a higher date of death valuation.
3. The planned disposition of the property by the estate or heirs. If, for example, no sale or other taxable disposition is envisioned, a higher income tax basis usually holds little attraction. Even though the property will not be disposed of in a taxable exchange, a high income tax basis could make good sense if the property is depreciable, depletable, or amortizable in the hands of the estate or heirs.
4. The nature of any gain to be recognized by the estate or heirs. A higher basis may mean more if the property will generate ordinary income rather than long-term capital gain. This would be particularly important if the long-term capital gain deduction is reinstated.
5. The income tax bracket of the estate or heirs.

A direct correlation exists in terms of the effect that the increase in death value will have on income tax basis (refer to variable 1). Since the basis becomes whatever value was used for death tax purposes, every dollar of increased valuation means a dollar of additional basis.

How Conclusive Is the Value Used for Estate Tax Purposes?   Suppose a value is used for estate tax purposes and reflected on the estate tax return. At some future date, an heir sells some of the property included in the gross estate and, in computing the basis for gain or loss, believes the value used for estate tax purposes was incorrect. Is there any chance of success in arguing for a different value and thereby changing the income tax basis? The answer is yes, but with definite reservations.

An heir's tax motivation for challenging a lower valuation used for estate tax purposes should be discernable. If it can be proven that the value at the time of death was in excess of that reported, less gain might result on the later sale of the property. Even better, a higher value on the date of death may not, in the absence of fraud on the part of the executor, generate additional estate taxes because the statute of limitations on further assessments by the IRS has run. If the statute of limitations has not run, the heir might try for a higher income tax basis by having the estate tax valuation raised. However, this would necessitate the cooperation of the decedent's executor and the acceptance by the IRS of the new valuation. Whether or not an heir's challenge will succeed depends on a consideration of the following factors:

1. The value reflected on the estate tax return and accepted by the IRS is presumed to be correct.[37] Thus, the heir has the burden of rebutting the presumption.
2. To rebut the presumption of correctness, it would be important to determine by what means the property was originally valued. Did the valuation result from a mere unilateral determination by the IRS, or was it the result of carefully considered compromise between the estate and the IRS? The presumption would be more difficult for the heir to overcome in the latter instance.
3. Did the heir have a hand in setting the original value? If so, the doctrine of estoppel might preclude disputing such value. Under this doctrine, the courts might hold that the heir is now trying to obtain unfair advantage. Thus, the heir used or influenced the use of a lower value for estate tax purposes (thereby saving estate taxes) and now wants a higher value for income tax purposes (thereby saving on recognized gain).[38] The doctrine of estoppel is appropriately used because the IRS is prevented by the statute of limitations from assessing the additional estate taxes that would otherwise be payable if the proposed new value is allowed.[39] On the other hand, if the heir had no hand in the administration of the estate and took no part in determining the value used, it would appear that the heir should not be estopped when attempting to alter such value.
4. Even if the heir can avoid the application of the doctrine of estoppel, justification for a new value must be produced. Perhaps there now exists some evidence of value unknown or not available to the executor of the estate when the property was originally valued. But was this evidence known to the parties involved in the original valuation and thereby taken into account? If not, was it foreseeable? Remember that the valuation process does not involve hindsight but should consider only the factors reasonably available on the appropriate valuation date.

Valuation Problems with a Closely-Held Corporation

A previous section of this chapter considered the criteria used to arrive at a value for stocks and bonds for which there is no recognized market.[40] Special

---

37. Rev.Rul. 54–97, 1954–1 C.B. 113; *H.B. Levy*, 17 T.C. 728 (1951); and *Malcolm C. Davenport*, 6 T.C. 62 (1946).
38. In *William A. Beltzer*, 74–1 USTC ¶ 9373, 33 AFTR2d 74–1173, 495 F.2d 211 (CA–8, 1974) *aff'g.* 73–2 USTC ¶ 9512, 32 AFTR2d 73–5250 (D.Ct.Neb., 1973), the doctrine of estoppel was invoked against the taxpayer, since as the executor of the estate, he had been instrumental in setting the original value reported on the death tax return.
39. Sections 1311 through 1315 (Mitigation of Effect of Limitations and Other Provisions) discussed in Chapter 14, which permit the statute of limitations to be disregarded under certain conditions, would not be applicable here, because different taxpayers (the estate and the heir) and different taxes (the estate tax and the income tax) are involved.
40. These criteria are set forth in Reg. § 20.2031–2(f) as supplemented by Rev.Rul. 59–60, 1959–1 C.B. 237.

attention is necessary, however, to certain concepts peculiar to this area that can carry a marked impact on value.

Valuation Approaches.   If a high value is to be avoided, the issue of goodwill has to be satisfactorily resolved. Particularly if the corporation's record of past earnings is higher than usual for the industry, the IRS is apt to claim the presence of goodwill as a corporate asset. As an indication of what this could mean, consider the following illustration:

Example 40   At the time of death, D owned 70% of the stock of D Corporation, with the remaining 30% held by various family members. Over the past five years, D Corporation has had average net profits of $100,000, and on the date of D's death, the book value (i.e., corporate net worth) of the corporation's stock was $250,000. If the IRS determined 8% to be the appropriate rate of return, one approach to the valuation of D Corporation stock would yield the following result:

Average net profit for the past five years	$100,000
8% of the $250,000 book value	20,000
Excess earnings over 8%	$ 80,000
Value of goodwill (5 × $80,000)	$400,000
Book value	250,000
Total value of the D Corporation stock	$650,000

Thus, the IRS might contend that the stock be included in D's gross estate at 70 percent of $650,000, or $455,000. If the estate wishes to argue for a lower valuation, relevant factors might include any of the following:

1. The average net profit figure for the past five years (i.e., $100,000) may not be representative. Perhaps it includes some extraordinary gains that normally do not occur or are extraneous to the business conducted by the corporation. An example might be a windfall profit for a particular year because of an unusual market situation. Or, suppose the corporation recognized a large gain from an appreciated investment held for many years. The figure may fail to take into account certain expenses that normally would be incurred but for some justifiable reason have been deferred. In a family business during periods of expansion and development, it is not uncommon to find an unusually low salary structure. Profits might be considerably less if the owner-employees of the business were being paid the true worth of their services.

2. The appropriate rate of return for this type of business may not be eight percent. If higher, there would be less goodwill because the business is not as profitable as it seems.

3. If D had been a key person in the operation of D Corporation, could it be possible that some or all of any goodwill developed by the business is attributed to his or her efforts? If so, is it not reasonable to assume that such goodwill might be seriously impaired by D's death?

Aside from the issue of goodwill, the valuation of closely-held stock should take other factors into account. For example, it would be relevant to consider the percentage of ownership involved. If the percentage represents a minority interest and the corporation has a poor dividend-paying record, a substantial discount might be in order.[41] The justification for such a discount would be the general inability of the holder of the minority interest to affect corporate policy, particularly with respect to the distribution of dividends. At the other extreme is an interest large enough to represent control, either actual or effective. Considered alone, a controlling interest would call for a higher valuation.[42]

A controlling interest, however, might be such that the disposition of the stock within a reasonable period of time after the valuation date could have a negative effect on any market for such shares. Known as the "blockage rule," this concept recognizes what may happen in terms of per unit value when a large block of shares is marketed at one time.[43] Most often, it is applied to stock for which there is a recognized market. The blockage rule will permit a discount from the amount at which smaller lots are selling on or about the valuation date.[44] The blockage rule could have a bearing on the valuation of other assets, but its application appears better suited to stocks and securities.[45]

Because most stock in closely-held corporations does not have a recognized market, a discount for lack of marketability may be in order. The discount recognizes the costs that would have to be incurred in creating a market for such shares to effectuate their orderly disposition.[46] Such a discount could be significant when one considers typical underwriting expenses and other costs attendant to going public.

Resolving the Valuation Problem for Stock in Closely-Held Corporations. Since the valuation of closely-held stock is subject to so many variables, planning should be directed toward bringing about some measure of certainty.

Example 41 D wants to transfer some of his stock in Z Corporation to a trust formed for his children. He also would like to make a substantial contribution to his alma mater, State University. At present, the stock of Z Corporation is owned entirely by D and has never been traded on any market or otherwise sold or exchanged. Z Corporation's past operations have proved profitable, and Z has established a respectable record of dividend distributions. Based on the best available information and taking into account various adjustments (e.g., discount for lack of marketability), D feels each share of Z Corporation stock possesses a fair market value of $120. □

---

41. See, for example, *Jack D. Carr,* 49 TCM 507, T.C. Memo. 1985–19.
42. See, for example, *Helvering v. Safe Deposit and Trust Co. of Baltimore, Exr. (Estate of H. Walters),* 38–1 USTC ¶ 9240, 21 AFTR 12, 95 F.2d 806 (CA–4, 1938), *aff'g.* 35 B.T.A. 259 (1937), in which the court stated ".... the influence of the ownership of a large number of shares upon corporate control might give them a value in excess of prevailing market quotations...."
43. Reg. § 20.2031–2(e).
44. See, for example, *Estate of Robert Damon,* 49 T.C. 108 (1967).
45. In *Estate of David Smith,* 57 T.C. 650 (1972), the estate of the now-famous sculptor argued for the application of the blockage rule to 425 sculptures included in the gross estate.
46. See, for example, *Estate of Mark S. Gallo,* 50 TCM 470, T.C.Memo. 1985–363. In this case, the taxpayer also argued that a bad product image (i.e., the Thunderbird, Ripple, and Boone's Farm brands) would depress the value of the stock. Since the trend was towards better wines, association with cheaper products had a negative consumer impact.

Of course, it would be easy enough for D to make a gift of some of the stock to the trust set up for his children and use the $120 per share valuation. What assurance is there the IRS will accept this figure? If it does not and if it is successful in increasing the fair market value per share, D could end up with additional gift tax liability. Although D cannot guarantee this will not happen, he could hedge against any further gift tax liability. Concurrently with the gift of stock to the trust formed for his children, D could make an outright transfer of some of the shares to S.U., thereby generating an income tax deduction. D would base the income tax deduction on the same value used for gift tax purposes.[47] If the IRS later raises the value and assesses more gift tax, D could file an amended income tax return, claim a larger charitable contribution deduction, and obtain an offsetting income tax refund. To carry out this hedge, the amount of Z Corporation stock D would have to donate to S.U. would depend on a comparison of D's gift tax and income tax brackets for the year of the transfers. It should be noted that no gift tax liability would be incurred for the stock transferred to S.U. by virtue of the charitable deduction allowed for gift tax purposes by § 2522 (discussed in Chapter 11).

The Buy and Sell Agreement and Valuation. The main objective of a buy and sell agreement is to effectuate the orderly disposition of a business interest without running the risk of such interest falling into the hands of outsiders. Moreover, if properly designed and executed, a buy and sell agreement can ease the problems of estate liquidity and valuation.

Two types of buy and sell agreements exist: the entity and the cross-purchase arrangements. Under the entity type, the business itself (i.e., partnership or corporation) agrees to buy out the interest of the withdrawing owner (i.e., partner or shareholder). For a corporation, this normally takes the form of a stock redemption plan set up to qualify for income tax purposes under either § 302(b) or § 303.[48] Under the cross-purchase type of buy and sell agreement, the surviving owners (i.e., partners or shareholders) agree to buy out the withdrawing owner (i.e., partner or shareholder).

Example 42 R, S, and D are equal and unrelated shareholders in T Corporation, and all three share in T's management. All agree to turn in their stock to the corporation for redemption at $100 per share in the event any one of them withdraws (by death or otherwise) from the business. Five years later, D dies and the estate redeems the stock from T Corporation at the agreed-upon price of $100 per share. □

Example 43 Assume the same facts as in Example 42, except the agreement is the cross-purchase type under which each shareholder promises to buy a share of the withdrawing shareholder's interest. When D dies, the estate sells the stock in T Corporation to R and S for $100 per share. □

---

47. The use of fair market value as the measure of the charitable contribution deduction presumes the Z Corporation stock, if sold by D, would yield long-term capital gain. See § 170(e).
48. The taxpayer wishes to have the distribution treated as being in exchange for stock rather than as dividend. Refer to Chapter 4.

Will the $100 per share paid to D's estate determine the amount to be included in D's gross estate? The answer is yes, subject to the following conditions:

1. The $100 per share price was reasonable when established. In this connection, one must look to the value of the stock when the agreement was made and not when executed (i.e., five years later).
2. The decedent's estate was legally obligated to dispose of the stock at $100 per share.
3. The decedent was bound by the agreement as to lifetime transfers. Thus, had D decided to sell the stock before death, the stock would have to be offered first to T Corporation (Example 42) or to R and S (Example 43) for $100 per share.[49]

Meeting these conditions and establishing the $100 per share value for death tax purposes is an ideal way to solve an otherwise difficult valuation problem. Unless properly handled, however, the fixed price approach (e.g., $100 per share) might work an inequity to some of the parties. Although the price might have been reasonable when the agreement was drawn up, what if a substantial change in the value of the business interest takes place by the time the agreement becomes effective? Referring to Example 43, suppose the value of a share of T Corporation stock increases from $100 to $150. D's estate must sell the stock for $100. Therefore, is there any doubt that R and S have obtained an unfair economic advantage? The possible inequity might be relieved by avoiding a fixed price commitment and substituting some type of formula that would better take into account business fluctuations (e.g., book value, capitalization of earnings). But even if the fixed price feature is to be retained, a sound approach would be to reset the price at periodic intervals. Thus, the agreement could require the parties to reevaluate the price every two years. A procedure could be established whereby the reevaluation will be carried out by qualified appraisers not possessing an interest in the business and mutually acceptable to the shareholders of T Corporation.

Problem Materials

Discussion Questions

1. In 1919, M made a gift to D (M's daughter) of the family sterling silver. In 1970, D made a gift of the same property to G (D's daughter). Because of unusual medical expenses, G is forced to sell the silver in 1988. In determining G's gain, what role does valuation play?

2. Discuss the relevance of the following in defining "fair market value" for Federal gift and estate tax purposes:

   a. § 2031(b).

   b. The definition contained in Reg. § 20.2031–1(b).

---

49. Reg. § 20.2031–2(h) and *Estate of Mabel G. Seltzer,* 50 TCM 1250, T.C.Memo. 1985–519.

   c. A forced sale price.

   d. The location of the property being valued.

   e. The sentimental value of the property being valued.

   f. The wholesale price of the property.

   g. Tangible personalty sold as a result of an advertisement in the classified section of a newspaper.

3. What factors should be considered in the valuation of bonds of a closely-held corporation when selling prices and bid and asked prices are not available? In the valuation of stock in a closely-held corporation under similar circumstances?

4. At the time of his death, D held some notes receivable (face amount of $20,000 and accrued interest of $4,000) issued by his son for sums borrowed from D. In his will, D forgives the loans but not the accrued interest thereon.

   a. How should these items be handled for Federal estate tax purposes?

   b. For Federal income tax purposes?

5. D creates a trust, life estate to W, remainder to S upon W's death.

   a. Why is it necessary to value the life estate and the remainder interest separately?

   b. In this regard, would it matter if the transfer occurred in 1970? In 1982? In 1988? Explain.

6. Comment on the following relative to the valuation of life insurance and annuity policies:

   a. The annuity contract is not issued by a company regularly engaged in the sale of annuity contracts.

   b. The annuity contract is issued by a company regularly engaged in the sale of annuity contracts.

   c. The life insurance policy being valued is paid-up.

   d. The life insurance policy has been in force for some time, and further premium payments must be made to continue the policy.

   e. The "interpolated terminal reserve" of the policy.

7. What is the justification for the alternate valuation date (i.e., § 2032)?

8. In connection with the alternate valuation date (§ 2032), comment on the following:

   a. Its elective nature.

   b. How the election is made.

   c. Who makes the election.

   d. When the election is available.

   e. What assets the election covers.

   f. Effect on changes in value caused by a mere lapse of time.

   g. The treatment of income earned by property after the death of the decedent.

   h. A disposition by an executor of estate property *within* six months from the date of the decedent's death.

9. In each of the following independent situations, determine whether or not the alternate valuation date can be elected:

Decedent	Year of Death	Fair Market Value of the Gross Estate	
		Date of Death	Alternate Valuation Date
A	1988	$595,000	$580,000
B	1988	590,000	610,000
C	1986	510,000	490,000
D	1986	520,000	530,000

10. In Question 9, would your answer be different if A had made a taxable gift of $10,000 in 1976? A taxable gift of $10,000 in 1980?

11. In Question 9, why might C's estate not elect the alternate valuation date (presuming it is otherwise available)?

12. Contrast current use value with most suitable use value. Why might there be a difference between the two values?

13. What type of hardship does the special valuation method of § 2032A purport to ease?

14. Comment on the special valuation method in connection with the following:

    a. The 50% test and the 25% test.

    b. Qualifying property.

    c. The five-out-of-eight-years requirement.

    d. The qualifying heir.

    e. The $750,000 limitation.

    f. The recapture possibility.

15. Presuming the special valuation method is elected by an estate and the qualifying heir disposes of the property within a 10-year period, what will be the income tax basis of the property?

16. What are some of the shortcomings of the special valuation method?

17. Review the income tax basis rules applicable when a donee sells property received as a gift under the following conditions:

    a. The gift took place before 1921.

    b. The gift took place after 1920 and before 1977.

    c. The gift took place after 1976.

18. In 1948, F purchased a collection of rare coins and in 1972 gave the coins to S. S died in 1984, and the collection passed to G under S's will. In 1988, G sells the collection. In determining G's gain or loss for income tax purposes, is F's purchase price relevant? Why or why not?

19. What is meant by a step-up in basis as to property acquired from a decedent? A step-down in basis?

20. What effect, if any, will the death of a spouse have on the income tax basis of the surviving spouse's share of the community property? Explain.

21. S gives property to his widowed mother. Nine months after the gift, S's mother dies. Under her will, the same property returns to S. Comment on the tax ramifications of these transfers.

22. H gives property to his wife, W. Thirteen months after the gift, W dies. Under her will, the same property returns to H. What are the gift, estate, and income tax consequences?

23. Assume the same facts as in 22, except that W dies 10 months after the gift. Again, comment on the gift, estate, and income tax consequences.

24. Under § 691(c), the party who collects income in respect of a decedent is allowed an income tax credit for the estate tax attributable to the inclusion of the income in the gross estate. Is this a correct statement? Why or why not?

25. W, a widow, dies in 1988 without a will. At the time of her death, W owned a ranch that was being operated by her unmarried son, S. W's only other heir is her daughter D. D lives in the city, is married, and has four small children. S hopes to expand the ranch and improve the breeding stock of the herd.

    a. Do you anticipate any potential problems with these circumstances?

    b. Presuming some planning had preceded W's death, what might have been a more desirable testamentary scheme?

26. Section 6166 commonly is referred to as the "5-year deferral, 10-year installment payment" provision. Explain.

27. In connection with § 6166, comment on the following:

    a. The more-than-35% test.

    b. The definition of a closely-held business.

    c. The family attribution rules.

    d. The aggregation rules.

28. T, currently still alive, almost complies for her estate's election of § 6166. T is not concerned, however, because before her death she plans on giving away her life insurance policy. This, she believes, will allow her estate to meet the requirements of § 6166. Any comment?

29. Discuss the income tax consequences to the donor and the donee of gifts of the following types of property:

    a. Installment notes receivable.

    b. §§ 1245 and 1250 property.

30. Sometimes it may be advisable to resolve questionable estate tax valuation issues in favor of the higher possible values. Discuss this approach in light of the following factors:

    a. The estate tax bracket of the decedent.

    b. Whether the heirs plan to dispose of the property.

    c. The character of the asset in the hands of the heirs (e.g., depreciable property, capital assets).

    d. The income tax bracket of the heirs.

31. How conclusive is the valuation used for Federal income tax purposes in establishing the income tax basis of property to the heirs?

32. Comment on the following points in relation to the valuation of stock in a closely-held corporation:

    a. The deceased shareholder was a key employee of the corporation.

    b. The past earnings of the corporation include large and nonrecurring gains.

    c. The deceased shareholder held only a minority interest in the corporation.

    d. The deceased shareholder held a controlling interest in the corporation.

    e. The cost the corporation would incur in going public.

33. During the same year in which a donor gives stock in a closely-held corporation to family members, donations of some of the stock are made to a qualified charitable organization. In terms of tax planning, what might be accomplished by such a procedure?

34. Under what circumstances will a price specified in a buy and sell agreement be effective in valuing the interest in a closely-held business for death tax purposes?

Problems

1. When V died in 1988 she owned 1,000 shares of Y Corporation. The stock was traded in an over-the-counter market. The nearest trades before and after V's death were as follows:

	Mean Selling Price
Five days before V's death	$ 40 (per share)
Four days after V's death	36 (per share)

    Presuming the alternate valuation date is not elected, at what value should the Y Corporation stock be included in V's gross estate?

2. Under the terms of M's will, S (M's son) is entitled to receive an annuity of $30,000 payable annually for life. The annuity is to be paid from M's estate and is freely transferable. When S reaches age 60, he gives the annuity to D, his daughter who is age 38. Using the appropriate table from Appendix A, determine the value of the transfer from S to D under the following assumptions:

    a. The gift occurred in 1982.

    b. The gift occurred in 1988.

3. F creates a trust with property valued at $500,000. Under the terms of the trust, G (a female, age 45) receives a life estate and H (a male, age 13) receives the remainder interest. Determine the value of the gifts under each of the following assumptions:

    a. The creation of the trust took place in early 1983.

    b. The creation of the trust took place in 1988.

4. R transfers $300,000 in trust. Under the terms of the trust instrument, income is payable to S (a male, age 13) for 12 years, remainder to D (a female, age 36). Determine the value of the gifts under the following assumptions:

    a. The trust was created in 1981.

    b. The trust was created in 1988.

5. M (a female, age 65) creates a trust with property worth $600,000. Under the terms of the trust, M retains a life estate with the remainder interest passing to D (M's daughter) upon M's death. M dies in 1988 when the value of the trust is $900,000 and D is age 45.

    a. Determine the value of the gift, if any, if the trust was created in 1975.

    b. Determine the value of the gift, if any, if the trust was created in 1984.

6. Assume the same facts as in Problem 5. How much, if any, of the trust is included in M's gross estate? Refer to Chapter 11 if necessary.

7. On the date of his death, E owned a patent (fair market value of $600,000) with a remaining life of 12 years. Six months later, the patent possessed a fair market value of $580,000.

   a. If the alternate valuation date is elected, at what value will the patent be included in E's gross estate?

   b. Under (a), what would be the result if the patent is sold by the executor for $590,000 four months after E's death?

8. At the time of her death, F held rental property worth $400,000 on which rents of $12,000 had been accrued. Six months later, the property is worth $405,000. By this time, the rents of $12,000 have been paid and an additional $8,000 accrued. How much should be included in F's gross estate if the alternate valuation date is not elected? If the alternate valuation date is elected?

9. Comment on the following statements relating to § 2032A:

   a. Section 2032A will apply even if the qualifying property is willed by the decedent to a nonfamily member.

   b. If § 2032A applies, current use value (as opposed to most suitable use value) can be used for the qualifying property but not to exceed a limit on the adjustment of $1,000,000.

   c. The special use valuation method cannot be used in setting the valuation of a lifetime gift.

   d. Full recapture of the benefit of the special use valuation method would not occur if the qualifying heir were to sell the property 10 years after the decedent's death.

   e. Recapture occurs only if the qualifying property is sold.

   f. In any recapture situation, an income tax basis adjustment is required.

   g. Lifetime gifts of nonqualifying assets may help in satisfying the 50% and 35% requirements of § 2032A.

   h. In satisfying the 50% and 35% requirements, the qualifying property is to be valued at most suitable use value.

10. F gives stock to D at a time when the stock has a fair market value of $80,000. The stock was acquired by F 10 years before the gift at a cost of $10,000. Determine D's income tax basis for gain or loss under each of the following assumptions:

    a. The gift occurred before 1921.

    b. The gift occurred after 1920 but before 1977. F paid a gift tax of $4,000 on the transfer.

    c. The gift occurred after 1976. F paid a gift tax of $4,000 on the transfer.

11. In the current year, M gives stock to S at a time when the stock has a fair market value of $90,000. The stock was acquired by M four years ago at a cost of $100,000. As a result of the transfer, M incurred and paid a gift tax of $5,000. Determine S's gain or loss if the stock is sold later for:

    a. $75,000.

    b. $95,000.

    c. $105,000.

12. In 1980, M gives publicly traded stock to S at a time when the stock has a fair market value of $300,000. The stock was acquired by M 10 years ago at a cost of $100,000. As a result of the transfer, M incurred and paid a gift tax of $18,000. Determine S's gain or loss if S sells the stock in 1988 for:

a. $200,000.

b. $110,000.

c. $330,000.

13. At the time of his death in 1987, H was married to W and both were residents of the State of Nevada. Among their assets, H and W held community property with the following cost and value attributes:

	Adjusted Basis to H and W	Fair Market Value	
		Date of Death	Alternate Valuation Date
Depreciable real estate	$ 50,000	$400,000	$420,000
Stock in X Corporation	300,000	600,000	550,000
Stock in Y Corporation	250,000	340,000	330,000

Under H's will, all property H owns passes to W.

a. How much is included in H's gross estate if the date of death value is used?

b. If the alternate valuation date is elected?

c. What will be W's income tax basis in the property under (a)? Under (b)?

d. Which choice would be preferable?

14. W dies in 1988 and is survived by H, her husband. Except for stock in Z Corporation which is bequeathed to a qualified charitable organization, W's will provides that all of her property shall pass to H. Relevant information concerning her estate, including cost and value attributes, follows:

	Adjusted Basis to W	Fair Market Value	
		Date of Death	Alternate Valuation Date
Adjusted gross estate (including the stock in Z Corporation)	$300,000	$900,000	$850,000
Stock in Z Corporation	60,000	70,000	100,000

a. Is the election of the alternate valuation date available?

b. What will be H's income tax basis in the property he receives from W?

15. In March 1987, T gives to D the following securities:

Item	Basis to T	Fair Market Value
Stock in R Corporation	$70,000	$20,000
Stock in S Corporation	40,000	80,000

D dies in February 1988, at which time the securities have a fair market value as follows: $30,000 (R Corporation) and $90,000 (S Corporation). Assume that no gift tax resulted from the transfer, D's estate does not elect the alternate valuation date, and D's will passes the securities to T. What income tax basis will T have in the stock of R Corporation? Of S Corporation?

16. In April 1987, T gives D a house (basis of $50,000 and a fair market value of $150,000) to be used as her personal residence. As a result of the transfer, T incurs and pays a gift tax of $9,000. Before her death in March 1988, D installs a swimming pool in the

backyard at a cost of $10,000. The residence is worth $170,000 on the date of D's death, and D's estate does not elect the alternate valuation date. Determine the income tax basis of the property to the heir based on the following assumptions:

a. Under D's will, the residence passes to T.

b. Under D's will, the residence passes to S (D's son).

17. Before his death, D sold a parcel of unimproved real estate held as an investment (basis of $30,000) for $90,000, receiving $10,000 in cash and a 12% interest-bearing note payable in five annual installments of $16,000 each. In reporting the gain from the sale, D did not elect out from the installment method (i.e., § 453). Before his death in the current year, D collected one installment of $16,000 (plus interest) as it came due. The remaining installments (plus interest) are collected by either D's estate or D's heirs. The note possesses a fair market value of $60,000 on the date of D's death, and the alternate valuation date is not elected.

a. Discuss D's income tax consequences in the year of sale.

b. Discuss D's income tax consequences for the year in which D collected the first $16,000 installment.

c. What are the death tax consequences upon D's death?

d. What are the income tax consequences to the estate and heirs upon the collection of the remaining installments?

18. Indicate whether the following statements related to the extension of time when the estate consists largely of an interest in a closely-held business (§ 6166) are true or false:

a. No interest need be paid for the first five years.

b. The value of the farm or other closely-held business must be more than 35% of the gross estate.

c. Four percent is the rate charged on the delayed payments up to the first $1,000,000 of estate value.

d. If the interest consists of stock in a corporation, the corporation cannot have more than 15 shareholders.

e. The estate of a partner cannot qualify unless at least 20% of the capital interest in the partnership is included in the gross estate.

f. Annual installment payments of the deferred estate tax liability are to be made over a period of 15 years.

g. Acceleration of deferred payments will occur if the interest is disposed of prematurely.

h. In satisfying the more-than-35% test, interests in more than one business cannot be aggregated.

19. Last year, D sold real estate (basis of $80,000) to P (an unrelated party) for $200,000, receiving $40,000 in cash and P's notes for the balance. The notes carry a 10% rate of interest and mature annually at $16,000 each year over a period of 10 years. D did not elect out of the installment method as to reporting the gain on this sale. Before any of the notes mature and when the notes have a total fair market value of $150,000, D gives them to S. Disregarding the interest element, what are D's income tax consequences as a result of the gift?

20. Assume the same facts as in Problem 19, except that P is D's son. Disregarding the interest element, what are D's income tax consequences as a result of the gift?

Research Problems

Research Problem 1.   At the time of his death, D held 100 percent of X Corporation, the stock of which has never been traded.   Under D's will the stock is to pass as follows: 51 percent to W (D's surviving spouse) and 49 percent to D's adult children.   On audit by the IRS of the Form 706 filed by the estate, the parties stipulate (i.e., agree) that the correct value of the total X Corporation stock is $2,000,000.   They disagree, however, on the value that should be assigned on the 51 percent passing to W.   The IRS contends that the value of this interest is $1,020,000, while the estate argues that this amount is too low.

   a. Why the controversy?

   b. Support the position of the IRS.

   c. Support the position of the estate.

Partial list of research aids:

Reg. § 20.2031–2(f).

Estate of Dean A. Chenoweth, 88 T.C. 1577 (1987).

Research Problem 2. For many years, the shares of X Corporation were held as follows:

Owner	Number of Shares
Mrs. T	60
Q	20
R	20

Neither Q nor R is related to each other or to Mrs. T.

In late 1985, Mrs. T is contacted by a group of investors who want to acquire control of X Corporation. While preliminary negotiations are in progress for the sale of the stock, Mrs. T creates four irrevocable trusts, to each of which she transfers 15 shares of the stock. Mrs. T's son is designated as the trustee of all trusts, with a different grandchild named as the beneficiary of each trust.

In early 1986, the trusts created by Mrs. T sell the shares of X Corporation to the group of investors for $400 each. Shortly thereafter, the investors acquire the remaining shares held by Q and R for $250 each.

On a timely filed gift tax return, Mrs. T reports the transfers to the four trusts. The gift tax paid by Mrs. T is based on a value of $250 per share.

   a. Justify Mrs. T's position on the valuation of the stock for gift tax purposes.

   b. How could the IRS dispute this determination?

   c. Could Mrs. T suffer any income tax consequences from these transactions? Explain.

Partial list of research aids:

§ 644.

Driver v. U.S., 76–2 USTC ¶ 13,155, 38 AFTR2d 76–6315 (D.Ct.Wis., 1976).

Blanchard v. U.S., 68–1 USTC ¶ 12,567, 23 AFTR2d 69–1803, 291 F.Supp. 348 (D.Ct. Iowa, 1968).

Research Problem 3. In 1977, D established a trust with 3,000 shares of X Corporation. Under the terms of the trust instrument, income is payable to S (D's son, age 20) for life, remainder to D or his estate. Although a local bank is designated as the independent trustee, such trustee is precluded from exchanging or selling the X Corporation stock. For each of the 10 years preceding the transfer in trust, X Corporation had paid an average dividend on its stock of 3%. Neither D nor the trustee has any control, directly or indirectly, over the management and operation of X Corporation. The stock of X Corporation is traded on the American Stock Exchange and was quoted at $50 per share when the transfer to the trust occurred and $80 per share on the date of D's death.

At the time of his death in 1986, D was receiving payments of $800 per month from a noncommercial annuity contract issued by his former employer. Under the terms of the contract, W (D's wife) is entitled to receive reduced payments of $400 per month for the rest of her life. At the time of D's death, W was age 45 and recuperating from recent surgery.

    a. What are the gift tax implications of D's transfer in trust in 1977?

    b. What are the estate tax implications as to the reversionary interest in the trust on D's death in 1986?

    c. What are the estate tax implications as to the annuity on D's death in 1986?

Partial list of research aids:

§§ 2033, 2039, and 6163.

Reg. §§ 20.2031–7(f) and 25.2512–9(f).

Thomas E. Jones, Jr., 36 TCM 380, T.C.Memo. 1977–87.

Rev.Rul. 77–195, 1977–1 C.B. 295.

Rev.Rul. 66–307, 1966–2 C.B. 429.

Research Problem 4. On June 1 of the current year, D entered into a contract to sell real estate for $100,000 (adjusted basis of $20,000). The sale was conditioned on a rezoning of the property for commercial use. A $5,000 deposit placed in escrow by the purchaser was refundable in the event the rezoning was not accomplished. After considerable controversy, the application is approved on November 10 and two days later, the sum of $95,000 is paid to D's estate in full satisfaction of the purchase price. D died unexpectedly on November 1.

    a. Discuss the estate and income tax consequences of this set of facts if it is assumed that the sale of the real estate occurred after D's death.

    b. Before D's death.

    c. When do you think the sale occurred? Why?

Partial list of research aids:

§§ 691 and 1014.

George W. Keck, 49 T.C. 313 (1968) *rev'd.* in 69–2 USTC ¶ 9626, 24 AFTR2d 69–5554, 415 F.2d 531 (CA–6, 1969).

Trust Company of Georgia v. Ross, 68–1 USTC ¶ 9133, 21 AFTR2d 311, 392 F.2d 694 (CA–5, 1967).

Research Problem 5. At the time of his death, D left an estate that consisted of, among other assets, a farm and a hardware business. The farm had a special use valuation of $400,000 but a present use value of $60,000. By itself, the farm comprised 42% of the adjusted value of the gross estate. Combined with the hardware business, however, the relative value of both moved to 53%. Although the farm included real estate, the hardware business did not, since it had been operated on leased premises. Thus, the value of the hardware business was entirely made up of personalty (e.g., inventory). Predicated on the assumption that the conditions of § 2032A were satisfied, the executor of D's estate valued the farm at $60,000 for estate tax purposes. Upon audit by the IRS, § 2032A was deemed inapplicable and the value of the farm was raised to $400,000. Which party is right, and why?

13 Income Taxation of Trusts and Estates

Objectives

Develop working definitions with respect to trusts, estates, beneficiaries, and other parties.

Identify steps by which to determine the accounting and taxable income of the trust or estate and the related taxable income of the beneficiaries.

Illustrate the uses and implications of distributable net income.

Examine effects of statutory restrictions on accounting periods and methods available to trusts and estates and on the taxation of distributions from accumulation trusts.

Present the special rules that apply to trusts that sell appreciated property received as a gift, that accumulate income, and over which the creator (grantor) of the trust retains certain rights.

An Overview of Subchapter J

Chapters 11 and 12 discussed the transfer tax provisions of the Internal Revenue Code. Several of the valuable income and estate tax planning techniques considered therein involved the use of the trust entity. Moreover, the very nature of estate taxation necessarily entails the estate of the decedent. It is now appropriate to cover the income tax treatment of trusts and estates.

The income taxation of trusts and estates is governed by Subchapter J of the Internal Revenue Code, §§ 641 through 692. Similarities will be apparent between Subchapter J and the income taxation of individuals (e.g., the definitions of gross income and deductible expenditures), partnerships (e.g., the conduit principle), and S corporations (e.g., the conduit principle and the trust as a separate taxable entity). Several important new concepts will be introduced, however, including the determination of distributable net income and the tier system of distributions to beneficiaries.

The primary concern of this chapter is the income taxation of estates and ordinary trusts. Grantor trusts are discussed to a limited extent in a later section of the chapter. Special trusts, such as alimony trusts,[1] trusts to administer the requirements of a court in the context of a bankruptcy proceeding, and qualified retirement trusts,[2] are beyond the scope of this text.

What Is a Trust?

The Code does not contain a definition of a trust. However, the Regulations explain that the term "trust," as used in the Code, refers to an arrangement created by a will or by an *inter vivos* (lifetime) declaration, through which trustees take title to property for the purpose of protecting or conserving it for the beneficiaries.[3]

Typically, then, the creation of a trust involves at least three parties: the *grantor* (sometimes referred to as the settlor or donor), whose selected assets are transferred to the trust entity; the *trustee*, who may be either an individual or a corporation and who is charged with the fiduciary duties associated with the trust agreement; and the *beneficiary*, whose rights to receive property from the trust are defined by applicable state law and by the trust document. In some situations, however, fewer than three persons may be involved, as specified by the trust agreement. For instance, an elderly individual who no longer can manage his or her own property (e.g., because of ill health) could create a trust under which he or she was both the grantor and the beneficiary so that a corporate trustee could be charged with management of the grantor's assets. In another situation, the grantor might designate himself or herself as the trustee of the trust assets. For example, a parent who wants to transfer selected assets to a minor child might use a trust entity to assure that the minor does not waste the property. By identifying himself or herself as the trustee, the parent would retain virtual control over the property that is transferred.

---

1. § 682.
2. § 401.
3. Reg. § 301.7701–4(a).

Under the general rules of Subchapter J, however, the trusts just described are not recognized for income tax purposes. When only one party is involved (i.e., when the same individual is grantor, trustee, and sole beneficiary of the trust), Subchapter J rules do not apply and the entity is ignored for income tax purposes.

Other Definitions

When the grantor transfers title of selected assets to a trust, those assets become the *corpus* (body), or principal, of the trust. Trust corpus, in most situations, earns *income*, which may be distributed to the beneficiaries or accumulated for the future by the trustee, as the trust instrument directs.

In the typical trust, the grantor creates two types of beneficiaries: one entitled to receive the accounting income of the trust and one who will receive trust corpus that remains at the termination of the trust entity. Those beneficiaries in the former category hold an *income interest* in the trust, and those in the latter category hold a *remainder interest* in the trust's assets. If the grantor retains the remainder interest, such interest is known as a *reversionary interest* (i.e., corpus reverts to the grantor when the trust entity terminates).

As identified by the trust document, the term of the trust may be for a specific number of years (i.e., for a *term certain*) or it may be until the occurrence of a specified event. For instance, a trust could be created that would exist (1) for the life of the income beneficiary—in this case, the income beneficiary is known as a *life tenant* in trust corpus; (2) for the life of some other individual; (3) until the income or remainder beneficiary reaches the age of majority; or (4) until the beneficiary, or another individual, marries, receives a promotion, or reaches some specified age.

The trustee may be required to distribute the accounting income of the entity according to a distribution schedule specified in the agreement. However, the trustee can be given a greater degree of discretion with respect to the timing and nature of such distributions. If the trustee can determine, within guidelines that may be included in the trust document, either the timing of the income or corpus distributions or the specific beneficiaries who will receive them (from among those identified in the agreement), the trust is referred to as a *sprinkling trust* (i.e., the trustee can "sprinkle" the distributions among the various beneficiaries). As discussed in Chapters 11 and 12, family-wide income taxes can be reduced when such income is received by those who are subject to lower marginal income tax rates. Thus, if the trustee is given a sprinkling power, the income tax liability of the family unit can be manipulated via the trust agreement.

For purposes of certain provisions of Subchapter J, a trust must be classified as either a *simple trust* or a *complex trust*. A simple trust is one that (1) is required to distribute its entire trust accounting income to designated beneficiaries every year, (2) has no beneficiaries that are qualifying charitable organizations, and (3) makes no distributions of trust corpus during the year. A complex trust is any trust that is not a simple trust.[4] These criteria are applied to the trust every year. Thus, every trust will be classified as a complex trust in

4. Reg. § 1.651(a)–1.

the year in which it terminates (i.e., because it will be distributing all of its corpus during that year).

What Is an Estate?

An estate is created upon the death of every individual. This entity is charged to collect and conserve all of the individual's assets, satisfy all of his or her liabilities, and distribute the remaining assets to the heirs identified by state law or the will.

In the typical case, the creation of an estate involves at least three parties: the *decedent*, all of whose probate assets are transferred to the estate for disposition; the *executor* or *executrix* (the latter is a female), who is appointed under the decedent's valid will (or the *administrator* or *administratrix*, if no valid will exists); and the *beneficiaries* of the estate, who are to receive assets or income from the entity, as the decedent has indicated in the will. The executor or administrator holds the fiduciary responsibility to operate the estate as directed by the will, applicable state law, and the probate court.

It is important to recognize that the assets that constitute the probate estate are not identical to those that constitute the gross estate for transfer tax purposes (refer to Chapter 11). Indeed, many of the gross estate assets do not enter the domain of the *probate estate* and thus are not subject to disposition by the executor or administrator. For instance, property held by the decedent as a joint tenant passes to the survivor(s) by operation of the applicable state's property law rather than through the probate estate. Proceeds of life insurance policies on the life of the decedent, over which the decedent held the incidents of ownership, are not under the control of the executor or administrator. Rather, the designated beneficiaries of the policy receive the proceeds outright under the insurance contract.

An estate is a separate taxable entity. Thus, taxpayers may find it profitable, under certain circumstances, to prolong the estate's existence. This situation is likely to arise when the heirs are already in a high income tax bracket. Therefore, the heirs would prefer to have the income generated by the estate assets taxed at the estate's lower marginal income tax rates. However, the tax authorities have recognized this possibility of shifting income to lower-bracket taxpayers. The Regulations caution that if the administration of an estate is unduly prolonged, the estate will be considered terminated for Federal income tax purposes after the expiration of a reasonable period for the performance by the executor of all duties of administration.[5]

↑ undefined time

Nature of Trust and Estate Taxation

Estates and trusts are separate taxable entities, and their income taxation is governed by Subchapter J of the Internal Revenue Code. In general, the taxable income of a trust or an estate is taxed to the entity or to its beneficiaries to the extent that each has received the accounting income of the entity. Thus, Subchapter J creates a modified conduit principle relative to the income taxation of

---

5. Reg. § 1.641(b)–3(a).

trusts, estates, and their beneficiaries. Whoever receives the accounting income of the entity, or some portion of it, is liable for the income tax thereon.

Example 1   Beneficiary A receives 80% of the accounting income of Trust Z. The trustee accumulated the other 20% of the income at her discretion under the trust agreement and added it to trust corpus. A is liable for income tax on no more than the amount of the distribution, while Trust Z is liable for the income tax on the accumulated portion of the income. □

Filing Requirements

The fiduciary is required to file a Form 1041 (U.S. Fiduciary Income Tax Return) in the following situations:[6]

—For an estate that has gross income for the year of $600 or more.

—For a trust that either has any taxable income or, if there is no taxable income, has gross income of $600 or more.

Although the fiduciary is responsible for filing Form 1041 and paying any income tax due, he or she has no personal liability for the tax. In general, the IRS must look to the assets of the estate or the trust for the tax due. The fiduciary may become personally liable for such tax if excessive distributions of assets have been made (e.g., payment of debts, satisfaction of bequests) and therefore render the entity unable to pay the tax due.[7] An executor or administrator may obtain from the IRS a discharge from such personal liability.[8] Taking advantage of this procedure would be highly advisable before making any substantial distributions of estate assets.

The fiduciary return (and any related tax liability) is due no later than the fifteenth day of the fourth month following the close of the entity's taxable year. The return should be filed with the Internal Revenue Service Center for the region in which the fiduciary resides or has his or her principal place of business.

Tax Accounting Periods, Methods, and Payments

An estate or trust may use many of the tax accounting methods available to individuals. The method of accounting used by the grantor of a trust or the decedent of an estate does not carry over to the entity.

An estate has the same election available to any new taxpayer regarding the choice of a tax year. Thus, the estate of a calendar year decedent dying on March 3 could select any fiscal year or report on a calendar year basis.[9] If the latter is selected, the estate's first taxable year would include the period from March 3 to December 31. More importantly, if the first or last tax years are

---

6. § 6012(a).
7. Reg. § 1.641(b)–2(a).
8. § 6905 and the Regulations thereunder.
9. § 441.

short years (i.e., less than one calendar year), income for such years need not be annualized.

To eliminate the possibility of deferring the taxation of fiduciary-source income simply by the use of a fiscal tax year, § 645 requires that all trusts (other than charitable and tax-exempt trusts) adopt a calendar tax year for taxable years that begin after 1986.

Trusts and certain estates are required to make estimated Federal income tax payments using the same quarterly schedule that applies to individual taxpayers.[10] This requirement applies to estates only with respect to tax years that end two or more years after the date of the decedent's death.

In addition, if the trustee so designates on the fiduciary income tax return that is filed on or before the sixty-fifth day following the close of the applicable trust tax year, an estimated income tax payment made by a trust can be assigned to a specified beneficiary of the entity. Under this rule, such a payment will be treated under § 643(g) as though it had been a timely filed fourth-quarter estimated tax payment of the beneficiary. No such election is available with respect to an estate.

The two-year estimated tax exception for estates undoubtedly recognizes the liquidity problems that an executor often faces during the early months of the administration of the estate. Note, however, that the language of the Code does not assure that an estate whose existence measures less than 24 months will never be required to make an estimated tax payment.

Example 2   X died on March 15, 1988. Her executor elected a fiscal year for the estate ending on July 31. Estimated tax payments will be required from the estate starting with the tax year that begins on August 1, 1989. ☐

Tax Rates and Personal Exemption

A compressed tax rate schedule applies to estates and trusts. In addition to being subject to the regular income tax, an estate or trust may be subject to the alternative minimum tax imposed on tax preference items.[11] Trusts also may be subject to a special tax imposed by § 644 on gains from the sale or exchange of certain appreciated property. The rules with respect to this special tax are discussed in more detail in later sections of the chapter.

Both trusts and estates are allowed a personal exemption in computing the fiduciary tax liability. All estates are allowed a personal exemption of $600. The exemption available to a trust, however, depends upon the type of trust involved. A trust that is required to distribute all of its income currently is allowed an exemption of $300. All other trusts are allowed an exemption of only $100 per year.[12]

The classification of trusts as to the appropriate personal exemption is similar but not identical to the distinction between simple and complex trusts. The classification as a simple trust is more stringent.

---

10. § 6654(l).
11. § 55.
12. § 642(b).

Example 3   Trust X is required to distribute all of its current accounting income to Ms. A. Trust Y is required to distribute all of its current accounting income, one-half to Mr. B and one-half to State University, a qualifying charitable organization. The trustee of Trust Z can, at her discretion, distribute the current accounting income or corpus of the trust to Dr. C. None of the trusts makes any corpus distributions during 1988. All of the accounting income of Trust Z is distributed to Dr. C in 1988.

Trust X is a simple trust; it will receive a $300 personal exemption for 1988. Trust Y is a complex trust; it will receive a $300 personal exemption. Trust Z is a complex trust; it will receive a $100 personal exemption. □

Taxable Income of Trusts and Estates

Generally, the taxable income of an estate or trust is computed in a manner similar to that used for an individual. Subchapter J does, however, present several important exceptions and special provisions that distinguish the computation of taxable income for such entities. Thus, a systematic approach to this taxable income calculation is necessary. Figure I illustrates the computation method followed in this chapter.

Figure I   Accounting Income, Distributable Net Income, and Taxable Income of the Entity and Its Beneficiaries

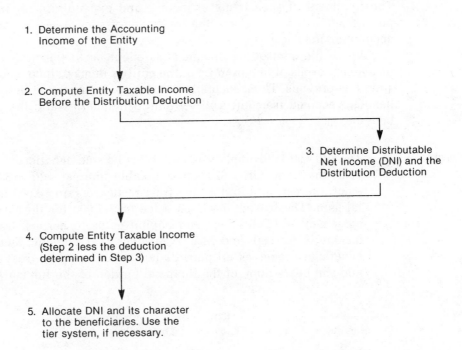

1. Determine the Accounting Income of the Entity

2. Compute Entity Taxable Income Before the Distribution Deduction

3. Determine Distributable Net Income (DNI) and the Distribution Deduction

4. Compute Entity Taxable Income (Step 2 less the deduction determined in Step 3)

5. Allocate DNI and its character to the beneficiaries. Use the tier system, if necessary.

Entity Accounting Income

The first step in determining the taxable income of a trust or estate is to compute the entity's accounting income for the period. Although this prerequisite is not apparent from a cursory reading of Subchapter J, a closer look at the Code reveals a number of references to the income of the entity.[13] Wherever the term "income" is used in Subchapter J without some modifier (e.g., *gross* income or *taxable* income), the statute is referring to the accounting income of the trust or estate for the appropriate tax year.

Thus, a definition of entity accounting income is critical to an understanding of the Subchapter J computation of fiduciary taxable income. Under state law, entity accounting income is the amount that the income beneficiary of the simple trust or estate is eligible to receive from the entity. Most importantly, the calculation of such accounting income is virtually under the control of the grantor or decedent (through a properly drafted trust agreement or will). If the document has been drafted at arm's length, a court will enforce a fiduciary's good-faith efforts to carry out the specified computation of accounting income.

By allocating specific items of income and expenditure either to the income beneficiaries or to corpus, the desires of the grantor or decedent are put into effect. For instance, the typical document allocates to income any receipts of interest, dividends, rents, and royalties; the net profits from a business owned by the trust or estate; and most stock dividends, especially those less than or equal to six percent of the underlying stock. Moreover, the document usually allocates to income a portion of the fiduciary's fees and investment commissions and the operating expenses of the entity's business interests. Conversely, the agreement or will typically allocates to corpus a portion of the fiduciary's fees and investment commissions, depreciation allowances relative to the business assets of the entity, casualty losses associated with the entity property, and the capital gains and losses relative to the trust's investment assets. The treatment of such items of income and expenditure for taxable income purposes does not determine the treatment of such items in computing entity accounting income.

Where the controlling document is silent as to the proper allocation to income or corpus of one or more of the entity's items of income or expenditure, state law prevails. Thus, such allocations are an important determinant of the benefits received from the entity by its beneficiaries and the timing of such benefits.

Example 4   The A Trust is a simple trust. Mrs. B is its sole beneficiary. In the current year, the trust earns $20,000 in taxable interest and $15,000 in tax-exempt interest. In addition, the trust recognizes an $8,000 long-term capital gain. The trustee assesses a fee of $11,000 for the year. If the trust agreement allocates fees and capital gains to corpus, trust accounting income is $35,000, and Mrs. B receives that amount. Thus, the income beneficiary receives no immediate benefit from the trust's capital gain, and she bears none of the financial burden of the fiduciary's fees.

---

13. For example, see §§ 651(a)(1), 652(a), and 661(a)(1).

Interest income	$ 35,000
Long-term capital gain	± 0*
Fiduciary's fees	± 0*
Trust accounting income	$ 35,000

* Allocable to corpus

Example 5   Assume the same facts as in Example 4, except that the trust agreement allocates the fiduciary's fees to income. The trust accounting income is $24,000, and Mrs. B receives that amount.

Interest income	$ 35,000
Long-term capital gain	± 0*
Fiduciary's fees	−11,000
Trust accounting income	$ 24,000

* Allocable to corpus

Example 6   Assume the same facts as in Example 4, except that the trust agreement allocates to income all capital gains and losses and one half of the trustee's commissions. The trust accounting income is $37,500, and Mrs. B receives that amount.

Interest income	$ 35,000
Long-term capital gain	+ 8,000
Fiduciary's fees	− 5,500*
Trust accounting income	$ 37,500

* One-half allocable to corpus

Gross Income

The gross income of an estate or trust is similar to that of an individual. Section 641 provides that fiduciary gross income includes the following:

1. Income that is to be distributed currently.
2. Income accumulated or held for future distribution under the terms of the will or trust.
3. Income that, at the discretion of the fiduciary, may be either distributed to the beneficiaries or accumulated on their behalf.

Although all of the foregoing items may represent gross income to the estate or trust, an offsetting distribution deduction may be allowed for item 1 and, to the extent paid or credited to the beneficiary, for item 3.

In determining the gain or loss to be recognized by an estate or trust upon the sale or other taxable disposition of assets, the rules for basis determination are similar to those that apply to other taxpayers. Thus, the basis of property to an estate received from a decedent is determined under § 1014 (refer to Chapter 12 for a more detailed discussion). Property received as a gift (the usual case in trust arrangements) is controlled by § 1015. Property purchased by the trust from the grantor receives the grantor's basis, increased by any gain recognized by the grantor on the transfer.

Property Distributions.   In general, no gain or loss is recognized by the entity upon its distribution of property to a beneficiary, pursuant to the provisions of the will or trust document. In this regard, the beneficiary of the distribution assigns to the distributed property a basis equal to that of the estate or trust. Moreover, the distribution absorbs distributable net income (DNI) and qualifies for a distribution deduction (both of which are explained in subsequent sections of this chapter) to the extent of the lesser of the distributed asset's basis to the beneficiary or the asset's fair market value as of the distribution date.[14]

Example 7   The H Trust distributes a painting, basis of $40,000 and fair market value of $90,000, to beneficiary K. K's basis in the painting is $40,000. The distribution absorbs $40,000 of H's DNI, and H may claim a $40,000 distribution deduction relative to the transaction. □

Example 8   Assume the same facts as in Example 7, except that H's basis in the painting is $100,000. K's basis in the painting is $100,000. The distribution absorbs $90,000 of H's DNI, and H may claim a $90,000 distribution deduction. □

A trustee or executor can elect to recognize gain or loss with respect to all of its in-kind property distributions for the year. If such an election is made, the beneficiary's basis in the asset is equal to the asset's fair market value as of the distribution date. In addition, the distribution absorbs DNI and qualifies for a distribution deduction to the extent of the asset's fair market value. Note, however, that § 267 can restrict a trust's deduction for such losses.

Example 9   The G Estate distributes an antique piano, basis to G of $10,000 and fair market value of $15,000, to beneficiary K. The executor elects that G recognize the related $5,000 gain on the distribution. Accordingly, K's basis in the piano is $15,000 ($10,000 basis to G + $5,000 gain recognized). Absent such an election, G would recognize no gain, and K's basis in the piano would be $10,000. □

Example 10   Assume the same facts as in Example 9, except that G's basis in the piano is $18,000. The executor elects that G recognize the related $3,000 loss on the distribution. Accordingly, K's basis in the piano is $15,000 ($18,000 − $3,000). Absent such an election, G would recognize no loss, and K's basis in the piano would be $18,000. □

Income in Respect of a Decedent.   The gross income of a trust or estate includes income in respect of a decedent (IRD).[15] For a cash basis decedent,

---

14. § 643(e).
15. § 691 and the Regulations thereunder. The concept of IRD was introduced in Chapter 12.

IRD includes accrued salary, interest, rent, and other income items that were not constructively received before death. For both cash and accrual basis decedents, IRD includes, for instance, death benefits from qualified retirement plans and deferred pay contracts, income from a partnership whose tax year does not end with the death of the deceased partner, and collections of installment notes receivable.

The tax consequences of income in respect of a decedent can be summarized as follows:

1. The fair market value of the right to IRD on the appropriate valuation date is included in the decedent's gross estate.[16] Thus, it is subject to the Federal estate tax.[17]
2. The decedent's basis in the property carries over to the recipient (i.e., the estate or heirs). There is no step-up or step-down in the basis of IRD items.
3. Gain or loss is recognized to the recipient of the income, measured by the difference between the amount realized and the adjusted basis of the IRD in the hands of the decedent. The character of such gain or loss depends upon the treatment that it would have received had it been realized by the decedent before his or her death. Thus, if the decedent would have realized capital gain, the recipient must do likewise.
4. Expenses related to the IRD (such as interest, taxes, and depletion) that properly were not reported on the final income tax return of the decedent may be claimed by the recipient if the obligation is associated with the IRD. These items are known as *expenses in respect of a decedent*. They are deductible for both Federal estate and income tax purposes.

Example 11   K died on July 13, of the current year. On August 2, the estate received a check (before deductions) for $1,200 from K's former employer; this was K's compensation for the last pay period of his life. On November 23, the estate received a $45,000 distribution from the qualified profit sharing plan of K's employer, the full amount to which K was entitled under the plan. Both K and the estate are calendar year cash basis taxpayers.

The last salary payment and the profit sharing plan distribution constitute IRD to the estate: K had earned such items during his lifetime, and the estate had an enforceable right to receive each of them after K's death. Consequently, the gross estate includes $46,200 with respect to these two items. However, the income tax basis to the estate for these items is not stepped up (i.e., from zero to $1,200 and $45,000, respectively) upon distribution to the estate.

The estate must report gross income of $46,200 for the current tax year with respect to the IRD items. Technically, the gain that is recognized upon the receipt of the IRD is $46,200 [$1,200 + $45,000 (amounts realized) − $0 (adjusted basis)]. □

16. § 2033.
17. To mitigate the effect of double taxation (i.e., imposition of both the estate tax and the income tax), § 691(c) allows the recipient an income tax deduction for the estate tax attributable to the income.

Although this result (i.e., that the IRD is included both in K's gross estate and in the gross income of the estate) may appear to be harsh, recall that it is similar to that which applies to all of a taxpayer's earned income: The amount is subject to income tax upon its receipt, and to the extent that it is not consumed by the taxpayer before death, it constitutes an element of the gross estate.

Example 12   Assume the same facts as in Example 11, except that K is an accrual basis taxpayer. IRD now includes only the $45,000 distribution from the qualified retirement plan. K's last paycheck was included in the gross income of his own last return (i.e., January 1 through date of death). Since the $1,200 salary was already properly recognized under K's usual method of tax accounting, it does not constitute IRD, and it is not gross income when it is received by the executor. □

Example 13   Assume the same facts as in Example 11. K's last paycheck was reduced by $165 for state income taxes that were withheld by the employer. The $165 tax payment is an expense in respect of a decedent, and it is allowed as a deduction *both* on K's estate tax return *and* on the estate's income tax return. □

Ordinary Deductions

As a general rule, the taxable income of an estate or trust is similar to that of an individual. Thus, deductions are allowed for ordinary and necessary expenses paid or incurred in carrying on a trade or business;[18] for the production or collection of income; for the management, conservation, or maintenance of property; and in connection with the determination, collection, or refund of any tax.[19] Reasonable administration expenses, including fiduciary fees and litigation costs in connection with the duties of administration, also qualify for a deduction under § 212.

Expenses attributable to the production or collection of tax-exempt income are not deductible.[20] The amount of the disallowed deduction is found by using an apportionment formula, based upon the composition of the income elements of trust accounting income for the year of the deduction. This apportionment of the § 212 deduction is made without regard to the trust accounting income allocation of such expenses to income or to corpus. The deductibility of the fees is determined strictly by the Code (i.e., under §§ 212 and 265), and the allocation of expenditures to income and to corpus is controlled by the trust agreement or will or by state law.

Example 14   The S Trust operates a business and invests idle cash in marketable securities. Its sales proceeds for the current year are $180,000. Expenses for wages, cost of sales, and office administration are $80,000. Interest income recognized is $20,000 from taxable bonds and $50,000 from tax-exempt bonds. The trustee claims a $35,000 fee for its activities. Accord-

---

18. § 162.
19. § 212.
20. § 265.

ing to the trust agreement, $30,000 of this amount is allocated to the income beneficiaries and $5,000 is allocated to corpus.

Sales income	$180,000
Cost of sales	– 80,000
Interest income ($50,000 is exempt)	+ 70,000
Fiduciary's fees, as allocated	– 30,000
Trust accounting income	$140,000

The sales proceeds are included in the gross income of the trust under § 61. The costs associated with the business are deductible in full under § 162. The taxable income is included in S's gross income under § 61, but the tax-exempt income is excluded under § 103. The fiduciary's fees are deductible by S under § 212, but a portion of the deduction is lost because of the § 265 prohibition against deductions for expenses incurred in the generation of tax-exempt income.

Specifically, 50/250 of the fees of $35,000 can be traced to tax-exempt income, and $7,000 of the fees is nondeductible. Note that for purposes of this computation, only the income elements of the current trust accounting income are included in the denominator. Moreover, the allocation of portions of the fees to income and to corpus is irrelevant for this calculation. Computation of the disallowed deduction for fiduciary's fees is as follows:

$$\$35,000^* \text{ (total fees paid)} \times \frac{\$50,000^{**} \text{ (exempt income elements of trust accounting income)}}{\$250,000^{**} \text{ (all income elements of trust accounting income)}}$$

$$= \$7,000 \text{ (amount disallowed)}$$

* All of the fees, and not just those that are allocated to income, are deductible by the trust under § 212.
** The numerator and denominator of this fraction are not reduced by expense items allocable to income (e.g., cost of sales).

Under § 642(g), amounts deductible as administration expenses or losses for death tax purposes (under §§ 2053 and 2054) cannot be claimed by the estate for income tax purposes unless the estate files a waiver of the death tax deduction. Although these expenses cannot be deducted twice, they may be allocated as the fiduciary sees fit between Forms 706 and 1041; they need not be claimed in their entirety on either return.[21] As discussed earlier, this prohibition against double deductions does not extend to expenses in respect of a decedent, which expenses are deductible both for estate tax purposes and on the income tax return of the recipient of the IRD.

Trusts and estates are allowed cost recovery deductions. However, such deductions are required to be apportioned among all of the parties involved. An estate is allowed a deduction for depreciation, depletion, and amortization,

21. Reg. § 1.642(g)–2.

to be apportioned among the estate and the heirs on the basis of the estate's accounting income allocable to each.[22]

Example 15   L and M are the equal income beneficiaries of the N Trust. Under the terms of the trust agreement, the trustee has complete discretion as to the timing of the distributions from N's current accounting income. The trust agreement allocates all depreciation expense to income. In the current year, the trustee distributes 40% of the current trust accounting income to L, and she distributes 40% of the income to M; thus, 20% of the income is accumulated. The depreciation deduction allowable to N is $100,000. This deduction is allocated among the trust and its beneficiaries on the basis of the distribution of current accounting income: L and M can each claim a $40,000 deduction, and the trust can deduct $20,000. ☐

Example 16   Assume the same facts as in Example 15, except that the trust agreement allocates all depreciation expense to corpus. L and M can each still claim a $40,000 depreciation deduction, and N retains its $20,000 deduction. The Code assigns the depreciation deduction proportionately to the recipients of current entity accounting income. Allocation of depreciation to income or to corpus is irrelevant in determining which party can properly claim the deduction. ☐

On a sale by a trust of property received by transfer from the grantor, the amount of depreciation subject to recapture includes the depreciation claimed by the grantor before the transfer of the property to the trust. However, depreciation recapture potential disappears at death. Thus, when an entity receives depreciable property from a decedent, the recapture potential is reduced to zero.

Example 17   J transferred an asset to the S Trust via a lifetime gift. The asset's total depreciation recapture potential was $40,000. If S sells the asset at a gain, ordinary income not to exceed $40,000 will be recognized by the trust. Had J transferred the asset after his death to his estate through a bequest, the $40,000 recapture potential would have disappeared. ☐

Deductions for Losses

An estate or trust is allowed a deduction for casualty or theft losses that are not covered by insurance or other arrangement. Such losses may also be deductible by an estate for Federal death tax purposes under § 2054. As a result, an income tax deduction will not be allowed to an estate unless the death tax deduction is waived.[23]

The net operating loss deduction is available for estates and trusts. The carryback of a net operating loss may reduce the distributable net income of

---

22. §§ 167(h) and 611(b)(3) and (4).
23. See Reg. § 1.642(g)–1 for the required statement waiving the estate tax deduction. In addition, see Reg. §§ 1.165–7(c) and 1.165–8(b), requiring that such a statement be filed to allow an income tax deduction for such losses.

the trust or estate for the carryback year and therefore affect the amount taxed to the beneficiaries for that year. In computing a net operating loss, the estate or trust cannot take into account deductions for charitable contributions or for distributions to beneficiaries. Moreover, any of a trust's income or deductions that are assignable to the grantor (see the later discussion of grantor trusts) cannot be considered.[24]

Certain losses realized by an estate or trust also may be disallowed, as they are for all taxpayers. Thus, the wash sales provisions of § 1091 disallow losses on the sale or other disposition of stock or securities when substantially identical stock or securities are acquired by the estate or trust within the prescribed 30-day period. Likewise, § 267 disallows certain losses, expenses, and interest with respect to transactions between related taxpayers. Under § 267(b), the term "related taxpayers" includes, in addition to other relationships, the following:

—A grantor and a fiduciary of any trust.

—A fiduciary of a trust and a fiduciary of another trust, if the same person is a grantor of both trusts.

—A fiduciary and a beneficiary of the same trust.

—A fiduciary of a trust and a beneficiary of another trust, if the same person is a grantor of both trusts.

—A fiduciary of a trust and a corporation, more than 50 percent in value of the outstanding stock of which is owned, directly or indirectly, by or for the trust or by or for a person who is a grantor of the trust.

Except for the possibility of unused losses in the year of termination, the net capital losses of an estate or trust cannot be deducted by a beneficiary.[25] They are to be used only on the fiduciary income tax return. The tax treatment of these losses is the same as that for individual taxpayers.

Charitable Contributions

An estate or complex trust is allowed a deduction for contributions to charitable organizations under the following conditions:

1. The contribution must be made pursuant to the will or trust instrument.
2. The recipient must be a qualified organization. For this purpose, qualified organizations include the same charities that qualify individual and corporate donors for the deduction, except that estates and trusts are permitted a deduction for contributions to certain foreign charitable organizations.
3. Generally, the contribution must be paid in the tax year claimed, but a fiduciary can treat amounts paid in the year immediately following as a deduction for the preceding year.[26] This rule treats estates and complex trusts more liberally than it does either individuals or corporations.

---

24. § 172 and Reg. § 1.642(d)–1.
25. § 642(h).
26. § 642(c)(1) and Reg. § 1.642(c)–1(b).

4. In addition, estates are allowed a deduction for amounts permanently set aside for charitable purposes, regardless of when the charity actually receives the contribution.[27]

Estates and complex trusts are not subject to a limitation on the extent of their deductible charitable contributions for the year (e.g., to a percentage of taxable or adjusted gross income), as are individuals and corporations. Nonetheless, the contribution may not fully qualify for a deduction by the entity.[28] Specifically, the deduction is limited to amounts included in the gross income of the entity in the year of the contribution. A contribution is deemed to have been made proportionately from each of the income elements of entity accounting income. Thus, in the event that the entity has tax-exempt income, the contribution is deductible only to the extent that the income elements of entity accounting income for the year of the deduction are included in the entity's gross income. This rule is similar to that used to limit the § 212 deduction for fiduciary fees and other expenses incurred to generate tax-exempt income. However, if the will or trust agreement requires that the contribution be made from a specific type of income or from the current income from a specified asset, the document will control (i.e., the allocation of the contribution to taxable and tax-exempt income will not be required).

Example 18   The K Trust has gross rental income in 1988 of $80,000, expenses attributable to the rents of $60,000, and tax-exempt interest from state bonds of $20,000. Under the trust agreement, the trustee is directed to pay 30% of the annual trust accounting income to the United Way, a qualifying organization. Under this provision, the trustee pays $12,000 to the charity in 1989 (i.e., 30% × $40,000). The charitable contribution deduction allowed for 1988 is $9,600 [($80,000/$100,000) × $12,000]. □

Example 19   Assume the same facts as Example 18, except that the trust instrument also requires that the contribution be paid from the net rental income. The agreement controls, and the allocation formula need not be applied. Thus, the entire $12,000 is allowed as a charitable deduction for 1988. □

Deduction for Distributions to Beneficiaries

The modified conduit approach of Subchapter J is embodied in the deduction allowed to trusts and estates for the distributions made to beneficiaries during the year. When the beneficiary receives a distribution from the trust, some portion of that distribution may be subject to income tax on his or her own return. At the same time, the distributing entity is allowed a deduction for some or all of the distribution. Thus, the modified conduit principle of Subchapter J is implemented. A good analogy to this operation can be found in the taxability of corporate profits distributed to employees as taxable wages. The

27. This provision also is available to a few trusts. See § 642(c)(2).
28. Reg. §§ 1.642(c)–3(b) and (c).

corporation is allowed a deduction for the payment, but the employee has received gross income in the form of compensation.

A critical value that is used in computing the amount of the entity's distribution deduction is *distributable net income* (DNI). DNI serves several functions as it is defined in Subchapter J:

1. DNI is the maximum amount of the distribution on which the beneficiaries could be taxed.[29] *DNI forms ceiling for taxes*
2. DNI is the maximum amount that can be used by the entity as a distribution deduction for the year.[30]
3. The makeup of DNI carries over to the beneficiaries (i.e., the items of income and expenses will retain their DNI character in the hands of the distributees).[31] *→ beneficiaries*

Subchapter J presents a circular definition, however, with respect to DNI. The DNI value is necessary to determine the entity's distribution deduction and therefore its taxable income for the year. Nonetheless, the Code defines DNI as a modification of the entity's taxable income itself. Thus, using the systematic approach to determine the taxable income of the entity and of its beneficiaries, as enumerated in Figure I (earlier in the chapter), one first must compute *taxable income before the distribution deduction*, modify that amount to determine DNI and the distribution deduction, return to the calculation of *taxable income*, and apply the deduction that has been found.

Taxable income before the distribution deduction includes all of the entity's items of gross income, deductions, gains, losses, and exemptions for the year. Therefore, in computing this amount, one must (1) determine the appropriate personal exemption for the year and (2) account for all of the other gross income and deductions of the entity.

The next step in Figure I is the determination of *distributable net income*, computed by making the following adjustments specified to the entity's *taxable income before the distribution deduction:* [32]

1. Add back the personal exemption.
2. Add back *net* tax-exempt interest. To arrive at this amount, reduce the total tax-exempt interest by any portion paid to or set aside for charitable purposes and by related expenses not deductible under § 265.
3. Add back the entity's *net* capital losses.
4. Subtract any net capital gains taxable to the entity (those that are allocable to corpus). In other words, the only net capital gains included in distributable net income are those attributable to income beneficiaries or to charitable contributions.

---

29. §§ 652(a) and 662(a).
30. §§ 651(b) and 661(c).
31. §§ 652(b) and 662(b).
32. These and other (less common) adjustments are detailed in § 643.

Since taxable income before the distribution deduction is computed by deducting all of the expenses of the entity (whether they were allocated to income or to corpus), distributable net income will be reduced by expenses that are allocated to corpus. The effect of this procedure is to reduce the taxable income of the income beneficiaries, even though the actual distributions to them exceed DNI, because the distributions are not reduced by expenses allocated to corpus. Aside from this shortcoming of Subchapter J, DNI offers a good approximation of the current-year economic income available for distribution to the entity's income beneficiaries.

Because distributable net income includes the net tax-exempt interest income of the entity, that amount must be removed from DNI in computing the distribution deduction. Moreover, with respect to estates and complex trusts, the amount actually distributed during the year may include discretionary distributions of income and distributions of corpus permissible under the will or trust instrument. Thus, the distribution deduction for estates and complex trusts is computed as the lesser of (1) the deductible portion of DNI or (2) the amount actually distributed to the beneficiaries during the year. In this regard, however, full distribution always is assumed by a simple trust, relative to both the entity and its beneficiaries, in a manner similar to the partnership and S corporation conduit entities.

Example 20   The Z Trust is a simple trust. Because of severe liquidity problems, its 1988 accounting income was not distributed to its sole beneficiary, M, until early in 1989. Z still is allowed a full distribution deduction for, and M still is taxable upon, the entity's 1988 income in 1988. □

Example 21   The P Trust is required to distribute its current accounting income annually to its sole income beneficiary, Mr. B. Capital gains and losses and all other expenses are allocable to corpus. In 1988, P incurs the following items:

Dividend income	$25,000
Taxable interest income	15,000
Tax-exempt interest income	20,000
Net long-term capital gains	10,000
Fiduciary's fees	6,000

1. The 1988 trust accounting income is $60,000; this includes the tax-exempt interest income, but not the fees or the capital gains, pursuant to the trust document. B receives $60,000 from the trust for 1988.
2. Taxable income before the distribution deduction is computed as follows:

Dividend income	$25,000
Interest income	15,000
Net long-term capital gains	10,000
Fiduciary's fees (40/60)	(4,000)
Personal exemption	(300)
Total	$45,700

The tax-exempt interest is excluded under § 103. Only a portion of the fees is deductible, because some of the fees are traceable to the tax-exempt income. The trust receives a $300 personal exemption, because it is required to distribute its annual trust accounting income.

3. DNI and the distribution deduction are computed in the following manner:

Taxable income before the distribution deduction (from above)		$45,700
Add back: Personal exemption		300
Subtract: Net long-term capital gains of the trust		(10,000)
Add back: Net tax-exempt income—		
Tax-exempt interest	$20,000	
Less disallowed fees	(2,000)	18,000
Distributable net income		$54,000
Distribution deduction (DNI $54,000 — Net tax-exempt income $18,000)		$36,000

4. Finally, return to the computation of the 1988 taxable income of the P Trust. Simply, it is:

Taxable income before the distribution deduction	$45,700
Minus: Distribution deduction	36,000
Taxable income, P Trust	$ 9,700

A simple test should be applied at this point to assure that the proper figure for the trust's taxable income has been determined. On what precisely is P to be taxed? P has distributed to Mr. B all of its gross income except the $10,000 net long-term capital gains. The $300 personal exemption reduces taxable income to $9,700. ☐

Example 22 The Q Trust is required to distribute all of its current accounting income equally to its two beneficiaries, Ms. F and the Universal Church, a qualifying charitable organization. Capital gains and losses and depreciation expenses are allocable to the income beneficiaries. Fiduciary fees are allocable to corpus. In the current year, Q incurs fiduciary fees of $18,000 and the following:

(1) Rental income	$100,000
Depreciation expense (rental income property)	− 15,000
Other expenses related to rental income	− 30,000
Net long-term capital gains	+ 20,000
Accounting income, Q Trust	$ 75,000

(2) Taxable rental income	$100,000
Depreciation deduction	0
Rental expense deductions	(30,000)
Net long-term capital gains	20,000
Fiduciary's fees	(18,000)
Personal exemption	(300)
Charitable contribution deduction	(37,500)
Taxable income before the distribution deduction	$ 34,200

Since Q received no tax-exempt income, a deduction is allowed for the full amount of the fiduciary's fees. Q is a complex trust, but since it is required annually to distribute its full accounting income, a $300 exemption is allowed. The trust properly does not deduct any depreciation for the rental property. The depreciation deduction is available only to the recipients of the entity's accounting income for the period. Thus, the deduction will be split equally between Ms. F and the church. Such a deduction probably is of no direct value to the church, since the church is not subject to the income tax. The trust's charitable contribution deduction is based upon the $37,500 that the charity actually received (i.e., one half of trust accounting income).

(3) Taxable income before the distribution deduction	$34,200
Add back: Personal exemption	300
Distributable net income	$34,500
Distribution deduction	$34,500

The only adjustment necessary to compute DNI is the adding back of the trust's personal exemption, as there is no tax-exempt income. Furthermore, Subchapter J requires no adjustment relative to the charitable contribution. Thus, DNI is computed only from the perspective of Ms. F, who also received $37,500 from the trust.

(4) Taxable income before the distribution deduction	$ 34,200
Minus: Distribution deduction	34,500
Taxable income, Q Trust	$ (300)

Perform the simple test (referred to above) to assure that the proper taxable income for the Q trust has been computed. All of the trust's gross income has been distributed to Ms. F and the charity. As is the case with most trusts that distribute all of their annual income, the personal exemption is "wasted" by the Q Trust. □

Tax Credits

An estate or trust may claim the foreign tax credit allowed under § 901 to the extent that it is not allocable to the beneficiaries.[33] Similarly, other credits must be apportioned between the estate or trust and the beneficiaries on the basis of the entity accounting income allocable to each.

Taxation of Beneficiaries

The beneficiaries of an estate or trust receive taxable income from the entity under the modified conduit principle of Subchapter J. As just discussed, distributable net income determines the maximum amount that could be taxed to the beneficiaries for any tax year. In addition, the constitution of the elements of DNI carries over to the beneficiaries (e.g., net long-term capital gains retain their character when they are distributed from the entity to the beneficiary).

The timing of any tax consequences to the beneficiary of a trust or estate presents little problem, except when the parties involved use different tax years. A beneficiary must include in gross income an amount that is based upon the distributable net income of the trust for any taxable year or years of the trust or estate ending with or within his or her taxable year.[34]

Example 23   An estate uses a fiscal year ending on March 31 for tax purposes. Its sole income beneficiary is a calendar year taxpayer. For the calendar year 1989, the beneficiary reports whatever income was assignable to her for the entity's fiscal year April 1, 1988, to March 31, 1989. If the estate is terminated by December 31, 1989, the beneficiary also must include any trust income assignable to her for the short year. This could result in a bunching of income in 1989. □

Distributions by Simple Trusts

The amount taxable to the beneficiaries of a simple trust is limited by the trust's distributable net income. However, since DNI includes net tax-exempt income, the amount included in the gross income of the beneficiaries could be less than DNI. Moreover, when there is more than one income beneficiary, the elements of DNI must be apportioned ratably according to the amount required to be distributed currently to each.

Example 24   For the current calendar year, a simple trust has ordinary income of $40,000, a long-term capital gain of $15,000 (allocable to corpus), and a trustee commission expense of $4,000 (payable from corpus). Its two in-

---

33. § 642(a)(1).
34. §§ 652(c) and 662(c).

come beneficiaries, A and B, are entitled to the trust's annual accounting income, based on shares of 75% and 25%, respectively. Although A receives $30,000 as his share (75% × trust accounting income of $40,000), he will be allocated DNI of only $27,000 (75% × $36,000). Likewise, B is entitled to receive $10,000 (25% × $40,000), but she will be allocated DNI of only $9,000 (25% × $36,000). The $15,000 capital gain is taxed to the trust. ☐

        ↳ goes to corpus

Distributions by Estates and Complex Trusts

A problem arises with respect to distributions from estates and complex trusts when there is more than one beneficiary who receives a distribution from the entity during the year and the controlling document does not require a distribution of the entire accounting income of the entity.

Example 25   The trustee of the W Trust may distribute the income or corpus of the trust at his discretion in any proportion between the two beneficiaries of the trust, Ms. K and Dr. L. Under the trust instrument, Ms. K must receive $15,000 from the trust every year. In the current year, the trust's accounting income is $50,000 and its distributable net income is $40,000. The trustee pays $15,000 to Ms. K and $25,000 to Dr. L. ☐

How is W's distributable net income to be divided between Ms. K and Dr. L? Several arbitrary methods of allocating the DNI between the beneficiaries can be devised, but Subchapter J resolves the problem by creating a two-tier system to govern the taxation of beneficiaries in such situations.[35] The tier system determines precisely which distributions will be included in the gross income of the beneficiaries in full, which will be included in part, and which will not be included at all.

Income that is required to be distributed currently, whether or not it is distributed, is categorized as a *first-tier distribution*. All other amounts properly paid, credited, or required to be distributed are considered to be *second-tier distributions*.[36] First-tier distributions are taxed in full to the beneficiaries to the extent that distributable net income is sufficient to cover these distributions. If the first-tier distributions exceed distributable net income, however, each beneficiary is taxed only on a proportionate part of the DNI. Second-tier distributions are not taxed if the first-tier distributions exceed DNI. However, if both first-tier and second-tier distributions are made and the first-tier distributions do not exceed distributable net income, the second-tier distributions are taxed to the beneficiaries proportionately to the extent of the "remaining" DNI.

The following formula is used to allocate DNI among the appropriate beneficiaries when only first-tier distributions are made and those amounts exceed DNI:

---

35. §§ 662(a)(1) and (2).
36. Reg. §§ 1.662(a)–2 and –3.

$$\frac{\text{First-tier distributions to the beneficiary}}{\text{First-tier distributions to all noncharitable beneficiaries}} \times \text{Distributable net income (without deduction for charitable contributions)} = \text{Beneficiary's share of distributable net income}$$

In working with this formula, amounts that pass to charitable organizations are not considered.

When both first-tier and second-tier distributions are made and the first-tier distributions exceed distributable net income, the above formula is applied to the first-tier distributions. In this case, none of the second-tier distributions are taxed, because all of the DNI has been allocated to the first-tier beneficiaries.

If both first-tier and second-tier distributions are made and the first-tier distributions do not exceed the distributable net income, but the total of both first-tier and second-tier distributions does exceed DNI, the second-tier beneficiaries must recognize income as follows:

$$\frac{\text{Second-tier distributions to the beneficiary}}{\text{Second-tier distributions to all beneficiaries}} \times \text{Remaining distributable net income (after first-tier distributions and charitable contributions)} = \text{Beneficiary's share of distributable net income}$$

Charitable contributions are taken into account at this point.

Example 26   The trustee of the G Trust is required to distribute $10,000 per year to both Mrs. H and Mr. U, the two beneficiaries of the entity. In addition, she is empowered to distribute other amounts of trust income or corpus at her sole discretion. In the current year, the trust has accounting income of $60,000 and distributable net income of $50,000. However, the trustee distributes only the required $10,000 each to Mrs. H and to Mr. U. The balance of the income is accumulated, to be added to trust corpus.

In this case, only first-tier distributions have been made, but the total amount of such distributions does not exceed DNI for the year. Although DNI is the maximum amount that must be included by the beneficiaries for the year, no more can be included in gross income by the beneficiaries than is distributed by the entity. Thus, Mrs. H and Mr. U each may be subject to tax on $10,000 as their proportionate shares of G's DNI. ☐

Example 27   Assume the same facts in Example 26, except that distributable net income is $12,000. Mrs. H and Mr. U each receive $10,000, but they cannot be taxed in total on more than DNI. Thus, each is taxed on $6,000 [DNI of $12,000 × ($10,000/$20,000 of the first-tier distributions)]. ☐

Example 28   Return to the facts described in Example 25. Ms. K receives a first-tier distribution of $15,000. Second-tier distributions include $20,000 to Ms. K and $25,000 to Dr. L. W's distributable net income is $40,000. The DNI is allocated between Ms. K and Dr. L as follows:

(1) First-tier distributions
  To Ms. K $15,000 DNI
  To Dr. L   0
 Remaining DNI = $25,000
(2) Second-tier distributions
  To Ms. K $11,111 DNI (20/45 × $25,000)
  To Dr. L $13,889 DNI (25/45 × $25,000)

Example 29 Assume the same facts as in Example 28, except that accounting income is $80,000 and DNI is $70,000. The DNI is allocated between Ms. K and Dr. L as follows:

(1) First-tier distributions
  To Ms. K $15,000 DNI
  To Dr. L   0
 Remaining DNI = $55,000
(2) Second-tier distributions
  To Ms. K $20,000 DNI
  To Dr. L $25,000 DNI

Example 30 Assume the same facts as in Example 28, except that accounting income is $18,000 and DNI is $12,000. The DNI is allocated between Ms. K and Dr. L as follows:

(1) First-tier distributions
  To Ms. K $12,000 DNI
   (i.e., limited to the DNI ceiling)
  To Dr. L   0
 Remaining DNI = $0
(2) Second-tier distributions
  To Ms. K $0 DNI
  To Dr. L $0 DNI

Example 31 The Y Estate is required to distribute its current income as follows: 50% to A, 25% to B, and 25% to C (a qualifying charitable organization). During the current year, it has accounting income of $40,000 and distributable net income (before any charitable contributions) of $27,000. Pursuant to the governing instrument, the following amounts are paid out: $20,000 to A (50% × $40,000), $10,000 to B, and $10,000 to C. A must include $18,000 in gross income [($20,000/$30,000) × $27,000], and B must include $9,000 [($10,000/$30,000) × $27,000]. Note that the distribution to the charitable organization was not considered in allocating distributable net income to the first-tier beneficiaries (i.e., the denominator of the fraction is only $30,000).[37] □

Example 32

The will that created the V Estate requires that $20,000 be distributed annually to Mrs. V. If any accounting income remains, it may be accumulated or it may be distributed to Miss V or to W College, a qualifying charitable organization. In addition, the executor of the estate may invade corpus for the benefit of Mrs. V, Miss V, or the college. In the current year, the accounting income of the estate is $35,000 and DNI (before any charitable contributions) is $25,000. The executor pays $30,000 to Mrs. V and $10,000 each to Miss V and to the college. The DNI is to be allocated among the beneficiaries as follows:

---

(1) First-tier distributions
    To Mrs. V $20,000 DNI
    To Miss V   –0–
    To charity   –0–
    Remaining DNI = $0
    ($25,000 DNI — first-tier distributions $20,000
                 — charitable contributions $10,000)

The charitable contribution does not reduce the exposure to DNI for the first-tier distribution, but it is applied in computing the DNI that remains for the second-tier distributions.

---

(2) Second-tier distributions
    To Mrs. V $0 DNI
    To Miss V $0 DNI

□

Separate Share Rule. For the sole purpose of determining the amount of distributable net income for a complex trust with more than one beneficiary, the substantially separate and independent shares of different beneficiaries in the trust are treated as *separate trusts*.[38] The reason for this special rule can be illustrated as follows:

Example 33

Under the terms of the trust instrument, the trustee has the discretion to distribute or accumulate income on behalf of G and H (in equal shares). The trustee also has the power to invade corpus for the benefit of either beneficiary to the extent of that beneficiary's one-half interest in the trust. For the current year, the distributable net income of the trust is $10,000. Of this amount, $5,000 is distributed to G and $5,000 is accumulated on behalf of H. In addition, the trustee pays $20,000 from corpus to G. Without the separate share rule, G would be taxed on $10,000 (the full amount of the DNI). With the separate share rule, G is taxed on only $5,000 (his

---

37. Reg. § 1.662(a)–2(e) (Ex. 2).
38. Reg. § 1.663(c)–1(a).

share of the DNI) and receives the $20,000 corpus distribution tax-free. The trust will be taxed on H's $5,000 share of the DNI that is accumulated.

□

The separate share rule is designed to prevent the inequity that otherwise would result if the corpus payment were treated under the regular rules applicable to second-tier beneficiaries. Referring to Example 33, the effect of the separate share rule is to produce a two-trust result: one trust for G and one for H, each with DNI of $5,000.

Character of Income

Consistent with the modified conduit principle of Subchapter J, various classes of income (e.g., dividends, long-term capital gains, tax-exempt interest) retain the same character for the beneficiaries that they had when they were received by the entity. However, if there are multiple beneficiaries *and* if all of the distributable net income is distributed, a problem arises with respect to the allocation of the various classes of income among the beneficiaries. Distributions are treated as consisting of the same proportion of each class of the items that enter into the computation of DNI as the total of each class bears to the total DNI of the entity. This allocation does not apply, however, if the terms of the governing instrument specifically allocate different classes of income to different beneficiaries or if local law requires such an allocation.[39] Expressed as a formula, this generally means the following:

$$\frac{\text{Beneficiary's total share of DNI distributed}}{\text{Total DNI distributed}} \times \frac{\text{Total of DNI element deemed distributed (e. g., tax-exempt interest)}}{} = \frac{\text{Beneficiary's share of the DNI element}}{}$$

If the entity distributes only a part of its distributable net income, the amount of a particular class of distributable net income that is deemed distributed must first be determined. This is done as follows:

$$\frac{\text{Total distribution}}{\text{Total distributable net income}} \times \frac{\text{Total of a particular class of distributable net income}}{} = \frac{\text{Total of the DNI element deemed distributed (e. g., tax-exempt interest)}}{}$$

Example 34   The B Trust has distributable net income of $40,000, including the following: $10,000 of taxable interest, $10,000 of tax-exempt interest, and $20,000 of dividends. The trustee distributes, at her discretion, $8,000 to M and $12,000 to N, both noncharitable beneficiaries. The amount of each element of distributable net income that is deemed distributed will be $5,000 of taxable interest [($20,000 total distributed/$40,000 DNI) × $10,000 taxable interest in DNI], $5,000 of tax-exempt interest [($20,000/$40,000) × $10,000], and $10,000 of dividends [($20,000/$40,000) × $20,000]. M's share of this income is $8,000, made up of $2,000 of taxable interest [($8,000 DNI received by M/$20,000 total DNI distributed) × $5,000 taxable interest distributed], $2,000 of tax-exempt interest [($8,000/$20,000) × $5,000], and $4,000 of dividends [($8,000/$20,000) × $10,000]. The remain-

---

39. Reg. § 1.662(b)–1.

ing amount of each income item deemed distributed is N's share: $3,000 of taxable interest, $3,000 of tax-exempt interest, and $6,000 of dividends. □

Example 35   Continue with the facts of Example 34. The character of the income that flows through to beneficiaries M and N is effective for all other Federal income tax purposes. For instance, the $2,000 exempt interest allocated to M will be used in computing the taxable portion of any Social Security benefits M receives. Similarly, the $15,000 taxable interest and dividend income allocated to N can be used to increase the amount of investment interest expense deductible by N in the year of the flow-through, as it is treated as portfolio income to the same extent as that received directly by the taxpayer. □

Special Allocations.   Under certain circumstances, the parties may modify the character-of-income allocation method set forth above. Such a modification is permitted only to the extent that the allocation is required in the trust instrument and only to the extent that it has an economic effect independent of the income tax consequences of the allocation.[40]

Example 36   Return to the facts described in Example 34. Assume that the beneficiaries are elderly individuals who have pooled their investment portfolios and avail themselves of the trustee's professional asset management skills. Suppose that the trustee has the discretion to allocate different classes of income to different beneficiaries and that she designates all of N's $12,000 distribution as being from the tax-exempt income. Such a designation *would not be recognized* for tax purposes; the allocation method of Example 34 must be used.

Suppose, however, that the trust instrument stipulated that N was to receive all of the income from tax-exempt securities, because only N contributed the exempt securities to trust corpus. Pursuant to this provision, the $10,000 of the nontaxable interest is paid to N. This allocation is recognized, and $10,000 of N's distribution is tax-exempt. □

Losses in the Termination Year

The ordinary net operating and capital losses of a trust or estate do not flow through to the entity's beneficiaries, as would such losses from a partnership or an S corporation. However, in the year in which an entity terminates its existence, the beneficiaries do receive a direct benefit from the loss carryovers of the trust or estate.[41]

Net operating losses and net capital losses are subject to the same carryover rules that otherwise apply to an individual (i.e., net operating losses can be carried back three years and then carried forward 15 years; net capital losses can be carried forward only, and for an indefinite period by the entity). However, if the entity incurs a net operating loss in the last year of its existence, the excess of deductions over the entity's gross income is allowed to the

---

40. Reg. § 1.652(b)–2(b). This is similar to the § 704(b) requirement for partnerships.
41. Reg. §§ 1.642(h)–1 and –2.

beneficiaries (i.e., it will flow through to them directly). This net loss will be available as a deduction *from* adjusted gross income in the beneficiary's tax year with or within which the entity's tax year ends in proportion to the relative amount of corpus assets that each beneficiary receives upon the termination of the entity but subject to the two-percent-of-AGI floor.

Moreover, any carryovers of the entity's other net operating and net capital losses flow through to the beneficiaries in the year of termination in proportion to the relative amount of corpus assets that each beneficiary receives. The character of the loss carryover is retained by the beneficiary, except that a carryover of a net capital loss to a corporate beneficiary always is deemed to be short-term. Beneficiaries who are individuals can use these carryovers as deductions *for* adjusted gross income.

Example 37   The E Estate terminates on December 31, 19X4. It had used a fiscal year ending July 31. For the termination year, the estate incurred a $15,000 net operating loss. In addition, the estate had an unused net operating loss carryover of $23,000 from the year ending July 31, 19X1, and an unused net long-term capital loss carryover of $10,000 from the year ending July 31, 19X3. D receives $60,000 of corpus upon termination, and Z Corporation receives the remaining $40,000. D and Z are calendar year taxpayers.

D can claim an itemized deduction of $9,000 [($60,000/$100,000) $\times$ $15,000] for the entity's net operating loss in the year of termination. This deduction is subject to the 2%-of-AGI floor on miscellaneous itemized deductions. In addition, D can claim a $13,800 deduction *for* adjusted gross income in 19X4 (60% $\times$ $23,000) for the other net operating loss carryover of E, and she can use $6,000 of E's net long-term capital loss carryover with her other 19X4 capital transactions.

Z Corporation receives ordinary business deductions in 19X4 for E's net operating losses: $6,000 for the loss in the year of termination and $9,200 for the carryover from fiscal 19X1. Moreover, Z can use the $4,000 carryover of E's net capital losses to offset against its other 19X4 capital transactions, although the loss must be treated as short-term.

With respect to both D and Z, the losses flow through in addition to the other tax consequences of E that they received on July 31, 19X4 (i.e., at the close of the usual tax year of the entity), under Subchapter J. Moreover, if the loss carryovers are not used by the beneficiaries in calendar year 19X4, the short year of termination will exhaust one of the years of the usual carryover period (e.g., D can use E's net operating loss carryover through 15 years). ☐

Special Tax Computation for Trusts

Congress enacted § 644 to discourage the transferring of appreciated property to a trust, which then would sell the property and thereby shift the gain on the appreciation of the asset to the trust's lower tax rates. This provision imposes a special tax on trusts that sell or exchange property at a gain within two years after the date of its transfer in trust by the transferor. The special tax applies, however, only if the fair market value of the property at the time of the initial transfer exceeded the adjusted basis of the property immediately after the transfer] (i.e., after any applicable adjustment for gift taxes paid).

The tax imposed by § 644 is equal to the amount of additional income tax that the transferor would have been required to pay (including any alternative minimum tax) had the gain been included in his or her gross income for the tax year of the sale. Note, however, that the tax applies only to an amount known as *includible gain*. Such gain is the lesser of the following:

—The gain recognized by the trust on the sale or exchange of any property.

—The excess of the fair market value of such property at the time of the initial transfer in trust by the transferor over the adjusted basis of such property immediately after the transfer.[42]

Several situations exist wherein the tax will not be imposed. For instance, the tax will not apply to the sale or exchange of property (1) acquired by the trust from a decedent or (2) that occurs after the death of the transferor.

Example 38   On July 1, 1988, G created an irrevocable trust with a transfer of 200 shares of Z Corporation stock. At the time of the transfer, the stock was a capital asset to G. It had a fair market value of $30,000; its basis to the trust was $20,000. On October 1, 1988, the trust sold the stock for $35,000. Section 644 will apply, because the stock was sold at a gain within two years after its transfer in trust *and* its fair market value at the time of the initial transfer exceeded its adjusted basis to the trust immediately after the transfer. The trust must report a § 644 gain of $10,000 [i.e., the lesser of its gain recognized on the sale ($15,000) or the appreciation in the hands of G]. This $10,000 is taxed to the trust at G's 1988 income tax rates on a net capital gain. The remaining $5,000 of the gain is taxed to the trust under the usual Subchapter J rules. □

Example 39   Assume the same facts as in Example 38, except that the fair market value of the stock at the time of the transfer was $18,000. Section 644 will not apply to the subsequent sale by the trust, since the fair market value of the stock on that date was less than the stock's basis to the trust. Note also that the § 644 tax would not apply in Example 38 if the stock were sold either at a loss or more than two years after the date of its initial transfer to the trust. □

The Throwback Rule

To understand the purpose and rationale of the throwback provision, one must review the general nature of taxation of trusts and their beneficiaries. The usual rule is that the income from trust assets will be taxed to the trust itself or to the beneficiary, but not to both. Generally, then, a beneficiary is not taxed on any distributions in excess of the trust's distributable net income. Thus,

42. §§ 644(b) and (d)(2).

trustees of complex trusts might be tempted to arrange distributions in such a manner that would result in minimal income tax consequences to all of the parties involved. For instance, if the trust is subject to a lower marginal income tax rate than are its beneficiaries, income could be accumulated at the trust level for several years before it is distributed to the beneficiaries. In this manner, the income that would be taxed to the beneficiaries in the year of distribution would be limited by the trust's DNI for that year. Further tax savings could be achieved by the use of multiple trusts, because the income during the accumulation period would be spread over more than one taxpaying entity, thereby avoiding the graduated tax rates.

To discourage the use of these tax minimization schemes, the Code has, since 1954, contained some type of *throwback rule*. Because of this rule, a beneficiary's tax on a distribution of income accumulated by a trust in a prior year will approximate the increase in the beneficiary's tax for such a prior year that would have resulted had the income been distributed in the year that it was earned by the trust. The tax as so computed, however, is levied for the actual year of the distribution. In essence, the purpose of the throwback rule is to place the beneficiaries of complex trusts in the same nominal tax position as would have existed had they received the distributions during the years in which the trust was accumulating the income.

A detailed description of the application of the throwback rule is beyond the scope of this text. However, some basic terms and concepts are presented in the following sections to familiarize the reader with the applicable statutory provisions and their purpose.

Basic Terms

An understanding of the throwback rule requires the definition of two important terms: (1) *undistributed net income* and (2) *accumulation distribution*. Undistributed net income is defined in § 665(a) as the distributable net income of the trust reduced by first-tier and second-tier distributions and the income tax paid by the trust on any remaining undistributed DNI. Accumulation distribution is defined in § 665(b) as any distribution from a trust for a particular year in excess of the trust's DNI for the year.

The throwback rule applies only to complex trusts that do not distribute all current accounting income. Thus, the rule does not apply to estates or simple trusts. Moreover, the rule applies only in years when the complex trust makes an accumulation distribution. When this occurs, the distribution is "thrown back" to the earliest year in which the trust had any undistributed net income. The accumulation is thrown back to succeeding years sequentially until it is used up. Accumulation distributions may not be thrown back to years before 1969. Moreover, distributions of accounting income, capital gains that are allocable to corpus, and income accumulated before the beneficiary attained age 21 are not subject to the throwback procedure.[43]

Because of the effect of the throwback rule, the beneficiary may be required to pay an additional income tax in the year of the accumulation distribution. The tax due for this year will be the sum of the tax on the beneficiary's

---

43. §§ 665(b) and (e).

taxable income (without the accumulation distribution) and the tax on the accumulation distribution.[44] The trust may not claim a refund (i.e., if the tax that it paid exceeded that which would have been paid by the beneficiary).[45]

Example 40   In 1983, the T Trust was subject to a marginal Federal income tax rate of 19%, while its sole income beneficiary, O, was subject to a 33% marginal rate. O encouraged the trustee to accumulate $7,500 of the trust's DNI, which totaled $10,000. The balance of the DNI was distributed to O. If T's tax on this accumulation, after credits, is $1,200, T's undistributed net income for 1983 is $6,300 [$10,000 (DNI) − $2,500 (distribution of income) − $1,200 (taxes paid)].

By 1988, O's marginal rate had fallen to 15%, and O encouraged the trustee to distribute to him, in that year, an amount equal to the 1988 DNI of $12,000 plus the $6,300 that had been accumulated, after taxes, in 1983. When the trustee complied with O's wish, she made an accumulation distribution of $6,300.

The tax on the accumulation distribution is levied upon O in 1988. O's additional tax will approximate what O would have paid in 1983 had the trust distributed its full DNI in that year (i.e., the $6,300 accumulation distribution will be subject to approximately a 33% tax rate and not to O's prevailing 15% rate). □

Although no interest or penalty is due with the tax on the accumulation distribution, the additional tax clearly discourages the manipulation of trust distributions to split taxable income among entities for tax avoidance purposes.

Tax on Accumulation Distribution

The tax imposed on the accumulation distribution is determined by adding a fraction of the distribution to the beneficiary's taxable income for three of the five immediately preceding tax years (excluding both the year of the highest taxable income and the year of the lowest taxable income).[46] The fraction is calculated by dividing the accumulation distribution by the number of years in which it was earned by the trust. Once the additional tax on the adjusted taxable income for the three years is determined, the beneficiary must calculate an average additional tax for each of the three years and multiply it by the number of years over which the trust earned the income. The result is the tax on the accumulation distribution.

The Sixty-Five Day Rule

Amounts paid or credited to the beneficiaries in the first 65 days of the trust's tax year may be treated as paid on the last day of the preceding taxable year.[47] Use of this provision offers the trustee some flexibility in timing distributions so that trust accumulations, and the resulting throwback procedures, can be avoided.

---

44. § 668(a).
45. § 666(e).
46. § 667(b). For further details on calculating the tax, see instructions to Schedule J (Form 1041).
47. See Reg. § 1.663(b)–2 for the manner and timing of such an election.

Grantor Trusts

A series of special statutory provisions contained in §§ 671 through 679 of the Code applies when the grantor of the trust retains beneficial enjoyment or substantial control over the trust property or income. In such an event, the grantor is taxed on the trust income, and the trust is disregarded for income tax purposes. The person who is taxed on the income is allowed to claim on his or her own return, any deductions or credits attributable to the income.

These special rules concern only the Federal income tax treatment of the trust. Another part of the Code deals with the Federal estate and gift tax consequences of such incomplete transfers (refer to Chapters 11 and 12). There is no complete correlation among the operation of these different Federal taxes. Clearly, however, such taxes restrict the grantor's ability to redirect the income recognized from trust corpus to the trust or its beneficiaries.

Reversionary Trusts

For many years, taxpayers have used the so-called Clifford trust vehicle as a way to assign gross income to other taxpayers who presumably are subject to lower income tax rates. Although the surest method of assigning income to other parties is to make a permanent transfer of the underlying assets to the transferee (e.g., by gift or sale), few potential donors are willing to part with a sizeable portion of the income-producing assets that they often have spent a lifetime accumulating.

The Code had allowed the use of the Clifford trust, under which the donor can part with the income-producing asset for only a temporary time period (defined in § 673 as greater than 10 years), during which any gross income that is earned would be taxed to the income beneficiary of the trust (i.e., at the donee's lower rates). Upon the termination of the trust or upon the death of the income beneficiary, the trust assets reverted to the grantor. Accordingly, the Clifford trust has offered a means by which one can temporarily assign income to those in more favorable tax brackets without a permanent transfer of the income-producing property.

This Code-sanctioned opportunity has allowed taxpayers to accumulate a fund with which a child could, for example, purchase a business or enter college or graduate school simply because of the ability of the redesignated taxpaying entity (i.e., the child) to compound additional funds at the IRS's expense. Similarly, if the income beneficiary of the Clifford trust were an elderly parent of the taxpayer, support for the parent's retirement period could accumulate at a faster rate, chiefly because of the lower income tax rates that apply to the parent.

The Tax Reform Act (TRA) of 1986 severely limited the future use of a Clifford trust as an effective income-shifting device. The change repealed the § 673 exception from grantor trust status for trusts whose donor holds a reversionary interest that satisfies the time period.

The TRA of 1986 provisions apply only with respect to assets transferred to the now-tainted reversionary trusts after March 1, 1986. Thus, the anticipated income-shifting results are still effective for funded Clifford trusts that existed on that date. Subsequent transfers to existing trusts and newly created reversionary trusts, however, are subject to the new limitations.

A Clifford-style income assignment can be made after March 1, 1986, with respect to a trust in which the donor holds a reversionary interest in either of two situations. Gross income of such a trust will be taxed at the income beneficiary's lower rates if (1) at the date of the creation of the trust the value of the grantor's reversionary interest does not exceed five percent of the fair market value of the assets that are transferred to the trust or (2) the grantor's reversion relates to a trust whose income beneficiary is a lineal descendant of the donor, where his or her reversion occurs solely as a result of the death of the income beneficiary prior to the latter's reaching age 21. Each of these exceptions is granted to allow the trust to include safeguard measures with respect to the unanticipated early death of the income beneficiary.

Creation of a reversionary trust is subject to the Federal gift tax. If the grantor dies before the income interest expires, the present value of the reversionary interest is included in his or her gross estate under § 2033; thus, a Federal estate tax could also result.

Powers Retained by the Grantor

Sections 674 through 677 contain other restrictions as to the extent of the powers over the trust that the grantor can retain without incurring grantor trust status upon the entity. Thus, a violation of any of these provisions means that the income of the trust will be taxed to the grantor (i.e., the usual Subchapter J rules will not apply to the trust).

Section 674 provides that the grantor will be taxed on the income therefrom if he or she retains (1) the beneficial enjoyment of corpus or (2) the power to dispose of the trust income without the approval or consent of any adverse party. An adverse party is any person having a substantial beneficial interest in the trust who would be affected adversely by the exercise or nonexercise of the power that the grantor possesses over the trust assets.[48]

Section 674(b) stipulates several exceptions to this broad rule and enumerates a number of important powers that will *not* cause income to be taxed to the grantor:

—To apply the income toward the support of the grantor's dependents (except to the extent that it actually is applied for this purpose).[49]

—To allocate trust income or corpus among charitable beneficiaries.

—To invade corpus on behalf of a designated beneficiary.

—To postpone temporarily the payment of income to a beneficiary.

—To withhold income from a beneficiary during his or her minority or disability.

—To allocate receipts and disbursements between income and corpus.[50]

---

48. §§ 672(a) and (b). See Reg. § 1.672(a)–1 for examples of adverse party situations.
49. § 677(b).
50. See Reg. § 1.674(b)–1 for a further discussion of these exceptions and for examples illustrating their applicability.

The retention by the grantor or a nonadverse party of certain administrative powers over the trust will cause the income therefrom to be taxed to the grantor. Such powers include those to deal with trust income or corpus for less than full and adequate consideration and to borrow from the trust without providing adequate interest or security.[51]

The grantor of a trust will be taxed on the trust's income if he or she (or a nonadverse party) possesses the power to revoke the trust.[52] In addition, a grantor may be taxed on all or part of the income of a trust when, without the consent of any adverse party, the income is or, at the discretion of the grantor or a nonadverse party (or both), the income may be

—Distributed to the grantor or the grantor's spouse.

—Held or accumulated for future distribution to the grantor or the grantor's spouse.

—Applied to the payment of premiums on insurance policies on the life of the grantor or the grantor's spouse.[53]

Moreover, trust income accumulated for the benefit of someone whom the grantor is *legally obligated* to support will be taxed to the grantor but only to the extent that it actually is applied for such purpose.[54]

Example 41   F creates an irrevocable trust for his children, with a transfer of income-producing property and an insurance policy on the life of M, F's wife. During the year, the trustee applies $3,000 of the trust income in payment of the premiums on the policy covering M's life. F is taxed on $3,000 of the trust's income. ☐

Example 42   M creates an irrevocable accumulation trust. Her son, S, is the life beneficiary, remainder to any grandchildren. During the year, the trust income of $8,000 is applied as follows: $5,000 toward S's college tuition and other related educational expenses and $3,000 accumulated on S's behalf. If, under state law, M has an obligation to support S and this obligation includes providing a college education, M is taxed on the $5,000 that is so applied. ☐

Concept Summary

1. Estates and trusts are temporary entities created to locate, maintain, and distribute assets and to satisfy liabilities according to the wishes of the decedent or grantor as expressed in the will or trust document.

---

51. See Reg. § 1.675–1(b) for a further discussion of this matter.
52. § 676.
53. § 677(a).
54. § 677(b).

2. Generally, the estate or trust acts as a conduit of the taxable income that it receives. Thus, to the extent that such income is distributed by the entity, it is taxable to the beneficiary. Taxable income retained by the entity is taxable to the entity itself.

3. The entity's accounting income first must be determined. Accounting conventions that are stated in the controlling document or, lacking such provisions, in state law allocate specific items of receipt and expenditure either to income or to corpus. Income beneficiaries typically receive payments from the entity that are equal to this accounting income amount.

4. The taxable income of the entity is computed using the computational scheme in Figure I. The entity usually recognizes income in respect of a decedent. Deductions for fiduciary's fees and for charitable contributions may be reduced if the entity received any tax-exempt income during the year. Depreciation deductions are assigned proportionately to the recipients of accounting income. Upon election, realized gain or loss on assets that properly are distributed in kind can be recognized by the entity.

5. A distribution deduction, computationally derived from distributable net income (DNI), is allowed to the entity. DNI is the maximum amount on which entity beneficiaries can be taxed. Moreover, the constitution of DNI is assigned to the recipients of the distributions.

6. Additional taxes are levied under Subchapter J to discourage (1) the transfer of appreciated assets to a lower-bracket estate or trust that quickly disposes of the assets in a taxable exchange, (2) the accumulation of trust income at the lower marginal tax rates of the entity followed by a subsequent distribution of the accumulation to beneficiaries, and (3) the retention of excessive administrative powers by the grantor of a trust when the gross income therefrom is taxed to a lower-bracket beneficiary.

✓ Tax Planning Considerations

Many of the tax planning possibilities for estates and trusts have been discussed in Chapters 11 and 12. However, there are several specific tax planning possibilities that should help to minimize the income tax effects on estates and trusts and their beneficiaries. These items are discussed in the following sections in connection with postmortem tax planning and the use of trusts as income tax savings devices. Several examples illustrating the interrelationship among income, gift, and estate taxes are included.

Income Tax Planning for Estates

As a separate taxable entity, an estate can select its own tax year and accounting methods. The executor of an estate should consider selecting a fiscal year, because this will determine when beneficiaries must include income distributions from the estate in their own tax returns. Beneficiaries must include the income for their tax year with or within which the estate's tax year ends. Proper selection of the estate's tax year thus could result in a smoothing out of income and a reduction of the income taxes for all parties involved.

Caution should be taken in determining when the estate is to be terminated. If a fiscal year had been selected for the estate, a bunching of income to the beneficiaries could occur in the year in which the estate is closed. Although prolonging the termination of an estate can be effective for income tax planning, keep in mind that the IRS carefully examines the purpose of keeping the estate open. Since the unused losses of an estate will pass through to the beneficiaries, the estate should be closed when the beneficiaries can enjoy the maximum tax benefit of such losses.

The timing and amounts of income distributions to the beneficiaries also present important tax planning opportunities. If the executor can make discretionary income distributions, he should evaluate the relative marginal income tax rates of the estate and its beneficiaries. By timing such distributions properly, the overall income tax liability can be minimized. Care should be taken, however, to time such distributions in light of the estate's distributable net income.

Example 43   For several years before his death on March 7, D had entered into annual deferred compensation agreements with his employer. These agreements collectively called for the payment of $200,000 six months after D's retirement or death. To provide a maximum 12-month period within which to generate deductions to offset this large item of income in respect of a decedent, the executor or administrator of the estate should elect a fiscal year ending August 31. The election is made simply by filing the estate's first tax return for the short period of March 7 to August 31. ☐

Example 44   B, the sole beneficiary of an estate, is a calendar year cash basis taxpayer. If the estate elects a fiscal year ending January 31, all distributions during the period of February 1 to December 31, 1987, will be reported on B's tax return for calendar year 1988 (due April 15, 1989). Thus, any income taxes that result from a $50,000 distribution made by the estate on February 20, 1987, will be deferred until April 15, 1989. ☐

Example 45   Assume the same facts as in Example 44. If the estate is closed on December 15, 1988, the distributable net income for both the fiscal year ending January 31, 1988, and the final tax year ending December 15, 1988, will be included in B's tax return for the calendar year 1988. To avoid the effect of this bunching of income, the estate should not be closed until calendar year 1989. ☐

Example 46   Assume the same facts as in Example 45, except that the estate has a substantial net operating loss for the period February 1 to December 15, 1988. If B is subject to a high income tax rate for calendar year 1988, the estate should be closed in that year so that the excess deductions will be passed through to its beneficiary. However, if B anticipates being in a higher tax bracket in 1989, the termination of the estate should be postponed. ☐

Example 47   Review Examples 28 through 30 carefully. Note, for instance, the flexibility that is available to the executor or administrator with respect to the timing of second-tier distributions of income and corpus of the estate. To illustrate, if Dr. L is subject to a high tax rate, distributions to this beneficiary should be minimized except in years when DNI is low. In this manner, Dr. L's exposure to gross income from such distributions can be controlled so that most of the distributions that Dr. L receives will be free of income tax. □

In general, those beneficiaries who are subject to high income tax rates should be made beneficiaries of second-tier (but not IRD) distributions of the estate. Most likely, these individuals will have less of a need for an additional steady stream of (taxable) income, and the income tax savings with respect to these parties can be relatively large. Moreover, a special allocation of tax-favored types of income and expenses should be considered so that, for example, tax-exempt income can be directed more easily to those beneficiaries in higher income tax brackets.

Income Tax Planning with Trusts

The great variety of trusts provides the grantor, trustee, and beneficiaries with excellent opportunities for tax planning. Many of the same tax planning opportunities that are available to the executor of an estate are available to the trustee. For instance, the distributions from a trust are taxable to the trust's beneficiaries to the extent of the trust's distributable net income. Thus, if income distributions are discretionary, the trustee can time such distributions to minimize the income tax consequences to all parties. Remember, however, that the throwback rule applies to complex trusts. Consequently, the timing of distributions may prove to be of a more limited benefit than is available with respect to an estate, and it could result in a greater nominal tax than if the distributions had been made annually. The trustee of a complex trust should thus consider the 65-day rule, which permits the trust to treat distributions made within 65 days of the end of its tax year as if they were made on the last day of such year. Proper use of this provision could help the trustee in both minimizing the overall income tax consequences and avoiding the throwback rule for the beneficiaries.

Tax Year and Payment Planning.   TRA of 1986 reduced the benefits that arise from the traditional, tax-motivated use of trusts and estates through its revisions of the rate schedules that apply to such entities. Specifically, the familiar technique that encourages the accumulation within the entity of the otherwise taxable income of the trust or estate may no longer produce the same magnitude of tax benefits that were available under a more progressive tax rate schedule. Because the lower marginal rates of the trust are exhausted more quickly and are very similar to those that apply to the potential beneficiaries (indeed, they may be higher for the trust), the absolute and relative values of such an income shift are reduced.

Example 48   The C Trust is required to distribute one half of its current accounting income annually to its sole income beneficiary, S. Capital gains and losses are allocable to corpus. During the current taxable year, the trust incurs the following items:

Dividend income	$ 50,000
Taxable interest income	30,000
Tax-exempt interest income	40,000
Net long-term capital gains	20,000
Fiduciary's fees	12,000
Trust accounting income	108,000
Distributable net income	108,000

The Federal income tax incurred by the trust, based upon the nominal 1986, 1987, and 1988 rates, is as follows:

Taxable Income	1986	1987	1988
Dividend income	$50,000	$50,000	$50,000
Interest income	30,000	30,000	30,000
Net long-term capital gains	20,000	20,000	20,000
Long-term capital gains deduction	(12,000)	NONE	NONE
Fiduciary's fees			
(80/120 × $12,000)	(8,000)	(8,000)	(8,000)
Personal exemption	(100)	(100)	(100)
Distribution deduction			
($54,000 × $72,000/$108,000)	(36,000)	(36,000)	(36,000)
Taxable income	$43,900	$55,900	$55,900
Tax liability	$13,796 [1]	$19,832 [2]	$15,652 [3]

(1) $8,184.30 + [42% × ($43,900 − $30,540)]
(2) $4,143 + [38.5% × ($55,900 − $15,150)]
(3) 28% × $55,900

Two other observations are pertinent with respect to the compressed marginal tax rate schedule that applies to fiduciaries after 1986.

1. The effective value of the entity's 15 percent bracket is only $650. Thus, the costs alone of planning to utilize this rate may exceed the eventual tax savings derived from such use. For example, there may no longer be a significant benefit to establishing a number of different trusts to take advantage of the graduated rates, since the costs associated with establishing and administering the trusts may exceed the $650 per trust tax savings.
2. The timing of trust distributions themselves will continue to be important to the planner, however, since the rate differences between the entity and its beneficiaries might be as much as 18 percentage points at any one time (i.e., 33% for the beneficiary — 15% for the entity). Consequently, it still may be a good idea to provide for a sprinkling power in the trust instrument.

The new law does not eliminate completely the use of reversionary trusts as income-shifting devices. However, it does lengthen considerably the period of time for which the income interest must be established. Under the old law, the income interest could not revert within 10 years. Under the new law, the equivalent period is more than 31½ years. Consequently, for all practical purposes, the use of reversionary trusts to shift income to lower tax brackets in the familiar manner will be reduced sharply.

Life Insurance Trusts. In some cases, contrary to traditional tax planning caveats, the classification of a trust as a grantor trust may be welcomed by the taxpayers, especially if the grantor is subject to a higher income tax rate than are the income beneficiaries. This is most likely to occur where an irrevocable life insurance trust resembles the so-called Super Trust (i.e., it is an irrevocable, "defective" grantor trust) that appears to be effective for estate tax, but *not* for income tax, purposes.

If the trust holds whole life insurance, for example, and a policy loan is initiated by the trustee under the terms of which the borrowed cash surrender value is used to pay the premiums, the related interest deductions with respect to the policy loan will be available to the grantor, to whom they are the most valuable. This opportunity will be most attractive when the life insurance trust holds (by choice or necessity) few other income-producing assets, the nondeductibility provisions of §§ 264 and 265 do not apply, and the grantor can claim a major portion of the interest as an itemized or investment interest deduction.

Distributions of In-Kind Property

The ability of the trustee or executor to elect to recognize the realized gain or loss relative to a distributed noncash asset allows the gain or loss to be allocated to the optimal taxpayer.

Example 49   The Y Estate distributed some stock, basis of $40,000 and fair market value of $50,000, to beneficiary L. Y is subject to a 15% marginal income tax rate, and L is subject to a 33% marginal rate. The executor of Y should elect that the entity recognize the related $10,000 realized gain, thereby subjecting the gain to Y's lower marginal tax rate and reducing L's future capital gains income. □

Example 50   Assume the same facts as in Example 49, except that Y's basis in the stock is $56,000. The executor of Y should *not* elect that the entity recognize the related $6,000 loss, thereby shifting the $56,000 basis and the potential loss to L's higher marginal tax rates. □

Problem Materials

Discussion Questions

1. What is the importance of the accounting income of a trust or estate in determining its taxable income?

2. When must an income tax return be filed for an estate? A trust? When could the fiduciary be held liable for the income tax due from an estate or trust?

3. What is the general scheme of the income taxation of trusts and estates? How does the modified conduit principle relate to this general approach?

4. Under what circumstances could an estate or trust be taxed on a distribution of property to a beneficiary?

5. What is income in respect of a decedent? What are the tax consequences to a recipient of income in respect of a decedent?

6. How must an estate or trust treat its deductions for cost recovery? How does this treatment differ from the deductibility of administrative expenses or losses for estate tax purposes?

7. What happens to the net operating loss carryovers of an estate or trust if the entity is terminated before the deductions can be taken? How can this provision be used as a tax planning opportunity?

8. Discuss the income tax treatment of charitable contributions made by an estate or trust. How does this treatment differ from the requirements for charitable contribution deductions of individual taxpayers?

9. What is distributable net income? Why is this amount significant in the income taxation of estates and trusts and their beneficiaries?

10. Distinguish between first-tier and second-tier distributions from estates and complex trusts. Discuss the tax consequences to the beneficiaries receiving such distributions.

11. What is the separate share rule? Why would this rule be of particular significance to a beneficiary who receives both first-tier and second-tier distributions?

12. How must the various classes of income be allocated among multiple beneficiaries of an estate or trust?

13. Under what circumstances would special allocations of particular classes of income to specific beneficiaries be recognized for income tax purposes?

14. What is the purpose of the special tax imposed on trusts by § 644? When is the tax applicable? How can it be avoided?

15. What is the throwback rule? When is it applicable? Why was such a rule adopted?

16. What is the 65-day rule, and under what circumstances can it be useful as a tax planning opportunity?

17. What is a reversionary trust? How can such a trust be established to insure that the income will not be taxed to the grantor?

18. What powers can be retained by the grantor of a trust without causing trust income to be taxed to the grantor?

19. Under what circumstances may the grantor be taxed on all or part of the income of a trust? How might state law help to avoid taxation to the grantor?

20. Discuss the tax planning opportunities presented by the ability of an estate to select a noncalendar tax year.

Problems

1. Indicate for which tax year must the following entities first make estimated Federal income tax payments:

	Entity	Entity Created	Entity Tax Year End
a.	Trust	1–1–88	12–31
b.	Trust	6–1–88	12–31
c.	Estate	1–1–88	12–31
d.	Estate	6–1–88	12–31
e.	Estate	6–1–88	7–31

2. The P Trust operates a welding business. Its current-year ACRS deductions properly amounted to $35,000. P's accounting income was $150,000, of which $80,000 was distributed to first-tier beneficiary Q, $60,000 was distributed to second-tier beneficiary R, and $10,000 was accumulated by the trustee. R also received a $15,000 corpus distribution. P's distributable net income was $52,000. Identify the treatment of P's cost recovery deductions.

3. The J Trust incurred the following items in 1988 using the cash basis of tax accounting:

Taxable interest income	$40,000
Tax-exempt interest income	35,000
Long-term capital gains	25,000
Fiduciary's fees	10,000

The trustee distributed $12,000 to a qualified charitable organization in 1989, designating such payment as from 1988 accounting income. The trust instrument allocates capital gains and fiduciary fees to income. Compute J's 1988 charitable contribution deduction.

4. Assume the same facts as in Problem 3, except that capital gains are allocated to corpus.

5. Assume the same facts as in Problem 4, except that the trust instrument directs that all charitable contributions be paid from J's taxable interest income.

6. The W Trust distributes $40,000 cash and a plot of land, basis of $15,000 and fair market value of $22,000, to its sole beneficiary, X. W's current-year distributable net income is $95,000. For each of the following independent cases, indicate (1) the amount of W's DNI deemed to be distributed to X, (2) W's distribution deduction for the land, and (3) X's basis in the land:

   a. No § 643(e) election is made.

   b. The trustee makes a § 643(e) election.

   c. Same as (a), except that W's basis in the land is $26,000.

   d. Same as (b), except that W's basis in the land is $26,000.

7. Assume the same facts as in Problem 6, except that W is an estate.

8. The X Trust had the following sources of income for the year:

Dividends from a domestic corporation	$150,000
Taxable interest	75,000
Long-term capital gains	15,000
Tax-exempt interest	60,000
Total	$300,000

The trustee's commission for the year amounted to $20,000.

   a. How much of the trustee's commission is allocable to tax-exempt income?

   b. Can such amount be deducted by the trust?

9. The Q Estate uses a fiscal year ending August 31 for Federal income tax purposes. For the year ending August 31, 1988, the estate had accounting income of $80,000 and distributable net income of $76,000. The estate has an unused net operating loss carryover of $40,000 from 1984. Its sole beneficiary, Mrs. Q, recognized an unusually low amount of taxable income from her other 1988 activities. The IRS is applying pressure to terminate the estate on December 31, 1988. What would be the tax conse-

quences of such a termination to the estate and to Mrs. Q? Should the executor attempt to keep the estate open into 1989?

10. The LMN Trust is a simple trust that correctly uses the calendar year for tax purposes. Its three income beneficiaries (L, M, and N) are entitled to the trust's annual accounting income in shares of one-third each. For the current calendar year, the trust has ordinary income of $60,000, a long-term capital gain of $18,000 (allocable to corpus), and a trustee commission expense of $6,000 (allocable to corpus).

    a. How much income is each beneficiary entitled to receive?

    b. What is the trust's distributable net income?

    c. What is the trust's taxable income?

    d. How much will be taxed to each of the beneficiaries?

11. Assume the same facts as in Problem 10, except that the trust instrument allocates the capital gain to income.

    a. How much income is each beneficiary entitled to receive?

    b. What is the trust's distributable net income?

    c. What is the trust's taxable income?

    d. How much will be taxed to each of the beneficiaries?

12. D dies on February 21, 1987. The executor elects the deferred tax payment schedule of § 6166 (refer to Chapter 12). With respect to D's estate, consider the following statements:

    1. A fiscal year can be used by the estate for 1987.

    2. A fiscal year can be used by the estate for 1997.

    3. The estate's income tax liability for 1987 is subject to estimated tax payments.

    4. The estate's income tax liability for 1997 is subject to estimated tax payments.

    Which of the statements is true?

    a. 1, 2, and 4

    b. 1 and 2

    c. 3 and 4

    d. 1, 2, 3, and 4

13. A trust is required to distribute $20,000 annually to its two income beneficiaries, A and B, in shares of 75% and 25%, respectively. If trust income is not sufficient to pay these amounts, the trustee is empowered to invade corpus to the extent necessary. During the current year, the trust has distributable net income of $12,000, and the trustee distributes $15,000 to A and $5,000 to B.

    a. How much of the $15,000 distributed to A must be included in her gross income?

    b. How much of the $5,000 distributed to B must be included in his gross income?

    c. Are these distributions considered to be first-tier or second-tier distributions?

14. Under the terms of the trust instrument, the trustee has discretion to distribute or accumulate income on behalf of W, S, and D in equal shares. The trustee also is empowered to invade corpus for the benefit of any of the beneficiaries to the extent of their respective one-third interest in the trust. In the current year, the trust has distributable net income of $48,000. Of this amount, $16,000 is distributed to W and $10,000 is distributed to S. The

remaining $6,000 of S's share of DNI and D's entire $16,000 share are accumulated by the trust. Additionally, the trustee distributes $20,000 from corpus to W.

a. How much income is taxed to W?

b. To S?

c. To D?

d. To the trust?

15. During the current year, an estate has $60,000 of distributable net income composed of $30,000 in dividends, $20,000 in taxable interest, and $10,000 in tax-exempt interest. The trust's two noncharitable income beneficiaries, S and T, receive $20,000 each.

a. How much of each class of income will be deemed to have been distributed?

b. How much of each class of income is deemed to have been distributed to S? To T?

16. The trustee of the M Trust is empowered to distribute accounting income and corpus to the trust's equal beneficiaries, Mr. P and Dr. G. In the current year, the trust incurs the following:

Taxable interest income	$40,000
Tax-exempt interest income	60,000
Long-term capital gains—allocable to corpus	35,000
Fiduciary's fees—allocable to corpus	12,000

The trustee distributed $25,000 to P and $28,000 to G.

a. What is M's trust accounting income?

b. What is M's distributable net income?

c. What is the amount of taxable income recognized by P from these activities? By G? By M?

17. Ms. D contributes 100 shares of Y Corporation stock to an irrevocable trust on July 1, 1986, income to her son, remainder to her grandson in 12 years. D's basis in the stock is $40,000; the fair market value of the stock at the date of the transfer is $300,000. On June 20, 1988, the trust sells the stock on the open market for $175,000. What is the amount of gain or loss recognized by the trust on the sale? How is the tax computed, and who is liable for it? How would the recognized gain have been treated had the stock been sold for $415,000?

18. Describe a tax planning situation that a tax adviser properly would suggest for each of the following independent cases:

a. A grantor trust be created.

b. Trust accumulations be made, even though the tax on accumulation distributions will be levied on the eventual payments.

c. A transfer of an appreciated asset to a trust be made, even though the § 644 tax will be levied on the entity.

19. In each of the following independent cases, determine whether the grantor of the trust will be taxed on the trust income:

a. G transfers property in trust, income payable to W (his wife) for life, remainder to his grandson. G's son is designated as the trustee.

b. G transfers income-producing assets and a life insurance policy to a trust, life estate to his children, remainder to his grandchildren. The policy is on the life of G's wife, and the trustee (an independent trust company) is instructed to pay the premiums with income from the income-producing assets. The trust is designated as the beneficiary of the policy.

c. G transfers property in trust. The trust income is payable to G's grandchildren, as W (G's wife) sees fit. W and an independent trust company are designated as trustees.

d. G transfers property in trust, income payable to W (G's ex-wife), remainder to G or his estate upon W's death. The transfer was made in satisfaction of G's alimony obligation to W. An independent trust company is designated as the trustee.

20. For each of the following independent statements, indicate whether the tax attribute is applicable only to estates (E), only to complex trusts (T), to both estates and complex trusts (B), or to neither (N):

a. Unrestricted selection of taxable year.

b. The entity's income tax liability may be paid in quarterly installments.

c. The entity must file an income tax return if its gross income for the year is $600 or more.

d. The entity must use the cash method of reporting its income and deductions.

e. The entity is entitled to a personal exemption of $300.

f. A special income tax may be imposed on gains from the sale or exchange of certain appreciated property.

g. In the year of termination, the entity's net operating loss carryovers will be passed through to the beneficiaries.

h. The entity's fiduciary is generally free to select the date of the entity's termination.

i. The entity's deduction for charitable contributions is not subject to a percentage limitation.

j. Distributions from the entity may be subject to the throwback rule.

21. S is the sole income beneficiary of a well-endowed trust. She believes that the trustee should be accumulating the trust accounting income that is being earned so that S can receive it after she retires and, presumably, when she will be subject to a lower income tax rate. S presently is subject to a 40% combined state and Federal rate. Describe how the throwback rule inhibits the trustee from manipulating the timing of income distributions in this manner for each of the following independent cases:

a. S is age 45.

b. S is age 15.

c. The trust allocates capital gains to income.

d. The entity is the estate of S's father.

22. W wishes to transfer some of the income from his investment portfolio to his daughter, age 6. W wants the trust to be able to accumulate income on his daughter's behalf and to meet any excessive expenses associated with the daughter's prep school and private college education. Furthermore, W wants the trust to protect his daughter against his own premature death without increasing his Federal gross estate. Thus, W provides the trustee with the powers to purchase insurance on his life and to meet tuition, fee, and book expenses of his daughter's education. The trust is created in 1987. A whole life insurance policy with five annual premium payments is purchased during that year. The trustee spends $10,000 for the daughter's college expenses in 1999 (but in no other year). W dies in 2005. Has the trust been tax-effective?

23. The O Trust has generated $40,000 in depreciation deductions for the year. Its accounting income is $21,000. In computing this amount, pursuant to the trust document,

depreciation was allocated to corpus. Accounting income was distributed at the trustee's discretion: $15,000 to Mr. H and $6,000 to Ms. J.

   a. Compute the depreciation deductions that H, J, and O may claim.

   b. Same as (a), except that depreciation was allocated to income.

   c. Same as (a), except that the trustee distributed $6,000 each to H and to J and retained the remaining accounting income.

   d. Same as (a), except that O is an estate (and not a trust).

24. Describe the income tax effects of the transfer of the following assets to the indicated fiduciary entities:

	Entity	Tax Attribute
a.	Trust	Depreciation recapture potential
b.	Estate	Depreciation recapture potential
c.	Trust	Deferred installment note income
d.	Estate	Deferred installment note income

Comprehensive Tax Return Problem

Prepare the 1987 Fiduciary Income Tax Return (Form 1041) for the Kathryn Anne Thomas Trust. In addition, determine the amount and character of the income and expense items that each beneficiary must report for 1987 and prepare a Schedule K–1 for Harold Thomas.

The 1987 activities of the trust include the following:

Office building rental income	$600,000
Rental expenses	
Management	85,000
Utilities and maintenance	375,000
Taxes and insurance	115,000
Straight-line cost recovery	200,000
Taxable interest income	100,000
Tax-exempt interest income	50,000
Net long-term capital gains	265,000
Fiduciary's fees	120,000

Under the terms of the trust instrument, depreciation, net capital gains and losses, and one third of the fiduciary's fees are allocable to corpus. The trustee is required to distribute $60,000 to Harold every year. In 1987, the trustee distributed $60,000 to Harold and $35,000 to Patricia Thomas. No other distributions were made.

The trustee, Wisconsin State National Bank, is located at 3100 East Wisconsin Avenue, Milwaukee, WI 53201. Its employer identification number is 84–7602487.

Harold lives at 9880 East North Avenue, Shorewood, WI 53211. His identification number is 498–01–8058.

Patricia lives at 6772 East Oklahoma Avenue, St. Francis, WI 53204. Her identification number is 499–02–6531.

Research Problems

Research Problem 1. Thanks to a recent speech that you gave to the Kiwanis Club, Y has been convinced of the tax-saving opportunities that are presented by the creation of trusts. He recognizes that a great deal of income can be shifted to the marginal income tax rates that apply to his three children, and he is willing to give up as much control over the trust corpus assets as is necessary to avoid a grantor trust classification.

Y is very enthusiastic about trusts—so much so, that he instructs you to place $30,000 into each of 12 trusts for each of his children. These 36 trusts would be administered separately by you, as trustee, but they would differ only in the assets that are used to fund them and in the termination date specified in the trust instrument. Specifically, one of each child's 12 trusts is scheduled to terminate annually, beginning in 15 years. Can the proliferation of multiple trusts, given the same grantor, the same trustee, the same beneficiaries, but different corpus assets and termination dates, be accepted under prevailing tax law?

Partial list of research aids:

Code § 643(f).

Estelle Morris Trusts, 51 T.C. 20 (1968).

Edward L. Stephenson Trust, 81 T.C. 283 (1983).

Research Problem 2. Your client has come to you for some advice regarding gifts of property. She has just learned that she must undergo major surgery, and she would like to make certain gifts before entering the hospital. On your earlier advice, she had established a plan of lifetime giving for four prior years. Consider each of the following assets that she is considering to use as gifts to family and friends. In doing so, evaluate the income tax consequences of having such property pass through her estate to the designated legatee.

  a. She plans to give a cottage to her son to fulfill a promise made many years ago. She has owned the cottage for the past 15 years and has a basis in it of $30,000 (fair market value of $20,000).

  b. Since she has $100,000 of long-term capital losses that she has been carrying forward for the past few years, she is considering making a gift of $200,000 in installment notes to her daughter. Her basis in the notes is $100,000, and the notes' current fair market value is $190,000.

  c. She has promised to make a special cash bequest of $25,000 to her grandson in her will. However, she does not anticipate having that much cash immediately available after her death. She requests your advice concerning the income tax consequences to the estate if the cash bequest is settled with some other property.

Research Problem 3. At a recent seminar entitled "Estate and Income Tax Planning After Tax Reform," you hear a speaker assert, "The Clifford Trust is dead as of March 1, 1986." Because you had become so familiar with the Clifford Trust and used it in conjunction with several of your clients, you wonder whether the speaker has not overstepped her bounds. Evaluate the propriety of the speaker's comment. Restrict your research to trusts created or assets transferred to such trusts after March 1, 1986.

14 Tax Administration and Practice

Tax Administration

To provide quality tax consulting services, it is necessary to understand how the IRS is organized and how its various administrative groups function. For example, a taxpayer may object to a proposed deficiency assessment resulting from an IRS audit. The tax specialist must be familiar with IRS administrative appeal procedures to make a fully informed decision concerning appeal of the deficiency.

Organizational Structure

The responsibility for administering the tax laws rests with the Treasury Department. The Internal Revenue Service, as part of the Department of the Treasury, has been delegated the operational aspects of enforcing the tax law.

Key positions within the IRS organizational chart and the major responsibilities of these positions are summarized in Figures I and II. An organizational chart depicting the interrelationship of the positions described in Figures I and II appears in Figure III.

IRS Procedure—Letter Rulings

Rulings that are issued by the National Office represent a written statement of the position of the IRS concerning the tax consequences of a course of action contemplated by the taxpayer. Letter (i.e., individual) rulings do not have the force and effect of law, but they do provide guidance and support for taxpayers in similar transactions. The IRS will issue rulings only on uncompleted, actual (rather than hypothetical) transactions or on transactions that have been completed before the filing of the tax return for the year in question.

The IRS will not, in certain circumstances, issue a ruling. It will not rule in cases that essentially involve a question of fact.[1] For example, no ruling will be issued to determine whether compensation paid to employees is reasonable in amount and therefore allowable as a deduction.[2]

A letter ruling simply represents the current opinion of the IRS on the tax consequences of a particular transaction with a given set of facts. IRS rulings are not immutable. They are frequently declared obsolete or are superseded by new rulings in response to tax law changes. However, revocation or modification of a ruling is usually not applied retroactively to the taxpayer who received the ruling if he or she acted in good faith in reliance upon the ruling and if the facts in the ruling request were in agreement with the completed transaction. The IRS may revoke any ruling if, upon subsequent audit, the agent finds a misstatement or omission of facts or substantial discrepancies between the facts in the ruling request and the actual situation. A ruling may be relied upon only by the taxpayer who requested and received it and must be attached to the tax return for the year in question.

Issuance of letter rulings benefits both the IRS and the taxpayer. The IRS ruling policy is an attempt to promote a uniform application of the tax laws. In

---

1. Rev.Proc. 88–1, I.R.B. No. 1, 7.
2. Rev.Proc. 88–3, I.R.B. No. 1, 29.

Figure I   Organization of the IRS National Office

	Duties
1. Commissioner of Internal Revenue	Appointed by the President. Establishes policy, supervises the activities of the entire IRS organization, and acts in an advisory capacity to the Treasury on legislative matters.
2. Deputy Commissioner	Provides overall coordination and direction, advises the Commissioner in planning and controlling IRS policies and programs, and provides line supervision over three (3) Associate Commissioners and seven (7) Regional Commissioners.
3. Associate Commissioners A. Operations	Advises the Commissioner on policy matters affecting operations and is responsible for the operating functions (among which are approval and examination of employee plans and exempt organizations, investigation of criminal fraud, examination of tax returns, collection of delinquent accounts, and the tax information program). Under the supervision of this Associate Commissioner are four (4) Assistant Commissioners.
B. Policy and Management	Advises on policy matters affecting agency administration and is responsible for the administrative functions (among which are tax forms and publications design, printing, and distribution; personnel and administration; training and employee development; management information systems; and fiscal management). Three (3) Assistant Commissioners are under the supervision of this Associate Commissioner.
C. Data Processing	Principal adviser on and serves as spokesperson for the data processing functions (among which are designing, developing, testing, and maintaining computer software used; processing of tax returns and information documents; accounting for all revenues collected by the Service; and maintaining master files of all taxpayer accounts). There are two (2) Assistant Commissioners under the supervision of this Associate Commissioner.
4. Chief Counsel	Defends the IRS in the Tax Court and participates with the Department of Justice in other tax litigation, reviews rulings, prepares proposed Regulations, and is charged with the Corporation Tax Division, Individual Tax Division, and Appeals Division.

addition, other benefits may accrue to the government through the issuance of rulings. Rulings may reduce the volume of litigation or number of disputes with revenue agents that would otherwise result, and they give the IRS an awareness of the significant transactions being consummated by taxpayers.

From the taxpayer's point of view, an advance ruling reduces the uncertainty of potential tax consequences resulting from a proposed course of ac-

Figure II Organization of the IRS Field Organization

Duties

1. Regional Commissioners (7)

2. District Directors (63)

3. Service Centers (10)

1. Establish regional standards, programs, and policies and have final settlement authority in the administrative appeal procedure for disputed tax deficiencies.

2. Establish primary contact with taxpayers; collect delinquent taxes; perform audit work, including the selection of taxpayers for audit; issue determination letters to taxpayers.

3. Serve as primary centers for tax return processing work, including selection of returns for audit.

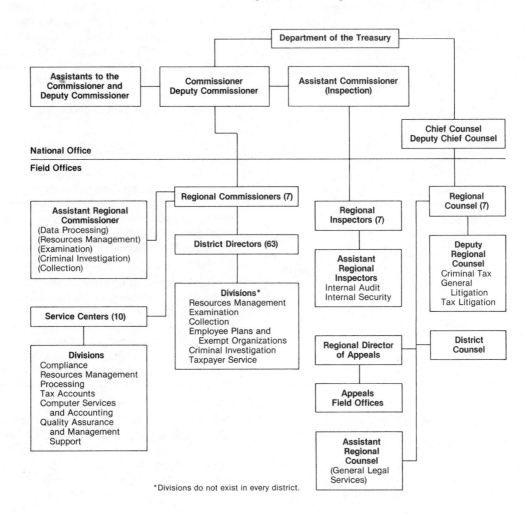

*Divisions do not exist in every district.

tion. Taxpayers frequently request a letter ruling before the consummation of a tax-free corporate reorganization because of the severe tax consequences that would result if the reorganization is subsequently deemed to be taxable. Liquidations, stock redemptions, and transfers to controlled corporations under § 351 are other sensitive areas in which taxpayers want confirmation.

Figure III Internal Revenue Service National Office Organization

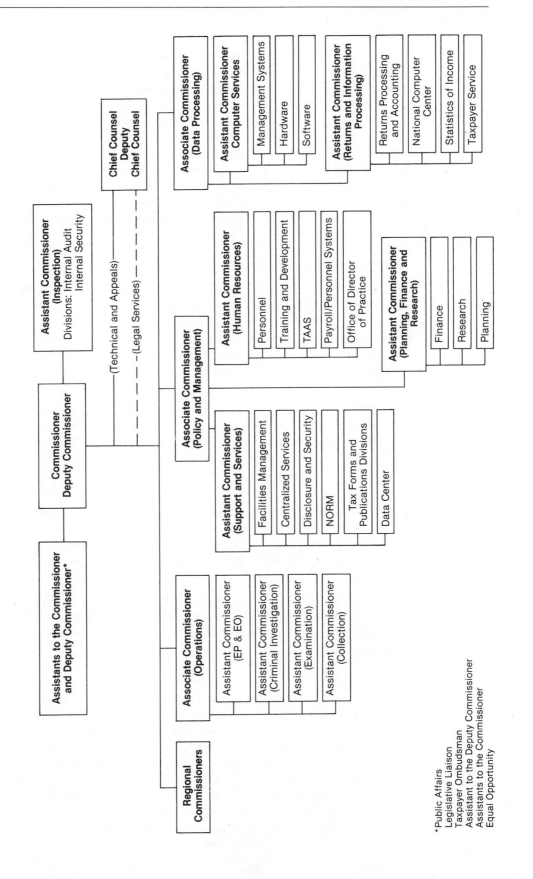

*Public Affairs
Legislative Liaison
Taxpayer Ombudsman
Assistant to the Deputy Commissioner
Assistants to the Commissioner
Equal Opportunity

Letter rulings that are of both sufficient importance and general interest may be published as Revenue Rulings (in anonymous form) and thus made available to all taxpayers. As noted in Chapter 1, Revenue Rulings are released weekly in the *Internal Revenue Bulletin* and later consolidated in permanent form in the *Cumulative Bulletin.*

In general, all unpublished letter rulings, determination letters, and technical advice memoranda are now open to public inspection once identifying details and certain confidential information have been deleted. Letter rulings and technical advice memoranda now are reprinted and published by Prentice-Hall and Commerce Clearing House and are available in the document retrieval services, WESTLAW, LEXIS, and PHINet. The general availability of such materials assists in the conduct of tax research and planning.

IRS Procedure—Additional Issuances

In addition to issuing unpublished letter rulings and published rulings and procedures, the IRS issues determination letters and technical advices.

A determination letter is issued by the District Director for a completed transaction when the issue involved is covered by judicial or statutory authority, regulations, or rulings. A determination letter is issued for various death, gift, income, excise, and employment tax matters.

Example 1   T Corporation recently opened a car clinic and has employed numerous mechanics. The corporation is not certain if the mechanics are to be treated as employees or as independent contractors for withholding and payroll tax purposes. T Corporation may request a determination letter from the appropriate District Director. □

Example 2   Assume the same facts as in Example 1. T Corporation would like to establish a pension plan that qualifies for the tax advantages of §§ 401 through 404. To determine whether the plan qualifies, T Corporation can request and obtain a determination letter from the IRS. □

Example 3   A group of physicians plans to form an association to construct and operate a hospital. The determination letter procedure is appropriate to ascertain the group's status—either subject to the Federal income tax or tax-exempt. □

Technical advice is rendered by the National Office to the District Director and/or Regional Commissioner in response to the specific request of an agent, Appellate Conferee, or District Director. The taxpayer may ask that a request for technical advice be made if an issue in dispute is not treated by the law or precedent and/or published rulings or Regulations. Technical advice also is appropriate when there is reason to believe that the tax law is not being administered consistently by the IRS. For example, a taxpayer may inquire why an agent proposes to disallow a certain expenditure when agents in other districts permit the deduction. Technical advice requests arise from the audit process, while ruling requests are issued before any IRS audit.

Administrative Powers of the IRS

Examination of Records.   For the purpose of determining the correct amount of tax due, the Code authorizes the IRS to examine the taxpayer's books and records and to summon those persons responsible to appear before the IRS and, when they appear, to produce the necessary books and records.[3] Taxpayers are required to maintain certain recordkeeping procedures and retain those records that are necessary to facilitate the audit. Therefore, the taxpayer and not the IRS has the burden of proof to substantiate any item on the tax return that is under examination. It should be noted that the files, workpapers, and other memoranda of a tax practitioner may be subpoenaed, since the courts have not extended to CPAs the privileged communication doctors and lawyers sometimes possess with respect to their clients.

Assessment and Demand.   The Code permits the IRS to assess a deficiency and to demand payment for the tax.[4] However, no assessment or effort to collect the tax may be made until 90 days following the issuance of a statutory notice of a deficiency (i.e., a 90-day letter). The taxpayer is therefore given 90 days to file a petition to the U.S. Tax Court that effectively prevents the deficiency from being assessed or collected pending the outcome of the case.[5]

Certain exceptions to this assessment procedure should be noted:

—The IRS may issue a deficiency assessment without waiting 90 days if mathematical errors on the return incorrectly state the tax at less than the true liability.

—If the IRS believes the assessment or collection of a deficiency is in jeopardy, it may assess the deficiency and demand immediate payment.[6] The taxpayer is able to stay the collection of the jeopardy assessment by filing a bond for the amount of the tax and interest. This action will prevent the sale of any property that has been seized by the IRS.

Following assessment of the tax, the IRS will issue a notice and demand for payment. The taxpayer is usually given 10 days following the notice and demand for payment to pay the tax.

IRS Collection Procedures.   If the taxpayer neglects or refuses to pay the tax after the receipt of the 10-day notice and demand letter, a lien develops in favor of the IRS upon all property (whether realty or personalty, tangible or intangible) belonging to the taxpayer. This lien, commonly referred to as a statutory lien, is not valid until the IRS files Form 668 (Notice of Federal Tax Lien Under Internal Revenue Laws).

The levy power of the IRS is very broad. It allows the IRS to garnish (i.e., attach) wages and salary and to seize and sell all nonexempt property *by any means*. Also, the IRS can make successive seizures on any property owned by the taxpayer until the levy is satisfied. Property that is exempt from levy is

---

3. § 7602.
4. § 6212.
5. § 6213.
6. § 6861.

basically limited to living necessities such as wearing apparel, personal effects, tools of a trade, unemployment benefits, child support payments, certain pension payments, and the first $75 per week in wages (plus $25 per week for the taxpayer's spouse and each dependent). However, in exceptional cases, an extension in the payment of a deficiency will be granted to prevent undue hardship.[7]

If property is transferred and the tax is not paid, the subsequent owners of the property may be liable for the tax. This pursuit of the tax liability against succeeding owners is referred to as transferee liability. For example, if an estate is insolvent and unable to pay the estate tax, the executor or the beneficiaries may be liable for such payment.[8]

The Audit Process

Selection of Returns for Audit.   The IRS uses the Discriminant Function System (DIF) as a starting point in the selection of tax returns for audit (i.e., examination). This selection procedure utilizes mathematical formulas to select tax returns that are most likely to contain errors and yield substantial amounts of additional tax revenues upon audit. Despite the use of computer selection processes, the ultimate selection of returns for audit is still conducted by the classification staff within the Audit Division of the IRS.

The IRS does not openly disclose all of its audit selection techniques. However, the following observations can be made regarding the probability of a return's selection for audit:

—Certain groups of taxpayers are subject to audit more frequently than others. These groups include individuals with gross income in excess of $50,000, self-employed individuals with substantial business income and deductions, and cash businesses where the potential for tax evasion is high.

Example 4   T owns and operates a liquor store on a cash-and-carry basis. As all of T's sales are for cash, T might well be a prime candidate for an audit by the IRS. Cash transactions are easier to conceal than those made on credit. □

—If a taxpayer has been audited in a past year and such audit led to the assessment of a substantial deficiency, a return visit by the IRS is to be expected.

—An audit might materialize if information returns (e.g., Form W–2, Form 1099) are not in substantial agreement with the income reported on the taxpayer's return. Over the years, the IRS has been able to correlate an increasing number of information returns with the returns filed by taxpayers. Obvious discrepancies do not necessitate formal audits but usually can be handled by correspondence with the taxpayer.

—If an individual's itemized deductions are in excess of norms established for various income levels, the probability of an audit is increased. Also, certain

---

7. § 6161(b).
8. § 6901.

types of deductions (e.g., casualty and theft losses, office in the home, tax-sheltered investments) are sensitive areas, since the IRS realizes that many taxpayers will determine the amount of the deduction incorrectly or may not be entitled to the deduction at all.

—The filing of a refund claim by the taxpayer may prompt an audit of the return.

—Certain returns are selected on a random sample basis [known as the Taxpayer Compliance Measurement Program (TCMP)] to develop, update, and improve the DIF formulas (see above). TCMP is the long-range research effort of the IRS designed to measure and evaluate taxpayer compliance characteristics. TCMP audits are tedious and time-consuming, since the taxpayer generally is asked to verify most or all items on the tax return.

—Information is often obtained from other sources (e.g., other government agencies, news items, informants). The IRS can pay rewards to persons who provide information that leads to the detection and punishment of those who violate the tax laws. Such rewards are discretionary by a District Director and will not exceed 10 percent of the taxes, fines, and penalties recovered as a result of such information.[9]

Example 5   T reports to the police that while he was out of town his home was burglarized and one of the items taken was a shoe box containing cash of $25,000. A representative of the IRS reading the newspaper account of the burglary might well wonder why someone would keep such a large amount of cash in a shoe box at home. □

Example 6   After 15 years, B is discharged by her employer, Dr. F. Shortly thereafter, the IRS receives a letter from B informing it that Dr. F keeps two sets of books, one of which substantially understates his cash receipts. □

Many individual taxpayers mistakenly assume that if they do not hear from the IRS within a few weeks following the filing of the return or if they have received a refund check, no audit will be forthcoming. As a practical matter, most individual returns are examined within two years from the date of filing. If not, they generally remain unaudited. All large corporations are subject to annual audits; and in many instances, tax years will remain open for long periods, since the taxpayer may agree to extend the statute of limitations pending settlement of unresolved issues.

Verification and Audit Procedures.   The tax return is initially checked for mathematical accuracy. A check is also made for deductions, exclusions, etc., that are clearly erroneous. An obvious error would be the failure to comply with the 7.5 percent limitation on the deduction for medical expenses. In such cases, the Service Center merely sends the taxpayer revised computations and a bill for the corrected amount of tax if the error results in additional tax liability. As previously noted, taxpayers usually are able to settle such matters

---

9. § 7623 and Reg. § 301.7623–1.

through direct correspondence with the IRS without the necessity of a formal audit.

Office audits are conducted by a representative (designated tax technicians) of the District Director's Office either in the office of the IRS or through correspondence. Individual returns with few or no items of business income are usually handled through the office audit procedure. In most instances, the taxpayer will be required merely to substantiate a deduction, credit, or item of income that appears on the return. An individual may have claimed medical expenses that are in excess of a normal amount for taxpayers on a comparable income level. The taxpayer will be asked to present documentation in the form of cancelled checks, invoices, etc., for the items in question. Note the substantiation procedure here that is absent from the mathematical check and simple error discovery process previously mentioned.

The field audit procedure is commonly used for corporate returns and for returns of individuals engaged in business or professional activities. This type of audit generally entails a more complete examination of a taxpayer's transactions. By way of contrast, an office audit usually is directed towards fewer items and is therefore narrower in scope.

A field audit is conducted by IRS agents at the office or home of the taxpayer or at the office of the taxpayer's representative. It is common practice for tax firms to hold conferences with IRS agents in the firm's office during the field audit of a corporate client. The agent's work may be facilitated by a review of certain tax workpapers and discussions with the taxpayer's representative relative to items appearing on the tax return.

Upon a showing of good cause, a taxpayer may request and obtain a reassignment of his or her case from an office to a field audit. The inconvenience and expense involved in transporting records and other supporting data to the agent's office may constitute good cause for reassignment.

Settlement with the Revenue Agent. Following the audit, the IRS agent may either accept the return as filed or recommend certain adjustments. The Revenue Agent's Report (RAR) is reviewed by the agent's group supervisor and the Review Staff within the IRS. In most instances, the agent's proposed adjustments are approved. However, it is not uncommon for the Review Staff or group supervisor to request additional information or to raise new issues.

Agents must adhere strictly to IRS policy as reflected in published rulings, Regulations, and other releases. The agent cannot settle an unresolved issue based upon the probability of winning the case in court. Usually, issues involving factual questions can be settled at the agent level, and it may be advantageous for both the taxpayer and the IRS to reach agreement at the earliest point in the settlement process. For example, it may be to the taxpayer's advantage to reach agreement at the agent level and avoid any further opportunity for the IRS to raise new issues.

A deficiency (an amount in excess of tax shown on the return or tax previously assessed) may be proposed at the agent level. The taxpayer might wish to pursue to a higher level the disputed issues upon which this deficiency is based. The taxpayer's progress through the appeal process is discussed in subsequent sections of this chapter.

If agreement is reached upon the proposed deficiency, Form 870 (Waiver of Restrictions on Assessment and Collection of Deficiency in Tax) is signed by the taxpayer. One advantage to the taxpayer of signing Form 870 at this point is that interest stops accumulating on the deficiency 30 days after the form is filed.[10] When this form is signed, the taxpayer effectively waives his or her right to the receipt of a statutory notice of deficiency (90-day letter) and to subsequent petition to the Tax Court. In addition, it is no longer possible for the taxpayer to go to the Appeals Division. The signing of Form 870 at the agent level generally closes the case. However, since Form 870 does not have the effect of a closing agreement, even after the taxpayer pays the deficiency, the taxpayer may subsequently sue for refund of the tax in a Federal District Court or in the Claims Court. Further, the IRS is not restricted by Form 870 and may assess additional deficiencies if deemed necessary.

The Taxpayer Appeal Process

If agreement cannot be reached at the agent level, the taxpayer receives a copy of the Revenue Agent's Report and a transmittal letter, which is commonly referred to as the 30-day letter. The taxpayer is granted 30 days to request an administrative appeal. If an appeal is not requested, a statutory notice of deficiency will be issued (90-day letter).

If an appeal is desired, an appropriate request must be made to the Appeals Division. Such request must be accompanied by a written protest except in the following cases:

—The proposed tax deficiency does not exceed $10,000 for any of the tax periods involved in the audit.

—The deficiency resulted from a correspondence or office audit (i.e., not as a result of a field audit).

The Appeals Division is authorized to settle all tax disputes based on the hazards of litigation. Since the Appeals Division has final settlement authority until a statutory notice of deficiency (90-day letter) has been issued, the taxpayer may be able to obtain a percentage settlement. In addition, an overall favorable settlement may be reached through a "trading" of disputed issues. The Appeals Division occasionally may raise new issues if the grounds are substantial and of significant tax impact.

Both the Appeals Division and the taxpayer have the right to request technical advice from the National Office of the IRS. When technical advice is favorable to the taxpayer, the Appeals Division is bound by such advice. However, if the technical advice is favorable to the IRS, the Appeals Division may nevertheless settle the case based on the hazards of litigation.

In a hazard of litigation situation, the facts are known but the application of the law to such facts may be uncertain. Also, there could be some question about establishing the facts with clear certainty, as might be the case when the taxpayer or a witness is not expected to give convincing testimony. Another possibility might involve situations where the facts are so ambiguous that they could, by different interpretation, lead to contrary tax results.

---

10. § 6601(c).

Example 7   At the time of the audit of T, the corporation that T controls had advances outstanding to T in the amount of $80,000. The IRS field agent held that these advances were constructive dividends to T (refer to the discussion in Chapter 4). Some facts point toward this result (e.g., the corporation is closely-held, T has made no repayments, and the loan balance has increased over several years). Other facts, however, appear to indicate that these advances are bona fide loans (e.g., the advances are evidenced by a written instrument with interest provided for, T has the independent means of repayment, and the corporation has a good dividend-paying record). The Appeals Division and taxpayer's representative assess the hazards of litigation as being 50% for each side. Thus, if T chose to take the issue to court, she would have an even chance of winning or losing her case. Based on this assessment, both sides agree to treat $40,000 of the advance as a dividend and $40,000 as a bona fide loan. The agreement enables T to avoid $40,000 of dividend income (i.e., the loan portion) and saves her the cost of litigating the issue.   □

By going to the Appeals Division, therefore, the taxpayer in Example 7 was able to obtain a satisfactory settlement otherwise unobtainable from the agent.

If agreement cannot be reached with the Appeals Division, the IRS issues a statutory notice of deficiency (90-day letter), which gives the taxpayer 90 days to file a petition with the Tax Court. (See Figure IV for a review of the income tax appeal procedures, including the consideration of claims for refund.) After the case has been docketed in the Tax Court, the taxpayer has the opportunity to arrange for possible pretrial settlement with the Regional Counsel of the IRS (the attorney who will represent the United States in the Tax Court trial). The Appeals Division settlement power is transferred to the Regional Counsel when the case is docketed for a Tax Court trial after the issuance of the statutory notice of deficiency.

Taxpayers who file a petition with the U.S. Tax Court have the option of having their case heard before the informal Small Claims Division if the amount of the deficiency or claimed overpayment does not exceed $10,000.[11] If the Small Claims Division is used, neither party may appeal the case, and the decisions of the Small Claims Division are not treated as precedents for other cases.

The economic costs of a settlement offer from the Appeals Division should be weighed against the costs of litigation and the probability of winning the case. Consideration should be given to the impact of such settlement upon the tax liability for future periods in addition to the years under audit.

If a settlement is reached with the Appeals Division, the taxpayer is required to sign Form 870AD. Interest will stop running on the deficiency when the Form 870AD is accepted by the Appeals Division. The IRS considers this settlement to be binding upon both parties, absent fraud, malfeasance, concealment, or misrepresentation of material fact. The question of whether this settlement form is binding upon the taxpayer (whether settlement prevents the

11. § 7463(a).

Figure IV

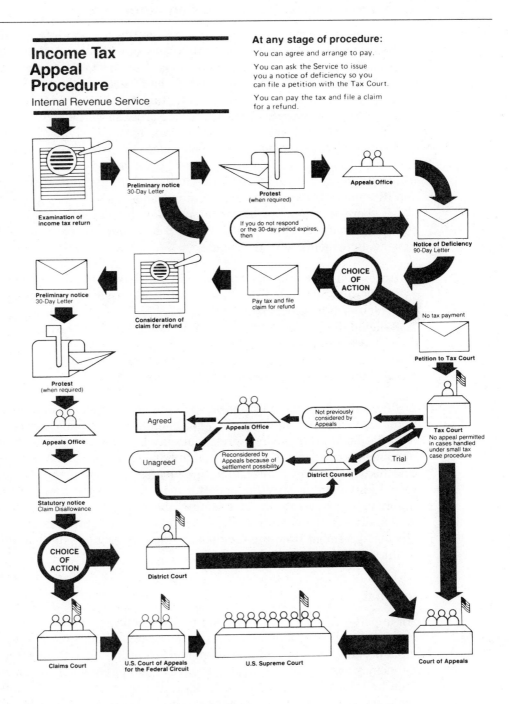

Income Tax Appeal Procedure
Internal Revenue Service

At any stage of procedure:
You can agree and arrange to pay.

You can ask the Service to issue you a notice of deficiency so you can file a petition with the Tax Court.

You can pay the tax and file a claim for a refund.

taxpayer from filing a subsequent refund claim and suit for refund) has been litigated with conflicting results.[12]

12. Compare *Stair v. U.S.,* 75–1 USTC ¶ 9463, 35 AFTR2d 75–1515, 516 F.2d 560 (CA–2, 1975), with *Unita Livestock Corp. v. U.S.,* 66–1 USTC ¶ 9193, 17 AFTR2d 254, 355 F.2d 761 (CA–10, 1966).

Offers in Compromise and Closing Agreements

The Code provides specific authority for the IRS to negotiate a compromise if there is doubt in the taxpayer's ability to pay the tax.[13] If the taxpayer is financially unable to pay the total amount of the tax, a Form 656 (Offer in Compromise) must be filed with the District Director or the IRS Service Center. The IRS investigates the claim by evaluating the taxpayer's financial ability to pay the tax. In some instances, the compromise settlement will include an agreement for final settlement of the tax through payments of a specified percentage of the taxpayer's future earnings. The District Director must obtain approval from the IRS Regional Counsel if the amount involved exceeds $500. This settlement procedure usually entails lengthy periods of negotiation with the IRS and is generally used only in extreme cases.

If there is doubt as to the amount of tax liability involved, a closing agreement may be appropriate. The IRS has enumerated situations in which closing agreements will be issued: [14]

1. An executor or administrator requires a determination of the tax liability either to facilitate the distribution of estate assets or to relieve himself or herself of fiduciary responsibility.
2. A liquidating corporation needs a determination of tax liability to proceed with the process of dissolution.
3. A taxpayer wishes to close returns on an annual basis.
4. Creditors demand evidence of the tax liability.

A closing agreement is binding on both the government and the IRS, except upon a subsequent showing of fraud, malfeasance, or misrepresentation of a material fact.[15] The closing agreement may be added to Form 870 in reaching agreement upon the entire amount of tax due for a year under audit, used when disputed issues carry over to future years, and employed to dispose of a dispute involving a specific issue for a prior year or a proposed transaction involving future years. If, for example, the IRS is willing to make substantial concessions in the valuation of assets for death tax purposes, it may require a closing agreement from the recipient of the property to establish the tax basis of the assets for income tax purposes.

Interest

An important consideration for the taxpayer during negotiations with the IRS is the interest that accrues upon overpayments, deficiency assessments, and unpaid taxes. A taxpayer can effectively stop the accrual of interest upon a deficiency assessment by signing Form 870 and paying the tax. This action can then be followed by a suit in a Federal district court or the Claims Court for recovery of the amount of the tax payment. If the Tax Court is selected as a forum, the tax usually is not paid and interest continues to accrue.

---

13. § 7122.
14. Rev.Proc. 68–16, 1968–1 C.B. 770.
15. § 7121(b).

Determination of the Interest Rate. Several years ago, Congress began to recognize that the interest rate applicable to Federal tax underpayments and overpayments should be made more realistic in terms of what occurs in the business world. Accordingly, the Code was changed to authorize the IRS to adjust the percentage every two years to conform with commercial rates. A later amendment changed the guidelines to provide for annual adjustments (as of each January 1) based on the average prime rate for the preceding September. Further legislation went one step further to sanction semiannual adjustments as of January 1 and July 1 of each year.

To make the interest rates even more reflective of the marketplace, TRA of 1986 provides for a quarterly determination of such rates. Thus, the rates that are determined during January are effective for the following April through June. The interest rates are to be based on the Federal short-term rates as published periodically by the IRS in Revenue Rulings appearing in the *Internal Revenue Bulletin*. They are based on the average market yield on outstanding marketable obligations of the United States with remaining maturity of three years or less. This is the mechanism for arriving at short-term Federal rates, which are used to test the adequacy of interest in certain debt instruments issued for property and certain other obligations.

TRA of 1986 further changes the parity that previously existed between tax deficiencies and refunds. Now, underpayments are subject to the Federal short-term rates plus three percentage points, and overpayments carry the Federal short-term rates plus two percentage points. Consequently, the rate for tax deficiencies will be one percentage point higher than the rate for tax refunds.[16] For the first quarter of 1988, interest on tax deficiencies has been set at 11 percent, and interest on refunds will be 10 percent. Prior interest rates are summarized in Figure V.

Figure V is not of mere historical interest. In cases of deficiency assessments or claims for refund, interest is computed in accordance with the rates in effect during the period involved.

Example 8 T, a calendar year taxpayer, is audited by the IRS in March 1988 and is assessed a deficiency for the return he timely filed for calendar year 1984. Since interest begins to run from the due date of the return (April 15, 1985, in T's case), the applicable rates are 13%, 11%, 10%, 9%, 10%, and 11%. □

For assessments where the statute of limitations is not applicable (e.g., no return was filed or fraud was involved—see later in the chapter), determining the interest element could prove to be a mathematical nightmare.

Example 9 T, a calendar year taxpayer, did not file a gift tax return (Form 709) for a taxable gift made in 1974. On audit by the IRS in late 1987, she is assessed a deficiency. The interest computation on the deficiency would have to cover the full range of Figure V. □

Computation of the Amount of Interest. Prior law required that any interest on a deficiency or a refund be determined using the simple-interest method.

---

16. § 6621.

Figure V Prior Interest Rates

	Rates		
Applicable Period	Underpayments	Overpayments	Both Underpayments and Overpayments
October 1, 1987, thru December 31, 1987	10%	9%	—
January 1, 1987, thru September 30, 1987	9	8	—
July 1, 1986, thru December 31, 1986	—	—	9%
January 1, 1986, thru June 30, 1986	—	—	10
July 1, 1985, thru December 31, 1985	—	—	11
January 1, 1985, thru June 30, 1985	—	—	13
July 1, 1983, thru December 31, 1984	—	—	11
January 1, 1983, thru June 30, 1983	—	—	16
February 1, 1982, thru December 31, 1982	—	—	20
February 1, 1980, thru January 31, 1982	—	—	12
February 1, 1978, thru January 31, 1980	—	—	6
February 1, 1976, thru January 31, 1978	—	—	7
July 1, 1975, thru January 31, 1976	—	—	9
Before July 1975	—	—	6

For interest accruing after 1982, current law requires that the amount be compounded daily.[17] Depending on the interest rate applicable, the daily compounding approach conceivably could double the principal amount over a period of five years or so. Consequently, this change in the method of computing interest should not be taken lightly.

The IRS has prepared and made available tables through which the daily compounded amount can be determined. Such tables will ease the burden of those who prepare late returns where additional taxes are due.[18]

The old rule (i.e., the simple-interest method) continues to apply to the penalty on underpayments of estimated tax by individuals and corporations. However, the quarterly interest rate adjustments (discussed above) will have to be used in arriving at the amount of the underpayment of estimated tax penalty.

---

17. § 6622.
18. These tables can be found in Rev.Proc. 83–7, 1983–1 C.B. 583.

IRS Deficiency Assessments. Interest usually accrues from the unextended due date of the return until 30 days after the taxpayer agrees to the deficiency by signing Form 870. If the taxpayer does not pay the amount shown on the IRS's "notice and demand" (tax bill) within 10 days, interest again accrues on the deficiency. However, no interest is imposed upon the portion of the tax bill that represents interest on the previous deficiency.

The accumulated earnings tax (§ 531) is imposed on corporations that accumulate beyond the reasonable needs of the business rather than pay dividends to the shareholders (refer to Chapter 7). In the past, interest was imposed only when the IRS assessed and demanded payment of the tax. Under TRA of 1986, interest will begin to run on the § 531 tax from the due date (without regard to extensions) of the income tax return for the year the tax is initially imposed. This amendment shall apply to returns the due date for which (determined without regard to extensions) is after December 31, 1985.

Example 10   Z Corporation, a calendar year taxpayer, files its 1983 income tax return on March 1, 1984. Z Corporation's 1983 Form 1120 is audited in 1985, the § 531 tax is assessed, and demand for payment is made on August 1, 1985. Since prior law applies, interest begins to run as of August 1, 1985.   □

Example 11   Q Corporation, a calendar year taxpayer, files its 1986 income tax return on March 1, 1987. Q Corporation's 1986 Form 1120 is audited in 1988, the § 531 tax is assessed, and demand for payment is made on August 1, 1988. Since the new law applies, interest begins to run as of March 15, 1987 (the due date of the return).   □

Refund of Taxpayer's Overpayments. If the overpayment is refunded to the taxpayer within 45 days after the date the return is filed or is due, no interest is allowed. Interest is authorized, however, when the taxpayer files an amended return or makes a claim for refund of prior year's tax (e.g., when net operating loss or investment tax credit carrybacks result in refunds of prior year's tax payments).

In the past and in light of high interest rates of up to 20 percent (refer to Figure V), it has proven advantageous for many taxpayers to delay filing various tax returns that lead to refunds. Thus, the IRS was placed in the unfortunate role of providing taxpayers with a high-yield savings account. Amendments to the tax law are intended to end this practice. The gist of the amendments is to preclude any interest accruing on a refund until such time as the IRS is properly notified of the refund.

Specifically the current law places taxpayers applying for refunds in the following described positions:

—When a return is filed after the due date, interest on any overpayment accrues from the date of filing. However, no interest will be due if the IRS makes the refund within 45 days of the date of filing.

Example 12   T, a calendar year taxpayer, files her return for 1986 on December 2, 1987, such return reflecting an overwithholding of $2,500. On June 10, 1988, T receives a refund of her 1986 overpayment. Under these circumstances, the interest on T's refund began to accrue on December 2, 1987. □

Example 13   Assume the same facts as in Example 12, except that the refund is paid to T on January 8, 1988 (rather than June 10, 1988). No interest would be due, since the refund was made within 45 days of the filing of the return. □

—In no event will interest accrue on an overpayment unless the return that is filed is in "processible form." Generally, this means that the return must contain enough information to enable the IRS to identify the taxpayer and to determine the tax (and overpayment) involved.

—In the case of a carryback (e. g., net operating loss, capital loss, certain tax credits), interest on any refund will begin to accrue on the due date of the return (disregarding extensions) for the year in which such carryback arises. Even then, however, no interest will accrue until a return is filed or, if already filed, the IRS pays the refund within 45 days.

Example 14   X Corporation, a calendar year taxpayer, incurs a net operating loss during 1987 which it can carry back to tax year 1984 for a refund. On December 27, 1988, it files a Form 1139 (Corporate Application for Tentative Refund) claiming the refund. The earliest that interest can begin to accrue in this situation is March 15, 1988, but since the return was not filed until December 27, 1988, the later date controls. If, however, the IRS pays the refund within 45 days of December 27, 1988, no interest is due. □

Penalties

A penalty is treated as an addition to the tax liability rather than a possible deductible interest expense. Some taxpayers mistakenly believe that penalties are deductible and do not fully appreciate the consequences of actions that trigger the imposition of such penalties.

Failure to File and Failure to Pay.   For a failure to file a tax return by the due date (including extensions), a penalty of five percent per month (up to a maximum of 25 percent) is imposed on the amount of tax shown as due on the return.[19]

For a failure to pay the tax due as shown on the return, a penalty of one half of one percent per month (up to a maximum of 25 percent) is imposed on the amount of the tax. A comparable penalty is assessed if the taxpayer fails to pay a deficiency assessment within 10 days.

In all of these cases, a fraction of a month counts as a full month. Also note that these penalties relate to the net amount of the tax due.

Example 15   T, a calendar year self-employed taxpayer, prepays $18,000 for income taxes during 1987. Her total tax liability for 1987 proves to be $20,000. Without obtaining an extension from the IRS, she files her Form 1040 in

19. § 6651(a).

early August of 1988 and encloses a check for the balance due of $2,000. The failure to file and the failure to pay penalties apply to the $2,000. □

During any month in which both the failure to file penalty and the failure to pay penalty apply, the failure to file penalty is reduced by the amount of the failure to pay penalty.[20]

Example 16   R files his tax return 10 days after the due date. Along with the return he remits a check for $3,000, which is the balance of the tax R owes. Disregarding the interest element, R's total penalties are as follows:

Failure to pay penalty (½ of 1% × $3,000)		$ 15
Plus:		
Failure to file penalty (5% × $3,000)	$150	
Less failure to pay penalty for the same period	15	
Failure to file penalty		135
Total penalties		$150

□

In Example 16, note that the penalties for one full month are imposed even though R was delinquent by only 10 days. Unlike the method used to compute interest, any part of a month is treated as a whole month.

Because the existing penalty for failure to file may not serve as a significant enough deterrent when the tax due is small or the delay in filing is short, the law was amended to provide for a minimum penalty. The minimum penalty is the *lesser* of $100 or the amount of tax still due.

The minimum penalty will apply only if the return is not filed within 60 days (with allowed extensions) of its due date. A showing of reasonable cause will excuse its imposition.

The minimum penalty is not in addition to the regular failure to file penalty. It merely is in lieu of such penalty in the event that a higher amount is the result.

When the minimum failure to file penalty applies, the amount of the failure to file penalty (when applicable) is not reduced by the failure to pay penalty. Rather, both penalties apply concurrently, and the combined total is due and owing.

Example 17   T, a calendar year individual taxpayer, files her 1987 return 70 days after its due date. T did not obtain an extension of time for filing her return, and such return reflects additional income tax due of $300. The regular penalty for T's delinquency would have been $45 (as determined under the procedure used in Example 16 using three months). Through the application of the minimum penalty, T's failure to file penalty will be $100. To

---

20. An exception exists to the double imposition rule when the IRS has issued a notice and demand for payment, 10 days have expired, and payment has not taken place by the following month.

this must be added a failure to pay penalty of $4.50 [1.5% (0.5% per month for three months) × $300], for total penalties of $104.50. ☐

These penalties can be avoided upon a showing by the taxpayer that the failure to file and/or failure to pay was due to reasonable cause and not due to willful neglect. The Code is silent on what constitutes reasonable cause, and the Regulations do little to clarify this important concept.[21] Court decisions, however, do set some specific criteria, summarized as follows:

—The reliance by the taxpayer on the advice of a *competent* tax adviser given in good faith, provided the facts are fully disclosed to the adviser and he or she considered that the specific question represents reasonable cause.[22] No reasonable cause was found, however, where the taxpayer delegated the filing task to another, even if such person were an accountant or an attorney.[23]

—Not qualifying as reasonable cause includes lack of information on the due date of the return,[24] illness that does not incapacitate a taxpayer from completing a return,[25] refusal of the taxpayer's spouse to cooperate for a joint return,[26] and ignorance or misunderstanding of the tax law.[27]

As previously noted, an extension of time granted by the IRS will avoid the failure to file penalty. It will not, however, exonerate the taxpayer from the failure to pay penalty. But if a taxpayer, for whatever reason, is not in a position to complete the return, how is he or she able to determine the tax liability? The Regulations mercifully provide some latitude in resolving this quandary. If the extension is of the "automatic" four-month variety, the penalty for failure to pay will not be imposed if the additional tax liability due is no greater than 10 percent of the tax shown on the return.[28]

Example 18 S, a calendar year taxpayer, is self-employed and during 1987 makes quarterly payments of estimated taxes of $40,000. In early April of 1988, she applies for and obtains a four-month extension for filing her 1987 income tax return. In late May of 1988, S completes her 1987 return and delivers it to the IRS along with a check covering the additional tax that is due of $3,900. Under these circumstances, S has circumvented both the failure to file and the failure to pay penalties. She will, however, owe interest on the $3,900 that was paid late. ☐

---

21. Reg. § 301.6651–1(c)(1) likens reasonable cause to the exercise of "ordinary business care and prudence" on the part of the taxpayer.
22. *Estate of Norman Bradley*, 35 TCM 70, T.C.Memo. 1974–17.
23. *U.S. v. Boyle*, 85–1 USTC ¶ 13,602, 55 AFTR2d 85–1535, 105 S.Ct. 687 (USSC, 1985).
24. *Beck Chemical Equipment Co.*, 27 T.C. 840 (1957).
25. *Jacob Gassman*, 26 TCM 213, T.C.Memo. 1967–42, and *Babetta Schmidt*, 28 T.C. 367 (1957). Compare *Estate of Kirchner*, 46 B.T.A. 578 (1942).
26. *Electric and Neon, Inc.*, 56 T.C. 1324 (1971).
27. *Stevens Brothers Foundation, Inc.*, 39 T.C. 93 (1965).
28. Reg. § 301.6651–1(c)(3)(i). The Regulation is premised on the assumption that satisfying the 10% rule constitutes reasonable cause.

When the 10 percent rule is not satisfied, the failure to pay penalty will be imposed on the *full* amount due.

Example 19   Assume the same facts as in Example 18, except that S's additional tax liability proved to be $5,000 (rather than $3,900). In this event, a failure to pay penalty will be imposed on the full $5,000 that was paid late.   □

Negligence Penalty.   Prior law provided a negligence penalty of five percent when the underpayment of tax was due to negligence or intentional disregard of rules and regulations (but without intent to defraud). For interest and dividend payments supported by information returns, taxpayers had to meet a higher standard. Here, the penalty was automatically imposed unless clear and convincing evidence was presented that no negligence was involved. The negligence penalty applied only to underpayment of income taxes, gift taxes, and the windfall profits tax.

TRA of 1986 generally redrafts the negligence penalty to make it clearer and more comprehensible. One element of that redrafting involves the provision of a definition of negligence. The amendment includes within the scope of negligence both any failure to make a reasonable attempt to comply with the provisions of the Code as well as any careless, reckless, or intentional disregard of rules and regulations.

TRA of 1986 also expands the scope of the special negligence standard currently applicable to failures to include in income interest and dividends shown on information returns.[29] This standard now will cover failures to account for amounts required to be reported on *all* information returns.

TRA of 1986 expands the scope of the negligence penalty by making it applicable to *all* taxes under the Code. Congress also made it clear that the negligence penalty is to be imposed on the entire amount of the underpayment.

Example 20   T underpaid $10,000 in income taxes, and the portion attributable to negligence was $2,000. The amount of the penalty is $500 (5% × $10,000) and not $100 (5% × $2,000).   □

To further discourage taxpayer noncompliance, a nondeductible addition-to-tax penalty is imposed that is equal to 50 percent of the interest attributable to that portion of the payment relating to negligence.

Example 21   Assume the same facts as in Example 20 with the added stipulation that interest on the $10,000 deficiency amounts to $1,000 ($200 of which related to the $2,000 portion attributable to negligence). T's total negligence penalty is determined as follows:

---

29. § 6653(a) as amended by TRA of 1986. Since the amendments to the negligence penalty apply only to returns due (determined without regard to extensions) after December 31, 1986, pre-TRA of 1986 rules will continue to be relevant for a number of years.

Regular negligence penalty (5% × $10,000)	$500
Penalty imposed on the interest due as a result of the negligence (50% × $200)	100
Total negligence penalty	$600

Fraud Penalty. A 75 percent penalty is imposed on any underpayment resulting from fraud on the part of the taxpayer.[30] Known as the civil fraud penalty, the burden of proof *is upon the IRS* to show by a preponderance of the evidence that the taxpayer had a specific intent to evade a tax.

Once the IRS has established that any portion of an underpayment is attributable to fraud, the entire underpayment is treated as so attributable except to the extent that the taxpayer establishes that any portion of the underpayment is not attributable to fraud. Thus, once the IRS has initially established that fraud has occurred, the taxpayer then bears the burden of proof to show the portion of the underpayment that is not attributable to fraud.

Although the Code and the Regulations do not provide any assistance in ascertaining what constitutes civil fraud, it seems clear that mere negligence on the part of the taxpayer (however great) will not suffice. In this regard, consideration has to be given to the particular facts involved. Fraud has been found in cases where there have been manipulation of the books,[31] substantial omissions from income,[32] and erroneous deductions.[33]

Parallel with the negligence penalty, 50 percent of the interest on a civil fraud assessment will constitute an additional penalty. The penalty is imposed only on that portion of the underpayment attributable to fraud.

Example 22 T underpaid his income tax for 1987 by $90,000. Assume that the IRS can prove that $60,000 of the underpayment was due to fraud. On the other hand, T can prove that $30,000 of the underpayment was not due to fraud. If the total interest on the underpayment amounts to $18,000, the civil fraud penalty would be computed as follows:

Civil fraud penalty (75% × $60,000)	$45,000
Penalty imposed on the interest due as a result of the fraud [$60,000/$90,000 × $18,000 = $12,000 × 50%]	6,000
Total fraud penalty	$51,000

---

30. § 6653(b). Before TRA of 1986, the fraud penalty was 50%. Since the amendment to the fraud penalty applies only to returns due (determined without regard to extensions) after December 31, 1986, the 50% penalty amount will be used for some time. As noted later in the chapter, fraudulent returns carry no statute of limitations.
31. *Dogget v. Comm.,* 60–1 USTC ¶ 9342, 5 AFTR2d 1034, 275 F.2d 823 (CA–4, 1960).
32. *Harvey Brodsky,* 21 TCM 578, T.C.Memo. 1962–105.
33. *Lash v. Comm.,* 57–2 USTC ¶ 9725, 51 AFTR 492, 245 F.2d 20 (CA–1, 1957).

If the underpayment of tax is partially attributable to negligence and partially attributable to fraud, the negligence penalty (which generally applies to the entire underpayment of tax) does not apply to any portion of the underpayment with respect to which a fraud penalty is imposed.

In addition to civil fraud penalties, the Code contains numerous criminal sanctions that carry varying monetary fines and/or imprisonment. The difference between civil and criminal fraud is one of degree. A characteristic of criminal fraud is the presence of willfulness on the part of the taxpayer. Thus, § 7201 dealing with attempts to evade or defeat a tax contains the following language:

> Any person who *willfully* attempts in any manner to evade or defeat any tax imposed by this title or the payment thereof shall, in addition to other penalties provided by law, be guilty of a felony and, upon conviction thereof, shall be fined not more than $100,000 ($500,000 in the case of a corporation), or imprisoned not more than five years, or both, together with the costs of prosecution. [Emphasis added.]

As to the burden of proof, the IRS must show that the taxpayer was guilty of willful evasion "beyond the shadow of any reasonable doubt." Recall that in the civil fraud area, the standard applied to measure culpability was "by a preponderance of the evidence."

Substantial Understatements of Tax Liability.   An understatement penalty[34] is designed to strike at middle and high income taxpayers who play the so-called audit lottery, that is, those who take questionable and undisclosed positions on their tax returns in the hope that the return will not be selected for audit. Of course, a disclosure of such positions would have called attention to the return and increased the probability of audit.

A substantial understatement of a tax liability transpires when the understatement exceeds the larger of 10 percent of the tax due or $5,000. (Note: The monetary ceiling for corporations is $10,000.) The understatement to which the penalty applies is 10 percent of the difference between the amount of tax required to be shown on the return and the amount of tax actually shown on the return.

The penalty can be avoided under any of the following circumstances:

—The taxpayer has "substantial authority" for such treatment.

—The relevant facts affecting the treatment are adequately disclosed in the return or in a statement attached thereto.

—The taxpayer has reasonable cause and acts in good faith.

---

34. § 6661(a).   Before legislation enacted in 1986, the penalty was 10%. At this point, some confusion exists as to what the increase will be. TRA of 1986 says 20% (effective for returns filed after 1986), but the Omnibus Budget Reconciliation Act of 1986 specifies 25% and applies the increase to penalties assessed after October 21, 1986. The IRS has announced that it will follow the latter, more stringent, legislation.

The broad criteria utilized as a means of avoiding the penalty undoubtedly provide taxpayers with little, if any, concrete safe harbors. However, "substantial" is to be tested by looking to the taxpayer's position and not to the contrary authority.

The further quandary exists as to what will constitute adequate disclosure. Although "adequate disclosure" is not a new concept, it remains to be seen whether past interpretations will carry over to this penalty area.

Penalty for Overvaluation.   The tax law provides for a graduated addition to tax for certain income tax valuation or basis overstatements.[35] The penalty applies only to the extent of any income tax underpayment of at least $1,000 that is attributable to such overvaluation (or basis overstatement) and only if the taxpayer is an individual, a closely-held corporation, or a personal service corporation.

When a valuation (or basis) overstatement exists, the following percentages are to be used to determine the applicable addition to tax:

If the valuation claimed is the following percentage of the correct valuation	The applicable percentage is
At least 150% but not more than 200%	10%
More than 200% but not more than 250%	20%
More than 250%	30%

Charitable contributions of property automatically fall under the 30 percent applicable percentage amount.

Example 23   In 1984, T purchased a painting for $10,000. In early 1987 and when the painting is worth $20,000 (as later determined by the IRS), T donates the painting to an art museum. Based on the appraisal of a cousin who is an amateur artist, T deducts $40,000 for the donation on a timely filed return for 1987. Since T was in a 38½% bracket, overstating the deduction by $20,000 resulted in a tax underpayment of $7,700 for 1987. □

Because the overvaluation resulted from a charitable contribution, the applicable percentage becomes 30 percent. Thus, the penalty is $2,310 [30% × $7,700 (the underpayment that resulted from using $40,000 instead of $20,000)].

If a charitable contribution had not been involved in Example 23, the overvaluation would still have been 200 percent [$40,000 (value used) compared to $20,000 (true value)], but the applicable percentage would have been 10 percent (see preceding table). The penalty, therefore, would have been 10 percent of the underpayment of $7,700, or $770.

If the taxpayer can establish that there was a reasonable basis for the valuation claimed on the return and the claim was made in good faith, the IRS

---

35. § 6659.

can waive all or part of the penalty. It is doubtful that Example 23 would constitute the type of situation where the IRS might choose to waive the penalty. For an item of art this valuable, relying on the appraisal of a relative who is an amateur artist does not seem to represent a good faith attempt at compliance.

Penalty for Undervaluation.   Until 1984, there was no penalty for undervaluation. Now a penalty deals with the valuation of property used in determining the Federal gift tax (as reported on Form 709) and the Federal estate tax (as reported on Form 706). The penalty materializes when the tax underpayment is $1,000 or more due to undervaluation of assets transferred and applies to returns filed after 1984.[36]

The following percentages are to be used to determine the applicable addition to tax:

If the valuation claimed is the following percentage of the correct valuation	The applicable percentage is
50% or more but not more than 66⅔%	10%
40% or more but less than 50%	20%
Less than 40 percent	30%

The IRS is authorized to waive the penalty if the taxpayer can prove that a reasonable basis existed for the valuation used and that he or she acted in good faith.

Failure to Pay Estimated Taxes.   A penalty is imposed for a failure to pay estimated income taxes. The penalty applies to individuals and corporations and is based on the rate of interest in effect for deficiency assessments.[37] Effective for tax years beginning after December 31, 1986, the penalty also applies to trusts and certain estates that are now required to make estimated tax payments.

For individuals, the penalty is not imposed if the tax due for the year (less any amounts withheld) is less than $500. For corporations, the threshold amount is the same as for individuals (refer to Chapter 2).

The penalty generally can be avoided if the quarterly payments were based on one fourth of the lesser of 90 percent of the current year's tax or 100 percent of the preceding year's tax (even if none was due).[38] Quarterly payments are to be made on or before the fifteenth day of the fourth month (i.e., April 15 for a calendar year taxpayer), sixth month, ninth month, and the first

---

36. § 6660.
37. §§ 6654 and 6655. Sections 6654(a) and 6655(a) refer to the penalty as "an addition to the tax" (i.e., the income tax, self-employment tax). Since these so-called additions to the tax have the characteristics of penalties, they have been classified as such in the text.
38. The previous safe harbor was 80% of the current year's tax liability. The change applies to tax years beginning after December 31, 1987.

month of the following year. With corporations, the last quarterly payment is accelerated and must be made by the twelfth month of the same year.

The penalty is levied on the amount of the underpayment for the period of the underpayment. Payments of estimated tax are credited against unpaid installments in the order in which the installments are required to be paid. As to employees, an equal part of withholding is deemed paid on each due date.

In computing the penalty, Form 2210 (Underpayment of Estimated Tax by Individuals) or Form 2220 (Underpayment of Estimated Tax by Corporations) is used.

False Information with Respect to Withholding. The Federal income tax system is based on a pay-as-you-go approach, an important element of which involves withholding procedures on wages. One way employees could hope to avoid the operation of the withholding procedure was to falsify the information provided to the employer on Form W–4 (Employee Withholding Allowance Certificate). For example, by overstating the number of exemptions, income tax withholdings could have been cut or completely eliminated.

To encourage compliance, the tax law imposes a civil penalty of $500 when a taxpayer claims withholding allowances based on false information. The criminal penalty for willfully failing to supply information or for willfully supplying false or fraudulent information in connection with wage withholding is a fine of up to $1,000 and/or up to one year of imprisonment.[39]

Failure to Make Deposits of Taxes and Overstatements of Deposits. When the business is not doing well or cash flow problems develop, there is a great temptation on the part of employers to "borrow" from Uncle Sam. One way this can be done is to fail to pay over to the IRS the amounts that have been withheld from the wages of employees for FICA and income tax purposes. Needless to say, the IRS does not appreciate being denied the use of such funds and has a number of weapons at its disposal to discourage the practice. Some of these penalties are summarized as follows:

—A penalty of 10 percent of any underdeposited amount not paid on or before the prescribed due date, unless it can be shown that the failure is due to reasonable cause and not to willful neglect.[40]

—A penalty of 25 percent of any overstated deposit claim unless such overstatement is due to reasonable cause and not to willful neglect.

—Various criminal penalties.[41]

—A 100 percent penalty if the employer's actions are willful.[42] The penalty is based on the amount of the tax evaded, not collected, or not accounted for or paid over. Since the penalty is assessable against the "responsible person" of the business, it could be that more than one party may be vulnerable (e.g., the president and treasurer of a corporation). Although the IRS might assess

39. §§ 6682 and 7205.
40. § 6656.
41. See, for example, § 7202 (willful failure to collect or pay over a tax).
42. § 6672.

the penalty against more than one person, it cannot collect more than the 100 percent due.

In addition to these penalties, the actual tax due must be remitted. An employer remains liable for the amount that should have been paid over even though the withholdings have not been taken out of the wages of its employees.[43]

Statute of Limitations

A statute of limitations defines the period of time during which one party may pursue against another party a cause of action or other suit allowed under the governing law. Failure to satisfy any requirement provides the other party with an absolute defense should he or she see fit to invoke the statute. Inequity would result if there were no statute limiting action. Permitting the lapse of an extended period of time between the initiation of a claim and its pursuit could place the defense of such claim in jeopardy. Witnesses may have died or disappeared; records or other evidence may have been discarded or destroyed.

In terms of Federal tax consequences, it is important to distinguish between the statute of limitations on assessments by the IRS and the statute applicable to refund claims by a taxpayer.

Assessment and the Statute of Limitations. In general, any tax that is imposed must be assessed within three years of the filing of the return (or, if later, the due date of the return).[44] Some exceptions to this three-year limitation follow:

—If no return is filed or a fraudulent return is filed, assessments can be made at any time. There is, in effect, no statute of limitations.

—If a taxpayer omits an amount of gross income in excess of 25 percent of the gross income stated on the return, the statute of limitations is increased to six years. The courts have interpreted this extended period of limitations rule to include only those items affecting income and not the omission of items affecting cost of goods sold.[45] In addition, gross income includes capital gains in the *gross* income amount (i.e., not reduced by capital losses).

Example 24 During 1983, T (an individual taxpayer) had the following income transactions (all of which were duly reported on his timely filed return):

---

43. § 3403.
44. §§ 6501(a) and (b)(1).
45. *The Colony, Inc. v. Comm.,* 58–2 USTC ¶ 9593, 1 AFTR2d 1894, 78 S.Ct. 1033 (USSC, 1958).

Gross receipts		$ 480,000
Less cost of goods sold		(400,000)
Net business income		$ 80,000
Capital gains and losses—		
Capital gain	$36,000	
Capital loss	12,000	24,000
Total income		$ 104,000

T retains your services in 1988 as a tax consultant. It seems that he inadvertently omitted some income on his 1983 return and he wishes to know if he is "safe" under the statute of limitations. The six-year statute of limitations would apply, putting T in a vulnerable position only if he omitted more than $129,000 on his 1983 return [($480,000 + $36,000) × 25%]. ☐

—The statute of limitations may be extended by mutual consent of the District Director and the taxpayer.[46] This extension covers a definite period and is made by signing Form 872 (Consent to Extend the Time to Assess Tax). The extension is frequently requested by the IRS when the lapse of the statutory period is imminent and the audit has not been completed. In some situations, the extensions may apply only to unresolved issues. This practice often is applied to audits of corporate taxpayers and explains why many corporations have "open years."

Special rules relating to assessment are applicable in the following situations:

—Taxpayers (corporations, estates, etc.) may request a prompt assessment of the tax.

—The period for assessment of the personal holding company tax is extended to six years after the return is filed only if certain filing requirements are met.

—If a partnership or trust files a tax return (a partnership or trust return) in good faith and a later determination renders it taxable as a corporation, such return is deemed to be the corporate return for purposes of the statute of limitations.

—The assessment period for capital loss, net operating loss, and investment credit carrybacks is generally related to the determination of tax in the year of the loss or unused credit rather than in the carryback years.

If the tax is assessed within the period of limitations, the IRS has six years from the date of assessment to collect the tax.[47] However, if the IRS issues a statutory notice of deficiency to the taxpayer, who then files a Tax Court petition, the statute is suspended on both the deficiency assessment and the

---

46. § 6501(c)(4).
47. § 6502(a).

period of collection until 60 days after the decision of the Tax Court becomes final.[48]

Refund Claims and the Statute of Limitations.   To receive a tax refund, the taxpayer is required to file a valid refund claim. The official form for filing a claim is Form 1040X for individuals and Form 1120X for corporations. A refund claim must follow certain procedural requirements. If it does not, the claim may be rejected with no consideration of its merit. These procedural requirements include the following:

—A separate claim must be filed for each taxable period.

—The grounds for the claim must be stated in sufficient detail.

—The statement of facts must be sufficient to permit IRS appraisal of the merits of the claim.

The refund claim must be filed within three years of the filing of the tax return or within two years following the payment of the tax if this period expires on a later date.[49] In most instances, the three-year period is relevant for determining running of the statute of limitations. To be allowed, a claim must be filed during this period.

Certain exceptions are incorporated in the Code that can inadvertently reduce the benefits of the refund claim.[50]

Example 25   On March 10, 1985, T filed his 1984 income tax return reflecting a tax of $10,500. On July 11, 1986, he filed an amended 1984 return showing an additional $3,000 of tax which was then paid. On May 20, 1988, he filed a claim for refund of $4,500. Assuming T is correct concerning the claim for refund, how much tax can he recover? The answer is only $3,000. Because the claim was not filed within the three-year period, T is limited to the amount he actually paid during the last two years. One might note that T would be entitled to interest on the $3,000 from July 11, 1986 (the date of the overpayment), to a date not more than 30 days before the date of the refund check (subject to the 45-day rule discussed earlier in the chapter).
□

Example 26   D had $10,000 withheld in 1984. Because of heavy itemized deductions, D assumed she had no further tax to pay for the year. For this reason and because of the exigencies of business, and without securing an extension, she did not file her 1984 return until June 9, 1985. Actually, the return showed a refund of $600, which D ultimately received. On May 3, 1988, D filed a $4,000 claim for refund of her 1984 taxes. How much, if any, of the $4,000 may D recover? None. Although the time limitation was met (i.e., the claim was filed within three years of the filing of the return), the amount limitation was not. A refund cannot exceed the amount paid within three years preceding the filing of the claim, and for this purpose,

48. § 6503(a)(1).
49. §§ 6511(a) and 6513(a).
50. § 6511(b).

D's withholdings were deemed paid as of April 15, 1985. Had D requested and obtained an extension covering the filing of her 1984 return, the claim for refund would have been timely, and taxes paid would have exceeded the refund claimed. ☐

The tax law sets forth special rules for claims relating to bad debts and worthless securities. A seven-year period of limitations applies in lieu of the normal three-year rule.[51] The extended period is provided in recognition of the inherent difficulty associated with identification of the exact year a bad debt or security becomes worthless.

Refund claims relative to capital or net operating loss carrybacks may be filed within three years after the time for filing the tax return (including extensions) for the year of the loss. The IRS will accelerate the processing of a refund from a net operating loss carryback if Form 1045 (applicable to individuals) or Form 1139 (applicable to corporations) is utilized. But this special procedure is available only if the form is filed within the year following the year of the loss. In other cases, a Form 1040X or Form 1120X should be used.

If the taxpayer's refund claim is rejected by the IRS, a suit for refund generally may be filed six months after the filing of the claim.[52] This suit is filed in a Federal district court or in the Claims Court.

Mitigation of the Statute of Limitations.   Sections 1311 through 1315 contain a set of complex rules designed to preclude either the IRS or a taxpayer from taking advantage of the statute of limitations when to do so would be inequitable. Simply stated, these Sections prevent the use of the statute as a means of obtaining a double benefit by maintaining an inconsistent position.

Example 27   In 1984, T Corporation inadvertently claimed as a deduction a $10,000 expenditure that should have been charged to a capital account and depreciated over a period of 10 years. In 1988, and after the statute of limitations has run on tax year 1984, T Corporation cannot begin claiming depreciation on this asset. If it does, the IRS can force T Corporation to make an adjustment for 1984, eliminating the inappropriate portion of the $10,000 deduction. ☐

Example 28   In 1982, U Corporation makes a $20,000 distribution to its sole shareholder, V. On audit of V's income tax return for 1982, the IRS deems the distribution to be fully covered by U Corporation's earnings and profits and forces V to recognize the $20,000 as dividend income. In 1988, V sells his stock for $80,000 more than his investment therein. Can the IRS now claim that V has a gain of $100,000 because the 1982 distribution really was a return of capital (thereby forcing V to reduce his stock basis and increase his gain by $20,000)? No. This would be the assumption of an inconsistent position by the IRS and would be inequitable to V. ☐

---

51. § 6511(d)(1).
52. § 6532(a)(1).

Tax Practice

The Tax Practitioner

Definition. What is a tax practitioner? What service does the practitioner perform? To begin defining the term "tax practitioner," one should consider whether the individual is qualified to practice before the IRS. Generally, practice before the IRS is limited to CPAs, attorneys, and persons who have been enrolled to practice before the IRS (termed "enrollees"). In most cases, enrollees are admitted to practice only if they take and successfully pass a special examination administered by the IRS. CPAs and attorneys are not required to take this examination and are automatically admitted to practice if they are in good standing with the appropriate licensing board regulating their profession.

Persons other than CPAs, attorneys, and enrollees may, however, be allowed to practice before the IRS in limited situations. Circular 230 (issued by the Treasury Department and entitled "Rules Governing the Practice of Attorneys and Agents Before the Internal Revenue Service") permits the following notable exceptions:

—A taxpayer may always represent himself or herself. A person also may represent a member of his or her immediate family if no compensation is received for such services.

—Regular full-time employees may represent their employers.

—Corporations may be represented by any of their bona fide officers.

—Partnerships may be represented by any of the partners.

—Trusts, receiverships, guardianships, or estates may be represented by their trustees, receivers, guardians, or administrators or executors.

—A taxpayer may be represented by whoever prepared the return for the year in question. However, such representation cannot proceed beyond the agent level.

Example 29   T, an individual, is currently undergoing audit by the IRS for tax years 1985 and 1986. She prepared the 1985 return herself but paid Z Company, a bookkeeping service, to prepare the 1986 return. Z Company may represent T in matters concerning only 1986. However, even with respect to 1986, Z Company would be unable to represent T at an Appeals Division proceeding. T could, of course, represent herself, or she could retain a CPA, attorney, or enrollee to represent her in matters concerning both years under examination. ☐

Rules Governing Tax Practice.   Circular 230 further prescribes the rules governing practice before the IRS. As applied to CPAs, attorneys, and enrollees, the following rules are imposed:

—A requirement to make known to a client any error or omission the client may have made on any return or other document submitted to the IRS.

—A duty to submit records or information lawfully requested by the IRS.

—An obligation to exercise due diligence as to accuracy in the preparation and filing of tax returns.

—A restriction against unreasonably delaying the prompt disposition of any matter before the IRS.

—A restriction against charging the client "an unconscionable fee" for representation before the IRS.

—A restriction against representing clients with conflicting interests.

Anyone can prepare a tax return or render tax advice, regardless of his or her educational background or level of competence. Likewise, there is nothing to preclude the "unlicensed" tax practitioner from advertising his or her specialty, from directly soliciting clients, or from otherwise violating any of the standards of conduct controlling CPAs, attorneys, or enrollees. Nevertheless, there do exist some restraints that govern all parties engaged in rendering tax advice or preparing tax returns for the general public.

—If the party holds himself or herself out to the general public as possessing tax expertise, he or she could be liable to the client if services are performed in a negligent manner. At a minimum, the measure of such damage would be any interest and penalties the client incurs because of the practitioner's failure to exercise due care.

—If someone agrees to perform a service (e.g., preparation of a tax return) and subsequently fails to do so, the aggrieved party may be in a position to obtain damages for breach of contract.

—The IRS requires all persons who prepare tax returns for a fee to sign as preparer of the return.[53] Failure to comply with this requirement could result in penalty assessment against the preparer.

—The Code prescribes various penalties for the deliberate filing of false or fraudulent returns. Such penalties are applicable to a tax practitioner who either was aware of the situation or actually perpetrated the false information or the fraud.[54]

—Code § 7216 prescribes penalties for tax practitioners who disclose to third parties information they have received from clients in connection with the preparation of tax returns or the rendering of tax advice.

Example 30   T operates a tax return preparation service. His brother-in-law, B, has just taken a job as a life insurance salesman. To help B find contacts, T furnishes B with a list of the names and addresses of all of his clients who report adjusted gross income of $10,000 or more. T is in violation of § 7216 and is subject to penalties. □

—All non-attorney tax practitioners should avoid becoming engaged in activities that constitute the unauthorized practice of law. If they engage in this

---

53. Reg. § 1.6065–1(b)(1). Rev.Rul. 84–3, 1984–1 C.B. 264, contains a series of examples as to when a person will be deemed to be a preparer of the return.
54. § 7206.

practice, action could be instituted against them in the appropriate state court by the local or state bar association. What actions constitute the unauthorized practice of law are undefined, and the issue remains an open question upon which reasonable minds can easily differ.

Legislative Penalties.   The following penalties also are provided under the Code:

1. A $100 penalty with respect to each return or claim for refund if the tax return preparer understates the taxpayer's liability and such understatement is due to the negligent or intentional disregard of rules and regulations.[55] The term "rules and regulations" includes the Code, Regulations, and published rulings. It should be noted that a preparer has not negligently or intentionally disregarded the rules and regulations if he or she in good faith and with a reasonable basis takes the position that a rule or regulation does not accurately reflect the Code.
2. A $1,000 ($10,000 for corporations) penalty per return or document is imposed against persons who aid in the preparation of returns or other documents that they know will result in understatement of tax liability. Aiding does not include clerical assistance in the preparation process. This penalty will not be imposed if the preparer penalty (refer to item 1) is invoked.[56]
3. A $500 per return penalty will be assessed on the preparer if the understatement of tax is due to a willful understatement of the taxpayer's tax liability. For example, a willful understatement occurs where a preparer disregards information furnished by the taxpayer in an attempt to wrongfully reduce the tax liability.
4. A $25 penalty is assessed against the preparer for failure to sign a return or furnish the preparer's identifying number and a $50 penalty is assessed for failure to retain a copy or list of taxpayers for whom returns or claims for refund have been prepared.
5. A $25 penalty is assessed if the preparer fails to furnish a copy of the return or claim for refund to the taxpayer unless the failure is due to reasonable cause and not due to willful neglect.[57]
6. A $500 penalty may be assessed if a preparer endorses or otherwise negotiates a check for refund of tax issued to the taxpayer.

Guidelines for the Imposition of the Negligence Penalty.   In connection with preparer penalties under § 6694(a) (refer to item 1), Rev.Proc. 80–40 provides guidelines as to what constitutes the negligent disregard of rules and regulations.[58] These guidelines are illustrated in a series of Revenue Rulings and are discussed in the following paragraphs.[59]

In determining whether the penalty under § 6694(a) is to be asserted, all of the relevant facts and circumstances of each case will be taken into account.

---

55. § 6694.
56. § 6701.
57. § 6695.
58. 1980–2 C.B. 774.
59. Rev.Rul. 80–262 (1980–2 C.B. 375), Rev.Rul. 80–263 (1980–2 C.B. 376), Rev.Rul. 80–264 (1980–2 C.B. 377), Rev.Rul. 80–265 (1980–2 C.B. 377), and Rev.Rul. 80–266 (1980–2 C.B. 378).

One such factor is the nature of the error causing the understatement. Was the provision that was misapplied or not discovered so complex, uncommon, or highly technical that a competent preparer of tax returns of the type at issue might reasonably be unaware or mistaken as to its applicability? Would a general review of the return have disclosed the error to the preparer? An isolated mathematical or clerical error ordinarily reflects no more than mere inadvertence and will not result in the imposition of the penalty.

Example 31   A taxpayer furnished T, the income tax return preparer, with all of the Forms 1099–INT (Statement for Recipients of Interest Income) that he had received. T failed to list the amount shown on one of the Forms 1099–INT on Schedule B of Form 1040. The omission was inadvertent and was the only error T made in preparing the return. Also, the error resulted in an understatement of tax liability that was not substantial. Under these circumstances, the negligence penalty will not be imposed on T. ☐

Example 32   Assume the same facts as in Example 31, except that T correctly listed all of the amounts shown on the Forms 1099–INT on Schedule B but made an error in totaling the separate amounts. Again, the error led to an understatement of tax liability that was not substantial. As was true with Example 31, the negligence penalty will not be imposed. ☐

The results reached in Examples 31 and 32 would have been different if the error had been substantial or so conspicuous that it should have been discovered by the preparer.

The IRS also will consider the frequency of errors. A pattern of errors on a return is presumptive of negligence and generally will result in the assertion of the penalty even though no one error would have done so.

Example 33   Assume the same facts as in Example 31, except that T fails to list the amounts shown on two of the Forms 1099–INT. Also, as was true in Example 32, T makes an error in totaling the separate amounts. Further, T used the wrong Tax Table in determining the tax. Although the errors resulted in an understatement of tax liability that was not substantial, the negligence penalty will be imposed on T. ☐

The IRS also will consider the materiality of errors. An error resulting in a material understatement may be greater indication of negligence than a similar error resulting in a less material understatement. But even where all of the relevant facts and circumstances suggest that the return was negligently prepared, the penalty generally will not be asserted if the following is true:

—The preparer's normal office practice indicates that the error in question rarely would occur.

—The normal office practice was followed in preparing the return in question.

Examples of normal office practice include a system to promote accuracy and consistency in the preparation of returns (e.g., a checklist), a method for obtaining the necessary information from the taxpayer, examining the prior year's return, and review procedures. The normal office practice of the preparer will not be relevant where the error is flagrant or either a pattern of errors occurs on a particular return or an error is repeated on numerous returns.

Example 34   Due to an oversight, T, an income tax return preparer, failed to report a substantial minimum tax liability resulting from a net capital gain deduction shown on the client's 1986 return. This was the only error on the return. To show that the normal office practice was to correctly apply the minimum tax provisions, T had a checklist reflecting that such tax had to be taken into account. Also, T's working papers indicated that the checklist had been reviewed. Considering T's knowledge, the internal procedures for review, and other facts and circumstances, the indications were that this error rarely would occur. In this type of situation, T will not be liable for the negligence penalty. ☐

The negligence penalty generally will not apply where a preparer in good faith relies without verification on information furnished by the client. Thus, the preparer is not required to audit, examine, or review books and records, business operations, or documents or other evidence in order to verify independently the client's information. However, the preparer may not ignore the implications of information either furnished by the taxpayer or that actually was known. Furthermore, the preparer shall make reasonable inquiries if the information furnished appears to be incorrect or incomplete.

Example 35   T prepared the Federal income tax returns for S and S Corporation (wholly owned by S) for tax year 1986. T was not the auditor of S Corporation and had no knowledge of any loans by S to S Corporation. Although T deducted the interest paid by S Corporation to S on Form 1120, she did not report any interest income on S's Form 1040. The information provided by S Corporation to T did not reflect who received the interest payment, and the information furnished by S did not reveal the receipt of such payment. Under these conditions, T will not be subject to the negligence penalty. ☐

Example 36   Assume the same facts as in Example 35, except that the information provided by S Corporation revealed that S was the payee of the interest. Here, the penalty applies. ☐

Some provisions of the Code [e.g., § 274(d)] require the existence of specific facts and circumstances (e.g., the maintenance of specific documents) before a deduction may properly be claimed. In such cases, the preparer should make appropriate inquiries to determine the existence of such facts and circumstances before claiming a deduction.

Example 37   T prepared a tax return for a client in which he deducted business entertainment expenditures. T did not make any inquiries of the client concerning whether or not such expenditures satisfied the substantiation requirements of § 274(d). On later audit by the IRS, it was revealed that no such substantiation existed, and the deduction was disallowed. Although T was unaware of the true facts when the return was prepared, the negligence penalty will be imposed. ☐

Example 38   Assume the same facts as in Example 37, except that T made the inquiry and was assured of the existence of the required substantiation by the client. Here, the negligence penalty will not apply to T. ☐

Ethical Considerations—"Statements on Responsibilities in Tax Practice"

Tax practitioners who are CPAs or attorneys must abide by the codes or canons of professional ethics applicable to their respective professions. The various codes and canons have much in common with and parallel the standards of conduct set forth in Circular 230. Tax practice is greatly affected by the prohibition against designation of a specialty. With some exceptions at the state bar association level, an attorney or a CPA cannot indicate on letterhead, business cards, or other approved listing that he or she specializes in tax matters or that his or her practice is limited to this field. From this standpoint, attorneys and CPAs are unlike physicians and dentists who have developed and effectively utilized an elaborate system of specialization.

In the belief that CPAs engaged in tax practice required further guidance in the resolution of ethical problems, the Tax Committee of the AICPA began issuing periodic statements on selected topics. The first of these "Statements on Responsibilities in Tax Practice" was released in 1964. Some of the statements that have been issued to date are summarized as follows:

—A CPA should sign as the preparer of a Federal tax return only if he or she is satisfied that reasonable effort has been made to provide appropriate answers to the questions on the return that are applicable to the taxpayer. When such questions are left unanswered, the reason for such omissions should be stated. The possibility that an answer to a question might prove disadvantageous to the taxpayer does not justify its omission. Likewise, it does not justify omitting the reason the question was not answered.

—A CPA may sign a return containing a departure from the treatment of an item on a prior year's tax return that was made pursuant to an administrative proceeding with the IRS. The departure need not be disclosed on the return.

Example 39   Upon audit of T Corporation's income tax return for 1987, the IRS disallowed $20,000 of the $100,000 salary paid to its president and sole shareholder on the grounds of unreasonable compensation [§ 162(a)(1)]. You are the CPA who has been engaged to prepare T Corporation's income tax return for 1988. Again the corporation paid its president a salary of $100,000 and chose to deduct this amount. Because you are not bound in 1988 by what the IRS deemed reasonable for 1987, the full $100,000 can be claimed as a salary deduction. ☐

—A CPA may prepare tax returns involving the use of estimates if such use is generally acceptable or if, under the circumstances, it is impractical to obtain exact data. When estimates are used, they should be presented in such a manner as to avoid the implication of greater accuracy than exists. The CPA should be satisfied that estimated amounts are not unreasonable under the circumstances.

—A CPA should promptly advise a client upon learning of an error in a previously filed return or upon learning of a client's failure to file a required return. The advice can be oral or written and should include a recommendation of the corrective measures, if any, to be taken. The error or other omission should not be disclosed to the IRS without the client's consent. If the past error is material and is not corrected by the client, the CPA may be unable to prepare the current year's tax return. Such might be true if the error has a carryover effect that precludes the correct determination of the tax liability for the current year.

Example 40   In connection with the preparation of a client's 1988 income tax return, you discover the final inventory for 1987 was materially understated. First, you should advise the client to file an amended return for 1987 reflecting the correct amount in final inventory. Second, if the client refuses to make this adjustment, you should consider whether the error will preclude you from preparing a substantially correct return for 1988. Because this will probably be the case (the final inventory for 1987 becomes the beginning inventory for 1988), you should withdraw from the engagement. If the error is corrected by the client, you may proceed with the preparation of the tax return for 1988. You should, however, assure yourself that the error is not repeated. □

—When the CPA is representing a client in an administrative proceeding with respect to a return in which there is an error known to the CPA that has resulted or may result in a material understatement of tax liability, he or she should request the client's agreement to disclose the error to the IRS. Lacking such agreement, the CPA may be compelled to withdraw from the engagement.

—In providing tax advice to a client, the CPA must use judgment to assure that the advice reflects professional competence and appropriately serves the client's needs. No standard format or guidelines can be established to cover all situations and circumstances involving written or oral advice by the CPA. The CPA may communicate with the client when subsequent developments affect advice previously provided with respect to significant matters. However, he or she cannot be expected to assume responsibility for initiating such communication, except while assisting a client in implementing procedures or plans associated with the advice provided. The CPA may undertake this obligation by specific agreement with his or her client.

—In preparing a return, the CPA ordinarily may rely on information furnished by the client. The CPA is not required to examine or review documents or other evidence supporting the client's information in order to sign the return as preparer. Although the examination of supporting data is not required, the CPA should encourage clients to provide such supporting data when appropriate. The CPA should make use of the client's returns for prior years whenever feasible. The implications of information known to the CPA cannot be ignored, and accordingly, the CPA is required to make reasonable inquiries when the information as presented appears to be incorrect or incomplete. If a CPA prepares a Federal tax return, the return should be signed by the CPA with no modification of the preparer's declaration.

Example 41 A CPA can normally take a client's word concerning the validity of dependency exemptions. But suppose a recently divorced client wants to claim his three children (of whom he does not have custody) as dependents. You must act in accordance with § 152(e)(2) in preparing the return, and this will require a waiver by the custodial parent. Without this waiver, you should not claim the dependency exemptions on your client's tax return. □

Example 42 While preparing a client's income tax return for 1988, you review his income tax return for 1987. In comparing the dividend income reported on the 1987 Schedule B with that received in 1988, you note a significant decrease. Further investigation reveals the variation is due to a stock sale in 1988 which, until now, was unknown to you. Thus, the review of the 1987 return has unearthed a transaction that should be reported on the 1988 return. □

The foregoing statements merely represent guides to action and are not part of the AICPA's Code of Professional Ethics. But because the statements are representative of standards followed by members of the profession, a violation thereof might indicate a deviation from the standard of due care exercised by most CPAs. The standard of due care is at the heart of any suit charging negligence that is brought against a CPA.

✓ Tax Planning Considerations

Strategy in Seeking an Administrative Ruling

Determination Letters. In many instances, the request for an advance ruling or a determination letter from the IRS is a necessary or desirable planning strategy. The receipt of a favorable ruling or determination reduces the risk associated with a transaction when the tax results are in doubt. For example, the initiation or amendment of a pension or profit sharing plan should be accompanied by a determination letter from the District Director. Otherwise, on subsequent IRS review, the plan may not qualify and the tax deductibility of contributions to the plan will be disallowed. In some instances, the potential tax effects of a transaction are so numerous and of such consequence that to proceed without a ruling is unwise.

Letter Rulings. It may not, in some cases, be necessary or desirable to request an advance ruling. For example, it is generally not desirable to request a ruling if the tax results are doubtful and the company is committed in any event to completion of the transaction. If a ruling is requested and negotiations with the IRS indicate that an adverse determination will be forthcoming, it is usually possible to have the ruling request withdrawn. However, the National Office of the IRS may forward its findings, along with a copy of the ruling request, to the District Director. In determining the advisability of a ruling request, consideration should be given to the potential exposure of other items in the tax returns of all "open years."

A ruling request may delay the consummation of a transaction if the issues are novel or complex. Frequently, a ruling can be processed within three months, although in some instances a delay of a year or more may be encountered.

Technical Advice. In the process of contesting a proposed deficiency with the Appeals Division, consideration should be given to a request for technical advice from the National Office of the IRS. If such advice is favorable to the taxpayer, it is binding on the Appeals Division. The request may be particularly appropriate when the practitioner feels that the agent or Appeals Division has been too literal in the interpretation of an IRS ruling.

Considerations in Handling an IRS Audit

As a general rule, attempts should be made to settle disputes at the earliest possible stage of the administrative appeal process. It is usually possible to limit the scope of the examination by furnishing pertinent information requested by the agent. Extraneous information or fortuitous comments may result in the opening of new issues and should therefore be avoided. Agents usually appreciate prompt and efficient response to inquiries, since their performance may in part be judged by their ability to close or settle assigned cases.

To the extent possible, it is advisable to conduct the investigation of field audits in the practitioner's office rather than in the client's office. This procedure permits greater control over the audit investigation and may facilitate the agent's review and prompt closure of the case.

Many practitioners feel that it is generally not advisable to have clients present at the scheduled conferences with the agent, since the client may give emotional or gratuitous comments that impair prompt settlement. If the client is not present, however, he or she should be advised of the status of negotiations. It should be clear that the client is the final authority with regard to any proposed settlement.

The tax practitioner's workpapers should include all research memoranda, and a list of resolved and unresolved issues should be continually updated during the course of the IRS audit. Occasionally, agents will request access to excessive amounts of accounting data for the purpose of engaging in a so-called fishing expedition. Providing blanket access to working papers should be avoided. Workpapers should be carefully reviewed to minimize opportunities for the agent to raise new issues not otherwise apparent. It is generally advisable to provide the agent with copies of specific workpapers upon request. An accountant's workpapers are not privileged and may therefore be subpoenaed by the IRS.

In unusual situations, a Special Agent may appear to gather evidence in the investigation of possible criminal fraud. When this occurs, the taxpayer should be advised to seek legal counsel to determine the extent of his or her cooperation in providing information to the agent. Also, it is frequently desirable for the tax adviser to consult personal legal counsel in such situations. If the taxpayer receives a Revenue Agent's Report (RAR), it generally indicates that the IRS has decided not to initiate criminal prosecution proceedings. The IRS usually does not take any action upon a tax deficiency until the criminal matter has been resolved. If, for whatever reasons, the criminal action is dropped, the 75 percent civil fraud penalty normally will be assessed.

Litigation Considerations

During the process of settlement with the IRS, the taxpayer must assess the economic consequences arising from possible litigation. Specifically, it is necessary to weigh the probability of winning in court with the costs of settlement (i.e., legal and court costs). In some instances, taxpayers become overly emotional and do not give adequate consideration to the economic and psychological costs of litigation.

Signing of Form 870 or Form 870–AD precludes the use of the Tax Court as a forum for future litigation. In such event, the taxpayer's only recourse is to pay the taxes and sue for a refund upon denial of a claim for refund. The Tax Court was established originally to permit taxpayers the opportunity to litigate issues without first paying the tax on the deficiency. Some taxpayers, however, prefer to litigate the case in a Federal district court or the Claims Court, since the payment of tax effectively stops the running of interest on the deficiency.

In the selection of a proper tax forum, consideration should be given to the decisions of the various courts in related cases. The Tax Court will follow the decisions of Courts of Appeals if the court is one to which the taxpayer may appeal.[60] For example, if an individual is in the Fifth Court of Appeals that has issued a favorable opinion on the same issue that currently confronts the taxpayer, the Tax Court will follow this opinion with respect to the taxpayer's case, even if previous Tax Court decisions have been adverse.

If the issue involves a question in which equity is needed, strategy may dictate the choice of a Federal district court (where a jury trial is obtainable) or the Claims Court, which has frequently given greater weight to equity considerations than to strict legal precedent.

Penalties

As previously discussed, penalties are imposed upon a taxpayer's failure to file a return or pay a tax when due. These penalties can be avoided if the failure is due to reasonable cause and not due to willful neglect. Reasonable cause, however, has not been liberally interpreted by the courts and should not be relied upon in the routine type of situation.[61] A safer way to avoid the failure to file penalty would be to obtain from the IRS an extension of time for filing the return. Although an extension of time for filing does not normally excuse the

---

60. *Jack E. Golsen,* 54 T.C. 742 (1970).
61. *Dustin v. Comm.,* 72–2 USTC ¶ 9610, 30 AFTR2d 72–5313, 467 F.2d 47 (CA–9, 1972), *aff'g.* 53 T.C. 491 (1969).

failure to pay penalty, it will do so in the case of the automatic four-month variety if the 90 percent rule has been satisfied (refer to Example 18).

Since it is not deductible for income tax purposes, the penalty for failure to pay estimated taxes can become quite severe. Often trapped by this provision are employed taxpayers with outside income. Such persons may forget about such outside income and place undue reliance on the amount withheld from wages and salaries as being adequate to cover their liability. For such persons, not only does April 15 provide a real shock (i.e., in terms of the additional tax owed) but a penalty situation may have evolved. One possible way for an employee to mitigate this problem (presuming the employer is willing to cooperate) is described as follows:

Example 43   T, a calendar year taxpayer, is employed by X Corporation and earns (after withholding) a monthly salary of $4,000 payable at the end of each month. T also receives income from outside sources (i.e., interest, dividends, and consulting fees). After some quick calculations in early October of 1988, T determines that he has underestimated his tax liability for 1988 by $7,500 and will be subject to the penalty for the first two quarters of 1988 and part of the third quarter. T, therefore, completes a new Form W–4 in which he arbitrarily raises his income tax withholding by $2,500 a month. X Corporation accepts the Form W–4, and as a result, an extra $7,500 is paid to the IRS on T's account for the payroll period from October through December 1988. ☐

The reason T avoids any penalties for the underpayment in Example 43 for the first three quarters is that withholding of taxes is allocated over the year involved. Thus, a portion of the additional $7,500 withheld in October–December is assigned to the January 1–April 15 period, the April 16–June 15 period, etc.[62] Had T merely paid the IRS an additional $7,500 in October, this would not have affected the penalty for the earlier quarters.

Statute of Limitations on Refund Claims

Avoiding the Statute of Limitations.   A refund claim must be filed within the statutory period of limitations (usually within three years from the time the return was filed). The failure to file a refund claim within this period will prevent the recovery of previous overpayments of tax.

Suppose a matter is pending that, upon being resolved, could have an impact on a taxpayer's own situation. Although the taxpayer may not be personally involved in the controversy, a favorable outcome would result in a refund. By the time the issue is settled, however, any such claim might be barred by the statute of limitations. To prevent this from happening, the taxpayer should consider filing what is known as a "protective claim for refund." This will keep the statute of limitations from running until such time as the IRS acts upon the claim. The IRS will hold up on either approving or denying the claim until the pending matter is decided.

---

62. § 6654(g).

Example 44   For the past few years, T has been paying a special Federal excise tax on crude oil. A lower court just held that this tax is unconstitutional. Because the amount of revenue at stake is considerable and large numbers of taxpayers are involved, the U.S. Supreme Court agrees to hear the appeal by the IRS. To freeze the running of the statute until the Supreme Court makes its decision, T files claims for refund for all open years in which she has paid the excise tax. Thus, T has protected herself from the statute of limitations in the event the tax is held to be unconstitutional. On the other hand, she loses nothing if the tax is found to be constitutional and her claim for refund is denied, since the tax has already been paid. □

A protective claim for refund also may be advisable in situations where the controversy has not reached the litigation stage.

Example 45   X Corporation is a shareholder in Y Corporation. Over the years, X Corporation has made advances to Y Corporation, and such transactions have been treated as bona fide loans by the parties. Annually, therefore, Y Corporation has been deducting interest expense, and X Corporation has been recognizing interest income. Upon audit of Y Corporation, the IRS is threatening to disallow Y Corporation's interest expense deduction on the grounds that the advances were not loans but represented contributions to capital. Consequently, the purported interest payments are really nondeductible dividend distributions. Based on these facts, X Corporation might be well advised to file protective claims for refund for all open years. These claims would be predicated on the assumption that if dividends are the ultimate result, X Corporation should be allowed a dividends received deduction. Keep in mind that interest income is fully taxed, while dividends received by a corporate shareholder enjoy preferential treatment. □

Voluntary Extension of the Statute of Limitations.   If the IRS is unable to complete its audit within the period before the expiration of the statute of limitations, the taxpayer may be asked to agree to an extension of time for assessment by signing Form 872 (Consent to Extend the Time to Assess Tax). It may be unwise to agree to this extension, since the IRS may subsequently assess a larger overall deficiency. Failure to agree to the extension of time, however, could force the IRS to issue a statutory notice of deficiency. This could cause the statutory notice to be unduly weighted against the taxpayer, since it may contain many adjustments that otherwise could have been resolved had the IRS been permitted more time to consider the matter.

Problem Materials

Discussion Questions

1. Why is it necessary for a tax practitioner to be familiar with the IRS organization and its administrative appeal procedures?

2. Why does the IRS issue rulings solely on uncompleted actual transactions or upon transactions that have been completed before the filing of the tax return?

3. Under what circumstances will a ruling be revoked by the IRS and applied retroactively to the detriment of the taxpayer?

4. During the course of your research of a tax problem, you find that another company received a favorable unpublished (letter) ruling approximately two years ago based on facts similar to your situation. What degree of reliance may be placed upon this ruling?

5. Under what circumstances might the request for an advance ruling be considered a necessity? Are there situations in which a ruling should not be requested? Why?

6. In what situations might a taxpayer seek a determination letter?

7. What purpose does a request for technical advice serve?

8. What, if any, is the relationship between DIF and TCMP?

9. A taxpayer is fearful of filing a claim for refund for a prior year because he is convinced that the claim will cause an audit by the IRS of that year's return. Please comment.

10. In March of 1988, T receives a refund check from the IRS for the amount of overpayment she claimed when she filed her 1987 return in January. Does this mean that her 1987 return will not be audited? Explain.

11. Comment on the following:

    a. An RAR.

    b. Form 870.

    c. The 30-day letter.

    d. The 90-day letter.

12. If a taxpayer wishes to go to the Appeals Division of the IRS, when is a written protest required?

13. What is meant by the term "hazards of litigation"?

14. Can the IRS agent settle cases based on the hazards of litigation?

15. Is it possible or desirable to "trade" unresolved issues with the Appeals Division?

16. How may the running of interest on a deficiency assessment be stopped?

17. V, a calendar year taxpayer, files her 1987 income tax return on February 9, 1988, on which she claims a $1,200 refund. If V receives her refund check on May 2, 1988, will it include any interest? Explain.

18. Why may it be desirable to settle with the agent rather than to continue by appealing to a higher level within the IRS?

19. For the completion and filing of his 1987 income tax return, R retains the services of a CPA. Because of a particularly hectic tax season, the CPA does not complete and file the return until June of 1988. Does this exculpate R under the reasonable cause exception from the failure to file and pay penalties? Would it make any difference if R were entitled to a refund for 1987?

20. What bearing should the interest rate currently in effect have on each of the following situations:

    a. Whether a taxpayer litigates in the U.S. Tax Court or the Claims Court.

    b. The penalty for underpayment of estimated taxes.

    c. The negligence penalty.

21. Describe each of the following items:

    a. A closing agreement.

    b. An offer in compromise.

22. Frequently, tax litigation involves unresolved questions relating to several years before the current year. How is it possible for the IRS to assess a deficiency for these years, since the statute of limitations expires three years from the date of filing of the tax return?

23. In connection with the negligence penalty that might be imposed on the preparers of tax returns, comment on the significance of each of the following:

    a. A substantial error.

    b. An inconspicuous error.

    c. A pattern of frequency of errors.

    d. The preparer's normal office practice.

    e. No verification by the preparer of information furnished by the client.

24. Certain individuals have stated that the preparation of a tax return by a qualified professional lends credibility to the return. Therefore, CPAs and attorneys should act in an impartial manner in the preparation of tax returns and should serve the overall enforcement needs of society for the administration of tax justice. Should a tax professional be an "umpire" or an "advocate"? Explain.

25. T, a vice president of Z Corporation, prepared and filed the corporate Form 1120 for 1986. This return is being audited by the IRS in 1988.

    a. May T represent Z Corporation during the audit?

    b. Can such representation continue beyond the agent level (e.g., before the Appeals Division)?

26. In 1986, S sold his business to B. Pursuant to an agreement between them, $40,000 of the selling price of $250,000 was allocated to the inventory of the business. In 1988 and upon final audit of S's 1986 income tax return, the IRS contends that the inventory should have been valued at $60,000. (This would have the effect of increasing S's ordinary income from the sale by $20,000.) What should B do under these circumstances?

27. During the course of an audit, the IRS agent requests a mutual extension of the statute of limitations for certain tax years. The agent states that this action is necessary to permit the completion of the audit. What are some of the pros and cons related to the signing of Form 872?

Problems

1. T, a calendar year taxpayer, does not file her 1987 return until June 3, 1988. At this point, she pays the $3,000 balance due on her 1987 tax liability of $30,000. T did not apply for and obtain any extension of time for filing the 1987 return. When questioned by the IRS on her delinquency, T asserts: "If I was too busy to file my regular tax return, I was too busy to request an extension."

    a. Is T liable for any penalties for failure to file and for failure to pay?

    b. If so, compute such penalties.

2. R, a calendar year taxpayer, was unable to file his 1987 income tax return on or before April 15, 1988. He did, however, apply for and obtain an automatic extension from the

IRS. On May 11, 1988, R delivers his completed return to the IRS and remits the $5,000 balance due on his 1987 tax liability of $41,000.

a. Determine R's penalty for failure to file.

b. For failure to pay.

c. Would it make any difference as to your answers to (a) and (b) if R's tax liability for 1987 were $51,000 (instead of $41,000)? Explain.

3. S, a calendar year individual taxpayer, files his 1987 return 65 days after its due date. S did not obtain an extension for filing his return, and such return reflects additional income tax due of $500. Based on this information and disregarding the interest factor, how much more does S owe the IRS?

4. Assume the same facts as in Problem 3, except that the additional income tax due was $80 (rather than $500). Based on these new facts and disregarding the interest element, how much more does S owe the IRS?

5. R, a calendar year individual taxpayer, files her 1986 return on January 11, 1988. R did not obtain an extension for filing her return, and such return reflects additional income tax due of $3,800.

a. What are R's penalties for failure to file and to pay?

b. Would your answer to (a) change if R, before the due date of the return, had retained a CPA to prepare the return and it was the CPA's negligence that caused the delay?

6. U underpaid his taxes for 1987 in the amount of $10,000, such underpayment being attributable to negligence. If the interest on the underpayment was $2,200, what is U's total negligence penalty?

7. Assume the same facts as in Problem 6, but only $5,000 of the $10,000 underpayment was attributable to negligence. What is U's total negligence penalty?

8. V underpaid his taxes for 1985 in the amount of $100,000, of which $80,000 was attributable to civil fraud. If the interest on the underpayment was $12,000, what is V's total civil fraud penalty?

9. Assume the same facts as in Problem 8, but the year of the underpayment is 1988 (not 1985). What is V's total civil fraud penalty?

10. In 1985, T made a charitable contribution of property which he valued at $20,000. This amount was claimed by T as a deduction on his 1985 income tax return filed in 1986. What was T's overvaluation penalty if the real value of this donated property was $8,000? (Assume T was in a 50% income tax bracket.)

11. In 1983, T Corporation purchased 10% of the stock in X Corporation for $100,000. In 1985, X Corporation made a cash distribution to its shareholders of $500,000 ($50,000 of which was received by T Corporation). Since all parties were convinced that X Corporation had no earnings and profits at the time of the distribution, no dividend income was recognized by any of the shareholders. After the statute of limitations had expired, the IRS correctly determined that the distribution was fully covered by earnings and profits and should have been reported by the shareholders as dividend income. In 1990, T Corporation sells its stock investment in X Corporation for $250,000.

a. How much gain should T Corporation recognize as a result of the sale?

b. If T Corporation recognizes a gain of $150,000 as a result of the sale, does the IRS have any recourse?

12. When T accepted employment in 1987 with X Corporation he completed a Form W–4 listing 14 exemptions. Since T was single and had no dependents, he misrepresented his situation on Form W–4. What penalties, if any, might the IRS impose upon T?

13. What is the applicable statute of limitations in each of the following independent situations:

    a. No return was filed by the taxpayer.

    b. A corporation is determined to have been a personal holding company for the year in question.

    c. For 1983, the XYZ Associates filed a Form 1065 (i.e., a partnership return). In 1988, the IRS determined that the organization was not a partnership in 1983 but was, in fact, a corporation.

    d. In 1983, T incurred a bad debt loss that she failed to claim.

    e. On his 1983 return, a taxpayer inadvertently omitted a large amount of gross income.

    f. Same as (e), except that the omission was deliberate.

    g. For 1983, a taxpayer innocently overstated her deductions by a large amount.

14. During 1983, T (an individual calendar year taxpayer) had the following transactions, all of which were properly reported on a timely filed return:

Gross receipts		$ 960,000
Cost of goods sold		(800,000)
Gross profit		$ 160,000
Capital gains and losses—		
Capital gain	$ 72,000	
Capital loss	(24,000)	48,000
Total income		$ 208,000

    a. Presuming the absence of fraud on T's part, how much of an omission from gross income would be required to make the six-year statute of limitations apply?

    b. Would it matter in your answer to (a) if cost of goods sold had been inadvertently overstated by $100,000?

15. On April 3, 1985, T filed his 1984 income tax return reflecting a tax of $40,000. On June 30, 1986, he filed an amended 1984 return showing an additional $12,000 tax, which was then paid. On May 20, 1988, he filed a claim for refund of $18,000.

    a. Assuming T is correct concerning the claim for refund, how much tax can he recover?

    b. For what period is the interest payable on T's refund?

16. Ms. T had $40,000 withheld in 1984. Because of heavy itemized deductions, she figured that she had no further tax to pay for the year. For this reason and because of personal problems, and without securing an extension, she did not file her 1984 return until July 1, 1985. Actually, the return showed a refund of $2,400, which Ms. T ultimately received. On May 10, 1988, Ms. T filed a $16,000 claim for refund of her 1984 taxes.

    a. How much, if any, of the $16,000 may Ms. T recover?

    b. Would it have made any difference if Ms. T had requested and secured from the IRS an extension of time for filing her 1984 tax return?

17. R's Federal income tax returns (i.e., Form 1040) for the past three years (1985–1987) were prepared by the following persons:

Preparer	1985	1986	1987
R	X		
S		X	
T			X

S is R's next-door neighbor and owns and operates a pharmacy. T is a licensed CPA and is engaged in private practice. In the event R is audited and all three returns are examined, comment on who may represent R before the IRS at the agent level. At the Appeals Division.

18. Indicate whether the following statements are true or false (Note: SRTP = Statements on Responsibilities in Tax Practice):

a. When a CPA has reasonable grounds for not answering an applicable question on a client's return, a brief explanation of the reason for the omission should not be provided, because it would flag the return for audit by the IRS.

b. In preparing a taxpayer's return for 1987, a CPA finds out that the client had 50% of his medical expense deduction claimed for 1985 disallowed on audit by the IRS. The CPA should feel bound by the prior administrative proceeding in determining his client's medical expense deduction for 1987.

c. If the client tells you that she had contributions of $500 for unsubstantiated cash donations to her church, you should deduct an odd amount on her return (e.g., $499), because an even amount (i.e., $500) would indicate to the IRS that her deduction was based on an estimate.

d. Basing an expense deduction on the client's estimates is not acceptable under the SRTP.

e. If a CPA knows that his or her client has a material error in a prior year's return, he or she should not, without the client's consent, disclose the error to the IRS.

f. If a CPA's client will not correct a material error in a prior year's return, the CPA should not prepare the current year's return for the client.

g. If a CPA discovers during an IRS audit that his or her client has a material error in the return under examination, he or she should immediately withdraw from the engagement.

h. If a CPA renders tax advice to the client in early 1987, the client should be able to rely on such advice until April 15, 1988. (The client prepared her own tax return.)

i. The SRTP have the same force and effect as the AICPA's Code of Professional Ethics.

Research Problems

Research Problem 1. For tax years 1971–1975, T filed fraudulent income tax returns. In 1977, however, he filed nonfraudulent amended returns and paid the additional basic taxes shown thereon. In 1983, the IRS issues notices of deficiency, asserting liability under § 6653(b) for additions to tax on account of fraud. T invoked the three-year statute of limitations as a defense to the assessment. Which side will prevail? Why?

Research Problem 2. E Corporation was formed in early 1978, did business for a short while, and is currently without assets. H was a director, minority shareholder, treasurer, and executive vice president of E Corporation from its creation to the date of his resignation on

September 12, 1978. H was responsible for E Corporation's day-to-day operations, although J, the majority shareholder and CEO, had the final say on the resolution of more important matters. At the start of his tenure with E Corporation, H himself determined on several occasions which of the bills were to be paid. In May of 1978, he caused $8,000 in back taxes to be paid to the IRS on behalf of J's predecessor partnership (with which H had no connection). J became extremely upset with H's action and ordered H not to pay any more money to the IRS. In fact, J relieved H of his duties for several weeks.

Upon being reinstated, H was instructed by J not to pay any more bills without J's prior approval. Although J generally told H which creditors he should pay and when, H did issue small checks without J's approval on a number of occasions. From May 12, 1978, to July 6, 1978, H was the only authorized signatory on the main checking account of E Corporation and wrote most of the company's checks. From July 6, 1978, until September 7, 1978, H and C (the comptroller and an employee working under H's supervision) were the only authorized signatories on this account. The bank required only one signature on checks drawn on this account.

E Corporation incurred employment tax liability for the second, third, and fourth quarters of 1978 in the amount of $30,388.53. These taxes included Federal income taxes withheld from employees, the employee portion of FICA taxes withheld from the employees, and the employer portion of FICA taxes. H was aware that the taxes were due and owing to the IRS, at least in some amount, as early as June of 1978.

At some point during the summer of 1978, H contacted a senior IRS official who was also a deacon at his church and asked what he should do about E Corporation's unpaid taxes. Allegedly, the official suggested that H write a letter to the IRS explaining the situation. H did not immediately follow this advice but continued fulfilling his duties at E Corporation throughout the summer. In this connection, he wrote at least 36 checks to creditors other than the IRS.

In his resignation letter to J, H expressed concern over the unpaid taxes (estimated to be in excess of $30,000). This letter was followed by a letter to the IRS, placing it on notice as to the situation. At the time these letters were written, E Corporation still had a substantial amount of money on deposit at the bank as well as substantial assets in the form of inventories and accounts receivable. The IRS did not move to collect the taxes until over two years later. By that time, E Corporation was without assets.

The IRS issued assessments in the amount of the unpaid taxes under § 6672(a) against both H and J. Unfortunately, the IRS was unable to effect personal service on J but pursued the assessment against H. After paying a portion of the amount involved, H sued for a refund in the District Court. The IRS counterclaimed for the balance of the unpaid assessment. How should this controversy be resolved?

Research Problem 3. B became a CPA in 1964 and has practiced public accounting since 1965. In 1979, he was hired by the accounting firm of GW who had, among other clients, R Corporation and R (the sole shareholder of R Corporation). In 1979, B was assigned the accounts of R Corporation and R and was designated to be the preparer of their 1978 income tax returns. In the past, GW had adopted the practice of sending a data questionnaire to its individual income tax clients that was to be completed by the client and returned to the firm or used by the client as a guide in collecting the information necessary for the firm to prepare the returns. Such a questionnaire was not used by B when he prepared R's individual income tax return. Instead, the information necessary was supplied to B by R Corporation's bookkeeper. Such information was reconciled by B with R's prior return, processed, and eventually timely filed with the IRS. B also prepared and filed the Form 1120 for R Corporation based on a trial balance sheet submitted by the same bookkeeper. Unknown to B, R Corporation (due to high interest rates) had changed its borrowing policy. Instead of financing its operations through banking institutions, the credit source became R. Thus, an interest deduction of $15,000 was claimed on R Corporation's Form 1120 but was not reported as income on R's Form 1040. When B prepared the returns for the same clients as to tax year 1979, the same procedure was followed. Thus, as to the omitted interest income, history repeated itself. When the IRS caught the oversight, it assessed the $100 tax preparer penalty against B for both 1978 and 1979. How should this matter be resolved?

Research Problem 4. T's 1976 tax return listed his address as being in Allentown, Pennsylvania. Twelve days before the three-year statute of limitations was to expire, T orally notified the IRS of his new address in Niles, Michigan. That same day, the IRS mailed to T at the new address a Form 872 to extend the statute of limitations for 1976. T signed and mailed the Form 872, but the form was not received by the IRS before the expiration of the three-year period. On the last day of the limitation period, the IRS mailed a statutory notice of deficiency (90-day letter) to T at his old address. The U.S. Postal Service forwarded the notice to T at the new Niles address. Within 90 days of the mailing of the notice, T filed a timely petition with the U.S. Tax Court. In his petition, T made a motion to dismiss for lack of a timely notice of deficiency. How should this controversy be resolved?

Research Problem 5. Dr. P executed a single Form 872 that purported to extend the period for assessment for his 1974, 1975, and 1977 taxable years to June 30, 1981. Before accepting this form, and at a time at least 55 days before the expiration of the period for assessment, the IRS struck through the reference to the 1977 taxable year. The IRS did not seek the consent of Dr. P to this alteration, and when Dr. P received the modified Form 872, he called the IRS, vented his anger, and repudiated the change. The IRS issued a statutory notice of deficiency on March 27, 1981. Is the notice of deficiency valid? Why or why not?

Research Problem 6. Shortly before the statute of limitations was about to expire on a net operating loss carryback, T conferred with a nearby IRS office to obtain taxpayer assistance. The agent gave T several copies of Form 1045 (Application for Tentative Refund from Carryback of Net Operating Loss, Unused Investment Credit). One of these was properly completed by T and duly mailed to and received by the District Director two days before the expiration of the statute of limitations. Five days later, T received a form letter from the District Director's office informing him that he had used the wrong form and should, instead, file Form 1040X. The letter enclosed T's completed Form 1045. On the same day, T completed Form 1040X and sent it by registered mail to the District Director. One month thereafter, T received notice that his claim was barred by the statute of limitations. What are T's rights under the circumstances?

Research Problem 7. The heirs of an estate engaged an attorney to handle its probate and relied upon him to perform all necessary acts. In turn, the attorney arranged to have an assistant of his named administrator and depended upon him to timely file the death tax return. Such return was not timely filed, and no explanation was presented for the failure to do so. Is the estate liable for the addition to tax under § 6651(a)?

Research Problem 8. While working in an abandoned garage, T finds $2,438,110 in old currency which he turns over to the local authorities. After a lengthy series of legal actions (to which T is not a party), the money is identified as belonging to a convicted mobster and is turned over to the IRS in part payment of his delinquent taxes. The IRS rewards T with a cash payment of approximately 1.32% of the amount of currency he found. T feels he has been cheated, and he files suit in the U.S. Claims Court for the difference between 1.32% and 10%. Does T have a chance?

Appendix A
Tax Rates and Tables

Income Tax Rates—Individuals
1987 Tax Rate Schedules

Single Taxpayers (Schedule X)

If taxable income is:		The tax is:	Of the Amount Over
Over	But Not Over		
$ 0	$ 1,800	$ 0 + 11%	$ 0
1,800	16,800	198 + 15%	1,800
16,800	27,000	2,448 + 28%	16,800
27,000	54,000	5,304 + 35%	27,000
54,000	—	14,754 + 38.5%	54,000

Heads of Household (Schedule Z)

If taxable income is:		The tax is:	Of the Amount Over
Over	But Not Over		
$ 0	$ 2,500	$ 0 + 11%	$ 0
2,500	23,000	275 + 15%	2,500
23,000	38,000	3,350 + 28%	23,000
38,000	80,000	7,550 + 35%	38,000
80,000	—	22,250 + 38.5%	80,000

Married, Filing Joint (Schedule Y)

If taxable income is:		The tax is:	Of the Amount Over
Over	But Not Over		
$ 0	$ 3,000	$ 0 + 11%	$ 0
3,000	28,000	330 + 15%	3,000
28,000	45,000	4,080 + 28%	28,000
45,000	90,000	8,840 + 35%	45,000
90,000	—	24,590 + 38.5%	90,000

Married, Filing Separate (Schedule Y)

If taxable income is:		The tax is:	Of the Amount Over
Over	But Not Over		
$ 0	$ 1,500	$ 0 + 11%	$ 0
1,500	14,000	165 + 15%	1,500
14,000	22,500	2,040 + 28%	14,000
22,500	45,000	4,420 + 35%	22,500
45,000	—	12,295 + 38.5%	45,000

Fiscal-year taxpayers will use the same 1987 blended rate schedules as calendar-year taxpayers for taxable years beginning in 1987.

1988 Tax Rate Schedules

Single [Sec. 1(c)]:

If taxable income is:	The tax is:
Not over $17,850	15% of taxable income.
Over $17,850	$2,677.50, plus 28% of the excess over $17,850.

Head of Household [Sec. 1(b)]:

If taxable income is:	The tax is:
Not over $23,900	15% of taxable income.
Over $23,900	$3,585, plus 28% of the excess over $23,900.

Married, Filing Joint Return and Qualifying Widow(er) [Sec. 1(a)]:

If taxable income is:	The tax is:
Not over $29,750	15% of taxable income.
Over $29,750	$4,462.50, plus 28% of the excess over $29,750.

Married, Filing Separately [Sec. 1(d)]:

If taxable income is:	The tax is:
Not over $14,875	15% of taxable income.
Over $14,875	$2,231.25, plus 28% of the excess over $14,875.

Rate Adjustment. Beginning in 1988, taxable income within certain ranges is subject to an additional 5% tax. This 5% rate adjustment phases out the benefit of the 15% tax rate. The applicable ranges of taxable income to which the additional tax (phaseout of 15% rate) applies are shown for each filing status in the following chart:

Filing Status	Taxable Income	
	(a) More Than	(b) But Not More Than
Married filing joint return and Qualifying widow(er)	$71,900	$149,250
Head of household	61,650	123,790
Single	43,150	89,560
Married filing separately	35,950	113,300

Phaseout of Personal Exemption. Beginning in 1988, the amount claimed as a deduction for personal exemptions will be phased out at a 5% rate once taxable income exceeds the amount in column (b) of the chart above for your filing status. Each increase of $10,920 of income above that amount will phase out the value of one personal exemption.

The amount of income subject to the 5% rate for the phaseout of the benefit of personal exemptions is the lesser of the taxable income in excess of the amount in column (b), or the number of exemptions claimed multiplied by $10,920.

Income Tax Rates—Estates and Trusts

Tax Year 1987

Taxable Income	Tax on Excess	Tax on Previous Brackets
Up to $500	11%	$ 0
$501–$4,700	15	55
$4,701–$7,550	28	685
$7,551–$15,150	35	1,483
Over $15,150	38.5	4,143

Tax Years 1988 and After

Taxable Income	Tax on Excess	Tax on Previous Brackets
Up to $5,000	15%	$ 0
Over $5,000	28	750
$13,000–$26,000	5*	

* Additional tax, "phases out" the fifteen percent bracket

Income Tax Rates—Corporations

Tax Year 1986

Taxable Income	Rate
$ 1—$ 25,000	15%
25,001— 50,000	18
50,001— 75,000	30
75,001— 100,000	40
over $ 100,000	46
$1,000,000—$1,405,000	5*

* Additional tax, "phases out" the lower marginal brackets

Tax Years Beginning After 6/30/87 **

Taxable Income	Rate
$ 1—$ 50,000	15%
50,001— 75,000	25
over $ 75,000	34
$100,000—$335,000	5*

* Additional tax, "phases out" the lower marginal brackets
** For fiscal year corporations, the proration rules of § 15 apply.

Unified Transfer Tax Rates

For Gifts Made and For Deaths After 1976 and Before 1982

If the amount with respect to which the tentative tax to be computed is:	The tentative tax is:
Not over $10,000	18 percent of such amount.
Over $10,000 but not over $20,000	$1,800, plus 20 percent of the excess of such amount over $10,000.
Over $20,000 but not over $40,000	$3,800, plus 22 percent of the excess of such amount over $20,000.
Over $40,000 but not over $60,000	$8,200, plus 24 percent of the excess of such amount over $40,000.
Over $60,000 but not over $80,000	$13,000, plus 26 percent of the excess of such amount over $60,000.
Over $80,000 but not over $100,000	$18,200, plus 28 percent of the excess of such amount over $80,000.
Over $100,000 but not over $150,000	$23,800, plus 30 percent of the excess of such amount over $100,000.
Over $150,000 but not over $250,000	$38,800, plus 32 percent of the excess of such amount over $150,000.
Over $250,000 but not over $500,000	$70,800, plus 34 percent of the excess of such amount over $250,000.
Over $500,000 but not over $750,000	$155,800, plus 37 percent of the excess of such amount over $500,000.
Over $750,000 but not over $1,000,000	$248,300, plus 39 percent of the excess of such amount over $750,000.
Over $1,000,000 but not over $1,250,000	$345,800, plus 41 percent of the excess of such amount over $1,000,000.
Over $1,250,000 but not over $1,500,000	$448,300, plus 43 percent of the excess of such amount over $1,250,000.
Over $1,500,000 but not over $2,000,000	$555,800, plus 45 percent of the excess of such amount over $1,500,000.
Over $2,000,000 but not over $2,500,000	$780,800, plus 49 percent of the excess of such amount over $2,000,000.
Over $2,500,000 but not over $3,000,000	$1,025,800, plus 53 percent of the excess of such amount over $2,500,000.
Over $3,000,000 but not over $3,500,000	$1,290,800, plus 57 percent of the excess of such amount over $3,000,000.
Over $3,500,000 but not over $4,000,000	$1,575,800, plus 61 percent of the excess of such amount over $3,500,000.
Over $4,000,000 but not over $4,500,000	$1,880,800, plus 65 percent of the excess of such amount over $4,000,000.
Over $4,500,000 but not over $5,000,000	$2,205,800, plus 69 percent of the excess of such amount over $4,500,000.
Over $5,000,000	$2,550,800, plus 70 percent of the excess of such amount over $5,000,000.

▬▬ Unified Transfer Tax Rates

For Gifts Made and For Deaths in 1982

If the amount with respect to which the tentative tax to be computed is:	The tentative tax is:
Not over $10,000	18 percent of such amount.
Over $10,000 but not over $20,000	$1,800, plus 20 percent of the excess of such amount over $10,000.
Over $20,000 but not over $40,000	$3,800, plus 22 percent of the excess of such amount over $20,000.
Over $40,000 but not over $60,000	$8,200, plus 24 percent of the excess of such amount over $40,000.
Over $60,000 but not over $80,000	$13,000, plus 26 percent of the excess of such amount over $60,000.
Over $80,000 but not over $100,000	$18,200, plus 28 percent of the excess of such amount over $80,000.
Over $100,000 but not over $150,000	$23,800, plus 30 percent of the excess of such amount over $100,000.
Over $150,000 but not over $250,000	$38,800, plus 32 percent of the excess of such amount over $150,000.
Over $250,000 but not over $500,000	$70,800, plus 34 percent of the excess of such amount over $250,000.
Over $500,000 but not over $750,000	$155,800, plus 37 percent of the excess of such amount over $500,000.
Over $750,000 but not over $1,000,000	$248,300, plus 39 percent of the excess of such amount over $750,000.
Over $1,000,000 but not over $1,250,000	$345,800, plus 41 percent of the excess of such amount over $1,000,000.
Over $1,250,000 but not over $1,500,000	$448,300, plus 43 percent of the excess of such amount over $1,250,000.
Over $1,500,000 but not over $2,000,000	$555,800, plus 45 percent of the excess of such amount over $1,500,000.
Over $2,000,000 but not over $2,500,000	$780,800, plus 49 percent of the excess of such amount over $2,000,000.
Over $2,500,000 but not over $3,000,000	$1,025,800, plus 53 percent of the excess of such amount over $2,500,000.
Over $3,000,000 but not over $3,500,000	$1,290,800, plus 57 percent of the excess of such amount over $3,000,000.
Over $3,500,000 but not over $4,000,000	$1,575,800, plus 61 percent of the excess of such amount over $3,500,000.
Over $4,000,000	$1,880,800, plus 65 percent of the excess of such amount over $4,000,000.

Unified Transfer Tax Rates

For Gifts Made and For Deaths in 1983

If the amount with respect to which the tentative tax to be computed is:	The tentative tax is:
Not over $10,000	18 percent of such amount.
Over $10,000 but not over $20,000	$1,800, plus 20 percent of the excess of such amount over $10,000.
Over $20,000 but not over $40,000	$3,800, plus 22 percent of the excess of such amount over $20,000.
Over $40,000 but not over $60,000	$8,200, plus 24 percent of the excess of such amount over $40,000.
Over $60,000 but not over $80,000	$13,000, plus 26 percent of the excess of such amount over $60,000.
Over $80,000 but not over $100,000	$18,200, plus 28 percent of the excess of such amount over $80,000.
Over $100,000 but not over $150,000	$23,800, plus 30 percent of the excess of such amount over $100,000.
Over $150,000 but not over $250,000	$38,800, plus 32 percent of the excess of such amount over $150,000.
Over $250,000 but not over $500,000	$70,800, plus 34 percent of the excess of such amount over $250,000.
Over $500,000 but not over $750,000	$155,800, plus 37 percent of the excess of such amount over $500,000.
Over $750,000 but not over $1,000,000	$248,300, plus 39 percent of the excess of such amount over $750,000.
Over $1,000,000 but not over $1,250,000	$345,800, plus 41 percent of the excess of such amount over $1,000,000.
Over $1,250,000 but not over $1,500,000	$448,300, plus 43 percent of the excess of such amount over $1,250,000.
Over $1,500,000 but not over $2,000,000	$555,800, plus 45 percent of the excess of such amount over $1,500,000.
Over $2,000,000 but not over $2,500,000	$780,800, plus 49 percent of the excess of such amount over $2,000,000.
Over $2,500,000 but not over $3,000,000	$1,025,800, plus 53 percent of the excess of such amount over $2,500,000.
Over $3,000,000 but not over $3,500,000	$1,290,800, plus 57 percent of the excess of such amount over $3,000,000.
Over $3,500,000	$1,575,800, plus 60 percent of the excess of such amount over $3,500,000.

Unified Transfer Tax Rates

For Gifts Made and For Deaths after 1983 and before 1993

If the amount with respect to which the tentative tax to be computed is:	The tentative tax is:
Not over $10,000	18 percent of such amount.
Over $10,000 but not over $20,000	$1,800, plus 20 percent of the excess of such amount over $10,000.
Over $20,000 but not over $40,000	$3,800, plus 22 percent of the excess of such amount over $20,000.
Over $40,000 but not over $60,000	$8,200, plus 24 percent of the excess of such amount over $40,000.
Over $60,000 but not over $80,000	$13,000, plus 26 percent of the excess of such amount over $60,000.
Over $80,000 but not over $100,000	$18,200, plus 28 percent of the excess of such amount over $80,000.
Over $100,000 but not over $150,000	$23,800, plus 30 percent of the excess of such amount over $100,000.
Over $150,000 but not over $250,000	$38,800, plus 32 percent of the excess of such amount over $150,000.
Over $250,000 but not over $500,000	$70,800, plus 34 percent of the excess of such amount over $250,000.
Over $500,000 but not over $750,000	$155,800, plus 37 percent of the excess of such amount over $500,000.
Over $750,000 but not over $1,000,000	$248,300, plus 39 percent of the excess of such amount over $750,000.
Over $1,000,000 but not over $1,250,000	$345,800, plus 41 percent of the excess of such amount over $1,000,000.
Over $1,250,000 but not over $1,500,000	$448,300, plus 43 percent of the excess of such amount over $1,250,000.
Over $1,500,000 but not over $2,000,000	$555,800, plus 45 percent of the excess of such amount over $1,500,000.
Over $2,000,000 but not over $2,500,000	$780,800, plus 49 percent of the excess of such amount over $2,000,000.
Over $2,500,000 but not over $3,000,000	$1,025,800, plus 53 percent of the excess of such amount over $2,500,000.
Over $3,000,000 *	$1,290,800, plus 55 percent of the excess of such amount over $3,000,000.

*For large taxable transfers (generally in excess of $10 million) there is a phase-out of the graduated rates and the unified tax credit.

Unified Transfer Tax Rates

For Gifts Made and For Deaths After 1992

If the amount with respect to which the tentative tax to be computed is:	The tentative tax is:
Not over $10,000	18 percent of such amount.
Over $10,000 but not over $20,000	$1,800, plus 20 percent of the excess of such amount over $10,000.
Over $20,000 but not over $40,000	$3,800, plus 22 percent of the excess of such amount over $20,000.
Over $40,000 but not over $60,000	$8,200, plus 24 percent of the excess of such amount over $40,000.
Over $60,000 but not over $80,000	$13,000, plus 26 percent of the excess of such amount over $60,000.
Over $80,000 but not over $100,000	$18,200, plus 28 percent of the excess of such amount over $80,000.
Over $100,000 but not over $150,000	$23,800, plus 30 percent of the excess of such amount over $100,000.
Over $150,000 but not over $250,000	$38,800, plus 32 percent of the excess of such amount over $150,000.
Over $250,000 but not over $500,000	$70,800, plus 34 percent of the excess of such amount over $250,000.
Over $500,000 but not over $750,000	$155,800, plus 37 percent of the excess of such amount over $500,000.
Over $750,000 but not over $1,000,000	$248,300, plus 39 percent of the excess of such amount over $750,000.
Over $1,000,000 but not over $1,250,000	$345,800, plus 41 percent of the excess of such amount over $1,000,000.
Over $1,250,000 but not over $1,500,000	$448,300, plus 43 percent of the excess of such amount over $1,250,000.
Over $1,500,000 but not over $2,000,000	$555,800, plus 45 percent of the excess of such amount over $1,500,000.
Over $2,000,000 but not over $2,500,000	$780,800, plus 49 percent of the excess of such amount over $2,000,000.
Over $2,500,000	$1,025,800, plus 50 percent of the excess of such amount over $2,500,000.

▬▬▬ Estate Tax Rates (before 1977)

(A) Taxable estate equal to or more than—	(B) Taxable estate less than—	(C) Tax on amount in column (A)	(D) Rate of tax on excess over amount in column (A)
			Percent
0	$ 5,000	0	3
$ 5,000	10,000	$ 150	7
10,000	20,000	500	11
20,000	30,000	1,600	14
30,000	40,000	3,000	18
40,000	50,000	4,800	22
50,000	60,000	7,000	25
60,000	100,000	9,500	28
100,000	250,000	20,700	30
250,000	500,000	65,700	32
500,000	750,000	145,700	35
750,000	1,000,000	233,200	37
1,000,000	1,250,000	325,700	39
1,250,000	1,500,000	423,200	42
1,500,000	2,000,000	528,200	45
2,000,000	2,500,000	753,200	49
2,500,000	3,000,000	998,200	53
3,000,000	3,500,000	1,263,200	56
3,500,000	4,000,000	1,543,200	59
4,000,000	5,000,000	1,838,200	63
5,000,000	6,000,000	2,468,200	67
6,000,000	7,000,000	3,138,200	70
7,000,000	8,000,000	3,838,200	73
8,000,000	10,000,000	4,568,200	76
10,000,000		6,088,200	77

Gift Tax Rates (before 1977)

(A) Amount of taxable gifts equal to or more than—	(B) Amount of taxable gifts less than—	(C) Tax on amount in column (A)	(D) Rate of tax on excess over amount in column (A)
			Percent
0	$ 5,000	0	$2\frac{1}{4}$
$ 5,000	10,000	$ 112.50	$5\frac{1}{4}$
10,000	20,000	375.00	$8\frac{1}{4}$
20,000	30,000	1,200.00	$10\frac{1}{2}$
30,000	40,000	2,250.00	$13\frac{1}{2}$
40,000	50,000	3,600.00	$16\frac{1}{2}$
50,000	60,000	5,250.00	$18\frac{3}{4}$
60,000	100,000	7,125.00	21
100,000	250,000	15,525.00	$22\frac{1}{2}$
250,000	500,000	49,275.00	24
500,000	750,000	109,275.00	$26\frac{1}{4}$
750,000	1,000,000	174,900.00	$27\frac{3}{4}$
1,000,000	1,250,000	244,275.00	$29\frac{1}{4}$
1,250,000	1,500,000	317,400.00	$31\frac{1}{2}$
1,500,000	2,000,000	396,150.00	$33\frac{3}{4}$
2,000,000	2,500,000	564,900.00	$36\frac{3}{4}$
2,500,000	3,000,000	748,650.00	$39\frac{3}{4}$
3,000,000	3,500,000	947,400.00	42
3,500,000	4,000,000	1,157,400.00	$44\frac{1}{4}$
4,000,000	5,000,000	1,378,650.00	$47\frac{1}{4}$
5,000,000	6,000,000	1,851,150.00	$50\frac{1}{4}$
6,000,000	7,000,000	2,353,650.00	$52\frac{1}{2}$
7,000,000	8,000,000	2,878,650.00	$54\frac{3}{4}$
8,000,000	10,000,000	3,426,150.00	57
10,000,000		4,566,150.00	$57\frac{3}{4}$

Table for Computation of Maximum Credit for State Death Taxes

(A) Adjusted Taxable Estate* equal to or more than—	(B) Adjusted Taxable Estate* less than—	(C) Credit on amount in column (A)	(D) Rates of credit on excess over amount in column (A)
			Percent
0	$ 40,000	0	None
$ 40,000	90,000	0	0.8
90,000	140,000	$ 400	1.6
140,000	240,000	1,200	2.4
240,000	440,000	3,600	3.2
440,000	640,000	10,000	4.0
640,000	840,000	18,000	4.8
840,000	1,040,000	27,600	5.6
1,040,000	1,540,000	38,800	6.4
1,540,000	2,040,000	70,800	7.2
2,040,000	2,540,000	106,800	8.0
2,540,000	3,040,000	146,800	8.8
3,040,000	3,540,000	190,800	9.6
3,540,000	4,040,000	238,800	10.4
4,040,000	5,040,000	290,800	11.2
5,040,000	6,040,000	402,800	12.0
6,040,000	7,040,000	522,800	12.8
7,040,000	8,040,000	650,800	13.6
8,040,000	9,040,000	786,800	14.4
9,040,000	10,040,000	930,800	15.2
10,040,000		1,082,800	16.0

* Adjusted Taxable Estate = Taxable Estate − $60,000

Valuation Tables

(After 1970 and before December 1, 1983)

Table A–6%

	Male				Female		
1 Age	**2** Annuity	**3** Life Estate	**4** Remainder	**1** Age	**2** Annuity	**3** Life Estate	**4** Remainder
0	15.6175	.93705	.06295	0	15.8972	.95383	.04617
1	16.0362	.96217	.03783	1	16.2284	.97370	.02630
2	16.0283	.96170	.03830	2	16.2287	.97372	.02628
3	16.0089	.96053	.03947	3	16.2180	.97308	.02692
4	15.9841	.95905	.04095	4	16.2029	.97217	.02783
5	15.9553	.95732	.04268	5	16.1850	.97110	.02890
6	15.9233	.95540	.04460	6	16.1648	.96989	.03011
7	15.8885	.95331	.04669	7	16.1421	.96853	.03147
8	15.8508	.95105	.04895	8	16.1172	.96703	.03297
9	15.8101	.94861	.05139	9	16.0901	.96541	.03459
10	15.7663	.94598	.05402	10	16.0608	.96365	.03635
11	15.7194	.94316	.05684	11	16.0293	.96176	.03824
12	15.6698	.94019	.05981	12	15.9958	.95975	.04025
13	15.6180	.93708	.06292	13	15.9607	.95764	.04236
14	15.5651	.93391	.06609	14	15.9239	.95543	.04457
15	15.5115	.93069	.06931	15	15.8856	.95314	.04686
16	15.4576	.92746	.07254	16	15.8460	.95076	.04924
17	15.4031	.92419	.07581	17	15.8048	.94829	.05171
18	15.3481	.92089	.07911	18	15.7620	.94572	.05428
19	15.2918	.91751	.08249	19	15.7172	.94303	.05697
20	15.2339	.91403	.08597	20	15.6701	.94021	.05979
21	15.1744	.91046	.08954	21	15.6207	.93724	.06276
22	15.1130	.90678	.09322	22	15.6587	.93412	.06588
23	15.0487	.90292	.09708	23	15.5141	.93085	.06915
24	14.9807	.89884	.10116	24	15.4565	.92739	.07261
25	14.9075	.89445	.10555	25	15.3959	.92375	.07625
26	14.8287	.88972	.11028	26	15.3322	.91993	.08007
27	14.7442	.88465	.11535	27	15.2652	.91591	.08409
28	14.6542	.87925	.12075	28	15.1946	.91168	.08832
29	14.5588	.87353	.12647	29	15.1208	.90725	.09275
30	14.4584	.86750	.13250	30	15.0432	.90259	.09741
31	14.3528	.86117	.13883	31	14.9622	.89773	.10227
32	14.2418	.85451	.14549	32	14.8775	.89265	.10735
33	14.1254	.84752	.15248	33	14.7888	.88733	.11267
34	14.0034	.84020	.15980	34	14.6960	.88176	.11824
35	13.8758	.83255	.16745	35	14.5989	.87593	.12407
36	13.7425	.82455	.17545	36	14.4975	.86985	.13015
37	13.6036	.81622	.18378	37	14.3915	.86349	.13651
38	13.4591	.80755	.19245	38	14.2811	.85687	.14313
39	13.3090	.79854	.20146	39	14.1663	.84998	.15002
40	13.1538	.78923	.21077	40	14.0468	.84281	.15719
41	12.9934	.77960	.22040	41	13.9227	.83536	.16464
42	12.8279	.76967	.23033	42	13.7940	.82764	.17236
43	12.6574	.75944	.24056	43	13.6604	.81962	.18038
44	12.4819	.74891	.25109	44	13.5219	.81131	.18869
45	12.3013	.73808	.26192	45	13.3781	.80269	.19731
46	12.1158	.72695	.27305	46	13.2290	.79374	.20626
47	11.9253	.71552	.28448	47	13.0746	.78448	.21552
48	11.7308	.70385	.29615	48	12.9147	.77488	.22512
49	11.5330	.69198	.30802	49	12.7496	.76498	.23502
50	11.3329	.67997	.32003	50	12.5793	.75476	.24524
51	11.1308	.66785	.33215	51	12.4039	.74423	.25577
52	10.9267	.65560	.34440	52	12.2232	.73339	.26661
53	10.7200	.64320	.35680	53	12.0367	.72220	.27780
54	10.5100	.63060	.36940	54	11.8436	.71062	.28938
55	10.2960	.61776	.38224	55	11.6432	.69859	.30141

Valuation Tables

(After 1970 and before December 1, 1983, *cont.*)

Table A-6%

Male				Female			
1 Age	2 Annuity	3 Life Estate	4 Remainder	1 Age	2 Annuity	3 Life Estate	4 Remainder
56	10.0777	.60466	.39534	56	11.4353	.68612	.31388
57	9.8552	.59131	.40869	57	11.2200	.67320	.32680
58	9.6297	.57778	.42222	58	10.9980	.65988	.34012
59	9.4028	.56417	.43583	59	10.7703	.64622	.35378
60	9.1753	.55052	.44948	60	10.5376	.63226	.36774
61	8.9478	.53687	.46313	61	10.3005	.61803	.38197
62	8.7202	.52321	.47679	62	10.0587	.60352	.39648
63	8.4924	.50954	.49046	63	9.8118	.58871	.41129
64	8.2642	.49585	.50415	64	9.5592	.57355	.42645
65	8.0353	.48212	.51788	65	9.3005	.55803	.44197
66	7.8060	.46836	.53164	66	9.0352	.54211	.45789
67	7.5763	.45458	.54542	67	8.7639	.52583	.47417
68	7.3462	.44077	.55923	68	8.4874	.50924	.49076
69	7.1149	.42689	.57311	69	8.2068	.49241	.50759
70	6.8823	.41294	.58706	70	7.9234	.47540	.52460
71	6.6481	.39889	.60111	71	7.6371	.45823	.54177
72	6.4123	.38474	.61526	72	7.3480	.44088	.55912
73	6.1752	.37051	.62949	73	7.0568	.42341	.57659
74	5.9373	.35624	.64376	74	6.7645	.40587	.59413
75	5.6990	.34194	.65806	75	6.4721	.38833	.61167
76	5.4602	.32761	.67239	76	6.1788	.37073	.62927
77	5.2211	.31327	.68673	77	5.8845	.35307	.64693
78	4.9825	.29895	.70105	78	5.5910	.33546	.66454
79	4.7469	.28481	.71519	79	5.3018	.31811	.68189
80	4.5164	.27098	.72902	80	5.0195	.30117	.69883
81	4.2955	.25773	.74227	81	4.7482	.28489	.71511
82	4.0879	.24527	.75473	82	4.4892	.26935	.73065
83	3.8924	.23354	.76646	83	4.2398	.25439	.74561
84	3.7029	.22217	.77783	84	3.9927	.23956	.76044
85	3.5117	.21070	.78930	85	3.7401	.22441	.77559
86	3.3259	.19955	.80045	86	3.5016	.21010	.78990
87	3.1450	.18820	.81130	87	3.2790	.19674	.80326
88	2.9703	.17872	.82178	88	3.0719	.18431	.81569
89	2.8052	.16831	.83169	89	2.8808	.17285	.82715
90	2.6536	.15922	.84078	90	2.7068	.16241	.83759
91	2.5162	.15097	.84903	91	2.5502	.15301	.84699
92	2.3917	.14350	.85650	92	2.4116	.14470	.85530
93	2.2801	.13681	.86319	93	2.2901	.13741	.86259
94	2.1802	.13081	.86919	94	2.1839	.13103	.86897
95	2.0891	.12535	.87465	95	2.0891	.12535	.87465
96	1.9997	.11998	.88002	96	1.9997	.11998	.88002
97	1.9145	.11487	.88513	97	1.9145	.11487	.88513
98	1.8331	.10999	.89001	98	1.8331	.10999	.89001
99	1.7554	.10532	.89468	99	1.7554	.10532	.89468
100	1.6812	.10087	.89913	100	1.6812	.10087	.89913
101	1.6101	.09661	.90339	101	1.6101	.09661	.90339
102	1.5416	.09250	.90750	102	1.5416	.09250	.90750
103	1.4744	.08846	.91154	103	1.4744	.08846	.91154
104	1.4065	.08439	.91561	104	1.4065	.08439	.91561
105	1.3334	.08000	.92000	105	1.3334	.08000	.92000
106	1.2452	.07471	.92529	106	1.2452	.07471	.92529
107	1.1196	.06718	.93282	107	1.1196	.06718	.93282
108	.9043	.05426	.94574	108	.9043	.05426	.94574
109	.4717	.02830	.97170	109	.4717	.02830	.97170

Valuation Tables

(After 1970 and before December 1, 1983, *cont.*)

Table B–6%

1 Number of Years	2 Annuity	3 Term Certain	4 Remainder	1 Number of Years	2 Annuity	3 Term Certain	4 Remainder
1	0.9434	.056604	.943396	31	13.9291	.835745	.164255
2	1.8334	.110004	.889996	32	14.0840	.845043	.154957
3	2.6730	.160381	.839619	33	14.2302	.853814	.146186
4	3.4651	.207906	.792094	34	14.3681	.862088	.137912
5	4.2124	.252742	.747258	35	14.4982	.869895	.130105
6	4.9173	.295039	.704961	36	14.6210	.877259	.122741
7	5.5824	.334943	.665057	37	14.7368	.884207	.115793
8	6.2098	.372588	.627412	38	14.8460	.890761	.109239
9	6.8017	.408102	.591898	39	14.9491	.896944	.103056
10	7.3601	.441605	.558395	40	15.0463	.902778	.097222
11	7.8869	.473212	.526788	41	15.1380	.908281	.091719
12	8.3838	.503031	.496969	42	15.2245	.913473	.086527
13	8.8527	.531161	.468839	43	15.3062	.918370	.081630
14	9.2950	.557699	.442301	44	15.3832	.922991	.077009
15	9.7122	.582735	.417265	45	15.4558	.927350	.072650
16	10.1059	.606354	.393646	46	15.5244	.931462	.068538
17	10.4773	.628636	.371364	47	15.5890	.935342	.064653
18	10.8276	.649656	.350344	48	15.6500	.939002	.060998
19	11.1581	.669487	.330513	49	15.7076	.942454	.057546
20	11.4699	.688195	.311805	50	15.7619	.945712	.054288
21	11.7641	.705845	.294155	51	15.8131	.948785	.051215
22	12.0416	.722495	.277505	52	15.8614	.951684	.048316
23	12.3034	.738203	.261797	53	15.9070	.954418	.045582
24	12.5504	.753021	.246979	54	15.9500	.956999	.043001
25	12.7834	.767001	.232999	55	15.9905	.959433	.040567
26	13.0032	.780190	.219810	56	16.0288	.961729	.038271
27	13.2105	.792632	.207368	57	16.0649	.963895	.036105
28	13.4062	.804370	.195630	58	16.0990	.965939	.034061
29	13.5907	.815443	.184557	59	16.1311	.967867	.032133
30	13.7648	.825890	.174110	60	16.1614	.969686	.030314

Valuation Tables

(After November 30, 1983)

Table A–10%
Single Life, Unisex, Showing the Present Worth of an Annuity,
of a Life Estate, and of a Remainder Interest
[Reg. §§ 20.2031–7(f) and 25.2512–5(f)]

1 Age	2 Annuity	3 Life Estate	4 Remainder	1 Age	2 Annuity	3 Life Estate	4 Remainder
0	9.7188	0.97188	0.02812	55	8.0046	.80046	.19954
1	9.8988	.98988	.01012	56	7.9006	.79006	.20994
2	9.9017	.99017	.00983	57	7.7931	.77931	.22069
3	9.9008	.99008	.00992	58	7.6822	.76822	.23178
4	9.8981	.98981	.01019	59	7.5675	.75675	.24325
5	9.8938	.98938	.01062	60	7.4491	.74491	.25509
6	9.8884	.98884	.01116	61	7.3267	.73267	.26733
7	9.8822	.98822	.01178	62	7.2002	.72002	.27998
8	9.8748	.98748	.01252	63	7.0696	.70696	.29304
9	9.8663	.98663	.01337	64	6.9352	.69352	.30648
10	9.8565	.98565	.01435	65	6.7970	.67970	.32030
11	9.8453	.98453	.01547	66	6.6551	.66551	.33449
12	9.8329	.98329	.01671	67	6.5098	.65098	.34902
13	9.8198	.98198	.01802	68	6.3610	.63610	.36390
14	9.8066	.98066	.01934	69	6.2086	.62086	.37914
15	9.7937	.97937	.02063	70	6.0522	.60522	.39478
16	9.7815	.97815	.02185	71	5.8914	.58914	.41086
17	9.7700	.97700	.02300	72	5.7261	.57261	.42739
18	9.7590	.97590	.02410	73	5.5571	.55571	.44429
19	9.7480	.97480	.02520	74	5.3862	.53862	.46138
20	9.7365	.97365	.02635	75	5.2149	.52149	.47851
21	9.7245	.97245	.02755	76	5.0441	.50441	.49559
22	9.7120	.97120	.02880	77	4.8742	.48742	.51258
23	9.6986	.96986	.03014	78	4.7049	.47049	.52951
24	9.6841	.96841	.03159	79	4.5357	.45357	.54643
25	9.6678	.96678	.03322	80	4.3659	.43659	.56341
26	9.6495	.96495	.03505	81	4.1967	.41967	.58033
27	9.6290	.96290	.03710	82	4.0295	.40295	.59705
28	9.6062	.96062	.03938	83	3.8642	.38642	.61358
29	9.5813	.95813	.04187	84	3.6998	.36998	.63002
30	9.5543	.95543	.04457	85	3.5359	.35359	.64641
31	9.5254	.95254	.04746	86	3.3764	.33764	.66236
32	9.4942	.94942	.05058	87	3.2262	.32262	.67738
33	9.4608	.94608	.05392	88	3.0859	.30859	.69141
34	9.4250	.94250	.05750	89	2.9526	.29526	.70474
35	9.3868	.93868	.06132	90	2.8221	.28221	.71779
36	9.3460	.93460	.06540	91	2.6955	.26955	.73045
37	9.3026	.93026	.06974	92	2.5771	.25771	.74229
38	9.2567	.92567	.07433	93	2.4692	.24692	.75308
39	9.2083	.92083	.07917	94	2.3728	.23728	.76272
40	9.1571	.91571	.08429	95	2.2887	.22887	.77113
41	9.1030	.91030	.08970	96	2.2181	.22181	.77819
42	9.0457	.90457	.09543	97	2.1550	.21550	.78450
43	8.9855	.89855	.10145	98	2.1000	.21000	.79000
44	8.9221	.89221	.10779	99	2.0486	.20486	.79514
45	8.8558	.88558	.11442	100	1.9975	.19975	.80025
46	8.7863	.87863	.12137	101	1.9532	.19532	.80468
47	8.7137	.87137	.12863	102	1.9054	.19054	.80946
48	8.6374	.86374	.13626	103	1.8437	.18437	.81563
49	8.5578	.85578	.14422	104	1.7856	.17856	.82144
50	8.4743	.84743	.15257	105	1.6962	.16962	.83038
51	8.3874	.83874	.16126	106	1.5488	.15488	.84512
52	8.2969	.82969	.17031	107	1.3409	.13409	.86591
53	8.2028	.82028	.17972	108	1.0068	.10068	.89932
54	8.1054	.81054	.18946	109	.4545	.04545	.95455

Valuation Tables

(After November 30, 1983, *cont.*)

Table B–10%
Table Showing the Present Worth of an Annuity for a Fixed Term of Years, of an Income Interest for a Fixed Term of Years, and of a Remainder Interest, Postponed for a Fixed Term of Years
[Reg. §§ 20.2031–7(f) and 25.2512–5(f)]

1 Number of Years	2 Annuity	3 Term Certain	4 Remainder	1 Number of Years	2 Annuity	3 Term Certain	4 Remainder
1	.9091	.090909	.909091	31	9.4790	.947901	.052099
2	1.7355	.173554	.826446	32	9.5264	.952638	.047362
3	2.4869	.248685	.751315	33	9.5694	.956943	.043057
4	3.1699	.316987	.683013	34	9.6086	.960857	.039143
5	3.7908	.379079	.620921	35	9.6442	.964416	.035584
6	4.3553	.435526	.564474	36	9.6765	.967651	.032349
7	4.8684	.486842	.513158	37	9.7059	.970592	.029408
8	5.3349	.533493	.466507	38	9.7327	.973265	.026735
9	5.7590	.575902	.424098	39	9.7570	.975696	.024304
10	6.1446	.614457	.385543	40	9.7791	.977905	.022095
11	6.4951	.649506	.350494	41	9.7991	.979914	.020086
12	6.8137	.681369	.318631	42	9.8174	.981740	.018260
13	7.1034	.710336	.289664	43	9.8340	.983400	.016600
14	7.3667	.736669	.263331	44	9.8491	.984909	.015091
15	7.6061	.760608	.239392	45	9.8628	.986281	.013719
16	7.8237	.782371	.217629	46	9.8753	.987528	.012472
17	8.0216	.802155	.197845	47	9.8866	.988662	.011338
18	8.2014	.820141	.179859	48	9.8969	.989693	.010307
19	8.3649	.836492	.163508	49	9.9063	.990630	.009370
20	8.5136	.851356	.148644	50	9.9148	.991481	.008519
21	8.6487	.864869	.135131	51	9.9226	.992256	.007744
22	8.7715	.877154	.122846	52	9.9296	.992960	.007040
23	8.8832	.888322	.111678	53	9.9360	.993600	.006400
24	8.9847	.898474	.101526	54	9.9418	.994182	.005818
25	9.0770	.907704	.092296	55	9.9471	.994711	.005289
26	9.1609	.916095	.083905	56	9.9519	.995191	.004809
27	9.2372	.923722	.076278	57	9.9563	.995629	.004371
28	9.3066	.930657	.069343	58	9.9603	.996026	.003974
29	9.3696	.936961	.063039	59	9.9639	.996387	.003613
30	9.4269	.942691	.057309	60	9.9672	.996716	.003284

Appendix B

Tax Forms

Form **709**

(Rev. January 1987)

Department of the Treasury
Internal Revenue Service

United States Gift (and Generation-Skipping Transfer) Tax Return

(Section 6019 of the Internal Revenue Code) (For gifts made after December 31, 1981, and before January 1, 1989)

Calendar year 19 _____

▶ **For Privacy Act Notice, see the Instructions for Form 1040.**

OMB No. 1545-0020
Expires 12-31-89

Part 1.—General Information

1 Donor's first name and middle initial	2 Donor's last name	3 Social security number
4 Address (number and street)		5 Domicile
6 City, state, and ZIP code		7 Citizenship

	Yes	No
8 If the donor died during the year, check here ▶ ☐ and enter date of death _____ , 19 _____		
9 If you received an extension of time to file this Form 709, check here ▶ ☐ and attach the Form 4868, 2688, 2350, or extension letter.		
10 If you (the donor) filed a previous Form 709 (or 709-A), has your address changed since the last Form 709 (or 709-A) was filed?		
11 Gifts by husband or wife to third parties.—Do you consent to have the gifts (including generation-skipping transfers) made by you and by your spouse to third parties during the calendar year considered as made one-half by each of you? (See instructions.)		

(If the answer is "Yes," the following information must be furnished and your spouse is to sign the consent shown below. If the answer is "No," skip lines 12–17 and go to Schedule A.)

12 Name of consenting spouse	13 Social security number

	Yes	No
14 Were you married to one another during the entire calendar year? (See instructions.)		
15 If the answer to 14 is "No," check whether ☐ married ☐ divorced or ☐ widowed, and give date (see instructions) ▶		
16 Will a gift tax return for this calendar year be filed by your spouse?		

17 **Consent of Spouse**—I consent to have the gifts (and generation-skipping transfers) made by me and by my spouse to third parties during the calendar year considered as made one-half by each of us. We are both aware of the joint and several liability for tax created by the execution of this consent.

Consenting spouse's signature ▶   Date ▶

Part 2.—Tax Computation

1	Enter the amount from Schedule A, line 15	1
2	Enter the amount from Schedule B, line 3	2
3	Total taxable gifts (add lines 1 and 2)	3
4	Tax computed on amount on line 3 (see Table A for the current year in separate instructions)	4
5	Tax computed on amount on line 2 (see Table A for the current year in separate instructions)	5
6	Balance (subtract line 5 from line 4)	6
7	Enter the unified credit from Table B (see instructions)	7
8	Enter the unified credit against tax allowable for all prior periods (from Sch. B, line 1, col. (c))	8
9	Balance (subtract line 8 from line 7)	9
10	Enter 20% of the amount allowed as a specific exemption for gifts made after September 8, 1976, and before January 1, 1977 (see instructions).	10
11	Balance (subtract line 10 from line 9)	11
12	Unified credit (enter the smaller of line 6 or line 11)	12
13	Credit for foreign gift taxes (see instructions)	13
14	Total credits (add lines 12 and 13).	14
15	Balance (subtract line 14 from line 6) (do not enter less than zero)	15
16	Generation-skipping transfer taxes (from Schedule C, Part 4, col. H, total)	16
17	Total taxes (add lines 15 and 16)	17
18	Gift and generation-skipping transfer taxes prepaid with extension of time to file	18
19	If line 18 is less than line 17, enter BALANCE DUE (see instructions)	19
20	If line 18 is greater than line 17, enter AMOUNT TO BE REFUNDED	20

Please attach the necessary supplemental documents; see instructions.

Under penalties of perjury, I declare that I have examined this return, including any accompanying schedules and statements, and to the best of my knowledge and belief it is true, correct, and complete. Declaration of preparer (other than donor) is based on all information of which preparer has any knowledge.

Donor's signature ▶   Date ▶

Preparer's signature
(other than donor) ▶   Date ▶

Preparer's address
(other than donor) ▶

Please attach check or money order here

For Paperwork Reduction Act Notice, see page 1 of the separate instructions to this form.

Form **709** (Rev. 1-87)

Form 709 (Rev. 1-87)   Page **2**

SCHEDULE A   Computation of Taxable Gifts

Part 1.—Gifts Subject Only to Gift Tax. *Gifts less political organization, medical, and educational exclusions—see instructions*

A Item number	B Donee's name and address and description of gift. If the gift was made by means of a trust, enter trust's identifying number below and attach a copy of the trust instrument. If the gift was securities, enter the CUSIP number(s), if available.	C Donor's adjusted basis of gift	D Date of gift	E Value at date of gift	
1					

Part 2.—Gifts Subject to Both Gift Tax and Generation-Skipping Transfer Tax. **You must list the gifts in chronological order.** *Gifts less political organization, medical, and educational exclusions—see instructions*

A Item number	B Donee's name and address and description of gift. If the gift was made by means of a trust, enter trust's identifying number below and attach a copy of the trust instrument. If the gift was securities, enter the CUSIP number(s), if available.	C Donor's adjusted basis of gift	D Date of gift	E Value at date of gift	
1					

Part 3.—Gift Tax Reconciliation

1	Total value of gifts of donor (add column E of Parts 1 and 2) (see instructions)	1		
2	One-half of items _____ attributable to spouse (see instructions)	2		
3	Balance (subtract line 2 from line 1)	3		
4	Gifts of spouse to be included (from Schedule A, Part 3, line 2 of spouse's return—see instructions) .	4		
	If any of the gifts included on this line are also subject to the generation-skipping transfer tax, check here ▶ ☐ and enter those gifts also on Schedule C, Part 1.			
5	Total gifts (add lines 3 and 4)	5		
6	Total annual exclusions for gifts listed on Schedule A (including line 4, above) (see instructions) . .	6		
7	Total included amount of gifts (subtract line 6 from line 5)	7		

Deductions (see instructions)

8	Gifts of interests to spouse for which a marital deduction will be claimed, based on items _____ of Schedule A . . .	8			
9	Exclusions attributable to gifts on line 8	9			
10	Marital deduction—subtract line 9 from line 8	10			
11	Charitable deduction, based on items _____ to _____ less exclusions .	11			
12	Total deductions—add lines 10 and 11		12		
13	Subtract line 12 from line 7		13		
14	Generation-skipping transfer taxes payable with this Form 709 (from Schedule C, Part 4, col. H, Total)		14		
15	Taxable gifts (add lines 13 and 14). Enter here and on line 1 of the Tax Computation		15		

(If more space is needed, attach additional sheets of same size.)

Form 709 (Rev. 1-87)　　　　　　　　　　　　　　　　　　　　　　　　　　　　　　　　　Page **3**

SCHEDULE A	**Computation of Taxable Gifts** (continued)

16 Terminable Interest (QTIP) Marital Deduction. (See instructions.)

☐ ◄ Check here if you elected, under the rules of section 2523(f), to include gifts of qualified terminable interest property on line 8, above. Enter the item numbers (from Schedule A) of the gifts for which you made this election ► _____

SCHEDULE B	**Gifts From Prior Periods**

Did you (the donor) file gift tax returns for prior periods? (If "Yes," see instructions for completing Schedule B below.)　　☐ Yes　☐ No

A Calendar year or calendar quarter (see instructions)	B Internal Revenue office where prior return was filed	C Amount of unified credit against gift tax for periods after December 31, 1976	D Amount of specific exemption for prior periods ending before January 1, 1977	E Amount of taxable gifts

1 Totals for prior periods (without adjustment for reduced specific exemption)　**1**

2 Amount, if any, by which total specific exemption, line 1, column (D), is more than $30,000　．　．　．　．　**2**

3 Total amount of taxable gifts for prior periods (add amount, column (E), line 1, and amount, if any, on line 2). (Enter here and on line 2 of the Tax Computation on page 1.)　．　．　．　．　．　．　．　．　．　．　．　．　**3**

SCHEDULE C	**Computation of Generation-Skipping Transfer Tax**

Part 1.—Generation-Skipping Transfers

A Item No. (from Schedule A, Part 2, col. A)	B Value (from Schedule A, Part 2, col. E)	C Split Gifts (enter ½ of col. B) (see instructions)	D Subtract col. C from col. B	E Annual Exclusion Claimed	F Subtract col. E from col. D	G Grandchild Exclusion Claimed	H Net Transfer (subtract col. G from col. F)
1							
2							
3							
4							
5							
6							
7							
8							

If you elected gift splitting and your spouse was required to file a separate Form 709 (see the instructions for Split Gifts), you must enter all of the gifts shown on Schedule A, Part 2, of your spouse's Form 709 here. In column C, enter the item number of each gift in the order it appears in column A of your spouse's Schedule A, Part 2. We have preprinted the prefix "S-" to distinguish your spouse's item numbers from your own when you complete column A of Schedule C, Part 4. In column D, for each gift, enter the amount reported in column C, Schedule C, Part 1, of your spouse's Form 709.	Split gifts from spouse's Form 709 (enter number)	Value included from spouse's Form 709					
	S-						
	S-						
	S-						
	S-						
	S-						
	S-						
	S-						
	S-						
	Total grandchild exclusions claimed on this return. Must equal total of column D, Schedule C, Part 2　．　．　．　．　．　．　．　．　．　．　．　．　．　．　．　．						

(If more space is needed, attach additional sheets of same size.)

Form 709 (Rev. 1-87)   Page **4**

SCHEDULE C	Computation of Generation-Skipping Transfer Tax (continued)

Part 2.—Grandchild Exclusion Reconciliation

Name of Grandchild	A Maximum Allowable Exclusion	B Total of Exclusions Claimed on Previous Returns	C Exclusion Available for This Return (subtract col. B from col. A)	D Exclusion Claimed on this Return	E Exclusion Available for Future Returns (subtract col. D from col. C)
	$2,000,000				
	$2,000,000				
	$2,000,000				
	$2,000,000				
	$2,000,000				
	$2,000,000				
	$2,000,000				
	$2,000,000				

Total grandchild exclusions claimed on this return. Must equal total of column G, Part 1

Part 3.—GST Exemption Reconciliation (Code section 2631)

1	Maximum allowable exemption	1	$1,000,000
2	Total exemption used for periods before filing this return	2	
3	Exemption available for this return (subtract line 2 from line 1)	3	
4	Exemption claimed on this return (from Part 4, col. C total, below)	4	
5	Exemption elected for transfers not shown on Part 4, below. You must attach a Notice of Allocation. (See instructions.)	5	
6	Add lines 4 and 5	6	
7	Exemption available for future transfers (subtract line 6 from line 3)	7	

Part 4.—Tax Computation

A Gift No. (from Schedule C, Part 1)	B Net transfer (from Schedule C, Part 1, col. H)	C GST Exemption Allocated	D Divide col. C by col. B	E Inclusion Ratio (subtract col. D from 1.000)	F Maximum Gift Tax Rate (see instructions)	G Applicable Rate (multiply col. E by col. F)	H Generation-Skipping Transfer Tax (multiply col. B by col. G)
1							
2							
3							
4							
5							
6							
7							
8							

| Total exemption claimed. Enter here and on line 4, Part 3, above. May not exceed line 3, Part 3, above . . . . . | | **Total generation-skipping transfer tax.** Enter here, on line 14 of Schedule A, Part 3, and on line 16 of the Tax Computation on page 1 . . . . | |

(If more space is needed, attach additional sheets of same size.)

Form **1120-A**

Department of the Treasury
Internal Revenue Service

U.S. Corporation Short-Form Income Tax Return
To see if you qualify to file Form 1120-A, see instructions.

`1235`

OMB No. 1545-0890

For calendar 1987 or tax year beginning _____, 1987, ending _____, 19 ___

1987

See Instructions for list of principal business:	**A** Activity	Use IRS label. Otherwise, please type or machine print	Name	**D** Employer identification number (EIN)	
	B Product or service		Number and street	**E** Date incorporated	
	C Code		City or town, state, and ZIP code	**F** Total assets (See Specific Instructions.)	

	Dollars	Cents
	$	

G Check method of accounting: **(1)** ☐ Cash **(2)** ☐ Accrual **(3)** ☐ Other (specify) . ▶ _____

H Check applicable boxes: **(1)** ☐ Initial return **(2)** ☐ Change in address

Income

1a	Gross receipts or sales _____ **b** Less returns and allowances _____ Balance ▶	1c	
2	Cost of goods sold and/or operations (see instructions).	2	
3	Gross profit (line 1c less line 2)	3	
4	Domestic corporation dividends subject to the Section 243(a)(1) deduction	4	
5	Interest	5	
6	Gross rents	6	
7	Gross royalties	7	
8	Capital gain net income (attach separate Schedule D (Form 1120))	8	
9	Net gain or (loss) from Form 4797, line 18, Part II (attach Form 4797)	9	
10	Other income (see instructions)	10	
11	TOTAL income—Add lines 3 through 10	11	

Deductions
(See Instructions for limitations on deductions)

12	Compensation of officers (see instructions).	12	
13a	Salaries and wages _____ **b** Less jobs credit _____ Balance ▶	13c	
14	Repairs	14	
15	Bad debts (see instructions)	15	
16	Rents	16	
17	Taxes	17	
18	Interest	18	
19	Contributions (see instructions for 10% limitation)	19	
20	Depreciation (attach Form 4562) . . . . . [20] _____		
21	Less depreciation claimed elsewhere on return . . . . [21a] _____	21b	
22	Other deductions (attach schedule)	22	
23	TOTAL deductions—Add lines 12 through 22	23	
24	Taxable income before net operating loss deduction and special deductions (line 11 less line 23) . . .	24	
25	**Less: a** Net operating loss deduction (see instructions) . . . . . [25a] _____		
	b Special deductions (see instructions) . . . . . [25b] _____	25c	

Tax and Payments

26	Taxable income (line 24 less line 25c).	26	
27	**TOTAL TAX** (from Part I, line 6 on page 2)	27	
28	**Payments:**		
a	1986 overpayment allowed as a credit . . . . _____		
b	1987 estimated tax payments . . . . _____		
c	Less 1987 refund applied for on Form 4466 . . . (_____)		
d	Tax deposited with Form 7004 . . . . _____		
e	Credit from regulated investment companies (attach Form 2439) _____		
f	Credit for Federal tax on gasoline and special fuels (attach Form 4136) . . .	28	
29	Enter any **PENALTY** for underpayment of estimated tax—Check ▶ ☐ if Form 2220 is attached . .	29	
30	**TAX DUE**—If the total of lines 27 and 29 is larger than line 28, enter AMOUNT OWED	30	
31	**OVERPAYMENT**—If line 28 is larger than the total of lines 27 and 29, enter AMOUNT OVERPAID . .	31	
32	Enter amount of line 31 you want: **Credited to 1988 estimated tax** ▶ _____ Refunded ▶	32	

Please Sign Here

Under penalties of perjury, I declare that I have examined this return, including accompanying schedules and statements, and to the best of my knowledge and belief, it is true, correct, and complete. Declaration of preparer (other than taxpayer) is based on all information of which preparer has any knowledge.

▶ _____ _____ ▶ _____
Signature of officer   Date   Title

Paid Preparer's Use Only

Preparer's signature	▶ _____	Date _____	Check if self-employed ▶ ☐	Preparer's social security number _____
Firm's name (or yours if self-employed) and address	▶ _____		E.I. No. ▶ _____	
			ZIP code ▶ _____	

For Paperwork Reduction Act Notice, see page 1 of the instructions.

Form **1120-A** (1987)

Form 1120-A (1987)   Page 2

Part I Tax Computation (See Instructions.)   Enter EIN ▶

1	Income tax (See instructions to figure the tax. Enter lesser of this tax or alternative tax from Schedule D.) Check if from Schedule D ▶ ☐	1
2	Credits. Check if from: ☐ Form 3800 ☐ Form 3468 ☐ Form 5884 ☐ Form 6478 ☐ Form 6765 ☐ Form 8586	2
3	Line 1 less line 2	3
4	Tax from recomputing prior-year investment credit (attach Form 4255)	4
5	Alternative minimum tax (see instructions—attach Form 4626)	5
6	Total tax—Add lines 3 through 5. Enter here and on line 27, page 1	6

Additional Information (See instruction F.)

I Was a deduction taken for expenses connected with:

(1) An entertainment facility (boat, resort, ranch, etc.)? Yes ☐ No ☐

(2) Employees' families at conventions or meetings? Yes ☐ No ☐

J Did any individual, partnership, estate, or trust at the end of the tax year own, directly or indirectly, 50% or more of the corporation's voting stock? (For rules of attribution, see section 267(c).) If "Yes," complete (1) and (2) . . . . Yes ☐ No ☐

(1) Attach a schedule showing name, address, and identifying number.

(2) Enter "highest amount owed;" include loans and accounts receivable/payable:

(a) Enter highest amount owed by the corporation to such owner during the year ▶

(b) Enter highest amount owed to the corporation by such owner during the year ▶

K Enter the amount of tax-exempt interest received or accrued during the tax year ▶

L (1) If an amount for cost of goods sold and/or operations is entered on line 2, page 1, complete (a) through (c):

(a) Purchases ▶

(b) Additional sec. 263A costs (see instructions) ▶

(c) Other costs (attach schedule) ▶

(2) Do the rules of section 263A (with respect to property produced or acquired for resale) apply to the corporation? . . . Yes ☐ No ☐

M At any time during the tax year, did you have an interest in or a signature or other authority over a financial account in a foreign country (such as a bank account, securities account, or other financial account)? (See instruction F for filing requirements for Form TD F 90-22.1.) . . . . Yes ☐ No ☐

If "Yes," write in the name of the foreign country ▶

N During this tax year was any part of your accounting/tax records maintained on a computerized system? . . . . Yes ☐ No ☐

O Enter amount of cash distributions and the book value of property (other than cash) distributions made in this tax year ▶

Part II Balance Sheets

		(a) Beginning of tax year		(b) End of tax year	
Assets	1 Cash				
	2 Trade notes and accounts receivable				
	a Less: allowance for bad debts	(	)	(	)
	3 Inventories				
	4 Federal and state government obligations				
	5 Other current assets (attach schedule)				
	6 Loans to stockholders				
	7 Mortgage and real estate loans				
	8 Depreciable, depletable, and intangible assets				
	a Less: accumulated depreciation, depletion, and amortization	(	)	(	)
	9 Land (net of any amortization)				
	10 Other assets (attach schedule)				
	11 Total assets				
Liabilities and Stockholders' Equity	12 Accounts payable				
	13 Other current liabilities (attach schedule)				
	14 Loans from stockholders				
	15 Mortgages, notes, bonds payable				
	16 Other liabilities (attach schedule)				
	17 Capital stock (preferred and common stock)				
	18 Paid-in or capital surplus				
	19 Retained earnings				
	20 Less cost of treasury stock	(	)	(	)
	21 Total liabilities and stockholders' equity				

Part III Reconciliation of Income per Books With Income per Return (Must be completed by all filers)

1 Enter net income per books

2 Federal income tax

3 Income subject to tax not recorded on books this year (itemize)

4 Expenses recorded on books this year not deducted in this return (itemize)

5 Income recorded on books this year not included in this return (itemize)

6 Deductions in this tax return not charged against book income this year (itemize)

7 Income (line 24, page 1). Enter the sum of lines 1, 2, 3, and 4 less the sum of lines 5 and 6

Form **1120**	**U.S. Corporation Income Tax Return**		OMB No. 1545-0123
Department of the Treasury Internal Revenue Service	For calendar 1987 or tax year beginning _____ , 1987, ending _____ , 19 ____ ▶ For Paperwork Reduction Act Notice, see page 1 of the instructions.		**1987**

Check if a—	Use IRS label. Other-wise please print or type.	Name	D Employer identification number
A Consolidated return ☐			
B Personal Holding Co. ☐		Number and street	**E** Date incorporated
C Business Code No. (See the list in the instructions.)		City or town, state, and ZIP code	**F** Total assets (See Specific Instructions.)

G Check applicable boxes: (1) ☐ Initial return (2) ☐ Final return (3) ☐ Change in address

		Dollars	Cents

Income

1a Gross receipts or sales _____ **b** Less returns and allowances _____ Balance ▶	**1c**		
2 Cost of goods sold and/or operations (Schedule A)	**2**		
3 Gross profit (line 1c less line 2)	**3**		
4 Dividends (Schedule C)	**4**		
5 Interest	**5**		
6 Gross rents	**6**		
7 Gross royalties	**7**		
8 Capital gain net income (attach separate Schedule D)	**8**		
9 Net gain or (loss) from Form 4797, line 18, Part II (attach Form 4797) .	**9**		
10 Other income (see instructions—attach schedule).	**10**		
11 TOTAL income—Add lines 3 through 10 and enter here . . . . . . ▶	**11**		

Deductions (See Instructions for limitations on deductions)

12 Compensation of officers (Schedule E)	**12**		
13a Salaries and wages _____ **b** Less jobs credit _____ Balance ▶	**13c**		
14 Repairs	**14**		
15 Bad debts (see instructions)	**15**		
16 Rents	**16**		
17 Taxes	**17**		
18 Interest	**18**		
19 Contributions (**see instructions for 10% limitation**)	**19**		
20 Depreciation (attach Form 4562) **20**			
21 Less depreciation claimed in Schedule A and elsewhere on return . **21a**	**21b**		
22 Depletion	**22**		
23 Advertising	**23**		
24 Pension, profit-sharing, etc., plans	**24**		
25 Employee benefit programs	**25**		
26 Other deductions (attach schedule)	**26**		
27 TOTAL deductions—Add lines 12 through 26 and enter here · · · · · · ▶	**27**		
28 Taxable income before net operating loss deduction and special deductions (line 11 less line 27) ·	**28**		
29 **Less: a** Net operating loss deduction (see instructions) **29a**			
b Special deductions (Schedule C) **29b**	**29c**		
30 Taxable income (line 28 less line 29c)	**30**		
31 **TOTAL TAX** (Schedule J)	**31**		

Tax and Payments

32 Payments: **a** 1986 overpayment credited to 1987			
b 1987 estimated tax payments			
c Less 1987 refund applied for on Form 4466 . . (	)		
d Tax deposited with Form 7004			
e Credit from regulated investment companies (attach Form 2439) .			
f Credit for Federal tax on gasoline and special fuels (attach Form 4136) .	**32**		
33 Enter any **PENALTY** for underpayment of estimated tax—check ▶ ☐ if Form 2220 is attached .	**33**		
34 **TAX DUE**—If the total of lines 31 and 33 is larger than line 32, enter AMOUNT OWED	**34**		
35 **OVERPAYMENT**—If line 32 is larger than the total of lines 31 and 33, enter AMOUNT OVERPAID	**35**		
36 Enter amount of line 35 you want: **Credited to 1988 estimated tax** ▶ Refunded ▶	**36**		

Please Sign Here

Under penalties of perjury, I declare that I have examined this return, including accompanying schedules and statements, and to the best of my knowledge and belief, it is true, correct, and complete. Declaration of preparer (other than taxpayer) is based on all information of which preparer has any knowledge.

▶ _____ _____ ▶ _____
  Signature of officer   Date   Title

Paid Preparer's Use Only

Preparer's signature ▶	Date	Check if self-employed ☐	Preparer's social security number
Firm's name (or yours, if self-employed) and address ▶		E.I. No. ▶	
		ZIP code ▶	

Form 1120 (1987)   Page **2**

Schedule A Cost of Goods Sold and/or Operations (See instructions for line 2, page 1.)

1 Inventory at beginning of year	1	
2 Purchases	2	
3 Cost of labor	3	
4a Additional section 263A costs (see instructions)	4a	
b Other costs (attach schedule)	4b	
5 Total—Add lines 1 through 4b	5	
6 Inventory at end of year	6	
7 Cost of goods sold and/or operations—Line 5 less line 6. Enter here and on line 2, page 1	7	

8a Check all methods used for valuing closing inventory:

(i) ☐ Cost (ii) ☐ Lower of cost or market as described in Regulations section 1.471-4 (see instructions)

(iii) ☐ Writedown of ''subnormal'' goods as described in Regulations section 1.471-2(c) (see instructions)

(iv) ☐ Other (Specify method used and attach explanation.) ▶ _____

b Check if the LIFO inventory method was adopted this tax year for any goods (if checked, attach Form 970) . . . . . . ☐

c If the LIFO inventory method was used for this tax year, enter percentage (or amounts) of closing inventory computed under LIFO . . . . | 8c |

d Do the rules of section 263A (with respect to property produced or acquired for resale) apply to the corporation? . . ☐ Yes ☐ No

e Was there any change (other than for section 263A purposes) in determining quantities, cost, or valuations between opening and closing inventory? If ''Yes,'' attach explanation . . . . . . ☐ Yes ☐ No

Schedule C Dividends and Special Deductions (See Schedule C instructions.)

	(a) Dividends received	(b) %	(c) Special deductions: multiply (a) × (b)
1 Domestic corporations subject to section 243(a) deduction (other than debt-financed stock)		see instructions	
2 Debt-financed stock of domestic and foreign corporations (section 246A)		see instructions	
3 Certain preferred stock of public utilities		see instructions	
4 Foreign corporations and certain FSCs subject to section 245 deduction		see instructions	
5 Wholly owned foreign subsidiaries and FSCs subject to 100% deduction (sections 245(b) and (c))		100	
6 Total—Add lines 1 through 5. See instructions for limitation			
7 Affiliated groups subject to the 100% deduction (section 243(a)(3))		100	
8 Other dividends from foreign corporations not included in lines 4 and 5			
9 Income from controlled foreign corporations under subpart F (attach Forms 5471)			
10 Foreign dividend gross-up (section 78)			
11 IC-DISC or former DISC dividends not included in lines 1 and/or 2 (section 246(d))			
12 Other dividends			
13 Deduction for dividends paid on certain preferred stock of public utilities (see instructions)			
14 Total dividends—Add lines 1 through 12. Enter here and on line 4, page 1 . ▶			
15 Total deductions—Add lines 6, 7, and 13. Enter here and on line 29b, page 1 . . . . ▶			

Schedule E Compensation of Officers (See instructions for line 12, page 1.)
Complete Schedule E only if total receipts (line 1a, plus lines 4 through 10, of page 1, Form 1120) are $150,000 or more.

(a) Name of officer	(b) Social security number	(c) Percent of time devoted to business	Percent of corporation stock owned		(f) Amount of compensation
			(d) Common	(e) Preferred	
		%	%	%	
		%	%	%	
		%	%	%	
		%	%	%	
		%	%	%	
		%	%	%	
		%	%	%	

Total compensation of officers—Enter here and on line 12, page 1 . . . .

Form 1120 (1987) Page **3**

Schedule J   Tax Computation (See instructions.)

1   Check if you are a member of a controlled group (see sections 1561 and 1563) . . . . ▶ ☐

2   If line 1 is checked, see instructions. If your tax year includes June 30, 1987, complete both a and b below. Otherwise, complete only b.

a *(i)* \$ _____*(ii)* \$ _____*(iii)* \$ _____*(iv)* \$ _____

b*(i)* \$ _____*(ii)* \$ _____

3   Income tax (see instructions to figure the tax; enter this tax or alternative tax from Schedule D, whichever is less). Check if from Schedule D ▶ ☐ **3**

4a	Foreign tax credit (attach Form 1118)	**4a**	
b	Possessions tax credit (attach Form 5735)	**b**	
c	Orphan drug credit (attach Form 6765)	**c**	
d	Credit for fuel produced from a nonconventional source (see instructions)	**d**	
e	General business credit. Enter here and check which forms are attached ☐ Form 3800 ☐ Form 3468 ☐ Form 5884 ☐ Form 6478 ☐ Form 6765 ☐ Form 8586	**e**	

5   Total—Add lines 4a through 4e **5**

6   Line 3 less line 5 . . . . **6**

7   Personal holding company tax (attach Schedule PH (Form 1120)) **7**

8   Tax from recomputing prior-year investment credit (attach Form 4255) . . . **8**

9a   Alternative minimum tax (see instructions—attach Form 4626) **9a**

b   Environmental tax (see instructions—attach Form 4626) **9b**

10   Total tax—Add lines 6 through 9b. Enter here and on line 31, page 1 . . . . **10**

Additional Information (See instruction F.)

	Yes	No
H Did the corporation claim a deduction for expenses connected with:		
(1) An entertainment facility (boat, resort, ranch, etc.)? . . .		
(2) Living accommodations (except employees on business)? . .		
(3) Employees attending conventions or meetings outside the North American area? (See section 274(h).)		
(4) Employees' families at conventions or meetings?		
If "Yes," were any of these conventions or meetings outside the North American area? (See section 274(h).)		
(5) Employee or family vacations not reported on Form W-2? . .		
I (1) Did the corporation at the end of the tax year own, directly or indirectly, 50% or more of the voting stock of a domestic corporation? (For rules of attribution, see section 267(c).) . .		
If "Yes," attach a schedule showing: (a) name, address, and identifying number; (b) percentage owned; (c) taxable income or (loss) before NOL and special deductions of such corporation for the tax year ending with or within your tax year; (d) highest amount owed by the corporation to such corporation during the year; and (e) highest amount owed to the corporation by such corporation during the year.		
(2) Did any individual, partnership, corporation, estate, or trust at the end of the tax year own, directly or indirectly, 50% or more of the corporation's voting stock? (For rules of attribution, see section 267(c).) If "Yes," complete (a) through (d) . . .		
(a) Attach a schedule showing name, address, and identifying number. Enter percentage owned ▶ _____		
(b) Was the owner of such voting stock a person other than a U.S. person? (See instructions.) **Note:** *If "Yes," the corporation may have to file Form 5472.* . . .		
If "Yes," enter owner's country ▶ _____		
(c) Enter highest amount owed by the corporation to such owner during the year ▶ _____		
(d) Enter highest amount owed to the corporation by such owner during the year ▶ _____		
Note: *For purposes of I(1) and I(2), "highest amount owed" includes loans and accounts receivable/payable.*		

	Yes	No
J Refer to the list in the instructions and state the principal:		
Business activity ▶ _____		
Product or service ▶ _____		
K Was the corporation a U.S. shareholder of any controlled foreign corporation? (See sections 951 and 957.) . .		
If "Yes," attach Form 5471 for each such corporation.		
L At any time during the tax year, did the corporation have an interest in or a signature or other authority over a financial account in a foreign country (such as a bank account, securities account, or other financial account)?		
(See instruction F and filing requirements for form TD F 90-22.1.)		
If "Yes," enter name of foreign country ▶ _____		
M Was the corporation the grantor of, or transferor to, a foreign trust which existed during the current tax year, whether or not the corporation has any beneficial interest in it?		
If "Yes," the corporation may have to file Forms 3520, 3520-A, or 926.		
N During this tax year, did the corporation pay dividends (other than stock dividends and distributions in exchange for stock) in excess of the corporation's current and accumulated earnings and profits? (See sections 301 and 316.).		
If "Yes," file Form 5452. If this is a consolidated return, answer here for parent corporation and on Form 851, Affiliations Schedule, for each subsidiary.		
O During this tax year did the corporation maintain any part of its accounting/tax records on a computerized system?		
P Check method of accounting:		
(1) ☐ Cash **(2)** ☐ Accrual		
(3) ☐ Other (specify) ▶ _____		
Q Check this box if the corporation issued publicly offered debt instruments with original issue discount . . . . . ☐		
If so, the corporation may have to file Form 8281.		
R Enter the amount of tax-exempt interest received or accrued during the tax year ▶ _____		
S If you are a member of a controlled group, enter the amount of taxable income for the entire group ▶ _____		

Form 1120 (1987)

Schedule L Balance Sheets		Beginning of tax year		End of tax year	
Assets		(a)	(b)	(c)	(d)
1 Cash					
2 Trade notes and accounts receivable . . .					
a Less allowance for bad debts					
3 Inventories					
4 Federal and state government obligations . .					
5 Other current assets (attach schedule) . . .					
6 Loans to stockholders					
7 Mortgage and real estate loans					
8 Other investments (attach schedule) . . .					
9 Buildings and other depreciable assets . . .					
a Less accumulated depreciation					
10 Depletable assets					
a Less accumulated depletion					
11 Land (net of any amortization)					
12 Intangible assets (amortizable only)					
a Less accumulated amortization					
13 Other assets (attach schedule)					
14 Total assets					
Liabilities and Stockholders' Equity					
15 Accounts payable					
16 Mortgages, notes, bonds payable in less than 1 year					
17 Other current liabilities (attach schedule) . .					
18 Loans from stockholders					
19 Mortgages, notes, bonds payable in 1 year or more					
20 Other liabilities (attach schedule)					
21 Capital stock: a preferred stock					
b common stock					
22 Paid-in or capital surplus					
23 Retained earnings—Appropriated (attach schedule)					
24 Retained earnings—Unappropriated . . .					
25 Less cost of treasury stock		(	)	(	)
26 Total liabilities and stockholders' equity . .					

Schedule M-1 Reconciliation of Income per Books With Income per Return You are not required to complete this schedule if the total assets on line 14, column (d), of Schedule L are less than $25,000.				
1 Net income per books		7 Income recorded on books this year not included in this return (itemize)		
2 Federal income tax		a Tax-exempt interest $ _____		
3 Excess of capital losses over capital gains . .		_____		
4 Income subject to tax not recorded on books this year (itemize) _____		8 Deductions in this tax return not charged against book income this year (itemize)		
_____		a Depreciation $ _____		
5 Expenses recorded on books this year not deducted in this return (itemize)		b Contributions carryover $ _____		
a Depreciation $ _____		_____		
b Contributions carryover $ _____		9 Total of lines 7 and 8		
_____		10 Income (line 28, page 1)—line 6 less line 9 .		
6 Total of lines 1 through 5				

Schedule M-2 Analysis of Unappropriated Retained Earnings per Books (line 24, Schedule L) You are not required to complete this schedule if the total assets on line 14, column (d), of Schedule L are less than $25,000.				
1 Balance at beginning of year		5 Distributions: a Cash		
2 Net income per books		b Stock		
3 Other increases (itemize) _____		c Property		
_____		6 Other decreases (itemize) _____		
_____		_____		
_____		7 Total of lines 5 and 6		
4 Total of lines 1, 2, and 3		8 Balance at end of year (line 4 less line 7)		

SCHEDULE PH
(Form 1120)

Department of the Treasury
Internal Revenue Service

Computation of U.S.
Personal Holding Company Tax

▶ Attach to your tax return.

OMB No. 1545-0123

·19**87**

Name

Employer identification number

Part I—Computation of Undistributed Personal Holding Company Income

Additions	1	Taxable income before net operating loss deduction and special deductions (Form 1120, line 28—see instructions for line 1)	1
	2	Contributions deducted in figuring line 1 (Form 1120, line 19)	2
	3	Excess expenses and depreciation under section 545(b)(6) (Schedule A, line 2)	3
	4	Total—Add lines 1 through 3	4
Deductions	5	Federal and foreign income, war profits, and excess profits taxes not deducted in figuring line 1 (attach schedule)	5
	6	Contributions deductible under section 545(b)(2) (see line 6 instructions for limitation)	6
	7	Net operating loss for the preceding tax year (deductible under section 545(b)(4))	7
	8a	Net capital gain (from separate Schedule D (Form 1120), line 10) . 8a	
	b	**Less:** Income tax on this net capital gain (see section 545(b)(5)—attach computation) 8b	8c
	9	Amounts used or irrevocably set aside to pay or retire qualified indebtedness (see instructions for line 9)	9
	10	Deduction for dividends paid (other than dividends paid after the end of the tax year (Schedule B, line 5))	10
	11	Total—Add lines 5 through 10	11
	12	Subtract line 11 from line 4	12
	13	Dividends paid after the end of the tax year (other than deficiency dividends defined in section 547(d)) but not more than the smaller of line 12 or 20% of Schedule B, line 1	13
	14	Undistributed personal holding company income—Subtract line 13 from line 12. (Foreign corporations—see instructions for line 14.)	14
Tax	15	Personal holding company tax (enter 38.5% of line 14 here and on: Schedule J (Form 1120), line 7; or the proper line of the appropriate tax return)	15

Part II—Information Required Under Section 6501(f). If the information on income and stock ownership is not submitted with the corporation's return, the limitation period for assessment and collection of personal holding company tax is 6 years.

Personal Holding Company Income

1	Dividends			1
2a	Interest	2a		
b	**Less:** Amount excluded under section 543(b)(2)(C) (attach schedule)	2b		2c
3	Royalties (other than mineral, oil, gas, or copyright royalties)			3
4	Annuities			4
5a	Rents	5a		
b	**Less:** Adjustments described in section 543(b)(2)(A) (attach schedule)	5b		5c
6a	Mineral, oil, and gas royalties	6a		
b	**Less:** Adjustments described in section 543(b)(2)(B) (attach schedule)	6b		6c
7	Copyright royalties (see instructions for an exception for certain computer software royalties)			7
8	Produced film rents			8
9	Compensation received for use of corporation property by shareholder			9
10	Amounts received under personal service contracts and from their sale			10
11	Amounts received from estates and trusts			11
12	Total personal holding company income—Add lines 1 through 11			12

For Paperwork Reduction Act Notice, see page 1 of Form 1120 instructions.

Schedule PH (Form 1120) 1987

Schedule PH (Form 1120) 1987   Page **2**

Stock Ownership   Enter the names and addresses of the individuals who together owned directly or indirectly at any time during the last half of the tax year more than 50% in value of the outstanding stock of the corporation.

(a) Name	(b) Address	Highest percentage of shares owned during last half of tax year	
		(c) Preferred	(d) Common
		%	%
		%	%
		%	%
		%	%
		%	%

Schedule A   **Excess of Expenses and Depreciation Over Income From Property Not Allowable Under Section 545(b)(6) (See instruction for line 3.)**

(a) Kind of property	(b) Date acquired	(c) Cost or other basis	(d) Depreciation	(e) Repairs, insurance, and other expenses (section 162) (attach schedule)	(f) Total of columns (d) and (e)	(g) Income from rent or other compensation	(h) Excess (col. (f) less col. (g))
1							

2   Total excess of expenses and depreciation over rent or other compensation. Enter here and on line 3, page 1.
Note: *Attach a statement showing the names and addresses of persons from whom rent or other compensation was received for the use of, or the right to use, each property.*

Schedule B   **Deduction for Dividends Paid (See instruction for line 10.)**

1	Taxable dividends paid (do not include dividends considered as paid in the preceding tax year under section 563, or deficiency dividends as defined in section 547)	1	
2	Consent dividends (attach Forms 972 and 973)	2	
3	Taxable distributions—Add lines 1 and 2	3	
4	Dividend carryover from first and second preceding tax years (attach computation)	4	
5	Deduction for dividends paid—Add lines 3 and 4. Enter here and on line 10, page 1	5	

Form **4626**	**Alternative Minimum Tax—Corporations**	OMB No. 1545-0175
Department of the Treasury Internal Revenue Service	**(including environmental tax)** ▶ See separate instructions. ▶ Attach to Forms 1120, 1120-A, etc.	**1987**

Name as shown on tax return	Employer identification number

1	Taxable income before net operating loss deduction	**1**	
2	**Adjustments:** (see instructions)		
a	Depreciation of property placed in service after 1986.	2a	
b	Mining exploration and development costs paid or incurred after 1986	2b	
c	Long-term contracts entered into after 2/28/86	2c	
d	Pollution control facilities placed in service after 1986	2d	
e	Installment sales of certain property	2e	
f	Circulation expenses (personal holding companies only)	2f	
g	Merchant marine capital construction funds	2g	
h	Section 833(b) deduction (Blue Cross, Blue Shield, and similar type organizations only)	2h	
i	Basis adjustment	2i	
j	Certain loss limitations	2j	
k	Tax shelter farm loss (personal service corporations only)	2k	
l	Passive activity loss (closely held corporations and personal service corporations only)	2l	
m	Total adjustments (combine lines 2(a) through 2(l))	**2m**	
3	**Tax preference items:**		
a	Accelerated depreciation of real property placed in service before 1987	3a	
b	Accelerated depreciation of leased personal property placed in service before 1987 (personal holding companies only)	3b	
c	Amortization of certified pollution control facilities placed in service before 1987 . .	3c	
d	Appreciated property charitable deduction	3d	
e	Tax-exempt interest from private activity bonds issued after August 7, 1986	3e	
f	Intangible drilling costs	3f	
g	Depletion.	3g	
h	Reserves for losses on bad debts of financial institutions	3h	
i	Total tax preference items (add lines 3(a) through 3(h))	**3i**	
4	Combine lines 1, 2(m), and 3(i).	**4**	
5	Adjusted net book income of corporation	5	
6	If line 5 is more than line 4, enter difference; otherwise enter zero	6	
7	Multiply line 6 by 50% (.5)	**7**	
8	Add line 4 and line 7	**8**	
9	Alternative tax net operating loss deduction. (Do not enter more than 90% of line 8.)	**9**	
10	Alternative minimum taxable income (subtract line 9 from line 8)	**10**	
11	Enter $40,000 (Controlled corporations, see instructions.)	**11**	
12	Enter $150,000 (Controlled corporations, see instructions.)	**12**	
13	Subtract line 12 from line 10 . If zero or less, enter zero	**13**	
14	Multiply line 13 by 25% (.25)	**14**	
15	Exemption. Subtract line 14 from line 11. If zero or less, enter zero	**15**	
16	Subtract line 15 from line 10. If zero or less, enter zero	**16**	
17	Multiply line 16 by 20% (.2)	**17**	
18	Alternative minimum tax foreign tax credit	**18**	
19	Tentative minimum tax (subtract line 18 from line 17)	**19**	
20	Income tax before credits minus foreign tax credit	**20**	
21	Alternative minimum tax (subtract line 20 from line 19). Enter on your tax return on the line identified as alternative minimum tax	**21**	
22	Environmental tax (subtract $2,000,000 from line 8, and multiply the result, if any, by .12% (.0012)). Enter on your tax return on the line identified as environmental tax (Controlled corporations, see instructions.) . .	**22**	

For Paperwork Reduction Act, see separate instructions.

Form **4626** (1987)

Form **1120S**	**U.S. Income Tax Return for an S Corporation**	OMB No. 1545-0130

Form **1120S**
Department of the Treasury
Internal Revenue Service

U.S. Income Tax Return for an S Corporation
For the calendar year 1987 or tax year beginning _____, 1987, ending _____, 19 ____
▶ For Paperwork Reduction Act Notice, see page 1 of the instructions.

1987

A Date of election as an S corporation

Use IRS label. Otherwise, please print or type.

Name

Number and street (P.O. Box number if mail is not delivered to street address)

City or town, state, and ZIP code

C Employer identification number

B Business code no. (see Specific Instructions)

D Date incorporated

E Total assets (see Specific Instructions)
Dollars / Cents
$

F Check applicable boxes: (1) ☐ Initial return (2) ☐ Final return (3) ☐ Change in address (4) ☐ Amended return

G Check this box if this is an S corporation subject to the consolidated audit procedures of sections 6241 through 6245 (see instructions) . . . . ▶ ☐

H Was this corporation in operation at the end of 1987 (see instructions)? . . . . Yes ☐ No ☐

I How many months in 1987 was this corporation in operation (see instructions)? . . . . ▶

Caution: Include **only** trade or business income and expenses on lines 1a through 21. See the instructions for more information.

Income

1a Gross receipts or sales _____ b Less returns and allowances _____ Balance ▶ | 1c
2 Cost of goods sold and/or operations (Schedule A, line 7). . . . . . . | 2
3 Gross profit (subtract line 2 from line 1c) . . . . | 3
4 Net gain (or loss) from Form 4797, line 18 (see instructions) . . . . | 4
5 Other income (see instructions—attach schedule). . . . . . | 5
6 TOTAL income (loss)—Combine lines 3, 4 and 5 and enter here . . . . ▶ | 6

Deductions (See instructions for limitations.)

7 Compensation of officers . . . . | 7
8a Salaries and wages _____ b Less jobs credit _____ Balance ▶ | 8c
9 Repairs. . . . . | 9
10 Bad debts (see instructions) . . . . . . | 10
11 Rents . . . . | 11
12 Taxes . . . . | 12
13 Deductible interest expense not claimed or reported elsewhere on return (see instructions) . . | 13
14a Depreciation from Form 4562 (attach Form 4562). | 14a
  b Depreciation reported on Schedule A and elsewhere on return . . | 14b
  c Subtract line 14b from line 14a . . . . . . | 14c
15 Depletion (**Do not deduct oil and gas depletion.** See instructions.) . . | 15
16 Advertising . . . . . . | 16
17 Pension, profit-sharing, etc. plans . . . . | 17
18 Employee benefit programs . . . . | 18
19 Other deductions (attach schedule) . . . . | 19
20 TOTAL deductions—Add lines 7 through 19 and enter here . . . ▶ | 20
21 Ordinary income (loss) from trade or business activity(ies)—Subtract line 20 from line 6 . . | 21

Tax and Payments

22 Tax:
a Excess net passive income tax (attach schedule) . . . . | 22a
b Tax from Schedule D (Form 1120S) . . . . | 22b
c Add lines 22a and 22b | 22c
23 Payments:
a Tax deposited with Form 7004 . . . . | 23a
b Credit for Federal tax on gasoline and special fuels (attach Form 4136) | 23b
c Add lines 23a and 23b | 23c
24 **TAX DUE** (subtract line 23c from line 22c). See instructions for Paying the Tax . . . ▶ | 24
25 **OVERPAYMENT** (subtract line 22c from line 23c). . . . . ▶ | 25

Please Sign Here

Under penalties of perjury, I declare that I have examined this return, including accompanying schedules and statements, and to the best of my knowledge and belief, it is true, correct, and complete. Declaration of preparer (other than taxpayer) is based on all information of which preparer has any knowledge.

▶ Signature of officer Date ▶ Title

Paid Preparer's Use Only

Preparer's signature ▶ Date Check if self-employed ▶ ☐ Preparer's social security number

Firm's name (or yours if self-employed) and address ▶ E.I. No. ▶ ZIP code ▶

Form **1120S** (1987)

Form 1120S (1987)   Page **2**

Schedule A	**Cost of Goods Sold and/or Operations** (See instructions for Schedule A.)		

1	Inventory at beginning of year	**1**	
2	Purchases	**2**	
3	Cost of labor	**3**	
4a	Additional section 263A costs (attach schedule)	**4a**	
b	Other costs (attach schedule)	**4b**	
5	Total—Add lines 1 through 4b	**5**	
6	Inventory at end of year	**6**	
7	Cost of goods sold and/or operations—Subtract line 6 from line 5. Enter here and on line 2, page 1	**7**	

8a Check all methods used for valuing closing inventory:

   (i) ☐ Cost

   (ii) ☐ Lower of cost or market as described in Regulations section 1.471-4 (see instructions)

   (iii) ☐ Writedown of ''subnormal'' goods as described in Regulations section 1.471-2(c) (see instructions)

   (iv) ☐ Other (Specify method used and attach explanation) ▶ --

  b Check this box if the LIFO inventory method was adopted this tax year for any goods (if checked, attach Form 970) . . . . . ☐

  c If the LIFO inventory method was used for this tax year, enter percentage (or amounts) of closing
   inventory computed under LIFO   **8c**

  d Do the rules of section 263A (with respect to property produced or acquired for resale) apply to the corporation? . . . . ☐ Yes   ☐ No

  e Was there any change (other than for section 263A purposes) in determining quantities, cost, or valuations between
   opening and closing inventory? (If ''Yes,'' attach explanation.) . . . . ☐ Yes   ☐ No

Additional Information Required		Yes	No
J	Did you at the end of the tax year own, directly or indirectly, 50% or more of the voting stock of a domestic corporation? (For rules of attribution, see section 267(c).)		

    If ''Yes,'' attach a schedule showing:

    (1) Name, address, and employer identification number;   **(3)** Highest amount owed by you to such corporation during the year; and

    (2) Percentage owned;   **(4)** Highest amount owed to you by such corporation during the year.

       (Note: *For purposes of J(3) and J(4), ''highest amount owed'' includes loans and accounts receivable/payable.)*

K Refer to the listing of business activity codes at the end of the Instructions for Form 1120S and state your principal:
   Business activity ▶ ----------------------------; Product or service ▶ -----------------------------

L Were you a member of a controlled group subject to the provisions of section 1561? . . . .

M Did you claim a deduction for expenses connected with:

   (1) Entertainment facilities (boat, resort, ranch, etc.)? . . . .

   (2) Living accommodations (except for employees on business)? . . . .

   (3) Employees attending conventions or meetings outside the North American area? (See section 274(h).) . . . .

   (4) Employees' families at conventions or meetings? . . . .

       If ''Yes,'' were any of these conventions or meetings outside the North American area? (See section 274(h).)

   (5) Employee or family vacations not reported on Form W-2? . . . .

N At any time during the tax year, did you have an interest in or a signature or other authority over a financial account in a foreign country (such as a bank account, securities account, or other financial account)? (See instructions for exceptions and filing requirements for form TD F 90-22.1.) . . . .

   If ''Yes,'' enter the name of the foreign country ▶ ---

O Were you the grantor of, or transferor to, a foreign trust which existed during the current tax year, whether or not you have any beneficial interest in it? If ''Yes,'' you may have to file Forms 3520, 3520-A, or 926 . . . .

P During this tax year did you maintain any part of your accounting/tax records on a computerized system? . . . . . .

Q Check method of accounting: **(1)** ☐ Cash   **(2)** ☐ Accrual   **(3)** ☐ Other (specify) ▶ --------------------

R Check this box if the S corporation has filed or is required to file **Form 8264,** Application for Registration of a Tax
   Shelter . . . . ▶ ☐

S Check this box if the corporation issued publicly offered debt instruments with original issue discount . . . . . ▶ ☐
   If so, the corporation may have to file Form 8281, Information Return for Publicly Offered Original Issue Discount Instruments.

T If section 1374 (new built-in gains tax) applies to the corporation, enter the corporation's net unrealized built-in gain as defined in section 1374(d)(1) (see instructions) ▶

Designation of Tax Matters Person

The following shareholder is hereby designated as the tax matters person (TMP) for the tax year for which this tax return is filed:

Name of designated TMP ▶	Identifying number of TMP ▶
Address of designated TMP ▶	

Schedule K	Shareholders' Shares of Income, Credits, Deductions, etc. (See Instructions.)		
	(a) Distributive share items	**(b) Total amount**	

Income (Losses) and Deductions

1	Ordinary income (loss) from trade or business activity(ies) (page 1, line 21)	**1**	
2a	Gross income from rental real estate activity(ies). **2a**		
b	Minus expenses (attach schedule) **2b**		
c	Balance: net income (loss) from rental real estate activity(ies).	**2c**	
3a	Gross income from other rental activity(ies) **3a**		
b	Minus expenses (attach schedule) **3b**		
c	Balance: net income (loss) from other rental activity(ies)	**3c**	
4	Portfolio income (loss):		
a	Interest income	**4a**	
b	Dividend income	**4b**	
c	Royalty income	**4c**	
d	Net short-term capital gain (loss) (Schedule D (Form 1120S)).	**4d**	
e	Net long-term capital gain (loss) (Schedule D (Form 1120S))	**4e**	
f	Other portfolio income (loss) (attach schedule)	**4f**	
5	Net gain (loss) under section 1231 (other than due to casualty or theft)	**5**	
6	Other income (loss) (attach schedule)	**6**	
7	Charitable contributions (attach schedule)	**7**	
8	Section 179 expense deduction (attach schedule)	**8**	
9	Expenses related to portfolio income (loss) (attach schedule) (see instructions)	**9**	
10	Other deductions (attach schedule)	**10**	

Credits

11a	Jobs credit (attach Form 5884)	**11a**	
b	Low-income housing credit (attach Form 8586)	**11b**	
c	Qualified rehabilitation expenditures related to rental real estate activity(ies) (attach schedule) . .	**11c**	
d	Credits related to rental real estate activity(ies) other than on lines 11b and 11c (attach schedule)	**11d**	
e	Credit(s) related to rental activity(ies) other than on lines 11b, 11c, and 11d (attach schedule) . .	**11e**	
12	Other credits (attach schedule)	**12**	

Tax Preference and Adjustment Items

13a	Accelerated depreciation of real property placed in service before 1987	**13a**	
b	Accelerated depreciation of leased personal property placed in service before 1987 . . .	**13b**	
c	Depreciation adjustment on property placed in service after 1986	**13c**	
d	Depletion (other than oil and gas)	**13d**	
e	(1) Gross income from oil, gas, or geothermal properties	**13e(1)**	
	(2) Gross deductions allocable to oil, gas, or geothermal properties	**13e(2)**	
f	Other items (attach schedule)	**13f**	

Investment Interest

14a	Interest expense on investment debts	**14a**	
b	(1) Investment income included on lines 4a through 4f, Schedule K	**14b(1)**	
	(2) Investment expenses included on line 9, Schedule K	**14b(2)**	

Foreign Taxes

15a	Type of income _____		
b	Name of foreign country or U.S. possession _____		
c	Total gross income from sources outside the U.S. (attach schedule)	**15c**	
d	Total applicable deductions and losses (attach schedule)	**15d**	
e	Total foreign taxes (check one): ▶ ☐ Paid ☐ Accrued	**15e**	
f	Reduction in taxes available for credit (attach schedule)	**15f**	
g	Other (attach schedule)	**15g**	

Other Items

16	Total property distributions (including cash) other than dividend distributions reported on line 18, Schedule K	**16**	
17	Other items and amounts not included in lines 1 through 16, Schedule K, that are required to be reported separately to shareholders (attach schedule).		
18	Total dividend distributions paid from accumulated earnings and profits contained in other retained earnings (line 26 of Schedule L)	**18**	

Form 1120S (1987)   Page **4**

Schedule L	Balance Sheets	Beginning of tax year		End of tax year	
	Assets	(a)	(b)	(c)	(d)
1	Cash				
2	Trade notes and accounts receivable				
a	Less allowance for bad debts				
3	Inventories				
4	Federal and state government obligations				
5	Other current assets (attach schedule)				
6	Loans to shareholders				
7	Mortgage and real estate loans				
8	Other investments (attach schedule)				
9	Buildings and other depreciable assets				
a	Less accumulated depreciation				
10	Depletable assets				
a	Less accumulated depletion				
11	Land (net of any amortization)				
12	Intangible assets (amortizable only)				
a	Less accumulated amortization				
13	Other assets (attach schedule)				
14	Total assets				
	Liabilities and Shareholders' Equity				
15	Accounts payable				
16	Mortgages, notes, bonds payable in less than 1 year				
17	Other current liabilities (attach schedule)				
18	Loans from shareholders				
19	Mortgages, notes, bonds payable in 1 year or more				
20	Other liabilities (attach schedule)				
21	Capital stock				
22	Paid-in or capital surplus				
23	Accumulated adjustments account				
24	Other adjustments account				
25	Shareholders' undistributed taxable income previously taxed				
26	Other retained earnings (see instructions). Check this box if the corporation has subchapter C earnings and profits at the close of the tax year ▶ ☐ (see instructions)				
27	Total retained earnings per books—Combine amounts on lines 23 through 26, columns (a) and (c) (see instructions)				
28	Less cost of treasury stock		( )		( )
29	Total liabilities and shareholders' equity				

Schedule M	Analysis of Accumulated Adjustments Account, Other Adjustments Account, and Shareholders' Undistributed Taxable Income Previously Taxed (If Schedule L, column (c), amounts for lines 23, 24, or 25 are not the same as corresponding amounts on line 9 of Schedule M, attach a schedule explaining any differences. See instructions.)

		Accumulated adjustments account	Other adjustments account	Shareholders' undistributed taxable income previously taxed
1	Balance at beginning of year			
2	Ordinary income from page 1, line 21			
3	Other additions			
4	Total of lines 1, 2, and 3			
5	Distributions other than dividend distributions			
6	Loss from page 1, line 21			
7	Other reductions			
8	Add lines 5, 6, and 7			
9	Balance at end of tax year—Subtract line 8 from line 4			

SCHEDULE K-1 **(Form 1120S)** Department of the Treasury Internal Revenue Service	**Shareholder's Share of Income, Credits, Deductions, etc.** For calendar year 1987 or tax year beginning _____, 1987, and ending _____, 19 ____ ▶ **For Paperwork Reduction Act Notice, see page 1 of Instructions for Form 1120S.**	OMB No. 1545-0130 **1987**	

Shareholder's identifying number ▶	Corporation's identifying number ▶
Shareholder's name, address, and ZIP code	Corporation's name, address, and ZIP code

A (1) Shareholder's percentage of stock ownership for tax year (see instructions for Schedule K-1) . . . .▶ _____ %
  (2) Number of shares owned by shareholder at tax year end . . . .▶

B Internal Revenue Service Center where corporation filed its return ▶

C Tax shelter registration number (see Instructions for Schedule K-1) . . . . ▶

D Did the shareholder materially participate in the trade or business activity(ies) of the corporation? (See instructions for Schedule K-1. Leave the check boxes blank if there are no trade or business activities.) . . . . ☐ Yes ☐ No

E Did the shareholder actively participate in the rental real estate activity(ies) of the corporation? (See instructions for Schedule K-1. Leave the check boxes blank if there are no rental real estate activities.) . . . . ☐ Yes ☐ No

F If (1) question D is checked "No" or income or loss is reported on line 2 or 3 and (2) the shareholder acquired corporate stock after 10/22/86, check here ▶ ☐ and enter the shareholder's weighted percentage increase in stock ownership for 1987 (see instructions for Schedule K-1) . . . . ▶ _____ %

G If question D is checked "No" and any activity referred to in question D was started or acquired by the corporation after 10/22/86, check here ▶ ☐ and enter the date of start up or acquisition in the date space on line 1. Also, if an activity for which income or loss is reported on line 2 or 3 was started after 10/22/86, check the box and enter the start up date in the date space on line 2 or 3.

H If the short tax year shown above was a result of a change in tax year required by section 1378, check here . . . .▶ ☐

Caution: *Refer to Shareholder's Instructions for Schedule K-1 before entering information from Schedule K-1 on your tax return.*

		(a) Distributive share items	(b) Amount	(c) Form 1040 filers enter the amount in column (b) on:
Income (Losses) and Deductions	1	Ordinary income (loss) from trade or business activity(ies). Date:_____		See Shareholder's Instructions for Schedule K-1 (Form 1120S).
	2	Income or loss from rental real estate activity(ies). Date: _____		
	3	Income or loss from rental activity(ies) other than line 2 above. Date: _____		
	4	Portfolio income (loss):		
	a	Interest		Sch. B, Part I, line 2
	b	Dividends		Sch. B, Part II, line 4
	c	Royalties		Sch. E, Part I, line 5
	d	Net short-term capital gain (loss)		Sch. D, line 5, col. (f) or (g)
	e	Net long-term capital gain (loss)		Sch. D, line 12, col. (f) or (g)
	f	Other portfolio income (loss).		(Enter on applicable line of your return.)
	5	Net gain (loss) under section 1231 (other than due to casualty or theft).		Form 4797, line 1
	6	Other income (loss) (attach schedule)		(Enter on applicable line of your return.)
	7	Charitable contributions.		See Form 1040 Instructions.
	8	Section 179 expense deduction (attach schedule)		See Shareholder's Instructions for Schedule K-1 (Form 1120S).
	9	Deductions related to portfolio income (loss) (attach schedule) . . .		
	10	Other deductions (attach schedule)		
Credits	11a	Jobs credit		Form 5884
	b	Low-income housing credit		Form 8586, line 8
	c	Qualified rehabilitation expenditures related to rental real estate activity(ies) (attach schedule)	/////	See Shareholder's Instructions for Schedule K-1 (Form 1120S).
	d	Credits related to rental real estate activity(ies) other than on lines 11b and 11c (attach schedule)	/////	
	e	Credits related to rental activity(ies) other than on lines 11b, c, and d (attach schedule)	/////	
	12	Other credits (attach schedule)		
Tax Preference and Adjustment Items	13a	Accelerated depreciation of real property placed in service before 1987	/////	Form 6251, line 5a
	b	Accelerated depreciation of leased personal property placed in service before 1987.		Form 6251, line 5b
	c	Depreciation adjustment on property placed in service after 1986 . .		Form 6251, line 4g
	d	Depletion (other than oil and gas)		Form 6251, line 5h
	e	(1) Gross income from oil, gas, or geothermal properties		See Form 6251 Instructions.
		(2) Gross deductions allocable to oil, gas, or geothermal properties . .		
	f	Other items (attach schedule)		See Shareholder's Instructions for Schedule K-1 (Form 1120S).

	(a) Distributive share items	(b) Amount	(c) Form 1040 filers enter the amount in column (b) on:
Investment Interest	**14a** Interest expense on investment debts		Form 4952, line 1
	b (1) Investment income included on Schedule K-1, lines 4a through 4f .		See Shareholder's Instructions for Schedule K-1 (Form 1120S).
	(2) Investment expenses included on Schedule K-1, line 9		
Foreign Taxes	**15a** Type of income ▶..		Form 1116, Check boxes
	b Name of foreign country or U.S. possession ▶.............................		Form 1116, Part I
	c Total gross income from sources outside the U.S. (attach schedule) . .		Form 1116, Part I
	d Total applicable deductions and losses (attach schedule).		Form 1116, Part I
	e Total foreign taxes (check one): ▶ ☐ Paid ☐ Accrued		Form 1116, Part II
	f Reduction in taxes available for credit (attach schedule)		Form 1116, Part III
	g Other (attach schedule)		See Form 1116 Instructions.
Other Items	**16** Property distributions (including cash) other than dividend distributions reported to you on Form 1099-DIV		See Shareholder's Instructions for Schedule K-1 (Form 1120S).
	17 Amount of loan repayments for "Loans from Shareholders"		

		A	B	C	
Property Subject to Recapture of Investment Credit	**18** Properties:				
	a Description of property (State whether recovery or non-recovery property. If recovery property, state whether regular percentage method or section 48(q) election used.).				Form 4255, top
	b Date placed in service .				Form 4255, line 2
	c Cost or other basis . .				Form 4255, line 3
	d Class of recovery property or original estimated useful life .				Form 4255, line 4
	e Date item ceased to be investment credit property				Form 4255, line 8

19 Supplemental information for lines 1 through 18 that is required to be reported separately to each shareholder (attach additional schedules if more space is needed):

_____

_____

_____

_____

_____

_____

_____

_____

_____

_____

_____

_____

_____

_____

_____

Supplemental Schedules

Form **1065**	**U.S. Partnership Return of Income**	OMB No. 1545-0099

▶ **For Paperwork Reduction Act Notice, see Form 1065 Instructions.**

Department of the Treasury
Internal Revenue Service

For calendar year 1987, or fiscal year beginning _____, 1987, and ending _____ 19 ___

19 87

A Principal business activity	Use IRS label. Other- wise, please print or type.	Name	D Employer identification number
B Principal product or service		Number and street (or P.O. Box number if mail is not delivered to street address)	E Date business started
C Business code number		City or town, state, and ZIP code	F Enter total assets at end of tax year $

G Check accounting method: **(1)** ☐ Cash **(2)** ☐ Accrual **(3)** ☐ Other
H Check applicable boxes: **(1)** ☐ Final return **(2)** ☐ Change in address
(3) ☐ Amended return

		Yes	No
I	Number of partners in this partnership ▶ _____		
J	Is this partnership a limited partnership (see the Instructions)? . .		
K	Is this partnership a partner in another partnership?		
L	Are any partners in this partnership also partnerships? . . .		
M	Does the partnership meet **all** the requirements shown in the Instructions for **Question M**?		
N	Was there a distribution of property or a transfer (for example, by sale or death) of a partnership interest during the tax year? If "Yes," see the Instructions concerning an election to adjust the basis of the partnership's assets under section 754		

		Yes	No
O	At any time during the tax year, did the partnership have an interest in or a signature or other authority over a financial account in a foreign country (such as a bank account, securities account, or other financial account)? (See the Instructions for exceptions and filing requirements for Form TD F 90-22.1.) If "Yes," write the name of the foreign country. ▶ _____		
P	Was the partnership the grantor of, or transferor to, a foreign trust which existed during the current tax year, whether or not the partnership or any partner has any beneficial interest in it? If "Yes," you may have to file Forms 3520, 3520-A, or 926 .		
Q	Was this partnership in operation at the end of 1987? . . .		
R	Number of months in 1987 that this partnership was in operation ▶ _____		
S	Check this box if the partnership has filed or is required to file Form 8264, Application for Registration of a Tax Shelter . . . . ☐		
T	Check this box if this is a partnership subject to the consolidated partnership audit procedures of TEFRA. (See page 7 of the Instructions.) . . . . . ☐		

Caution: *Include only trade or business income and expenses on lines 1a–21 below. See the instructions for more information.*

Income

1a	Gross receipts or sales $ _____ **1b** Minus returns and allowances $ _____ Balance ▶	1c	
2	Cost of goods sold and/or operations (Schedule A, line 7)	2	
3	Gross profit (subtract line 2 from line 1c)	3	
4	Ordinary income (loss) from other partnerships and fiduciaries (attach schedule) . . .	4	
5	Net farm profit (loss) (attach Schedule F (Form 1040))	5	
6	Net gain (loss) (Form 4797, line 18)	6	
7	Other income (loss)	7	
8	**TOTAL** income (loss) (combine lines 3 through 7)	8	

Deductions *(see instructions for limitations)*

9a	Salaries and wages (other than to partners) $ _____ **9b** Minus jobs credit $ _____ Balance ▶	9c	
10	Guaranteed payments to partners	10	
11	Rent	11	
12	Deductible interest expense not claimed elsewhere on return (see Instructions)	12	
13	Taxes	13	
14	Bad debts	14	
15	Repairs	15	
16a	Depreciation from Form 4562 (attach Form 4562) $ _____ **16b** Minus depreciation claimed on Schedule A and elsewhere on return $ _____ Balance ▶	16c	
17	Depletion (***Do not deduct oil and gas depletion.***)	17	
18a	Retirement plans, etc.	18a	
b	Employee benefit programs	18b	
19	Other deductions (attach schedule)	19	
20	**TOTAL** deductions (add amounts in column for lines 9c through 19)	20	
21	Ordinary income (loss) from trade or business activity(ies) (subtract line 20 from line 8) . . .	21	

Please Sign Here

Under penalties of perjury, I declare that I have examined this return, including accompanying schedules and statements, and to the best of my knowledge and belief, it is true, correct, and complete. Declaration of preparer (other than taxpayer) is based on all information of which preparer has any knowledge.

▶ _____ Signature of general partner

▶ _____ Date

Paid Preparer's Use Only

Preparer's signature ▶	Date	Check if self-employed ▶ ☐	Preparer's social security no.
Firm's name (or yours if self-employed) and address ▶		E.I. No. ▶	
		ZIP code ▶	

Form 1065 (1987)   Page **2**

Schedule A	Cost of Goods Sold and/or Operations		

1	Inventory at beginning of year	**1**	
2	Purchases minus cost of items withdrawn for personal use	**2**	
3	Cost of labor	**3**	
4a	Additional section 263A costs (see instructions)	**4a**	
b	Other costs (attach schedule)	**4b**	
5	Total (add lines 1 through 4b)	**5**	
6	Inventory at end of year	**6**	
7	Cost of goods sold (subtract line 6 from line 5). Enter here and on page 1, line 2	**7**	

8a Check all methods used for valuing closing inventory:

    (i) ☐ Cost

    (ii) ☐ Lower of cost or market as described in regulations section 1.471-4

    (iii) ☐ Writedown of "subnormal" goods as described in regulations section 1.471-2(c)

    (iv) ☐ Other (specify method used and attach explanation) ▶ --- ☐

  b Check if the LIFO inventory method was adopted this tax year for any goods (if checked, attach Form 970) . . . . . ☐

  c Do the rules of section 263A (with respect to property produced or acquired for resale) apply to the partnership? . . . ☐ **Yes** ☐ **No**

  d Was there any change (other than for section 263A purposes) in determining quantities, cost, or valuations between opening and closing inventory? If "Yes," attach explanation . . . . ☐ **Yes** ☐ **No**

Schedule H	Income (Loss) From Rental Real Estate Activity(ies)		

1 In the space provided below, show the kind and location of each rental property. Attach a schedule if more space is needed.

Property A ---

Property B ---

Property C

Rental Real Estate Income		Properties			Totals (Add columns A, B, C, and amounts from any attached schedule)	
		A	**B**	**C**		
2 Gross Income	**2**				**2**	
Rental Real Estate Expenses						
3 Advertising	**3**					
4 Auto and travel	**4**					
5 Cleaning and maintenance . .	**5**					
6 Commissions	**6**					
7 Insurance	**7**					
8 Legal and other professional fees	**8**					
9 Interest expense	**9**					
10 Repairs	**10**					
11 Taxes	**11**					
12 Utilities	**12**					
13 Wages and salaries	**13**					
14 Depreciation from Form 4562	**14**					
15 Other (list) ----------------- ----------------- -----------------						
16 Total expenses. Add lines 3 through 15	**16**				**16**	
17 Net income (loss) from rental real estate activity(ies). Subtract line 16 from line 2. Enter total net income (loss) from all properties on Schedule K, line 2	**17**				**17**	

Form 1065 (1987)   Page **3**

Schedule K	Partners' Shares of Income, Credits, Deductions, etc.		
	(a) Distributive share items		**(b) Total amount**

Income (Loss)	1 Ordinary income (loss) from trade or business activity(ies) (page 1, line 21)	**1**	
	2 Net income (loss) from rental real estate activity(ies) (Schedule H, line 17)	**2**	
	3a Gross income from other rental activity(ies) . . . . . . **3a** $		
	b Minus expenses (attach schedule) . . . . **3b** $		
	c Balance net income (loss) from other rental activity(ies) . . . . ▶	**3c**	
	4 Portfolio income (loss):		
	a Interest income	**4a**	
	b Dividend income	**4b**	
	c Royalty income	**4c**	
	d Net short-term capital gain (loss) (Schedule D, line 4)	**4d**	
	e Net long-term capital gain (loss) (Schedule D, line 9)	**4e**	
	f Other portfolio income (loss) (attach schedule)	**4f**	
	5 Guaranteed payments	**5**	
	6 Net gain (loss) under section 1231 (other than due to casualty or theft)	**6**	
	7 Other (attach schedule)	**7**	
Deduc-tions	8 Charitable contributions (attach list)	**8**	
	9 Expense deduction for recovery property (section 179)	**9**	
	10 Deductions related to portfolio income (do not include investment interest expense) . . .	**10**	
	11 Other (attach schedule)	**11**	
Credits	**12a** Credit for income tax withheld	**12a**	
	b Low-income housing credit (attach Form 8586)	**12b**	
	c Qualified rehabilitation expenditures related to rental real estate activity(ies) (attach schedule)	**12c**	
	d Credit(s) related to rental real estate activity(ies) other than 12b and 12c (attach schedule)	**12d**	
	e Credit(s) related to rental activity(ies) other than 12b, 12c, and 12d (attach schedule) . .	**12e**	
	13 Other (attach schedule)	**13**	
Self-Employ-ment	**14a** Net earnings (loss) from self-employment	**14a**	
	b Gross farming or fishing income	**14b**	
	c Gross nonfarm income	**14c**	
Tax Preference Items	**15a** Accelerated depreciation of real property placed in service before 1/1/87	**15a**	
	b Accelerated depreciation of leased personal property placed in service before 1/1/87	**15b**	
	c Depreciation adjustment on property placed in service after 12/31/86	**15c**	
	d Depletion (other than oil and gas)	**15d**	
	e (1) Gross income from oil, gas, and geothermal properties	**15e(1)**	
	(2) Deductions allocable to oil, gas, and geothermal properties	**15e(2)**	
	f Other (attach schedule)	**15f**	
Invest-ment Interest	**16a** Interest expense on investment debts	**16a**	
	b (1) Investment income included on lines 4a through 4f, Schedule K	**16b(1)**	
	(2) Investment expenses included on line 10, Schedule K	**16b(2)**	
Foreign Taxes	**17a** Type of income -------------------------------------		
	b Foreign country or U.S. possession ----------------------		
	c Total gross income from sources outside the U.S. (attach schedule)	**17c**	
	d Total applicable deductions and losses (attach schedule)	**17d**	
	e Total foreign taxes (check one): ▶ ☐ Paid ☐ Accrued	**17e**	
	f Reduction in taxes available for credit (attach schedule)	**17f**	
	g Other (attach schedule)	**17g**	
Other	18 Attach schedule for other items and amounts not reported above. See Instructions . . .		

Form 1065 (1987)   Page **4**

Schedule L   Balance Sheets

(See the Instructions for Question M Before Completing Schedules L and M.)

Assets	Beginning of tax year		End of tax year	
	(a)	**(b)**	**(c)**	**(d)**
1 Cash				
2 Trade notes and accounts receivable				
a Minus allowance for bad debts				
3 Inventories				
4 Federal and state government obligations . . .				
5 Other current assets (attach schedule)				
6 Mortgage and real estate loans				
7 Other investments (attach schedule)				
8 Buildings and other depreciable assets				
a Minus accumulated depreciation				
9 Depletable assets				
a Minus accumulated depletion				
10 Land (net of any amortization)				
11 Intangible assets (amortizable only).				
a Minus accumulated amortization				
12 Other assets (attach schedule)				
13 **TOTAL** assets.				
Liabilities and Capital				
14 Accounts payable				
15 Mortgages, notes, bonds payable in less than 1 year				
16 Other current liabilities (attach schedule)				
17 All nonrecourse loans				
18 Mortgages, notes, bonds payable in 1 year or more				
19 Other liabilities (attach schedule)				
20 Partners' capital accounts.				
21 **TOTAL** liabilities and capital				

Schedule M   Reconciliation of Partners' Capital Accounts

(Show reconciliation of each partner's capital account on Schedule K-1 (Form 1065), Question I.)

(a) Capital account at beginning of year	**(b)** Capital contributed during year	**(c)** Income (loss) from lines 1,2, 3c, and 4 of Sch. K	**(d)** Income not included in column (c), plus nontaxable income	**(e)** Losses not included in column (c), plus unallowable deductions	**(f)** Withdrawals and distributions	**(g)** Capital account at end of year

Designation of Tax Matters Partner

The following general partner is hereby designated as the tax matters partner (TMP) for the tax year for which this partnership return is filed:

Name of designated TMP ▶ _____   Identifying number of TMP ▶ _____

Address of designated TMP ▶ _____

SCHEDULE K-1 (Form 1065) Department of the Treasury Internal Revenue Service	**Partner's Share of Income, Credits, Deductions, etc.** For calendar year 1987 or fiscal year beginning _____, 1987, and ending _____ , 19 ____ .	OMB No. 1545-0099 **1987**

Partner's identifying number ▶ _____

Partnership's identifying number ▶ _____

Partner's name, address, and ZIP code

Partnership's name, address, and ZIP code

A(1) Is this partner a general partner? . . . ☐ Yes ☐ No
If "yes" to Question A(1):
(2) Did this partner materially participate in the trade or business activity(ies) of the partnership? (See page 12 of the Form 1065 Instructions. Leave blank if no trade or business activities). . . . ☐ Yes ☐ No
(3) Did this partner actively participate in the rental real estate activity(ies) of the partnership? (See page 13 of the Form 1065 Instructions. Leave blank if no rental real estate activities). . . . ☐ Yes ☐ No
B Partner's share of liabilities
Nonrecourse. . . . . $ _____
Other . . . . $ _____
C What type of entity is this partner? ▶

D Enter partner's percentage of: **(i)** Before decrease or termination   **(ii)** End of year
Profit sharing . . . . . . _____%   _____%
Loss sharing . . . . . . _____%   _____%
Ownership of capital . . _____%   _____%
E IRS Center where partnership filed return ▶ _____
F Tax Shelter Registration Number ▶ _____
G(1) Did the partner's ownership interest in the partnership increase after Oct. 22, 1986? . . . . . ☐ Yes ☐ No
If yes, attach statement. (See page 13 of the Form 1065 Instructions.)
(2) Did the partnership start or acquire a new activity after Oct. 22, 1986? . . . . ☐ Yes ☐ No
If yes, attach statement. (See page 14 of the Form 1065 Instructions.)
H Check here ▶ ☐ if this Schedule K-1 is for a short tax year required by section 706(b).

I Reconciliation of partner's capital account:

(a) Capital account at beginning of year	(b) Capital contributed during year	(c) Income (loss) from lines 1, 2, 3, and 4 below	(d) Income not included in column (c), plus nontaxable income	(e) Losses not included in column (c), plus unallowable deductions	(f) Withdrawals and distributions	(g) Capital account at end of year

Caution: *Refer to attached Partner's Instructions for Schedule K-1 (Form 1065) before entering information from this schedule on your tax return.*

	(a) Distributive share item	(b) Amount	(c) 1040 filers enter the amount in column (b) on:
Income (Loss)	**1** Ordinary income (loss) from trade or business activity(ies)		⎫ (See Partner's Instructions for Schedule K-1 (Form 1065))
	2 Income or loss from rental real estate activity(ies)		
	3 Income or loss from other rental activity(ies)		⎭
	4 Portfolio income (loss):		
	a Interest		Sch. B, Part I, line 2
	b Dividends		Sch. B, Part II, line 4
	c Royalties		Sch. E, Part I, line 5
	d Net short-term capital gain (loss)		Sch. D, line 5, col. (f) or (g)
	e Net long-term capital gain (loss)		Sch. D, line 12, col. (f) or (g)
	f Other portfolio income (loss) (attach schedule)		(Enter on applicable lines of your return)
	5 Guaranteed payments		⎱ (See Partner's Instructions for Schedule K-1 (Form 1065))
	6 Net gain (loss) under section 1231 (other than due to casualty or theft)		
	7 Other (attach schedule)		(Enter on applicable lines of your return)
Deductions	**8** Charitable contributions		See Form 1040 Instructions
	9 Expense deduction for recovery property (section 179)		⎫ (See Partner's Instructions for Schedule K-1 (Form 1065))
	10 Deductions related to portfolio income		
	11 Other (attach schedule)		⎭
Credits	**12a** Credit for income tax withheld		See Form 1040 Instructions Form 8586, line 8
	b Low-income housing credit		
	c Qualified rehabilitation expenditures related to rental real estate activity(ies) (attach schedule)		
	d Credit(s) related to rental real estate activity(ies) other than 12b and 12c (attach schedule)		⎰ (See Partner's Instructions for Schedule K-1 (Form 1065))
	e Credit(s) related to rental activity(ies) other than 12b, 12c, and 12d (attach schedule).		
	13 Other credits (attach schedule)		

For Paperwork Reduction Act Notice, see Form 1065 Instructions.   **Schedule K-1 (Form 1065) 1987**

Schedule K-1 (Form 1065) (1987)   Page **2**

(a) Distributive share item		(b) Amount	(c) 1040 filers enter the amount in column (b) on:
Self-employment	**14a** Net earnings (loss) from self-employment		Sch. SE, Part I
	b Gross farming or fishing income		} (See Partner's Instructions for Schedule K-1 (Form 1065))
	c Gross nonfarm income		
Tax Preference Items	**15a** Accelerated depreciation of real property placed in service before 1/1/87		Form 6251, line 5a
	b Accelerated depreciation of leased personal property placed in service before 1/1/87		Form 6251, line 5b
	c Depreciation adjustment on property placed in service after 12/31/86		Form 6251, line 4g
	d Depletion (other than oil and gas)		Form 6251, line 5h
	e (1) Gross income from oil, gas, and geothermal properties . . .		See Form 6251 Instructions
	(2) Deductions allocable to oil, gas, and geothermal properties . . .		See Form 6251 Instructions
	f Other (attach schedule)		(See Partner's Instructions for Schedule K-1 (Form 1065))
Investment Interest	**16a** Interest expense on investment debts		Form 4952, line 1
	b (1) Investment income included in Schedule K-1, lines 4a through 4f .		} (See Partner's Instructions for Schedule K-1 (Form 1065))
	(2) Investment expenses included in Schedule K-1, line 10		
Foreign Taxes	**17a** Type of income _____		Form 1116, Check boxes
	b Name of foreign country or U.S. possession _____		Form 1116, Part I
	c Total gross income from sources outside the U.S. (attach schedule) .		Form 1116, Part I
	d Total applicable deductions and losses (attach schedule)		Form 1116, Part I
	e Total foreign taxes (check one): ▶ ☐ Paid ☐ Accrued		Form 1116, Part II
	f Reduction in taxes available for credit (attach schedule)		Form 1116, Part III
	g Other (attach schedule)		See Form 1116 Instructions
Other	**18** Other items and amounts not included in lines 1 through 17g and 19 that are required to be reported separately to you		(See Partner's Instructions for Schedule K-1 (Form 1065))

Property Subject to Recapture of Investment Credit	**19** Properties:	**A**	**B**	**C**	
	a Description of property (State whether recovery or nonrecovery property. If recovery property, state whether regular percentage method or section 48(q) election used.) .				Form 4255, top
	b Date placed in service .				Form 4255, line 2
	c Cost or other basis . .				Form 4255, line 3
	d Class of recovery property or original estimated useful life .				Form 4255, line 4
	e Date item ceased to be investment credit property				Form 4255, line 8

Other Information Provided by Partnership:

_____

_____

_____

_____

_____

_____

Form **1041**

Department of the Treasury
Internal Revenue Service

U.S. Fiduciary Income Tax Return

For the calendar year 1987 or fiscal year

beginning _____ , 1987, and ending _____ , 19 ___

OMB No. 1545-0092

1987

Check applicable boxes:
- ☐ Decedent's estate
- ☐ Simple trust
- ☐ Complex trust
- ☐ Grantor type trust
- ☐ Bankruptcy estate
- ☐ Family estate trust
- ☐ Pooled income fund
- ☐ Initial return
- ☐ Amended return
- ☐ Final return

Name of estate or trust (grantor type trust, see instructions)

Name and title of fiduciary

Address of fiduciary (number and street)

City, state, and ZIP code

Check if this is for a short taxable year under section 645 ▶ . . . . ☐

Employer identification number

Date entity created

Nonexempt charitable and split-interest trusts, check applicable boxes (see instructions):
- ☐ Described in section 4947(a)(1)
- ☐ Not a private foundation
- ☐ Described in section 4947(a)(2)

Income

1	Dividends	**1**
2	Interest income	**2**
3	Income (or losses) from partnerships, other estates or other trusts (see instructions)	**3**
4	Net rent and royalty income (or loss) (attach Schedule E (Form 1040)).	**4**
5	Net business and farm income (or loss) (attach Schedules C and F (Form 1040))	**5**
6	Capital gain (or loss) (attach Schedule D (Form 1041))	**6**
7	Ordinary gain (or loss) (attach Form 4797)	**7**
8	Other income (state nature of income)	**8**
9	**Total** income (add lines 1 through 8) . . . . ▶	**9**

Deductions

10	Interest **10**	
11	Fiduciary fees **11**	
12	Charitable deduction (from Schedule A, line 6) **12**	
13	Attorney, accountant, and return preparer fees **13**	
14	Other deductions (including taxes) (attach schedule) **14**	
15	**Total** (add lines 10 through 14) . . . . ▶	**15**
16	Adjusted total income (or loss) (subtract line 15 from line 9)	**16**
17	Income distribution deduction (from Schedule B, line 17) (see instructions) (attach Schedule K-1 (Form 1041)).	**17**
18	Estate tax deduction (including generation-skipping transfer taxes) (attach computation) . . .	**18**
19	Exemption	**19**
20	**Total** (add lines 17 through 19) . . . . ▶	**20**
21	Taxable income of fiduciary (subtract line 20 from line 16) . . . . ▶	**21**

Computation of Tax

Please attach check or money order here

22	**Tax:** ☐ **a** Tax rate schedule or ☐ Schedule D ....; **b** Other tax...............; Total ▶	**22c**
23	**Credits:** **a** Foreign tax.............................; **b** Nonconventional fuel...............; Total ▶	**23c**
24	**Credits:** ☐ Form 3800 ☐ Form 3468 ☐ Form 5884 ☐ Form 6478 ☐ Form 6765 ☐ Form 8586	**24**
25	**Total** (add lines 23c and 24) . . . . ▶	**25**
26	**Balance** (subtract line 25 from line 22c)	**26**
27	Recapture of investment credit (attach Form 4255).	**27**
28	Alternative minimum tax (attach Form 8656)	**28**
29	**Total** (add lines 26 through 28) . . . . ▶	**29**
30	**Credits: a** Form 2439.................; **b** Form 4136.................; **c** Form 6249 ....; Total ▶	**30d**
31	**Payments: a** 1987 estimated tax payments ▶	
	b Paid with extension of time to file (attach Form 2758) ▶ ....; **c** Withheld ▶ ....; Total ▶	**31d**
32	**Total** (add lines 30d and 31d) . . . . ▶	**32**
33	**Balance of tax due** (subtract line 32 from line 29) (see instructions)	**33**
34	**Overpayment** (subtract line 29 from line 32)	**34**
35	Amount of line 34 to be: **a** Credited to your 1988 estimated tax ▶	
	b Treated as paid by trust beneficiaries (Attach Form 1041-T) ▶ .... **Refunded** ▶	**35c**
	Check ▶ ☐ if Form 2210 (2210F) is attached (see instructions) **Penalty: $**	

Please Sign Here

Under penalties of perjury, I declare that I have examined this return, including accompanying schedules and statements, and to the best of my knowledge and belief, it is true, correct, and complete. Declaration of preparer (other than fiduciary) is based on all information of which preparer has any knowledge.

▶ _____

▶ Signature of fiduciary or officer representing fiduciary   Date

Paid Preparer's Use Only

Preparer's signature ▶	Date	Check if self-employed ▶ ☐	Preparer's social security no.
Firm's name (or yours if self-employed) and address ▶		E.I. No. ▶	
		ZIP code ▶	

For Paperwork Reduction Act Notice, see page 1 of the instructions.

Form **1041** (1987)

Form 1041 (1987)   Page 2

SCHEDULE A.—Charitable Deduction—*Do not complete for a simple trust or a pooled income fund.*
(Write the name and address of each charitable organization to whom your contributions total $3,000 or more on an attached sheet.)

1 Amounts paid or permanently set aside for charitable purposes from current year's gross income	1	
2 Tax-exempt interest allocable to charitable distribution (see instructions)	2	
3 Balance (subtract line 2 from line 1)	3	
4 Enter the net short-term capital gain and the net long-term capital gain of the current tax year allocable to corpus paid or permanently set aside for charitable purposes	4	
5 Amounts paid or permanently set aside for charitable purposes from gross income of a prior year (see instructions)	5	
6 Total (add lines 3, 4, and 5). Enter here and on page 1, line 12	6	

SCHEDULE B.—Income Distribution Deduction

1 Adjusted total income (Enter amount from page 1, line 16.) (If net loss, enter zero.)	1	
2 Adjusted tax-exempt interest (see instructions)	2	
3 Net gain shown on Schedule D (Form 1041), line 17, column (a) (If net loss, enter zero.)	3	
4 Enter amount from Schedule A, line 4	4	
5 Long-term capital gain included on Schedule A, line 1	5	
6 Short-term capital gain included on Schedule A, line 1	6	
7 If the amount on page 1, line 6, is a capital loss, enter here as a positive figure	7	
8 If the amount on page 1, line 6, is a capital gain, enter here as a negative figure.	8	
9 Distributable net income (combine lines 1 through 8)	9	
10 If a complex trust, amount of income for the tax year determined under the governing instrument (accounting income) 10		
11 Amount of income required to be distributed currently (see instructions)	11	
12 Other amounts paid, credited, or otherwise required to be distributed (see instructions)	12	
13 Total distributions (add lines 11 and 12). (If greater than line 10, see instructions.)	13	
14 Enter the total amount of tax-exempt income included on line 13	14	
15 Tentative income distribution deduction (subtract line 14 from line 13)	15	
16 Tentative income distribution deduction (subtract line 2 from line 9)	16	
17 Income distribution deduction (Enter the smaller of line 15 or line 16 here and on page 1, line 17.) . . .	17	

Other Information

	Yes	No
1 If the fiduciary's name or address has changed, enter the old information ▶		
2 Did the estate or trust receive tax-exempt income? (If "Yes," attach a computation of the allocation of expenses.) . . . Enter the amount of tax-exempt interest income ▶		
3 Did the estate or trust have any passive activity loss(es)? (If "Yes," enter the amount of any such loss(es) on **Form 8582**, Passive Activity Loss Limitations, to figure the allowable loss.)		
4 Did the estate or trust receive all or any part of the earnings (salary, wages, and other compensation) of any individual by reason of a contract assignment or similar arrangement?		
5 At any time during the tax year, did the estate or trust have an interest in or a signature or other authority over a financial account in a foreign country (such as a bank account, securities account, or other financial account)? (See the Instructions for exceptions and filing requirements for Form TD F 90-22.1 . . . . If "Yes," enter the name of the foreign country ▶		
6 Was the estate or trust the grantor of, or transferor to, a foreign trust which existed during the current tax year, whether or not the estate or trust has any beneficial interest in it? (If "Yes," you may have to file Form 3520, 3520-A, or 926.) . .		
7 Check this box if this entity has filed or is required to file **Form 8264**, Application for Registration of a Tax Shelter. . ▶ ☐		
8 Check this box if this entity is a complex trust making the section 663(b) election . . . . ▶ ☐		
9 Check this box if a section 643(e)(3) election is made (attach Schedule D (Form 1041)) . . . . ▶ ☐		
10 Check this box if the decedent's estate has been open for more than 2 years (see instructions) . . . . ▶ ☐		

SCHEDULE J
(Form 1041)

Department of the Treasury
Internal Revenue Service

Information Return
Trust Allocation of an Accumulation Distribution
(I.R.C. Section 665)
▶ File with Form 1041.

OMB No. 1545-0092

19**87**

Name of trust	Employer identification number

Part I **Accumulation Distribution in 1987**

For definitions and special rules, see the regulations under sections 665-668 of the Internal Revenue Code.
See the Form 4970 instructions for certain income minors may exclude and special rules for multiple trusts.

1 Enter amount from Schedule B (Form 1041), line 12, for 1987	**1**	
2 Enter amount from Schedule B (Form 1041), line 9, for 1987 . . . . **2**		
3 Enter amount from Schedule B (Form 1041), line 11, for 1987 . . . . **3**		
4 Distributable net income for 1987 (subtract line 3 from line 2. If line 3 is more than line 2, enter zero) . . .	**4**	
5 Accumulation distribution for 1987 (subtract line 4 from line 1)	**5**	

Part II **Ordinary Income Accumulation Distribution (Enter the applicable throwback years below.)**

If the distribution is thrown back to more than five years (starting with the earliest applicable tax year beginning after December 31, 1968), attach additional schedules. (If the trust was a simple trust see regulations section 1.665(e)-1A(b).)		Throwback year ending 19	Throwback year ending 19	Throwback year ending 19	Throwback year ending 19	Throwback year ending 19 ....
6 Distributable net income (see instructions)	**6**					
7 Distributions (see instructions).	**7**					
8 Undistributed net income (subtract line 7 from line 6) . . .	**8**					
9 Enter amount from line 25 or line 31, Part III, as applicable .	**9**					
10 Subtract line 9 from line 8 . .	**10**					
11 Enter amount of prior accumulation distributions thrown back to any of these years	**11**					
12 Subtract line 11 from line 10 .	**12**					
13 Allocate the amount on line 5 to the earliest applicable year first. Do not allocate an amount greater than line 12 for the same year (see instructions) .	**13**					
14 Divide line 13 by line 10 and multiply result by line 9 . . .	**14**					
15 Add lines 13 and 14	**15**					
16 Tax-exempt interest included on line 13 (see instructions). . .	**16**					
17 Subtract line 16 from line 15 .	**17**					

For Paperwork Reduction Act Notice, see page 1 of the Instructions for Form 1041.   Schedule J (Form 1041) 1987

Schedule J (Form 1041) 1987   Page **2**

Part III Taxes Imposed on Undistributed Net Income (Enter the applicable throwback years below.)

If more than five throwback years are involved, attach additional schedules. If the trust received an accumulation distribution from another trust, see the regulations under sections 665-668 of the Internal Revenue Code.

If the trust elected the alternative tax on capital gain, **OMIT** lines 18 through 25 **AND** complete lines 26 through 31.		Throwback year ending 19	Throwback year ending 19	Throwback year ending 19	Throwback year ending 19	Throwback year ending 19 ....
(The alternative tax on capital gain was repealed for tax years beginning after December 31, 1978.)						
18 Tax (see instructions)	18					
19 Net short-term gain (see instructions)	19					
20 Net long-term gain (see instructions)	20					
21 Total net capital gain (add lines 19 and 20)	21					
22 Taxable income (see instructions)	22					
23 Enter percent (divide line 21 by line 22, but not more than 100%)	23	%	%	%	%	%
24 Multiply amount on line 18 by percent on line 23	24					
25 Tax on undistributed net income (subtract line 24 from line 18. Enter here and on line 9)	25					
If the trust did not elect the alternative tax on long-term capital gain, do **NOT** complete lines 26 through 31.						
26 Tax on income other than long-term capital gain (see instructions)	26					
27 Net short-term gain (see instructions)	27					
28 Taxable income less section 1202 deduction (see instructions)	28					
29 Enter percent (divide line 27 by line 28, but not more than 100%)	29	%	%	%	%	%
30 Multiply amount on line 26 by percent on line 29	30					
31 Tax on undistributed net income (subtract line 30 from line 26. Enter here and on line 9)	31					

Part IV Allocation to Beneficiary

Complete Part IV for each beneficiary. If the accumulation distribution is allocated to more than one beneficiary, attach an additional Schedule J with Part IV completed for each additional beneficiary. If more than five throwback years are involved, attach additional schedules.

Beneficiary's name		Identifying number		
Beneficiary's address (number and street including apartment number or rural route)		Enter amount from line 13 allocated to this beneficiary **(a)**	Enter amount from line 14 allocated to this beneficiary **(b)**	Enter amount from line 16 allocated to this beneficiary **(c)**
City, state, and ZIP code				
32 Throwback year 19	32			
33 Throwback year 19	33			
34 Throwback year 19	34			
35 Throwback year 19	35			
36 Throwback year 19	36			
37 Total (add amounts on lines 32 through 36)	37			

| SCHEDULE K-1 (Form 1041) Department of the Treasury Internal Revenue Service | **Beneficiary's Share of Income, Deductions, Credits, etc.—1987** for the calendar year 1987, or fiscal year beginning ...., 1987, ending ...., 19 ..... Complete a separate Schedule K-1 for each beneficiary. | OMB No. 1545-0092 1987 |

Name of estate or trust ▶

| Beneficiary's identifying number ▶ | Estate's or trust's employer identification number ▶ |
| Beneficiary's name, address, and ZIP code | Fiduciary's name, address, and ZIP code |

A. 4-Year Proration.—Fiduciary: Check here ▶ ☐ if this Schedule K-1 is for a short taxable year required by section 1403 of the Tax Reform Act of 1986. **Beneficiary:** If this box is checked, you must prorate all column (b) amounts shown below (except for line 9a) over a four-year period beginning with this tax year. (See the instructions on the other side of this schedule.)

(a) Allocable share item	(b) Amount	(c) Calendar year 1987 Form 1040 filers enter the amounts in column (b) on:
1 Dividends		Schedule B, Part II, line 4
2a Net short-term capital gain (or loss)		Schedule D, line 5, column (f) or (g)
b Net long-term capital gain (or loss)		Schedule D, line 12, column (f) or (g)
3 Interest		Schedule B, Part I, line 2
4a Other taxable income:		
(1) Rental, rental real estate, and business income from activities acquired before 10/23/86		(see instructions)
(2) Rental, rental real estate, and business income from activities acquired after 10/22/86		(see instructions)
(3) Other income		Schedule E, Part III, column (e) or (f)
b Depreciation (including cost recovery) and depletion:		
(1) Attributable to line 4a(1)		(see instructions)
(2) Attributable to line 4a(2)		(see instructions)
(3) Attributable to line 4a(3)		Schedule E, Part III, column (e)
c Amortization deductions:		
(1) Attributable to line 4a(1)		(see instructions)
(2) Attributable to line 4a(2)		(see instructions)
(3) Attributable to line 4a(3)		Schedule E, Part III, column (e)
5 Estate tax deduction (including generation-skipping transfer taxes) (attach computation)		Schedule A, line 25
6 Excess deductions on termination (attach computation)		Schedule A, line 21
7 Distributable Net Alternative Minimum Taxable Income		See Form 6251, line 4q instructions
8 Foreign taxes (list on a separate sheet)		Form 1116 or Schedule A (Form 1040), line 7
9 Other (itemize):		
a Trust payments of estimated taxes credited to you		Include on page 2, line 55, Form 1040
b Tax-exempt interest		Enter on page 1, line 9, Form 1040
c		
d		(Enter on applicable line
e		of appropriate tax form)
f		
g		
h		

For Paperwork Reduction Act Notice, see page 1 of the instructions for Form 1041.

Schedule K-1 (Form 1041) 1987

Instructions for Beneficiary Filing Form 1040

General Instructions

Name, Address, and Identifying Number.—Your name, address, and identifying number, the estate or trust name, address, and identifying number should have been entered on the Schedule K-1 you received.

Tax Shelters.—If you receive a copy of **Form 8271,** Investor Reporting of Tax Shelter Registration Number, and other tax shelter information from the estate or trust, or if the estate or trust is a tax shelter required to register under section 6111, see the Instructions for Form 8271 to determine your reporting requirements.

Errors.—If you believe the estate or trust has made an error on your Schedule K-1, notify the fiduciary of the estate or trust and ask for a corrected Schedule K-1. Do not change any items on your copy. Be sure that the estate or trust sends a copy of the corrected Schedule K-1 to the IRS.

4-Year Proration.—Section 1403 of the Tax Reform Act of 1986 requires most trusts to adopt the calendar year as their taxable year in 1987. Fiscal year trusts will accomplish this conversion by filing a short year 1987 Form 1041 that ends on December 31, 1987. Therefore, if you are the beneficiary of a former fiscal year trust, you should receive two Schedule K-1s for 1987. The first will be for the full fiscal year that ends in 1987, and the second will be for the short taxable year that ends on December 31, 1987.

For the short year, you must prorate each of the amounts (except line 9a) shown on the short year's Schedule K-1 over a four-year period beginning with 1987. This alleviates the bunching of income arising from the change in taxable years. The prorated amounts for the short year are to be added together with the items shown on the full fiscal year Schedule K-1 you received. These combined amounts are to be entered on your 1987 tax return as indicated in column (c) of the two Schedule K-1s.

Thus, if the fiduciary checked the box on line A to indicate that this Schedule K-1 is filed for a short tax year, you must prorate all of the column (b) amounts (except line 9a) for the short year in the following manner:

For 1987, enter one-fourth of the amounts shown in column (b) (except line 9a) on your Form 1040, and its schedules, or other forms, as shown in column (c). For 1988, 1989, and 1990, enter one-fourth of the amounts shown in column (b) of this 1987 Schedule K-1 on your Form 1040, and its schedules, or other forms, that you will file for each of those years. In order to make the proper entries for these future years, you should retain the 1987 short year Schedule K-1 in your records.

The line references to Form 1040 and its schedules shown on this Schedule K-1 are valid for 1987 only. For the 1988 through 1990 tax years, consult the Form 1040 and Schedule K-1 that will be issued for each of those years to determine where to enter the 1987 amounts prorated to those years.

Specific Instructions

Line 2. Capital Gains.—Report the amount from line 2a (Schedule K-1) on your Schedule D (Form 1040), line 5, column (f) or (g). Report the amount from line 2b (Schedule K-1) on your Schedule D (Form 1040), line 12, column (f) or (g). If there is an attachment to this Schedule K-1 that reports a disposition of a rental, rental real estate, or passive business activity, see the instructions to Form 8582 for information on the treatment of dispositions of interests in a passive activity.

Lines 4a–4c.—New Code section 469 provides rules that limit deductions and credits derived from passive activities to the income derived from passive activities and the tax imposed on any net income from such activities. A trade or business activity in which you, as beneficiary of an estate or trust, DO NOT materially participate is a passive activity.

You are treated as materially participating in an activity only if you are involved in the operations of the activity on a regular, continuous, and substantial basis.

All rental activities are considered to be passive activities, regardless of participation. However, section 469 provides a special rule for rental real estate activities in which you actively participate. Generally, you are allowed to deduct up to $25,000 of these losses against non-passive income.

If this Schedule K-1 shows income (line 4a), or deductions (lines 4b or 4c) from trade or business activities of the estate or trust in which you do not materially participate, or from rental activities of the estate or trust, you generally must complete **Form 8582,** Passive Activity Loss Limitations, to figure the allowable amount of loss to report on your Form 1040.

Depreciation and amortization deductions from a rental real estate activity of the estate or trust reported on lines 4b(1) or (2) or 4c(1), or (2) may be eligible for the $25,000 allowance if you actively participate in the activity. The $25,000 allowance is figured on Form 8582.

The limitations of section 469 are figured on Form 8582 after combining passive activity amounts from all sources (including the estate or trust). An overall loss from passive activities generally may not offset income such as salary, interest, dividends, and non-passive business activity income. Credits attributable to a passive activity generally are limited to tax attributable to passive activities. There is also a special phase-in rule for 1987 that allows you to deduct 65% of your total passive activity loss attributable to activities acquired before October 23, 1986. See the instructions for Form 8582 on how to combine passive activity amounts, how to apply the passive loss rules if you have an overall passive activity loss, and how to compute the amount of any passive activity loss you can deduct.

You do not have to complete Form 8582 if all of the following conditions are met:

(a) This Schedule K-1 is not accompanied by an attachment that summarizes the results of more than one passive activity;

(b) You have no income or deductions from other passive activities; and

(c) The income shown on lines 4a(1) or (2) is greater than the deductions attributable to such income shown on lines 4b(1) or (2); or 4c(1) or (2).

Line 9a.—For purposes of computing any underpayment and penalty on **Form 2210,** Underpayment of Estimated Tax by Individuals, you should treat the amount entered on line 9a as an estimated tax payment made on January 15, 1988. You should not prorate this estimated tax payment to future tax years even if the 4-year proration box is checked.

Line 9b.—If any tax-exempt interest is entered on this line by the estate or trust, then you should report it on Form 1040, line 9. Beginning in 1987, every person required to file a return must report any tax-exempt interest income received.

Lines 9c–h.—The amount of gross farming and fishing income is included in "Other taxable income" on line 4. This income is also separately stated on line 9 to assist you in determining if you are subject to a penalty for underpayment of estimated tax.

• *Individual Beneficiaries.*—Report the amount of gross farming and fishing income on Schedule E (Form 1040), Part VI, line 43.

• *Beneficiaries That Are Estates or Trusts.*—Beneficiaries that are estates or trusts must pass through the amount of gross farming and fishing income included on line 9 of their Schedule K-1s to line 9 of their beneficiary's Schedule K-1s on a pro rata basis.

Note: *The fiduciary's instructions are contained in the Form 1041 instructions.*

Form **8656**

Department of the Treasury
Internal Revenue Service

Alternative Minimum Tax— Fiduciaries

► See separate instructions.
► Attach to Forms 1041 or 990-T.

OMB No. 1545-1024

19**87**

Name as shown on tax return	Identifying number

1	Total income (from line 9, Form 1041)		**1**
2a	Interest—see instructions	**2a**	
b	Fiduciary fees (from line 11, Form 1041)	**2b**	
c	Charitable deduction (from line 12, Form 1041)	**2c**	
d	Other—see instructions	**2d**	
3	Total (add lines 2a through 2d)		**3**
4	Line 1 less line 3		**4**
5	Adjustments:		
a	Depreciation of property placed in service after 1986	**5a**	
b	Circulation and research and experimental expenditures paid or incurred after 1986.	**5b**	
c	Mining exploration and development costs paid or incurred after 1986 . .	**5c**	
d	Long-term contracts entered into on or after 3/1/86	**5d**	
e	Pollution control facilities placed in service after 1986	**5e**	
f	Installment sales of certain property	**5f**	
g	Basis adjustment	**5g**	
h	Loss limitations—see instructions	**5h**	
i	Total adjustments (add lines 5a through 5h)		**5i**
6	Tax preference items:		
a	Accelerated depreciation of real property placed in service before 1987 . .	**6a**	
b	Accelerated depreciation of leased personal property placed in service before 1987	**6b**	
c	Amortization of certified pollution control facilities placed in service before 1987	**6c**	
d	Appreciated property charitable deduction—see instructions	**6d**	
e	Incentive stock options.	**6e**	
f	Tax-exempt interest on specified private activity bonds	**6f**	
g	Intangible drilling costs.	**6g**	
h	Depletion	**6h**	
i	Reserves for losses on bad debts of financial institutions	**6i**	
j	Total tax preference items (add lines 6a through 6i)		**6j**
7	Add lines 4, 5i, and 6j		**7**
8	Alternative tax net operating loss deduction. (Do not enter more than 90% of line 7.)		**8**
9	Distributable net alternative minimum taxable income (DNAMTI) (line 7 less line 8)		**9**
10	Income distribution deduction—see instructions		**10**
11a	Estate tax deduction (from line 18, Form 1041).	**11a**	
b	Exemption—see instructions	**11b**	
c	Fiduciary's share of alternative minimum taxable income (line 9 less lines 10, 11a, and 11b)		**11c**
	Note: *If line 11c is less than $20,000, you are not liable for the alternative minimum tax. **Do not** complete this form.*		
12	Exemption amount	**12**	$20,000	
13	Phase-out of exemption amount	**13**	$75,000	
14	Line 11c less line 13 (If zero or less, enter zero.).		**14**
15	Multiply line 14 by 25% (.25).		**15**
16	Line 12 less line 15 (If zero or less, enter zero.)		**16**
17	Line 11c less line 16		**17**
18	Multiply line 17 by 21% (.21).		**18**
19	Alternative minimum tax foreign tax credit		**19**
20	Tentative minimum tax (line 18 less line 19)		**20**
21a	Regular tax before credits (see instructions)	**21a**	
b	Section 644 tax (if any, from line 22b, Form 1041).	**21b**	
c	Add lines 21a and b.		**21c**
22	Alternative minimum tax (line 20 less line 21c). Enter here and on line 28, Form 1041, or line 13a, Form 990-T		**22**

For Paperwork Reduction Act Notice, see page 1 of the instructions.

Form **8656** (1987)

Appendix C
Glossary of Tax Terms

The words and phrases appearing below have been defined to reflect their conventional use in the field of taxation. Such definitions may therefore be incomplete for other purposes.

A

Accelerated cost recovery system. A method whereby the cost of a fixed asset is written off for tax purposes. Instituted by the Economic Recovery Tax Act of 1981, the system places assets into one of various recovery periods and prescribes the applicable percentage of cost that can be deducted each year. In this regard, it largely resolves the controversy that used to arise with prior depreciation procedures in determining estimated useful life and in predicting salvage value. § 168.

Accelerated depreciation. Various methods of depreciation that yield larger deductions in the earlier years of the life of an asset than the straight-line method. Examples include the double-declining balance and the sum-of-the-years' digits methods of depreciation. §§ 167(b)(2) and (3).

Accounting method. The method under which income and expenses are determined for tax purposes. Major accounting methods are the cash basis and the accrual basis. Special methods are available for the reporting of gain on installment sales, recognition of income on construction projects (i.e., the completed contract and percentage-of-completion methods), and the valuation of inventories (i.e., last-in, first-out and first-in, first-out). §§ 446–474. See also *accrual basis, cash basis, completed contract method, percentage of completion method,* etc.

Accounting period. The period of time, usually a year, used by a taxpayer for the determination of tax liability. Unless a fiscal year is chosen, taxpayers must determine and pay their income tax liability by using the calendar year (i.e., January 1 through December 31) as the period of measurement. An example of a fiscal year is July 1 through June 30. A change in accounting periods (e.g., from a calendar year to a fiscal year) generally requires the consent of the IRS. Some new taxpayers such as a newly formed corporation, are free to select either an initial calendar or fiscal year without the consent of the IRS. §§ 441–443. See also *annual accounting period concept.*

Accrual basis. A method of accounting that reflects expenses incurred and income earned for any one tax year. In contrast to the cash basis of accounting, expenses need not be paid to be deductible nor need income received to be taxable. Unearned income (e.g., prepaid interest and rent) generally is taxed in the year of receipt regardless of the method of accounting used by the taxpayer. § 446(c)(2). See also *accounting method, cash basis,* and *unearned income.*

Accumulated adjustments account. An account that comprises an S corporation's post–1982 income, loss and deductions for the tax year (including nontaxable income and nondeductible losses and expenses). After the year-end income and expense adjustments are made, the account is reduced by distributions made during the tax year.

Accumulated earnings credit. A reduction allowed in arriving at accumulated taxable income in determining the accumulated earnings tax. See also *accumulated earnings tax* and *accumulated taxable income.*

Accumulated earnings tax. A special tax imposed on corporations that accumulate (rather than distribute) their earnings beyond the reasonable needs of the business. The accumulated earnings tax and related interest, is imposed on accumulated taxable income in addition to the corporate income tax. §§ 531–537.

Accumulated taxable income. The base upon which the accumulated earnings tax is imposed. Generally, it is the taxable income of the corporation as adjusted for certain items (e.g., the Federal income tax, excess charitable contributions, the dividends received deduction) less the dividends paid deduction and the accumulated earnings credit. § 535.

Accumulating trusts. See *discretionary trusts.*

Acquiescence. Agreement by the IRS on the results reached in most of the Regular decisions of the U.S. Tax Court sometimes abbreviated *acq.* or *A.* See also *nonacquiescence.*

Acquisition. See *corporate acquisition.*

ACRS. See *accelerated cost recovery system.*

Ad valorem tax. A tax imposed on the value of property. The more common ad valorem tax is that imposed by states, counties and cities on real estate. Ad valorem taxes can, however, be imposed on personal property, as well. See also *personalty.*

Add-on minimum tax. Before the Tax Equity and Fiscal Responsibility Act of 1982, an add-on minimum tax covered both corporate and noncorporate taxpayers. As applied to individuals, the add-on minimum tax was 15 percent of the tax preference items (reduced by the greater of $10,000 or one-half of the income tax liability for the year). For taxable years beginning after 1982, the add-on minimum tax is repealed as to individuals. In its place, Congress expanded the scope of the alternative minimum tax. Similarly, the add-on tax with respect to corporate taxpayers is repealed as of 1986, and an alternative minimum tax applies. See also *alternative minimum tax.*

Adjusted basis. The cost or other basis of property reduced by depreciation allowed or allowable and increased by capital improvements. Other special adjustments are provided for in § 1016 and the Regulations thereunder. See also *basis.*

Adjusted gross estate. The gross estate of a decedent reduced by § 2053 expenses (e.g., administration, funeral) and § 2054 losses (e.g., casualty). The determination of the adjusted gross estate is necessary in testing for the extension of time for installment payment of estate taxes under § 6166. See also *gross estate.*

Adjusted gross income. A tax determination peculiar to individual taxpayers. Generally, it represents the gross income of an individual, less business and certain personal expenses, and less any appropriate capital gain or loss adjustment. See also *gross income.*

Adjusted ordinary gross income. A determination peculiar to the personal holding company tax imposed by § 541. In testing to ascertain whether a corporation is a personal holding company, personal holding company income divided by adjusted ordinary gross income must equal 60 percent or more. Adjusted ordinary gross income is the corporation's gross income less capital gains, § 1231 gains, and certain expenses. Adjusted ordinary gross income is defined in § 543(b)(2) and the Regulations thereunder. See also *personal holding company income.*

Adjusted taxable estate. The taxable estate reduced by $60,000. The adjusted taxable estate is utilized in applying the table of § 2011 for determining the limit on the credit for state death taxes paid that will be allowed against the Federal estate tax. See also *taxable estate.*

Administration. The supervision and winding up of an estate. The administration of an estate runs from the date of an individual's death until all assets have been distributed and liabilities paid. Such administration is conducted by an administrator or an executor.

Administrator. A person appointed by the court to administer (i.e., manage or take charge of) the assets and liabilities of a decedent (i.e., the deceased). Such person may be a male (administrator) or a female (administratrix). See also *executor.*

AFTR. Published by Prentice-Hall, *American Federal Tax Reports* contain all of the Federal tax decisions issued by the U.S. District Courts, U.S. Claims Court, U.S. Court of Appeals, and the U.S. Supreme Court.

AFTR2d. The second series of the *American Federal Tax Reports,* dealing with 1954 and 1986 IRC case law.

Alimony. Alimony deductions result from the payment of a legal obligation arising from the termination of a marital relationship. Designated alimony payments generally are included in the gross income of the recipient and are deductible *for* AGI by the payor.

Allocable share of income. Certain entities receive conduit treatment under the Federal income tax law. This means the earned income or loss is not taxed to the entity, but such amounts are allocated to the owners or beneficiaries thereof regardless of the magnitude or timing of corresponding distributions. That portion of the entity's income that is taxed to the owner or beneficiary is the allocable share of the entity's income or loss for the period. Such allocations are determined by (1) the partnership agreement relative to the partners, (2) a weighted-average stock ownership computation relative to shareholders of an S corporation, and (3) the controlling will or trust instrument relative to the beneficiaries of an estate or trust.

✓**Alternate valuation date.**   Property passing from a person by death may be valued for death tax purposes as of the date of death or the alternate valuation date. The alternate valuation date is six months from the date of death or the date the property is disposed of by the estate, whichever comes first. The use of the alternate valuation date requires an affirmative election on the part of the executor or administrator of the estate. The election of the alternate valuation date is not available unless it decreases the amount of the gross estate *and* reduces the estate tax liability.

Alternative minimum tax (AMT).   Presently, taxpayers are not subject to an add-on minimum tax but are covered by an alternative minimum tax. Simply stated, the AMT is a fixed percentage of alternative minimum taxable income (AMTI). AMTI generally starts with the taxpayer's adjusted gross income (for individuals) or taxable income (for other taxpayers). To this amount, the taxpayer (1) adds designated preference items (e.g., the appreciation on charitable contribution property), (2) makes other specified adjustments (e.g., to reflect a longer, straight-line cost recovery deduction), (3) subtracts certain AMT itemized deductions for individuals (e.g., interest incurred on housing but not taxes paid), and (4) subtracts an exemption amount (e.g., $40,000 on an individual joint return). The taxpayer must pay the greater of the resulting AMT (reduced by only the foreign tax credit and a reduced investment credit) or the regular income tax (reduced by all allowable tax credits). See also *add-on minimum tax.*

Amortization.   The tax deduction of the cost or other basis of an intangible asset over the asset's estimated useful life. Examples of amortizable intangibles include patents, copyrights, and leasehold interests. The intangible goodwill cannot be amortized for income tax purposes because it possesses no estimated useful life. As to tangible assets, see *depreciation.* As to natural resources, see *depletion.* See also *estimated useful life* and *goodwill.*

Amount realized.   The amount received by a taxpayer upon the sale or exchange of property. The measure of the amount realized is the sum of the cash and the fair market value of any property or services received, by the taxpayer, plus any related debt assumed by the buyer. Determining the amount realized is the starting point for arriving at realized gain or loss. The amount realized is defined in § 1001(b) and the Regulations thereunder. See also *realized gain or loss* and *recognized gain or loss.*

Annual accounting period concept.   In determining a taxpayer's income tax liability, only those transactions taking place during a particular tax year are taken into consideration. For reporting and payment purposes, therefore, the tax life of taxpayers is divided into equal annual accounting periods. See also *accounting period* and *mitigation of the annual accounting period concept.*

Annual exclusion.   In computing the taxable gifts for any one year, each donor may exclude the first $10,000 of a gift to each donee. Usually, the annual exclusion is not available for gifts of future interests. § 2503(b). See also *election to split gifts* and *future interest.*

Annuitant.   The party entitled to receive payments from an annuity contract. See also *annuity.*

✓**Annuity.**   A fixed sum of money payable to a person at specified times for a set period of time or for life. If the party making the payment (i.e., the obligor) is regularly engaged in this type of business (e.g., an insurance company), the arrangement is classified as a commercial annuity. A private annuity involves an obligor that is not regularly engaged in selling annuities (e.g., a charity or family member).

Anticipatory assignment of income.   See *assignment of income.*

Appellate court.   For Federal tax purposes, appellate courts include the Courts of Appeals and the Supreme Court. If the party losing in the trial (or lower) court is dissatisfied with the result, the dispute may be carried to the appropriate appellate court. See also *Court of Appeals* and *trial court.*

Arm's length.   The standard under which unrelated parties would carry out a particular transaction. Suppose, for example, X Corporation sells property to its sole shareholder for $10,000. In testing whether $10,000 is an arm's length price, one would ascertain the amount for which the corporation could have sold the property to a disinterested third party.

Articles of incorporation.   The legal document specifying a corporation's name, period of existence, purpose and powers, authorized number of shares, classes of stock, and other conditions for operation. These articles are filed by the organizers of the corporation with the state of incorporation. If the articles are satisfactory and other conditions of the law are satisfied, the state will issue a charter recognizing the organization's status as a corporation.

Assessment.   The process whereby the IRS imposes an additional tax liability. If, for example, the IRS audits a taxpayer's income tax return and finds gross income understated or deductions overstated, it will assess a deficiency in the amount of the tax that should have been paid in light of the adjustments made. See also *deficiency*.

Assignment of income. A procedure whereby a taxpayer attempts to avoid the recognition of income by assigning to another the property that generates the income. Such a procedure will not avoid the recognition of income by the taxpayer making the assignment if it can be said that the income was earned at the point of the transfer. In this case, usually referred to as an anticipatory assignment of income, the income will be taxed to the person who earns it.

Association. An organization treated as a corporation for Federal tax purposes even though it may not qualify as such under applicable state law. What is designated as a trust or a partnership, for example, may be classified as an association if it clearly possesses corporate attributes. Corporate attributes include centralized management, continuity of existence, free transferability of interests, and limited liability. § 7701(a)(3).

At-risk amount. The taxpayer has an amount at risk in a business or investment venture to the extent that it has subjected personal assets to the risks of the business. Typically, the taxpayer's at-risk amount includes (1) the amount of money or other property that the investor contributed to the venture for the investment, (2) the amount of any of the entity's liabilities for which the taxpayer personally is liable and that relate to the investment, and (3) an allocable share of nonrecourse debts incurred by the venture from third parties in arm's length transactions, with respect to real estate investments.

At-risk limitation. Generally, a taxpayer can deduct losses relative to a trade or business, S corporation, partnership, or investment asset only to the extent of the at-risk amount.

Attribution. Under certain circumstances, the tax law applies attribution rules to assign to one taxpayer the ownership interest of another taxpayer. If, for example, the stock of X Corporation is held 60 percent by M and 40 percent by S, M may be deemed to own 100 percent of X Corporation if M and S are mother and son. In such a case, the stock owned by S is attributed to M. Stated differently, M has a 60 percent direct and a 40 percent indirect interest in X Corporation. It can also be said that M is the constructive owner of S's interest.

Audit. Inspection and verification of a taxpayer's return or other transactions possessing tax consequences. See also *correspondence audit, field audit,* and *office audit*.

B

Bailout. Various procedures whereby the owners of an entity can obtain the entity's profits with favorable tax consequences. With corporations, for example, the bailout of corporate profits without dividend consequences might be the desired objective. The alternative of distributing the profits to the shareholders as dividends generally is less attractive, since dividend payments are not deductible. See also *preferred stock bailout*.

Bargain sale or purchase. A sale of property for less than the fair market value of such property. The difference between the sale or purchase price and the fair market value of the property must be accounted for in terms of its tax consequences. If, for example, a corporation sells property worth $1,000 to one of its shareholders for $700, the $300 difference probably represents a constructive dividend to the shareholder. Suppose, instead, the shareholder sells the property (worth $1,000) to his or her corporation for $700. The $300 difference probably represents a contribution by the shareholder to the corporation's capital. Bargain sales and purchases among members of the same family may lead to gift tax consequences. See also *constructive dividends*.

Basis. The amount assigned to an asset for income tax purposes. For assets acquired by purchase, basis would be cost (§ 1012). Special rules govern the basis of property received by virtue of another's death (§ 1014) or by gift (§ 1015), the basis of stock received on a transfer of property to a controlled corporation (§ 358), the basis of the property transferred to the corporation (§ 362), and the basis of property received upon the liquidation of a corporation (§§ 334 and 338). See also *adjusted basis*.

Beneficiary. A party who will benefit from a transfer of property or other arrangement. Examples include the beneficiary of a trust, the beneficiary of a life insurance policy, and the beneficiary of an estate.

Bequest. A transfer by will of personal property. To bequeath is to leave such property by will. See also *devise* and *personal property*.

Blockage rule. A factor to be considered in valuing a large block of stock. Application of this rule generally justifies a discount in the fair market value, since the disposition of a large amount of stock at any one time may depress the value of such shares in the market place.

Bona fide. In good faith, or real. In tax law, this term is often used in connection with a business purpose for carrying out a transaction. Thus, was there a bona fide business purpose for a shareholder's transfer of a liability to a controlled corporation? § 357(b)(1)(B). See also *business purpose*.

Book value. The net amount of an asset after reduction by a related reserve. The book value of accounts receivable, for example, would be the amount of the receivables less the reserve for bad debts.

Boot. Cash or property of a type not included in the definition of a nontaxable exchange. The receipt of boot will cause an otherwise taxfree transfer to become taxable to the extent of the lesser of the fair market value of such boot or the realized gain on the transfer. For example, see transfers to controlled corporations under § 351 (b) and like-kind exchanges under § 1031(b). See also *like-kind exchange* and *realized gain or loss*.

Brother-sister corporations. More than one corporation owned by the same shareholders. If, for example, C and D each own one-half of the stock in X Corporation and Y Corporation, X and Y are brother-sister corporations.

B.T.A. The Board of Tax Appeals was a trial court that considered Federal tax matters. This Court is now designated as the U.S. Tax Court.

Burden of proof. The requirement in a lawsuit to show the weight of evidence and thereby gain a favorable decision. Except in cases of tax fraud, the burden of proof in a tax case generally is on the taxpayer. See also *fraud*.

Business bad debts. A tax deduction allowed for obligations obtained in connection with a trade or business that have become either partially or completely worthless. In contrast with nonbusiness bad debts, business bad debts are deductible as business expenses. § 166. See also *nonbusiness bad debts*.

Business purpose. A justifiable business reason for carrying out a transaction. It has long been established that mere tax avoidance is not an acceptable business purpose. The presence of a business purpose is crucial in the area of corporate reorganizations and certain liquidations. See also *bona fide*.

Buy and sell agreement. An arrangement, particularly appropriate in the case of a closely-held corporation or a partnership, whereby the surviving owners (i.e., shareholders or partners) or the entity (i.e., corporation or partnership) agrees to purchase the interest of a withdrawing owner (i.e., shareholder or partner). The buy and sell agreement provides for an orderly disposition of an interest in a business and may aid in setting the value of such interest for death tax purposes. See also *cross-purchase buy and sell agreement* and *entity buy and sell agreement*.

C

Calendar year. See *accounting period*.

Capital asset. Broadly speaking, all assets are capital except those specifically excluded by the Code. Major categories of non-capital assets include property held for resale in the normal course of business (i.e., inventory), trade accounts and notes receivable, and depreciable property and real estate used in a trade or business (i.e., § 1231 assets). § 1221. See also *capital gain* and *capital loss*.

Capital contribution. Various means by which a shareholder makes additional funds available to the corporation (i.e., placed at the risk of the business) without the receipt of additional stock. Such contributions are added to the basis of the shareholder's existing stock investment and do not generate income to the corporation. § 118.

Capital expenditure. An expenditure that should be added to the basis of the property improved. For income tax purposes, this generally precludes a full deduction for the expenditure in the year paid or incurred. Any cost recovery in the form of a tax deduction would come in the form of depreciation, depletion, or amortization. § 263.

Capital gain. The gain from the sale or exchange of a capital asset. See also *capital asset*.

Capital loss. The loss from the sale or exchange of a capital asset. See also *capital asset*.

Cash basis. A method of accounting that reflects deductions as paid and income as received in any one tax year. However, prepaid expenses that benefit more than one tax year (e.g., prepaid rent and prepaid interest) usually must be spread over the period benefited rather than deducted in the year paid. § 446(c)(1). See also *constructive receipt of income*.

Cash surrender value. The amount of money that an insurance policy would yield if cashed in with the insurance company that issued the policy.

CCH. Commerce Clearing House (CCH) is the publisher of a tax service and of Federal tax decisions (i.e., USTC series).

C corporation. A regular corporation governed by Subchapter C of the Code. Distinguished from S corporations, which fall under Subchapter S of the Code. See also *S corporation*.

Centralized management. A concentration of authority among certain persons who may make independent business decisions on behalf of the entity without the need for continuing approval by the owners of the entity. It is a characteristic of a corporation, since day-to-day business operations are handled by appointed officers and not by the shareholders. Reg. § 301.7701–2(c). See also *association*.

Cert. den. By denying the Writ of Certiorari, the U.S. Supreme Court refuses to accept an appeal from a U.S. Court of Appeals. The denial of certiorari does not, however, mean that the U.S. Supreme Court agrees with the result reached by the lower court. See also *certiorari*.

Certiorari. Appeal from a U.S. Court of Appeals to the U.S. Supreme Court is by Writ of Certiorari. The Supreme Court need not accept the appeal and usually does not (i.e., *cert. den.*) unless a conflict exists among the lower courts that must be resolved or a constitutional issue is involved. See also *cert. den.*

Cf. Compare.

Civil fraud. See *fraud*.

Claims Court. A trial court (i.e., court of original jurisdiction) that decides litigation involving Federal tax matters. Previously known as the U.S. Court of Claims, appeal from the U.S. Claims Court is to the Court of Appeals for the Federal Circuit.

Clifford trust. A grantor trust whereby the grantor (i.e., creator) of the trust retains the right to possess again the property transferred in trust (i.e., a reversionary interest is retained) upon the occurrence of an event (e.g., the death of the beneficiary) or the expiration of a period of time. Unless the requirements of § 673 are satisfied, the income from the property placed in trust will continue to be taxed to the grantor. See also *grantor trust* and *reversionary interest*.

Closely-held corporation. A corporation, the stock ownership of which is not widely dispersed. Rather, a few shareholders are in control of corporate policy and are in a position to benefit personally from such policy.

Collapsing. To disregard a transaction or one of a series of steps leading to a result. See also *step-transaction approach, substance vs. form,* and *telescoping*.

Common law state. See *community property*.

Community property. The states with community property systems are Louisiana, Texas, New Mexico, Arizona, California, Washington, Idaho, Nevada, and Wisconsin. The rest of the states are classified as common law jurisdictions. The difference between common law and community property systems centers around the property rights possessed by married persons. In a common law system, each spouse owns whatever he or she earns. Under a community property system, one-half of the earnings of each spouse is considered owned by the other spouse. Assume,

for example, H and W are husband and wife and their only income is the $50,000 annual salary H receives. If they live in New York (a common law state), the $50,000 salary belongs to H. If, however, they live in Texas (a community property state), the $50,000 salary is divided equally, in terms of ownership, between H and W. See also *separate property*.

Completed contract method. A method of reporting gain or loss on certain long-term contracts. Under this method of accounting, gross income and expenses are recognized in the tax year in which the contract is completed. Reg. § 1.451–3. See also *percentage of completion method*.

Complex trusts. Complex trusts are those that are not simple trusts. Such trusts may have charitable beneficiaries, accumulate income, and distribute corpus. §§ 661–663. See also *simple trusts*.

Concur. To agree with the result reached by another, but not necessarily with the reasoning or the logic used in reaching such a result. For example, Judge R agrees with Judges S and T (all being members of the same court) that the income is taxable but for a different reason. Judge R would issue a concurring opinion to the majority opinion issued by Judges S and T.

Condemnation. The taking of property by a public authority. The taking is by legal action, and the owner of the property is compensated by the public authority. The power to condemn property is known as the right of eminent domain.

Conduit concept. An approach the tax law assumes in the tax treatment of certain entities and their owners. The approach permits specified tax characteristics to pass through the entity without losing their identity. Under the conduit concept, for example, long-term capital losses realized by a partnership are passed through as such to the individual partners. The same result does not materialize if the entity is a regular corporation. Varying forms of the conduit concept are applicable for partnerships, trusts, estates, and S corporations.

Consent dividends. For purposes of avoiding or reducing the penalty tax on the unreasonable accumulation of earnings or the personal holding company tax, a corporation may declare a consent dividend. In a consent dividend, no cash or property is distributed to the shareholders, although the corporation obtains a dividends paid deduction. The consent dividend is taxed to the shareholders and increases the basis in their stock investment. § 565.

Consolidated returns. A procedure whereby certain affiliated corporations may file a single return, combine the tax transactions of each corporation, and arrive at a single income tax liability for the group. The election to file a consolidated return is usually binding on future years. See §§ 1501–1505 and the Regulations thereunder.

Consolidation. The combination of two or more corporations into a newly created corporation. Thus, A Corporation and B Corporation combine to form C Corporation. A consolidation may qualify as a nontaxable reorganization if certain conditions are satisfied. §§ 354 and 368(a)(1)(A).

Constructive dividends. A taxable benefit derived by a shareholder from the shareholder's corporation, although such benefit was not designated as a dividend. Examples include unreasonable compensation, excessive rent payments, bargain purchases of corporate property, and shareholder use of corporate property. Constructive dividends generally are a problem limited to closely-held corporations. See also *bargain sale or purchase, closely-held corporation,* and *unreasonable compensation.*

Constructive ownership. See *attribution.*

Constructive receipt of income. If income is unqualifiedly available although not physically in the taxpayer's possession, it will be subject to the income tax. An example would be accrued interest on a savings account. Under the constructive receipt of income concept, such interest will be taxed to a depositor in the year available rather than the year actually withdrawn. The fact that the depositor uses the cash basis of accounting for tax purposes makes no difference. See Reg. § 1.451–2. See also *cash basis.*

Continuity of life or existence. The death or other withdrawal of an owner of an entity will not terminate the existence of such entity. This is a characteristic of a corporation, since the death or withdrawal of a shareholder will not affect the corporation's existence. Reg. § 301.7701–2(b). See also *association.*

Contributions to the capital of a corporation. See *capital contribution.*

Contributory qualified pension or profit sharing plan. A plan funded with both employer and employee contributions. Since the employee's contributions to the plan will be subject to the income tax, a later distribution of such contributions to the employee will be free of income tax. See also *qualified pension or profit sharing plan.*

Controlled group. A controlled group of corporations is required to share the lower-level corporate tax rates and various other tax benefits among the members of the group. A controlled group may be either a brother-sister or a parent-subsidiary group.

Corporate acquisition. The takeover of one corporation by another if both parties retain their legal existence after the transaction. An acquisition can be effected via a stock purchase or through a tax-free exchange of stock. See also *corporate reorganization* and *merger.*

Corporate liquidation. Occurs when a corporation distributes its net assets to its shareholders and ceases its legal existence. Generally, a shareholder recognizes capital gain or loss upon such liquidation of the entity regardless of the corporation's balance in its earnings and profits account. However, the distributing corporation recognizes gain and loss on assets that it distributes to shareholders in kind.

Corporate reorganization. Occurs, among other instances, when one corporation acquires another in a merger or acquisition, a single corporation divides into two or more entities, a corporation makes a substantial change in its capital structure or a corporation undertakes a change in its legal name or domicile. The exchange of stock and other securities in a corporate reorganization can be effected favorably for tax purposes if certain statutory requirements are followed strictly. Such tax consequences include the nonrecognition of any gain that is realized by the shareholders except to the extent of boot received. See also *corporate acquisition* and *merger.*

Corpus. The main body or principal of a trust. Suppose, for example, G transfers an apartment building into a trust, income payable to W for life, remainder to S upon W's death. Corpus of the trust is the apartment building.

Correspondence audit. An audit conducted by the IRS by mail. Typically, the IRS writes to the taxpayer requesting the verification of a particular deduction or exemption. The completion of a special form or the remittance of copies of records or other support is all that is requested of the taxpayer. See also *audit, field audit,* and *office audit.*

Court of Appeals. Any of 13 Federal courts that consider tax matters appealed from the U.S. Tax Court, a U.S. District Court, or the U.S. Claims Court. Appeal from a U.S. Court of Appeals is to the U.S. Supreme Court by Writ of Certiorari. See also *appellate court* and *trial court.*

Credit for prior transfers. The death tax credit for prior transfers applies when property is taxed in the estates of different decedents within a 10-year period. The credit is determined using a decreasing statutory percentage, with the magnitude of the credit decreasing as the length of time between the multiple deaths increases.

Criminal fraud. See *fraud.*

Cross-purchase buy and sell agreement. Under this type of arrangement, the surviving owners of the business agree to buy out the withdrawing owner. Assume, for example, R and S are equal shareholders in T Corporation. Under a cross-purchase buy and sell agreement, R and S would contract to purchase the other's interest should that person decide to withdraw from the business. See also *buy and sell agreement* and *entity buy and sell agreement.*

Current earnings and profits. A corporate distribution is deemed to be first from the entity's current earnings and profits and then from accumulated earnings and profits. Shareholders recognize dividend income to the extent of the earnings and profits of the corporation. A dividend results even if the entity has generated a positive current earnings and profits amount concomitant with a larger negative balance in accumulated earnings and profits.

Current use valuation. See *special use value.*

Curtesy. A husband's right under state law to all or part of his wife's property upon her death. See also *dower.*

D

Death benefit. A payment made by an employer to the beneficiary or beneficiaries of a deceased employee on account of the death of the employee. Under certain conditions, the first $5,000 of such payment will not be subject to the income tax. § 101(b)(1).

Death tax. A tax imposed on property transferred by the death of the owner. See also *credit for prior transfers, estate tax,* and *inheritance tax.*

Decedent. An individual who has died.

Deduction. The Federal income tax is not imposed upon gross income. Rather, it is imposed upon net income. Congressionally identified deductions are subtracted from gross income to arrive at the tax base taxable income.

Deductions in respect of a decedent. Deductions accrued to the point of death but not recognizable on the final income tax return of a decedent because of the method of accounting used. Such items are allowed as deductions on the estate tax return and on the income tax return of the estate (Form 1041) or the heir (Form 1040). An example of a deduction in respect of a decedent is interest expense accrued up to the date of death by a cash basis debtor.

Deferred compensation. Compensation that will be taxed when received and not when earned. An example is contributions by an employer to a qualified pension or profit sharing plan on behalf of an employee. Such contributions will not be taxed to the employee until they are distributed (e.g., upon retirement). See also *qualified pension or profit sharing plan.*

Deficiency. Additional tax liability owed by a taxpayer and assessed by the IRS. See also *assessment* and *statutory notice of deficiency.*

Deficiency dividends. Once the IRS has established a corporation's liability for the personal holding company tax in a prior year, the tax may be reduced or avoided by the issuance of a deficiency dividend under § 547. The deficiency dividend procedure is not available in cases where the deficiency was due to fraud with intent to evade tax or to a willful failure to file the appropriate tax return [§ 547(g)]. Nor does the deficiency dividend procedure avoid the usual penalties and interest applicable for failure to file a return or pay a tax.

Deficit. A negative balance in the earnings and profits account.

Demand loan. A loan payable upon request by the creditor rather than on a specific date.

Depletion. The process by which the cost or other basis of a natural resource (e.g., an oil or gas interest) is recovered upon extraction and sale of the resource. The two ways to determine the depletion allowance are the cost and percentage (or statutory) methods. Under the cost method, each unit of production sold is assigned a portion of the cost or other basis of the interest. This is determined by dividing the cost or other basis by the total units expected to be recovered. Under the percentage (or statutory) method, the tax law provides a special percentage factor for different type of minerals and other natural resources. This percentage is multiplied by the gross income from the interest to arrive at the depletion allowance. §§ 613 and 613A.

Depreciation. The write-off for tax purposes of the cost or other basis of a tangible asset over the asset's estimated useful life. As to intangible assets, see *amortization.* As to natural resources, see *depletion.* See also *estimated useful life.*

Depreciation recapture. Upon the disposition of depreciable property used in a trade or business, gain or loss is measured by the difference between the consideration received (i.e., the amount realized) and the adjusted basis of the property. Before the enactment of the depreciation recapture provisions of the Code, any such gain recognized could be § 1231 gain and usually qualified for long-term capital gain treatment. The recapture provisions of the Code (e.g., §§ 1245 and 1250) may operate to convert some or all of the previous § 1231 gain into ordinary income. The justification for depreciation recapture is that it prevents a taxpayer from converting a dollar of deduction (in the form of depreciation) into deferred income (§ 1231 gain taxed as a long-term capital gain). The depreciation recapture rules do not apply when the property is disposed of at a loss or via a gift. See also *Section 1231 gains and losses.*

Determination letter. Upon the request of a taxpayer, a District Director will comment on the tax status of a completed transaction. Determination letters are most frequently used to clarify employee status, determine whether a retirement or profit sharing plan qualifies under the Code, and determine the tax-exempt status of certain nonprofit organizations.

Devise. A transfer by will of real estate. See also *bequest.*

Disclaimer. The rejection, refusal, or renunciation of a claim, power, or property. Section 2518 sets forth the conditions required to avoid gift tax consequences as the result of a disclaimer.

Discretionary trusts. Trusts under which the trustee or another party has the right to accumulate (rather than pay out) the income for each year. Depending on the terms of the trust instrument, such income may be accumulated for future distributions to the income beneficiaries or added to corpus for the benefit of the remainderperson. See also *corpus, income beneficiary,* and *remainderperson.*

Disproportionate. Not pro rata or ratable. Suppose, for example, X Corporation has two shareholders, C and D, each of whom owns 50 percent of its stock. If X Corporation distributes a cash dividend of $2,000 to C and only $1,000 to D, the distribution is disproportionate. The distribution would have been proportionate if C and D had received $1,500 each.

Disregard of corporate entity. To treat a corporation as if it did not exist for tax purposes. In such event, each shareholder would account for an allocable share of all corporate transactions possessing tax consequences. See also *entity.*

Dissent. To disagree with the majority. If, for example, Judge B disagrees with the result reached by Judges C and D (all of whom are members of the same court), Judge B could issue a dissenting opinion.

Distributable net income (DNI). The measure that determines the nature and amount of the distributions from estates and trusts that the beneficiaries thereof must include in income. DNI also limits the amount that estates and trusts can claim as a deduction for such distributions. § 643(a).

Distributions in kind. A transfer of property "as is." If, for example, a corporation distributes land to its shareholders, a distribution in kind has tak-

en place. A sale of land followed by a distribution of the cash proceeds would not be a distribution in kind of the land. As to corporate liquidations, see § 336 for one type of distribution in kind.

District Court. A Federal District Court is a trial court for purposes of litigating Federal tax matters. It is the only trial court for which a jury trial can be obtained. See also *trial court.*

Dividend. A nondeductible distribution to the shareholders of a corporation. A dividend constitutes gross income to the recipient if it is from the current or accumulated earnings and profits of the corporation.

Dividends received deduction. A deduction allowed a corporate shareholder for dividends received from a domestic corporation. The deduction usually is 70 percent of the dividends received, but it could be 80 or 100 percent depending upon the ownership percentage held by the payee corporation. §§ 243–246.

Domestic corporation. A corporation created or organized in the United States or under the law of the United States or any state or territory. § 7701(a)(4). Only dividends received from domestic corporations qualify for the dividends received deduction (§ 243). See also *foreign corporation.*

Domicile. A person's legal home.

Donee. The recipient of a gift.

Donor. The maker of a gift.

Dower. A wife's right to all or part of her deceased husband's property. It is a concept unique to common law states as opposed to community property jurisdictions. See also *curtesy.*

E

Earned income. Income from personal services. Distinguished from passive, portfolio, and other unearned income. See § 911 and the Regulations thereunder.

Earnings and profits. Measures the economic capacity of a corporation to make a distribution to shareholders that is not a return of capital. Such a distribution will result in dividend income to the shareholders to the extent of the corporation's current and accumulated earnings and profits.

Election to split gifts. A special election for Federal gift tax purposes whereby husband and wife can treat a gift by one of them to a third party as being made one-half by each. If, for example, H (the husband) makes a gift of $20,000 to S, W (the wife) may elect to treat $10,000 of the gift as coming from her. The major advantage of the election is that it enables the parties to take advantage of the nonowner spouse's (W in this case) annual exclusion and unified credit. § 2513. See also *annual exclusion*.

Eminent domain.   See *condemnation*.

Employee stock ownership plan (ESOP).   A type of qualified profit sharing plan which invests in securities of the employer. In a noncontributory ESOP the employer usually contributes its shares to a trust and receives a deduction for the fair market value of such stock. Generally, the employee recognizes no income until the stock is sold after its distribution to him or her upon retirement or other separation from service. See also, *qualified pension or profit sharing plan*.

En banc.   The case was considered by the whole court. For example, only one of the 19 judges of the U.S. Tax Court will hear and decide a tax controversy. However, when the issues involved are unusually novel or of wide impact, the case will be heard and decided by the full Court sitting *en banc*.

Encumbrance.   A liability, such as a mortgage. If the liability relates to a particular asset, the asset is encumbered.

Entity.   An organization or being that possesses separate existence for tax purposes. Examples are corporations, partnerships, estates, and trusts. See also *disregard of corporate entity*.

Entity accounting income.   Entity accounting income is not identical to the taxable income of a trust or estate, nor is it determined in the same manner as would be the entity's financial accounting income. The trust document or will determines whether certain income, expenses, gains, or losses are allocated to the corpus of the entity or to the entity's income beneficiaries. Only those items that are allocated to the income beneficiaries are included in entity accounting income.

Entity buy and sell agreement.   A buy and sell agreement whereby the entity is to purchase the withdrawing owner's interest. When the entity is a corporation, the agreement generally involves a stock redemption on the part of the withdrawing shareholder. See also *buy and sell agreement* and *cross-purchase buy and sell agreement*.

Escrow.   Money or other property placed with a third party as security for an existing or proposed obligation. C, for example, agrees to purchase D's stock in X Corporation but needs time to raise the necessary funds. The stock is placed by D with E (i.e., the escrow agent) with instructions to deliver it to C when the purchase price is paid.

Estate.   The assets and liabilities of a decedent.

Estate tax.   A tax imposed on the right to transfer property by death. Thus, an estate tax is levied on the decedent's estate and not on the heir receiving the property. See also *death tax* and *inheritance tax*.

Estimated useful life.   The period over which an asset will be used by a particular taxpayer. Although such period cannot be longer than the estimated physical life of an asset, it could be shorter if the taxpayer does not intend to keep the asset until it wears out. Assets such as goodwill do not have an estimated useful life. The estimated useful life of an asset is essential to measuring the annual tax deduction for depreciation and amortization.

Estoppel.   The process of being stopped from proving something (even if true) in court due to prior inconsistent action. It is usually invoked as a matter of fairness to prevent one party (either the taxpayer or the IRS) from taking advantage of a prior error.

Excise tax.   A tax on the manufacture, sale, or use of goods or on the carrying on of an occupation or activity, or a tax on the transfer of property. Thus, the Federal estate and gift taxes, are, theoretically, excise taxes.

Executor.   A person designated by a will to administer (i.e., manage or take charge of) the assets and liabilities of a decedent. Such party may be a male (executor), female (executrix), or a trust company (executor). See also *administrator*.

Exemption.   An amount by which the tax base is reduced for all qualifying taxpayers. Individuals can receive personal and dependency exemptions, and taxpayers apply an exemption in computing their alternative minimum taxable income. Often, the exemption amount is phased out as the tax base becomes sizable.

Exemption equivalent.   The maximum value of assets that could be transferred to another party without incurring any Federal gift or death tax because of the application of the unified tax credit.

F

Fair market value.   The amount at which property would change hands between a willing buyer and a willing seller, neither being under any compulsion to buy or to sell and both having reasonable knowledge of the relevant facts. Reg. § 20.2031–1(b).

Federal Register.   The first place that the rules and regulations of U.S. administrative agencies (e.g., the U.S. Treasury Department) are published.

F.2d. An abbreviation for the Second Series of the *Federal Reporter,* the official series in which decisions of the U.S. Claims Court and of the U.S. Court of Appeals are published.

F.Supp. The abbreviation for *Federal Supplement,* the official series in which the reported decisions of the U.S. Federal District Courts are published.

Fiduciary. A person who manages money or property for another and who must exercise a standard of care in such management activity imposed by law or contract. A trustee, for example, possesses a fiduciary responsibility to the beneficiaries of the trust to follow the terms of the trust and the requirements of applicable state law. A breach of fiduciary responsibility would make the trustee liable to the beneficiaries for any damage caused by such breach.

Field audit. An audit conducted by the IRS on the business premises of the taxpayer or in the office of the tax practitioner representing the taxpayer. See also *audit, correspondence audit,* and *office audit.*

First-in, first-out (FIFO). An accounting method for determining the cost of inventories. Under this method, the inventory on hand is deemed to be the sum of the cost of the most recently acquired units. See also *last-in, first-out (LIFO).*

Fiscal year. See *accounting period.*

Flat tax. In its pure form, a flat tax would eliminate all exclusions, deductions, and credits and impose a tax on gross income.

Foreign corporation. A corporation that is not organized under the laws of one of the states or territories of the United States. § 7701(a)(5). See also *domestic corporation.*

Foreign tax credit or deduction. A U.S. citizen or resident who incurs or pays income taxes to a foreign country on income subject to U.S. tax may be able to claim some of these taxes as a deduction or a credit against the U.S. income tax. §§ 27 and 901–905.

Form 706. The U.S. Estate Tax Return. In certain cases, this form must be filed for a decedent who was a resident or citizen of the United States.

Form 709. The U.S. Gift Tax Return. See Appendix B for a specimen form.

Form 709–A. U.S. Short Form Gift Tax Return.

Form 870. The signing of Form 870 (Waiver of Restriction on Assessment and Collection of Deficiency in Tax and Acceptance of Overassessments) by a taxpayer permits the IRS to assess a proposed deficiency without needing to issue a statutory notice of deficiency (90–day letter). This means the taxpayer must pay the deficiency

and cannot file a petition to the U.S. Tax Court. § 6213(d).

Form 872. The signing of this form by a taxpayer extends the period during which the IRS can make an assessment or collection of a tax. In other words, Form 872 extends the applicable statute of limitations. § 6501(c)(4).

Form 1041. U.S. Fiduciary Income Tax Return, required to be filed by estates and trusts. See Appendix B for a specimen form.

Form 1065. U.S. Partnership Return of Income. See Appendix B for a specimen form.

Form 1120. U.S. Corporation Income Tax Return. See Appendix B for a specimen form.

Form 1120–A. U.S. Short-Form Corporation Income Tax Return. See Appendix B for a specimen form.

Form 1120S. U.S. Small Business Corporation Income Tax Return, required to be filed by S corporations. See Appendix B for a specimen form.

Fraud. Tax fraud falls into two categories: civil and criminal. Under civil fraud, the IRS may impose as a penalty an amount equal to 75 percent of the underpayment [§ 6653(b)]. Fines and/or imprisonment are prescribed for conviction of various types of criminal tax fraud (§§ 7201–7207). Both civil and criminal fraud require a specific intent on the part of the taxpayer to evade the tax; mere negligence is not enough. Criminal fraud requires the additional element of willfulness (i.e., done deliberately and with evil purpose). In practice, it becomes difficult to distinguish between the degree of intent necessary to support criminal, rather than civil, fraud. In either situation, the IRS has the burden of proving fraud. See also *burden of proof.*

Free transferability of interests. The capability of the owner of an entity to transfer his or her ownership interest to another without the consent of the other owners. It is a characteristic of a corporation, since a shareholder usually can freely transfer the stock to others without the approval of the existing shareholders. Reg. § 301.7701–2(e). See also *association.*

Fringe benefits. Compensation or other benefits received by an employee that are not in the form of cash. Some fringe benefits (e.g., accident and health plans, group term life insurance) may be excluded from the employee's gross income and thus are not subject to the Federal income tax.

Future interest. An interest that will come into being at some future point in time. It is distinguished from a present interest, which is already in existence. Assume, for example, that D tranfers securities to a newly created trust. Under the terms of the trust instrument, income from the securities is to be paid each year to W for her life, with the securities passing to S upon W's death. W has a present interest in the trust, since she is currently entitled to receive the income from the securities. S has a future interest, since he must wait for W's death to benefit from the trust. The annual exclusion of $10,000 is not allowed for a gift of a future interest. § 2503(b). See also *annual exclusion* and *election to split gifts*.

G

General partner. A partner who is fully liable in an individual capacity for the debts of the partnership to third parties. A general partner's liability is not limited to the investment in the partnership. See also *limited partner*.

General power of appointment. See *power of appointment*.

Gift. A transfer of property for less than adequate consideration. Gifts usually occur in a personal setting (such as between members of the same family). They are excluded from the income tax base but may be subject to a transfer tax.

Gift splitting. See *election to split gifts*.

Gift tax. A tax imposed on the transfer of property by gift. Such tax is imposed upon the donor of a gift and is based on the fair market value of the property on the date of the gift.

Gifts within three years of death. Some taxable gifts made after 1981 automatically are included in the gross estate of the donor if death occurs within three years of the gift. § 2035.

Goodwill. The reputation and built-up business of a company. For accounting purposes, goodwill has no basis unless it is purchased. In the purchase of a business, goodwill generally is the difference between the purchase price and the value of the assets acquired. The intangible asset goodwill cannot be amortized for tax purposes. Reg. § 1.167(a)–3. See also *amortization*.

Grantor. A transferor of property. The creator of a trust is usually designated as the grantor of the trust.

Grantor trust. A trust under which the grantor retains control over the income or corpus (or both) to such an extent that such grantor will be treated as the owner of the property and its income for income tax purposes. The result is to make the income from a grantor trust taxable to the grantor and not to the beneficiary who receives it. §§ 671–677. See also *Clifford trust* and *reversionary interest*.

Gross estate. The property owned or previously transferred by a decedent that will be subject to the Federal death tax. Distinguished from the probate estate, which is property actually subject to administration by the administrator or executor of an estate. §§ 2031–2046. See also *adjusted gross estate* and *taxable estate*.

Gross income. Income subject to the Federal income tax. Gross income does not include all economic income. That is, certain exclusions are allowed (e.g., interest on municipal bonds). For a manufacturing or merchandising business, gross income usually means gross profit (i.e., gross sales or gross receipts less cost of goods sold). § 61 and Reg. § 1.61–3(a). See also *adjusted gross income* and *taxable income*.

Gross up. To add back to the value of the property or income received the amount of the tax that has been paid. For gifts made within three years of death, any gift tax paid on the transfer is added to the gross estate. § 2035.

Group term life insurance. Life insurance coverage permitted by an employer for a group of employees. Such insurance is renewable on a year-to-year basis and typically does not accumulate in value (i.e., no cash surrender value is built up). The premiums paid by the employer on such insurance are not taxed to the employees on coverage of up to $50,000 per person. § 79 and Reg. § 1.79–1(b).

Guaranteed payments. Payments made by a partnership to a partner for services rendered or for the use of capital to the extent that such payments are determined without regard to the income of the partnership. Such payments are treated as though they were made to a nonpartner and thus are usually deductible by the entity.

Guardianship. A legal arrangement under which one person (i.e., a guardian) has the legal right and duty to care for another (i.e., the ward) and his or her property. A guardianship is established because of the ward's inability to legally act on his or her own behalf [e.g., because of minority (i.e., he or she is not of age) or mental or physical incapacity].

H

Head of household. An unmarried individual who maintains a household for another and satisfies certain conditions set forth in § 2(b). Such status enables the taxpayer to use a set of income tax rates that are lower than those applicable to other unmarried individuals but higher than those applicable to surviving spouses and married persons filing a joint return.

Heir. A person who inherits property from a decedent.

Hobby. An activity not engaged in for profit. The Code restricts the amount of losses that an individual can deduct with respect to hobby activities so that such transactions cannot be used to offset income from other sources. § 183.

Holding period. The period of time during which property has been held for income tax purposes. The holding period is significant in determining whether gain or loss from the sale or exchange of a capital asset is long-term or short-term. § 1223.

H.R. 10 plans. See *Keogh plans.*

Hot assets. This term refers to unrealized receivables and substantially appreciated inventory under § 751. When hot assets are present, the sale of a partnership interest or the disproportionate distribution of such assets can cause ordinary income to be recognized.

I

Imputed interest. For certain long-term sales of property, the IRS has the authority to convert some of the gain from the sale into interest income if the contract does not provide for a minimum rate of interest to be paid by the purchaser. The application of this procedure has the effect of forcing the seller to recognize less long-term capital gain and more ordinary income (i.e., interest income). § 483 and the Regulations thereunder.

Incident of ownership. An element of ownership or degree of control over a life insurance policy. The retention by an insured of an incident of ownership in a life insurance policy will cause the policy proceeds to be included in the insured's gross estate upon death. § 2042(2) and Reg. § 20.2042–1(c). See also *gross estate* and *insured.*

Includible gain. Section 644 inposes a special tax on trusts that sell or exchange property at a gain within two years after the date of its transfer in trust by the transferor. The provision applies only if the fair market value of the property at the time of the initial transfer exceeds the adjusted basis of the property immediately after the transfer. The tax imposed by § 644 is the amount of additional tax the transferor would have to pay (including any minimum tax) had the gain been included in the transferor's gross income for the tax year of the sale. However, the tax applies only to an amount known as *includible gain.* This is the lesser of the following: The gain recognized by the trust on the sale or exchange of any property. The excess of the fair market value of such property at the time of the initial transfer in trust

by the transferor over the adjusted basis of such property immediately after the transfer.

Income beneficiary. The party entitled to income from property. In a typical situation, A is to receive the income for life with corpus or principal passing to B upon A's death. In this case, A is the income beneficiary of the trust.

Income in respect of a decedent. Income earned by a decedent at the time of death but not reportable on the final income tax return because of the method of accounting that appropriately is utilized. Such income is included in the gross estate and will be taxed to the eventual recipient (i.e., either the estate or heirs). The recipient will, however, be allowed an income tax deduction for the estate tax attributable to the income. § 691.

Income shifting. Occurs when an individual tranfers some of his or her gross income to a taxpayer who is subject to a lower tax rate, thereby reducing the total income tax liability of the group. Income shifting produces a successful assignment of income. It can be accomplished by transferring income-producing property to the lower-bracket taxpayer to an effective trust for his or her benefit or by transferring ownership interests in a family partnership or in a closely-held corporation.

Incomplete transfer. A transfer made by a decedent during lifetime which, because of certain control or enjoyment retained by the transferor, will not be considered complete for Federal estate tax purposes. Thus, some or all of the fair market value of the property transferred will be included in the transferor's gross estate. §§ 2036–2038. See also *gross estate* and *revocable transfer.*

Incorporated pocketbook. For individuals in high income tax brackets, it often was advantageous to transfer income-producing property (e.g., stocks and bonds) to a specially created corporation. In this manner, the income from such property would be shifted to the corporation and taxed at a lower rate. The incorporated pocketbook approach led to the enactment of the penalty tax on personal holding companies.

Individual retirement account (IRA). Individuals with earned income are permitted to set aside up to 100 percent of such income per year (not to exceed $2,000) for a retirement account. The amount so set aside can be deducted by the taxpayer and will be subject to income tax only upon withdrawal. The Code limits the amount of this contribution that can be deducted *for* AGI depending upon (1) whether the taxpayer or spouse is an active participant in an employer-provided qualified retirement plan and (2) the magnitude of the taxpayer's AGI before the IRA contribution is considered. § 219. See also *simplified employee pensions*.

Inheritance tax. A tax imposed on the right to receive property from a decedent. Thus, theoretically, an inheritance tax is imposed on the heir. The Federal estate tax is imposed on the estate. See also *death tax* and *estate tax*.

In kind. See *distributions in kind*.

Installment method. A method of accounting enabling a taxpayer to spread the recognition of gain on the sale of property over the collection period. Under this procedure, the seller computes the gross profit percentage from the sale (i.e., the gain divided by the selling price) and applies it to each payment received to arrive at the gain to be recognized. § 453.

Insured. A person whose life is the subject of an insurance policy. Upon the death of the insured, the life insurance policy matures and the proceeds become payable to the designated beneficiary. See also *life insurance*.

Intangible asset. Property that is a "right" rather than a physical object. Examples are patents, stocks and bonds, goodwill, trademarks, franchises, and copyrights. See also *amortization* and *tangible property*.

Inter vivos transfer. A transfer of property during the life of the owner. Distinguished from testamentary transfers, wherein the property passes at death.

Interest-free loans. Bona fide loans that carry no interest (or a below-market rate). If made in a nonbusiness setting, the imputed interest element is treated as a gift from the lender to the borrower. If made by a corporation to a shareholder, a constructive dividend could result. In either event, the lender may have interest income to recognize. § 7872.

Internal Revenue Code. The collected statutes that govern the taxation of income, property transfers, and other transactions in the United States and the enforcement of such provisions. Enacted by Congress, the Code is amended frequently, but it has not been reorganized since 1954. Because of the extensive revisions to the statutes that occurred with respect to the Tax Reform Act of 1986, Title 26 of the U.S. Code is now known as the Internal Revenue Code of 1986.

Interpolated terminal reserve. The measure used in valuing insurance policies for gift and estate tax purposes when the policies are not paid-up at the time of their transfer. For an illustration of the application of this method see Reg. § 20.2031–8(a)(3), Ex. (3).

Intestate. No will exists at the time of death. Under such circumstances, state law prescribes who will receive the decedent's property. The laws of intestate succession generally favor the surviving spouse, children, and grandchildren and then move to parents and grandparents and to brothers and sisters.

Investment income. Consisting of virtually the same elements as portfolio income, a measure by which to justify a deduction for interest on investment indebtedness. See also *investment indebtedness* and *portfolio income*.

Investment indebtedness. Debt incurred to carry or incur investments by the taxpayer in assets that will produce portfolio income. Limitations are placed upon interest deductions that are incurred with respect to such debt (i.e., generally to the corresponding amount of investment income).

Investment tax credit. A special tax credit equal to 6 or 10 percent of the qualified investment in tangible personal property used in a trade or business. Expired as of the end of 1985.

Investment tax credit recapture. When § 38 property is disposed of or ceases to be used in the trade or business of the taxpayer, some of the investment tax credit claimed on such property may be recaptured as additional tax liability. The amount of the recapture is determined by reference to § 47(a). See also *investment tax credit* and *Section 38 property*.

Involuntary conversion. The loss or destruction of property through theft, casualty, or condemnation. Any gain realized on an involuntary conversion can, at the taxpayer's election, be deferred for Federal income tax purposes if the owner reinvests the proceeds within a prescribed period of time in property that is similar or related in service or use. § 1033.

IRA. See *individual retirement account*.

Itemized deductions. Certain personal and employee expenditures allowed by the Code as deductions from adjusted gross income. Examples include certain medical expenses, interest on home mortgages, and charitable contributions. Itemized deductions are reported on Schedule A of Form 1040.

J

Jeopardy assessment. If the collection of a tax appears in question, the IRS may assess and collect the tax immediately without the usual formalities. The IRS can terminate a taxpayer's taxable year before the usual date if it feels that the collection of the tax may be in peril because the taxpayer plans to leave the country. §§ 6851 and 6861–6864.

Joint and several liability. Permits the IRS to collect a tax from one or all of several taxpayers. A husband and wife who file a joint income tax return usually are collectively or individually liable for the full amount of the tax liability. § 6013(d)(3).

Joint tenancy. The undivided ownership of property by two or more persons with the right of survivorship. Right of survivorship gives the surviving owner full ownership of the property. Suppose, for example, B and C are joint owners of a tract of land. Upon B's death, C becomes the sole owner of the property. As to the death tax consequences upon the death of a joint tenant, see § 2040. See also *tenancy in common* and *tenancy by the entirety.*

Joint venture. A one-time grouping of two or more persons in a business undertaking. Unlike a partnership, a joint venture does not entail a continuing relationship among the parties. A joint venture is treated like a partnership for Federal income tax purposes. § 7701(a)(2).

K

Keogh plans. A designation for retirement plans available to self-employed taxpayers. They are also referred to as H.R. 10 plans. Under such plans a taxpayer may deduct each year up to either 20 percent of net earnings from self-employment or $30,000, whichever is less.

L

Lapse. The expiration of a right either by the death of the holder or upon the expiration of a period of time. Thus, a power of appointment lapses upon the death of the holder if such holder has not exercised the power during life or at death (i.e., through a will).

Last-in, first-out (LIFO). An accounting method for valuing inventories for tax purposes. Under this method, it is assumed that the inventory on hand is valued at the cost of the earliest acquired units. § 472. See also *first-in, first-out (FIFO).*

Layperson. Nonmember of a specified profession.

Leaseback. The transferor of property later leases it back. In a sale-leaseback situation, for example, R sells property to S and subsequently leases such property from S. Thus, R becomes the lessee and S the lessor.

Legacy. A transfer of cash or other property by will.

Legal age. The age at which a person may enter into binding contracts or commit other legal acts.

In most states, a minor reaches legal age or majority (i.e., comes of age) at age 18.

Legal representative. A person who oversees the legal affairs of another; for example, the executor or administrator of an estate or a court appointed guardian of a minor or incompetent person.

Legatee. The recipient of property under a will and transferred by the death of the owner.

Lessee. One who rents property from another. In the case of real estate, the lessee is also known as the tenant.

Lessor. One who rents property to another. In the case of real estate, the lessor is also known as the landlord.

LEXIS. An on-line database system, produced by Mead Data Services, by which the tax researcher can obtain access to the Internal Revenue Code, Regulations, administrative rulings, and court case opinions.

Life estate. A legal arrangement under which the beneficiary (i.e., the life tenant) is entitled to the income from the property for his or her life. Upon the death of the life tenant, the property is transferred to the holder of the remainder interest. See also *income beneficiary* and *remainder interest.*

Life insurance. A contract between the holder of a policy and an insurance company (i.e., the carrier) under which the company agrees, in return for premium payments, to pay a specified sum (i.e., the face value or maturity value of the policy) to the designated beneficiary upon the death of the insured. See also *insured.*

Lifetime exemption. See *specific exemption.*

Like-kind exchange. An exchange of property held for productive use in a trade or business or for investment (except inventory and stocks and bonds) for other investment or trade or business property. Unless nonlike-kind property (i.e., boot) is received, the exchange is nontaxable. § 1031. See also *boot.*

Limited liability. The liability of an entity and its owners to third parties is limited to the investment in the entity. This is a characteristic of a corporation, since shareholders generally are not responsible for the debts of the corporation and, at most, may lose the amount paid in for the stock issued. Reg. § 301.7701–2(d). See also *association.*

Limited partner. A partner whose liability to third–party creditors of the partnership is limited to the amount invested by such partner in the partnership. See also *general partner* and *limited partnership.*

Limited partnership. A partnership in which some of the partners are limited partners. At least one of the partners in a limited partnership must be a general partner. See also *general partner* and *limited partner.*

Liquidating distribution. A distribution by a partnership or corporation that is in complete liquidation of the entity's trade or business activities. Typically, such distributions generate capital gain or loss to the investors without regard, for instance, to the earnings and profits of the corporation or to the partnership's basis in the distributed property. They can, however, lead to recognized gain or loss at the corporate level.

Liquidation. See *corporate liquidation.*

Long-term capital gain deduction. Before 1987, noncorporate taxpayers were allowed a deduction *for* AGI to the extent of 60 percent of the net long-term capital gains that they recognized during the year.

Long-term capital gain or loss. Results from the sale or other taxable exchange of a capital asset that had been held by the seller for more than one year or from other transactions involving statutorily designated assets, including § 1231 property and patents.

Lump-sum distribution. Payment of the entire amount due at one time rather than in installments. Such distributions often occur from qualified pension or profit sharing plans upon the retirement or death of a covered employee.

M

Majority. See *legal age.*

Malpractice. Professional misconduct; an unreasonable lack of skill.

Marital deduction. A deduction allowed against the taxable estate or taxable gifts, upon the transfer of property from one spouse to another.

Market value. See *fair market value.*

Merger. The absorption of one corporation by another under which the corporation being absorbed loses its legal identity. X Corporation is merged into B Corporation, and the shareholders of X Corporation receive stock in B Corporation in exchange for their stock in X Corporation. After the merger, X Corporation ceases to exist as a separate legal entity. If a merger meets certain conditions, it will be nontaxable to the parties involved. § 368(a)(1)(A). See also *corporate acquisition* and *corporate reorganization.*

Minimum tax. See *add-on minimum tax* and *alternative minimum tax.*

Minority. See *legal age.*

Mitigation. To make less severe. See also *mitigation of the annual accounting period concept* and *mitigation of the statute of limitations.*

Mitigation of the annual accounting period concept. Various tax provisions that provide relief from the effect of the finality of the annual accounting period concept. For example, the net operating loss carryover provisions allow the taxpayer to apply the negative taxable income of one year against a corresponding positive amount in another tax accounting period. See also *annual accounting period concept.*

Mitigation of the statute of limitations. A series of tax provisions that prevents either the IRS or a taxpayer from obtaining a double benefit from the application of the statute of limitations. It would be unfair, for example, to permit a taxpayer to depreciate an asset previously expensed, but which should have been capitalized, if the statute of limitations prevents the IRS from adjusting the tax liability for the year the asset was purchased. §§ 1311–1315. See also *statute of limitations.*

Monetary bequest. A transfer by will of cash. It is often denoted as a pecuniary bequest.

Mortgagee. The party who holds the mortgage; the creditor.

Mortgagor. The party who mortgages the property; the debtor.

Most suitable use value. For gift and estate tax purposes, property that is transferred normally is valued in accordance with its most suitable or optimal use. Thus, if a farm is worth more as a potential shopping center, the value as a shopping center will control even though the transferee (i.e., the donee or heir) continues to use the property as a farm. For an exception to this rule concerning the valuation of certain kinds of real estate transferred by death, see *special use value.*

Multi-tiered partnerships. See *tiered partnerships.*

N

Necessary. Appropriate and helpful in furthering the taxpayer's business or income-producing activity. §§ 162(a) and 212. See also *ordinary.*

Negligence. Failure to exercise the reasonable or ordinary degree of care of a prudent person in a situation that results in harm or damage to another. Code § 6653(a) imposes a penalty on taxpayers who show negligence or intentional disregard of rules and Regulations with respect to the underpayment of certain taxes.

Net operating loss. To mitigate the effect of the annual accounting period concept, § 172 allows taxpayers to use an excess loss of one year as a deduction for certain past or future years. In this regard, a carryback period of three years and a carryforward period of fifteen years currently is allowed. See also *mitigation of the annual accounting period concept.*

Net worth method. An approach used by the IRS to reconstruct the income of a taxpayer who fails to maintain adequate records. Under this method the gross income for the year is estimated as the increase in net worth of the taxpayer (i.e., assets in excess of liabilities) with appropriate adjustment for nontaxable receipts and nondeductible expenditures. The net worth method often is used when tax fraud is suspected.

Ninety-day letter. See *statutory notice of deficiency.*

Nonacquiescence. Disagreement by the IRS on the result reached by the U.S. Tax Court in a Regular Decision. Sometimes abbreviated *nonacq.* or *NA.* See also *acquiescence.*

Nonbusiness bad debts. A bad debt loss incurred not in connection with a creditor's trade or business. Such loss is classified as a short-term capital loss and will be allowed only in the year the debt becomes entirely worthless. In addition to family loans, many investor losses fall into the classification of nonbusiness bad debts. § 166(d). See also *business bad debts.*

Noncontributory qualified pension or profit sharing plan. A plan funded entirely by the employer with no contributions being made by the covered employees. See also *qualified pension or profit sharing plans.*

Nonliquidating distribution. A payment made by a partnership or corporation to the entity's owner is a nonliquidating distribution when the entity's legal existence does not cease thereafter. If the payor is a corporation, such a distribution can result in dividend income to the shareholders. If the payor is a partnership, the partner usually assigns a basis in the distributed property that is equal to the lesser of the partner's basis in the partnership interest or the basis of the distributed asset to the partnership. In this regard, the partner first assigns basis to any cash that he or she receives in the distribution. The partner's remaining basis, if any, is assigned to the noncash assets according to their relative bases to the partnership.

Nonrecourse debt. Debt secured by the property that it is used to purchase. The purchaser of the property is not personally liable for the debt upon default. Rather, the creditor's recourse is to repossess the related property. Nonrecourse debt generally does not increase the purchaser's at-risk amount.

Nonseparately stated income. The net income of an S corporation that is combined and allocated to the shareholders. Other items, such as capital gains and charitable contributions, that could be treated differently on the individual tax returns of the shareholders are not included in this amount but are allocated to the shareholders separately.

O

Obligee. The party to whom someone else is obligated under a contract. Thus, if C loans money to D, C is the obligee and D is the obligor under the loan.

Obligor. See *obligee.*

Office audit. An audit conducted by the IRS in the agent's office. See also *audit, correspondence audit,* and *field audit.*

On all fours. A judicial decision exactly in point with another as to result, facts, or both.

Optimal use value. Synonym for most suitable use value.

Ordinary. Common and accepted in the general industry or type of activity in which the taxpayer is engaged. It comprises one of the tests for the deductibility of expenses incurred or paid in connection with a trade or business; for the production or collection of income; for the management, conservation, or maintenance of property held for the production of income; or in connection with the determination, collection, or refund of any tax. §§ 162(a) and 212. See also *necessary.*

Ordinary and necessary. See *necessary* and *ordinary.*

Ordinary gross income. A concept peculiar to personal holding companies and defined in § 543(b)(1). See also *adjusted ordinary gross income.*

P

Partner. See *general partner* and *limited partner.*

Partnership. For income tax purposes, a partnership includes a syndicate, group, pool, or joint venture, as well as ordinary partnerships. In an ordinary partnership, two or more parties combine capital and/or services to carry on a business for profit as co-owners. § 7701(a)(2). See also *limited partnership* and *tiered partnerships.*

Passive investment income. As defined in § 1362(d)(3)(D), passive investment income means gross receipts from royalties, certain rents, dividends, interest, annuities, and gains from the sale or exchange of stock and securities. With certain exceptions, if the passive investment income of a corporation exceeds 25 percent of the corporation's gross receipts for three consecutive years, S status is lost.

Passive loss. Any loss from (1) activities in which the taxpayer does not materially participate, (2) rental activities, or (3) tax shelter activities. Net passive losses cannot be used to offset income from nonpassive sources. Rather, they are suspended until the taxpayer either generates net passive income (and a deduction of such losses is allowed) or disposes of the underlying property (at which time the loss deductions are allowed in full). Landlords who actively participate in the rental activities can deduct up to $25,000 of passive losses annually. However, this amount is phased out when the landlord's AGI exceeds $100,000. Passive loss limitations are phased in beginning in 1987. See also *portfolio income.*

Pecuniary bequest. A bequest of money to an heir by a decedent. See also *bequest.*

Percentage depletion. See *depletion.*

Percentage of completion method. A method of reporting gain or loss on certain long-term contracts. Under this method of accounting, the gross contract price is included in income as the contract is completed. Reg. § 1.451–3. See also *completed contract method.*

Personal and household effects. Items owned by a decedent at the time of death. Examples include: clothing, furniture, sporting goods, jewelry, stamp and coin collections, silverware, china, crystal, cooking utensils, books, cars, televisions, radios, stereo equipment, etc.

Personal holding company. A corporation that satisfies the requirements of § 542. Qualification as a personal holding company means a penalty tax will be imposed on the corporation's undistributed personal holding company income for the year.

Personal holding company income. Income as defined by § 543. Such income includes interest, dividends, rents (in certain cases), royalties (in certain cases), income from the use of corporate property by certain shareholders, income from certain personal service contracts, and distributions from estates and trusts. Such income is relevant in determining whether a corporation is a personal holding company and is therefore subject to the penalty tax on personal holding companies. See also *adjusted ordinary gross income.*

Personal property. Generally, all property other than real estate. It is sometimes designated as personalty when real estate is termed realty. Personal property can also refer to property not used in a taxpayer's trade or business or held for the production or collection of income. When used in this sense, personal property could include both realty (e.g., a personal residence) and personalty (e.g., personal effects such as clothing and furniture). See also *bequest.*

Personalty. Personalty is all property that is not attached to real estate (i.e., realty) and is movable. Examples of personalty are machinery, automobiles, clothing, household furnishings, inventory, and personal effects. See also *ad valorem tax* and *realty.*

P–H. Prentice-Hall is the publisher of a tax service and of Federal tax decisions (i.e., AFTR and AFTR2d series).

PHINet. An on-line database system, produced by Prentice-Hall Information Services, by which the tax researcher can obtain access to the Internal Revenue Code, Regulations, administrative rulings, and court case opinions.

Portfolio income. Income from interest, dividends, rentals, royalties, capital gains, or other investment sources. Net passive losses cannot be used to offset net portfolio income. See also *passive loss* and *investment income.*

Power of appointment. A legal right granted to someone by will or other document that gives the holder the power to dispose of property or the income from property. When the holder may appoint the property to his or her own benefit, the power usually is designated as a general power of appointment. If the holder cannot benefit himself or herself but may only appoint to certain other persons, the power is a special power of appointment. For example, assume G places $500,000 worth of securities in trust granting D the right to determine each year how the trustee is to divide the income between A and B. Under these circumstances, D has a special power of appointment. If D had the further right to appoint the income to himself, he or she probably possesses a general power of appointment. For the estate tax and gift tax effects of powers of appointment, see §§ 2041 and 2514. See also *testamentary power of appointment.*

Preferred stock bailout. A process wherein the issuance, sale, and later redemption of a preferred stock dividend was used by a shareholder to obtain long-term capital gains without any loss of voting control over the corporation. In effect, therefore, the shareholder was able to bail out corporate profits without suffering the consequences of dividend income treatment. This procedure led to the enactment by Congress of § 306 which, if applicable, converts the prior long-term capital gain on the sale of the stock to ordinary income. Under these circumstances, the amount of ordinary income is limited to the shareholder's portion of the corporation's earnings and profits existing when the preferred stock was issued as a stock dividend. See also *bailout.*

Present interest. See *future interest.*

Presumption. An inference in favor of a particular fact. If, for example, the IRS issues a notice of deficiency against a taxpayer, a presumption of correctness attaches to the assessment. Thus, the taxpayer has the burden of proof of showing that he or she does not owe the tax listed in the deficiency notice. See also *rebuttable presumption.*

Previously taxed income (PTI). Before the Subchapter S Revision Act of 1982, the undistributed taxable income of an S corporation was taxed to the shareholders as of the last day of the corporation's tax year and usually could be withdrawn by the shareholders without tax consequences at some later point in time. The role of PTI has been taken over by the accumulated adjustments account. See also *accumulated adjustments account.*

Principal. Property as opposed to income. The term is often used as a synonym for the corpus of a trust. If, for example, G places real estate in trust with income payable to A for life and the remainder to B upon A's death, the real estate is the principal, or corpus, of the trust.

Pro se. In a pro se situation, a taxpayer represents himself or herself before the court without the benefit of counsel.

Probate. The legal process wherein the estate of a decedent is administered. Generally, the probate process involves collecting a decedent's assets, liquidating liabilities, paying necessary taxes, and distributing property to heirs. These activities are carried out by the executor or administrator of the estate, usually under the supervision of the state or local court of appropriate jurisdiction.

Probate court. The usual designation for the state or local court that supervises the administration (i.e., probate) of a decedent's estate.

Probate estate. The property of a decedent that is subject to administration by the executor or administrator of an estate. See also *administration.*

Prop.Reg. An abbreviation for Proposed Regulation. A Regulation may first be issued in proposed form to give interested parties the opportunity for comment. When and if a Proposed Regulation is finalized, it is designated as a Regulation (abbreviated Reg.).

Pro rata. Proportionately. Assume, for example, a corporation has 10 shareholders, each of whom owns 10 percent of the stock. A pro rata dividend distribution of $1,000 would mean that each shareholder would receive $100.

PTI. See *previously taxed income.*

Public policy limitation. A concept developed by the courts precluding an income tax deduction for certain expenses related to activities deemed to be contrary to the public welfare. In this connection, Congress has incorporated into the Code specific disallowance provisions covering such items as illegal bribes, kickbacks, and fines and penalties. §§ 162(c) and (f).

Q

Qualified pension or profit sharing plan. An employer-sponsored plan that meets the requirements of § 401. If these requirements are met, none of the employer's contributions to the plan will be taxed to the employee until distributed to him or her (§ 402). The employer will be allowed a deduction in the year the contributions are made (§ 404). See also *contributory qualified pension or profit sharing plan, deferred compensation,* and *noncontributory pension or profit sharing plan.*

Qualified terminable interest property (QTIP). Generally, the marital deduction (for gift and estate tax purposes) is not available if the interest transferred will terminate upon the death of the transferee spouse and pass to someone else. Thus, if H places property in trust, life estate to W, and remainder to their children upon W's death, this is a terminable interest that will not provide H (or H's estate) with a marital deduction. If, however, the transfer in trust is treated as qualified terminable interest property (i.e., the QTIP election is made), the terminable interest restriction is waived and the marital deduction becomes available. In exchange for this deduction, the surviving spouse's gross estate must include the value of the QTIP election assets, even though he or she has no control over the ultimate disposition of the asset. Terminable interest property qualifies for this election if the donee (or heir) is the only beneficiary of the asset during his or her lifetime and receives income distributions relative to the property at least annually. As to gifts, the donor spouse is the one who makes the QTIP election. As to property transferred by death, the executor of the estate of the deceased spouse has the right to make the election. §§ 2056(b)(7) and 2523(f).

R

RAR. A Revenue agent's report, which reflects any adjustments made by the agent as a result of an audit of the taxpayer. The RAR is mailed to the taxpayer along with the 30–day letter, which outlines the appellate procedures available to the taxpayer.

Realized gain or loss. The difference between the amount realized upon the sale or other disposition of property and the adjusted basis of such property. § 1001. See also *adjusted basis, amount realized, basis,* and *recognized gain or loss.*

Realty. Real estate. See also *personalty.*

Reasonable needs of the business. The usual justification for avoiding the penalty tax on unreasonable accumulation of earnings. In determining the amount of taxable income subject to this tax (i.e., accumulated taxable income), § 535 allows a deduction for "such part of earnings and profits for the taxable year as are retained for the reasonable needs of the business." § 537.

Rebuttable presumption. A presumption that can be overturned upon the showing of sufficient proof. See also *presumption.*

Recapture. To recover the tax benefit of a deduction or a credit previously taken. See also *depreciation recapture* and *investment tax credit recapture.*

Recapture potential. A measure with respect to property which, if disposed of in a taxable transaction, would result in the recapture of depreciation (§§ 1245 or 1250), deferred LIFO gain, or deferred installment method gain.

Recognized gain or loss. The portion of realized gain or loss subject to income taxation. See also *realized gain or loss.*

Regulations. The U.S. Treasury Department Regulations (abbreviated Reg.) represent the position of the IRS as to how the Internal Revenue Code is to be interpreted. Their purpose is to provide taxpayers and IRS personnel with rules of general and specific application to the various provisions of the tax law. Regulations are published in the *Federal Register* and in all tax services.

Related parties. Various Code Sections define related parties, and often include a variety of persons within this (usually detrimental) category. Generally, related parties are accorded different tax treatment from that which applies to other taxpayers who would enter into similar transactions. For instance, realized losses that are generated between related parties are not recognized in the year of the loss. However, these deferred losses can be used to offset recognized gains that occur upon the subsequent sale of the asset to a nonrelated party. Other uses of a related-party definition include the conversion of gain upon the sale of a depreciable asset into all ordinary income (§ 1239) and the identification of constructive ownership of stock relative to corporate distributions, redemptions, liquidations, reorganizations, and compensation.

Remainder interest. The property that passes to a beneficiary after the expiration of an intervening income interest. If, for example, G places real estate in trust with income to A for life and remainder to B upon A's death, B has a remainder interest. See also *life estate* and *reversionary interest.*

Remainderperson. The male or female holder of a remainder interest (usually as to property held in trust). Under a will, the remainderperson is the party who will receive what is left of the decedent's property after all specific bequests have been satisfied. If, for example, D dies and her will leaves $10,000 in cash to A and the remainder of the estate to B, the remainderperson is B.

Remand. To send back. An appellate court may remand a case to a lower court, usually for additional fact finding. In other words, the appellate court is not in a position to decide the appeal based on the facts determined by the lower court. Remanding is abbreviated "rem'g."

Reorganization. See *corporate reorganization.*

Return of capital. When a taxpayer reacquires financial resources that he or she previously had invested in an entity or venture, the return of his or her capital investment itself does not increase gross income for the recovery year. A return of capital may occur with respect to an annuity or insurance contract, the sale or exchange of any asset, or a distribution from a partnership or corporation.

Revenue neutral. A change in the tax system that results in the same amount of revenue. Revenue neutral, however, does not mean that any one taxpayer will pay the same amount of tax as was previously the case. Thus, as a result of a tax law change, corporations could pay more taxes, but the excess revenue will be offset by lesser taxes on individuals.

Revenue Procedure. A matter of procedural importance to both taxpayers and the IRS concerning the administration of the tax laws is issued as a Revenue Procedure (abbreviated Rev.Proc.). A Revenue Procedure is first published in an Internal Revenue Bulletin (I.R.B.) and later transferred to the appropriate Cumulative Bulletin (C.B.). Both the Internal Revenue Bulletins and the Cumulative Bulletins are published by the U.S. Government Printing Office.

Revenue Ruling. A Revenue Ruling (abbreviated Rev.Rul.) is issued by the National Office of the IRS to express an official interpretation of the tax law as applied to specific transactions. Unlike a Regulation, it is more limited in application. A

Revenue Ruling is first published in an Internal Revenue Bulletin (I.R.B.) and later transferred to the appropriate Cumulative Bulletin (C.B.). Both the Internal Revenue Bulletins and the Cumulative Bulletins are published by the U.S. Government Printing Office.

Reversed (Rev'd.). An indication that a decision of one court has been reversed by a higher court in the same case.

Reversing (Rev'g.). An indication that the decision of a higher court is reversing the result reached by a lower court in the same case.

Reversionary interest. The property that reverts to the grantor after the expiration of an intervening income interest. Assume, for example, G places real estate in trust with income to A for 11 years, and upon the expiration of this term, the property returns to G. Under these circumstances, G holds a reversionary interest in the property. A reversionary interest is the same as a remainder interest, except that, in the latter case, the property passes to someone other than the original owner (e.g., the grantor of a trust) upon the expiration of the intervening interest. See also, *Clifford trust, grantor trust,* and *remainder interest.*

Revocable transfer. A transfer of property whereby the transferor retains the right to recover the property. The creation of a revocable trust is an example of a revocable transfer. § 2038. See also *incomplete transfer.*

Rev.Proc. Abbreviation for an IRS Revenue Procedure. See *Revenue Procedure.*

Rev.Rul. Abbreviation for an IRS Revenue Ruling. See *Revenue Ruling.*

Right of survivorship. See *joint tenancy.*

S

Schedule PH. A tax form required to be filed by corporations that are personal holding companies. The form must be filed in addition to Form 1120 (U.S. Corporation Income Tax Return).

S corporation. The designation for a small business corporation. See also *Subchapter S.*

Section 38 property. Property that qualified for the investment tax credit. Generally, this included all tangible property (other than real estate) used in a trade or business. § 48.

Section 306 stock. Preferred stock issued as a nontaxable stock dividend which, if sold or redeemed, would result in ordinary income recognition. § 306(c). See also *preferred stock bailout.*

Section 306 taint. The ordinary income that would result upon the sale or other taxable disposition of Section 306 stock.

Section 1231 assets. Depreciable assets and real estate used in a trade or business and held for the appropriate holding period. Under certain circumstances, the classification also includes timber, coal, domestic iron ore, livestock (held for draft, breeding, dairy, or sporting purposes), and unharvested crops. § 1231(b). See also *Section 1231 gains and losses.*

Section 1231 gains and losses. If the combined gains and losses from the taxable dispositions of § 1231 assets plus the net gain from business involuntary conversions (of both § 1231 assets and long-term capital assets) is a gain, such gains and losses are treated as long-term capital gains and losses. In arriving at § 1231 gains, however, the depreciation recapture provisions (e.g., §§ 1245 and 1250) are first applied to produce ordinary income. If the net result of the combination is a loss, such gains and losses from § 1231 assets are treated as ordinary gains and losses. § 1231(a). See also *depreciation recapture* and *Section 1231 assets.*

Section 1244 stock. Stock issued under § 1244 by qualifying small business corporations. If § 1244 stock becomes worthless, the shareholders may claim an ordinary loss rather than the usual capital loss.

Section 1245 property. Property subject to the recapture of depreciation under § 1245. For a definition of § 1245 property, see § 1245(a)(3). See also *depreciation recapture* and *Section 1245 recapture.*

Section 1245 recapture. Upon a taxable disposition of § 1245 property, all depreciation claimed on such property after 1962 will be recaptured as ordinary income (but not to exceed recognized gain from the disposition).

Section 1250 property. Real estate subject to the recapture of depreciation under § 1250. For a definition of § 1250 property, see § 1250(c). See also *depreciation recapture* and *Section 1250 recapture.*

Section 1250 recapture. Upon a taxable disposition of § 1250 property, some of the depreciation or cost recovery claimed on the property may be recaptured as ordinary income.

Separate property. In a community property jurisdiction, separate property is that property that belongs entirely to one of the spouses. Generally, it is property acquired before marriage or acquired after marriage by gift or inheritance. See also *community property.*

Sham. A transaction without substance that will be disregarded for tax purposes.

Short-term capital gain or loss. Results from the sale or other taxable exchange of a capital asset that had been held by the seller for one year or less or from other transactions involving statutorily designated assets, including nonbusiness bad debts.

Simple trusts. Simple trusts are those that are not complex trusts. Such trusts may not have a charitable beneficiary, accumulate income, or distribute corpus. See also *complex trusts.*

Simplified employee pensions. An employer may make contributions to an employee's individual retirement account (IRA) in amounts not exceeding the lesser of 15 percent of compensation or $30,000 per individual. § 219(b)(2). See also *individual retirement account.*

Small business corporation. A corporation that satisfies the definition of § 1361(b), § 1244(c)(2), or both. Satisfaction of § 1361(b) permits an S election, and satisfaction of § 1244 enables the shareholders of the corporation to claim an ordinary loss on the worthlessness of stock.

Special power of appointment. See *power of appointment.*

Special use value. An option that permits the executor of an estate to value, for death tax purposes, real estate used in a farming activity or in connection with a closely-held business at its current use value rather than at its most suitable or optimal use value. Under this option, a farm would be valued at its value for farming purposes even though, for example, the property might have a higher value as a potential shopping center. For the executor of an estate to elect special use valuation, the conditions of § 2032A must be satisfied. See also *most suitable use value.*

Specific bequest. A bequest of ascertainable property or cash to an heir of a decedent. Thus, if D's will passes his personal residence to W and grants $10,000 in cash to S, both W and S receive specific bequests.

Specific exemption. For transfers made before 1977, each donor was allowed a specific exemption of $30,000. Available for the lifetime of a donor, the exemption could be used to offset any taxable gifts made. Section 2521 was repealed by the Tax Reform Act of 1976.

Specific legatee. The recipient of designated property under a will and transferred by the death of the owner.

Spin-off. A type of reorganization wherein, for example, A Corporation transfers some assets to B Corporation in exchange for enough B stock to represent control. A Corporation then distributes the B stock to its shareholders.

Split-off. A type of reorganization wherein, for example, A Corporation transfers some assets to B Corporation in exchange for enough B stock to represent control. A Corporation then distributes the B stock to its shareholders in exchange for some of their A stock.

Split-up. A type of reorganization wherein, for example, A Corporation transfers some assets to B Corporation and the remainder to Z Corporation in return for which it receives enough B and Z stock to represent control of each corporation. The B and Z stock is then distributed by A Corporation to its shareholders in return for all of their A stock. The result of the split-up is that A Corporation is liquidated, and its shareholders now have control of B and Z Corporations.

Sprinkling trust. When a trustee has the discretion to either distribute or accumulate the entity accounting income of the trust and to distribute it among the trust's income beneficiaries in varying magnitudes, a sprinkling trust exists. The trustee can "sprinkle" the income of the trust.

Standard deduction. A minimum amount allowed to individual taxpayers as a deduction *from* AGI to minimize recordkeeping responsibilities. An additional standard deduction amount is allowed to taxpayers who are either blind or age 65 or older. A limited standard deduction is allowed to a taxpayer who is claimed as a dependent on another's tax return.

Statute of limitations. Provisions of the law that specify the maximum period of time in which action may be taken on a past event. Code §§ 6501–6504 contain the limitation periods applicable to the IRS for additional assessments, and §§ 6511–6515 relate to refund claims by taxpayers.

Statutory depletion. See *depletion.*

Statutory notice of deficiency. Commonly referred to as the 90-day letter, this notice is sent to a taxpayer upon request, upon the expiration of the 30–day letter, or upon exhaustion by the taxpayer of his or her adminstrative remedies before the IRS. The notice gives the taxpayer 90 days in which to file a petition with the U.S. Tax Court. If such a petition is not filed, the IRS will issue a demand for payment of the assessed deficiency. §§ 6211–6216. See also *deficiency* and *thirty-day letter.*

Step-down in basis. A reduction in the income tax basis of property.

Step-transaction approach. Disregarding one or more transactions to arrive at the final result.

Assume, for example, that the shareholders of A Corporation liquidate the corporation and thereby receive cash and operating assets. Immediately after the liquidation, the shareholders transfer the operating assets to newly formed B Corporation. Under these circumstances, the IRS may contend that the liquidation of A Corporation be disregarded (thereby depriving the shareholders of capital gain treatment). What may really have happened is a reorganization of A Corporation with a distribution of boot (ordinary income) to A's shareholders. If this is so, there will be a carryover of basis in the assets transferred from A Corporation to B Corporation.

Step-up in basis. An increase in the income tax basis of property. The classic step-up in basis occurs when a decedent dies owning appreciated property. Since the estate or heir acquires a basis in the property equal to the property's fair market value on the date of death (or alternate valuation date if available and elected), any appreciation is not subject to the income tax. Thus, a step-up in basis is the result, with no income tax consequences.

Stock attribution. See *attribution.*

Stock redemption. Occurs when a corporation buys back its own stock from a specified shareholder. Typically, the corporation recognizes any realized gain or loss on the noncash assets that it uses to effect a redemption, and the shareholder obtains a capital gain or loss upon receipt of the purchase price.

Subchapter C corporation. A regular corporation subject to the rules in Subchapter C (§§ 301–386) of the Internal Revenue Code. Distinguished from an S corporation, which is governed by Subchapter S of the Code.

Subchapter S. Sections 1361–1379 of the Internal Revenue Code. An elective provision permitting certain small business corporations (§ 1361) and their shareholders (§ 1362) to elect to be treated for income tax purposes in accordance with the operating rules of §§ 1363–1379. Of major significance is the fact that S corporations usually avoid the corporate income tax and corporate losses can be claimed by the shareholders.

Substance vs. form concept. A standard used when one must ascertain the true reality of what has occurred. Suppose, for example, a father sells stock to his daughter for $1,000. If the stock is really worth $50,000 at the time of the transfer, the substance of the transaction is probably a gift of $49,000.

Substantial economic effect. Partnerships are allowed to allocate items of income, expense, gain, loss, and credit in any manner that is authorized in the partnership agreement, provided that such allocation has an economic effect aside from the corresponding tax results. The necessary substantial economic effect is present, for instance, if the post-contribution appreciation in the value of an asset that was contributed to the partnership by a partner were allocated to that partner for cost recovery purposes.

Surviving spouse. When a husband or wife predeceases the other spouse, the survivor is known as a surviving spouse. Under certain conditions, a surviving spouse may be entitled to use the income tax rates in § 1(a) (i.e., those applicable to married persons filing a joint return) for the two years after the year of death of his or her spouse. For the definition of a surviving spouse for this purpose, see § 2(a).

Survivorship. See *joint tenancy.*

T

Tangible property. All property that has form or substance and is not intangible. See also *intangible asset.*

Tax benefit rule. A rule that limits the recognition of income from the recovery of an expense or loss properly deducted in a prior tax year to the amount of the deduction that generated a tax saving. Assume, for example, that last year T (an individual) had medical expenses of $3,000 and adjusted gross income of $30,000. Because of the 7.5 percent limitation, T was able to deduct only $750 of these expenses [i.e., $3,000 − (7.5% × $30,000)]. If, in this year, T is reimbursed by his insurance company for $900 of these expenses, the tax benefit rule limits the amount of income from the reimbursement to $750 (i.e., the amount previously deducted with a tax saving).

Tax Court. The U.S. Tax Court is one of three trial courts of original jurisdiction that decide litigation involving Federal income, death, or gift taxes. It is the only trial court where the taxpayer must not first pay the deficiency assessed by the IRS. The Tax Court will not have jurisdiction over a case unless the statutory notice of deficiency (i.e., 90-day letter) has been issued by the IRS and the taxpayer files the petition for hearing within the time prescribed.

Tax on unearned income of a child under age 14. Passive income, such as interest and dividends, that is recognized by such a child is taxed *to him or her* at the rates that would have applied had the income been incurred by the child's parents, generally to the extent that such income exceeds $1,000. The additional tax is assessed regardless of the source of the income or the income's underlying property. If the child's parents are divorced, the custodial parent's rates are used. The

Tax preference items. Those items that may result in the imposition of the alternative minimum tax. §§ 55–58. See also *add-on minimum tax* and *alternative minimum tax*.

Tax year. See *accounting period*.

Taxable estate. Defined in § 2051, the taxable estate is the gross estate of a decedent reduced by the deductions allowed by §§ 2053–2057 (e.g., administration expenses, marital, charitable, and ESOP deductions). The taxable estate is the amount that is subject to the unified transfer tax at death. See also *adjusted taxable estate* and *gross estate*.

Taxable gift. Defined in § 2503, a taxable gift is the amount of the gift that is subject to the unified transfer tax. Thus, a taxable gift has been adjusted by the annual exclusion and other appropriate deductions (e.g., marital and charitable).

Taxable income. The tax base with respect to the prevailing Federal income tax. Taxable income is defined by the Internal Revenue Code, Treasury Regulations, and pertinent court cases. Currently, taxable income includes gross income from all sources except those specifically excluded by the statute. In addition, taxable income is reduced for certain allowable deductions. Deductions for business taxpayers must be related to a trade or business. Individuals also can deduct certain personal expenses in determining their taxable incomes. See also *gross income*.

Tax-free exchange. Transfers of property specifically exempted from income tax consequences by the tax law. Examples are a transfer of property to a controlled corporation under § 351(a) and a like-kind exchange under § 1031(a).

Tax-option corporation. See *Subchapter S*.

T.C. An abbreviation for the U.S. Tax Court used to cite a Regular Decision of the U.S. Tax Court.

T.C. Memo. An abbreviation used to refer to a Memorandum Decision of the U.S. Tax Court.

Telescoping. To look through one or more transactions to arrive at the final result. It is also designated as the *step-transaction approach* or the *substance vs. form concept* (see these terms).

Tenancy by the entirety. Essentially, a joint tenancy between husband and wife. See also *joint tenancy* and *tenancy in common*.

Tenancy in common. A form of ownership whereby each tenant (i.e., owner) holds an undivided interest in property. Unlike a joint tenancy or a tenancy by the entirety, the interest of a tenant in common does not terminate upon that individual's death (i.e., there is no right of survivorship). Assume, for example, B and C acquire real estate as equal tenants in common, each having furnished one-half of the purchase price. Upon B's death, his one-half interest in the property passes to his estate or heirs, not to C. For a comparison of results, see also *joint tenancy* and *tenancy by the entirety*.

Terminable interest. An interest in property that terminates upon the death of the holder or upon the occurrence of some other specified event. The transfer of a terminable interest by one spouse to the other may not qualify for the marital deduction. §§ 2056(b) and 2523(b). See also *marital deduction*.

Testamentary disposition. The passing of property to another upon the death of the owner.

Testamentary power of appointment. A power of appointment that can be exercised only through the will (i.e., upon the death) of the holder. See also *power of appointment*.

Thin capitalization. When debt owed by a corporation to the shareholders becomes too large in relation to the corporation's capital structure (i.e., stock and shareholder equity), the IRS may contend that the corporation is thinly capitalized. In effect, this means that some or all of the debt will be reclassified as equity. The immediate result is to disallow any interest deduction to the corporation on the reclassified debt. To the extent of the corporation's earnings and profits, interest payments and loan repayments are treated as dividends to the shareholders.

Thirty-day letter. A letter that accompanies a revenue agent's report issued as a result of an IRS audit of a taxpayer (or the rejection of a taxpayer's claim for refund). The letter outlines the taxpayer's appeal procedure before the IRS. If the taxpayer does not request any such procedures within the 30–day period, the IRS will issue a statutory notice of deficiency (the 90–day letter). See also *statutory notice of deficiency*.

Tiered partnerships. An ownership arrangement wherein one partnership (the parent or first tier) is a partner in one or more partnerships (the subsidiary/subsidiaries or second tier). Frequently, the first tier is a holding partnership and the second tier is an operating partnership.

Trade or business. Any business or professional activity conducted by a taxpayer. The mere ownership of rental or other investment assets does not constitute a trade or business. Generally, a trade or business generates relatively little passive investment income.

Transfer tax. A tax imposed upon the transfer of property. See also *unified transfer tax.*

Transferee liability. Under certain conditions, if the IRS is unable to collect taxes owed by a transferor of property, it may pursue its claim against the transferee of such property. The transferee's liability for taxes is limited to the extent of the value of the assets transferred. For example, the IRS can force a donee to pay the gift tax when such tax cannot be paid by the donor making the transfer. §§ 6901–6905.

Treasury Regulations. *See Regulations.*

Trial court. The court of original jurisdiction; the first court to consider litigation. In Federal tax controversies, trial courts include U.S. District Courts, the U.S. Tax Court, and the U.S. Claims Court. See also *appellate court, Claims Court, District Court,* and *Tax Court.*

Trust. A legal entity created by a grantor for the benefit of designated beneficiaries under the laws of the state and the valid trust instrument. The trustee holds a fiduciary responsibility to manage the trust's corpus assets and income for the economic benefit of all of the beneficiaries.

Trustee. An individual or corporation that takes the fiduciary responsibilities under a trust.

U

Undistributed personal holding company income. The penalty tax on personal holding companies is imposed on the corporation's undistributed personal holding company income for the year. The adjustments necessary to convert taxable income to undistributed personal holding company income are set forth in § 545.

Unearned income. Income received but not yet earned. Normally, such income is taxed when received, even for accrual basis taxpayers.

Unified transfer tax. A set of tax rates applicable to transfers by gift and death made after 1976. § 2001(c).

Unified tax credit. A credit allowed against any unified transfer tax. §§ 2010 and 2505.

Uniform Gift to Minors Act. A means of transferring property (usually stocks and bonds) to a minor. The designated custodian of the property has the legal right to act on behalf of the minor without requiring a guardianship. Generally, the custodian possesses the right to change investments (e.g., sell one type of stock and buy another), apply the income from the custodial property to the minor's support, and even terminate the custodianship. In this regard, however, the custodian is acting in a fiduciary capacity on behalf of the minor. The custodian could not, for example, appropriate the property for his or her own use, because it belongs to the minor. During the period of the custodianship, the income from the property is taxed to the minor. The custodianship terminates when the minor reaches legal age. See also *guardianship* and *legal age.*

Unrealized receivables. Amounts earned by a cash basis taxpayer but not yet received. Because of the method of accounting used by the taxpayer, such amounts have no income tax basis. When unrealized receivables are distributed to a partner, they generally convert a transaction from nontaxable to taxable, or they convert otherwise capital gain to ordinary income.

Unreasonable compensation. Under § 162(a)(1) a deduction is allowed for "reasonable" salaries or other compensation for personal services actually rendered. To the extent compensation is "excessive" (i.e., "unreasonable"), no deduction is allowed. The problem of unreasonable compensation usually is limited to closely-held corporations, where the motivation is to pay out profits in some form that is deductible to the corporation. Deductible compensation therefore becomes an attractive substitute for nondeductible dividends when the shareholders also are employed by the corporation.

USSC. An abbreviation for the U.S. Supreme Court.

U.S. Tax Court. See *Tax Court.*

USTC. Published by Commerce Clearing House, *U.S. Tax Cases* contain all of the Federal tax decisions issued by the U.S. District Courts, U.S. Claims Court, U.S. Courts of Appeals, and the U.S. Supreme Court.

V

Value. See *fair market value.*

Vested. Absolute and complete. If, for example, a person holds a vested interest in property, such interest cannot be taken away or otherwise defeated.

Voting trust. A trust that holds the voting rights to stock in a corporation. It is a useful device when a majority of the shareholders in a corporation cannot agree on corporate policy.

W

Wash sale. A loss from the sale of stock or securities that is disallowed because the taxpayer has, within 30 days before or after the sale, acquired stock or securities substantially identical to those sold. § 1091.

WESTLAW. An on-line database system, produced by West Publishing Company, by which the tax researcher can obtain access to the Internal Revenue Code, Regulations, administrative rulings, and court case opinions.

Writ of Certiorari. See *certiorari*.

Appendix D-1

Table of Code Sections Cited

[See Title 26 U.S.C.A.]

Appendix D-2

Table of

Regulations Cited

Appendix D-3

Table of Revenue Procedures and Revenue Rulings Cited

Appendix E
Table of Cases Cited

Subject Index

E